Contemporary
Literary Criticism

Guide to Gale Literary Criticism Series

For criticism on	Consult these Gale series
Authors now living or who died after December 31, 1999	*CONTEMPORARY LITERARY CRITICISM (CLC)*
Authors who died between 1900 and 1999	*TWENTIETH-CENTURY LITERARY CRITICISM (TCLC)*
Authors who died between 1800 and 1899	*NINETEENTH-CENTURY LITERATURE CRITICISM (NCLC)*
Authors who died between 1400 and 1799	*LITERATURE CRITICISM FROM 1400 TO 1800 (LC)* *SHAKESPEAREAN CRITICISM (SC)*
Authors who died before 1400	*CLASSICAL AND MEDIEVAL LITERATURE CRITICISM (CMLC)*
Authors of books for children and young adults	*CHILDREN'S LITERATURE REVIEW (CLR)*
Dramatists	*DRAMA CRITICISM (DC)*
Poets	*POETRY CRITICISM (PC)*
Short story writers	*SHORT STORY CRITICISM (SSC)*
Black writers of the past two hundred years	*BLACK LITERATURE CRITICISM (BLC)* *BLACK LITERATURE CRITICISM SUPPLEMENT (BLCS)*
Hispanic writers of the late nineteenth and twentieth centuries	*HISPANIC LITERATURE CRITICISM (HLC)* *HISPANIC LITERATURE CRITICISM SUPPLEMENT (HLCS)*
Native North American writers and orators of the eighteenth, nineteenth, and twentieth centuries	*NATIVE NORTH AMERICAN LITERATURE (NNAL)*
Major authors from the Renaissance to the present	*WORLD LITERATURE CRITICISM, 1500 TO THE PRESENT (WLC)* *WORLD LITERATURE CRITICISM SUPPLEMENT (WLCS)*

ISSN 0091-3421

Volume 148

Contemporary Literary Criticism

Criticism of the Works
of Today's Novelists, Poets, Playwrights,
Short Story Writers, Scriptwriters, and
Other Creative Writers

Jeffrey W. Hunter
SENIOR EDITOR

Tom Burns
ASSISTANT EDITOR

GALE GROUP

THOMSON LEARNING

Detroit • New York • San Diego • San Francisco
Boston • New Haven, Conn. • Waterville, Maine
London • Munich

STAFF

Library of Congress Catalog Card Number 76-46132
ISBN 0-7876-5217-2
ISSN 0091-3421
Printed in the United States of America

10 9 8 7 6 5 4 3 2 1

Contents

Preface

Named "one of the twenty-five most distinguished reference titles published during the past twenty-five years" by *Reference Quarterly*, the *Contemporary Literary Criticism* (*CLC*) series provides readers with critical commentary and general information on more than 2,000 authors now living or who died after December 31, 1999. Volumes published from 1973 through 1999 include authors who died after December 31, 1959. Previous to the publication of the first volume of *CLC* in 1973, there was no ongoing digest monitoring scholarly and popular sources of critical opinion and explication of modern literature. *CLC*, therefore, has fulfilled an essential need, particularly since the complexity and variety of contemporary literature makes the function of criticism especially important to today's reader.

Scope of the Series

CLC provides significant passages from published criticism of works by creative writers. Since many of the authors covered in *CLC* inspire continual critical commentary, writers are often represented in more than one volume. There is, of course, no duplication of reprinted criticism.

Authors are selected for inclusion for a variety of reasons, among them the publication or dramatic production of a critically acclaimed new work, the reception of a major literary award, revival of interest in past writings, or the adaptation of a literary work to film or television.

Attention is also given to several other groups of writers—authors of considerable public interest—about whose work criticism is often difficult to locate. These include mystery and science fiction writers, literary and social critics, foreign authors, and authors who represent particular ethnic groups.

Each *CLC* volume contains individual essays and reviews taken from hundreds of book review periodicals, general magazines, scholarly journals, monographs, and books. Entries include critical evaluations spanning from the beginning of an author's career to the most current commentary. Interviews, feature articles, and other published writings that offer insight into the author's works are also presented. Students, teachers, librarians, and researchers will find that the general critical and biographical material in *CLC* provides them with vital information required to write a term paper, analyze a poem, or lead a book discussion group. In addition, complete biographical citations note the original source and all of the information necessary for a term paper footnote or bibliography.

Organization of the Book

A *CLC* entry consists of the following elements:

- The **Author Heading** cites the name under which the author most commonly wrote, followed by birth and death dates. Also located here are any name variations under which an author wrote, including transliterated forms for authors whose native languages use nonroman alphabets. If the author wrote consistently under a pseudonym, the pseudonym will be listed in the author heading and the author's actual name given in parenthesis on the first line of the biographical and critical information. Uncertain birth or death dates are indicated by question marks. Single-work entries are preceded by a heading that consists of the most common form of the title in English translation (if applicable) and the original date of composition.

- A **Portrait of the Author** is included when available.

- The **Introduction** contains background information that introduces the reader to the author, work, or topic that is the subject of the entry.

- The list of **Principal Works** is ordered chronologically by date of first publication and lists the most important works by the author. The genre and publication date of each work is given. In the case of foreign authors whose works have been translated into English, the English-language version of the title follows in brackets. Unless otherwise indicated, dramas are dated by first performance, not first publication.

- Reprinted **Criticism** is arranged chronologically in each entry to provide a useful perspective on changes in critical evaluation over time. The critic's name and the date of composition or publication of the critical work are given at the beginning of each piece of criticism. Unsigned criticism is preceded by the title of the source in which it appeared. All titles by the author featured in the text are printed in boldface type. Footnotes are reprinted at the end of each essay or excerpt. In the case of excerpted criticism, only those footnotes that pertain to the excerpted texts are included.

- A complete **Bibliographical Citation** of the original essay or book precedes each piece of criticism.

- Critical essays are prefaced by brief **Annotations** explicating each piece.

- Whenever possible, a recent **Author Interview** accompanies each entry.

- An annotated bibliography of **Further Reading** appears at the end of each entry and suggests resources for additional study. In some cases, significant essays for which the editors could not obtain reprint rights are included here. Boxed material following the further reading list provides references to other biographical and critical sources on the author in series published by Gale.

Indexes

A **Cumulative Author Index** lists all of the authors that appear in a wide variety of reference sources published by the Gale Group, including *CLC*. A complete list of these sources is found facing the first page of the Author Index. The index also includes birth and death dates and cross references between pseudonyms and actual names.

A **Cumulative Nationality Index** lists all authors featured in *CLC* by nationality, followed by the number of the *CLC* volume in which their entry appears.

A **Cumulative Topic Index** lists the literary themes and topics treated in the series as well as in *Literature Criticism from 1400 to 1800, Nineteenth-Century Literature Criticism, Twentieth-Century Literary Criticism,* and the *Contemporary Literary Criticism* Yearbook, which was discontinued in 1998.

An alphabetical **Title Index** accompanies each volume of *CLC*. Listings of titles by authors covered in the given volume are followed by the author's name and the corresponding page numbers where the titles are discussed. English translations of foreign titles and variations of titles are cross-referenced to the title under which a work was originally published. Titles of novels, dramas, nonfiction books, and poetry, short story, or essay collections are printed in italics, while individual poems, short stories, and essays are printed in roman type within quotation marks.

In response to numerous suggestions from librarians, Gale also produces an annual cumulative title index that alphabetically lists all titles reviewed in *CLC* and is available to all customers. Additional copies of this index are available upon request. Librarians and patrons will welcome this separate index; it saves shelf space, is easy to use, and is recyclable upon receipt of the next edition.

Citing *Contemporary Literary Criticism*

When writing papers, students who quote directly from any volume in the Literary Criticism Series may use the following general format to footnote reprinted criticism. The first example pertains to material drawn from periodicals, the second to material reprinted from books.

Alfred Cismaru, "Making the Best of It," *The New Republic* 207, no. 24 (December 7, 1992): 30, 32; excerpted and reprinted in *Contemporary Literary Criticism,* vol. 85, ed. Christopher Giroux (Detroit: The Gale Group, 1995), 73-4.

Yvor Winters, *The Post-Symbolist Methods* (Allen Swallow, 1967), 211-51; excerpted and reprinted in *Contemporary Literary Criticism,* vol. 85, ed. Christopher Giroux (Detroit: The Gale Group, 1995), 223-26.

Suggestions are Welcome

Readers who wish to suggest new features, topics, or authors to appear in future volumes, or who have other suggestions or comments are cordially invited to call, write, or fax the Managing Editor:

Managing Editor, Literary Criticism Series
The Gale Group
27500 Drake Road
Farmington Hills, MI 48331-3535
1-800-347-4253 (GALE)
Fax: 248-699-8054

Acknowledgments

The editors wish to thank the copyright holders of the excerpted criticism included in this volume and the permissions managers of many book and magazine publishing companies for assisting us in securing reproduction rights. We are also grateful to the staffs of the Detroit Public Library, the Library of Congress, the University of Detroit Mercy Library, Wayne State University Purdy/Kresge Library Complex, and the University of Michigan Libraries for making their resources available to us. Following is a list of the copyright holders who have granted us permission to reproduce material in this volume of *CLC*. Every effort has been made to trace copyright, but if omissions have been made, please let us know.

COPYRIGHTED MATERIAL IN *CLC*, VOLUME 148, WAS REPRODUCED FROM THE FOLLOWING PERIODICALS:

American Historical Review, v. 80, October, 1975 for a review of "Metahistory: The Historical Imagination in Nineteenth-Century Europe" by Michael Ermarth; v. 93, October, 1988 for a review of *"The Content of the Form": Narrative Discourse and Historical Representation* by Dominick Lacapra. Reproduced by permission of the publisher and the respective authors.—*American Journal of Psychiatry,* v. 149, December, 1992 for a review of *A Dream of Mind: Poems* by Robert Michels. Copyright © 1992, the American Psychiatric Association. Reprinted by permission of the publisher and the author.—*The Bloomsbury Review,* September-October, 1993 for an interview with Rudolfo A. Anaya by Ray Gonzalez. Copyright © by Owaissa Communications Company, Inc. 1998. Reproduced by permission of the author.—*Canadian Historical Review,* v. LVI, 1975. © University of Toronto Press 1975. Reproduced by permission of the University of Toronto Press Incorporated.—*Chicago Tribune Books,* December 31, 1995 for "The Poems of Stanley Kunitz Confront 'The Great Simplicities'" by A.V. Christie. Tribune Media Services, Inc. All rights reserved. Reproduced by permission of the author.—*Chicago Tribune,* December 22, 1985 for "Stanley Kunitz Shares Next-to-Last Poems, Essays with Readers" by James Idema. © 1985 Tribune Media Services, Inc. All rights reserved. Reproduced by permission of the author.—*The Christian Science Monitor,* v. 60, September 6, 1968; v. 61, February 24, 1969 for "Alan Sillitoe–the Novelist as a Poet" by Victor Howes. © 1969 by Victor Howes; v. 63, October 7, 1971 for a review of "A Start in Life" by Victor Howes. © 1971 by Victor Howes; v. 69, August 4, 1977; March 6, 1987; August 10, 2000. © 1968, 1977, 1987, 2000 The Christian Science Publishing Society. All rights reserved. Reproduced by permission from The Christian Science Monitor and respective author.—*CLIO,* v. 29, Winter, 2000. © 2000 by Purdue Research Foundation. Reproduced by permission of the author.—*College Literature,* v. 27, Fall, 2000. Copyright © 2000 by West Chester University. Reproduced by permission. –*Comment,* v. CXXXVI, September, 1980 for "The Ineluctable Signature of Stanley Kunitz" by Peter Stitt. Reproduced by permission of the author.—*Comparative Literature,* v. XXX, Spring, 1978. © copyright 1978 by University of Oregon.— *Contemporary Literature,* v. XV, Winter, 1974; v. XXIX, Summer, 1988; v. XXXIII, Summer, 1992. © 1974, 1988, 1992 by the Board of Regents of the University of Wisconsin System. Reproduced by permission of The University of Wisconsin Press.—*Encounter,* v. LIV, April, 1980 for "On American Poetry" by Alan Brownjohn. © 1980 by Alan Brownjohn. Reproduced by permission of the author.—*Film Quarterly,* v. 11, 1983 for *"The Loneliness of The Long Distance Runner and Chariots of Fire"* by Sophia B. Blaydes and Philip Bordinat. © 1983 by The Regents of the University of California. Reproduced by permission of the authors.—Stitt, Peter, "A Variegation of Styles: Inductive, Deductive, and Linguistic," in *The Georgia Review,* v. XXXVII, Winter, 1983, pp. 894-905; Kitchen, Judith "Skating on Paper," in *The Georgia Review,* v. XLVII, Fall, 1993, pp. 578-95; "The Ladybug and the Universe" in *The Georgia Review,* v. L, Summer, 1996. Copyright, 1993, 1996 by the University of Georgia. Reproduced by permission. Copyright, 1983, by the University of Georgia. Reproduced by permission of the author.—*The Gettysburg Review,* v. 5, Spring, 1992. Reproduced by permission.— *History and Theory,* v. XXVII, October, 1980; v. XIX, December, 1980; v. 32, October, 1993; v. 36, December, 1997; v. 37, May, 1998; v. 39, October, 2000. Copyright © 1980, 1993, 1997, 1998, 2000 by Wesleyan University. Reproduced by permission of Blackwell Publishers.—*The Hudson Review,* v. XXXVII, Spring, 1984; v. XLVIII, Summer, 1995. Copyright © 1984, 1995 by The Hudson Review, Inc. Reproduced by permission.—*International Studies in Philosophy,* v. XXIV, Spring, 1992 for "Fiction and History: A Common Core?" by L. B.Cebik. Reproduced by permission of the author.— *Journal of American Studies,* v. 23, April, 1989. © Cambridge University Press 1989. Reproduced with the permission of Cambridge University Press and the author.—*Journal of Contemporary History,* v. 31, January, 1996 for "Searching for an Audience: The Historical Profession in the Media Age–A Comment on Arthur Marwick and Hayden White" by Wulf Kansteiner; for "Narrative History as a Way of Life" by Geoffrey Roberts; for "History and Metahistory: Marwick Versus White" by Beverley Southgate. Reproduced by permission of the publisher and the respective authors.—*Journal of Modern History,* v. 72, September, 2000 for a review of "Figural Realism: Studies in the Mimesis Effect" by Allan Megill. Copyright © 2000 by The University of Chicago. Reproduced by permission of the author.—*Journal of Modern Literature,*

Literary Criticism Series Advisory Board

Rudolfo Anaya
1937-

(Full name Rudolfo Alfonso Anaya) American novelist, short story writer, children's writer, poet, essayist, playwright, and critic.

The following entry presents an overview of Anaya's career through 1999. For further information on his life and works, see *CLC,* Volume 23.

INTRODUCTION

One of the most influential authors in Chicano literature, Anaya has been acclaimed for his skillful utilization of realism, fantasy, and myth in his novels that explore the experiences of Hispanics in the American Southwest. Critics have noted that Anaya's unique style was profoundly influenced by his fascination with the mystical nature of Spanish-American *cuentos,* or folk tales, in the oral tradition. Anaya first established his literary reputation with his acclaimed debut novel, *Bless Me, Ultima* (1972). Anaya's preoccupation with myth and folklore—including his unique negotiation between mystical and realistic depictions of indigenous New Mexican life in the twentieth century—extends his prose beyond regional fiction and toward a more universal portrayal of human experience. Anaya's departure from the highly politicized tone of the Chicano writing of the 1960s distinguishes him from his peers, and the complexity of his characters breaks from the stereotypical portrayal of those in the Chicano community as simple, working peasants.

BIOGRAPHICAL INFORMATION

Anaya was born on October 30, 1937, in Pastura, New Mexico. He spent his childhood in the village of Santa Rosa, New Mexico, and moved to Albuquerque as an adolescent. His hospitalization for a spinal injury in his childhood was a formative experience that he revisited fictionally in *Tortuga* (1979), a novel about a young boy burdened with a body cast. After briefly attending business school, Anaya earned a B.A. and M.A. in English, as well as an M.A. in counseling, from the University of New Mexico in Albuquerque. After college, he worked as a public school teacher and a counselor. Anaya eventually returned to the University of New Mexico as a professor of English, where he helped found the well-known creative writing journal *Blue Mesa Review.* Anaya has since retired from teaching to work as a full-time writer. His literary honors include the Premio Quinto Sol national Chicano literary award for *Bless Me, Ultima,* the Before Columbus

Foundation American Book Award for *Tortuga,* and the PEN-West Fiction Award for *Alburquerque* (1992). He has also received grants from the National Endowment for the Arts, the National Chicano Council of Higher Education, and the Kellogg Foundation. Anaya's major novels have been translated into several languages, garnering him international critical attention.

MAJOR WORKS

Anaya's writing is strongly influenced by the oral tradition of storytelling inherent to his Hispanic roots. His strict Catholic upbringing and the *llano* (open plain) of rural New Mexico are two major themes in his writing; his works continually refer to both as "havens" from which his characters are often exiled. His novels and stories attempt to structurally replicate the dynamic nature of storytelling. They are ordered organically, by natural and psychological cycles, instead of constructing plots that focus on external or historical events. Anaya repeatedly employs dream imagery to obscure the gap between the unconscious and the conscious. This allows both realms of analysis to be subjected to an artistic ambiguity more often associated with poetry or folklore than the realistic novel. Other archetypal images and themes frequently emerge in Anaya's work, emphasizing nature, faith, and the alienating effects of modern capitalism. The figures of the witch and the *curandera*—a healer who uses traditional herbal remedies—appear in many of Anaya's stories, and comprise the dual roles of the title character of *Bless Me, Ultima.* Young Antonio Márez, the novel's protagonist, sees Ultima, an old woman, as a representation of a dwindling way of life. Ultima also acts as a living reminder of Antonio's childhood, his ancestral roots, and the way that modern North American urban life rejects faith and mysticism. The quest for self-knowledge and the reconciliation between old and new American cultures in *Bless Me, Ultima* is variously reworked in *Heart of Aztlán* (1976), *Tortuga,* and in many of Anaya's short stories. While the setting of *Bless Me, Ultima* is predominantly rural, *Heart of Aztlán* deals with more urban and political landscapes. The novel traces the experiences of the Chávez family following their move from a small village in Mexico to the Barelas barrio in Albuquerque, New Mexico. The reactions of the family members to urban life—ranging from drug addiction and violence to a sacralization of the rural homeland—illustrates the myriad pressures that Chicanos face as they adjust to modernity, technology, and capitalism. *Tortuga* details the recovery of a sixteen-year-old boy following a paralyzing accident. Anaya uses the boy's physical healing to show the tranquility of self-knowledge and the importance of physical and mental well-being on a communal level. The health of the greater community is symbolized by a hospital for crippled children, the primary setting of the novel. Anaya has contended that *Bless Me, Ultima, Heart of Aztlán,* and *Tortuga* "are a definite trilogy in my mind. They are not only about growing up in New Mexico, they are about life."

In the 1990s, Anaya wrote four mystery thrillers—*Alburquerque, Zia Summer* (1995), *Rio Grande Fall* (1996), and *Shaman Winter* (1999). Like his previous fictional "trilogy," these works expand upon his analysis of life in the New Mexican *barrio* while at the same time telling compelling detective stories. In addition to his novels and short stories in *The Silence of the Llano* (1982), Anaya has also published children's fiction, including *Farolitos for Abuelo* (1998) and *My Land Sings* (1999); poetry in *The Adventures of Juan Chicaspatas* (1985) and *An Elegy on the Death of Cesar Chavez* (2000); a travel journal, *A Chicano in China* (1986); and several plays, radio scripts, and essays reflecting on contemporary Chicano life.

CRITICAL RECEPTION

Bless Me, Ultima has generated more critical reaction than any other novel in contemporary Chicano literature. Critics of this work have found Anaya's story unique, his narrative technique compelling, and his prose both meticulous and lyrical. The reception of *Heart of Aztlán,* however,

was less enthusiastic. Although many critics have approved of the novel's mythic substructure, some commentators have found Anaya's intermingling of myth and politics confusing. *Tortuga* has also prompted a mixed critical response. Some commentators, extolling the novel's structural complexity and innovative depiction of Chicano life, have proclaimed *Tortuga* Anaya's best work; other critics have denigrated the novel as melodramatic and unrealistic. The works in Anaya's second series—*Alburquerque, Zia Summer, Rio Grande Fall,* and *Shaman Winter*— are widely regarded to be more commercial novels and were less well-received that his original, unofficial "trilogy" (*Ultima, Heart,* and *Tortuga*). Anaya's novels continue to be studied and analyzed with an intensity accorded to few other Hispanic writers. Praised for their universal appeal, his works have been translated into a number of languages. Of Anaya's international success, Antonio Marquez has written, "It is befitting for Anaya to receive the honor and the task of leading Chicano literature into the canons of world literature. He is the most acclaimed and the most popular and universal Chicano writer, and one of the most influential voices in contemporary Chicano literature."

PRINCIPAL WORKS

Bless Me, Ultima (novel) 1972
Heart of Aztlán (novel) 1976
Tortuga (novel) 1979
The Silence of the Llano (short stories) 1982
The Legend of La Llorona (novel) 1984
The Adventures of Juan Chicaspatas (poetry) 1985
A Chicano in China (nonfiction) 1986
The Farolitos of Christmas: A New Mexican Christmas Story (juvenilia) 1987
Lord of the Dawn: The Legend of Quetzalcóatl (legends) 1987
Alburquerque (novel) 1992
The Anaya Reader (prose, essays, and plays) 1995
Zia Summer (novel) 1995
Jalamanta: A Message from the Desert (novel) 1996
Rio Grande Fall (novel) 1996
Farolitos for Abuelo [illustrated by Edward Gonzales] (juvenilia) 1998
My Land Sings: Stories from the Rio Grande [illustrated by Amy Cordova] (short stories) 1999
Shaman Winter (novel) 1999
An Elegy on the Death of Cesar Chavez [illustrated by Gaspar Enriquez] (poetry) 2000
Roadrunner's Dance [illustrated by David Diaz] (juvenilia) 2000

CRITICISM

Jane Rogers (essay date Spring–Summer 1977)

SOURCE: "The Function of the *La Llorona* Motif in Rudolfo Anaya's *Bless Me, Ultima,*" in *Latin American Literary Review,* Vol. V, No. 10, Spring–Summer, 1977, pp. 64–69.

[*In the following essay, Rogers examines the archetypal themes of passage, longing, and deadly seduction in* Bless Me, Ultima, *drawing attention to the symbolism and imagery of the "la llorona" myth.*]

In *The Odyssey,* Circe warns the homeward-bound Odysseus of the menace of the Sirens, who, surrounded by the mouldering skeletons of men, lure and bewitch the unaware man with the music of their song. Yet just beyond their lovely voices—that Odysseus escapes by having himself lashed to the mast of his ship—lurks peril, a choice between annihilation on the sheer cliffs of the Wandering Rocks or a meeting with the double menace of Scylla and Charybdis, the former hideously fishing for a passersby with her twelve dangling feet, the latter but a bow's shot distance away threatening to suck men down into the deep waters near the foot of a luxurious fig tree. Certain death is the fate of the man who succumbs to the sweet lure of the sirens. The peril of life, and yet the promise of home, is the alternative.

A similar theme is developed by Rudolfo Anaya's use of the *la llorona* motif in **Bless Me, Ultima.** In the novel, Antonio, symbolically both Christ and Odysseus, moves from the security and from the sweet-smelling warmth of his mother's bosom and kitchen out into life and experience. As he weighs his options—priesthood and the confinement represented by the farms of the Lunas' or the Marezes' freedom on the pagan sea of the llano—and as he grows from innocence to knowledge and experience, the *la llorona* motif figures both on a literal mythological level and as an integral part of Antonio's life.

As "literal" myth, *la llorona* is the wailing woman of the river. Hers is the "tormented cry of a lonely goddess" that fills the valley in one of Antonio's dreams. *La llorona* is "the old witch who cries along the river banks and seeks the blood of boys and men to drink."[1] This myth is closely related to Cico's story of the mermaid.[2] The mermaid is the powerful presence in the bottomless Hidden Lakes. Her strange music is a "low, lonely murmuring . . . like something a sad girl would sing." (p. 109) Cico relates that all that had kept him from plunging into the bottomless lake when he heard the sound was the Golden Carp, whose appearance caused the music to stop. Not that the singing was evil, he relates, but "it called for me to join it. One more step and I'da stepped over the ledge and drowned in the waters of the lake—" (p. 109) Cico continues with the story of the shepherd taken by the mermaid. A "man from Mejico," working on a neighboring ranch, not having heard the story about the lakes, had taken his sheep to water there. Hearing the singing, he ran back to town and swore he had seen a mermaid.

> "He said it was a woman, resting on the water and singing a lonely song. She was half woman and half fish—He said the song made him want to wade out to the middle of the lake to help her, but his fear had made him run. He told everyone the story, but no one believed him. He ended up getting drunk in town and swearing he would prove his story by going back to the lakes and bringing back the mer-woman. He never returned. A week later the flock was found near the lakes. He had vanished—"
>
> (p. 109)

As an integral part of Antonio's life, the *la llorona* motif emerges in his experiences with nature. *La llorona* is the ambivalent *presence* of the river, which Antonio fears and yet with which he senses a sharing of his own soul and a mystic peace. *La llorona* speaks in the owl's cry and in the dove's cou-rou. Even the dust devils of the llano bear *la llorona*'s signature, embracing Antonio in swirling dust as the gushing wind, which imprints evil on his soul, seems to call his name:

> Antonioooooooooooooooo . . .
>
> (p. 52)

But more significantly for Antonio, the *la llorona* motif emerges in his relationship with his mother and in the imagery of the women in the novel. It is the primary image associated with the mother, Maria. Her frequent extended calls of "Antonioooooooo," like that of the whirlwind, reflect the wailing call of the *la llorona* of Tony's dream:

> *La llorona* seeks the soul of Antonioooooooooo . . .
>
> (p. 24)

In the same dream, Tony hears his "mother moan and cry because with each turning of the sun her son [is] growing old . . ." (p. 24) On his first day of school Antonio awakens with a sick feeling in his stomach, both excited and sad because for the first time he will be away from the protection of his mother. As he enters the kitchen his mother smiles, then sweeps him into her arms sobbing, "My baby will be gone today." (p. 50) At Ultima's stern but gentle persistence, Antonio is separated from his mother, yet as he leaves, following the sisters Deborah and Theresa up the goat path, he hears his mother "cry" his name. Maria, as she prays around the Virgin's altar for Antonio and his three older brothers, is *la llorona*. On the return of Andrew, Eugene, and Leon from the war, Maria alternately sobs and prays until Gabriel complains, "Maria, . . . but we have prayed all night!" (p. 58) Mother and Virgin both assume the mournful aspect of *la llorona* in one of Antonio's dreams just prior to the three brothers' return:

> Virgen de Guadalupe, I heard my mother cry, return my sons to me.
>
> Your sons will return safely, a gentle voice answered.
>
> Mother of God, make my fourth son a priest.
>
> And I saw the virgin draped in the gown of night standing on the bright, horned moon of autumn, and she was in mourning for the fourth son.
>
> (p. 43)

Similarly, the *la llorona* motif is echoed in the tolling of the church bells and in the imagery of the mourning, lonely women as they are called to mass on the morning following Lupito's death. "Crying the knell of Lupito," the bell "tolled and drew to it the widows in black, the lonely, faithful women who came to pray for their men." (p. 32)

La llorona emerges in the patterns of imagery that surround the episode at Rosie's on the day of the Christmas pageant and of Narciso's death. The "single red light bulb" which shines at the porch door over the "snow-laden gate of the picket fence" is "like a beacon inviting weary travelers in from the storm." Light shines through the drawn shades, and from "somewhere in the house a faint melody" seeps out and is "lost in the wind." Antonio knows he must get home before the storm worsens, yet he is compelled to linger "at the gate of the evil women." The music and laughter intrigue him. His ears "explode with a ringing noise," and he is paralyzed to flight. (p. 155) Instead, he must remain to learn that he himself has lost his innocence. The cry of the sirens prevails over Andrew, too, as the red-painted woman calls him from the back of the house:

"Androoooooo. . . ."

(p. 156)

When Andrew is summoned by Narciso, it is the giggling girl, her voice "sweet with allurement" that holds Andrew back. He fails to assume the responsibility that would have meant help for Narciso. Instead he succumbs to the allure of the siren.

Wherever it emerges in the novel, the *la llorona* motif harbors ambivalence. *La llorona* invites with music and warmth, and she offers security. Yet, like the mermaid in the hidden lakes, *la llorona* threatens death. For Antonio, his mother offers warmth, fragrance, security. But his own maturity demands that he deny it. To succumb would mean the death of his own manhood and who, like the fate of William Blake's Thel, unwilling to accept the consequences of the generative life of experience, withdraws to an original state of primal innocence. Yet this world holds an even darker fate for her because it becomes at once prison and paradise, a state of natural innocence and a state of ignorance.[3] This is the choice Antonio must make. He moves from the fragrance and the warmth and the security of his mother's kitchen, from the reassurance of her call, out into the world of experience, the world of school and his companions.

Antonio is introduced into the inferno of school life by Red, who leads him on the first day into the dark, cavernous building, its radiators snapping with steam and its "strange, unfamiliar smells and sounds that seemed to gurgle from its belly." (p. 53) Antonio races the Kid and Time across the bridge to and from school as the years pass and he matures chronologically. With the tutoring of Samuel he learns of the Golden Carp which is to provide apocalyptical knowledge and understanding, an illumina-

tion which burdens him with doubt and responsibility. Cico leads Antonio to Narciso's magic garden where he tastes of the fruit—the golden carrot—and to El Rito Creek where he at last experiences the Golden Carp, the "sudden illumination of beauty and understanding," an understanding he anticipated but later failed to find in the ritual of the Holy Communion. Coincident with his vision of the carp, Antonio doubts his own Christian God when he suddenly realizes that Ultima's power had succeeded in curing his Uncle Lucas where the Christian God had failed.

Antonio sees the powers of good and evil contend in Ultima, who serves as his guide through life, and in the dark, diabolic Tenorio. He experiences the deaths of Lupito, of Narciso, and of the angelic and heretical Florence. He sees his brother Andrew deny his responsibility at the summons of the girl at Rosie's, of *la llorona*. Andrew remains to indulge in pleasure, yet the knowledge that he has failed in his responsibility to Narciso drives him, finally, away into the death, the world of lost wanderings, of his other brothers, Eugene and Leon.

The experience at Rosie's is equally ambivalent for Antonio. He is at once lured and repulsed. It marks for him the beginning of a ritual death as he becomes abruptly aware of his own loss of innocence.

I had seen evil, and so I carried the evil within me. . . . I had somehow lost my innocence and let sin enter into my soul, and the knowledge of God, the saving grace, was far away.

(p. 158)

The illness which follows is a "long night" as Ultima sits by "powerless in the face of death."

A long, dark night came upon me in which I sought the face of God, but I could not find Him. Even the Virgin and my Saint Anthony would not look at my face.

. . . In front of the dark doors of Purgatory my bleached bones were laid to rest.

(p. 167)

But, unlike Andrew's death, Antonio's experience at Rosie's becomes one that leads to death and ultimate rebirth. Antonio recovers from his illness, and though the events of the spring, of catechism and first communion, do not provide the enlightenment he finds with the carp, Antonio is a new man. His life has changed; he feels older. He faces directly the question of the existence of evil, and he is ready to accept his father's explanation that "most of the things we call evil are not evil at all; it is just that we don't understand those things and so we call them evil. And we fear evil only because we do not understand it." (p. 236) Antonio learns to accept the greater reality of life, that he is both Marez and Luna, that he does not have to choose one but can be both. He accepts his father's explanation that the understanding he failed to find in the Holy Communion will come with life. He comes to realize that one's dreams are "usually for a lost childhood." (p.

237) More importantly, he learns from Ultima that "the tragic consequences of life can be overcome by the magical strength that resides in the human heart." (p. 237)

Antonio spends the summer working on the farms with his uncles in El Puerto. Finally, as he struggles to get back to Guadalupe and his family to warn Ultima of Tenorio's threat when his second daughter dies, Antonio encounters *la llorona* once more:

> With darkness upon me I had to leave the brush and run up in the hills, just along the tree line. . . . Over my shoulder the moon rose from the east and lighted my way. Once I ran into a flat piece of bottom land, and what seemed solid earth by the light of the moon was a marshy quagmire. The wet quicksand sucked me down and I was almost to my waist before I squirmed loose. Exhausted and trembling I crawled onto solid ground. As I rested I felt the gloom of night settle on the river. The dark *presence* of the river was like a shroud, enveloping me, calling to me. The drone of the grillos and the sigh of the wind in the trees whispered the call of the soul of the river.
>
> Then I heard an owl cry its welcome to the night, and I was reminded again of my purpose. The owl's cry re-awakened Tenorio's threat . . .
>
> (p. 243–44)

Free of the call of *la llorona,* of the "dark *presence* of the river" which called to him, Antonio runs "with new resolution." He runs "to save Ultima" and "to preserve those moments when beauty mingled with sadness and flowed through [his] soul like the stream of time." Antonio leaves the river and runs across the llano feeling a new lightness, "like the wind" as his strides "carried [him] homeward." (p. 244) No longer does he feel the pain in his side, the thorns of the cactus or the needles of yucca that pierced his legs and feet. Yet Antonio knows his childhood is over as the report of Tenorio's rifle shatters it "into a thousand fragments." (p. 245)

Antonio has come home to himself. He has eluded the death call of *la llorona,* and as he buries the owl, Ultima's spirit, he takes on the responsibility of the future in which he knows he must "build [his] own dream out of those things which were so much a part of [his] childhood." (p. 248) Antonio has avoided annihilation on the sheer cliffs of the Wandering Rocks—the fate of his brothers—and he has moved through the narrow strait and evaded the menace of Scylla and Charybdis as he comes to face the reality of his manhood.

Notes

1. Rudolfo A. Anaya, *Bless Me, Ultima* (Berkeley, Calif.: Quinto Sol, 1972), p. 23. All quotations from *Bless Me, Ultima* are from this edition; page numbers will henceforth be cited in parentheses within the text.

2. Joseph Campbell, *The Masks of God: Primitive Mythology,* notes the association between the water im-

age in mythology and "goddesses, mermaids, witches, and sirens," who may represent either the "life-threatening" or "life-furthering" aspect of the water. The use of water imagery to represent the theme of rebirth, Campbell says, is a "mythological universal" imprinted at the moment of birth when "the congestion of blood and sense, of suffocation experienced by the infant before its lungs commence to operate give rise to a brief seizure of terror, the physical effects of which . . . tend to occur, more or less strongly, whenever there is an abrupt moment of fright. . . . The birth trauma, as an archetype of transformation, floods with considerable emotional effect the brief moment of loss of security and threat of death that accompanies any crisis of radical change. In the imagery of mythology and religion this birth (or more often rebirth) theme is extremely prominent; in fact every threshold passage—not only this from the darkness of the womb to the light of the sun, but also those from childhood to adult life and from the light of the world to whatever mystery of darkness may lie beyond the portal of death—is comparable to a birth and has been ritually represented, practically everywhere, through an imagery of re-entry into the womb." (New York: Viking Press, 1959), pp. 61–62.

3. See Harold Bloom's commentary on "The Book of Thel" in *The Poetry and Prose of William Blake,* ed. David V. Erdman, (Garden City, N.Y.: Doubleday, 1965), pp. 807–08.

Antonio Márquez (essay date 1982)

SOURCE: "The Achievement of Rudolfo A. Anaya," in *The Magic of Words: Rudolfo A. Anaya and His Writings,* edited by Paul Vassallo, University of New Mexico Press, 1982, pp. 33–52.

[*In the following essay, Márquez discusses Anaya's contribution to Chicano literature and provides an overview of the central themes, artistic aims, and critical reception of* Bless Me, Ultima, Heart of Aztlán, *and* Tortuga.]

The homage to Rudolfo Anaya comes at an appropriate time. Recently, *The New York Times Book Review* belatedly granted him national status. Moreover, Anaya's work is on the verge of international recognition. The growing interest in Anaya and other Chicano writers in Latin America and Europe, attended by the expected translations of **Bless Me, Ultima** into German and Polish, opens new vistas for Chicano literature. Just as **Bless Me, Ultima** (and Tomás Rivera's *Y No Se Lo Tragó La Tierra*) formed the vanguard of modern Chicano prose, Anaya's work is at the vanguard that promises to liberate Chicano literature from the confines of "ethnic" or "regionalist" literature. It is befitting for Anaya to receive the honor and the task of leading Chicano literature into the canons of world literature. He is the most acclaimed and the most popular and universal Chicano writer, and one of the most influential voices in contemporary Chicano literature.

Anaya's literary career has been energetically diverse: novelist, essayist, folklorist, short-story writer, and playwright. Not slighting this admirable diversity, Anaya's major contribution has been as a novelist, and his reputation and achievement largely rest on *Bless Me, Ultima, Heart of Aztlán,* and *Tortuga.* Therefore, this survey focuses on Anaya's novels. It is a conspectus that will exclude critical examination of the plots, characters, folklore, legends, extensive symbolism, and other particulars that animate his novels. An accompanying bibliography notes the numerous articles, theses, and dissertations that have provided exegeses on these aspects of Anaya's fiction. In fact, concomitant with his role as the most acclaimed Chicano writer, his work (especially *Bless Me, Ultima*) has inspired the largest body of criticism in contemporary Chicano literature. This essay, then, is a general assessment of Anaya's position in Chicano literature, the critical reception of his work, and the nature of his achievement and reputation.

It was *Bless Me, Ultima* (1972) that vaulted Anaya to a stellar position in Chicano literature and a significant place in American literature. The subsequent novels, *Heart of Aztlán* (1976) and *Tortuga* (1979), solidified his reputation. To assess the significance of Anaya's work one must first consider its place in Chicano literary history. The appearance of *Bless Me, Ultima* was auspicious and rather startling. It stood in stark contrast to the shrill polemics that emerged from the political cauldron of the 1960s and attempted to pass for literature. *Bless Me, Ultima,* a muted and subtle work that dissuaded politics, projected reams of symbols and archetypes, and fused realism and fantasy, demonstrated that it was a painstakingly crafted novel. There appeared in the often woolly perimeters of Chicano fiction a singularly accomplished novel. To appreciate this accomplishment one only has to view his predecessors. José Antonio Villarreal's *Pocho,* Raymond Barrio's *The Plum Plum Pickers,* and Richard Vásquez's *Chicano,* for example, were important literary expressions of Chicano life, but they were marred as novels. All too often stilted and amateurish, they lacked novelistic invention or artistry. In the early 1970s two works appeared that marked a significant break from formulaic "social protest literature." These two works, Rivera's *Y No Se Lo Tragó La Tierra* and Anaya's *Bless Me, Ultima,* initiated the maturity and diversification of contemporary Chicano fiction. Quite different in theme and form, they were distinguished by their structural complexity and innovative exploration of Chicano life. Informed with the experimental techniques of William Faulkner and especially of Juan Rulfo, Rivera brought an eviscerating realism and existentialist thematics to Chicano fiction. On the other hand, Anaya's novel opened new vistas with its richly poetic vein and mythic configurations. Equally important, they brought a greater honesty and authenticity to the portrayal of Chicano life and countered stereotypic literature on the Chicano. *Bless*

Me, Ultima forcefully dramatized that "Chicanos are not simple, fun-loving, tradition-bound, lovable non-achievers or other mythical stereotypes such as those produced by John Steinbeck, but, rather, complex individuals like those found in any society."[1] In a similar vein, Daniel Testa, who has provided the most astute criticism on *Bless Me, Ultima,* concluded his critical study with praise for Anaya's large accomplishment and promising talent: "As a creative writer and spokesman for the Hispano-mestizo minority, who for too long has struggled in the backwaters of American life, Anaya gives every indication of invigorating the cultural growth of his people and verifying the existence of an inner force and power in their daily lives."[2]

Although some critics were irritated by its "affectations" and "artistic naivete," *Bless Me, Ultima* was generally well-received and enthusiastically acclaimed in some quarters. It was deservedly praised for its fine storytelling, superb craftsmanship, and the artistic and philosophic dignity that it brought to Chicano literature. However, the joy of discovery often took injudicious turns; some critics celebrated *Bless Me, Ultima* as "an American classic" and carelessly and erroneously placed Anaya among Faulkner and Joyce. Fortunately, most assessments of *Bless Me, Ultima* were sensible and gave the work and its author their due worth. Martin Bucco exemplifies the judicious criticism:

> To be sure, if Anaya is not a world voice, he is at least a valuable new one, gifted and youthful, his creative consciousness suggesting, establishing, creating . . . the serious Mexican-American regional novel need not atrophy simply because it does not coincide with mass taste or with the complex art of Joyce, Gide, and Faulkner.[3]

The most common refrain was that *Bless Me, Ultima* "achieved something that few pieces of Chicano literature have; that is, simply, that it stands by itself as a novel, with the 'Chicano' added later. . . ."[4] The emphasis on *Bless Me, Ultima*'s primary achievement as a novel and its secondary trait of ethnicity is an appropriate criterion. Ultimately, the novel's success rests on Anaya's imaginative mythopoesis and his careful and loving attention to the craft of fiction. The latter quality leads to a larger issue. Anaya from the start has seen himself, and rightly so, as an artist. He has vigorously made clear that he is not an apologist, polemicist, or literary ideologue, and he has frequently spoken out against the "politicization" of art: "I think any kind of description or dictation to the artist as a creative person will ruin his creative impulse. . . . The best writers will deal with social responsibility and the welfare of the people indirectly—as opposed to direct political statement or dogma."[5]

Anaya's aestheticism and his avoidance of doctrinaire politics have been the major targets of his detractors. And his detractors, mostly academic critics and ideologues of the marxist stripe, found ample ground in *Heart of Aztlán* for their contentions. The general attack is that Anaya's archaism and myth-making are vague abstractions that have no bearing on existing and pressing issues. In a recent panel discussion with other Chicano writers and academics, Anaya offered this explanation of his mythopoesis:

> I define myth as the truth in the heart. It is the truth that you have carried, that we as human beings have carried all of our history, going back to the cave, pushing it back to the sea. It seems to me that what happens at a certain time with people is that in order to come to a new conscious awareness they need to separate necessarily from a social, political context.[6]

Anaya subsequently took the critical brunt of the colloquium. One participant voiced a common complaint about Anaya's fiction: "I think that his idea of truth in the heart is very, very abstract." Another participant was rankled by the lack of practicality in Anaya's myth-making: ". . . looking back to the man with ultimate wisdom . . . won't answer the problem that's facing us directly and that's never answered." Alurista, a major Chicano poet and Anaya's most testy adversary in this exchange, questioned Anaya's archaism and concluded: "Necesitamos un mito más racional que confronte las necesidades contemporáneas, y que confronte el enemigo del espíritu del hombre [We need a more rational myth that will confront contemporary necessities, and that will confront the enemy of the human spirit.]"[7] This confrontation is used as an example of the numerous occasions where Anaya has been taken to task and prompted to defend his work. One can plausibly assume that Anaya by now is weary of these polemical confrontations and indifferent to the criticism that argues that he has failed to become a "committed" and "relevant" Chicano writer.

The controversy found specific grounds in *Heart of Aztlán.* The critical reception was divided and often delusive: its champions were charmed by the mythic substructure and poetic correspondences, but ignored its technical discrepancies; its detractors damned the confusing mixture of politics and metaphysics, but ignored the frequent moments of lyrical and poignant introspection. Some readers cloyed the novel and made heady assessments: "In *Heart of Aztlán* a prose-writer with the soul of a poet, and a dedication to his calling that only the greatest artists ever sustain—is on an important track, the right one, the only one."[8] On the other hand, some critics were vexed by the novel's diffused narrative line and vague morality:

> Can insight into the existence of a spiritual bond destroy oppression and end exploitation? Can the feeling of a shared communal soul destroy the chains of steel that bind the people? Is there not some other ingredient necessary in addition to a spiritual feeling of love? Has contact with the myths provided a real tool to correct social injustice?[9]

There was much blather over Anaya's exotic metaphysics and fuzzy political notions, but very few readers pinpointed the chief failing of *Heart of Aztlán.* The crux of the matter was suggested by Bruce-Novoa in a brief preface to an interview with Anaya: "*Ultima* produced expectations that *Heart of Aztlán* did not satisfy. Not that the introduction of blatantly political topics is a fault in and of itself—no, it is a matter of the craftsmanship, not of the themes, and *Heart,* for whatever reason, is less polished, less accomplished."[10] Precisely, the novel's detriment was its lack of craftsmanship. *Heart of Aztlán* stands out as a blemish in the Anaya canon because its disjointed and amorphous style contrasts with the meticulous, controlled, and carefully executed prose of Anaya's other works. Ostensibly, it was an experiment that sought to combine mythic elements and a socioeconomic theme. It attempts to balance and form a correlation between the myth of Aztlán (presented in numerous symbols and archetypes) and barrio life in Albuquerque in the 1950s (presented in realistic details of socioeconomic conditions and the labor struggles of the time). But it is a literary mixed-bag rather than a cohesive work of fiction. Apparently, Anaya placed himself in a difficult novelistic stratagem in trying to work two discordant plots and themes. Anaya has commented on the technical problems involved in transforming Clemente from a drunken wastrel to a spiritual visionary that leads a labor struggle armed with love and mysticism:

> It's most difficult, because he's caught up in a very realistic setting and then how in hell do you take him into his visionary trip that I attempted to do with Clemente. I suppose I could have done it in a dream, I could have done it in some kind of revelation, and I chose to do it instead through Crispín and the old woman, the keeper of the rock.[11]

Anaya's telling comments on the "visionary trip" that leads to the novel's rather forced resolution suggest that Anaya was not confident or totally clear about the execution of the novel. Culling this candid moment of autocriticism, Anaya offered a more telling admission that shed light on his most common liability: his occasional rhetorical excesses and cutesy mannerisms. He explains his playful manner:

> I get a kick out of doing things that I know people will respond to, especially critics. In *Heart of Aztlán* I did something that was really too cutesy . . . 'The sun sucked the holy waters of the river, and the turtle-bowl sky ripped open with dark thunder and fell upon the land. South of Aztlán the golden bear drank his fill and tasted the sweet fragrance of the drowned man's blood. That evening he bedded down with the turtle's sisters and streaked their virgin robes with virgin blood. . . . Oh wash my song into the dead man's soul, he cried, and soak his marrow dry.' That's part of that. I get carried away.[12]

Apart from the convoluted narration, Anaya touches on a pointed issue. All too often, he is "cutesy" and "gets carried away" in purple prose.

The critical reception of *Tortuga* is less defined. At the present, the criticism on Anaya's third novel consists of a scattering of reviews. So far the reception of *Tortuga* has been favorable. The cursory reviews have noted the strong narrative line, the striking realism, and the novel's powerful theme. However, the connecting elements in the trilogy and Anaya's maturation have not been considered. Foremost, there is an integrity and cohesiveness to *Tortuga* that were lacking in *Heart of Aztlán*. Apart from containing the rudiments of Anaya's fiction—a mythopoeic cluster of images and symbols, it discloses sharper insight and accommodation of realistic situations. Notably, Anaya returns to first-person narrative point of view, which seems to be more conformable to his style. We can gather that Anaya in *Heart of Aztlán* was stretching out and experimenting with new ways of telling a story. The return to the narrative technique of *Bless Me, Ultima* makes *Tortuga* a smooth and lucid novel which is free of the vagaries that made *Heart of Aztlán* less than successful. It can also be noted that Anaya returns to the exploration of "memory and imagination." These two elements gave *Bless Me, Ultima* a magical resonance. *Tortuga* achieves a similar effect with its Proustian overture and memory-laden images: "I awoke from a restless sleep. For a moment I couldn't remember where I was . . . Upon waking it was always the same; I tried to move but the paralysis held me firmly in its grip." (1) And later: "The words struck chords and a remembrance of things past would flood over me and in my imagination I would live in other times and other places. . . ." (54)

Tortuga, which has neither achieved the popularity and critical acclaim of *Bless Me, Ultima,* nor received the brickbats leveled at *Heart of Aztlán,* is in several respects Anaya's most accomplished novel. True, there are still rhetorical excesses and inconsistencies in the lyrical voice. When measured and used to enlarge a character's sensibility, the lyricism is quite effective: "I followed her gaze and through her eyes I saw the beauty she described, the beauty I had not seen until that moment. The drabness of winter melted in the warm, spring light, and I saw the electric acid of life run through the short green fuses of the desert plants and crack through the dark buds to brush with strokes of lime the blooming land." (166) Here Anaya magically employs his poetic gift to catch an expressive moment. In the lesser moments, the lyrical manner is too self conscious and rhapsodic. For example, at one point Anaya indulges in hackneyed Homeric metaphors:

> The daughter of the sun awoke to weave her blanket with pastel threads. Her soft, coral fingers worked swiftly to weave the bits of turquoise blue and mother of pearl into the silver sky. She had but a moment in which to weave the tapestry that covered her nakedness, because behind her the sun trumpeted, awoke roaring alive with fire and exploded into the sky, filling the desert with glorious light and scattering the mist of the river and the damp humours of the night. Dawn blushed and fled as the sun straddled the mountain, and the mountain groaned under the welcomed light. The earth trembled at the sight.
>
> (27)

At such moments, one wishes that Anaya had been more restrained. Happily, such passages are few and the greater part of the narrative is enriched with vibrant lyricism.

Moreover, *Tortuga* is the product of Anaya's increasing prowess as a novelist, and one can conjecture that Anaya esteems it as his best work. His third novel demonstrates, notwithstanding the discrepancy noted above, that Anaya has conscientiously worked at his craft. In brief, it is a more disciplined and carefully executed novel. And it presents a stronger correspondence to the "real-world" of human suffering and failure. The intention was stated even before the novel was finished: ". . . It will deal with the kind of crippling of life that we have created in our society, where love is no longer the predominant feeling that we have for one another. Once love is not the feeling that dictates our social interaction with each other, then we cripple people."[13] *Tortuga* intensely dramatizes this condition. The novel is set in a children's hospital, and it relentlessly and graphically describes horrible diseases, amputations, and the nerve-shattering cries of pain and despair. Appropriately, it also extensively explores the battered psyches of society's "throwaway children." By far, it is Anaya's most sober work and it discloses a compelling tragic sense. Whereas the tragic sense was often weakened by obtrusive sentimentality in the earlier novels, in *Tortuga* it is sustained and rivets a truth about the unconscionable disposal of human beings. This is not to suggest that the tragic sense overwhelms the novel and renders it a dark and pessimistic work. To be clarified later, Anaya's mythopoesis and his faith in the regenerative power of love deny victory to the forces of death. Rather, it is meant to emphasize Anaya's large compassion for human suffering and to credit his moral vision—which refuses to tolerate the absence of love and humaneness in the world.

Mythopoesis—myth and the art of myth-making—is the crux of Anaya's philosophical and artistic vision. Precisely, Anaya's archetypal imagination is rooted in an archaism that reveres the wisdom of the past and sees this ancient wisdom as a means toward the spiritual fulfillment of humanity. It is also informed by the conviction that myth is an eternal reservoir that nourishes the most creative and the most universal art. Anaya's aesthetic credo is in accord with Northrop Frye's distinction that "myth is a form of verbal art, and belongs to the world of art. Unlike science, it deals, not with the world that man contemplates, but with the world that man creates."[14] Anaya, well-versed in mythic literature and the theory of archetypes, has repeatedly defended the validity of myth and archetypes:

> One way I have of looking at my own work . . . is through a sense that I have about primal images, primal imageries. A sense that I have about the archetypal, about what we once must have known collectively. What we all share is a kind of collective memory. . . . It simply says that there was more harmony, there was more a sense that we knew we are dust. That we had been created from it, that we were in touch with it, that we danced on it, and the dust swirled around us, and it grew the very kind of basic stuff that we need to exist. That's what I'm after. My relationship to it.[15]

Anaya's comment, of course, echoes Jung's "collective unconscious," and there are striking similarities to Jung's thoughts in *Modern Man in Search of a Soul*:

. . . there is a thinking in primordial images—in symbols which are older than historical man; which have been ingrained in him from earliest times, and, eternally living, outlasting all generations, still make up the groundwork of the human psyche. It is only possible to live the fullest life when we are in harmony with these symbols; wisdom is a return to them.[16]

Similarly, Anaya shares with Jung, Mircea Eliade, and other contemporary exponents of mythopoetics a concern for the demythicization of human consciousness and the fragmentation of the human psyche. Anaya gives emphasis to terms like *polarity, duality,* and *dichotomy* in describing the spiritual and psychic debility which he sees as characteristic of modern existence:

What did archaic men do that we cannot do? Archaic man could communicate with both worlds. Where does dualism and polarity come from? We can say it comes from social reality and the dialectic. I disagree. I say it comes from our spiritual self, a disharmonizing force. Our civilizing and socializing influence has made us not as unified, not as harmonious, as archaic man. To go back and get in touch, and to become more harmonious, we go back to the unconscious and we bring out all of the symbols and archetypals that are available to all people.[17]

Anaya's conviction that harmony and the reconciliation of elemental forces are needed for spiritual fulfillment leads to the holistic philosophy that forms the thematic core of his three novels. His trio of seers—Ultima in *Bless Me, Ultima,* Crispín in *Heart of Aztlán,* and Salomón in *Tortuga*—are agents of reconciliation and harmony. The oneness of things is repeatedly stated in multiple images and thematic motifs. In *Bless Me, Ultima,* a parable of good and evil in which discordant elements create dissension and violence, harmony is the greatest good. It is noteworthy that Anaya, through mythopoesis, encompasses the particular and the universal. In Antonio, the narrator and central character of the novel, Anaya projects the immemorial struggle for identity and self-knowledge. Antonio endures the rite of passage that takes him from childhood to adolescence, from innocence to incipient knowledge, and into the complex world of human affairs. His passage leads him to experience *la tristeza de la vida,* the truism that human existence is often a sad and tragic enterprise. The spiritual source that enables Antonio to overcome the disillusionment and the tragedies of life is Ultima. She brings to Antonio a holistic creed and the ultimate truth (the pun on *última,* the last and the ultimate of things, is charming and unobtrusive) that the greatest wisdom resides in the human heart. In a dream sequence, Ultima whispers to Antonio the direction that he must take toward true knowledge: "You have been seeing only parts, she finished, and not looking beyond into the great cycle that binds all." (112) Through Ultima's teachings and example, Antonio finds the moral and spiritual strength to reconcile the familial differences, the religious contraries, and the other polarities that serve as the novel's thematic conflict. The dichotomies are unified and the narrative converges in ringing affirmation: ". . . I made strength from everything that had happened to me, so that in the end even the final tragedy could not defeat me. And that is what Ultima tried to teach me, that the tragic consequences of life can be overcome by the magical strength that resides in the human heart." (237) The novel ends with a celebration of love—the unifying principle of human existence.

The conclusion of *Bless Me, Ultima* is unabashedly sentimental, and introduces an ethical prescription that is reiterated and intensified in *Heart of Aztlán* and *Tortuga.* Starting with the novel's title, *Heart of Aztlán* works the same thematic metaphor to describe the inner force that will lead to the discovery of an ancient and profound truth. The quest for *Aztlán* is, in effect, a search for the peace and harmony that have been lost throughout history and that loss has removed Chicano people from their identity and purpose. The pristine truth is that the Chicano can *return* to Aztlán; it has always existed, but people became blind to its magical presence. In an epiphany (one of Anaya's favorite devices), Clemente, like Antonio in *Bless Me, Ultima,* discovers the mythic power of Aztlán:

Time stood still, and in that enduring moment he felt the rhythm of the heart of Aztlán beat to the measure of his own heart. Dreams and visions became reality, and reality was but the thin substance of myth and legends. A joyful power coursed from the dark womb-heart of the earth into his soul and he cried out I AM AZTLAN!

(131)

True to the holistic concept that nerves Anaya's fiction, Clemente sees his place in the cosmic scheme of things and unifies the elements that previously had created alienation and confusion. Again it leads to the recognition of the superior force of love and the rejection of hatred and violence: "The real fire of heaven is not the fire of violence, it is the fire of love!" (207) The sentimental conclusion was effective in *Bless Me, Ultima,* but in *Heart of Aztlán* it is close to being a platitude. And here is where Anaya risked critical fire in suggesting that love is the answer to the oppression and injustice suffered by Chicanos.

Laced with mythopoeic images and symbols, *Tortuga* works similar metaphysical and ethical themes. Centered on a sixteen-year-old boy nicknamed "Tortuga"—due to his crippling paralysis and the "turtle cast" which he has to wear, the novel amplifies his anguish and alienation as he bitterly turns away from life and loses faith in divine providence—and himself. The resurrecting agent is Salomón, a seer and mythic figure who discloses *the path of light* (the way to reconciling wisdom and the spiritual fulfillment of the individual). Although he is a terminally-ill patient (and dies like Ultima in a similarly poignant scene), he is an abundant reservoir of spirituality and is the force that leads Tortuga to the recognition of life's value. He instructs Tortuga to appreciate and affirm the beauty of life: ". . . life is sacred, yes, even in the middle of this wasteland and in the darkness of our wards, life is sacred. . . ." (42) Like his predecessors, Salomón embodies a holistic metaphysic and celebrates the oneness of life: ". . . we're all bound together, one great force binds us all, it's the light of the sun that binds all life, the mountain and the desert, the plains and the sea." (102) The expected truism that love is the force that binds human life is dramatically (perhaps melodramatically) announced: "That's what Salomón had said. That love was the only faith which gave meaning to our race across the beach. The path of the sun was the path of love. I needed to love!" (150) Culling tropes from Eliot and other modern poets who have metaphorically described the spiritual sterility of our times, Anaya dovetails the narrative to Tortuga's realization that Salomón had left him a legacy of regenerative mythopoesis: "We must create out of our ashes. Our own hero must be born out of this wasteland, like the phoenix bird of the desert he must rise again from the ashes of our withered bodies. . . . He must walk in the path of the sun . . . and he shall sing the songs of the sun." (160) Tortuga nobly meets the task. Like Antonio in **Bless Me, Ultima,** he becomes a singer of songs; he will become a poet that will transmit the magical wisdom inherited from Ultima, Crispín, and Salomón. And, of course, he will sing songs of love. The concluding sentences of the novel describe Tortuga's homeward bound journey. His singing voice fills the bus and streams across the majestic expanse of the New Mexico desert. And Salomón's loving encouragement reverberates across the closing page: "Sing a song of love, Tortuga! Oh yes, sing of love!"

The avenue for Anaya's accomplishment in expanding and invigorating the Chicano novel has been myth and the mythopoeic art. Here lies the core of his novelistic invention. His archetypal imagination richly mines indigenous materials, fuses them with poetic images and symbols, and connects the past and the present to make something new from the old. On a smaller scale, Anaya possesses the gift and achieves the art credited to one of the twentieth-century exemplars of mythopoesis, Thomas Mann: "In a narrative tone that recalls the past, he reveals what we find disturbing in the present. He is at once old and new, and his gift is the mingling of the mythic and the present moment."[18]

At one point in **Tortuga,** Salomón explains the mythologizing behind his stories: "Each carries a new story, but all these stories are bound to the same theme . . . *life is sacred.*" (42) Similarly, each of Anaya's novels presents a new story, but they are bound by one central theme: life is sacred and the love of life is the greatest human accomplishment. Anaya cherishes the kinder moments of the human race and sings a song that seeks to bind humanity. There is much truth in his song, and there is a largeness of heart in the man and his work. Anaya's work is eloquent testament that art can teach us to recognize our humanity. It is an exemplary achievement.

Notes

1. Rolando Hinojosa, "Mexican-American Literature: Toward an Identification," *Books Abroad,* 49, No. 3 (Summer 1975): 422–30.

2. Daniel Testa, "Extensive/Intensive Dimensionality in Anaya's *Bless Me, Ultima,*" *Latin American Literary Review,* V, No. 10 (Spring–Summer 1977): 70–78.

3. Martin Bucco, "A Review of *Bless Me, Ultima,*" *Southwestern American Literature,* 2, No. 3 (Winter 1972): 153–54.

4. Dyan Donnelly, "Finding a Home in the World," *Bilingual Review,* 1, No. 1 (January–April 1974): 113–18.

5. David Johnson and David Apodaca, "Myth and the Writer: A Conversation with Rudolfo Anaya," *New America,* 3, No. 3 (Spring 1979): 76–85.

6. "Mitólogos y Mitómanos," *Maize: Xicano Art and Literature Notebooks,* 4, Nos. 3–4 (Spring–Summer 1981): 6–23.

7. Ibid., passim.

8. Karl Kopp, "A Review of *Heart of Aztlán,*" *La Confluencia,* 1, Nos. 3–4 (July 1977): 62–63.

9. María López Hoffman, "Myth and Reality: *Heart of Aztlán,*" *De Colores,* 5, Nos. 1–2 (1980): 111–14.

10. Bruce-Novoa, *Chicano Authors: Inquiry by Interview* (Austin: University of Texas Press, 1980), p. 184.

11. "Myth and the Writer: A Conversation with Rudolfo Anaya," 82.

12. Ibid., 83.

13. Ibid., 84.

14. Northrop Frye, "Myth, Fiction and Displacement," *Myth and Myth Making,* ed. Henry A. Murry (New York: George Braziller, 1960), p. 164.

15. "Myth and the Writer: A Conversation with Rudolfo Anaya," 79.

16. C. G. Jung, *Modern Man in Search of a Soul,* trans. W. S. Dell and Cary F. Baynes (New York: Harcourt, Brace & Co., 1947), pp. 129–30.

17. "Mitólogos y Mitómanos," 12.

18. Wright Morris, *About Fiction* (New York: Harper & Row, 1975), p. 145.

Rudolfo Anaya with John Crawford (interview date May 1986)

SOURCE: "Rudolfo Anaya," in *This is about Vision: Interviews with Southwestern Writers,* edited by William Balassi, John F. Crawford, and Annie O. Eysturoy, University of New Mexico Press, 1990, pp. 83–93.

[*In the following interview, originally conducted in May 1986, Anaya comments on his formative influences, the development of Chicano literature, his interest in mythol-*

ogy, and the problems of cultural identity and political consciousness in Bless Me, Ultima, Heart of Aztlán, *and* Tortuga.]

Rudolfo Anaya—novelist, short story writer, oral historian, editor, and college professor—has spoken frequently of his relationship to the *llano,* the harsh rangeland of eastern New Mexico, and his role as a groundbreaking Chicano novelist of the 1970s. Born in 1937, he grew up in Santa Rosa, New Mexico, where he attended school through the eighth grade. He moved with his parents to Albuquerque to complete his schooling at Washington Junior High and Albuquerque High School (1956), and then went on to the University of New Mexico, where he received a B.A. and M.A. in English literature. After graduation he wrote laboriously. He borrowed the backdrop of his best-known novel, **Bless Me, Ultima** (1972), from his early years in Santa Rosa. "Part of the land structure, the river, the llano, the hills, are there. Some of the church, the school, and the bridge is there. It seemed the major symbology that I work with was there but it had to be extracted, distilled through the creative process." Hailed as one of the first major Chicano novelists, he went on to write two more books in succession: **Heart of Aztlán** (1976), a story of a family's hard migration from the llano to Albuquerque, and **Tortuga** (1979), the tale of the recovery of a paralyzed boy in a children's hospital deep in the desert. He also began to produce an ongoing series of anthologies, marking him as uniquely generous towards younger writers. He still lives in Albuquerque, where he is professor of English at the University of New Mexico and edits the literary magazine *Blue Mesa Review.* This interview with John Crawford took place in his office in May 1986.

[Anaya:] One of the most interesting experiences about coming to Albuquerque in the fifties was coming from a very small rural town into a big city *barrio* and being thrown into a completely different life-style. Recently, while attending the Writers of the Purple Sage Conference, it occurred to me that almost every writer there had shared a similar experience. No one lives in a small town any more; nearly all of us are city writers. Although I had all my upbringing in that small town, the majority of my life has been spent in the big city now. That's kind of shocking—we write about our roots that are close to the land, and then we get slapped with this new reality.

[*Crawford:*] *In your novels there's a double move, from the llano to the small towns and then to the big city.*

I think it's a progression that has happened in New Mexico. Historically, after World War II you have that exodus from the small towns into the metropolitan areas, especially from the Mexican working community. The new professions were being opened up, the GI Bill was sending some of the veterans to the university, and my writing reflects that historical pattern.

In **Heart of Aztlán** *it sounds like the small factories were opening up in New Mexico and they were exploiting cheap labor where they could find it, and that would be a reason also.*

Absolutely.

One particular way I remember you writing about the space you grew up in had to do with interior space: the public library in Santa Rosa.

I would visit it periodically, starting at an early age, when I was in grade school. It was a little one-room library actually placed on top of the fire house on the first floor, where there was an old beaten up fire truck used on a volunteer basis when there was a fire in the town. We climbed up those rickety steps to the little room that was the library. That interests me too, you know, looking back at what was formative in my love of books.

In your novels the formative influences seem to be the figures who represent wisdom and knowledge, like Ultima and Crispin. Were there real people like that in your life who would serve such a function, or are those characters a sort of metaphor or composite?

I think it was a little bit of each. In our Hispanic culture there is a great deal of respect given to older people—and growing up in the forties as I did, the relationships that we had with older people were ones of trust. We listened to what they said and we learned from them. And there were specific people that I knew and held in awe. These fabulous *vaqueros* would come in from the llano and my father or brothers and I would visit them; to me, they were almost mythological figures, bigger than life. I think I felt the same way about teachers, because it was normal in our culture to be taught by anyone who was older and to give him or her respect. So when I came to write my novels, which basically have to do with a search for meaning or an archetypal journey, the person who can guide the hero turns out to be the older person not only out of the structure of myth as we know it but out of my background, out of my life. Those older people played very important roles. We believed that *curanderas* could cure; we saw them do it. We believed that there were evil powers that came to be represented by witches, because we lived in the universe where we saw those powers work.

And also that things were animated with life, like Tortuga the mountain. There were places that had power.

Most definitely. I think it's Clemente in **Heart of Aztlán** who recalls, "I remember there were times and certain places in the llano where I grew up where I would stand at this place and have a feeling of elation, a feeling of flying"—that's interesting, because there are *cuentos* or folk tales where you get these little stories about people who can fly—so in your mind you think, where does this power come from? Is it the power of imagination that we as a communal group are given by those older, wiser people, or can it actually be? So it was very interesting to deal with the power that the earth has to animate us—we *are* animated by the power of the earth—it is in Native American terms our Mother—it nurtures us, it gives us spirit and sustenance, and I guess if we're attuned enough or sensitive enough it can give us different *kinds* of powers. And so, coming out of that kind of complex universe where I grew up thinking of all these places, the river and the hills, having this life to them, this animation, it was very good not only for my growing up but for the imagination, getting fed by that very spiritual process that was in the natural world around me.

That must have come to you first in the cuentos *themselves, the stories you would have heard while growing up. When did you start taking an interest in myth outside your own culture—was that in college—and where did this interest lead you?*

It was probably when I was an undergraduate here at UNM. We were guided to read Greek mythology. I wasn't really making the connections because I was looking at it as stories that had to do with another time and place. I think it wasn't until I turned more toward Native American mythology that I began to see that there are these points of reference that world myths have, that somehow speak to the center of our being, and connect us—to other people, to the myth, to the story, and beyond that to the historic process, to the communal group.

You have a way of making the myths take on very specific roles in the novels. I'm thinking of the incredible way that the mountain and the boy interplay at the beginning of **Tortuga,** *where the mountain actually moves and something in the boy moves. It must have taken a great deal of trial and error to find out artistic ways to make the myths connect up with the plots of the stories you were working. They seem highly integrated, in* **Tortuga** *especially.*

I would hope that by **Tortuga** they would seem integrated, because it was my third novel and I had been consumed by that process long enough, and possibly also had learned a little bit about how to write a novel.

I have been told, when I travel around the country and read, that there haven't been that many American writers interested in the role of myth and in making myth work in contemporary settings—but I think now we see more and more writers doing that. All the Native American writers tend to do that, fuse their sense of myth into their stories but at least for awhile it's been rather new to people.

The other thing that people seem to remark on is that not too many writers are lyrical novelists—you know, **Ultima** opens with a great deal of lyricism, a song of invocation almost, if not to the Muse then to the Earth, because Antonio says "In the beginning she opened my eyes and then I could see the beauty of my landscape, my llano, the river, the earth around us."[1] There are other examples in American literature when that happens, but certainly it's been one of my preoccupations. I think the sense of diction and syntax and rhythms of language that come out of having grown up in a Spanish-speaking world, and the act of transferring that to English, creates a "fresh ripple" in people's sensibilities as they read this new language, this

conversion of Hispanic language and world view into English. They may be a little shocked at the onset, but most people who get past it find it's refreshing, it's new.

I was especially struck by the freshness of the language in the Christmas play scene in **Ultima** *and when the children go to the theater in* **Tortuga**—*partly, I think, because these are scenes of rebellion against the norms of authority and partly because these are children in their spontaneity. There is such vitality in these scenes, where one set of cultural and social expectations crosses another. I suppose when you were writing* **Ultima** *there wasn't much like that in prose, even in Chicano prose.*

No, there wasn't—actually, I had read absolutely no Chicano prose during all my school years, including my university years. There were a few novels out there, and I suppose if you were into research you could have found diaries and newspapers, or in folklore you could have read the *cuentos,* but contemporary Chicano prose wasn't born until the mid-sixties during the Chicano movement, and so I think in a sense what we did in the sixties was to create the model itself, or as I have phrased it elsewhere, we set about to build a house and in the sixties we built a foundation. From that comes what we're seeing now in the eighties, an incredible amount of production and writing and unique forms and styles of writing. But all of that was new; it was new to me. In fact, in the sixties when I first began to work, I used Anglo American writers as role models. But I really couldn't get my act together until I left them behind. They had a lot to teach me and I don't underestimate that—you're learning whether you're reading a comic book or Hemingway or Shakespeare or Cervantes—but I couldn't tell my story in their terms. And it wasn't until I said to myself, let me shift for myself, let me go stand on my earth, coming out of my knowledge, and tell the story then and there—that's where Ultima came in. She opened my eyes as she opens Antonio's eyes at the beginning of the book, for the first time; so I sat down to write the story **Bless Me, Ultima,** thinking in Spanish though I wrote it in English. And it worked, because I was creating what to me was a reflection of that real universe that I knew was there.

It seems tremendously integrated—not only as to myth and plot, as we were just discussing, but the style. I know you said you put it through several drafts; it looks as if it just sprang out of heaven that way. That must have taken an enormous amount of work.

At least seven drafts *is* a lot of work. And then there is a concern for what you just said, that integration, that consistency that you don't want to give up in any one place, and a kind of conscious/subconscious working and interrelating of the myths and the symbols so that they all make a consistent pattern, like weaving a beautiful Navajo rug, you know? It's consistent because it reflects not only the particular person who does the weaving, but all the communal history that went into those symbols and those colors.

There also you have the sense of the llano, probably best described there of the three books—and also the farming communities and the towns. And there's a juxtaposition of one against the other, shown in the conflicts of the two families. Was that from your own background? Were both sides of that conflict present within your own family?

Yes, in fact, my mother is from a farming community and my father did most of his work as a *vaquero*—what you would call a cowboy or a sheepherder—out on the llano in the ranches; so there was the antagonism between the *llaneros* and the farmers in my family.

I love the way the farmers are people of few words. When they are talking to Antonio they will communicate in a few sentences what they have been thinking about all day. That seems to be true of farmers everywhere.

Yeah, I think it is a characteristic, isn't it, of people who work with the earth to have imbued in them a sense of patience. On the other hand, they also have their own storytelling, and I remember visiting those farms along Puerta de Luna, where my grandfather had a farm, and late at night people would gather around and begin to tell stories. But the tradition was kind of different. The *llaneros* (*vaqueros* to me) would always be the loud men; they made a lot of noise, they were rough, they were gruff, they laughed more and probably drank more, so what you learned from the respective groups was very different, had its own flavor. . . .

There's a strong sense in **Ultima** *that the life experience cuts against some of the aspects of traditional Catholicism, so that there seems to be a sort of striving to supplant or transform it into a kind of world religion based on experience, especially mystical experience. Am I right about this? And did you encounter resistance from traditional Catholics for that message in the book?*

I've never felt there was any resistance or opposition. I think quite the contrary, a lot of readers who are Catholic have seen an accurate portrayal of the church at least as it was in those times—you're talking now about forty years later, and things have changed. But I think it's fair to say that what goes on in the novel also reflects my attempt to get an understanding of the Native American tradition and those other religions that are not Catholic and not based in the Christian mythology.

Especially from the indio.

Especially from the *indio*. And again, not to give up the one tradition for the other, but to see if those points of reference I talked about can be reached, whether from my Catholic world I knew as a child or my exploration of the Native American world that is also part of me or the worlds that I read of in other mythologies, such as Buddhism. And so I think for me to look only in my Catholic background was too limiting, and *Bless Me, Ultima* begins to explore new ground.

I was struck by the richness of choices that Antonio has at the end of the novel. He has many things to think about, reconcile, bring together.

Well, his universe begins to get constricted. I think Antonio's life is—as he begins to see that he is losing the innocence of childhood—it possibly reflects the life of the Hispanic community in New Mexico, in the sense that we too began to lose that age when the only thing that affected us happened within our family or our village. The world was changing around us and was going to bring a lot of new and positive things to us, but also some threats. And we had a lot of decisions to make. Pretty quick.

There's a thread of continuity in the books—literally, the same family is mentioned first in **Ultima,** *is the whole subject of* **Aztlán,** *and the boy carries on in* **Tortuga**—*but also, there is the thread of another kind of continuity. It seems to me that the three books are a trilogy, and in the third book is an overall interpretation you can bring— what the boy is going through personally somehow involves the whole culture, and his success, his survival, is a very important thing: an achievement for everyone.*

It's strange that no one has ever said that, you know. And I agree with your interpretation, because it seems to me that one of the important things I was doing in *Tortuga* was taking the main character and trying to make him well again after he had been crippled by life, by the circumstances that occur in *Heart of Aztlán.* And I felt that as much or more than any other character I had ever created, Tortuga was Everyman of the Chicano culture, that indeed the culture was under assault, and that the paralysis reflected in Tortuga was that paralysis that had set on the community. Tortuga has not only to get well, he has to perform still more heroic tasks in the future; not only that, the Mexican American community has to find ways of breaking out of its bondage, its paralysis.

It's also true that there are people from other cultures in the hospital who are also afflicted. . . .

Yes, and in this respect I think the novel should acquire some kind of universal meaning, because what we have created of our modern society can paralyze all of us— those of us from minority groups get displaced more and used more, but I think if we are not careful the same forces that cripple us can do it to everyone. So you have in the hospital, even if they are never completely identified by ethnic group, representatives of all of them.

In all three novels, the power of love is the redeemer in some sense. In **Tortuga** *it's very much a literal one: It's sexual love, it's also working together—there's a wonderful sense of the people pulling together in a more collective spirit within the room he's in; there's real affection between the boys there—in fact, that seems to be the dominant message that your novels carry. . . .*

I think you're right. Though I have lived in and explored the existential universe, I have come back to a communal universe. I grew up in that tradition, I left it in some of my wanderings, and I returned to it; and what the tradition of the community has to teach us is what I've already alluded to—respect, love for the family and for the village that is the community. I think that's where the power of love comes in. I feel it has sustained all those Indian and Mexican pueblos that have occupied this region for such a long time; they must have had it as they came together and formed their bond—a bond not only of tradition and language and culture and heritage, but of love. That's how they were able to survive, and that's how they will be able to survive in the presence of all those powers that can cripple and kill us, you see.

In **Heart of Aztlán** *there is also that spirit of coming together, within the community established in Albuquerque, in the various parts of the* barrio *whatever the difficulty of the circumstances.*

One of the things that some critics have viewed as a failure in **Heart of Aztlán** has been that no structure, no political structure with a given political ideology, is put into place. But I guess my feeling is that while those structures may come into being, if they're not shored up by some common respect and a common goal that we have as human beings, they don't last long. And I do see their importance—they're the way we get things done in today's world. But I was more interested, I guess, in following the other side of that coin, and that is can we really get together as a community—not because of what's in it for me, but because of that old sense of value that has sustained all communities on earth throughout history. And to me, the element of love must play a large role in it.

That brings me to a political question. You had clearly stated ten years ago that you didn't feel Chicano literature was strongest when it was narrowly addressed to political struggle and resistance. Ten years ago, the climate was very politically charged. What do you think about this now?

What I have come to see is that there is even more need now for what we call a political stance, in our poetry and our novels. That seems to be a big change from where I was ten years ago. I guess I thought then that the literature we were writing would be very good for our community, one more place where we could reflect on our history and our identity and move on from there, and that we didn't have to overwhelm the reader with "message," so to speak; we didn't have to hit the reader over the head with ideology. I think that's principally the reason I wasn't in tune with the political writings of the Chicano movement at the time. I felt all too often that the ideology came up short— all too often it was only a Marxist ideology—and, too, I tended to see in writers whose main concern was message a lack of aesthetic attention to what they were practicing, what they were learning to be. They didn't really want to be writers, they wanted to be politicians, and I think there's two different animals there. Can you get those two together in the same work? Can a very good writer who has learned

and paid attention and practiced his craft communicate his political feelings about the society? I think yes; I feel stronger about that now than I did then. I still think it's probably the hardest kind of writing to do, because you tend to put the reader off. The reader wants story and you're talking message; the reader may quickly leave you. But it is important in this country, especially when you speak of our community, the Southwest. We have not only the story to write, we also have to remind our people about their history and their traditions and their culture and their language, things that are under that threat that we talked about right now, and liable to disappear if we don't look closely at ourselves in a historical process—and part of analyzing that historical process is not only story and myth and legend and tradition, it's a political space we occupy. How have we occupied it? How have we been used in that political space?

Recently I've played around with an essay in which I talk about writing in colonial space, which is a political concept, right? How do we feel as a minority group, a clearly recognizable ethnic group, when we have to respond to colonial space—how do we carve out our own identity? This is what the Chicano movement was all about, trying to create within colonial space the space for our own community, our literature. And that process is tied into the political process.

So in a sense you're always tied into it—I think my three novels are. The fact that they don't clearly call for one specific ideology may be interpreted as a critical fault in a political novel, but I didn't set out to write political novels. Though I do see their importance.

I think probably the novel that I'm writing now, which is again set in Albuquerque, is my analysis of my contemporary world, the present, today: What role do the different cultures of New Mexico play vis-à-vis each other? how is the Southwest changing? what is the concept of the Sunbelt all about? who is coming here and why are tremendous investments being made across the Southwest? what do they mean to our communities that have been here a long time? I think probably the only way we respond to some of these questions, critical questions if we're going to exist as a culture, *is* in novels that carry that social-political impact and perhaps allow the public to think on those questions that are crucial. But I'm still of the opinion that you do that through a well told story.

I've noticed there seem to be affinities between the ideas you're expressing and the writings of magic realism in Central and South America—being political in the broadest sense, describing what is happening in the Americas, and doing it with art—not leaving it to rhetoric. Do you have any direct relationships with Marquez or Fuentes or. . . .

No, I haven't. If I were more inclined to go around visiting with writers, I would have found ways, but I'm not. I have one short story called **"B. Traven Is Alive and Well**

in Cuernavaca" which begins something like this: "I don't go to Mexico to meet writers; I go to write!"

I want to go back to **Tortuga.** *It seems to me it's the most political novel you've done because it's the most concentrated on this extended metaphor we've been talking about—because that hospital is also a prison. The Indian boy that gets out dies very soon. It's as if people have been cut off from the land so that in going back to it, it becomes dangerous.*

Yeah . . . the idyllic and pastoral llano and river valley of ***Bless Me, Ultima*** becomes the cancerous desert, the blinding sandstorms that you have to cross to get back home, the frozen mountain in midwinter that the Indian boy has to cross and that kills him. So even the land has almost become an antagonist, whereas before it was the nurturing mother. We get the sense of the unnatural storms, radiation, death in the desert, grasses described as brittle, and that's all part of the extended metaphor, the reflection of what we are doing to ourselves, what we are doing to our earth.

One thing you did in that book struck me in a very personal way, because I spent some time myself in children's hospitals. It's where you talk about pain. You say that for someone who's had a great deal of pain, it's very hard to avoid things like drugs and alcohol later, because pain is a high and you get used to it. That's a very clear insight. When I read that I thought, "This guy has been there." You must have known something about that experience to be able to write that way.

Yeah, well, I spent a summer in one of those hospitals and that's where the germ of the novel comes from—the experience, some of the characters, and some of the things that he went through. Around that is the reflection of what we are doing to ourselves and to the earth. It does have the hope in it that my characters seem to keep looking around—there must be *somebody* out there who I can make contact with—like the persons I knew in childhood who were a little wiser and more solid because they were sharing themselves. And even though the rest of the landscape alternates between the dead desert with the sandstorms and the frozen mountains around the hospital on the west side, the springs of the mountain are still running, there is still hope, it's not too late, and you can go there and you can bathe and be made whole. But there's very little of that left, you know. And we've got to touch base with it pretty quick. Otherwise, living in this region that has so much potential to it, because it's a very special corridor in this country, the Rio Grande Valley and the cultures that have been here for thousands of years—it's a very special place—if we don't realize that, we're going to lose part of the hope that this region has to offer us and the people in it.

We might end with one other question about that. It seems to me that some of the most responsible writers, as well as some of the best, from the three cultures here have written

about this sense of place in one way or another—I'm thinking of Edward Abbey, who's really a westerner; Leslie Silko and Simon Ortiz; certainly yourself; and several others who have addressed it in a big way, in novels. What do you think the prospects are for this multicultural work becoming a national forum that people can begin to see as a model for such statements?

I think that has already happened. I see any number of regions around the country that are in a sense turning inward and looking at themselves and producing wonderfully gifted writers. I'm not sure that we in the Southwest caused that forum; the times themselves are calling for a truly representative speaking to each other, letting down some of these false borders that we've had between us. I think that's a very positive thing. What's happening in this country—if we are part of it, much more power to us—is that if we are able to take our different perspectives of how the world ought to be—alerted to the fact that there are people out there who thrive on destroying—and share these perspectives, you know, communicate among groups, then we have something to offer the whole country and the world. The world *is* interested; that's one thing that is conveyed to me every time a visitor comes through here. They've locked into the Southwest as a place going through a very interesting experiment—it has to do with how people can live with each other, can share—and this is as important to the whites and the Maori of New Zealand as it may be to the Catalonians and the Basques, the Nicaraguans and the Misquitos, you know what I mean? It's important to us to realize that we are a center of focus—a lot of people are looking at us, and we can do something very positive with all the changes that are coming across this land, or we can blow it. And I tend to want to work more on the positive things that are going on here, so that we can learn from each other.

Note

1. The first paragraph of *Bless Me, Ultima* begins:

   Ultima came to stay with us the summer I was almost seven When she came the beauty of the llano unfolded before my eyes, and the gurgling waters of the river sang to the hum of the turning earth. The magical time of childhood stood still, and the pulse of the living earth pressed its mystery into my living blood . . .

Robert M. Adams (review date 26 March 1987)

SOURCE: "Natives and Others," in *New York Review of Books,* March 26, 1987, pp. 32–36.

[*In the following excerpt, Adams explores the issue of ethnic identity in* Bless Me, Ultima.]

Nobody in Santa Fe really belongs there unless his line stretches back, by one genealogical trapeze act or another, to the seventeenth century; so my wife and I—native New

Yorkers both—have adapted without strain to being outsiders and aliens. Who doesn't feel like a transplant in America? Here there's nothing else to be. It's an oasis culture; nobody gets much more than his minimal quota of earth, air, and water, and who needs more? Every so often, just to make contact with our fellow transients, we drive down the valley of the Rio Grande to the flat marshlands of Bosque del Apache, south of Socorro, some 140 miles from our house in Santa Fe. Into these wide lagoons and stagnant pools thousands of wild fowl come every year to spend the winter months—visitors, like ourselves, with strong memories of northern places and deeper forests, but content for the time being with a for-the-time-being existence. There are Canada geese, sandhill cranes, a few rare whooping cranes, multitudes of mallard, teal, and a dozen other species whose names I don't know. To stand under the cloud of wings when five thousand wild white geese explode into the air all at once in a storm of honkings and flappings is an experience to stir the blood.

One can drive west from Socorro next day to the plains of San Augustin where stands the Very Large Array. It is a set of twenty-seven giant saucer-shaped receivers painted stark white and mounted on railroad tracks. They are designed to "see" electronically into the outermost regions of the cosmos—to collect infinitesimal impulses from inconceivably vast galaxies at a distance in light-years before which the imagination faints. From some of these outermost galaxies the entire array of telemetering devices receives in the course of a solid year a total amount of energy equivalent to a single snowflake falling on the surface of the earth. Yet by electronic enhancement the machines of the installation can print on a postcard the image of two galaxies, each millions of light-years across, and both at a distance from our little speck of dust too inconceivably enormous to be expressed. There is no reason why the bird refuge and the astronomical array should seem to be making complementary statements; and almost certainly what they say to me is not what they will say to someone else. But the double experience has always seemed to me purifying and exalting.

Daily life in our part of the world imposes odd perspectives too. In filling out certain bureaucratic forms I am occasionally asked to define my ethnic background—the form allows it to be either "Native American," "Hispanic," or "Other." Given those three options, it isn't hard to figure out where I belong; but putting oneself down as "Other" is always a little jarring. "Anglos" in New Mexico are a very loose category indeed. Orientals are automatically Anglo; a PTA member will also be heard to say, "We have four Anglos in our school, two of them black." Hispanics are divided by the length of their stay here: wetbacks and illegals (*Mojados*), old settlers (*Manitos*), and a tiny, almost hypothetical minority who have some connection with Spain itself.

Indians are divided among tribe, language groups, different pueblos, and an assimilated, often urban population the extent of which is anybody's guess. (In certain lines of commercial endeavor a tinge of Indian blood is a great advantage: Fritz Scholder, a foremost "Indian" painter, is one-fourteenth Indian, i.e., one of his eight great-grandparents belonged to a California tribe.) Local Indians often have Hispanic as well as Indian names; they combine, in a fashion that satisfies them completely, Roman Catholicism with the rites and rituals of their own basically animistic religion. Living on reservations, the land of which they jealously guard (they are in addition forbidden by federal law to sell it), they show one face to the white world around them, and live among themselves a life of their own, about which they are very secretive. The reasons for secrecy are not hard to imagine. I recall the story of an early anthropologist who, in company with his wife, was interrogating the elders of the Hopi tribe on their religious beliefs. The questions were probing, incisive, logical; the answers polite, evasive, and uninformative. At last the enraged wife, coming to her husband's help, unfurled a parasol, and began beating the "informants" over the head. They *would* tell her husband their most intimate thoughts, they *must!* . . .

Much of Hispanic cultural life seems just as resolutely attached to the past. Not only is the reconquest of New Mexico reenacted annually, the folk festivals retell aspects of the nativity story every year, sometimes in language so traditional that the performers themselves have trouble understanding it. Every Christmas time, the stories of *Los Tres Reyes Magos,* of *Los Pastores,* or of *Las Posadas* are produced by neighborhood groups in the small towns and barrios of New Mexico. Stars of the show are, predictably, the devil, who grimaces, capers, and menaces to the shrill terror of small children in the audience, and the Virgin Mary, who is bound to be the prettiest girl available—no jokes allowed. It is a pageant, not a drama, all the more welcome as it is more familiar. Outdoors as well, people are reminded everywhere of the ancient story by little fires burning before people's houses wherever the householder wants to signal that the Christ child is welcome. The little fires—a few sticks of piñon—are *luminarias,* whatever the terminology may be in less careful parts of the world; the little paper bags weighted with sand, enclosing a candle, and set outdoors as Christmas decorations, are properly *farolitos.*

Rudolfo Anaya, who teaches at the University of New Mexico, is a leading Hispanic writer, largely because of his widely appreciated fiction, **Bless Me, Ultima,** published in 1972 by Tonatiuh International of Berkeley, California. More a series of semi-attached sketches than a consecutive novel, this book presents a nostalgic picture of life in a group of small eastern New Mexico villages during and just after World War II. Dramatic interest is provided by a running feud between the black forces of Tenorio Trementina abetted by his witch daughters—and the Ultima of the title, who is an idealized "curandera," halfway between a white witch and a saint. The story's events are described as from a great distance, they take place in a largely closed world, and the conflict of magics, hexes, and folklore cures is taken with complete seriousness by all concerned; thus the story gives a strong impression of long ago and far away.

Mr. Anaya's narrator in this fiction is a precocious child in elementary school who is having some familiar problems with divine providence and some less easily defined problems in choosing between the models provided by his father's people (nomadic) and his mother's (agricultural). With the aid of some too tangible help from Joyce's *Portrait of the Artist,* young Antonio Márez gropes his way toward a meditative distancing, if not a resolution, of his problems. "Sometime in the future I would have to build my own dream out of those things that were so much a part of my childhood." The book is in effect a *Bildungsroman* with most of the *Bildung* presented as a promissory note. John Nichols's *Milagro Beanfield War* (currently being reduced to a movie) is a novel about Hispanic life with problems of its own; talky and episodic, it's too melodramatic. But it's tough and funny in a here-and-now way, and it is worth setting against Anaya's nostalgic and credulous vision of the Hispanic outback.

A. Robert Lee (essay date 1990)

SOURCE: "Ethnic Renaissance: Rudolfo Anaya, Louise Erdrich, and Maxine Hong Kingston," in *The New American Writing: Essays on American Literature since 1970,* edited by Graham Clarke, St. Martin's Press, 1990, pp. 139–64.

[*In the following excerpt, Lee discusses the rise of American ethnic literature in the 1960s and focuses on Anaya's* Bless Me, Ultima *as an example of Chicano literature and its emphasis on cultural identity, tradition, and displacement.*]

Ethnic art *is* the American mainstream. . . .

—Ishmael Reed, Interview, 'The Third Ear,' B.B.C. Radio 3, April 1989[1]

Growing up ethnic is surely the liveliest theme to appear in the American novel since the closing of the frontier. . . .

—John Skow, reviewing Amy Tan, *The Joy Luck Club, Time,* 27 March 1989[2]

1

A vogue it may currently appear. But can it be doubted that ethnicity has ever been other than a key ingredient in American culture? One thinks of founding racial encounters: Columbus sighting his 'gentle' Arawak Indians in the 1490s and they him, Cortés imposing Spanish imperial rule upon Aztec Mexico and the American southwest after arriving at Mexico City in 1519, or those first twenty enslaved Africans being deposited in Jamestown in 1619 from a reputed Dutch man-of-war.[3] One thinks, subsequently, of the great ensuing waves of European immigra-

tion, each the bearer of a culture in its own right yet each to be made over into a new hyphenation with America— Anglos, Irish, Scots, Germans, Slavs, Italians, Scandinavians, Jews out of Russia and Poland. To these has to be added the Asian diaspora, from the early Chinese who spoke of San Francisco as 'The Gold Mountain' to the Japanese to the latter-day Korean and Vietnamese. The process in no way abates.

There would emerge, too, a now familiar body of ethnic debate. Was America melting-pot or mixing bowl, a W.A.S.P. hegemony or a genuine quilt of all peoples?[4] Yet however long-standing or endemic the issue of ethnicity in America, it was in the 1960s as never before that it took on new prominence, new assertion. For during that turbulent decade and thereafter ethnic America, and above all non-European ethnic America, re-announced itself. The process was political, economic, a bid for long-overdue empowerment. It was also cultural, a major and continuing surge of imaginative self-expression.

To cite the 1960s from an ethnic or racial perspective of necessity first means a reference-back to the call for redress by black America. No clearer index of change offered itself than the use of Black for Negro, the latter discarded as belonging to a time about to pass and to a more traditional and quiescent racial equation. Other changes, however, were nothing if not dramatic—the Civil Rights marches, the push for voter registration in the Dixie South, the long hot summers, the city burnings from New Jersey to Watts and from Atlanta to Detroit, and the emergence of Black Power groups like the Panthers and Muslims. Tragically, too, there was the litany of assassinations, whether Jack and Bobby Kennedy, or Medgar Evers, or Martin Luther King, or Malcolm X, or George Jackson. Yet as the legislation got on the books, as a pantheon of new black leadership emerged, and as the American media increasingly took note of its black population, few doubted that an end to any supposed one-standard America lay in prospect.

Artists, film-makers, musicians, journalists, sports stars and comics all played their part, supplying fresh codes and images of American blackness. Literary figures, in especial, contributed. A fiction begun in names like those of Ralph Ellison and James Baldwin has continued through into the generation of Ishmael Reed, James Alan McPherson and even beyond. A line of writing by Afro-American women has come to prominence, Ann Petry and Paule Marshall from an earlier time and Toni Morrison, Alice Walker and Gayl Jones from among their successors. New departures in poetry, theatre and film have made their impact, as has a rich vein of autobiographical work stretching from Malcolm X to LeRoi Jones/Amiri Baraka and from Eldridge Cleaver to Maya Angelou. Then, too, there was the galvanizing effect of Alex Haley's *Roots* (1976), both the novel and the spectacularly widely viewed T.V. series. Whether 'Black' truly had become 'Beautiful' as the slogan ran, it had without a doubt called time on past assumptions. Not without cause has there been talk of a Second Renaissance of Afro-American art and ideas.[5]

But central as was this black efflorescence, it tended to eclipse others. Hispanic or Brown America lay in waiting, demographically the largest impending minority in America: Puerto Ricans in New York, *emigré* Cubans in Florida, Chileans, Salvadoreans, Argentinians and others in flight from dictatorship, and, above all, Mexican-Americans or Chicanos. These latter not only arose out of a profoundly non-Anglo tradition—Aztec-Spanish, Catholic, border Mexican—but out of their own variety of American Spanish and bilingualism. Theirs, too, was another geography, California, Texas, Arizona, New Mexico, Colorado and southern Utah, not to mention another set of cultural styles from foodways to low-rider cars. Equally, they could look back upon their own interpretation of history, be it the Mexican-American War (1846–48), Mexican Independence (1910), the Sleepy Lagoon and Zoot Suit Riots (1943), or the continuing influx across the Rio Grande. The 1960s meant César Chávez and the struggle of his U.F.W. (founded in 1962) to fight the grape-picking wars. They also meant Corky González and the Denver Crusade for Justice and José Angel Gutiérrez and La Raza Unida of Texas. They even came to mean the increasing recognition of a Chicano input into general American usage—*Aztlán* as the mythical homeland of the Chicano people and words like *la raza* (literally 'the race'), *mestizo* (someone of mixed Indian and Spanish blood) and *pachuco* (young male Chicano). In literary-cultural terms they also meant nothing less than a Chicano Renaissance: Luis Valdez's *Teatro Campesino,* or the fiction of Tomás Rivera, Rudolfo Anaya, Ron Arias and others, or the poetry of Alurista and Bernice Zamora, or Richard Rodriguez's controversial autobiography *Hunger of Memory* (1982). Thus as *The Milagro Beanfield War, East LA* and *Stand and Deliver* win out in their depictions of Chicano life on American cinema screens, there can be little doubt that *Chicanismo,* too, has established new rights to attention.[6]

Blacks and Chicanos were to find their counterparts among the Indians of America. Reservation-based or urban, they in their turn felt moved to call time on their past demoralization. Typical was the replacement of the name 'Indian' itself with 'Native-American,' another break with white nomenclature. Typical, too, were events like the challenge of the National Indian Youth Council and the American Indian Movement (A.I.M., founded in 1969) to the traditional powers of the Bureau of Indian Affairs; or the occupations and land claims in Alcatraz, Taos, Maine and Massachusetts; or the seizure in 1973 by Sioux activists of the historic village of Wounded Knee in the Pine Ridge Reservation of South Dakota; or the emergence of a militant new generation of leaders like Dennis Banks and Russell Means. To hand, also, were manifestos and re-interpretations like Vine Deloria's *Custer Died for Your Sins* (1969) and *Behind the Trail of Broken Treatises* (1974). Non-Indian scholarship likewise took up the call, none more so than Leslie Fielder's *The Return of the Vanishing American* (1968), an analysis of the hidden 'Red America' within both high and popular American culture, and Dee Brown's *Bury My Heart at Wounded Knee* (1970),

a history which examines the brutal cost to the Indian of the Winning of the West with its white triumphalist myth of frontier and settlement.[7] Brown took as his departure-point the 'graves of the dead' as the Shawnee chief, Tecumseh, once put it. All of this was to have its literary manifestation, nothing less than another genuine contemporary American renaissance. In quick order appeared fiction like: *House Made of Dawn* (1968) by the Kiowa, N. Scott Momaday; *Seven Arrows* (1972) by the Cheyenne, Heyemeyohsts Storm; *Winter in the Blood* (1974) by the Blackfoot, James Welch; *Ceremony* (1978) by the Laguna, Leslie Marmon Silko; and, to be sure, the Chippewa-inspired story-telling of Louise Erdrich. To these has to be added the poetry of talent like Gerald Vizenor, Simon Ortiz, Gail Tremblay and Joy Harjo. Once again, a new ethnic and cultural contract was being sought with America.[8]

Asian-Americans were to have their day slightly later, in the 1980s. Theirs, too, like 'Hispanic' has been a composite name, in need of clear particularization into Chinese-American, Japanese-American and the like.[9] America's Chinese have had to fight off a more than usually entrenched set of popular-culture stereotypes, those of coolie, cook and launderer. Sax Rohmer's Fu Manchu and Earl Derr Biggers's Charlie Chan respectively bequeathed greatly influential images of 'bad' and 'good' Chinese, as likewise did Chop-Chop in the massively popular cartoon series *Blackhawk* (1941–84).[10] Against these odds and the daemonology of 'Red China,' a new and largely West Coast flowering has been under way. So, at least, would be the evidence of the memoir work of Maxine Hong Kingston (her first novel, *Tripmaster Monkey,* is currently announced), the drama of Frank Chin—especially *The Chickencoop Chinamen* (1972) and *The Year of The Dragon* (1974)—and novels like *Homebase* (1979) by Shawn Wong, *Thousand Pieces of Gold* (1981) by Ruthanne Lum McCunne, and latterly, *The Joy Luck Club* (1989) by Amy Tan. Similarly Japanese-Americans have had to contend against the inherited stigmas of Pearl Harbour, the Pacific islands wars, and their removal to Californian and other 'relocation' camps during World War II. That story, and more, has been told by the likes of Monica Sone, Hisaye Yamamoto and Toshio Mori. Furthermore, the Asian-American literary roster grows, as can be witnessed in the ongoing fiction and essays of the Filipino-American, Carlos Bulosan (*America is in the Heart* (1946, 1973) as notably as any), or in a novel like *Clay Walls* (1986) by the Korean-American, Kim Ronyoung, or in *Blue Dragon White Tiger* (1978) by the Vietnamese-American, Tran Van Dinh.[11] *Time* magazine, even if its focus was business and yuppiedom rather than culture, did no more than mirror another ethnic cycle of change when it gave over a whole issue in mid-1988 to Asian America.[12]

Anaya, Erdrich, Kingston: these three names, then, must do composite duty. They have every cause to be taken wholly on their own terms, powerful imaginations each. Yet as, respectively, Chicano, Native-American and Chinese-American, they also have drawn profoundly and quite inescapably from their different ethnic legacies. In each case, too, they have lived both within and yet at an angle from what passes as 'mainstream' America, a truly hyphenated or joint cultural citizenry as it were. In imagining 'ethnically,' thereby, they offer the paradox of having written into being an America the nation barely knew itself to be, another and yet the same America.

2

A historic first presence in the American southwest, a landscape as much of custom and language as of place, and the interplay of an ancestral Aztec legacy with a missionary-derived Catholicism—it hardly surprises that Chicano fiction has been so taken up with its communal past. Few Chicanos, writers or otherwise, have not pondered their pre-Columbian origins (for the most part it is carried in their facial appearance and skin colour), or the antiquity of their own legends and religion, or the push westwards and north into a supposed Yankee El Dorado. That consciousness, certainly, has pressed hard behind the landmarks of the achievement, novels like José Antonio Villarreal's *Pocho* (1959), generally acknowledged as the first Chicano novel and which portrays the Rubio family's bitter migration into California, or John Rechy's *City of Night* (1963), in line with his other fiction essentially a novel of homosexual transience but which also reflects his early Chicano and Texas origins, or Tomás Rivera's *. . . y no se lo tragó la tierra* (*. . . and the earth did not part,* 1970), a story-cycle set in Texas and unfolded through the persona of an unnamed child as a conflict of Chicano and Anglo cultures (rightly it has been compared with Joyce's *Dubliners* and Anderson's *Winesburg, Ohio*), or, of late, Ron Arias's *The Road to Tamazunchale* (1987), a fantastical dream novel told as the last words of Don Fausto, a dying Chicano elder who looks back from the Los Angeles *barrio* upon his community's meaning and inheritance.[13] To these has to be added a body of *literatura chicanesca,* writing about Chicano life by non-Chicanos, of which indisputably the foremost since the Robert Redford film version has been John Nichols's *The Milagro Beanfield War* (1976)—the first in a New Mexico trilogy.[14]

Within this frame, Rudolfo Anaya has equally laid down his own terms of reference and nowhere more so than in the novel which continues most to secure his reputation, *Bless Me, Ultima* (1972).[15] Set in the rural New Mexico of World War II, it tells the rite of passage of 8–year-old Antonio Márez—Tony as he will become with anglicization—an evocation by turns tender and fierce of a unique Chicano childhood. For into its telling, Anaya brilliantly imports a whole stock of dynastic history, myth and belief, that of a people caught at the turning-point between a Mexican-hispanic past and an American-hispanic future. Presiding over the whole is the shamanistic figure of Ultima, known also as La Grande, a *curandera* or healer-sage under whose guiding kindliness Antonio falls. An inspired fusion of eventfulness and dream, the historic and the ceremonial, *Bless Me, Ultima* also yields its own Portrait of the Artist, the boy's emerging measure of his

inheritance subtly rewoven into a first-person work of memory. Anaya's subsequent two novels, *Heart of Aztlán* (1976) and *Tortuga* (1979), the former which deals with the transition of a rural family into the urban *barrio* of Barelas in Albuquerque and the latter with the path into recovery and self-independence of a crippled boy (*tortuga,* tortoise, refers to his hospital plaster cast), may indeed represent a certain drop in power. But they share with *Bless Me, Ultima,* which deservedly won the prestigious Second Annual Premio Quinto Sol, a belief in the as yet still untold reaches of Chicano life.

'Every morning I seem to awaken with a new experience and dreams strangely mixed in me.' So Antonio looks back on his self-proclaimed 'magical' New Mexico upbringing, caught as he is between the Márez legacy of his father, one of *vaquero* or herdsman life on the *llano* (flatlands), and the Luna legacy of his mother, one of homestanding and cultivation of the land. Márez as against Luna might also be said to signify male and female principles, *conquistador* as against settler and homemaker. If, too, Gabriel hopes his son will reincarnate a nomadic past glory, his wife hopes the boy will become a priest and farmer like one of her own first ancestors. For *Bless Me, Ultima* portrays nothing if not worlds in transition. Gabriel Márez has moved in from the *llano* to the *pueblo,* works not with horses and cattle but in a highway repair crew, and if he looks backwards to the myth of his ancestors he also seeks to look forwards to his family's eventual (though unlikely) migration to California. A larger frame is also provided by the reference to the Second World War. Nearby lies Los Alamos (The Poplars), the testing site for the first atomic bomb and the instance of a technology at quite the other end of the time spectrum to that which has produced the Márez and Luna clans. Transition, too, is registered in the enlistment of Antonio's three brothers, eventual returnee GIs who come from battles in Japan and Germany not to stay but to become drifters seeking an easy pleasure in Las Vegas (The Lowlands). Aztec, Mexican or New Mexican as may be the sub-stratum of Antonio's land and history, yet, too, another transition pends—that brought on by his beginning studies of English, the pull of Yankee America for his cultural allegiance.

The novel's essential transitions, however, occur in terms of the boy himself, 'experience' and 'dream' indeed 'strangely mixed'. In the former column, Anaya has Antonio witness the arrival in the family home of Ultima, his father's story-telling and drinking, intervals working the land with his mother's relatives at El Puerto, his first schooling, and the tugs and tensions of early boyhood friendship. He also witnesses four dramatically told deaths: that of Lupito, a war-veteran mentally damaged in Japan who shoots Chávez, the sheriff, and who typifies a madness imported from 'the outside'; that of Narciso, the town's basically harmless drunk killed by Tenorio Trementina who believe Ultima a *bruja* or witch responsible for the death of one of his daughters but for whom Narciso has only gratitude and love; that of Florence, a boy who drowns and with whom Antonio has struck up a bond of private sympathy and ritual; and that of Ultima herself, who teaches him that death can be continuity and restoration as well as separation. He also undergoes a cycle of childhood fevers and acts of witness as when he sees the Lupito killing or is assailed by an avenging Tenorio astride his horse or sees Ultima cure with secret herbs a member of the Téllez family. Yet, wonderfully conceived and patterned as these events are, they in effect serve as supports to even deeper transitions taking place within Antonio Márez's inward being.

In these, dream and myth play key rôles, most of all in connection with Ultima. Antonio dreams of his own birth and '*the old woman*' who delivered him ('*Only I will know his destiny,*' Ultima announces); he dreams several times of his three brothers, fugitive elder presences who strike out in directions he slowly realizes he cannot follow; he dreams of Tenorio's dead daughter ('*my dream-fate drew me to the coffin*'), a vision with Macbethian overtones of witchery and magic; and, above all, he dreams of the legend of the Golden Carp, a huge fish which swims about the waters flowing beneath and about his *pueblo* and which is protected and half-worshipped by his friends Samuel and Cisco. The carp exists in fact and fantasy, a literal river fish but also a source of legend. Samuel explains how, in communal myth, the carp incarnates a protector-god, the deity of land and people:

> . . . he went to the other gods and told them that he chose to be turned into a carp and swim in the river where he could take good care of his people. The gods agreed. But because he was a god they made him very big and colored him the color of gold. And they made him the lord of all the waters of the valley.

The carp, thus, mediates a world of fact and superstition, actuality and dream. And, for Antonio, it also supplies a counter to the Catholicism in which Father Byrne and the church have begun giving him instruction. A dilemma thus arises for the boy: which offers the better theology, an Indian animism or the Christianity of the Easter Week against which are set the later parts of the novel? Whichever Antonio's choice, both now co-exist as resources in the boy's nascent creative psyche.

So, too, and in overwhelming fashion, does Ultima. No obscure peyote or psychedelic cultist out of Carlos Castaneda, she is truly *una última,* one of the last of an ancient order. A Catholic believer, she nonetheless incarnates a oneness with prior and non-Christian stores of knowledge, the spirituality of the natural order. Not that Anaya turns her into mere formula or symbol; far from it. He depicts her as a credibly live presence, a bearer of the past but also for Antonio at least a major figure of his present. More still to the point, perhaps, she will be a crucial remembered presence in his future. From the start, too, he understands the meaning of the owl as her titular emblem ('with Ultima came the owl'), a totem whose every successive cry heralds a major turn not only in her life but his own. It is the owl which attacks Tenorio in his first at-

tempt to destroy Ultima and puts out his eye; the owl which accompanies her on her every mission; and the owl which when finally killed by Tenorio signals also her own inevitable death. Antonio acts both as her apprentice and her memorialist. She so in addition calls out his rising creative-imaginative sympathies, his artist's ability to see *curandera* and owl at once literally and figuratively yet without the slightest undue contradiction.

No account of *Bless Me, Ultima,* too, can pass over lightly Anaya's passionate sense of New Mexico not simply as region or place but as a storehouse of past Chicano identity. He himself has spoken of its hold for him in interview:

> [The] landscape plays a major rôle in the literature that I write. In the beginning, it is an empty, desolate, bare stage; then, if one looks closely, one sees life—people gather to tell stories, to do their work, to love, to die. In the old days the sheep and cattle ranchers gathered in that small village, which had a train station, watering station for the old coal-burning trains. It was prosperous; they were good times. Then after the visit or the business at hand is done, the people disappear back into the landscape and you're left as if alone, with the memories, dreams, stories, and whatever joys and tragedies they have brought to you.[16]

Bless Me, Ultima clearly arose out of this store of 'memories, dreams [and] stories,' a triumph both for what they so palpably have given to him but which by the same token he has given back to them.

Notes

1. Broadcast 18 April 1989, and repeated 23 April 1989. The interviewer was the present writer.

2. Skow's review continues: 'The Chinese-American culture is only beginning to throw off . . . literary sparks, and Amy Tan's bright, sharp-flavored first novel belongs on a short shelf dominated by Maxine Hong Kingston's remarkable works of a decade ago, *The Woman Warrior* and *China Men*'—*Time,* 27 March 1989.

3. See, respectively: Angie Debo, *A History of the Indians of the United States* (Norman: University of Oklahoma Press, 1970); Julian Samora and Patricia Vendel Simon, *A History of the Mexican-American People* (Notre Dame, Indiana: University of Notre Dame Press, 1977), and Lerone Bennet, Jr., *Before the Mayflower: A History of the Negro in America 1619–1964,* rev. edn. (Baltimore, Maryland: Penguin Books, 1966).

4. For a provocative contemporary cultural discussion of these issues see Werner Sollers, *Beyond Ethnicity: Consent and Descent in American Culture* (New York: Oxford University Press, 1986).

5. The following offer accounts of this achievement: James M. McPherson, Laurence B. Holland, James M. Banner, Nancy J. Weiss and Michael D. Bell

(eds.), *Blacks in America: Bibliographical Essays* (New York: Doubleday, 1971); Roger Rosenblatt, *Black Fiction* (Cambridge, Massachusetts: Harvard University Press, 1974); Addison Gayle, Jr., *The Way of the New World: The Black Novel in America* (New York: Anchor/Doubleday, 1975); Michael S. Harper and R. E. Stepto (eds.), *Chants of Saints: A Gathering of Afro-American Literature, Art and Scholarship* (Urbana, Illinois: Illinois University Press, 1979); Robert Stepto, *From Behind the Veil: A Study of Afro-American Narrative* (Urbana, Illinois: Illinois University Press, 1979); A. Robert Lee (ed.) *Black Fiction: New Studies in the Afro-American Novel* (London: Vision Press, 1980); C. W. E. Bigsby, *The Second Black Renaissance: Essays in Black Literature* (Westport, Connecticut: Greenwood Press, 1980); A. Robert Lee, *Black American Literature Since Richard Wright* (British Association of American Studies Pamphlet No. 11, 1983); Keith E. Byerman, *Fingering the Jagged Grain: Tradition and Form in Recent Black Fiction* (Athens, Georgia: University of Georgia Press, 1985); and John F. Callaghan, *In the Afro-American Grain: The Pursuit of Voice in Twentieth-century Black Fiction* (Urbana, Illinois: University of Illinois Press, 1988).

6. On Chicano history and politics, see especially: Matt S. Meier and Feliciano Rivera, *The Chicanos: A History of Mexican Americans* (New York: Hill and Wang, 1972); Rodolfo Acuna, *Occupied America: The Chicano's Struggle Towards Liberation* (San Francisco: Canfield Press, 1972); Marcia T. García *et al* (eds.), *History, Culture and Society: Chicano Studies in the 1980s* (Ypsilanti, Michigan: Bilingual Press/Editorial Bilingüe, National Association of Chicano Studies, 1983); John A. García *et al* (eds.), *The Chicano Struggle: Analyses of Past and Present Efforts* (Ypsilanti, Michigan: Bilingual Press/Editorial Bilingüe, National Association of Chicano Studies, 1984); Alfredo Mirandé, *The Chicano Experience: An Alternative Perspective* (Notre Dame, Indiana: University of Notre Dame Press, 1985); Rodolfo O. de la Garza, Frank D. Bean, Charles M. Bonjean, Ricardo Romo and Rodolfo Alvarez (eds.), *The Mexican American Experience* (Austin, Texas: University of Texas Press, 1985); and Renate von Bardeleben, Dietrich Briesemeister and Juan Bruce-Novoa (eds.), *Missions in Conflict: Essays on U.S.: Mexican Relations and Chicano Culture* (Tubingen: Gunter Narr Verlag, 1986). For the Chicano literary renaissance, see: Ed Ludwig and James Santibañez (eds.), *The Chicanos: Mexican American Voices* (Baltimore, Maryland: Penguin Books, 1971); Francisco A. Lomelí and Donaldo W. Urioste, *Chicano Perspectives in Literature: A Critical and Annotated Bibliography* (Albuquerque, New Mexico: Pajarito Publications, 1976); Francisco Jiménez (ed.), *The Identification and Analysis of Chicano Literature* (Binghampton, New York: Bilingual Press/Editorial Bilingüe, National Association of Chicano Studies,

1979); Juan Bruce-Novoa, *Chicano Authors: Inquiry by Interview* (Austin, Texas: University of Texas Press, 1980); Juan Bruce-Novoa, *Chicano Poetry: A Response to Chaos* (Austin, Texas: University of Texas Press, 1982); Salvador Rodríguez del Pino, *La Novela Chicana Escrita en Español: Cinco Autores Comprometidos* (Ypsilanti, Michigan: Bilingual Press/Editorial Bilingüe, National Association of Chicano Studies, 1982); Jorge A. Huerta, *Chicano Theater: Theme and Forms* (Ypsilanti, Michigan: Bilingual Press/Editorial Bilingüe, National Association of Chicano Studies, 1982); Charles M. Tatum, *Chicano Literature* (Boston, Twayne Publishers, 1982); Robert G. Trujillo and Andrés Rodríguez, *Literatura Chicana: Creative and Critical Writings Through 1984* (Oakland, California: Floricanto Press, 1985); Luis Leal, *Aztlán y México: Perfiles Literarios e Históricos* (Binghampton, New York: Bilingual Press/Editorial Bilingüe, National Association of Chicano Studies, 1985); Cordelia Candelaria, *Chicano Poetry: A Critical Introduction* (Westport, Connecticut: Greenwood Press, 1986); Julio A. Martínez and Francisco A. Lomelí (eds.), *Chicano Literature: A Reference Guide* (Westport, Connecticut: Greenwood Press, 1986); and Carl R. Shirley and Paula W. Shirley, *Understanding Chicano Literature* (Columbia: University of South Carolina, 1988).

7. Leslie Fiedler, *The Return of the Vanishing American* (New York: Stein and Day, 1968); Dee Brown, *Bury my Heart at Wounded Knee: an Indian History of the American West* (New York, Holt, 1970).

8. For general accounts of this renaissance, see Jack W. Marken (ed.), *The American Indian Language and Literature* (Illinois: A.M.H. Publishing Corporation, Goldentree Bibliography, 1978); Robert F. Berkhover, Jr., *The White Man's Indian: Images of the American Indian from Columbus to the Present* (New York: Knopf, 1978); Charles R. Larson, *American Indian Fiction* (Albuquerque, New Mexico: University of New Mexico Press, 1978); Paula Gunn Allen (ed.), *Studies in American Indian Literature* (New York: Modern Language Association of America, 1983); Kenneth Lincoln, *Native American Renaissance* (Berkeley and Los Angeles: University of California Press, 1983); Brian Swann (ed.), *Smoothing the Ground: Essays on Native American Oral Literature* (Berkeley and Los Angeles: University of California Press, 1983); Arnold Krupat, *For Those Who Come After: A Study of Native American Autobiography* (Berkeley and Los Angeles: University of California Press, 1985); and Brian Swann and Arnold Krupat (eds.), *Recovering the Word: Essays on Native American Literature* (Berkeley and Lost Angeles: University of California Press, 1987).

9. For a relevant background, see H. Brett Melendy, *Chinese and Japanese Americans* (Boston: Twayne Publishers, 1972; reprinted New York: Hippocrene Books, 1984).

10. A most useful pamphlet which deals with these and other comic-strip ethnic stereotypes is: Charles Hardy and Gail F. Stern (eds.), *Ethnic Images in the Comics* (Philadelphia, Pennsylvania: Balch Institute for Ethnic Studies, 1986). See, also, Eugene Franklin Wong, *Visual Media Racism: Asians in the American Motion Pictures* (New York: Arno Press, 1978).

11. See, especially, Amy Tachiki, Eddie Wong, Franklin Odo, with Betty Wong (eds.), *Roots: An Asian American Reader* (Los Angeles: U.C.L.A. Asian American Studies Center, 1971); Kay-yu and Helen Palubinska (eds.), *Asian American Authors* (Boston: Houghton Mifflin, Co., 1972); Frank Chin, Jeffery Paul Chan, Lawson Fusso Inada and Shawn Hsu Wong (eds.), *Aiiieeee! An Anthology of Asian-American Authors* (Washington, D.C.: Howard University Press, 1974); Elaine H. Kim, *Asian American Literature: An Introduction to the Writings and their Social Context* (Philadelphia: Temple University Press, 1982); and King-Kok Cheung and Stan Yogi (eds.), *Asian American Literature, An Annotated Bibliography* (New York: Modern Language Association of America, 1988).

12. *Time,* 31 August 1988.

13. To these I would add: Raymond Barrio, *The Plum Pickers* (1969), Richard Vásquez, *Chicano* (1970), Miguel Méndez, *Peregrinos de Aztlán* (*Pilgrims of Aztlan,* 1971), Oscar Zeta Acosta, *The Autobiography of a Brown Buffalo* (1972), Alexandro Morales, *Caras Viejas y Vino Nuevo* (*Old Faces and New Wine,* 1975), Rolando Hinojoso, *Klail City y sus Alrededores* (*Klail City and its Environs,* 1976), and Nash Candelaria, *Memories of the Alhambra* (1977).

14. The other two are *The Magic Journey* (1976) and *The Nirvana Blues* (1978).

15. *Bless Me, Ultima* (Berkeley, California: Quinto Sol Publications, 1972); *Heart of Aztlán* (Berkeley, California: Editorial Justa, 1976); and *Tortuga* (Berkeley, California: Editorial Justa, 1979). Among Anaya's other main publications should be included his several anthologies: *Cuentos: Tales from the Hispanic Southwest* (Santa Fe, New Mexico: Museum of New Mexico Press, 1980) and (co-ed. Antonio Marquez), *Cuentos Chicanos: A Short Story Anthology* (Albuquerque, New Mexico: University of New Mexico Press, 1984); his play *The Season of la Llorona* (produced by El Teatro de la Companía de Albuquerque, October 1979); his travel-narrative *A Chicano in China* (Albuquerque, New Mexico: University of New Mexico Press, 1986); his collection *The Silences of the Llano: Short Stories* (1982); and his various essays and stories published in magazines like *Bilingual Review/Revista Bilingüe, Escolios, Agenda, Rocky Mountain Magazine, Grito del Sol* and *South Dakota Review.*

16. Juan Bruce-Novoa (ed.), *Chicano Authors: Inquiry by Interview* (op. cit.), pp. 184–85.

Rudolfo Anaya with R. S. Sharma (interview date 7 April 1992)

SOURCE: "Interview with Rudolfo Anaya," in *Prairie Schooner,* Vol. 68, No. 4, Winter, 1994, pp. 177–87.

[*In the following interview, originally conducted in 1992, Anaya discusses the state of Chicano literature in the United States, as well as his own literary aims, cultural concerns, and identity as a Chicano writer.*]

> *This interview was taped on April 7, 1992 in his office at the University of New Mexico. R. S. Sharma teaches in the Department of English, Osmania University, Hyderabad, India.*

[*Sharma:*] *Rudy, I am in this country to learn about the writers. You are one of the major voices of Chicano writing and, in fact, one of the pioneers. What exactly is meant by Chicano writing and Chicano literature?*

[Anaya:] We are very glad that you can be with us. Welcome to the University of New Mexico in Albuquerque. [Anaya's recent novel is titled **Alburquerque.** He insists on using the original spelling of the city, la villa de Alburquerque.] The Chicano movement began in the mid-1960s in California and in the Southwest, and in other places where there were Mexican-American communities. It was designated as the Chicano movement because the Mexican-American community was looking for a word, a label, that would most closely fit our identity—our present identity. And so they took the word Chicano from *Mexicano*; Me-shi-cano became Chicano. Embodied in that word was a sense of pride, a sense of revolution, a sense that we had to create our own destiny, a sense that we could not leave that destiny in the hands of Anglo-America; we had a history and a heritage and a language to preserve, to be proud of and to study.

That history had not been presented to us in the educational system. For me, Chicano means taking our destiny into our own hands. We are Hispano in the sense that we are a Spanish-speaking group; we are Mestizos in the sense that we are Mexicanos who came up (either recently, or in the last generation, or many years ago) from Mexico. Our ancestors came through Mexico and became part of the Mexican mestizo (a blending of the European with the Native Americans). In my case, my ancestors settled here along the Río Grande and for many centuries learned from, lived with, and intermarried with the Pueblo Indians. So Chicano also meant taking pride in the indigenous Native American roots that are a part of us.

Well, the question of tradition. Which tradition would you like yourself to be associated with? The European tradition, so-called American tradition, or the Spanish tradition in literature? Or would you like to create a tradition of your own?

You said in your lecture last week that India is, in many ways, an eclectic country. That it draws from many traditions and maybe that's its strength. I see myself as an eclectic person. I can draw from many traditions. If we are really to know ourselves, we have to rely on the vast storehouse of humanity, not just one narrow path. As a matter of fact, that's been the problem in this country. In the United States, Anglo-America has insisted on the tradition of *one* path to follow. (The melting pot, you see.) It doesn't fit. It doesn't work and it creates damage and harm.

You also hit the nail on the head when you said, "Would you like to create a position of your own?" I think that is what the Chicano movement has done. We have looked at our heritage and our history and re-analyzed it to create a Chicano literature. So, for the first time through the publication of books that go out to society and to the world, we created a literature from our own community, from our roots. And in it we are speaking of our identity, our history, our language, the oppression that we have suffered, and we were pointing to the future. The sense of identity is what we would like to see in our community—to revitalize it, to give it pride, and to become, in a sense, this multicultural eclectic group that can draw from many streams of thought.

You have talked about bilingualism. And Chicanismo as a bilingual culture. Now, do you have problems with that? Do you think culture is language specific? If it is language specific which would you prefer, English or Spanish?

One definition of culture is language specific: the language is the soul of the culture and if you lose the language, you lose the soul. I grew up speaking Spanish in a small village here in New Mexico. I spoke Spanish the first six years of my life, until I went to school. I didn't know a word of English. My grandparents and my parents spoke only Spanish, most of my family, most of the neighbors in that small village spoke Spanish. I still retain a great deal of my New Mexican Spanish and I speak it. Chicano youth of today are changing to English. I write now in English, as you know. I think what we can portray of our culture is now in the *content* of the story, the poem, or the play—in the content we can carry our culture and its values forward, even though the language is English. I would not like to see the Spanish language lost. I think we should preserve it, and I think this country should wake up and realize that being bilingual or multilingual is an asset and teach more language, but at the same time we're struggling with this very real contemporary problem: we have to do our best in English and see if the content will carry forth in that language.

Is the Chicano movement just a cultural movement? Are you just seeking cultural pluralism, or are you also seeking political pluralism? Do you have a politicalism now?

Yes, we have a political agenda; it was especially evident in the early years of the Chicano movement. There were many ideologies that were presented to the Chicano community, ranging from Marxism to cultural nationalism, the myth of Aztlán, for example, and its power to perhaps regenerate and gather the community together again. Wrapped up in those ideologies were the ideals of more representation, better jobs, better health protection for farm workers, and other workers. We sought entry into post-secondary education, and we wanted an education that was relevant to our children in the lower grades. We desperately needed professors and administrators in secondary education and at the university level. All that was part of a very definite political agenda. Part of that political agenda was a parallel stream: the cultural movement. We returned to Mexican music, Mexican art and created Chicano literature, Chicano theater, motion pictures, and one of the most lasting attributes of the Chicano movement, Chicano literature. The Chicanos found their voice and began to publish in small presses, to create from the beginnings in 1965 a few books, and now twenty years later, hundreds of books and a whole new generation of writers, a whole new generation of women writers— Chicanas who are lending their perspective to Chicano literature.

Would you prefer a Chicano existence within the corporate life of the U.S. or would you like to be associated with life in Mexico?

During the early days of the Chicano movement in the early 1970s I was traveling a lot to Mexico, almost every summer, and I was learning the culture and beginning also to speak more and more Spanish. I also studied the history and mythology, because I have made a great deal of use of mythology in my work. I like myth, I like the oral tradition that comes from the people and works its way into the novels. So, I was reflecting on the importance of that indigenous experience, whatever it is about me that is Mexicano. I filled myself up with those experiences, bringing them back with me to New Mexico where I was writing my novels.

My identity right now is tied to the Chicano identity. I can work in the Anglo-American world. I have been a professional teacher, secondary and also in the elementary, and the post-secondary schools at the university level. I can live in that world, I can work in it, I understand it. I could probably, after a very short time, also survive in Mexico, but my reality is here. My reality is in the United States as a person who has a particular history and heritage. Out of that heritage grew an identity that is strong, authentic, and proud. The United States should wake up and realize that those of us who are from different cultural groups want to keep up our identity within those groups, and we have every right to that identity.

You can see that I have a dark skin and features that don't fit the Anglo-American features, and you know that I was born here in New Mexico, my roots are here, so I demand to have a right to that identity. I can live in many cultures, and I can be multicultural and multilingual and still enjoy this identity. You see, the mainstream has tried to take that identity away from us. It didn't work. It caused too many problems and hardships and it ruined too many lives. People have to be free to choose their identity, so they can be fulfilled, so they can be liberated as authentic human beings.

The line of color, even in Mexico is not very well defined. In your writing you have recognized the Indian heritage as part of the Chicano heritage. Maybe as an American you have more in common with Anglo-America than with Mexico?

I probably do. Because I was born and raised in this country. I am a product of its school system, I am a product of an English department at the university and majoring in English language and literature, and the psyche and the history and the popular culture and the racism of this country, so I am a product of this country. I don't deny that. And as you say, probably more so than of Mexico. I have lived here all my life. But I still have to create my own identity, and I want to preserve my Nuevomexicano culture and its values.

You are a writer. Who do you write for?

Sometimes I write for the world, and sometimes I write for the Chicano community and sometimes that community is very specific. Sometimes I write for the Nuevo Mexi-canos, the New Mexicans. Sometimes I will write either a scene or a passage thinking of a particular person enjoying that passage. Writing is a communication of my life to everyone. I am very much a part of this Southwest region. So I don't know if my work would strike a chord of recognition in India. But I hope it would, you see, because that's one of my goals, to write for everyone.

Yes. If literature did not have that universal element it will not register beyond its very immediate context. Many American ethnic writers are received very well in India, primarily because they have a great deal of feeling and emotion in their writing which is somehow missing in the mainstream. There is a great deal of experimentation with form.

I would add to that that it's not only our emotion and our passion for writing, we are also presenting to the United States and to the world a particular world view.

What is that world view?

For me, it's part European, it's part Anglo-American, it's part New Mexican, and it was formed in my childhood: the way of life that my parents and my grandparents lived, which was life in a small New Mexico village, a pastoral way of life with sheep, cattle, small farms along the river, very religious and spiritual. Religious and Catholic. Spiritual in the sense of oneness with the universe and the love of the earth which comes from the Native American traditions. A very communal approach to life, values of respect for the old, a very deep attachment to the earth that not only has to do with the pastoral lifestyle but, I

think, it has to do with that Native American experience that the Mexicans learned in the Rio Grande. The earth is the mother that nurtures us all with the grains and fruit which we receive. Add the fact that historically we were colonized in the mid-nineteenth century by the United States and you have added a brand new dimension to the world view of the Mexicano. And when two distinct world views and cultures meet, you get an added dimension to life not always pleasant. Sometimes borrowing and sometimes sharing and sometimes growing with each other, but also very often an oppressive situation which I think some Chicanos would insist is the true definition of Chicano. That dialectic between the Chicano and the Anglo-American.

Your work also grows from a strong house of myths and you're also creating myths. What are they?

They are a way to understand the truth or to get to the truth. We want to understand the myths that all people have created on Earth, the spiritual myths of all communal groups. And maybe eventually we will learn the central storehouse of mythology. They're another way of looking at philosophy, spiritual thought, and wisdom. In my case they have to do with an indigenous experience. You know my book **Lord of the Dawn,** about Quetzalcóatl? It's based on a Mexican legend. I also have an interest in the cuentos (the oral tradition) of my culture. Native American myths resonate in me. They tell me something about myself. So I like to work those ideas into my novels.

Since the publication of your first novel you have done many other novels. Has your perspective as a Chicano writer changed?

I would hope so. I am still very tied to the original idea I had of writing a literature that relates to my community, a literature that describes our experience—in which people can recognize themselves. My perspective has not changed. I have been labeled a regional writer. That used to bother me—it doesn't bother me anymore. Because I see the importance of the work that I'm, that we're, doing.

The label "regional writer" was perceived, and is still perceived, as limiting. But you have the literature of the East, the whole range of writers; you have the literature of the South.

There is a whole world view wrapped up in the South that is defined by their history and their language and how they evolved. And we know so little about it. So we go to the writers and try to understand it. Through the literature we get a sense of their history. Someone said very recently, no one ever called Eugene O'Neill an ethnic writer. Of course he was, but he got incorporated into the canon, so it's much easier to marginalize us or pigeonhole us and put us to the side and say "Oh, those are the ethnic writers," as if we didn't know anything. That's the problem of not ac-cepting a more eclectic, multicultural point of view. Because then you don't give credit to each community and what it produces. To me that is hypocritical. As Chicanos we are here, and we are going to remain here and we're going to remain an active, creative people. The country will have to listen to us. We're going to make a difference.

Yes, I think there is a greater response to diversity in this country at the moment.

There is also a reaction. While we have more people aware of diversity, and more classes in the universities, there is this big reaction against it. So we have to deal with both sides. The new openness and the old status quo.

In India we have fourteen constitutionally recognized languages with their own literature. So we are familiar with the phenomenon of diversity; literary diversity, which you are not. Our students, when they read Chicano writers, or American Indian writers, still think of them as American writers. Are you happy with that kind of perception?

Yes, that's the way they see us in the beginning. But I think they have to dig deeper and realize the struggle that we've had within the society. We had to create our own literature and to create our own small presses. It hasn't been easy, you see. So, it's all right for your students to accept us that way, but also they have to know our history.

It would not appear to be true in your case considering that your first novel itself sold, if I'm right, more than a million.

No, no, not a million. I think we're at 300,000.

That's quite a reasonable sale for a first novel.

It's astounding in terms of book sales in this country. **Bless Me, Ultima** was published in 1972, it's now 1992, twenty years later . . . it's being used in high school, universities, around the world. I think many people still talk about it as a small press phenomenon. I'm very pleased. Now the publication houses of the United States are opening up a little bit to Chicano works. I see now that some of our writers are publishing with Doubleday, or Norton, or New Directions.

You mean there is a general acceptance of minority writing now in this country?

In a limited way. Afro-American writing has had an acceptance for quite a while, published by the big trade publishers. A few Native American writers have had that acceptance, and are recognized. Chicano writers are still on the tail end. I would say it's only been in the past few years that major trade publishers will look at a Chicano writer or publish them. So, the general acceptance is still not there.

Who do you think are the major Chicano writers now?

Maybe I'll give you a bibliography. That way you can look through the names. I think it's dangerous to talk about the *major* writers when we ourselves are struggling to get all the writers of our culture out and published. There has to be real concern to make sure that women within our culture have access to publication, and that homosexuals and gays have access to publication. That people who have not been able to share in that process have access. I think there is a new generation of young writers some of whom are gaining in importance. We are going to have Denise Chávez here on Friday, Ray González, Luis Urrea. José Montoya is still writing in California, one of the members of the old generation, but still very active. I can go on and on. There is now more of a gathering of other Latino writers in the United States. I think you're going to see the Puerto Ricans and the Cubans really come into the forefront and begin to learn about us and about each other. Virgil Suarez, down in the South is doing an anthology and he published my work, and he wants to come to New Mexico to make a connection with us. He's a Cuban-American writer. The new Latino literature is going to be very exciting in the next five or ten years.

But you will be still writing about the American experience. From a different perspective.

No, we will be writing—I will be writing about my experience *within* the American experience. There's a difference.

I have read about Chicano writers. Chicano poets. Women writing about literature, and I felt that many of them are writing the same way in which other women were writing than, say, different ethnic groups. Anything universal about this women's writing?

I think if you talk to the Chicana writers their universal response has to do with their struggle in a world that has been defined by men, and as literature has been defined by men, and largely taught and propagated by men. They have that common element. They are now presenting their own voice, which is a new voice, very much like the Chicano male writers presented their voice in the '60s and early '70s.

The ethnic writer wants to be heard. But you want something more than simply being heard by an all-American audience.

Well, isn't that idea of communication crucial to writing? In the beginning was the word, God wanted to be heard. Nothing wrong with a writer wanting to be heard. Because being heard means being able to create in the face of chaos (or in the case of oppression) your own identity. What is heard is your voice and your voice says, I too am a human being! I, too, belong to the human race and I have hopes and fears and aspirations: listen to me! I think that is a very important element of why we dare to write.

I think there is too much reliance on the past in much of the ethnic writing. Too much reliance on past history. Do you think there is a possibility of looking beyond the past into the future?

Writers writing about the future write science fiction, but I don't know too many ethnic writers writing science fiction. There's nothing wrong if your past has never been told, to tell it. We're trying to express our history, our community, our language, our language of the street, our bilingual language, everything that is us because it's never been told. This is what's exciting! We are concerned with the present and the future. That's where our children are going to live, and we have to give them skills to live in that world. But very many of us, or maybe I'll speak for myself, look at life now and into the future and don't see the things I value. Life is getting more violent, more war, more greed, and we are creating technologies that enslave us instead of help us. So why shouldn't I look at values that came from my past, that speak to the human being and my needs, not only as a person but as a spiritual person? Nothing wrong with that. We read world literature and the classics and philosophy, not only contemporary literature, because history gives us clues to the search we have for our identity.

I didn't mean there was anything wrong in that pursuit. How do you relate to the present?

My novel, **Alburquerque,** looks at my city, Albuquerque, New Mexico, at the traditional cultures of the Rio Grande, at the Chicano, Native American, and what's happening all around us in the city. Change, new people coming here, new industry, money, politics, what all these have to do with my life and my community. The majority of the work that I see coming out now looks at and analyzes our present situation.

There's too much reliance, also, on myths and folklore. What do you think about form? Myth and folklore are very important ingredients of your form, of Chicano literature. Are there any new experimentations in form?

Oh yes. Tremendous amounts of experimentation at the very beginning of the Chicano movement. Poets and writers were writing bilingual poetry, trilingual poetry, or poetry in four or five languages, English, Spanish, Black rhythm, Mexican Nahuatl, Indian, and our street Pachuco talk. [Nahuatl is the native language spoken in Central Mexico and Pachuco is the argot of the Mexican American (Chicano) zoot-suiters of the 1940s. Both languages are still spoken today.] Don't tell me that's not experimentation! It's been there from the beginning! In my own early novel, although it's a traditional story set in a small town in New Mexico, the Spanish language comes across as a crucial ingredient. Some of the newer writers now are very interested in experimenting with style. (Juan Felipe Herrera and Francisco Alarcon are examples.) My own interest is still a more conventional approach to the novel because I want to communicate with my community. That's important to me, so I don't see my role as a stylist. My work comes from the oral tradition, mythology, magical realism, the community, all adapted to fiction.

I gather that the literacy percent is very low among the Chicano community. Do you think lots of people read the literature?

I think many read, but unfortunately the history of the Mexican American people in this country tells us we have not had access to education. We have been a working people.

We have worked in farms and factories. Quite frankly, the generation after World War II and then my generation after the Korean War is the first Chicano generation to have widespread access to education. A small group of us became educated. Now we have a slightly larger group, the present generation, but it's still very low in comparison to the total society. So yes, literacy is a major concern in getting our stories, our poetry, and our theater out to our community. It is a major concern for me.

Do you have a kind of central body of Chicano writers? Something like the national association of Chicano writers?

No. We have a National Association of Chicano Studies that meets once a year. Writers are asked to read and present panels on their work and we meet each other. We really don't have a national association of Chicano writers. It's a good idea.

What are the major journals devoted to Chicano writing?

Las Americas from Arte Público Press and *The Bilingual Review* from the Hispanic Research Center in Tempe, Arizona State University, *La Confluencia* from Colorado.

Do you think a Chicano writer can live well by writing?

No. As a matter of fact very few writers can live well, even to say, pay their rent and have food on the table, by writing. Most writers in this country do another job.

Do you feel satisfied as a writer? With your role as a writer?

Extremely satisfied. I think it's the best life that the fates (el destino) could have granted.

I see that you have a large array of honors. What is your ultimate ambition?

I don't have an ultimate. I have now a project to write four novels based on the city of Albuquerque. I have written about the idea of change, people trying to change New Mexico into their own image and the harm that comes to people already here. I've finished the second one, **Zia Summer,** about storehousing of nuclear waste in New Mexico. I'm working on the third one. So I would say short-term it's to finish this quartet of novels.

Are there writers writing plays, drama? Do you have a tradition of Chicano drama?

Yes. We have a long tradition. In the old Mexicano newspapers of the Southwest, literature was included. And theater troops from Mexico used to come up and perform theater. We have folk theater and dances in the pueblos. And, now we have the Chicano movement, teatro. Luis Valdez was very important in Chicano theater, and he's gone on to make movies. Jorge Huerta is very well known. We have here in Albuquerque a bilingual theater company that has produced some of my plays, and the plays of other writers, not only from the state but international writers. A good theater movement, struggling but good.

Thank you very much. I avoided asking you more universal questions, criticisms and theory because I wanted you to talk basically to reach out to the students and teachers.

Well, it's also best, because, as you know, I think of myself as a writer.

Kevin McIlvoy (review date 30 August 1992)

SOURCE: "Celebrating the Old Ways," in *Los Angeles Times Book Review,* August 30, 1992, p. 8.

[*In the following review, McIlvoy offers a positive assessment of* Alburquerque.]

Alburquerque is an archetypal story of a young man's initiation into self-acceptance and, finally, kinship with others. The truth offered in Rudolfo Anaya's newest novel is deceptively simple: *Tu eres tu.* You are who you are.

In *Bless Me, Ultima, Heart of Aztlán, Tortuga, Silence of the Llano,* and his works of nonfiction, this extraordinary storyteller has always written unpretentiously but provocatively about identity. Every work is a "fiesta," a ceremony preserving but reshaping old traditions that honor the power within the land and *la raza,* the people. One account in *Alburquerque* explains:

> It was in the fiestas of the people that I discovered the essence of my people, the Mexican heritage of my mother. There is a chronicle of life in the fiestas, beginning with baptism. *La fiesta bautismo.* I painted the *padrinos* at church as they held the baby over the font for the priest to bless *el niño* with holy water. In the faces of the *padrino* and *madrina* I saw and understood the godparents' role. The *padrinos* would become the child's second parents, and the familial kinship in the village or the barrio would be extended. *La familia* would grow.

The exhilarating fiesta of *Alburquerque* is a splendid reading experience set in the contemporary city of Albuquerque, which, we learn, might have kept its original spelling if not for the Anglo stationmaster in the 1880s who remembered to paint both q's but could not remember both r's. In mixed admiration and disdain New Mexicans describe Albuquerque by saying, "It's not Santa Fe."

Albuquerque, they mean, has not yet become a parody of itself but, for the sake of "economic development," it soon could.

At a time when the future identity of the city seems to be exclusively in the hands of the politicians and other power brokers, a young ex-Golden Gloves champion, Abran Gonzalez, tries to solve the mysteries of his own past and future. He has very little information at hand, only cryptic legends about his dead mother, Cynthia Johnson. He has, as well, some of her paintings. Abran has been told that "she painted an honesty into the *Hispanos* that's never been done before. Same faces you see on the street today, or in the villages. The gringo painters can't do that. Not a one can get the soul of the people. She did. In her paintings you look into the soul of this land."

All the strands of Abran's life story, he finds, are held by others who, after his mother's death, withhold information about the personality of his mother and the identity of his real father. He struggles to learn more about his mother and father's choice to give him up for adoption. As he takes hold of more strands he is pulled across personal borders into new awareness: "He was a child of this border, a child of the line that separated white and brown. *La raza* called people like him 'coyote.'"

A poignant element of the novel concerns how Abran's friend, Joe Calabasa, a "coyote" of Santo Domingo Indian and Mexican blood, unselfishly involves himself in Abran's search. Through these parts of the story new definitions of community emerge. Abran and Joe learn together the ways in which community and family might once more be linked by a lasting connection to "the earth and the rhythms of the people."

He falls in love with Lucinda, whose family, like Abran's, has old roots in the Albuquerque community. What results from meeting and coming to know Lucinda's family is an understanding of the community's identity that becomes more important to him than his individual identity.

Alburquerque is unflinchingly honest in its portrayal of class lines and ethnic lines, but it is also convincingly optimistic—even in 1992, in the golden age of cynicism. How is that possible?

One answer is that Anaya treats the contemporary value of the old ceremonies, the fiestas that have inexplicably lasted: the cleaning of the *acequia* on the Santo Domingo pueblo, the pilgrimage to the church at Chimayo, the healing methods of the *curanderas* like Nana and dòna Tules, the stories retold by the old people like Juan Oso and by the new storytellers like Ben Chavez. In his patient, respectful portrayal of these ceremonies in *Alburquerque,* Anaya seems to passionately argue for them to be allowed to continue. The novel itself is a tribute to how storytelling traditions should be allowed to change and develop. Room must be made for all the ceremonies to co-exist in urban New Mexico, especially in cities like Albuquerque and Santa Fe—which Lucinda calls "Santa Fantasy."

When Anaya writes of these ceremonies, the prose shimmers like the air of northern New Mexico, dense with golden dust and pollen. An entry from Abran's mother's diary recalls the haunting fiesta of *la matanza* (the killing of hogs for winter meat). After the young people have been unable to muster strength or wisdom enough to gracefully act their parts in the very old, brutal drama, the patriarch of the family, don Pedro, takes charge:

> When don Pedro had come face-to-face with the pig, he raised his hammer, and with the speed of a matador, there was a brief glint in the sunlight, the arc of his arm, a dull thud, and the pig jerked back and stiffened. The kill was complete and clean.
>
> It had taken all the old man's strength to make the kill, but he had done it with grace. There was no loud thunder of the rifle, no crying children or barking dogs, just a clean kill. We stood hypnotized as don Pedro dropped to his knees in front of the quivering pig. Two of the men held the pig by the ears as don Pedro plunged the knife into the pig's heart. The blood flowed swiftly.
>
> . . . When don Pedro withdrew the knife it seemed to come out spotless, unbloodied, and his hands were clean. Then the old man stood, and a shudder of fatigue passed through his frail body. He took a deep breath, and then sipped from the tin cup of water his wife handed him. He smiled at her, and when he looked at us, there was a serene beauty in his face.

The minor characters in this disturbing, memorable story-within-the-story, don Pedro and tia Ramona, are among many vivid figures who collectively make up the personality of the community. In *Albuquerque* the community itself, with its contradictory history of physical brutality and spiritual beauty, is as vital a character as Abran.

The author is less successful in distinctively portraying the subplot of political satire involving the mayoral competition between Frank Dominic, Marisa Martinez, and Walter Johnson. They are ruthless, ruthless, and ruthless, respectively. The battles between them are replays of familiar Southwestern political power struggles involving land grants and water rights. This mayoral race culminates in predictable melodrama; however it ultimately does nothing to diminish the quiet, rewarding surprises throughout *Alburquerque.*

Like his friend, Ben Chavez, Abran Gonzalez discovers in the "violence and fear . . . at the core of every city" the healing effects of public and private ceremony. *Alburquerque* invites the reader into a fiesta: a cleansing, blessing journey of simple steps through old and complex paths.

Jordan Jones (review date Fall 1992)

SOURCE: A review of *Alburquerque,* in *Review of Contemporary Fiction,* Vol. 12, No. 3, Fall, 1992, pp. 201–02.

[*In the following review, Jones offers a favorable assessment of* Alburquerque.]

At the age of twenty-one, Abrán González—the former Golden Gloves boxer and pride of the Albuquerque barrio—discovers at the deathbed of his birth mother Cynthia Johnson that he was adopted and is half Anglo. This revelation begins Abrán's quest for his father, which forms the center of a magical book that heals like the hands of a *curandera* shaman.

Alburquerque fairly brims with considerations of origins. The title reclaims the city's original spelling, lost when an Anglo stationmaster dropped the first *r* on the railroad sign. Abrán's search for his own beginnings thrusts him into Cynthia's high-society world. He meets Frank Dominic, one of Albuquerque's richest powerbrokers, Ben Chávez, a Latino novelist, and Marisa Martínez, Albuquerque's beautiful and committed mayor. These people and others help teach Abrán how to be himself—most do so by positive example; Frank Dominic does so by negative example. (Even Dominic is obsessed with origins; he fancies himself a descendant of the Duke of Alburquerque.) In the course of the novel, Abrán learns that, despite seeming ethnic complexity, he is who he is. As Doña Tules says to Abrán, "Tú eres tú."

Anaya is at his visionary best in creating magical realist moments that connect people with one another and the earth. Cynthia Johnson's diary describes a certain "la matanza" (ceremonial killing of hogs) botched by young men who had lost their connection to life and the earth: "It was a ceremony, the taking of the animal's life to provide meat for the family. The young men needed to be reminded that it was not sport, it was a tradition." Joe, Abrán's half-Indian, half-Mexican friend, woke up in Vietnam while about to kill a man: "'I couldn't kill him. It would've been wrong, the old man wasn't a deer, he was a man.'" These visionary moments become, in the course of the book, ever more magical and curative, transforming the characters into nothing more nor less than themselves.

Rudolfo Anaya with Ray González (interview date March 1993)

SOURCE: "Songlines of the Southwest: An Interview with Rudolfo A. Anaya," in *Conversations with Rudolfo Anaya,* edited by Bruce Dick and Silvio Sirias, University Press of Mississippi, 1998, pp. 153–60.

[*In the following interview, originally conducted in 1993 and published in* The Bloomsbury Review, *Anaya addresses his retirement from the University of New Mexico, his writing projects, the lasting influence of* Bless Me, Ultima, *and his views on contemporary Chicano literature.*]

This interview was conducted in March 1993 during Anaya's visit to The Guadalupe Cultural Arts Center in San Antonio, Texas.

[*González:*] *You're retiring from teaching at the University of New Mexico and want to devote more time to your writing and other interests. At the same time your novel* **Alburquerque** *is reaching a larger audience. It's going to appear in a mass paperback edition along with* **Bless Me, Ultima.** *Do you feel all these things show that you are reaching a new phase in your long career as a writer?*

[Anaya:] That's a very good way to put it: a new phase. I don't view leaving the University of New Mexico and teaching as retirement. I view it more as the mid-career change, to do a lot of writing and other things, like reading. I want to do more essays. So I think it's just a shift of energy into new areas.

You are one of the first Chicanos to get recognition with **Bless Me, Ultima** *in the early seventies, before the whole idea of multiculturalism meant a larger audience and more opportunities for Latino writers. Who do you think your audience was twenty to twenty-five years ago? Has it changed much? Are there more publishing venues than twenty years ago?*

Bless Me, Ultima, was published in 1972, the same time that the multicultural efforts in education and publishing began. At that time **Bless Me, Ultima** had two audiences: one, the Chicano community, because they had not had contemporary fiction to read by living Chicano writers; two, white America found an interest not only in the culture I was portraying but also the worldview that was portrayed in my work. The audiences are still the same. There is a growing audience in the Chicano community that wants to read its writers, and certainly in twenty years we've built up that audience. It's more aware, and it's searching for new writers. The rest of the country has developed a tremendous interest in the cultural differences we present in our work. I also think an international audience has grown—there's an interest in Europe, in Mexico. I've gotten translations in Poland and Russia, for example. The cultural nucleus of family that we represent as Chicanos in the U.S. has so many fascinating and interesting aspects to it, that appeals to an international audience. That to me is a growing component.

When you were doing your early writing in the sixties and seventies, did you feel alone as a writer? Was there an external community back then or do you feel that now, with the higher attention on Chicano writers, there is more of a community?

Definitely, I felt very much alone as a writer. I was writing in Albuquerque, New Mexico, and teaching part time in grade school, then high school. I thought at the time, and I still do, that Chicano writers twenty years ago were composing the first models and aesthetics of what would be Chicano literature, for better or worse. I'll leave that to historical judgement. So we had that kind of isolation. We didn't have other contemporary works around us. It was the beginning of the whole Chicano movement.

In my case, I didn't have enough examples, especially in the novel. We had *Pocho* by Villareal, but even that we

hadn't read. We really had to compose a style of our own, a sense of community, our sense of storytelling and the *cuentos, corridos,* the give and take of *familia.* We had to evolve that model that we would eventually present as our literature. The aspect that was not lonely was more of a subconscious energy; the Chicano movement itself. Literary movements are formed by this subconscious energy that is going on. You may not be aware of it, but you are being energized by it. By the time I hit the press in 1972 with **Bless Me, Ultima,** Quinto Sol was publishing Rolando Hinojosa and Tomás Rivera. Estela Portillo was also publishing. Out of that we created the base of contemporary Chicano literature.

Do you think that today **Bless Me, Ultima** *offers its audience a chance to interpret the book differently than perhaps readers did twenty years ago?*

I think that question could be better answered by critics from my point of view. They are still looking at the same things. In other words, teachers will tell me what their students think, or I'll get a group of letters from students, or I'll go to a high school and visit students. They are very interested in the life of Antonio, how he grew up, how it relates to them. They are interested in that element of our culture that is spiritual, that has to do with healing resources and with our long tradition of using the earth and its resources not only to feed ourselves but to heal us. All of that has come into a kind of fruition, and people are very interested. They still find the same kind of interest in **Bless Me, Ultima,** after all these years.

Even though there are more novels today by Chicano writers, the subject matter of **Bless Me, Ultima** *is not found in too many of them. More of these contemporary novels are about urban life. The spiritual quest you offer in* **Bless Me, Ultima** *is harder to find in younger Chicano writers. Do you have any ideas of why that might be?*

I think the movement from the rural to the urban setting is very natural. Chicanos have moved out of the farms, ranches, and small villages into urban settings. On the other hand, I insist that if there are universal values, that make us the community that we are, we have to take those universal values into the urban setting. Otherwise urban novels will reflect only chaos, violence, and disorientation of the contemporary urban setting. It's good too that writers reflect part of the realities as they try to give it meaning—as in **Alburquerque**—by not forgetting those roots. The roots of our universality as so deep and embedded in such a beautiful, indigenous tradition. Their fingers stretch back into Iberian and North African and Mediterranean traditions. We haven't begun to tap the deeper meaning of what constitutes our consciousness. That's what I find exciting—contemporary writers who will pay attention to what we can eventually call our *alma,* our soul, and reflect that in their work. There is so much to be done that we need dozens of writers poised to create the second phase of the Chicano movement, *una nueva onda.* We see it happening in the younger writers today. If we are going to reflect only on the disorientation and the chaos, then the question is, What do we reflect to our community? Part of my role as a writer is to reflect the deeper meaning of our universal experiences.

We've talked off and on about how there are more opportunities for younger Chicano writers. Do you ever wonder whether having more publishers going after their work, more agents, more reading and writing programs, take away from the sense of community among the writers? Can they get back to their people, or is there such competitiveness within the market that it removes the writers from their community?

I think it's natural in the evolution of any community to be caught up in the desires of the society at large. In many respects, its about time our writers had opportunities to publish with trade publishers that can distribute works to a wider audience. We write to communicate, and that communication somehow has to be gotten out. My only concern is that some of the publishers still view the Chicano community as one that really doesn't have depth of meaning, one still largely invisible to the American eye, invisible to white America. Exploitation may come about because they are now under pressure to publish the work of this community, which is big and growing. With the given world economics of this hemisphere, it is acquiring a force. We have to be careful not to join hands in that exploitation. We need our writers to be published and distributed. We need to make more movies, we need to get our music and art out because of our rich heritage. We have to remember one of our first jobs as Chicano artists is to try to reflect our own community and our own deeper reality of who we are as Chicanos.

You've written a number of other novels and several books of nonfiction, yet, **Bless Me, Ultima,** *and its legacy are always with you and with readers and scholars of Chicano literature who know the history of the genre. How do you see yourself moving beyond that book and legacy, even though it's going to be a part of your biography forever? Has it been hard to live with that book and yet go on to other work?*

Quite the contrary. Every author should be so lucky to have a first novel stay around twenty years. I see it as a blessing that I was able to write it in those early years while I was wrapped up in trying to find my soul within and the soul of my community, that I could pull enough together in one story to reflect that. People have told me that I'm lucky to hit that once in a lifetime. I was convinced as a young writer that what I wanted to do was go on and write, to try all kinds of genres, attitudes and attempts at storytelling. I've done nonfiction, travel journals, plays, and children stories. I learn more about myself and about writing by the constant exploration in those other areas. I'm darned glad I have a *Bless Me, Ultima* at the middle passage in my life. I can pay attention to a lot of things I want to write about. That's a very comfortable place to be.

When you read novels by other Chicano writers, especially younger ones, do you feel there is a sense of personal search or do you feel they are too busy reflecting on what's going on now, trying to be a part of the market and getting recognition? How do you approach these newer Chicano novels?

As I said earlier, I think it's part of a natural evolution to have this new bursting out, this flowering, this *nueva onda,* if you want to call it that, of young writers, especially a lot of women writers who are finding their voices. The only way we learn about ourselves is from a diversity of voices. You can't learn from one person. Even in the origin of our culture, we pay attention more to village elders as opposed to one chief priest. So we have that tradition, and new writers are the new chorus of the community. Being here, I was reflecting on how different San Antonio is from Albuquerque. We have to recognize that within the community we have these regional differences. We pay attention to different parts of our lives that have to do with the region and the landscape. We need the poets from San Francisco to read in New Mexico, and we need the writers from San Antonio to also read in New Mexico. They need us. That chorus is going to present a truer picture of who we are. In terms of the market, it is unwise for young writers to be fooled into exploitation by a market simply because it is there. Writing is an art. To me it's almost a sacred calling that we have. We are in the sense those new elders. We have to be careful that what we say is not exploited.

Albuquerque and the Southwest have been settings for a number of your books. In recent years, so-called border literature has been getting more recognition. Writers like Arturo Islas, Aristeo Brito, Denise Chávez, and yourself have been writing about this area. Why do you think there has been such a focus on the Southwest by novelists?

The ones you named live there. It is our turf, our *tierra.* One thing that makes writers strong is when they look at that field of energy, that *tierra* that has nurtured their body and their soul. It makes sense to write what you know.

Your most recent novel, **Alburquerque,** *tells a different kind of history, of a familiar place to many people who either know New Mexico or have been to the area who like the Southwest. In many ways, it ties into your other novels like* **Tortuga** *and* **Heart of Aztlán** *because it continues to create and document a way of life that even many Chicano audiences may not be aware of. I sense* **Alburquerque** *is a very important novel in your career. It's gathered many things from your earlier work and put them into this story. How do you see the new book?*

It is important in my career. You are right in saying it gathers the strands out of my first three novels. It is also quite a change in style for me. The lyricism I had as a young writer is not as prevalent. I saw myself moving into a new style by which to communicate to my community. Attacking political themes was something I hadn't done before. They certainly fit into the power struggles going on in the urban settings of the Southwest. The themes include problems of urban development that as an indigenous culture we have to deal with, and the growth of high technology in laboratories. The whole question will be with us forever—water usage, who owns, who dominates water usage, and how. In the West, it is a very important part of our lives. I'm in a new time and space. At the same time, I see that it has its roots planted in what is still *nuevo Mexicano*. The book is about what it means to me to be *nuevo Mexicano*.

Was it difficult to combine autobiographical details and the history of the area with these current political and environment problems? How did you come up with a story that preserves that past as you take on current issues about growth in New Mexico?

It was difficult in the sense that I worked on the novel for ten years. That may be indicative of the process I was going through. I was doing a lot of other things: anthologies, writing plays, editing, doing a few children's stories. But I constantly worked on *Alburquerque* during those years. The changes in subject matter and style were not easy. They were earned.

You have also edited a number of anthologies and continue to publish The Blue Mesa Review. *What made you go beyond the normal life of a writer to become an editor and work with different writers?*

I have been fortunate since I first published in 1972. I owe some of my time and energy to the writing community. Anthologies are a way of bringing new voices out and publishing them. The anthologies I did were for small presses, and there was no money to be earned. I did them so the presses would be able to publish another book. It's giving back part of my good fortune to the writing community.

When I talk to other Chicano writers about what's going on in publishing now, with a growing audience, your name comes up when we ask who are the writers who need to be read, who are the writers you need to talk to and find out what it takes to survive. People who talk to you and read your books learn some of the things that you've gone through. You are now one of the elders you mentioned earlier, one of the first ones who broke ground for those of us today. Are you still learning things yourself, or are you just passing things on to other writers?

Every day I sit down in front of my computer to write something new or revise something. I'm learning. If I weren't learning every day, I wouldn't be writing. The process for me is one of self-illumination. My goal is clarity. That's the basis of my worldview and was taught to me by my ancestors. It's my way of being in touch with the community, the earth, the universe. That process is good whether you are an eighteen-year-old writing your first short story or fifty-five and working on a new novel.

People call me up and send me manuscripts. I try to help as much as I can because it's again part of that return. They may be at a level where they need a lot of help. I'm willing to give as much as I can. Chicano writers by and large are still not coming out of the MFA creative writing programs. We're still largely self taught. We need to help each other a lot. The most important thing you can give a young writer is an editorial vision about what the work has in it, how it can be improved, what you see happening. If I were going to set up a program to help young Chicano writers, I would set up a mentorship program between young and older writers so that they could work together for six months to a year. The give and take is helpful.

In the beginning of the interview we talked about your being in an important place in your career—reading, getting away from teaching, finding more time for the other things. Are there any projects or goals you have not reached yet?

I have in mind a quartet of novels: *Alburquerque* is the first one, *Zia Summer* is the second one. I've already written it. I'm starting now to work on the third one. The goal of a quartet is brand new, and it's going to take a long time. I want to shift a bit of attention into developing stories for children, because one of the most crucial areas where we can give our sense of community is to the *niños*, to the young people. It's a responsibility that we have. I also want to continue to travel and do readings. Maybe spend more time in my apple orchard.

You've been in New Mexico your entire life, and you've produced a body of work mainly set in New Mexico. You've taught there and continue to create there. You are a writer who has a real sense of place. That's hard to find in a lot of writers today. Is there anything about home that means the most to you as you look back on your career?

If you study the map, you will find there are certain migration routes that are used along what we call the *frontera*. Our ancestors used these routes because they were what the aborigines of Australia called the "songlines of the earth," the songlines of *la Madre Tierra's* memory. The Río Grande valley and the Sangre de Cristo mountains in New Mexico for me are those kinds of places on earth. There is a great deal of spirituality attached to places. The sense of the memory of my ancestors and the memory of the earth is what gives me my power to write and reflect upon it. So I can't see uprooting myself in search of something new when it's right at my back door. Or I would say my door that faces east where the sun comes up every morning over the Sandia Mountains.

Feroza Jussawalla (review date Winter 1994)

SOURCE: A review of *Alburquerque,* in *World Literature Today,* Vol. 68, No. 1, Winter, 1994, p. 125.

[*In the following review, Jussawalla offers a positive assessment of* Alburquerque, *but notes that it does not measure up to Anaya's* Bless Me, Ultima.]

Rudolfo Anaya's **Bless Me, Ultima** is probably the best novel I have ever read. It has had a powerful impact on my thinking about differences in cultures and how we can bring them together through our own spirituality. Every semester I find some excuse to teach it, whether in children's literature, in my "Introduction to Fiction" courses, or in composition classes. **Alburquerque** is not such a novel and frankly does not measure up to **Ultima**'s greatness. It is, however, a touching story, one I could not put down once I had started it. Through some passages I wept copiously. Anaya is that kind of writer—gut-wrenching, tear-jerking, and one who leads you to an examination of your own life. If through **Alburquerque** he could get half the residents of Albuquerque, New Mexico, to examine their lives, as he led me to examine mine, he would fulfill his calling as a shaman and bring healing to our multicultural world.

Alburquerque is about Abran Gonzalez, an ex-Golden Gloves boxing champion who is the son of Cynthia Johnson and her Hispanic high-school boyfriend Ben Chavez. Cynthia, the daughter of a powerful white businessman, is forced to give up Abran shortly after his birth. Her father cannot stand the thought of his colleagues thinking that "Walter Johnson's daughter had lain with a Mexican kid and had a baby." Cynthia gives up the child to her childless maid to raise him. The novel begins as Abran receives a letter from Cynthia, his birth mother, while she is dying of cancer at an Albuquerque hospital. His adoptive mother finally tells him her story but does not know who the father is. Abran reaches his birth mother's bedside minutes too late, and thus his quest for his father begins. In his search to learn who his real father is, Abran allows himself to be used by the cunning Dominic, who talks him into a prize fight through which Dominic hopes to raise money and to increase his own popularity as a candidate for mayor of Albuquerque in a forthcoming election. As Abran is being pounded in the ring, his girlfriend and the man he does not know is his father, Ben Chavez, go ringside to tell him he does not need to fight any more, that Chavez is his father. The knowledge having given him a second wind, Abran wins the fight.

Like its predecessor, **Alburquerque** portrays a quest for knowledge. Here, however, it is a much more intimate knowledge which in the long run leads to the kind of over-arching knowledge that Antonio in **Bless Me, Ultima** struggles to attain: "Tu eres tu, a free spirit come to create his destiny in the world." **Alburquerque** is a novel about many cultures intersecting at an urban, power- and politics-filled crossroads, represented by a powerful white businessman, whose mother just happens to be a Jew who has hidden her Jewishness ("the crypto Jews of New Mexico"), and a boy from the barrio who fathers a child raised in the barrio but who eventually goes on to a triumphant assertion of his cross-cultural self.

William Clark (essay date 21 March 1994)

SOURCE: "The Mainstream Discovers Rudolfo Anaya," in *Publishers Weekly,* March 21, 1994, p. 24.

[*In the following essay, Clark discusses the enduring success of* Bless Me, Ultima, *and Anaya's increasing mainstream popularity and recognition.*]

What may be most striking about the six-title, six-figure book deal that New Mexico author Rudolfo Anaya recently concluded with Warner Books is that this major recognition has been so slow in coming.

Long hailed as one of the founding fathers of Chicano literature, described in the *New York Times Book Review* as "the novelist most widely known and read in the Latino community," in *Newsweek* as "the most widely read Mexican-American" period, Anaya is, as *Newsweek* also points out, "celebrated in the West and barely known back East." But all that is about to change, beginning in April, when Warner will simultaneously publish mass market paperback and color-illustrated hardcover editions of **Bless Me, Ultima,** Anaya's classic Chicano coming-of-age novel. This is the first hardcover appearance ever of the highly acclaimed 1972 work.

Though the players in this deal decline to give precise figures, Susan Bergholz, Anaya's New York agent, characterizes it as "a significant six-figure arrangement." A series of three contracts were settled between November 1992 and late 1993, calling for the appearance of five more books in the next three years.

In September, Warner will release a mass market paperback of Anaya's 1992 novel **Alburquerque** and a Spanish edition of **Bless Me, Ultima**—this publisher's first Spanish-language book, in a translation purchased from the Mexican house of Grijalbe. **The Anaya Reader,** composed of short fiction, essays and possibly a play or two, is scheduled for trade paperback publication in April 1995. Two new murder-mysteries will follow in hardcover—**Zia Summer** in June '95 and **Rio Grande Fall** in summer '96. And, as icing on that rich literary cake, last year Anaya also sold Hyperion a pair of children's books.

The quantity and diversity of this material, its mix of old and new, is partly what makes Anaya's Warner deal so unusual, notes Bergholz. "For a publisher to say, 'We want to take you on as an author, with all your different masks,' used to happen a lot years ago, but doesn't often happen now. It was a gutsy thing to do."

To Anaya, Warner's commitment is emblematic of a dramatic shift in attitudes since the early '70s, when only academic publishers would accept Chicano writers. "We had nowhere else to go . . . it was extremely hard. But each community has art to offer, and now we've come to a place in American history where we celebrate that," says Anaya, who, at 56, has lived his entire literary life in Albuquerque.

For 19 years, until his retirement in 1993, he taught creative writing and Chicano literature at the University of New Mexico, whose press issued several of his later works. Since the appearance over two decades ago of *Bless Me, Ultima*—which, published by a small California press called Quinto Sol, has sold more than 300,000 copies in 21 printings—Anaya has continued to produce at a prolific rate.

"This author has a huge following, was poised to launch into the mainstream," says Warner editor Colleen Kapklein, who initiated negotiations. "We saw him as having a strong track record, and he was taking a new direction in his work—telling more commercial stories, wanting to reach a wider audience—a direction we'd want him to take. There was a lot of good timing in this deal."

That timing also has to do, she says, with changes in the publishing industry linked to the debate about multiculturalism. "The industry has become much more open regarding what it can sell; you reach more readers if you publish more kinds of books, and readers are more open to different kinds of books." With nice poetic justice, the success of several younger Latino writers, such as Ann Castillo and Sandra Cisneros, for whom Anaya provided inspiration and a role model, has helped create the climate for their mentor's breakthrough.

But there's further serendipity. Bergholz and Anaya connected in May 1992, and the agent soon floated their proposal for a package of books to a dozen publishers, all of whom expressed interest in parts of the package, but not in the whole vision. Meanwhile, Kapklein, who hadn't yet been contacted, saw the *Publishers Weekly* review of Anaya's novel *Alburquerque* and called Bergholz to discuss paperback rights. When she learned that *Bless Me, Ultima* was also available, along with two new novels, she swung into action and within three months a contract was in place for the initial phase of the deal.

Anaya is a quiet, reserved man, but this new arrangement, with its promise of national distribution, coming as it does just when he's finally able to devote all his time to writing, clearly gives him deep satisfaction. "What a writer wants is to communicate with people," he says simply. "The other part of it—me going on writing, doing the things that interest me, following inclinations about where the work is leading me—will remain the same."

"But it's a whole new ball game."

Ray González (review date 18 July 1994)

SOURCE: "Desert Songs," in *Nation*, July 18, 1994, pp. 98–101.

[*In the following excerpt, González examines the lasting achievement of* Bless Me, Ultima *and Anaya's significance as a groundbreaking Chicano writer.*]

After twenty-two years as the most important and influential Chicano novel ever written, although available only from a small press, Rudolfo Anaya's *Bless Me, Ultima* has been reprinted in hardcover and mass-market editions by Warner Books. A timeless work of youth and rites of passage, Tonatiuh-Quinto Sol's edition sold more than 300,000 copies in two decades of classroom use and word-of-mouth readership. Despite Anaya's impact as a storyteller and mentor for many Chicano writers and the fact that he is one of the best fiction writers in the United States, it has taken all this time for his work to reach a mass audience. Up to now, his books have appeared through small and university presses, which meant consistent publication but limited distribution. This was the norm for the majority of Chicano writers until recently. With the boom in Latino literature in the late 1980s and its present flowering, many younger Latino writers—I'm thinking of Cristina Garcia, Julia Alvarez, Dagoberto Gilb and Denise Chavez, for example—will not have to "pay dues" for the length of time that Anaya has. The most recent example of this is Luis Alberto Urrea. His memoir *Across the Wire: Life and Hard Times on the Mexican Border* (Anchor) was a best seller, and *In Search of Snow,* his first novel, enjoys the backing of HarperCollins.

The reason such marketing considerations have to be a part of examining these two novels is that the context in which Chicano fiction is received is changing as more work is available on a larger scale. Anaya is enjoying a period of prosperity in his career, though he never stopped writing and has endured for decades; Urrea, a talented essayist novelist and poet who is one of the hottest Chicano writers around now, is almost automatically a "mainstream" property early in his career. *In Search of Snow* is an ideal novel for the nineties because Urrea does not have to restrict himself to "Chicano" themes, or even characters. It is also an interesting contrast to *Bless Me, Ultima* because Anaya's famous characters of the boy Antonio Márez and Ultima, the *curandera* (healer), created the legacy and the world in which Urrea has his story take place.

Both novels revolve around male characters and how they come of age. Antonio grows up in the mythical town of Guadalupe, New Mexico, in a time when strong family ties were the key source in the education of a young boy. His mysterious dreams and his discovery of the natural world of the *llano* (plain), the desert, owls and the sheer isolation of life in the Southwest will strengthen his spiritual bonds to his family and to his own future. He is blessed to be brought up and guided by Ultima, one of the last *curanderas,* whose ties to a pagan past meant she had to pass her dying secrets to Antonio.

As one of the first bilingually canted novels, with its heavy use of Spanish phrases, *Bless Me, Ultima* set the stage for the unique Chicano genre of Catholic-pagan fiction. The now-familiar elements include a supernatural environment, a questioning of traditional Christian values and the presence of a strong mother figure to perplex and guide the young protagonist through his life. Early in the novel Antonio admits:

I was happy with Ultima. . . . I learned from her that there was a beauty in the time of day and in the time of night, and that there was peace in the river and in the hills. She taught me to listen to the mystery of the groaning earth and to feel complete in the fulfillment of its time. My soul grew under her careful guidance.

Anaya encompassed his native New Mexico landscape in this work, which turned out to be in sharp contrast with the more contemporary urban settings of later Chicano novels. While he was writing about the power of family myths and Antonio was learning the many names for the earth, other Chicano writers were dealing with the barrio, political protest in Vietnam-era America and confrontations in the streets. As a result, the formal style and unfolding beauty of the language in *Bless Me, Ultima* isolated it from the direction a majority of Chicano writers took in the seventies and eighties.

Reading this book decades after it was written, it is clear that Antonio's apprenticeship at the hands of Ultima is part of the natural evolution of Mexican-American culture. The boy's awareness of good and evil still reverberates in our hearts: Now, with gang death loyalty the only kind of love and brotherhood known to many young boys, Ultima's visionary gifts and Antonio's yearning for them are needed more than ever. This is Anaya's ultimate triumph as a writer and a leader in our community.

After all these years, *Bless Me, Ultima* endures because Anaya had the vision to see and capture the past, the present and the future of his people in one work of art. It is a difficult task to accomplish in fiction, yet Anaya did it with the same rare magnitude Gabriel García Márquez effected in *One Hundred Years of Solitude*. *Bless Me, Ultima* is our Latin American classic because of its dual impact—it clearly defines Chicano culture as founded on family, tradition and the power of myth. Through Antonio and Ultima, we learn how to identify these values in the midst of the dark clouds of change and maturity. *Bless Me, Ultima* also shows that, like García Márquez, Anaya recognizes that the Latino world is fluid and mysterious and can only be re-created by playing with time and the unpredictable environment that surreal-religious forces create in the lives of all, the young and the elderly, the isolated and the social, the powerful and the weak. . . .

The central messages of *Bless Me, Ultima* and *In Search of Snow* may be quite different, but this shows an evolving quality: These novels stand like opposing bookends in the historical and psychic shape of the Mexican-American experience, meaning this literature is succeeding in encompassing the choices we have as a culture, as writers, and as a people coming from the same landscape to redefine our spiritual and familial needs.

William Clark (essay date 5 June 1995)

SOURCE: "Rudolfo Anaya: 'The Chicano Worldview,'" in *Publishers Weekly*, June 5, 1995, pp. 41–42.

[*In the following essay, Clark provides an overview of Anaya's life, literary career, and growing recognition as a founding father of contemporary Chicano literature.*]

From the large, east-facing windows of his home high on the mesa west of Albuquerque, N.M., Rudolfo Anaya commands a sweeping panorama of the Rio Grande Valley. The city where this legendary 57–year-old Chicano author has lived his varied and prolific literary life spreads out below, threaded by the sinuous bosque, the forest of giant cottonwoods, that flanks the Great River.

"River of dreams, river of cruel history, river of borders, river that was home," Anaya calls this artery of water, so vital to the arid landscape of New Mexico, in his novel *Alburquerque.* It is a region that, with its unique, centuries-old Hispanic culture—part Spanish, part Native American—he has made inimitably his own.

Anaya's father was a vaquero from Pastura, a horseman who worked cattle and sheep on the big ranches of this region; his mother came from a farming family in the Hispanic village of Puerto de Luna in the Pecos Valley. The windswept wildness and solitude of the llano, the plains, and the settled domesticity of the farm—"Those are the two halves of my nature," says Anaya, a short, wiry man, quiet and reserved, with curly graying hair and a thick mustache reminiscent of Pancho Villa's that dominates his strong, rugged features, the face of the ranchero he might well have become.

"Much is in the blood," he continues in his soft, resonant voice, "because the blood has memory, memory that has been imprinted, encoded, from the past—the whispers of the blood are stories. The rational mind works in tandem with that information; in fact, its job is to bring that to light, to tell us who we are." Beyond the valley and the city's eastern sprawl, the Sandia Mountains rise in a sheer escarpment that marks the point of the sun's daily rebirth, an event that has deep spiritual significance for Anaya.

The sun is indeed the central symbol of *Zia Summer,* the new novel from Warner Books—and this versatile writer's first outing in the murder-mystery genre. The Zia is an ancient Pueblo Indian sun symbol, and it provides key clues in Anaya's tale of Albuquerque PI Sonny Baca, who, in solving the murder of his cousin, confronts a terrorist cult and the threat posed by the transport and disposal of nuclear waste.

Zia Summer is the second of a quartet of seasonal novels that began in 1992 with Anaya's *Alburquerque* (the original spelling of the city's name), whose protagonist, a young barrio boxer in search of his true Chicano identity, helps thwart a grandiose real-estate development scheme that threatens the traditional life of the region's old Hispanic and Indian communities.

Sonny Baca will return in *Rio Grande Fall,* the already-completed third book in this series, due out next year from

Warner. That mystery deals with, among other matters, the pressing social problem of homelessness, Anaya says. He prefers not to speak of the final novel of his quartet, which is now in progress, beyond noting that Sonny will once again do battle with the eco-terrorist villain he first encountered in *Zia Summer.*

QUEST FOR A CULTURAL IDENTITY

But, underpinning Anaya's most recent novels—with their new emphasis on contemporary social issues and the more accessible style he says he's consciously adopted—are the themes he has consistently probed since his first book, the seminal Chicano coming-of-age novel, *Bless Me, Ultima,* appeared in 1972: spirituality and healing; Chicano tradition and myth; the sacredness of the land; the role of shaman-like figures as mentors and guides; and the quest for personal, communal and cultural identity.

Though published by a small academic press, *Bless Me, Ultima* sold more than 300,000 copies in 21 printings before Warner finally brought out the first hardcover edition in 1994. Told with lyric magic realism, steeped in the traditional lifeways and folklore of New Mexico's rural Latino culture, the novel established Anaya's reputation as one of the founding fathers of Chicano literature.

Addressing matters that mirror not only Anaya's own life but also the experience of Chicanos throughout the Southwest, his next novel, *Heart of Aztlán* (Editorial Justo Publications, 1976) brought a rural Nuevo Mexicano family to Albuquerque and depicted their painful struggle to maintain the values of their Mexican-American culture within the new context of the urban barrio. His third novel, *Tortuga* (Editorial Justo, 1979), examined pain, loss and healing in a different way—through the experience of a boy hospitalized with a severe back injury like the one Anaya himself endured as a teenager, the result of a diving accident.

"I think of myself as a novelist," Anaya muses, "but from the beginning, I wanted to try many things." In the dozen years between *Tortuga* and the appearance of his next full-length novel, *Alburquerque,* he published a volume of short stories, *The Silence of the Llano* (Quinto Sol, 1982), two novellas and several plays; produced a book-length Chicano mock-epic poem and the travel journal *A Chicano in China* (Univ. of New Mexico, 1986); and wrote a steady stream of essays. One of his children's stories of that period, *The Farolitos of Christmas,* is due out from Hyperion in December, and Warner has just released a wide-ranging anthology, *The Anaya Reader.*

This productive career has brought Anaya more than a score of honors, among them the Premio Quinto Sol national Chicano literary award for *Bless Me, Ultima,* the PEN-West Fiction Award for *Alburquerque,* and a National Endowment for the Arts fellowship. His lectures and readings have taken him throughout the U.S. and far abroad—a long way from the tiny village of Pastura on the plains of

east-central New Mexico, where he was born, and the nearby Pecos River town of Santa Rosa, where he grew up.

Anaya's family left rural New Mexico when he was in the eighth grade and moved to Albuquerque, where he attended high school and went on to study English and American literature at the University of New Mexico, earning a bachelor's degree in 1963, then an M.A. in 1968. Though he began writing *Bless Me, Ultima* in 1963, he was also teaching in the Albuquerque public schools and attending graduate school part-time; he spent seven years perfecting that book. He was working, he says, "in a vacuum," not yet involved with the Chicano movement then gaining momentum in the Southwest, of which he would soon become one of the most eloquent voices.

WORK WITHOUT PRECEDENTS

"With as much literature as I'd read and studied," Anaya recalls, "when it came time to treat my own experience, other novels in the American experience didn't work as models. I had to find my own voice, my own expression, my own forms, working with my own materials, values, culture. What I set out to do—which is what every writer does—was to create a universe, one that had its roots in the Nuevo Mexicano experience. I just plunged into the material and tried to give it form, structure. I wanted to take those people I had known and make them breathe again."

History would show that he succeeded masterfully, but getting this new work out—couched in the bilingual, Spanish-English form that Anaya pioneered and has pursued throughout his career—proved, to say the least, difficult.

"It was extremely hard," he says. "I sent the book to dozens of trade publishers over a couple of years and found no interest at all. The mainstream publishers weren't taking anything Chicano and we had nowhere to go. For us, living in a bilingual world, it was very normal to allow Spanish into a story written in English—it's a process that reflects our spoken language—but [in approaching mainstream publishers] I was always called on it. Without the small academic, ethnic and university presses, we'd never have gotten our work published intact."

Keeping faith in his work through those years of rejection, Anaya ultimately gleaned the address of one such obscure press, Quinto Sol Publications in Berkeley, Calif., from a magazine, and sent off his manuscript—which was accepted immediately and published in 1972.

But, even as his reputation as the "godfather" of the Chicano novel grew, Anaya would continue to publish exclusively with small presses for over two decades. In 1992, he met New York literary agent Susan Bergholtz and, in part because of her longstanding advocacy of Latino writers, signed with her—the first and only agent he's ever had. Together, they developed a proposal for a package of books, a mix of old and new work, and, by late 1993, Bergholtz had settled a series of contracts with Warner for the publication of illustrated hardcover, paperback and Spanish editions of **Bless Me, Ultima** and a paperback edition of **Alburquerque** in 1994, as well as **The Anaya Reader** and the three novels featuring Sonny Baca. That major recognition at last placed Anaya, after 20 years, squarely in the world of mainstream publishing, with access to the broad public he's always wanted.

Throughout his career, Anaya supported his family and his writing through work as a teacher and academic counselor. From 1974 until his retirement in 1993, he was a professor at the University of New Mexico, specializing in creative writing and Chicano literature—a field in which his own widely anthologized work has become standard fare. That long commitment to education connects with the idea of mentorship that is a consistent theme in his writing (most of his protagonists have spiritual guides) and which is, he says, "in a sense, the role of the writer."

Anaya has provided a groundbreaking model for a whole generation of Latino writers, and his UNM students have included the likes of Chicana novelist and playwright Denise Chavez. "There seems to be a new wave in Chicano literature and visual art—it's booming, and Chicanos are coming into their own," Anaya says, with one of the grins that frequently light up his face, hints of the strain of humor that pervades his work. "Any community, to be known, needs many voices to describe it, and that's what's happening."

For two or three hours each weekday morning, Anaya, working on his computer, continues to add his voice to that vibrant chorus, pursuing his life's work in the adobe home he and Patricia—his wife of 29 years, who is also a writer—designed for themselves two decades ago. In his small study, a glass door faces the Rio Grande Valley, and one book-lined wall bears a row of santos, the statues of saints that are so much a part of Nuevo Mexicano life.

"The place where I work is very important, hard to duplicate," he says. "It's where all the characters gather; they're used to this little room, comfortable visiting me here." For Anaya, the process of fiction is "part meditation, part bringing up ideas that have been fermenting, but a lot of it involves characters speaking to you and forcing you to write their stories. There's no preconceived story line—the characters come alive and say: here's my story."

In this "centered, sacred space," Anaya will, he says, typically draft a novel within a year, then revise extensively through five or six drafts—each of them read by Patricia, his "frontline editor"—as he hones language, fills out characters, sharpens his focus. "What I've wanted to do is compose the Chicano worldview—the synthesis that shows our true mestizo identity—and clarify it for my community and for myself," Anaya says. "Writing for me is a way of knowledge, and what I find illuminates my life."

A. Robert Lee (essay date 1996)

SOURCE: "*Chicanismo* as Memory: The Fictions of Rudolfo Anaya, Nash Candelaria, Sandra Cisneros, and Ron Arias," in *Memory and Cultural Politics: New Approaches to American Ethnic Literatures,* edited by Amritjit Singh, Joseph T. Skerrett Jr., and Robert E. Hogan, Northeastern University Press, 1996, pp. 320–39.

[*In the following excerpt, Lee explores the complex matrix of historical, geographic, and cultural legacies that underlies Chicano identity, as well as the significance of memory and remembrance in Chicano literature, particularly in* Bless Me, Ultima.]

> To John J. Halcón and María de la Luz Reyes
>
> For those of us who listen to the Earth, and to the old legends and myths of the people, the whispers of the blood draw us to our past.
>
> —Rudolfo A. Anaya, **A Chicano in China**
>
> Mexican, the voice in his deep dream kept whispering. Mejicano. Chicano.
>
> —Nash Candelaria, *Memories of the Alhambra*
>
> I'm a story that never ends. Pull one string and the whole cloth unravels.
>
> —Sandra Cisneros, "Eyes of Zapata"
>
> I might say that I studied Spanish and Hispanic literature . . . because I had to know more about my past, my historical past.
>
> —Ron Arias in Bruce-Novoa, *Chicano Authors*

Four Chicano storytellers, four calls to legacy. No less than other American cultural formations, *chicanismo* invites a play of memory coevally personal and collective. If one begins with the historical sediment, the substrata that have made up Chicano culture, it is first to underscore the human passage involved, those transitions from past to present that its novelists, poets, and dramatists have so remembered when making imagined worlds out of actual ones.

The Olmecs and Mayans provide a founding repository, passed-down legends, belief systems, alphabets, and an architecture. *Los aztecas* and the European intrusion of Hernán Cortés in turn bequeath the very memory of *mestizaje,* a first joining to be endlessly repeated through time. Mexican Independence in 1821, the Texas-Mexican War of 1836, the Mexican-American War of 1846–1848, and above all the Mexican Revolution of 1910–1917 again make for history as iconography, fact as also inward memory. Villa and Zapata, for their parts, supply the epic names, substance, and yet, as always, shadow. Seen from the 1960s and beyond, and to a population burgeoning by both birth rate and immigration, it comes as no surprise that *Aztlán* has found new currency, a term of rally and consciousness, yet always a remembrance, a reference back to *chicanismo*'s first homeland.[1]

Memory, thus, for virtually every Chicano/a, has meant a dramatic crossply, Nezahualicóyotl and Moctezuma invoked alongside *Los Reyes Católicos,* or La Malinche, La Llorona, and La Virgen de Guadalupe alongside Cortés, Coronado, and Cabeza de Vaca. It has meant overlapping *cuentos* of war and peace, from the *aztecas* to the conquistadores, or from the Alamo of the Mexican-American conflict to the Los Alamos of the atomic bomb. It looks to the transition whereby *Alto México* became the "American" Southwest of New Mexico, Arizona, Colorado, California, and Texas. *Brujería* and *curanderismo,* likewise, carry a folk pastness into a later Catholicism of First Communions and Mass. So rich a human "text" has increasingly found its literary equivalent, memory as the pathway into a renaissance of Chicano word and narrative.

In the same way as a Chicano legacy invokes the rural, a *campesino* life of crops and herding and festival, so does it invoke the urban. Barrios from East Los Angeles to Houston, Albuquerque to Denver, bear witness to the history of an estimated 60 percent of Chicanos who have now moved into the cities. If Harlem for African Americans carries the residues of both Dixie and Manhattan, then an East Los Angeles or Houston for Chicanos looks back to both *el campo* and the exhilarations and losses of inner-city life.

One refraction lies in popular culture, whether mariachi bands or Los Lobos, mural art or low-rider cars, work songs or "Latin" rap. Memory, at times nostalgia, it can be admitted, runs right through the cultural rebirth of the 1960s, from the music of Ritchie Valens to the *actos* of Luis Valdez's Teatro Campesino, with, in train, the singing of Linda Ronstadt, the comedy of Cheech Marin, and the screenwork and directing of Edward James Olmos. In this latter respect, films like *La Bamba, Zoot Suit, The Milagro Beanfield War, Stand and Deliver, American Me, Blood In, Blood Out* (coscripted by Jimmy Santiago Baca), and even television's once mooted *El Pueblo/L.A.,* for all their resemblance to the contemporary, could not have been more permeated by pastness, the appeal to shared recollection.

In like manner there has been the view of Chicano community, even in poverty, as in and of itself a kind of memorial art form, an inherited pageant of culture and custom. In this, Chicano foodways bear an especially ancestral insignia—a now familiar menu of *chile, frijoles, enchiladas, mole, chimichangas,* or *tamales.* If, however, a single token of legacy were needed, it would surely be found in the *ristras* hanging in almost every Chicano home.

In common with its *nuyorriqueño* and *cubano-americano* counterparts, *chicanismo* also involves a past held inside two seemingly parallel but actually deeply unparallel languages.[2] For under American auspices English has long emerged as the language of power, leaving Spanish as the assumed lesser idiom, a signifier of illiteracy or migrant outsiderness. Even so, this is anything but to suggest that the two languages have not been historically symbiotic. Chicano Spanish, for its part, may resort to the street or vernacular *caló* of *pachucos, vatos,* and *chulas,* but it also abounds with borrowed anglicisms like *watchar la tele* or *kikear* (the drug habit). American English has in mirror fashion long made its own borrowings, like *barrio* and the all-serving *gringo,* as well as farm or ranch borrowings, like *lasso, adobe, bronco, cinch,* or *sombrero.* Endless repetition on television and other commercials of food terms like *taco, tortilla,* and *nacho* has made quite as marked an impact, one language's "history" remembered (or more aptly misremembered) inside another.

In the case of anglicization, Chicano memory has been stirred in another way as well. In categories like Hispanic or, depending on the user, even the more generally favored Hispano or Latino, many have heard the carryover of a note of condescension. "Ethnic" likewise arouses suspicion, a WASP hegemony's self-appointed rubric for patronage of minority culture. The English Only campaigns, now under way in more than twenty states, recapitulate the same discriminatory process. Here, in all its historic loading, is but the latest effort to make the language as well as the general sway of Anglo culture the presumed standard for America at large. Does not, then, an accusing politics of memory lie behind a reaction like "English Yes, But Only, No"?

A *corrido,* or folk song, like "The Ballad of Gregorio Cortez," adapted for the screen by PBS in 1982 from Américo Paredes's version with Edward James Olmos in the title role, nicely points up the discrepancy.[3] The tale of a "Mexican" smallholder in the Texas of 1901 falsely accused of horse theft, it turns on how the word *horse* in English can translate into Spanish as both masculine and feminine, namely *caballo* and *yegua.* At issue, however, is infinitely more than a quirk of philology. The ballad speaks on the one hand to Gregorio Cortez's Mexican Chicano ancestry, and on the other, to the Anglo hegemony that lies behind the Texas Rangers who pursue him and the Yankee judge and court that try him for the murder of the sheriff. What is involved here is the remembrance of two value systems, two misreadings across the cultural divide. Much as English and Spanish might seem to have been saying the same thing, the gap has been symptomatic, and in this case, fatal.

Similar discrepancies in fact underlie a whole array of "popular" versions of American history. No better instance offers itself than the Siege of the Alamo (1836), and in its wake, the defeat of Santa Anna at San Jacinto. Told one way, the Siege has come to signify Anglo triumphalism. Where more so than in John Wayne's 1960 Hollywood version with its "Lone Star State" hurrahs and featuring James Bowie and William B. Travis as the truest of patriot martyrs? Told in another way, did not Santa Anna's attack on the Alamo represent a timely resistance, a counterforce to Yankee expansionism? Such a perspective, going against the grain, appears in Jesús Salvador Trevino's television film of 1982, *Seguín.*

These splits and divergences in memory extend more generally to the American Southwest and West, not least when they double as *el norte*. From a mainstream viewpoint, the link is to Manifest Destiny, an *indigenista,* tribal-Chicano world preordained to be won and settled. A Mexican or tribal viewpoint, however, speaks of colonized land, stolen *tierra* or *patria*. Counterversions of the Mexican Revolution similarly arise, on the one hand the Red plot, the Bolshevism so warningly reported (and then not reported) by, say, the Hearst press, and on the other hand the heroizing popular revolution of the Institutional Revolutionary Party (known as the PRI) and leftist recollection in general.

Sleepy Lagoon and the Zoot-Suit riots of 1942–1943 also yield their twofold interpretations. Were the assaults of a largely white Southern navy in wartime Los Angeles "straight" racism or, more obliquely, the fascination of one uniformed group (Anglo, English-speaking, Bible-Protestant, military) with its also uniformed opposite (Latin, Spanish-speaking, sexually knowing, baroque)?[4] How, subsequently, should one remember 1960s movements like César Chávez's United Farm Workers, especially the 1968 grape boycott, José Angel Gutiérrez's La Raza Unida in Texas, and "Corky" Gonzales's Crusade for Justice in Denver? Do they best refer back to mainstream labor politics (in Chávez's case, on account of the alliances with Filipino and other Asian workers) or, when linked back into the wartime *bracero* programs, to a wholly more discrete Chicano politics?

Nor, however collective the memory, does *chicanismo* yield some unconflicted view of itself. The class hierarchy, for instance, created by the conquistadores who devastated Moctezuma's Aztecs, has had its modern footfalls, still based on blood, skin color, landedness, and, as often, family name. Old *chicanismo* plays against new, especially between certain New Mexico dynasties and those of a supposedly inferior birthright. Does this also not call up the disdain of Spanish-born *gachupines* for colonial-born *criollos* or Creoles, and theirs, in turn, for *los indios* (especially *genízaros*—Indians forced to lose their tribal language and to speak only Spanish), for mestizos, and for *negros* (a distinct but Spanish-speaking black population)?[5]

Just as a missionary-begun Catholicism largely took over from Aztec and other cosmologies (though obliged to coexist with vernacular practices like *curanderismo*), so did evangelical Protestantism increasingly make inroads into that same Catholicism.[6] This, and the impact of Latin American liberation theology, has led to increasing doubts about the church's attitude to family, women, birth control, divorce, and authority in general. How are Chicanas, especially, to "remember" Catholicism? As spiritual sanctuary or as yet another patriarchy able to oppress with its gendered rules of conduct?

Another major contradiction lies in the continuing pull of California. It has, undoubtedly, promised betterment, the dream of *abundancia,* whatever the risk of repeated deportations by *la migra*. Somewhere in this persists the remembered myth of *el dorado,* the continuing lure of *Las*

Siete Ciudades de Cíbola. But California has notoriously also flattered to deceive. Chicano unemployment has soared, as have high school dropout rates, *barrio* poverty and crime, and the wars of attrition with the police and courts. Yet as the continuing surge of cross-border migration bears out, and despite each amnesty over residence papers, California remains history both made and still in the making.[7]

Imagining and reimagining the past may well be, in L. P. Hartley's apt and rightly celebrated phrase, to visit a "foreign country"—especially in an America notoriously obsessed with the future. Yet Chicanos, no doubt having known the flavors of defeat as well as those of triumph, have had good reason to dwell there. Whether it was the conquistador regime, a border as redolent of human flight as *El Río Grande,* the history by which *Tejas* was reconstituted as Texas, or the duality of California as promise and yet denial, the prompt to memory has been always ongoing. For it is the memory that serves as solvent for each generation's telling of *la raza,* and nowhere more so than in the ongoing body of fiction of what rightly has become known as *chicanismo*'s literary renaissance.[8]

Certainly that has been the case for Anaya, Candelaria, Cisneros, and Arias, however differently they have styled their uses of memory. Indeed, the Chicano tradition can virtually be said to have thrived on the shaping energies of remembrance, a present told and reinvented in the mirrors of the past. This is true especially for one of the seminal novels of *chicanismo*. José Antonio Villarreal's *Pocho* (1959) not only offers the life of its writer-protagonist, Richard Rubio, as a portrait of the artist, it also locates that life within the history of migration from Mexico to southern California—thus memory as collective in scope yet specific, a single trajectory.[9]

In a story cycle as delicately imagistic as Tomás Rivera's ". . . Y no se lo tragó la tierra"/And the Earth Did Not Part (1971),[10] another kind of memory holds sway, that of a single migrant-labor year of a Chicano dynasty headed for "Iuta" (Utah) in which all other similar years and journeys are to be discerned. Raymond Barrio's *The Plum Plum Pickers* (1971) makes for a linking memorialization,[11] this time set in the Santa Clara Valley during the Reagan governorship. Its very accusations of labor exploitation and racism lie in remembrance. In *Peregrinos de Aztlán* (1974),[12] Miguel Méndez takes a more vernacular direction—the memories of Loreto Maldona, car washer in Tijuana—as an anatomy of border life, of poverty and dreams, nationality and *mestizaje*. For his part, Alejandro Morales in *Caras viejas y vino nuevo* (1975),[13] translated as *Old Faces and New Wine* in 1981, transposes *barrio* Los Angeles into a kind of working archive, a city of inheritances and the present-day told in its own imaginative right as at once then and now.

In *Klail City y sus alrededores* (1976),[14] as in the rest of the "Klail" series, Rolando Hinojosa subjects Belken County to Faulknerian rules, a south Texas Chicano and white "mythical kingdom" invoked as through a lattice of multicultural (and bilingual) recollection. Daniel Cano's *Pepe Rios* (1991) attempts historical fiction of an older kind,[15] the Mexican Revolution as an epilogue to colonialism and yet a prologue to *chicanismo*. Arturo Islas looks to memory as myth in *The Rain God* (1984),[16] the portrait of a Tex-Mex dynasty descended in the aftermath of the Mexican Revolution from the escaping but always imperturbable matriarch Mama Chona. In all these different modes of using *chicanismo* as memory, fiction lays claim to a special kind of authority, a heritage of time and voice given its own dialogic measure.

Memory has equally shaped an increasingly emergent Chicana fiction, in whose ranks Sandra Cisneros has been little short of a luminary. Isabella Ríos's *Victuum* (1976),[17] through the psychism of its narrator, Valentina Ballesternos, renders womanist history as a kind of ongoing dream script. Ana Castillo's *The Mixquiahuala Letters* (1986) creates an epistolatory,[18] and teasingly self-aware, feminist novel of women's friendship that also explores the pasts of America and Mexico, a historic *mestizaje* again taken up in her fantasia, *Sapogonia* (1990), and in her New Mexico almanac-memoir, *So Far from God* (1993).[19] Cherrié Moraga's storytelling (and essay work), of which the anthology she co-edited with Gloria Anzaldúa, *This Bridge Called My Back: Writings by Radical Women of Color* (1981), and her *Loving in the War Years* (1983) and *The Last Generation* (1993) can be thought symptomatic, yields another remembrance, that of the "silence" that, by historic writ, has surrounded lesbian life in a culture so given to patriarchy.[20]

Literatura chicanesca, non-Chicano writing about Chicano life and culture, affords another styling of memory in John Nichols's *The Milagro Beanfield War* (1974).[21] However specifically set in the 1970s or local the story, its drama of contested water rights again calls up an inlaid older history of Indian, Mexican, and Anglo conflict that, across four centuries, took New Mexico from a Spanish colony to a territory to America's forty-seventh state. Joe Mondragón finds himself fighting Ladd Devine and his Miracle Valley Recreation Area Development for the right to irrigate his land. In fact, what Nichols portrays tacitly is the fight for the Chicano heritage in which the bean field acts as a trope for the very soil, the nurturing medium, of a whole people's history. Nichols's novel and the Redford-Esparza movie of 1988 (with its appropriately multiethnic cast of Ruben Blades, Carlos Riquelme, Sonia Braga, and Christopher Walken) can so play "fact" against *el mundo de los espíritus,* the historicity of the past as open to a figural or any other kind of access.

Chicano autobiography as a related kind of "fiction" has been wholly as various in its uses of memory, whether Oscar Zeta Acosta's rambunctious, Beatnik-influenced narratives of the 1960s, *The Autobiography of a Brown Buffalo* (1972) and *The Revolt of the Cockroach People* (1973), or Richard Rodriguez's elegiac, if controversially assimilationist, *Hunger of Memory* (1981) and *Days of*

Obligation (1992), or Linda Chavez's radically conservative manifesto, *Out of the Barrio* (1991), or Ray Gonzalez's El Paso "border" history, the lyric and pertinently titled *Memory Fever* (1993).[22]

For as these texts, too, "remember" (even those of an assimilationist bent) so, like the novels and stories they accompany, they inevitably contest and dissolve mainstream decreation of *chicanismo*. Perhaps, overall, Frances A. Yates's notion of "memory theatre" applies best—the forms of the past, however obliquely, always to be remembered and re-remembered in the forms of the present.[23]

"Some time in the future I would have to build my own dream of those things which were so much a part of my childhood." So does the narrator of Rudolfo Anaya's **Bless Me, Ultima** (1972) reflexively look back to the pending *cuentista* or authorial self who will write that childhood, that past, into being.[24] The note, for Anaya, is typical, one of retrospect, pastness, and memory as a textualized weave of events actual and imaginary, which, if less persuasively, also runs through his subsequent novels, **Heart of Aztlán** (1976), **Tortuga** (1979), and **Alburquerque** (1992).[25]

The novel typically begins in remembrance. "The magical time of childhood stood still," says Antonio Márez at the outset. He repositions himself as the seven-year-old raised in the 1940s Spanish-speaking New Mexico who finds himself pulled between the *vaquero,* herdsman, Márez clan on his father's side and the farmer-cultivator Luna clan on his mother's. But he also acknowledges the writer-in-waiting who will learn to appropriate as his own the shamanism, the *brujería,* of Ultima, the *anciana* and *curandera* invited by his parents to spend her last days with the family.

Anaya enravels each inside the other, a Chicano childhood as literal event, in Antonio's case often the most traumatic kind, and a drama of inner fantasy and imagining. "Experience" and "dream," he rightly recollects, "strangely mixed in me." This blend makes the imagined landscape of **Bless Me, Ultima** not a little Proustian, a New Mexico there on the map and yet personalized and sacralized by personal remembrance.

One contour, thus, has the adult Antonio recalling his ill-matched parents, his sisters, Deborah and Theresa, and the three absentee brothers with their eventual disruptive return from the wars in Europe and Japan. It looks back to the Spanish of the home, the English of school, the latter having anglicized him from Antonio to Tony. It summons back his parents' competing hopes for him: his father's dream of a new beginning in California and his mother's hope that he will enter the priesthood. He sees, too, as he could not have done in childhood, the irony of a horseman father now asphalting the highways as if to seal in, to inhume, the very *tierra* his family once proudly herded.

Yet another contour remembers the dreamer child within, drawn to the *indio* myths of earth, mountain, and river and to the legend of the Golden Carp—a creation myth of a god-protector of the village—in which he comes to believe under the tutelage of his friends Samson and Cisco. The center of all these memories, however, has to be Ultima—ancient, as her name implies, midwife at his birth, explainer of his *pesadillas,* or nightmares, teacher of herbs and flora, and martyr who at the cost of her own death has brought down the murderer Tenorio Trementina. Her grave, whose secret celebrant he becomes, serves the novel in two ways: as a figuration of both his past and his future, his legacy and at the same time his destiny.

Antonio thus finds himself irresistibly drawn in memory to her bag of potions, her nostrums, her deific owl with its links to a Christly dove or an Aztec eagle, and her very aroma. But if she signifies for him as at once guardian angel, muse, and the very anima of *chicanismo,* he, for his part, plays the perfect apprentice, the word maker with his own eventual kind of *brujería.*

This double weave, the memory of the "facts" of his history and of his first prompts to imagination, determines the whole novel. He thinks back to the deaths he has witnessed: Lupito, who, unhinged by his Asian war experiences, shoots at the sheriff only to invite his own destruction; Narciso, the harmless drunk who, all too true to his name, is killed by Trementina; Florence, the drowned boyhood friend who first guided him to the Golden Carp; and Ultima herself. Each death "happens," or "happened," but each, equally, goes on "happening" in his own chambers of memory, to await transcription by the memoirist he will become.

The back-and-forth movement of memory also encloses Jason's Indian, the unspeaking sentinel to a pre-conquistador past; like the carp and the owl, he embodies the tribal and vernacular folk past as against the Holy Weeks, Communions, and Masses of Father Byrne's parish church. There is a sheen, a membrane, that also settles over the novel's place-names, notably Los Alamos, as indeed the Poplars, but also, the irony of which is anything but lost on Anaya, as the atomic test site. More domestically, for Antonio, "El Puerto" ("refuge," "harbor") as the home of the Lunas and "Las Pasturas" ("pasture") as that of the Márez family resonate with equal effect—even as they pass into time past. Memory, in other words, in all its overlapping and coalescing kinds, also yields mixed emotional fare for the narrator-memoirist, pain and warmth, breakage as well as love.

But "build my own dream" ***Bless Me, Ultima*** does, a landmark portrait of childhood's dream itself told as a dream. The spirit of the dream derives, overwhelmingly, from Ultima, her creativity carried by the narrator from childhood to adulthood, from first associations to written word. For the memory of her, as of his family, of his land, and of all the voices and myths that have made up his legacy of *chicanismo,* cannot be thought other (such is Anaya's triumph) than Antonio Márez's memory—and memorialization—of himself.

Notes

1. The following usefully address Chicano history and politics: George I. Sánchez, *Forgotten People: A Study of New Mexicans* (Albuquerque, N.M.: C. Horn, 1940); Carey McWilliams, *North from Mexico: The Spanish-Speaking People of the United States* (New York: Greenwood Press, 1948); Matt S. Meier and Feliciano Rivera, *The Chicanos: A History of Mexican-Americans* (New York: Hill and Wang, 1972); Rodolfo Acuña, *Occupied America: The Chicano's Struggle Towards Liberation* (San Francisco: Canfield Press, 1972); Richard Griswold de Castillo, *The Los Angeles Barrio, 1850–1890: A Social History* (Berkeley: University of California Press, 1979); Marcia T. García et al., eds., *History, Culture and Society: Chicano Studies in the 1980s* (Ypsilanti, Mich.: Bilingual Press/Editorial Bilingüe, National Association of Chicano Studies, 1984); Alfredo Mirandé, *The Chicano Experience: An Alternative Perspective* (Notre Dame, Ind.: University of Notre Dame Press, 1985); Rodolfo O. de la Garza et al., eds., *The Mexican American Experience* (Austin, Tex.: University of Texas Press, 1985); and Renate von Bardeleben, Dietrich Briesemeister, and Juan Bruce-Novoa, eds., *Missions in Conflict: Essays on US-Mexican Relations and Chicano Culture* (Tübingen: Gunter Verlag, 1986).

2. See Andrew D. Cohen and Anthony F. Beltramo, eds., *El Lenguaje de los Chicanos: Regional and Social Characteristics Used by Mexican-Americans* (Arlington, Va.: Center for Applied Linguistics, 1975); also Dogoberto Fuentes and José A. López, *Barrio Language Dictionary: First Dictionary of Caló* (Los Angeles, Calif.: Southland Press, 1974).

3. Américo Paredes, *"With His Pistol in His Hand": A Border Ballad and Its Hero* (Austin, Tex.: University of Texas Press, 1979).

4. A persuasive interpretation of these events is found in Mauricio Mazón, *The Zoot-Suit Riots: The Psychology of Symbolic Annihilation* (Austin, Tex.: University of Texas Press, 1984).

5. For the implications of this nomenclature, see Alfred Yankauer, "Hispanic/Latino—What's in a Name?" and David E. Hayes-Bautista and Jorge Chapa, "Latino Terminology: Conceptual Bases for Standardized Terminology," both in *American Journal of Public Health* 77, no. 1 (1987): 61–68. I am grateful to Dr. Arthur Campa of the School of Education, University of Colorado at Boulder, for directing me to these references.

6. A symptomatic publication would be Freddie and Ninfa García, *Outcry in the Barrio* (San Antonio, Tex.: Freddie García Ministries, 1988).

7. Perhaps the most provocative history remains Acuña, *Occupied America.*

8. For bearings on this achievement, see Joseph Sommers and Tomás Ybarra-Frausto, *Modern Chicano*

Writers: A Collection of Critical Essays (Englewood Clitts, N.J.: Prentice-Hall, 1979); Juan Bruce-Novoa, *Chicano Authors: Inquiry by Interview* (Austin, Tex.: University of Texas Press, 1980); Juan Bruce-Novoa, *Chicano Authors: A Response to Chaos* (Austin, Tex.: University of Texas Press, 1982); Salvador Rodríguez del Pino, *La Novela Chicana Escrita en Español: Cinco Autores Comprometidos* (Ypsilanti, Mich.: Bilingual Press/Editorial Bilingüe, National Association of Chicano Studies, 1982); Charles M. Tatum, *Chicano Literature* (Boston: Twayne, 1982); Robert G. Trujillo and Andrés Rodríguez, *Literatura Chicana: Creative and Critical Writings through 1984* (Oakland, Calif.: Floricanto Press, 1985); Luis Leal et al., eds., *A Decade of Chicano Literature, 1970–1979: Critical Essays and Bibliography* (Santa Barbara, Calif.: Editorial La Causa, 1982); Houston Baker, ed., *Three American Literatures: Essays in Chicano, Native American, and Asian-American Literatures for Teachers of American Literature* (New York: Modern Language Association, 1982); Luis Leal, *Aztlán y México: Perfiles Literarios e Históricos* (Binghamton, N.Y.: Bilingual Press/Editorial Bilingüe, National Association of Chicano Studies, 1985); Marta Ester Sánchez, *Contemporary Chicana Poetry* (Berkeley, Calif., University of California Press, 1985); Maria Herrera-Sobek, ed., *Beyond Stereotypes: The Critical Analysis of Chicana Literature* (Binghamton, N.Y.: Bilingual Press/Editorial Bilingüe, 1985); Julio A. Martínez and Francisco A. Lomelí, eds., *Chicano Literature: A Reference Guide* (Westport, Conn.: Greenwood Press, 1986); Cordelia Candelaria, *Chicano Poetry: A Critical Introduction* (Westport, Conn.: Greenwood Press, 1985); Vernon E. Lattin, ed., *Contemporary Chicano Fiction: A Critical Survey* (Binghamton, N.Y.: Bilingual Press/Editorial Bilingüe, 1986); Carl R. Shirley and Paula W. Shirley, *Understanding Chicano Literature* (Columbia, S.C.: University of South Carolina Press, 1988); Francisco A. Lomelí and Carl R. Shirley, eds., *Chicano Writers First Series, Dictionary of Literary Biography,* vol. 82 (Detroit, Mich.: Bruccoli Clark Layman, 1989); Asunción Horno-Delgado et al., eds., *Breaking Boundaries: Latina Writing and Critical Readings* (Amherst, Mass.: University of Massachusetts Press, 1989); Ramón Saldívar, *Chicano Narrative: The Dialectics of Difference* (Madison, Wis.: University of Wisconsin Press, 1990); and Héctor Calderón and José David Saldívar, eds., *Criticism in the Borderlands: Studies in Chicano Literature, Culture, and Ideology* (Durham: Duke University Press, 1991).

9. José Antonio Villarreal, *Pocho* (New York: Doubleday, 1959).

10. Tomás Rivera: *". . . Y no se lo tragó la tierra"/And the Earth Did Not Part* (Berkeley, Calif.: Quinto Sol Publications, 1971).

11. Raymond Barrio, *The Plum Plum Pickers* (Sunnyvale, Calif.: Ventura Press, 1969; rpr., with introduction and bibliography, Binghamton, N.Y.: Bilingual Press/ Editorial Bilingüe, 1984).

12. Miguel Méndez, *Peregrinos de Aztlán* (Tucson, Ariz.: Editorial Peregrinos, 1974).

13. Alejandro Morales, *Caras viejas y vino nuevo* (México: J. Mortiz, 1975).

14. Rolando Hinojosa, *Klail City y sus alrededores* (La Habana: Casa de las Américas, 1976); *Generaciones y semblazas,* trans. Rosaura Sánchez (Berkeley, Calif.: Justa Publications, 1978). Author's English version: *Klail City* (Houston, Tex.: Arte Público Press, 1987).

15. Daniel Cano, *Pepe Rios* (Houston, Tex.: Arte Público Press, 1991).

16. Arturo Islas, *The Rain God* (New York: Avon Books, 1984, 1991).

17. Isabella Ríos, *Victuum* (Ventura, Calif.: Diana-Etna, 1976).

18. Ana Castillo, *The Mixquiahuala Letters* (Binghamton, N.Y.: Bilingual Press/Editorial Bilingüe, 1986).

19. Ana Castillo, *Sapogonia* (Houston, Tex.: Bilingual Press/Editorial Bilingüe, 1990) and *So Far from God* (New York: W. W. Norton, 1993).

20. Cherrié Moraga et al., eds., *Cuentos: Stories by Latinas* (New York: Kitchen Table/Women of Color Press, 1983); Cherrié Moraga and Gloria Anzaldúa, eds., *This Bridge Called My Back: Writings by Radical Women of Color* (Watertown, Mass.: Persephone Press, 1981); Cherrié Moraga, *Loving in the War Years: lo que nunca pasó por los labios* (Boston: South End Press, 1983); Cherrié Moraga, *The Last Generation* (Boston: South End Press, 1993).

21. John Nichols, *The Milagro Beanfield War* (New York: Holt, Rinehart, 1974). The rest of the trilogy comprises *The Magic Journey* (New York: Holt, Rinehart, 1978) and *The Nirvana Blues* (New York: Holt, Rinehart, 1981).

22. Oscar Zeta Acosta, *The Autobiography of a Brown Buffalo* (San Francisco: Straight Arrow, 1972) and *The Revolt of the Cockroach People* (San Francisco: Straight Arrow, 1973); Richard Rodriguez, *Hunger of Memory* (Boston: Godine, 1981) and *Days of Obligation: An Argument with My Mexican Father* (New York: Viking Penguin, 1992); Linda Chavez: *Out of the Barrio* (New York: Basic Books, 1991); and Ray Gonzalez, *Memory Fever* (Seattle, Wash.: Broken Moon Press, 1993).

23. Frances A. Yates, *The Art of Memory* (Chicago: University of Chicago Press, 1966). Some of these implications of "memory" I have explored elsewhere. See A. Robert Lee, *"The Mill on the Floss*: 'Memory' and the Reading Experience," in Ian Gregor, ed., *Reading the Victorian Novel: Detail into Form* (London: Vision Press, 1980).

24. Rudolfo Anaya, *Bless Me, Ultima* (Berkeley, Calif.: Quinto Sol Publications, 1972).

25. Rudolfo Anaya, *Heart of Aztlán* (Berkeley, Calif.: Editorial Justa Publications, 1976); *Tortuga* (Berkeley, Calif.: Editorial Justa Publications, 1979); and *Alburquerque* (Albuquerque, N.M.: University of New Mexico Press, 1992).

Works Cited

Acosta, Oscar Zeta. *The Autobiography of a Brown Buffalo.* San Francisco: Straight Arrow, 1972.

———. *The Revolt of the Cockroach People.* San Francisco: Straight Arrow, 1973.

Acuña, Rodolfo. *Occupied America: The Chicano's Struggle Towards Liberation.* San Francisco: Canfield Press, 1972.

Anaya, Rudolfo A. *Alburquerque.* Albuquerque, N.M.: University of New Mexico Press, 1992.

———. *Bless Me, Ultima.* Berkeley, Calif.: Quinto Sol Publications, 1972.

———. *A Chicano in China.* Albuquerque, N.M.: University of New Mexico Press, 1986.

———. *Heart of Aztlán.* Berkeley, Calif.: Editorial Justa Publications, 1976.

———. *Tortuga.* Berkeley, Calif.: Editorial Justa Publications, 1979.

Arias, Ron. *The Road to Tamazunchale.* Reno, Nev.: West Coast Poetry Review, 1975. Reprint, Albuquerque, N.M.: Pajarito Publications, 1978.

Baker, Houston, ed. *Three American Literatures: Essays in Chicano, Native American, and Asian-American Literatures for Teachers of American Literature.* New York: Modern Language Association, 1982.

Barrio, Raymond. *The Plum Plum Pickers.* Sunnyvale, Calif.: Ventura Press, 1969. Reprint, with introduction and bibliography, Binghamton, N.Y.: Bilingual Press/Editorial Bilingüe, 1984.

Bruce-Novoa, Juan. *Chicano Authors: Inquiry by Interview.* Austin, Tex.: University of Texas Press, 1980.

———. *Chicano Authors: A Response to Chaos.* Austin, Tex.: University of Texas Press, 1982.

Calderón, Héctor, and José David Saldívar, eds. *Criticism in the Borderlands: Studies in Chicano Literature, Culture, and Ideology.* Durham: Duke University Press, 1991.

Candelaria, Cordelia. *Chicano Poetry: A Critical Introduction.* Westport, Conn.: Greenwood Press, 1985.

Candelaria, Nash. *Inheritance of Strangers.* Binghamton, N.Y.: Bilingual Press/Editorial Bilingüe, 1985.

———. *Memories of the Alhambra.* Palo Alto, Calif.: Cibola Press, 1977. Reprint, Ypsilanti, Mich.: Bilingual Press/Editorial Bilingüe, 1977.

Cano, Daniel. *Pepe Rios.* Houston, Tex.: Arte Público Press, 1991.

Castillo, Ana. *The Mixquiahuala Letters.* Binghamton, N.Y.: Bilingual Press/Editorial Bilingüe, 1986.

———. *Sapogonia.* Houston, Tex.: Bilingual Press/Editorial Bilingüe, 1990.

———. *So Far From God.* New York: W. W. Norton, 1993.

Chavez, Linda. *Out of the Barrio.* New York: Basic Books, 1991.

Cisneros, Sandra. *The House on Mango Street.* Houston, Tex.: Arte Público, 1983. Revised edition, New York: Vintage Books, 1989.

———. *Woman Hollering Creek and Other Stories.* New York: Random House, 1991.

Cohen, Andrew D., and Anthony F. Beltramo, eds. *El Lenguaje de los Chicanos: Regional and Social Characteristics Used by Mexican-Americans.* Arlington, Va.: Center for Applied Linguistics, 1975.

de la Garza, Rodolfo O., et al., eds. *The Mexican American Experience.* Austin, Tex.: University of Texas Press, 1985.

Fuentes, Carlos. *Cambio de Piel.* México: Joaquín Mortiz, 1967.

Fuentes, Dogoberto, and José A. López. *Barrio Language Dictionary: First Dictionary of Caló.* Los Angeles, Calif.: Southland Press, 1974.

García, Freddie, and Nina García. *Outcry in the Barrio.* San Antonio, Tex.: Freddie García Ministries, 1988.

García, Marcia T., et al., eds. *History, Culture, and Society: Chicano Studies in the 1980s.* Ypsilanti, Mich.: Bilingual Press/Editorial Bilingüe, National Association of Chicano Studies, 1984.

Gonzalez, Ray. *Memory Fever.* Seattle, Wash.: Broken Moon Press, 1993.

Griswold de Castillo, Richard. *The Los Angeles Barrio, 1850–1890: A Social History.* Berkeley: University of California Press, 1979.

Hayes-Bautista, and Jorge Chapa. "Latino Terminology: Conceptual Bases for Standardized Terminology." *American Journal of Public Health* 77, no. 1 (1987): 61–68.

Herrera-Sobek, María, ed. *Beyond Stereotypes: The Critical Analysis of Chicana Literature.* Binghamton, N.Y.: Bilingual Press/Editorial Bilingüe, 1985.

Hinojosa, Rolando. *Generaciones y semblazas.* Translated by Rosaura Sánchez. Berkeley, Calif.: Justa Publications, 1978.

———. *Klail City y sus alrededores.* La Habana: Casa de las Américas, 1976. Translated by Rolando Hinojosa as *Klail City.* Houston, Tex.: Arte Público Press, 1987.

Horno-Delgado, Asunción, et al., eds. *Breaking Boundaries: Latina Writing and Critical Readings.* Amherst, Mass.: University of Massachusetts Press, 1989.

Islas, Arturo. *The Rain God.* New York: Avon Books, 1984, 1991.

Lattin, Vernon E., ed. *Contemporary Chicano Fiction: A Critical Survey.* Binghamton, N.Y.: Bilingual Press/ Editorial Bilingüe, 1986.

Leal, Luis. *Aztlán y México: Perfiles Literarios e Históricos.* Binghamton, N.Y.: Bilingual Press/Editorial Bilingüe, National Association of Chicano Studies, 1985.

Leal, Luis, et al, eds. *A Decade of Chicano Literature, 1970–1979: Critical Essays and Bibliography.* Santa Barbara, Calif.: Editorial La Causa, 1982.

Lee, A. Robert. *"The Mill on the Floss*: 'Memory' and the Reading Experience." In *Reading the Victorian Novel: Detail into Form,* edited by Ian Gregor. London: Vision Press, 1980.

Lomelí, Francisco A., and Carl R. Shirley, eds. *Chicano Writers, First Series,* vol. 82. Detroit, Mich.: Bruccoli Clark Layman, 1989.

Martínez, Julio A., and Francisco A. Lomelí, eds. *Chicano Literature: A Reference Guide.* Westport, Conn.: Greenwood Press, 1986.

Mazón, Mauricio. *The Zoot-Suit Riots: The Psychology of Symbolic Annihilation.* Austin, Tex.: University of Texas Press, 1984.

McWilliams, Carey. *North from Mexico: The Spanish-Speaking People of the United States.* New York: Greenwood Press, 1948.

Meier, Matt S., and Feliciano Rivera. *The Chicanos: A History of Mexican-Americans.* New York: Hill and Wang, 1972.

Mendez, Miguel. *Peregrinos de Aztlán.* Tucson, Ariz.: Editorial Peregrinos, 1974.

Mirandé, Alfredo. *The Chicano Experience: An Alternative Perspective.* Notre Dame, Ind.: University of Notre Dame Press, 1985.

Moraga, Cherríe. *The Last Generation.* Boston: South End Press, 1993.

———. *Loving in the War Years: lo que nunca pasó por los labios.* Boston: South End Press, 1983.

Moraga, Cherríe, and Gloria Anzaldúa, eds. *This Bridge Called My Back: Writings by Radical Women of Color.* Watertown, Mass.: Persephone Press, 1981.

Moraga, Cherríe, et al., eds. *Cuentos: Stories by Latinas.* New York: Kitchen Table Women of Color Press, 1983.

Morales, Alejandro. *Caras viejas y vino nuevo.* México: J. Mortiz, 1975.

Nichols, John. *The Magic Journey.* New York: Holt, Rinehart, 1978.

———. *The Milagro Beanfield War.* New York: Holt, Rinehart, 1974.

———. *The Nirvana Blues.* New York: Holt, Rinehart, 1981.

Paredes, Américo. *"With His Pistol in His Hand": A Border Ballad and Its Hero.* Austin, Tex.: University of Texas Press, 1979.

Ríos, Isabella. *Victuum.* Ventura, Calif.: Diana-Etna, 1976.

Rivera, Tómas. *". . . Y no se lo tragó la tierra"/And the Earth Did Not Part.* Berkeley, Calif.: Quinto Sol Publications, 1971.

Rodriguez, Richard. *Days of Obligation: An Argument with My Mexican Father.* New York: Viking Penguin, 1992.

———. *Hunger of Memory.* Boston: Godine, 1981.

Rodríguez del Pino, Salvador. *La Novela Chicana Escrita en Español: Cinco Autores Comprometidos.* Ypsilanti, Mich.: Bilingual Press/Editorial Bilingüe, National Association of Chicano Studies, 1982.

Saldívar, Ramón. *Chicano Narrative: The Dialectics of Difference.* Madison, Wis.: University of Wisconsin Press, 1990.

Sánchez, George I. *Forgotten People: A Study of New Mexicans.* Albuquerque, N.M.: C. Horn, 1940.

Sánchez, Marta Ester. *Contemporary Chicana Poetry.* Berkeley, Calif.: University of California Press, 1985.

Shirley, Carl R., and Paula W. Shirley. *Understanding Chicano Literature.* Columbia, S.C.: University of South Carolina Press, 1988.

Sommers, Joseph, and Tomás Ybarra-Frausto. *Modern Chicano Writers: A Collection of Critical Essays.* Englewood Cliffs, N.J.: Prentice-Hall, 1979.

Tatum, Charles M. *Chicano Literature.* Boston: Twayne, 1982.

Trujillo, Robert G., and Andrés Rodriguez. *Literature Chicana: Creative and Critical Writings through 1984.* Oakland, Calif.: Floricanto Press, 1985.

Villarreal, José Antonio. *Pocho.* New York: Doubleday, 1959.

von Bardeleben, Renate, Dietrich Briesemeister, and Juan Bruce-Novoa, eds. *Missions in Conflict: Essays on US-Mexican Relations and Chicano Culture.* Tübingen: Gunter Narr Verlag, 1986.

Yankauer, Alfred. "Hispanic/Latino—What's in a Name?" *American Journal of Public Health 77,* no. 1 (1987): 15–17.

Yates, Frances A. *The Art of Memory.* Chicago: University of Chicago Press, 1966.

Pilar Bellver Saez (review date Spring 1996)

SOURCE: A review of *Zia Summer,* in *World Literature Today,* Vol. 70, No. 2, Spring, 1996, p. 403.

[*In the following review, Saez offers a positive assessment of* Zia Summer.]

Zia Summer, Rudolfo Anaya's latest novel, is a detective story that develops the themes of cultural identification and survival. The murder of Gloria Dominic triggers a literary quest that leads Sonny Baca, an amateur Chicano private eye and Gloria's cousin, to uncover a terrorist plot to turn the city into a nuclear wasteland. Set against the background of New Mexico in the 1990s, a time of growth in the West, the story examines the perils of rapid and culturally blind economic change. At the same time, it warns the Mexican-American community to preserve "the old ways" in the face of instability generated by an unequal modernization.

Anaya's novel is an original contribution to the murder-mystery genre. As in the classic detective story, the plot hinges on an unsolved mystery: the strange murder of a woman, her blood drained, and the symbol of the Zia sun scratched around her navel. The work also shares with the hard-boiled detective novel of the 1940s a sense of social and political crisis. Like other popular dicks of the time, Sonny Baca, an honest but clumsy anybody, must find his way through a labyrinth of murder, political corruption, and greed, all against the background of the city's campaign for mayor.

Zia Summer, however, departs from the classic detective genre in significant ways. The harsh rapid dialogue of the hard-boiled classics gives way here to a language of poetic resonance and to a slow-moving narration that makes room for rich descriptions of the New Mexico desert. Don Eliseo, an Albuquerque old-timer, connects Sonny with his cultural past and teaches him respect and love for the beliefs and ways of his Mexican and Indian ancestors. Like characters encountered in previous works by this author (Ultima in **Bless Me, Ultima** or Crispin in **Heart of Aztlán**), he introduces into the narration a mythical world view that becomes central to the hero's resolution of the conflict. Moreover, far from fulfilling the stereotype of the individualistic detective who only relies upon a personally developed value system, Sonny Baca seeks in the collective wisdom of Don Eliseo and in the love and food of his girlfriend Rita the spiritual, mental, and physical energy necessary to solve the case. Becoming aware of his Hispanic past, Sonny comes to understand Gloria's murder as a symptom of the loss of a sense of unity with nature, brought about by modernization and misappropriation of the ancient cultural symbols by a new power-thirsty elite.

The detective in **Zia Summer** is on a quest not only to discover the murderer but also to find his cultural identity. Albuquerque, and more specifically the old Hispanic Alburquerque, becomes the true protagonist of this story. Anaya's focus on culture and history in the long run shifts attention away from the traditional whodunit focus of the detective novel; by the end, the unmasking of the murderer is no surprise and, ultimately, not important in itself. Anaya skillfully transforms the traditional detective novel into a novel that addresses the broader question of Mexican-American identity.

Farhat Iftekharuddin (essay date Summer 1996)

SOURCE: "Gender Roles in Rudolfo Anaya's *The Silence of the Llano*,"[1] in *Journal of Modern Language,* Vol. 20, No. 1, Summer, 1996, pp. 121–28.

[*In the following essay, Iftekharuddin examines traditional Hispanic conceptions of gender and the portrayal of women as temptresses and victims of sexual violence in Anaya's short fiction.*]

A noticeable feature in Mexican American literature is the suggestion, at once implicit and explicit, that culture, history, and setting are the decisive factors determining identity and destiny. The shared history of two nations—Mexico and the United States—which is the inheritance of Mexican Americans, provides evidence to support this suggestion and also marks a partial focus for Mexican American literature. Nearly three hundred years of subjugation under Spanish rule has left indelible marks on Mexicans. Pure Indian bloodlines have given way to generations of *mestizos* (the mixed offspring of Indian and Spanish blood); the building of Spanish churches atop great pyramids and above hundreds of temples has placed Christianity astride the ancient pre-Columbian gods, thus nearly obliterating (or, at least, disguising) old beliefs. One obvious result of such a process of oscillating from self-rule to subjugation back to self-rule, of shifting from a polytheistic to a monotheistic faith, is loss of identity. In its more recent history, Mexico's loss of nearly half of its territory to the United States has only accentuated the problem of identity among its inhabitants. *Mestizos* and *Criollos* (descendants of Europeans alone) alike acquired under their new rulers novel classifications: "Mexicanos" in California, "Tejanos" in Texas, and "Nuevo Mexicanos" or "Hispanos" in New Mexico. Such general problems also become personal; through the evolutionary psychological process called "scripting," external problems of subjugation and persecution became internal to this ethnic body. As a result, the already male dominant order among Hispanics has become even more persecutory. Thus, while Mexican-American writers enjoy the enviable resources of their intricate past—from cultures that have left behind them an art and an architecture that are testaments to human ingenuity—they also have the complex task of redefining themselves. Authors such as Rudolfo Anaya have felt the urgency to recreate their identity, to begin anew, particularly by addressing that cultural variant of the concept of primogeniture that subjugates women.

The works of Rudolfo Anaya—**Bless Me Ultima, Tortuga,** and **The Silence of the Llano**—deal primarily with this search for the self. They explore the defeats and triumphs of Mexican-Americans through the love/hate interactions of his male and female characters. As these characters attempt to reveal themselves both in their relationships to one another and in their singularity as individuals, they also battle to understand themselves, to understand the call of the "ancients" that courses through their veins. Thus, they are preoccupied with the myths that force them into rituals which may ultimately connect them to their past. Such a connection is imperative to self-definition. "Myth," as Anaya himself has defined it, "is our umbilical connection to the past, to the shared collective memory."[2] It is this "shared collective memory," which "resid[es] in the blood,"[3] that Anaya's male and female characters alike attempt to share with us. In the story **"The Silence of the Llano,"** for example—from the collection of stories of the same name—we meet Rafael, who lives on the vast expanse of the llano, the plains surrounded by mountains. Rafael leads a solitary existence, traveling occasionally to town "to swap stories"[4] and to "break the hold of the silence" (p. 4) of the llano. This is the land of his forefathers; it is the land of his hurt. At fifteen, he buried his parents following a blizzard that took their lives. Rafael's lonely existence changes as he meets and marries his beautiful wife, Rita, and brings her back to the llano. He tills the arid soil, plants trees, makes a garden, and impregnates his wife. Seasons change; a daughter is born; and Rita dies following childbirth. Rafael abandons his daughter, who is raised by the midwife whom he had called in to save his wife. This tragedy, instead of cementing a closer unity between father and daughter, creates a breach of communication that lasts for sixteen years: the garden dies; the child grows up, reaches puberty, and is raped by outsiders. Following this violation, Rafael communicates with his daughter, names her Rita, and turns the soil of the garden one more time. In this story, Anaya weaves the llano and his characters into an enigmatic mass. The llano is harshly silent and possessive. Its expanse hides human history; its solitude captures human souls; its silence mutes human tongues. It is the symbol of the shifting, ever-changing quality of its inhabitants, a microcosm reflecting their emptiness, the distance and isolated self, their fears and their challenges. The townspeople "whispered that the silence of the llano had taken Rafael's soul" (p. 3), but they also know that it is home which beckons him. Rafael flees not to town in order to survive the loss of his wife but deep into the llano.

The isolation of the llano provides Anaya with the playing field that his characters use to resolve their passions and their innermost fears without outside intervention or interference. Both father and daughter are tethered to the gravitational center of the llano, and that is their unnatural yet mutual bond. Here the roles of male and female are played out to resolution. Rafael abandons his daughter because, at the primary level, she is, to him, symbolic of lost love (the death of his wife) rather than the reflection of the mother. But there is also an implicit sinister undertone: the Hispanic male's fear of the female, as temptress, the source of animal attraction that gnaws away at social defenses. Both father and daughter contend with this subliminal perversion as they sleep in close proximity. As the girl reaches puberty and feels the "warm flow

between her legs" (p. 16), she becomes "aware of her father" sleeping "on the bed at the other side of the room" (pp. 16–17). Her breasts grow; her hips widen; and she understands "the great mystery of birth which she had seen take place around the llano" (p. 17). As she observes the hen with her chicks, she realizes that "there is life in the eggs" (p. 17) and remembers seeing "the great bull mount one of the cows" (p. 17). In her dreams, "she saw the face of the man who lived there" and "was to be called father" (p. 20). She is awakened by the cry of the owl, and so is her father, but "each lay awake, encased in their solitary silence, expecting no words, but aware of each other as animals are aware when another is close by" (p. 21). The daughter is aware that "the coyote was drawing near" (p. 21). Then come the outsiders, followed by rape.

Rafael rushes home, drawn by the "cloud of dust" (p. 21), and finds his daughter virtually naked. She points to the "stain of blood" (p. 23) on the sheet and raises her hand, calling out for the first time "Rafael" (p. 23); he notices "the curves of her breast rising and falling" (p. 23), and he flees, riding his horse hard. The dream, the outsiders, the rape, and the name "Rafael" merge into a macabre synthesis. Male figures—father/rapist—become inseparable even as the mythological harbinger of bad omen, the owl, sounds a prophetic warning that fails to protect her. Thus, the girl becomes a victim of her anatomical weakness; as Octavio Paz laments in *The Labyrinth of Solitude*, "despite the vigilance of society, woman is always vulnerable. . . . [T]he misfortune of her open anatomy exposes her to all kinds of dangers, against which neither personal morality nor masculine protection is sufficient." Ironically, the girl, as a result of being orphaned, abandoned, and raped, now qualifies for what Paz calls the "compensation mechanism" available in the myth of the "long-suffering Mexican woman."[5] This "compensation mechanism" operates in Rafael when "the ghost of his wife . . . the beauty of her features . . . [blur] into the image of the girl" (p. 24). The female duality of mother as giver of life and as temptress is also resolved here. The possibility of incest is countered by the rape, freeing Rafael from viewing his daughter as temptress. What remains is the merged image of mother/daughter, which provides Rafael with a religious escape.

Among Hispanics, according to Alan Riding, the myth of the long-suffering woman is "exemplified" by the pure image of the Virgin of Guadalupe as "personified by each" Hispanic's "own mother."[6] Therefore, the process of rejuvenation begins when Rafael names his daughter Rita, after her mother. The girl herself has undergone self-purification: "she bathed her shoulders in the cold water, bathed her body in the moonlight" (p. 25). Both Myth and religion are involved in this purification. As Rafael brings his daughter into existence by the act of naming, "a new dawn" (p. 25) appears in the east. Genesis, thus re-established, also forces a new form of communication between father and daughter, between male and female. Since Rita has grown up in virtual silence, she is unfamiliar with the language of her father, the language of males that nearly destroyed her. She recalls only the sounds of a select number of words that she has heard as a child from the mid-wife, Doña Rufina. Rita spoke them "aloud just to hear the sound they made as they burst from her lips, 'Lumbre' . . . 'Agua' . . . 'Tote'" (p. 18). Language and action, thus transferred in matrilineal form, subvert the traditional concept of patriarchal dominance and transference of language. Rafael must now learn to converse with Rita on her own terms; he must learn to "imitate the call of wild doves . . . and wild sparrows" (pp. 18–19).

On the llano, a new man/woman relationship begins. The silence of the llano that had taken Rafael's soul is retrieved a second time by a female, first by his wife and now by his daughter. At the birth of his daughter, Rafael had felt betrayed, both because his wife had died giving birth to his child, but also because the birth of a daughter raises the question of his masculinity: a female issue cannot continue the family name. His misfortunes had led him to brood that "he was a man who could not allow himself to dream" (p. 16), but he escapes from this self-pity and undergoes a vital transformation in his acceptance of his daughter. He promises to "turn the earth," and he asserts that "the seeds will grow" (p. 28).

The indignity of women at the hands of men is even more vivid in the story **"The Road to Platero."** This is the story of Carmelita, who is raped by her father, now her husband, and bears a son from that sexual violence. The setting is again the desolate llano. Carmelita's horrifying experience has left her a bitter woman. She oscillates between memories of her father's love and her father's violence. She had been at one time "his jewel, his angel, his only daughter."[7] The terrible irony is that this is Carmelita's dream of what a father ought to be. The unfortunate reality is that to her father, Carmelita was and still is woman to be violently possessed. The females in this large family of vaqueros are reduced to animal levels. Carmelita's son recalls: "of all the women in Platero, my mother is the youngest. She is thin, her hair is long and black, her skin is smooth. . . . I have seen the vaqueros admire the sleek, beautiful mares and I have seen them look at my mother" (p. 34). As the vaqueros return home along the country road, riding their stallions, their women scurry to the windows, and "in the corral the mares paw the ground nervously" (p. 33). Except for the boy, the men and women know Carmelita's dark secret. The women remain silent, and the men drink for courage and to forget.

There are two images for Carmelita of the man who has fathered her son: one that remembers him as "a real caballero," and the other as the one who violated her and her dreams. Because of this violence, the father loses identity for her and remains nameless. (As does "Mr." in Alice Walker's *The Color Purple*.) Carmelita refers to this "m[a]n-creature" simply as "he" or "him" or "the man." Her father/husband is aware of this loss of his identity; he is aware that as the daughter died in the rape, so did he. This is an insult to his masculinity and renders him spiritually and morally impotent. Unable to forget, and having lost respect and identity, the father/husband attempts to

relieve his guilt onto Carmelita: "'your sin is too dark to be forgiven . . . your sin is the sin of hell, and you will do penance by serving me forever,'" he tells her (p. 37). The male in this repetitive cycle of violence is trapped in the sins of his fathers. Carmelita's whispered love to her son is a warning and an assertion of this fact. "'I have submitted to that beast,' she tells the boy, 'only to protect you my son, but you are a man like any other man. Will, you, too raise your spurs and rake your mother's flanks when you are grown?'" (p. 33).

Carmelita, like Rita, is the long-suffering woman. But, unlike Rita, her reconciliation with her father is violent. The story begins with a metaphysical triangulation: "'Love came, death came, then you were born, my little son . . . '" (p. 31), a tragic continuum which renders women inferior to men. Carmelita stoically resigns herself to this state of inferiority as she tells her son, "'yes, we are slaves of our fathers, our husbands, our sons . . . and you, my little one, my life, you will grow to be a man . . . '" (p. 33). She realizes that this is more a curse on her son than a blessing, and in her resignation she finds the source of redemption. As she kills her father/husband, exclaiming, "'Now for you, my son'" (p. 39), Carmelita herself dies from a deep spur wound to her throat. Her sacrifice provides her son with a new beginning, as "peace" settles over the llano, and the "horseman who haunted the road" (p. 39) to Platero disappears.

In the role of the long-suffering woman, both Rita and Carmelita provide credence to Octavio Paz's observation that to Hispanic men the "inferiority" of women "is constitutional and resides in their sex, their submissiveness, which is a wound that never heals."[8] Women, thus dehumanized, are naturally destined to be violated. In this process of continued sexual violation, men themselves are caught in the web of their ancient gods. The Aztec hero Huitzilopochtli was "born in an instant" from the woman Coatlicue ("snake skirt"), who already had four hundred sons and one daughter who was their leader. Huitzilopochtli decapitates his sister with a snakehead scepter, thus achieving triumph over female authority and becoming protector of the wandering Mexicas.[9] According to the version of the myth in the *Popol Vuh,* "Why the Earth Eats the Dead," the Aztec god Quetzalcoatl created the earth by quartering Hungry Woman.[10] In a variant of the myth of the Corn Woman's Marriage, the woman bears a son who grows up and marries his own sister, and the world is populated by their incestuous offspring.[11] Even the coyote that both Rafael and his daughter recognize before the rape has its origin in the myth of the trickster Kauyumari. In order to control the reproductive process of females, Kauyumari (meaning "coyote" or "wolf"), at the command of the sun god, places "teeth in the women's vaginas" (*la vagina dentada*). As a result, the men—including Kauyumari—are mutilated. However, the coyote Kauyumari's sexual desire is "so great that his missing organ promptly regenerates."[12] In order to survive future castration, the coyote clears away the teeth in the woman's vagina with "a blunt instrument, usually a stick of wood."[13]

Imbedded in such mythologized violence against women is the power that they have always held over men and their male gods. Women are both mothers, originators of the world, and temptresses whose vaginas are traps that fathers, husbands, and sons fall victim to. The violence perpetuated against Rita (the daughter) and Carmelita by the "men-creatures" (**"Road,"** p. 32) is a perverted and futile attempt at subjugation. In fact, such painful experiences strengthen their resolve, their resiliency. Through suffering, Hispanic women become "invulnerable,"[14] and they "remain," as Riding points out, "the pivot of the family."[15] Rafael's daughter, Rita, does win her father's recognition, and Carmelita's act of parricide suggests the end of male violence. Her sacrifice promises a better future for her boy.

While the female child acquires first stoicism and then strength from suffering, the male child battles for an identity independent of the female, be she mother, wife, or lover. His search for selfhood forces him into the community of men or "tribes," as in the case of the young boy in **"Salomon's Story."** Salomon leaves the pastoral beauty of his father's land and joins a group of youngsters who call themselves "a tribe."[16] He is an initiate in this fraternity, and the initiation requires that he kill the first animal that the tribe encounters. Salomon and the tribe venture into "unknown territory" (p. 57) along the river bank and eventually encounter a "giant river turtle" (p. 56). He is handed the tribal knife and following frenzied cries of "'Kill it,'" he severs the head. But their celebration is short lived; the turtle rises and moves towards the river. Salomon thrusts his hand in the gaping hole of this female turtle in a desperate attempt to turn it over but is driven backward into the river by the power of the creature. As the turtle disappears into the depths from which it came, the tribe abandons the young initiate. Salomon "left the river, free of the tribe, but unclean and smelling of death. That night the bad dreams came, and then paralysis" (p. 61). Salomon responds to what he calls his "destiny" (p. 55). He has left his father, "a good man" who "kept the ritual of the seasons, marked the path of the sun and the moon across the sky, and . . . prayed each day that the order of things not be disturbed" (p. 55). But it had been a "wild urge" in his "blood" that "drove" him from his father (p. 55). In killing the turtle, Salomon violates the "order of things"; he disconnects the continuum of life, the primeval link between water and earth represented by the turtle. Unwittingly, he is guilty of usurping the gods of his own mythology: According to one Mesoamerican myth, the gods, in order to fertilize the earth, engaged in bloodletting around a turtle altar,[17] and the ancient Mayans believed that the maize god was resurrected through the turtle shell.[18] The young hunter pays through paralysis to atone for his unconscious transgression; like Tieresias, he is "forced by the order of [his] destiny" (p. 56) to be a storyteller. **"Salomon's Story"** is fatalistic; Salomon is "doomed" when he answers his "wild urge." He cannot acquire an identity independent of patriarchal control, and any attempt to do so can lead only to tragedy.

However, seen within the context of the novel ***Tortuga,*** from which **"Salomon's Story"** has been extracted, the message may seem less disquieting. The characters in this novel are grotesques, disfigured and crippled children waiting out their lives in a hospital. Into this scene, a young boy arrives paralyzed from a broken back. He acquires the name Tortuga—"turtle"—when the doctor puts him in a hard body cast with only his legs and arms protruding. Lying on his back in a state of metamorphosis, the young boy comes to symbolize the paralysis of all the children as they struggle to prevail against a vast, meaningless, and unresponsive world. Viewed as a turtle, however, he is a symbol of life, of time and history. Tortuga's body cast—covering his breast and back—is analogous to the ephod worn by the high priest of Israel (I Samuel, 2:18), who was God's spokesman of justice and judgment (Exodus, 28:15). Salomon makes Tortuga the audience for his story, the spokesman who must tell the others of the "meaning of life and death" (p. 38). By attaching himself to Tortuga, the only patient who eventually walks out of the hospital, Salomon finally breaks from his "forsaken . . . initiation" (p. 58). The fatalistic vision of life is exchanged for one of hope and the future. Tortuga himself begins anew: on his way to his parents' house, he stops at the home of his love, Ismelda, the actual catalyst in his healing process.

Anaya's stories are not an indictment of Mexican-American culture. Rather, they provide images that are part of their collective memory. Anaya's "men-creatures" of the Llano remind us of Samuel Ramos' description of the *pelado* in his book *Profile of Man and Culture in Mexico*: to the *pelado*, his "sexual organ becomes symbolic of masculine force."[19] "It suggests . . . the idea of power. From this he has derived a very impoverished concept of man. Since he is, in effect, a being without substance, he tries to fill his void with the only suggestive force accessible to him: that of the male animal."[20] In provoking this recollection of the male as animal, Anaya asserts the fact that the future is not an isolated moment in time; it is linked to the past. Only by addressing the neurosis of the past can the perfections sought for the future be achieved. Anaya believes that "history moves us toward perfection through small epiphanies."[21]

In his story the **"Silence of the Llano,"** his male character does experience an epiphanic realization. In finally recognizing his daughter as a part of himself to be loved and not coveted, he breaks from the ranks of the "men-creatures," from the *pelado*. Rafael realizes, as Paul Smith points out in *The Body Hispanic,* that "the ground on which man takes up his position is, inevitably, woman."[22] If the paradoxical nature of woman as mother and temptress troubles Hispanic men, this lack of understanding also reveals their own contradictory nature. Rosalind Coward in *Female Desire* states that there has been intense investigation into the enigmatic nature of women, when "in reality," it is "men's bodies, men's sexuality which is the true 'dark continent' of . . . society."[23] Perhaps in the past of Mexicans, "a mute and ancient past" as Carlos Fuentes terms it,[24] confronting this contradictory aspect of men's sexuality was not an option. But in Anaya's stories, it is. Both male and female characters in his stories are forced into confronting their individual sexuality, and in the process they create new beginnings. The men realize that the women cannot be muted through oppressive acts. Parricide is not an option but an exigency of life necessary to counter the perditious effects of sexual violence. Recognizing each other and attempting to overcome the traditional dichotomy between the sexes are part of the sexual dialectics of Anaya's stories.

Notes

1. Farhat Iftekharuddin, "Gender Roles in Rudolfo Anaya's *The Silence of the Llano*," *Journal of Modern Literature*, XX, 1 (Summer 1996), pp. 121–128. © Foundation for Modern Literature, 1996.

2. Rudolfo Anaya, "Aztlan: A Homeland Without Boundaries," *Aztlan: Essays on the Chicano Homeland*, eds. Rudolfo A. Anaya and Francisco A. Lomeli (University of New Mexico Press, 1991), p. 236.

3. Anaya, *Aztlán*, p. 236.

4. Rudolfo Anaya, "The Silence of the Llano," *The Silence of the Llano: Short Stories* (TQS Publications, 1982), p. 3. All subsequent references will be cited parenthetically.

5. Octavio Paz, *The Labyrinth of Solitude and the Other Mexico, Return to the Labyrinth of Solitude, Mexico and the United States, The Philanthropic Ogre*, trans. Lysander Kemp, Yara Milos, and Rachel Phillips Belash, (Grove Weidenfeld, 1985), p. 38.

6. Alan Riding, *Distant Neighbors: A Portrait of the Mexicans*, (Vintage, 1986), p. 8.

7. Rudolfo Anaya, "The Road to Platero," *The Silence of the Llano*, p. 32. All subsequent references will be cited parenthetically.

8. Octavio Paz, *The Labyrinth of Solitude*, p. 30.

9. John Bierhorst, *The Mythology of Mexico and Central America* (William Morrow, 1990), p. 159.

10. Bierhorst, p. 149.

11. Bierhorst, p. 169.

12. Bierhorst, p. 169.

13. John Bierhorst, *The Mythology of North America* (William Morrow, 1985), p. 125.

14. Octavio Paz, *The Labyrinth of Solitude*, p. 3.

15. Riding, p. 9.

16. Rudolfo Anaya, "Salomon's Story." *The Silence of the Llano*, 1982, p. 55. All subsequent references will be cited parenthetically.

17. Mary Miller and Karl Taube, eds. *The Gods and Symbols of Ancient Mexico and the Maya: An Il-* lustrated Dictionary of Mesoamerican Religion (Thames and Hudson, 1993), p. 75.

18. Karl Taube, *The Legendary Past: Aztec and Maya Myths* (University of Texas Press, 1993), p. 67.

19. Samuel Ramos, *Profile of Man and Culture in Mexico,* trans. Peter G. Earle (University of Texas Press, 1962). p. 59.

20. Ramos, p. 61.

21. Anaya, *Aztlán*, p. 241.

22. Paul Julian Smith, *The Body Hispanic: Gender and Sexuality in Spanish and Spanish American Literature* (Clarendon Press, 1989), p. 5.

23. Rosalind Coward, *Female Desire: How They Are Sought, Bought and Packaged* (Grove Weidenfeld, 1985), p. 227.

24. Carlos Fuentes, "How I Started to Write," *Myself With Others: Selected Essays* (Farrar, Straus and Giroux, 1988), p. 9.

William Anthony Nericcio (review date Autumn 1996)

SOURCE: A review of *Jalamanta*, in *World Literature Today*, Vol. 70, No. 4, Autumn, 1996, pp. 957–58.

[*In the following review, Nericcio offers an unfavorable assessment of* Jalamanta.]

In January of 1996 a writer for *Publishers Weekly,* that chronicler of esthetically noteworthy textual effluvia, fell to reviewing Rudolfo Anaya's **Jalamanta**. The less-than-exhilarated reviewer found it "a sharp departure from the yeasty realism that won [Anaya] a large readership," ultimately labeling it a "preachy New Age parable" with "lofty sentiments" which become "somewhat platitudinous with repetition." I wish I could be as gentle.

Far and away, this is Anaya's most misbegotten literary experiment. Warner Books' publicity hacks remind us on the book's dust jacket how **Jalamanta** comes from a scribe Tony Hillerman dubbed the "godfather and guru of Chicano literature"; they only succeed at increasing the disappointment. No **Bless Me, Ultima, Jalamanta** offers its readers a visit to a dystopic, mystical, allegorical terrain trod before by Frank Herbert and Carlos Castaneda. Juxtaposed as such, it does not come off very well.

Anaya's novel is set in and around a fictional "Seventh City of the Fifth Sun" and tells the story of Fatimah and her love, the exiled rebel teacher Jalamanta, né Amado. While waiting thirty long years for his return, Fatimah and her people live the sorry life of exploited exiles, "people who many years ago had revolted against the authorities," "outcast[s] from their homes in the city." The enemy are brownshirted forces of order, "authorities" who use "sacred books to oppress."

Dominant motifs in Anaya's morality play include lights and veils, hence the telling name "Jalamanta," "he who strips away the veils that blind the soul"—an important issue, we know, as Anaya reminds us repeatedly: dark is bad; light is good. No sartorial Beau Brummel he, Jalamanta's only material accessory is a "weathered staff made from the twisted roots of a desert tree, crowned by the carved heads of two entwined snakes." Said staff once again resounding Anaya's binary emphases.

Speaking of binaries, Jalamanta has two boyhood friends: "Santos," a saintly (get it?) friend who "spends his time reading holy books"; and "Iago," Jalamanta's betrayer, a "wine merchant" whose "ways are secretive." An Iago as traitor—how novel! As the book slowly paces toward its tragic, totally anticipated climax, you almost wish Jalamanta had sat through a performance of Shakespeare's *Othello* during his exile. Surely Jalamanta should know that trusting one's fate to a man named Iago is like mortgaging your house through a loan shark. Anaya's other bad guys are no more subtle. Take "Vende," a representative of the central authorities, who "dresse[s] in a brown uniform and black boots" with a "cap sewn [with] an insignia of three skulls." *Vende* translates as "sell" or "he sells." Selling, bad; veils, bad; light, love, and truth, good. This is the structure of Anaya's experiment.

Jalamanta's patient lover Fatimah is a "healer"—no doubt echoing for fans of Anaya and of his singularly important first novel the memory of Ultima, the *curandera* in **Bless Me, Ultima.** I have read **Bless Me, Ultima,** written about **Bless Me, Ultima,** and Fatimah, you are no Ultima. Consider this: most of the book, Fatimah (Our Lady of?) waits around for Jalamanta and then quietly supports his absurdly monomaniacal quest. No day job, Jalamanta's whole vocation is that of "seeker." In his own words: "I have wandered in the desert seeking the truth."

Other problems derail Anaya's fable. At times, the writing is this side of a Barbara Cartland romance; Fabio would be at home on the cover of the paperback version. Imagine Harlequin Books inviting Castaneda or Herbert to author novels for them and you might not be surprised at some of the following riffs: "I offer you the kiss of life," [Jalamanta] said, feeling the surge of love flowing between them, the energies of their souls becoming a filament of light in the stream of sunlight." The romantic scenes are hard to get through—one motif, the Holy Grail, is used to an extent surpassed only by the comedy troupe Monty Python, and that was for comedy. One sample suffices: "[Fatimah] was the Holy Grail of [Jalamanta's] dreams."

In the end Jalamanta brings about his own arrest by declaring that by allowing our souls to be filled with light, we are "becoming god." As might be anticipated, the brown-shirted authorities are not too keen on this kind of blasphemy; neither are they so finely attuned to the allegorical nature of Jalamanta's doublespeak. They take him at his word and throw him in chains. The final chapter of the novel is aptly named "Betrayal." There Anaya's

readers witness Iago's inevitable betrayal of Jalamanta to the authorities. A teacher and wise sage man, he should have seen it coming.

Speaking of allegory, *betrayal* here can read in two ways, for the term aptly characterizes "guru" Anaya's treatment of his readers. While cynical, I am not so churlish as to suggest the book has *no* redeeming qualities; when Jalamanta reminds us how "the germ of creation lies in chaos," one dreams of what might have been if the novel itself could have more chaos.

In recent years Anaya has tried his hand at detective fiction, travel narrative, and now, with **Jalamanta,** ethereal allegory—he certainly cannot be accused of resting on his laurels. While we should champion this restless spirit which drives Anaya to new prose and fictional forms, we should also not be surprised when this restlessness leads our godfather down the wrong back alley.

Theresa M. Kanoza (essay date Summer 1999)

SOURCE: "The Golden Carp and Moby Dick: Rudolfo Anaya's Multi-Culturalism," in *MELUS,* Vol. 24, No. 2, Summer, 1999, pp. 159–71.

[*In the following essay, Kanoza presents a thematic analysis of* Bless Me, Ultima *and Herman Melville's* Moby-Dick, *contending that there are "thematic and tonal links" between the two novels.*]

In **Bless Me, Ultima,** Rudolfo Anaya presents a world of opposites in the New Mexican village of Guadalupe. The parents of the young protagonist Antonio have strikingly different temperaments, as dissimilar to each other as the backgrounds from which they hail. Maria Luna Marez, the pious daughter of Catholic farmers from the fertile El Puerto valley, steers her son toward the priesthood and a ministry in an agrarian settlement. Gabriel Marez, Antonio's adventurous father, is descended from a long line of nomadic horsemen; he expects his son to share his wanderlust, and he hopes that as compadres they will explore the vanishing *llano* (plains). The thrust of Anaya's *bildungsroman,* however, is not that maturation necessitates exclusionary choices between competing options, but that wisdom and experience allow one to look beyond difference to behold unity.

Historic continuity and spiritual harmony are recurrent strains in much of Anaya's work as he often laments man's weakened connection to the earth, to the past, and to the myths that reveal the proper balance of the cosmos. In **"The Myth of Quetzalcoatl,"** Anaya criticizes the heavy toll which economic and political realities exact from the fragile landscape of the Southwest and its ancient cultures, but, a conciliator, he also cites some merit in change. Rather than condemning or shunning innovation, as do many who, like Anaya, want to protect an endangered heritage, he advocates a measured application of modernization. "Technology may serve people," he reminds those whom he claims are wont to retrench in the old ways, but "it need not be the new god" (198). Likewise, informed engagement in the legislative process, a political reality of the here-and-now, can serve the cause of preserving the landscape and the cultures it sustains. Anaya urges that just as the present can safeguard the past, historical awareness can "shed light on our contemporary problems" (198). He reaches back through the centuries to the Toltec civilization of Tula to bring instructive parallels to bear on current rapacious materialism in the United States (199). As a writer, Anaya practices the rich admixing across time and space that he preaches, for his novels of the American Southwest blend diverse cultural strains. In *Bless Me, Ultima* he draws deeply on Native American mythology and Mexican Catholicism,[1] and, though the novel is written in conventional English that the protagonist deems a "foreign tongue" (53), the prose is to be read as a translation of the Spanish which most characters speak. When his characters use English, they typically engage in code-switching.[2]

Bless Me, Ultima has earned acclaim for its "cultural uniqueness" and is lauded for such distinctive Chicano features as its use of Aztec myth and symbol, its thematic emphasis on family structures, and its linguistic survivals. Furthermore, Anaya is renowned as one of the "Big Three" of the Chicano canon, alongside Tomás Rivera and Rolando Hinojosa (Sommers 146–47). Set in a sacred place imbued with a spiritual presence and long inhabited by indigenous peoples, his book presents a world where the Anglo is of little consequence to its strong Chicano characters.[3]

Yet this highly celebrated ethnic novel also reveals the strong imprint of Anglo-American belles-lettres. Many critics observe Anaya's reliance upon James Joyce's *Portrait of the Artist as a Young Man* to relate the anguished rites of passage of his own protagonist.[4] Both Antonio Marez and Stephen Dedalus ask bold questions about the nature of good and evil as they examine their roles within the families and Church that circumscribe their lives. William Faulkner, John Steinbeck, and Katherine Anne Porter, among others, have also been cited as literary influences on Anaya.[5] But in a novel that uncovers shared tenets among seemingly discordant worldviews by an author who prizes cross-cultural connections, Anaya goes even further afield in choosing his literary models. *Bless Me, Ultima,* lauded as a masterpiece of the margins, also evokes that text which is most often cited as the epitome of the white, northeastern literary paradigm—Herman Melville's *Moby-Dick.*[6] Both novels tap into biblical and mythological archetypes as their main characters plumb the mysteries of creation. In their quests for experience, knowledge, and mastery, the protagonists in each book break religious taboos and push the limits of human awareness as they try to fathom the unknowable mind of God. In fact, both novels have drawn similar criticism for their weighty, abstract subject matter and for their individualist rather than social focus.[7]

But to detect a Melvillian influence in *Bless Me, Ultima* is not to charge Anaya with being derivative, nor is it a backhanded attempt to "prove" the universality of the traditional canon by asserting that it presciently accommodates the Chicano experience. For in many ways, Anaya's book testifies to the triumph of the Chicano cosmology. As presented by Melville, the negative romantic and "sick soul,"[8] the world is a place of horror and despair; Anaya, revealing his Jungian bent as he taps into the collective unconscious, finds vigor, beauty, and order there.[9] Indeed, Anaya's text reads as though he, along with Ishmael, has survived the wreck of the *Pequod* but that he has lived to articulate the harmonies of the universe which Melville's sailors could not recognize. In *Bless Me, Ultima,* Anaya reconciles into a unified whole the dichotomies which loom chaotic and rend the cosmos in *Moby-Dick.*

Both Melville's Ishmael and Antonio Marez, the schoolboy protagonist of *Bless Me, Ultima,* are novices. Generally untrained in the ways of whaling, Ishmael proves to be a quick study after signing on as a deckhand aboard the *Pequod.* He is ostensibly in pursuit of whales and then more specifically *the* whale, after Ahab commandeers the crew to his own vengeful mission. But more significantly Ishmael pursues experience and wisdom, goals which make him a milder version of the blasphemous Ahab, who lashes out at the God-head to avenge his own human limitations. Antonio, also seeking to understand the complexity of life, tracks a fish of his own, the legendary golden carp, the avatar of an Aztec nature-god.[10] By sighting the river-god which swims the waters that surround Antonio's village and by pondering its history of sacrifice for the salvation of others, Antonio hopes to learn the secrets of the universe. His journey into paganism is an exhilarating quest but one which induces guilt and anxiety as he breaks the first commandment of his Christian faith.

Guadalupe, an isolated village that is set apart from the greater New Mexican landmass by a river which encircles it, is at once as insular and internally diverse as the *Pequod,* the island ship which sails the world's oceans. Melville's sailors represent widely differing nationalities and religious beliefs: Ahab is a Quaker-turned-atheist, and Ishmael a Presbyterian; the harpooners are described as heathens, Queequeg as a Polynesian idolater and cannibal, Daggoo as a "gigantic, coal-black negro-savage," and Tashtego an "unmixed Indian" (107). Of Ahab's secret East Indian crew, Fedallah, a Parsee, is a fire-worshiper. Although not as wildly diverse, a varied constituency also comprises Antonio's world. Besides the stark differences in the mores and temperaments of the peaceful farmers who are his maternal relatives and his raucous, rootless paternal uncles who ride the *llano,* Antonio finds sharp contrasts among his friends. Catholic and Protestant classmates taunt each in the schoolyard about their conflicting beliefs of heaven and hell, while those secretly faithful to the cult of the golden carp, such as Cico, Samuel, and Jason, are contemptuous of these arcane concerns. Children of no particular religious persuasion, some of whom are eerily animal-like in appearance and endowed with preternatural strength and speed, watch the squabbles in amusement. All are terrified by the three Trementina sisters, who are legendary for practicing black magic.

Both Melville and Anaya ascribe a mystical, seductive beauty to the natural world—or more specifically to bodies of water—for, as Ishmael explains, "meditation and water are wedded for ever" (13). In "Loomings," the first chapter of *Moby-Dick,* Ishmael describes the magnetic pull of the ocean. Seeking a spiritual sustenance not found in the commerce that occupies them during the workweek, "crowds of water-gazers" gather at the wharfs during their leisure. Ishmael pronounces these "thousands upon thousands of mortal men fixed in ocean reveries" (12) to be narcissists, for they seek in their reflections thrown back by the mirror-like "rivers and oceans . . . the ungraspable phantom of life . . . the key to it all" (14). Ishmael, of course, is no exception to these questers. Hoping to learn the secrets of the "wonder-world," he says he is drawn to the whaling voyage by "a portentous and mysterious monster [that] raised all my curiosity" (16).

Later in "The Mast-Head" when Ishmael is assigned watch high above the ship's deck, he experiences the dangerous allure of pantheism. As a meditative man surrounded by the glory of the universe, he fears he could lose himself both literally and figuratively in the beauty of nature.

> Lulled into such an opium-like listlessness of vacant, unconscious reverie is this absent-minded youth by the blending cadence of waves with thoughts, that at last he loses his identity; takes the mystic ocean at his feet for the visible image of that deep, blue bottomless soul, pervading mankind and nature; and every . . . undiscernible form, seems to him the embodiment of those elusive thoughts that only people the soul by continually flitting through it. In this enchanted mood, the spirit ebbs away to whence it came; becomes diffused through time and space. . . .
>
> (140)

To yield rationality to revery, Ishmael cautions, is to lose one's footing and plummet to the sea; to merge with the natural world is to surrender one's distinct identity. He concludes his warning with the stern note, "heed it well, ye Pantheists" (140), and Melville proves that it is advice best followed. In "The Life-Buoy," a subsequent chapter, a crew member who passes into a "transitional state" while posting lookout from the crow's nest falls to his death in the sea.

A pantheistic-like spirituality is an equally strong contender for the religious affections of the soul-searchers in *Bless Me, Ultima.* Anaya handily debunks the merits of dogmatic Catholicism in the cold and ineffectual Irish priest whose sole method of reaching his first communicants is a meaningless catechism. The children respond by rote but have no deeper understanding of the faith to which they are being indoctrinated; Father Byrnes neither encourages nor facilitates any fuller awareness. Antonio's pathologically devout mother, though honest and loving, is further testament to the Church's ineffectuality and harm. A fearful, superstitious woman for whom religious devotion means passivity, she is the epitome of weakness that Melville derides in Roman Catholicism as "feminine . . . submission and endurance" (315).

Worship of nature—wild, free, and seemingly benevolent—is an attractive alternative to the Catholicism which many in Antonio's world find stifling. (The parish church, in fact, is described as dark, dank, and musty). But Anaya, like Melville, also conveys the danger of a spirituality derived from nature. When the cult member Cico seeks to convert Antonio to his pagan beliefs, he is careful to caution the initiate about the possible hazards that loom in a mystical merger with the natural world. Like Ishmael, Cico is a "water-gazer," one who is drawn to the river by its "strange power [and] *presence*" (**Bless** 108). He recounts to Antonio that he became spellbound while perched on an overhanging cliff high above the hidden lake, and that he only narrowly resisted the strange music that beckoned him to the depths below: "It wasn't that the singing was evil," Cico explains. "It was just that it called for me to join it. One more step and I'da stepped over the ledge and drowned in the waters of the lake" (109).

Actual fatalities follow Cico's close call. Narciso, a cult member (whose name echoes the narcissists who gaze into the water to find their bearings at the outset of *Moby-Dick*), is, like the drowning victim of Melville's "Life-Buoy," trapped in his own "transitional state." Pegged as the pathetic but good-hearted town drunk who has lost control over his faculties, Narciso is eventually murdered by the villainous Tenorio Trementina. Another casualty of nature-worship is Florence, Antonio's friend, whose tortured boyhood has destroyed his faith in God. Though scornful of the limitations and cruel paradoxes of Catholicism, Florence is no simple heretic. He searches for "a god of beauty, a god of here and now . . . a god who does not punish" (228). He is drawn to the lake, much as Antonio and Cico are, but, unable to resist the beckoning water, he drowns. Florence's death dive is described as an underwater exploration that lasts too long.

In seeking to resurrect the spirit of the land and the power of ancient myth, Anaya is certainly sympathetic to Cico, the believer in "many gods . . . of beauty and magic, gods of the garden, gods in our own backyards" (227). Yet when Cico counsels Antonio to renounce Christ, whom he calls a jealous deity that would instruct his priests to kill the golden carp, Anaya does not endorse this exclusionary vision. For though Cico observes the link between the natural and the divine, he does not recognize the affinity between Christianity and the indigenous spirituality. The kinship of Christ with the nature-god, who transformed himself into a carp so as to live among and protect his people who were likewise transformed into fish as punishment for their sins, is lost on Cico.

With his blindered vision, Cico is reminiscent of those Melville characters who also reduce the complex unity of the world to polarities. Richard Slotkin has named "consummation" as the main thrust of *Moby-Dick,* a merger conveyed through such metaphors as the Eucharist, marriage, and, more literally, the hunt. But he explains that, finally, Melville delivers no such consolation since his characters achieve no lasting spiritual balance or cosmic bonding. Ishmael, for example, heeds too well his own warning to pantheists. While he warns that mysticism can leach away individuality, he also bemoans social interdependence as one of life's "dangerous liabilities" (271).[11]

Ahab, like Cico, is unable to reconcile seeming opposites; like Ishmael, he perverts the notion of unity. If Ahab sees a "common creaturehood" with Moby Dick, his own self-loathing forces him to destroy what he perceives as an extension of himself (545). And if Moby Dick is an avatar of God and the wound it inflicts is a punishment, the whale represents the power which Ahab covets and can attain only by subduing. For the monomaniacal sea captain, there is no co-existing with the white whale, no possibility that Moby Dick is a mediator between the human and the divine. Ahab believes he must either kill the whale, or be killed by it. His binary vision makes him hopelessly paranoid: what he cannot fully understand he construes as malign and warranting pre-emptive destruction.[12]

It is Ultima, an ironic counterpart to Ahab in their shared capacity as mentors, who teaches Antonio to look beyond difference to recognize transcendent parallels. Though their respect for life varies greatly and, indeed, their world-views clash, the *curandera* (medicine woman) of the New Mexican *llano* and the captain of the *Pequod* are similarly enigmatic and powerful figures. Their marred outward appearances attest to their intense engagement with life— Ahab with his ivory leg and the scar that runs the length of his body and Ultima with her shrunken frame and wizened face. Both are cut off from family. Ahab was orphaned before his first birthday, and as an adult he chooses Moby Dick and the sea over the wife and infant son he leaves in New England. Ultima, aged and apparently childless, is homeless until Antonio's father Gabriel moves her from the unsheltered *llano* into his home in Guadalupe.

The most significant parallel the two share is their own hybridity from which they draw their awe-inspiring strength. Captains Bildad and Pelag, the *Pequod*'s owners, aptly sum up Ahab's contradictory nature. "He's a grand, ungodly, god-like man. . . . Ahab's been in colleges, as well as 'mong the cannibals" (76). "Old Thunder" vows to lash out at the sun should it insult him, a threat he later carries out by smashing the quadrant that requires him to rely on the heavens to determine his bearings in the sea. Yet he clearly "has his humanities," as when he consoles the crazed Pip or recalls the warm home he has left behind. He is vulnerable too, dwarfed and deformed as he is by his uncontrollable obsession. Such dualities within Ahab do not comport well; they are in constant conflict and drive him to war with the universe. His internal chaos

manifests itself in his fractious nature, which causes him to perceive a fragmented outer world. He will brook no compromise nor accede to any mediation: Moby Dick is pure evil and Ahab must destroy him, or lose his life trying.

Ultima is not without her own dark side, since she too encompasses dualities. "La Grande," as she is called, is part saint but also part witch. Her ability to cast out demons and to remove curses derives from her own acquaintance with evil. Yet her dualities do not taint or confound her; they complement her. In fact, her understanding of evil enhances her capacity for goodness. Recognizing that the disparate elements of creation work in concert, she instructs Antonio to respect rather than to fear difference, for "we fear evil only because we do not understand it" (236). Her universe, in all its splendid diversity, is coherent, not chaotic.

In the broad sweep of Ultima's vision, cooperation rather than competition is the driving force of the cosmos. For her, pagan and Christian precepts are not mutually exclusive. Whereas Cico counsels Antonio to renounce the Christian trinity as impostors so that he might pledge his faith to the golden carp, Ultima, who also worships the golden carp, integrates her heterogenous beliefs. As Cordelia Candelaria observes, Ultima's spirit, embodied in the owl which always hovers near her, suggests at once Christ as dove and Quetzalcoatl as eagle (*Chicano Literature* 39). There is no hypocrisy or sacrilege as she joins Maria in praying to the Virgin of Guadalupe, nor in her attendance at Sunday mass with the Marez family. Yet as much as she is a companion to the devout Maria, she is the compatriot of Gabriel, the begrudging Catholic and restive villager. He is unfulfilled by the Church and reluctant to join Maria in praying the rosary. Instead he draws spiritual sustenance from the *llano,* where he finds "a power that can fill a man with satisfaction." Ultima, who participates in Catholic rituals but whose faith is never dictated by dogma, shares Gabriel's reverence for the untamed plains and responds in kind to his praise for the land: "and there is faith here . . . a faith in the reason for nature being, evolving, growing" (220). The merger of her pagan and Christian beliefs is complete in her answer to Antonio's plea, which is the title of the novel. As she offers her blessing, she adopts the cadence of the Catholic benediction and invokes her own secular, benevolent triune: "I bless you in the name of all that is good and strong and beautiful" (247).

As Ultima's apprentice, Antonio learns that Christianity and native mythology are compatible. Initiated into the awareness that the whole is comprised of its many parts, he resolves as well the conflicting agenda his parents set for him. When Antonio dreams that he is being riven by his parents as each issues a self-interested plan for his future, Ultima intercedes on his behalf. Maria claims that her son is a true Luna, a child of the moon who was baptized by the holy water of the Church and thus destined for a vocation as a priest; Gabriel counters that the boy, like all Marez men, is a product of the restless salt-water sea, and that he is therefore meant to ride the plains. Ultima refutes his parents' false and limiting dichotomies to reveal an underlying mystical holism:

> You both know . . . that the sweet water of the moon which falls as rain is the same water that gathers into rivers and flows to fill the seas. Without the waters of the moon to replenish the oceans there would be no oceans. And the same salt waters of the oceans are drawn by the sun to the heavens, and in turn become again the waters of the moon.
>
> (113)

Ultima's insight into the harmony of the universe is the understanding which Ahab lacks. Her cosmology features no aspect of creation as foreign, superfluous, or malign, for each has a contributing and complementary role. "The waters are one," she tells the relieved Antonio. "You have been seeing only parts . . . and not looking beyond into the great cycle that binds us all" (113). Just as Antonio comes to comprehend the kinship of the golden carp and Christ,[13] he realizes the obvious—that as the offspring of his mismatched parents he is living proof that opposites can integrate. As Ultima's eventual successor, he will grant his mother's wish for a priest by ministering to the needs of others and by mediating between the earthly and the spiritual; and, blending his Christianity with pagan mysticism, he will fulfill his father's desire for an heir who is in touch with the supernatural forces of the land.

The union achieved in Antonio Marez is always thwarted in *Moby-Dick*. Aboard the *Pequod*, co-mingling is misconstrued as a blurring of identity that threatens the extinction of the self, or as a dominion over another. Queequeg's taste for human flesh and Stubb's relish for freshly killed whale meat further perverts the Eucharist into cannibalism. Suggestions of fertility and fruition merely tease, as in the crew members' coming together to manipulate the spermaceti in "A Squeeze of the Hand," a pleasurable and erotic bonding but one that is ultimately frustrating and unproductive.

That Ahab works against rather than with nature is clear in his uneasy alliance with the instruments by which he navigates the seas, such as the quadrant that he destroys and the compass which reverses itself. The interchange over the ship's log and line, tools for gauging speed and direction, further reveals that he is out of sync with the dynamism of the universe. When the rotten line snaps and the log is lost, Ahab announces that he "can mend all" (427). The claim is self-delusory, since Ahab, having denied the synergism in the complex world around him, cannot forge the vital nexus he desires. In proposing to "mend the line" as he reaches out to Pip, who then urges that they "rivet these two hands together; the black one with the white" (428), Ahab suggests that he will continue and fortify his lineage through crossbreeding. But the union will not hold: the partners are not of sound mind as they take their vows. One is "daft with strength, the other daft with weakness." Reeling in the broken line as Ahab departs with his young black "mate," the Manxman prophetically observes, "here's the end of the rotten line. . . . Mend it, eh? I think we had best have a new line altogether" (428). The prognosis for any new hybrid "line" is grim, since Ahab persists in seeing the world as inexorably oppositional: He dies pursuing the whale that he maintains is wholly evil, the ship and crew go down, and Ishmael, the lone survivor, is left afloat on a coffin until the *Rachel*, on its own death watch, picks him up.

When in *Bless Me, Ultima* the townspeople of Guadalupe object to the sacrilegious over-reaching of science as manifest in the atomic bomb tests that are conducted south of their town, they could easily be describing Ahab's quest for omniscience. "Man was not made to know so much," they contend. "[T]hey compete with God, they disturb the seasons, they seek to know more than God Himself. In the end, that knowledge they seek will destroy us all" (183). Ahab, dissatisfied with what he deems his lowly place in the universe, seeks mastery through destruction. In contrast, Antonio, who, like Ahab, pursues and attains wisdom, is not antagonistic in his search for knowledge. He comes to luxuriate in the synchronized workings of the world, for he credits Ultima with having taught him to "listen to the mystery of the groaning earth and to feel complete in the fulfillment of its time." Through her he learns that his "spirit shared in the spirit of all things" (14).

Communion in *Moby-Dick* is perverted by a murderous urge; man's relationship to nature and to God is adversarial, and his goal is destruction or the absorption of another. True "marriage," Richard Slotkin asserts, occurs only when there is a mutual acceptance of each by the other, in which neither is destroyed (554). *Bless Me, Ultima* achieves this beneficent reciprocity. In tune with the cosmic harmonies, Antonio joins together diverse and discordant beliefs, temperaments, and values, for he realizes that he can "take the llano and the river valley, the moon and the sea, God and the golden carp—and make something new" (236). His communion is neither conquest, as it is for Ahab, nor the cancellation of the self, which Ishmael fears; it is true consummation.

In *Bless Me, Ultima,* Anaya's method is his message. The worldview which Antonio achieves by reconciling a host of opposites is repeated in Anaya's own literary multiculturalism. Influenced by Biblical and Indian mythology, Spanish lore, and the traditional canon, Anaya reveals his pluralistic cultural consciousness. He attains the "integrity of memory" which coheres across boundaries of time, ethnicity, and ideology.[14] Such mutually respectful and beneficial co-existence is the mode of being that Anaya advocates for Chicano literature in the United States, even as he seeks a broad readership for his work.[15] Chicano writing need not be self-sequestered nor shunted aside by others under a dubious celebration of "difference" to be legitimated, nor should it be stripped of distinguishing characteristics so as to gain entry into the traditional canon. "I believe that Chicano literature is ultimately a part of U.S. literature," Anaya maintains, continuing to see the whole as the sum of its parts. "I do not believe that we have to be swallowed up by models or values or experimentation within contemporary U.S. literature. We can present our own perspective. . . . But ultimately it will be incorporated into the literature of this country" (Bruce-Novoa 190). The thematic and tonal links between *Moby-Dick* and **Bless Me, Ultima**—as well as their divergent outlooks and resolutions—attest to cross-cultural interconnections amid rich heterogeneity.

Notes

1. Carmen Salazar Parr explains that, more specifically, the Indian lore reflects Nahuatl thought, that of the Mexican and Central American tribes (139).

2. Translating and discussing "Degradacion y Regeneracion en *Bless Me, Ultima*," by Roberto Cantu, Cordelia Candelaria notes Cantu's more grim observation about language use in the novel. Claiming that Antonio undergoes a loss of spirituality, Cantu cites a progressive absence of Spanish after Antonio enrolls in school as evidence of this decline. See "Anaya, Rudolfo Alfonso," *Chicano Literature* 47.

3. The setting of *Bless Me, Ultima* is often regarded as a world apart, a separate and protected enclave. The German critic Horst Tonn, however, detects the encroaching Anglo presence—in the highway that runs near the idyllic town of Guadalupe, in the tours of military duty which Antonio's three older brothers must serve during World War II, and in the atomic bomb tests run close to the Marez's New Mexican village.

4. Raymund Paredes's "The Evolution of Chicano Literature" and Robert M. Adams's "Natives and Others" explore Anaya's ethnic distinctiveness as well as the influence of Anglo-American writers upon his work.

5. Candelaria notes the influence of Faulkner's Yoknapatawpha stories in the way characters from *Bless Me, Ultima* return in *Heart of Aztlán* (1976). In Anaya's third novel, *Tortuga* (1979), Candelaria finds echoes of the persistent turtle from *The Grapes of Wrath* and of Katherine Anne Porter's use of a hospital as a microcosm of humanity in *Ship of Fools*. See "Anaya, Rudolfo Alfonso, *Chicano Literature*.

6. Anaya's graduate work in the 1960's emphasized the traditional canon, and he cites an abiding interest in American Romanticism. See Juan Bruce-Novoa, "Rudolfo A. Anaya," *Chicano Authors* 188.

7. Paul Lauter maintains that literature of the American Renaissance is tantamount to escapist fiction in its portrayals of single (white) males striking out for a frontier of some sort—the sea, the woods, the prairie. Many minorities, he reminds us, faced the other side of the adventure, invasion. Lauter contends that for them, "individual confrontations with whales or wars

were never central, for the issue was neither metaphysics nor nature but the social constructions called 'prejudice,' and the problem was not soluble by or for individuals . . . but only through a process of *social* change" (16). Hector Calderon uses Anaya and *Bless Me Ultima* as examples of a too-heavy emphasis on meditative abstractions and individualistic introspection. Antonio's egocentrism, Calderon claims, comes at the expense of a collective vision (112–13).

8. See William James for a discussion of the opposing temperaments, sick souls and healthy minds.

9. Candelaria discusses Anaya's use of Jungian themes in "Anaya, Rudolfo Alfonso," *Chicano Literature* 36–39. In "Rudolfo A. Anaya," *Dictionary of Literary Biography* she is critical of Anaya's penchant for happy endings, which, she charges, gloss over unpleasant or grim realities. Anaya's search, Candelaria contends, "always finds its uplifting grail of enlightenment and happiness. Alienation, irony, ambiguity, and the myriad uncertainties of a dynamic cosmos, whether ancient or modern, seem to lie beyond the boundaries of his fictive universe" (34).

10. Herminio Rios and Octavio Ignacio Romano connect the myth of the golden carp to Atonatiuh, the first cosmic catastrophe in Nahuatl cosmology (ix).

11. On numerous occasions Queequeg and Ishmael are happily in sync and mutually served by each other, as in "The Monkey Rope" for example. Yet Ishmael remains ambivalent at best about their interdependence. Consider D. H. Lawrence's reading of Ishmael's casual regard for Queequeg after bunking with him at the Spouter-Inn in "A Bosom Friend": "You would think this relation with Queequeg meant something to Ishmael. But no. Queequeg is forgotten like yesterday's newspaper. Human things are only momentary excitements or amusements to the American Ishmael" (147–48).

12. See Slotkin's discussion of Ahab's Puritanical response to the spirit of nature, which allows only two lines of action: he can either be nature's captive or its destroyer (547–48).

13. Vernon Lattin, rather than seeing Antonio's accommodation of Christianity and pantheism, contends that Antonio rejects the Church to embrace the pagan gods. Likewise, Raymund Paredes sees Antonio affecting no reconciliation of his parents' conflicting ambitions for him. He maintains that "at the end of the novel, Antonio rejects the confining traditionalism of the Lunas in favor of the Marez's doctrine of personal freedom" (101).

14. Explaining the "integrity of memory" and its role in canon revision, Annette Kolodny urges Americanists to dissociate themselves temporarily from reassuringly well-known texts to become immersed in the unfamiliar. The result she foresees is an awareness

made full by interconnections and new decipherings previously unrecognized.

15. William Clark explains that Anaya, "wanting to reach a wider audience," has recently completed a six-title contract with Warner Books. The mass marketing deal includes paperback and color-illustrated hard-cover editions of *Bless Me, Ultima* (24).

Works Cited

Adams, Robert M. "Natives and Others." Rev. of *Bless Me, Ultima,* by Rudolfo A. Anaya. *New York Review of Books* 26 March 1987: 32.

Anaya, Rudolfo A. *Bless Me, Ultima.* Berkeley: Tonatiuh-Quinto Sol International, 1975.

————. "The Myth of Quetzalcoatl in a Contemporary Setting: Mythical Dimensions/Political Reality." *Western American Literature* 23 (1988): 195–200.

Bruce-Novoa, Juan. "Canonical and Noncanonical Texts: A Chicano Case Study." *Redefining American Literary History.* Eds. A. LaVonne Brown Ruoff and Jerry W. Ward, Jr. New York: MLA, 1990. 196–209.

————. ed. "Rudolfo A. Anaya." *Chicano Authors: Inquiry by Interview.* Austin: U of Texas P, 1980. 183–202.

Calderon, Hector. "The Novel and the Community of Readers: Rereading Tomás Rivera's *Y no se lo trago la tierra.*" *Criticism in the Borderlands: Studies in Chicano Literature, Culture, and Ideology.* Eds. Hector Calderon and Jose David Saldivar. Durham: Duke UP, 1991. 97–113.

Candelaria, Cordelia. "Anaya, Rudolfo Alfonso." *Chicano Literature: A Reference Guide.* Eds. Julio A. Martinez and Francisco A. Lomeli. Westport: Greenwood, 1985.

————. "Rudolfo A. Anaya." *Dictionary of Literary Biography: Chicano Writers, First Series.* Eds. Francisco A. Lomeli and Carl R. Shirley. Vol. 82. Detroit: Gale Research, 1989.

Clark, William. "The Mainstream Discovers Rudolfo Anaya." *Publishers Weekly* 21 March 1994: 24.

James, William. *Writings, 1902–1910/William James.* New York: Viking, 1987.

Kolodny, Annette. "The Integrity of Memory: Creating a New Literary History of the United States." *American Literature* 57 (1985): 291–307.

Lattin, Vernon. "The Quest for Mythic Vision in Contemporary Native American and Chicano Fiction." *American Literature* 50 (1979): 625–40.

Lauter, Paul. "The Literatures of America: A Comparative Discipline." *Redefining American Literary History.* Eds. A. LaVonne Brown Ruoff and Jerry W. Ward, Jr. New York: MLA, 1990. 9–34.

Lawrence, D. H. *Studies in Classic American Literature.* 1923. New York: Viking, 1961.

Melville, Herman. *Moby-Dick.* 1851. Eds. Harrison Hayford and Hershel Parker. New York: Norton, 1967.

Paredes, Raymund. "The Evolution of Chicano Literature." *MELUS* 5.2 (1978): 71–110.

Parr, Carmen Salazar. "Current Trends in Chicano Literary Criticism." *The Identification and Analysis of Chicano Literature.* Ed. Francisco Jimenez. New York: Bilingual P / Editorial Bilingue, 1979. 134–42.

Rios, Herminio and Octavio Ignacio Romana. Foreword. *Bless Me, Ultima.* By Rudolfo A. Anaya. Berkeley: Quinto Sol, 1972. ix.

Slotkin, Richard. *Regeneration Through Violence: The Mythology of the American Frontier, 1600–1860.* Middletown: Wesleyan UP, 1973. 538–65.

Sommers, Joseph. "Critical Approaches to Chicano Literature." *The Identification and Analysis of Chicano Literature.* Ed. Francisco Jimenez. New York: Bilingual Press/Editorial Bilingue, 1979. 143–52.

Tonn, Horst. "*Bless Me, Ultima*: A Fictional Response to Times of Transition," *Aztlan: A Journal of Chicano Studies* 18.1 (1987): 59–67.

Margarite Fernández Olmos (essay date 1999)

SOURCE: "*Bless Me, Ultima,*" in *Rudolfo A. Anaya: A Critical Companion,* Greenwood Press, 1999, pp. 25–44.

[*In the following essay, Olmos provides an overview of the major themes, narrative techniques, and critical interpretations of* Bless Me, Ultima.]

In Rudolfo Anaya's first novel he turned to his life experiences for inspiration. The story of the awakening of the consciousness of a young boy growing up in a small New Mexico town shortly after World War II closely parallels the author's own life (see chapter 1 herein). At the same time, however, **Bless Me, Ultima** is a highly original work with a unique story and a universal appeal that established Anaya's international reputation. This chapter will focus on his best-known novel, a work of poetic beauty and richness that introduces the themes and motifs that have become the hallmark of Anaya's writing.

Narrative Strategies

How can a story told from the vantage point of a seven-year-old boy express profound insights and complex ideas? **Bless Me, Ultima** accomplishes the task by being an extended flashback—that is, by assuring the reader from the very beginning that the events described, although seemingly occurring in the present, in fact occurred at an earlier time. The narrator is, therefore, by implication, an adult. Anaya is able to maneuver this tension of the older implied narrator and the younger voice of the child-protagonist Antonio Márez by carefully re-creating the reactions of a small boy. Antonio's comments reflect the expected limitations of a child of that age. For Antonio, World War II is a "far-off war of the Japanese and the Germans," for example, and other historical events are explained in an equally simple, age-appropriate manner.

The reader is informed that Ultima, a respected midwife, came to stay with Antonio Márez and his family the summer that he was almost seven years old. Her arrival marks a beginning—"the beginning that came with Ultima" (1)—and, indeed, Antonio's story begins and ends with her. Subsequent references in the same chapter to a time "long after Ultima was gone and I had grown to be a man" (13) affirm the fact that, although the story is presented in the voice of a young boy, the events are actually those of a remembered youth. Time and chronology assume additional significance; time is described as "magical," it "stands still" and is linked with the character of Ultima. She represents origins and beginnings. Her very name implies extremes and the extent of time and distance that Antonio will travel on his passage from innocence into awareness.

Bless Me, Ultima is an accessible novel despite its grounding in Chicano folk culture and myth and its occasional use of Spanish. It follows a linear, or straightforward, story development, a plotline that is clearly defined, and avoids the more experimental prose styles of other writers. Levels of narration are delineated for the reader by the use of italics, a device Anaya employs frequently. Antonio's dream sequences, for example, are separated from the rest of the narration by italics, indicating a different dimension of consciousness. The first chapter serves important functions in plot development and structure. It gently guides the reader toward essential story elements such as setting, characters, and historical background, and it introduces the major conflicts that will form the basis for the dramatic tension throughout the novel. The technique of foreshadowing, which can often provide structural and thematic unity to a work, first appears in the introductory chapter.

"Foreshadowing" refers to the device of hinting at events to come; later events are therefore prepared for or shadowed forth beforehand, building suspense and reader expectation. In *Bless Me, Ultima* foreshadowing ranges from statements that openly indicate future events to symbolic premonitions in dreams that suggest them. After Antonio's home is described in Chapter One as a place that offers the young boy a unique vantage point from which to observe family incidents, he refers to the tragedy of the sheriff's murder that has yet to occur, the anguish of his brothers' future rebellion against their father, and the many nights when he will see Ultima returning from her moonlit labors gathering the herbs that are folk healer's remedies. Ultima, who rarely speaks and whose words are therefore significant, states that "there will be something" between herself and Antonio, suggesting a strong and important relationship yet to come. But the most effective foreshadowing technique is found in Antonio's dream sequences throughout the novel, the first of which occurs

in Chapter One. These sequences express the dread and anxiety of his inner world but are also frequently premonitions of the future. Antonio's dreams provide both a structural and thematic framework for the novel as they illustrate past events and suggest future conflicts.

SETTING

The setting is of particular importance in this novel, as it is in most of Anaya's fiction. Nature is part of the magic that will teach young Antonio that seemingly incarnate elements are actually living beings, whose beauty and value the young boy will discover with Ultima's help—a river that sings, land that impresses its mysteries into the narrator's "living blood" (1). The setting, the world of nature in rural New Mexico, assumes a significance similar to that of a character in terms of its influence on people and events. Since setting is of paramount importance in so much of Anaya's work, the landscape, the environment, the forces of nature, the *llano* (plains) of New Mexico all combine to create a powerful sense of place that produces an experience Anaya has referred to as an "epiphany," a sudden flash of enlightenment or a revealing intuition often occasioned by something trivial or apparently insignificant. This is the type of experience we observe in Antonio, for example, in several scenes in which he allows himself to be transformed by opening his eyes to the beauty of the simple objects in his natural environment. Anaya has occasionally described this experience using a term invented by the poet Gerard Manley Hopkins, "inscape," by which is meant a type of mystical illumination or insight into the fundamental order and unity of all of creation.

CULTURAL CONTEXT

Family history and New Mexican history are inextricably linked in *Bless Me, Ultima.* Antonio's father, Gabriel Márez, teaches the young boy about his past, which is tied to the Spanish colonial period of the region. Gabriel is a *vaquero,* or cowboy, but this is more than just an occupation: it is a "calling" that has united Antonio's father and his paternal ancestors to the New Mexican plains, described as vast as the oceans. (Indeed, Antonio's father's surname, Márez, derives from the Spanish word *mar,* meaning the sea.) Social and economic changes in the state severely curtailed the free-spirited, aggressive lifestyle of the vaqueros, however, when Anglo settlers took control of the land. The novel refers to such background information as part of the process of Antonio's education concerning his family's past. These facts also serve to provide readers with the cultural and historical foundation that will broaden their appreciation of events in the novel.

Antonio's mother, María Luna, is also linked with local culture but from a different perspective, as her own surname, Luna, implies. (The Lunas are a people of the moon, tied to the land as farmers.) The Lunas represent a different tradition within the rural U.S. Hispanic culture of the Southwest: the farming tradition—settled, tranquil, modest, devout, tied to old ways and customs. María had convinced her husband to leave the village of Las Pasturas and a lifestyle she considered coarse and wild, to move the family to the town of Guadalupe, where better opportunities existed for their children. The move separates Gabriel from the other vaqueros and the free llano life he loves. He becomes a bitter man who drinks to soothe his hurt pride and his loneliness. The differences between these two cultures form the basis for the first major conflict affecting Antonio's family. These tensions, as we will discover in others throughout the work, are presented as dichotomies: Márez/Luna, vaquero/farmer, free-spirited/settled. Antonio must find a balance in these divided forces, which tug at him from opposite directions.

The first dream sequence in Chapter One illustrates his anxieties. Antonio describes a dream in which he witnesses his own birth assisted by an old midwife. After he is born she wraps up the umbilical cord and the placenta as an offering to the Virgin of Guadalupe, the patron saint of the town (and of Mexicans and Mexican Americans in general). In his dream Antonio observes a terrible quarrel between the two branches of his family. The Lunas hope that the baby will become one of them, or possibly even a priest (his mother's fervent hope); the Márez uncles smash the symbolic offerings of fruits and vegetables brought by the mother's clan, replacing them with their own emblematic gifts of a saddle, a bridle, and a guitar. They hope Antonio will follow their free-spirited ways.

Both families frantically attempt to take hold of the placenta, hoping to control the baby's destiny by disposing of it in their own allegorical fashion. The Lunas want to bury it in the fields, tying the boy to the earth; the Márez family wishes to burn it and scatter the ashes freely to the winds of the llano. The families nearly come to blows over the issue until the old midwife steps in, claiming her rights as the person who brought the young life into the world to dispose of the afterbirth herself.

That old midwife is Ultima, the *curandera,* or folk healer, who eventually comes to live in their home. One issue upon which both parents agree is their obligation to provide and care for the elders, respecting customs and traditions. Therefore, when Antonio's father discovers that Ultima will be living alone in the llano as people abandon the village of Las Pasturas, he and Antonio's mother decide to invite her into their household in gratitude for her years of service to them and the community. Ultima is a respected figure, referred to as "La Grande," the old wise one. Outside of the family, however, Ultima is feared by some. Her healing powers are suspect, and she is considered a *bruja,* or witch. The suggestion of witchcraft brings a shudder of fear to Antonio and is a warning to the reader as well; the idea that witches can heal but can also place and lift curses with evil powers is another example of Anaya's foreshadowing of things to come.

Ultima is associated with ancient traditions and wisdom; in *Bless Me, Ultima* she is also equated with the forces of nature. Her meeting with Antonio is accompanied by a whirlwind, an oft-repeated motif representing magical power and/or a warning of danger. As in traditional witch stories, Ultima is identified with a specific animal—in this case an owl. The animal is reputed to be a disguise assumed by witches, but Ultima's owl does not frighten Antonio. On the contrary, her owl protects, defends, and soothes him, an observation legitimized by another of Antonio's dreams in which the owl flies the Virgin of Guadalupe on its wings to heaven.

LANGUAGE

From the very first pages of the novel, Anaya interjects the Spanish language into the narration, in the form of individual words, characters' names, local references, and, on occasion, entire sentences of dialogue, as well as the chapter numeration. This interjection is accomplished with a naturalness that avoids interrupting the flow of the story. Spanish words are not italicized or differentiated in any way from the rest of the text, nor are there footnotes or a glossary to define them; rather, they are explained in a subtle, unobtrusive manner where appropriate. Occasionally an English equivalent will appear in sentences after a Spanish term has been introduced, or an explanatory phrase will clarify some term for those unfamiliar with the language. In several instances the syntax and phrasing of some of the dialogue in English sounds like a literal translation from Spanish. The bilingual use of language is limited but nonetheless effective in creating a distinctive tone in the novel. It is rationalized in the first chapter when Antonio affirms that the older people of his community speak exclusively in Spanish and that he himself learned English only after attending school (10). The use of Spanish is a carefully and minutely crafted device that is accepted by the reader as natural and logical, something not unexpected.

DREAM SYMBOLISM

Throughout ***Bless Me, Ultima*** Antonio's dreams serve several functions: they sometimes anticipate events to come, but more important they are an index to the main character's emotional and psychological development. Anaya has skillfully blended the external plot events with Antonio's frequent introspective musings and his world of dreams, a combination of personal experience, fantasy, and mythical legend. The blending is often achieved by the main character himself; reflecting on the importance of his dreams, Antonio will interpret their significance in the narratives that follow them. After the second dream in Chapter Two, which ends with his mother crying because Antonio is growing old (26), for example, the narrator begins the following chapter remarking on his fleeting youth (27), repeating the same message of his growing maturity. Indeed, Anaya leaves little to the reader's imagination regarding the interpretation of Antonio's dreams and other plot elements. The narrator often regulates our reading of the work by commenting on events and repeating their message. Comments such as "That is what Ultima meant by building strength from life" (247) ensure that the reader will remain on the right track.

Antonio's dreams pervade his waking hours; each influences to some degree his conduct and attitude. In Chapter Nine, for instance, aware that his brothers frequent "Rosie's house," the town brothel, Antonio's musings on his brothers' behavior mirror his own apprehensions with regard to women and sexuality, innocence and the concept of sin. The young boy represses his disturbing feelings by transferring them to a dream about his brothers' restlessness as they experience the restraints of a small town and their parents' aspirations. Their behavior is rationalized in the novel, in great part, by their lineage; the notion of blood and heredity is a motif throughout *Bless Me, Ultima.* Just as Gabriel's aggressiveness and María's gentle, subdued manner are understood as hereditary qualities in the "blood," Antonio's brothers' attitudes and actions are attributed to their father's character: "The Márez blood draws them away from home and parents" (72). Antonio's mother attempts to link his destiny with that of a Luna ancestor, a priest who supposedly established Guadalupe generations earlier. In his dream Antonio's brothers declare him to be a Luna who, for their mother's sake, will become a farmer-priest like their maternal ancestor. The dream sequences serve as good examples of the cross-weaving of the external and internal conflicts that drive the plot.

PLOT DEVELOPMENT

After her arrival in the home of Antonio's family, Ultima settles into a bucolic life. All the family members benefit from her presence: Antonio's mother is happy to share her days with another adult female, his sisters' chores are lessened with Ultima's assistance, and Antonio's father has someone to whom he can relate his frustrated dreams of moving westward to California with his older sons. World War II has taken them from his side, upsetting his plans. Antonio enjoys Ultima's presence as well; she is his mentor in the ways of nature and spirituality. This time of innocent joy gives way, however, to his first terrible experience of violence and death, to which Ultima's owl will sound a warning cry, as it does whenever it senses danger that could affect the family.

The dramatic events that propel the evolution of the main story (the external events that effect change in Antonio) are initiated dramatically in Chapter Two with the murder of the town sheriff, Chávez, and the revenge taken against his murderer, Lupito. Lupito is a disturbed man whose mind has been traumatized by war. His senseless killing of the sheriff incenses the men of the town, who form a search party to capture and punish the culprit. Hiding in bushes near the river, Antonio observes them. Despite attempts to sway the group, the men kill Lupito and thereby rouse Antonio's first doubts of conscience. Issues of right and wrong, guilt and innocence, the concept of God and justice are thoughts that assail his young, impressionable mind. This is the first of four tragic deaths that Antonio will encounter in a brief space of time. Ultima's influence is felt here too in the presence of her owl, which accompanies Antonio and calms his fears, temporarily dispelling his anxieties.

As in most novels of the coming-of-age genre, a significant element of the young narrator's development is his or her relationship with peers. School and a social network form a crucial component of the type of knowledge a young child will require to survive and flourish beyond the family orbit. Antonio is successful at making friends, among them Jason Chávez, Samuel, and Cico, who introduce him to a world of native legend and a type of spirituality and morality outside of official, established religion. The catechism lessons he studies in order to receive the sacrament of First Communion in the Catholic Church conflict with the folk traditions he learns from his friends. They propose an alternative religiosity and code of morality based on indigenous beliefs and offer a contrasting pagan deity to his family's devout Christianity. In Chapter Nine the boys relate the well-guarded secret of the golden carp (a secret known to few children and only to adults who, like Ultima, are "different"). The story is first told to Jason by the only Indian in town, a character referred to simply as "Jason's Indian." The legend holds that the carp had once been a god. The people who lived in that earlier time had sinned, and their punishment was to become fish. Loving his people, the god also became a fish to swim among them and protect them. The waters of the rivers and lakes that surround the town of Guadalupe hold other secrets as well, including that of a mermaid, a siren whose singing pulls those who hear it into the dark waters of the Hidden Lakes (115–117).

These stories create more religious dilemmas for Antonio, adding to his already confused spirituality. As in previous circumstances, Antonio confronts and partially resolves these conflicts in his dreams. In one dream the waters of the mermaid and the golden carp transform themselves into the stormy waters of his parents' fierce struggle over his future. The sweet water of the placid Luna moon tries to claim his loyalty, while his father rages that the salt water of the oceans is what truly binds him as a Márez. The conflict grows into a cosmic storm that threatens to destroy everything until Ultima intercedes. She brings peace to the dream (and to Antonio's tortured psyche) as she clarifies the meaning for Antonio, explaining that the moon and seas are not divided or distinct, but are, in fact, part of a holistic cycle of oneness, each replenished by the other.

Antonio's early doubts regarding established religion and conventional beliefs are heightened in Chapter Ten when the devoutly Catholic Lunas turn to Ultima to cure a family member who had been cursed by the three daughters of Tenorio Trementina, the town barber and owner of a run-down saloon. The women are believed to be witches and are referred to as "cohorts of the devil." María's brother Lucas had inadvertently witnessed one of their demonic rituals and had confronted them. Their evil powers bring him to death's door, and Ultima is summoned when Western medicine and the Catholic priest fail to break the spell. This chapter is one of the most effective in terms of creating an atmosphere of suspense and mystery. The narrator reiterates words that suggest wickedness and fear:

sinister signs, Black Masses, the appearance of devils, and an "early horned moon" combine with familiar clichés regarding female witchcraft (for example, dancing with the devil, vulnerability to bullets etched with a sign of the cross, ritual sacrificing of animals, the use of dolls to create harmful spells). The drive to the Luna farm, normally a pleasant journey, is now "filled with strange portents," the atmosphere of the family home is "deathly quiet," and even the weather responds to psychic forces (90–91).

When Ultima confronts Tenorio and requests that his daughters cease their evil curse on Antonio's uncle or accept the consequences of their actions, a mournful whirlwind provides the background to the scene: the sky grows dark, blocking out the sun to produce an atmosphere described as "unnatural" (94–95). These and many other details contribute to the suspense that builds up to the process of the cure itself, a type of exorcism in which Ultima, with Antonio serving as his bewitched uncle's spiritual double, will rid Lucas of the evil curse. The three days that Antonio will suffer along with his uncle and his symbolic death and rebirth to save another are all part of Antonio's spiritual challenges. More powerful than the three witches and even more powerful than the priest and doctors, Ultima's faculties extend to retribution as well. Tenorio's daughters will pay for their crimes. One by one they fall ill and die. Ultima will be accused of witchcraft herself and put to the test by Tenorio and his friends, but her power is greater, and she is vindicated. Ultima's actions, however, set in motion the chain of events that will eventually lead to her own death at Tenorio's hands.

Chapter Fourteen combines many different plot elements that build toward the climax and contribute to the outcome of Antonio's ultimate understanding of himself. The chapter begins with Antonio's return to school, where he has found acceptance and a sense of belonging. It contains a rare note of humor in the depiction of the school Christmas play. A terrible blizzard prevents the girls of the school from attending and playing their assigned roles. The boys substitute grudgingly. The production is a calamity but ends in good-humored bedlam.

The relief of tension is short lived, however. Another of Tenorio's daughters falls ill, and he repeats his vow to kill Ultima and Narciso, a friend of the family. After school Antonio braves the blizzard alone and heads for home. He witnesses an argument between Tenorio and Narciso, who leaves to warn Ultima of the danger. Not realizing that he is being observed by Antonio, Narciso stops on his way at Rosie's brothel to warn Antonio's brother, Andrew, of Tenorio's plans. This scene adds to Antonio's confusion: Why does Narciso search for Andrew in such a place? Which Márez is Narciso calling for at the door? Could his own father be inside? In a prior dream Andrew had told Antonio that he would not enter Rosie's until his young brother had lost his innocence. Had young Antonio's experiences of death and violence, of magical cures and pagan gods, opened the path for sin to enter his soul? His crisis is exacerbated by his brother's appearance by the

side of a young prostitute who convinces Andrew to remain with her instead of assisting Narciso. Still hidden by the storm, the boy observes Tenorio ambush Narciso and murder him.

Antonio runs home and informs his parents, succumbing to a fever and a terrible *pesadilla* (nightmare); his apocalyptic, end-of-the-world dream is one of the novel's most vivid. The main character's sense of confused guilt and terror fuses with figures and events from his past life in a chaotic frenzy. The thunderous voice of a vengeful God frightens the boy, who relives in his dream the murder, satanic rituals, and other forms of wickedness, as well as terrifying biblical tortures. The nightmare will end in resolution, however, effected by the healing power of nature. The golden carp swallows everything—good and evil—taking with it all the pain and strife of humanity. Antonio's subconscious discovers order and harmony in nature and native mythology.

Subsequent events in the novel continue to test the young boy's faith in God and humanity and the belief system he has been raised to maintain. In Chapters Seventeen and Eighteen the catechism lessons he must take fail to satisfy his spiritual needs. When a friend, Florence, challenges Antonio's religious beliefs, schoolmates force Antonio to play the role of priest to punish Florence for his ideas. In several other instances Antonio inadvertently finds himself in that same role: "Bless me" are the final words he hears from Lupito before his violent death near the river, and Narciso's dying wish is for Antonio to hear his confession. The religious event that Antonio had so anticipated is disappointing; all the doubts he believed would be answered with the experience of First Communion receive no reply: "The God I so eagerly sought was not there, and the understanding I thought to gain was not there" (222).

Tenorio's threats against Ultima continue, but his evil extends to others as well. In Chapter Twenty a curse has been placed on a family that seeks Ultima's assistance. Stones rain from the sky on the Téllez family home, which even the priest's blessings were unable to prevent. Ultima determines that the curse was laid on a *bulto* (ghost) that haunts the house. The curse is linked in the novel with historical abuses against the indigenous peoples of the region. Ultima explains that the area was once the land of the Comanche Indians. Displaced by the Spaniards and Mexicans, three Indians had raided Téllez's grandfather's flocks for food and were hanged as punishment. As their bodies were not accorded a customary burial, their wandering souls can be used to harm others. Tenorio's daughters have awakened the Indian ghosts of the past to harm the Téllez family, but with Ultima's guidance a ceremonial cremation gives the Comanche spirits rest and eliminates the curse. Events such as these add to Antonio's anxieties and undermine his faith in God, who was not able to free the Téllez family from the curse.

The reappearance of the golden carp in the lake, however, soothes his worries: "Seeing him made questions and worries evaporate, and I remained transfixed, caught and caressed by the essential elements of sky and earth and water" (237). Antonio would like to share this feeling of tranquillity and illumination, "the beginning of adoration of something simple and pure" (238), with Florence, who had been alienated from Catholicism and spirituality by his own life experiences, but the protagonist will not get that opportunity. That same day Florence drowns in a tragic swimming accident in a forbidden section of the lake.

Antonio's family sends him to the Luna farm to rest from his terrible experiences and spend the summer assisting his uncles, a time he describes as "the last summer I was truly a child" (250). A heart-to-heart talk with his father during their trip to the farm brings them closer to an understanding, but trouble will reach Antonio even in this tranquil environment. Tenorio's second daughter has died, and he resolves again to take his vengeance. This time, however, he will attack Ultima's owl realizing that it is her very spirit.

After attempting to kill Antonio with his stallion, Tenorio makes for the boy's home. Antonio tries to warn Ultima, but he is too late. Tenorio points his rifle first at Antonio, but Ultima's owl takes the bullet in his place, mortally wounding her. "That shot destroyed the quiet, moonlit peace of the hill, and it shattered my childhood into a thousand fragments that long ago stopped falling and are now dusty relics gathered in distant memories" (258). Another attempt to destroy Antonio brings Tenorio's death, as he himself is killed by one of Antonio's uncles. The novel ends with Ultima's final blessing on the young boy, who gives her owl the burial Ultima has requested. The reader is left with the impression that Antonio will go on, better able to understand himself and find the answers he so wishes to discover.

CHARACTERIZATION

Bless Me, Ultima tells the story of an important relationship between a young boy and an old woman who helps him discover the beauty and complexity in life and in himself. As both protagonist and narrator, Antonio gradually reveals himself to the reader through his own words and through his dreams; he is both an evolving character and a narrating voice. Ultima, on the other hand, is revealed to us more by her actions and by the other characters' reactions to them. Many of the important events of the novel center on her. Her importance as a character is more functional: her character advances thematic concerns and helps to expose Antonio's qualities. Although less developed than Antonio's character, Ultima is integral to the novel nonetheless. As stated before, **Bless Me, Ultima** begins and ends with Ultima, and the relationship between her and Antonio propels the process of the boy-hero's development as a character.

Inquisitive and courageous, sensitive and thoughtful, Antonio's character evolves on several levels: on the objective, external plane his character passes through a variety of experiences, some typical of most young boys, some highly unusual. Many of his experiences can be compared to those of other rural Hispanic children in the U.S. Southwest of a certain era: he is raised in a Spanish-speaking home where traditions are maintained and respected; he confronts an Anglo-oriented school system where he is linguistically and culturally socialized into mainstream society; he is indoctrinated into the Catholic religion even as he is surrounded by competing influences.

Other experiences are less typical and even extraordinary: in a short period of time Antonio confronts violence and murder, tragic death, witchcraft, and supernatural phenomena. He will actively participate in ritual healing and even experience a symbolic death and rebirth as a part of his spiritual and psychological maturation. What Antonio cannot face or understand on a conscious level is deciphered in his dreams. His doubts and uncertainties are echoed on the subconscious level and occasionally resolved there as well. His reactions to these events as expressed in his dreams are the most revealing insights into the growth and evolution of the character, providing a thematic framework of his gradual transformation.

As noted earlier, Antonio's first dream is of his own birth; both his biological mother and his spiritual mother (Ultima) are present. The dreams that follow reflect concerns about family and fear of losses (of people and illusions) that prepare him for his passage into adulthood and individuality. The critic Vernon E. Lattin divides the nine remaining dreams that follow the birth sequence into groups that reveal the path to Antonio's destiny ("'Horror of Darkness'" 51–57). Dreams three (45), five (70), and seven (140) reflect the fear of loss: Antonio foresees that he will not become the priest his mother had hoped for, his innocence will be lost as he faces the temptations of sexuality, and the vision of Ultima in her coffin foreshadows the loss through death of his spiritual mother. Dreams two (25), four (61), and nine (235) reflect anxieties concerning Antonio's brothers and the larger world beyond, foreshadowing the experience of loss that he must assimilate in order to attain adulthood. In dreams two and four Antonio's brothers confront their own destinies beyond the family. With Antonio's help they can face the dangers of the treacherous river, but Antonio comes to realize that he cannot always assist these giants of his dreams, and by dream nine he resigns himself to the fact that they are lost to him and to his parents. Like the souls of the Comanche spirits calmed by Ultima's ritual cremation, the souls of his brothers are put to rest in Antonio's anguished psyche.

Dreams six (119), eight (172), and ten (243) are considered by Lattin and other critics as the most significant, "the dreams most homologous with the experience of the sacred, and as they present the dark night of the soul, they prepare the soul for its rebirth" (Lattin, "'Horror of Darkness'" 55). Dream six is the calm of reconciliation after the storm, an important step in solving Antonio's dilemma of good versus evil. The eighth dream becomes progressively more violent as despair and destruction are vividly communicated to the young boy: his home is set afire, his family is destroyed, Ultima is beheaded by an angry mob, and all life around him disintegrates. From this cosmic nothingness, regenerative powers emerge. Although Antonio's final dream, the tenth, is filled with the terror of death, the reader senses that he is now more prepared to accept and understand the realities of life. Having by now witnessed so much of Ultima's healing power, the messages of her teachings and of his own dreams have revealed themselves to him. Toward the novel's end he reflects: "And that is what Ultima tried to teach me, that the tragic consequences of life can be overcome by the magical strength that resides in the human heart" (249).

Ultima, as previously noted, is a less developed character than Antonio, but she is crucial nonetheless. At once a stabilizer and a catalyst for growth and change, the story revolves around the transference of her knowledge and worldview to Antonio. In Ultima Anaya has created a fascinating character who embodies the combination of indigenous traditions, ancient beliefs, and shamanic healing. Ultima is seer and natural scientist, teacher and herbal doctor. Despite her never having married or having had children of her own, she is a symbolic mother figure representing the mysteries of life, death, and transformation.

Ultima is a conciliatory force in the novel, guiding Antonio between the extremes of his parents and the myriad other tensions he must attempt to resolve. Respected as "una mujer que no ha pecado" (a woman who has not sinned) she is also feared. Her skills were acquired from a renowned healer, "the flying man of Las Pasturas," and hence many consider her a bruja. Ultima's characterization goes beyond the usual expectations regarding gendered roles for men and women because she is a curandera; she is afforded a place in the public world not usually given to women in traditional patriarchal cultures. Her power comes in part from her knowledge of herbal remedies, spiritual healing, and magical rituals. Her spiritual approach comes from numerous sources: from modern medicine, time-honored Native-American curative practices, Christianity, and pagan traditions. The complexity of this character derives from these differing sources that are blended in her. Ultima represents a Mexican/Amerindian tradition that has often been preserved precisely by women curanderas. Though uncommon in U.S. letters, curanderas have been a part of the Hispanic tradition for centuries and are familiar characters for many Hispanic readers.

Although somewhat ambiguous as to Ultima's status as a bruja, the novel clearly distinguishes between good and evil witches in its portrayal of Tenorio Trementina's three daughters. We learn of their practices through other characters. Tenorio himself is a troublemaker, his daughters bad-tempered and ugly. These characters are more stereotypical depictions of witches, participating in evil rituals with the devil, concocting terrible curses and brews, capable of assuming animal forms. Being labeled a bruja, however, is life threatening here, as evidenced in Tenorio's attempts to have Ultima declared a witch. A bruja is hated and feared even to the point of murder.

Tenorio and his daughters, along with other characters in the novel outside of Antonio and Ultima, are more functional than integral. They are one-dimensional and, in some cases, like that of the evil witches, little more than stereotypes. Some characters also serve an allegorical function, representing stages in Hispanic history in the region, recalling that the first Spanish settlers who arrived in the 1600s created a self-sufficient ranching and farming economy. In particular, the Márez side of Antonio's family epitomizes the early Spanish explorers, and the Lunas correspond to the brief Mexican period in New Mexico's history (Critics believe that the reference to the Luna farmer-priest ancestor who settled the town is an allusion to the historical figure of Father José A. Martinez, a New Mexican clergyman in the nineteenth century who played a key role in the Taos revolt of 1846.)

THEMES

Given the density of symbolism, myth, and cultural references in *Bless Me, Ultima,* it is not surprising that the novel has inspired a variety of critical responses. On the most fundamental level the novel's major theme is the coming-of-age and self-realization of a young Hispanic boy in New Mexico. Other topics are the quest for personal and cultural identity, the significance of Chicano tradition and myth in spirituality and healing, and the role of mentors and guides in psychological and spiritual growth and development. Ultima fulfills that role in Antonio's life; her intimate knowledge of nature and healing introduces him to the sources that will facilitate his understanding of himself and his world. The varied elements in the novel that determine who the boy-hero will eventually become have prompted numerous and diverse readings of the novel.

Bless Me, Ultima emphasizes the protagonist's need to reconcile the opposites in his life. The novel offers numerous conflicts the young boy must confront and presents them as seemingly irreconcilable dichotomies. The most evident is the clash between his father's pastoral lifestyle and his mother's farming tradition. The differences between the two are repeated throughout the novel, underscored by their very surnames—Márez and Luna. Other striking examples are the conflicts between male and female, good and evil (personified in the beneficent mother figure Ultima versus the evil father Tenorio), love and hate, town and country, a Christian God versus the golden carp, and so forth.

Ultima's role is that of mediator, from the first dream in which she resolves the dispute between the two families who wish to control Antonio's destiny to the dream in which she reconciles the dichotomy of the waters of the sea and the moon by reminding Antonio that "the waters are one." Antonio, however, is also a mediator, searching for a middle ground, attempting to please both parents in the house they built in a space in-between them—not quite in the fertile valley but at the edges of the llano. The boy's chores will please both mother and father: he feeds the animals but also tries to create a garden from the rugged soil of the plains.

Some critics have also noted the message of reconciliation, synthesis, and harmony that is apparent in the novel. Conflicts and imbalances find a solution in harmony, balance, and a message of oneness; synthesis resolves opposites and mediates differences. Generally the balance and mediation is brought about by Ultima or Antonio; in other instances the wisdom of nature itself restores harmony.

Some readings of the novel portray it as a nostalgic text, romanticizing an era that has little relevance for contemporary Chicano readers, who are largely urban and for whom the conflicts among rural Hispanic traditions are issues of the past. Other critics disagree. For Horst Tonn, *Bless Me, Ultima* can be read on another level at which "the novel constitutes a significant response to relevant issues of the community. In broad terms, these issues are identity formation, mediation of conflict, and utilization of the past for the exigencies of the present" (*"Bless Me, Ultima*: Fictional Response" 2). At the time Anaya was writing his work the society of the United States was experiencing a crisis of values similar to that portrayed in the novel in the mid-1940s. The theme of the pressure of change portrayed in the novel that Tonn identifies is underscored in the scene in which the townspeople react to the detonation of the first atomic bomb near Alamogordo, New Mexico, in 1945: "They compete with God, they disturb the seasons, they seek to know more than God Himself. In the end, that knowledge they seek will destroy us all" (190).

The disruptive effects of World War II on veterans and their families, as well as the internal migration from rural areas to the cities, have their counterpart in the social upheavals of the 1960s, when Chicanos participated in movements for social change and began to question their cultural values and identities. *Bless Me, Ultima* proposes responses to the contemporary crisis of values based on the need for healing and reconciliation. Just as Antonio and Ultima function as mediators, healing a community suffering from strife and disruption, "the novel itself can be said to share in and contribute to a mediation process at work in the Chicano community during the 1960s and early 1970s" (Tonn, *"Bless Me, Ultima*: Fictional Response" 5). Juan Bruce-Novoa agrees that *Bless Me, Ultima* is truly a novel reflective of its era. In the midst of conflict and violence, some present at the time proposed the alternative responses of "love, harmony, and the brotherhood of all creatures in a totally integrated ecology of resources. . . . *Bless Me, Ultima* belongs to the counterculture of brotherhood based on respect for all creation" ("Learning to Read" 186).

ALTERNATIVE READING: ARCHETYPAL MYTH CRITICISM

An analysis of *Bless Me, Ultima* based on myth theory and criticism emphasizes the developing dream life of its protagonist and Anaya's expressed affinity for myth (see chapters 1 and 2 in this book). Myth theory and criticism examine such questions as the origin and nature of myth and the relationship between myth and literature. Scholars and critics who have attempted to respond to these issues have done so from such diverse disciplines as philosophy, psychology, anthropology, linguistics, folklore, and political science.

The ideas of psychiatrist Carl G. Jung have inspired many literary critics, particularly in the field of archetypal criticism. Although often used synonymously with myth criticism, archetypal criticism has a distinct history, evolving specifically from Jung's theory of archetypes. As was noted earlier in chapter 2, Jung was a student of Sigmund Freud, who referred to dreams as "the royal road to the unconscious." For Freud dreams reflected individual unconscious wishes and desires. Jung, on the other hand, believed that the recurrence of enduring symbols in dreams reflected a more universal and collective unconscious (inherited feelings, thoughts, and memories shared by all humans). He referred to the patterns of psychic energy that originate in the collective unconscious (and are normally manifested in dreams) as "archetypes" (the prime models upon which subsequent representations are based). The Jungian approach to mythology, therefore, is based on a belief of a common human access to the collective unconscious. Mankind in the modern world would encounter in dreams the same types of figures that appear in ancient and primitive mythology.

Jung described several of these archetypes specifically. Among them are the Shadow, the archetype of inherent evil; the Anima, the feminine principle that has multiple manifestations including the Earth Mother, the Good Mother, and its opposite, the Terrible Mother; and the Wise Old Man, who represents the enlightener, the master, the teacher. Often critics will use the term more loosely, referring to characters as archetypes to indicate that they represent universal principles. Rudolfo Anaya is well versed in these theories and has reflected on their validity: "One way I have in looking at my own work . . . is through a sense that I have about primal images, primal imageries. A sense that I have about the archetypal, about what we once must have known collectively" (Johnson and Apodaca, "Myth and the Writer" 422).

Bless Me, Ultima offers ample opportunities for archetypal interpretations. The archetypal feminine principle—the intuitive, loving, life-affirming protector and nurturer—can be attributed to Ultima, the Good Mother/Earth Mother, and on another level to the Virgin of Guadalupe, who appears often in Antonio's dreams and is his mother's spiritual protector. The Terrible Mother—the frightening female figure, emasculating and life threatening—

corresponds to La Llorona, the legendary mother who destroyed her own children and threatens those of others. Female characters are presented as contrasts: Tenorio's daughters are the evil counterparts of Ultima's beneficent magic. The female temptress, representing female sexuality, appears on several levels: on the idealistic plane in the sirens and mermaids that lure men into dangerous waters but also in the prostitutes that work in Rosie's brothel, who cause men to stray from their rightful path. The archetypal Shadow is illustrated in numerous places, most obviously in the form of evil that Tenorio embodies, but the novel also teaches that evil can reside within people, hidden at a deeper level. Antonio's dreams, for example, force him to confront his own sinful temptations and self-doubts that must be overcome if he is to evolve and grow.

Antonio's character has been interpreted as that of the classic boy-hero who must successfully complete the universal rite of passage of separation, initiation, and return. He must depart the comforts of his mother's hearth and cross the bridge into the wide world of the town, with its perils and challenges. His trials will extend from witnessing Lupito's murder to actively participating in his uncle's ritual exorcism, during which he sacrifices himself for the sake of another. After three days of agony he will emerge as if reborn, a new, more mature boy who can reconcile himself with his father and mother and the world around him. Ultima provides him with the symbolic tools (her pouch of herbs) and the spiritual weapons (her teachings) that will assist him in this development.

A Jungian approach to **Bless Me, Ultima** could run the risk of leading to a static, unchanging mythical perception, however, one that certainly would not be faithful to Anaya's views on mythology. For the author mythology is not simply a refashioning or retelling of ancient or universal tales and patterns. Myths should speak to our contemporary lives, give significance to a community. Historically constructed over generations, myths can help us understand contemporary realities and conditions. A more dynamic approach to myth criticism in **Bless Me, Ultima** is described by Enrique Lamadrid as "an ongoing process of interpreting and mediating the contradictions in the everyday historical experience of the people" ("Myth as Cognitive Process" 103). In the novel this is manifested in the oppositions (for example, good versus evil, love versus hate) that are mediated by Ultima and Antonio. Their role is to reconcile these contradictions to arrive at harmony and synthesis and, in keeping with the original role of myth, resolve the internal schisms of their community.

A myth criticism interpretation of **Bless Me, Ultima** should bear in mind, however, that Anaya describes a specific culture, a particular belief system. An analysis of the character of Ultima may reflect universal principles, but it must be remembered that Ultima, as a shaman/curandera, represents an actual vocation, that of a healer or spiritual leader, a role with a useful and important function in an authentic culture. The role of the shaman and that of the

curandera are often indistinguishable. Both can resort to dreams and visions for help and guidance; both practice medical, magical, and spiritual arts. A specialist in the use of spells and incantations as well as herbal remedies, the shaman is believed to have the power to change her or his human form into that of an animal or spirit (see discussion of shamanism in chapter 8 herein). The curative practices of a curandera are intertwined with religious beliefs and respect for nature. Disharmony and imbalance cause a disruption of health; healing is a return to oneness and harmony with nature.

These alternative healing values have endured for centuries and continue to provide contemporary answers to age-old questions. **Bless Me, Ultima** demonstrates that myth criticism and a culturally specific approach to a work of literature need not be mutually exclusive. Anaya's novel is historically relevant and magical, both ancient and contemporary.

FURTHER READING

Criticism

Barrientos, Tanya. "Rudolfo Anaya's Simmering Mystery Is a Recipe that Failed." *Chicago Tribune* (25 September 1996): 3.

> Barrientos offers a negative assessment of *Rio Grande Fall*.

Davis-Undiano, Robert Con. Review of *Shaman Winter*, by Rudolfo Anaya. *Hispanic* 12, Nos. 1–2 (January–February 1999): 106.

> Davis-Undiano offers a positive assessment of *Shaman Winter*.

Espinoza, Marth. "A Passion for History." *Hispanic* 12, No. 9 (September 1999): 64.

> Espinoza provides an overview of Anaya's life, work, and achievements.

Klett, Rex E. Review of *Rio Grande Fall*, by Rudolfo Anaya. *Library Journal* (1 September 1996): 213.

> Klett offers a brief positive assessment of *Rio Grande Fall*, calling the novel "a thrilling adventure."

Lamadrid, Enrique. "The Dynamics of Myth in the Creative Vision of Rudolfo Anaya." In *Pasó por Aquí: Critical Essays on the New Mexican Literary Tradition, 1542–1988*, edited by Erlinda Gonzales-Berry, pp. 243–54, University of New Mexico Press, 1989.

> Lamadrid examines Anaya's synthesis of archetypal and cultural themes in his fiction, particularly in *Bless Me, Ultima*.

Leslie, Roger. Review of *My Land Sings: Stories from the Rio Grande,* by Rudolfo Anaya. *Booklist* 95, No. 22 (August 1999): 2043.

>Leslie offers a brief positive assessment of *My Land Sings: Stories from the Rio Grande.*

Nelson, Antonya. "Turf Wars in New Mexico." *New York Times Book Review* (29 November 1992): 22.

>Nelson offers a generally positive assessment of *Alburquerque.*

Perera, Victor. "Parable for Our Times: 'Jalamanta' Is More Spiritual than Story." *Washington Post* (20 February 1996): D2.

>Perera derides *Jalamanta*'s lack of story and didactic tone.

Peters, John. Review of *An Elegy on the Death of Cesar Chavez,* by Rudolfo Anaya. *Booklist* (15 December 2000): 811.

>Peters offers a brief positive review of *An Elegy on the Death of Cesar Chavez.*

Review of *An Elegy on the Death of Cesar Chavez,* by Rudolfo Anaya. *Publishers Weekly* (20 November 2000): 68.

>The critic offers a mixed assessment of *An Elegy on the Death of Cesar Chavez,* arguing that the work "gets bogged down in flowery metaphors."

Rose, David James. Review of *Bless Me, Ultima,* by Rudolfo Anaya. *Hispanic* 7, No. 8 (September 1994): 90.

>Rose offers an unfavorable assessment of *Bless Me, Ultima.*

Taylor, Paul Beekman. "Chicano Secrecy in the Fiction of Rudolfo A. Anaya." *Journal of the Southwest* 39, No. 2 (Summer 1997): 239–65.

>Taylor examines Anaya's dual use of Spanish and English in his fiction and the underlying themes and cultural meanings that are mediated and obscured by such linguistic contexts, offering different perspectives for Chicano and Anglo readers.

Additional coverage of Anaya's life and career is contained in the following sources published by the Gale Group: *Authors and Artists for Young Adults,* **Vol. 20;** *Contemporary Authors,* **Vols. 45–48;** *Contemporary Authors Autobiography Series,* **Vol. 4;** *Contemporary Authors New Revision Series,* **Vols. 1, 32, and 51;** *Contemporary Novelists; Dictionary of Literary Biography,* **Vols. 82 and 206;** *DISCovering Authors Modules: Multicultural Authors* **and** *Novelists; Hispanic Literature Criticism,* **Vol. 1;** *Hispanic Writers,* **Vol. 1;** *Literature Resource Center; Major 20th-Century Writers,* **Editions 1 and 2; and** *Novels for Students,* **Vol. 12.**

Stanley Kunitz
1905-

(Full name Stanley Jasspon Kunitz; has also written under the pseudonym Dilly Tante) American poet, editor, essayist, translator, and critic.

The following entry presents an overview of Kunitz's career through 2000. For further information on his life and works, see *CLC*, Volumes 6, 11, and 14.

INTRODUCTION

Revered as an elder statesman of American poetry, Kunitz has produced a distinguished body of work that spans generations and continues to win acclaim for its virtuosity and insight. Kunitz won the Pulitzer Prize for *Selected Poems, 1928–1958* (1958), the National Book Award for *Passing Through* (1995), and, at age ninety-five, was named poet laureate of the United States beginning in 2000. Kunitz is well-known for the nonconformity of his style, and critics seldom draw direct comparisons between him and his contemporaries, although they do note his relationship with his protégé Theodore Roethke. In the 1930s and 1940s, while the experimental verse of T. S. Eliot and Ezra Pound enjoyed wide popularity, Kunitz's work reflected the dense formalism of seventeenth-century metaphysical poets such as John Donne and George Herbert. Kunitz's verse has gradually become less autobiographical and formal over the years, evolving by the 1970s into a poetic style that combines metric complexity with lucid form.

BIOGRAPHICAL INFORMATION

Kunitz was born in Worcester, Massachusetts, in 1905, several weeks after his father, Soloman, committed suicide. This event haunted Kunitz in his formative years and it informs much of his early poetry, which focuses on themes of death and orphanhood. Raised by his mother, Yetta Jasspon Kunitz, a Lithuanian immigrant and entrepreneur who took over the family business, Kunitz's childhood was marked by his love of reading. His literary and academic prowess allowed him to obtain a scholarship to Harvard, where his poetic and linguistic talents were recognized and encouraged. After graduating from Harvard *summa cum laude* in 1926 and earning a master's degree in English, Kunitz worked briefly as a newspaper reporter in Worcester, Massachusetts. One of his first positions after college involved editing the letters of Bartolomeo Vanzetti, who was executed in the United States with Nicola Sacco in 1927 under the charge of anarchy.

Kunitz's efforts to prevent what many perceived as an unjust execution were unsuccessful, and this experience contributed to his lifelong advocacy of political freedom. Kunitz later forged a successful career as an editor of literary reference works while working for the H. W. Wilson Company in New York. He inaugurated two important series of reference books: the *Wilson Library Bulletin* and the *Authors Biographical Series*. Following the publication of his collection *Intellectual Things* (1930), Kunitz gradually focused his attention on writing poetry, but remained a working editor and translator for most of his career. Kunitz also held the position of poetry professor at Bennington College in Vermont, Columbia University in New York, the University of Washington, and Queens College, New York. Though he eschewed the confinement of an academic career, Kunitz has been recognized as an important mentor for many poets, notably Roethke and Louise Glück. He served as general editor of the "Yale Series of Younger Poets," published by Yale University Press, from 1969 to 1977. During World War II, Kunitz was drafted, although his identification as a nonaffiliated pacifist excused him from active duty. He is a founder of the Fine Arts Work Center in Provincetown, a community that sponsors young artists and writers. Kunitz's impact on the artistic community was honored by the publication of *A Celebration of Stanley Kunitz on His Eightieth Birthday* (1986), a volume of poems, essays and letters edited by Stanley Moss.

MAJOR WORKS

Kunitz's early poetry collections, *Intellectual Things, Passport to the War* (1944) and *Selected Poems, 1928–1958,* earned him a reputation as an intellectual poet. Reflecting Kunitz's admiration for the English metaphysical poets John Donne and William Blake, these intricate poems, rich in metaphor and allusion, were recognized more for their craft than their substance. *The Testing-Tree* (1971), with its conversational tone, loose form, and short lines, marked a departure to a simpler, more open style for Kunitz. In a *Publishers Weekly* article, Kunitz commented on his two styles: "My early poems were very intricate, dense and formal. . . . They were written in conventional metrics and had a very strong beat to the line. . . . In my late poems I've learned to depend on a simplicity that seems almost nonpoetic on the surface, but has reverberations within that keep it intense and alive. . . ." The change in Kunitz's style was reflected in his treatment of his most major recurring themes. Critics have noted that Kunitz has been more inclined to expose his personal feelings in his later work, particularly with regard to the suicide of his father. Poems such as "The Portrait," "Open the Gate," and "Father and Son"—which focus on a son's quest to know his father—show Kunitz to be more willing to confront his personal trauma than he was in his earlier verse. Critics have also focused on Kunitz's interest in the narrow balance between life and death, which Kunitz describes as "a rather terrifying thought that is at the root of much of my poetry." Kunitz's exploration of such serious themes has drawn acclaim from several critics, although many note that his tone has become more optimistic in his later collections such as *Next-to-Last Things* (1985) and *Passing Through.*

CRITICAL RECEPTION

Critics have overwhelmingly praised Kunitz's poetry, calling him "difficult" and "obtuse" at times, but these terms are used approvingly. The critical reverence for Kunitz's poetry often emphasizes the characteristic mysterious nature of his verse. In 1930, William Rose Benét found *Intellectual Things* "modern and yet very old, intricate and metaphysical and yet undeniably full of the true seer." Many recent critics suggest that Kunitz's poetry has improved over time, although he is still primarily placed within a generation of older poets. According to Jay Parini, "the restraints of [Kunitz's] art combine with a fierce dedication to clarity and intellectual grace to assure him of a place among the essential poets of his generation, which

includes Roethke, [Robert] Lowell, [W. H] Auden, and [Richard] Eberhart." However, Kunitz's initial works prompted scant critical attention, and it was not until he was awarded the Pulitzer Prize that critics began to take any significant interest in his poetry. Still, academic critics have been much less receptive to Kunitz than his peers. For many years, general critical consensus held that Kunitz was too imitative, lacking any recognizable style of his own. Many reviewers felt that in his early works, Kunitz was a derivative practitioner of the modernist-metaphysical mode, and in his later works, he switched to the confessional mode made popular by such poets as Lowell and John Berryman. In recent years, Kunitz has been praised for the power and intensity of his lyric poems, while continuing to be admired for his meticulous attention to the subtleties of sound and sense. Kunitz has continued to be recognized by his peers as an important voice in contemporary American poetry.

PRINCIPAL WORKS

Intellectual Things (poetry) 1930

Living Authors: A Book of Biographies [editor; as Dilly Tante] (nonfiction) 1931

Authors Today and Yesterday: A Companion Volume to "Living Authors" [editor; with Howard Haycraft] (nonfiction) 1933

The Junior Book of Authors: An Introduction to the Lives of Writers and Illustrators for Young Readers [editor; with Howard Haycraft] (nonfiction) 1934; revised edition, 1951

British Authors of the Nineteenth Century [editor; with Howard Haycraft] (nonfiction) 1936

American Authors, 1600–1900: A Biographical Dictionary of American Literature [editor; with Howard Haycraft] (nonfiction) 1938

Twentieth Century Authors: A Biographical Dictionary [editor; with Howard Haycraft; with Vineta Colby] (nonfiction) 1942; first supplement, 1955

Passport to the War: A Selection of Poems (poetry) 1944

British Authors before 1800: A Biographical Dictionary [editor; with Howard Haycraft] (nonfiction) 1952

Selected Poems, 1928–1958 (poetry) 1958

European Authors, 1000–1900: A Biographical Dictionary [editor; with Vineta Colby] (nonfiction) 1967

The Testing-Tree (poetry) 1971

Poems of Anna Akhmatova [translator; with Max Hayward] (poetry) 1973

The Coat without a Seam: Sixty Poems, 1930–1972 (poetry) 1974

The Terrible Threshold: Selected Poems, 1940–1970 (poetry) 1974

A Kind of Order, A Kind of Folly: Essays and Conversations (essays and interviews) 1975

The Lincoln Relics (poetry) 1978

The Poems of Stanley Kunitz, 1928–1978 (poetry) 1979

The Wellfleet Whale and Companion Poems (poetry) 1983

Next-to-Last Things: New Poems and Essays (poetry and essays) 1985

Passing Through: Later Poems, New and Selected (poetry) 1995

The Collected Poems of Stanley Kunitz (poetry) 2000

CRITICISM

Stanley Kunitz with Cynthia Davis (interview date 9 March 1972)

SOURCE: "An Interview with Stanley Kunitz,"[1] in *Contemporary Literature,* Vol. 15, No. 1, Winter, 1974, pp. 1–14.

[*In the following interview, conducted in 1972, Kunitz discusses his formative influences and approach to writing poetry, his artistic development and changing existential and mythopoetic concerns, and his views on the significance of poetry and the place of the poet in contemporary society.*]

[*Davis:*] *Mr. Kunitz, you said once to a group of students studying your poetry that no one has the "right answers" in interpretation, and that after it's published the poem belongs as much to them as to you. Are you generally reluctant to explain your poems?*

[Kunitz:] I often don't really know what a poem means, in rational terms. There are so many currents that flow into the poem, of which the poet himself can't be totally aware. Years after you have written a poem, you come back to it and find something you didn't know was there. Sometimes, I grant, a poet can be helpful about a specific image or an obscure portion of his poem.

Do you think it's helpful to talk about the circumstances that led to your writing a poem?

If they can be recalled, they may, in some cases, prove illuminating. But, as a general rule, the poem ought to have released itself from the circumstances of its origin.

Is that related to the idea of myth—poetry as myth?

Yes, it's that, but it's also related to my feeling that the poem has to be found beyond the day, that it requires a plunge into the well of one's being, where all one's key images lie. The occasion for a poem, which may have been something quite casual, is not the true source of the poem—it has only helped to trigger the right nerves.

When I asked about myth, I was thinking of the idea that I find in the poems of **The Coat without a Seam** *especially, the idea that myth is something constant that can be* expressed in many different kinds of circumstances, but that goes beyond circumstances—even beyond the individual. So a great poem speaks to everyone because all share a common condition.

Jung spoke of archetypal images that go beyond the individual persona and that pertain to the collective history of the race.

Is that a reason for your use of dream and hallucination in the poetry—to reach that archetypal material?

I think of dream as an actual visitation into that world, as a clue to secrets of which one is only faintly aware in ordinary consciousness.

But you wouldn't agree with the "psychic automatism" of the surrealists?

No. Because I think a poem is a combination of unconscious and conscious factors. One is trying to reach a level of transcendence; at the same time, one has to keep a grip on language, not to let it run away with itself. Automatic writing is such a bore!

Is your use of metaphysical techniques—exploiting the metaphor in extended conceits—one of the ways of exercising that conscious control over language, giving form to the raw materials of the unconscious mind?

The image leads you out of yourself into a world of relatives. The beautiful risk to take is to extend the image as far as you can go, until it turns in upon itself. The danger is in jumping off into absurdity, but that's part of the risk.

Perhaps we can consider some of these questions by talking about changes in your development. You eliminated almost half of the poems in **Intellectual Things** [*hereafter cited as* **IT**] *(1930) in later volumes. Was that because they were technically unsuccessful, or because you no longer agreed with the ideas you expressed in them?*

My main feeling was that they were immature. Maybe I felt a little embarrassed reading them, so I thought it would be better to drop them, that's all.

I felt that many of the poems in that book placed much greater emphasis on the power of the intellect than later poems. I'm thinking of poems like **"Mens Creatrix"** (**IT**, *p. 16*), *in which you seem to talk about the superiority of the intellect over the emotions. I wondered if perhaps one of the reasons for elimination of such poems was that you had changed your emphasis.*

I doubt it. Certainly when I was writing the poems in **Intellectual Things,** I meant to demonstrate, if I could, not that the poem was a cerebral exercise, but the contrary, that the intellect and the passions were inseparable—which is the whole point of the Blake epigraph to the book, "The tear is an intellectual thing."

Then why the poems in which you talk about putting away passion, or subduing it by intellectual power?

It's not a question of putting it away or rising above it. Remember, I'm thinking back a good many years, so that I wouldn't swear to this—but my recollection is that my characteristic figure at this stage, in speaking of mind and heart, was of each devouring and being devoured by the other, an act of mutual ingestion. In **"Beyond Reason"** (*IT*, p. 62) I spoke of taming the passions "with the sections of my mind"—as though it were a sort of dog food—but then I wanted to "teach my mind to love its thoughtless crack."

One of the poems that impressed me on this theme was "Motion of Wish" (**IT,** *p. 52*).

I'll take a look at it and see whether you're right or not. . . . Yes, I think the lines you were thinking of were ". . . wish may find / Mastery only in the mind." This poem I haven't looked at in so long, but as I read it now, I see these lines as the key to understanding of the poem: ". . . mariners eat / One lotus-moment to forget / All other moments, and their eyes / Fasten on impossible surprise." And then the end: "A man may journey to the sun, / But his one true love and companion / Sleeps curled in his thoughtful womb. / Here will the lone life-traveler come / To find himself infallibly home." But you have to consider here that the mind is the eater of the passions, and the passions rest in that mind, so that what one is asserting is a sense of the unity of all experience, not a separation.

And the mind contains that sense of unity.

Yes. The mind stands for the whole experiential and existential process. I think that the confusion here is to think that when I talk of mind in this volume, that I'm talking about brain. I'm not talking about brain; I'm talking about the whole process of existence.

What about poems like "Very Tree" (**IT,** *p. 21*), *where it seems that what you're saying is that you perceive the essence of the tree—its treeness—and discard its particulars? That the particulars are not important?*

One of my great influences was Plato, and I was very deep in Platonic lore, especially at this period of my first work. The theme is the idea of tree, treeness, as opposed to the shadow of the idea.

But you're not really suggesting that particulars of experience are unimportant?

You arrive at universals through the perception—the clear perception—of what Blake called "Minute Particulars."

These earlier poems are much more abstract than your later work, aren't they?

I suppose so. That may have been the Platonic influence, as much as anything else that I can think of.

Did you become dissatisfied with that kind of approach?

As I became more of a political being, I wanted to fasten my poems to the reality of the day. I turned away from poems that began with the grandeur of generality. I wanted to find the general through breaking the kernel of particulars.

Is this why, in **Passport to the War** *[hereafter cited as* **PW**] *(1944), you make so many references to contemporary events? As concretions for your general themes?*

Don't you think that is possibly simply the result of maturing a bit and having more experience of the world? At the time of writing **Intellectual Things,** I was in my early twenties and was an innocent in so many ways. I had developed intellectually more than I had emotionally or experientially.

This volume, especially, the war poetry, seems very different even from your later poetry.

It was my darkest time.

Do you still have the same feelings about the conditions of the modern world and what it does to man?

I've never stopped being a dissenter. I have no use for a superior technology that breeds hatred, injustice, inequality, and war.

What do you think the poet's position should be in relationship to that kind of society?

Number one, he must not become a subscribing member of it. Since the beginning of the Industrial Revolution, the poet has been the prophetic voice of a counterculture. Poetry today speaks more directly to the young than ever before because they recognize its adversary position.

Then you think it's more difficult to be a poet now than it was before the nineteenth century?

The poet before the Industrial Revolution could identify himself with State or Church, but he certainly has not been able to do so since. That's why he is a creature apart.

You often talk about guilt in **Passport to the War.** *Sometimes it's played upon by society, but sometimes you seem to say that everyone carries a load of guilt around with him. What is this guilt caused by and directed at?*

When I speak of **"The Guilty Man"** (*PW*, p. 27), I don't mean someone who has sinned more than anybody else. I mean the person who, simply by virtue of being mortal, is in a way condemned; he's mortal and he's fallible, and his life is inevitably a series of errors and consequences. Since he cannot really see the true path—it is not given to him to see it, except in moments of revelation—he is denied the rapture of innocence.

Like Original Sin?

Without the theological furniture.

Is this related to the existentialist idea of the fear of freedom?

I was making noises like an existentialist before I knew what it was to be one. I keep on trying to record my sense of being alive, which means in practice my sense, from moment to moment, of living and dying at once, a condition of perpetual crisis.

*In particular, when I read **"The Fitting of the Mask"** (**PW**, p. 28), I thought of Sartre's "bad faith": the attempt to conceal one's own being from oneself.*

If we did not wear masks, we should be frightened of mirrors.

*You say in **"Night Letter"** (**PW**, p. 9) that you "believe in love" as the salvation from this fear of one's own being and from the evils of modern society. Are you speaking primarily of love for mankind or personal love?*

Abstract love is not love at all. One expresses love in relation to another—that's the germinal node. I don't really care much for people who are always talking about love for mankind and hate their neighbors.

*The treatment of the love theme is another difference I found between the first volume and later ones. In **Intellectual Things,** the love poetry is often about relationships that fail; it isn't until the later poetry that you really celebrate fulfilling relationships.*

That's more or less to be expected. After all, the disasters of early love are legendary and part of one's education. For that reason, among others, poets in their youth tend to be melancholy. "When I was young," said Yeats, "my Muse was old; now that I am old, my Muse is young."

It wasn't, then, that you had a more pessimistic conception of the relationship?

I've always been an optimist about love. Three marriages are the proof.

*I'd like to talk a little about **Selected Poems** [hereafter cited as **SP**]. Perhaps we could begin with a poem that seems central to that volume, **"The Approach to Thebes"** (**SP**, p. 31). That poem ends with these lines: ". . . I met a lovely monster, / And the story's this: I made the monster me." Is this just acceptance of one's fate?*

More than that. . . . I have a theory about monsters. I remember, a few years ago, telling Mark Rothko, who was a dear friend of mine, that every genius is a monster. Mark thought about that for sometime, and then, with the typical vanity of an artist, said, "You mean I'm a monster?" I replied, "Well, I'm not talking about anybody in this room." But of course I was. The adversary artist in our time pays a price, in human terms, for his excess of ego and sensibility. He has had to sacrifice too much; he is poisoned by ambition; and he carries too big a load of griefs and shames—that's the hunch on his back. You're not likely to find him open, generous, or joyous. Rothko, incidentally, killed himself by slashing his wrists not long after our discussion. I have a poem about him, entitled **"The Artist,"** in *The Testing-Tree.*

And the burden of monsterdom is placed on mythic heroes, too?

Yes.

There's one mythic hero that you seem to consider more than others, and that's Christ. Why is the Christian myth more important in your poetry than other myths?

Because it shakes me more. It is the supreme drama of guilt and redemption. I have no religion—perhaps that is why I think so much about God.

When you speak of myth in poetry, you mean a re-creation of the human drama embodied in religious myths such as this?

Poetic myth is nourished by all the great traditions.

Then you are saying that all myths attempt to do the same thing, to tell the same story.

All myths are the same myth; all metaphors are the same metaphor. When you touch the web of creation at any point, the whole web shudders.

And poetry has the same function as myth?

Metaphorically.

You draw many parallels between the poet and the mythic hero. Do you, like so many poets, see the poet as supreme example of affirmative action, of what a man can be?

As I said a while back, he can be a monster. But ideally he is the last representative free man, in that he is beholden to nobody but himself and his own vision of truth. Almost anybody else you can think of is beholden to others: the pastor to his congregation, the politician to the public, the actor to his audience. But the poet, since he is not a commodity, is more blessed than others—he can strive toward the absolute purity of his art.

Aren't you beholden to your publisher and your readers, at least in some measure financially?

No. I don't think so. One manages to survive. If I felt for a moment that I had to write lies in order to publish, I would stop publishing. It wouldn't matter that much. I could still go on writing.

You're especially concerned with the question of what it is to be a poet in **"The Coat without a Seam,"** *and nearly all of the poems in that section are new in* **Selected Poems.** *Why is it that you became more concerned with poems about poetry in that volume?*

I'm not sure that I did. Periodically one tries to redefine and reassert one's vocation—not always in obvious terms. Wallace Stevens made a career out of doing precisely that. "Poetry," he wrote, "is the subject of the poem." As you rightly perceived, I keep trying to relate poetic function with mythic or heroic destiny.

You note that relationship in other sections, too, in poems like **"Green Ways"** *(SP, p. 5).*

I wonder whether you caught the logic of the various sections in the *Selected Poems.* They were meant to indicate my primary thematic concerns.

Perhaps you would talk about a couple of those sections; for example, "The Terrible Threshold."

That title—"The Terrible Threshold"—comes, of course, from one of the poems, **"Open the Gates"** (*SP*, p. 41), where the poet sees "The end and the beginning in each other's arms." I think of the poems in this section as visionary experiences, culminating in a moment of illumination.

In speaking to a group of students studying **"Prophecy on Lethe"** *(SP, p. 61), you said that that moment was one of fleeting awareness, and that you couldn't state what that awareness was of. If you can't state what you see in that moment of epiphany. . . .*

I don't have to state it. The awareness is in the poem, not in my memory of it. Come to think of it, I don't even remember what the last lines were!

"With your strange brain blooming as it lies / Abandoned to the bipeds on the beach; / Your jelly-mouth and, crushed, your polyp eyes."

I see all those death images piled up on that shore. The key word, the transcendental word, for me is "blooming."

There's a movement there toward a sense of identity, isn't there? First an anonymous figure floating on the stream, and at the end you speak directly to the "you."

Death-in-Life. Life-in-Death. The glory of the senses. . . .

This is what I was trying to get at: I saw the poem as, at least partially, a myth of the birth of consciousness, moving from a Being-in-Itself state—unconscious and no perception—to that sense of identity that you have because you're conscious. And of course, a sharper awareness of your own sensuous perceptions. I don't know whether that would be valid or not.

Thanks—I'll buy it. It just occurs to me that there's a comparable evolution in my later poem, **"Green Ways."** I hadn't seen the affinity before.

And part of the point of **"Green Ways"** *is that it is the duty of the conscious being to accept his consciousness, isn't it?*

More than that, he must affirm his vegetable and mineral existence, as well as his animal self.

Not discarding them with consciousness, then.

Accepting them, in the fullness of the life-process.

Could you talk a little about "The Serpent's Word" section also?

Those are love poems, or deal with the love experience. The phrase is always the key to the section that it heads; here it's from the line: "Who taught me the serpent's word, but yet the word." Which takes us back to the Garden of Eden.

In **"The Dark and the Fair"** *(SP, p. 33), the source of that line, there's a Fair Lady and another Dark Lady, and the Dark Lady replaces the Fair. The Dark Lady is from the past; is she symbolic of the Fall?*

She's Lilith, in the poem.

There is another poem in "The Serpent's Word" that I find more difficult than most, **"As Flowers Are"** *(SP, p. 10).*

That poem records the changes in a field through the seasons. And at the same time, it offers by implication a metaphor of the aspects of love. From week to week each species of flower, each hue, struggles to gain possession of the field.

Is that the "war" of the flowers?

Yes. The yellows and whites of spring yield to the hot tones of summer, a riot of colors. The chill nights bring the lavenders in; and, with the first frost, the whole field turns bronze. It's a parable, I suppose.

I think I see it now.

It's not so difficult, if you listen to the music.

You've said that in an open society, poetry tends to become hermetic, more difficult, and very private. Do you think this is true of your own poetry?

The important question is, do I still think we live in an open society. Certainly America seems to me less open than it was. And certainly my work has undergone a sea-change. Robert Lowell wrote something to the effect that I've broken with my "passionately gnarled" earlier style and am writing in a language that "even cats and dogs can understand." Perhaps in my age I've managed to untie some of the knots of my youth. I want to say what I have to say without fuss. I want to strip everything down to essentials.

You talked about some of these ideas in **Passport to the War,** *and that volume also had a more open style than the first one.*

Poets are always wanting to change their lives and their styles. Of the two, it's easier to change the life.

In that last volume, **The Testing-Tree** *(1971), you included several of your translations of other authors. Why did you pick those particular ones?*

Obviously because I liked them as poems. And because they seemed to have an affinity with my own work. For example, I've been working on the poems of Anna Akhmatova for several years—they make up my next book. I've been so absorbed in her verse that it would be surprising if I hadn't been affected by it. Incidentally, I tend to think of a book as a composition, a joining of parts into an architectural whole, not just a throwing-together of the poems as written. A book ought to have an interior logic: these few translations seemed to me to fit into the logic of this particular book. I deliberately excluded scores of others.

Are they fairly strict translations?

Close, but not slavishly close. Translating poetry is an exercise in paradox. "Be true to me!" says the poem to its translator. And in the next breath, "Transform me, make me new!" If you follow the original, word for word, and lose the poetry—as you must, if you insist on a literal rendering—your translation is a dud. But if you find the poetry in a free act of the imagination, it's a lie. I'm reminded of the citizen in Kafka's aphorism who's fettered to two chains, one attached to earth, the other to heaven. No matter which way he heads, the opposite chain pulls him back with a jolt. That's pretty much the condition of the translator.

Do you read the originals yourself?

My knowledge of Russian is rudimentary. Though my parents came from Russia, I am not a Russian linguist or scholar. So I nearly always translate with somebody whom I can depend on for roots and connotations and allusions. Max Hayward helped me with Akhmatova, as he did before with Voznesensky.

Did you do many translations earlier?

A few . . . from French, Spanish, and Italian. I included one of my Baudelaire translations in **Selected Poems.** He was important to me.

You spoke of the "internal logic" of a volume of poetry. Does **The Testing-Tree** *have a definite logic for its sections, as* **Selected Poems** *does?*

A logic, but less definite, perhaps. I shuffled those poems all around. The first section is the overture, anticipating the main themes. Section two is dominated by poems of place; three, political; four deals with the role and character of the artist.

The title poem seems most like your earlier poems in theme.

Not in form, certainly. But that and **"King of the River"** go back to the mythic.

Were they written earlier?

No. Quite late.

Would you say, then, that your themes are the same, that you're just expressing them in a different way?

A man's preoccupations and themes aren't likely to change. What changes is the extent to which he can put the full diversity of his moods and interests and information into his poems. Formal verse is a highly selective medium. A high style wants to be fed exclusively on high sentiments. Given the kind of person I am, I came to see the need for a middle style—for a low style, even, though that may be outside my range.

I was interested in Robert Lowell's review of **The Testing-Tree** *because I thought that he was saying, among other things, that the new poetry was more like his, more like confessional poetry.*

I've always been an intensely subjective poet. There's never been any shift from that.

The sort of open description of autobiographical detail that appears in your last volume is generally considered confessional poetry.

Confession is a private matter. Most so-called confessional poetry strikes me as raw and embarrassing—bad art.

Do you think you've been influenced by any of the confessional poets? Lowell and Roethke?

In the first place, you mustn't call Roethke a confessional poet. He would have vomited at the thought. We were friends for thirty years, till his death, swapping manuscripts and criticism. My friendship with Lowell dates from the publication of my **Selected Poems** in 1958. **Intellectual Things** had brought Roethke and me together—he was still unpublished. But these are more than literary friendships. In these long and deep associations it's idle to discuss who influences whom. Friendship is a sustained act of reciprocity. We have all been touched by our interchange. Vulnerable human beings affect each other; that's all there is to it.

You wouldn't then put yourself in any group?

Now or at any stage, I can't imagine to what group I could possibly be attached. A one-to-one relationship is the limit of my herd instinct.

What earlier poets would you say influenced you greatly?

Donne and Herbert and Blake were my first major influences—Donne and Herbert stylistically, Blake prophetically. I must have learned something, too, from Wordsworth's "Prelude" and his "Intimations of Immortality." For awhile I steeped myself in Keats and Tennyson. After that, almost nobody until Hopkins overwhelmed me during my college years. And Yeats, of course, whom I consider to be the great master of the poem in English in this century. I suppose Eliot to a degree, though I opposed him, quarreling with his ideas, his criticism, and what I thought of as his poverty of sympathy. His theory of the depersonalization of poetry struck me as false and destructive. My work didn't fit into that picture of his at all. Both Roethke and I felt from the beginning that the Eliot school was our principal adversary. We fought for a more passionate art. Nevertheless I was so aware of his existence that even in a negative way I was influenced by him. So was Roethke. That Eliot rhythm had an hypnotic effect.

I'd like to go back for a moment to the question we discussed earlier, your differences from confessional poets. Your latest volume is certainly more directly autobiographical than the others. Rosenthal justifies the use of autobiographical material in confessional poetry by the poet's assumption that the literal self is important and that it becomes symbolic of the world—what happens to the self is what the modern world does to man. How does your idea of poetry differ from that?

I phrase it differently. I say that the effort is to convert one's life into legend, which isn't quite the same thing. Secrets are part of the legend. My emphasis isn't on spilling everything. It's on the act of transformation, the ritual sense, the perception of a destiny.

Is it possible to see these mythic connections even if you're not a poet?

I'm not contending that the poet is set apart from others. On the contrary, he is more like others than anybody else—that's his nature. It's what Keats meant by negative capability, the predisposition to flow into everyone and everything. A poetry of self-indulgence and self-advertisement is produced by the egotistical sublime—Keats's phrase again—and is simply ugly. God knows a poet needs ego, but it has to be consumed in the fire of the poetic action.

Then your view is almost the reverse of the confessional one; you begin with a general idea of the human condition.

The only reason you write about yourself is that this is what you know best. What else has half as much reality

for you? Even so, certain details of your life can be clouded by pain, or fear, or shame, or other complications, that induce you to lie, to disguise the truth about yourself. But the truth about yourself is no more important than the truth about anybody else. And if you knew anybody else as well as you know yourself, you would write about that other.

Note

1. The interview was conducted on March 9, 1972, at Mr. Kunitz's home in New York. Mr. Kunitz kindly consented to read and edit the interview. Poems quoted are identified by page number with the following abbreviations: *IT—Intellectual Things* (New York: Doubleday, 1930); *PW—Passport to the War* (New York: Henry Holt, 1944); *SP—Selected Poems, 1928–1958* (Boston: Little, Brown, 1958); *TT—The Testing-Tree* (Boston: Little, Brown, 1971).

Robert Weisberg (essay date Spring 1975)

SOURCE: "Stanley Kunitz: The Stubborn Middle Way," in *Modern Poetry Studies,* Vol. 6, No. 1, Spring, 1975, pp. 49–73.

[*In the following essay, Weisberg provides an overview of Kunitz's artistic development and poetic style, drawing attention to his metaphysical concerns, creative vision, and the influence of T. S. Eliot and W. A. Auden.*]

"The easiest poet to neglect is one who resists classification."[1] Had he spoken of himself, Stanley Kunitz might rather have said that we neglect the poet who becomes classified too early and too narrowly. Since a brief, if sympathetic, article by Jean Hagstrum in 1958,[2] Kunitz's impressive canon has aroused no critical interest. Instead, he has been dubiously honored, by almost universal agreement, as a strange phenomenon called the "poet's poet," and the only recent study of him, by Marjorie Perloff in the *Iowa Review,* explicitly sustains this official view.[3] In what sense is Kunitz "the poet's poet"? The title first assumes that his verse is of minor interest in itself, but that his literary relationships as peer and mentor have merited him a grateful, if condescending, nod from the historians of contemporary poetry. More specifically, the title has generally implied fixed critical views of the nature of his verse. In his early work as represented in *Selected Poems* he is a skillful but derivative practitioner of the modernist-metaphysical mode, limited in subject, a bit abstruse in imagery, and interesting chiefly as a technician. In the late poems in *The Testing-Tree* he is again the skillful derivative, this time as a late convert to the confessional mode.

We will see the real Kunitz when we look askance at our categories of classification. It seems absurd, but may be necessary, to say that his career as a sane, mature, and stable eye in the storm of modern literary lives is no reason to slight his work. The notion that his field of vision is narrow is challenged by his own remark about political poetry: "An age in crisis needs more than ever to be made aware of the full range of human possibility." We must ask whether narrowing his material may, ironically, have helped us to widen that range. And if we avoid the self-fulfilling prophecy of typing the late poems as pallid confessionals, we might see that there are magnificent autobiographical poems, like his **"King of the River,"** which "derive" from a tradition of personal poetry far older than that born in 1959 with Robert Lowell's *Life Studies*. We may come to see Kunitz as a still point in the turning world of recent poetry, a poet whose dynamic order will remind us of what subject matter may be worth a poet's excluding.

What has been seen as the safe path of the "poet's poet" has been a stubborn middle way. Kunitz has felt no need to encompass the extremes of his contemporaries when he can remain at their point of intersection. He need not journey all the way to either hell or Byzantium to dramatize the condition of the poet caught in between: to deny this is to assume an ethic and aesthetic of Faustian aspiration which he would say destroys more good poetry than it creates, because it destroys good poets. Kunitz lives among the classic paradoxes of modern literature and has learned that a sane irony produces a poetry as useful as the most audacious plumbing and soaring.

Born in 1905, Kunitz emerged as a poet in one of the dourest literary periods in America, a time of the odd convergence of such literary influences as T. S. Eliot's, and such philosophical influences as Marx's and Freud's. W. H. Auden is the mediator between these influences and a large if loose group of young American poets who came of age between the wars, and whose pre-war poetry now, in retrospect, seems so stylized in its cultivated, impersonal, and often ideological despair. In **"The Dark and the Fair,"** Kunitz recalls a literary gathering (it ideally would have included Randall Jarrell, Delmore Schwartz, Karl Shapiro, Lowell, and Theodore Roethke) and sums up its mood:

> A roaring company that festive night;
> The beast of dialectic dragged his chains,
> Prowling from chair to chair in the smoking light,
> While the snow hissed against the windowpanes.
>
> Our politics, our science, and our faith
> Were whiskey on the tongue; I being rent
> By the fierce divisions of our time, cried death
> And death again, and my own dying meant.

This recalls a whole mode of poetry most obvious in the painfully psychological, probing poems of the first Auden volume, and such Jarrell poems as "The Winter's Tale" that follow. In them the poet, having absorbed a lot of Freud and Marx (in the sense of analytic approach if not actual ideology) attempts a hawk's-eye survey of a somber pre-war world and sees nothing but life-denial. It is revealing that even here, the poet finds the source of this vision in personal depression and not in the results of comprehen-

sive social analysis. Kunitz offers a poem quite directly in this mode in **"Night Letter"**;

> I suffer the twentieth century,
> The nerves of commerce wither in my arm:
> Violence shakes my dreams; I am so cold,
> Chilled by the persecuting wind abroad,
> The oratory of the rodent's tooth,
> The slaughter of the blue-eyed open towns,
> And principle disgraced, and art denied.
> My dear, it is too late for peace. . . .

"Night Letter" embodies attitudes of its moment in its arch, world-weary tone, its often contrived yearning for a "faith, and especially its agonizing debate with history as Satan. ("Gerontion" is the great model here.) It is certainly close to the early poems of Schwartz, to Shapiro's bitter social ironies, and even, without the acrobatics of style, to the Lowell of *Lord Weary's Castle*. It was a generation, in its self-conscious anti-Romanticism, all too ready to adopt the Romantic youthful pose of exhausted cynicism tinged with rootless religious idealism. Those most deeply involved in this mode, of course, sought release from it after the war's conclusion induced in America a sense of relief and security; the free-form and ultimately the confessional followed the impersonally cynical in our poetic history.

Kunitz's membership in this group needs qualification. Despite sharing the tone and diction, he shows little inclination toward any ideology or faith-based view of the world (as Auden ultimately does), and he only slowly, if at all, follows the path of confessional liberation of Lowell and Jarrell, for example. Yet, years later, he still clings to some of the central concerns of this group, especially the burden of the past (though for him it is *always* personal, never collectively historical) and the possibilities of healing what Eliot decried as our dissociation of sensibility in a verse that fuses an active critical intelligence and a Romantic temperament. Perhaps this makes Kunitz the truest member of this group, again, the still point at its center, a subtle guide to the development of contemporary poetry amidst the extremer tendencies of his fellows.

Selected Poems, 1928–1958 is organized, the poet tells us, not by chronology, but by similarities of "argument," of theme. Two outstanding themes appear in it, and perhaps a third emerges to unite the two. The first theme unifies a great number of poems that make the agonies of love a metaphor of mortality in general. The poet pictures these agonies through complex metaphysical imagery as a wound, or, more often, a festering disease from which we may seek escape into pure vision, but to which we return as the *felix culpa* of poetry: love and life are a venereal disease. The second major theme is that of generation, of the poet's three-phase struggle with his past. First, the poet tries to escape the responsibility that the ghosts of the past place on him; then he ecstatically embraces them in a transcendent illumination; and finally, as in the first theme, rejecting a rarefied vision for the salvation he finds in the fecund ditch of life, he learns to "endure" (a central word in Kunitz) the agonies of the generative process. This does not mean to make peace with the past by transcending time, but to make peace with time itself. Ultimately, the wound and the generative process are one, and it is the poet's job to celebrate them.

It is the poems of the first theme that undoubtedly caused critics to type Kunitz as an extreme formalist, but it is important to see a substantial change within them even in *Selected Poems.* We might say that Kunitz does begin with poems that *do* all too self-consciously offer themselves as reincarnations of John Donne:

> And even should I track you to your birth
> Through all the cities of your mortal trial,
> As in my jealous thought I try to do,
> You would escape me—from the brink of earth
> Take off to where the lawless auroras run,
> You with your wild and metaphysic heart.
> My touch is on you, who are light-years gone.
> We are not souls but systems, and we move
> In clouds of our unknowing. . . .

("**The Science of the Night**")

Kunitz here displays the typical dilemma of his generation—and excess of sheer stylistic talent all too vulnerable to string influence—as if he were too enthusiastically filling Eliot's request for a re-association of sensibility. The burden of talent and influence produces an immensely interesting and rich lyric which yet seems to stifle the poet's true voice, as if an almost unconscious insincerity may have been the curse attached to the Eliot-Auden inheritance. At other times we may feel the poet fully to blame for conceiving himself as the restorer of the Elizabethan World Picture:

> So intricately is this world resolved
> Of substance arched on thrust of circumstance,
> The earth's organic meaning so involved
> That none may break the pattern of his dance; . . .

("**So Intricately Is This World Resolved**")

The problem is that at the base of a good metaphysical yoking-conceit must be some sort of conflict between an order and a violence, and if the violence is insufficiently realized in the poem, if it seems just a tame, cultivated violence and not the genuine violence of a convincing emotional experience, the order in the conceit will seem more clever than dynamic.

But as *Selected Poems* progresses, a more sincere voice does emerge in the poems of this first theme; a more forceful, less genteel, violence of language reveals a genuine emotional core, and Kunitz seems to achieve the difficult synthesis he may well have thought Eliot was asking for. He manages to bring to his immediate experience a Renaissance sense of wit and decorum, including metrical formality, and use it to express and contain his personality, not suppress it through derivative stylization. We might even imagine him in these poems conducting a secret argument with Eliot. The poet has acknowledged himself a respect-

ful adversary of Eliot: "His definition of poetry as an objective act, a depersonalized performance, was contrary to my own conviction that art and life were bound together. I sought a more passionate voice. And I scorned his politics." Kunitz undoubtedly is wrong in seeing a crude art-life split in Eliot, but he takes Eliot at his word in making a poetry of intelligence and emotion possible again, very close to the original Renaissance model. This is opposite to what Eliot did in his own verse, which was to transform the metaphysical mode so thoroughly into modernist-free verse as to make the metaphysical influence more a critical catalyst than a true poetic model.

The new voice emerges gradually. We see in "**No Word**" still the almost excessively thick imagery, yet the wit in this poem conceals a contemporary, common subject—the "no word" is the telephone call that does not come—and so the metaphysical style begins to connect with a true experience:

> No message. May the mothering dark,
> Whose benediction calms the sea,
> Abater of the atrocious spark
> Of love and love's anxiety,
> Be kind; and may my self condone,
> As surely as my judge reprieves,
> This heart strung on the telephone,
> Folded in death, whom no voice revives.

At the end here, the poet moves toward Eliot in weaving an object of common experience into the conceit, and the effect is startling and emotionally convincing. Recalling Eliot's distinction between the "rhetorics" of Henry James and John Milton, we might see the twists and turns of the verse approaching the vacillations of an active emotional mind, and not just self-consciously elaborating the conceit. The woman of the poem remains as remote as in "**The Science of the Night**"—but remote as a real woman might be to a man, and not, as in the previous poem, remote merely because abstract. Here she is simply distant and cold, and takes on some implied substance through the poet's own tension.

We see another advance in "**The Words of the Preacher.**" The diction is no more contemporary, and in some ways the emotional experience no more precise. But the poem has an *energy* that other of Kunitz's metaphysical lyrics lack. And so it succeeds as one of Ezra Pound's early experiments in traditional forms succeeds, by investing the form with new vigor and whole, yet being, in a sense, a purely imitative poem. Equally important though, the poem begins to develop the disease conceit that will dominate the rest of the volume:

> Taking infection from the vulgar air
> And sick with the extravagant disease
> Of life, my soul rejected the sweet snare
> Of happiness; declined
> That democratic bait, set in the world
> By fortune's old and mediocre mind.
>
> To love a changing shape with perfect faith
> Is waste of faith; to follow dying things

With deathless hope is vain; to go from breath
To breath, so to be fed
And put to sleep, is cheat and shame—because
By piecemeal living a man is doomed, I said.

This verbal energy, or, more specifically, this invigorating sense of a speaking voice, is precisely what most imitative verse lacks. Many poems of the thirties compound the weakness by seeming uncertain of *who* is speaking at all. The potential energy in a good "homage" may be dissipated by the poet's anxiety to force sincerity, and the result is the insincerity we have seen already. Here, the poet displays a rare Pound-like sense of play with the metaphysical style. The poem deals with his serious theme, yet borrows from the early Pound the redeeming power of play in rejuvenating the old form. This sense of play is a significant movement for Kunitz, for the poems get richer as they turn from a forced Elizabethan elegance to the sharper emotional thrust that is more natural to him.

For Kunitz, the *felix culpa* is man's attachment to this "extravagant disease" (the metaphor has the metaphysical *vigor* of such Yeats metaphors as "dying animal" and "fecund ditch"), and like W. B. Yeats, he gradually lays claim to this middle ground, this scrimmage of mortality between nihilism and rarefied vision as the distinct arena of his poetry. Kunitz's best poems refuse to decorate the physical life with Elizabethan elegance, or transcend it for a permanence he finds all the more threatening. Again, the poems are strongest where the commitment to this mortal arena is most honest, where the metaphysical images heighten rather than tame the tension.

Three poems stand out in particular, and it might be well to begin with **"By Lamplight,"** which, with revealing irony, may well evoke from a sensitive but incautious reader the odd notion that a poem written decades ago is "Plathian":

> Welcome, eccentric life,
> Attracted to my star,
> Let there be festival
> Perverse and singular.
> Let any drop of poison
> Grow legs and crawl and eat:
> The malice of unreason
> A man can tolerate.
> The stumblers and the clowns
> Are wired with their will
> To live, to live, to live:
> They do not mean to kill.
> Sweet beetles, comrade moths,
> The bonfires in your head
> Are neither coals of hell
> Nor the rose in the marriage-bed.
> I heard all summer long
> (Dance, monsters, hairy forms!)
> The idiot on the leaf
> Babbling of the dust and storms,
> And in this rough heart made
> A little thin-legged song
> Out of my greening blood
> To swell the night's harangue.

The synthesis of order and violence becomes, for Kunitz, not just the *felix culpa* of diseased mortality, but the growth of poetry itself. The poem is, in origin, simply the meditation of the midnight poet on the gross insect life orbiting around his lamp. This insect life becomes for him the "hairy forms," the "festival" of perverse mortality which he not only welcomes into his brain, but makes his poetry of. The disease image is repeated at the end, almost as an image of a kind of festering mental gangrene, but the grossness of physicality is absorbed into the thoroughly healthy, unmorbid vigor of the poem. Kunitz chooses here the middle ground between "the coals of hell" and "the rose in the marriage-bed"—his territory is absolute neither in extreme damnation nor perfected symbolic harmony. It is only after acknowledging this powerful embrace of reality that the rhymed (often slant-rhymed) and well-varied iambic trimeter, which encloses the aberrant circles of the insects, should be noted for the poem's formal success.

We can begin, then to understand the common misconception of Kunitz. The violence of his theme is not over-cultivated; he is rarely a gardener poet, and as seen, in the best short poems, the violence is anything but elegant. It is simply that he lives, or once lived, in a very symbolic universe, so that we are offered little of the *explicit* private or public material of violence that we have come to expect in contemporaries. Kunitz, in fact, is a devout romantic in his adherence to the natural world as his model for human experience, though he has successfully transformed nature from Wordsworthian harmony and sublimity to the modern disfigurement he must deal with, especially by dealing more with *man's* body than with earth's body. So it is a very conscious, controlled limitation of explicit subject matter, rather than any over-refinement, that may make the poems seem genteel to the contemporary ear: The disease of mortality in Kunitz *is* a disease; but the poet has decided that the more he documented it, the less he would make music of it.

A more striking example of this balance is **"Off Point Lotus,"** a poem which as well as any in Kunitz demonstrates the inadequacy of using the label "confessional" to measure the personal. The poem is wholly and impressively personal in the sense that a reader knowing nothing of the poet's life will still intuit that it has been written out of a private experience and that the reader will need no explicit evidence of that experience. His intuition will derive, rather, from the thoroughly uncontrived verve with which the Odysseus myth is taken up, and from the lucid connections the poem makes to others in the volume to establish itself as a stage in the construction of a coherent poetic character:

> Three years I lolled in that country of the girls,
> Thick with their wine, their loose idolatry,
> Nor saw that I was only prince of gulls,
> Nor heard the ambiguous whisper of the sea.
>
> Used . . . used! Eating their morphine leaf,
> I breathed a cloud of self-congratulations
> To pillow me, while my boat slapped on the wharf
> And a gang of spiders scribbled invitations.

All right, my bully-boys, you who connived
My fall, I thank you for your dirty part,
I kiss you for each lie you took to wife
And for that salt you packed around my heart.

Good-bye, old things, I am forever lost!
My crazy vessel dances to the rail,
Sea-drunken since I left that barbarous coast,
The stain of anger spreading on my sail.

The manipulation of tone is the great strength of this poem, and tone is just that factor which makes a self-consciously mythic or conventional poem "personal" in the Kunitz sense.

Again, referring to the earlier metaphysical lyrics, we can recall a somber archness disturbingly in excess of the experience as it is offered to us in the poems. Here, the harshness is distributed on both sides of the lotus experience: the self-irony of "lolled," in the subtle shift to a confident irony toward his seducers in the third stanza. Kunitz alludes to the disease theme in the rather painful salt image and in the blood-wine stain at the end, but the infection of carnal and liquorous ecstasy becomes his moving force and even his emblem on the sail. He does not offer these figures as pre-contrived conceits, as a more obvious metaphysical poet would. Rather, they are not conceits at all: they emerge from the emotional logic of the poem's imagery. Again, keeping half an eye on the triumphant **"King of the River,"** it is the subordination of a rich—and thoroughly traditional—symbolic material to an original and active mind and heart caught moving through the contours of our fundamental experiences that characterizes the best Kunitz poems. Once this symbolic material has been established as the "connecting tissue" of the volume, we can, as if with libretto in hand, sway to the diverse emotional music.

One wants to say that **"Hermetic Poem"** is so "Roeth-kean," until one realizes how well it epitomizes this first theme of Kunitz:

The secret my heart keeps
Flows into cracked cups.

No saucer can contain
This overplus of mine:

It glisters to the floor,
Lashing like lizard fire

And ramps upon the walls
Crazy with ruby ills.

Who enters by my door
Is drowned, burned, stung and starred.

The reader suffers the four fates of the poem not in any indulgent disarray of poetic effects, but in a controlled perilous journey of a sensibility through appetite, to pain, to poetry.

Much as the first theme is of a journey through pain, the second is a journey through guilt; pain and guilt are the loci of the poetry. In this theme of guilt we may see a parallel development from an agonizing awareness, to a magniloquent vision of transcendence, and finally to a middle ground that does not undermine the vision but balances it with a subtler possibility of enduring a bitter, but liberating, tension between the guilt and the vision. Thus may the development be seen in bare outline, but as with the first theme, a very close reading of the poems reveals a complicated journey in and out of these three phases, with an emerging emphasis on the last phase toward the end of the volume and in the finest poems in *The Testing-Tree.*

As the pain came from love, so the guilt comes from time, and in **"The Signal from the House,"** the poet boldly announces the theme, and immediately casts it into its central metaphor. His "father's house" is the repository of ghosts who fail him, as we shall see, in not offering him a clear spiritual heritage, in not giving him a Word to take into the future, and whom he fails in his refusal or inability to make peace with them. The poems of what we might thus call the generation theme oscillate between these two failures, but it is the latter failure that provides the drama for this first announcement:

I said to the watcher at the gate,
"They also kill who wait."

I cried to the mourner on the stair,
"Mother, I hate you for those tears."

To mistress of the ruined hall,
The keeper of the sacred heart,

I bought the mind's indifference
And the heavy marble of my face.

For those who were too much with me
Were secretly against me:

Hostages to the old life,
Expecting to be ransomed daily

And for the same fond reason
From the deep prison of their person.

Their lantern shining in the window
had signaled me, like a cry of conscience,

Insisting that I must be broken
Upon the wheel of the unforsaken.

Aside from being another example of a work intensely personal while in no clear way being confessional, the poem succeeds as a conscious metaphysical conceit where earlier ones failed, in that again, it energizes an old form: here what we might call the dramatic reversal structure of such a George Herbert poem as "The Collar." The reversal arises from the speaker's defiant but uncertain attitude toward the dead, exemplified by his attitude to the mourners, whom he chides for mediating between him and the father he wants to forget but cannot. He resists identifying with the mourners—who are imagined as respectful worshippers as well as the bereaved—and adopts the pose of "marble indifference."

The action significantly connects with the well-known poem **"The Thief,"** in which Kunitz ultimately rejects the marble past of Rome for the squalid and fertile modern city that stands on its ruins. In **"The Signal from the House,"** the same pose is offered only to be shown in its futility. The undertone of guilt and paranoia at the center of the poem turns suddenly at the end to a direct acknowledgement of the wheel, the medieval torture of time to which he is committed. The father-haunted-house metaphor is woven into the metaphors of the sacred chapel and of the psychological kidnapping, and all merge in the final torture which the poet presents in impressive understatement. Here, as in the next poem of the theme, we begin with an ironic Miltonic echo, which reminds us at the end, that the poet must join those "waiting," enduring the responsibilities the unburied dead foist on us.

Now it is just this stance of serving and waiting that **"Open the Gates"** contradicts, and it is important to see this as a very deliberate contradiction, as Kunitz establishes the opposite pole of the theme. **"Open the Gates"** is a poem of visionary impatience with time, a storming of the door out of the haunted house and into heaven, and though its goal is rejected by later poems, it still stands as a brilliant, terse revelation of a *possibility*. Even if modified later, this possibility by its power, still maintains a constant valence in Kunitz's mind. Without this poem as opposite pole, even **"King of the River"** might be weakened in its dramatic placement in his canon:

> Within the city of the burning cloud,
> Dragging my life behind me in a sack,
> Naked I prowl, scourged by the black
> Temptation of the blood gone proud.
>
> Here at the monumental door,
> Carved with the curious legend of my youth,
> I brandish the great bone of my death,
> Beat once therewith and beat no more.
>
> The hinges groan: a rush of forms
> Shivers my name, wrenched out of me.
> I stand on the terrible threshold, and I see
> The end and the beginning in each other's arms.

The past, personal as well as cultural, is even more clearly a guilty burden in this poem. Kunitz creates an impersonal sense of visionary possibility of unity rising out of the personal theme of **"The Signal from the House,"** which is reiterated in the sense of skulking guilt and shame at the end of the first stanza here. An earlier poem, **"Among the Gods,"** had platonically celebrated "the sound / Of matter pouring through eternal forms," as if the music of that cascade will be his true poetry. In **"Open the Gates,"** in the final metamorphosis of the concluding scene of St. Augustine's *Confessions* into a brilliant, Yeatsian sexual metaphor, the process reverses, and the forms ecstatically

rush *out* of the speaker, and he stands, purged, before "the terrible threshold" through which he sees time embraced into a unity. The commitment to physicality in such poems as **"Among the Gods"** seems coldly abstract compared to the sexual excitement of the return to Platonic purity in **"Open the Gates,"** his **"Byzantium."**

The struggle with time and guilt continues in such well-known poems as **"For the Word Is Flesh"** and **"Father and Son,"** and in **"Goose Pond,"** where the poet literally returns to his childhood, his juncture with the past, the "detritus of his birth, / The rusted hoop, the broken wheels," until "He meets his childhood beating back / To find what furies made him man." **"Goose Pond"** gives us no new clues, but serves to sustain the search, for the poem promises that time has not died, that some life can be extracted from the past, however threatening. But **"Goose Pond"** also deliberately misleads us for a moment, by offering the seemingly irrefutable idea that memory is a key to redemption in or from time. Indeed, it begins to suggest that all past clues have misled us, the visionary, the hopeless, and resigned, as well as the Bacchic descent into the present in **"The Thief,"** though this last brings us close to the truth of the two lyrics in which the poet finds his deepest meaning. For in **"The Scourge"** and **"Last Words,"** he lays out a principle of endurance, which rejects memory as sterile and vision as quixotic and finally sterile too; here the poet reaches a mature recognition of the need to commit himself to time, and to the mystery of the process of generation that will give sons who may understand him no more than he understood his father; the sustenance of generation itself will become his main value.

"Last Words" is a self-colloquy on the theme of transience, and like **"The Scourge,"** it resolves into a new maturity of acceptance. He arises "from sleep's long pillow" at the end of the imagined journey of life, and it is worth noting that we have here neither the apocalyptic jump out of the time of **"Open the Gates"** nor the desolate waste of time of the "father" poems:

> The colors of the world are permanent
> Despite the bleach of change. Pure stain on stain,
> The bow of light's eternal forms is bent
> Across steep heaven in the general brain.

The color of stain, of mortal suffering, subtly blends into Platonic purity, and "stain on stain" becomes the figure of the sequence of generation, which he sees now not as a blind reproductive cycle, but as a grand Lawrentian rainbow. In the third stanza, he chides himself for the melodramatic lament, "Who cries, The beautiful, the proud, are fallen! / (O silly child it was myself that cried.)" And we see how at the end the personal stain becomes the pure form of stain when it merges into a "general pattern," when he sees mortal suffering as, not the agony of the individual, but as a stage in the history of his race:

Our little strength, our beauty, and our pride

Are for the race to keep; we can discover
Secrets with our broken skulls; our dead feet run
Under the lid of earth that closes over
The generations marching to the sun.

The affirmation requires a faith—a faith in the impercep-
tible, buried pattern of generation that gives meaning to
our experience: as in Eliot's "bedded axle-tree," the history of the race is enacted in a chthonic movement, and it
may take the battering of our skulls, literally or figuratively,
to merge with that movement. But Kunitz affirms that the
movement is there, and as the generations march to the
sun, I think we see the sun not as the sudden apocalypse
out of time, but as the light of truth which guides our
generational progress. It is neither a blind nitrogen cycle
of the race, nor Yeats's Nietzschean recurrence, but a
stately dance to the music of time.

"The Scourge" also pits melodrama against faithful acceptance, and perhaps even more successfully, because of
the lucid opposition of the two voices in the poem. We
have a debate between "heart" and what we might call
"self," parallel in some ways to Yeats's great dialogue,
where, too, a self suggesting wholeness of vision must
defend itself against a soul-heart that mournfully or
melodramatically demands death:

My heart felt need to die,
Our dusty time had come;
I said, "Endure the lie,
The waste, the tedium."

My heart sank to his knees,
Schooled in the tragic style,
But I, being out of heart,
Whipped him another mile,

And not because I cared
To let that actor go,
But only that I feared
His eternal No, No, No.

We see the poet, with brilliant simplicity, putting the poetry
of high vision into the perspective to which it has been
tending all along as Kunitz possesses his poetic middle
way: the "heart" is first, a mere actor, second, by implication, a "hypochondriac" of the kind described in **"For the
Word Is Flesh,"** and finally, and this is crucial for Kunitz,
less a voice of affirmation than of nihilism, a denier that
the World is flesh. But the self makes its point by allowing
the heart to enact its melodrama of visionary nihilism,
with surprising results:

Beyond the covered bridge
The crooked road turned wild;
He rose at the season's edge,
Passionate and defiled,

Plucking the remnant leaf
Stained with the only good,
While all my children leaped
Out of the glowing wood.

This great ending is clearly a response to the challenge of
"Open the Gates." Instead of an embrace of beginning
and end, we get a burst into an infinite future. Like the
speaker of **"Open the Gates,"** the heart jumps across the
threshold toward death, yet here it is not a "monumental
door," but a crooked road and a covered, obscured passage. And instead of beating the cold bone of death, the
poet re-enacts the plucking of the golden bough. Only, the
gold is the stain of the blood of generation, "the only
good," and the gush of blood is the gush of the generations marching again to the sun. The great achievement of
"The Scourge" is to establish an ethic of endurance in a
poetic vision which is really more violently thrilling than
the vision of apocalypse he is implicitly rejecting.

Selected Poems, Kunitz tells us, is classified into themes
and arguments, and the absence of chronological structure
teases us into abstracting a line of development that the arrangement of poems may obscure. As such, having
discerned the two basic themes of disease and generation,
we may have to add a third, not just to tie our two themes
into a conclusion, but to account for a number of impressive poems which fall in between or outside these themes.
Let us call it the theme of monstrosity.

Kunitz has explicitly defined for us a concept of the
contemporary artist as a potential monster:

What is it in our culture that drives so many artists and
writers to suicide—or, failing that, mutilates them
spiritually? At the root of the problem is the cruel
discrepancy between the values of art and the values of
society, which makes strangers and adversaries out of
those who are most gifted and vulnerable. The artist
who turns in on himself, feeds off his own psyche, ag-
grandizes his bruised ego, is on the way to monsterdom. Ambition is the fire in his gut. No sacrifice is
judged too great for his art. At a certain point the
becomes a nexus of abstract sensations and powers,
beyond the realm of the personal.

He then refers to two poems in particular, **"Approach to
Thebes,"** and **"The Artist,"** from ***The Testing-Tree,*** which
elaborate this notion. The Oedipus figure of the latter poem
lives to tell his story, and so, though "spiritually mutilated"
by his incest with his "flagrant source" (the pun suggests,
in terms of the generation theme, the dangers of the beginning and the end embracing), survives as a poet to
bequeath his monstrous legend to his posterity. And such
would be a tolerable notion of the role of the poet, as be-
queather except we see a more terrifying picture of the
poet as monster in Mark Rothko's suicide in **"The Artist,"** and most especially in an amazing poem that Kunitz
does not mention, **"Prophecy on Lethe."**

Echo, the beating of the tide,
Infringes on the blond curved shore;
Archaic weeds from sleep's green side
Bind skull and pelvis till the four
Seasons of the blood are unified.

Anonymous sweet carrion,
Blind mammal floating on the stream

Of depthless sound, completely one
In the cinnamon-dark of no dream—
A pod of silence, bursting when the sun

Clings to the forehead, will surprise
The gasping turtle and the leech
With your strange brain blooming as it lies
Abandoned to the bipeds on the beach;
Your jelly-mouth and, crushed, your polyp eyes.

A poem like this may explain why the poet resists what he calls elsewhere "the Faustian dog that chews my penitential bones," why he resists a poetry of visionary prophecy, to which he is clearly attracted, why he sets against the great monsters of poetry such figures as William Carlos Williams and Boris Pasternak "who were whole, who excelled in their humanity, who fulfilled themselves in the life as well as in the work." It explains, in fact, the whole middle way of Kunitz's poetry, a refusal to embrace "the Truth" so violently that he will ruin himself into abstracted monsterhood—the danger being, of course, that it *is* the truth that he fears. But the poet is honest enough to acknowledge what he is willing and not willing to do, and **"Prophecy on Lethe"** suggests that he has come close enough to the terror of the truth to know what he would choose to keep clear of.

"Prophecy" makes monstrosity much more precise and suicidal than **"Approach to Thebes."** It alludes to the myth of Echo and Narcissus and makes the poet a bit of each, doomed to inwardness, reduced to two separate parts: a carrion and a voice. Like Oedipus, the implicit poet figure bequeaths a poetic legend to posterity. The bequest turns out to be his own frightening monster-self, tossed on the shore of normal reality from the sea of Truth—inward truth—that the self has descended to. It is swollen, decayed, contorted; it has seen some Medusa, and it cannot tell the story but only offer itself as a warning. Yet the warning cannot even be heard or understood, since the animal imagery or the poem pictures the poet as having passed into a wholly new species, inexplicable to "the bipeds on the beach." He has passed, in fact, all the way through poetry to silence, the visionary embrace having separated itself from the voice it left underwater. Instead of the beginning and the end in each other's arms, we get the "skull and pelvis" bound and blurred beyond human recognition and denied voice and vision. The heroic poet has been harmonized into grotesquerie. Kunitz acknowledges that not every poet can be a monster, that it "takes a special kind of greatness," such as Sylvia Plath had, and here we have the poet's refusing to join what has become the post-confessional suicidal school. We can only say that if it seems he lacks that "greatness," his poetry is ennobled nevertheless by the way he refuses to desire it.

So perhaps the truest final note of *Selected Poems* comes in the wry realism of **"Revolving Meditation,"** which tries to put poetry into a perspective of the larger question of the whole, healthy life, arguing that there may be something "beyond all this fiddle."

Imagination makes
Out of what stuff it can,
An action fit
For a more heroic stage
Than body ever walked on.
I have learned,
Trying to live
With this perjured quid of mine,
That the truth is not in the stones,
But in the architecture;

Kunitz is willing to risk that his poetry may suffer the consequences of his believing that mere is something worth more than poetry, though it is that risk which ironically produces many of his best poems. To those who cry for a leap into the Truth, he responds:

But I fly towards Possibility, . . .

Careless that I am bound
To the flaming wheel of my bones,
Preferring to hear, as I
Am forced to hear,
The voice of the solitary
Who makes others less alone,
The dialogue of lovers,
And the conversation of two worms
In the beam of a house,
Their mouths filled with sawdust.

We can relate the worm-riddled house to the Broken Tower here, and see the poet making what he can of the decaying process, which is also the march of pure stain upon stain toward the sun. He wants poetry to bring him fulfillment *in* life, not beyond or beneath it.

The Testing-Tree shows us some of that fulfillment in the possibilities of poetry once the struggle with "the brave god" has been relaxed, the battles for the truth over. **"The Artist,"** the poem on Rothko, provides us with a bridge to Kunitz's latest volume, since it reassures us that the poet is now beyond any interest in self-consumption:

At last he took a knife in his hand
and slashed an exit for himself
between the frames of his tall scenery.
Through the holes of his tattered universe
the first innocence and the light
came pouring in.

It takes a full appreciation of the early Kunitz to receive the full ironic bite of those lines. The artist here is denied even the grotesque legacy of **"Prophecy on Lethe"**; he achieves not even destruction, but pure dissolution. *The Testing-Tree* is the offering of a poet who has learned—and hopefully taught—his lesson, and the appealing personal—*not* confessional—warmth of the volume is a model of what a deliberately, maturely limited aesthetic can produce.

"Illumination," which in some ways recapitulates **"Open the Gates,"** uses a light tone to make a serious new point about the possibilities of vision—in fact, to deliberately deepen the ambivalence of the value and feasibility of the visionary embrace he once tried so resolutely to assert. The poet here, with obvious irony, catalogs the ills of his life:

> the parent I denied,
> the friends I failed,
> the hearts I spoiled,
> including at least
> my own left ventricle—

Then, with even subtler irony, the illumination is promised, but not delivered. And yet the poem leaves him—and us—with the strangest feeling that perhaps the illumination was accomplished—but not as intended:

> "Dante!" I cried
> to the apparition
> entering from the hall,
> laureled and gaunt,
> in a cone of light.
> "Out of mercy you came
> To be my Master
> and my guide!"
> To which he replied:
> "I know neither the time
> nor the way
> nor the number on the door . . .
> but this must be my room,
> I was here before."
> And he held up in his hand
> the key,
> which blinded me.

This poem subsumes all the conflicts about vision shaping the earlier poetry in a healthy irony exactly opposed to the deadly irony of his Auden-influenced work. Having moved among extremes of feeling and thought, the poet has created as the great sanity and health-inducing element of his poetry the manipulation of tone as the great limiter and negotiator among extremes. There is a lessened risk here; after all, **"The Artist"** did see a light the poet cannot allow into this poetry. But Kunitz finds ample poetic freedom in dramatizing the vicissitudes of the mind and heart tracing out their boundaries, and his subtlest and most mature manipulation of tone is also his most lucid map of the geography of the mind and heart, and finally the richest poem of his career.

"King of the River" fuses the emotional intensity of the early poems with the terse and yet conversational style of the other poems of this volume. It is his most distilled statement and most finely crafted lyric. Ironically, both Kunitz and Lowell (in "Waking Early Sunday Morning") have been moved by Yeats to write about *salmon*. Yeats, a great influence on the early poems, may be seen as an antagonist here. "Sailing to Byzantium" itself is, of course, ambivalent in its nostalgia and desire for the fish-filled sensual river of generation—or we might say simply its nostalgia *for* desire. But the thrust of Yeats's poem is to assert the primacy of monuments of unaging intellect as the right goal of the imagination. Kunitz, in effect, is

reconstituting Yeats's "Dialogue of Self and Soul" and throwing it in the face of Byzantium, by actively committing himself to corruption. The bruised, battered human muscle of Kunitz's poem, "glazed with madness," is only slightly less grotesque in physical form than the polyp-eyed corpse of **"Prophecy on Lethe,"** yet it becomes a figure not of terror, but of heroic endurance and imagination. The poet embraces, not the dissolving of the beginning into the end, but his constant oscillation on the "two-way ladder / between heaven and hell." And the waving orchestration of the poem, parallel to the coiling and uncoiling of this generative human muscle, celebrates the same ambiguities of his attitude toward time and eternity. Kunitz renews Yeats's "fecund ditch" in his "orgiastic pool," and the rapid and almost grotesque birth, copulation, and aging to ward death of the salmon becomes the happiest metaphor of the poet's career. As in **"The Illumination,"** where he subsumed the dilemma over vision, here he perfectly dramatizes the tensions of nostalgia and desire in the contours of the verse—in the "if-but-then" sequence which builds irony into the very structure of the poem:

> If the power were granted you
> to break out of your cells,
> but the imagination fails
> and the doors of the senses close
> on the child within,
> you would dare to be changed,
> as you are changing now,
> into the shape you dread
> beyond the merely human.

The finest irony of all is that the visionary poet fails to see that the shape he aspires to assume, he may be assuming all his life. To be visionary for Kunitz is to want orgiastic death, which is what we are having all along if we will slow down our senses to notice. Normal experience is all the orgy toward death a poet needs, and all the monstrosity he can afford. We are going nowhere as rapidly and as grandiloquently as we need to, so to endure is to be as apocalyptic as we need be.

Notes

1. This and all subsequent quoted comments of Kunitz are extracted from "Imagine Wrestling with an Angel: An Interview with Stanley Kunitz," Robert Boyers, interviewer, in *Salmagundi* (Spring-Summer, 1973), pp. 71–83. Quotations from Kunitz's poems are from: *Selected Poems, 1928–1958* (Boston, 1958). *The Testing-Tree* (Boston, 1970).

2. "The Poetry of Stanley Kunitz," in Edward S. Hungerford, *Poets in Progress* (Evanston, 1962).

3. "The Testing of Stanley Kunitz," *Iowa Review* 3 (Winter, 1972).

Andrew Motion (review date 2 November 1979)

SOURCE: "Dazzling," in *New Statesman*, November 2, 1979, pp. 686–87.

[*In the following review of* The Poems of Stanley Kunitz, 1928–1978, *Motion finds shortcomings in Kunitz's early work, though cites redeeming qualities in his later poetry.*]

[W. B.] Yeats is usually cited as the exception who proves the rule that most poets, after peaking somewhere in their 30s, steadily deteriorate as they get older. And Yeats, it seems, is mainly responsible for making Stanley Kunitz another such odd-man-out. If the early work in *The Poems of Stanley Kunitz, 1928–1978* is anything to go by, its author's development was severely retarded by admiration for Innisfree and its environs. In recent years, however, he's stopped winding himself in 'the bright thread of a dream,' and turned his back on myth kitties. The first third of the book—it's arranged in reverse chronology—is consistently unillusioned and contains the rewards of half a century's effort to establish a durably sincere style and poetic personality.

But even while discovering his greatest strengths as a pragmatic realist, Kunitz is tormented by some aspects of his original romanticism. Inflated rhetoric and exaggerated self-consciousness are still liable to compromise him when he writes with an entirely straight face. He's obviously aware of this problem himself—'I am not what I was,' he says in **'The Layers,'** 'though some principle of being / abides'—and has adopted an increasingly wry tone of humour to cure it. This isn't used to evade seriousness, but to register its unavoidably preposterous, embarrassing and comic aspects. In doing so it enlarges the human application of poems like **'River Road'** or **'Signs and Portents,'** and thereby enlists a greater degree of sympathy than his earlier and more unremitting gravities.

Vernon Young (review date 22 November 1979)

SOURCE: "It Makes You Wonder," in *New York Review of Books,* November 22, 1979, pp. 39–41.

[*In the following review, Young provides an overview of Kunitz's literary contributions and analyses of several exemplary poems from* The Poetry of Stanley Kunitz, 1928–1978.]

While some poets can be read exclusively in their poems, without our having recourse to anything else written by them, or without our knowing anything of their biography, this is not the case with Stanley Kunitz. Mr. Kunitz has been for many years of a long life a busy man of letters; his achievements as editor, teacher, reviewer, and translator are worthy ones. Yet these are, perhaps, less dramatic qualifications for fame than having died young or become a political activist or written a manifesto denouncing all American poets influenced by T. S. Eliot.

To report that Mr. Kunitz has published five volumes of poems (the present one [The Poems of Stanley Kunitz, 1928-1978] includes new poems which he calls **"The Layers"**), that he received the Pulitzer Prize for his 1928–1958 collection, that he has been Consultant to the Library of Congress, lectured at several universities, and ably translated poems by Akhmatova and Voznesensky: all this, though it locates him for those who are casual readers of poetry and endows his name with intellectual respectability, is, in some sense, inadequate.

Stanley Kunitz is not a monumental poet, nor is he a spectacular one; he is notable for his intelligence, and intelligence tends to wait a longer time for recognition or acquires it within a relatively limited circle. If Mr. Kunitz had never written a poem, he would be a hero in my books for having been the co-editor of *Twentieth Century Authors,* a reference work I have hunted in vain to buy since I first discovered it on the shelves of the Royal Library in Stockholm. An encyclopedic record of its subject, crammed with personal histories frequently supplied by the authors represented, it has refreshing critical estimates that support or challenge the reputations enshrined. There is no publication to replace it, no other biographical dictionary known to me which is at the same time so copious, anecdotal, and judicious. These volumes are not listed on the credits page of the book under review, perhaps because Mr. Kunitz himself may not value them as highly as I do.

Among his other valuable contributions, in my opinion, are certain short reviews which are included in a book of his essays and conversations entitled *A Kind of Order, A Kind of Folly* (Little, Brown, 1975). These are seldom longer than six pages, sometimes only three; they are a relief from much of the exegetical pomposity around us. In small compass Kunitz manages to capture the qualities of, among others, Wallace Stevens, Conrad Aiken, Robinson Jeffers, Marianne Moore, Louise Bogan, Randall Jarrell, and, above all, Theodore Roethke, whose work he has since written about with strong insight.

The record stands, honorable and useful. If there have been moments, either in his verse or in his prose, when Mr. Kunitz has appeared to prefer the consuming blaze to the measured view, he has confessed sooner or later, that such has not been his fate, save within the domain of metaphor.

> Formal verse is a highly selective medium. A high style wants to be fed exclusively on high sentiments. Given the kind of person I am, I came to see the need for a middle style—for a low style, even, though that may be outside my range.

By a low style, I infer that he means a form of address more idiomatic than any he has himself used.

Among the earliest poems represented here (from the 1930 collection) is one called **"I Dreamed that I Was Old,"** in which the poet was already shedding a histrionic tear for the wisdom which he felt confident he would later acquire—"in stale declension / Fallen from my prime, when company / Was mine, cat-nimbleness, and green invention. . . ." Obviously he was then deciding that sweet as are the green inventions and the visceral energies of youth, the crown of life is not ecstasy but wisdom. If I say that the intellectual bent which led him into the complementary duties of teaching and criticism is a marked feature of his poetry, I am not implying that his verse is lacking in sensuousness or conflict, only that in it Apollo has the upper hand to Dionysus. Three poems, from three periods of his work, will better epitomize what I want to point out than a spate of short quotations.

"Father and Son" (in the 1944 volume) was, I take it, a decisive poem in his development, wherein, whatever else is going on, the pursuit of the lost father is described with intense anguish and is finally relinquished. From its lyrical opening,

> Now in the suburbs and the falling light
> I followed him, and now down sandy road
> Whiter than bone-dust, through the sweet
> Curdle of fields, where the plums
> Dropped with their load of ripeness . . .

it rises to a clamor of dependence and invocation:

> At the water's edge, where the smothering ferns lifted
> Their arms, "Father!" I cried, "Return! You know
> The way. . . .
>   Instruct
> Your son, whirling between two wars,
> In the Gemara of your gentleness,
> For I would be a child to those who mourn
> And brother to the foundlings of the field
> And friend of innocence and all bright eyes.
> O teach me how to work and keep me kind."

If the poem had ended there we might have justifiably regarded it as poised between sentiment and *schmalz*. The two lines that in fact and beautifully terminate it—

> Among the turtles and the lilies he turned to me
> The white ignorant hollow of his face

—staunch the flow, seal the wound, cancel the outcry, save the poem.

Thereafter, the most effective poems are those in which the personal lament is diverted during the course of the recital by an abrupt shift of attention or by a willed inclusion of qualifying details—as in **"The Thief,"** where, having been robbed of his wallet in Rome, the poet fats his revenge by mingling imprecation with a cold eye cast at the history which, in the form of lantern slides, had seduced him into going to Rome in the first place.

> But the past that tempted me, the frozen pure,
> Was a pedagogic lie. All's motion here,
> And motion like emotion is impure,
> A flower flawed by mutability,
> Religion by its ruins, and yet thereby
> More lovely and more graced, perhaps
> More true.

Losing ground in his argument, he revises his description, relating the cynical present to the voluptuary past:

> . . . the assassin motorcyclists charge,
> Wolves prowl in the streets under arcades of bells,
> Tiberius grovels through his dungeon halls
> Dreaming of boy-sized fishes in his bath.

He fails to resolve his anger at the situation—it cannot be resolved except by time—but he resolves the *poem,* with an adroitly uncompromised finale that retains to the last the belligerence of his dialogue with "Mater Cloaca."

> Here in my blistered room
> Where the wind flaps my ceiling like a sail
> (A miracle, no doubt, to be left at that!)
> I recognize the gods' capricious hand
> And write this poem for money, rage, and love.

Kunitz's most impressive poem is, I think, **"The Approach to Thebes,"** a judgment which I don't impose on other readers as, "objective" (if objectivity is either important or possible). I happen to admire poems in which a personal agony is transformed by assimilation in a historical—or mythic, it's the Oedipus story—setting. The opening lines are as close to a baroque diction as Kunitz ever wrote; every modifier is unusual and irrevocable.

> In the zero of the night, in the lipping hour,
> Skin-time, knocking-time, when the heart is pearled
> And the moon squanders its uranian gold,
> She taunted me, who was all music's tongue,
> Philosophy's and wilderness's breed,
> Of shifting shape, half jungle-cat, half-dancer,
> Night's woman-petaled, lion-scented rose. . . .

With regrets that I can't quote all the splendor of the poem, I cut to the end of the first section, where the compensatory satisfaction is followed, in the next passage, by the traditional judgment:

> I can bear the dishonor now of growing old.
> Blinded and old, exiled, diseased, and scorned—
> The verdict's bitten on the brazen gates.

Then comes, line by line, the reversal, the crescendo of self-revelation.

> Children, grandchildren, my long posterity,
> To whom I bequeath the spiders of my dust,
> Believe me, whatever sordid tales you hear,
> Told by physicians or mendacious scribes,
> Of beardless folly, consanguineous bust,
> Fomenting pestilence, rebellion, war,
> I come prepared, unwanting what I see,
> But tied to life. On the royal road to Thebes
> I had my luck, I met a lovely monster,
> And the story's this: I made the monster me.

I'd call that wholly successful as poetic impersonation and moral subtlety. And it is allied with what seems to me to be the central obsession in Kunitz's poetry, if obsession is an appropriate figure for verse that respects "the need for a middle style": the conviction that at some strategic moment, which only the self knows, the poet (the artist) must "[slash] an exit for himself"—that is, from the ordered medium and the dissimulation, in order to express (and in this context he quotes Ortega y Gasset) "the terror of facing single-handed . . . the ferocious assaults of existence." From a later collection (***The Testing-Tree,*** 1971), **"The Artist"** crucially embodies the strategy.

> His paintings grew darker every year.
> They filled the walls, they filled the room;
> eventually they filled his world—
> all but the ravishment.
> When voices faded, he would rush to hear
> the scratched soul of Mozart
> endlessly in gyre.
> Back and forth, back and forth,
> he paced the paint-smeared floor,
> diminishing in size each time he turned,
> trapped in his monumental void,
> raving against his adversaries.
> At last he took a knife in his hand
> and slashed an exit for himself
> between the frames of his tall scenery.
> Through the holes of his tattered universe
> the first innocence and the light
> came pouring in.

Clearly, the setting of this poem derived from Kunitz's infatuation with nonfigurative painters, though the subject of the poem need not be limited to that reference. The many compliments this poet-critic has produced for prominent painters must have flattered them, but Kunitz's art criticism has remained literary, and I fear that he contributed more than his share to that transcendental vocabulary enlisted to praise the canvases of Mark Rothko.

Concerning the poem itself, as aesthetic doctrine; the extent to which liberation—or "innocence and the light"—may be purchased by slashing an exit, and plucking bright honor from the pale-faced moon, is arguable. I don't myself believe the unpaintable can be painted (God knows they've tried it) or the last unspeakable word spoken. I don't think Stanley Kunitz believes so either. I think he appreciates the rhetoric of freedom in aesthetic gestures because it has a political ring. In his practice, as I have noted, he observes the central amenities. This is to say: he prefers lucidity to excruciating difficulty (note that **"The Approach to Thebes"** is grounded on iambic pentameter and that **"The Artist,"** neither spasmodic nor vehement, consists of six complete sentences in sequential order); he shows a classical respect for the pulse of nature in art (he has stated, "For the poet, even breathing comes under the heading of prosody"); and he almost invariably judges the experience in the poem, even while he is conveying it. Conspicuous, in the most convincing of Stanley Kunitz's poems, is the tension produced in them by a controlled inhibition of the passion that threatens to break through.

Alan Brownjohn (review date April 1980)

SOURCE: "Contour Lines," in *Encounter,* Vol. LIV, No. 4, April, 1980, pp. 62–66.

[*In the following excerpt, Brownjohn offers a positive assessment of* The Poems of Stanley Kunitz, 1928–1978.]

It's been easy for English readers to tell which selected American poets have been most influential on this side of the Atlantic in recent years; harder to know who they have been selected *from*. There is (there almost always has been) a dearth of good, explanatory anthologies, even those with axes to grind; so the map of present-day American poetry is difficult to draw. Its two poles are clearly marked, because they are the places at which English poets leaning towards the United States have been most eager to cluster: around the "avant-garde" at one end and the "academic," "Europeanised" poets at the other. (The categories are gross simplifications, but they have been only too usable for English poets—and they do in fact relate quite plausibly to that basic division into redskins and palefaces.) But the land between the poles is wide and indistinct, a terrain where vaguely respected names appear like distant cities, too shadowy for their age, geography or customs to be made out with any certainty.

The best we get is occasional shafts of light on this scene, often in the form of guilty reminders of what we have allowed ourselves to miss. Stanley Kunitz's collected poems [***The Poems of Stanley Kunitz, 1928–1978***], for example, is a remarkable achievement by any standards; his anti-chronological arrangement of the poems allows the reader to choose between beginning with new poems "and stepping back to my start"; or to try out the experiment of reading a book backwards. The last pages of the book contain work (just contemporary with late Hart Crane and just after most of John Crowe Ransom) of considerable formal gravity and command, a little severe on its own romantic inclinations, yet already impressively confident. Further back, in the poems of the war years and after, his range widens, to include the sensuous, the ironical, and the disquieting ("'Rover!' I call my fourfoot home, / Whose only language is a growl; / Dig up old bones, but he won't come / That chose the world; it is more foul.") And back further still, towards the present, Kunitz is drawing into his own work some of the strengths of the European poets he is translating with unobtrusive distinction, Mandelstam and Ungaretti among them. In the present, at the end of the book which is really the beginning, he is writing in a flexible yet controlled free verse hammered out of years of dedication to the hard graft of formal versification: something suited equally to scenes from the American past (and occasionally the landscape of today) and to personal meditations on age and death.

Such a control, so traditional a kind of meticulous calculation, is not the point at all for certain American poets who have adopted a different kind of discipline. Since the deaths during the last three years of Robert Lowell, Allen Tate and Elizabeth Bishop, writers such as Kenneth Koch, John Ashbery and John Hollander can almost be advanced into a "senior" generation; but, to the astonishment and disappointment of their admirers in Britain, they remain for most readers in this country part of the great undiscovered territory. Read their work aloud in groups of knowledgeable aspirants (I have done this often in creative writing workshops in the English outback) and you raise only bewilderment, at best, among those who can take, say, Ginsberg at one extreme, and Wilbur at the other. Clearly something very new and unfamiliar is going on, so it's necessary to discount it for its eccentricity, or its flippant approach to serious matters like the shaping of imaginative effusions into proper forms, or its occasionally extravagant length. It's a poetry which puzzles, and disturbs, and calls out defences. So the chances are it might be good.

Peter Stitt (review date September 1980)

SOURCE: "The Ineluctable Signature of Stanley Kunitz," in *Poetry,* Vol. CXXXVI, No. 6, September, 1980, pp. 347–51.

[*In the following review of* The Poems of Stanley Kunitz, 1928–1978, *Stitt argues that Kunitz's greatest strength lies in his high-minded rhetorical style, rather than the "middle" or "low" style associated with confessional poetry and Kunitz's professed democratic sympathies.*]

Although Stanley Kunitz was awarded the Pulitzer Prize in 1959 for his *Selected Poems,* he is best known for the revolution in his style which occurred with the poems of *The Testing-Tree,* published in 1971. Robert Lowell (echoing virtually all the criticism devoted to Kunitz since that time) praised the volume for reflecting what he called "the drift of the age," a movement away from tortured formality towards prosaic relaxation, away from metaphor and indirection towards clarity, the literal truth, Kunitz himself explained the change in this way: "A high style wants to be fed exclusively on high sentiments. Given the kind of person I am, I came to see the need for a middle style—for a low style, even, though that may be outside my range." The statement correctly assumes that the voice of a poem ought in some way to reflect the personality of the poet; the style, after all, is the man.

I think we have a generally accurate notion of the kind of man Stanley Kunitz is. Much of his poetry is politically based, and his stance is consistently democratic; he sides with the people against the tyrants. He has, in short, far greater affinity with the middle or low than with the high. But it is a curious fact that the flattest, least satisfying—even least characteristic—poems in this volume [*The Poems of Stanley Kunitz, 1928–1978*] are the political poems and the translations (which are themselves almost exclusively political, coming from such writers as Akhmatova, Mandelstam, and Yevtushenko). Among the rest of the more recent poems, the weakest are consistently those that most adamantly display the low or middle style; such poems as **"Words for the Unknown Makers," "My Sisters,"** and **"Journal for My Daughter"** are simple, clear, literal and trivial, obvious, boring. In point of fact,

Kunitz is at his best today, and has always been at his best, when writing in an elevated, rhetorical style.

The trouble with Kunitz's justification of his change in method lies in its first sentence, where the poet describes what he is rejecting: "A high style wants to be fed exclusively on high sentiments." We will soon be looking at the high style, but for now must ask—what are high sentiments? Kunitz makes his early work sound like a series of lofty moral maxims, suitable for high-toned greeting cards or Victorian tea parties. In truth, the elevation visible in his strongest poems comes not from their high sentiments but from the powerful range of emotions which they enunciate. I would amend the sentence to read thus: Powerful emotions in verse are best presented through a powerful and rhetorical style. Whatever his social and political commitments, Kunitz is not a man of tepid emotions, and his more tranquil and reflective poems, which appear most frequently in his later work, virtually disappear under the fog of their blandness. For example, these lines from **"My Sisters"**:

> I had two sisters once
> with long black hair
> who walked apart from me
> and wrote the history of tears.
> Their story's faded with their names,
> but the candlelight they carried,
> like dancers in a dream,
> still flickers on their gowns
> as they bend over me
> to comfort my night-fears.

The lines were chosen for quotation because they do contain some emotion and some life; not enough, however, to transform the poem into anything more than a touching exercise in remembrance.

For contrast, let us look at another of the most recent poems—**"The Knot,"** which in fact opens this volume:

> I've tried to seal it in,
> that cross-grained knot
> on the opposite wall,
> scored in the lintel of my door,
> but it keeps bleeding through
> into the world we share.
> Mornings when I wake,
> curled in my web,
> I hear it come
> with a rush of resin
> out of the trauma
> of its lopping-off.
> Obstinate bud,
> sticky with life,
> mad for the rain again,
> it racks itself with shoots
> that crackle overhead,
> dividing as they grow.
> Let be! Let be!
> I shake my wings
> and fly into its boughs.

This powerful lyric is dramatic in tone, and takes its strength from the skillful manipulation of several poetic devices. Perhaps the first thing that strikes the reader is the insistence of the rhythm; the lines are loosely iambic and vary from three beats to two beats in length. The stress pattern is made more prominent through heavy use of assonance, consonance, and internal rhyme. The individual sentences open with strong, dramatic phrases and end abruptly, always at the end of a line.

In the way it handles meaning, the poem is not literal, not direct, not in any way plain; it is, rather, firmly grounded in the suggestive obliquity of metaphor. The message, to which Kunitz has a strong emotional commitment, concerns growth, rebirth, freedom, a release back into life from dormancy. The painted-over knot is (against reality) allowed this process, in part through the agency of the speaker's dream. As for the speaker himself, his role is presented in terms of a sleeping caterpillar ("curled in my web") that emerges to "shake my wings / and fly." The story the poem tells is archetypal, even mythic, and is very similar to that told inmost of Kunitz's best poems. He has described the pattern himself, with great accuracy: ". . . my impulse towards form generally tends to move along the lines of certain ineluctable archetypes, particularly those of death and rebirth, the quest, and the night-journey (or descent into the underworld). In all three patterns— which may be consubstantial—the progress is from a kind of darkness into a kind of light." This pattern (the three paths are indeed consubstantial) is especially prominent in the earlier work. When it is absent from the later work, the poems suffer from a lack of both thematic and artistic intensity; and when it is present there, as in **"The Knot,"** we suddenly see the true consistency in this man's art and life.

Kunitz's poems are delivered in an impressively authoritative voice; issues are heightened and generalized as in, say, the King James Bible. We could almost think at times that we were listening to one of the Old Testament prophets or chroniclers. An important part of this effect is owing to the narrative form in which the poems are cast; they are spoken almost in the form of parables. This quality is apparent in the opening lines of many poems, as we are plunged into what looks to be a timeless story of universal relevance. For example, each of these passages is the opening to a different poem:

> Time swings her burning hands
> I saw him going down
> Into those mythic lands . . .

> Soul of my soul, in the ancestral wood
> Where all the trees were loosened of their leaves
> I strayed . . .

> Within the city of the burning cloud,
> Dragging my life behind me in a sack,
> Naked I prowl . . .

> Concentrical, the universe and I
> Rotated on God's crystal axletree . . .

Often, the ensuing poem will turn out to have only the portentous tone and form of a parable; what actually is described may be altogether more mundane, as in the poem—utterly typical of Kunitz—**"No Word"**:

> Through portal and through peristyle
> Her phantom glides, whose secret mouth,
> The absence of whose flagrant smile,
> Hangs on my chimney like a wreath of cloud.

> I prod the coals; my tortured faith
> Kneels in the blaze on melting paws;
> Jeweled with tears, the lonely beast
> Bequeaths me irony and claws.

> No message. May the mothering dark,
> Whose benediction calms the sea,
> Abater of the atrocious spark
> Of love and love's anxiety,

> Be kind; and may my self condone,
> As surely as my judge reprieves,
> This heart strung on the telephone,
> Folded in death, whom no voice revives.

The apocalyptic tone of the poem—a common tone in Kunitz—issues from a not-very-exceptional situation: the death is that of a love affair; the complaint is that the beloved does not, will not, telephone. What gives the poem its considerable energy is the emotion of the speaker, which Kunitz translates into rhetoric and metaphor. We note in passing his heavy reliance on adjectives—general in his poems—"secret mouth," "flagrant smile," "tortured faith," "melting paws," "lonely beast," "mothering dark," "atrocious spark"—a technique that would ruin a plainer poem.

Kunitz learned his trade largely from the seventeenth-century British metaphysical poets—Donne and Herbert to be sure, but also their more baroque followers, Crashaw, Vaughan, Carew. In many passages illustrating this debt, we are reminded of another debt as well. Theodore Roethke was an early admirer of Kunitz; throughout the life of the younger, and more famous, poet, they nurtured one another with their work. It isn't always easy to say who influenced whom, but in lines like these from Kunitz, the similarities are nakedly evident:

> Air thickens to dirt.
> Great hairy seeds that soar aloft
> Like comets trailing tender spume
> Break in the night with soft
> Explosions into bloom.
> Where the fleshed root stirs . . .

There is a hyperbolic quality to most of Kunitz's work, as the passages I have quoted surely show. His love of rhetoric, metaphor, parable, the lushness of imagery and sound, is forever pushing him to the extreme edge of the possibilities of language. Such excess is of his essence, and shows his singularity. He has never been short on self-knowledge, and has always had the wisdom to keep faith in himself, his voice. When nearly all the participants in a symposium on the poem **"Father and Son"** objected strenuously to one of its lines—"The night nailed like an orange to my brow"—Kunitz defended himself at some length, and concluded: "Such moments in a poem, evident only by the pressure building behind them, can never fully explain themselves, but the poet must take his risk with them as an article of faith. In the end, for whatever it may be worth, they constitute his signature." We can only be grateful to Stanley Kunitz for the courage he has shown throughout his career. The risks he has taken have ever sprung from inner necessity; they have the stamp of personal rightness upon them. Such is their undeniable signature.

Cynthia A. Davis (essay date Spring 1981)

SOURCE: "Stanley Kunitz and the Transubstantial World," in *Literary Review,* Vol. 24, No. 3, Spring, 1981, pp. 413–26.

[*In the following essay, Davis provides an overview of Kunitz's poetic development in* Intellectual Things, Passport to the War, The Testing-Tree, Selected Poems, *and* The Poems of Stanley Kunitz. *Davis refutes the view of Kunitz as a derivative poet, drawing attention to his recurring archetypal images, technical skill, and effort to mediate between personal experience and universal myth.*]

Stanley Kunitz once said, "The originality of any poet consists to a considerable degree in finding those key images which forever haunt him, which make him different from others."[1] The recent publication of *The Poems of Stanley Kunitz, 1928–1978* (Little, Brown and Company, 1979) offers the opportunity to trace those images in development throughout Kunitz's long career, to find the obsessions that produce them, and to judge them in the context of the poetry as a whole. Almost all of his published poems appear here, beginning with new poems in the opening section, **"The Layers,"** and moving back in time through sections corresponding to his four previous American volumes.[2] The new poems themselves strike a retrospective note: **"The Knot"** opens the volume with description of a reappearing knothole, "Obstinate bud, / sticky with life," and the title poem of **"The Layers"** concludes the section, "I am not done with my changes."

The promise of recurrence and growth is well-chosen as frame to this section and as introduction to all the poetry. Kunitz has described his "key images" as "certain ineluctable archetypes, particularly those of death and rebirth, the quest, and the night-journey (or descent into the underworld)."[3] Those patterns do indeed recur in Kunitz's poetry. But they are best understood through his overriding concern: the relation between experience and expression. This concern produces the themes of myth, language, and poetry itself; it regulates the shifting forms of the "ineluctable archetypes"; and it drives Kunitz's development through the stages of his poetic career. As he investigates the possibilities of speech, poetry, and myth, he alternates in emphasis, but he always recognizes the

same struggle: to match fact to idea, life to archetype, and event to meaning. To follow his relentless pursuit of "the word" that can achieve that integration, we must read *Poems* backwards, following Kunitz's growth chronologically.

Kunitz has always been a "formal" poet, preferring musical effects, rhythmic and ringing phrases. That control may have contributed to his minor status among critics, who tend to regard him as competent but limited, even timid in vision and expression. His first volume, *Intellectual Things* (1930), helped to create this impression; while they certainly show Kunitz's talent, these poems are of the kind that can easily become stalled in an over-refined, over-intellectualized stage. Yvor Winters criticized their "excessively facile statement," "perceptive numbness" and "claptrap meter,"[4] and some of those criticisms are justified. These poems often seem quite derivative in form and simplistic in thought; worse, they are sometimes nearly impenetrable in their substitution of clever phrasing for clear idea. A stanza from **"Particular Lullaby"** can illustrate this point:

> The ebb of spirit from the vase
> Of woman is the hurt extreme
> Of conscious breath. Bewilder your thighs,
> Wrap your long thought in a dream.

Kunitz's own dissatisfaction with his beginnings is reflected in his exclusion of nine of the fifty poems in *Intellectual Things* from the new collection. (None from succeeding volumes are omitted.) But these poems of a very young man are not total failures. Most of them do avoid "claptrap meter," and most display what Zabel called a "melodic gift"[5]; occasional obscurities do not ruin a generally thoughtful approach.

The problems are, in fact, not so much technical as philosophical. *Intellectual Things* is largely concerned with apocalyptic and revelatory moments; there are almost no "realistic"—much less ordinary—situations in the poems. The visions often focus on language as a creative force. In **"When the Dead Arise,"** for example, "this maggoty dumb earth / Pronounces verbs erect and vertebrate"; in **"Single Vision,"** the "language of my marrow" contains "forms . . . instant to my will." The Thomas-like speaker of **"Poem"** says, "And I spoke the corn, / And I cried the clover up, with the dewy mouth of my mirth." Such experiences show an ideal union of subject and object, human and world, so that language becomes what it represents. But that perfect moment of "the word" seems to occur only in death, birth, or dream. These are the "ineluctable archetypes"; but they lack force except at the very limits of human life. And they bring only temporary satisfaction. As in **"Geometry of Moods,"** the moment of mental purity often fails:

> Concentrical, the universe and I
> Rotated on God's crystal axletree,
>
> I core of the world, a bead in a ball of glass
> So pure that only Nothing could be less.

Oh the earth ensphered me, liberal and warm,
When the curve of heaven was her sleeping arm.

Now cubical upon a fractured pole
It creaks, scraping the circle of my soul.

The problem is in the source of revelation: despite its religious tone, *Intellectual Things* celebrates only the power of the human mind. That ought to concentrate the poetry on human life, but in fact it causes a conflict that Kunitz is not yet prepared to handle: he praises the eternal and essential nature of thought without accepting the limitations of the individual, temporal thinker. He is painfully aware of those limitations, and even opens with a picture of the problem:

Dissolving in the chemic vat
Of time, man (gristle and fat),
Corrupting on a rock in space
That crumbles, lifts his impermanent face
To watch the stars, his brain locked tight
Against the tall revolving night.

                                        ("Change")

Unfortunately, at this stage Kunitz is less interested in resolving the conflict than in escaping it. He sets up the polar opposites so that he can opt for one pole—the mental one. Thus the "quest" always leads away from experience into dream or thought.

The language of *Intellectual Things* is that of abstract reason, dominated by references to human skills and sciences like geometry and sculpture, and spoken by an anonymous and generalized persona. Speech patterns are formal, often stilted, corresponding to regular rhythm and rhyme. These poems are celebrations of control; "the word" they offer is conscious and analytical. And they emphasize the superiority of mental life in image as well as diction. Natural images are always imaginatively opposed to, or transformed into, artifacts and ideas whose permanence exposes the inadequacy of the dying world. Reductive processes consistently deny particularity and vitality, as **"Very Tree"** exemplifies:

Forget the tube of bark,
Alliterative leaves,
Tenacious like a hand
Gnarled rootage in the dark
Interior of land.
                    . . . . .

Here is a timeless structure wrought
Like the candelabrum of pure thought,
Stripped of green root and leaf,
Getting no seed to sprout, . . .

What sensory details remain evoke an atmosphere that is pure, bare, cold, hard; these are qualities attached throughout the volume to the mental world:

Brain, be ice,
A frozen bowl of thought,

Pure radius of the marble eye
That is time's central spot:
In cold eternal calm
Chasten the trembling thigh.

All these effects, like the explicit subject matter, contribute to Kunitz's air of grappling with the problems of mental creation to the exclusion of direct sensuous experience. He is trying to achieve the integrating word not by balancing self and world, but by subsuming the world, imposing his will on it. His later rejection of that narrow position shows even in the titles of the poems omitted from the new collection; they suggest the emphasis on abstraction (**"Thumb-Nail Biography," "Any History," "A Daughter of the Sun Is She," "Promenade on Any Street"**) and the attack on natural and particular life (**"Rape of the Leaf," "Dissect This Silence," "Thou Unbelieving Heart," "Sad Song," "Invasions"**). But at this stage any ambivalence is only suggested, in the potentially negative qualities assigned to the mental world and in the repeated failure to sustain control. The young Kunitz explicitly sees life as "disease," "infection," "rot"; he desires to transcend that state in the purity of the Idea. But many of the most powerful poems are passionate with the failure to transcend. For every poem in which the adventurer comes to the "thoughtful womb" of the mind (**"Motion of Wish"**), there is another reminding us that "life escapes closed reason" (**"Organic Bloom"**). That "escape" is usually tragic at this stage; Kunitz talks about "teach[ing] my mind to love its thoughtless crack" (**"Beyond Reason"**), but cannot yet do it. Despite the Blakean epigraph—"For the tear is an intellectual thing"—his homage to particular life is the recognition of necessity, not true love. He sees that life is not reason, but keeps trying to make the exchange. That is why these poems are concrete without being at all sensuous: the young Kunitz longs for Platonic purity even as he sees its difficulty in a world of appearances.

In *Passport to the War* (1944), the uneasiness about cloistered mental life blossoms into bitter paranoia. The inability to achieve "language of my marrow" appears repeatedly, in frustrated attempts at communication—unanswered questions, broken syntax, lapses into silence. But now the failure is not due to imperfect life; it is caused by sterile intellect. The "dialect of love," now lost in the war (**"Welcome the Wrath"**), is replaced by "language of the wound"—agonized protest—or by corrupted language—"news" that ignores human suffering (**"The Hemorrhage"**), abstract labels and categories (**"My Surgeons"**), "the oratory of the rodent's tooth" that fits a dishonest world (**"Night Letter"**: originally "the weasel's tooth"). In newly concrete situations, a new persona emerges—still anonymous, but now speaking for suffering humanity. This speaker, bitter and cynical, calls for rebellion.

The poems of *Passport to the War* have an obvious political dimension, based on World War II and more generally on post-industrial society. But they are also a clear extension of the earlier poems; Kunitz breaks out of his over-intellectualized position by turning his images back on themselves, to reveal the dangers of abstract "purity." Now human skills and sciences create a tyrannical Pavlovian world (**"Reflection by a Mailbox"**); analysis and abstraction become tools for deadly dissection (**"My Surgeons"**). Imaginative metamorphosis is replaced by mad hallucination (**"Night Letter"**); artifacts are "marble faces" or fixed masks of ignorance and fear (**"Father and Son," "The Fitting of the Mask"**). And the bare, cold, regular, and infertile milieu of earlier poems now clearly implies the sterility of the isolated intellect. *Intellectual Things* celebrated the purity of mental creation, always threatened by imperfect temporal life. *Passport to the War* shows what results when mental life denies that outer reality. "The gesture made is woven in the sleeve," says **"The Harsh Judgment,"** echoing the image of clothes-become-man running throughout the volume. The denial of the inseparability of thought and action has created the sick world.

There is still some hope—the belief in love of **"My Surgeons,"** the "pity penny" of **"The Tutored Child,"** the defiance of **"Welcome the Wrath"** and **"Night Letter."** Natural images take on new power through association with instinct, emotion, and identity; for example, the image of man becoming tree in **"The Illusionist"** and **"Invocation"** shows an escape into the non-rational self, an evasion of self-knowledge, but it has a potential much greater than the stripped image of **"Very Tree,"** because it retains its living quality. Even more positive images depict natural passionate life in opposition to mechanical forms. Two in particular suggest the way out of *Passport*'s painful world repeated images of blood and fire turn pain into purgation, support choice with feeling. Thus in **"Invocation"** the poet unites the early theme of creative shaping with a new sense of natural energy; speaking to a "Circler" who can draw form from loss, he describes the "one incendiary vein"

> I have defended, purified, to slake
> You in the burning, whose daemonic beak
> The casp of bone about my heart O break!

Such hopes, though, are still largely confined to fiery liberation and purgative bloodletting—violence meeting a violent world. These are vigorous, concrete, passionate poems. But they are bitter at the failure of the quest for the saving word, both personally and universally. Their bitterness provoked one critic to comment, "They are the poems of a sick man in a sick world."[6] Not until his next volume could Kunitz combine his early passion for thought and form with the later appreciate on of immediacy and motion, and find a joyous "word."

Selected Poems, 1928–1958 marks a new stage for Kunitz, and manifests a new mastery of poetic form. (This section in *Poems* is called "This Garland, Danger," from a line in **"Green Ways."**) Kunitz won the Pulitzer Prize for this volume, and his own recognition of its significance shows in his inclusion of poems from the two earlier books. His arrangement of the poems by theme obscures his development, but emphasizes the constancy of concern; and the new poems themselves mark a similar consolidation. They still use false or weak speech as corollary to failed vision—"Perception blunted as one's syntax fails" (**"The Thief"**)—and oppose that failure to instinctive expression—"There's grammar in my bones!" (**"Grammar Lesson"**)—but they do not try to achieve "the word" by "subduing" the passions or by irrational defiance. Instead, a new "word" combines passionate being with conscious communication. The speaker of **"Green Ways,"** for example, first pleads for instinctive inarticulate union with the natural world, but finally accepts the burden of conscious awareness relieved, expressed, and symbolized by language: "Let me proclaim it—human be my lot!" In **"Among the Gods,"** the poet says of the gods, representatives of eternal truth,

> Huge blocks of language, all my quarried love,
> They justify, and not in random poems,
> But shapes of things interior to Time,
> Hewn out of chaos when the Pure was plain.

"The word," then, expresses man's halfway position, tied to pure spirit and to imperfect but vital physical life. Articulation can console for the fallen state—"the serpent's word, but yet the word" (**"The Dark and the Fair"**). More, it is "the language that saves" (**"Sotto Voce"**), for articulated knowledge produces the redeeming myth; in **"A Spark of Laurel,"** articulation becomes incarnation, combining universal and particular by resurrecting the individual story in myth:

> Ha! Once again I heard
> The transubstantial word
> That is not mine to speak
> Unless I break, I break;
>
> The spiral verb that weaves
> Through the crystal of our lives,
> Of myth and water made
> And incoherent blood; . . .

"The word," then, is myth, the union of particular action with universal thought. Like *Intellectual Things,* the new pieces in *Selected Poems* are dominated by religious, mythic, and artistic language. But while *Intellectual Things* used that language to separate mental from physical life, the new poems connect intellectual systems to particular experience to create new and complex modes of apprehension, as in the awed "astronomy" of **"The Science of the Night"**:

> My touch is on you, who are light-years gone.
> We are not souls but systems, and we move
> In clouds of our knowing
>   like great nebulae.
> Our very motives swirl and have their start
> With father lion and with mother crab.

Images of balance and symmetry no longer censor, but reinforce sensuous experience, as do mythic allusions. The "ineluctable archetypes" come into their own, developed in detail as well as outline. The importance of living the archetype is now equal to the understanding of it. So in **"The Approach to Thebes,"** Oedipus meets his fate, saying, "And the story's this: I made the monster me." That acceptance of all the aspects of experience dominates *Selected Poems,* as "the word" becomes not intellectual, but "transubstantial." And within what are still quite regular forms, new variations in tone and diction reveal the range of life that myth can capture—from a whimsical song for a mouse (**"The Waltzer in the House"**) to solemn chants and tender love poems. Technical virtuosity does not overwhelm the poems; their form is like that of the beloved in **"The Unwithered Garland"**: "Her grace is not of any part, / But selfhood's self, its very motion."

Kunitz reaches a peak in *Selected Poems,* a command of the musical and magical potential of poetry that makes him a glorious singer. But he continues to grow; *The Testing-Tree* (1972) startled reviewers in its apparent wrenching away from the early philosophical and musical style toward what they saw as "confessional" and literal poetry. Kunitz does indeed try new ways in *The Testing-Tree,* but they are again understood best as an outgrowth of the earlier work. The theme of language as indicator of perception continues, but the word is again made new as Kunitz turns back to the limits of the individual perspective. Now he shows less the essentiality of myth than the inability of an individual story to reach the status of myth, or even of complete expression.

Such a theme naturally demands concrete illustration, and in *The Testing-Tree* persona and scene take on their greatest definition. Poems are spoken by or tell of specific individuals, sometimes historical personages like Bonhoeffer (**"Around Pastor Bonhoeffer"**), sometimes fictional but carefully individualized characters, most often Kunitz himself. Each character has an appropriate language, from Bonhoeffer's religious idiom to the child's fairytale perspective in **"Journal for My Daughter"** or the young Kunitz's mixture of reverence and childish arrogance in **"The Testing-Tree"**:

> then sprinted lickety-
>   split on my magic Keds
>   from a crouching start,
>
>   . . . . .
>
>   with no one where to deny
> when I flung myself down
>   that on the given course
>   I was the world's fastest human.

But of course the sense of limitation requires, beyond specific situation and persona, a hint of larger meaning. *The Testing-Tree* is shot through with a sense of the discrepancy between appearance and meaning, between individual understanding and a greater intuition. Hence the frequent use of childhood experience: speaking as child or as remembering adult, Kunitz can reveal the inadequacy of the childish articulation, or even of the adult sense of

symbolic parallel: "I am looking for the trail. / Where is my testing-tree? / Give me back my stones!" Historical characters can also show limited vision, like Dante in **"The Illumination"** when asked for guidance:

> To which he replied:
> "I know neither the time
> nor the way
>
> nor the number on the door . . .
> but this must be my room,
> I was here before."

These poems are clear and concrete, even more so than *Selected Poems*; but their literalness defeats absolute certainty, even as their feeling lifts them above random event. The prophet-like figure of **"Journal for My Daughter"** expresses unsatisfied desire; **"The Customs-Collector's Report"** is a pathetic tale of confused last words; the love note of **"After the Last Dynasty"** is a set of questions; and even Bonhoeffer's "omega" expresses the finality of terror rather than certainty. Ordinary events and expressions must take on disproportionate significance, like the "red Masonic hat / and a walking stick" that represent a lost father in **"Three Floors,"** or the commonplace metaphors of the astronaut in **"The Flight of Apollo."** Conversely, narrow certainty of meaning is deflated by the glimpse of a "blue unappeasable sky" in **"Robin Redbreast,"** or by the "innocence and the light" outside the enclosed world of **"The Artist."** Even the recurrent vocabularies of history and nature, that might suggest systems of meaning, remain undeveloped. So Kunitz finally fulfills his early dictum that "Life escapes closed reason."

Reviewers who read these as "confessional" poems have criticized their tentative air as "an occasional uncertainty as to how to transfigure the object, how to find the appropriate detail that makes a remembered incident come alive" or that "can endow a private incident or public event with universal significance."[7] But Kunitz's focus is on the uncertainty of universal significance, the impossibility of such a transparent view. The circumstances that incarnate meaning also obscure it; they distort reality by limiting it. The flawed expression parallels the divided consciousness. In fact, the weakest parts of *The Testing-Tree* are often *overly* explicit statements (e.g., the assertive endings of **"The Magic Curtain"** and **"River Road"**). Poems that leave open the gap between experience and myth, like **"Three Floors,"** are moving in the felt discrepancy between fact and meaning: the hat and stick are clearly presented as symbols inadequate to the boy's need, and therefore make the father's absence more poignant, as is the boy's feeling:

> Bolt upright in my bed that night
> I saw my father flying;
> the wind was walking on my neck,
> the windowpanes were crying.

"The Mound Builders" offers an image for what Kunitz attempts in *The Testing-Tree.* At Ocmulgee National

Monument, the poet thinks of the "seven-layered world" of the mound, the layers of civilization extending from tribes now in "museums of prehistory" to modern Macon. The thought of former lives allows a sense of myth—an understanding of the "millennial ordeal" that links one life to another. But it does not cancel out the immediate life that opens the poem. Standing on the latest layer, the poet seeks to know previous ones—to inform present life by connection with the buried past and the buried self. Distressed by modern "spoilers of the air," he finds consolation, not escape by transcendence, but support from natural ("the prevalence of green / and the starry chickweed of the fields") and human continuity.

Kunitz uses a similar image in the newest poems; in **"The Layers,"** he describes a celestial admonition to "Live in the layers, / not on the litter." And he enforces that theme by a return to myth and dream. These poems are clearly not "confessional"; those that do deal with Kunitz's personal life or family avoid the literal level of *The Testing-Tree.* In **"Quinnapoxet,"** for example, the poet encounters his long-dead parents while fishing; in **"The Unquiet Ones,"** they "glide" into his dreams, "dark emissaries / of the two-faced god." His sisters write "the history of tears" (**"My Sisters"**). In such cases, the lost past returns, but particular experience has become "ineluctable archetype," its forms more important emotion of *The Testing-Tree,* we get what lay behind them—the glimpse of a deeper and darker meaning.

In poems that show the adult Kunitz in the midst of experience (**"The Quarrel," "Route Six"**), the poet is much quicker to interpret the event. This is not so much a denial of the limited meanings in *The Testing-Tree* as an accumulation of them; the retrospective (though rarely nostalgic) note in **"The Layers"** comes from the collection of experiences and summary of their meanings. Now the explained scene can lead to (though not *be*) a metaphor or conclusion that helps define the Self. The individual event could not be the myth; but more and more it can participate in the myth. So, in **"The Quarrel,"** an angry word "weighs less than a parsley seed, / but a road runs through it / that leads to my grave." Or on one journey to the Cape, "Twenty summers roll by." The traveller of **"The Layers"** looks back to see his "abandoned camp-sites," no longer present but necessary to his journey. The backward look allows a sense of pattern much less arbitrary than the abstractions of *Intellectual Things*; the shape of one's life finally begins to emerge.

Other people, in contrast, seem less knowable now. In *The Testing-Tree,* the sense of individual limits did not prevent Kunitz's entry into the world according to Bonhoeffer; in fact, that narrowed vision was essential to definition by means of language and image. Now Kunitz holds back more, defining others through their products and possessions. We discover a slave through his cigarstore Indian, nineteenth-century women through their handicrafts (**"Words for the Unknown Makers"**); we approach Lincoln by looking at the contents of his pockets (**"The Lincoln Relics"**). These forms of acting on the world may show us others more honestly than the attempt at empathy. But the two approaches are not as contradictory as they might seem. The poet of *The Testing-Tree* felt the narrowness of an individual perspective, and so balanced his own with others'; but he stayed within the boundaries of one view at a time. The poet of **"The Layers"** extends his meanings to myth, recovering an earlier sense of significance and structure; but he cannot do so on the basis of personal experience alone. So he reminds us of the reality of others—not only as limited perceivers, but like himself as artists. They are known by the intersection of their lives with the perceivable world, by the objects they handle and the artifacts they produce. The art object may be dangerous if it cuts the artist off from the "terrible storm" or the calls of his "twisted brother" outside the ivory tower (**"The Crystal Cage"**). But it can also be a means of communication with others, a form that links different experiences—one's own, or many people's. So the cigarstore Indian is the "surrogate and avatar" of its maker, expressing a freedom he can only desire; and a conventional funeral scene expresses "common tears" and so suggests a reality beyond its "narrow gate" (**"Words for the Unknown Makers"**).

Art, of course, is especially important, with myth and love, and other intentional links of form to meaning. But even apparently random reality can provide a link. The poet is moved by the Lincoln relics, "what he carried next to his skin, / what rocked to his angular stride, / partook of his man-smell, / shared the intimacy of his needs." And this personal touch, not just "his legend and his fame," recovers Lincoln as a reality. The poem ends with the gap between the evanescent, external physical reality and the mythic meaning:

> He steps out from the crowd
> with his rawboned, warty look,
> a gangling fellow in jeans
> next to a plum-colored sari,
> and just as suddenly he's gone.
> But there's that other one
> who's tall and lonely.

For the first time, both modes of knowledge seem equally important. We do not get to one "through" the other, do not sacrifice one to the other; we have a simultaneous perception of Lincoln the man and Lincoln the legend, each enriching the other.

"What of the Night?" offers a similar view. In part 1, the poet sinks into himself "like a stone / dropped down a well." In the "slime" and "brackish life," he finds a pure myth,

> as when pilot angels
> with crystal eyes and streaming hair
> rode planets through the shies,
> and each one sang
> a single ravishing note
> that melted
> into the music of the spheres.

But in part 2 he is awakened by a "night-bell" calling him to the outer world, for an obscure, perhaps pointless, mission. Resisting the call, he says,

> Oh I should be the one
> to swell the night with my alarm!
> When the messenger comes again
> I shall pretend in a childish voice
> my father is not home.

The self's pure vision, already located in "brackish life," is further balanced by the ambiguous demand of the world. We know that, whatever his protestations, Kunitz does not deny its call, for his tender concern rings through his work. He now fulfills the promise of *Intellectual Things*: the radiance and order of the inner world suffuse these poems. But instead of escape into the "frozen bowl of thought," here his vision illuminates a world of particular experience, which in turn invigorates and tests the ideal. So in **"Firesticks,"** the mythic quest goes "into the mind's white exile," but follows "down history's long roads." And **"The Layers"** concludes these new poems with a promise of "changes" that will continue the discovery of the eternal myth beneath the masks of particulars.

Poems recalls *Selected Poems* most clearly in its retrospective nature, its air of summary and consolidation. But we can see in *Poems* how far Kunitz has come from the metaphysical patterns of *Intellectual Things,* through the bitter attacks of *Passport to the War,* Kunitz moves on to assertion, then confession, and finally to a sense of self that is both vigorous and open. Starting with a narrow exercise of will, he learns to recognize the mutual importance of fact and idea. The change is apparent technically too. Kunitz has always had a good ear, but the language is now more adequate to the music, the situation to the idea; and the poem's rhythms, here and in *The Testing-Tree,* are more subtle (usually two- and three-stress lines) and more conversational. These new poems do have weaknesses: sometimes the old tendency to belabor the point shows through in an unnecessary admonition at poem's end (e.g., **"The Catch"**). At the other extreme, there is an occasional "untransfigured" detail—a situation either too obscure (as in **"My Sisters"**) or too mundane (**"The Quarrel"**) to bear its weight of meaning. The summary note of *Poems* makes such problems more important than the modesty of *The Testing-Tree.* Usually, however, meaning and event are carefully matched and carefully distinguished as well. Kunitz has alternated between these poles throughout his career, stressing myth and meaning in *Intellectual Things* and *Selected Poems,* turning to fact and experience in *Passport to the War* and *The Testing-Tree. Poems* shows how closely those poles are related, and in **"The Layers"** displays their coexistence.

There is no question that Kunitz has been influenced by his times; his career has followed the poetic development of the age. But to view him as merely a derivative poet is quite unfair to his achievement. He has a sense of music in a time when much poetry is deaf to rhythm and sound; his most conversational poems are rich with harmony and echo. He has a gift for the haunting phrase and image that once earned him the title of "surrealist" poet; the "key images which forever haunt him"—the lost father, the journey and descent, the loss and phantom reappearance—haunt us too. And to the ear and imagination he has added an eye ever keener as the years go on. He has taught himself to see a suffering world, and the individuals in it; and he has refused to see all as a commentary on himself alone. Putting the personal experience beside the universal myth, he finds the "word" for both, one that shows the power and the limits of each side. Kunitz is not a prolific poet, nor an "experimental" one. For fifty years, he has gone on writing careful, intelligent, and passionate defenses of the human condition. These poems may not startle, but they last.

Notes

1. Kunitz in David Lupher, "Stanley Kunitz on Poetry: A Yale Lit Interview," *Yale Literary Magazine,* 136, 3 (May 1968), p. 9.

2. A collection published in England, *The Terrible Threshold: Selected Poems, 1940–1970* (London: Martin Secker and Warburg Limited, 1974), contained poems already published in the first four American collections.

3. Kunitz in Anthony Ostroff, ed., *The Contemporary Poet as Artist and Critic* (Boston: Little, Brown and Company, 1964), p. 79.

4. Yvor Winters, "The Poetry of Stanley Kunitz," *New Republic,* 63, (4 June 1930), p. 77.

5. Morton Dauwen Zabel, "Prelude to Adventure," *Poetry,* 36, 4 (July 1930), p. 220.

6. A. J. M. Smith, "Language of the Wound," *Poetry,* 64, 3 (June 1944), p. 166.

7. Marjorie G. Perloff, "The Testing of Stanley Kunitz," *Iowa Review,* 3, 1 (Winter 1972), pp. 102, 103.

Gregory Orr (essay date 1985)

SOURCE: "Introduction: Life into Legend," in *Stanley Kunitz: An Introduction to the Poetry,* Columbia University Press, 1985, pp. 1–48.

[*In the following essay, Orr provides an analysis of the recurring images and personal symbolism in Kunitz's poetry, drawing particular attention to the significance of legend, quest, and parent-child motifs related to the poet's search for self-identity and meaning.*]

When Stanley Kunitz' magnificent fourth book of poems, *The Testing-Tree,* was published in 1971, it was hailed by Robert Lowell on the front page of the *New York Times Book Review.* As Kunitz' books make their appearance, it seems inevitable that he will be generally accorded that status which he has long since earned in the eyes of fellow poets—that of a major poet of the dramatic lyric. Yet the immediate chorus of praise and the excitement in the literary world that greeted *The Testing-Tree*'s appearance was followed by the relative critical neglect that has persistently haunted Kunitz' achievement as a poet.

Kunitz writes sparingly—on the average his books have appeared at fourteen-year intervals. In his words, he writes "only those poems that *must* be written, that force themselves into being." As a result, the transitional poems often don't get written, and each poem can represent, or appear to represent, a new departure. But transitional poems are dear to the hearts of critics and readers alike; they are often the bridges between major poems that allow us to perceive more quickly the patterns of concern and theme.

Curiously, we demand of a major poet not simply great poems but a great vision. In terms of the dramatic lyric, this great vision involves the sense of a distinct personality encountering, those particular mysteries of existence that most compel its energy and utterance. Paradoxically, the very excellence and integrity of Kunitz' individual poems have had the effect of obscuring the larger vision and continuity that guarantee his status as a major poet. The appearance of his collected volume, *The Poems of Stanley Kunitz, 1928–1978,* gives us the perspective we need to see the pattern and wholeness of Kunitz' oeuvre. The themes of identity and of the self's quest for autonomy and intensity of being emerge as the principle constellations in which each fine poem is a separate star.

In this Introduction I will be moving rapidly across the body of Kunitz' work, seeking those thematic and stylistic continuities that make his poetry more complex and coherent than that of many lyric poets. In identifying and emphasizing these underlying structures, I will be quoting only briefly from individual poems. Finally, it is these individual poems, their integrity and intensity, that determine Kunitz' stature as a poet.

The necessarily theoretical nature of this chapter will result in a temporary neglect of the individual poems, which will, I hope, be remedied by the subsequent chapters where we will move chronologically through Kunitz' books, examining individual poems in some depth.

A Few Assertions

Kunitz is a poet of the dramatic lyric who strives to dramatize the themes and contradictions of his life. He distrusts the didactic impulse in poetry—the impulse to summarize, interpret, or otherwise comment upon the dramas he presents. Keats is perhaps Kunitz' favorite poet, yet in his introduction to his edition of *The Poems of Keats*, Kunitz does not hesitate to chide him for a lapse into didacticism:

> No matter how you read, "'Beauty is truth, truth beauty'—that is all / Ye know on earth, and all ye need

to know," the lines have a thematic and didactic smack to them. Keats has a finer aesthetic perception in one of his letters when he refers to the reality of aethereal things, and names them: "such as existences of Sun Moon & Stars and passages of Shakespeare," or when, on another occasion, he asserts, "The Imagination may be compared to Adams' dream—he awoke and found it truth." (*A Kind of Order, A Kind of Folly* [hereafter cited as *Order/Folly*], p. 69)

Kunitz would approve of Yeats' remark that we cannot know the truth, we can only embody it. He might further add that we can dramatize the truth as an encounter, a "drama in a nutshell" (**"Revolving Meditation,"** p. 143). Kunitz speaks of the poet's need to "polarize his contradictions." These contradictions are polarized in order to enact a dramatic encounter whose events *are* its meaning.

Kunitz is a poet of irrational or nonrational intelligence, although he is aware of irrationality's dangers:

> Irrationality may well be the safest of all disguises for the modern artist—the Mask, or Persona, that permits him the greatest freedom of expression with a certain degree of immunity; though there is a danger, to be sure, that the Mask may eventually usurp the Face. (*Order/Folly* p. 7)

The irrational or nonrational intelligence that structures his poems takes many forms, but the alchemical ambition that marshals these forms remains consistent: to convert life into legend.

That which is to be alchemized is the self as much as the life. Through the transformation of self into language he wants to "test existence at its highest pitch—what does it feel like to be totally one's self" (*Order/Folly,* p. 17). Such a transformation also has aspects of the heroic quest; Kunitz speaks of "submitting to the ordeal of walking through the fires of selfhood into a world of archetypal forms" (*Order/Folly,* p. 13). It is the poem itself that enacts that transformative ordeal. The enterprise is the same as that of Keats when Keats speaks of this world as a "vale of soul-making."

When Kunitz proposes "converting life into legend" as a formula for his poetic enterprise, he is in part making an assertion about the lyric poet's awareness of larger structures and principles of continuity in his work. That notion of the lyric which sees each poem as an epiphanic moment crystallized in language yet isolated from all other such moments does not appeal to Kunitz. The word "legend" in the formula emphasizes a consistent narrating thread that runs through the individual poems.

"Legend" is Kunitz' attempt to make of the lyric poet's enterprise an open-ended quest whose themes, goals, and events become representative human dramas. Kunitz' legends are based in private experience; yet, translated and dramatized, they acquire universality: the quest for love, for authenticity and autonomy, for intensity of being.

The concept of the "key image" provides a second structural continuity to Kunitz' work. Basically, the key image has its source in the poet's childhood and manifests itself again and again in the poetry. Its recurrence elevates it to the status of a symbol in the poet's personal mythology and at the same time provides at the image level the continuity which legend provides at the narrative level.

The third factor of continuity in Kunitz' poetry is the self, the dramatized "I" who is the protagonist of the poems. This self is the central and centralizing persona of the dramatic lyric. The self quests, seeks meaning. Sometimes the self journeys through a horizontal landscape emblematic of the life lived inside time. At other times, the self responds to the transcendental impulse so powerful in the lyric and seems to spiral above a crucial incident or event, held by the event's centripetal power yet striving to rise up to view it from a different perspective.

These two selves, the journeying self and the spiraling self, are both valid for Kunitz. The spiraling self acknowledges the power of recurring themes in our lives and the necessity to confront them again and again. The spiraling self is most appropriately linked to the recurring key images. The journeying self acknowledges another truth: that we convey our past with us as we enter a future whose events we cannot predict. The journeying self is appropriately linked to the narrative thrust of the legends.

These continuities of narrative, image, and self are necessary in order to overcome a critical bias that seeks to minimize the scope and ambition present in the work of a major lyric imagination. Perhaps the most demeaning manifestation of this bias is the belief that the lyric poet's highest ambition is to appear in an anthology. It is necessary to propose a countertruth: to assert that in some cases, as with Kunitz' work, it is possible to say that *all* a lyric poet's poems are one poem, that the work as a whole partakes of the same impulse toward unity and coherence that shapes language and event into the individual poem.

THE LEGENDS AND THE QUEST

Kunitz has frequently spoken of the theme of the son's quest for the father, which is indeed a central part of his work. But in fact, his work focuses on several distinct quests or legends, each having its unique narrative thrust. These legends are linked to each other in various ways, and they also have a common motive: the quest for identity.

When we speak of a quest for identity that originates in lived experience and that involves a son's search for his father, we have entered the territory of psychology. In the lived life, identity is determined largely in terms of family relationships, and it is here that the other legends emerge.

A retrospective reading of Kunitz' poetry reveals three figures who are primary poles of his imaginative existence: father, mother, and beloved. These three figures imply an "I" whose identity emerges in relation to them.

The first two relationships are father—son and mother—son. From these two, a further relationship emerges: that of man (grown son) and beloved.[1]

Kunitz will dramatize the primary concerns of his life and work in terms of legends based on these three primary relationships.

The first legend I will call the "father legend." The two female figures represent a more complex interaction. Until very late in the work, the powerful figure of the mother is liable to appear in the same poem as the beloved. This fact has great significance and constitutes a legend of its own: the mother/beloved legend. There are also numerous poems in which the lover/beloved appears without the mother, and when it seems appropriate I will refer to them as one of two variations of this legend: the beloved legend or the beloved/muse legend.

In the early poetry, the figure of the beloved is idealized and frequently related to the courtly love tradition in a way that the contemporary reader may find archaic. But equally, the later Kunitz of *The Testing-Tree* presents some of the most fully realized, dignified, and convincing figures of women in poetry written by men. What remains constant and consistent throughout is Kunitz' belief that love has the power to transform us—a power he embodies in the figure of the beloved.

Besides the father legend and the mother/beloved legend, there is a third major legend of identity that emerges most strongly in Kunitz' later work. But, if the other legends have their origins in psychology, the third legend seems rooted in metaphysics. I will call it the "legend of being" or the "quest for being itself." This third legend tends to make its appearance in early poems as a final transformation of the father legend. It exists in such later poems as **"King of the River," "The Layers,"** and **"The Knot"** as an autonomous legend that is the triumphant and culminating expression of Kunitz' imagination.

THE SOURCES

Certain key facts and figures from his youth provide the basic material for Kunitz' alchemical transformation of life into legend. In a 1971 interview with Selden Rodman, Kunitz presents the bare bones of the life situation that so affected his work. His immigrant parents were from grain merchant families who lived in Luthuanian Russia, though he was never to learn for sure the real birthplace of his father:

> Perhaps my father, who killed himself six weeks before I was born, came from East Prussia: I've never known much about him because my mother made it a forbidden subject. Why he killed himself wasn't clear. The dress manufacturing business they'd started together was going bankrupt; but there must have been another woman, too, or mother wouldn't have made the subject taboo. Not even his name could be mentioned. Mother was a great seamstress—and business woman—so after the double catastrophe she opened a little dry goods

store and for years worked day and night to pay off the debts—though she wasn't obliged to legally.

I was farmed out, or in the hands of nursemaids . . . I was lonely and fatherless, but my father *had* left a library—fairly substantial sets of Dickens, Thackeray, Tolstoi and the like. . . .

My two sisters died young. Mother was just forty when I was born. When I was eight, she married again. My stepfather taught me most of what I know about love and gentleness. He was an Old World scholar, of no practical help to my mother, but she revered his learning and the sweetness of his character. She anticipated the modern liberated woman, being perfectly capable of managing by herself what had developed into a flourishing business, based on her dress designs—I can still see the loft with its cutting tables and long rows of girls bent over their electric sewing machines. Mother never trusted anybody else to repair the machines when they were out of order. But she was always tired at the end of the day. When my stepfather died suddenly in my fourteenth year, my world was shattered. It didn't leave me with much sense of family. . . .

What finally destroyed her was that she couldn't bear to fire anyone. So she went bankrupt again in the Depression, and that was the end of her business career. She had fought for money and power, and she had failed—for which she could not forgive herself. She died, alert and intransigent, in the early Fifties at the age of eighty-six.[2]

The directness and clarity of this presentation only become available to Kunitz late in his life. The overriding theme of Kunitz' work is identity—the struggle to discover and dramatize "what furies made him man" (**"Goose Pond,"** p. 120). These forces find their locus in his childhood circumstances. Throughout Kunitz' long career, these primary family figures (father, mother, son) and the dramatic situations they enact are what draw out his deepest emotional and imaginative responses.

The Mother and the Beloved

Although the quest for the father is often spoken of as the major thematic thrust of Kunitz' work, the motive and priority must be sought in the mother—son relationship. The figure that emerges from Rodman's biographical interview is of a remarkably powerful, competent, and unyielding mother. In order to locate the quest for identity at one of its origins, we must comprehend the situation of a boy who is left fundamentally alone with a powerful mother. His biological father is mysteriously absent, and there is a taboo against his very name. In order to establish his autonomy and identity, Kunitz must break out of the orbit created by his mother's gravitational power. When the legend concerning the mother—son relationship does make one of its infrequent appearances in the early poems, the figure of the mother is consistently seen as powerfully destructive of or inhibiting the son's quest for autonomy. She is also, in the early poems, repeatedly linked to the beloved, especially in poems of failed love as **"Poem"** (*Intellectual Things*) or **"The Signal from the House"** (*Selected Poems*):

I cried to the mourner on the stair,
"Mother, I hate you for those tears."

(p. 156)

In terms of the quest for identity, the beloved is a goal, the mother is an obstacle to that goal.

Freud, in his essay, "A Prevalent Form of Degradation in Erotic Life," talks about the role of the mother at that time in a young man's life when he chooses a love object in the world. Freud contends that the mother is always the actual first love object and that the beloved is a surrogate. He maintains that at this point the young man separates love into two components: a "tender," idealizing impulse and a "sensuous," sexual impulse. These two components cannot be reunited into the figure of the mother lest incest-fear incapacitate the young man.

What happens in a great deal of Kunitz' work *is* strongly related to the mother, but the effect is different from that suggested by Freud's model. In Freud's essay, the mother is a rock against which the young man's libido flows and separates into two streams ("tender" and "sensuous") which cannot be reunited. In early Kunitz, it is as if the libido is never given any expression in the external world. In an early poem, **"So Intricately Is This World Resolved,"** Kunitz proposes that the man cannot or must not act in the world of sexual impulse, that love not only cannot be consummated but cannot be acted upon:

O lover,
Lift no destroying hand; let fortune pass
Unchallenged, beauty sleep; dare not to cover
Her mouth with kisses by the garden wall,
Lest, cracking in bright air, a planet fall.

(p. 228)

In many of the poems of *Intellectual Things,* the libidinal energy thus frustrated of expression animates an inner world, an interior landscape, and creates a condition of erotic solipsism. In these poems, language itself becomes charged with the energy and actions of sexual event, but the arena is interior to the self: in **"Mens Creatrix,"** the brain becomes a "mental womb" which will be "cleaved" by a "rhythmic Spike of Light" (p. 202).

While language and mental events become charged with sexual energy, the figure of the beloved in the early love poems becomes or remains an idealized figure from literary tradition rather than a recognizably flesh-and-blood creature. She is "love's incarnate form" or "a dove-soft nimble girl" and acts in an interiorized landscape that in no way corresponds to the external world. The result in the early work is twofold: a love poetry in which the object is idealized in such a way as to transcend any human particularity; and a poetry about poetry itself—or about mental processes—which is charged with sensual intensity.

In terms of the quest for identity, Kunitz must struggle to overcome his own inhibitions and emotional contradictions and his mother's prohibitions in relation to the beloved. One movement in this theme is from the interior, enclosed world of *Intellectual Things* (1930) outward toward a recognizable external landscape and a recognizable, if tortured, relationship between self and other in *Passport to the War* (1944).

On the psychological level, the mother/beloved legend culminates and is resolved in **"The Magic Curtain"** (*The Testing-Tree,* 1971). As in **"Poem,"** and **"The Signal from the House,"** the mother and the beloved are both present in the same poem and the same drama, but here they are present so that the boy can choose the beloved (a governess) in a way that affirms a tender, sensuous love and also affirms his identity as distinct from the mother's:

> "I'll never forgive her," mother said,
> but as for me, I do and do and do.
>
> (**"The Magic Curtain,"** p. 68)

The beloved triumphs over the mother (at a human level); love triumphs over negations; forgiveness over "never forgiving."

On the metaphysical level, the mother/beloved legend culminates and is resolved in **"A Spark of Laurel,"** where the powerful and erotic female figure that has dominated many of the poems in *Selected Poems* is recognized as reconciling mother and beloved (ideal and passionate love) and her ambiguous identity is seen as the very source of poetry: the muse, who is "'Mother and mistress, one'" (**"A Spark of Laurel,"** final lines, p. 147).

THE FATHER AND THE SPIRIT FATHER

"To find the father is to find oneself."

(Interview, 1978)[3]

If, in the early work of *Intellectual Things* and *Passport to the War,* the beloved is a goal toward which the speaker/ self moves with great intensity, then the other main goal is the father. In the figure of the father we are dealing with a fusion of the biological father, whose suicide before Kunitz' birth made his name taboo, and the gentle and loving stepfather who died suddenly when Kunitz was fourteen. The term "father" in any discussion of Kunitz' work should be understood to mean the fusion of the *pain* of the beloved stepfather's sudden death with the *imagery* and *mystery* of the biological father's suicide. In all Kunitz' poems the father is dead, but this fact in no way undercuts his reality; in fact, it heightens his reality at the psychological level. In Kunitz' memory, as we have seen, both fathers are associated with books or scholarship, and they are characterized in the poems as being loving and yet mysteriously absent or elusive. They are also, and this point is critical, perceived as being actual or potential allies in Kunitz' quest for identity and his related effort to break free of the power of the maternal. The father is a goal of the identity quest in much the same way that the beloved is:

> And I will go, unburdened, on the quiet lane
> Of my eternal kind, till shadowless
> With inner light I wear my father's face.
>
> (**"Vita Nuova,"** p. 236)

Jung, in his essay "Freud and Jung—Contrasts," criticizes Freud for his overemphasis on the child's relation to the parents; he sees it finally as an entangling, sterile relationship from which Freud offers no means of escape, no avenue for growth. Jung claims to see in the universal cultural phenomenon of initiation rites, a human impulse toward rebirth and as such a release from "the boring and sterile family drama." Such a rebirth is a movement beyond the biological toward the spiritual. Such a reborn person sees that the Spirit is Father and Nature is Mother.

Behind the biological father stands the Spirit Father, behind the biological mother stands the Nature Mother. Throughout the poems of son and father, Kunitz' Spirit Father is ambiguous (he is helper and haunter, guide and ghost), but he is Spirit from the outset and the goal of the son's quest.

Perhaps Kunitz so quickly identifies father with Spirit because his biological father is absent and therefore transparent.[4] Not so the figure of the mother. As Freudian biological mother, she is an opaque and powerful figure standing between young Kunitz and the beloved. As Jung's Nature Mother she is associated with the decay that overtook the father. This decay is linked with vegetation; the mother "buries" humans like seeds:

> In the year of my mother's blood, when I was born,
> She buried my innocent head in a field, because the
>   earth
>
> Was sleepy with the winter. And I spoke the corn
>
> (**"Poem,"** p. 198)

Frequently, as in the following poem, animal ("carrion") and vegetative ("a pod") nature overlap in the recurring image of a ripening that is merely prelude to a bursting and rotting:

> Anonymous sweet carrion,
> Blind mammal floating on the stream
> Of depthless sound, completely one
> In the cinnamon-dark of no dream—
> A pod of silence, bursting when the sun
>
> Clings to the forehead,
>
> (**"Prophecy on Lethe,"** p. 209)

In **"Organic Bloom"** the human brain is seen as a grotesque water lily:

> Enormous floats the brain's organic bloom
> Till, bursting like a fruit, it scatters doom.
>
> (p. 234)

In the poems of *Intellectual Things,* Kunitz sees the relationship of spirit to nature as a war, a struggle in which the father is always threatened with "a second perishing" (**"For the Word Is Flesh"**). What will free Kunitz' poetry from this struggle is a twofold imaginative transformation: the embracing of nature as a *cyclical* (death—decay—rebirth) rather than linear (death and then decay) process; and the location of the Spirit Father *in* nature rather than *against* it:

> O father in the wood,
> Mad father of us all,
> King of our antlered wills

> (**"The Way Down,"** p. 137)

Although Kunitz seeks and even pursues the figure of the father, he also needs to confront him in order to be free of a father "whose indomitable love / Kept me in chains" (**"Father and Son,"** p. 157). In the early poems of *Intellectual Things,* the Spirit Father either succumbs to decay or represents a transcendence of physical conditions which fails to accommodate the central phenomenon of death. When he is at last located in cyclical nature in **"The Way Down"** (*Selected Poems*),

> Where the fleshed root stirs,
> Marvelous horned strong game,
> Brine-scaled, dun-caked with mould,
> Dynastic thunder-bison, Asian-crude,
> Bedded in moss and slime,
> Wake

> (p. 136)

then indeed, as Heraclitus says (and the poem's title indicates), "The way down and the way up are one and the same."

This reconciliation of Spirit and Nature represents a major advance in Kunitz' quest for identity. The Nature of *Selected Poems* and after is a Nature whose cyclical renewals offer hope, and the father, who represents great positive power and potential guidance for the son, is identified with this new conception of Nature. Kunitz' abiding love of the natural world links with his idealization of the father. In later Kunitz, Nature is Father Nature—its renewals are expressed in the phallic imagery of male potency.

THE THIRD LEGEND

The first two major legends of Kunitz' poetry (the father legend and the mother/beloved legend) can be understood and appreciated at a psychological level without being confined or reduced to that level. The poems of these legends depict the way a strong male identity is formed through imaginative interaction with the figures of father, mother, and beloved. But the third legend goes beyond the issue of individual identity, shifting from psychology to metaphysics, from identity to being. The third legend could be called the legend of being itself, or "the quest of being for yet more intense being"—for the secret of its own mystery, which is understood as a journey that has no goal and finds its meaning in the journey itself.

The third legend can be understood also as the human adventure—the absurd heroics of human grandeur—the journey for the journey's sake, but at the highest level of risk and intensity. One of Kunitz' favorite metaphors for this is the journey into space. Perhaps this metaphor gripped him first when, as a cub reporter for the *Worcester Telegram,* he was sent to interview Robert Goddard, the father of modern rocketry, who was sending aloft curious missiles from pastures near Clark University. Young Kunitz heard him say, "In your lifetime, man will walk on the moon," and he never got over the grandeur of Goddard's imagination. **"The Flight of Apollo"** is the best embodiment of this version of the quest for its own sake. It is a hymn to the quest, but also an exploration of its motives—"Earth was my home, but even there I was a stranger. . . . Think of me as nostalgic, afraid, exalted" (p. 48).

At the core of the legend of being is the fact of our mortality and our awareness of it. Perhaps it is this that places the emphasis on journey and process rather than on any goal. Kunitz himself best expresses the fundamental dynamic of the legend of being: "The hard and inescapable phenomenon to be faced is that we are living and dying at once. My commitment is to report the dialogue" (*Order/Folly,* p. 123).

The supreme poem of this third legend is **"King of the River,"** where Kunitz seeks a nonhuman creature to commune with: a salmon. This creature is noble (he is king of the river), and he represents the ultimate metaphysical paradox of consciousness itself, beyond all individual identity, but *within* mortality where "'The only music is time, / the only dance is love'" (p. 54).

The legend of being emphasizes process, movement, metamorphosis. Its characteristic images are those of the journey and of transcendent phallic shapes that represent pure, renewable energy questing onward without purpose, but finding meaning in the ecstasy of the process itself. We find this transcendent phallus in the rocket ship of space exploration, but even more centrally in **"The Knot"** where it is the "Obstinate bud, / sticky with life" (p. 1) that becomes a tree of life, or in **"King of the River"** where it is the male salmon, a "Finned Ego" thrashing upriver to spawn and die.

But a relentless forward thrusting is by no means the only characteristic movement of this legend. Sometimes the journeying self is aware of two countermovements within it: one that pulls toward the past (Kunitz calls it "nostalgia") and the other that pulls the self forward (Kunitz' term is "desire"). The forward thrusting of the phallic self is present in "desire" and in "will." But the backward motion is equally strong and has its role to play in the journey:

> I look behind,
> as I am compelled to look
> before I can gather strength
> to proceed on my journey

> (**"The Layers,"** p. 35)

The title of another poem, **"Revolving Meditation,"** brings us from the journeying self to the spiraling self. The spiraling self involves a revolving motion around a center. The spiral is an emblem for the obsessive self and the obsessive theme in Kunitz' poetry: for the poem and the self that circle or revolve above a set of images or a subject—returning to them again and again:

> How much I disapprove of it!
> How little I love it!
> Though, contrariwise,
> Can there be
> Anything half as dear?

> (p. 143)

The self spirals above the image or subject, trying to transform it, to convert life into legend, to "find the drama in a nutshell."

LOVE AND ART

When Kunitz speaks to the child of a marriage that is ending, he describes himself as "Your father, in whom two ambitions rave, / Like stations wrangling on the foreign wave / For spheres of influence." Such a father "loathes the heart that blends / His guilty love; but the quarrel never ends" (**"The Tutored Child,"** p. 155). In a companion poem later in the same book, he addresses the child's mother, whose accusing question: **"What Have You Done?"** was originally the poem's title. In the second poem the "two ambitions" of **"The Tutored Child"** are identified and fused in the transformed heart:

> From my angry side O child,
> Tumbles this agate heart,
> Your prize, veined with the root
> Of guilty life,
> From which flow love and art.

> (**"The Reckoning,"** p. 183)

"Love and art" are the two ways Kunitz seeks his identity. When, in the central poem, **"The Testing-Tree,"** the boy Kunitz enacts a ritual of three stones thrown at a sacred oak tree target, the goals for which he strives are the same:

> I played my game for keeps—
>
> for love, for poetry,
>   and for eternal life—
>   after the trials of summer.

> (p. 91)

THE KEY IMAGE

The key image is the single most important element in Stanley Kunitz' work. The clearest definitions Kunitz himself provides occur in a lecture given at the Library of Congress on May 12, 1975, and printed by the Library as the essay **"From Feathers to Iron"**:

> One of my convictions is that at the center of every poetic imagination is a cluster of key images which go back to the poet's childhood and which are usually associated with pivotal experiences, not necessarily traumatic. . . . That cluster of key images is the purest concentration of the self, the individuating node, the place where the persona starts. . . . In Keats's case, one can learn more about his quiddity by pursuing images of fever and of ooze than by analysing his literary sources. A critical property of key images is that they are unalterable, being good for a lifetime.

and in a 1977 interview with *Columbia* magazine:

> [*Interviewer:*] *You've spoken of a poet's finding his center, could you talk about that?*
>
> [Kunitz:] I'll try. You have at the center of your being a conglomeration of feelings, emotions, memories, traumas that are uniquely yours, that nobody else on earth can duplicate. They are the clue to your identity. If you don't track them down, lay claim to them, bring them out into the light, they'll eventually possess you, they'll fester, or erupt into compulsive behavior. The farther you stray from your center, the more you will be lost. That's one of the teachings of Lao-tzu. When you're there, at the existential core, you'll know it. Hopkins said in one of his letters that he could taste himself, and the taste was more distinctive than the taste of ale or alum, or the smell of walnutleaf or camphor. You can tell the poets who are working at their center by the distinctiveness of their voice, their constellation of key images, their instantly recognizable beat.

> (p. 5)

When Kunitz proposes such an important role for the cluster of key images, he is affirming the fact that his is a symbolic, associative intelligence rather than a conceptual, discursive one. For Kunitz, even at his most allusive, Christianity and Neo-platonism are sources of images for impulses and emotions, not philosophical or religious perspectives.

In Kunitz' work, key images can be verbs (e.g., flow, throb, pulse, turn, burst) as well as nouns (e.g., wound, house, threshold, tree, heart). The meanings of these key images emerge both *intensively* in the context of the particular poem and *extensively* in their various (and sometimes metamorphosed) recurrences throughout the life's work.

KEY IMAGES THROUGH TIME: THE WOUND AND THE HOUSE

One way of understanding how a key image functions in Kunitz' work as a whole is to trace its occurrences in the poems chronologically. Although a key image may be, to use Kunitz' phrase, "good for a lifetime," it is far from static. For example, during the course of the work, the wound image, perhaps the most important of Kunitz' key images, evolves and metamorphosizes, appearing also as a hurt, a stain, a scald, or a burn.

In the early poems of *Intellectual Things,* this image cluster centered on "wound" is linked to the mortality that so haunts the volume. It makes its first, earliest appearance as "hurt" (an abstraction) and as "stain":

> The blessing in this conscious fruit, the hurt
> Which is unanswerable, fill the brow
> With early death.
>
> **("Beyond Reason,"** p. 235)

> The shape confronting me upon the stair
> (Athlete of shadow, lighted by a stain
> On its disjunctive breast—I saw it plain—)
>
> **("Master and Mistress,"** p. 233)

The stain of the second poem is associated with a ghost/apparition. The hurt of the first is associated with the brow. In later poems, the hurt will become less abstract, more violent and concrete, and increasingly associated with the head and brow. At the outset it is an image soiled by mortality, but it is held at a distance, abstracted and intellectualized, even resisting its own physical implications. Later, this stain of mortality will reappear as a "mudstain" the son promises to wipe from the father's corpse (**"Father and Son"**). In a poem called **"The Pivot,"** the following strange image occurs:

> he leaves behind
> A faunlike head upon a tray,
> Spear buried in the mind.
>
> (p. 205)

In an early poem about the process of poetry, **"Mens Creatrix,"** a "rhythmic Spike of Light" was said to "cleave" the brain.

Without being reductive we can assert that this pervasive set of images is linked to the father's suicide as imagined by the son. since the suicide is the central fact of Kunitz' imaginative life, that from which all else flows, it is perhaps appropriate to skip from the first book to the fourth book and present the pivotal poem of the entire oeuvre, **"The Portrait."** In this poem the personal, biographical source of Kunitz' being is presented with the extraordinary simplicity and understatement characteristic of his later work (it appears in *The Testing-Tree,* published when Kunitz was 66):

> My mother never forgave my father
> for killing himself,
> especially at such an awkward time
> and in a public park,
> that spring
> when I was waiting to be born.
> She locked his name
> in her deepest cabinet
> and would not let him out,
> though I could hear him thumping.
> When I came down from the attic
> with the pastel portrait in my hand
> of a long-lipped stranger
> with a brave moustache
> and deep brown level eyes,
> she ripped it into shreds

> without a single word
> and slapped me hard.
> In my sixty-fourth year
> I can feel my cheek
> still burning.
>
> (p. 86)

"The Portrait" is the first poem to mention the father's death as a suicide. When we consider that children turn to their parents, the source of their being, for answers to their identity, the implications of a father who kills himself while the son is in the womb are indeed disturbing. This self-willed contradiction of life by one's own life-source is sufficient (when fused with the beloved stepfather's sudden death) to send Kunitz' life down a curious path. He must seek the father; he must confront this contradiction of life at his life's source, a contradiction whose image is the wound.

Among other significant information about Kunitz' life, **"The Portrait"** tells us that his father committed suicide in a public park and that all mention of the father and the event were prohibited by Kunitz' mother. This leads us to a crucial speculation: that the young Kunitz must *imagine* the method of suicide and that he imagines it as a revolver shot to the head (though drowning is not impossible and ponds and lakes are also key images associated with the father's death). Looking backward from **"The Portrait,"** we can recognize that the plot of an earlier poem, **"The Hemorrhage,"** closely parallels the actual circumstances of the father's suicide and that the wound is the centralizing image:

> The people made a ring
> Around the man in the park.
> He was our banished king
> Of blames and staunchless flows,
> Exhibitor of the dark
> Abominable rose;
>
> Our chief, returned at last
> From exile, with the grim
> Stamina of the lost,
> To show his sovereign hurt.
>
> (p. 163)

The hurt, the hemorrhage, the "staunchless" flow are powerful images both for the source of Kunitz' trauma and the power of that trauma to persist and constantly threaten his own being.

Without attempting to define or confine the meaning of the key image of wound, we can assert the following: it is connected to mortality; it is frequently located at the forehead or brow; it is connected to the father; and ultimately it becomes a link between father and son: a badge of shared suffering that each wears, a legacy from father to son that unites them. This last aspect of the image is seen in embryonic form in the orange/nail image of **"Father and Son,"** becomes a legacy in the burning cheek of the final lines of **"The Portrait,"** and achieves its final role as an emblem of communion in the very late poem **"Quinnapoxet,"** where the son signals to the father's ghost in the poem's final image:

> I touched my forehead
> with my swollen thumb
> and splayed my fingers out—
> in deaf-mute country
> the sign for father.

(p. 5)

In **"Quinnapoxet"** the speaker dreams a wound (a "gashed" and swollen thumb) and then sees the apparition of his two parents approaching. Like **"The Portrait,"** it is a poem of the family triad, one where we see very clearly the negating power of the mother over Kunitz' sense of self:

> "Why don't you write?" she cried
> from the folds of her veil.
> "We never hear from you."
> I had nothing to say to her.

(pp. 4–5)

Here, the mother is imagined as a barrier between son and father (now that death is no longer the barrier, death having been imaginatively overcome in **"The Way Down"**). The son signals to the father with his wound; wound to wound, they commune. The "swollen thumb" has to do with a phallic life-force, a life-force hurt into being, yet potent.

"Quinnapoxet" is the culmination of the father legend— Kunitz has gone as far as he can go in psychological terms and in the context of son—mother—father. In **"The Knot,"** the father legend (symbolized by the "bleeding" knot wound) yields to the legend of pure being (symbolized by the phallic tree of life). The metamorphosis (or regeneration) of wound into phallus is that point at which we pass from psychology to metaphysics, from a hymn to the father to a hymn in praise of pure being and its power to renew itself and us with it.

A less spectacular, but equally important set of key images that relate to the legend of pure being is that of "house" or "home." House/home represents the backward motion of being (nostalgia) just as the phallic rocketship, tree of life, and "Finned Ego" of the salmon represent its forward motion (desire).

How does the image of house/home relate to nostalgia? By investigating the image of house/home we uncover the power of context in determining the meaning of a key image. Considered without a specific dramatic context, one might well assume that house/home had positive meanings related to security, domestic intimacy, and belongingness. But in Kunitz' poetry these positive qualities are constantly undercut in such a way as to establish a fundamental aspect of his vision: that security and stability in the physical and emotional or social worlds are illusions.

He establishes and undermines the positive aspects of the image at the same time. The most revealing instance of this is in **"Father and Son."** In this poem the son has pursued the father's ghost across a dream landscape, hoping at last to catch him and confront him with his needs for guidance in the world. The pursuing son anguishes over the opening words to this crucial encounter:

> How should I tell him my fable and the fears,
> How bridge the chasm in a causal tone,
> Saying, "The house, the stucco one you built,
> We lost."

(p. 157)

The father, whose presence would give stability to a son's identity, had the power to "build a house"—to create a surrounding stability and security. The house that the father built his survivors have lost.

Here we see the essence of Kunitz' dilemma in the father legend: he is in awe of a father he never knew. He feels a son's intense need for fathering and guidance. One image of the father's mythic power is the house he built, and when the son looks back into the past, he does so with *longing*. He wants, impossibly, the dead father to return— "'Father,' I cried, 'Return! You know / The way.'" As long as Kunitz associates the house with the lost father, he sees it in the distant past.

In the poem that immediately precedes **"Father and Son,"** we see the image of the house connected to the mother/ beloved legend, and thus the image acquires other meanings. In this poem, **"The Signal from the House,"** the house is associated negatively with both the mother and the beloved, people who "were too much with" the speaker and therefore "secretly against" him. He seeks to abandon them and the house in order to embark on a journey and to escape "the old life." The signal of the title calls him back "like cry of conscience" to what he knows to be his destruction. If the house was built by the father, it is inhabited by the mother. The son, in order to grow, must leave the house and embark on his journey; if he actually yields to the backward, nostalgic pull of the house, he accedes to his own self-destruction.

Although the house/home image is strongly linked with the past and pastness, it most truly belongs with poems of the legend of being, where homelessness is connected to desolation and solitude as a condition of being. At the mythic level this is the story of our eviction from Eden, our first home. In **"Robin Redbreast,"** where one of the poem's primary strategies is to identify the bird's situation and the speaker's, we see Kunitz making connections between Eden, the self's desolation and insecurity, and the house image:

> It was the dingiest bird
> you ever saw, all the color
> washed from him, as if
> he had been standing in the rain,
> friendless and stiff and cold,

since Eden went wrong.
In the house marked For Sale,
where nobody made a sound,
in the room where I lived
with an empty page . . .

(p. 56)

In another poem of the legend of being, **"The Flight of Apollo,"** the poem's primary movement is the outward journeying of adventurous desire, but the opening lines establish Kunitz' special sense of home as a precondition of the quest—"Earth was my home, but even there I was a stranger" says the astronaut, and later "think of me as nostalgic, afraid, exalted." The astronaut's journey is one of the purest forms of the legend of being, and its source is a home that is not a home.

When Kunitz dramatizes the legend of being as a male salmon, the "King" of the river journeying upriver to spawn and die, house/home becomes "kingdom," and the poem's final paradox again concerns home and homelessness as a state of being:

> he is not broken but endures,
> limber and firm
> in the state of his shining,
> forever inheriting his salt kingdom,
> from which he is banished
> forever.

("King of the River," p. 54)

In one sense this "salt kingdom" is the ocean he is journeying away from, upriver, and up fish ladders over dams. Earlier in the same poem, through the image of a ladder, Kunitz links the salt kingdom/home *behind* the salmon to nostalgia:

> If the heart were pure enough,
> but it is not pure,
> you would admit
> that nothing compels you
> any more, nothing
> at all abides,
> but nostalgia and desire,
> the two-way ladder
> between heaven and hell.

(pp. 53–54)

We have here the fundamental dynamic of the legend of being. A backward urge toward "house/home" that is called "nostalgia" and is either illusory or, if acted upon, dangerous. And a forward urge called "desire" whose movement is the journey and whose image is often phallic as in the "Finned Ego" of the male salmon. Desire in the legend is not desire for some object or goal, but is simply an index of the intensity of being itself: "'*What do I want of my life? / More! More!*'" (**"Journal for My Daughter,"** p. 42).

The overriding image is of the self's journey, but the backward glance of nostalgia that I have discussed earlier

is as much a condition of being as the restless forward journey into the unknown.

We can speculate that for a key image to work successfully in a body of poetry, it must be rooted in personal experience. Among literary modes of thought, the key image (a variant of symbol) has a peculiar power of verticality: it can function with equal authority at different levels of being or reference. Kunitz demonstrates his awareness of these different levels of being or reference that the key image has simultaneous access to when he remarks apropos of the key image "pond" in his work, "As far as I am concerned, the pond in Quinnapoxet, Poe's 'dank tarn of Auber,' and the mere in which Beowulf fights for his life with Grendel and the water-hag are one and the same" (*Order/Folly,* p. 125). Similarly, if we glance briefly to the side and recall Kunitz' ambition of "converting life into legend" (life and legend being two parallel levels of being), we can see that the image of the wound functions in one context (say, **"The Portrait"**) at the literal level of the lived life, and in another context it functions at a universal, legendary level as the wound of mortality and human suffering.

The Spiral and the Journey: Two Forms of Self

The central and centralizing figure of all lyric poetry is the dramatized self. In trying to understand the nature of the dramatized self in Kunitz' work and how it functions, we gradually become aware that there are two distinct concepts of the self and that they are ultimately complimentary. Like the wave and particle theories of light, neither of which alone explains the phenomenon of light, both concepts of self are needed by Kunitz in order to let him tell his whole story.

The first is the concept of the spiraling self. The spiraling self represents our human impulse to return again and again to a particular issue. The spiraling self circles over this recurrent issue with a funneling motion that goes either higher (wider arcs) or lower (narrower), depending on whether the self is trying to rise above the issue or approach it more closely. Whether the self is ascending or descending, its purpose is the same: to arrive at a different level of being from which to view the same issue. To understand an old problem at a different level of being is to arrive at a new understanding of the problem.

The spiraling self acknowledges also the centripetal power of certain themes, images, or events (sometimes traumas) in human life: certain moments we return to again and again seeking release, transcendence, transformation, clarity. These powerful moments are none other than Kunitz' key images and are dominated by the powerful figures that often stand behind them: mother, father, beloved.

When we spoke earlier about the figures of Spirit and Nature behind the father and mother, we might also have spoken in terms of the spiraling self. The Spirit Father is at the same position on the spiral as the biological father, only on a higher level of being. When I say "higher" or "lower," I am not speaking evaluatively; lower simply means closer to the key image and its source in lived experience. Higher speaks about the self's impulse to deal with an event at the level of archetype or myth or by means of substitution and displacement—an impulse still anchored to its source in the world of experience.

The second self is the journeying self. If the spiraling self has a vertical impulse around a central key image, then the journeying self has a linear, horizontal movement. Here meaning concentrates in the figure of the self, the "I," as it journeys through the landscape of the poem. This self has a history in terms of pastness ("nostalgia" is its emotional coloring) and an impulse toward the onward journey (which it understands as "desire"). This self has an urgent, linear sense of time and of mortality. The journeying self is the one most adapted to the legend of being as it unfolds in the later poems, but often, as in **"The Layers,"** both "selves" function together to create the fullest story.

THE CONSTELLATION AND THE SPIRALING SELF

When Kunitz speaks about key images that recur throughout a poet's work, one might easily arrive at the notion of obsession. One could argue that the history of important lyric poetry from, say, Sappho or Petrarch on is a history of obsessed poets whose obsessions are thematically profound. But there are certain negative connotations to the word obsession which should be confronted, connotations of narrowness and spiritual stasis or fatalism. These negative connotations might seem appropriate to a poet such as Sylvia Plath whose vision of the world might image the cluster of key images as a kind of interiorized astrological fatalism as in the final lines of her poem "Words":

> While
> From the bottom of the pool, fixed stars
> Govern a life.

> (from *Ariel*)

But Stanley Kunitz' poetry is a poetry of survival, questing, and renewal through imagination. If Kunitz' poetry errs in its view of things, it errs deliberately on the side of the heroic:

> I am your man on the moon, a speck of
> megalomania, restless for the leap toward
> island universes pulsing beyond where the
> constellations set.

> (**"The Flight of Apollo,"** p. 48)

The question becomes: how does the concept of a cluster of key images accommodate itself to movement and growth? The answer is: through the spiraling self. The spiraling self can be imagined as a funneling movement above a still center composed of the cluster of key images: a funneling movement above a constellated stillness of images. If the key image can represent the grim fixity of fate,

then the spiraling self is motion, movement, possibility circling above fixity and seeking to transform it.

We find real warrant for the notion of a dynamic spiral in the work itself:

> The spiral verb that weaves
> Through the crystal of our lives,
> Of myth and water made
> And incoherent blood . . .

> (**"A Spark of Laurel,"** p. 146)

We see the spiral motion self-consciously present in the poem title, **"Revolving Meditation,"** whose opening lines enact the ambivalence of the spiraling self toward its own obsessions:

> How much I disapprove of it!
> How little I love it!
> Though, contrariwise,
> Can there be
> Anything half as dear?

> (p. 143)

and whose later lines show the marriage of free will and compulsion that characterize the self that has yielded to the power of recurring images in order to unlock the mystery of their meaning:

> Preferring to hear, as I
> Am forced to hear . . .

> (p. 145)

In this poem, Kunitz revolves around trauma seeking a way out, seeking a way to make the *circle* of endless repetition into a *spiral* of higher levels of consciousness (life become legend). In **"Night Letter,"** we encounter "the spiral of a soul balanced on a stone" (p. 161).

In a late poem, **"The Illumination,"** Dante appears to Kunitz in a vision, standing in a spiral-like "cone of light" (p. 45). When the bewildered Dante speaks he says, "I was here before," and thus touches on a central truth of the spiraling self: the need to repeat a significant act or image in order to reach its meaning. Dante himself is both a spirit guide to Kunitz (a precursor poet who converted life into legend in his *Vita Nuova*) and a Spirit Father: Kunitz' own, long-sought father at a higher level of being. Dante's "cone of light" and his return tell us about the spiraling self and its desire to transform.

If we were to inquire what image is at the center of Kunitz' funnel of self at its narrowest, we might follow another image of the spiral:

> The gestures made is woven in the sleeve,
> The spiral echo sinks into the grain.

> (**"The Harsh Judgment,"** p. 165)

The image here is of the knot in wood. It is a variant of the wound/mortality image in Kunitz: one that is heavily fated and static in this context. Kunitz' late poem **"The Knot"** enacts a triumph of renewal and affirmation over this fatal image that is both the father's death wound and all human mortality. Here the knot of "trauma" is not fixed and unalterable, for out of the very wound itself, renewal and regeneration occur:

> I hear it come
> with a rush of resin
> out of the trauma
> of its lopping-off.
> Obstinate bud,
> sticky with life.
>
> (p. 1)

The spiraling self encounters a phenomenon again and again—hoping to transform it. The wisdom of *repetition* in regard to hard things is a lesson the natural world teaches in the late poem, **"The Mulch"**:

> A man with a leaf in his head
> watches an indefatigable gull
> dropping a piss-clam on the rocks
> to break it open.
> Repeat. Repeat.
>
> (p. 55)

Later in the same poem we hear:

> "Try! Try!" clicks the beetle in his wrist

We are involved not only in the repetition of actions but the repetition of words—a favorite stylistic device in Kunitz. This phrasal repetition that occurs throughout Kunitz' work is closely linked to incantation and the magical use of language as a means of transformation:

> Ha! Once again I heard
> The transubstantial word
> That is not mine to speak
> Unless I break, I break.
>
> (**"A Spark of Laurel,"** p. 146)

THE JOURNEYING SELF

There is a second, equally central version of the self in Kunitz' work, one that complements the spiraling self but discloses its own meanings and possibilities. The journeying self might be the one Kunitz is referring to when he speaks of the strategy of certain modern artists: "A few dare to submit themselves to the ordeal of walking through the fires of selfhood into a world of archetypal forms" (*Order/Folly,* p. 13). This version of the self emphasizes process, movement—images of journey that are linear as opposed to spiraling.

We encounter the journeying self at the very outset. In a poem from the first book, the speaker feels the need to leave a house and, in the final lines, embark on a journey:

> And I shall go
> By silent lanes and leave you timeless here.
>
> (**"In a Strange House,"** p. 232)

The final poem of this book, **"Vita Nuova,"** echoes these lines—"And I will go, unburdened, on the quiet lane / Of my eternal kind." **"Vita Nuova"** takes its title from Dante's poem of spiritual rebirth after loss. It establishes the quest as a central structural device of individual poems as well as a theme for the work as a whole.

In **"Vita Nuova"** the journey is specifically concerned with the father. Later, the journey becomes an image for a metaphysical gesture:

> But I fly towards Possibility,
> In the extravagantly gay
> Surprise of a journey,
> Careless that I am bound
> To the flaming wheel of my bones
>
> (**"Revolving Meditation,"** p. 145)

In the image of the flaming wheel, fate (the spiral flattened to the closed repetition of circle) impinges on the freedom and optimism of the journey metaphor.

Journey in Kunitz is related to quest—to the heroic self encountering the basic conditions of its personal destiny (as in **"The Approach to Thebes,"** where an omniscient Oedipus journeys to the city) or the impersonal hugeness of the universe, as in **"The Flight of Apollo,"** where the astronaut speaks:

> Earth was my home, but even there I was a stranger. This mineral crust. I walk like a swimmer. What titanic bombardments in those old astral wars! I know what I know: I shall never escape from strangeness or complete my journey. Think of me as nostalgic, afraid, exalted. I am your man on the moon, a speck of megalomania, restless for the leap toward island universes pulsing beyond where the constellations set.
>
> (p. 48)

The ultimate imperative of the journey is courage:

> It is necessary to go
> through dark and deeper dark
> and not to turn.
>
> (**"The Testing-Tree,"** p. 92)

The journey is recognized in later Kunitz poetry as the appropriate governing metaphor for the legend of being: it is the truest story of our consciousness. The salmon on his journey upriver to spawn and die is an image of ourselves, our creature selves. He is pulled forward by desire, pulled backward in imagination by nostalgia, but he *exists* "in the state of his shining"—that is: in the active intensity of the journey itself. There is no rest, and no goal. Finally, even death is regarded as "the threshold of the last great mystery"—a mere marker the heroic journeyer will pass and pass beyond:

> no doubt the next chapter
> in my book of transformations
> is already written.

I am not done with my changes.

(**"The Layers,"** p. 36)

"The Layers" is no doubt the penultimate poem of the journey. It begins:

> I have walked through many lives,
> some of them my own,
> and I am not who I was,
> though some principle of being
> abides, from which I struggle
> not to stray.

(p. 35)

In the midst of this poem celebrating the journey of self, we find a precise image of the spiral (here partly repudiated by the ambiguous adjective "scavenger") and the static constellation of key images which the spiral moves above:

> and the slow fires trailing
> from the abandoned camp-sites,
> over which scavenger angels
> wheel on heavy wings.

(p. 35)

The dominant journey image returns:

> Yet I turn, I turn,
> exulting somewhat,
> with my will intact to go
> wherever I need to go,
> and every stone on the road
> precious to me.

(pp. 35–36)

This journey has purpose, if only in its own courageous acceptance of the process itself, and is contrasted with a purposeless and meaningless form of journey in which "I roamed through wreckage."

Kunitz has always arranged the sequence of his poems within a book with the utmost care. It is therefore significant that the first poem in a very late book is a major poem of the vertically rising spiraling self (**"The Knot"**) and the final poem is metaphorically governed by the journeying self (**"The Layers"**).

Because the journey takes place inside history and time, it has an implied beginning and end. Kunitz tends to focus his poems in mid-journey, even when the end is foreknown as in **"The Approach to Thebes."** Why? At one level Kunitz is deeply fatalistic—"the verdict's bitten on the brazen gates," Oedipus says of his future (**"The Approach to Thebes,"** p. 112). It is possible to say that death ends all journeys—and against the tension of that fate, Kunitz protests with the power of imagination to transform or the self itself to metamorphose. Out of the great negation comes the heroic affirmation of being:

> Let be! Let be!
> I shake my wings
> and fly into its boughs.

(**"The Knot,"** p. 1)

The human self journeys from beginning to end. But because of imagination, we are both more and less than human: we can descend to the creature self or fly upward as the angel/bird/winged demon of the final lines of **"The Knot."** In other words, the vertical nature of the spiraling self is not simply linked to trauma's recurrence but also to the way the imagining self eludes its fate in time.

SURVIVAL AND SELF

In Kunitz' work the questing self is a self determined to survive against the odds of "the hurt / Which is unanswerable [and] fill[s] the brow / with early death" (**"Beyond Reason"**). The themes of identity and a surviving self merge in later Kunitz:

> My name is Solomon Levi,
> the desert is my home,
> my mother's breast was thorny,
> and father I had none.
>
> The sands whispered, *Be separate,*
> the stones taught me, *Be hard.*
> I dance, for the joy of surviving,
> on the edge of the road.

(**"An Old Cracked Tune,"** p. 87)

In this poem's persona we recapitulate the characteristics of the parental dynamic in Kunitz' imaginative life: the rejecting mother, the almost mythically absent father, and the psychic consequences for the son's identity—the ambiguous lessons of isolation and "hardness." But the final resolution is again one of affirmation: the sheer act of survival becomes a joy and a motive for being.

In the later work, intensity of being and intensity of desire fuse and become the animating force of the surviving self, as seen in **"Journal for My Daughter,"** where Kunitz depicts himself as a "white-haired prowler" haunting his daughter's dreams and life:

> the folded message in his hands
> is stiff with dirt and wine-stains,
> older than the Dead Sea Scrolls.
> Daughter, read:
> *What do I want of my life*?
> *More! More*!

(p. 42)

Or in the climactic incantation of **"The Knot"** where the repeated exclamation exists paradoxically as both a plea for the life force to desist and an affirmation of that very life force in all its intensity: "Let be! Let be!"

For Kunitz the quest for identity involves encounters with such painful aspects of the human condition as suffering, trauma, fear, loss, rejection, and mortality: those aspects of the human condition that most threaten the self and its search for meaning. These aspects are encountered in the arena of the dramatic lyric and a representative struggle ensues, out of which the self emerges as the human embodiment of being. A touchstone for the self's encounter with negating forces might be a statement by Paul Tillich, which Kunitz quotes in his 1977 *Columbia* magazine interview: "the self-affirmation of a being is stronger the more non-being it can take into itself" (p. 5).

THE PRIVATE AND THE PERSONAL IN LYRIC POETRY

When Baudelaire speaks of the poet as a kind of "public dreamer," he is describing both the nature of a kind of lyric poem and the curious burdens it puts on the poet and the facts of the poet's life. If the dream is a model for the process and the product of a certain kind of lyric imagination, then how is the lyric poem to be reconciled to a higher order than the self? Kunitz has endorsed Gerard Manley Hopkins' statement that he desires a poetry which retains "the taste of self," and his own program, the "conversion of life into legend," is a precise statement of such a poet's task in expanding the implications of lyric poetry without denying the central, centralizing reality of the self.

A major lyric poet such as Baudelaire, Rilke, or Yeats gambles on his ability to dramatize the personal issues of the life in such a way that we as readers gain access to them and yet they retain the tension and intensity of private crisis. An important audience aspect of this endeavor is *curiosity*: we want to know about other lives; we want to hear stories about other lives. The power of curiosity can operate in the poet's favor almost as a magical spell when the story is presented in compelling language as in Coleridge's "The Rime of the Ancient Mariner":

> He holds him with his glittering eye—
> The Wedding-Guest stood still,
> And listens like a three years' child:
> The Mariner hath his will.
>
> The Wedding-Guest sat on a stone:
> He cannot choose but hear.

The other aspect, which rests with the poet, is his ability to exteriorize the drama of the life and give it aesthetic structure. It is a test of the power of this kind of lyric poet's imagination—whether or not he can dramatize the private tensions, crises, images, and events of his life in such a way as to make them meaningful and accessible to others.

Yeats succeeded in assimilating facts and events of another person's life into the ongoing themes of his poetry: Maude Gonne is a dramatics persona in his work and undergoes even further imaginative transformation to appear as Helen of Troy. In Baudelaire we see mythological structures and references, but we also see a version of "warring opposites" or "polarized contradictions" (the ideal and the real world; the dream and the reality of "The Double Room" of *Paris Spleen*), a strategy that also appears in early Kunitz. One of the main functions of literary allusion (e.g., the Neoplatonic and Christian references in early

Kunitz) is as a storehouse of publicly accessible images that can mediate between the poet's private world and the public world of the reader.

Privacy ultimately translates as failure in lyric poetry. The poem must be rooted deeply in the personal, and yet some level of universality of human experience must be posited and located, either consciously or unconsciously, by the poet in the work. The poem must go from the level of life to the level of legend.

In one of Kunitz' rare commentaries on a poem of his own (**"Father and Son"**), we have a lucid statement of the connection between life and legend (i.e., poem) that is central to his ethos as a poet:

> I do not propose to launch into a full-scale autobiography here, but I am ready to say that all the essential details of the poem are true, as true as dreams are, with their characteristic fusions, substitutions, and dislocations.
>
> *(Order/Folly,* p. 124.)

We have here the meeting of outer and inner reality, life and legend. We also have the dream as a model for the transformation process (what Kunitz calls "conversion"). The process is complex, involving fusion, substitutions, and dislocations: the powerful processes of the associative imagination that are central to Kunitz' art. These processes are irrational but intelligent; as Freud believes, dreaming is that mode of thought employed by the mind when it is asleep.

To say that such a poet is egocentric or narcissistic is to miss the point and the purpose of such poetry. The "I" of such a poem is also a transformed "I," a dramatized figure whose movement through the language of the poem is a representative human quest for meaning in a particular set of circumstances. Such a poet cannot escape the power of certain events in his life, but he can transform, through imagination, these events in such a way that they crystallize and constitute meaning.

One may be, as Auden says of Yeats, "hurt into poetry"— but poetry is hurt transformed. Kunitz is hurt into his quest, and the quest discloses level upon level of meaning as it spirals outwards from its source in pain. Lines of Yeats on the power of imagination and self-transformation seem relevant here:

> *The friends that have it I do wrong*
> *When ever I remake a song,*
> *Should know what issue is at stake:*
> *It is myself that I remake.*[5]

The dramatic lyric poet knows that the "I" of the poems is not limited by the conditions of the "I" of the life: the poet's quest is to remake the "I" into that form of meaning known as the poem. The self, the "I" of the poems, is the figure that enacts the drama, but the poet's belief is in imagination (which transforms) and in poetry itself. What poetry accomplishes is the embodiment of the transformed life beyond oblivion and change, in the crystallized permanence of form and the eternal present of its telling.

The dramatized lyric I am describing consists of at least three parts: *the life,* those subjective and objective facts to which the poet is compelled to be faithful; *the legend,* that level of the human story that is shared and is in some way universal or archetypal; and *conversion,* the dynamic process that transforms life into legend and which poets are prone to call imagination. Life and legend, when successfully functioning in a poem, are parallel levels of being. A curious thing about the dramatic lyric is that we do not find it satisfying or compelling if it takes place entirely on the level of legend; it must have what Hopkins called "the taste of self."

In connection with conversion, a quotation from Kunitz serves to emphasize the lyric poet's faith in the power of magical language (here the key image) and his personal yet universally comprehensible motive: "It's curious how certain images out of the life—not necessarily the most spectacular—keep flashing signals from the depths, as if to say: 'Come down to me—and be reborn!'" (**Order/Folly,** p. 305.)

Kunitz' poems often ponder or enact the process of transformation and are consciously concerned with spiritual renewal through transforming imagination. Such a poem will sometimes contain the dross (the "litter") in order to transform it at poem's end, as in **"Revolving Meditation"** or **"My Surgeons,"** both from *Selected Poems.* Keats' notion, expressed in a letter of May, 1819, that this world is not a "vale of tears," as religion misconceives it to be, but "a vale of soul-making" speaks directly to the poet's self-appointed task of self-transformation and spiritual growth through imagination.

FORM AND THE DRAMATIC LYRIC: STORY,
SYMBOL, AND SELF

A poet whom I respect a great deal once announced to me that "all personal tragedy is in fact metaphysical tragedy." I responded that to me the converse seemed true: "All metaphysical tragedy is in fact personal tragedy." The two of us represented two profoundly differing temperaments; his abstracted the tragic encounters of his personal life; mine personalized phenomena which, tragic or not, are part of the human condition. I thought at the time that these temperaments could not be reconciled, could not coexist in one consciousness or one poetry.

Kunitz, in his best work, resolves themes on both a personal, psychological level and a metaphysical level, and with equal authority. When the legend of the beloved and mother is followed forward through Kunitz' work, it culminates psychologically in **"The Magic Curtain"**— where the beloved replaces the mother and love and forgiveness replace angry intransigence. At the metaphysical level, it resolves itself in **"A Spark of Laurel,"** where "mother and mistress" are recognized as one, and identi-

fied as the source of tragic (fatal) poetry; siren and Clytemnestra: the dark, compelling muse.

If **"The Magic Curtain"** resolves itself as *story* (the human, linear level), then **"A Spark of Laurel"** resolves itself as *symbol* (the transcendent, vertical gesture). Story and symbol are the two central forms of meaning available to poetry structured by nonrational intelligence.

When Tolstoy remarks that "all happy families resemble one another," he is acknowledging the necessary and experienced link between disharmony and story. Where there is no disharmony, no discrete centers of energy, there can be no interesting story. The *drama* of the dramatic lyric necessitates conflict and contraries. When in "The Marriage of Heaven and Hell" Blake says, "Without Contraries is no progression. Attraction and Repulsion, Reason and Energy, Love and Hate, are necessary to Human Existence," we might add that they are necessary to human story as well. At the formal level, the contraries of story polarize language: make it tense, intensify it. Without the tension-creating quality of disharmonious story, language would simply dribble down the page.

In Kunitz' poetry, the drama can be an interior drama such as the primordial conflict of heart—mind, or some other polarity such as memory versus oblivion. When it is external, it might be that most ancient of dramas: he—she. The main point is that a fundamental structure of the dramatic lyric is that of a story in which two centers of energy (often two characters, sometimes a character and a landscape or object) enact a drama that polarizes and intensifies language while the story moves through time (down the page) toward some resolution of its conflict. A lyric poet who fails to discover or posit this essential underlying framework of contraries may be forced to exaggerate the sensuous, nondiscursive aspects of language (e.g., "The Lost Son" of Roethke or many of the poems of Hart Crane).

We often speak of a poet's gifts, certain innate talents that discipline and experience can develop but cannot substitute for. Among the most frequently mentioned are a "good ear" (i.e., a sensitivity in hearing and employing sounds), a gift for metaphors, and a feel for compelling rhythms. I would assert that, in the case of the dramatic lyric, a gift for formal unity should be included in the list of talents or gifts the ideal poet is blessed with. If we acknowledge the existence of organic form as Coleridge defines it, we must account for it as an innate predisposition and possession of the poet's consciousness, not just of the individual poems the poet produces.

In the dramatic lyric, the gift for formal unity is inextricably tied up with the self. The self is that central, centralizing force that constellates all the elements of language and experience into that peculiar form of meaning called the poem. The image I would use for this "self" and its role is derived from chemistry: it is possible under certain conditions to create a supersaturated chemical solution in which molecules are held in suspension and do not precipitate out. When a piece of string is lowered into a beaker of this liquid, the molecules cling to and crystallize around the string. That string is the self lowered into the supersaturated solution of the unconscious: language clings to it in forms as absolute and precise as the internal structure of each crystal, yet as seemingly random as the attachment of one crystal cluster to the next along the string.

The self is a given quality of consciousness, a gift. The lyric poet possesses it and *must* possess it in order to create lyric poetry that has the unity and wholeness we require of all art. Like all gifts and talents, it is possessed in greater degree by some poets than by others, some lack it almost entirely and strive to compensate for it through learned skills.

Keeping in mind one of Kunitz' definitions of the key image ("You have at the center of your being a conglomeration of feelings, emotions, memories, traumas that are uniquely yours, that nobody else on earth can replicate. They are the clue to your identity"), we can say that for a lyric poet the self means having access to a lifetime's key images, images which form the structures of consciousness and the structures of poems.

It is difficult to say exactly where and how this self exists in the life of the poet. It is certainly not the ordinary ego-I of the poet's daily existence. Perhaps we can locate and ponder it best by studying the transformed "I" that enacts the drama of the poem, because it is there—in the poem—that we see the self as the active, formative, form-giving principle of the lyric. Even when the "I" is not overtly present in the poem, the self is present: each word is its footprint in the snow of the page. To return to the earlier image—even when the self is not manifest, it must be there *within* the language of the poem, just as the string is present within its sheath of crystals.

Notes

1. Having proposed a psychological model for the underlying structure of Kunitz' work, it is necessary to say that we need not adopt any particular theory of identity development through the interaction of family members. By the time Kunitz left high school for college in 1922, he had already read Freud. In his essays and interviews, Kunitz rarely mentions psychological figures or theories, although when Jung's name was brought up by an interviewer, Kunitz mentioned being favorably impressed by an essay on individuation.

2. Selden Rodman, *Tongues of Fallen Angels* (New York: New Directions, 1974), 99. 96–98.

3. "The Poetry Miscellany," *Salmagundi* (1978), 8:30.

4. As Schiller says in his description of the elegiae mode in poetry. "The content of poetic lamentation can therefore never be an external object, it must

always be only an ideal, inner one, even if it grieves over some loss in actuality, it must first be transformed into an ideal loss" (*The Naive and Sentimental in Poetry*).

5. William Butler Yeats, *The Collected Works in Verse and Prose of William Butler Yeats* (Stratford-on-Avon: 1908), vol. 2, unpaged proem. This is the only appearance of this poem previous to the Variorum Edition.

James Idema (review date 22 December 1985)

SOURCE: "Stanley Kunitz Shares 'Next-to-Last' Poems, Essays with Readers," in *Chicago Tribune,* December 22, 1985, p. 39.

[*In the following review, Idema offers a favorable assessment of* Next-to-Last Things.]

There is an appropriateness, somehow, in turning to **Next-to-Last Things** in this, the waning of the year. It is that kind of book. Portrait of the artist as an old man. One pictures the 80–year-old poet rummaging among the scraps of his late harvest, musing over what to reject, what to save, fretting over a word or phrase that at the moment seems somehow vagrant, smiling to himself at the felicitousness of "Seedcorn and Windfall" under which he groups the lesser pieces at the end, reluctant finally to let anything go. The penultimate title of the book rings wistful. It seems to say, I'm not quite finished.

"To a poet of my age," he writes, "each new poem presents itself in a double aspect, as a separate entity demanding to be perfected and, conversely, as an extension of the lifework, to which it is joined by invisible psychic filaments. In this latter aspect, all the poems of a lifetime can be said to add up to a single poem . . . one that is never satisfied with itself, never finished."

There is beauty and wisdom in this modest book, although its ultimate success may be measured by how many readers it sends to the bookstores in search of more comprehensive Kunitz collections. Having **The Poems of Stanley Kunitz, 1928–1978** at hand while reading **Next-to-Last Things** is helpful, even essential. The new book contains only a dozen short poems; the bulk of the text consists of essays and reflections on life and on poets and poetry—Whitman, Keats and Lowell most prominently—with several references to poems of his own that are not included. Particularly in an interview that appeared in a 1982 issue of Paris Review and is reproduced here, significant works from the poet's long but comparatively unprolific career are discussed in specific detail. Assuming the general reader's familiarity with them is assuming too much.

On the other hand, while there are rich rewards to be had from searching out vintage Kunitz in previous collections, perusing this slim new sampler is not without its own pleasures. The poems that open the book are leaner than those from the early and middle years, narrower on their pages. "I've tried to squeeze the water out of my poems," Kunitz says in the interview. Some of them are serene and melancholy, as you might expect. Most reflect the sky-and-weather environment of his Provincetown summer home, where he is most comfortable confronting "the great simplicities." But the best ones are full of action and vivid imagery. **"Raccoon Journal,"** for all its humorous celebration of this precocious night prowler, has a preternatural ring to it, while **"The Wellfleet Whale,"** without being the slightest bit obvious, is full of the wonder and dread of Herman Melville.

There aren't many poets of Kunitz's generation still productive; still around, even. Robert Penn Warren comes most readily to mind. But I am more reminded of Robert Frost (though he would be 110 if he were still alive!), particularly in the discussions of the nature of poetry, its basic properties. Both poets insisted that an independent life-force is part of a good poem's essence. Frost noted "a course of lucky events" that a poem takes, "finding its own name as it goes" before it "ends in a clarification of life . . . a momentary stay against confusion."

Kunitz says in the Paris Review interview: "A poem has secrets that the poet knows nothing of. It takes on a life and a will of its own. It might have proceeded differently—toward catastrophe, resignation, terror, despair—and I still would have to claim it."

Thomas D'Evelyn (essay date 6 March 1987)

SOURCE: "Stanley Kunitz: 'American Freethinker,'" in *Christian Science Monitor,* March 6, 1987, p. B2.

[*In the following essay, D'Evelyn provides an overview of Kunitz's career and discusses the poem "Day of Foreboding" from* Next-to-Last Things.]

Put aside the Pulitzer Prize (1959). Put aside the years as consultant in poetry to the Library of Congress, the praise for his translations from Andrei Voznesensky and Anna Akhmatova, the prestige of editing the "Yale Series of Younger Poets," the election to the 50–member American Academy of Arts and Letters in 1975, the chancellorship of the Academy of American Poets, the years spent in the echoing classrooms of major universities.

Put aside the generations of poets he has survived, especially the tormented one identified with his friend Robert Lowell. Put aside the still-fresh laurels of the Bollingen Prize in Poetry, awarded him last month, along with New York State's Walt Whitman Citation of Merit for Poets.

"*Great events are about to happen. . . .*" So begins a little poem from Stanley Kunitz's most recent book, *Next-to-*

Last Things (the Atlantic Monthly Press, Boston, 1985). As poems go, it's a modest-looking thing, almost archaic-sounding, maybe a translation from Old English. It helps put things into perspective.

In a way, Kunitz always goes with the flow: traditional forms in the early poetry, when they were popular; looser-looking ones since the '60s.

In a way, Kunitz had to go with the flow. After graduating *summa cum laude* and winning prizes and taking his master's from Harvard (he says he apprenticed with Alfred North Whitehead), he was denied a teaching position because "Anglo-Saxons would resent being taught English by a Jew." He went home—Worcester, Mass.—and became a reporter on the Worcester Telegram.

After the Sacco-Vanzetti trial and executions, he quit and carried Vanzetti's letters to New York in search of a publisher. The Red scare made it impossible. He got a job editing literary biographies, was married and moved to the country, was drafted (a non-affiliated pacifist), and didn't teach his first class, at Bennington College, Vt., until 1946. So Kunitz is not a creature of the academy.

Recently he discussed the origins of a poem he published in 1944. It's called **"Fathers and Sons."** It's about the way sons turn away from fathers, toward their own futures. He doesn't mention the fact that his father committed suicide in a public park some months before he was born. He says, "I had no intimation then that the theme that had been given to me would soon be haunting the imagination of a whole generation of poets." He goes through some sample poems, then turns back to Homer for "a more constructive archetype." The modesty ("the theme that has been *given to me*") and the long view are typical.

Kunitz's intellectual independence goes back to his mother. She was, he says, "one of the pioneer businesswomen, a dress designer and manufacturer." He does not recall being kissed by her during his childhood. He never doubted her "fierce pride" in his academic and literary accomplishments. Her heroes were Bernard Shaw and Bertrand Russell.

Kunitz calls himself "an American freethinker."

Kunitz's recent poems at their best are like pieces of driftwood. Shaped by enormous impersonal forces, they seem to have been deposited on the page, stripped and worn, polished by wind, sun, water, rock, time: by history, intellectual and natural.

In **"Day of Foreboding,"** the laconic style is deceptive. The rhythmic flatness—a waste to an English ear—gains sculptural relief by the brevity and, wholeness of each line.

At closer range, "unprecedented" is comic-tragic: That's where, after the thick irony of the opening, the poem takes off. The gnomic line "My bones are a family in their tent" may recall Kunitz's early love of Yeats. But it stands, alone, and has been nicely prepared for by the word "picked"!

"Uncertain"—flat, again—is almost dogmatic. Still, it's the climax. The emotion of the poem crests there, to break and withdraw in the last line, the short line made almost infinitely long, and quite moving, by the little word "long."

This is more than Kunitz's fabled skill. This is wisdom, bleached of transcendentalism, yet drenched in "transformation and transcendence," which Kunitz calls the "two infallible touchstones of the poetic art."

"Day of Foreboding" puts his long, not uneventful life in perspective by turning toward the future.

Like other poems in *Next-to-Last Things,* it makes me think of that old saw Hamlet quotes: "the readiness is all."

Elizabeth Kastor (essay date 12 May 1987)

SOURCE: "Stanley Kunitz: The Poetic Adversary," in *Washington Post,* May 12, 1987, pp. D1, D6.

[*In the following essay, Kastor presents an overview of Kunitz's career and accomplishments, and reports Kunitz's comments on his work and the role of the poet.*]

Stanley Kunitz has always written deep into the night and through to morning and, when desperate publishers plead for an overdue essay from the 81–year-old poet, as they lately have been, the nights grow even longer. Over the last three, he has slept less than six hours. "The world's quiet then," says Kunitz. "I feel that splendid isolation, which is fructifying, replenishing."

And he does somehow manage to look replenished by those nights filled with writing, nights that have, over the last six decades, made him a dean of the poetic scene and won him the 1959 Pulitzer Prize for poetry and, this year, the Bollingen Prize. He will read at the Folger Shakespeare Library tonight at 8.

Isolation has been a constant in Kunitz's life, from a lonely childhood, scarred by his father's suicide just before Kunitz's birth and spent in a house where birthdays were not celebrated and "I would not admit I cared / that my friends were given parties," to the years writing in the isolation of the country, through decades of little popular or critical recognition. And if for the last several decades he has received the accolades of the established literary world—including appointment as consultant in poetry at the Library of Congress in the '70s—he remains a gracious yet defiant man who says he is closer to today's younger poets than those of his own generation—"I feel they're too old"—and has patterned his intellectual life on the model of William Blake.

"Blake stood very much for what I have aspired to stand for," says Kunitz, who selected the contents for *The Essential Blake,* a newly released pocket-sized book designed to make the often intimidating British poet more accessible. "He was a radical intelligence. He opposed the king. He applauded the French and American revolutions. He was *violent* in his feelings about child labor, the exploitation of women. This was the background and some of it seeps into the poems. He was a maverick outside literary circles, unappreciated in his lifetime. He's a hero, and meanwhile, he was writing these marvelous poems."

The poet, Kunitz feels, must continue to stand in that "adversarial relationship."

"The most elementary of our adversarial relationships are in terms of the power of the state, which has never been so great in the history of mankind," he says. "That power can destroy us all. It's a terrible power to entrust to people who are not spiritually great, that's all there is to it. You see it in the callousness, self-aggrandizement, insensitivity to the plight of the poor. In the general level of ethical conduct, the state has become an abomination. The Vietnam war—I was very hot about that, as I am about our policy in Nicaragua. All such difficulties lead one to feel more and more separated from the heads of state and the conduct of the state.

"The poet can't change anything, but the poet can demonstrate the power of the solitary conscience. It's an example. Any gain, even the conquest of a small part of oneself, is a triumph."

In his 1976 poem "The Lincoln Relics" Kunitz wrote:

Mr. President,
in this Imperial City,
awash in gossip and power,
where marble eats marble
and your office has been defiled,
I saw the piranhas darting
between the rose-veined columns,
avid to strip the flesh
from the Republic's bones.

"This is part of the whole problem—so-called—of modern poetry," he says. "It's true it has lost its general audience. It isn't that there aren't readers. There are some, but they are isolated. Your only constituents as a poet are in the university world, the college world. That's too limited. It's stultifying in a way that mature persons in society, those who are our leaders know nothing about poetry, don't read it. I think they are damaged because they don't stretch their imaginations."

A small man in an overlarge brown suit, Kunitz sits in an unceasingly gray, boxy Washington hotel room. Venetian blinds clack; the spring wind is rushing to get in. Back in his Greenwich Village solarium, Kunitz's plants are blossoming, and in Provincetown his carefully nurtured garden waits for the summer arrival of the poet and his wife, painter Elise Asher.

"I really need some green around me or I perish," he says, smiling. "Nothing makes me as happy as to get out there and grub with my hands. It is very important to have an understanding of the body, a love of the body, a whole enjoyment of one's physical self as much as one's mind."

And the advice he gives beginning poets is imbued with such sentiments. Know more than poetry, says the man who for years worked as a newspaper reporter, edited reference books, served in the Army in World War II and never sought a tenured position at the universities where he taught.

"I've never accepted tenure because I don't believe in it," he says. "I don't think that poets ought to become academicians. I also feel that kind of security and responsibility to an institution is a threat to the imagination, to the free play of the imagination."

Kunitz was born in Worcester, Mass. After graduating from Harvard *summa cum laude,* he was indirectly informed that he would not be welcome to stay on as a teaching assistant because Christian students would bridle at being taught by a literature teacher who was Jewish. He left Harvard and in 1930 published his first book of poems, *Intellectual Things.* Heavily influenced by the 17th-century metaphysical poets, Kunitz wrote short poems thick with metaphor and came to be known for his mastery of craft—for what seemed to some an overreliance on craft. Poet and friend Michael Ryan has described that early poetry as taking "the risk of pitching the tone too high for human ears, the language becoming so dense that the act of reading becomes an act of translation."

"I always get angry," Kunitz says, laughing, about the inevitable questions about his dedication to craft. "I wasn't trying merely to be clever and to juggle ideas and ironies. I was, even in those very earliest poems, really trying to find out who I am, where I am going, why I am here. I still ask the same questions."

But if the questions stayed the same, the tone and form changed in the late '50s and early '60s. With *The Testing-Tree,* published in 1971, his style grew more colloquial, still rich but less obscure, and the stories and pain of his childhood began to appear explicitly in the poems.

In **"Three Floors,"** collected in *The Testing-Tree,* he wrote:

> Under the roof a wardrobe trunk
> whose lock a boy could pick
> contained a red Masonic hat
> and a walking stick.
>
> Bolt upright in my bed that night
> I saw my father flying

the wind was nothing on my neck,
the windowpanes were crying.

"If I didn't change, I'd become a terrible bore, even to myself," Kunitz says, That's what I mean about entering into the experiential world—every new adventure of the heart or the mind modifies your state of being.

"The difficulty is that to change one's style is an arduous task. I think in one of my speeches I say it's easier to change one's life than to change one's style. You tend to repeat the patterns of your expression and even your mannerisms, syntax, your prosodic pattern and the rest. But if it no longer excites . . . All you know is you're dissatisfied if you're going through the same paces again. There has to be some sort of leap, a leap of the soul, really. So you can have joy in it again."

In **"The Layers,"** Kunitz wrote:

> In my darkest night
> when the moon was covered
> and I roamed through wreckage,
> a nimbus-clouded voice
> directed me:
> "Live in the layers,
> not on the litter."
> Though I lack the art
> to decipher it,
> no doubt the next chapter
> in my book of transformations
> is already written.
> I am not done with my changes.

And now, Kunitz is taking the leap once more. He is now working on poems that he says "return to song, just pure song . . . I'm in the midst right now of a shift. I can't define it yet, but that's why I'm working on these songs. I think something is emerging out of them that will be recognizably different, and yet a continuation."

Kunitz once said, "I feel that I am not only living now, but also in other times, past and future. Now is one of the locations of my life, but so is my childhood and, beyond that, the childhood of the race. Even my own death is part of my occupation."

In **"Passing Through—on my Seventy-Ninth Birthday,"** Kunitz addresses his wife, who has brought birthday celebrations into his life.

> Sometimes, you say, I wear
> an abstracted look that drives you
> up the wall, as though it signified
> distress or disaffection.
> Don't take it so to heart.
> Maybe I enjoy not-being as much
> as being who I am. Maybe
> it's time for me to practice
> growing old. The way I look
> at it, I'm passing through a phase:
> gradually I'm changing to a word.
> Whatever you choose to claim
> of me is always yours;

nothing is truly mine
except my name. I only
borrowed this dust.

Calvin Bedient (review date Winter 1988)

SOURCE: "The Wild Braid of Creation," in *Sewanee Review,* Vol. XCVI, No. 1, Winter, 1988, pp. 137–49.

[*In the following excerpt, Bedient discusses aspects of "strangeness" and the imagery of animals and elements in* Next-to-Last Things.]

In poetry strangeness is essential, whether of word, figure, or development. It is inseparable from the intense concentration that justifies special linear and rhythmic dispositions of language; these dispositions, in turn, cast an eclipse-strange light back on the words. Prose is daylight, poetry entering or emerging from the dark of the moon. . . .

I have written as if strangeness ought to be potent in poetry—both strong and fertile. What of the authority of Stanley Kunitz, who seems to imply otherwise when he asks what at his age (the date was 1977, when he was seventy-two) is "left for you to confront but the great simplicities. . . . I want to write poems that are natural, luminous, deep, spare. I dream of an art so transparent that you can look through and see the world"?

The thirteen poems in *Next-to-Last Things: New Poems and Essays* (more strictly, twelve poems, for the prose piece **"Tumbling of Worms"** should not be passed off as a poem) are "natural" seeming enough for artifacts, and fairly luminous, deep, and spare. And the strangest, **"The Abduction,"** is an early work. Nonetheless all the poems resonate with strangeness, for Kunitz is as aware as anyone that poetry is rooted in the gestural life of the physical mind, and that "the body, in its genetic code, holds the long odyssey of the race," indeed that "poems rise out of the swamps of the hindbrain, 'the old brain,' dragging their amphibian memories behind them" (I quote from one of the fine essays in the new book, *The Wisdom of the Body*). [Dennis] Schmitz's woman soaking off animal blood in the stream, and [Colin Way] Reid's Daphne drinking and rising rootedly, are, in this regard, allegorical illustrations.

In such instances poetry implicitly declares its filiations with the realm of the animals and the elements. Tactilely so, when Kunitz says of two snakes surprisingly "entwined / in a brazen love-knot" in chilling September, "At my touch the wild / braid of creation / trembles." The oxymoron of "wild braid" and the generalizing possessive "of creation" constitute the necessary, archaizing imaginative wildness. Again **"Raccoon Journal"** creates a frisson through evocations of manic hoots and dark encroachments ("On the back door screen / a heavy furpiece hangs, / spreadeagled, breathing hard . . ."). The theriophobic

sexual menace implicit in "spreadeagled, breathing hard" is instinctively right. For Kunitz the physical "creation" still bristles with primitive messages; more than an irate gardener beset by raccoons, he's a throwback to the green man.

He knows that loneliness, too, is essentially strange. The loneliness both of the creative artist and of the aged man. On this subject the best of the new poems are **"The Image-Maker"** and **"The Long Boat."** The first, typically a bit uneven, is superb at the close:

> Seductive Night! I have stood
> at my casement the longest hour,
> watching the acid wafer
> of the moon slowly dissolving
> in a scud of cloud, and heard
> the farthest hidden stars
> calling my name.
> I listen, but I avert my ears
> from Meister Eckhart's warning:
> *All things must be forsaken.*
> *God scorns*
> *to show Himself among images.*

The conceptual wild braid of "Seductive Night!" and "acid wafer" is brilliant; less so, but interestingly complex, and helping to save the one weak segment (the sentimental "heard / the farthest hidden stars / calling my name"), is the superposition on the bidding stars of the forbidding Meister Eckhart. **"The Long Boat"** is almost equally ambivalent about the seduction of the cosmic edge of loneliness, the temptation to disappear back into the elements. A boat snaps its moorings, the subject tries "at first to wave / to his dear ones on shore, / but in the rolling fog / they had already lost their faces." Overcome with tiredness, he is

> content to lie down
> with the family ghosts
> in the slop of his cradle,
> buffeted by the storm,
> endlessly drifting.
> Peace! Peace!
> To be rocked by the Infinite!
> As if it didn't matter
> which way was home;
> as if he didn't know
> he loved the earth so much
> he wanted to stay forever.

On the one hand a blood-draining, [Samuel] Menashe-like allegiance to "family ghosts," and on the other the contrary persistence of an image-maker. The language is plain, the lineation casual (which is what Kunitz means by "natural"), and even imitatively supine. Both are bobbingly related to the commonplace. But, equally important, both are buoyed by the fantastic element of fable, the strangeness of what at once is and is not itself: a strangeness like that the human mind feels before the distorting mirror of the animal world, or before the curiously familiar and unfamiliar elements. Before the slop of the cradle. Before the knowledge that it doesn't matter which way is home.

The summoned and seductive strangeness in poetry is the shivering invisible body in the denims of the words—a body that is other to the conscious mind and to ordinary uses of language; a body that, the curious twists of history aside, is animal or vegetal or elemental, and already passing back into the stream.

Stanley Kunitz with Peter Stitt (interview date May 1990)

SOURCE: "An Interview with Stanley Kunitz," in *Gettysburg Review*, Vol. 5, No. 2, Spring, 1992, pp. 193–209.

[*In the following interview, conducted in 1990, Kunitz discusses his early life, formative experiences, education, beginnings as a poet, literary relationships, and his approach to writing and experiencing poetry.*]

Stanley Kunitz, who will turn eighty-seven on July 29, 1992, is the reigning dean of American poets. Not only is he still writing, but he is writing as well today as he ever has, as is evident from the new poem, **"Chariot,"** published below. The third child of Solomon Z. Kunitz and Yetta Helen Jasspon, Stanley Kunitz was born and raised in Worcester, Massachusetts. He earned his B.A. from Harvard in 1926 and his M.A. in 1927; at his first graduation, he won the coveted Lloyd McKim Garrison Medal for Poetry, was awarded highest honors, and was elected Phi Beta Kappa. After graduation, Kunitz worked briefly for the *Worcester Telegram* and then, from 1928 to 1943, served as editor of the *Wilson Library Bulletin*. His first book, ***Intellectual Things*** (1930), was praised both for its "fresh utterance" and for its "intricate and metaphysical" style. From 1943 to 1945 Kunitz served in the Air Transport Command of the United States Army, and in 1944 he published his second volume, ***Passport to the War.***

A Guggenheim Fellowship awarded in 1945 allowed Kunitz to live in Santa Fe, New Mexico, for a year, and in the autumn of 1946, at the urging of Theodore Roethke, he returned to academia by beginning a three-year teaching stint at Bennington College in Vermont. Since then he has regularly taught at many places, but—by design—only on a year-to-year basis, and never with tenure. While Kunitz was filling in for Roethke as poet-in-residence at the University of Washington (1955–56), he taught the young James Wright. His ***Selected Poems*** was published in 1958 and won for him the Pulitzer Prize in 1959. Kunitz began his twenty-two-year association with Columbia University in 1963, and in 1968 he helped to organize the Fine Arts Work Center in Provincetown, Massachusetts; he will work there again this summer, for the twenty-fifth consecutive year.

In 1967 Kunitz visited Russia as part of a cultural exchange program, reading his poems and lecturing. Thus began his deep commitment to the poetries of oppressed peoples: his translations of Anna Akhmatova and Andrei Voznesensky are particularly notable. When ***The Testing-Tree*** was published in 1971, Kunitz was praised for revising and enlivening one of the most-recognizable styles in American poetry. He himself explained that "as a young poet I looked for what Keats called 'a fine excess,' but as an old poet I look for spareness and rigor and a world of compassion." The publication of ***The Poems of Stanley Kunitz, 1928–1978*** in 1979 won for Kunitz the Lenore Marshall Prize, signalling his ascension to the top of his field. When ***Next-to-Last Things: New Poems and Essays*** was published in 1985, critics responded by saying that "Mr. Kunitz is a living treasure" whose spirit "is sensual and mythic, cosmic in its deep searchings for connections between the worlds of nature and man"; he is "the finest living American poet."

With his wife Elise Asher, Stanley Kunitz spends his winters in New York City and his summers in Provincetown; his flower garden is both one of his great passions and one of the primary attractions of Cape Cod. He visited Gettysburg College on the twelfth and thirteenth of March, 1990, to read his poems and to visit classes in creative writing and contemporary American poetry. The interview was conducted in his apartment in New York on the third of May, 1990.

[*Stitt:*] *What sort of childhood did you have?*

[Kunitz:] As I look back on it, my main impression is of how lonely I was. Aside from school, where of course I did have a degree of companionship, it was a childhood without much company outside the household itself, largely because, for so much of that time, we were living far out at the edge of the city without any neighbors. My main refuge was the woods that lay behind the house, where I wandered every day. That is where I invented the game I write about in **"The Testing-Tree."** I would throw three rocks at the tree, and the results would determine my fate. In retrospect I realize that those three throws of the stone against the patriarchal oak reveal much of the meaning of my life, at that point and in the future. If I hit the target with only one stone, somebody would love me. If I hit it twice, I should be a poet. And if I hit it three times, I should never die. That was the game, and I think it expresses my deepest yearnings.

How old were you at that time?

I must have been in my early teens. Thirteen or fourteen.

It is interesting that you should have wished to be a poet at that age. When were you first conscious that this was your desire?

It is hard for me to define exactly. I was writing from the very beginning, from the moment I went to school. Writing was what gave me the most gratification. I was also reading omnivorously. Every week I would walk to the public library, about three and a half miles from where we lived, and I would pick out this great bundle of books. The librarian would say, "Now, Stanley, you are permitted to take only five books, no more. That's the limit." So I would wrestle with the problem of which five books out of this big bundle I should take. The regulation was that you could do this only once a week; I do not know why there was such a limitation. But I would always be back a day or two later, wanting five more books. So eventually she consented to bend the rules and let me have those extra books. Then I would trudge all the way home and devour them. My taste was indiscriminate. I did not know what I was reading—I just grabbed anything that caught my eye.

I take it this was going on even before you were twelve.

Yes, it started early. I still have—on yellow sheets of sketch paper—a collection of short stories I wrote at the age of eleven, recounting my adventures in the far north. All of them are very detailed, very tragic and desperate. They are about survival. I am mushing through snow and ice with my team of huskies. We are lost in this terrible storm, and one by one they start dropping off, dying of the cold. Finally, there is just one left and we sort of keep each other warm. No doubt I was influenced by Jack London.

That is a lonely story, a story without companions, and it reminds me of another great loneliness in your life. A moment ago you referred to the "testing-tree" as a "patriarchal" tree. I am aware that you grew up in a single-parent home. How aware were you as a child of the absence of your father? How aware were you of how he left you?

I do not remember exactly how or when I learned that he had committed suicide a few weeks before I was born. There must have been a prior state of innocence, but I cannot recall it. It is as though I had plucked the knowledge of his death out of the air.

My most vivid memories are of stumbling by accident on a few bits of information. In my tenth or eleventh year, I was rummaging in the attic among old garments and trunks and some odd pieces of furniture. In one of the trunks I found my father's Masonic robes—apparently he was a thirty-second degree Mason—and some documents pertaining to his membership in that order. I have written about this discovery—which I kept secret then—in my poem **"Three Floors."**

On another occasion, something far more dramatic happened. Rummaging again in the attic, I came across a pastel portrait that I knew immediately, intuitively, was a portrait of my father. I brought it down to show to my mother. Her instant reaction was to slap me and tear the likeness into shreds. This was out of anger, I am sure, but not anger directed at me. My mother wanted to erase my father out of her memory. She never referred to him, never spoke the slightest word of him. And that one gesture was the only manifestation of her emotion about him that I ever saw. I never dared question her, dreading the

consequence. This of course made him all the more mysterious and important to me. I was compelled to create a mythical father to replace the real father I never had. This mythical being is the one who has dominated my imagination and my poems through all the years.

Did anybody else in the family ever mention him?

The only person I could talk to was my older sister. She was only six when he disappeared, so her memories were limited. I tried to pump her for information, but she had little to offer. The detail that I remember most clearly relates to my father's funeral. At the cemetery, when my mother became hysterical and tried to leap into the grave, our family physician—whose name was Dr. Nightingale, all so mythic—restrained her and said, "Be quiet! Don't forget, you have a lot to do with this." Now that is my sister's story, I do not know how accurate. Late in my mother's life, actually forty-six years after my father's death, I persuaded her to write an informal memoir. She was able to describe her life, in exact detail, up to the moment of her marriage, but at that point she froze. She could not write another word.

Let me go back to what you were saying about your early reading and writing. Was Worcester the sort of community that would support that kind of activity on the part of a very young man?

It was hardly an ideal environment. The Worcester that I knew was largely an immigrant city. It was built on seven hills, like ancient Rome—as the town fathers liked to boast—and each hill was inhabited by a different ethnic group: Irish, Swedes, Armenians, Italians, Jews, etc. Each group was isolated from the others. In fact, you were apt to encounter animosity and even some violence if you strayed into the wrong neighborhood. I bitterly resented the all-too-visible signs of parochialism and sectarianism and vowed to make my escape at the first opportunity. Sherwood Anderson's *Winesburg, Ohio,* with its depressing picture of the frustrations of small-town existence, was a book that reinforced my determination.

In high school, I founded a literary magazine called *The Argus,* in which I published early poems and other writings. In the old WASP section of Worcester, there was a group called The Browning Society, staunch survivors of what had once been a flourishing network of chapters. I have no idea how it came about, but as a young poet and editor I was granted the privilege of joining them. The elderly ladies of the Society, in their prim hats and long dresses, drank tea and discussed the poetry of Robert Browning in reverential terms. That was my first taste of the literary life, that invitation of The Browning Society.

Let me add that despite the reservations I have expressed about the Worcester environment, I remain forever grateful for the quality and breadth of instruction. I received in the local schools, particularly at Classical High, a sort of magnet school, though the term hadn't been invented yet.

I still treasure the hand-inscribed copy of *Bartlett's Familiar Quotations* that the faculty presented to me at graduation. No prize since then has meant as much to me. Those teachers, I believe, were superior to almost any you would find today in the public school system. I'm not even sure you could find their equivalent in the private sector.

Was there a special teacher at Classical High School who encouraged your poetry?

One such teacher was Perry Howe, the coach of the debating and declamation teams. In those days debating and declaiming were taken very seriously—there were inter-school competitions in both categories, and silver cups were given to the winning teams. I was chosen captain of teams that successfully defended Classical's championship record. These were big events, held in the main auditorium of the city, with overflow audiences of students and parents in attendance. One of our first debates was on the subject of granting suffrage to women; fortunately, we drew the right side. Perry Howe helped me to overcome my native shyness and taught me how to project my voice.

I am indebted most of all of Martin Post, whom students joked about because of his love of poetry. One day he tossed aside the textbook from which he was reading to us a set of soporific quatrains—you know, the kind of didactic verse they fed to youngsters then—and reached into his pocket, saying, "I want you to hear some real poetry." That was my introduction to Robert Herrick: "Get up! get up for shame! . . . / Get up, sweet slug-a-bed and see / The dew-bespangling herb and tree." And those other unforgettable lines: "Whenas in silks my Julia goes, / Then, then, methinks, how sweetly flows / That liquefaction of her clothes." I had never heard such delightful music. Right after school I dashed to the public library on Elm Street and took home Herrick's poems. I have been smitten with them ever since.

In another session of his class, Martin Post went over to the piano, struck a sequence of bass notes, and asked us, "What color did you hear?" In the midst of the snickers, when I saw that nobody else was tempted to respond, I raised my hand. The bottom notes, I said, were black, but a bit higher in the scale they moved toward the purple. Then Mr. Post put me to the test with the high, tinkling notes at the other end of the keyboard. I told him the topmost notes sounded white or crystal, moving downward toward the yellow. He turned to me and said, "Stanley, you're going to be a poet." Years later I read about the new findings by psychologists in their study of sensory perception. At birth all our five senses are fused; their differentiation is a developmental process. So that synaesthesia, the translation of one sense into the language of another, is tantamount to a return to a state of innocence. It is one of the great metaphorical resources of the poetic imagination. What was it Emily Dickinson wrote?: "To the bugle, every color is red." I don't know where Martin Post got his information.

Tell me something more about the magazine you founded, The Argus. *How long did that go on and how much writing did you do for it?*

I must have been a sophomore when I started it. Publication continued for a good many years after my departure. Eventually the school shut down: classical education was no longer considered to be essential. Somewhere I have a file of *The Argus* tucked away. Among my contributions, I can recall, were parodies of Poe's "Raven" and Longfellow's "Excelsior." I suppose that parody was my way of learning metrics, as effective a discipline as any I know of. Perhaps, too, I was already beginning to distance myself from the nineteenth century worthies who dominated the literary landscape.

How did you happen to go to Harvard after high school?

This was the period in which there were heavy restrictions on the number of Jews in the colleges. Even as valedictorian of my class, I had no assurance of being admitted to the college of my choice, especially since I needed financial assistance. The Principal of Classical High School, Kenneth Porter, had his heart set on my going to Amherst, but failed to persuade his alma mater to accept me. Fortunately, Harvard—which I scarcely dared dream of—came through with the grant of a handsome scholarship. This despite its notorious two per cent quota.

I recall that you were an English major at Harvard. Did you receive any encouragement there as a writer?

In my second year I took a course in composition with visiting professor Robert Gay. His requirement was the submission of a one-page typed manuscript every day, Monday to Friday, on any topic of our choice—an heroic assignment, since he read and commented on every paper. After a month or so, he wrote on one of my papers, "You are a poet—Be one!" That was an even clearer signal than Martin Post had given me, and I tried, as best I could, to apply myself accordingly. In my senior year I was awarded the Garrison Medal in Poetry. During my graduate year, 1927, I took a course in versification with Robert Hillyer, but not with any appreciable benefit, since I resisted the mechanics of his approach to prosody.

Alfred North Whitehead came to Harvard, from England, while I was still an undergraduate. I knew his work and was eager to study with him, but his only offering was in advanced mathematical theory and philosophy. When I inquired about auditing his lectures, I was told that as an English major with inadequate scientific background I did not qualify. So I went to Whitehead himself. He examined my record and asked, "Why do you want to study with me?" I replied, in the firmest tones I could command, "Because I admire your work extravagantly and because I hope to be a poet." He looked at me in some astonishment and said, "You're in."

But I ended up bearing no great love for Harvard. This is an old story now, but I don't want it forgotten. After graduating *summa cum laude,* I assumed I would be asked to stay on as a teaching assistant. When I inquired of my counselor why I had not been approached, he said that he had wondered about it himself and would discuss the matter with the head of the department, Professor John Livingston Lowes, who was famous for his book on Coleridge and his course on the Romantic poets. He came back, looking embarrassed, and delivered his message, carefully giving each syllable equal weight: "What I've been told is simply this—'Our Anglo-Saxon students would resent being taught English by a Jew.'" That really shocked me. I felt crushed and angry. At that point I abandoned all thought of an academic career. How could I foresee then that eventually I would thank heaven for having been deflected from that course? After I received my master's, I left Harvard for good. During the previous summers I had been working as a cub reporter on the *Worcester Telegram.* Now I returned to Worcester as a full-fledged member of the staff and a few months later became assistant Sunday feature editor.

How did all that come about?

At Harvard, since I needed to supplement my scholarship income, I applied to Captain Roland Andrews, editor of the *Worcester Telegram,* for summer employment. It did not strike me as absurd that, in order to impress him with my qualifications for a job as cub reporter, I enclosed an essay I had written on James Joyce. This must have been in 1924, shortly after the publication in Paris of *Ulysses,* a book judged then and for an entire decade to be obscene and unfit for American consumption. I still wonder what an old-school conservative New Englander could have made of my panegyric. Nevertheless, I got a letter back from Captain Andrews saying, "You certainly can write. There's a job waiting for you. Come in whenever you are ready."

My major assignment on the *Telegram* was to report on the last-ditch effort to save Nicola Sacco and Bartolemeo Vanzetti from the electric chair. Like tens of thousands of others, I passionately believed that this pair of Italian immigrants had been condemned to die, not because they were proven guilty of murder during the course of a payroll robbery in South Braintree, Massachusetts, but because of their radical politics. Their case became the cause of a whole generation of writers and artists, who joined the demonstrations in the streets. Edna St. Vincent Millay wrote a poem of outrage whose title, "Justice Denied in Massachusetts," was picked up as a battle cry. I was sent to interview the judge of the trial, Judge Webster Thayer, a mean, little, frightened man who hated what he called "these anarchistic bastards." In the end, all the efforts to reverse the conviction or to secure clemency failed. Sacco and Vanzetti were executed in August 1927. It seemed to me the closing of a chapter. After consulting with members of the defense organization, the Committee for Justice, I decided to leave my job and go to New York in the hope of finding a publisher for Vanzetti's proud and eloquent letters, the ones he wrote in prison. A few months later I

arrived in Manhattan and made the rounds, beating on every publisher's door. But my mission was a failure. Because of the Red scare, nobody would touch so controversial a project. Besides, I was young and unknown, just the wrong person to enlist support for this risky enterprise. The letters needed and, luckily, found a better advocate in the person of Felix Frankfurter, whose sponsorship insured that a dead man's voice, his poignant broken English, would yet be heard. As for me, I had to face the hard reality that I was jobless in a strange city, without friends or prospects.

As I recall, you ended up working for The H. W. Wilson Company, the great library publisher.

It was not what I had hoped for, but it was my last resort. That was 1928, and the Depression was coming on. I tried every literary publisher and newspaper in New York. The letters from my editor in Worcester to the editors of the *Times* and the *Herald Tribune* did not get me past the reception desk. Finally, when I was virtually penniless and did not know how I could survive, I spotted a blind ad in the *Times* for a "correspondent"—whatever that might mean—at a publishing house. That led me eventually to the sprawling plant of The H. W. Wilson Company, uptown is the Washington Heights area, near the Yankee Stadium. The Wilson Company is the leading publisher of reference works for the library profession, *The Reader's Guide to Periodical Literature, The Cumulative Book Index,* and countless other invaluable tools. The founder and president, an entrepreneurial Scotsman, who had started the business in the back room of his Minneapolis bookstore, was still in charge, running the show like a family shop. Halsey W. Wilson was obviously impressed with my credentials and indicated I might be the right person for the job. I asked what the job involved, and he said writing letters. When I expressed some diffidence about this prospect, he commented, "Well, maybe we can find something better for you. I'll let you know in a week." True to his word, he called to offer me the job, for twenty-eight dollars a week. I had been earning forty in Worcester, so I did not think this was great progress. Nevertheless, I told him I would report for work the following Monday. In the meantime, Alfred Knopf called me up—I had been to see him, and he had not been very encouraging. But now he said, "I think, on later consideration, that we can use you." I said, "I' sorry, but I've given my word." Maybe that was a great mistake. Who knows what might have happened if I had gone to the great house of Knopf?

So were you a correspondent, did you work at home?

I was given a desk in a vast loft with people sitting at open desks; there were no enclosures of any kind. It was like going back to the nineteenth century, to a Dickensian world. Even the president—well, he had some filing cabinets stacked around him, but otherwise nothing separated him from his staff of several hundred employees, most of them doing indexing of various kinds. When I came in for work on the first day, one of the editors approached me and asked who I was. I told her my name and introduced myself as a new employee. She said, "You'll have to punch in on the time clock." I recoiled in absolute horror: "Oh no, I can't do that." She said, "Everybody punches the time clock." I stood my ground: "Nobody told me." She said, "Well, you'll have to see Mr. Wilson."

"What is the trouble?" he asked. When I told him, he said, "Everybody does it. Nobody has ever complained." I asked him, "Do you punch a time clock?" He replied, "No, but I'm the president!" I said, "Well, I'm only me, but it goes against my grain." We looked at each other for a few minutes. At last he said, "If I make an exception for you, it would not be good for my relations with other people in the office. But I'll tell you what: suppose somebody else punches the time clock for you, and you don't have anything to do with it." I said, "That suits me." Looking back, I can only marvel at his tolerance and patience.

Then I sat at my solid oak desk for three long days, and nothing happened. Nobody gave me any work to do, not even a single letter to answer. I was a correspondent who didn't seem to exist. Was this a test of some sort? When Kafka appeared in translation some years later, I had a sense of déjà vu reading him. It was embarrassing for me to have to go back to Mr. Wilson to complain how useless I felt, but he gave no sign of being vexed or surprised. "What would you like to do?" he asked. I had been studying the firm's operations and did not have to hunt for a reply. My first suggestion was the publication of a library periodical that—without repeating the details now—would be livelier and more literary than the trade competition. My other proposal went something like this: "It's amazing that there's no standard reference work available in this country, or anywhere for that matter, on contemporary world authors. I visualize an illustrated series of books on writers, presenting biographical, critical, and bibliographical information for ready reference, in encyclopedic format." "Go ahead," said Mr. Wilson. "Let's see what you can do." So that was how the *Wilson Library Bulletin, Twentieth Century Authors,* and the whole multi-volumed Wilson Author Series got their start. They are still flourishing, but of course I am no longer connected with them. That's ancient history.

I take it that you were also working on your poetry at this time?

I was working on the poems that constituted my first book, writing them at night and feeling good when they began to appear in various magazines, including *Poetry, The Nation, The Dial, Commonweal,* and *The New Republic.* Early in 1929 I put my poems together and sent them in the mail to the biggest publishing house in the country then: Doubleday, Doran. Only a few weeks later I had a telephone call from an editor who identified himself as Ogden Nash; he had read my poems with pleasure and wanted to congratulate me on the acceptance of my manuscript. Would I please come in to talk things over?

So that is how I got my first book published. I felt that I was fortune's child. By the time **Intellectual Things** came out, in the spring of 1930, I was abroad.

What was Ogden Nash like?

Soft-spoken and amiable, keeping his witty persona under wraps—but I never got to know him well. I should explain that my foreign adventure was made possible by a free-lance arrangement with Mr. Wilson. Living abroad then was extraordinarily cheap. I remained in France and Italy for about a year.

Did you return then to The H. W. Wilson Company?

Yes, but not for long. My taste of freedom had spoiled me for office routine. I decided to move to a run-down farm in outer Connecticut that could be acquired for a pittance. "I suppose this will be goodbye," I said to Mr. Wilson. He paused for a moment before replying: "Not necessarily. There is always the U.S. mail. We can send manuscripts and other materials, and you can continue to do your work in the country, just as you did in Europe." But then he added, "Of course, you'll have to take a cut in salary." I was back, financially, where I had started. Nevertheless, I felt enormously relieved.

You mentioned your sense of isolation from any kind of literary community in your early days. Was that isolation absolute?

Not by this time. But keep in mind that in those days there were no creative writing programs, no poetry readings, few arts organizations or fellowships. Poets tended to work in isolation unless they were motivated to meet by a convergence of political passions. The old established writers were, as a rule, indifferent or hostile to the new upstart generation. If I have spent so much of my life trying to build a sense of community among writers and artists, it is largely because I know from experience how much the lack of it means. And yet I realize as well that I have been luckier through the years than most and am accordingly grateful for the many acts of friendship and generosity and hospitality that have eased my journey. In 1928, when I still thought of myself as a stranger in New York, I was invited, out of the blue, to be a guest at Yaddo. This was shortly after it had opened its doors as an artists' colony. I was one of the first to enjoy its lavish hospitality.

Really? How did that come about?

I suppose that without realizing it, I was beginning to acquire some sort of underground reputation. More to the point, I was seeing a girl who knew Lewis Mumford, and I believe she told him about me and showed him some of my poems. He and Alfred Kreymborg were editing a publication called *The American Caravan,* which collected the new writing of the day. They asked me to contribute to it, and they also recommended me to Yaddo.

What was Yaddo like then?

It was still shaping itself, and there were not many people there. The guests included Kreymborg himself—rather an avuncular figure in contemporary poetry at that time, editor of an avant-garde magazine called *Others.* One special attraction to me was a poet in her thirties, Helen Pearce, a great beauty, whom I courted and later married, disastrously. Then there was the playwright Hatcher Hughes and a painter named Carl Schmitt. Only two others, I think. I was by far the youngest there. It was a fateful visit, though it lasted only two or three weeks, when I had my encounter with a ghost, an incident that has become part of the Yaddo legend.

A ghost?

Yes. Here's what happened. Yaddo is a big, baronial estate, and the great house, with its old-world, stone architecture, built for the ages, could be the setting for a Gothic novel. My bedroom was upstairs in the spacious tower room. One night, while I was lying in bed reading, I heard something scratching at the casement window. It must be the scraping of a branch, I thought, and went back to my book. The scratching continued. I rose, went over to the window, and looked out on the silent landscape. There was nothing suspicious in sight. I went back to bed and turned off the light. It was well after midnight. The moment I stretched out, the scratching began again, growing louder and louder. I got up again and again found nothing. I used all my willpower to ignore what was happening, even putting a pillow over my head, but the noise sifted through, clawing at my ears. I gave up trying to sleep and sat up straight in bed.

Suddenly, the wall I was facing became eerily luminous, and a mottled shape appeared on it—a winged creature, suspended from a pendulum, which kept swinging back and forth in a wide arc. The tempo of the scratching on the casement accelerated, the pendant bird swung faster and faster, and the glowing wall began to pulse. I was spellbound, terrified.

And then I heard the glass shatter! Everything went wild.

In panic I turned on the bedside light. The wall showed me its usual blank face; the closed casement was perfectly intact. I crept out of bed and fled downstairs. I lay down on the sofa in front of the enormous stone fireplace and spent the rest of the night there.

In the morning I went back to my room, where everything looked serene. I was too shaken to reveal my story. Then at breakfast, Elizabeth Ames, the founding director of Yaddo, said to me, "Stanley, wouldn't you like to make a tour of the painting gallery? You'll be interested, I'm sure, in the family treasures." Like everything else at Yaddo, the paintings—mostly nineteenth-and early twentieth-century portraits—belonged to the estate of Spencer and Katrina Trask. The tour consisted largely of anecdotes about the subjects of the portraits, several of them illustrious or wealthy friends of the Trasks. I was only half-listening

when at one point I found myself standing mesmerized—I did not know why—in front of a portrait of a delicate young girl. "Who is that?" I asked. "The daughter of the Trasks," said Mrs. Ames. "She was at the center of the great tragedy of their marriage." And she continued: "One summer evening this lovely child disappeared. She was last seen walking down the path to the pond at the foot of the rose garden. When they instigated a search for her, they found her floating among the lilies; she had fallen in and drowned." I had a premonition of the answer, but I asked the question, "Can you tell me where she slept?" Mrs. Ames said, "Yes, in your room." I thanked her, packed my bags, and left Yaddo.

How did you happen to meet Theodore Roethke?

In the late thirties, when I was living in Bucks County, Pennsylvania—this was after the breakup of my marriage with Helen Pearce—Ted drove down in his jalopy from Lafayette College, where he was teaching, and knocked at my door. He was wearing a voluminous raccoon coat, and he had my book, **Intellectual Things**—much of which he knew by heart—under his arm.

He was very large, very formidable, and he stood on the doorstep reciting lines out of my poems. Then he said, "May I come in? I'd like to talk with you." With an introduction like that, he was more than welcome. Of course, he had also brought his own poems with him in manuscript. He was working on the poems that were to constitute his first volume, which I titled for him, *Open House.* It was clear to me from the start that Ted was a force of nature, a real poet. The poems he was writing then were by no means great—they were quite formal, somewhat imitative, and restricted in range. But there were signs everywhere of his ultimate destiny.

He was the first poet I had met whose passion for poetry was like mine—who had the same rather terrifying immersion in the poetic medium and who had read everybody. Through the years we learned a lot from each other, though I, being a little older and having already published, was certainly at first in the position of being more his mentor than he was mine. Later he was to open doors of the imagination for me, particularly during the period when he erupted into the poems of *The Lost Son.* To me those were the most important poems written by anyone in my generation.

I would like to turn more toward talking about your own poetry. You have said something elsewhere that intrigues me. I think this might have to do with poetry, but maybe not. Apparently you played the violin as a child, and then you gave it up—because you resisted playing other people's music.

That's right.

Would you have kept it up if you could have played your own music?

I doubt it. My deep, sensuous delight in language made me feel that this was the art I was born for. Once I became absorbed in poetry, I lost interest in playing the violin.

Perhaps the connection would be between the way a violin-ist can physically feel the music and the way you feel about language.

All the arts, in varying degree, are somehow connected with the human body. The violin tucked under the chin—what an intimate and comforting sensation! I must tell you about my teacher, Margaret MacQuade, who invested so much hope in me. She had been a favorite pupil of the famous Belgian virtuoso Eugène Ysaÿe, and he had presented her with one of his violins, saying, "Pass it on some day to your best student." I still have that violin—a beautiful, old, Italian instrument—and I feel guilty about its lying there in my closet, abandoned and unused. Perhaps I have made amends by trying to pass on to some of the gifted young poets who have worked with me the sense of having inherited, if only metaphorically, the equivalent of Ysaÿe's violin.

You once said, "The language of the poem must do more than convey experience, it must embody it." Does that mean for you the physicality of language?

Definitely. The poems that mean most to me are the ones to which I respond physically as well as intellectually or aesthetically. When we say that we are moved or stirred or shaken by a poem we are describing a kinaesthetic response to fields of verbal energy. In the dynamics of poetry, all the sounds are actions. It is as though some intrinsic gesture of the soul itself were being expressed through the resonances of language. In that context the marriage of sense with sound seems to me to be a deep metaphysical action.

Is this why you love the Metaphysical poets so much, and why your own work has been grouped with that of the new metaphysical poets?

I don't care much for these groupings. Through the various stages of my work, I've been put into some rather strange company. But seriously, I'm inclined to think of myself less as a metaphysical than as an existential poet. To me, the struggle of words to be born, to arrive at the level of consciousness, is like the struggle of the self to become a person. I think that what the poet is trying to do is to bring words out from the darkness of the self into the light of the world. That is like the primordial act of creation, what Coleridge meant when he spoke of the repetition in the finite mind of the infinite I AM.

As you were talking about the physicality of the language, which would seem to imply the necessity of a rich verbal texture, it occurred to me to ask if you have that same feeling about your more recent poems, those beginning with **The Testing-Tree.**

Some years ago, in commenting on my later work, I said I was trying to write poems with a surface so simple and

transparent that you could look through them and see the world. I didn't mean to suggest that I had lost interest in the orchestration of the world within. Texture is more than a superficial phenomenon and is not to be confused with the maintenance of a high style. My main concern is with psychic texture, which is a deeper and more complex thing.

When you compose your poems, is there that same sense of actual physical engagement?

I have never known how to compose poems except by saying them. The problem always has been to discover a rhythm on which I can ride. When that happens, I am on my way. A poem springs to life when its energy begins to flow from one's deepest wells.

In my interview with him, James Wright quoted you as having said to him when he was a young poet: "You've got to get down into the pit of the self, the real pit, and then you have to find your own way to climb out of it. And it can't be anybody else's way. It has to be yours."

Very sound advice!

Do you write regularly, say a little bit every day?

No.

How do you know when it is time to write a new poem?

I have never been able to sit down and write a poem as an act of will. My poems seem to have wills of their own. They keep their own schedules secret, and they don't answer the phone. They usually come to me at night with a phrase or image that starts troubling my sleep, gradually hooking up with other words and images, often counter-images, searching—as I've already indicated—for a controlling rhythm. It's a slow process.

Have you ever had poems come to you ready-made, a kind of spontaneous perfect composition?

Miracles happen now and then, but not if you count on them.

I am going to name a few poems and see if you have anything to say about the story behind the poem or its genesis: **"End of Summer."**

That's one I happen to have written about. It dates back to the time I was living in Bucks County. I was hoeing in the corn field when I heard a clamor in the sky—it was the season for the wild Canadian geese to be flying south. Great v-shapes, constellations of them. Something in that calling of the birds disturbed me. I dropped my hoe, ran into the house, and started to write. After the geese delivered their message to me, they flew out of the poem. They told me to make an important decision, to change my life, and I did. It is a poem about migration.

How about the poem **"No Word"***?*

That's simple. I don't believe anyone has ever asked me about it before. I was waiting for a telephone call from someone who meant a lot to me, and the call did not come. Well, it did finally come, but too late.

How about "Open the Gates"?—Jim Wright's favorite of your poems.

"Open the Gates" originated in a dream. The landscape suggests the cities of the plain, Sodom and Gomorrah, from which I am fleeing—at least that was my interpretation on waking. In the climactic action, the monumental door I knock on is the door of revelation. Many of my poems speak of a quest, the search for the transcendent, a movement from darkness into light, from the kingdom of the profane into the kingdom of the sacred. As a rule, I don't feel I'm done with a poem until it passes from one realm of experience to another.

Your interest in politics is profound, as we see in your devotion to poets who have lived under totalitarian governments. But your poems are never overtly political.

Well, almost never. I maintain that to live as a poet in this society is to make a definite political statement. The politics is inherent in the practice of the art, as well as in the life. At the same time I feel that poetry resists being used as a tool. The truth is that we are suffering from an excess of political rhetoric and a dearth of the compassionate imagination.

Michael Ryan (essay date 1993)

SOURCE: "Life between Scylla and Charybdis," in *Interviews and Encounters with Stanley Kunitz,* edited by Stanley Moss, Sheep Meadow Press, 1993, pp. 128–36.

[*In the following essay, Ryan offers an analysis of Kunitz's poem "My Sisters" and discusses Kunitz's views on the social, moral, and personal significance of poetry.*]

> The life of a poet is crystallized in his work, that's how you know him.
>
> —Stanley Kunitz

This is one of the poems by Stanley Kunitz I love the most:

"My Sisters"

*Who whispered, souls have shapes?
So has the wind, I say.
But I don't know,
I only feel things blow.*

I had two sisters once
with long black hair
who walked apart from me
and wrote the history of tears.
Their story's faded with their names,

but the candlelight they carried,
like dancers in a dream,
still flickers on their gowns
as they bend over me
to comfort my night-fears.

Let nothing grieve you,
Sarah and Sophia.
Shush, shush, my dears,
now and forever.

The poem is beyond comment, or underneath it, at least in the language of criticism, which is "a kind of translation," as Eudora Welty says, "like a headphone we can clamp on at the U.N. when they are speaking the Arabian tongue." **"My Sisters"** resists this translation exceptionally well because its Arabic is silence—the silences of the past, of lost time, death, and eternity. These are different silences, I think, and one of the accomplishments of the poem is that it differentiates them, it makes them distinct and present and felt as such, and then gathers them into that tender, heartbreaking final sentence—"Shush, shush," a comforting gesture, a wish for silence as relief from sadness or grief or a child's night-fears (and so calling back to stanza two), a wish for silence as relief from frailty and mortality. Just as the past becomes present (through the agency of "the candlelight they carried" that "still flickers"), and the comforted finally becomes the comforter (and vice versa), that last gesture transforms the preceding silences into one silence that includes not only the poem's characters but also its readers. At least this reader. It makes me feel the intimate texture of the simple, inexhaustible fact that—as Kunitz put it in an interview—"we are living and dying at the same time."

The way it does this is primarily nondiscursive, through structure, movement, music, and drama. "The best part" of a poem, Frost said, is "the unspoken part." Almost all of **"My Sisters"** is unspoken in this sense, like Hardy's "During Wind and Rain," which so exceeds its commonplace idea, that human beings are mortal, by embodying its emotional truth in structure and rhythm, refrain and variation, in the voice that begins each stanza and begins the poem, "They sing their dearest songs," and the voice that invariably answers and closes the poem, "Down their carved names the rain-drop plows."

"My Sisters" has two voices, too, but their function and relationship are very different from those of Hardy's poem. The voice of the first stanza frames the rest of **"My Sisters"** like one of Vermeer's half-opened windows that filter and admit the light in which everything appears at once palpable and numinous. It strikes me as a voice out of nowhere, from the wilderness of inner space, not the same "I" that speaks the second and third stanzas but given terrestrial life by the second "I." "There is an aspect of one's existence that has nothing to do with personal identity, but that falls away from self, blends into the natural universe," Kunitz wrote in *A Kind of Order, A Kind of Folly.* This, I believe, is the first "I" of **"My Sisters,"** appropriately distinguished by italics from the personal "I" who has memories and affections and a life in time; one of the dramatic undercurrents of the poem is probably *their* blending together "into the natural universe" of silence.

In any case, the first line—"*Who whispered, souls have shapes?*"—sets the tone. It echoes in my ear "Who said, 'Peacock Pie'?"—the beginning of a strange, wonderful poem by a strange, sometimes wonderful poet, Walter de la Mare, who is much loved in England and mostly unread in the United States. De la Mare's is another poem in two voices, one that questions and one that replies, a mechanical arrangement meant to go nowhere, unlike **"My Sisters,"** which moves great distances gracefully "like dancers in a dream." **"My Sisters"** is, in fact, a miracle of movement, traveling from the impersonal undervoice of the opening to the intimate direct address of the ending, invariably immediate and increasingly dramatic. Is it this movement over the fluid three-beat lines marked by irregular rhymes and half-rhymes which makes the form feel like a membrane that can barely contain an overwhelming grief and sweetness? The way the three-beat line is used is a joy to look at closely. The second sentence of the second stanza, besides being a wonder syntactically and lodging in the dramatic image so it won't be forgotten, is cut into lines of extraordinary rhythmical beauty and function. "Like dancers in a dream" is the pivotal line of the six-line sentence. The return to the strict iambic trimeter after the rhythmical variation of the previous three lines physiologically and psychologically brings the line home. The satisfaction of the rhythmical expectation mounting since the last strict iambic trimeter ("who walked apart from me") is bonded to content, and the image of the "dancers in a dream" acquires the authority of that satisfaction. "Like dancers in a dream" also immediately reestablishes the ground beat, the rhythmical context for the lines following it. "Still flickers on their gowns"—another iambic trimeter—reinforces this, but unlike the previous three lines it isn't end-stopped, a subtle variation, but enough with the line's slightly increased duration to echo the ground beat yet still keep the rhythm fluid. Now, in the next line, when the second beat occurs before it "should"— "as they *bend* over me"—that moment takes on terrific emphasis, even if, especially if, this emphasis is registered subconsciously while we are attending to the drama, the meaning of the words. The gesture of bending becomes palpable beneath its description or representation.

Also, the subconscious rhythmical effect is so powerful at that moment, it keeps us locked in the remembered scene to a degree that makes the astonishing move into direct address after the stanza-break feel simple and natural. This kind of pivot or "turn"—what Petrarch called the "volta" between the octave and sestet of the sonnet—seems inherent to poetic form, and there are all sorts of turns in all sorts of poems, but this one, because of its marriage of solidity and wildness, seems to me inspired: "Let nothing grieve you, / Sarah and Sophia." And, by saying the names, the story that had "faded with their names" is restored; the sisters are given life, as in a ritual of the dead, at least for

the ritualistic, rhythmic time of the poem. Their silence is shaped and, in the poem's last gesture, accepted and honored.

A great deal could be written about how the last stanza uses the established iambic trimeter to depart from it, but I want to look at only two lines, both examples of foreshortening but of different kinds. The first line—"Let nothing grieve you"—has three beats but a syllable missing in a strategic position. The unexpected silence extends the long vowel of "grieve"; because of the metrical pattern, the word literally must be given more time than it normally takes to say it, just as the syllable "you" acquires a stronger stress than it would have in conversation. If there were an unstressed syllable between "grieve" and "you," for example, "Let nothing grieve for you," the glide of the long ë—Emily Dickinson's favorite vowel, like a scream— wouldn't require extension because the sound would be encased in the iambic trimeter. As it is, the held note makes a very affecting music.

And the last line of the poem, working within and against the metrical grid, is even more effective and affecting: "Now and forever." Period. Two stresses and a feminine ending. In the ensuing silence after the last, unstressed syllable, after all those three-beat lines, the final beat never comes. Its absence is palpable, as if the silence itself were stressed, an endless incompletion, a longing for something missing, something lost.

The wealth of mystery in the poem, a good part of which is acquired through its rhythm and music, is not obscured by the slightest mystification. Its depths are discovered and displayed in a language absolutely simple and clear, words, as Wittgenstein said, "like film on deep water." Kunitz himself said in *The Paris Review* interview: "I dream of an art so transparent you can look through and see the world." He surely has already accomplished this, and much more, in **"My Sisters."**

Stanley Kunitz was eighty last July. As much as a young poet could learn about writing poetry from his poems, he or she could learn about the vocation of poetry from his prose. The book to mark his birthday appropriately includes poems and essays. But his life with poetry has not been confined to writing. For Kunitz, poetry is a spiritual discipline, a way of being and knowing oneself and the world, and he has purposefully presented himself as an example in a century when it has probably never been harder to live a poet's vocation and never been easier to cultivate a poet's "career," pathetic as such a "career" is next to those valued by corporate society.

In this regard, though his style was initially suffused with Hopkins and the Metaphysical Poets, the figure of John Keats in his "vale of Soul-making" has been Kunitz's main spiritual guide. In **"The Modernity of Keats,"** first published in 1964, he wrote that Keats's "technique was not an aggregate of mechanical skills, but a form of spiritual testimony." And this observation is recast as

Kunitz's central assumption a decade later in the foreword to *A Kind of Order, A Kind of Folly*: "One of my unshakeable convictions has been that poetry is more than a craft, important as the craft may be: it is a vocation, a passionate enterprise, rooted in human sympathies and aspirations."

Theoretically, it may appear that this vocation could be a private affair between the poet and his or her own soul, as it surely was for Emily Dickinson and for Hopkins, though even in the latter case this was not necessarily by choice. Hopkins wrote to his friend Dixon in 1878: "What I do regret is the loss of recognition belonging to the work itself. For as to every moral act, being right or wrong, there belongs, of the nature of things, reward or punishment, so to every form perceived by the mind belongs, of the nature of things, admiration or the reverse." And, later in the same letter, more from the gut than from the Jesuit: "Disappointment and humiliation embitter the heart and make an aching in the very bones."

How many poets have sooner or later been poisoned by this bitterness? It's clearly from the desire and need for an audience that disappointment and humiliation and worse have inevitably come. Yet even if this desire and need were eliminated in the poet's heart, "Art is social in origin" (as Jane Ellen Harrison says bluntly in *Ancient Art and Ritual*), and poetry still retains its fundamental social character, even when the difference between the sale of five thousand copies, of a volume of poems, which is unusual, and fifty thousand copies, which is almost unheard of, is the difference between minute fractions of one percent of the population. In response, poetry can and sometimes has become hermetic, opaque, precious, and prosaic; it can become difficult—as Eliot said it *must* be in this century—like a child suffering from lack of attention and love. It can refuse to give pleasure, even to the poet who writes it. And the figure of the poet may become the *poète maudit*, Gérard de Nerval walking his lobster on a leash and hanging himself with a shoelace, dandified, flippant—or doomed, as in the sad incarnation of Delmore Schwartz in an essay entitled "The Vocation of the Poet in the Modern World":

> In the unpredictable and fearful future that awaits civilization, the poet must be prepared to be alienated and indestructible. He must dedicate himself to poetry, although no one else seems likely to read what he writes; he must be indestructible as a poet until he is destroyed as a human being.

In the absence of an audience, are the available choices either killing the poetry or killing the poet? It's interesting and moving to watch how poets have tried to negotiate this Scylla and Charybdis in their lives and ideas and work. In his "Preface to *Lyrical Ballads* (1800)," Wordsworth internalizes the conflict between the poet and a culture which has abandoned him because his original social function is served by more efficient institutions and technology. Wordsworth tries to rescue the poet's social role by asserting that "the Poet binds together by passion

and knowledge the vast empire of human society, as it is spread over the whole earth, and over all time." Yet, in the same essay, having imagined this grand audience out of the thinnest air, he admits that, in fact, the Poet's "own feelings are his stay and support."

For poets since the Industrial Revolution, Wordsworth articulates the predicament, but his solution is a formula for solipsism or, as Keats charitably called it, the "Wordsworthian or egotistical sublime." Grandiosity ("the vast empire," etc.) and isolation ("his own feelings are his stay and support") can only feed and increase each other, and, if their marriage is insular, can only breed bombast. They can kill the poet's soul and consequently his art, and can even become—as in the case of Delmore Schwartz and the dominant figures of Kunitz's generation—a risk to his life.

This danger is exactly what Whitman is addressing in this great passage from his "Preface" to the 1855 edition of *Leaves of Grass*:

> The soul has that measureless pride which consists in never acknowledging any lessons but its own. But it has sympathy as measureless as its pride and the one balances the other and neither can stretch too far while it stretches in company with the other. The inmost secrets of art sleep with the twain.

The poet's "own feelings are his stay and support" for Whitman, too, but his "measureless pride," essential to enduring the lack of an audience and its economic and psychological implications, is offset by a "sympathy as measureless" for other people and even for other things outside of the self. This is the crucial counterweight to the solipsism that is Whitman's explicit currency, and from the tension between then he makes his poetry: "The inmost secrets of art sleep with the twain." Tested by poverty and loneliness to the degree that, as Kunitz quotes him in **"At the Tomb of Walt Whitman,"** he sometimes felt his poems "in a pecuniary and worldly sense, have certainly wrecked the life of their author," the balance of "measureless" pride and sympathy is nonetheless the key to Whitman's spiritual discipline and probably to his survival.

It is also a remarkably accurate description of Stanley Kunitz. His poetry, his character, and his ideas are born of these polarities. From his new book, *Next-to-Last Things*:

> If it were not for [the poet's] dream of perfection, which is the emblem of his life-enhancing art, and which he longs to share with others, generations of men and women would gradually sink into passivity, accepting as their lot second-rate or third-rate destinies, or worse. If one is to be taught submission, in the name of progress or national security, it is redemptive to recall the pride of one [Keats] who averred that his only humility was toward "the eternal Being, the Principle of Beauty, and the Memory of great Men."

The paradox, of course, is that a "life-enhancing art" which the poet "longs to share with others" isn't subject to the modification, opinion, or response of any other human being—"the eternal Being, the Principle of Beauty, and the Memory of great Men" being ideas—much less of any audience at large. And if the idea of the poet's preventing "generations" from sinking "into passivity" sounds like Wordsworth, in an earlier essay and somewhat different mood, Kunitz, shows himself to be fully aware of the hazards of such "measureless pride":

> One of the dangers of poetry, certainly, is grandiosity. Let us not deceive ourselves: a poet isn't going to change the world with even the most powerful of his poems. The best he can hope for is to conquer a piece of himself.

In Kunitz's view, the spiritual discipline of poetry implies and incorporates the poet's social function. The poet is "an embodiment of resistance":

> resistance against universal apathy, mediocrity, conformity, against institutional pressures to make everything look and become alike. This is why he is so involved with contraries.

He is "the representative free man of our time":

> The poet, in the experience of his art, is a whole person, or he is nothing. . . . He is uniquely equipped to defend the worth and power and responsibility of individuals in a world of institutions.

Consequently, and most pointedly:

> The poet speaks to others not only through what he says but through what he is, his symbolic presence, as though he carried a set of flags reading Have a Heart, Let Nothing Get By, Live at the Center of Your Being. His life instructs us that it is not necessary, or even desirable, for everyone to join the crowds streaming onto the professional or business highway, pursuing the bitch goddess.

In other words (though a paraphrase is hardly needed), the poet's vocation has an important social function even if his poetry is drowned out by the noise of TV, movies, commercials, and factories spuming forth new products. It's a vocation inherently subversive to corporate ideology, spoken symbolically and by example:

> Poets are subversive, but they are not really revolutionaries, for revolutionaries are concerned with changing others, while poets want first of all to change themselves.

If those dedicated to social change through civil disobedience spend a lot of time in jail, the poet's dedication to changing himself implies a life of internal exile in a society built for profit, in—as Ronald Reagan calls it—"the age of the entrepreneur." Kunitz's most recent statement, in *The Paris Review* interview, is also his most urgent:

> Evil has become a product of manufacture, it is built into our whole industrial and political system, it is be-

ing manufactured every day, it is rolling off the assembly line, it is being sold in the stores, it pollutes the air. . . .

> Perhaps the way to cope with the adversary is to confront him in ourselves. We have to fight for out little bit of health. We have to make our living and dying important again. And the living and dying of others. Isn't this what poetry is about?

In this light, a poem as apparently apolitical as **"My Sisters"** takes on political content and becomes a political gesture, ineffective as it may be against the million movies and TV programs in which life is sentimentalized and death is trivialized. The political nature of poetry has no more to do with subject than with its rendering, in making us feel living and dying are more important than property and "the national interest," in using language clearly and accountably, unlike the way politicians and commercials use it. Insofar as the poet's vocation is a public act, it can be an act of conscience with a social function, though the border between public and publicity in this media culture needs constant checking. If the vocation of poetry Kunitz describes were arranged in a line, it would look like his characterization of "the power of the mind": "to transform, to connect, to communicate"—the first ("to transform") being the poet's relation to himself in his spiritual discipline, the second ("to connect") his relation to the world and to others, and the third ("to communicate") his social function, both through his poetry and his "symbolic presence." Of course, it isn't a line. It's all these at once.

This outline of Kunitz's ideas really is "a kind of translation" from "the Arabian tongue" of his prose. He certainly never presents them this systematically. They have more vitality and nuance combined with his many other convictions, concerns, and affections. Reading his essays, I get a transfusion of his indomitable spirit, his "fierce hold on life," which is much more important to me than my agreement. There are excellent reasons, for the sake of the poetry itself, to try to rescue its social function, even when from all appearances it has none. Poets from Horace to Sidney to Eliot have tried to do so, finding themselves at the edge of exile within the versions of civilization in which they lived. For Kunitz, poetry is a manifestation of hope and life, for the culture as well as for the individual— this is the source of its power and poignance. He argues for the essential seriousness of poetry, and for clarity and depth and music at a time when intelligent critics, perhaps unconsciously reflecting the political atmosphere, indulge triviality and obscurity and praise superficial linguistic invention.

> In the best poetry of out time—but only the best—one is aware of a moral pressure being exerted on the medium in the very act of creation. By "moral" I mean a testing of existence at its highest pitch—what does it feel like to be totally oneself?; an awareness of others beyond the self; a concern with values and meaning rather than with effects; an effort to tap the spontaneity that hides in the depths rather than what forms on the surface; a conviction about the possibility of making

right and wrong choices. Lacking this pressure, we are left with nothing but a vacuum occupied by technique.

In exactly this sense, Kunitz's example to poets of my generation is a moral example, put forward consciously with an awareness of the hazards of doing so. He has said, "The poet's first obligation is survival," by which he means spiritual as well as literal, knowing from experience the conflicts between the two for a poet in this culture: "No bolder challenge confronts the modern artist than to stay healthy in a sick world."

Visiting Stanley Kunitz a few years ago, during a difficult period, I made the standard complaints about the poet's life that anyone who has been around poets has heard a thousand times. That means he had heard them a hundred thousand times, and maybe even voiced them once or twice when he was living in absolute obscurity on almost nothing, as he did for over twenty years. But he listened until I was finished, and then replied, "But, Michael, poetry is something you give to the world." If I'm ever able, as Chekhov said, "to squeeze the slave's blood out of my veins," this is the type of blood I would replace it with.

Susan Mitchell (essay date 1993)

SOURCE: "A Visit to the Poet's Studio," in *Interviews and Encounters with Stanley Kunitz,* edited by Stanley Moss, Sheep Meadow Press, 1993, pp. 144–54.

[*In the following essay, Mitchell reflects on the organic processes, universal revelations, and "ecstatic" voice in Kunitz's poetry, particularly that in* Next-to-Last Things.]

A couple of months ago during a long night of insomnia that seemed the price paid for my recent dislocation from New England to South Florida, I reread Dante's *Vita Nuova* and Stanley Kunitz's *Next-to-Last Things* (The Atlantic Monthly Press, 1985). It was not only the fact that, once again, I was starting my life over that returned me to Dante and, for that matter, to Kunitz whose poems bear witness to his own powerful drive for spiritual renewal and transformation. I chose these writers because I had read them so often I knew they would give me an alternative to geographic place: they were a familiar intellectual soil I was already rooted in and a soil made all the more hospitable by my own numerous underlings, asterisks, personal jottings penciled in margins. Here, said each marking, was a place I had stopped and thought and dreamed before. As I settled into that long reading, first one, then the other book spread open in my lap, the night itself opened up around me. Nights in South Florida, I was to learn that night, are not really dark, but different shades of blue. When I glanced up from my reading, there was the swimming pool, clearly visible, an eerie pale blue in the artificial light of the courtyard; and beyond the swimming pool and the rustling date palms, a deep water canal, sometimes navy, sometimes a muddy violet—colors not so much seen as sensed whenever a rhythmic slap of waves

against the dock signaled the passing of a boat on its way to the Intracoastal. My move to Florida has coincided with the start of the rainy season, and at intervals during that night, torrents of rain would suddenly gush, plummet, and pour in columns so thick it was hard to tell whether the rain was falling or growing up from the earth, stalactite or stalagmite?—and then as abruptly as it had begun, the rain would stop. Sometimes a bird let fall long plumes of song, though with the source of the singing invisible, it seemed as if the air had become saturated with music, as well as with water, and at intervals had to spill down in trills and rivulets of song. Other times, birdsong arced, then dropped like a flare, the music momentarily illuminating the farthest reaches of the night: I was seeing all the way to the Keys where Florida trails off into dots and dashes—the geographic impulse tapering into archipelagoes, into the Dry Tortugas where the state finally dives into wild waters of the Atlantic or else lifts on a sudden updraft, soaring with the black frigate birds above the last malarial outpost, Fort Jefferson, where Dr. Samuel Mudd, guilty of setting the broken leg of Lincoln's assassin, wrote long letters home to Maryland and his wife.

During that night I felt lost within the enormous flatness of Florida, a terrain so filled with water—lakes, swamps, inlets, rivers, irrigation canals—that from the air, much of the state appears in continual motion; and at the same time, I felt the proud possessor of a geography that seemed to contract as easily as it could expand: the state suddenly reduced to that hand-sized piece I loved to snap into the jigsaw puzzle map of the United States I was given for my ninth birthday—Florida, an exciting Benadryl pink against the deep wooden blue of the Atlantic. It was within this shifting terrain that I read *Next-to-Last Things,* a book which is itself unusually concerned with shape shifting. "I will try to speak of the beauty of shapes," says Socrates in a passage from Plato's *Philebus* that provides the epigraph for the book's first section of thirteen poems. The shapes Socrates has in mind are the primal lineaments of the natural world and geometry: "straight lines and curves and the shapes made from them by the lathe, ruler or square." With this passage, we are close to the Platonic notion of ideal forms, those primordial figures from which the concrete, sensuous world is copied. And with ideal forms, we are in the studio where creation begins.

What Henry James called "the sacred mystery of structure" has always been of crucial importance for Kunitz. Accumulative, circular, dialectical—these, he told his poetry workshop students at Columbia University, are the three basic patterns that shape meaning in poems. As Kunitz explained each fundamental pattern, I felt as if the keys to the universe had just been handed over to me. And, in a way, they had. For these structures inform not only works of art, but also the natural world, and are probably a part of the human brain in the way that the dark spot that draws the bee deep inside the flower is probably a part of the bee's eye. In *Next-to-Last Things,* shapes abound, sometimes as dimly felt presences—

Out there is childhood country,
bleached faces peering in
with coals for eyes.

                                                    ("The Abduction")

Other times as distinct, recognizable forms—

On the back door screen
a heavy furpiece hangs,
spreadeagled, breathing hard,
hooked by prehensile fingers,
with its pointed snout pressing in,
and the dark agates of its bandit eyes
furiously blazing. Behind,
where shadows deepen, burly forms
lumber from side to side

                                                    ("Raccoon Journal")

But it is not the shapes of living figures, or even the shapes of phantasms, that preoccupy Kunitz in this book. What fascinates him is the shape of human consciousness, the shifting shapes of the poet's mind at work, its "rush of forms"—that place of becoming I think of as the poet's studio.

As early as his first book, *Intellectual Things* (1930), Kunitz was concerned with mind, and in a tightly packed sonnet, entitled **"Organic Bloom,"** he expressed three ideas which were to turn up again and again in his work, though it is only now in *Next-to-Last Things* that these ideas are fully explored. Listen, first, to the early sonnet:

The brain constructs its systems to enclose
The steady paradox of thought and sense;
Momentously its tissued meaning grows
To solve and integrate experience.
But life escapes closed reason. We explain
Our chaos into cosmos, cell by cell,
Only to learn of some insidious pain
Beyond the limits of our charted hell,
A guilt not mentioned in our prayers, a sin
Conceived against the self. So, vast and vaster
The plasmic circles of gray discipline
Spread outward to include each new disaster.
Enormous floats the brain's organic bloom
Till, bursting like a fruit, it scatters doom.

To begin with, this sonnet shows Kunitz attempting to find visual shapes for mental processes. In another poem from the same book, **"This Very Tree,"** Kunitz speaks of "the candelabrum of pure thought," and in still another, **"Mens Creatrix,"** he writes, "Brain, be ice, / A frozen bowl of thought." Second, **"Organic Bloom"** shows Kunitz connecting processes of thought with organic processes that work in cycles: like fruit, the thinking processes appear to ripen—then burst. In another poem from *Intellectual Things,* **"Motion of Wish,"** the wish, which is "sprung from the brain," goes "through evolutions of the seed." Like the Creation of the Lurianic Kabbalah which works on a triple rhythm of contracting, bursting apart, and healing, the creative process for Kunitz is combustive, culminating in explosion. And there is another important

connection with Kabbalistic tradition. In Lurianic thought, the vessels of Creation break because what God has to say, His name, is too strong for His words; in **"Organic Bloom,"** the brain bursts because, like the vessels of Creation, it is unable to contain its own thinking processes. Which brings me to my third point. **"Organic Bloom"** pictures the mind continually evading and escaping itself, paradoxically extending beyond its own contours. While in this early poem the mind's expansiveness takes a Freudian form, with forgotten—or repressed—guilt and sin relegated to regions of mind still uncharted, nearly fifty years later, Kunitz's fascination with inclusiveness turns up again, this time stripped of all psychoanalytic thinking. In a conversation with Chris Busa, reprinted in this volume, Kunitz says: "I sometimes think I ought to spend the rest of my life writing a single poem whose action reaches an epiphany only at the point of exhaustion, in the combustion of the whole life, and continues and renews, until it blows away like a puff of milkweed." When I read this passage, I immediately thought of **"Organic Bloom."** As in that early poem, the thinking process, for Kunitz, is still organic, its rhythms comparable to the cycles of plant life. There is been the same combustive energy, the thinking process exploding, blowing away "like a puff of milkweed." And finally, there is the same desire for inclusiveness, a need to record the mental processes of a lifetime in a single poem. Kunitz himself has observed: "Occasionally, I am astonished to find, through all the devious windings of a poem, that my destination is something I've written months or years before, embedded in a notebook or recorded on a crumpled scrap of paper, perhaps the back of an envelope. That is what the poem, in its blind intuitive way, has been seeking out. The mind's stuff is wonderfully patient" (*A Kind of Order, A Kind of Folly*).

But while the model Kunitz proposes for a single poem is reminiscent of **"Organic Bloom"** in some ways, in other respects it is very different. Where the sonnet stressed the compactness of the brain, the more recent model emphasizes the vast realms of space human consciousness contains—and not only because this single poem would follow the action of the whole life. Kunitz has replaced the image of fruit with the image of the milkweed pod. When milkweed explodes, the seed-bearing puffs do not blow away all at once; they lift into the air at rhythmic intervals, blowing away gradually, fitfully. And the journey they trace in the air includes not only the puffballs but the spaces between their eruptions; just as in passages of music where there are many rests, the pauses are meant to be heard and the listener must feel the musicians playing the silences as well as the notes. When, in his conversation with Busa, Kunitz talks of organizing his poems spatially—"I follow the track of the eye—it's a track through space"—I see those puffs of milkweed, the intervals between them. Poets' models, the blueprints or maps for poems they hope to write, are peculiar because they tend to combine qualities that are essentially incompatible. In a poem that has always impressed me as Elizabeth Bishop's own aesthetic model, she describes a monument that would certainly never stand, but that brings together through its architectural peculiarities contradictory elements in her own style, which combines the exotic with the domestic, the highly ornate with the plain:

> Then on the topmost cube is set
> a sort of fleur-de-lys of weathered wood,
> long petals of board, pierced with odd holes,
> four-sided, stiff ecclesiastical.

("The Monument")

And there is a poem by A. R. Ammons, "The Arc Inside and Out," which reconciles in the image of "periphery enclosing our system with / its bright dot," Ammons's own opposing needs: the minimalist need for "the impoverished diamond" and the "heap shoveler's" need for sheer "plentitude." Kunitz's model implies a need to give form to consciousness itself—to stand somehow outside the workings of his own mind so that he can discover the shape of what is essentially elusive because it is in a continual state of becoming; or, as Kunitz succinctly stated the paradox in an early poem, **"Change"**— "Becoming, never being, till / Becoming is a being still." Combustive, agitated, explosive—Kunitz's model is primarily kinesthetic, the whole life danced out, with the image of the milkweed giving visual form to a process that is at first felt inside the body as rhythm. "Even before it is ready to change into language," Kunitz says, "a poem may begin to assert its buried life in the mind with word-less surges of rhythm and counter rhythm. Gradually the rhythms attach themselves to objects and feelings" (*A Kind of Order, A Kind of Folly*). To discover the rhythms by which the mind beats out its thoughts, to find the pattern in what is continually moving, dying and renewing— all this is implied by Kunitz's model for a poem that would record the combustion of the whole life. Unlike other models of artistic inclusiveness—Marcel Duchamp's *Box in a Valise* (1941), for example, which contains miniature reproductions of nearly all his works—Kunitz's model is not stationary, but in motion: it pulses with thought.

As I read Kunitz's *Next-to-Last Things* during my long night of insomnia, it seemed to me that the single poem whose action continues and renews until it blows away like a puff of milkweed was quite possibly this book. For one thing, *Next-to-Last Things* has "world enough, and time" to be that poem, more world and time than any of Kunitz's previous books. Though its first section is made up of only thirteen poems, that section alone enacts a drama that moves simultaneously through three different levels of time—personal, mythical, and creative. With the first poem, **"The Snakes of September,"** the speaker is in a garden that could be Kunitz's own garden at 32 Commercial Street, but we are also reminded of that other mythical Garden by two snakes entwined "in a brazen love-knot," as if defiant of the Fall. With the last poem, **"The Wellfleet Whale,"** there is again a personal experience drawn from Kunitz's own life, his encounter with a fin back whaler, foundered and dying on well fleet beach, an encounter which appears to be a manifestation of a greater mythical event. Because many phrases in the poem—phrases like "news of your advent," "keepers of the nightfall watch," "hour of desolation," and "huge lingering passion"—allude to Christ's Passion and because the tourists and souvenir hunters who crowd around the whale, carving initials in its flanks and peeling strips of its skin, recall the crowds of Christs's tormentors depicted in the great Renaissance paintings by Brueghel and Bosch, this poem, like the first in this section, enacts a mythical as well as a personal drama: a drama that takes in the grand sweep of Christian time from the Creation to the Passion—and also redefines one aspect of that drama, the Fall. For Kunitz, the Fall does not seem to be caused either by human pride or human yearning for more knowledge (Kunitz is too fearless a transgressor of limits to accept such interpretations). Rather, the Fall is displaced from the Garden, which remains defiantly innocent, to the scene of Christ's death on the cross; that is, the Fall coincides with the loss of our greatest human ideals, with the loss of those figures that, like the whale—"pure energy incarnate / as nobility of form"—embody beauty, majesty, grace, with the loss of those ideal forms that thrill us, stirring our wonder and awe. When the speaker of **"The Wellfleet Whale"** expresses his sense of loss—"You have become like us, / disgraced and mortal"—I feel as if a curtain has suddenly been ripped, as if the very fabric of life has been torn. Whatever the reader is going to do with this profoundly disturbing revelation will require time, and therefore the book wisely provides no more poems. Instead of comfort, it offers the reader another mode of thinking entirely: the second half of the book consists of a rich variety of prose genres—essay, memoir, conversation, and journal entry—all sustaining a kind of fugal dialogue with one another, as well as with the poems in the opening section. While several memoirs extend the poet's personal history with rich remembrances of close friends, the poet Robert Lowell and the artist Philip Guston, and even take the reader back to Kunitz's childhood with the story of his mother, Yetta Helen Dine, the major thrust of the prose, it seems to me, is toward an exploration of the creative process, as particularized in Kunitz's own experiences. Not only do several of the essays explore the origins of some of Kunitz's poems, but through the inclusion of so many different prose forms, this section seems to embody the creative impetus of the thinking process itself, as mind continually finds new shapes to renew itself. From the more intuitive thinking of the earlier poems, this section shifts to the more cognitive, more rational thinking of the essay. From the more extroverted thinking of conversation and interview, to the more introspective thinking of the journal. These forms of thinking even vary as to how much silence—or space—they include, with the more fragmented journal entries awash in silence, a veritable archipelago of thoughts where mind trails off into the wild waters just beyond the limits of rational thinking, into what Kunitz might call "clouds of our unknowing." As in this journal entry: "When the Tzartkover Rabbi, celebrated in Hasidic lore, was asked his reason for failing to preach torah for a long time, he gave as his answer: 'There are seventy ways of reciting Torah. One of them is through silence.'" By contrast, the conversation with Busa, which incidentally provides the best interview of Kunitz that I know of, is tightly packed, the voices of poet and interviewer spiraling around one another, braiding into intricate patterns of thought which suddenly unravel into a new design.

Because the book's second section not only explores the creative process as a discussable subject, but also embodies that process through its own shape shifting, certain poems in the first section, which themselves are concerned with poetic composition, are suddenly reactivated by the prose pieces. The reader goes back to **"The Round,"** a poem which dramatizes through its own circular structure the poet's cyclic activity, his daily round, with its deep immersions in writing; as the poem closes, the speaker is scribbling on the blotted page the very words that began the poem—"Light splashed." What Kunitz envisioned in an early poem—"The end and the beginning in each other's arms" (**"Open the Gates"**)—is now fulfilled through the form of **"The Round,"** which, like the mythical uroborus, that circular snake which grasps its own tail in its mouth, wraps around itself. **"The Wellfleet Whale"** provides another look at the creative process. The poem begins with a journal entry, not a simulated journal entry, but a real excerpt which can be found in an earlier collection of Kunitz's prose pieces, *A Kind of Order, A Kind of Folly*. Beginning with the journal account allows Kunitz to overcome certain technical problems: for example, it frees him to plunge immediately into a lyrical address to the whale because he can count on the journal notation to ground the reader in all the necessary narrative information. But the journal-entry beginning also accomplishes something else. It allows the reader to discover those places where the poem has changed and transformed the original anecdote. As the reader compares the journal's account of Kunitz's encounter with the whale with the poem's account, reading re-creates the process of poetic composition, that wonderful period of indeterminacy where even the poem's structure is in a state of flux. To discover that the poem has substituted a *we* for the first person singular point of view of the journal is to reach that place in the creative process where a decision was made, where the possibility of a crowd scene suggestive of the crowds that milled around the dying Christ may first have occurred to the poet. Where the journal entry is anecdotal, verging on insight, the poem is interpretative, and the world it presents charged with meaning.

I suspect that it is the way in which the second section of *Next-to-Last Things* returns us to the poems of the first section, inviting us to read those poems through its own interest in the creative process, that finally provides the comfort which **"The Wellfleet Whale"** at first denies. As Yeats wisely understood, "All things fall and are built again, / And those that build them again are gay." The second section invites us to enter into the history of the poems in the first section, to explore the layers of experience they shape and transform: to reread **"The Abduction,"** this time knowing something about its origins in Kunitz's reading on UFO adventures; to return even to a poem from an earlier book, **"Green Ways,"** this time with

the knowledge of Keats's influence on Kunitz's imagination. To read the poems in this way is to unsettle them, to return them to that place of pure becoming, that "terrible threshold" where the poet hears "a rush of forms" (**"Open The Gates"**). *Next-to-Last Things* is more filled with process, with the action of the mind, with poems caught in the act of becoming than any other Kunitz book, which is my other reason for thinking that this book is the combustion of a whole life. Most poets feel regret over what gets left out of their poems, and Kunitz, I think, is no exception. "Language overwhelms the poet in a shapeless rush," he writes. "It's a montage, an overlapping of imagery, feelings, thoughts, sounds, sensations, which have not yet submitted to regimentation" (*A Kind of Order, A Kind of Folly*). The shapeless rush has energy, excitement, vigor: the mouth filled with the poem in all its rich simultaneity, none of the wild feathers plucked. Some of the greatest poets have tried to preserve in their poems the shifting shapes of pure becoming when the poem dazzles with kaleidoscopic possibilities. Chaucer's dream poems, for example, appear to simulate early, rougher stages of their own composition, thus recording, or seeming to record, a series of broken-off attempts: they grow around these earlier versions the way a tree grows around its own rings. But it was especially Dante who sought to preserve the emotional state that accompanied the writing of those poems addressed to Beatrice. That strange book, the *Vita Nuova,* alternates between sections of poetry and sections of prose, with the prose sections describing the circumstances of poetic composition. Since these circumstances often place a feverish, love-sick Dante at celebrations, banquets, and funerals where he is surrounded by shifting crowds of young women, Beatrice's friends, finally, those crowds which keep reforming, flowing into new shapes, become a metaphor for Dante's state of creative flux and seem as much a part of the poet's visionary experience, his own teeming mind, as a part of his quotidian experience. So imperceptibly do vision and reality shade into one another in the *Vita Nuova* that at times it is impossible to tell them apart. Dante keeps the reader positioned at that edge where the creative impulse keeps surging up, an edge so fine it is like an imaginary number, the square root of minus one, that symbol i which Leibniz called "an amphibian between being and nonbeing."

Perhaps it was my reading the *Vita Nuova* during the same night that I read Kunitz's book that made me especially sensitive to what I had missed on previous readings: the way so many of the poems in *Next-to-Last Things* seem to catch the very moment when they were first heard or glimpsed or sensed. The poems straddle that edge where the nonverbal rush of forms is first translated into words. Listen to the beginnings of two of the poems, **"The Snakes of September,"**

> All summer I heard them
> rustling in the shrubbery
> outracing me from tier
> to tier in my garden,
> a whisper among the viburnums,
> a signal flashed from the hedgerow,

a shadow pulsing
in the barberry thicket.

and now **"The Image-Maker,"**

> A wind passed over my mind,
> insidious and cold.
> It is a thought, I thought,
> but it was only its shadow.
> Words came,
> or the breath of my sisters,
> with a black rustle of wings.

The poems begin at the threshold of perception where seeing and hearing scorn the sense organs. Such poems upset the reader's orientation, for there is always more *out there,* they suggest, than the reader at first supposed. To a great extent, it is the forms and shapes that keep looking in at the poems's speakers, like the "heavy furpiece" pressed to the screen door in **"Raccoon Journal"** and "the bleached faces peering in / with coals for eyes" in **"The Abduction,"** that make the reader so keenly aware of realms of space that keep growing vast and vaster, realms that elude human knowledge. But another, perhaps more important factor, is the way the poem's speakers keep pressing for a knowledge of their world that continually escapes them:

> Some things I do not profess
> To understand, perhaps
> not wanting to, including
> whatever it was they did
> with you or you with them
> that timeless summer day
> when you stumbled out of the wood,
> distracted, with your white blouse torn
> and a bloodstain on your skirt.

The woman described in the opening lines of **"The Abduction"** now lies beside the poem's speaker, as mysterious, as unknowable as the UFOs that perhaps abducted her into outer space—or the men, "a dumb show retinue / in leather shrouds" who, more probably, gang-raped her. All the speaker has to offer the reader—and himself—are what the woman he loves has pieced together with him over the years; that is to say, what he has to offer are interpretations of an event that may itself be a fiction. "What do we know," the speaker concludes, "beyond the rapture and the dread?" What do we know, in other words, beyond the emotions stirred up by our own versions of the world, our own myths? With the concluding question, inner space becomes as vast and unknowable as outer space. And like the man depicted in **"The Long Boat,"** whose "boat has snapped loose / from its moorings," the reader is also set adrift, "rocked by the Infinite!"

When I started to read *Next-to-Last Things,* I had expected to hear a voice I already knew, the generic Kunitz made familiar by all the particular encounters I have had with him—as his student at Columbia University, as a fellow at the Fine Arts Work Center, as audience at many of his poetry readings. Instead, I heard someone or something else, a thrilling presence, disembodied as the bird song

that kept erupting into my long night of insomnia. In a fascinating exchange that is preserved in Busa's interview of Kunitz, poet and interviewer distinguish between "the varied voice of personality, the voice that speaks in the context of a dramatic situation," and the voice of incantation, made up of sound and rhythm. The voice I heard that night was neither the voice of personality nor the incantatory voice, but a more impersonal, universal presence that seemed to sound from the beauty of shapes, from the primordial structures of the thinking process itself. I call this the ecstatic voice, and by ecstatic, I do not mean what I think many people mean when they use that word incorrectly as a synonym for euphoric. I am using ecstatic in its root sense to mean standing outside of or apart from or beyond one's usual self or one's usual sense of the world. The ecstatic voice articulates the shifting shapes of pure becoming, of mind exceeding itself, and is kin to the grand, protean structures of the natural world; those thunderheads that pile up on the horizon during Florida's rainy season, cumulonimbus balanced on cumulonimbus, mountainous altars to abundance, altars so affluent they can afford to spend themselves in further expansions, puffing up into anvil-shaped towers, until suddenly the altar topples, itself the sacrifice, spilling down as rain. While I sensed the ecstatic voice everywhere in *Next-to-Last Things,* I heard it especially in **"The Image-Maker,"** a poem that seems miraculous to me in the way it moves at the very limits of consciousness, and in its closing lines, even extends a little beyond those limits through the sheer efforts of envisioning them:

> I listen, but I avert my ears
> from Meister Eckhart's warning:
> *All things must be forsaken.*
> *God scorns*
> *to show Himself among images.*

Though the image-maker averts his ears from the master's warning, the reader of the poem, who now conceives of an imageless form of thinking, who probes its possibility, feels as if some boundary has just been transgressed. Perhaps the poem has led the reader to imagine life after death, a realm of shapes so pure they scorn particulars. Wherever the reader has been led, it is not a place visited before. The brain has just advanced into its own uncharted territory, paradoxically exceeding its own limits.

Phoebe Pettingell (review date 9–23 October 1995)

SOURCE: "Survivors' Stories," in *New Leader,* October 9–23, 1995, pp. 14–15.

[*In the following review, Pettingell offers a positive assessment of* Passing Through.]

Stanley Kunitz has proved to be the survivor of his generation of poets. Born the same decade as Langston Hughes, Theodore Roethke, W. H. Auden, and Robert Penn Warren, Kunitz continues, at 90, to flourish as a writer. To mark his latest chronological milestone, Norton has published his ninth collection of verse, ***Passing Through: Later Poems, New and Selected.*** The book brims with the enthusiasm and energy we have come to expect from its author. True, Kunitz' themes can be dark. He views many subjects with irony, sometimes outright skepticism, occasionally outrage. What most impresses itself on the reader, however, is his imagination: perpetually curious, eager for fresh revelation. In **"The Round,"** he confesses, "I can scarcely wait for tomorrow when a new life begins for me, / as it does each day. . . ."

Passing Through opens with Kunitz' brief affirmation of the craft he has practiced for seven decades: "In an age defined by its modes of production, where everybody tends to be a specialist of sorts," he writes, "the [poet] ideally is that rarity, a whole person making a whole thing." Against the widespread belief that literature is merely self-referential, and "poetry makes nothing happen," Kunitz champions verse as "spiritual testimony, the sign of the inviolable self consolidated against the enemies within and without that would corrupt or destroy human pride and dignity." Disturbed "that 20th century American poets seem largely reconciled to being relegated to the classroom," he declares: "It would be healthier if we could locate ourselves in the thick of life, at every intersection where values and meaning cross, caught in the dangerous traffic between self and universe."

The poems that follow live up to those pronouncements. **"Around Pastor Bonhoeffer"** evokes the heroism of the eponymous German pastor and ethicist, who was martyred by the Nazis, to exemplify the kind of engagement with real problems Kunitz admires. Dietrich Bonhoeffer joined the plot to kill Hitler even though it meant lying, dissembling, and putting both his family and himself in danger. He resolved to "risk his soul in the streets / . . . in God's name cheating, pretending, / playing the double agent, / choosing to trade / the prayer for the deed." The poet holds up the churchman for being willing to face the ambiguities and pain of existence head-on, to forgo the ideal of holiness and make the sacrifice involved in dirtying his hands with a necessary act. Kunitz similarly transforms an old anti-Semitic music hall song into a paean to Jewish endurance. At the end of **"An Old Cracked Tune"** the speaker asserts, "I dance, for the joy of surviving."

"Words for the Unknown Makers" (written on the occasion of the Whitney Museum's 1974 American Folk Art exhibition) glories in slaves who carved cigar store Indians and little girls who worked intricate samplers, in traveling portrait painters and Shaker artisans, and in the legions of women who quilted, stenciled, embroidered, hooked rugs, or wove. All "pass from their long obscurity, through the gate that separates us from our history, a moving rainbow-cloud of witnesses in a rising hubbub." By leaving us creative expressions of themselves, each tells us something about ourselves, about the human desire to make a splash of color on the drab fabric of the ordinary, to joyously defy adversity, even heartbreak.

Amplifying his theme—"the telling of the stories of the soul"—Kunitz includes some of his resonant translations of Osip Mandelstam and Anna Akhmatova. Like his own poems, they show people willing to risk their freedom and the well-being of those dearest to them in order to win a greater liberty, and to speak out for those who cannot or dare not.

Along with its social statements, this collection offers much that is appealing on the author's childhood. **"The Magic Curtain"** brings back the wonder created by early movie palaces. **"The Testing-Tree"** recalls the imaginative games Kunitz created in boyhood, several of which unconsciously reproduced ancient rituals. A schoolboy terror—that the earth would be destroyed by a celestial object—is remembered in **"Halley's Comet."** **"My Mother's Pears"** chronicles the day Kunitz helped plant a tree that still produces fruit eight decades later.

The poet's sense of connectedness to nature extends to the animal kingdom. Some of the most endearing passages in ***Passing Through*** concern "Jonathan, the last of the giant tortoises on wind-beaten St. Helena," who sulks like the exiled Napoleon; raccoons at the poet's Provincetown, Massachusetts home; snakes mating "in a brazen love-knot"; and fierce-looking tomato hornworms who turn out, at least as Kunitz envisions them, to have more in common with us than one might think at first.

The finest of these animal poems, **"The Wellfleet Whale,"** was inspired by a 1966 encounter with one of the gargantuan mammals when it beached itself on Cape Cod. Kunitz conveys both the awe inspired by the creature in its agony, and the growing sense of kinship felt by those who stood around it during its slow death listening to its eerie rumblings and wails, helpless to relieve the suffering:

> Toward dawn we shared with you
> your hour of desolation,
>   the huge lingering passion
>   of your unearthly outcry,
>   as you swung your blind head
>   toward us and laboriously opened
>   a bloodshot, glistening eye,
> in which we swam with terror and recognition.

Just as the dying whale captures the beauty and fear of being alive, Stanley Kunitz' humanism illuminates ***Passing Through.*** On his 90th birthday he has given us a wonderful present.

A. V. Christie (review date 31 December 1995)

SOURCE: "The Poems of Stanley Kunitz Confront 'The Great Simplicities,'" in *Chicago Tribune Books,* December 31, 1995, p. 4.

[*In the following review, Christie offers a positive assessment of* Passing Through.]

Yes, lately we've been intrigued by a poetry infused with the postmodern, by its skeptical deconstructions and complexities. But how it refreshes and affirms to reconnect with a voice, an aesthetic, that risks caring.

"What is there left to confront but the great simplicities? I never tire of birdsong and sky and weather. . . . I dream of an art so transparent that you can look through and see the world," states Stanley Kunitz in the opening comments to his *Passing Through: Later Poems, New and Selected.*

Winner of this year's National Book Award, *Passing Through* is Kunitz's ninth collection and coincides with the celebration of his 90th birthday. Leave the metadiscourse to some other generation, Kunitz is "in league with that ounce of heart / pounding in my palm" (**"Robin Redbreast"**).

The volume brings together most of Kunitz's best poems from the later years and includes several new poems that engage with his abiding themes: time's legacies, nature and loss. He here displays the kind of intelligence and precision that hone the lyric moment. Throughout the wide sweep of years we see this rare lyric sensibility at work, as Kunitz purely sketches an instant in time, making a "noble, dissolving music" from a cross-grained knot in the opposite wall, a day spent fishing at Quinnapoxet, a dragonfly or a quarrel. His brief poem **"The Catch"** is perfect example of the purity of his epiphanies and their intensity of vision:

> "It darted across the pond / toward our sunset perch, / weaving in, up, and around / a spindle of air, / this delicate engine / fired by impulse and glitter, / swift darning-needle, / gossamer dragon, / less image than thought, / and the thought come alive. / Swoosh went the net / with a practiced hand. / 'Da-da, may I look too?' / You may look, child, / all you want. / This prize belongs to no one. / But you will pay all / you life for the privilege, / all your life."

But Kunitz's world is not merely a world of lyric beauty and natural enticements, of "blue-spiked veronica" and his "late bloomers / flushed with their brandy"—Kunitz keeps a lush, seaside garden of wide renown. Aware of poetry's place through the "millennial ordeal," he insists that poetry "is ultimately mythology, the telling of the stories of the soul. This would seem to be an introverted, even solipsistic, enterprise, if it were not that these stories recount the soul's passage through the valley of this life—that is to say, its adventure in time, in history."

Kunitz's poems go beyond personal history and the testimony of individual spirit. They speak as witness to history's greater deeds and misdeeds. In poems like **"The Lincoln Relics"** and **"The Mound Builders,"** Kunitz offers quiet commentary on those moments compelling and threatening to humanity, from the disgrace of Richard Nixon to nuclear testing. In **"Around Pastor Bonhoeffer"** about the German pastor (co-conspirator in a failed plot to murder Hitler), Kunitz writes in the persona of the pastor:

". . . if you permit / this evil, what is the good / of the good of your life?"

A luminous and deep accounting of the times to which he has belonged, Kunitz's poetry reminds us that the best art stakes its claim in crossroads territory, at the resonant intersection of the private and the public. And in these later poems we do sense a voice that has crossed from world to world.

Everywhere are the figures of such journeys: Orpheus, Proteus and the Wellfleet Whale in the remarkable poem of the same name:

> You prowled down the continental shelf, / guided by the sun and stars / and the taste of alluvial silt / on your way southward / to the warm lagoons, / the tropic of desire / where the lovers lie belly to belly / in the rub and nuzzle of their sporting; / and you turned, like a god in exile, / out of your wide primeval element, / delivered to the mercy of time. / Master of the whale-roads, / let the white wings of the gulls / spread out their cover. / You have become like us, / disgraced and mortal.

We sense, too, a voice looking back on what it has made: "I walk into the woods I made / my dark and resinous blistered land, / through the deep litter of the years" (**"River Road"**). The speaker in **"The Long Boat"** lies down, absolved of a life's burdens that suggest Kunitz's own: "conscience, ambition, and all that caring."

What Kunitz has made has been always generous and full of ardor. In the book's final poem, **"Touch Me,"** he asks what makes the engines of the crickets go, what makes a life go, and answers "Desire, desire, desire." This desire for the world and its details has distinguished Kunitz's poetry. He may invoke Orpheus, whose music brought the trees to blossom, but many readers will be left with an image of Kunitz himself as the lamplighter in his **"Lamplighter: 1914,"** the man who raises an orange flame and touches the lamps "one by one, / till the whole countryside bloomed."

Stanley Kunitz with Bill Moyers (interview date 1995)

SOURCE: "Stanley Kunitz," in *The Language of Life: A Festival of Poets,* by Bill Moyers, edited by James Haba, Doubleday, 1995, pp. 239–55.

[*In the following interview, Kunitz discusses formative events in his life and career, his approach to writing poetry, the origin of several of his poems, and the significance of poetry for the artist and society.*]

Stanley Kunitz begins his ninetieth year with a new collection of luminous, life-affirming poems. Still wrestling with basic themes—"the world's wrongs and the injustice of time"—and still joyfully rearranging the sounds of language as he does the flowers in his garden, Kunitz has received nearly every honor bestowed upon a poet, including the Pulitzer Prize in 1959 and appointments as consultant in poetry to the Library of Congress (now called poet laureate) and poet laureate of New York. He was a founder of the Fine Arts Work Center in Provincetown. Massachusetts, and of Poets House in New York City. He is also a chancellor of the Academy of American Poets.

[*Moyers:*] *Do you remember the first time you truly experienced words, somehow, as part of your being?*

[Kunitz:] I used to go out into the woods behind our house in Worcester, Massachusetts, and shout words, any words that came to me, preferably long ones, just because the sound of them excited me. "Eleemosynary," I recall, was one of my favorites. "Phantasmagoria" was another.

I grew up in the South where Lincoln was not as revered as he was elsewhere. I remember the sound of that language, even to this moment:

> George Washington was a great big boss,
> He rode himself around on a big white horse.
> Abraham Lincoln was a goddamn fool,
> He rode himself around on a skinny old mule.

When I was in the fourth grade, my teacher, Miss McGillicuddy, had assigned us a composition on George Washington to celebrate his birthday. I still remember my sensational beginning: "George Washington was a tall, petite, handsome man." Whether or not I suspected what "petite" meant, I found it too elegant to resist. Miss McGillicuddy, whose French vocabulary may have been no better than mine, thought my composition was fabulous and every year from that point on into the next generation she used to read it to her new classes as a literary model. I spent a good part of my childhood exploring language, trying to find a new word every day in the unabridged Century Dictionary that was one of our household's prized possessions. And I haunted the public library. The librarian said sternly, "Five books. That's the limit you can take, Stanley. Five for the week." When I came back in a couple of days, she insisted I couldn't read that much so fast, I convinced her I had, and wangled permission to haul away five more. She was really a kind soul.

Were these books of poetry?

Some were. Of course, my taste in poetry was indiscriminate. Tennyson and Whittier and Longfellow and James Whitcomb Riley and Robert Service all seemed to offer equal enchantments. When I was graduated from elementary school, as class valedictorian, the poem I chose to recite for the occasion was Kipling's "Recessional":

> Lord God of Hosts, be with us yet,
> Lest we forget—lest we forget!

By then I knew that language was tremendously important to me. I already felt drawn to the community of poets.

Once in East Africa on the shore of an ancient lake, I sat alone and suddenly it struck me what community is. It's gathering around the fire and listening to somebody tell a story.

That's probably how poetry began, in some such setting. Wherever I've traveled in the world, I've never felt alone. Language is no barrier to people who love the word. I think of poets as solitaries with a heightened sense of community.

But, Stanley, is your community limited to other poets?

I should be sad if that were true.

Have you ever changed a poem you wrote long ago?

There are a few old poems I've tinkered with, correcting a word here or a phrase there that was obviously wrong, but I think it's foolhardy to attempt radical revisions of early work. You are no longer the poet who wrote those lines in his troubled youth. Time itself is stitched into the fabric of the text.

What has happened to the music of poetry? Why does poetry now simply lie there on the printed page, which you have called "a very cold bed"?

One of the problems with poetry in the modern age is that it's become separated from the spoken word. When you ask students to read a poem aloud, you find they have no idea of the rhythm of the language, its flow, inflection, and pitch. They do not understand that stress and tonality are instruments of meaning. Is the fault wholly theirs? Poetry has strayed far from its origins in song and dance. With its gradual retreat into print and, currently, into the academy, it is in danger of becoming a highly technical and specialized linguistic skill. It has already lost most of its general listening audience.

Is it possible that the rock musician is the poet of our day?

It's a commentary on the state of our culture that the vast audience for rock and other varieties of pop seems to be quite satisfied at that level of communication. It doesn't feel a need for poetry. That disturbs me because poetry explores depths of thought and feeling that civilization requires for its survival. What does it signify that the mass of our adult population cares as little for the poets of the great tradition as it does for the moderns? The consoling thought is that children are still impressionable and ready to receive poetry, ready to make it part of their lives. But that's before they are spoiled. Our educational system had failed us in that respect, among others.

I think back on the poems I read in high school—Shelley, Keats, and Byron. They rhymed. They had meter. That's not true anymore.

Certainly it's easier to remember verse that has a fixed rhyme scheme, a regular beat, and a standard length of line. Much of the pleasure we derive from the poetry of the past, regardless of its quality, is due to the fulfillment of expectations. But that's precisely the kind of aesthetic satisfaction that the most representative and seminal imaginations of this century taught us to question. Right now we seem to be entering a more conservative phase, but I'm not ready to greet the dawn of a neoclassical age.

Do people quote your poems?

Not by the tens of thousands, but I've heard of some who do. Perhaps it's relevant to note that I was trained in the metrical tradition or, rather, I trained myself, since there were no creative writing programs in those days. At a later stage I became a lapsed formalist, choosing to write by and for the ear, without preimposed conditions. I trust the ear to let my rhythms go where they need to go. The ear is the best of prosodists.

These lines of yours come to mind—I wish you'd comment on them.

> I dance, for the joy of surviving,
> on the edge of the road.

That's the ending of **"An Old Cracked Tune,"** a poem that had its origin in a scurrilous street song remembered from my youth. The butt of the song's mockery was a stereotypically avaricious and conniving Jewish tailor. The very first line—the one I appropriated—went: "My name is Solomon Levi." It didn't occur to me until later that Solomon was my father's given name and that he was a Levite, a descendant of the priestly house of Levi. When the line from that odious song popped into my head, I wondered, "Can I redeem it?" And so I wrote the poem.

"An Old Cracked Tune"

My name is Solomon Levi,
the desert is my home,
my mother's breast was thorny,
and father I had none.

The sands whispered, Be separate,
the stones taught me, Be hard.
I dance, for the joy of surviving,
on the edge of the road.

You must have been repelled by the anti-Semitism.

It hurt me and left a scar. The bigotry of this country early in the century cut deep into our social fabric. And it persists to this day, as an ugly racist infection. I'm not implying that this was in mind when I started to write that poem. Poems don't tell you why you need to write them. Perhaps you write them in order to find out why. My driving impulse was to embrace a wounded name.

Why did you call the poem **"An Old Cracked Tune"***?*

I've never thought about it—the title came with the poem. "Old tune" must allude to the source of the poem, as well

as to its being a sort of ancestral song. "Cracked" tells something about the speaker's age and voice and maybe about his state of mind.

Do you remember the original lyrics?

No. Only the first line and "zip-zip-zip" out of the refrain. The one person on earth, to my knowledge, who remembers that song is Richard Wilbur.

The poet.

Yes, and he can sing several stanzas of it—more, I guess, than I've ever wanted to remember. He may have heard it at Harvard years after I did.

Anti-Semitism cost you a teaching position at Harvard.

According to the illustrious head of the English Department in 1927, the year of my M.A., Harvard's Anglo-Saxon students would resent being taught English literature by a Jew.

What did you do?

I left Harvard in a state of rage and confusion. After a brief start as reporter for the *Worcester Telegram,* my hometown paper, I came to New York—this was on the eve of the Great Depression—and went to work for the H. W. Wilson publishing firm. There I became editor of the *Wilson Library Bulletin* and initiated a series of biographical dictionaries that are still standard works of literary reference. In 1930 Doubleday published ***Intellectual Things,*** my first book of poems.

What did you mean when you said you wanted to "redeem" the man in the poem?

I hoped to restore his dignity by identifying with him. Like him, the poet in our society is a marginal character, dancing on the edge of the road, not in the middle where the heavy traffic flows. Maybe one of the secrets of survival is to learn *where* to dance.

You took something bitter and turned it into something joyous.

Poetry has a great digestive system and can consume and recycle almost anything. It is the poet's persona that gives meaning to the process. For years I've been telling young poets that the first important act of the imagination is to create the person who will write the poems. And that's not the end of it. We have to invent and reinvent who we are until we arrive at the self we can bear to live with and die with. Art demands of the artist the capacity for self-renewal. Without it, art withers. And, of course, so does the life.

There is an erotic quality to poetry—creative and recreative. Do you make love to the word?

Every new poem is like finding a new bride. Words are so erotic, they never tire of their coupling. How do they renew themselves? In their inexhaustible desire for combinations and recombinations.

Is it hard work to write a poem?

Is it *hard*? I think poetry is the most difficult, the most solitary, and the most life-enhancing thing that one can do in the world.

What makes it such a struggle?

Because in our daily lives we enslave words, use them and abuse them, until they are fit for only menial tasks and small errands.

You have to kill a lot of clichés, don't you?

You have to remove the top of your head and plunge into the deep waters of the buried life in order to come up with words that are fresh and shining. Poetry isn't written on schedule. A poem that occupies less than a page may take days, weeks, months—and still want more attention to set it right. You know, that's not very practical in the world's terms.

The world is so meagerly supportive of the poet. How do you keep going?

A poet has to be cunning in the world's ways, too. Poets who flunk their lessons in the art of survival either drop out or die young. Above all, we need to buy time, meditation time, but not at the world's price. One of the strategies I've learned is to stay alive when the rest of the world is asleep. When I shut the door of my study, the clocks stop ticking. A few minutes seem to pass, and suddenly it's dawn.

On what are you meditating?

You don't choose the subject of meditation, *it* chooses you. But you have to put yourself into a state of readiness. You have to move into areas of the self that remain to be explored, and that's one of the problems of maturing as a poet. By the age of fifty, the chances are that you've explored all the obvious places. The poems that remain for you to write will have to come out of your wilderness.

Wilderness?

Yes, the untamed self that you pretend doesn't exist, all that chaos locked behind the closet door, those memories yammering in the dark. . . .

You have said that certain images are "key images." Are these memories of childhood?

Usually so. I believe that at the center of every poetic imagination is a cluster of images associated with pivotal moments. That cluster is the key to one's identity, the pur-est concentration of the self. Poetry happens when new images of sensations are drawn into the gravitational field of the old life.

In **"Three Floors,"** *which is one of my favorite poems, you are remembering your childhood.*

"Three Floors"

Mother was a crack of light
and a gray eye peeping;
I made believe by breathing hard
that I was sleeping.

Sister's doughboy on last leave
had robbed me of her hand;
downstairs at intervals she played
Warum on the baby grand.

Under the roof of a wardrobe trunk
whose lock a boy could pick
contained a red Masonic hat
and a walking stick.

Bolt upright in my bed that night
I saw my father flying;
the wind was walking on my neck,
the windowpanes were crying.

That poem is one of several stemming from the suicide of my father a few weeks before I was born. My mother kept just a few of his relics in a trunk in the attic, including a red Masonic hat and a walking stick, which figure in the poem. The time was World War I, when I was about ten. Another poem, **"The Portrait,"** returns me to that attic, discovering a portrait of my father. When I brought it down to show to my mother, she tore it up.

And your mother slapped you for finding it, as the poem says?

Yes.

"The Portrait"

My mother never forgave my father
for killing himself,
especially at such an awkward time
and in a public park,
that spring
when I was waiting to be born.
She locked his name
in her deepest cabinet
and would not let him out,
though I could hear him thumping.
When I came down from the attic
with the pastel portrait in my hand
of a long-lipped stranger
with a brave moustache
and deep brown level eyes,
she ripped it into shreds
without a single word
and slapped me hard.
In my sixty-fourth year

> I can feel my cheek
> still burning.

Do you think she slapped you because you found the portrait or because she held you responsible for your father's death?

Her anger was directed at him, not at me. She wanted to expunge his memory. No mention of him ever crossed her lips.

For a long time you did not write about it.

In **"Father and Son,"** written in my mid-thirties, I pursue and ultimately confront his image. It was an act of liberation for me.

Of whom is the portrait a portrait? Your father, your mother, yourself? Or is it the portrait of an experience, a memory?

You are perfectly right to imply that it is more than my father's portrait.

How do dreams play a role in the creating of poetry?

In their fluidity and illogic, dream images readily translate into poetry. Everything in **"Quinnapoxet,"** for example, came to me in a dream—not the words, but all the images.

"Quinnapoxet"

> I was fishing in the abandoned reservoir
> back in Quinnapoxet,
> where the snapping turtles cruised
> and the bullheads swayed
> in their bower of tree-stumps,
> sleek as eels and pigeon-fat.
> One of them gashed my thumb
> with a flick of his razor fin
> when I yanked the barb
> out of his gullet.
> The sun hung its terrible coals
> over Buteau's farm: I saw
> the treetops seething.
>
> They came suddenly into view
> on the Indian road,
> evenly stopping
> past the apple orchard,
> commingling with the dust
> they raised, their cloud of being,
> against the dripping light
> looming larger and bolder.
> She was wearing a mourning bonnet
> and a warp of shining taffeta.
> "Why don't you write?" she cried
> from the folds of her veil.
> "We never hear from you."
> I had nothing to say to her.
> But for him who walked behind her
> in his dark worsted suit,
> with his face averted
> as if to hide a scald,

> deep in his other life,
> I touched my forehead
> with my swollen thumb,
> and splayed my fingers out—
> in deaf-mute country
> the sign for father.

Two people come into view, and a woman says, "Why don't you write?" The other is wearing a burial suit. Is he your father?

That's the image.

You salute him. That is a reconciliation?

The recognition of a bond. As if to say, we belong to each other.

And you dreamed this.

From beginning to end. Then I began exploring what I had dreamed. In an illustrated article on sign language for the deaf I found the hand gesture I had made in my dream. It is the most reverential of all the signs for father.

Do you think there's special wisdom in dreams?

Poets have always loved the language of dreams—it's so full of secrets.

Do you sometimes think you're carrying on a conversation with ancestors you never knew?

The arts, by their nature, are our means of conducting that dialogue. Where is the history of the race inscribed, if not in the human imagination? One of my strongest convictions is that poetry is ultimately mythology, the telling of the stories of the soul. We keep asking Gauguin's famous set of questions, "Where do we come from? Who are we? Where are we going?" The echo that mocks us comes from the Stone Age caves. The poem on the page is only a shadow of the poem in the mind. And the poem in the mind is only a shadow of the poetry and the mystery of the things of this world. So we must try again, for the work is never finished I don't think it's absurd to believe that the chain of being, our indelible genetic code, holds memories of the ancient world that are passed down from generation to generation. Heraclitus speaks of "mortals and immortals living in their death, dying into each other's lives."

*The other night, at your reading, young people were approaching, and they had very special applause for **"End of Summer."***

"End of Summer"

> An agitation of the air,
> A perturbation of the light
> Admonished me the unloved year
> Would turn on its hinge that night.

I stood in the disenchanted field
Amid the stubble and the stones,
Amazed, while a small worm lisped to me
The song of my marrow-bones.

Blue poured into summer blue,
A hawk broke from his cloudless tower,
the roof of the silo blazed, and I knew
that part of my life was over.

Already the iron door of the north
Clangs open: birds, leaves, snows
Order their populations forth,
And a cruel wind blows.

That poem came to me in mid-life when I was living in Bucks County, Pennsylvania. The occasion is still vivid in my mind. I was out in the field, hoeing down an old standard of corn. Suddenly I heard a commotion overhead. A flock of wild geese, streaking down from the north, rattled the sky with their honking. I stood in the field, gazing upward with a sense of tumult and wonder, for something had been revealed to me: the story of migration had become my story. At that moment I made one of the most important decisions of life. I dropped my hoe and ran into the house and started to write this poem. It began as a celebration of the wild geese. Eventually the geese flew out of the poem, but I like to think they left behind the sound of their beating wings.

Why did you use the word "perturbation" in the second line, "A perturbation of the light"? Why not "commotion" or "disturbance" or "flurry"?

There's more wingbeat in "perturbation." I might add that the rhythm is intentionally persistent, relying largely on the interplay between open and closed vowels.

An agitation of the air,
A perturbation of the light
Admonished me the unloved year
Would turn on its hinge that night.

Did you speak the lines?

I *always* speak the lines. That's how I write my poems.

You said that you heard the geese and looked up and responded instantly with a decision. That couldn't have been an intellectual decision. Your body *said something to you which was triggered by the geese.*

I saw the writing in the sky. Don't forget that there were soothsayers in ancient times who practiced divination by studying the flight of birds.

I remember seeing your poem about the moonwalk, **"The Flight of Apollo,"** *in* The New York Times.

"The Flight of Apollo"

Earth was my home, but even there I was a stranger.
This mineral crust. I walk like a swimmer. What titanic

bombardments in those old astral wars! I know what I know: I shall never escape from strangeness or complete my journey. Think of me as nostalgic, afraid, exalted. I am your man on the moon, a speck of megalomania, restless for the leap toward inland universes pulsing beyond where the constellations set. Infinite space overwhelms the human heart, but in the middle of nowhere life inexorably calls to life. Forward my mail to Mars. What news from the Great Spiral Nebula in Andromeda and the Magellanic Clouds?

2

I was a stranger on earth.
Stepping on the moon, I begin
the gay pilgrimage to new
Jerusalems
in foreign galaxies.
Heat. Cold. Craters of silence.
The Sea of Tranquillity
rolling on the shores of entropy.
And, beyond,
the intelligence of the stars.

You have a long memory, for that was in 1969. The *Times* had asked me for a poem in tribute to man's first landing on the moon, and fortunately I had one at hand, having written it in the days before Apollo 11 was launched. When I saw the actual landing on TV, I felt I had already been there. There was no need to change a word. I've always been fascinated by space exploration, so that it seemed quite natural for me to imagine myself a stranger on earth seeking a new home in the skies. Eventually, I suppose, the human race will have to move from this planet and settle elsewhere in the galaxy, for this planet will die.

Beyond this planet, as you say in the poem, is "the intelligence of the stars."

Simply on the basis of probability. I cannot believe that planet Earth is the only blob of dirt in the firmament that supports life.

There is a man in one of your poems who "carries a bag of earth on his back," and it reminds me that you are a gardener who likes to work with his hands. What does gardening have to do with poetry?

It has *everything* to do with poetry. When I work in my garden I feel that it is myself being planted, nourished, reborn. I am enchanted with every step in the process of making things grow. In the grand view, I see gardening as a ritual drama, in which the whole cycle of death and rebirth is enacted annually. But that doesn't prevent me from undertaking the most lowly tasks and truly enjoying them, even weeding and grubbing. It strikes me that gardens and poems are equally unpredictable, given the vagaries of weather and imagination. A plant behaves beautifully one summer. The next summer it turns gross and invasive. Or languishes in the heat, disfigured and splotchy with mildew or succumbs to the voracious appetites of cutworms and beetles and slugs. In the civilization of the garden such specimens must be treated as outlaws. Out with them! The making of a garden requires the same kind of ruthlessness as the making of a poem.

I like the image of growing a garden as you grow a poem, as you grow a self. **"Passing Through,"** *the poem you wrote on your seventy-ninth birthday, implies a process of changing. In your later poems you write with much more simplicity and economy than in your early poems. Why is that?*

"Passing Through"

—on my Seventy-Ninth Birthday

Nobody in the widow's household
ever celebrated anniversaries.
In the secrecy of my room
I would not admit I cared
that my friends were given parties.
Before I left town for school
my birthday went up in smoke
in a fire at City Hall that gutted
the Department of Vital Statistics.
If it weren't for a census report
of a five-year-old White Male
sharing my mother's address
at the Green Street tenement in Worcester
I'd have no documentary proof
that I exist. You are the first,
my dear, to bully me
into these festive occasions.

Sometimes, you say, I wear
an abstracted look that drives you
up the wall, as though it signified
distress or disaffection.
Don't take it so to heart.
Maybe I enjoy not-being as much
as being who I am. Maybe
it's time for me to practice
growing old. The way I look
at it, I'm passing through a phase:
gradually I'm changing to a word.
Whatever you choose to claim
of me is always yours;
nothing is truly mine
except my name. I only
borrowed this dust.

In a curious way, age is simpler than youth, for it has fewer options. In the beginning, life seems to offer us infinite choices, a bewilderment of opportunities. We have no certainties about our destination, or a path that will lead us there. We might become a scientist, or a theologian, or a farmer, or a poet. Who knows? Every time we make a significant choice—affecting, let's say, our education, or career, or involvement with others—we reduce, exponentially, the number of choices left to us. Finally, we arrive at the realization that the only remaining choice of any consequence, if it can be considered a choice at all, is between living and dying. This simplifies, as it purifies, the operation of the mind. What could be more natural than for the mature imagination at sunset to move toward

economy of style and gravity of tone? When I read the late work of Hardy or Yeats, I get the distinct impression that the life of the poet is already passing into his poems.

Your once said that you were living and dying at the same time, but when you reach a certain age aren't you dying faster than you're living?

I prefer to say, as I do in **"Passing Through,"** that "gradually I'm changing to a word." The beauty of that transaction is that it involves a transfer of energy, not a loss. I'm conditioned to believe that the word is less perishable than its creator.

In another poem you ask, "What do I want of my life?" And you answer, "More! More!"

That's from an earlier poem—but I still subscribe to the sentiment.

Before we met today I was listening to Mozart's Piano Concert No.21 and I thought, that's *immortality. The musician has given way to the music. What about poetry?*

I follow Coleridge in believing that the sense of musical delight, together with the power of producing it, is the gift that marks the poet born. When Keats wrote in one of his letters, "I am certain of nothing but of the holiness of the heart's affections and the truth of imagination," he was defining for all of us the ground of that music. Let me tell you about a twelfth-century Chinese poet named Yang Wan-li, one of the four masters of Southern Sung poetry. One day he gathered his disciples around him and addressed them in this fashion: "Now, what is poetry? If you say it is simply a matter of words, I will say, 'A good poet gets rid of words.' If you say it is simply a matter of meaning, I will say, 'A good poet gets rid of meaning.' But, you say, if words and meaning are gotten rid of, where is the poetry? To this I reply, 'Get rid of words and meaning and there is still poetry.'"

Scholars have been wrestling with that test for centuries. I think that Yang is telling us that poetry is more than a product of human intelligence and craft. It is an intrinsic element of the beauty and mystery of existence, something we take in with the air we breathe. We take it in and then we give back some semblance of it in our art.

David Yezzi (review date 1996)

SOURCE: "To Turn Again," in *Parnassus*, Vol. 21, Nos. 1–2, 1996, pp. 215–29.

[*In the following positive review of* Passing Through, *Yezzi provides an analysis of recurring "key images" and archetypes in Kunitz's poetry and comments favorably on Kunitz's effort to construct a "personal mythology."*]

When asked by Christopher Busa in *The Paris Review* interview if he felt differently about translating the poems of Baudelaire, whom he could never know personally, than about translating the work of various contemporary poets, Stanley Kunitz replied "I know Baudelaire too." Taken literally, Kunitz's contention might set a more speculative imagination to flights of wild conjecture. ("All poets are contemporaries," he has said.) Think of the possible combinations of acquaintance that such time travel would allow. What species of exquisite naughtiness could Hart Crane and John Wilmot hatch, left to their own devices in the Ramble in Central Park? Allen Ginsberg would not think it strange to see Garcia Lorca pricing summer fruit or Whitman pawing the ground chuck in the fluorescence of a Berkeley grocery. Mightn't Ovid have benefited from Archibald MacLeish's diplomatic acumen in helping to grease his return to Rome from Tomis on the Black Sea? Literary gatherings would take on added luster: "Wystan, I'd like you to meet Quintus Horatius Flaccus—Oh, I see you're already acquainted." Such reveries aside, Kunitz has something more serious in mind. To say that one may know poets long dead implies a transubstantiation between the flesh-and-blood poet and his incarnation on the page; this mystery manifests itself in the dual meanings of *corpus*—the physical body, a body of work (the Greek *soma* splits the same way). For his part, Kunitz has long been aware of the numerous intersections between the life and the work: "The life of a poet is crystallized in his work, that's how you know him"; or, as he put it on another occasion, "A poet's collected work is his book of changes"; and, finally, this Jungian distillate, "[Poetry] has its source, deep under the layers of a life, in the primordial self."

At ninety, Stanley Kunitz has more layers to his life than most. Accumulated in those layers are the poems of nearly three quarters of a century, alongside which stand interviews and essays, the products of a mind occupied not only with poetry but the teaching of it. Traced accurately, Kunitz's pedagogical reach might encompass more contemporary American poets and poetry than any other living individual's; and, as his students and acolytes—Lucie Brock-Broido, Susan Mitchell, Louise Glück, and Michael Ryan among them—take on their own students (Brock-Broido now teaches in the Columbia writing program, where she once studied with Kunitz), his influence continues to grow exponentially. Marie Howe has said of his mentoring powers, "How can I tell you what he's taught us? I can't stand here and tell you that he fussed with my commas and line breaks. He changed my life. He changed the lives of so many of us." As many artists will attest, to work on technique is to work on the bugbears and shortcomings in the self; poetry is "interwoven with the tissue of the life." In Kunitz's Socratic phrasing from the preface to his most recent book, *Passing Through: Later Poems, New and Selected,* the poet puts it this way: "Through the years I have found this gift of poetry to be life-sustaining, life-enhancing, and absolutely unpredictable. Does one live, therefore, for the sake of poetry? No, the reverse is true: poetry is for the sake of

the life." If poetry and the life are inextricable, then there can be no summary division between Kunitz's work as teacher and his work as a poet. The heuristic impulse applies to the making of poems as to the teaching of them: both endeavors function as aides to discovery. While, of necessity, Kunitz's discussions of verse take on a character distinct from his poems, both are mined from the same vein. Where the poems are highly refined, their metal hammered to a near transparency, his broader, more sententious reflections on the writing life display both the raw materials and by-products of the verse. His numerous interviews trade phrases with the poems; poems crystallize journal entries and bits of conversation. Here we get a further sense of *soma*—the life/work as a whole organism as opposed to its discrete parts.

2. "I STAND ON THE TERRIBLE THRESHOLD"

In the title poem of **"The Layers,"** a section of new poems from ***The Poems of Stanley Kunitz, 1928–1978,*** published when he was in his seventies, the poet wrings the liquor from several of his apothegms quoted above:

> Yet I turn, I turn,
> exulting somewhat,
> with my will intact to go
> wherever I need to go,
> and every stone on the road
> precious to me.
> In my darkest night,
> when the moon was covered
> and I roamed through wreckage,
> a nimbus-clouded voice
> directed me:
> "Live in the layers,
> not on the litter."
> Though I lack the art
> to decipher it,
> no doubt the next chapter
> in my book of transformations
> is already written.
> I am not done with my changes.

Here, Kunitz animates the life/work connection through metaphor. Each phase of the life marks a chapter recorded in a "book of transformations." (All poets live contemporaneously; their quickening takes place on the page.) The final line of the poem, a credo of sorts, sounds as a refrain in Kunitz's interviews; with it he refers at once to himself and his art. This is powerful juju from a septuagenarian poet, who fifteen or so years down the line may now look back and see that he was right: His changes are not finished, and the ethos behind this continuous transformation shows no sign of flagging.

A telling facet of the poet's outlook glitters from **"The Layers."** Not only is change continual for Kunitz, but often his changes are "already written." Compare this generosity of spirit with T. S. Eliot, who is middle age could already envision a state where one "do[es] not hope to turn again." (Kunitz states his turning not once but twice in the poem.) As A. David Moody suggests, Eliot, in

"Ash-Wednesday" resigns the "hope of a renewal of youth's joy and strength." For Kunitz, however, youth harbors the source of those primordial networks of images that give a poet the strength to live and write. Less a model than a foil, Eliot functions for Kunitz as a kind of influence manqué, someone to put his feet up against. Whereas the forty-year-old Eliot indulges his hopelessness, the seventy something Kunitz exults from deep within the layers of the life.

This striking affirmation notwithstanding, Kunitz's sterling optimism, more of the hard-won variety than the cock-eyed kind, remains burnished. Here is the first half of **"The Layers"** leading up to the poem's pivotal line with its insistent "turn"s:

> I have walked through many lives,
> some of them my own,
> and I am not who I was,
> though some principle of being
> abides, from which I struggle
> not to stray.
> When I look behind,
> as I am compelled to look
> before I can gather strength
> to proceed on my journey,
> I see the milestones dwindling
> toward the horizon
> and the slow fires trailing
> from the abandoned camp-sites,
> over which scavenger angels
> wheel on heavy wings.
> Oh, I have made myself a tribe
> out of my true affections,
> and my tribe is scattered!
> How shall the heart be reconciled
> to its feast of losses?
> In a rising wind
> the manic dust of my friends,
> those who fell along the way,
> bitterly stings my face.

For the writer of a personal book of changes, the scope of **"The Layers"** could not be much broader. Far from milquetoast lyric composed to commemorate a fleeting observation, the poem assays life in its entirety, viewed back to front. At the center of the poem gapes a doorway dividing the past from the future, advantage point from which the poet may survey his surround; from this cusp Kunitz takes stock of his beginning and his end. Richard Jackson, in an interview with Kunitz, has pointed out the abundance of "thresholds" in the poems, as in **"Open the Gates"**: "I stand on the terrible threshold, and I see / The end and the beginning in each other's arms." Again an echo of Eliot clamors from the wings, but even more nearly we hear the lines of the anonymous Scots poem "Balled of Sir Patrick Spence," which Coleridge (another poet that Kunitz could claim to know) takes as an epigraph to his "Dejection: An Ode": "Late, late yestreen I saw the new Moon, / With the old Moon in her arms / And I fear, I fear, my master dear! / We shall have a deadly storm." Signs and portents.

A storm rises in **"The Layers"** as well, blowing the dust of "those who fell along the way" into the poet's eyes. The speaker stands between the jambs of "I turn, I turn," compelled to crane his neck in order to proceed forward. Behind, milestone dwindle into an expansive distance, slow fires trail; camps are abandoned, tribes scattered; the heart feasts on loss. The G-force on that tiny *yet* as it streaks into the atmosphere of the poem is nearly enough to squelch it. The turn is so tenuous starting out that it must be affirmed, gaining force in the repetition. Here the poet pivots in the doorway to peer forward again, but carrying the memory of what lies behind. Chilled in the penumbra of a recalled darkness, the speaker can exult only "somewhat," but the will to proceed remains intact. In the transformative light of the speaker's resolve, fate, that aloof prankster, appears robed like grace; at the close of the poem, the next chapter of the life "is already written," and in fact is being written as the poet peers past the lintel to utter at once a prophecy and a plea: "I am not done. . . ." A typographical representation of the poem would resemble one of Herbert's "Easter Wings." The panorama of the past narrows as the speaker approaches his peripety at the poem's center (looking back, angels—of history?—are scavengers on heavy wings); from there the view expands again, opening, however tentatively, to an assured future. Herbert, a poet to whom Kunitz has long acknowledged indebtedness, concludes his poem with this angelic feather: "Affliction shall advance the flight in me." Kunitz, in his, is similarly "compelled" to take stock of his afflictions before proceeding onward.

The next poem in *Passing Through,* from the 1985 collection, *Next-to-Last Things,* provides another point of intersection with Kunitz's more general poetic concerns. Noticing two garden snakes sliding among the conifers in his Provincetown plot, Kunitz murmurs:

> I should have thought them gone,
> in a torpor of blood
> slipped to the nether world
> before the sickle frost.
> Not so. In the deceptive balm
> of noon, as if defiant of the curse
> that spoiled another garden,
> these two appear on show
> through a narrow slit
> in the dense green brocade
> of a north-country spruce,
> dangling head-down, entwined
> in a brazen love-knot.
> I put out my hand and stroke
> the fine, dry grit of their skins.
> After all,
> we are partners in this land,
> co-signers of a covenant.
> At my touch the wild
> braid of creation
> trembles.

(from **"The Snakes of September"**)

Compare the end of this passage with its prose corollary, which Stanley Moss cites in his introduction to *Interviews and Encounters*: "All myths are the same, all metaphors are the same metaphor; when you touch the web of creation at any point, the whole web shudders." Poetry for Kunitz aspires to the status of myth, and by placing us squarely in the center of received myth **"Snakes"** serpentines toward the creation of a new, personal one ("the effort is to convert one's life into legend"). The scene proceeds through dualities, a constant division of ones into twos. Structurally, the poem divides in half on the *volta*-like sixteenth line; here we read that it's noon, the hour dividing ante- from postmeridian. "September" situates the speaker in an equinoctial month, and one supposes it to be the 23rd, the first day of the fall (read *the Fall*); for in a garden where netherworldly serpents are "defiant of the curse / that spoiled another garden," how could it be otherwise? The poem turns on "not so," after which twos repair into ones: The two snakes twine together; the poet partners with the serpents; they become "co-signers of a covenant." At Kunitz's deft handling of *covenant,* the whole web of Biblical myth shudders, from Adam to Moses to Jesus.

In the structural complexity of **"The Serpents,"** with its dense helix of images spiraling down through the poem, we may behold Kunitz's own braid/web of creation. If you prod one image in Kunitz, other poems register a reaction. "If we go deep enough," the poet explains, in his interview with Jackson, "we may discover the secret place where our key images have been stored since childhood. There are chains of other images attached to them, the accretions of the years. A single touch activates the whole cluster." This last bit is immediately recognizable as a second paraphrase of **"The Layers."** While many of Kunitz's poems rework the same "key images," poem calls to poem most explicitly in **"Touch Me"**:

> *Summer is late, my heart.*
> Words plucked out of the air
> some forty years ago
> when I was wild with love
> and torn almost in two
> scatter like leaves this night
> of whistling wind and rain.

The italicized first line echoes the poet's **"As Flowers Are,"** from *Selected Poems, 1928–1958,* the contents of which are sadly omitted from the current *Selected*:

> Summer is late, my heart: the dusty fiddler
> Hunches under the stone; these pummelings
> Of scent are more than masquerade; I have heard
> A song repeat, repeat, till my breath had failed.
> As flowers have flowers, at the season's height,
> A single color oversweeps the field.

Kunitz's images, his personal archetypes, surface and resurface throughout his lyrics; the effect can be understood, not by reading one poem as separate from another, but by considering the work—poetry and prose—as a whole. In midcareer the poet traded the masterly pentameters of **"As Flowers Are"** for the *sui generis* "functional stressing" present in the later poetry quoted thus far—a loose trimeter or tetrameter line with ample variation where the ear dictates the intervals. Early Kunitz, which comprises three volumes—*Intellectual Things* (1930), *Passport to the War* (1944), and the 1958 *Selected*—employs a syntax and vocabulary that to today's ear may seem wantonly mandarin. These, however, are among the poems that Yvor Winters recommended to his students at Stanford. For many of that generation, *Intellectual Things,* by the precocious twenty-five-year-old, with its fluent formalism and lush syntax, was a manual on how to write verse. In the mid-Thirties Theodore Roethke, who at that time had yet to publish a volume of his own, appeared on Kunitz's doorstep wearing a raccoon coat and sporting a copy of that arresting first book. Inside, after a few drinks, Roethke proceeded to pay homage by reciting several of the poems from memory.

Part of Kunitz's evolution has been to thin out the linguistic densities of his early work, finding instead a pellucidity of surface and diction; the complexities of the later poems are formed in the layers hidden from ready view, which Kunitz locates "below the floor of consciousness." Psychological richness replaces the early emphasis on prosodic richness. One may regret (as this reader does) the loss in Kunitz of the linguistic challenges of *Intellectual Things.* Formal brinkmanship, daring to go too far, while not always successful, can on occasion result in lines that lodge unassailably in the mind. If *Passing Through* were Kunitz's first book, would a young unknown show up with it committed to memory? Lines, yes; whole poems, no. Willfully weeding the poems of their surface mystery, Kunitz has labored to cultivate a mysterious interconnectedness in the inner tissue of a given poem and even between poems.

As the redeployment of the line from **"As Flowers Are"** suggests, while the early style may have developed into its virtual opposite—hermetic lines in received meters replaced by a "transparent" free verse—strings of recurring images endure, clinging in the web of the work *in toto*: "If you understand a poet's key images, you have a clue to the understanding of his whole work." "Key images" is a felicitous phrase considering the extent to which locks and keys and doors operate in Kunitz's poems as just these kind of clues:

> "Dante!" I cried
> to the apparition
> entering from the hall,
> laureled and gaunt,
> in a cone of light.
> "Out of mercy you came
> to be my Master
> and my guide!"
> To which he replied:
> "I know neither the time
> nor the way
> nor the number on the door . . .
> but this must be my room,
> I was here before."
> And he held up in his hand

the key,
which blinded me.

(from **"The Illumination"**)

Set in a Paris hotel, the poem depicts a private heart of darkness, one in which the poet finds himself disconsolate, alone in a foreign city, his funds sapped. In this self-imposed exile from his native soil, the poet's most formidable demons conspire to haunt him: the parent he has denied, the friend he's failed, the hearts he's spoiled ("including my own left ventricle"). Out of this slough, poet calls to poet. An edition of Dante's *Inferno,* with engravings by Gustave Doré, which Kunitz knew in his childhood, figures in several of the poems, both early and late. As much as the Florentine's chthonic epic, the accompanying images by the nineteenth-century French engraver found purchase with the poet at that formative age. Doré's first plate in the *Inferno,* a depiction of Dante cowering in that dark wood, renders the pilgrim much as Kunitz does in **"The Illumination"**: "in a cone of light." In the first Canto of the *Comedy,* the sun begins to rise, illuminating somewhat the savage wilderness and briefly bolstering Dante's spirits. Soon, Virgil, whom Dante calls *maestro,* appears. In **"The Illumination"** Kunitz paraphrases Dante's greeting in an address to *his* master; Alighieri's Paris incarnation, however, falters in his role as hoped-for Virgilian guide—he too is lost—and the key he proffers is blinding.

3. "The key which blinded me"

Each image within a given body of work operates as a valise containing not only denotative meaning but the connotations accrued from the poet's deployment of that image elsewhere; hence, the "green thought" in "The Garden" can be grasped only in terms of Marvell's use of "green" throughout the body of his poems. What, then, is this "key" that Kunitz refers to, and what is it that is locked? The image reappears in **"The Testing-Tree"**:

Once I owned the key
to an umbrageous trail
thickened with mosses
where flickering presences
gave me right of passage.

As in **"The Layers,"** the "flickering presences" of the past, in this case the spirits of Wampanoag Indians, provide Kunitz with right of passage, but, as he discovers in **"The Illumination,"** the specters of the past, seen in that poem as private failings, can withhold imprimatur; in any case, they must be dealt with. In the early poem **"Open the Gates,"** in which Doré's images loom large, the poet again confronts his past as a requirement for stumbling forward:

Within the city of the burning cloud,
Dragging my life behind me in a sack,
Naked I prowl, scourged by the black
Temptation of the blood grown proud.

Here at the monumental door
Carved with the curious legend of my youth . . .

Before being admitted, the poet must decipher the conundrum posed by his youth; the information he needs to untangle this curious legend—his life—he has carried with him on his back.

Depending from this chain of images rattles a passage from **"The Portrait,"** which Kunitz has called, along with **"The Layers,"** a poem of origins:

My mother never forgave my father
for killing himself,
especially at such an awkward time
and in a public park,
that spring
when I was waiting to be born.
She locked his name
in her deepest cabinet
and would not let him out,
though I could hear him thumping.

Locked as it is the deepest cabinet, the specter of the lost father lurks as the oldest and most powerful in Kunitz's poetry of personal legend. Perhaps it is the mother's willful internment of the memory of her husband (later in the poem, she tears up her son's pastel rendering of his father) that has caused this ghost to pace the floorboards of Kunitz's poetry. The father, however, as in the last line of **"Father and Son,"** often makes no reply; in answer to his son's entreaties for his return, the father offers only "the white ignorant hollow of his face." The image recalls Dante via Doré. In the *Vita Nuova,* a title Kunitz borrows for one of the poems written in his twenties, Dante employs his own "key" image: "Here me and then consider: am not I / The keep and key / Of all the torments sorrow can combine." Certainly this heartsick questioning lies in the same register as the description of the mother's locked cabinet with its grisly contents; it bespeaks the same desolate horror of that Paris hotel room; it feeds at the feast of losses glimpsed from the center of **"The Layers."**

4. "All myths are the same"

If there is a peculiarity, not quite a flaw, in Kunitz's later style of freighted imagery, it is the way a poem sometimes changes gears too quickly, leaving the reader behind, as the poem speeds on toward revelation. At the end of **"The Snakes of September,"** the poet moves from the particular to the universal, as the "wild braid of creation trembles" at his touch. The poem earns its conclusion on the level of meaning, but there is something overripe about that "wild." This rapid tonal shift to an ecstatic register jars, and for an instant our attention is diverted to the machinery of the poem working slightly too hard.

In his best work Kunitz achieves these grace notes while sacrificing nothing in the build up. **"The Wellfleet Whale,"** a jeweled tiara of a poem, crowns the poet's achievement, and restores some of the linguistic pomp of the early poetry. The poem carries a prose epigraph, a journal entry describing the poet's encounter with a whale stranded on the beach. The whale, now in its death throes, opens one prehistoric eye to gaze on the poet. While Kunitz's long poem should be read in full, this passage from the fifth and final section, carries the signature of the whole:

> Voyager, chief of the pelagic world,
> you brought with you the myth
> of another country, dimly remembered,
> where flying reptiles
> lumbered over the steaming marshes
> and trumpeting thunder lizards
> wallowed in the reeds.
> While empires rose and fell on land,
> your nation breasted the open main,
> rocked in the consoling rhythm
> of the tides. Which ancestor first plunged
> head-down through zones of colored twilight
> to scour the bottom of the dark?
> . . . . .
> Master of the whale-roads,
> let the white wings of the gulls
> spread out their cover.
> You have become like us,
> disgraced and mortal.

The poignancy of the apostrophe, another of the poet's characteristic moves, derives from its personification of the doomed Leviathan. As with the September snakes or the titular salmon in **"King of the River,"** this creature from the natural world provides the poet with an appropriate catalyst for verse. Through these beasts Kunitz may refer to the human animal: "You have become like us."

This suitability of the subject weds the suitability of the form; the concatenating tercets of **"The Wellfleet Whale,"** with their restless forward motion, provide Kunitz the sweep he needs to work this scene into the necessary tonalities, from the epic to the personal. By discarding inherited prosodic forms in his later poetry, Kunitz may be likened to a virtuoso who has left off playing from score and begun to improvise. Rather than grappling with standard measures, the poet relies on his own sense of a line's musicality to set the needed length and number of stresses. Echoing Blake, an abiding poetic forebear, and fellow seer, Kunitz notes, in an interview, "I must create a system myself or be enslaved by another man's." Freed from rigid metrical contracts, this poet may better find the unique vessel appropriate to each poem. Oddly, Kunitz works out his two finest poems, **"The Wellfleet Whale"** and **"The Testing-Tree,"** in the same pattern of tercets wrought in numbered sections. This expansive form heightens the music of Kunitz's line:

> You have your language too,
> an eerie medley of clicks
> and hoots and trills,
> location-notes and love calls,
> whistles and grunts. Occasionally,
> it's like furniture being smashed,
> or the creaking of a mossy door,
> sounds that all melt into a liquid
> song with endless variations,
> as if to compensate

> for the vast loneliness of the sea.
> Sometimes a disembodied voice
> breaks in as if from distant reefs,
> and it's as much as one can bear
> to listen to its long mournful cry,
> a sorrow without name, both more
> and less than human. It drags
> across the ear like a record
> running down.

(from **"The Wellfleet Whale"**)

Kunitz here submerges an *ars poetica*: "liquid song" sung "to compensate for the vast loneliness of the sea" could serve as the jacket blurb to this **Selected.** In the above passage we hear the whole symphony of Kunitz's musicianship: the pizzicato strings of "clicks and hoots and trills"; the legato horn of "location-notes and love calls"; the tympanic percussion of "a record running down." All of this elegiac music, ostensibly for the dying mammal on that Cape Cod beach, borrows certain measures from the poet's life: as with Margaret in Hopkin's "Spring and Fall," it is *Kunitz* that he mourns for, making **"The Wellfleet Whale,"** in its sweep and intimacy, the most far-reaching and potent of his many personal myths.

Part of the power of myths derives from our inability to pinpoint their exact meaning and message; they cannot be distilled to one-line thematic essence. Myth may be paraphrased, alluded to, stolen from, reworked, but its meanings resist the sound-bite; they are not fables with appended morals. In this sense, Kunitz's attempt to create a personal mythology, his legends of origin, has been wholly successful. More than isolated lyrics, the poems resonate, cross-pollinate, call to one another, and will not be reduced to incidental music. The dangers in writing a highly personal poetry of origins—dangers succumbed to by a number of Kunitz's epigones—include sentimentality and solipsism (the "who cares?" factor), which Kunitz's poems, happily, avoid. What registers instead emanates from the molten center of life-long experience, images transformed to poetry by their mystery and complexity, conveying human warmth, wisdom, and the poet's dearly held resolve to turn again, which is living itself.

Judith Kitchen (review date Summer 1996)

SOURCE: "The Ladybug and the Universe," in *Georgia Review*, Vol. L, No. 2, Summer, 1996, pp. 386–403.

[*In the following excerpt, Kitchen comments on the task of the reviewer and offers a favorable evaluation of* Passing Through, *including close readings of two poems, "Three Floors" and "Touch Me," from the volume.*]

Every Sunday morning we watch CBS's *Sunday Morning.* Well, almost every Sunday morning. With *The New York Times* waiting, I wait, somewhat impatiently, for the final minute of the show—that minute where Charles Kuralt used to say, "I leave you now near Omaha, on the banks of the Missouri," and the camera would simply sit there, looking at the long sweep of the river on a clear day in November with the sun lowering itself in the west. Then, a goose or two would come into the range of the lens, followed by more until the screen was filled with geese wheeling and banking, skein upon skein threading themselves through each other, the air filled with yelping as they came in to land. Or else he'd say, "I leave you in the mountains of Vermont," and the camera would start up close, focused on ice melting, so that a drop would slowly form, take on solidity and weight, tug at its own surface tension, elongate, then drop to the stream below—over and over, the accumulated shedding of winter until, finally, the camera would carefully pull back, and we'd see a rushing stream and then, at last, the mountains in the distance.

Those moments mattered. In a busy world—one in which we do all too little sitting in the middle of the forest, or standing at the edges of rivers—they put us in touch with ourselves. With the self who had once been the child on her stomach in the grass watching the precarious progress of a ladybug, or the adolescent suddenly struck by the ever expanding universe as ranges of hills unfolded before her and the wind made the only sound for miles around, lonesome and austere. You only need to have had one of those moments in your life—one clear, fixed point at which you fit yourself into the larger world—for that final minute of CBS *Sunday Morning* to matter. It gave you back to yourself, briefly, even as it took you somewhere new.

Things have changed a bit since Charles Osgood took over. For one thing, he comments more, can't seem to resist using words to tell us that here in the flatlands of eastern Washington we are likely to see what the Spokane saw long before the white man, etc. In other words, he directs our thoughts just at the moment when they should be most free to roam. And the camera has changed, too—more radically, and far more destructively. It's a nervous camera now. Instead of letting things come into the range of its lens, it takes on life as an active verb, flitting from branch to branch, flirting with nature. It pounces on its images—one recent Sunday I counted six different animals in less than a minute—then darts away in search of something more interesting. The eye cannot rest, cannot take in, cannot settle and savor. We are no longer participants, but spectators.

Sometimes an individual poem can act as the fixed lens of the static camera. It can put us back in touch with ourselves by inviting a sustained attention, transforming its subject by the quality of the attention being paid. Once we've entered its field of vision, that poem opens to us others by the same writer. A poem we encounter in the initial stages of becoming familiar with a writer's work can have predictive power; it acts as a genetic marker, a key to open the door. We see more *because of* that earlier poem; we are attuned to nuance that *comes from* that earlier poem. We assume a kind of direct lineage, an underlying sensibility that links one with the other.

Reviewers, almost by definition, look at an expanding universe: the world created by the poet as the poems accumulate. When we make a statement about a book, it is necessarily abstracted, defined by what we think the individual poems add up to. So we tend to forget that the way they add up is poem by poem, drop by drop, and that how we read the individual poem is the way we once looked so hard at the ladybug—with intense scrutiny, amazed curiosity, passionate response.

Interestingly, it seems to be possible to agree on the cumulative effect of a poet's work without agreeing on the particulars. Joseph Brodsky's essay "On Grief and Reason" (1994) takes a long, hard look at two poems by Robert Frost. Brodsky finds a dark vision in Frost that leads, in the end, to the isolation of the poet as maker: "he stands outside, denied re-entry, perhaps not coveting it at all. . . . And this particular posture, this utter autonomy, strikes me as utterly American." But on the way to a conclusion with which I concur, Brodsky fails to read the tone of "Come In" to such an extent that he gives the poem a particularly Catholic reading. I would venture to say that "repent" (which Brodsky would substitute for "lament") was not much in Frost's vocabulary. Yankee Protestantism would dictate an even darker reading of the poem—one where a recognition of nature's indifference eclipses any religious yearnings. And when Brodsky reads the "darkened parlor" in "Home Burial" as a metaphor for the grave instead of what it clearly is—a darkened parlor—he also takes himself (as reader) outside the time frame of the poem. The child's body is still in the parlor; the husband is outside digging the grave with an abandon that offends the wife; the reader of the poem is expected to understand the simultaneity of the events in order to preclude any tendency to "take sides." Frost stands *with* the reader; to make a metaphor would be to violate his impartiality, to force meaning. The greatness of "Home Burial" has always depended on its maker knowing "not to sing."

Both the mystery and the individuality of reviewing, it seems to me, lie in how the leap is made from the particular to the abstract. For each book, there must be several discrete moments of recognition: moments in which the poem itself acts as objective correlative, as an entry to the way the poet's world comes to meaning. You look through the viewfinder, adjust the focus, and click: the lens flies open to take in the world of someone else.

This is especially true when you are reading poets with an established body of work, poets whose work you have followed over the years. How easily your voice slides into theirs. Maybe you've heard them read in person, made some adjustments in how you hear. Maybe you've simply grown used to the cadence, the rhythm of their thoughts. But there was a time when the work was new, when you walked into a strange landscape and didn't know which way to turn. And what you did was what nearly all readers do: you let one poem speak to you so deeply that it speaks still, and goes on speaking.

"As one who was not predestined, either by nature or by art, to become a prolific poet, I must admit it pleases me that, thanks to longevity, the body of my work is beginning to acquire a bit of heft." This sentence, from the author's note to *The Poems of Stanley Kunitz, 1928–1978,* was written almost twenty years ago. Now his longevity is celebrated once again in *Passing Through,* marking the occasion of Kunitz's ninetieth birthday. This book collects the poems from three books (including a *Selected*) written after 1958. It also contains the long major poem **"The Wellfleet Whale,"** which appeared as a separate chapbook, as well as nine new poems. **"Three Floors,"** first published in *The Testing-Tree* in 1971, is one of those poems that serves as a lens; it speaks to—and through—the later poems.

"Three Floors"

Mother was a crack of light
and a gray eye peeping;
I made believe by breathing hard
that I was sleeping.

Sister's doughboy on last leave
had robbed me of her hand;
downstairs at intervals she played
Warum on the baby grand.

Under the roof a wardrobe trunk
whose lock a boy could pick
contained a red Masonic hat
and a walking stick.

Bolt upright in my bed that night
I saw my father flying;
the wind was walking on my neck,
the windowpanes were crying.

Over the solid warp of the poem—a strict stanzaic and rhythmical structure placed there to support the sweep of memory and imagination—the poem is a sea of shifting images and associations. In sixteen lines, Kunitz has peopled the house with ghosts. The small boy is literally caught in the middle between past (the loss of his father) and future (his sister's marriage, his own manhood). The poet re-creates the various claims on his affections as he presents the immediate moment of the poem—the darkness and the visionary sight of his father flying. The reader is drawn into the poem's emotional complex in such a way that childhood itself, with all its confusions, is awakened in memory.

"Three Floors" is a study in variation. Alternating between four- and three-stress lines (with slight differences in syllabic count), each stanza is at once familiar and surprising. There is a contrast between the strong masculine end rhymes of "hand/grand" and "pick/stick" and the haunting feminine rhymes of "peeping/sleeping" and "flying/crying." "Whose lock a boy could pick" is iambic trimeter, but the strong beat is muted so that each word must be read in a slower, more measured cadence. The child picks at the metaphorical lock of the family, hoping to discover his own identity.

The final couplet creates a sense of closure by returning to the strict meter of the poem and, at the same time, by

moving into the realm of fantasy. In this way, the make-believe sleep of the first stanza is contrasted with, and equated to, the wide-awake vision of the last. The poem thus feels complete in its metrical package even as it opens up a strange emotional world where nothing is quite what it seems. **"Three Floors"** itself has become a vehicle for the imagination, creating a father for the son. But even as the father is apprehended, he seems to be leaving. In a frenzy, the child perceives an elemental loss where the external world reflects his own amorphous grief. And behind loss is a question: *Warum*—why? The father's death, the mother's anger, the child's internalized conflict—nothing makes sense. Without an answer, the child is fated to ask this question throughout his life. The imaginative act, then, is seen as a way of discovering meaning, of making a divided house, however briefly, whole.

Twenty-five years ago, **"Three Floors"** harked back to a still earlier poem, **"Father and Son"** (1944), in which the poet searched for the lost father who had committed suicide before the son's birth—and found, at the bottom of a pond, "the white ignorant hollows of his face." But it also pointed to a companion piece in *The Testing-Tree,* **"The Portrait,"** in which the mother jealously, even angrily, denies the child any access to his dead father. But now, in 1996, **"Three Floors"** seems to prefigure the new and important final poem of *Passing Through.*

"Touch Me"

Summer is late, my heart.
Words plucked out of the air
some forty years ago
when I was wild with love
and torn almost in two
scatter like leaves this night
of whistling wind and rain.
It is my heart that's late,
it is my song that's flown.
Outdoors all afternoon
under a gunmetal sky
staking my garden down,
I kneeled to the crickets trilling
underfoot as if about
to burst from their crusty shells;
and like a child again
marveled to hear so clear
and brave a music pour
from such a small machine.
What makes the engine go?
Desire, desire, desire.
The longing for the dance
stirs in the buried life.
One season only,
    and it's done.
So let the battered old willow
thrash against the windowpanes
and the house timbers creak.
Darling, do you remember
the man you married? Touch me,
remind me who I am.

"Touch Me" connects directly to its antecedent, but it is a connection made as much by contrast as by similarity. What makes these two poems coalesce, for me, is sensibility—and the poet's desire to fix the moment in memory. Once again he is lying in bed, haunted by wind and rain, by the branches thrashing against the windowpanes. And once again he sees *through* to the heart of things. This time, however, the present is meditative as opposed to visionary. He reactivates the child whose questions haunted the earlier poem by recovering the child who paid attention to the crickets. Both poems contain the large underlying question of identity, but the later poem poses, first, the simple question of being.

Opening with a reference to a much earlier poem ("**As Flowers Are**"), "**Touch Me**" is a bit less formal than "**Three Floors**"; the structure is more subtle, its music even more varied, and its methods more sure. There are the same intricate rhymes—more a crochet than a weaving—slant rhymes that make a pattern like the fluid course of a soccer ball as the players work it down the field: "rain/flown/afternoon/down" and later "again/machine/done," or the initial "air" echoed in "clear/pour/desire, desire, desire" and then, as in a reprise, caught up again in "remember"—the operative word of the poem. But the ending is not elevated as in "**Three Floors**," where the poet tries to make language fill the void. In "**Touch Me**" he falters at the edge of the visionary, falters where the song has "flown," pulling back from the urge to fabricate in favor of the urge to resuscitate. At the exact moment when the earlier poem would have made the transformative leap, this one settles back. The poet forgoes rhyme and rhythm in favor of statement, a deflated kind of poetry that makes the end both terrible and moving: "Darling, do you remember / the man you married?"

The line break is crucial. Because if she remembers, then he has identity; if she remembers, she connects with the person who was "wild with love"; if she remembers, she is the link between the old man, his younger self, the child, the cricket, the very earth in which he has been gardening all afternoon. She connects him to his life through touch—the very thing that was withheld in "**Three Floors**." Even as he interrogates, he answers his own question: "remind," not "show."

The act (if it comes) will remind him of what has already been fulfilled. The gesture of *poetry* is superseded. "**Touch Me**" is a poem of completion and incompletion: poetry can only do so much, makes the link for the poet but it isn't sufficient. With great honesty and great vulnerability he admits to a need for another to restore him fully to a sense of himself, but it is a self rooted firmly in the present tense: "who I am." Such a simple poem (a study in monosyllables almost comparable to Frost's) for such a complex thought.

Speaking of poetry as a form of blessing, Kunitz tells us (in an introduction to *Passing Through,* which he calls "**Instead of a Foreword**") that "it would be healthier if

we could locate ourselves in the thick of life, at every intersection where values and meanings cross, caught in the dangerous traffic between self and universe." Time and again, as this volume shows, Kunitz locates himself at that intersection, still asking why and still discovering that, although it has "one season only," life is worth the living.

John Taylor (review date February 1997)

SOURCE: "Short Reviews," in *Poetry,* Vol. CLXIX, No. 4, February, 1997, pp. 291–93.

[*In the following review, Taylor offers a positive assessment of* Passing Through.]

[*Passing Through*] displays once again Stanley Kunitz's remarkable range and subtlety. Adding nine recent poems to work originally printed in *The Testing-Tree* (1971), *Next-to-Last Things* (1985) and "**The Layers**" (which appeared in the acclaimed 1979 edition of his collected poetry), Kunitz passes from retrospective appraisals of personal tragedy ("My mother never forgave my father / for killing himself . . . that spring / when I was waiting to be born") to haunting metaphysical allegories, such as his anthropomorphic portrayal, in "**King of the River,**" of a salmon almost consciously longing for metamorphosis and transcendence. Connecting many of these otherwise disparate poems are compelling themes of innocence and love—the loss of both, the search for both. Time and again the poet depicts himself, family members, acquaintances, even the Acropolic caryatids and the mummy of Ramses the Second (as in the ironic, erudite "**Signs and Portents**"), striving to recover states of purity or harmony.

No poem summarizes this endeavor better than the moving final one, "**Touch Me,**" in which an aged narrator—Kunitz was born in 1905—kneels "to the crickets trilling / underfoot as if about / to burst from their crusty shells." "Like a child again," the poet marvels "to hear so clear / and brave a music pour / from such a small machine." And so absorbed does he remain in this ephemeral phenomenon—"The longing for the dance / stirs in the buried life. One season only, / and it's done"—that eventually he must ask his beloved to "remind" him who he is. He is indeed a human being anchored, not in eternity, but rather in time. Yet hasn't his time-bounded wonder at the trilling somehow put him in touch with eternity?

This finely-crafted poetry raises this question. The poet is at once grateful for having been allowed to witness one of life's miracles and acutely aware that such experiences exacerbate the pain fostered by the knowledge of inescapable endings. In "**The Knot,**" for example, he praises the undying desire of a resin-oozing, cross-grained knot, imprisoned in the lintel of his door, to sprout "shoots / that crackle overhead, / dividing as they grow." Yet his cry "Let be!" is ultimately ambiguous (and for this reason, poignant), for it is in poetry alone that a man can "shake

[his] wings" and fly into the envisioned boughs. In **"The Abduction,"** a psychologically intricate poem about a woman's recurrent, ambivalent memory of being raped, Kunitz simply puts it this way: "What do we know / beyond the rapture and the dread?" He is by no means a despairing or an unconsolable poet, however, even when evoking "a murderous time" in which "the heart breaks and breaks / and lives by breaking." In any dichotomy pitting the certainty of having felt something extraordinary against the uncertainty of what the feelings signify, recollected rapture inevitably outbalances skepticism and gloom. In **"The Round,"** for example, he tellingly depicts himself "sitting in semi-dark / hunched over my desk / with nothing for a view / to tempt me / but a bloated compost heap"; yet in this downstairs "cell" he transforms into words the "curious gladness" that he had felt earlier that morning as "light splashed . . . on the shell-pink anemones." The conclusion of this insightful poem about the poetic process bespeaks a characteristic, quiet optimism: "I can scarcely wait till tomorrow / when a new life begins for me, / as it does each day."

The act of naming necessarily simplifies, indeed diminishes, the sudden, overwhelming original perception, saturated with sense stimulators; such are the limitations of language. Yet written words can nevertheless reclaim a semblance of the enrapturing moment from oblivion. Such a "moment," Kunitz observes in his brief preface, "is dear to us, precisely because it is so fugitive, and it is somewhat of a paradox that poets should spend a lifetime hunting for the magic that will make the moment stay." Sometimes the enchanting or bewitching past moment embodies an enduring duty that must be passed on. Kunitz recalls, for instance, how his night-fears would be assuaged by his candle-bearing sisters; now that they have died, he can return the tenderness in a lullaby: "Let nothing grieve you, / Sarah and Sophia. / Shush, shush, my dears, / now and forever."

Motivating these poems are multifarious falls from grace. Kunitz sometimes confesses to his own misdeeds or alludes to disruptive political events; he rarely rages, however, although occasionally he is sardonic. Instead, he summons his considerable delicacy of touch with regard to meter and discreet half-rhymes to explore his—our—"disgraced, mortal" predicament. These portentous adjectives qualify the unlucky, beached, dying "Wellfleet whale," the subject of another magnificent allegory set halfway between human society and a pristine natural world. The descriptions are scientifically precise, yet they build into troubling metaphors suggesting that—at birth, as it were—human beings are also cast up on coastal rocks and "delivered to the mercy of time." We, too, await our "hour of desolation" Perhaps, like the stranded whale, we, too, have brought with us "the myth / of another country, dimly remembered." Kunitz is at his most masterful when he opens up, as if through the thick wall of the material world, peepholes looking out onto such vistas.

Stanley Kunitz with Gary Pacernick (interview date Fall 1997)

SOURCE: "An Interview with Stanley Kunitz," in *Michigan Quarterly Review,* Vol. XXXVI, No. 4, Fall, 1997, pp. 646–54.

[*In the following interview, Kunitz comments on his life, work, creative inspiration, Jewish heritage, and the significance of poetry.*]

On Tuesday, December 5, 1995, I interviewed Stanley Kunitz in his spacious Greenwich Village apartment, crammed with books and plants and works of art. He had just returned from a reading in Cambridge, but had found time while on the train to write some answers to my questions and referred to these texts during the interview. In the spring of 1997 we had a follow-up discussion that led to a number of revisions and additions.

Stanley Kunitz was born in 1905 and has won many honors for his poetry, including the Pulitzer, Bollingen, and Lenore Marshall Prizes, and most recently the National Book Award for ***Passing Through: Later Poems, New and Selected.*** In 1993, he received the National Medal of Arts from President Clinton at a White House ceremony.

[*Pacernick:*] *Stanley, you have said to Bill Moyers that "poetry is the most difficult, the most solitary, and the most life-enhancing thing that one can do in the world." Can you elaborate, especially about what makes it such a life-enhancing activity?*

[Kunitz:] The experience of love and the creative act are the supreme expressions of the life force. They do more than express it; they refresh and renew it and give it back, magnified.

What have you found the hardest thing about being a poet? You're obviously saying that it's extremely important and beneficial, but I'm sure there are hard things about it.

Being a poet is more or less easy, but writing poems is difficult.

Are you talking about the formal challenge, are you talking about finding just the right word?

Making it right, in sound and sense; making it whole and true.

Are you the person who determines that? Do you feel that you, finally, are the person who knows whether the poem works?

In the long run I do. I try very hard not to be self-deceived.

What is the most enjoyable thing about being a poet for you?

The knowledge that there is nothing else I would rather do or be.

Here we are, almost at the end of the twentieth century with all these incredible technological changes, most significantly in the modes and process of communication. Is there any future for poetry in the new age?

The relevance of poetry is to the history of civilization, not to the progress of technology. Poets today can hope to do precisely what poets have always done, that is, tell the story of the human adventure, express what it feels like to be alive in this particular time, this particular place.

What does a poet need to know about craft, and are rhyme and meter still important enough to be part of a young poet's training?

I am never satisfied that I know enough about craft. I am still learning. But I think that it's important to stress that craft is not an end in itself, only a means. Only a means to gain control over language, to make it more sensitive to the modulations of one's thoughts and feelings, to improve its precision so that one won't have to tell lies.

You are someone who has written poetry of note both in traditional forms and in free verse. Do you think free verse can be taught, and is there anything coherent and plausible that one can say about writing free verse poetry?

In the first place, I don't think free verse is free. It has rather indeterminate principles, but at the least it must connect and cohere and establish a defining rhythmic pulse. As to whether traditional form is still essential, all I can say, out of my own experience, is that my early discipline in metrics and rhyme has been invaluable to me, even though I no longer tend to write in strict metrical patterns and prefer subtler internal harmonies to the click of rhyme. Incidentally, there were no graduate writing programs in my youth. I learned my craft by studying the poets around and before me.

What do you think inspired you to be a poet, and as part of that, were there poets who made you want to write poetry?

When Henry James, toward the end of his life, reflected on his long creative voyage, he identified his point of embarkation as the port of his loneliness. That is true of most of the poets I know. "A poem is solitary and on its way," said Paul Celan, the poet of the Holocaust. What sets it on its way is the search for a community.

Do you identify with any of your contemporaries in particular? Of course one thinks of Roethke and Lowell. Are there others?

I feel close to a whole tribe of poets, young and old, but in the act of writing a poem, I have always felt alone.

Do you have any favorite poems of your own? Which are they and why?

A new poem is always the one I feel closest to, if only for a while.

"The Wellfleet Whale" is different from most of your other poems. Was your writing process in that poem different from your usual procedure?

"The Wellfleet Whale" had a long gestation period. I knew from the beginning, in September 1966, when the whale foundered in Wellfleet Harbor, that it was a significant experience, and I experimented through the years with various ways of conveying what I saw and experienced. All of them were failures. During that interval, I had an opportunity on Cape Cod to study other beached whales, went out on sightseeing watches, and read whatever seemed to me even remotely pertinent, until I began to feel I was part of the civilization of the whale. Fifteen years after the event, I was able to pull it all together and write the poem.

You succeeded in converting all that information into a significant action. Can you comment on your guiding principle of organization?

In the end, I turned to Greek drama—specifically Sophoclean tragedy—to help me solve the problem of the poem's architecture. Jane Harrison's *Prolegomena* clarified for me the main structural elements in the development of the action, from agon to recognition scene. It's a poem that wants to be read aloud, preferably in the open air. I guess I'm really thinking of an ancient amphitheater.

You have translated Russian poets. How did you come to the Russian poets?

I came rather naturally to them. After all, my parents were raised in Eastern Europe. My mother's forebears, who were fugitives from Spain, wandered through central Europe until they settled in Lithuania at the time of the Inquisition. Despite this heritage, I never heard Russian or any foreign language spoken in our household during my childhood. My connection with the Russian poets dates from the early sixties, when Patricia Blake, then a correspondent for *Time,* and the Oxford scholar Max Hayward, the outstanding Slavist of that period, persuaded a number of friends and acquaintances to undertake translations of Andrei Voznesensky's poems for an edition in English of his *Antiworlds.* This was the book that made Andrei famous in the Soviet Union and eventually everywhere else. There were six of us in that list of translators, and none of us, including Auden and Wilbur, knew a word of Russian, but we felt confident that we could rely on Max's literal versions and, if needed, his interpretation of the text. I felt the same way a few years later, when Max and I collaborated on the poems of Akhmatova, an exceptionally important book for me.

Did the intimate contact with Akhmatova's poems affect your own work?

I hope I learned something from Akhmatova about the management of an open style and the possibility of breaking down the barrier between the public and private poem.

Perhaps I learned something more from the passion and humanity of her voice.

You recently won the National Book Award for poetry with the publication of **Passing Through,** *the poems of your later years, including your newest work. Thirty-six years before, in 1959, you received the Pulitzer Prize. Did that earlier recognition have a significant impact on you and your career as a poet?*

One doesn't write poetry for prizes, but I have to admit that the Pulitzer Prize actually changed the course of my life. It gave me self-confidence at a time when I needed it sorely. The manuscript for my *Selected Poems, 1928–1958* had been rejected by more publishers than I could bear to count before Atlantic accepted it. I had been through a bad period and I was tired of being called a "poet's poet." That sudden turn of the wheel did wonders for my morale.

Do you have any themes, concerns, subjects that matter a great deal to you and enter frequently into your work?

Actually, I never think about themes when I am writing my poems. In the usual course of events, my poems spring from the occasions of the day, something perceived as beautiful or terrible or true. When that perception attaches itself to language and rhythm, I know I am on my way, but not with any foreknowledge of my destination. Whenever I yield to the temptation to explicate one of my poems, I am astonished at all the secrets I find buried in the text. Poets are characterized less by their subject matter than by their tone of voice, their ground of feeling. When I was still at school, I picked up a volume of Keats's letters and discovered the passage in which he spoke of "the holiness of the heart's affections." More than seventy years later, those words still light the way for me.

As I look around your apartment, I see many striking works of art, including several by your wife Elise Asher. You have written about some of your artist friends. Would you comment on that relationship?

Like so many other poets, past and present, I have a feeling of kinship with painters and their art. During my youth in Worcester, my favorite haunts were the woods, the public library, and the local art museum, and it seemed almost inevitable that I should eventually marry into the world of painters. When that happened in the fifties in New York, I inherited Elise's friends and soon felt very much a part of the emerging generation of Abstract Expressionist painters just as they were preparing to step into the limelight. They were wonderful company—lively, articulate, ambitious, hard-working, hard-drinking, gregarious, outrageous, and ready at any hour to argue about anything. Eventually, of course, success and fame and hypertension took their toll. I'm thinking, in particular, of Rothko, de Kooning, Guston, and Kline—all of them gone now. But in the early years, they seemed to embody Blake's dictum that "energy is eternal delight," and their élan struck me as irresistible and contagious. Painters, I think, have a special gift for friendship.

Have you done any artwork yourself?

I am never happier than when I am working with my hands. In Provincetown, where we spend a good portion of the year, my toolroom and garden compete for attention with my study. If there's any odd job that needs to be done around the house, I treat it as a challenge. There was a period when I produced a number of collages and assemblages and wire sculptures, but that was when I could make a bit of free time available. These days I seem to be busier than ever.

Dante is a presence in your work. In **"The Illumination,"** *you address his apparition as "my Master and my guide." What is the source of your connection?*

My conversation, so to speak, with Dante began very early. Thanks to my immigrant parents, our house in Worcester was the only one in the neighborhood, as far as I knew, that could boast of an extensive library. It was there that I first encountered the plays of Shakespeare, each in a separate volume, bound in red cloth, with a critical preface and an appendix of historical sources. Other well-thumbed books that I recall were complete sets of Tolstoy, Dickens, and Thackeray; the poems of Browning, Tennyson, Wordsworth, Longfellow, and Whittier; a multi-volume set of classic histories, including Plutarch, Gibbon, Grote, and Prescott; the Century Dictionary, unabridged; Spinoza and Maimonides; and the Holy Bible, leather-bound, both Old and New Testaments, with red-ink passages and marginal glosses. But the book that enthralled me most in that library was a folio edition of Dante in Cary's translation, with the Gustave Doré illustrations. Those visual images of Hell took possession of my imagination. I used to sit in that library with this enormous folio on my lap (I was twelve years old or so), terrified by that vision of the underworld. I had nightmares. So Dante was with me at a most impressionable stage. Later, at Harvard, I studied *The Divine Comedy* with C. H. Grandgent, the famous Dante scholar.

The poet Gregory Orr, who has written a book about you, says the suicide of your father shortly before you were born is the central fact of your imaginative life, "that from which all else flows." Do you agree?

Certainly the most traumatic event through my formative years.

The poem **"The Knot,"** *which I find mysterious, does that have symbolic associations for you, and how did you come to write it?*

The poem's origin is quite simple, nothing mysterious about it. Over a period of years, in our place on the Cape, I couldn't help but notice a great swirling knot that kept bleeding through several layers of paint on the lintel of our bedroom door. And the more I studied it, the more I marveled at its persistence, as though it still had a buried life, a will to grow, to become branching pine again "out of the trauma of its lopping-off." As I lay in bed, only half-awake, it did not seem far-fetched to imagine flying into its boughs.

Another deep, difficult poem, **"The King of the River."** *What kind of disintegration takes place within the narrator?* "You would dare to be changed, / as you are changing now, / into the shape you dread / beyond the merely human." *Are you writing of madness there, or are you writing of some other kind of transforming experience?*

"King of the River" deals primarily with the aging process. The Pacific Northwest salmon gets done with it in only a few weeks. For humans, death is the most definitive of a long series of gradual transformations. That thought adds to the complication of feelings when I say in a later poem, **"The Layers"**: "I am not done with my changes."

Is **"An Old Cracked Tune"** *in some way suggestive of Jewish alienation and suffering for you?*

The very first line, "My name is Solomon Levi," is borrowed from an ugly, anti-Semitic street song recollected from my college days. Coincidentally, Solomon was my father's first name. According to what I have learned, he was a Levite, and so am I by inheritance descended from a tribe with a priestly function. Obviously, **"An Old Cracked Tune"** has some connection with my heritage. As for alienation and suffering, I believe that the people of the Diaspora carry the memory of exile in their blood. But don't forget that the singer of this poem closes it with a dance.

You were obviously raised to be conscious of Judaism as a religion.

I was raised in a Jewish community in Worcester. In our household the emphasis was never on religious practice, but on the ethical tradition. And so it still remains for me.

A tough question: Do you consider yourself a Jewish poet?

My sense is that the noun "poet" does not require a qualifying adjective, either Jewish or American or modern.

Didn't the Nazi death camps of World War II have a powerful effect on you?

Of course! Even Dante's vision of Hell hadn't prepared me for that monstrous reality.

It doesn't seem to enter into your poetry directly.

It's there, nevertheless, deep in the substratum of my poems. The one poem that seems to me great and terrible enough to evoke the smell of evil, the delirium, of the death camps is Celan's "Todesfugue." Only a survivor of he camps could have written it, one whose borrowed life ended in suicide. My most explicit approach to the genocidal horror of the Hitler years is my poem in honor of Dietrich Bonhoeffer, that true Christian, whose failed plot against the Führer led to his death by hanging—yes, in an extermination camp. I call it, **"Around Pastor Bonhoeffer."**

How would you characterize your faith? Is it an artistic faith, is it a religious faith?

I am a non-believer, but with strong religious impulses and yearnings.

Has the Bible influenced your poetry?

The Bible—Jewish and Christian, as I've already indicated—was one of the first books that I studied, page after page.

Here's big question. How does one face death and can poetry help?

One lives and dies simultaneously. It happens bit by bit, every day. I have tried to report that dialogue. In my childhood I dreaded going to sleep, because I was terrified at the thought of losing consciousness. I am less fearful of death in my nineties than I was in my teens, for the natural cycle has its own reasons, even its own dark beauty. In consider myself lucky to have been given this life.

America doesn't seem to listen to its poets. If America listened to its poets, what could it learn?

Our American culture has no poetry written into its origin. We inherited our poetry—mostly hymns and heroic couplets—from England, and we've tended, since the onset of the Industrial Age, to regard the medium itself as superfluous or frivolous, if not dangerous. Whitman clearly perceived that our myth, our great national myth, has to do with power, success, money; and he attempted to supersede it with a myth of Democracy and of himself as Democratic Man. And the truth is that he died unhappy, believing that he had failed, that his country had rejected him. We still need to understand that a nation that alienates itself from the creative imagination has already begun to wither.

You seem to agree with your mentor William Blake that the genius of the poetic imagination is the most important gift. What do you hope to still accomplish?

Oh, how do I know? I want to record whatever I feel most deeply. And I have plenty of unfinished business.

What is the most amazing thing about life?

Life itself is the most amazing thing in the universe!

What is the most amazing thing about your life?

Maybe it's that here I am, at this age, still loving this life as I did from the very beginning, and wanting more.

And finally, while many of your poems have an elegiac tone, you have survived and lived a long, rich life. Have you found light within the darkness?

Love and poetry are lights enough.

Fred Moramarco and William Sullivan (essay date 1998)

SOURCE: "Lost Worlds: Midcentury Revisions of Modernism," in *Containing Multitudes: Poetry in the United States Since 1950,* Twayne, 1998, pp. 1–36.

[*In the following excerpt, Moramarco and Sullivan discuss the historical context of mid-twentieth-century American poetry and provide an overview of Kunitz's literary career, thematic preoccupations, and the development of his poetic style.*]

"O world so far away! O my lost world!"

—Theodore Roethke, "Otto"

"How shall the heart be reconciled to its feast of losses?"

—Stanley Kunitz, **"The Layers"**

Major midcentury poets like Randall Jarrell, Robert Lowell, Elizabeth Bishop, Theodore Roethke, and Stanley Kunitz, born in the first two decades of the twentieth century and at the center stage of poetry by the fifties, inherited the heaviest of burdens. Not only did they work in the shadows of their towering predecessors—T. S. Eliot, Wallace Stevens, Robert Frost, W. H. Auden, E. E. Cummings, and William Carlos Williams, who were still publishing important work—but they were not free to carry out the modernist creed of making poetry new. By now classical modernists such as Allen Tate and New Critics such as John Crowe Ransom had already defined modern poetry and restricted both its vision and its aesthetic practices. Modern poetry, they believed, should acknowledge human fallibility, the perplexing nature of existence, as well as the decline of Western civilization and the singular value of art and tradition in a decadent age. It should be ironic, impersonal, complex, allusive, and carefully wrought. As if this cramped predicament were not enough, the American poet was becoming more isolated, less tied to a complacent audience rapidly turning to mass media for its culture.

History was equally unkind. By the end of the 1950s, these poets had witnessed the Great Depression; two world wars; the Holocaust, which resulted in the death of more than 6 million Jews; the dropping of the atomic bomb on Hiroshima and Nagasaki; the firebombing of cities in Germany and Japan; the specter of totalitarianism in Stalin's Russia; the intrigues of the Cold War; and, at home, the rise of the security state, McCarthyism, and the injustices of racism. The decade Robert Lowell characterized as "the tranquilized *Fifties*"[1] offered little hope for a "brave new world."

In addition, the poets' lives were often as bleak. Most of the major midcentury poets suffered either a personal or psychological loss in childhood that threatened their sense of identity, belonging, and well-being. Given their private and public histories, many fell victim to various addic-

tions, psychological breakdowns, shattered relationships and marriages, and extremely disruptive lives. A disproportionate number actually committed suicide. They were, seemingly, a cursed generation who had been born in the worst of times. Having lost their connection to a secure, comforting world, they struggled to write well and honestly and—literally—to remain alive in a hostile environment.

Out of this struggle came some very significant poetry that is often overlooked as readers pass quickly from the modernists to what Donald Allen called, in an important anthology, *The New American Poetry.* A closer look at these middle-generation poets reveals a group of artists who courageously faced the dislocations of their public and private lives in a manner more direct and more linked to contemporary events and to actual life than that of such classical modernists as John Crowe Ransom, Allen Tate, and Robert Penn Warren. For the new generation there is much less obliqueness, less insistence on "objective correlatives" (Eliot's term for poetic language that corresponds to particular emotional states) and corresponding myths and allusions; in place of these modernist literary values there is more emphasis on directly confronting the particulars of existence. These poets not only test the classical modernists' insistence that poetry must flee from the personal but actually move closer to what would become a central strain of contemporary American poetry: an insistence on the primacy of personal experience. As they wrote more candidly about individual experience and personal history, they also explored the possibilities of a more prosaic diction and less rigid rhythms than their predecessors had used. Their difficulties were many and often overwhelming; they are not to be seen as the last vestiges of a self-satisfied but exhausted movement but as a bridge to new territory in American poetry.

As James Breslin illustrates in *From Modern to Contemporary,*[2] earlier strains of modernism may have come to "The End of the Line"; however, in vision and form, a number of the midcentury poets pushed ahead, retaining what they found valuable in the earlier modernist models but also creating their own poetic worlds and constructs. The result, viewed after the heat of the battle between perceived traditionalists and innovators has cooled, is a body of work that is often moving and, presumably, lasting. . . .

STANLEY KUNITZ (B. 1905)

In 1935 Theodore Roethke arrived at Stanley Kunitz's doorsteps with a copy of *Intellectual Things* (1930), Kunitz's first published volume of poems. In that volume and those that followed, as well as his prose (*A Kind of Order, A Kind of Folly* [1975], and *Next-to-Last Things: New Poems and Essays* [1985]), the literary kinship between Kunitz and Roethke became clear: both were lost travelers seeking a new world.

Born and raised in Worcester, Massachusetts, the central event in Kunitz's life was the loss of his father, Solomon, who committed suicide by swallowing carbolic acid in a public park when his mother was pregnant with Kunitz.[3] His mother, Yetta, was so devastated by her husband's suicide that she refused to allow his name to be spoken in the house. forced to support a family of three (two daughters and Stanley) and rescue a bankrupt dressmaking business, she became, in Kunitz's words, "a pioneer businesswoman," who opened a dry goods store and sewed garments in the back room. Unfortunately, her business affairs, which kept her from her family, and her less than passionate nature—Kunitz can't recall ever being kissed by Yetta—made it certain that there would be little warmth from his mother. When Stanley was eight, Yetta married Mark Dine, a gentle and scholarly man Kunitz grew to love; however, he died when Kunitz was fourteen. This tragic childhood became Kunitz's major theme, his **"Old Cracked Tune,"** which is expressed by his speaker, Solomon Levi: "the desert is my home, / my mother's breast was thorny, / and father I had none" (87). Fate, circumstance, and tragedy, as in the Greek dramas, seemed to haunt the Kunitz household, and it was out of these dark autobiographical strands that he sought to transform his life into legend or chaos into myth and achieve "a new ordering of creation."[4]

This insistence that the poet treat his personal experience as myth differentiates Kunitz from Eliot and his followers who insisted that poetry be both mythic and impersonal. "From the beginning," Kunitz declares, "I was a subjective poet in contradiction to the dogma propounded by Eliot and his disciples that objectivity, impersonality, was the goal of art. Furthermore, I despised his politics" (*Next,* 89). Kunitz found it ironic that he would eventually be classified as a late convert to confessional or autobiographical poetry, since from the start his "struggle [had been] to use the life in order to transcend it, to convert it into legend" (89).

There is also a rhetorical mode of subjectivity in Kunitz's poetry that emerges in his quest to find a language and rhythm that not only communicates but, more important, also recreates past emotions and thoughts. It is not the I, the ego, that writes the poem, Kunitz declares, "but my cells, my corpuscles, translating into language the chemistry of a passion" (29). Thus, "the wisdom of the body" occurs when one thinks with one's senses and relies on the primitive, shamanistic, incantatory elements of language; for "poems rise out of the swamps of the hindbrain," (51) and "our best songs are body songs" (53). "Key images," Kunitz explains, also rise out of the poet's unconscious. These images uniquely mark each poet's work and come from a poet's "childhood and . . . are usually associated with pivotal experiences." This "cluster of key images is the purest concentration of the self, the individuating node, the place where the persona starts" (30). By "revisiting" one's pivotal childhood experiences, "one's state of . . . innocence," the poet hopes "to learn how to live with the child" (30) he once was. As Gregory Orr, poet and former student of Kunitz, points out in his critical study,[5] these images enable the reader to enter Kunitz's world.

The images of the wound in **"The Hemorrhage"** or the haunted house in **"In a Strange House"** suggest his lost world of innocence, the absence of father and mother, and his present state of alienation. The image of the journey, in **"The Layers,"** by contrast, suggests the need to move beyond a crippling nostalgia for the past and to transcend an unrelentingly painful existence. The paradox that "we are living and dying at once" is captured in these key images, and it is Kunitz's goal "to report the dialogue" (*Next,* 30).

This contrapuntal music of "nostalgia and desire" is recorded in the subjective "body-language" of the poet. Kunitz's belief in the physiological nature of poetry and his stress on the poet's breath links him to poets like Charles Olson and Robert Creeley. And like Robert Bly and James Wright, Kunitz draws his key images from the deep recesses of his mind, if not from the world of dreams itself. His poetry is not only autobiographical but also expressionistic and, at times, surrealistic. Like the abstract expressionist painters, or action painters, Kline, deKooning and like the poet Roethke, with whom he was friends, he views his work as a subjective "kind of action . . . every achieved metaphor . . . is a gesture of sorts, the equivalent of the slashing of a stroke on canvas" (107).

Given his very personal approach and early metaphysical style—his difficult syntax, complex metaphors, and numerous literary and historical allusions—it is little wonder that his first two volumes (***Intellectual Things*** [1930], ***Passport to War*** [1940]) were not in fashion in either the thirties, the decade of social reform, or the forties, when W. H. Auden's witty, elegant verse dominated the scene. When the confessional mode of the fifties did come about, few were aware that Kunitz had been writing highly personal poetry for nearly three decades. In an early poem, **"For the Word Is Flesh,"** for example, he laments his "O ruined father dead, long sweetly rotten / Under the dial . . ." and bitterly concludes "Let sons learn from their lipless fathers how / Man enters hell without a golden bough" (*Poems,* 190, 91).

By the time Kunitz published ***Intellectual Things*** (1930) he had earned his B.A., summa cum laude (1926), and his M.A. from Harvard (1927), and he had secured a job with the H. W. Wilson Company, a reference publisher in New York City, after being rejected for a teaching position at Harvard University because he was told by the English faculty that the "'Anglo-Saxon students would resent being taught English by a Jew'" (*Next,* 100). At Wilson's he began a long and distinguished career as an editor of *Authors Biographical Series* and of such important biographical series as ***Living Authors*** and ***Twentieth Century Authors.*** His career was disrupted in 1943 when he was drafted as a conscientious objector, shuttled to various training camps, and eventually assigned to the Air Transport Command at Gravely Point, Washington.

Kunitz has identified ***Passport to the War*** as his "bleakest book." For his "passport," or draft notice, plunged him into the dark night of history. These lines are from **"Night**

Letter," a poem addressed to his beloved: "I suffer the twentieth century, / . . . The slaughter of the blue-eyed open towns, / And principle disgraced, and art denied." The speaker informs his love that "The bloodied envelope addressed to you, / Is history, that wide and mortal pang" (*Poems*, 161). In **"Father and Son,"** one of his most famous and most analyzed poems, the speaker follows his ghostly father through a symbolic, dreamlike landscape that reeks of decay and death to the pond from which his father has come and to which he will return; here the son hopes to communicate with "the secret master of my blood" whose love "Kept me in chains." He rehearses the sins and failures he wishes to confess to his father and then desperately asks his father to come back to him. Then he pleads: "'O teach me how to work and keep me kind.'" The father, however, can only turn "The white ignorant hollow of his face" (157, 58) toward his son. There are no instructions, directions, or words from the fathers of history. The son must move beyond his obsession with his lost world represented by his suicidal father.

Selected Poems, 1928–1958 received numerous awards and established Kunitz as one of the most important mid-century poets; the volume contains a number of the most moving love poems and visionary poems of the period. They also show Kunitz to be an evolving poet: "I am not done with my changes" (36), he writes later in **"The Layers"** (1978), and certainly one of his more dramatic changes was the shift in style that took place in his fourth volume, *The Testing-Tree* (1971). Prior to this book, Kunitz's complex imagery, difficult syntax, and formal language created a texture that often proved too dense and tangled for many readers. Beginning with *The Testing-Tree*, however, Kunitz's verse becomes direct, immediate, and accessible as he narrates the particular events of his past and present life using a William Carlos Williams—like mode of diction, syntax, and rhythm. In **"Journal for My Daughter,"** for example, the informal nature of a journal is reflected in short, crisp lines and accessible diction as Kunitz renders in journal entries his experiences with his daughter: "I like the sound of your voice / even when you phone from school / asking for money" (41).

And in **"The Testing-Tree,"** composed in Williams's triadic or three-part line and his distinctly American diction, Kunitz sharply depicts his boyhood rituals in the fields and hills surrounding Worcester. This is his entry into the world of nature as he "followed in the steps / of straight-backed Massassoit" (90). It is here that he ritualistically tested his ability to hit an ancient and "inexhaustible oak" (a symbol of the durability of nature) with three rocks. Each successful throw would gain him a valued prize and accomplish his quest:

> In the haze of afternoon,
>   while the air flowed saffron,
>   I played my game for keeps—
>   for love, for poetry,
>   and for eternal life—
>   after the trials of summer.

(91)

The speaker, nearing death, is still haunted by his past as well as his own "murderous times" but knows his journey must continue. As a poet he recognizes that "It is necessary to go / through dark and deeper dark / and not to turn" (92). So he looks once again for his trail and also seeks again his "testing-tree" and his stones to test once more his ability to achieve love, art, and a vision of eternity.

Although Kunitz acknowledges that his basic rhythm "is essentially dark and grieving—elegiac" (*Next*, 96), there are clear notes of endurance, determination, acceptance, and even celebration that appear in these later poems. He is determined to "'Live in the layers / not on the litter'" (*Poems*, 36). No longer alienated or homeless, he embraces a world of snakes, worms, raccoons, and gardens as well as a world of human love, social justice, and poetry. Indeed, it can be said of Kunitz that "he loved the earth so much / he wanted to stay forever" (*Next*, 19). In his ninetieth year, Kunitz received the National Book Award for *Passing Through: Later Poems, New and Selected* (1995). The new poems in this collection range from his crystal-clear memories of his childhood days in Worcester (**"My Mother's Pears"** and **"Halley's Comet"**) to a very poignant love poem dedicated to his wife, Elise Asher.

For nearly seventy years, Kunitz has struggled to survive the personal and historical tragedies of his time and place. That struggle is recorded in ever-changing but always exquisitely crafted poetic forms. His work is simultaneously personal, representative of an age, and universal in its mythic nature. In addition, his lasting contributions as editor, essayist, translator of Russian poets, and mentor and advocate for younger poets speak to Kunitz's dedication to poetry and his long and distinguished career.

Notes

1. Robert Lowell, *Life Studies and For the Union Dead* (New York: Farrar, Straus and Giroux, 1967), 85.

2. James Breslin, *From Modern to Contemporary* (Chicago: University of Chicago Press, 1984). See chapter 1, pp. 1–22.

3. See "The Hemorrhage," originally titled "The Man in the Park," in Stanley Kunitz, *The Poems of Stanley Kunitz, 1928–1978* (Boston/Toronto: Atlantic Monthly Press, 1979), 163, 164.

4. Stanley Kunitz, *Next-to-Last Things: New Poems and Essays* (Boston/New York: Atlantic Monthly Press, 1985), 36.

5. Gregory Orr, *Stanley Kunitz: An Introduction to the Poetry* (New York: Columbia University Press, 1985), 21–41.

Linton Weeks (essay date 29 July 2000)

SOURCE: "Stanley Kunitz, 95, Becomes Poet Laureate for a New Century," in *Washington Post*, July 29, 2000, pp. C1, C5.

[*In the following essay, Weeks provides an overview of*

Kunitz's literary career and poetry upon his appointment as Poet Laureate of the United States.]

Stanley Kunitz, who once said that all poetry is born of love, is the country's newest poet laureate. And its oldest. He turns 95 today. The formal announcement will be made Monday by James Billington, Librarian of Congress.

"In my work, at this age," said Kunitz from his summer house in Provincetown, Mass., "this is gratifying and astonishing. I must say, I was not prepared for that call."

The nonagenarian is the 10th laureate in an impressive succession. He follows in the wake of Robert Penn Warren, Howard Nemerov, Mona Van Duyn, Rita Dove and Robert Hass. Robert Pinsky has been poet laureate for the last three years.

In a statement, Billington said that Kunitz "continues to be a mentor and model for several generations of poets, and he brings uniquely to the office of poet laureate a full lifetime of commitment to poetry."

Kunitz has been writing verse for a long time. His first poem appeared in 1930, the same year that T. S. Eliot published "Ash Wednesday." I've forgotten many of those early poems," Kunitz admitted. But he remembers others quite vividly.

He believes that an artist must reckon with the age in which he lives. "**The Layers,**" he said, "speaks to that."

From that poem:

> When I look behind,
> as I am compelled to look
> before I can gather strength
> to proceed on my journey,
> I see the milestones dwindling
> toward the horizon
> and the slow fires trailing
> from the abandoned camp-sites,
> over which scavenger angels
> wheel on heavy wings.

"I have known many of the great poets in the English language," he said. "At least I encountered a good portion of the best poets of the 20th century.

"And I follow what is being written today in the contemporary journals," he added. In fact, Kunitz is a founder of the Fine Arts Work Center in Provincetown, which offers residency programs to young poets and artists.

"Everything affects poetry," he said, "including rap. I don't doubt that the poetry of the future, as even today, is influenced by the rap culture—just as in the 19th century poets who really initiated the romantic movement were influenced by the street ballads."

Kunitz, who taught writing at Columbia University for years, has received just about every accolade available to a contemporary poet. He's won the Pulitzer Prize, the Bollingen Prize, the National Book Award and countless other trophies. He's been a senior fellow at the National Endowment for the Arts, the state poet of New York and a chancellor emeritus of the Academy of American Poets. He's even been the Library of Congress's poetry adviser before. From 1974 to 1976 he served as the consultant in poetry at the library. That position evolved into poet laureate.

Those years here were tumultuous, he recalled yesterday. He wrote a poem about being at the library during Watergate. In **"The Lincoln Relics,"** he speaks to the 16th president:

> Mr. President
> In this Imperial City,
> awash in gossip and power,
> where marble eats marble
> and your office has been defiled,
> I saw the piranhas darting
> between the rose-veined columns,
> avid to strip the flesh
> from the Republic's bones.
> Has no one told you
> how the slow blood leaks
> from your secret wound?

He has written 10 books of verse. He plans to write more. His collected poems will be published this fall. The one-year appointment requires very little of the title holder. Kunitz will make $35,000 a year, maintain an office at the library and preside over special occasions—a reading in the fall and a lecture in the spring. He will also be able to hold forth on matters poetic.

"Given my years," he admitted, "I will not be as active a poet laureate as Robert Pinsky has been."

Kunitz doesn't plan to live in Washington.

Other professors and poets cheered the tidings.

"He's a wonderful poet," offered David Gewanter, who teaches poetry at Georgetown University. "He can write wonderful short poems of nature that remind you of Robert Frost. And smart and wry poems about marriage, about life, about the ongoing negotiations of adults."

"That's astonishingly wonderful news," said Pulitzer Prize winner Henry Taylor, who teaches poetry at American University.

"What sets Kunitz apart from most people," he continued, "is his level of emotional intensity that historically has been difficult to maintain as one ages."

Taylor spoke of one of Kunitz's best known poems, **"Touch Me."**

An excerpt:

So let the battered old willow
thrash against the windowpanes
and the house timbers creak.
Darling, do you remember
the man you married? Touch me,
remind me who I am.

"It's cry from the heart," Taylor said, "about what it's like to be remarkably aged and be in love with the same woman one was in love with many years ago."

Kunitz has been married to poet and painter Elise Asher since 1958. Each has a daughter by another spouse.

"What the poet laureate can do," Taylor concluded, "is remind us, help us recognize, that poetry is part of our lives even when we don't think it is. Poetry is inescapable."

FURTHER READING

Criticism

Barber, David. Review of *Passing Through,* by Stanley Kunitz. *Atlantic Monthly* 277, No. 6 (June 1996): 113.
    Barber provides an overview of Kunitz's literary career and the development of his poetry.

Dove, Rita. "Poet's Choice." *Washington Post Book World* (1 October 2000): 12.
    Dove lauds Kunitz's appointment as Poet Laureate and extols the vitality and eloquence of his poetry.

Flint, R. W. Review of *Next-to-Last Things,* by Stanley Kunitz. *New York Times Book Review* (6 April 1986): 24.
    Flint offers a generally positive review of *Next-to-Last Things.*

Geeslin, Campbell. Review of *Next-to-Last Things,* by Stanley Kunitz. *People Weekly* (13 January 1986): 14.
    Geeslin offers a brief positive assessment of *Next-to-Last Things.*

Glück, Louise. "On Stanley Kunitz." *American Poetry Review* 14, No. 5 (September–October 1985): 27–28.
    Glück relates her personal debt to Kunitz, who served as her teacher and an indispensable mentor during her formative years.

Kunitz, Stanley with Leslie Kelen. "Stanley Kunitz: An Interview by Leslie Kelen." *American Poetry Review* 27, No. 2 (March–April 1998): 49–55.
    In this interview, which was compiled from conversations in 1991 and 1993, Kunitz discusses his formative experiences, the development of his poetry, contrasts and continuities in his body of work, and his preoccupations with myth, the parent-child relationship, and existential themes.

Moss, Stanley, ed. *A Celebration for Stanley Kunitz on His Eightieth Birthday.* Riverdale-on-Hudson, NY: Sheep Meadow Press, 1986, 159 p.
    This is a collection of essays and tributes dedicated to Kunitz.

————. *A Tribute to Stanley Kunitz on His Ninety-Sixth Birthday.* Riverdale-on-Hudson, NY: Sheep Meadow Press, 2001.
    This is a collection of critical and laudatory pieces dedicated to Kunitz.

Oliver, Mary. "Gathering Light." *Kenyon Review* VIII, No. 3 (Summer 1986): 129–35.
    Oliver offers a positive assessment of *Next-to-Last Things.*

Plummer, William. "New Beginnings: At 95, Fledgling Poet Laureate Stanley Kunitz Finds Fresh Words." *People Weekly* (30 October 2000): 159.
    Plummer provides an overview of Kunitz's life, work, and career, including his appointment as poet laureate.

Review of *The Collected Poems,* by Stanley Kunitz. *Publishers Weekly* (31 July 2000): 89.
    The critic offers a brief positive review of *The Collected Poems of Stanley Kunitz.*

Smith, Dinitia. "The Laureate Distilled, to an Eau de Vie." *New York Times* (2 August 2000): E1.
    Smith provides an overview of Kunitz's life and work.

Tabor, Mary B. W. "A Poet Takes the Long View, 90 Years Old." *New York Times* (30 November 1995): C13.
    Tabor profiles the life and work of Kunitz.

Additional coverage of Kunitz's life and career is contained in the following sources published by the Gale Group: *Contemporary Authors,* Vols. 41–44R; *Contemporary Authors New Revision Series,* Vols. 26, 57, and 98; *Contemporary Poets; Dictionary of Literary Biography,* Vol. 48; *DISCovering Authors* 3.0; *Literature Resource Center; Major 20th-Century Writers,* Editions 1 and 2; *Poetry Criticism,* Vol. 19; and *Poetry for Students,* Vol. 11.

Alan Sillitoe
1928-

English novelist, short story writer, essayist, poet, playwright, screenwriter, and author of children's literature.

The following entry presents an overview of Sillitoe's career through 1998. For further information on his life and works, see *CLC*, Volumes 1, 3, 6, 10, 19, and 57.

INTRODUCTION

One of England's most prolific contemporary authors, Sillitoe is known for his candid and compassionate depictions of British working-class life. He is part of a generation of writers known as the Angry Young Men—including John Wain and Kingsley Amis—whose defiant male protagonists fight against the deprivations and injustices of Britain's stringent class system. Although Sillitoe often portrays disillusioned characters who are either unemployed or trapped in unskilled occupations, his works utilize a realistic prose style, allowing the emotions and concerns of his characters to appeal to a universal audience.

BIOGRAPHICAL INFORMATION

Sillitoe was born in Nottingham, England, on March 4, 1928. His father, a tannery worker, was functionally illiterate and often unemployed. The family lived in poverty and at times went hungry. Sillitoe had to leave school at the age of fourteen to go to work in a bicycle factory. After several months he quit the factory to protest the low wages. A series of various industrial jobs followed until Sillitoe joined the Royal Air Force just before his eighteenth birthday. He served as a radio operator in Malaya for two years until he contracted tuberculosis and subsequently spent sixteen months recuperating in a military hospital. This extended hospital stay was the beginning of Sillitoe's literary life, as he immersed himself in reading. Sillitoe married American poet Ruth Fainlight in 1959 and relocated to France. Later, the couple moved again to the Spanish island of Majorca, where he studied the craft of writing, composing both fiction and poetry. Author Robert Graves was also living in Majorca at the time and greatly influenced and encouraged Sillitoe's work. Sillitoe returned to England in 1958. He has been a prolific writer, composing short stories, novels, screenplays, poetry, and nonfiction. Film versions were also made of his novel *Saturday Night and Sunday Morning* (1958) and his short stories "The Loneliness of the Long-Distance Runner" and "The Ragman's Daughter." He won the British Authors' Club

Prize for *Saturday Night and Sunday Morning* in 1958 and the Hawthornden Prize for his short story collection *The Loneliness of the Long-Distance Runner* (1959).

MAJOR WORKS

Much of Sillitoe's fiction revolves around working-class life in Nottingham, England. *Saturday Night and Sunday Morning* follows the life and loves of Arthur Seaton, a bored young factory worker whose daily existence is comprised of good wages, sexual adventures, and wild weekends at the neighborhood pub. His occasional fishing excursions and retreats to the countryside, as well as his rebellious nature and refusal to be worn down by an unfair system, save Arthur from embracing a wholly destructive lifestyle. Sillitoe's William Posters trilogy—*The Death of William Posters* (1965), *A Tree on Fire* (1967), and *The Flame of Life* (1974)—recounts the personal struggle of Mr. Frank Dawley. Reacting to signs marked "Bill Posters Will Be Prosecuted," Dawley invents a character named William Posters, who symbolizes the proletarian struggle for equality. *A Start in Life* (1970), Sillitoe's picaresque novel, tells the story of Michael Cullen, an unskilled worker who breaks out of his middle-class life by obtaining a job in real estate. When Cullen enters the world of crime, the novel becomes a thriller, replete with a gold-smuggling ring, twists, turns, and a host of secondary characters. By the end of the novel, Cullen vows to reform, but in the sequel, *Life Goes On* (1985), Cullen returns to his criminal life—this time as a courier in a heroin-trafficking operation. *Her Victory* (1982) traces the escape of a woman named Pam from her troubled marriage in Nottingham. After an attempt to commit suicide, she is saved by Tom, another isolated soul, and the two try to forge a new life together in Israel. The protagonists of *Last Loves* (1989) are typical examples of Sillitoe's defiant male characters. In the novel, George and Bernard, who served in Malaya during World War II, return there in an attempt to find insights into their past.

In addition to his novels, Sillitoe has written several collections of short stories. *The Loneliness of the Long-Distance Runner* is best known for its title story, which was adapted for film by Sillitoe himself. Set in a boys' reformatory, this piece revolves around a cross-country race. The story's adolescent narrator, Colin, seeks victory until he realizes that the race was conceived only to flaunt the reformatory's rehabilitation program to the region's governor. Although winning the race would gain Colin social acceptance, he intentionally loses and retains his self-respect. In the collection *Men, Women, and Children* (1973), Sillitoe explores issues of abandonment and betrayal. "Before Snow Comes" tells the story of Mark, a divorced man who falls in love with Jean, whose husband has deserted her. After he cares for her and her children emotionally and financially, she leaves him to reunite with her husband. Sillitoe has also authored several volumes of poetry, children's novels, and essays.

CRITICAL RECEPTION

Sillitoe has been a prolific writer of poetry, novels, and short stories, but he has not met with the same critical success in every genre. Sillitoe's poetry, for example, has not received wide critical acclaim; in fact, commentators complain that his poetry is filled with abstractions that can only be understood in the poet's own mind. In his review of Sillitoe's *Collected Poems* (1993), John Lucas argued, "Too many of these poems are muffled by dead language, inert rhythms and pointless stanza divisions, as though Sillitoe is determined to come on as a 'poet,' but has chosen to leave behind virtues that make him at his best a valuable writer of fiction." Although his subsequent collections did not achieve the success of *The Loneliness of the Long-Distance Runner*, Sillitoe's short fiction is generally considered superior to his novels. Reviewers have found fault with Sillitoe's later novels in particular, often asserting that the plots "fumble" or "miss their mark." Other critics maintain that Sillitoe can be too heavy-handed with his satire, especially when writing about white-collar

characters, whom he tends to caricature. Several critics applauded Sillitoe's portrayal of a female consciousness in *Her Victory*, although many feminists felt the character of Pam capitulates at the end of the novel and lacks the emotional growth of a truly emancipated character. Most reviewers have noted that Sillitoe's ability to realistically evoke the world of working-class Nottingham is his greatest strength as a fiction writer. Despite the overwhelming bleakness of his literary world, critics continue to praise Sillitoe for his proficiency at finding beauty and hope in a world of despair. Walter Sullivan described it as Sillitoe's "ability to perceive the rare stroke of beauty in the midst of drabness, the butterfly—if I may be permitted this ancient image—perched momentarily on the pile of dung."

PRINCIPAL WORKS

Without Beer or Bread (poetry) 1957
Saturday Night and Sunday Morning (novel) 1958
The Loneliness of the Long-Distance Runner (short stories) 1959
The Rats and Other Poems (poetry) 1960
Key to the Door (novel) 1961
The Ragman's Daughter and Other Stories (short stories) 1961
Road to Volgograd (nonfiction) 1964
The Death of William Posters (novel) 1965
The City Adventures of Marmalade Jim (juvenilia) 1967
A Tree on Fire (novel) 1967
Guzman, Go Home and Other Stories (short stories) 1968
Love in the Environs of Voronezh and Other Poems (poetry) 1968
A Start in Life (novel) 1970
Raw Material (memoirs) 1972
Men, Women, and Children (short stories) 1973
The Flame of Life (novel) 1974
Storm and Other Poems (poetry) 1974
Mountains and Caverns: Selected Essays (essays) 1975
The Widower's Son (novel) 1976
Pit Strike (play) 1977
The Incredible Fencing Fleas (juvenilia) 1978
Snow on the North Side of Lucifer (poetry) 1979
The Storyteller (novel) 1980
The Second Chance and Other Stories (short stories) 1981
Her Victory (novel) 1982
The Lost Flying Boat (novel) 1983
Down from the Hill (novel) 1984
Sun before Departure (poetry) 1984
Life Goes On (novel) 1985
Tides and Stone Walls (poetry) 1986
Nottinghamshire (nonfiction) 1987
Out of the Whirlpool (novel) 1987
The Open Door (novel) 1988
Last Loves (novel) 1989
Leonard's War: A Love Story (novel) 1991
Collected Poems (poetry) 1993

*Sillitoe authored a screenplay adaptation of *Saturday Night and Sunday Morning* in 1960, and a screenplay adaptation of *The Loneliness of the Long-Distance Runner* in 1961.

CRITICISM

Neil Millar (review date 6 September 1968)

SOURCE: "Fierce Burnings in Private Wildernesses," in *Christian Science Monitor,* Vol. 60, No. 240, September 6, 1968, p. 9.

[*In the following mixed review, Millar asserts that Sillitoe shows great skill in* A Tree on Fire, *but that the novel fails as great art.*]

Loud words shouted, soft words spat. A grunt in a mess of silence, a groan in a world's aching. A tree on fire, a house on fire, a nation on fire, a world not even watching.

A luminous fog of events. A glittering mist of words shot with little lightnings of epigram and swirled by sooty eddies of lust. The artist who despises those who don't understand him—and makes no effort to understand them. The artist as petty cheat and major victim; the artist as oaf, wit, clown, casual Casanova. The artist as disaster always about to happen, a kind of gray imminence; the artist as metaphysician and as tempestuous master of a tempestuous, teeming household. The artist as artist. The artist as Alan Sillitoe. Sillitoe as everyone.

This is a novel of ideas, and therefore every character tends to speak the author's thoughts and language. (Whether the author believes himself is a different matter.) It is the nature of such a book to be unnatural, and *A Tree on Fire* is sincerely artificial. Here the great action is mental because the novel assumes the primacy of mentality over matter. Not only is the human mind more interesting than the human body; it is more human. And certainly more wise; whenever the body interferes with the story it makes a fool of itself. This is a perceptive realism behind a nonrealistic drama.

The fatuity of the flesh is clearly demonstrated by both the artist Handley (and his assorted women) and the heroic Frank Dawley who seeks to find himself—or extinction—in fighting for the freedom of Algeria. Dawley leaves his women to fend for themselves while he goes on his death-or-Dawley mission in desert and mountain. Such

courage is selfish—perhaps because it is desperate. A brave man searching for himself "e'en in the cannon's mouth" may think he has found himself already, and may loathe what he found.

The artist is less heroic and more memorable, drawn larger than life and smaller than morality, honest only in his art. Yet some harsh generosity flickers about this hard-hating lover, ex-writer of begging letters. Handley is the rightful owner of new wealth, new fame, and these blessings threaten to break his marriage. He cherishes his long-loved wife as she cherishes him—enduringly, passionately, often savagely, with a kindness surpassing silence and a ready fury always likely to draw blood.

Some of the author's several tongues are snugly in his cheek: his message requires it. He writes on various levels: allegory and realism, parable and paradox. Most of the book is well worth reading once; some is worth reading and rereading: the skimmed-over surface tells little, but conceals treasure. From time to time the hurrying reader stumbles on what seems like a hummock of nothing: closer inspection may reveal that the mound is alive.

Mr. Sillitoe writes a poet's prose; he feels as a poet: injustices (except, perhaps, to women) sting him. *A Tree on Fire* is a work of great talent, although perhaps not a work of great art. Art is flame, shaped and shining against darkness; this book seems more like a brush fire on a brilliant day. But only a very gifted writer can make any sort of flame with ink.

Because of the allegory which infuses it, the book (like Samuel Beckett's play *Waiting for Godot*) rewards according to the perceptions brought to it. Like the play, it deals with wildernesses of the mind; unlike the play, its metaphysic seems to leave no room for deity looming and inscrutable in the infinite wings of the tiny human stage. For most of the characters there is no hint that perhaps, after all, a divine plan and a divine affection may somehow, somewhere, exist. Perhaps that is why in Mr. Sillitoe's valleys of despair, so few dry bones put on the living flesh of tenderness. The bush burns, burns, and is consumed.

Victor Howes (review date 24 February 1969)

SOURCE: "Alan Sillitoe—The Novelist as a Poet," in *Christian Science Monitor,* Vol. 61, No. 75, February 24, 1969, p. 9.

[*In the following review, Howes contends that Sillitoe focuses too much on specifics and not enough on life's universalities in the poems of* Love in the Environs of Voronezh.]

George Bernard Shaw once subdivided a group of his plays into "Plays Pleasant and Unpleasant." By almost anyone's critical standards, Alan Sillitoe's poems, *Love in the Environs of Voronezh,* would be classed as Poems Unpleasant.

Mr. Sillitoe employs an elliptical style, knotty, hard to unravel, like the speech of people who grudge their words and spit them out sparingly. His poems are filled with implicit violence: with knives, bullets, bombs, with verbs like "to savage," "to razor," "to rifle out and kill." His images seem to be forcibly held together by some subjective logic of the poet's own—a logic the reader can grasp only in subjective flashes of intuition. Cataclysm seems always to impend, as the images threaten to pull apart and leave us face to face with chaos.

Mr. Sillitoe is fascinated with the opposition of fire and ice. Characteristically he offers

> midnight-midday frostbitten forest fires
> Burning into the dust and honeymilk.
> And eating even the iron through.

And again,

> a fire engine races through
> A freak snowstorm . . .
> Will it skid into oblivion . . .
> And leave only the snow of heaven
> To put all fires out?

With Sillitoe one feels the impulse to say extravagant things, to squander words without any reserve of credit to back them up. He addresses himself, in one poem, to a "star that beats in me like a fish." In another, he confides, "I am a tree whose roots destroy me." He lullabies a baby with the words, "Goodnight sweet baby, sleep / Safe in the uplands of oblivion / Beyond the iced bite of the moon."

In the present collection, his third book of poetry, there are poems about the ways of love, mainly destructive; poems about animals, about the exploration of space, poems of withdrawal from, and occasionally return to, the world, poems about identity, dreams, survival.

Some deal with travel, inspired by a journey Mr. Sillitoe made to the Soviet Union. But whether they explore the world outside or within the poet scarcely matters, for both groups are marked and marred by the poet's preoccupation with the bizarre. The Eurasian landscape through which he moves becomes merely another symbol for his inner journey.

> Black ice smoulders all around . . .
> Ninety degrees of bitterness preserve
> Mosquito eggs. There is death
> From fire but not by ice
> As the list of winter
> Pulls into the mitten of the sun.

Alan Sillitoe is an English novelist of considerable reputation. Two of his books, *Saturday Night and Sunday Morning* and *The Loneliness of the Long-Distance Runner,*

have provided the bases of films. These are widely admitted for their sensitive depictions of English working-class life. Mr. Sillitoe has worked in Majorca under the direction of the poet and novelist, Robert Graves, and there is no question about his powers of language, or his power to write angry, tortured poems, filled with images of rejection and negation.

Furthermore, great art can be made from such materials: witness *Othello,* the satires of Swift and Pope, and many of the poems of Thomas Hardy, Robert Frost, Edwin Arlington Robinson. But for art there must be objectivity and aesthetic distance; there must be a sense of the larger life of humanity going on about its business, "eating," as W. H. Auden has put it, "or opening a window or just walking dully along."

Only fleetingly, as in the title poem, a celebration of a city rebuilt from its ashes, does Mr. Sillitoe show us that he glimpses life's continuities. For the most part he seems to be standing up too close to his canvas either to see it steadily or to see it whole.

Virginia Quarterly Review (review date Summer 1969)

SOURCE: A review of *Love in the Environs of Voronezh,* in *Virginia Quarterly Review,* Vol. 45, No. 3, Summer, 1969, p. 96–97.

[*In the following review, the critic maintains that Sillitoe's* Love in the Environs of Voronezh *exhibits "only flashes of authority."*]

The scant handful of successful poems in [*Love in the Environs of Voronezh*] is barely able to save it from a plunge into a totally monotonous performance. Too many of the poems are of the sort one finds monopolizing the worksheets of undergraduate poetry-writing classes, half-realized poems which neglect the possibilities of metaphor, dealing instead in uninspired abstractions, as in "We": "We-I have destroyed you / WE-I have finished you off / Torn you out of me," or employing trite images such as the mask in **"I Tell Myself"**: "I tell myself as if it's true / I wear an utterly complete disguise / Which is myself." Generally the poems lack richness of texture and syntactic variety. If Sillitoe could have maintained the sense of rhythm, the aural qualities, and the honesty of his title poem, he would have a truly skillful performance rather than one possessing only flashes of authority.

Times Literary Supplement (review date 18 September 1970)

SOURCE: "A Naturalist No More," in *Times Literary Supplement,* No. 3577, September 18, 1970, p. 1026.

[*In the following review, the critic argues that Sillitoe's* A Start in Life *is not as good as the author's earlier work.*]

In the stories in *The Loneliness of the Long-Distance Runner* (1959) and *The Ragman's Daughter* (1963) and in *Saturday Night and Sunday Morning,* which also began as sketches of life in Nottingham, Alan Sillitoe was able to recreate, in its own idiom, a whole vein of experience which had usually got into literature only as material for comic character stuff in the way of Alfred Doolittle in *Pygmalion* or for militant reportage in the way of Orwell's *Wigan Pier.* The life concerned is one of hard-grafting, in all sense of that word—of living in old rows of industrial housing, working in down-town factories, getting outlet and satisfaction through semi-licit or illicit pleasures, from screwing the overlooker's wife to shooting foxes on a Sunday.

The idiom matters as much as the experience. Its hard snap and unpredictable humour still crop up in his novel of 1965, *The Death of William Posters,* whose title (not really made good in the book) is based on the splendid joke that "Bill posters will be prosecuted" means the authorities have it in for a scapegoat called Posters. In this new novel [*A Start in Life*] that sort of voice can be still heard in snatches, like "Her middle name was Audrey, which she favoured most, Tawdry Audrey from Tibshelf, who got off the bus one Saturday night in Worksop market place."

This ability to root his art in the life of the poorly-off has made Sillitoe our outstanding portrayer of what Arthur Miller has called (in his classic introduction to his *Collected Plays*) "that sub-culture where the sinews of the economy are rooted, that darkest Africa of our society from whose interior only the sketchiest messages ever reach our literature or our stage." It is presumably what Raymond Williams means when he speaks (in *The English Novel*) about finding in Sillitoe and David Storey late "followers" of Lawrence, a "narrower, more jagged edge" of evoked communal experience. Sillitoe himself, in a recent *Guardian* interview and in his introduction to the Heritage of Literature edition of *Saturday Night,* has repudiated the label of "working-class writer." But the label is surely invidious only when it implies that the artist is dealing with a rather limited area that is somehow less human than other ways of life. What matters is that since, in *William Posters,* Sillitoe took to presenting the London middle-class scene, his touch has become fatally uncertain; whole tracts of his novels have been sketchy or forced; and he has resorted to literary modes which he cannot master.

A Start in Life is (yet again) about a man who breaks out of the hard-grafting life of the unskilled worker in the Midlands. The first seventy pages are (yet again) in the vein of the brutally breezy life-story told by the rogue male himself. But Sillitoe clearly signals his desire to break away from "regional" naturalism in the devices he resorts to. Narrative is interrupted for minor characters to tell their life-stories, in the manner of a Fielding novel: names are ludicrously fitting—Claudine Forks the husband-hungry Nottingham girl, Claud Moggerhanger the London racketeer, Bridgitte Appledore the rosy *au pair* girl from

Holland, and Kundt the womanizing journalist from Sedenborg in Sweden . . . This kind of thing, along with the deliberately unlikely meetings and reencounters and getaways, prompts the publishers to credit Sillitoe with "reviving the picaresque." He also "revives" Ian Fleming by bringing in a master criminal, who organizes big-time gold smuggling from inside an iron lung.

The result is inchoate. A thriller must be tightly plotted or it is nothing. A typical turning-point in *A Start in Life* is when the hero, quite implausibly, confides certain crucial details to a girl-friend. This might suit the deliberately cavalier linkings of picaresque, but here it jars horribly with a wholly different vein—the quite deep and subtle probings of psychological contrariness which Sillitoe is able to give the narrator when he is introspecting:

> If I had taken the pains to see, which wouldn't have been all that far beyond me, to the deepest recesses behind his eyes in which that picture lurked in black and grey and red, of his wife's head tilted in the mud and staring at some innocent barge going by in the moonlight, I might have saved her, and him. But I didn't because somehow my feet were no longer plugged into the earth, and my aerial was withered in its contact with heaven. It seemed I had been living underwater not to have known the truth of what was so obvious . . . I saw everything clear and sharp with the bare eye, but a lazy idleness inside kept a permanent clothbound foot on the deeper perceptions that blinded me from action.

His best work of some years ago and the force which he still fitfully commands continue to give Sillitoe a claim on our attention. But there is a chance that his talent may fray itself out for good unless he now makes himself become less headlong in his output, perhaps by holding back from easy identification with the rogue male and by weighing up more thoughtfully what it is that he has against our present way of life.

Victor Howes (review date 7 October 1971)

SOURCE: A review of *A Start in Life,* in *Christian Science Monitor,* Vol. 63, October 7, 1971, p. 7.

[*In the following review, Howes lauds Sillitoe's* A Start in Life *for its humor and comic characters.*]

In the spill-a-minute world of the animated cartoon, the comic hero by turns falls off a cliff, is knocked flat as a tortilla by a steamroller, is exploded by a giant firecracker, and in the next frame—always jauntily intact and in the finest of fettle—embarks upon still another pratfall.

Alan Sillitoe's latest novel [*A Start in Life*] has a hero like that. Obedient to a formula as old as the novel itself, Sillitoe's rogue male takes on the world with all the gusto of a Don Quixote assailing a windmill. Never mind how many times it flails him down, in the next episode he's up again and fighting.

Born out of wedlock, not knowing who his father is, Michael Cullen early opts for a career in real estate. His taste for extralegal activities quickly gets him sacked. With his ill-gotten profits, he buys a car and heads for London, where he intends to live by his wits. Drifting into a series of jobs, he finds employ first as a bouncer in a sleazy night club, then as chauffeur to London's biggest racketeer, finally as an international gold smuggler.

Cutting athwart his life of crime are the stories of his numerous love affairs. The girls Michael Cullen meets possess vocabularies that seem never to have included the word "no."

Briefly synopsized, *A Start in Life* cannot help sounding sordid. But what redeems the novel from sordor is Michael's unflagging high-spirits, the undercurrent of satiric social comment, and the beyond-good-and evil naiveté of Michael's narrative voice. "The pure of heart shall inherit the earth," he confides, "and what could be more pure of heart than a simple good-natured desire for money and an easy life that would harm none of my fellowmen?"

Michael's greatest resource is his resourcefulness. His gift for lies, for assumed identities, for improvising in tight situations make him a match for Odysseus, the master of all escape-artists. His ready way with women, his skill in handling children, his kindness to such downtrodden members of society as Almanack Jack, make him, in spite of his amorality, one of the most lovable *picaros* to come down the pike since Fielding's Tom Jones.

A Start in Life is a real lark, a picaresque novel brought into the age of the automobile and the airplane. Kidding the conventions of the chance meeting of old acquaintances, the long-lost father bit, and the happy ending with all sinners cheerily "cultivating their gardens," the novel portrays a shooting-gallery full of comic types.

Two of British novelist Sillitoe's previous fictions, *Saturday Night and Sunday Morning* and *The Loneliness of the Long-Distance Runner* have been made into films. *A Start in Life* cries out for cinematic rendition.

Russell Davies (review date 29 November 1974)

SOURCE: "Trouble at the Dacha," in *Times Literary Supplement,* No. 3795, November 29, 1974, p. 1336.

[*In the following review, Davies provides an unfavorable assessment of Sillitoe's* The Flame of Life.]

The Flame of Life completes a cycle which began in 1964 with *The Death of William Posters* and continued with *A Tree on Fire.* Bill Posters has been prosecuted far enough. Alan Sillitoe has taken some time getting round to this

conclusion, but he is able to present, in an author's note, a certificate of diligence: during the progress of the new book "three other novels were written, two books of short stories, two film-scripts, and a volume of poems."

This makes him very nearly as prolific as Albert Handley, the painter who lords it over his own rural commune almost to the end of this curious and garbled book. Albert is a creator/monster who seems to have grown out of the author's fears of self (the clues to identification include Albert's Schimmelpenninck cigars, a small tin of which is seen protruding from Mr Sillitoe's shirt pocket in the jacket photograph). He is a Gulley Jimson intoxicated by the privileges of a self-made man. Among the lower strata of the community the resonances are more variable and eccentric. The wildly frank breast-baring, the socialist/anarchist undertones of political debate, the climactic firing off of a revolver in the yard—these give the air of a Chekhovian dacha populated by disaffected remnants of the *IT* Home Affairs staff.

Amusing to contemplate in the abstract realm to which it belongs, this communal experience is a bore to live through page by page. The flame of life is choked off not only by the dull smoke of theory—the inmates of communes habitually waste much time wondering what is keeping them there—but also by the wet blanket of the author's presence. Mr Sillitoe has lived with this narrative so long that none of it "escapes" him, as it were: nothing takes fire from him and goes crackling off on its own. Thus even as the 300th page approaches, it is still difficult to tell the characters apart, to lend or withdraw moral support as the focus shifts, chapter by chapter. The intrusions of Albert are exaggeratedly welcome, for though his patron-bedding sexual bout with Lady Daphne Maria Fitz-Gerald Ritmeester in Chapter One is deeply bogus, it feeds on a lunatic rumbustiousness that has one looking forward to a repeat of this kind of behaviour. It never comes. This leaves only the internal ravings of the rest: Cuthbert, failed priest, nihilist and poseur; Dawley, revolutionary activist and insubstantial shade; Ralph, sobbing depressive and ultimate heir to a vast and vastly implausible fortune; Dean William Posters, pot-smoking heir to Mr Sillitoe's bad joke (see above); several women even less well differentiated than their consorts; and the dog, Eric Bloodaxe, howling gothically in the distance, where the reader would like to be. But Mr Sillitoe is cunning enough not to allow a moment's escape: one whiff of fresh air to clear the brain, and we'd realize that this material is incombustible.

Walter Sullivan (review date July 1975)

SOURCE: "Erewhon and Eros: The Short Story Again," in *Sewanee Review,* Vol. 83, No. 3, July, 1975, pp. 537–46.

[*In the following excerpt, Sullivan discusses the strengths and weaknesses of the stories in* Men, Women, and Children.]

. . . . The world of Alan Sillitoe and the characters who inhabit it are as different as they could possibly be from the glittering figures and the handsome landscapes of V. S. Pritchett. As readers of *Saturday Night and Sunday Morning* will remember, the sun seldom shines in Nottingham, and when it does break palely through the industrial haze, it illuminates crowded shabby houses, dripping gutters, weed-choked gardens. The people drink and fornicate, drink and commit adultery, drink and work when they have to, hating every moment they spend in the factory and most of the moments that they spend at home. Marriage itself in the Sillitoe canon appears as a kind of blight, the ceremony guaranteed to make unpalatable those things which when done out of wedlock appear to be fun. Speaking of Mark in **"Before Snow Comes,"** which is one of the best of the generally good stories in *Men, Women, and Children,* Sillitoe puts the case thus: "He had two brothers and two sisters, all of them married and all of them divorced, except one who was killed in a car crash. It wasn't that his family was unlucky or maladjusted, simply that they were normal and wholesome, just conforming like the rest of the world and following in the family tradition with such pertinacity that at the worst of times it made him laugh, and at the best it sent him out in carpet slippers on Sunday morning to buy a newspaper and read what was happening to other families."

The fictional possibilities of such a wasteland are obviously limited. Even in the world of [John] O'Hara's upper crust there are financiers and artists, professionals and heiresses, politicians and gangsters. But Nottingham is monolithic, unrelieved in its ugliness, and its citizens are cut from a common mould. Take them anywhere—to a borstal, to the army—and Nottingham goes with them: it is a way of life, a religion that admits no renegades. The wonder is how Sillitoe manages to write not only competent but occasionally brilliant fiction within such rigid limits. He succeeds because of his ability to perceive the rare stroke of beauty in the midst of drabness, the butterfly—if I may be permitted this ancient image—perched momentarily on the pile of dung.

I must be careful not to overstate the case. Most of *Men, Women, and Children* is about boredom and betrayal: husbands who leave their wives, wives who leave their husbands, parents who abandon their children, lovers of all kinds who prove untrue. The protagonist in **"Scenes from the Life of Margaret"** has trouble enough when the story opens, having been forsaken by her husband and left with three children. At the end she is once more pregnant and her lover has gone too. But it is Margaret alone among the patrons of a tearoom who will go—fruitlessly as it turns out—to the aid of a dying old man. Mark in **"Before Snow Comes"** is that rarest of all Nottingham citizens: he loves order. Another of Nottingham's deserted women becomes his mistress. He mends her broken fence, makes repairs on her house, saves his money to take her and her two children on holidays. But at the last she leaves him to go off with her returned husband and does not stop to say good-bye.

Finally there is **"A Trip to Southwell"** which is about a seventeen-year-old boy and a fifteen-year-old girl and their initiation into the grim patterns of adult existence. Mavis's older sister has already lost her virtue—if such an old-fashioned assertion can have any meaning when applied to Sillitoe's characters—and Alec is willing, even anxious, that Mavis should remain pure. She and Alec love: they kiss and fondle each other with innocent passion. Then he must go to Southwell, and when he returns she has fallen. Facing her from outside her doorway, he cannot tell whether she is pregnant. But the change in her is apparent and he is deeply hurt and still very much in love and inclined to blame himself for what has happened to her. He would marry her, regardless of whether or not she is to bear another's child, but she will not go out with him. The story ends on the note of his speculation: could the kisses he gave her have started the process which brought her to this?

Sillitoe's work is restricted to be sure. He would be a better writer if he knew more or if he allowed himself more space in which to operate. . . .

Frederick H. Guidry (review date 4 August 1977)

SOURCE: "Sillitoe Novel Traces a Soldier's Growth and Switch to Civilian Life," in *Christian Science Monitor,* Vol. 69, No. 177, August 4, 1977, p. 22.

[*In the following review, Guidry praises Sillitoe's use of the interior monologue in* The Widower's Son.]

A military man is Alan Sillitoe's newest hero [in *The Widower's Son*], opening up for the author a wide range of metaphor having to do with campaign and strategy, attack and defense, victory and defeat, as applied to personal relationships.

William Scorton, whose experience is chronicled here from his teens to his early fifties, has a character that appears to have been as much reinforced as created by military life. So it may be incorrect to blame the army for the downfall that temporarily wrecks his adjustment to civilian life. The role of master-gunner suited Scorton, put his aggressiveness to respectable use. But after 20 years, including some time as an officer, he was ready to explore the outer world. "I love you," he tells his wife, Georgina, assuring her with customary directness that she will not be hurt by the change. "The army phase of my life's ended. I want another to begin. I'm not the sort who rots away."

Georgina, a brigadier general's daughter, has good reason for doubts about the next phase of their life together. She knows the positive side of military service and its ability to provide purpose and structure for the individuals under its control. The author thus seems to have stacked the cards against his central characters—service children inadequately prepared for mid-life crises which are intensified in this instance by a sudden switch to civilian life.

But if army life provides the basic tone of this story, it is far from limiting. Scorton's musings, his struggles to do right, his puzzlement over aspects of the human condition, though couched often in terms of military experience and observation, are easily appreciated for their general aptness and poetical intensity.

Mr. Sillitoe's earlier novels include *Saturday Night and Sunday Morning* and *The Loneliness of the Long-Distance Runner.* He is an accomplished writer of evocative dialogue. But his most appealing passages are those of interior monologue—those impromptu gropings toward a coherent and satisfying view of life—typified by Scorton's thoughts while bicycling:

> There was no monotony in pedaling, as if the wheels worked a well to draw up thoughts from underground. Times had altered. People often felt this when they got older, but he had entered a state of calm beneficial chaos where regimentation of the spirit no longer had any place. . . . Nothing stays still—even my bicycle when I'm not thinking of pedaling. Chaos mustn't get the upper hand, though we don't want to get back to the brainless and soulless sort of order we had before.

Such blending of points of view—the author describing, his fictional creation ruminating, almost indistinguishably—bring the reader into subtle union with the very essence of the story: self-knowledge attaining ever higher levels.

Daniel J. Cahill (review date Spring 1982)

SOURCE: A review of *The Second Chance and Other Stories,* in *World Literature Today,* Vol. 56, No. 2, Spring, 1982, pp. 339–40.

[*In the following review, Cahill explores Sillitoe's affinity for depicting ordinary people in the stories comprising* The Second Chance.]

In a long and prolific career that goes back to the mid-1950s, Alan Sillitoe has proved himself to be one of the most incisive recorders of what life is really like for the working class of England today. His twenty-fifth book, *The Second Chance,* is a collection of short stories written during the past twenty years. All the stories have been previously published in various periodicals, but this collection has special value because it focuses upon the persistent affinity which Sillitoe displays for the plight and torment of ordinary people whose lives are without dreams of happiness. The author of *Saturday Night and Sunday Morning* and *The Loneliness of the Long-Distance Runner,* Sillitoe understands with the weight of deep personal experience the need for a second chance, the dim belief that tomorrow will be better.

The title story involves a bizarre longing to revive the dead. In southern England an elderly couple, the Baxters, who have lost their son Peter in the Battle of Britain, are

living out their days in unabated grief. One day the husband spies a young man in a hotel bar who bears a startling resemblance to the dead Peter. The young man and the Baxters need "a second chance," and the three form a complex alliance of feeling and adopted roles. The young man is really a cheap crook waiting to seize the best advantage of the Baxters. In a risky and suspenseful plot, Sillitoe turns the tables, and material and emotional greed topple each other. The plot owes something to Pinter in the metaphor of the intruder into house and heart. Sillitoe is at his very best as he explores the fear and abraded emotion of people feeding on each other.

In contrast to this novella-length narrative, all the remaining stories of the collection are brief, and the main intent of each seems to converge on several characters whose lives have crossed on the path of love. **"The Meeting"** and **"The Confrontation"** are among the best examples. These are stories which seem to rise out of Sillitoe's conviction that the lives of the most ordinary people may illustrate the grand compromise that is all our lives. No dreams are ever fulfilled, but always there remains the redeeming hope for "a second chance."

Joan Reardon (review date 21 November 1982)

SOURCE: "Complex People Plunge into Love," in *Los Angeles Times Book Review,* November 21, 1982, p. 6.

[*In the following laudatory review of* Her Victory, *Reardon asserts that "Sillitoe has reached a new level of craftsmanship and a degree of resonance that will outdistance his earlier work."*]

Trendy novels of consciousness and change often seem "self-help" books with their persistent directive to open windows to new experiences. So, while Alan Sillitoe's latest book might easily be read as a message "to reach out and touch someone," the novel does, in fact, deliver much more than the plot promises.

Her Victory is not limited to the simple story of a woman who had "married at 20 and had come out at 40 with her heart so bruised that it seemed as if she couldn't do anything except turn into a cabbage and rot in the earth." And the complexity of the novel's characters—seemingly ordinary people who must come to terms with their past in order to live in the present—cannot be ignored despite the deceptive commonplaceness of their names.

From beginning to end, the troubled and triumphant tale of Pam's escape—from life with George in Nottingham to her residence in Israel with Tom and their infant daughter—holds the reader's attention. But Pam's inner struggle with the "two people she was" is an unforgettable experience for anyone who has had to make those decisions that are usually irrevocable.

Pam's determination to leave her parental home and a satisfying job in order to marry George was her first decision. It proved disastrous. Walking out on her husband and son was her second. "Both decisions had affected her so profoundly that all she had ever learned had come out of them." Unable to bear the chill of loneliness and the nightmare of a return to George any longer, she attempts suicide in the London walk-up that she has made her home. The effort fails when she is rescued by a retired seaman who had taken up residence in the flat next door.

The narrative that follows—the story of a lonely man who "had battened down the hatches of [his] spirit during 30 years at sea"—complements Pam's own story. Tom's isolation, though different in kind and degree, is similar to hers. His past is hidden in the "documentary belongings" stored in his deceased aunt's apartment. Because Tom has saved Pam's life, she now can save his by helping him reconstruct his life, discover his mother in photographs and diaries, and eventually assume an identity that is both comfortable and true. In the long process of "sorting each other out," they forge a relationship that ultimately leads to a shared life in the Promised Land, a "romantic story" without a tragic end—but tragic, nonetheless.

Her Victory is a novel about "aloneness," a testimony to the subtle and not-so-subtle ways that a man and a woman can torture each other in the isolation of togetherness. Because Pam's domestic life with George was played out in scenes of insensitivity, psychological harassment and even physical attack, the "defining process of marriage" had unleashed the demons of violence in her own soul. To escape the past, to refuse to return when George and his brothers forcibly try to reclaim her, ill-prepares Pam for loving Tom. Their commitment is a long and difficult process involving an initiation into communal love with another woman. It is a personal victory before it becomes a shared one. And it is a riveting story.

With this book, Sillitoe has reached a new level of craftsmanship and a degree of resonance that will outdistance his earlier work. Hers is not the only victory. Sillitoe has won his own.

Sophia B. Blaydes and Philip Bordinat (essay date 1983)

SOURCE: "The Loneliness of the Long-Distance Runner and *Chariots of Fire*," in *Film Quarterly,* Vol. 11, No. 4, 1983, pp. 211–14.

[*In the following essay, Blaydes and Bordinat analyze the use of William Blake's "Jerusalem" in Sillitoe's* The Loneliness of the Long-Distance Runner *and Colin Welland's* Chariots of Fire.]

The evolution of great literature into popular culture is vividly seen in the films *The Loneliness of the Long-Distance Runner* (1962) and *Chariots of Fire* (1981) through their use of William Blake's lyric "And did those feet," commonly known as "Jerusalem." Written and

etched about 1804–1808, the poem is the conclusion to the "Preface" of Blake's prophetic book *Milton.* Arguing with Milton, Blake urges the English to free themselves from "either Greek or Roman models" that had "curb'd" Shakespeare and Milton, and he urges them instead to turn to their own inspiration and prophecy. He asks that the "Young Men of the New Age" be "just and true" to their "own Imaginations." Blake then introduces the poem:

> And did those feet in ancient time
> Walk upon England's mountains green?
> And was the holy Lamb of God
> On England's pleasant pastures seen?
>
> And did the Countenance Divine
> Shine forth upon our clouded hills?
> And was Jerusalem builded here
> Among those dark Satanic Mills?
>
> Bring me my Bow of burning gold:
> Bring me my Arrows of desire
> Bring me my Spear: O clouds unfold
> Bring me my Chariot of fire.
>
> I will not cease from Mental Fight.
> Nor shall my Sword sleep in my hand
> Till we have built Jerusalem
> In England's green & pleasant Land.[1]

By the 1880s the poem had become the motto of the Guild of St. Matthew's weekly paper. Set to music by Sir Hubert Parry in 1916, the combination of words and music became an anthem first for the men in World War I and after the war for the British Labour Party. By 1923 the words and music were published as a hymn for English congregations. More recently it has been brought before larger and more international audiences as the thematic background music for two highly successful British films: *Loneliness,* adapted by Alan Sillitoe from his short story by the same name and directed by Tony Richardson; and *Chariots,* written by Colin Welland, directed by Hugh Hudson, and produced by David Puttman.

Over the years the lyric has been transformed from an individualized, prophetic injunction to an anthem of popular culture. Each succeeding use of the lyric demonstrates the leveling of Blake's ironic statement into superficial messages that ignore some of the most subtle, ambiguous, and symbolic poetry available to us. The lyric seems now to mean whatever the age wishes. The poem is Blake's exhortation to the English to unshackle themselves. As Joseph Anthony Wittreich, Jr., recently observed, "Both Milton and Blake wished to return to original Christianity as it was laid down by Christ and his apostles," and, for both, "God awakens the spirit of imagination in the poet who, in turn, must awaken the same spirit in his audience."[2]

Written after the Industrial Revolution took hold in England, *Milton* and its prefatory lyric reflect Blakes's rejection of a social and economic milieu that almost destroyed the power and individuality of man. Emphasizing man's spirit and his mind, Blake reveals his abhorrence of war and his hatred of reason. As the prophet or God's instrument, Blake insisted he wrote "'from immediate dictation. . . . I dare not pretend to be any other than the secretary.'"[3] With the imagery and symbolism of Christ as the "holy lamb of God," Blake asks if the early English walked with Christ. He asks whether God's light shines now through the clouds that rest upon the English hills. Pursuing the image to its bitter moment, Blake then asks whether God's country was built among England's factories and mills. By the third stanza, Blake turns from a series of questions to declarative statements rich in power and purpose. With the weapons of war—a bow, arrows, a spear, and a chariot—Blake repeatedly excites the reader to follow him to the glory of God, but not through actual battle. Instead, the last stanza explains that the bow "of burning gold," the "Arrows of desire," the "Spear" that is revealed by the clouds, and the "Chariot of fire," are metaphors for the weapons of "mental fight." Blake's battle is at first personal with the emphasis on "my" until the last two lines of the poem, where he returns to the plural mode of the first two stanzas. He closes, asserting that the sword will not "sleep in my hand," until all of the English have succeeded in building "Jerusalem," symbolic now of freedom from the tyrannies of society, especially those that repress and destroy man's imagination and prophetic energy.

That meaning of Blake's poem was profoundly affected in 1915 or 1916 when Sir Hubert Parry set it to music. Perhaps because the song arose from a need to have an anthem of sorts during World War I, it became associated with nationalistic causes. Published in sheet form in 1916, the "tune . . . immediately and lastingly received popular approbation."[4] First sung at a concert in Albert Hall, it was adopted by the Federation of Music Competition Festivals as their anthem, but even more important, the song became a second national anthem by the 1920s.

Over the years the same words with which the poet rejected established institutions and beliefs have been ironically embraced by English political parties and churches, and have invested ceremonies with nationalistic fervor. While some occasions may indeed echo the spirit of the original, more often the poet's words have become ironic footnotes. Such is the cast in the two films *Loneliness* and *Chariots*. In each, Blake's lyric serves both as an inspiration and as an ironic counterpoint to the filmmakers' depictions. Coincidentally about running and winning, both films are more importantly about freedom and individuality. An examination of the two films reveals that Blake's words and the music to which those words were set become integral to the purposes of the filmmakers and that those purposes are ironically antithetical. Both use "Jerusalem," the earlier film, as an important, pervasive leitmotif, the latter as part of the title and as inspirational punctuation. In addition, neither film provides a clear understanding of Blake's poem.

In *Loneliness,* Colin Smith, a rebellious Nottingham youth, rejects the controls of the establishment by stealing a car

and robbing a bakery. He is caught and sent to a Borstal where his talent as a long-distance runner enables him to join the establishment. He need only win the challenge cup for the governor, who suggests to Smith, "The greatest honour a man could ever have would be to represent his country at the Olympics." Smith, angry young man that he is, rejects the opportunity. Having left his opponents far behind in the race, he stops a few yards short of the finish line and stares defiantly at the governor. Before a shocked crowd, he refuses to win. Smith has chosen to remain outside the establishment.

As in *Loneliness,* in *Chariots* the outsider defies the British establishment through running. The film depicts the true story of two outsiders. Harold Abrahams, who is Jewish, runs to exalt his people, and Eric Liddell, who is Scottish, runs to glorify his God. Here, as in *Loneliness,* characters reject establishment rules: Abrahams by hiring a professional coach, and Liddell by refusing to run on Sunday. Abrahams and Liddell hold to their convictions in the face of establishment pressures, and, ironically, they become national heroes by winning Olympic gold medals. Both *Loneliness* and *Chariots* depict outsiders who battle the establishment and win on their terms. Smith wins by losing and he remains outside the establishment; so did the angry young man of the nineteen sixties. Abrahams and Liddell, unlike Smith, win and become heroes, though, like Smith, they retain their integrity and identities as outsiders. Although both films use the hymn in different ways, they distort Blake's poem. In *Loneliness,* Tony Richardson, like Blake, protests against the way things are in England. Richardson and Alan Sillitoe in his screenplay answer Blake's rhetorical question, "And was Jerusalem builded here / Among those dark Satanic Mills?" with a resounding "No." Richardson introduces the hymn, with its twentieth-century, patriotic associations, as a leitmotif for the establishment. For example, the film opens with strings intoning "Jerusalem." Trumpets join in as a police van moves along a country road. The camera moves inside the van where it focuses on Smith, several other "new boys," and two guards. The hymn continues as the youths comment on their arrival at the Borstal with a mixture of fear and bravado. The hymn recurs when Smith rebels against the inept psychiatrist, when Smith reacts against the platitudes of the governor, who pompously states, "You play ball with us; we'll play ball with you," and when Smith resists the detective who promises lenience in exchange for a confession. Again "Jerusalem" is played when Smith's rival is beaten by the warders. Midway in the film, the words of the poem accompany the music, when the local minister leads the Borstal boys in a rousing chorus of the hymn. As the film ends and Smith is reprimanded by a warder, the soundtrack repeats the boys' chorus of the final quatrain of "Jerusalem."

The hymn produces a different irony in *Chariots* because the filmmakers intended to criticize the English establishment[5] through Abrahams, an intense Jew, and Liddell, a Scottish missionary. Both overcome or deny the establishment. In so doing, the protagonists seem to justify the use of Blake's poem in the film's title and as the hymn for the postlude, for *Chariots* does present "Men of a New Age." Yet neither runner is English establishment, and neither wins for England. Abrahams runs to rise above the anti-Semitic establishment: *"And run them off their feet!"*[6] Liddell is equally a man whose inner convictions take precedence over patriotism. In response to the Prince of Wales' request that England be placed before God, Liddell responds, "Sir, God knows I love my country. But I can't make that sacrifice" (p. 140). In neither case was the principal motivation of the two outsiders patriotic. Yet, "Jerusalem" majestically closes the film with the fervor of England's second national anthem.

While "Jerusalem" appears in both films, it performs different functions in them. In *Loneliness* it is the most pervasive and affecting part of the soundtrack, offset only by a jazz melody that accompanies Smith's most satisfying, euphoric moments when he is free and running. When Smith is most beset by the restrictions of the establishment, the soundtrack plays "Jerusalem." In *Chariots*, although the title arises from it, "Jerusalem" is less significant. Instead, the dominant music is an original melody that heightens the intensity of the races. The most obvious use of "Jerusalem" occurs at the end following the service for Abrahams after his death in 1978. Ironically, Blake's song here celebrates the death of an outsider with all the pomp and ceremony available to the establishment, but the irony is unintentional.

From a poem that urges a new Jerusalem to be won by mental fight, Blake's lyric has been transformed into a vehicle of easy ironies and emotional charges. The hymn in each film demands little thought and no familiarity with Blake's poem or his concern for personal freedom and inspiration. In *Loneliness* and in *Chariots,* it is used for irony and patriotic fervor. Perhaps it is a tribute to the power of the words and the ambiguities of the images in Blake's work that the poem can be so varied in its form and meaning. It becomes in *Loneliness* a powerful extension of the theme of the angry young man; it becomes in *Chariots* an evocative affirmation of the establishment; but it remains in Blake a powerful exhortation to his English readers to arm themselves for that mental fight of independence. The impact of popular culture on literature is often recognized, but where is it more clearly and ironically depicted than through the evolution of Blake's poem and its use in two successful films of our time?

Notes

1. *Blake: Complete Writing with Variant Reading,* ed. Geoffrey Keynes (London: Oxford Univ. Press, 1971), pp. 480–81.

2. *Angel of Apocalypse: Blake's Idea of Milton* (Madison: Univ. of Wisconsin Press, 1975), pp. 158, 183.

3. Allardyce Nicoll, *William Blake and His Poetry* (1922; rpt. New York: AMS, 1971), pp. 117–18.

4. *Companion to Congregational Praise,* eds. K. L. Parry and Erik Routely (London: Independent, 1953), p. 312.

5. James McCourt, "The New York Film Festival," *Film Comment,* 17 (1981), 61.

6. W. J. Weatherby, *Chariots of Fire* (New York: Dell, 1981), p. 33.

Valentine Cunningham (review date 6 November 1983)

SOURCE: "Biggles and the Murks," in *Observer,* November 6, 1983, p. 31.

[*In the following excerpt, Cunningham provides a favorable assessment of Sillitoe's* The Lost Flying Boat.]

Not all trite-seeming fictional packages disclose tosh when you unwrap them. A few sleuths actually turn out to be Grail-seekers, some ordinary Coral Islanders end up as Lords of the Flies. And the overt simplicities of Alan Sillitoe—this time a generous freight of boyish-looking adventure stuff—can prove most deceptive ones.

When Adcock, Sillitoe's wireless-operating narrator [in ***The Lost Flying Boat***], meets Bennett, the ex-RAF bomber-pilot who's urgently crewing up a flying-boat to go snatch a trove of German gold coins off an Antarctic island, he spots the man's cigars: Partagas. Or, as he notes (quick on the alphabetics), Saga Trap backwards. And saga modes certainly proliferate hereabouts. It's RAF Bigglesforth time as the great plane's clutch of doomy hards—'bespoke tragedians' they're called—heads out for every trouble that a rival gang, assorted 'gremlins' in the works, and this kind of Press on Remorseless, All In It Together, And Then There Were Five plot can sling at them.

But, it soon eventuates, they're flying into no mere saga trap. In fact, they're in a much more intriguing corner, a giant solipsistic container laden with their fears, violences, suspicions, and their good and bad recollections of the war. They thought they were escaping from nightmares of nights in Lancasters over Essen and Berlin, and putting their troubled peacetime marriages behind them. But whichever way they fly is confusing and hellish—especially for Sparks Adcock, accustomed to using human signs to codify, sort out, make plain, but condemned now to radio silences and mounting haziness on a flight into inexplicables, moral murks, a hermeneutics of darkness. Boy's Own hero meets frustrated semiotician. It's a rather dazzling convergence. . . .

David Craig (essay date 1984)

SOURCE: "The Roots of Sillitoe's Fiction," in *The British Working-Class Novel in the Twentieth Century,"* edited by Jeremy Hawthorn, Edward Arnold, 1984, pp. 95–110.

[In the following essay, Craig traces the development of Sillitoe's fiction throughout his career.]

> I've only to say I hate Nottingham, he thought with a silent ironic laugh, for all the years it's put on me to come into my mind as clear as framed photos outside a picture house.[1]

This sentence from Alan Sillitoe's third novel expresses the thoughts of a character, Brian Seaton, and not the author's own. Yet it does suggest Sillitoe's conflicting views of the city where he grew up—the seed-bed of his experience. When he was asked at the Lancaster Literature Festival in 1982 what his old community thought of him, his reply was: 'I was asked once to a reception given by the Soviet Cultural Attaché in London, and there I met the Mayor of Nottingham. He didn't want to talk to me. They don't like what I've done.' Revulsion from the squalor and harshness of the old place—a deep-laid sense of its normality and homeliness and vigour: these two clusters of feelings are forever surfacing and going under again in Sillitoe's imagination, heating to boiling-point and dying away again. Working-class Nottingham comprises the gamut of human nature. It is what a free spirit is driven to flee from. Both these 'incompatible' attitudes lie at the root of his vision.

This vision (by which I mean an author's whole sense of the world and its possibilities) abides fairly unchanged through Sillitoe's work for 20 years, from the writing of the episodes that became *Saturday Night and Sunday Morning* to several of the key stories in *Men, Women, and Children* and even the very recent *The Storyteller.* Here is what Dickens might have called a 'keynote' passage from *Saturday Night*:

> And trouble for me it'll be, fighting every day until I die. Why do they make soldiers out of us when we're fighting up to the hilt as it is? Fighting with mothers and wives, landlords and gaffers, coppers, army, government. . . . Born drunk and married blind, misbegotten into a strange and crazy world, dragged-up through the dole and into the war with a gas-mask on your clock, and the sirens rattling into you every night while you rot with scabies in an air-raid shelter. Slung into khaki at eighteen, and when they let you out, you sweat again in a factory, grabbing for an extra pint, doing women at the weekend and getting to know whose husbands are on the night-shift. . . .[2]

This would at once be recognizable as Sillitoe. The prose moves with a headlong energy felt in the impact of the alliteration, the choice of a word like 'rattling' where a kind of heartfelt violence matters more than objective accuracy, the wish to generalize or opinionate which comes out in phrases only just enough removed from cliché to create specific meanings.

Six years after that, in *The Death of William Posters,* Frank Dawley, factory worker on the run from his old life, says to a nurse who takes him in and gives him a meal:

> Most of my mates wanted an easier job, less hours, more pay, naturally. But it wasn't really work they

hated, don't think that. They didn't all want to be doctors or clerks, either. Maybe they just didn't like working in oil and noise, and then going home at night to a plate of sawdust sausages and cardboard beans, and two hours at the flicker-box with advertisements telling them that those sausages and beans burning their guts are the best food in the country. I don't suppose they knew what they wanted in most cases—except maybe not to be treated like cretins.[3]

This is a lucid, considered statement on behalf of his class. A little earlier in the same sequence, it has felt like this from the inside:

> He was on the main road after the soldier's lift, doing ninety and dashing around like a tomcat after its own bollocks, tart wild and pub crazy after a stretch of high-fidelity that he'd stood so long because he was temporarily dead, thinking: 'I go round in circles, as if in some past time I've had a terrible crash, and the more I drive in circles the more I'm bleeding to death. I don't feel this bleeding to death because it's slow and painless (almost as if it's happening to another man and I'm not even looking on, but am reading about it in a letter from a friend hundreds of miles away) but I know it's happening because my eyes get tired and I'm fed up to my spinal marrow, while the old rich marrow I remember is withering and turning black inside me. . . .'[4]

The rough, ribald vernacular ingredient in this is still very much Arthur Seaton but the imagery symbolizing personal depths is more prominent than before and may represent an effort to act on some profound advice that David Storey had offered in a review of *The Ragman's Daughter* two years before:

> In Sillitoe's work there is an ambiguity which is never resolved: the feeling that the revolution he would set up in society is in fact a revolution inside himself, and one which he has not yet acknowledged. Society— 'Them: The Rats'—is his externalising of something inside; a black and subtle aggression directed not against society but more truly against his own experience; his attempt to exorcise some incredible pain out there rather than within himself.[5]

In spite of this, the old ranting and railing at society, to say nothing of the old effort to define the real meanness in it, persists into the stories in *Guzman, Go Home,* especially **'Isaac Starbuck'**:

> He turned north into the patchwork country. A rabbit-hutch bungalow stood for sale in a rabbit-food field. He imagined it worth three thousand pounds. Could get it for a couple of quid after the four-minute warning. Five bob, perhaps, as the owner runs terrified for the woods, hair greying at every step—if I wanted to own property and get a better deal in heaven.
>
> Needle shivering at cold eighty, he felt something like love for the machine under him, the smooth engine swilled and kissed by oil, purring with fuel, cooled by the best water. Out of the rut of family, the trough of drink and the sud-skies of low-roofed factories. . . .[6]

Headlong he rushes past or away from the settled or average life, this hero (for the author allows little to qualify or resist him) who seethes with ungovernable energies that never find a way of gearing themselves to a fulfilling life.

These inseparable elements—the irrepressible urge to tear and break away, the feeling of unfulfilled personal powers—are as present as ever in **Men, Women, and Children,** especially in the earliest story and the latest, **'Before Snow Comes'** (1967) and **'The Chiker'** (1972). Mark, the hero of **'Before Snow Comes,'** hovers, as usual, on the border between settled, domestic life and an outcast limbo: he is divorced, and his love affair with Jean, a married woman, expires in a doomed way. At the core of his nature lies this typically embattled vision:

> He worked at a cabinet-making factory as a joiner, making doors one week and window frames the next, lines of window frames and rows of doors. The band-saws screamed all day from the next department like the greatest banshee thousand-ton atomic bomb rearing for the spot-middle of the earth which seemed to be his brain. Planing machines went like four tank engines that set him looking at the stone wall as if to see it keel towards him for the final flattening, and then the milling machines buzzing around like scout cars searching for the answers to all questions. . . . It was like the Normandy battlefield all over again when he was eighteen, but without death flickering about. Not that noise bothered him, but he often complained to himself of minor irritations, and left the disasters to do their worst. It was like pinching himself to make sure he was alive.[7]

A 'chiker' is a peeping Tom, and Ken, who does the chiking, is a middle-aged man who rankles and smoulders at other people's sexual lives (his daughter and her boyfriend on the settee, young couples on the common at night): 'Maybe all men of his age felt young enough to be their own sons. . . . Now he was in the same boat and felt as if, on his way up through the orphanage and army, marriage and factory, he'd not been allowed to grow older properly like some people he knew.'[8] So he hotches to break out and away, and empathizes with unattached young men going towards the station with luggage in their hands. But he himself is embedded in habitual living (he works as a waste-paper baler in a factory) and his deep-seated conflict between rootedness and escape is caught in the terrific closing sequence where he goes berserk at the canary singing in his living-room, shoves it in its cage onto the fire-grate, and starts to kindle a fire under it. But he lets the match burn his fingers, opens the cage door, and sits there sobbing as the bird stops singing: 'He looked blankly at the bird and the wide open door of its cage, but it seemed as if it would never make a move. It sat on its perch and kept quiet, waiting for him to shut it before beginning its song again.'[9]

So the man (always the man) yearns to escape and harks back to his roots. Only five years ago the urge outwards (or drift south) was still the tendency of **The Storyteller.**

> He didn't know what had got him into such daftness. Telling tales in pubs! And for money? Show your teeth when you laugh like that, you ginger-haired bastard. Donkey-head. He lived a mile away, so the story of his story might not reach home. In any case they would be so drunk at chucking-out time that they wouldn't remember much of what happened by Sunday morning. You live in hope, but you die in squalor. Maybe he'd leave home, and do it in Leicester. Never cack on your own doorstep. Move South to Northampton and, after a week or two at the pubs there, go and cheer up the car workers of Luton, which would be good practice for when he finally chucked himself into London.[10]

This novel, however, strikes me as forced and over-written: few of the story-teller's stories could conceivably be delivered in any actual lounge or public bar; and this is typical of the novels Sillitoe has written in the second part of his life, from **A Tree on Fire** through **A Start in Life** to **The Storyteller.** They tend to be horribly uncertain and fumbling, or lunging, in their touch. The Sillitoe who writes a sort of picaresque thriller set in the Home Counties in **A Start in Life** or a mixture of war novel and celebration of the Great Artist in **A Tree on Fire** no longer seems sure about what level he is working at or what voice to use. Characters are non-credible (e.g. John the mad radio genius in **A Tree on Fire**) even though the mode of the book is still apparently realism, and they are allowed to utter lengthy manifestos or self-advertisements in the guise of lifelike dialogue. When we are most insistently invited to treat them as incarnations of vitality or creativity, we can only back away from their overweening egoism, or the implausibility with which it is dramatized. At the same time—for the past 19 years—he has never set a larger work in his old home community (although he has continued to use it for perfectly sure-footed short stories). The question I will try to answer in this essay is: has Sillitoe failed to make himself at home in any way of life other than his original one? Or to put it another way: are there shortcomings in his talent which can be overlaid by the sheer intimate knowledge of a place and its people but become glaring when he has to rely more on invention and less on memory?

The working class (those who live by the sale of their labour-power and draw no income from surplus-value created by others) make up three-quarters of the population of countries like ours. Yet such is the chronic cultural imbalance that working-class experience has always bulked little in our literature (at least in printed books; in television film and drama things are rather better). Nevertheless, since the later fifties—since the coming-of-age of working-class offspring able to benefit from the results of the 1944 Education Act—the lives of the majority have at last been able to find outstanding imaginative interpreters, especially Sillitoe, David Storey, and Barry Hines.[11] The catch is that a writer's habits, the company he keeps and where he lives, are likely to distance him from his roots and move him into the milieu of the middle and upper-middle class (Census Class II, professional and managerial). This in turn can become the writer's subject but this depends on his or her adaptability. Lawrence, for example, was supremely quick at seizing on the essentials of an alien way of life—what would-be militant critics used to call 'betraying his class.' The examples of Hines and Storey are instructive in another way. Hines has worked steadily in veins known to him from his youth in Barnsley, in the West Riding, from his vision of how an undersized lad from a one-parent family could fulfil himself in his relationship with animals to his most recent novels about young people and women struggling to make a living in a country ridden by slump. For Hines, it *is* a matter of being loyal to a class: he sees it as political work to present the dilemmas and qualities of the unprivileged. Storey is much less political; his interests are more inward and psychological. Yet even he is more strictly focused on his old class— the coalfield workers and their families in the Wakefield area—than is Sillitoe. As recently as *Saville* (1976) Storey was still moved to spend the most detailed attention on the people from the little houses, who bike or bus to work underground—the milieu also of Hines's television plays and novel *The Price of Coal* (1977, 1979). Yet because a miner's child can climb the schooling ladder to a clean and 'respectable' job, Storey has equally shown the precise circumstances, and the strains, of this process, in the later parts of *Saville* and in *Pasmore* (1972). Sillitoe has his own version of this tendency to move out and away; as we have seen, it is never by that usual ladder of GCE passes, further education, and a white-collar job, nor by that other usual ladder or bridge, emigration (unless Frank Dawley's time in Algeria fighting for the FLN counts as that). Arthur Seaton, Isaac Starbuck, Ken the Chiker itch to take off (but never do) through a sheer chafing at the programmed life. No social path appears to open out before them. The most ambitious and sustained break-out, Frank Dawley's in the 'Bill Posters' trilogy, is purely lonely: he grafts a solidarity with the oppressed people of Algeria onto his inner escapism: 'You worked with those at the bottom in order to be reborn.'[12]

This contrast between Sillitoe and the others applies also to his view of the old home community. For Hines, it is simply there: his unblinking naturalism presents the life of the housing estates and the working men's clubs as just a mixture like any other, although we can infer a cutting-edge of solidarity with the workers from the advantage given to the anti-Royal wit of the miners in *The Price of Coal* and the undeceived dourness with which George Purse looks after his gentleman at the grouse shoot in *The Gamekeeper* (1975). For Storey the old home community is a milieu in which people (miners and their wives) have settled for half, in which they have, often literally, lain down under cramped and mean conditions and to some extent lost the power of living fully as a result.[13]

By contrast, Sillitoe has a much heartier relish and a more settled appreciativeness for the ordinary urban way of life than Hines or Storey. He also turns against it more bitterly. These 'incompatible' attitudes must now be looked into more closely.

Sillitoe's appreciation for the big Midland city in all its sprawl and shabbiness comes out at its purest in the well-being that all kinds of characters repeatedly feel when they are at home in it, for example Arthur Seaton just before being beaten up by Jack's soldier mates:

> His footsteps led between trade-marked houses, two up and two down, with digital chimneys like pigs' tits on the rooftops sending up heat and smoke into the cold trough of a windy sky. . . . Winter was an easy time for him to hide his secrets, for each dark street patted his shoulder and became a friend, and the gaseous eye of each lamp glowed unwinking as he passed. Houses lay in rows and ranks, a measure of safety in such numbers, and those within were snug and grateful fugitives from the broad track of bleak winds that brought rain from the Derbyshire mountains and snow from the Lincolnshire Wolds.[14]

In the most basic way the city is a shelter against the elements, and though Arthur's well-being here is inseparable from his sexual contentment, the environment is still crucial to his state of mind, as it is towards the end when the summer routine of fishing along the nearby canal bodies forth his ease in the coming marriage with Doreen:

> Another solitary man was fishing further along the canal, but Arthur knew that they would leave each other in peace, would not even call out greetings. No one bothered you: you were a hunter, a dreamer, your own boss, away from it all for a few hours on any day that the weather did not throw down its rain. Like the corporal in the army who said it was marvellous the things you thought about as you sat on the lavatory.[15]

In such places we feel—and it is a very rare feeling to get from literature—that the main protagonist can at the same time be both himself and part of the urban social norm. He doesn't necessarily have to separate himself from the mundane and average to be himself, to be fulfilled. Almost the opposite is true of all the other protagonists in this line of writing, from Paul Morel in *Sons and Lovers* to Pasmore and Saville, and Billy Casper in Hines's *A Kestrel for a Knave*.

This ability to be at ease in the city is not simplistic or sentimental on Sillitoe's part. In a fine early story, **'The Fishing-Boat Picture,'** the postman is presented throughout as comfortable in a dull way, not much bothered when his wife walks out on him, phlegmatically willing to welcome her back for weekly evening visits when her lover has died, and this is figured in the calm townscape mid-way through the story:

> I was at home, smoking my pipe in the backyard at the fag-end of an autumn day. The sky was a clear yellow, going green above the house-tops and wireless aerials. Chimneys were just beginning to send out evening smoke, and most of the factory motors had been switched off. The noise of kids scooting around lamp-posts and the barking of dogs came from what sounded a long way off.[16]

But Sillitoe knows the limitations of this readiness to make do, and when the postman has not quite been able to bring himself to invite her back, he senses his mistake and is left realizing (after her accidental early death) that he has failed:

> I began to believe there was no point in my life— became even too far gone to turn religious or go on the booze. Why had I lived? I wondered. I can't see anything for it. . . .
>
> I was born dead, I keep telling myself. Everybody's dead, I answer. So they are, I maintain, but then most of them never know it like I'm beginning to do. . . . Yes, I cry, but neither of us *did anything about it,* and that's the trouble.[17]

Sillitoe's people are workers to the core—not token or courtesy workers or abstract human natures with a few proletarian trimmings. They can at times feel their work to be part of themselves, as in a natural moment like this from **'Before Snow Comes'**:

> He would get clean steel nails and set out those laths and offshoot wasted planks from the trunks of great trees that he got cheap because one of his mates worked there, and brush off the sawdust lovingly from each one, feeling it collect like the wooden gold-dust of life in the palm of his hands and sift between the broad flesh of his lower fingers.[18]

Here Mark is working for himself, or for Jean (it is her garden), but his feeling for materials and processes springs from his whole working life and it is a feeling which in places grows outwards to the extent of making us feel that a person can be at home in a factory—can overcome the alienating effects of divided labour and distant management. At times this seems willed—done more to enforce a doctrine than to express something the author knows and is sure of from the bottom of himself, as when Frank argues with Myra in **The Death of William Posters**: "'All I believe in is houses and factories, food and power-stations, bridges and coalmines and death, turning millions of things out on a machine that people can use, people who also turn out millions of things that other people can use. It's no use harping back to poaching rights and cottage industries.'"[19] Is this not too flatly asserted as speech, too void of character or idiom? The same stiffness comes over the style when Frank, in the Algerian desert, likens his belonging to the freedom fighters' war-machine to his first experience of turning a metal part to the specifications on a blueprint, or when Brian at the end of **Key to the Door** looks forward to working in the same engineering shop as his dad and going to union meetings in the evening.[20] The test is in the quality of the language, and in this respect the long passage presenting the start of Arthur's week in the bicycle factory seems to me faultless:

> Arthur reached his capstan lathe and took off his jacket, hanging it on a nearby nail so that he could keep an eye on his belongings. He pressed the starter button, and his motor came to life with a gentle thump. Looking around, it did not seem, despite the infernal noise of hurrying machinery, that anyone was working with particular speed. He smiled to himself and picked up a glittering steel cylinder from the top box of a pile beside him, and fixed it into the spindle. He jettisoned his cigarette into the sud-pan, drew back the capstan, and swung the turret into its broadest drill. Two minutes passed while he contemplated the precise position of tools and cylinder; finally he spat onto both hands and rubbed them together, then switched on the sud-tap from the movable brass pipe, pressed a button that set the spindle running, and ran in the drill to a neat chamfer. Monday morning had lost its terror.[21]

This is the first passage I know of in our literature (nearly two centuries after the first power-loom was patented!) which evokes a factory-worker's experiences from the inside with the finesse that writers have given to all the others in the human range. The emotion suggested in the course of a very practical or technical passage is pleasure in the way things are and in being adept at them. The passage persuades me that a lively and feeling person can find that his own prowess or physical—mental needs are satisfied, at least for a time, by that industrial job. For five or six generations, since the start of the industrial revolution, our writers had figured the factory as Hell.[22] And certainly the full-fledged forms of mass production, on the moving assembly-line, make up a fairly monstrous system; the experience many Ford car workers have of it is summed up in sentences like 'The line here is made for morons' or 'Wind me up at 8 a.m. and that's that.'[23] But there are jobs and jobs within the factory. 'The factory' is no more to be stereotyped, as though it was all one and the same, than are 'the home' or 'marriage.' It is a vast theatre of the most various human skills and experiences. To do it justice we need, not a single black or blank stereotype (Hell), but a complicated picture rich in evidence from the grassroots.

Sillitoe is equivocal about these roots and tends to deny their relevance to his work. In an introduction he wrote for an edition of **Saturday Night and Sunday Morning** he refers to the 'so-called "working-class"' and goes on to say:

> The greatest inaccuracy was ever to call the book a 'working-class novel' for it is really nothing of the sort. It is simply a novel, and the label given it by most reviewers at the time it came out, even the intelligent ones who should have known better, was simply a way of categorizing a piece of work they weren't capable of assessing from their narrow class standpoint.[24]

Partly this is the resentment of a young writer at the patronage of people surprised that a novelist could spring from a line of factory workers. But only two years ago he could still write:

> I was amused when reviewers and journalists referred to me as a 'working-class' novelist. In spite of the stage on which I set many of my novels and stories I had ceased to be connected to that part of life from the moment I enlisted in the RAF. Before that time I hadn't heard the phrase, and wouldn't have known what it meant. Then when I became a writer I simply did what any other novelist does, which is to use the first 18 years of his or her life in order to begin writing novels and stories.[25]

To this, I believe, we have to answer 'Never trust the artist. Trust the tale,' and the tale of Sillitoe's worth trusting above any other I take to be **'The Good Women.'** It was first published in the *Daily Worker* from 26 May to 2 June 1962 and then (with significant small softenings of wording) in **The Ragman's Daughter.** One of its many strengths is that it centres on a character quite distinct from the author—an ordinary working-class mother—whereas in much of his fiction it is only the man, the impatient, overweening, anarchic man, who is fully created and the other characters are a foil to him. Liza Atkin is a woman learning to be militant. Her first experience shaped by politics comes over to her as purely personal: her elder son is killed in the Korean war by an American plane spreading napalm meant for the Communist lines near by. Her dogged sanity shows in her refusal to be funereal about him: 'Liza came down the street next day with a loaf of bread in her hand, biting a piece off now and again. . . . Months later Liza was walking along a lane near Wollaton, and remembered how, at the beginning of the war, Harry and Alf had been evacuated to Workshop. Harry had been sick all the way there on the bus, and she laughed now to think about it.' But she faces her pain squarely: 'Korea was a world, a word, as far off now as somebody else's dream, that had killed Harry, called him up and bombed him to ashes for no good reason, like when you have too many kittens you dunk some in a copper. It wasn't necessary, it was wrong, the bad thing to do.' When it thunders, she projects her rage into the storm: 'I don't know who to blame, she thought, but go on, rip and claw the effing world to pieces. Tear up that bleddy town, sling it to hell.'

Again the story is rare in Sillitoe's work in that Liza finds an outlet for her personal anguish: it transmutes into militancy. When she goes to work in the bike factory, she shows her independence by refusing to be a soft touch when a shop steward assumes he can recruit her for the union without even a minute's explanation, but when a strike is called against being put on short time, she exults in it because 'it was a way of doing damage to those who bossed the world about'—and because the best rank-and-file speaker at the meeting and the march reminds her of her dead son.

He makes two speeches, and they are crucial. Unlike any other political speeches in fiction (most notably the red-dawn rhetoric in Upton Sinclair's *The Jungle*), they are very well written, whether as trenchant expressions of a viewpoint or as dramatic imitations of public speaking in a vernacular:

> 'Well, they can give us that we want in this dispute (and they will, make no mistakes about it) and they can give us a raise when we force the boggers to it, but as far as I'm concerned, it'll be like them smallpox jabs I had. It wain't take. It's not a raise here and a bit of an improvement there that we want—none of it'll take. It's a whole bloody change'—his wide-apart fists gave a slow forceful turning motion as if at the wheel of some great ship and making a violent alteration in its course—'a turnover from top to bottom. . . .'

As the main narrative comes to an end, the prose balances wonderfully between evoking this particular woman's thoughts and a slightly more impersonal vision which gives us, more convincingly and clearly than anything else I know in the literature of our time, a definition of the impasse, the locked-up potential, which exists in our world:

> 'I knew we'd get what we wanted,' Liza said, exulting before those along the bench at how she had marched downtown with 2,000 men, as if inviting them to tease and remind her of it as often as they liked. Yet she felt that the strike had never really ended, that such a downing of tools meant little because instead of coming back to work they should have stayed out solid and gone on from there.

> Something other than the mere petty end of an industrial dispute lay beyond them, the half-felt, intangible presence of an abyss that needed crossing for everything to be settled once and for all. They had had enough, but Liza, passing the thousands of components through her gauges at the bench, recalled the tall young man speaking on the first day of the walk-out, and knew that he and many others scattered through the factory also considered that something else was in front of them, a great space of freedom and change not too far beyond the feet and eyes.[26]

To write so well about 'that part of life,' you cannot have 'ceased to be connected' with it. Your line through to it must be clear and many-fibred, even though it now consists of memories, language-habits, and, presumably, surviving family relationships, and not any longer of actual membership. Sillitoe's own wisest thoughts on the class question, at the level of explicit comment, occur in the Author's Note to **Men, Women, and Children** where he writes:

> I again use Nottingham and its county as my stage, though it is unnecessary to point out that the breadth of activity, of movement and suffering, is as intense and deep when undergone by the people on this stage as on any other . . . emotions have to be delineated in the minds of people who are not usually prone to describing them. The same emotions and feelings are of course felt by them as by more voluble and literate people. . . . [They] have the same sufferings as kings and queens, but their daily problems are more fundamental and tormenting.[27]

He has also said that the great problem for a writer starting out is 'to remain true to what he has'[28] and on the evidence of his work we have to say that what he has is an undying imaginative participation in the lives of the people he lived amongst for his first 19 years. It is because these were working-class people that it is necessary, and not misleading, to call him a working-class writer.

In **Men, Women, and Children** Sillitoe also says that 'Those complicated people who are less down to earth are in many ways easier to describe, or at least no more difficult.' His own practice suggests that for him this is actually not so. I question whether he has ever successfully created a character from the middle or upper-middle class. Yet his later novels have, inevitably, taken him in that direction. At the same time he has been trying out veins of boisterous, not to say frantic, picaresque. The result is this kind of image of artists, intellectuals, media people, and other types from 'Home Counties, Census Class II':

> One crumby pub was bunged up to the gills, but along the bar was a face I'd seen before. . . . He was a tall man, dressed in a high-necked sweater and an expensive tweed jacket, the sort of casual gear that must have cost far more than a good suit. His face was, I suppose, sensitive because of the thick lips, putty skin, and pale eyes. He wore a hat, but in spite of this I was struck by the length of his face and head, which did not however make him as ugly as it should have done. . . . it was sharp-eyed June who told me he was a writer by the name of Gilbert Blaskin.

This writer's conversation consists exclusively of far-fetched drivel, monologues elaborating the plot of his 'latest novel' and the like, and after one such sequence the hero (a refugee from the Midland working class, of course) puts him down as follows: 'I got up and put the coffee back on the stove, while he chewed the fat of his insane liver that lived off the fat of the land. I wished I'd been working in a factory so that I could have told him to belt up and get some real work done.'[29]

My criticism of this kind of thing is that it is too approximate and the authorial prompting too browbeating. Sillitoe doesn't have the satirist's gift of letting us see the precise features of the original just under the deformities of the cartoon. Whenever he touches at all on the lives of the white-collared, he is driven to violent caricature. This disfigures the whole part of the 'Bill Posters' trilogy which is set in England, particularly amongst the family of Albert Handley, the Great Painter, who stands for anarchic creativity. His wife's haranguing of a visiting Sunday-paper journalist is typical:

> 'There are some people to whom being an out-and-out bastard gives strength. Oh, I don't mean the weedy or puffy sort who never have the strength to be real bastards anyway, like you. But I mean the man who, not strong in the beginning, like Albert, soon finds himself becoming so when he gets money, and the *urge to be a swine gets into his blood*.'[30]

The context leaves us in no doubt that the Handleys embody Life, as against the half-life of almost everybody else, and the author tries to equip them with radical credentials which will complete their image as the last word in fearless authentic living. None of this has the least reality: Handley's eldest son, Richard (one of seven children), is at one point supposed to be sending the plans of 'secret bases' to Moscow rolled in a bundle of *New Statesmans*.[31] Satirist's licence? Yet, throughout, the Handleys triumph much too easily for us to feel that they are in any way placed or qualified by their creator. The feeling is that they embody what he has now come to be himself—a part of privileged, successful England yet still hankering to defy and discredit it.

The lesson would seem to be that if you are to do so, you must at least have become, imaginatively, master of the middle-class milieu in which you now find yourself. One touchstone for this is Storey: as we have seen, he has gone on cleaving more closely to his old class than has Sillitoe, yet when he has needed to present the owners, managers, and rulers, his touch has been unerring. Consider the subtlety with which the manipulations of Weaver, the works owner and rugby club director in *This Sporting Life*, are evoked by physical and dramatic means.[32] Or think of the truly sinister power (created by terse, low-key writing from which violent moments erupt) of those twin figures, Helen's husband in *Pasmore* and Newman in *A Temporary Life* (1973). Both are 'self-made men' (counterparts of Claud Moggerhanger in *A Start in Life*): without the least strain or excess Storey is able to establish them as black presences below the surface of the business world—representatives of those club-owners and property dealers who have taken recently to funding the British fascist parties, setting up connections with the Mafia-based drug trade, and so on.

The most complete touchstone is Lawrence—from the same part of England as Sillitoe, making the same moves as his career blossomed, earning the same equivocal standing in his old community. Lawrence shows a valuable self-knowledge in the letter where he remarks on one of his own working-class qualities, as he sees it, a 'jeering and purpleism,' which are also common in Sillitoe but given free rein, not understood self-critically. Both men curse strait-laced, habit-bound England in very similar terms so far as explicit comment goes. But here the resemblance ends. Lawrence feels to be as at home when he is characterizing the 'well-bred' intellectuals, mine-owners, and hostesses in *Women in Love,* for example, as he is when he is evoking the shabby-genteel life of Ursula and Gudrun's parents. Again, when he moves amongst the London smart set and their horse-riding county friends in *St. Mawr,* he is able to dramatize them satirically while not deforming or diminishing their reality as persons; he writes about this milieu with decisive sardonic criticism but not with animus (Leavis's valuable distinction[33]). For example, with that caricature of Gilbert Blaskin in *A Start in Life* compare this image of Rico, the dilettante painter son of an Australian baronet, being got at by his dissatisfied young wife ('moderately rich . . . Louisiana family, moved down to Texas'):

> 'Rico dear, you must get a horse.'

> The tone was soft and southern and drawling, but the overtone had a decisive finality. In vain Rico squirmed—he had a way of writhing and squirming which perhaps he had caught at Oxford. In vain he protested that he couldn't ride, and that he didn't care for riding. He got quite angry, and his handsome arched nose tilted and his upper lip lifted from his teeth, like a dog that is going to bite. Yet daren't quite bite.

> And that was Rico. He daren't quite bite. Not that he was really afraid of the others. He was afraid of himself, once he let himself go. He might rip up in an

eruption of life-long anger all this pretty-pretty picture of a charming young wife and a delightful little home and a fascinating success as a painter of fashionable, and at the same time 'great,' portraits: with colour, wonderful colour, and at the same time, form, marvellous form. He had composed this little *tableau vivant* with great effort. He didn't want to erupt like some suddenly wicked horse. . . .[34]

Lawrence is able to conceive of such a person psychologically even while he places him satirically as a social being. For Sillitoe, people from outside his old home community are nearly always butts. And this connects with the spasms of aggression when he tries to get Them in his sights—his gun-sights.[35] In spite of such violent squaring-up, and the constant use of 'Communism' like an incantation (no main character is ever a Communist but the cousins and uncles, off-stage, often are), it is very rare for Sillitoe to present a substantial conflict between Us and Them. (The clearly articulated industrial dispute in **'The Good Women'** is an exception, as is the Algeria section of the Frank Dawley trilogy). The more rebellious of the Us people are therefore left to fulminate in a kind of vacuum—to pedal round and round in the cycles of their rage without their energy being geared to anything much outside themselves. And Sillitoe seems not to know this clearly enough, which gives rise to the wild swipes at the white-collared and also to a great deal of overblown phrase-making, mixed metaphors, a diarrhoea of adjectives: as Storey puts it in that important early review, 'whenever passion fails, it's the words themselves that unsuccessfully he tries to whip along.'

The final thoughts of that review remain hard to dissent from, even though Sillitoe has produced another 20 years' work since then:

> Continually it's suggested that society alone inspires rebellion without any awareness that we are condemned to find in society very much of what we wish to find there. . . . If one is increasingly exasperated by Sillitoe's beating at those out there rather than at the thing inside it is because his particular pain—the agony that runs like an underground torrent through *Saturday Night and Sunday Morning*—is one that is so important and yet one that is rapidly being sentimentalised. He has shown us his gesture, and we've seen it; now let us hear the cry within.[36]

My own review of *A Start in Life* 14 years ago arrived at a kindred point when it said that Sillitoe's talent 'may fray itself out for good unless he now makes himself become less headlong in his output, perhaps by holding back from easy identification with the rogue male and by weighing up more thoughtfully what it is that he has against our present way of life.'[37] I still hope that he may try to explore the deeper, more psychological levels of experience, bosses' as well as workers,' in the industrial community with the intensity that he has been so good at focusing on its more outward incidents and characters.

Notes

1. Alan Sillitoe, *Key to the Door* (London, W. H. Allen, 1961), p. 241.

2. Alan Sillitoe, *Saturday Night and Sunday Morning* (London, W. H. Allen, 1958), p. 213.

3. Alan Sillitoe, *The Death of William Posters* (London, W. H. Allen, 1965), p. 44.

4. *Op. cit.,* p. 34.

5. David Storey, 'Which revolution?,' *The Guardian* (18 October 1963).

6. 'Isaac Starbuck,' in Alan Sillitoe, *Guzman, Go Home* (London, Pan Books, 1970), p. 114.

7. 'Before Snow Comes,' in Alan Sillitoe, *Men, Women, and Children* (London, W. H. Allen, 1973), p. 68.

8. 'The Chiker,' in Sillitoe, *Men, Women, and Children,* p. 146.

9. *Op. cit.,* p. 155.

10. Alan Sillitoe, *The Storyteller* (London, W. H. Allen, 1980), p. 37.

11. See my 'Sillitoe and the Roots of Anger,' in David Craig, *The Real Foundations* (London, Chatto and Windus, 1973), pp. 270–1, 277–9.

12. Alan Sillitoe, *A Tree on Fire* (London, W. H. Allen, 1979), p. 151.

13. See David Craig, 'David Storey's Vision of the Working Class,' in Douglas Jefferson and Graham Martin, eds., *The Uses of Fiction* (Milton Keynes, The Open University Press, 1982), pp. 126–9, 135–7.

14. Sillitoe, *Saturday Night,* p. 163.

15. *Op. cit.,* p. 210.

16. 'The Fishing-boat Picture,' in Alan Sillitoe, *The Loneliness of the Long-Distance Runner* (London, W. H. Allen, 1959), p. 85.

17. *Op. cit.,* pp. 94, 99.

18. Sillitoe, *Men, Women, and Children,* p. 67.

19. Sillitoe, *William Posters,* p. 259.

20. Sillitoe, *Tree on Fire,* p. 192; *Key to the Door,* pp. 444–5.

21. Sillitoe, *Saturday Night,* pp. 28–9.

22. See David Craig, 'Images of Factory Life,' *Gulliver II* 11 (1977), pp. 100–1; Craig, 'The Crowd in Dickens,' in Robert Giddings, ed., *The Changing World of Charles Dickens* (London, Vision Press, 1983), p. 87.

23. Huw Beynon, *Working for Ford* (London, Allen Lane/Penguin Education, 1973), pp. 114, 119.

24. Alan Sillitoe, *Saturday Night and Sunday Morning,* ed. David Craig (London, Longman, 1968), pp. viii, xii.

25. Alan Sillitoe, 'Writing and Publishing,' *London Review of Books* (1–14 April 1982).

26. Quoted from both versions: *Daily Worker* (26 May–2 June); Alan Sillitoe, *The Ragman's Daughter* (London, W. H. Allen, 1963), pp. 169–72, 182, 185–6.

27. Sillitoe, *Men, Women, and Children,* p. 10.

28. Special Correspondent, 'Alan Sillitoe,' *The Times* (6 February 1964).

29. Alan Sillitoe, *A Start in Life* (London, W. H. Allen, 1970), pp. 173, 184.

30. Sillitoe, *Tree on Fire,* p. 27.

31. *Op. cit.,* p. 41.

32. See Craig, 'Hear Them Talking To You,' in *The Real Foundations,* pp. 266–8.

33. F. R. Leavis, *D. H. Lawrence: Novelist* (London, Chatto and Windus, 1955), p. 276.

34. 'St Mawr,' in *The Tales of D. H. Lawrence* (London, Heinemann, 1934), pp. 561–2.

35. Sillitoe, *Saturday Night,* pp. 134–5; *The Loneliness of the Long-Distance Runner,* p. 33; *William Posters,* p. 315: 'The kick at his shoulder was the joy of life.'

36. Storey, 'Which revolution?.'

37. *The Times Literary Supplement* (14 September 1970).

Note

I list below books which include treatments of the working class by the principal authors discussed in the body of my article.

Patrick MacGill, *Children of the Dead End* (Dingle, Co. Kerry, Brandon Books, 1982; first published London, Herbert Jenkins, 1914).

Patrick MacGill, *Moleskin Joe* (London, Caliban Books, 1983; first published London, Herbert Jenkins, 1923).

Patrick MacGill, *The Rat-Pit* (Dingle, Co. Kerry, Brandon Books, 1982; first published London, Herbert Jenkins, 1915).

Michael McLaverty, *Call My Brother Back* (Swords, Co. Dublin, Poolbeg Press, 1979; first published London, Jonathan Cape, 1939).

Michael McLaverty, *Lost Fields* (Swords, Co. Dublin, Poolbeg Press, 1980; first published London, Longman, 1942).

Frank O'Connor (pseud. of Michael O'Donovan), *Collected Stories* (New York, Knopf, 1981).

Frank O'Connor, *Collection Three* (London, Macmillan, 1969).

Frank O'Connor, *Collection Two* (London, Macmillan, 1964).

Frank O'Connor, *The Cornet Player Who Betrayed Ireland and Other Stories* (Swords, Co. Dublin, Poolbeg Press, 1981).

Frank O'Connor, *An Only Child* (London, Macmillan: Knopf, New York, 1961).

Frank O'Connor, *The Saint and Mary Kate* (London, Macmillan, 1932).

Frank O'Connor, *The Stories of Frank O'Connor* (London, Hamish Hamilton, 1953).

James Stephens, *The Charwoman's Daughter* (Dublin, Gill and Macmillan, 1972; first published London. Macmillan, 1912).

James Stephens, 'Hunger,' in *Desire and Other Stories* (Swords, Co. Dublin, Poolbeg Press, 1981; first published as a booklet under the pseudonym 'James Esse,' Dublin, The Candle Press, 1918. Included in *Etched in Moonlight,* London, Macmillan, 1928).

Alan Sillitoe with Joyce Rothschild (interview date 24 April 1985)

SOURCE: "The Growth of a Writer: An Interview with Alan Sillitoe," in *Southern Humanities Review,* Vol. 20, No. 2, Spring, 1986, pp. 127–40.

[*In the following interview, Sillitoe discusses his creative process as well as the primary influences on his work.*]

Alan Sillitoe, recognized as one of England's foremost living writers, was born in 1928 in Nottingham, England, and grew up there in impoverished circumstances. His father was a tannery worker, often unemployed, who could neither read nor write. During the 1930s, in the worst years of the depression, the five Sillitoe children often went hungry, and the family moved from one overcrowded slum dwelling to another. At the age of fourteen, Alan Sillitoe left school to work in the Raleigh Bicycle Factory. Protesting what he considered an unfair wage, he quit the bicycle factory after a few months and moved on to a series of other factory jobs. In 1946, not quite eighteen years old, he joined the Royal Air Force and served as a radio operator in Malaya for two years.

Sillitoe contracted tuberculosis in Malaya and was forced to recuperate in a military hospital for sixteen months. By the time he received his military discharge (in 1950), he had decided to become a writer. Moving first to France and then to the Spanish island of Majorca, he spent the next eight years mastering his craft, working on both poetry and fiction.

His first success came in 1958 with the publication of *Saturday Night and Sunday Morning,* which received the British Authors' Club Prize. The publication of a short story collection, *The Loneliness of the Long-Distance Runner,* followed in 1959. It too won critical acclaim. Within the next several years, the successful films based on these two works brought fame to Sillitoe in the United

States as well as in England and increased the number of readers interested in his work.

Sillitoe left Majorca in 1958 to resume residence in England. He now lives in Kent with his wife, the American-born poet Ruth Fainlight. A prolific writer, Sillitoe has produced fourteen novels in the last twenty-five years, as well as four collections of short stories, six books of poetry, and a collection of essays. Sillitoe's recent works have received mixed reviews in the United States, but in Great Britain and throughout Europe his writing has continued to excite readers and earn the praise of literary critics.

At the time Alan Sillitoe first came to public notice, he was seen as one of "Britain's angry young men," a group of 1950s writers that included the playwright John Osborne and the novelists John Braine, John Wain, and Kingsley Amis. Called "angry" because of the hostility toward social institutions and norms that was evident in their work, these writers tended to be identified in the public mind with the disorderly young working-class males they had created as fictional protagonists. In the years following the 1950s, these writers—each an important figure on the British literary scene—pursued decidedly different goals. Today, in some ways, Sillitoe may be seen as the most clearly proletarian of them all; although his concerns have broadened and deepened, he remains an eloquent spokesman for the British laboring classes. Nor is his anger at certain forms of institutionalized oppression very much abated.

Yet, in Sillitoe's case, any simple description of allegiance is deceptive. His fiction affords a critical view of many working-class values. Furthermore, his commitment to individualism both in his life and in his work overrides the promptings of class loyalty. Like another product of Nottingham, D. H. Lawrence, Sillitoe in his fiction depicts characters developing "consciousness" and thereby facing up to their own individuality. For him, as for Lawrence, the ultimate truths of existence are to be found in the individual psyche and—in particular—in the wellsprings of desire that are located in the unconscious. For Sillitoe's protagonists, some measure of freedom comes almost inevitably as soon as the individual breaks through the barriers to psychic self-knowledge. With that freedom comes a rejection of restrictive group identifications.

In keeping with his individualistic commitment, Sillitoe's most defiant public action was to refuse to comply with the British census of 1971—a symbolic act of protest against governmental infringement of privacy, for which he was prepared to go to jail (although, as it happened, he received a fine instead). Over the years, Sillitoe has steadfastly refused to become part of the British establishment.

Looking back over Alan Sillitoe's impressive body of work, one can now see Arthur Seaton, the young trouble-making factory worker who is the protagonist of ***Saturday Night and Sunday Morning,*** as a type that recurs as a secondary character in later novels. Seaton begins as a charming rogue, but by the novel's end we find his spunky recalcitrance reduced to timid respectability. Twenty years ago critics were struck by this novel's socioeconomic determinism—viewed one way, Arthur Seaton is emasculated by a society that denies him any access to power. Yet one sees today that the novel may be read another way. In this second view, Seaton acquiesces too readily in the conditions that circumscribe his life. In Sillitoe's more recent fiction, the characters who are worthy of our respect manage to alter circumstances that they find to be untenable.

The precursor of Sillitoe's later individualist heroes is Colin Smith, the teenage-thief-turned-athlete described in the title story of the collection ***The Loneliness of the Long-Distance Runner.*** In that story, the plot turns on the emergence of "consciousness"—a combined physical, emotional, intellectual, and moral awareness—coming almost inevitably to a character who has become attuned (through long-distance running) to his body and psyche. Smith's refusal to win the race that others have trained him for and his opting to remain an outlaw are (in the context of the story) morally justifiable decisions. However, Colin Smith is not granted an enlarged perspective that might have enabled him to move freely in the world. In contrast, the male protagonists in such subsequent works as ***The Death of William Posters*** (1965), ***The Widower's Son*** (1976), ***The Storyteller*** (1979), and ***Down from the Hill*** (1984) do gain a widened perspective and are thereby empowered to move beyond the confines of working-class existence.

One of this author's strengths has been his ability to create complex, compelling female characters. It is thus not surprising that his 1982 novel with a woman as the central figure reveals Sillitoe at the peak of his descriptive and plot-generating powers. This novel, ***Her Victory,*** presents a complicated, but essentially affirmative view of male-female relationships. He is currently at work on another novel.

The interview recorded below took place at Auburn, Alabama, on April 24, 1985, in relaxed, informal circumstances.

[*Joyce Rothschild:*] *Mr. Sillitoe, some years ago you were cited (in the book on you by Allen Penner) as thinking of yourself as primarily a poet rather than a writer of fiction. Would you say the same thing about yourself today?*

[Alan Sillitoe:] I started writing poetry first as a very young man, and I continue to write poetry. But I suppose it doesn't meet all the needs of my psyche, and that's why I find myself writing fiction as well. I am a bit fearful of inquiring too deeply into my motives for writing—I don't want to know too much about my unconscious. However, I trust it as the source of whatever it is that makes me a writer.

Can you tell me something about how you began writing?

In a way, it was an accident, a result of my coming down with tuberculosis when I was stationed in Malaya as a young man in the Air Force. I was forced into the hospital and had to lie still for about a year. It was then that I began to read—of course I had read as a child, but I mean that now I began to read seriously and to think about what I was reading. I read everything I could get my hands on that year, starting with a translation of *The Odyssey,* which was the first thing I happened to take off the book trolley in the hospital. I didn't know anything about Homer, but I was enthralled by the story, so I asked if that fellow Homer had written anything else, and of course I was given *The Iliad.* I went on to Sophocles, Terence, and Greek and Roman history. All of this I read in the hospital that year when I was twenty. That reading changed my view of the world. As a consequence, I decided that I would try to be a writer. I had wanted a career in aviation, but now because of the tuberculosis I couldn't have that, and had to find something else to do. I was discharged from the Air Force with a small pension (enough to live on if one were very frugal), and I spent the next nine years or so living as frugally as I could—which in those days meant going abroad. I lived first in southern France and then in Majorca. During that time I read nearly everything that was worth reading, and I began to write, both poetry and fiction. Robert Graves, who was a famous poet by that time, was also living in Majorca. After I showed him some of my poems, he encouraged me to continue writing.

What have been the major influences on your fiction?

My early fiction was more or less a mixture of Aldous Huxley, D. H. Lawrence, and Dostoevsky—it was not very good, terribly derivative. I destroyed all that early work. But it was important for me to write all that in order to exorcise those influences and find my own voice. I keep the Bible by my bed, and I am always reading it, for the beauty of the prose. I also keep by my bed a book called *A Treasury of Yiddish Stories,* which my wife's father sent me as a gift many years ago. The stories in that book have been a great influence on my writing. I admire especially the Yiddish tales of Israel Joshua Singer (the brother of Isaac Bashevis Singer) and his great novel, *The Brothers Ashkenazi.* The Yiddish stories taught me a lot about the possibilities of storytelling. I learned from them that you don't have to follow a linear progression. You can wander a bit, which is more my style.

Have you been particularly influenced by any other authors?

Most of the books I read as a child were the usual juvenile fare, adventure stories that were not especially memorable. But I recall reading over and over again *Les Misérables,* by Victor Hugo. Something spoke to me in that book about the condition of my existence. Later, when I was a young man and had begun to write, I read D. H. Lawrence's novel *The Rainbow,* which is set in Nottinghamshire, where

I grew up. It was a revelation to me to read a book that was about places I knew. It suddenly occurred to me that I could write about my own life rather than write adventure stories that were impossibly romantic and had nothing to do with life as I knew it.

What is it that leads you to write a particular story?

I always start with a character. I become interested in a certain character, who might be inspired by a real person I know or sometimes a relative I have been told stories about. Sometimes I build the character on a fleeting glimpse of a person I saw only once. For instance some years ago my imagination was captured by the face of a woman of about forty whom I saw one day walking down the Portobello Road, near my home in London. Her face was not beautiful, but it interested me; she looked as though she was going through some sort of crisis. I began to imagine what sort of experiences had brought her to that particular part of London at the time I saw her, and out of that process of imagination came a novel, *Her Victory,* in which she was the central character.

I usually do not plan out a novel more than a chapter at a time. If you do that, there's more opportunity for spontaneity, that is, for allowing unexpected things to happen. Spontaneous things that happen are more truly representative of human nature than anything you might force in a story to make events follow a certain line. I may begin with an idea of how a story will end, but that idea will often change through what the characters have taught me.

You've often been considered a political writer. Do you consider that you write from a political perspective?

Well, the short answer is no. I've thought a lot about it, and one or two stories I've written directly from a political point of view, and in fact I don't think they have been very successful. One of them is a story called **"Pit Strike,"** which was based on the 1974 coalminers' strike in England. **"Pit Strike"** was in a book called *Men, Women, and Children*; the story was later made into a television film. The other story I think of as political is **"The Good Women,"** which appears in a book called *The Ragman's Daughter.* But, with possibly those exceptions, I have always refused to be drawn into politics. I think it's fatal for a writer or any artist. This is not to say that George Woodcock [a British-Canadian writer on political themes] and others like him are too political. I'm saying that it's not for me. If I tried to further a political cause by writing fiction, I would not get the best out of myself. It's a matter of expediency, really, almost as much as belief.

I'd like to follow up with a somewhat political question. Do you think the class system in England is going to last?

The class system in England is probably as solid as it ever was. I think it's the last thing that will go. As England sinks into the ocean, there will be a flag on top, the emblem of the class system—it'll be the last thing to go down. I don't say that on the glib assumption that it's a bad thing necessarily. It has a lot of charm, a rather cozy feeling for a lot of people. Not for me because I have never felt part of it. When I was a child in my sort of ghetto, I didn't realize that any other class existed, so I couldn't care about a class system. Then I went into the factory, where class doesn't exist—you simply work. It's mind-deadening work, and you're selling yourself for what you earn. When I went into the Air Force, there was a hierarchy, but not class. You were judged according to your accomplishments. When I came out of the Air Force, I had a pension and went to live as an expatriate in France and Spain.

So the class system never really crossed my consciousness. It comes into my work simply because it is in other people's lives about whom I write, but it never worried me. But I think the English people love it. If they didn't love it, they wouldn't have it, you know. I think it's there to stay. All I can say is good luck to them.

As you know, you've been characterized as an "angry" writer, one of the "angry young men." Would you comment on that?

I've never thought of myself as angry, particularly. In fact, I never write when I'm angry, or sad, or happy. I like to write when I'm feeling dispassionate and detached—so as to get things down right. As for being a member of a group called the "angry young men," I have never quite understood how that idea developed. When I was writing **Saturday Night and Sunday Morning** and the stories collected in **The Loneliness of the Long-Distance Runner,** I didn't know John Braine or Kingsley Amis or John Osborne and I hardly knew at all what they were writing. We're all very much unlike, as our subsequent work has shown. I don't think I have been influenced by any of them in a significant way.

Does it bother you that people want to talk about your fiction—the works you just mentioned—written twenty years or more ago?

No. I don't worry too much about that. I just put my head down and write.

I'd like to change the subject a bit, to explore the subject of your early life. Do you have any bitterness at the lack of education you received? Or do you think it was perhaps to your advantage?

I don't have any bitterness, no. I was always grateful that I was given as much education as I was. One learned how to read, one learned how to write, one learned the rudiments of geography and a few other things. In fact, given the resources they had and the raw material they had to deal with, I think the teachers were very dedicated—quite good, really. I was disappointed when I didn't pass the eleven-plus exam—the examination that determined whether or not you would go on in school and would be prepared for university. But I think it was out of the question anyway. I think out of this small school about two passed. You know when you're presented with I. Q. questions, everything looks like Chinese ideograms—unless your parents have gone into town to a bookshop and purchased a set of similar examination papers and have had you practice for weeks beforehand so that at least you're familiar with the form of the questions. But then, if I had passed as I wanted to, the question would have been who would pay for my uniform, who would pay for my books—my parents wouldn't have done it. My grandmother might have done it, but I'm not sure.

When I came out of the Air Force, I thought to myself, maybe I should go to the university now. So I spoke to someone who knew how to get in, and he said, "Well, okay. What you've got to do now is start learning Latin." Because in those days you had to pass an examination in Latin before you could get into the university. I had already started to write, and I thought that, well, I would just stay on as I was and write and see how much I would make of it. No, I was never bitter. Disappointed, that's something else, but not bitter. I think if I had been to a university I might have been writing clear English two or three years before I was. So I might have been published at the age of 27 instead of 30. And who is to say that my voice wouldn't have been stifled? I don't know. I think that if I had been to an American university, the chances are less that my voice would have been stifled. If I had been to an English one, I might have easily become ashamed of my background and hidden it and never gotten my real voice out.

I believe that you were too young to fight in World War II. Did you have any relatives who did fight?

I had more relatives who deserted. Many people deserted during the war. Some I knew just came home, burned their uniforms, and led a life of crime. They didn't want to fight. Oh, eventually they did fight. They were caught and went back into the army and acquitted themselves with sufficient honor. But, generally speaking, anyone who joined up was considered to be a fool, even in wartime.

But this didn't apply to me. I really wanted to join up. I volunteered when I was seventeen, right before the European War ended. Right up to the end, one didn't believe it would end. You thought it was here for good. You couldn't conceive of a time when there would be peace. And I thought that in a couple of years I would be in it with the rest of them. When the European War ended, I thought the Japanese War would be on for another two years, but it ended the same year. So I was let off the hook. I'm sure I would have been killed because I had volunteered for Air Crew and passed the Air Crew Selection Board because I had been a cadet for four years learning aviation. So I was pre-channeled to be a pilot on a carrier. I wanted to be a navigator, but they wouldn't take me as a navigator—I had to be a pilot. I wanted to be a navigator in a bomber over Germany so I could drop bombs—that was my idea, horrible as it sounds.

Was there much bombing in Nottingham?

Not very much. I think there was one raid when over 200 people were killed, but that wasn't considered much at all. There was always a bit of skirmishing going on because Nottingham was so near Derby, where there was a Rolls Royce aero-engine plant.

Do you think of World War II as an important experience? Did it change things in England at all?

It fundamentally changed England in some ways. But not to the extent that they'd cut their own throats by having some kind of bloody revolution. They didn't want things to alter unrecognizably. The war changed things to the extent that a vast improvement took place in everyone's lives. I mean that there is no connection between poverty today and the poverty that existed in the 1930s. That sort of poverty is unthinkable today. Nobody would put up with it. Today there are three million unemployed in England. They all draw some kind of dole. So they are being "bought off" from social unrest by the dole. Now, where is the money for the dole coming from?—from the North Sea oil revenues. Instead of using the North Sea oil revenues to finance a second technological revolution, they're using it to pay off the unemployed. So when the oil revenues disappear, and they have no more money to pay the unemployed, then there may be trouble.

It's interesting to me that you married an American, the poet Ruth Fainlight.

Well, there I am tempted to say it's just chance, which is what one says when there's no easy answer. I met Ruth in a second-hand bookshop in the town of Nottingham. She was just twenty, and I wasn't much older. I didn't know that she was an American. Her English accent was very good—she had been living in England since she was fifteen. I thought maybe she was from Canada. We got to know each other, and after a year or so we left everything and went to France. We thought we were going away for six months and came back six years later. We got married in 1959. We have a son, David, who's now twenty-three. He's a photographer, doing quite well on his own.

Do you read much contemporary writing?

They're not precisely contemporary, but I'm reading the memoirs of Hector Berlioz now, a chap I greatly admire. I seem to be reading all the time—something. Do you know William Kennedy, a writer from Albany, New York? He wrote *Ironweed* and *Legs,* which is about Legs Diamond. Those are wonderful novels, part of a trilogy, that I read recently. I tend to read a lot of American writing. When we were living in Majorca in the fifties, all the stuff was American. Styron, Salinger, Mailer—you name it, we were reading it. We weren't getting anything from England. The American lot had plenty of vigor—still does.

Your latest novel, **Down from the Hill**—*is it available in the United States?*

The British publisher is Granada. I'm not sure that the book is going to be published in the United States. The general reaction of the two or three American publishers that saw it was that it was a bit too English, too parochial, or whatever they call it. That was their reaction to **The Widower's Son,** as well. This is a similar type of novel, though it's shorter, only about 200 pages.

It's a simple story about a young boy of 17 who works in a factory. In the summer of 1945 he decides to go on holiday on his bicycle. He had planned to go with a friend, but the friend pulled out at the last minute, so he is on his own. This circuit of 300 to 400 miles which he does around the English Midlands takes place when he is at his absolute peak of consciousness. He works in a factory and is about to join up. He feels good, the world is wonderful, even the war in Europe has just ended. Also a few weeks before there had been a general election. Labor had just won a landslide victory. He feels this is a turning point, not only for him but for the whole country. That section of the novel, which is three-quarters of it, ends when he gets back to Nottingham.

The first part of the novel is in the first person, while the last part is in the third person. It has the same man some 38 years later, who is driving on the same circuit and recreating this earlier journey. And as he's going on his way, the news is coming through of Mrs. Thatcher's enormous landslide victory. It's one of those novels which is about the discovery of the past; but it's also about the realization that, in England at least, nothing changes.

Despite your disclaimers, then, you certainly seem to have a political outlook and definite allegiances.

Yes, of course, coming from the background that I do, I am always on the side of the workers. But I have come to see how complicated certain situations can be—like the coalminers' strike this past year—and to believe that often neither side is completely right.

I have not found much reference to religion in your early fiction, but in later work you sometimes seem to be wrestling with ideas about God—as though you can't entirely dispense with the notion of the existence of God. Would you care to comment?

My family when I was growing up was so poor that we were even below the "religion line." That is, we didn't go to any church. I was not raised with any religion. That was not unusual among people living in the Nottingham slums at a subsistence level. Probably as a result, I have never been much attracted to religion. But the idea of God is a powerful concept that no writer can entirely disregard. It has occurred to me that writing may be my way of coping with the ultimate questions of existence.

Which of your works of fiction are your favorites?

Raw Material is a book with anecdotal chapters about my four grandparents and my aunts and uncles, interwoven

with "philosophic" chapters in which the narrator speculates on the connections between lying and fiction. It is a
book I often read from when asked to give a public reading. Because it is so hard to say where the literal truth
changes to fiction, I have always thought that ***Raw Material*** should be classified as fiction, even though it could
also be called a memoir.

Basically, as a writer, one doesn't dwell too much on work
that is already written. Probably, out of my fiction, I like
best ***The Widower's Son*** and ***Her Victory.*** These are closest to my heart. They also took the most out of me to
write—each one nearly killed me. Perhaps they mean most
to me because they cost me so much to write. As I get
older, it gets harder to write, not easier. That's good. It
means that one's perceptions are more complex.

In **The Widower's Son,** *the main character, William Scorton, makes a crucial decision to leave the army, his career
up to then; it is a decision that costs him his marriage. I
found his decision surprising, given the fact he has been
brought up to be a career soldier and has obviously been
successful at it. Would you comment on Scorton's decision?*

If you remember, Scorton's wife, Georgina, has just had a
miscarriage, and he has taken her for a vacation to
Belgium, to view the battlefield at Bruges where he fought
during the war. He misguidedly decides—on impulse, just
after they have made love—that he must get out of the
army because if he doesn't the marriage is going to collapse. She's central to his life—the army is as well, but at
that point he veers over into her court. They've had a
troubled marriage, and this occurs to him as what he must
do to save it. But of course it doesn't turn out as he
anticipated.

*You don't think his decision was a rejection of what the
army represented?*

No, certainly not consciously. I think one acts basically
according to one's unconscious mind. Life would be in a
sense more satisfactory if you never had to make a decision because if you don't make a decision, then sooner or
later a decision is made for you. And that's the true decision.

I think at that time Scorton had no idea he was going to
leave the army, but it suddenly spoke out of him at that
particular point. By then, when he had said, "I'm going to
leave the army," he had committed himself, and pride and,
in a way, stupidity made it so that he couldn't go back.
And the more his wife objected to it, even less could he
go back. In other words, his subconscious, or fate, was
pushing him along a certain course. He had to get out of
the army because he was on a way to gaining his new life,
which was apparent by the end. That was the turning point
of the novel when he said, "I'm going to leave the army."
All the rest of his life he had been following the precepts
of his father. From that point on, it was decided by his

subconscious that "This isn't me, something's got to
change." He didn't consciously think that he might lose
Georgina as a consequence, but his subconscious decided
that he would damn well lose Georgina if that were the
price. Of course, the two of them were not meant for each
other, which was obvious from the beginning.

*In the course of breaking up with Georgina, William Scor-
ton has some kind of emotional breakdown. Do you think
he had to break down in order to change?*

Well, yes. Fundamentally, it seems to me, there's no
growth without great pain. It always takes some kind of
crisis for a human being to move into a new dimension of
awareness.

In **Her Victory,** *the main character is a woman of about
forty who makes an abrupt change in her life, like Scorton. She's a fairly ordinary woman who suddenly realizes
that she must leave her husband—he has been behaving
very badly to her, and that seems to be the reason she
must leave, but it's not the real reason, which is a need to
save her soul. So she flees to London and arrives without
money or friends—in a state of crisis. It is from that crisis,
a state of desperation really, that eventually her strength
emerges. The novel is about the victory she achieves.

*How aware are you of imagery and symbolism when you
write?*

I don't theorize when I write—or think about symbols and
such—that would be disastrous. I think about human beings. Later, sometimes, I can see patterns of imagery, but I
don't think about these when I am writing. Of course, one
does many drafts of a story or a novel and considers some
aspects of craftsmanship in later versions which one
doesn't earlier.

*Do you view the process of writing poetry as different from
the process of writing fiction?*

I see poetry as a quite separate and fundamental part of
me, very distinct from the fiction in that it comes only on
inspiration—rather than through the exercise of craft and
conscious encouragement as does fiction. Poetry writes
itself much more than fiction, but having said that, and
having the page (or so) of raw material in front of me, I
find that the work then begins. Whereas I often put a story
or a novel through as much as eight drafts, a poem can be
worked a score of times before real clarity of meaning
emerges, as it must before it can be considered finished.

I try never to be obfuscatory in anything, and certainly not
in poems—relying mainly on free verse rhythms. I studied,
and still study, prosody, and experiment occasionally in
traditional forms, but usually I use my own basic personal
(Biblical sometimes) free rhythms. I'm not saying that
poetry must be deadening in its simplicity, but I don't
think that one should be too esoteric to the extent that one
assumes the reader can apply all the footnotes and transla-

tions of foreign phrases. Maybe a poem needs to be read carefully a couple of times, but after that it should be fairly plain.

Do you read reviews of your work?

Yes.

Do you get helpful advice or ideas from them?

No, never. I read reviews. And I get irritated. If I get bad reviews, well, I don't care much. I suppose the publisher likes for you to get good reviews. If I get consistently good reviews, I think it is time to cut my throat because I feel that I am doing something wrong.

Would you tell us something about the novel you're currently writing?

The novel I'm working on now is about a man, some sort of writer, who comes from a background without consciousness. That is, he comes from an environment where people tend not to think about themselves, their choices, their lives—they don't have the habit of doing so. This man has become a writer, which means that he has become conscious in a way that people of his background usually are not. The novel is the story of how he got from the one place to the other. Obviously, there's a lot of my story in this, but it's not entirely about me.

William Hutchings (essay date Spring 1987)

SOURCE: "The Work of Play: Anger and the Expropriated Athletes of Alan Sillitoe and David Storey," in *Modern Fiction Studies,* Vol. 33, No. 1, Spring, 1987, pp. 35–47.

[*In the following essay, Hutchings examines the role of sports and the athlete in the work of Alan Sillitoe and David Storey.*]

"At the same time that factory work exhausts the nervous system to the uttermost," Karl Marx observed in *Das Kapital,* "it does away with the many-sided play of the muscles, and confiscates every atom of freedom, both in bodily and intellectual activity" (422). Nowhere has this observation been better exemplified than in the English novels of working-class life since the late 1950s. Whether toiling at lathes like Arthur Seaton in Alan Sillitoe's *Saturday Night and Sunday Morning* and Arthur Machin in David Storey's *This Sporting Life* or at a milling-machine like Smith's in *The Loneliness of the Long-Distance Runner,* the protagonists of such fiction typically find that their actions soon became automatic, reducing them as workers (and, more importantly, as human beings) to mere operative extensions of the factory's machinery in exactly the way that Marx described. For virtually all of these working-class protagonists, the body and its pleasures provide refuge from the workaday monotony, fragmentation, and dreariness of factory-bound life in a class-ridden

world. At the end of the week, having received their pay packets, they leave behind the factory with its noise and smells, eager to have "the effect of a week's monotonous graft in the factory . . . swilled out of [their] system[s]" in the "cosy world of pubs and noisy tarts" (Sillitoe, *Saturday Night* 7, 33) for which such novels are renowned. For many, however, sports provide an equally vital source of such pleasure—and, for those who play the pools or frequent the betting-shops, the prospect of supplementary profit or loss as well. To some fans, such as the narrator of Sillitoe's short story **"The Match,"** a team's dismal fortunes on the playing-field even presage a crisis in the day-to-day relationships of family life; to some athletes, such as the narrator of *This Sporting Life,* a team's collective endeavors provide a welcome release for the frustrations and pain that such personal relationships involve. Even to those who no longer play the game, like the middle-aged sportswriter who is the central character of Storey's novel *Present Times* (1984), the world of sport—with its clear rules and its unambiguous outcomes—provides a haven from the various cultural upheavals and controversies that rive the modern family as well as contemporary society as a whole.

For spectators and participants alike, the importance of the "game" extends far beyond the vicarious enjoyment of fans' team-loyalties and the athletes' personal accomplishments. Yet, as characters in Sillitoe's **The Loneliness of the Long-Distance Runner** and Storey's *This Sporting Life* and *The Changing Room* come to recognize, sport, play, and even the body itself have been expropriated by exactly the social "establishment" from which they are alienated. Turned into the "work" of professional rugby for Storey's characters and into officially mandated "games" in Sillitoe's novella, "play" and sport become dehumanizing, no longer fulfilling their original and essential recreational functions in the way that they did in earlier times. Although in both authors' works the characters' participation in sports affords them a certain personal satisfaction and fulfillment that life in the "real" world cannot provide, the fact of the athlete's expropriation not only provides a crucial symbol for the causes of the characters' alienation and anger but also has implications well beyond their particular time, class, and society.

Almost invariably in such fiction, the protagonist is repeatedly described as being *"big"*—a standard image of the worker in twentieth-century art of all forms, of course, from Soviet Socialist Realism to the murals of the W. P. A. Yet, as Sillitoe has pointed out in one of his essays in **Mountains and Caverns,** such a portrayal of a working-class protagonist had particular importance in England in the mid-1950s when

> working men [who were] portrayed in England by the cinema, or on radio and television, or in books were . . . presented in unrealistic terms . . . behaving in the same jokey but innocuous fashion. They lacked dignity in fiction because they lacked depth.

(37–38)

In stark contrast to Alfred Doolittle, Andy Capp, Alf Garnett, and countless others, Arthur Seaton and Arthur Machin tower over their parents and over their bosses at work—even though, symbolically, Seaton's "tall frame was slightly round shouldered from stooping day in and day out at his lathe" (*Saturday Night* 58); even Smith in *The Loneliness of the Long-Distance Runner* is *taller* than the other boys, though not specifically described as *big*. For many, such size reinforces an equally sizable ego: "it makes you feel good," Arthur Machin is told by the woman he loves; "it makes you feel big—you know how you like to feel big" (*This Sporting Life* 147). Through his success at Rugby League football, Arthur Machin finds both recognition and a source of supplementary income, both of which are means by which, he explains, he "kept his head above the general level of crap, and that . . . was the main thing" (18).

Beyond such fundamental considerations, however, the sport also provides an outlet for important emotions that cannot be expressed in his workaday world. Specifically, Storey's protagonist finds particular satisfaction in the arousal of

> a kind of anger, a savageness, that suited the game very well. . . . This wildness was essential to the way I played . . . [and] seemed to correspond to my personality. . . . [It was] a preliminary feeling of power. I was big, strong, and could make people realize it. I could tackle hard, and with the kind of deliberation I took a pride in later, really hurt someone. I was big. Big! It was no mean elation.
>
> (20)

Similarly, as Sillitoe's narrator runs across the chilly fields at dawn, he finds both an elation and a release for the anger that he feels for the "In-laws" of ostensibly respectable society:

> Them bastards over us aren't as daft as they most of the time look. . . . They're cunning, and I'm cunning. . . . If only "them" and "us" had the same ideas we'd get on like a house on fire, but they don't see eye to eye with us and we don't see eye to eye with them . . . the pig-faced snotty-nosed dukes and ladies—who can't add two and two together and would mess themselves like loonies if they didn't have slavies to beck-and-call. . . . [But] standing in the doorway in shimmy and shorts . . . I feel like the first bloke in the world. . . . And that makes me feel good, so as soon as I'm steamed up enough to get this feeling in me, I take a flying leap out of the doorway, and off I trot.
>
> (*Loneliness* 7–9)

Whether, like rugby, a particular sport requires a subordination of self to the collective endeavors of a team, or whether, like long-distance running, it allows free rein to the individual alone, each athlete finds—uniquely, through the experience of sports—an "alternate reality" into which the problems and anxieties of the everyday world no longer intrude.

Yet even though sports allow such outlets for the anger and frustrations that build up in their lives, the athletes in both novels soon find that they themselves—and, indeed, their respective sports as well—have been expropriated by the very same "establishment" that they rail against, so that (as a character in *This Sporting Life* complains) "a great game . . . [is being] spoiled by people who try and make it something else" (185). Specifically, in Storey's works it is being made a business, even an industry—with paid managers and owners whose interests do not necessarily coincide with those of their workers, the players. Before he has even signed his contract, Machin is told that he is now "property of the City" team (*This Sporting Life* 59), and he soon remarks that "they bought and sold players" like any other commodity or product. Consequently, the athletes can no longer be regarded *primarily* as human beings; their success or failure on the field becomes a matter that must be assessed in terms of profit and loss rather than any more "humane" values. Voluntarily co-opted as part of a system of paid performance for commercial entertainment, Machin soon realizes that he has not only been dehumanized but even reduced to the level of an animal:

> I was an ape. Big, awe-inspiring, something to see perform. . . . People looked at me as if I was an ape. Walking up the road like this they looked at me exactly as they'd look at an ape walking about without a cage . . . [a] thing to make them stare in awe, and wonder if after all . . . I might be human.
>
> (163–164)

On *and off* the playing field, no less than when he stands at his lathe in the factory, Machin has been dehumanized by the work of play. As a professional athlete—no less than as a factory worker—he is an operative cog in a commercial, mechanistic enterprise whose owner is far removed from the struggles and sufferings of those who toil on his behalf.

Although Smith in *The Loneliness of the Long-Distance Runner* is certainly not a professional athlete like Arthur Machin, he has been expropriated in exactly the same way by the "establishment" that runs the reformatory in which he is confined. The novella's opening line makes this expropriation unmistakably and emphatically clear: "As soon as I got to Borstal *they* made *me* a long-distance cross-country runner" (7; emphasis mine). During the weeks of his training for a championship race, Smith is repeatedly encouraged to "win *them* the Borstal Blue Ribbon Prize Cup for Long Distance Cross Country Running (All England)" by the borstal's governor—an "owner" who, like the capitalists caricatured in any form of agit-prop, is a "pot-bellied pop-eyed bastard" with a grey moustache and "lily-white workless hands" (11, 9). In fact, his relationship with Smith is defined in explicitly contractual terms, a *quid pro quo* befitting an employer and employee:

> "We want hard honest work and we want good athletics," he said as well. "And if you give us both these

things you can be sure we'll do right by you and send you back into the world an honest man."

(9)

Although Smith receives no remuneration of any kind for his efforts in the race (not even a quid in exchange for all of his *quo*), his running—no less than Arthur Machin's rugby—has clearly been made a form of contractual work rather than play. And like Machin, Smith finds this expropriation dehumanizing and compares himself to an animal (though his chosen simile is less unflattering than Machin's ape metaphor): "They give us a bit of blue ribbon and a cup for a prize after we've shagged ourselves out running or jumping, like race horses, only we don't get so well looked-after as race horses, that's the only thing" (8). Not even the cup and blue ribbon will be Smith's own because they will belong instead to the winning institution—a reform school *qua* factory whose product is "honest men"; its governor/manager never once suggests that the athlete should win for *himself*—that the laborer should receive the reward of his toil—or even that (altruistically) the sport can provide a sense of personal achievement and a satisfaction all its own whether he wins or not. Accordingly, Smith recognizes that the victory, which he is quite capable of achieving, "won't mean a bloody thing to me, only to him, and it means as much to him as it would mean to me if I picked up the racing paper and put my money on a hoss I didn't know, had never seen, and didn't care a sod if I ever did see" (12). Because Smith's athletic endeavors receive no recompense of any kind, whereas Arthur Machin's are at least a professionally contracted and compensated job, Sillitoe's protagonist is seemingly the more wholly expropriated of the two; yet, in cunningly subverting the plans of those who seek to keep him under their control, Smith is also the more defiant and independent of the pair.

Against all such attempts at dehumanization and expropriation, the narrators of both novels affirm the existence of an innately *human* alternative. However successful others may be in "owning" the athlete's body (which, like a factory's machine, is well-maintained, powerful, efficient, and smoothly functional), they can never control his mind, subdue his emotions, quash his spirit, or quell his independent will. Thus, as Smith contends, he retains a vital freedom of thought and feeling—an unsubduable psychological independence—that those around him fail to acknowledge and/or refuse to take into account:

I'm a human being and I've got thoughts and secrets and bloody life inside me that [the governor] doesn't know is there, and he'll never know what's there because he's stupid. . . . I can see further into the likes of him than he can see into the likes of me . . . and I'll win in the end even if I die in gaol at eighty-two because I'll have more fun and fire out of my life than he'll ever get out of his.

(12)

Relying on exactly the same "cunning" and the pleasures of "thinking" that Arthur Seaton cites in claiming "it's a

hard life if you don't weaken" (*Loneliness* 7; *Saturday Night* 34, 28, 32), Smith deliberately loses the race that he could easily win; in so doing, he unmistakably asserts a fundamental human freedom not to suborn himself, not to conform, and not to comply.

For Arthur Machin as well, the primacy of powerful and innately human "feelings" abrades against his "professional" obligations as an athlete—though the emotions involved are more adult (and more amatory) than the adolescent rebelliousness that fuels the defiance of Sillitoe's long-distance runner. Although the hard physical contact involved in professional rugby provides an ample outlet for his anger and frustration, and although the perquisites of being a celebrity (an expensive car, ostentatious dinners, public recognition) provide an ego-gratification that exceeds even the salary that he earns, his attempts to express more *tender* emotions cause much of the turmoil in his life. In the rough-and-tumble sometimes brutally violent world of the playing field, Arthur Machin excels and is appropriately rewarded; in the fragile often stormy relationship with the woman he loves, he encounters a pain no less acute—and no less real—than the pain caused by the physical injuries he gives and receives. Paradoxically, the strain that besets his loving relationship with Mrs. Hammond, the widow from whom he rents a room, is caused by the very same personal traits that contribute so much to his success at rugby: aggressiveness, recklessness, ruthlessness, and a certain impervious disregard for whoever or whatever might thwart his attempts to achieve his goals. As he gains more and more acclaim for exhibiting these traits in the game, he becomes increasingly insensitive in seeking an intimate relationship, until, in his frustration, the type of conduct that is appropriate and applauded on the field obtrudes in—and disrupts—the home as a sudden brutal outburst of domestic violence occurs.

Although the nature of his chosen sport itself inherently demands a number of his macho traits, such tendencies are accelerated by the fact that he is a paid *professional* who is economically (as well as socially and psychologically) rewarded for successfully behaving in this way. Accordingly, Arthur admits,

I was a hero . . . [but also] the big ape again, known and feared for its strength, frightened of showing a bit of soft feeling in case it might be weakness. . . . No feelings. It'd always helped to have no feelings. So I had no feelings. I was paid not to have feelings. It paid me to have none.

(*This Sporting Life* 163)

Nevertheless, as his frustrated love for Mrs. Hammond, his anger, and his grief over her death near the end of the novel demonstrate, powerful and vital human "feelings" have not been entirely suppressed despite the dehumanizing pressures that accompany the work of play. Through their resurgence, even in unpredictably and unacceptably explosive ways, such emotions clearly demonstrate that the athlete has not been *wholly* expropriated by the economic system that "owns" him. Rather than merely a well-functioning body that seems impervious to pain, Arthur Machin is a complex and fully *human* being with feelings that—like those of Sillitoe's long-distance runner—are not entirely subject to any form of *control*; he is, accordingly, a man rather than a mechanism, "A. Machin" rather than "a machine."

The fact that the pervasive influence of economics alters even the most fundamental meaning of the word "play" is particularly evident in *The Changing Room* (1972), Storey's ostensibly "plotless" drama. For the play's athletes and nonathletes alike (the players, the trainers, the team's owner, and even its janitor), the sport is a source of supplementary income—a commercial enterprise—rather than the source of enjoyment that "play" is traditionally held to be; the rugby match is a contractual rather than a wholly "voluntary" obligation, a form of *work* rather than *play*. Subtly but surely, the insidious influence of commercial "professionalism" becomes evident: the owner of the team does not watch it play, retiring to the locker room to warm himself and to enjoy a drink and conversation instead; the team's subsequent victory celebration commingles the players' satisfaction at their achievement and their relief that, in miserable weather and despite physical pain, another of their contractual performances has been completed. As Christopher Lasch has observed, economic concerns taint the basic nature of sports as

> the managerial apparatus makes every effort to eliminate the risk and the uncertainty that contributes so centrally to the ritual and dramatic success of any contest. When sports can no longer be played with appropriate abandon, they lose the capacity to raise the spirits of players and spectators, to transport them to a higher realm. Prudence and calculation, so prominent in everyday life but so inimical to the spirit of games, come to shape sports as they shape everything else.
>
> ("Corruption" 30)

Among players who can be sold or traded like commodities and retired by a decision of the owners, the whole concept of being a team is (as Lasch suggests) "drained of its capacity to call up local or regional loyalties" and therefore

> reduces itself (like the rivalry among the corporations themselves) to a struggle for shares of the market. The professional athlete does not care whether his team wins or loses (since losers share in the pot), as long as it stays in business.
>
> ("Letter" 40)

Although the athletes in Storey's work are "professional" in that they are paid for their participation in the sport, it is *not* their primary occupation (or "profession"); all also hold "regular" jobs in the world "outside." They play intensely and unrestrainedly, but they are by no means obsessed with winning—a subject they hardly mention among themselves; neither is there any concern about

"representing" their particular locality. The owner of the team gives a typical pregame speech inciting them on to victory, but he takes little actual interest in the game itself. The players, like workers aggrieved at the policies and practices of management, complain about the stinginess of the owners and want a "more hygienic" system of separate showers to replace the common bath. A distinction between the workers/players and the owners/management is thus clearly evident in *The Changing Room*; the intrusion of economic issues—including charges of corporate ("Club") stinginess, low compensation, and unhygienic conditions—has blurred the age-old distinction between "work" and "play."

Yet regardless of the compensation that any of the characters receive, the "realm" of sport remains vitally separate from their lives in the "outside" world and their jobs there. The essential reason for this is that, as Johan Huizinga remarked in *Homo Ludens,* "Play is not 'ordinary' or 'real' life. It is rather a stepping out of 'real' life into a temporary sphere of activity with a disposition all of its own" (8) wherein specific and binding rules are observed and administered by impartial officials and a definite hierarchy—in which each person is expected to perform a specific role and duty that he knows well—prevails. In fact, as Huizinga points out, "inside the playground an absolute and peculiar order reigns. . . . Play . . . creates order, *is* order. Into an imperfect world and into the confusion of life it brings a temporary, a limited perfection" (10). For players and spectators alike, the game offers a ritualistic reenactment of an unending struggle between competing forces; in Storey's play, the central conflict is between "us" and "them," the primary terms used to refer to the teams. Yet, as in *The Loneliness of the Long-Distance Runner,* this fundamental dichotomy provides a metaphor for much larger issues in the world "outside" the realm of games and "play." Within the microcosm that the artificial world of sports provides, such struggles are resolved with a certain finality at the end of the match; yet, paradoxically, there are no *final* victories. As in the macrocosm of the world "outside," the major struggles of self against other and "us" against "them" are never completely and unambiguously resolved; even at world championships and after tournament "finals," one hears "Wait until next year!"

Although their "play" is actually contractual "work," Storey's rugby players find that their experience as members of a team provides a personal satisfaction that their job in the "outside world" lack. As Christopher Lasch has pointed out,

> Modern industry having reduced most jobs to a routine, games in our society take on added meaning. Men seek in play the difficulties and demands—both intellectual and physical—which they no longer find in work. . . . Risk, daring, and uncertainty, important components of play, have little place in industry or in activities infiltrated by industrial methods, which are intended precisely to predict and control the future and to eliminate risk.
>
> ("Corruption" 40)

In the workplace, standardization and automation have supplanted individual craftsmanship and personal pride; as work is ever more deprived of personal responsibility and integrity, sports remain a haven in an increasingly mechanized, literally "heartless" world. Specifically, the experience of being a member of a *team* offers Storey's athletes a number of attributes that are seldom if ever found elsewhere in life: a functional and hierarchical "social" order in which each player knows his clearly defined "position"; a role suited to his particular skills, on which others rely and the success of the collective enterprise may well depend; authoritative rules; reliably impartial officials whose decisions are immediate and (usually) irreversible; "a temporary, a limited perfection"; personal autonomy and accountability; the opportunity to display carefully developed skills and individual judgment; and an unambiguous resolution that yet allows the prospect of a different (and, to the loser, more appealing) outcome on another day. All of these attributes share one all-important characteristic: *certainty*—the quality that is most absent in the modern age of doubt, anxiety, alienation, and anomie.

Among the players themselves, therefore, the experience of "belonging to" the team provides a temporary union that is forged through common purpose and shared endeavor. As they change their clothes and prepare to play the game, the athletes must set aside their various differences and the preoccupations of the outside world and assume new responsibilities and interdependencies as members of a team. Confirmed through wholly secular rituals that are unselfconsciously but unfailingly performed, this crucial "change" remains *beyond* the reach of those who have expropriated the game for purposes of their own, transforming it into an economic enterprise and commercial ceremony. Unlike traditional religious rituals, which confirmed a union and a significance lasting beyond the duration of the activity (and sustained the participants until their next involvement in the group), the wholly secular rituals of the changing room perform no such function; nevertheless, the lives of the players would clearly be less satisfying without them. Though the effects are both fleeting and impermanent, the athletes achieve an instance of order and unity that their lives in the outside world cannot provide.

Significantly, *This Sporting Life* ends in the locker-room rather than on the playing field itself because the latter is the site of the devalued commercial ritual that the game has become. As he joins in the players' postgame horseplay as a new team member undergoes an initiation with a ceremonial shower (a secular rite of passage), Arthur Machin achieves—through a renewal and confirmation of the team bond—a brief respite from the still-intense personal grief that he feels over the death of Mrs. Hammond. Like Paul Morel's decision to turn away from his self-absorbing grief at the conclusion of D. H. Lawrence's *Sons and Lovers,* Arthur Machin's action in the novel's final scene does not in any way deny the *intensity*—or the sincerity—of the grief he feels; yet by participating in the collective life of the team and taking part in one of its wholly private rituals, he too has "chosen life" rather than the death, personal isolation, darkness, and despair that are associated with the "outside" world.

Because long-distance running is an individual sport rather than a team effort, Sillitoe's Smith finds no such communal bond in the experience of sports, nor does he seek any such affirmation. Yet for him, too, the sport provides a haven from the factorylike regimentation and routine of borstal life, and it allows him to assert his individuality and self-reliance in a way that his workaday life in the "outside" world seldom affords. Unlike his job at the factory lathe, running allows him complete autonomy; success in the race—like success in his criminal activities—requires careful planning, agility, strategic maneuvering, and the assumption of risk. As Lasch points out, "risk, daring, and uncertainty, important components of play, have little place in industry or in activities infiltrated by industrial methods, which are intended precisely to predict and control the future and to eliminate risk" ("Corruption" 24). Because the sport has been expropriated by the governor and others like him, however, the rewards for taking such risk will not be his own. By deliberately refusing to win the race, Smith reaffirms the importance of daring, risk, unpredictability, and personal autonomy. Just as he was punished for his similar assertion of autonomy in his criminal activity, he is punished for having defied the authorities and violated their social norms—though he becomes a hero to the other boys, who recognize the significance of what he has done and understand the paradox that, under the circumstances of such expropriation that makes work out of play and attempts to dehumanize the worker/athlete into a mere mechanism, deliberately and defiantly to lose is to win.

Whereas Sillitoe's depiction of sports was not derived from any personal experience as an athlete (as he explains in **"The Long Piece"** in *Mountains and Caverns*), Storey's portrayal of the world of rugby-league football in *This Sporting Life* was based on his own first-hand experience as a member of a team. While a student at the Slade School of Art in London in 1953, Storey returned home each weekend to England's industrial north, where he played professional rugby for Leeds. Thus, he led a dual life, dividing his time between the physically demanding "public life" of a professional athlete and the private creative life of an art student; after each match, he would return to London to resume a type of life quite apart from (and perhaps incomprehensible to) the working-class teammates with whom he was regularly, though temporarily, united on the field of play. Years later, during an interview published in *Sports Illustrated,* he described the experience as follows:

> The pleasure to me is in the pitch of endeavor, sustaining it, going beyond it. In many ways I hated rugby, but it allowed people to do marvelous things. Often the real expression occurs at the point of physical and mental exhaustion. I recall one very hard game, played in pouring rain on a pitch that seemed to be 15 feet

deep in mud. My relations with the team were at their worst. I should have hated every minute of that match, but suddenly something almost spiritual happened. The players were taken over by the identity that was the team. We were genuinely transported.

(Duffy 69)

That the experience was "something *almost* spiritual" is a crucially precise phrase, suggesting Storey's conscious realization that a *truly* "spiritual" (that is, religious) experience cannot by definition arise from a wholly secular activity and cannot occur in a desacralized world.

The same evolution from participation to "spectatorship" shapes the histories of both sport and theater; yet, as Huizinga contended in *Homo Ludens,* so much of the ritual value of sports has been lost in modern times that "however important [the contest] may be for the players or spectators, it remains sterile . . . the old play-factor [having] undergone almost complete atrophy" as a result of "the fatal shift towards overseriousness" in sports "play" (198). Yet notwithstanding the devaluation of sport (and life) by professionalism and the less-than-heroic stature of modern man, the rugby match and related activities *do* manifestly provide something "real" in the players' lives. "The ancient connections between games, ritual, and public festivity," which Lasch described in his essay on "The Corruption of Sports," have been diminished but *not eradicated* because play retains "its capacity to dramatize reality and to offer a convincing representation of the community's values . . . rooted in shared traditions, to which [games] give objective expression" (30). Like the "sacred space" of traditional religions, the playground is, as Huizinga observed, "hallowed, within which special rules obtain. All are temporary worlds within the ordinary world, dedicated to the performance of an act apart" (10).

The fact that these terms are even *more* applicable to the activities of the locker room is fundamental to Storey's works: unlike the commercial public ceremony of the game itself, the "change" is *literally* "an act apart," occurring within a "temporary world within the ordinary world," a wholly secular sanctuary to which only those with proper "credentials" are allowed access and in which the players' particular and binding but nontraditional rituals are unselfconsciously performed. The significant action of the play is the temporary reaffirmation of what Huizinga termed "the feeling of being 'apart together' in an exceptional situation, of sharing something important, of mutually withdrawing from the rest of the world and rejecting the usual norms" (12). Despite his dour conclusion in the final chapter of *Homo Ludens* that the "ritual tie [having] now been completely severed sport has become profane, 'unholy' in every way, [having] no organic connection whatever with the structure of society" (197–198), Huizinga also maintained (in his first chapter) that vestigial formal elements of ritual and play survive today:

> The ritual act has all the formal and essential characteristics of play . . . particularly in so far as it transports the participants to another world. . . . A closed space

is marked out for [play], either materially or ideally, hedged off from the everyday surroundings. . . . Now the marking out of some sacred spot is also the primary characteristic of every sacred act. . . . *Formally speaking, there is no distinction whatever between marking out a space for a sacred purpose and marking it out for sheer play.* The turf, the tennis-court, the chess-court, and pavement hopscotch cannot formally be distinguished from the temple or the magic circle.

(18–20; emphasis mine)

Accordingly, the playing field is the profane world's counterpart of the "sacred space" of a theocentric culture. Yet much more than the public arena, the locker room constitutes a secular "holy of holies"—a "closed space" that may be entered only by those who are responsible for the performance of the public ritual that relies to a remarkable degree on "the feeling of being 'apart together'" that is fostered among them. As Lasch has observed, sports constitute the most efficacious modern means whereby both participants and observers may be (in Storey's phrase) "genuinely transported": "Among the activities through which men seek release from everyday life, games offer in many ways the purest form of escape. . . . They obliterate awareness of everyday reality, not by dimming that awareness but by raising it to a new intensity . . ." (Lasch, "Corruption" 24). Though none of the team members could articulate its significance, each finds in the experience of sports a personal renewal through the affirmation of the team bond—and a unity, transcendence, and significance that would be missing from his life otherwise. Storey's meticulous depiction of this event, "invisible" though it is, affords an insight into the athlete's experience *as an athlete* that is unique among the depictions of sports in modern literature.

The expropriation of the athlete is *not* exclusively economic, however, as Sillitoe's works reveal; its basis is more broadly social, having its origins in the power of one person or group to "have the whip-hand over" others (*Loneliness* 13), demanding allegiance to an institution, class, city, or state. Accordingly, in his essay on **"Sport and Nationalism"** in *Mountains and Caverns,* Sillitoe argued that "The Olympic torch is a flame of enslavement" for exactly this reason (84), expropriating athletes as champions of the state in much the same way that Storey's athletes become "property of the City." Against such dehumanization and what Sillitoe in *Her Victory* termed "the slavery of expectation" (392), both authors assert remarkably similar alternatives, though vaguely defined by both as just "feelings" and "thinking." Implicitly, these are a recognition of individuality and the inner self, persistent and defiant even in a mechanized world. For Arthur Machin, it is the belated recognition of the importance of his love for Mrs. Hammond; for Smith, as for Arthur Seaton, it is an affirmation of the unsubduable "thoughts and secrets and bloody life inside me" (*Loneliness* 12)— including the essential freedoms *not* to conform, *not* to "play along," *not* to win for others' sakes, and *not* to live by others' expectations and desires. Despite Marx's assertion to the contrary, both authors' works demonstrate that not "every atom of freedom" has been confiscated by those seeking to expropriate "the many-sided play of the muscles" in play as well as in work. In the anger and defiant self-assertion of their expropriated athletes—rather than in that of their counterparts still in the factories—Sillitoe and Storey alike have found a crucial symbol that not only embodies the predicament of people in a specific time, place, and class but also resonates throughout modern societies as well.

Works Cited

Duffy, Martha. "An Ethic of Work and Play." *Sports Illustrated* 5 Mar. 1973: 66–69.

Huizinga, Johan. *Homo Ludens: A Study of the Play Element in Culture.* Boston: Beacon, 1950.

Lasch, Christopher. "The Corruption of Sports." *The New York Review of Books* 28 April 1977: 24–30.

———. Letter/reply in "Corrupt Sports: An Exchange." *The New York Review of Books* 29 Sept. 1977: 40.

Marx, Karl. *Capital: A Critical Analysis of Capitalist Production.* Trans. from the third German ed. by Samuel Moore and Edward Aveling. Ed. Frederick Engels. London: Swan Sonnenschein & Lowery, 1872.

Sillitoe, Alan. *Her Victory.* London: Granada, 1983.

———. *The Loneliness of the Long-Distance Runner.* New York: NAL, 1959. 7–47.

———. "The Match." *The Loneliness of the Long-Distance Runner.* 105–113.

———. *Mountains and Caverns: Selected Essays by Alan Sillitoe.* London: Allen, 1975.

———. *Saturday Night and Sunday Morning.* New York: NAL, 1958.

Storey, David. *The Changing Room.* London: Cape, 1972.

———. *This Sporting Life.* 1960. New York: Avon, 1975.

———. *Present Times.* London: Cape, 1984.

Judith Grossman (review date 20 March 1988)

SOURCE: "Jilted by His Fairy Godmother," in *Los Angeles Times Book Review,* March 20, 1988, p. 2.

[*In the following review, Grossman offers tempered praise for Sillitoe's* Out of the Whirlpool.]

Alan Sillitoe's favored theme, since his debut in 1958 with *Saturday Night and Sunday Morning,* has always been the quest of a disadvantaged hero for the magical key to a better life. In *Out of the Whirlpool,* a new short novel, he offers an unsparing reconsideration of the terrors and delights of the poor boy suddenly become lucky. In the process, Sillitoe revisits his own roots—in 1950s Nottingham, England.

Nottingham is also the home territory of D. H. Lawrence. And in fact, *Out of the Whirlpool* resembles a minimalist replay of *Lady Chatterley's Lover,* with the conclusion gone sour. Instead of the romantic gamekeeper, we have Peter Granby, unskilled laborer in a furniture factory, age 19; and in place of the aristocratic lady of the woods, we have Eileen Farnsfield, the handsome, 40-ish widow of a suburban architect, who befriends Peter and hires him as caretaker.

It's a match made somewhere other than in heaven, yet for a while, the precarious balance in the relationship works. He gets a rewarding sexual partner, and wider experience of the world. She finds herself recovering a taste for life, enjoying Peter's sweet looks and open sexuality.

Since Peter's family seemed to have had no resources for nurturance beyond the bare survival level, and his mother died of cancer while he was in his early teens, the age difference suits him fine. In his imagination of happy endings, the fairy godmother makes the perfect bride. But Eileen knows better: She hasn't the maternal temperament, and besides, she's not about to make herself look ridiculous in the eyes of her upper-class friends. For her, caste rules apply.

The crisis between them, when it comes, is a sharp, violent battle whose outcome seems inevitable from the start. Yet there is renewed hope at the end in an alliance with a young West Indian woman. It may be the immigrants who will help resolve the ingrown class-conflicts.

Sillitoe has great sureness of touch with his environment here, even in passing glances at the decaying industrial landscape: "A pebble dash of ice and snow covered the old lime kilns near the canal, bricks scattered like pieces of thrown-away cake. You could see where the oven doors had been." He knows all the dog breeds of his neighborhoods and he knows exactly what passes for *haute cuisine* in Eileen's suburb (wine with the pot roast, cream on the dessert).

This highly specified vision is paired with a real compassion for the young victims of the urban underclass. They are, Sillitoe sees, victims not just of exclusion from mainstream benefits but also of the careless incompetence of their own brutalized elders. Bad fathering is not excused by circumstances. Nor are long-suffering women let off: They won't think or plan; they are selfishly content with trivial pleasures.

You feel, reading, that Sillitoe has earned a right to the anger that smolders here. But *Out of the Whirlpool* might have been a stronger work if the targets of his indignation were challenged more abrasively.

In substance, the book explores a gentle adolescent's furnishing of his heart and soul. On the other hand, its style, which is often graceless, denuded to the point of mutilation, reveals a profound disgust with the realities that are handled. The result is an impression of conflicting rather than complex purposes.

Peter Farmer's line illustrations capture the wispy appeal of the young hero, as well as the grotesqueness of his elders.

D. A. N. Jones (review date 18 May 1990)

SOURCE: "Never Go Back," in *Times Literary Supplement*, No. 4546, May 18, 1990, p. 535.

[*In the following review, Jones considers the realism and tragedy of Sillitoe's* Last Loves.]

As they grow older, men sometimes dream of revisiting foreign lands where they served as soldiers, when they were only twenty. The experience is likely to be disappointing and discouraging: it is a matter of nostalgia—the pain in a desire to return. [In *Last Loves,*] Alan Sillitoe has constructed a sombre story about two ex-servicemen, George and Bernard, revisiting Malaysia, where they fought against the "bandits" forty years ago when they were young hopefuls. Bernard is still a fairly hopeful man, self-assured, expecting to get his own way: he has been given this holiday trip by his kindly wife, as a sixtieth-birthday present, and she has also paid for George, his old Army friend, to accompany him. George is dour, thoughtful and quietly dissatisfied: he is a retired schoolteacher, recently divorced after an unsatisfactory marriage. Bernard, a comfortably ageing businessman, still looks (to George) quite handsome, proud and confident, as he seemed in his twenties, "showing that early photographs, albeit in black and white, and maybe even for that reason, did not lie." Bernard is quite happy to see himself in the mirror, but when he looks at recent photographs of himself, he becomes almost despondent.

Arrived in Malaysia, they take a taxi to visit Fort Perth, where they used to spend their leaves, sunning themselves on the beach. The area now houses a divisional headquarters of the Malaysian army and the elderly men are afraid to take photographs. "They'll think we're snapping military installations," says George. He feels that the young George, "the person of forty years ago, had died somewhere along the way. . . . And believing in all the formalities he had come back to bury him." Bernard had hoped to stand on the beach where once they photographed one another, wearing white tailor-made drill; but suddenly he too feels dead and their taxi seems a hearse. Looking at Malaysia and glossy, businesslike Singapore, Bernard concludes: "After forty years it was like seeing a film in Technicolor, a soulless remake of the original faded classic of black and white."

However, a subsequent chapter, pursuing this photographic imagery, finds George reflecting: "Memories of the old days made it impossible to forget why he was here, but the black and white film of then and the Technicolor production of now were slowly merging. Maybe by the time they left the difference would be minimal." This flicker of hope is stimulated by the inviting presence of a younger woman, an Englishwoman called Gloria, holidaying in Malaysia for similar nostalgic reasons: she is tracing memories of her dead father, a colonial official and subsequently a prisoner of war. In this mood, she attaches herself to the two old soldiers, particularly to George. Bernard does not object or express jealousy: he has enjoyed several discreet affairs during his comfortable marriage—and so (he presumes) has his kindly wife.

The story marches to its grim conclusion, skilfully prepared. The old soldiers are not acting their age. Their conversation, generally stodgy and bufferish, sometimes takes on a jaunty, barrack-room tone: their behaviour becomes imprudent and reckless. Rather bored by aeroplanes, taxis and grand hotels, with their practised smiles, Bernard finds a badly-built urinal and deliberately makes it collapse. George takes over the saddle from a pedi-cab driver and pedals away in dangerous exhaustion. They lead Gloria on a long, hot, hilly walk and then accept a lift on an earth-mover, clinging to the sides as it rattles and bumps. Finally, the three of them go to the edge of the jungle, where once George and Bernard battled with the enemy. One of the party, deeply depressed by bad news from home, gets lost—and another must search for the missing person, through the jungle in pounding rain. These incidents could have been presented as comic sketches; but although the author is sometimes witty, the story is not at all funny. It is more like a tragedy, realistic in its observation, about ordinary, ill-at-ease, rather dull people meeting their appointed doom. Sillitoe has thoughtfully used his experience to bridge the gulf between the 1940s and the 80s, between bold twenty-year-olds and soured sexagenarians, without patronizing either.

William Hutchings (review date Spring 1991)

SOURCE: A review of *Last Loves,* in *World Literature Today,* Vol. 65, No. 2, Spring, 1991, pp. 304–05.

[*In the following review, Hutchings offers a mixed assessment of Sillitoe's* Last Loves, *contending that the novel lacks the "complexity and mythical resonance" of earlier works.*]

Exactly forty years after their military stint in Malaya, George Rhoads and Bernard Missenden, lifelong friends who are the protagonists of Alan Sillitoe's *Last Loves,* return together to now-independent Malaysia on what is (at least initially) a sentimental journey, "a nostalgia tour to find out whether or not those faded black-and-white photographs stuck in the disintegrating sellotaped [sic] albums had any meaning." Though their quest for such insight and personal validation is initially thwarted in the nation's much-changed cities, where few vestiges of places they remember still remain, they realize that they must ultimately return to the islands' primordial jungle, the site of the most dangerous moments of their military career, a locale that has been virtually unaffected by the intervening years.

For Sillitoe too, their journey constitutes a literary "return": the Malayan jungle (the site of his own military service from 1947 to 1949) has figured repeatedly throughout his fiction, both as a literal setting and as a recurrent metaphor. The most autobiographical of Sillitoe's early novels, *Key to the Door* (1960), reaches its climax in that jungle—an existentially self-defining moment when its protagonist Brian Seaton must decide whether to kill a Malay insurgent, an "enemy" with whose cause he secretly sympathizes; his arduous ascent of the jungle-laden mountain known as Gunong Barat is equally an attempt to penetrate the complexities of his mind and soul. The jungle entanglements encountered in Sillitoe's work are thus not only physical but metaphysical as well. Even his characters who have never left England's industrial cities repeatedly characterize their world in "jungle" terms of essentially amoral struggle and strife: Arthur Seaton, for example, the factory-working (anti)hero of Sillitoe's first novel, *Saturday Night and Sunday Morning* (1958), insists, "It's a good [but also a *hard*] life if you don't weaken," a concise summary of the modern urban jungle's social Darwinist code.

Nevertheless, it is in the literal jungle of Malaysia that the long-standing friendship of George and Bernard receives its ultimate test, that painful truths are unexpectedly realized, that new insights and fulfillment are finally and fatally achieved. Self-described as formerly the "craziest bastards in the platoon," they indulge occasionally in the kind of antic disruptiveness for which Sillitoe's protagonists are renowned, though they do so primarily to prove themselves capable of being still rowdy after all these years. They are accompanied on their journey by a woman named Gloria, who has traveled from England to Malaysia to learn more about her father's life there as a prison administrator during the war; she is the most insightfully developed female character in Sillitoe's fiction since Pam Hargreaves, the protagonist of *Her Victory* (1982).

With the rather somber retrospectiveness that first appeared in Sillitoe's fiction in *The Widower's Son* (1976), *Last Loves* deftly and sympathetically depicts his characters' relatively mundane domestic lives as well as their search for a meaningful past; however, it lacks the complexity and mythic resonance of *The Storyteller* (1979) and *The Lost Flying Boat* (1983), individual novels from his later career that seem more likely to endure.

William Hutchings (essay date 1993)

SOURCE: "Proletarian Byronism: Alan Sillitoe and the Romantic Tradition," in *English Romanticism and Modern Fiction: A Collection of Critical Essays,* edited by Allan Chavkin, AMS Press, 1993, pp. 83–112.

[*In the following essay, Hutchings delineates how "Sillitoe's characters are . . . in many ways the modern-day working-class counterparts of the Byronic anti-hero."*]

> Camus came to the conclusion that, after all, the artist was a romantic. I began there. Where I am now I know exactly; but where I'm going I never shall know till I get there.
>
> Sillitoe, *A Tree on Fire*
> [hereafter cited as *ATOF*], chapter 2

Separated from the lives and times of the English romantics by approximately 150 years, living in the industrial cities in the north of England, the working-class protagonists of Alan Sillitoe's best-known fiction would at first appear to have little or nothing in common with literary characters from the romantic period—and least of all with the alienated but aristocratic personalities created by George Gordon, Lord Byron. Certainly, Sillitoe's characters lack any semblance of introspective melancholy or cosmic *Angst* associated with Byron's Childe Harold, for example, and they have had neither the benefits of advanced education nor the countless other opportunities afforded by aristocratic privilege and leisure. Nevertheless in a surprising number of ways, Sillitoe's early novels redefine the traditional romantic/Byronic anti-hero in specifically modern, working-class terms, despite the manifest differences that are attributable primarily to class, historical period, and economic privilege. Such fundamental differences between them notwithstanding, the avowedly iconoclastic attitudes of Sillitoe's working-class anti-heroes constitute, in effect, a form of proletarian "Byronism," characterized by (1) a heedless disdain for conventions of bourgeois propriety, (2) a willingness to flout society's conventional morality and (particularly) its sexual constraints, and (3) a rebelliousness against government and other forms of repressive authority, regimentation, and dehumanization. Thus, Sillitoe's characters are—unbeknownst to themselves—in many ways the modern-day working-class counterparts of the Byronic anti-hero.

Throughout Sillitoe's novels of the 1950's and 1960's, the romantically anti-heroic qualities of his protagonists become increasingly apparent, and their commitments to romantic ideals of revolution become increasingly radical as well as ever more overtly—and militantly—expressed. Whereas Arthur Seaton in *Saturday Night and Sunday Morning* [hereafter cited as *SN & SM*] (1958) expresses such rebelliousness only in occasional rhetoric, relatively innocuous acts of disruption of his factory's routine, raucous sexual escapades (worthy of Don Juan), and socially disruptive behavior, Smith in *The Loneliness of the Long-Distance Runner* (1959) takes direct if symbolic action to subvert the plans of what is, to him, a repressive regime that controls his life in the borstal where he is confined. In *Key to the Door* (1961), Brian Seaton secretly sympathizes with the Communist insurgents in Malaya, where he is stationed during World War II; at a crucial moment, he declines to shoot one of the rebels with whom he has a face-to-face encounter, thus helping to further (however passively) the revolution that his "enemy" supports. In *The Death of William Posters* [hereafter cited as *DWP*] 1965) and *A Tree on Fire* (1967), the struggle for Algerian independence is actively supported (at great risk to their own lives) by Sillitoe's protagonist Frank Dawley and his friend Shelley Jones, characters whose lives establish them—to a remarkable degree and in particular detail (though they are not poets)—as the twentieth-century's counterparts of Byron and Shelley themselves. However, in order to understand the full extent of Sillitoe's surprising affinity for (and literary assimilations of) the English romantic poets in general as well as Byron and Shelley in particular, one must first assess the centrality of his concept of romanticism in his particular world-view.

1

As Raymond Williams noted in an interview in the *New Left Review,* there has historically been a particular affinity between the English working class and the English romantic authors:

> It seems probable that the English working class was struggling to express an experience in the 1790s and 1830s which in a sense, because of the subordination of the class, its lack of access to means of cultural production, but also the dominance of certain modes, conventions of expression, was never fully articulated. If you look at their actual affiliations, what is striking is a great grasping at other writings. Working people used Shelley; they used Byron, of all people. . . . These works could only have been approximations or substitutes for their own structure of feeling.
>
> (164–165)

Yet, as Sillitoe's novels of the 1950's and 1960's reveal, the working-class "use" of a "structure of feeling" that was embodied in the works of Byron and Shelley—and, indeed, in romanticism in general—was not limited to the early nineteenth century.

During an interview with John Halperin published in 1979, Sillitoe contended that even in the late twentieth century "as long as writers are writing we're in a Romantic age rather than a Waste Land age" (Halperin 189). Though he has not elaborated on the remark and has not defined precisely what he means by a "Romantic age," a number of specifically romantic ideals found vigorous (if generally unremarked) reexpression in Sillitoe's early fiction. The contours of his "romanticism" are also apparent within the context of his most autobiographical book-length work, *Raw Material* [hereafter cited as *RM*](1972, rev. 1977, 1979):

1. For Sillitoe, as for so many of the romantics, being a writer involves an on-going and intensely personal quest for truth, which can be found only through the personal and particular. Thus, he contends,

> I am a writer because I do not know what or who I am, though in trying to find out I may by a fluke help others to know who they are. If so I trust it will persuade them to go on living and not despair about the fate of the world or themselves. You have to go beyond the limits of despair to reach the truth.
>
> (171)

Like Wordsworth, Sillitoe seeks to convey a more universal truth that transcends the particularities and details of his personal "raw material"; like Byron, he freely transmutes autobiographical experiences into fiction.

2. Like the Romantics, Sillitoe retains a faith in the perfectibility of mankind and "the better world I hope to see on earth," and he emphasizes the importance of "striv[ing] as I do to create [paradise] for everybody, to construct it in [one]self as an example for others" (*RM* 26)—in much the same way that Byron maintained "his indomitable search for an earthly Eden" (Marchand 354). *Road to Volgograd,* Sillitoe's adulatory (virtually Utopian) non-fiction account of his visit to the Soviet Union in 1963, characterized the "Workers' Paradise" as virtually the Writers' Paradise as well.[1] In his later (post-1970) writings, however, this quest for a newly-created "better world" is more often associated with the state of Israel.

3. Having been fascinated by maps even as a child, Sillitoe has long maintained the importance of travel, associating it with a concurrent *inward* quest or self-exploration—as in Wordsworth's *Prelude* and Byron's *Childe Harold's Pilgrimage,* among countless others. In *Key to the Door,* for example, Brian Seaton's quest culminates in Malaya during an attempt to ascend the mountain called Gunong Barat; in *The Death of William Posters* and *A Tree on Fire,* Frank Dawley becomes a "new man" in the deserts of Algeria during that nation's struggle for independence. "A man must travel, and turmoil, or there is no existence" Byron wrote in a letter of August 1820 (quoted in Marchand 331)—a sentiment with which Sillitoe would surely agree.

4. Even for Sillitoe's earliest protagonists, whose opportunities for travel have been severely limited (i.e., Arthur Seaton and Smith), the world of nature provides a welcome respite from the factory and the city, where (as for Wordsworth) the grimy world of "getting and spending"—and, especially, manufacturing—is "too much with us." Although Sillitoe is primarily an "urban" writer, who seems to share the disdain of one of his characters for those who "swoon and rapturize over wild flowers, and all the false crap of Lawrence and Powys and Williamson, [who constitute] the 'I am a wild beast and proud of it but still very sensitive . . . because my father was a bastard to my mother'" school of literature (*ATOF* 77), his characters often find particular solace (of whatever kind) out in nature. Arthur Seaton, for example, has one of his most memorable illicit trysts with another man's wife in the woodlands outside the city, and he does his best "thinking" while fishing at a favorite spot alongside a canal that

overlooks—but is not a part of—the urban landscape. For Smith, the fields across which he runs at dawn connote a freedom that is, obviously, quite the opposite of the restraint imposed by the borstal in which he is confined. Such freedom is especially lyrically evoked in the film version of *The Loneliness of the Long-Distance Runner* (1960, directed by Tony Richardson from Sillitoe's own screenplay); the film also adds a romantic interlude between Smith and his girlfriend at the seaside near Skegness which is not included in the novella. Nature is far more adversarial and untamed in *Key to the Door* and the William Posters trilogy, wherein the jungle and the desert (respectively) are the sites of their protagonists' struggles as well as their eventual hard-won insights. As *Raw Material* makes clear, the origins of Sillitoe's view of nature can be traced back to his childhood, as he lovingly evokes his grandparents' rural home, which he often visited as a child—a countryside locale that provides a stark contrast to industrial Nottingham, where he and his parents lived during the depression of the 1930's and the subsequent war.

5. Like his romantic forebears, Sillitoe insists that the emotions are far more important than reason, since

> Whatever is done to the heart, and whatever the heart does back, it must be trusted and obeyed absolutely. The only protector is your own heart. It will lead you into the wilderness, but carry you through peril and despair. And if it finally betrays you, you will only have lived in the way you were meant to live.
>
> (*RM* 75)

Nevertheless, with a typically romantic view of the inevitability of suffering, he insists that "the heart must be bruised before the truth comes out. How else can one find it?" (*RM* 40)

6. Like Wordsworth and Blake, Sillitoe maintains in *Raw Material* that "a child is a mystic, and what he lacks in intelligence and worldly knowledge he makes up for in earnestness and depth of feeling" (59). Although this assertion is a clear recapitulation of Wordsworth's paean to the child as a "Mighty Prophet! Seer blest! / On whom those truths do rest / That we are toiling all our lives to find" in his "Ode: Intimations of Immortality" (lines 114–116), its doctrine is seldom if ever apparent in Sillitoe's novels, where children seldom figure significantly. One notable exception, a boy known as Smog in *A Start in Life* (1970), is far from being "a six-years' Darling of a pygmy size!" ("Ode," line 86).

Although these contours of Sillitoe's beliefs establish him squarely within the romantic tradition, the *precise* extent of his knowledge of specific works cannot be as readily ascertained. The fact that he is, by his own admission, a voracious reader has frequently been overlooked in critical assessments of his works; apart from citing the picaresque elements of his novels and his place within the tradition of the "rogue's tale" from Defoe and Fielding onwards (a "low" and/or popular form of fiction, unlike more "seri-

ous" and "reputable" literary works), most critics have focused primarily on the importance of his working-class background and the Marxist implications of his writings.[2] Such assessments wrongly (if implicitly) assume that this self-taught writer—who had left school at the age of fourteen to work in a bicycle factory, having twice failed to win a scholarship to an English preparatory school—lacks any developed awareness of the literary tradition. Thus, for example, Anthony Burgess (who is surely among the most erudite and polymathic writers of the postmodern era) contends that Sillitoe's fiction, which he admires for its vitality and its Lawrentian "poetry of the body . . . [and] of the family," ultimately *lacks* "the discipline of art" (Burgess 149)—ostensibly an aesthetic deficiency that can be attributed at least in part to Sillitoe's presumed unawareness of the literary tradition and/or his lack of formal education. Yet in his essay for the *Contemporary Authors Autobiography Series,* Sillitoe remarks that, since he "had not gone through three years of university training on how to write essays or vivisect poems," his first novel was not "the composition of some pastiche, with a dash of cynicism and a peppering of false worldliness, plus the unthinking acceptance of everything that traditional society stands for" (380). Although he had always loved books during his childhood (when two of his favorites were novels of the French romantic period, Hugo's *Les Misérables* and Dumas's *The Count of Monte Cristo*), his "real" education had begun when, in Malaya during the Second World War, he was hospitalized with tuberculosis:

> I began to read whatever books seemed interesting on the library trolley which was pushed up to my bed two or three times a week. I had hardly read any adult matter before, and an endless feast began. . . . While quietly lying there I read, among other things, translations from all the Latin and Greek classics I could get my hands on, and as much English poetry as I could find. Another patient had an old school edition of Wordsworth's poems, and there was a section at the back on prosody, a subject I had never heard of before. In a week I had taken it in, and then sent off for Egerton Smith's classic work *The Principles of English Metre.*
>
> (379–80)

Despite the fact that Sillitoe has neither mentioned any particular favorites among their authors nor offered further details about specific books that he then read, one can safely assume that reasonably complete collections of all of the major romantic poets were among the books that were then available to him; in fact, for all the reasons cited above, their works seem to have been the most influential in shaping his literary (as opposed to his socioeconomic and/or political) world-view.

Toward the end of *Raw Material,* Sillitoe deplores "the descending death-trap ceiling of tight-arsed Victorian hypocrisy and repression" which "crushed for more than a hundred years" the vitality of earlier literature—including, presumably, that of the romantics, though he specifies "the generous and lecherous spirit of the eighteenth century" (178), to which his own picaresque novels—including *A*

Start in Life (1970) and its sequel *Life Goes On* (1985) as well as *Saturday Night and Sunday Morning*—have often been compared. Elsewhere, however, he alludes less obliquely to favorite romantic works: thus, for example, when alone at night in the outermost radio hut in the Malayan jungle (where Sillitoe himself served as a radio-operator during the Second World War), Brian Seaton sends Morse-coded transcriptions of Coleridge's "Kubla Khan," feeling "exhilarated in knowing that such a poem was filling the jungles and oceans of the Far East, coming, if anyone heard it, from an unknown and unanswerable hand." He also sends Keats's "'La Belle Dame Sans Merci' . . . singing hundreds of miles out into darkness, perhaps reaching the soul of the man who wrote it and maybe also touching the source of golden fire that sent down these words to him in the first place" (246). In his previous novels, however, any such "romantic" affinities were far less overt, although—when viewed in the context of his later writings—the incipient formation of Sillitoe's unique "proletarian Byronism" may yet be found in the portrayal of his defiant, rebellious, and "angry" young anti-heroes who gave new and vigorous voice to the "structure of feeling" of the modern English working class.

2

Whereas many of the protagonists created by the generation of working-class writers who became prominent in the mid-1950's and were known (misleadingly) as the "angry young men" have railed bitterly against society's injustices and/or sought to escape their proletarian backgrounds, Sillitoe's characters seem more comfortable with their working-class origins. Typically, they express neither the vituperative resentments of John Osborne's Jimmy Porter in *Look Back in Anger* (1956) nor a desire to "escape" or "rise" into the middle class like Joe Lampton in John Braine's *Room at the Top* (1959), among others. Yet, paradoxically, there is throughout Sillitoe's early writings an increasingly ardent—and intensely "romantic"—interest in an ideology of revolution. Without exception, the protagonists of his novels written between 1958 and 1967 are as strongly attracted by the idea of social revolution as their counterparts were in England's romantic period—and they are also increasingly actively engaged in helping to bring such radical changes about.

The first—and most wholly rhetorical—manifestation of this romantic/rebellious "spirit of feeling" occurs in *Saturday Night and Sunday Morning,* as Arthur Seaton proclaims that

> Once a rebel, always a rebel. You can't help being one. You can't deny that. And it's best to be a rebel so as to show 'em it don't pay to try to do you down. . . . It's a hard life if you don't weaken, if you don't stop that bastard government from grinding your face in the muck, though there ain't much you can do about it unless you start making dynamite to blow their four-eyed clocks [faces] to bits.
>
> (175)

Working at his lathe in the bicycle factory in Nottingham, twenty-one-year-old Arthur Seaton is confined in one of the "dark Satanic mills" that William Blake decried. The piece-work routine of factory life requires only actions that soon become automatic, in effect reducing him to a mere operative extension of the factory's machinery—exactly as Karl Marx described it in *Das Kapital*: "At the same time that factory work exhausts the nervous system to the uttermost, it does away with the many-sided play of the muscles, and confiscates every atom of freedom, both in bodily and intellectual activity" (422). Yet although Arthur's "tall frame was slightly round-shouldered from stooping day in and day out at his lathe" (58), it is patently clear that (despite Marx's hyperbole) NOT "every atom" of Arthur's energy is suborned by factory, despite the best efforts of its owners and managers: Arthur's rowdy behavior on and off the factory floor asserts the primacy of the body—of energy, and thus of life itself—against the demands for automaton-like conformity that the industrial system imposes and requires.

From the moment when, at the beginning of the first chapter, after having downed seven gins and eleven pints of ale in a drinking contest, Arthur Seaton tumbles headlong down a flight of stairs at the local pub on a raucous Saturday night, it is clear that—both literally and figuratively—he is a man of almost larger-than-life capacities. He is, in fact, a violator of all decorum, a despoiler of middle-class proprieties, and a seducer of other men's wives. Yet beyond the rowdy humor for which the novel is deservedly well-known, there is in Arthur Seaton the prototype of a decidedly *proletarian* hero who, despite his defiance of all traditional (middle-class) norms of "respect-ability," is in many ways the modern counterpart of earlier comic scapegraces—a character who not only engages in a variety of (mock-)heroic adventures but also (albeit reluctantly) by the novel's end proves himself capable of a certain "redemption" through surprisingly traditional means. In the beds of his various girlfriends and the "cosy world of pubs and noisy tarts" (33) in which, each weekend, "the effect of a week's monotonous graft in the factory was swilled out of [his] system in a burst of goodwill" (7), Arthur finds the pleasures and satisfactions that make his life worthwhile. Yet, for all his vaunted rebelliousness and exuberant iconoclasm, his primary means of resistance amount to little more than a defiant assertion of personal autonomy, a refusal to submit to regimentation and conformity, and the secret subversion of authority through "thinking" and "cunning."

This "thinking" and "cunning," which constitute his main defense, are precisely those qualities that (as Marx pointed out) the modern industrial worker is presumed not to need; given little or no opportunity to express such attributes on the job, he is therefore—erroneously—assumed not to possess them. As a result, any manifestation of such qualities becomes a form of subversion, a pleasure to be enjoyed for its own sake whatever the risk may be. Thus as Arthur maintains in the closing paragraphs of the novel,

> There's bound to be trouble in store for me every day of my life, because trouble it's always been and always will be. Born drunk and married blind, misbegotten

into a strange and crazy world, . . . working with rotten guts and an aching spine, and nothing for it but money to drag you back there every Monday morning.

Well, it's a good life and a good world, all said an done, if you don't weaken, and if you know that the big wide world hasn't heard from you yet, no, not by a long way, though it won't be long now.

(190)

Arthur's final affirmation that his is ultimately a *good* life is central to an understanding of both his character and his ideology of secret subversions. "Though no strong cause for open belligerence existed as in the bad days talked about, it persisted for more subtle reasons that could hardly be understood but were nevertheless felt," Sillitoe writes (53); it is, accordingly, a crucial part of the ethos (or Williams's "structure of feeling") in his working-class milieu. Thus, though Arthur contends that he would willingly blow up the factory with dynamite if given the opportunity (and handed the plunger by somebody else), he also remarks that it's "not that I've got owt against 'em, but that's just how I feel now and again. Me, I couldn't care less . . ." (34). Similarly, though he boasts that he voted for the communist candidate in the most recent election—and illegally used his father's voting card to do so, since "that's what all these loony laws are for . . . to be broken by blokes like me"—his motive in doing so was "to 'elp the losin' side" whose "poor bloke wouldn't get any votes" otherwise (31). Arthur Seaton is not a committed ideologue or a revolutionary zealot—for the simple reason that he is having too much fun otherwise.

Whereas Arthur Seaton's secret subversiveness is primarily expressed through his rhetoric rather than overt political action, the adolescent protagonist of **The Loneliness of the Long-Distance Runner** undertakes a defiant, public action that is, in effect, an existential commitment to subvert the plans of those in authority over him. As a self-described outlaw and outcast who is alienated from the normative values of the prevailing culture of his times, he—far more than Arthur Seaton—is Sillitoe's first *true* modern counterpart of the romantic anti-hero. Like Byron's Cain and countless others, he defines himself fundamentally and unrelentingly in adversarial terms—a fact that is established in the opening sentence of the story: "As soon as I got to Borstal, *they* made *me* a long-distance cross-country runner" (7; emphasis mine). The relationship between "them" and "me" (later, "us," including the other boys) is readily apparent, as is "their" power and "their" ability to define their young charges' lives. Significantly, Smith is given no say whatever in the matter; without being consulted in even a perfunctory way, he is *told* what he will be and given a training regimen that will, "they" confidently expect, "win *them* the Borstal Blue Ribbon Prize Cup for Long-Distance Cross-Country Running (All England)" (11; emphasis mine). Selected for his slender build, he is assessed with the objectivity of an odds-maker calculating the prospects of a race horse; thus, even from his initial moments in the borstal, "they" treat him as if he were a *thing* rather than a human being. Specifically, the

race horse metaphor is extended throughout the first of the story's three segments: Smith realizes that his victory in the race "means as much to [the governor of the borstal] as it would mean to me if I picked up the racing paper and put my bet on a hoss I didn't know, had never seen, and didn't care a sod if I ever did see" (12). Nor does he care about the perfunctory reward to be gained if he wins, "a bit of blue ribbon and a cup for a prize after we've shagged ourselves out running or jumping, like race horses, only we don't get so well looked-after as race horses, that's the only thing" (8). Smith's decision that he will deliberately lose the race, disclosed to the reader in the early pages of the story, is motivated primarily "because I'm not a race horse at all, and I'll let him know it" (12), asserting fundamentally *human* freedoms that the romantics also cherished: the freedom not to be dehumanized, not to suborn himself, not to conform, and not to comply.

Smith's "us-them" duality is further characterized as the fundamental opposition of "Out-laws" like himself and "In-laws" like the governor of the borstal and all other ostensibly "respectable" and law-abiding citizens. Though he recognizes that such people "have the whip-hand [another race horse metaphor] over blokes like me, and I'm almost dead sure it'll always be like that" (13), he defies and derides them with characteristic vigor:

> Them bastards over us aren't as daft as they most of the time look. . . . They're cunning, and I'm cunning. If only 'them' and 'us' had the same ideas we'd get on like a house on fire, but they don't see eye to eye with us and we don't see eye to eye with them . . . all the pig-faced snotty-nosed dukes and ladies—who can't add two and two together and would mess themselves like loonies if they didn't have slavies to beck-and-call. . . .

(7–8)

Like the forthright, earnest, and profane narrative of Holden Caulfield in J. D. Salinger's *The Catcher in the Rye* (1954), the frankness of which shocked readers in the 1950's, Sillitoe's vernacular style, diction, and rhythm in this novella stretched (and therefore helped to redefine) the "acceptable limits" of discourse in English fiction. Though seemingly non- (or sub-) literary by the prevailing standards of its day (no less than Wordsworth's diction and subject matter in *Lyrical Ballads*), Sillitoe's work accurately—and even lyrically—captured the language really used by young men, particularly when in a state of confinement.

Like Brendan Behan's autobiographical *Borstal Boy* (1958), **The Loneliness of the Long-Distance Runner** introduced readers to the realities of borstal life as seen through the eyes of a teenaged protagonist who, despite the anti-social acts of which he was convicted, proves himself to be an exuberant, irrepressible, and defiant anti-hero, expounding values that remain irreconcilable with the ideology of the prevailing culture but are none the less important for all that. With Orc-like energy, Smith defines himself *against* the entire respectable, staid, repressive, and "reasonable" In-law world; his foremost adversary is the (Urizen-like) Governor of the borstal, the nameless embodiment of all authority figures who exercise institutionalized control. Like Arthur Seaton, Smith assumes that "it's war between me and them," though he also asserts that "it's a good life . . . if you don't give in to coppers and Borstal-bosses and the rest of them bastard-faced In-laws" (11). Like Arthur, too, he relishes the "fun and fire" to be gotten out of life (12) and is not seriously interested in social or political issues, noting that "government wars aren't my wars; they've got nowt to do with me, because my own war's all that I'll ever be bothered about" (15). Nevertheless, as he runs across the chilly fields at dawn, Smith enjoys the solitude in nature, "feel[ing] like the first and last man on the world, both at once" (8). Away from the crowded dormitories and the class-ridden society of the outside world (where he worked at a factory milling-machine), he spends the time "doing a lot of thinking . . . and that's what I like" (10). Yet, predictably, he has no regrets about the activities that brought him to the reformatory, and he has no serious intentions of reforming his ways.

The final section of the story takes place during and after the race itself. Assuming the lead easily, he plans to lose the race deliberately when he is within sight of the goal line and being observed by not only his fellow confinees but also "the pop-eyed potbellied governor" and "a pop-eyed potbellied Member of Parliament who sat next to his pop-eyed potbellied whore of a wife" (33)—thus subverting the confident expectations that others have for him and frustrating their plans for his future and his life. In so doing, he not only repudiates the entire English "public school" ethos of sports (in which the governor and member of parliament, as representatives of their class, unquestioningly believe), but he also asserts—though he would not recognize it as such—an existential freedom to say no. Like other existential (and Byronic) heroes, he accepts full responsibility for his choice, well aware that his defiance will bring retaliation; although he is relegated to the hardest and dirtiest jobs in the borstal for the weeks remaining in his sentence, he remains a hero to the other boys.

Within the context of this existential self-definition, Smith's insistence on his own kind of "honesty" becomes clear. In choosing to *run* rather than to *race,* to set his own standards rather than to compete against (and thus define himself in terms of) others, he asserts the fundamental—and ultimately *romantic*—primacy of the self: he refuses to allow others to impose their conventional expectations on his behavior, thereby restricting his freedom. Like Huckleberry Finn—still another adolescent out-law from the ostensibly lower classes of society—Smith resists all attempts to "civilize" him, though he maintains that, despite his criminal record,

> . . . I *am* honest, that I've never been anything else but honest, and that I'll always be honest. . . . I think my honesty is the only sort in the world, and [the governor] thinks his is the only sort in the world as well.
>
> (13)

Smith's "honesty," like that of his romantic forebears, affirms the truth of feelings rather than propriety, of personal integrity and existential autonomy rather than "civilized" decorum and unthinking conformity. It also entails an acceptance of life's hardships and pain, represented by his father's "Out-law death" (43) from stomach cancer, refusing to be hospitalized, rejecting the doctors and their drugs, defiant until the last; in contrast, the governor and other In-laws are said to be "dead from the toenails up," and their counsel to "be honest . . . [is] like saying: Be dead, like me . . . and settle down in a cosy six pounds a week job" (13). The alternative is an exuberant *joie de vivre* that is effectively symbolized in the narrative's frequently lyrical descriptions of running (though Sillitoe himself was never an athlete himself, nor was confined in a borstal—as he responds to his most-frequently-asked questions); "I'll win in the end," Smith contends, "even if I die in gaol at eighty-two, because I'll have had more fun and fire out of my life than [the governor]'ll ever get out of his" (12).

Clearly, his running has been made a form of contractual work rather than play. Yet not even the cup and blue ribbon will be Smith's own, since they will belong to the winning institution—a reform school *qua* factory whose product is "honest men." Its governor/owner/manager never once suggests that the athlete should win for *himself*—that the laborer should receive the reward of his toil—or even that (altruistically) the sport can provide a sense of personal achievement and a satisfaction all its own whether he wins or not. Accordingly, Smith recognizes that the victory, which he is quite capable of achieving, "don't mean a bloody thing to me" (12). In cunningly subverting the plans of those who seek to keep him under their control for their own benefit, he affirms the existence of an innately *human* (and fundamentally *romantic*) alternative to the prevailing social and economic ethos: however successful others may be in "owning" the athlete's body (which, like a factory's machine, is powerful, well-maintained, efficient, and smoothly functional), they can never control his mind, subdue his emotions, quash his spirit, or quell his independent will. Thus, in making sure that *this* race is indeed "not to the swift," Smith proves that, in the words of the Book of Ecclesiastes, the more important "battle" is also "not to the strong."

3

In many ways, the publication of *The Death of William Posters* (1965)—the first volume of a trilogy that also includes *A Tree on Fire* (1967) and *The Flame of Life* (1974)—signified a new direction in Sillitoe's writing, although its affinities with romantic rebelliousness in general and Byronic attitudes in particular are more explicit than ever before. The trilogy is a far more ambitious and complex undertaking than any of his previous works, presenting the interconnected lives of three central characters in addition to numerous secondary ones, and its settings range from the world of London's avant-garde art galleries to the deserts of Algeria during its war for independence. The *Zeitgeist* of the 1960's and early 1970's pervades its diffuse plot as well: the "anger" of the earlier works, which had so startled readers in the staid 1950's, pales in comparison to the rage of the militants and ideologues of the later decade. Unlike the relatively innocuous "secret subversions" that are carried out by the central characters in *Saturday Night and Sunday Morning* and *The Loneliness of the Long-Distance Runner,* the rebellion that is joined by the protagonist of *The Death of William Posters* is an act of genuine political defiance rather than a symbolic (or token) gesture; the *literal* battles in which he fights require a far more serious existential and ideological commitment than Smith or Arthur Seaton would ever conceivably be called upon to make. Clearly, therefore, in writing the William Posters Trilogy, Sillitoe intended to reach beyond Nottingham and its narrow "cosy world of pubs and noisy tarts" (*SN&SM* 7) with which his fiction had become identified—and to extend the range and scope of his fiction by assaying more profound themes of art and politics, creating characters whose involvements and activities are more closely attuned to the ideological, social, and artistic upheavals of their times.

Whereas the earlier novels typically ended with their protagonists' arrival at the threshold of a significant and imminent transformation in their lives, *The Death of William Posters* begins with such a threshold being crossed: Frank Dawley, a twenty-seven-year-old working-class machine-operator, abandons his wife and child, his job in the factory, and his home for no apparent reason other than that "he had to leave, yet without knowing why" (48), having become simply and thoroughly sick of it all. Having sold his car to raise cash to support himself, he sets out with a knapsack to follow the open road toward self-discovery; fundamentally, it is a romantic quest, a search for moral and political answers on *how best to live.* Its first premise is a rejection of the spirit-stifling domestic conventionality that is represented by both his unhappy marriage and his soul-stifling job in the factory. Despite the familiar pattern of the alienated, lusty, brawling, working-class protagonist that was established in Sillitoe's earlier fiction, Frank Dawley is some ways quite different—and he makes clear his disdain for men like Arthur Seaton as he remembers "one of his Nottingham mates who, unless he got blind drunk, spewed his guts up, and was knocked to the ground in unequal fight, didn't feel he'd had a good time—the sort of thing that now seemed a waste of life to Frank Dawley" and, apparently, to his author too (150). In fact, Sillitoe parodies the entire tradition of ostensibly "angry young men" as another of his characters considers

> the voting Labour masses that still seemed to inhabit the North: cloth-capped, hardworking, generous and bruto, or that was the impression she got from reading a book (or was it books?) called *Hurry On Jim* by Kingsley Wain that started by someone with eighteen pints and fifteen whiskies in him falling downstairs on his way to the top.
>
> (*DWP* 143)

In her confusion, she conflates John Wain's *Hurry On Down* (1953), Kingsley Amis's *Lucky Jim* (1954), John Braine's *Room at the Top* (1957), and Sillitoe's own *Saturday Night and Sunday Morning* (1957) into one mega-"angry" novel—as if, in the public's mind, to have read one is to have read them all. Such a novel is, nevertheless, clearly quite different from the work that Sillitoe had undertaken in the William Posters trilogy.

There is, however, no "real" William Posters; he is, instead, a figment of Frank Dawley's imagination, a modern-day renegade like Robin Hood, an outlaw and outcast whose legendary misdeeds have confounded Nottingham officials (including, presumably, its sheriff) as well as authorities elsewhere, who inscribe on various public surfaces the warning that "Bill Posters Will Be Prosecuted." Throughout the years, Dawley has elaborated the legend, which, like many myths, is not entirely or explicably consistent. Initially, Frank is said to have "endow[ed] the slovenly Bill with the typical mentality of the workman-underdog, the put-upon dreg whose spiritual attributes he had been soaked and bombarded with all through his school, home, and working life" (13)—though such a character would surely be incapable of the (anti-)heroic deeds that are later attributed to him. Despite the claim that "Frank had fought [such influences] off, being like him in no single way at all" (13), he also contends that "maybe if [Bill] hadn't been persecuted . . . he'd have turned out a different man, been a bloke like me who'd got a job in a factory and . . . been a good worker for the union" (15). Yet, in his anti-authoritarian response to the threatened prosecution and persecution, Frank finds that "in some big way Bill Posters had also been responsible for his [Frank's] exploding out of life so far, leaving wife, home, job, kids and Nottingham's fair city where he had been born, bred and spiritually nullified" (13). When Bill and Frank have broken out of the old life, the anti-heroic aspects of the mythic, working-class figure become more apparent:

> He must know no rest, for they were still out to get him. . . . Bill was always in a hurry, travelling furtively, travelling light . . . But the great and marvellous thing was that they never got him! Bill had been on the run from birth and was more than a match for his persecutors . . . [who would] never catch Bill . . . for he was clever and . . . too smart to give himself away[, and] . . . infamous in these streets for generations. . . .
>
> (13–14)

Accordingly, in many ways William Posters is Frank Dawley's alter-ego, unfettered by domestic responsibilities and the mundane routine of a factory job, free to travel at will, clever enough to violate whatever laws and social conventions he dislikes, and cunning enough to thrive in defiance of all forms of authority. As such, he shares a number of the traits that characterized Sillitoe's earlier protagonists, with their unsubduability and their secret subversions, in which they take both pride and delight. Yet, for all this "outlaw" rebelliousness, William Posters (like Arthur

Seaton and even Smith) remains fundamentally *domestic,* which is *per se* a capitulation—in contrast to the genuinely revolutionary activity which Frank Dawley eventually undertakes in the deserts of Algeria.

Maintaining that "there's no place for me on this right little tight little island" (**DWP** 193), Frank admits that he is running away from himself to find himself. Accompanied by his lover Myra Bassingfield, whose husband died in a car crash while trying to run down the pair when making their escape together, he leaves England for the continent, travelling from Paris to Barcelona before going on to Majorca and Granada. On the steamer from Barcelona, he meets Shelley Jones, an American expatriate, a former advertising executive who gave up his job, trained in Cuba, and now travels the world giving covert aid to nationalist insurgencies and anti-imperial revolutionaries throughout the world; he is currently headed toward Tangier, from where he will be gun-running for the Algerian FLN in their struggle against the French. Frank readily agrees to become Shelley's co-driver, seizing the opportunity "to get out of his spiralled airtight shell and carry violence to the enemy camp" for the first time in his life (**DWP** 246). He thus commits himself to an outlaw action that William Posters would never have dared to undertake, being "too English for this world" of radical political commitment, having "never had a Bren [submachine gun] at his shoulder" (**DWP** 264, 265). The novel ends as Frank successfully takes part in his first ambush in the Algerian desert, the gun's "kick at his shoulder [being] the joy of life" (**DWP** 268). In effect, he has laid the ultimately ineffectual William Posters to rest by committing his life to the furtherance of militant, radical, and literally revolutionary change.

In much the same way that, in James Joyce's *Ulysses,* the seemingly mundane events in the life of Leopold Bloom on a June day in Dublin in 1904 recapitulate adventures of Ulysses that are recounted in Homer's *Odyssey,* Frank Dawley is in many ways the twentieth-century proletarian counterpart of George Gordon, Lord Byron during the portion of his life following his separation from his wife—a period that includes his final exile from England and his activities in support of the struggle for Greek independence. Although such correspondences are far less intricately detailed than those in Joyce's work, and although the differences between the two lives are manifest, the pattern that they constitute can hardly be coincidental; the parallels suggest not only a provocative concept of contemporary Byronism but help to account for some of Frank Dawley's actions that may seem at best only vaguely motivated otherwise. Thus, for example, the novel begins *immediately* after Frank Dawley has left his wife and family at the age of twenty-seven, the age at which Byron left his marriage; although Frank Dawley's reasons are not *specifically* explained, there is no suggestion of the type of lurid accusations that were brought by Lady Byron against her husband. Frank Dawley's involvement with other women also echoes Byron's own amorous entanglements (an affair with a nurse named Pat Shipley

precedes his relationship with Myra, who later bears his child). The more important parallels occur during Frank's self-imposed sojourn abroad, however—and even his resolution to flee forever "this . . . tight little island" (**DWP** 193) exactly echoes Byron's own, as the latter used the same phrase in a letter written late in 1816 (quoted in Marchand 260). Although Frank Dawley's travels take him through France and Spain rather than Switzerland and Italy as Lord Byron's had done, each journey ultimately leads to the battlefronts of the foremost national liberation movements of their times, in Algeria and Greece respectively.

Within this Byronic context of romantic revolutionism, Frank Dawley's initial meeting with the appropriately named Shelley Jones takes on added significance; like his namesake, Sillitoe's character of Shelley is younger than Frank, far more erudite and intellectual, and much more radical in his ardent commitment to international revolution. His effect on Frank is the same as that of the earlier Shelley on his friend Byron, which Leslie Marchand has described:

> Shelley, who [was] himself an ethereal presence, opened up wide vistas in Byron's mind . . . [through] the spell of [his] eloquence. . . . It was a novelty for Byron to find [in Shelley and his party] agreeable persons untrammeled by the conventions of society, well read and intelligent, with sensitive appreciation, ready to discuss any subject under the sun with speculative intensity.
>
> (Marchand 241–42)

It was, in fact, Shelley who rekindled Byron's interest in the Greek struggle for independence (Marchand 360). Sillitoe's Shelley, like his namesake, is a radical nonconformist in virtually every aspect of his personal life, and each has abandoned the security of his conservative backgrounds (in the Sussex gentry and on Madison Avenue, respectively) to devote himself to radically idealistic causes. Each is also an ardent follower of the foremost theorists of political revolution of his day—Godwin and the founders of the French revolution in the early nineteenth century, and Mao Tse-tung, Ngoyen Giap, Che Guevara, and Fidel Castro in the 1960's.

Like Byron in support of Italy's Carbonari in their attempt to "send the Barbarians of all nations back to their own dens" (Marchand 324) and in his aid to the Greek effort to overthrow the Turks—and, indeed, like Brian Seaton with his secret sympathies for the Malayan insurgents in **Key to the Door**—Frank Dawley supports the FLN's struggle against the French as a form of anti-imperialism and pro-nationalism. In the twentieth century, of course, these also coincide with a distinctively communist ideology that Byron—with his belief in "an aristocratic or gentlemanly leadership" as well as his "distrust of the mob and lack of sympathy for democratic or proletarian, or even middle-class, control or participation in government" (Marchand 321)—definitely would not have shared. Yet whereas Byron's support of the Greek cause was primarily financial (a type of contribution that Sillitoe's proletarian protagonist is unable to make), Frank Dawley's commitment to the revolution places his life in even more immediate jeopardy as he literally (i.e., physically) provides munitions to the guerrillas in their desert outposts, accompanying Shelley on their gun-running missions and taking part in firefights and acts of sabotage against the French. In so doing, he carries out the sort of direct action for which Byron longed when, as a leader of the Suliotes in 1824, he planned to lead a night raid against Turkish ships to damage their rigging and drive them onto the rocks (Marchand 434). Accordingly, *The Death of William Posters* ends with just such a night-time ambush against a French convoy, although the enemy "vessels" that are destroyed in the twentieth-century work are airplanes rather than ships. The novel ends with Frank Dawley in the desert in the aftermath of the battle, his fate unknown; it was shortly after Byron's planning the above-mentioned battle that he became ill and died.

Nevertheless, as the novel's title indicates, it is William Posters—not Frank Dawley—whose death occurs by the end of the book, and for him too there is a significant "Byronic" parallel. As Frank Dawley's adventurous but imaginary alter-ego, William Posters is a proletarian folk- (or mock-) hero who, despite obvious differences in class background, bears the same sort of relationship to his "creator" as Byron's variously imagined romantic outcasts and exiles bore to Byron himself. Like Childe Harold and others, William Posters is a quasi-autobiographical figure who "constituted his [creator's] secret life and his greatest pleasure and gave a quiet satisfaction to his days" (Marchand 271). Yet, paradoxically, he is also quintessentially *English* and thus unable to break through the social conventions that Frank Dawley has come increasingly to deplore. Thus, although William Posters is a self-styled rebel and outcast whose "secret subversions" earn him a certain anti-heroic notoriety, he (like Arthur Seaton) has never really questioned—or *seriously* threatened to undermine—the status quo in any radical or genuinely revolutionary way. In much the same way that, for Byron, exile became the essential first step in overcoming "the canting generalizations and pomposities of English poetry [and English life, as well as] . . . the fetters of British propriety" (Marchand 273), Frank Dawley must escape British factory life and William Posters' insufficiently radical, stolidly proletarian mentality, respectively:

> Thirty years had taught him nothing except that life was good but limited (the innerlife anyway that the society he'd been brought up in told him existed)—limited in everything, depth, space, decision, strength. . . . He felt at the forward point of the world. . . . The new man of the world must work and live as if he weren't going to be alive the next day. . . . It was a new way to live, and, even now, he was trying it, the first kick-off started the day he left the Nottingham world of moribund William Posters.
>
> (*DWP* 232)

In the exhilaration of the successful ambush and its aftermath, Frank finally repudiates William Posters as "that

soul-anchor . . . that snivelling muffle-capped man on the eternal run who'd never had a Bren at his shoulder" (*DWP* 263, 265). Although Frank Dawley is still *literally* on the run as a guerrilla, his actions are the result of a far more intense ideological commitment, on which he has staked his life, undertaking responsibilities for actions that are far more substantially subversive (if necessarily still secret) than any portrayed in Sillitoe's fiction heretofore.

When their story resumes in *A Tree on Fire,* Frank and Shelley are veterans of many successful acts of sabotage and desert skirmishes. While Shelley plans to board a ship and return with more arms from Morocco or Libya, Frank has resolved to "stay [on the Algerian front] while the fighting lasted, looking on his commitment as the great oceanic end of the line for him, the wide spaces of the world that he must allow himself to be swallowed by if he was to do any good in it" (126)—much as Byron regarded his support of the Greek cause. In Shelley, he recognizes "a nonchalant, easy-going man whose idealism and sense of purpose seemed so much nearer the bone than that which had impelled Frank to set out on this ideological adventure" (134), during which he has learned that "the freedom of the wide-open wilderness had no meaning, was a myth" since "nothing had been escaped from, only entered into . . . push[ing him] deeper into the prison of [him]self" (133). Although Sillitoe expressed his unequivocal disdain for the poetry of T. S. Eliot in his interview with John Halperin, his description of spiritual desolation and the desert as the site of a subsequent personal renewal invites comparison with *The Waste Land*: "to go into the desert meant emptying oneself of all that was bad in order that what should have been there in the first place could then enter" (*ATOF* 148), he contends, shortly after the insurrectionists have sought shelter from a dust-storm in the shadow of a (red?) rock (137). Specifically, Frank Dawley finds himself "in the transition from a life in which he had grown old to a new life in which he had not yet learned to live, needing . . . the heart and brain of a newborn man who now wanted to be on his own" (139); he is, in effect, the modern-day counterpart of the romantics' emergent "new man" (Orc-like, even Promethean), unshackled as a result of liberating, radical, and literally revolutionary societal change.

Like his romantic predecessor, Sillitoe's modern-day Shelley has devoted himself to "trying to prove that [he] can live alone, without man and without God" (his own version of *The Necessity of Atheism*), and he forfeits his life at an untimely age, having never wavered in his dedication "to the cause of helping people towards the togetherness of socialism" (142). Although his life ends in the desert from gangrene-infected wounds that he received in battle (rather than in a boating accident of the kind that killed his namesake), he dies visualizing the sea:

> If the wave broke, he would drown. It became olive-green, white cloud at the top. The black cloth fell over him again, and he saw no more sea.
>
> (186)

Like the drowned, Shelley Jones at his death "was unrecognizable, mouth black and torn from the grind of teeth, eyes unable to open" (181), and his death affects Frank Dawley with "a pouring out of sorrow and loneliness, heartache and despair" (188) that is as profound as Byron's grief over Shelley's demise.

Like Byron, too, Frank Dawley becomes gravely ill relatively shortly after Shelley's death—although, unlike his romantic predecessor, Sillitoe's protagonist survives his illness and returns to England and to his two families (i.e., his wife and children in Nottingham as well as Myra and the son he has never seen), for both of which he has come increasingly to yearn, as Byron did also while in Greece. Yet whereas Byron died without fulfilling any such desires for renewed contact with his family, Frank Dawley not only survives but also finally achieves a life-changing realization in the desert, enabling him to begin (yet again) a new spiritual quest, based on a recognition of personal responsibility:

> In the clarity of his mind he speculated on how many sins one had to commit before reaching the kingdom of heaven, how many good people abandon who had come to lean on you more heavily for support than you realized in your malformed desire to be free of them. Your life depended on people who needed you. Nancy and the children, Myra and their child . . .—he had abandoned them to help people whom he wanted to need him, but who, in reality, had learned well enough how to help themselves, a break with settled fate in order to control the circumstances of his own life.
>
> (201)

Following his nearly-fatal illness, Frank Dawley returns to England with plans not only to unite his two families but to join the chaotic commune-like existence of the large family of his long-time friend Albert Handley, a now-famous artist whom he had first met soon after setting out on his journey toward self-discovery. For all his resolve to return to personal domestic responsibility, Frank Dawley—like Albert Handley and his bizarre family—remains fundamentally determined to avoid "the bourgeois trap" (217). Nevertheless, his function as a modern-day Byronic revolutionary effectively comes to an end in the desert, just as Byron himself died in Greece with the goals of the (eventually successful) insurgency that he supported still unachieved.

Although the parallels between Frank Dawley and Lord Byron (and those between the two Shelleys) constitute the principal romantic parallels in the trilogy, there are other noteworthy romantic motifs and affinities in *A Tree on Fire*. Like Frank, Albert Handley characterizes himself as a "revolutionary by faith" (92), though he contends that "no artist has the right to go and fight for the oppressed peoples, etc." (109), since such an action would entail an abandonment of his "higher calling"; his art—like Frank's political commitment—is a product of the spiritual "unknown desert-emptiness that he'd stumbled into and taken the courage to cross" (90). Later, his reflections on

the chaos of his family life echo the romantic concept of the artist's internal and external *Sturm und Drang*:

> In the middle of a long great storm the ability to know was replaced by the necessity to act. It was chaos that decided what you could and would do, so that all you had to do was prepare for it, unless you were an artist, in which case every form of storm was already in you—everything.
>
> He looked for confirmation of this to his recent painting. . . .
>
> (119)

Like Gulley Jimson, the narrator-protagonist of Joyce Cary's *The Horse's Mouth* (1944), Albert Handley is a genial genius-cum-reprobate whose quasi-religious "primitive surrealistic realist" paintings (*DWP* 95) seem to have particular affinities with those of William Blake in the romantic period (and, perhaps, Stanley Spencer in more recent times).

The novel's most surprising—and most ironic—romantic obeisance occurs in its final chapters, which involve Albert's brother John, a war-deranged invalid who for fifteen years has confined himself to the family home, tirelessly transcribing Morse-coded radio-signals in the hope that, from out of the heavens, "they might one day yield a precise solution to the whole pattern of his life that he could fall down before and worship" (*ATOF* 66). Suddenly and without warning, after setting fire to his brother's house, he goes to rescue Frank Dawley and bring him back from Algeria. After finding him near death in an Algerian hospital and securing his passage home, John goes to Paris (the romantics' center of revolution, to which he too is now committed), convinced that a *new* revolutionary triumverate of "Energy, Imagination, and Intelligence were to replace the autocratic triumverate of Inertia, Stagnation, and Reaction" (351) which had, in turn, supplanted the romantics' cherished ideals of Liberty, Fraternity, and Equality among "the lumpen-bourgeoisie" (368). Yet, crossing the English channel from Calais, he places a revolver in his mouth and fires, as the

> stacks of loose papers in foolscap sheets [which are his] years of radio-logs . . . tak[en] down . . . in the hope of finding and hearing and recording for himself and everyone a message from some non-existent God or god-like fountain beyond all the layers of the stars that might contain the precious message of life that would fill him with energy, imagination, and intelligence. . . . The hundreds of sheets of paper covered with his neat writing scattered like . . . dead leaves. . . .
>
> (356)

This startling image obviously evokes the closing sonnet of Shelley's "Ode to the West Wind," with its hope for a revitalizing of the revolutionary spirit:

> Drive my dead thoughts over the universe
> Like withered leaves to quicken a new birth!

And by the incantation of this verse,
Scatter, as from an unextinguished hearth
Ashes and sparks, my words among mankind!
Be through my lips to unawakened Earth
The trumpet of a prophecy! O Wind,
If Winter comes, can Spring be far behind?

(lines 63–70)

John's transcriptions of radio-messages from the empyrean are the (devalued) modern counterparts of Shelley's neo-Platonism, and it is symbolically appropriate that his death, like Shelley's, occurs on a boat—with his brains as well as his words being scattered by his self-extinguishing (pistol-) fire. Yet, coming as it does at the end of the second novel of the trilogy, this overt obeisance to Shelley's poem might *also* herald a similarly hoped-for revolution—to which the many of the novel's readers in 1967, at the height of tumultuous international social upheaval that was then held to be the dawning of a new and Aquarian age, might plausibly have felt themselves to have been particularly well attuned.

In describing the trilogy in his 1985 essay for *Contemporary Authors Autobiography Series,* Sillitoe rather dismissively remarked that "the thousand pages of these three books deal with the political attitudes of the 1960s" (386)—and subsequently added that he "didn't really get into [his] stride as a writer until [his] midforties, marked by the publication of **The Widower's Son** (1976)," the novel that *followed* completion of the trilogy (388). "At that time," he adds, "there was a change of gear" (388), though its nature remains unspecified. In part, perhaps, the change involved abandoning his exploration of the political ideologies of revolution that figured so prominently in the trilogy and, less ardently, in the earlier works as well. Yet it is also possible that Sillitoe had "gotten into [his own] stride as a writer" by working out his relationship to the literary tradition in general and the romantic poets in particular, whose works and world-views pervade his writings to a degree that is far more extensive than recognized heretofore—denoting an "anxiety of influence" being worked through in the early novels, which (paradoxically) were recognized even from the outset as the expression of a new, vigorous, and vital literary voice that was also—and remains—uniquely his own.

Notes

1. In Sillitoe's brief discussion of *Road to Volgograd* in his autobiographical essay for the *Contemporary Authors Autobiography Series* (1985), however, he remarks that "at that time there seemed to be more freedom for the writer and artist (and therefore for everybody else) since before the Revolution, and my optimistic tone expressed it. Later visits showed me however that it was only a temporary change, and that the rigid orthodoxy of the Russian system was incapable of liberalisation. When I went as a tourist to Russia in September 1967 I gave a lecture at the Gorki Literary Institute, my theme being that of 'Freedom for the Writer.' It didn't go down very well

with the authorities, but the students liked it" (386). *Road to Volgograd* has not been reprinted since its initial publication.

2. See, for example, Allen R. Penner, Stanley S. Atherton, Peter Hitchcock, and Ronald D. Vaverka. For comprehensive bibliography of primary and secondary sources, see David Gerard.

Works Cited

Atherton, Stanley S. *Alan Sillitoe: A Critical Assessment.* London: W. H. Allen, 1979.

Burgess, Anthony. *The Novel Now: A Guide to Contemporary Fiction.* 1967; New York: Pegasus, 1970.

Gerard, David. *Alan Sillitoe: A Bibliography.* London: Mansell, 1988.

Halperin, John. "Interview with Alan Sillitoe." *Modern Fiction Studies* 25:2 (Summer 1979), 175–189.

Hitchcock, Peter. *Working Class Fiction in Theory and Practice: A Reading of Alan Sillitoe.* Ann Arbor: UMI Press, 1989.

Marchand, Leslie A. *Byron: A Portrait.* 1970; Chicago: U of Chicago P, 1979.

Marx, Karl. *Capital: A Critical Analysis of Modern Capitalist Production.* Trans. from the third German ed. by Samuel Moore and Edward Aveling. Ed. Frederick Engels. London: Swann Sonnenschein & Lowery, 1872.

Penner, Allen R. *Alan Sillitoe.* New York: Twayne, 1972.

Sillitoe, Alan. *The Death of William Posters.* 1965; London: Grafton Books, 1986.

———. *Key to the Door.* 1961; London: Grafton Books, 1986.

———. *The Loneliness of the Long-Distance Runner.* New York: NAL, 1959. 7–47.

———. *Raw Material.* 3rd rev. ed. London: Grafton Books, 1987.

———. *Road to Volgograd.* London: W. H. Allen, 1964.

———. *Saturday Night and Sunday Morning.* New York: NAL, 1958.

———. *A Tree on Fire.* 1967; London: Grafton Books, 1986.

———. Untitled autobiographical essay. *Contemporary Authors' Autobiography Series.* Ed. Adela Sarkissian. Detroit: Gale Research Co., 1985. Vol. 2, 371–389.

Vaverka, Ronald D. *Commitment as Art: A Marxist Critique of a Selection of Alan Sillitoe's Political Fictions.* Uppsala: U of Uppsala P, 1978.

Williams, Raymond. *Politics and Letters: Interviews with New Left Review.* London: Verso Editions, 1980.

John Lucas (review date 12 August 1994)

SOURCE: "Nurtured by the Wasteland," in *Times Literary Supplement,* No. 4767, August 12, 1994, p. 24.

[*In the following review, Lucas provides an unfavorable assessment of Sillitoe's* Collected Poems.]

In the preface to this ample volume, [**Collected Poems,**] Alan Sillitoe explains that it contains fewer than half the poems he has published during his writing career. "Fat and gristle," he calls the work he has discarded, adding that what he has chosen to include has been subjected to "extreme revision" and represents "the meat" of his achievement as a poet. It also "displays the emotional history" of Sillitoe's "heart and soul." I don't complain of such unguarded candour, however old-hat the phrasing may seem to be; nor is there reason to doubt that the pruning knife has been hard at work. What is to be regretted is that the cutting and re-writing haven't done much for the candour. Too many of these poems are muffled by dead language, inert rhythms and pointless stanza divisions, as though Sillitoe is determined to come on as a "poet," but has chosen to leave behind the virtues that make him at his best a valuable writer of fiction.

His first verse collection, **The Rats,** was written, he says, while he was working on **Saturday Night and Sunday Morning.** But where, in the poems, can you find any evidence of the ear for local speech, the vivid understanding of particular lives, that distinguish his novel? "The wasteland that seemed to Mr Eliot death / Nurtured me with passion, life and breath." Admittedly, the lines that follow these try to itemize how and why "The wasteland was my library and college," but they do so with such clumsy, reach-me-down vocabulary and rhymes that they quite undermine the claims the poet hopes to make for his unsentimental education. This is not so much candour as schlock.

Matters improve when he moves away from Nottingham, although he never shakes off the habit of slovenly writing. "A broad and solid oak exploded / Split by mystery and shock / Broken like bread / Like a flower shaken." Exploded *and* split? Broken *and* shaken? It's odd that Sillitoe should have a thing about trees and woods—several poems celebrate or "deal" with them—when he has so little regard for how they actually look or for their histories or the space they occupy. But then Sillitoe the poet hasn't much sense of any of these things. Perhaps for this reason one of the most interesting of his poems, called **"Lancaster,"** has for subject the displaced and displacing experience of being taken for a (peacetime) flight in a Second World War bomber:

> the botch of Leicester
> Railways of Rugby, the sandstone of Oxford
> The peace of Abingdon and the first view of
> the Thames,
> Canals and rivers of new reality, calico
> tablecloth

> Hiding all in me, unseen from my chosen
> seat.

The language is at best journalistic, but the sense of not belonging. "My place forever looking down and in," comes across as near to the writer's "heart and soul."

Unfortunately, the looking seldom amounts to more than tepid adjective-noun constructions. Even the poems Sillitoe has selected from **Tides and Stone Walls** offer very little by way of imagistic sharpness, and this is in spite of the fact that they were originally written to accompany work by the photographer Victor Bowley. "It's what the tide reveals / When it huffs and leaves / That means so much." Maybe, but given that we're never told what in fact is revealed, we have to take the claim on trust. Perhaps Sillitoe felt he couldn't and/or shouldn't try to compete with the photographs, and this is entirely understandable. But the sad truth is that left to themselves the poems drop into an incoherent mutter. "Bombs are the enemies of bricks"; "Blood makes history, / And desolation / A winter's day." Reading these and other poems that between them make up Sillitoe's **Collected,** you come to feel that it's the product of someone endlessly ill at ease with a medium he nevertheless cannot bring himself to do without.

Edward Blishen (review date 7 July 1995)

SOURCE: "A Life in Notts," in *Times Educational Supplement,* July 7, 1995, p. 12.

[*In the following review of* Life without Armour, *Blishen asserts that much of the information in the autobiography has been utilized in Sillitoe's novels and short stories.*]

He was looking out of the window—for once not writing, he seems to remember [in his autobiography **Life without Armour**], being in a vacant mood—when he saw a youngster in vest and shorts trotting past. He scribbled on a clean sheet of paper what he took to be the first line of a poem: "The loneliness of the long distance runner . . ." But no second line came, so he put it away, and got on with a long poem called **"The Rats."**

For eight years he had been trying to break into print. There'd been *The General's Dilemma,* a novel drawing on his passion for world politics and warfare. (At 15 he had set out to write a history of the war, alongside the dossier he was keeping on the illegal activities of his cousins: if his mother had not come across this last, the whole family might have ended up in prison, victims of the stubborn chronicler they'd spawned). There was *The Palisade,* and *Mr Allen's Island,* and much else: hope kept going by an agent as obstinate as himself.

Now he was in Bishop's Stortford, after six years abroad, largely in Majorca, where Robert Graves, having read one of the manuscripts, said: "Why don't you write something set in Nottingham? That's the place you know best." Though until he was 19 he had read only two adult novels, he had soon thereafter got on to DH Lawrence, that other local lad who had moved into Europe, towards the sun, and flowered there: and had begun by writing "something set in Nottingham."

Alan Sillitoe does not say if he was stirred by Graves's advice: but lately he had begun work on a novel with the tentative title *The Adventures of Arthur Seaton,* for which, with the unflinching cannibalism of the writer-in-waiting, he had drawn on several of his (of course, unpublished) short stories.

Arthur Seaton, hero of **Saturday Night and Sunday Morning,** as it ended up being called, was to be, extremely famously, a young man impatient with what he thought of as his enslavement to the lathe in the bicycle-making factory. Alan Sillitoe had worked at the same lathe, but with satisfaction: "The magic of turning out each separate object never left me."

Like Arthur Seaton, like the long distance runner (when at last that remarkable story wrote itself), he was marked by "an enduring disrespect for authority," which he attributed to the influence, this way or that, of his father, who had "the mind of a ten-year-old in the body of a brute." But he was endlessly patient, growlingly dogged, into the bargain: all along the years there are these photographs of him biting into his pipestem, the eyes reflecting the undivertable imagination within but being also stern, obdurate.

Sillitoe has told us much of all this in his fiction: and at first that seems a problem. There are stretches in the autobiography, spoken as the memoirist must speak them, as from a witness box, where I longed for what I thought of as the superior truthfulness of this or that short story or novel, spoken from the freer, warmer platform that the fictioneer occupies. But after a time one sees that the methodical trudge of the plain account of oneself has curiously valuable additions to offer.

Take the childhood. Sillitoe says he grew up as one of those referred to in Robert Graves's and Alan Hodges's *The Long Weekend* as "the unkillable poor." If it was a wonder that they were not killed by hard luck and penury, it was a wonder also that they did not kill each other. Sillitoe's father added to his streak of violence the frustrated fury of an illiterate. It is an example of the writer's refusal of self-pity that he says his father's hatred of his love of reading might have been a spur, and a reason to be grateful.

An early memory is of his mother making sure the blood from an injury inflicted by her husband dripped into a pail and not on the carpet. Sillitoe says, in his gruffest tone, that his was a paradise of a childhood compared to that of a Jewish boy or girl in the Warsaw ghetto. Yes, you want to say, of course: but this does not mean it was not awful to have to struggle up as children in Sillitoe's condition had to struggle up.

It is another valuable feature of the autobiography that it makes it plain how this determined child preserved himself. He had a passion for maps, and for the names of foreign places and people, and for the geography of the sky as well as that of the earth. He made his way forward via the Air Training Corps: became so good at navigation and the rest that he was accepted as a trainee pilot for the Fleet Air Arm, though later he withdrew: became an airfield controller.

All that, culminating in service in the RAF, has fed much of his fiction. But here we are helped to see clearly the young man who had perfected his armour against a world coldly ready to do him down. Intent here too on giving the strictest possible report on himself, Sillitoe says he had, out of what he thinks of as supineness and obtuseness, melted thought into action: he was not going to let the mind have much of a say, since this would lead to worry, and so to uncertainty: "And I wasn't having any of that."

But odd bits of experience were prising thought and action apart: music, for example, especially, for some reason, Bizet's *L'Arlesienne*; and among all the books he was reading, the two he'd come to know while still an adolescent, *Les Miserables* and *The Count of Monte Cristo.*

Then, to make it certain that his "not sufficiently unhappy state" should be fully, cruelly reformed, there was tuberculosis: "From wanting to be first-class everything I was suddenly defeated in an area where no trouble had been expected at all." This defeat, of course, was the first step towards a tremendous victory, when out of all that writing came the dramatic first success. Typically he says he was not dismayed when 15 years earlier his second attempt at the scholarship failed: as he puts it, he knew he was going to enter by way of the ceiling, not the cellar.

Not that he allowed any forward step to be easy. Tom Maschler would have taken **Saturday Night and Sunday Morning** for McGibbon and Kee, but wanted to edit it: and Sillitoe, having learned to write the hard way, was not going to be told by anyone how to revise his novel. Marvellous: though anyone reading him now, with whatever admiration, might wish he'd allowed editorship in respect of his addiction to the unrelated participle. (Alarmed, I imagine his teeth tightening on that pipestem).

His refusal to be thought of in any fashion that might be regarded as pigeonholing him makes him furious about being described as working class. He is a writer, he holds, like any other, one who happened to have emerged (receiving his first underwear ever at kitting out for the RAF) from awkward circumstances in down-town Nottingham. Again one thinks, yes of course: but read the short stories, especially the earlier ones in this selection, and try to think of some way of avoiding his wrath whilst putting the case that they offer remarkable views of the British working class just before, during and just after the Second World War.

What does Alan Sillitoe himself think of the difference between the platforms offered by fiction and autobiography (this autobiography, by the way, ending with the transformation in 1958 of the ugly duckling into the industrious swan: what followed, he says, disappointingly, would amount to a mere list of books produced).

When I rang him with the question the answer was instant. "In fiction," he said, "one always embellishes. Things have a patina that the imagination gives them." There was a slight pause. "Nothing in my fiction," he said, "is me."

Andy Croft (review date 21 July 1995)

SOURCE: "Don't Thee 'Tha' Me," in *New Statesman and Society,* Vol. 8, No. 362, July 21, 1995, p. 39.

[*In the following excerpt, Croft offers a positive review of* Life without Armour.]

The first book Alan Sillitoe ever owned, given to him when he was nine by a kindly teacher, included an extract from *The Count of Monte Cristo* in which Dantes escapes from the dungeons of the Chateau d'If; soon afterwards, he bought a second-hand copy of *Les Miserables.* "Between them they lit up my darkness with visions of hope and escape." One was a story of escape, the other of justice: "powerhouses buried in the heart which they helped to survive." In the terrible conditions of Sillitoe's childhood, both seemed more real than fictions. But it was Dumas' novel he took with him when he was evacuated to Worksop in 1939, and which shapes the narrative of *Life without Armour.*

Sillitoe soon learned to escape from the unhappiness of his parents' fights into books; from the Nottingham slums to the surrounding fields; and from the capstan lathe to dreams of flying. *Life without Armour* is a marvellous escape story: Sillitoe's long flight from TB, England, **"The Rats,"** literary failure, until he burst through the doors of success at last. "A kick having been aimed at the door, the whole structure was found to be rotten."

The idea of the door recurs throughout Sillitoe's work (**"Key to the Door," "The Open Door"**) and is one of the ways in which *Life without Armour* recalls his apprehension, as a young man, of the future—sometimes also a map, a mountain, a road, and a concrete wall.

Throughout the book, Sillitoe is in a state of constant excitement and impatience for life to begin. The first half deals with his life to 1948, looking forward to the time when he would begin writing; the second, with his struggles to write in the 1950s. He ends in 1961, the Hawthornden Prize and the triumphant filming of *Saturday Night and Sunday Morning* and *The Loneliness of the Long-Distance Runner.*

It's surprising place to stop, with the door swinging shut behind him, justified on the grounds that, thereafter, his life as a successful writer has been "too dull to write about." But following Sillitoe's early manuscripts as they bounce back is interesting enough, especially those later used in the two filmed works (and now collected with his other stories). If life beyond that door has been so much less interesting—if the huge impatience for living to begin has been squandered on 35 years of writing—we are entitled to wonder why, and to ask if it has been worth it.

Because he does not address these questions, parts of the book read like messages from a distant, long-exploded star, a golden age of working-class-writing—although Sillitoe would be the first to refuse the term. And so for a while it seemed, as a generation of novelists gate-crashed through the narrow door which he had helped to "blow off its hinges."

John Melmoth (review date 18 August 1995)

SOURCE: "Crime as a Buzz," in *Times Literary Supplement,* No. 4820, August 18, 1995, p. 22.

[*In the following review, Melmoth underscores the realism and humanity of Sillitoe's autobiography and collected stories.*]

Alan Sillitoe was never particularly taken with the "angry young man" label; more than thirty years later it still rankles. In fact *Life without Armour* reveals a bloody-minded aestheticism that has little to do with being famous for being fed up.

Many years ago, Sillitoe concludes, he faced up to the fact that it was not possible for him to work and live, and although his choice of work "was to be a mistake as far as my life was concerned, it was necessary because there was not enough energy in me to do both." The consequent immersion in his writing has meant that in his literary career a little experience has been made to go a long way. If you are too busy writing to experience new things to write about, then you can either bring new and self-referential worlds into being, or you can return again and again to the time before you were a writer. This is what Sillitoe does in his short stories. He only worked in a factory for a short period before the war, yet many of his stories are set against the rigours of factory life; he hasn't lived in Nottingham since he was a young man, but his imagination has continued to return there. His home town (like Joyce's Dublin) has become mythologized, stuck in time.

The second sentence of his autobiography suggests that he is unlikely to spend much time romanticizing his childhood: "With regard to my father, I have never been able to decide on the mental age at which he was stalled during much of his life . . . he sometimes seemed to have the mind of a ten-year-old in the body of a brute." His father was "short legged and megacephalic," illiterate, fussy and violent. His mother is depicted as weepy and ineffectual, resorting to occasional prostitution in order to bring money into the house. He was even sent to a school for mentally handicapped children, because there, at least, he would be properly fed. The squalor of this upbringing is captured with a novelistic verve that later sections of the book fail to match. Deprivation makes good copy; hard work and dedication—as ever—write white.

That such a child should grow up to be a writer is nothing less than amazing, proof positive that writers are born rather than made, By his early teens, Sillitoe was already beginning to relish his sense of difference and dramatize his predicament as that of a "courtier in the cage of an orangutan." And from this sense of difference came detachment and victory over the father who kept his family in brutish thrall. As Sillitoe's intellectual life takes off, his father simply ceases to figure much. Dismissed as "hopeless"—a key adjective—he dwindles to a kind of sullen impotence. The son has set out on a journey that the father is powerless to prevent.

The public library was the place of escape. Old maps, old Baedekers and *Guides Bleus* were voraciously consumed in an adolescent search for a "stable and desirable world beyond the one in which I was too firmly fixed." Sillitoe left school at fourteen and went to work in a factory and might have remained there, had he not joined the RAF at the end of the Second World War as an air-traffic controller and spent several years in Malaya. In 1948, he returned to Britain to be demobbed only to discover that he had TB. Paradoxically, illness proved the making of him, because for many years afterwards he received a military pension which financed his efforts to turn himself into a writer. The enormous success of his first novel, *Saturday Night and Sunday Morning* (1958), was followed by the sale of the film rights to *The Loneliness of the Long-Distance Runner.* And here the story ends, presumably on the grounds that what followed was essentially more of the same. Whatever else, *Life without Armour* is evidence that the best person to go to find out what it takes to be a writer is not always a writer. Certainly, Sillitoe's coyness—"I have always believed that a writer should show an interest in people from any background"—scarcely takes the argument much further.

As he ranges over his early life, it is possible to identify the exact moment when possible destinies intersected, the moment he chose art rather than life. Early in 1948, he was on duty in Malaya monitoring the air traffic in the region when, "On the standby radio at midnight the haunting music of Bizet's *L'Arlésienne Suite Number Two* came shortwaving through static out of some place in the Pacific, as if it had followed me halfway round the world from a summer's evening in Nottingham when I had heard it in the house alone and thought that my soul would burst." The moment was epiphanic and definitive; a revelation of the pleasures and values by which he would live.

The *Collected Stories* contains all his significant work in the genre, from 1959 until 1981. In the course of those twenty years, Sillitoe created a unique and uncompromising world of poverty and petty criminality, wrecked lives,

young mothers worn down before their time, children with pinched faces and no underwear. It is a world in which politics and culture (beyond the television, which is always flickering in the background, and the pub) play scant part. It is a hire-purchase world that smells of wet raincoats, unwashed clothes, cigarettes, cups of tea and cheap buns, hot oil, factory smoke, beans on toast. It is a world in which a "full and tolerable life" is a profoundly unattainable goal.

It has been Sillitoe's fate to be associated with his earliest work, typecast by early success. The first of the stories is also the most famous. Much of what was shocking about *The Loneliness of the Long-Distance Runner,* particularly the language, is frankly quaint. But it is still possible to see what the fuss was about. The unmediated voice of the boy who chooses to break the law, "It's a good life, I'm saying to myself, if you don't give in to coppers and Borstal-bosses and the rest of them bastard-faced In-laws"—depicts crime as a buzz, joyous and life-affirming respectability as creeping paralysis.

Other stories from the same period also celebrate outlawry. **"The Firebug"** is about the apprenticeship of an arsonist, who lights his first fire in the woods—"A stone of blood settled over my heart, but smoke and flame hypnotized me." **"The Ragman's Daughter"** is an account of the exploits of Nottingham's answer to Bonnie and Clyde. For Tony, Doris is the incarnation of loveliness and naughtiness. For them, criminality is not just an escape from the appalling conditions of ordinary life, it is more fun.

Not that respectability and conformity are entirely absent. **"The Fishing-Boat Picture"** musters what must be one of the least promising first sentences in the history of literature: "I've been a postman for twenty-eight years." His story is the usual one of an unlived life, of a woman who died. **"The Decline and Fall of Frankie Buller,"** one of the best stories, is about a big daft kid, who used to be leader of the local gang but who is now just another fearful man on the cusp of middle age.

By culture and circumstance, Sillitoe's characters are denied the possibilities of rational self-expression and are reduced to behavioural extremes out of sheer frustration. Domestic violence is an almost inevitable part of married life. In **"The Road,"** Ivan is taken on a day trip to Skegness by his parents, but the day turns bitter when his father beats his mother in public. In **"Revenge,"** the marriage does not get off to a particularly auspicious start, when the groom pulverizes the wedding presents with a poker. In **"The Meeting,"** the only way the husband and wife can suppress their anger is to pretend to be strangers. Not all the stories are set in the Midlands. However, even for a career exile, the lure of home is strong, and while **"The Rope Trick"** opens on a Greek island, it makes a rapid dash back to a Nottingham café on a wet afternoon.

Several pieces modishly sift through their own entrails. In **"Enoch's Two Letters,"** a young boy is left alone when his parents decide to leave one another on the same day. In **"The End of Enoch,"** the narrator is asked by the matron of the clinic where he has had an operation, if he will write a sequel. "Quite rightly," she cannot bear not knowing what happened. This is not an easy question for him to answer, since "there is rarely an end to any story."

Sillitoe maintains that the only gift he ever received from his father was a disrespect for all forms of authority, and he writes only on his own terms—extraordinarily self-sufficient, refusing to allow his work to be edited. The only acknowledged influence is Isaac Bashevis Singer, whose Yiddish stories taught him that "the poor lead vivid lives and suffer much . . . one has to write about their tribulations and follies as if one loves them." Whole swaths of human experience, especially those things that make life good in parts, are seriously under-represented. Nevertheless, Sillitoe finds in the lives and struggles of the urban poor, in a small part of the Midlands, clues about what it means to be human. Chipper he isn't, but as a cartographer of what he describes in one of the stories as "the spoiled territory of the heart, and the soiled landscape of the soul," he has a compelling claim to our attention.

James Urquhart (review date 30 January 1998)

SOURCE: "Excess Cappuccino," in *New Statesman,* Vol. 127, No. 489, January 30, 1998, pp. 47–8.

[*In the following mixed review, Urquhart comments on strengths and weaknesses of the stories in* Alligator Playground.]

Not much is left of Sillitoe's working Nottingham. The John Player tobacco factory has shut down, machine industries have relocated, pits have closed. But the social landscape holds some resonance of close-knit terraces and hard corner pubs fugged with beer fumes and noise; of large families with boorish, emotionally brutal men and their hard-bitten, enduring wives.

Sillitoe wrote of blue-collar Nottingham in his first novel, *Saturday Night and Sunday Morning* (1958); and his first short story collection, *The Loneliness of the Long-Distance Runner,* had the same undertow of violence and illicit behaviour. The runner, a Borstal boy, provided a manifesto for the author: honesty isn't about lawfulness, but about being true to your origins. Publishers at first rejected *Saturday Night* but Sillitoe continued to write of "ordinary people as I knew them" and, if this made him unpublishable, "then so be it."

In its perverse way, nothing could prove the rightness of his stubborn defence of honest writing better than **"Alligator Playground,"** the insubstantial novella that opens his latest collection. The plot involves thirtysomethings flopping limply at each other on the mudflats of London's literary crowd. A philandering publisher, Tom, works through wives and any bit of available skirt, before bed-ding a previously strident lesbian. Jo immediately renounces her Sapphic career, moves in with misogynistic Tom and bang! they have kids.

It's difficult to see Sillitoe's purpose with this cod bed-hopper. Any attempt at satire of promiscuous, self-important haste fails, since we care for neither the bland melodrama nor the glass-eyed caricatures trawled from London's fashionable waters. The author has, by pressing four marriages, three divorces and two deaths into less than 90 pages, sacrificed emotional gravity to action. The result has the circularity of a morality tale but lacks any sense of empathy or moral structure.

Happily the other eight tales restore faith. Sillitoe's great strength—teasing out the frail niceties of relationships—ensures that slender accounts of love and loss are washed with a poignancy that rarely encroaches on the sentimental. His capacity is wide—**"Ron Delph and His Fight with King Arthur"** touchingly recounts the anxieties of adolescence; **"A Matter of Teeth"** satisfyingly proclaims the justness of double infidelities. But there's also an economy with motifs: the events in both **"A Respectable Woman"** and **"Battlefields"** occur while driving through France, and we discover three coy couples "going the whole way in the darkest part of the wood" in this collection alone.

Sillitoe never quite achieves the intricate family relation-ships found in William Trevor's short stories, or the explicit dysfunctions of A L Kennedy or Helen Simpson. Here he tries different timbres of character and class, but the only true chord in **"Beggarland"** is Greta, the sassy au pair from "up north." It's as though Sillitoe isn't suf-ficiently interested in the urbane proprieties of her sniffy employers to make them interesting. Inevitably, perhaps, the strongest work reverts to familiar Nottingham terraces in **"Call Me Sailor"** and the autobiographical **"Ivy."**

Alligator Playground implies animal predation and a degree of lazy violence that is never fully realised in this collection. Three-quarters of Sillitoe's first novel was Saturday night, rolling passion with pints and punches until Seaton was lamped out on the pub floor. Forty years on, Sillitoe's Sunday morning is all newspapers and cap-puccino, but his middle classes are thirsting for more gal-vanising spirits.

Neil Powell (review date 16 October 1998)

SOURCE: "Nottingham Nights," in *Times Literary Supplement,* October 16, 1998, p. 24.

[*In the following negative review, Powell deems* The Broken Chariot *"a flawed novel."*]

In the opening pages of *The Broken Chariot,* Maud, a country vicar's daughter and the mother of the as yet unborn central character, is discovered reading *The Old*

Wives' Tale. Since this is just before 1914, Arnold Bennett's novel would have been recently published, but the reference is not there merely to authenticate a historical moment; it reminds us that Alan Sillitoe—with his attentiveness to provincial life, his fidelity to traditional forms of fiction and his sometimes cumbersome prose—is a consciously Bennett-like writer, and it hints at the nature of the book which follows.

The early chapters are discouraging. While tending her father's stalled and steaming car, the first of the novel's broken chariots, practical Maud meets and, during the First World War, marries Hugh Thurgarton-Strang; after the war, they end up in India and from there dispatch their son Herbert to a batty prep school in Sussex, which subliminally metamorphoses into an equally odd West Country public school, from where at the age of seventeen he rather implausibly runs away. It is a helter-skelter progress, full of abrupt lurches and awkward syntax, and it all happens in under thirty pages. Almost penniless, Herbert fetches up in Nottingham where—his defining stroke of good fortune—he at once finds a benign, if impoverished, father-figure in Isaac Frost, the first rounded character in the book and, perhaps, in Herbert's life. The novel's preliminary business done, the frantic pace relents and the narrative settles into its proper terrain.

Under Isaac's tutelage, Herbert Thurgarton-Strang becomes plain Bert Gedling: factory-worker, womanizer, National Serviceman and, in the late 1950s, fashionably proletarian novelist. There are obvious intersections here both with the author's life and with his earlier fiction: occasionally, these are disadvantageous, as when a cursory visit to Nottingham Goose Fair suffers by comparison with Sillitoe's wonderfully evocative story **"Noah's Ark,"** though the factory scenes are as sharply realized as ever. The army takes Herbert/Bert to Cyprus, where his narrow escape from a crashed lorry (another Phaeton image) leaves him with a rough, romantic facial scar as emblem of his double self; once back in Nottingham, he encounters a popular novelist and one of his admiring readers, with whom he has a mutually uncomprehending affair; and their negative example shapes his own literary ambitions, which must somehow combine Herbert's fluency with Bert's experience. Sillitoe seems here to aim for a satirical lightness—the publisher is a sententious fool and his dim whiz-kid editor is, ludicrously, an old-fashioned school-friend of Herbert's—but he is convincing when writing seriously about characters he admires: Herbert's mentor, Isaac; his Nottingham landlady, Mrs Denman; Archie, his rough drinking-partner, and Maud, his mother, who brings the book to its touchingly full-circle conclusion.

All the same, *The Broken Chariot* is a flawed novel. Messily written and negligently edited, it fails to reconcile a sometimes unruly comic surface with more portentous mythical or literary substrata; and in this, of course, it exactly resembles its main character, whose recurrent self-interrogations about his wilfully self-inflicted loss of identity threaten to become wearisome. If, despite these

difficulties, the novel is in the end readable and indeed admirable, this is largely thanks to Sillitoe's abundant generosity of spirit, his affectionate understanding of provincial urban society—"the glow of homeliness in the streets, the beer-smelling fagstink of friendly pubs, and the mateyness of the blokes at work"—and his eye for the telling descriptive detail: snowflakes "spinning down the panes in slow Catherine wheels," "high cauliflower clouds," "the Jaffa-orange" of the landlord's light bulb. Of these possibly unfashionable qualities, Arnold Bennett would surely have approved.

Stephen Daniels and Simon Rycroft (essay date 1998)

SOURCE: "Mapping the Modern City: Alan Sillitoe's Nottingham Novels," in *The Regional Novel in Britain and Ireland,* edited by K. D. M. Snell, Cambridge University Press, 1998, pp. 257–89.

[*In the following essay, Daniels and Rycroft discuss the importance of mapping and geography in Sillitoe's Nottingham novels, and how these novels portray the modernization of working-class neighborhoods during the first half of the twentieth century.*]

As a literary form, the novel is inherently geographical. The world of the novel is made up of locations and settings, arenas and boundaries, perspectives and horizons. Various places and spaces are occupied or envisaged by the novel's characters, by the narrator and by audiences as they read. Any one novel may present a field of different, sometimes competing, forms of geographical knowledge and experience, from a sensuous awareness of place to an educated idea of region and nation. These various geographies are coordinated by various kinds of temporal knowledge and experience, from circumscribed routines to linear notions of progress or transformation.[1]

From its formulation in the eighteenth century, the novel has been a speculative instrument for exploring and articulating those material, social and mental transformations we call modernisation. The novel was first associated with the transformation of London into a world metropolis, representing the capitalist city to its bourgeois citizens as 'accessible, comprehensible and controllable.'[2] Its scope was not confined to the city; early novelists charted transformations in the countryside and colonies too. The refinement of the novel as a genre was commensurate with the refinement of a number of geographical discourses, such as town planning, estate improvement, cartography and topographical painting, which surveyed and re-ordered the spaces of the modernising world.[3] From the time of Defoe, the novel has been fashioned and refashioned as an instrument for representing various geographies in different phases, forms and sites of modernisation.[4]

In this chapter we examine the geographies of novels by Alan Sillitoe set in and around Nottingham. We consider how the novels explore conflicts in the modernisation of working-class areas of the city from the 1920s to the 1950s, in particular the clearance of slums, the building of new housing estates and the emergence of a consumer culture. It was a time when the city corporation, proud of its progressive social and economic planning, promoted Nottingham as 'the modern city.' We focus on the geographies of the novels' Nottingham born male protagonists, local rebel Arthur Seaton in *Saturday Night and Sunday Morning* (1958), RAF conscript Brian Seaton in *Key to the Door* (1961) and *The Open Door* (1989) and internationalist guerilla Frank Dawley in *The Death of William Posters* (1965). These novels take us beyond transformations of mid-century Nottingham to transformations overseas, to the violent ending of colonial rule in Malaya and Algeria.

We situate these novels in terms of a number of Sillitoe's other writings: autobiography, travel writing, literary criticism, poetry, political journalism.[5] We also consider a range of other cultural discourses which bear upon the novels, including aerial photography, urban sociology, and classical mythology. Above all we wish to show the importance of maps, map reading and map-making to the geographies of the novels. This was the subject of an interview that we conducted with Alan Sillitoe in 1991 which provides a main source for this chapter.[6]

Firstly we will examine the issue of mapping in relation to Sillitoe's life and work, his literary influences and the modernisation of Nottingham. Secondly we will consider the connections between mapping, modernism and masculinity. The third and largest part of the chapter analyses the texts and contexts of the novels. Finally we compare the geographies of Nottingham in these novels with geographies of the city in official and academic publications of the time.

In this chapter we try to re-vision the relationship between 'geography and literature'[7] in a way which takes account of some recent developments in cultural geography and literary criticism.[8] We consider geography and literature not as the conjunction of two essentially distinct, coherent disciplines, or orders of knowledge—objective and subjective, real and imaginative, and so—but as a field of textual genres—the novel, the poem, the travel guide, the map, the regional monograph—with complex overlaps and interconnections. We have brought out both the worldliness of literary texts and the imaginativeness of geographical texts. The imaginativeness of texts consists in the images they express, in the way they construct, through modes of writing or composition, and however empirically, particular and partial views of the world. The worldliness of texts consists in the various contexts—biographical, economic, institutional, geographical—which are entailed by texts and make them intelligible.

MAPS AND THE MAN

Home is like a fortress of an army which prides itself on its mobility . . . Departing from the base, feet define

geography, the eyes observe and systematize it . . . As the base line in surveying is essential for the formation of a map and all points on it, so the connected points of birth, place, and upbringing are—for any person, and even more so for a writer—factors never to be relinquished.[9]

Alan Sillitoe was born and raised in the Radford area of Nottingham, a nineteenth-century working-class suburb to the west of the city centre. Sillitoe recalled the Radford of his childhood as a labyrinthine world:

Even when you knew every junction, twitchell and double entry (a concealed trackway which, connecting two streets, figured high in tactics of escape and manoeuvre) you never could tell when a gas lamp glowed that someone in the nearby dark was not using its light as an ambush pen. Neither did you know what waited behind the corner it stood on . . . You invented perils, exaggerated pitfalls, occasionally felt that you even called them up. Potholes became foxholes, and foxholes as often or not turned into underground caverns full of guns and ammunition, food, and later, more gold than Monte Cristo ever dreamed of. In such streets you could outdream everybody.[10]

As a child Sillitoe envisaged his neighbourhood in terms of the underground worlds of the novels which then dominated his reading: *The Count of Monte Cristo* and, more strongly still, *Les Misérables*.

Les Misérables took me through the prolonged crisis of childhood . . . I read the book again and again . . . till most of it was fixed firmly in . . . From an early age I was more familiar with the street names of Paris than those of London . . . Exotic though it was in many ways, *Les Misérables* seemed relevant to me and life roundabout . . . Gavroche, the street urchin who reminded me vividly of one of my cousins . . . the revolutionary fighting in the streets of Paris . . . when Jean Valjean rescues one of the wounded fighters from one of the about-to-be overrun barricades by carrying him through the sewers.[11]

The physiography of Nottingham, and its attendant folklore, gave credence to the Parisian connection. Under the city, carved out of a cave system, is a complicated network of chambers dating back to medieval times. These were used for storage, dwelling, gambling and, during the Second World War, as air raid shelters. Their occasional occupation throughout Nottingham's history by outlaws and rebels sustained a local mythology of a clandestine underworld, much like that of Paris as set out in *Les Misérables*.[12]

In *Les Misérables* the counterpoint of the underworld is the spacious, systematic new city planned by Baron Haussman for Napoleon III.[13] Haussman's plan was a city-wide vision which directly opposed the Parisian underworld, clearing poor districts to make way for a system of broad boulevards, public buildings, parks, parades and classical perspectives. It was a spectacular vision, planned from a height, in a new survey of the city from especially constructed towers, and best seen in panoramic views.[14]

Haussman's Paris is in many ways the vantage point of Hugo's novel. The narrator looks back to events of 1815–32 from the perspective of the 1860s, reconstructing, with the help of old maps, the social geography which Haussman erased. Hugo's 'aerial observer' does not always have a clear view, peering down into the 'silent, ominous labyrinth' of the insurrectionary districts (as the reader 'peered into the depths' of another 'labyrinth of illusion,' the conscience of the fugitive Valjean).[15] While sympathetic to the plight of *les misérables,* the novel tracks them with a consciously cartographic eye.

In Sillitoe's Nottingham novels, the urban underworld is similarly counterpointed by a newly planned, systematic, self-consciously modern city. From the 1920s, the City Corporation promoted Nottingham as 'the modern city' with 'wide thoroughfares, well-proportioned buildings, and an entire absence of the smoke and grime usually associated with industry . . . creating a broad spaciousness that other cities envy and seek to emulate.' In official guides and publications, the structure of this modern city was displayed in aerial photographs: the new city hall (the Council House) and civic square, bright new factories, broad boulevards and spacious suburban estates. The Corporation was particularly keen on the new aerodrome built outside the city, in 1928, the second in Britain to be licensed: 'the city of Nottingham has always been in the forefront in the matter of aviation.'[16]

During Sillitoe's youth the country beyond Radford—estate land developed with a mixture of parkland, plantations, collieries, allotments and cottages—was comprehensively modernised. The Corporation purchased a large swathe of this land and built a spacious zone of boulevards, public parks and housing estates. The 2,800 houses of the Aspley estate (1930–2) were intended for newly married couples from Sillitoe's Radford or to rehouse families from cleared slum areas. There was a school at the centre of the estate, a showpiece of the city's enlightened educational policy, but few other social facilities or places of work. The new working-class suburb contrasted pointedly with the old; its elegant curves, crescents and concentric circles served to emphasise the town's intricate network of terraces, back-streets and alleys.[17] Sillitoe's autobiographical story of childhood gang-fights is set on this modern frontier: 'Our street was a straggling line of ancient back-to-backs on the city's edge, while the enemy district was a new housing estate of three long streets which had outflanked us and left us a mere pocket of country in which to run wild.'[18]

Despite, or perhaps because of, the fact that his family remained in Radford, Sillitoe sought a heightened consciousness of Nottingham in a passion for maps as well as books. He taught himself to read maps as he learnt to read novels, and made maps as he learned to write. Born into a poor family, suffering the insecurities of chronic unemployment, Sillitoe 'latched onto maps in order to pull myself into the more rarefied and satisfying air of education and expansion of spirit.' Maps helped make

sense of Nottingham, clarified its character and development. And they connected the city to a wider world. 'The first time I saw a map I wanted to leave home.'[19] Sillitoe collected maps of all kinds. A large-scale estate map from his grandfather's cottage on the fringe countryside beyond Radford became a 'dream landscape' as this land began 'to be covered by houses and new roads.' An inch-to-the mile Ordnance Survey map of the Aldershot area marked with tactical exercises, a gift from a retired guardsman next door, 'gave a picture I could relate to the land in my own district. Every cottage and copse was marked, every lane and footpath.' At school he watched 'with wonder and fascination' as the teacher took a wheeled metal cylinder and rolled gleaming outlines of Europe or North America on the page, 'it was the action of a magic wand.'[20]

The magic of maps was not just conceptual but technical, maps as artefacts not just images. As a child Sillitoe made maps of all kinds, of both real and imaginary places, drawn on wallpaper, in the flyleaves of books, drawn 'with the same attention to detail as my lace-designer uncle put into his intricate patterns before they were set up on Nottingham machines.' Sillitoe esteemed maps as agents of modern, material transformation, 'a highway built where one had not existed before . . . a new town settled on the edge of sandy or forest wastes.'[21] Wartime conditions heightened Sillitoe's map consciousness. With signposts removed, and street maps torn out of city guides, the war 'turned everyone into a spy and me into my own surveyor.' With the aid of a War Office manual Sillitoe taught himself triangulation and 'with a simple compass and the expedient of pacing' made a detailed map of his neighbourhood.[22]

Failing a scholarship exam, Sillitoe left school at fourteen, to take a variety of factory jobs, including a spell as a lathe operator in the Raleigh bicycle factory at the end of his street, then turned over to war production, making components for aircraft engines. Here, especially through his membership of the Transport and General Workers Union, he acquired a political education. 'I found it impossible to work in a factory without believing that socialism was the ultimate solution for all life on this planet.'[23] Sillitoe also enlarged his local geographical knowledge. With his first wages he purchased a bicycle and explored as far as the Peak District and the Lincolnshire coast. In the absence of signposts a map was a necessity. In a Foreword to a history of the Raleigh company Sillitoe spelled out the benefits of the cyclist's vantage point, 'that it is often possible to see over the hedge at the horizon beyond. One can also stop and admire the view, or pause to consult a map with no trouble at all.'[24] It is the revelatory vantage point of regional survey recommended to young urban excursionists of the time, one enshrined in Ellis Martin's illustration of the cyclist on the cover of the Popular Edition One Inch Ordnance Survey Maps.[25]

During the war, Sillitoe joined the Air Training Corps based at the local aerodrome. Here he acquired a military-geographical education, learning radio-telegraphy, flight theory, meteorology and photogrammetry. The vertical viewpoint offered on training flights over Nottingham from a de-Haviland bi-plane was a revelation. The oblique panorama of the topographical observer gave way to a broader, more penetrating vision:

> This bird's eye snapshot appeared to be just as valuable as the dense intricacies that came with lesser visibility on the ground . . . It was easy to pick out factories and their smoking chimneys, churches and park spaces, the Castle and the Council House, as well as the hide-outs and well-trodden streets that had seemed so far apart but that now in one glance made as small and close a pattern as that on a piece of lace . . . From nearly two thousand feet the hills appeared flat, and lost their significance, but the secrets of the streets that covered them were shown in such a way that no map could have done the job better.[26]

During and immediately after the war, progressive experts, including professional geographers, hoped that increased flying experience and familiarity with aerial photography would re-order ordinary people's perceptions of the world and their place in it. In 1946 David Linton told the Geographical Association that

> the air view of the ground . . . has become a familiar thing to us all . . . Direct flying experience . . . has been extended to a great body of service personnel, ATC cadets and others, and war films and war photographs have brought some appreciation of the airman's point of view to virtually the whole adult population.[27]

The advantages of the airman's point of view were cumulative:

> As we leave the ground our visual and mental horizon expands, and we have direct perception of space-relations over an ever-widening field, so that we may see successively the village, the town, the region, in their respective settings. The mobility of the aircraft makes our range of vision universal . . . We may fly to the ends of the earth.[28]

This expanding field of vision was seen to be potentially one of international citizenship, connecting the local with the global in a new post-war world order.[29]

Sillitoe's internationalism maintained its leftward bearing. He saw his air-training as preparation for 'the fight against fascism,' but the war ended too soon for Sillitoe to participate and he was posted to Malaya by the RAF, to take part in the fight against communist insurgents in 1948. Here as a wireless operator he was required 'against my political beliefs' to give bearings to bombers trying to 'hunt out the communist guerillas in the jungle' and maintained his 'accustomed accuracy' with 'lessening enthusiasm.'[30]

In Malaya Sillitoe took up writing in a desultory way, 'odd poems and scraps of prose—generally concerned with the beauties of scenery—to pass away the fourteen-hour shifts in my radio hut at the end of the runway.'[31] Upon demobilisation, back in England, Sillitoe was

diagnosed as having tuberculosis and, in response, wrote voraciously. During eighteen months convalescence in an army camp Sillitoe began a 'feverish bout of urgent writing,' filling empty wireless logbooks with dozens of poems, sketches and bits of description, some of which were used in later published works. The most sustained of these pieces was a thirty-page narrative of a six-day jungle-rescue exercise he had navigated three months before in Malaya, based on a diary and maps of the area he had drawn up before embarking.[32] Sillitoe also read the canon of western literature, modern works like the novels of D. H. Lawrence and Dostoevsky as well as Latin and Greek classics newly available in Penguin paperback translations. At the same time, through a correspondence course, Sillitoe 'really got to grips with the proper science of surveying,' with a view to a career in 'the mundane occupation of making maps.' But 'as my writing took over my whole existence [so] I left off the studies in surveying' and set about the task 'of getting into the map of my own consciousness.'[33]

Returning to Nottingham in 1950, Sillitoe wrote a few short stories, some published in a local magazine, and a long novel, 'a vainglorious mish-mash of Dostoevsky, D. H. Lawrence and Aldous Huxley,' promptly rejected by a London publisher.[34] In a second-hand bookshop he met Ruth Fainlight, an American writer and poet and the woman he was to marry. Because of Sillitoe's illness, they decided to move to the sunnier climate of southern Europe, subsisting on Sillitoe's Air-Force pension. Expecting to be away for six months, they stayed six years, by which time Sillitoe had established his vocation as a writer.

In southern Europe Sillitoe and Fainlight 'were culturally severed from England.' 'The magazines we read, the people we met, the books we got hold of, came from Paris, or New York or San Francisco.'[35] Sillitoe was part of a great post-war migration to the Mediterranean of English writers and artists.[36] Robert Graves, then working on *The Greek Myths,* lived nearby in Majorca and gave Sillitoe and Fainlight access to his library. Sillitoe wrote some poems on classical heroes and a fantasy novel but Graves suggested he 'write a book set in Nottingham, which is something you know about.' From a series of unpublished short stories and sketches centring on the character of Arthur Seaton, 'a young anarchic roughneck,' Sillitoe completed the first draft of ***Saturday Night and Sunday Morning*** in 1956–7.[37] 'The factory and its surrounding area ascended with a clarity that might not have been so intense had I not looked out over olive groves, lemons and orange orchards . . . under a clear Mediterranean sky.'[38] Writing the novel, Sillitoe was reminded of the clear view of his first training flight over Nottingham, but felt, at the dawn of the space-age, launched further into orbit: 'I redrew my maps and made my survey as if from a satellite stationed above that part of the earth in which I had been born.'[39]

Sillitoe's cultural exile, and the sense of homeplace it sharpened, invites comparison with the local collier's son who, writing in southern Europe, defined Nottingham and its region as a literary landscape, D. H. Lawrence. In an essay on Lawrence Sillitoe regards his forbear's exile as a condition of his realistic grasp of the people and places of his upbringing, but notes that the longer Lawrence sojourned in sunny, southern landscapes, the more he 'began to lose his grip on local topography.' In *Lady Chatterley's Lover* Nottinghamshire was reduced to 'a sort of black-dream country that did not seem human or real.' Sustained exile incorporated Lawrence in that pastoral literary tradition which bewails the 'ruination of sweet and rural England' and nourishes an 'unreasonable hatred of the urban and industrial landscape.' Sillitoe also suggests something Oedipal in this 'unreasonable hatred,' the rejection of the masculine world of the mining country: 'he had to go to those places where the female spirit of the Virgin Mary was in the ascendant, where mother-worship of the Latins was the norm.' In contrast, Sillitoe maintained his grip on local topography, not just by returning to England, and occasionally to Nottingham, but by sustaining a documentary vision, not sliding from a strictly cartographic to a softly scenic idea of landscape. Mapping offered Sillitoe both a pre-literary definition of Lawrence's country and a way of keeping his forbear in his sights. Reading Lawrence, Sillitoe reaches for the one-inch maps which remind him of the cycle trips to the country he made as a boy, years before he realised that Lawrence had portrayed it in his novels. And the essay on Lawrence ends with an imaginative journey, viewing key places in his novels from various hilltops in and around Nottingham: 'such roaming is a constant wonder of triangulation, surveys that fix themselves in the heart and stay there.'[40]

Writing, Sillitoe is surrounded by maps, 'a street plan of Nottingham, a large-scale trench-map of the Gommecourt salient in 1916, marked by the advancing death-lines of the Sherwood Foresters, a relief chart of Deception Island, and a topographical map of Israel flanked by the Mediterranean and the Jordan River—different regions I cannot shut my eyes to.'[41] Sillitoe's study resembles an operations room. 'Just as a general needs maps upon which to plan his campaign,' Sillitoe declares, 'so an author requires them for his novels and stories.'[42]

For Sillitoe maps are not just a framework for writing, but a medium of citizenship.[43] On a visit to Leningrad in 1964 he admired the 'colourful, complex' map of the city hanging in Lenin's headquarters, 'a campaign street plan of the October rising,' a map that 'is sure to be looked at and studied on many a South American or Asian wall.' 'I could have followed its intricacies for many an hour. Every self-respecting man should, with a plan of the city he lives in, practice schemes for an insurrection in times of war or trouble, or for its defence should an insurrection ever come about.'[44]

On the same trip to the Soviet Union, Stalingrad is envisaged as a New Jerusalem in a modernist *mappa mundi*:

> I felt that Stalingrad was in the middle of the world, a place where the final battle between good and evil was

fought out. It was also the last battle of the Bolshevik Revolution, and may be the final decisive contest of the world, the turning point of humanity in its struggle between science and magic, science and barbarity.[45]

In a poem of 1964, Stalingrad is transposed onto Nottingham:

> A map of Stalingrad pinned on
> A plan of Nottingham
> For easy reference from crossbred stories:
> Coloured elbows of the Don and Volga
> Chase the tape worm artery of the Trent
> To merge in Stalinham and Nottingrad,
> Spartak and Calverton . . .
>
> Trent, the Volga and the Don run quiet
> Consistent river drawn to widening seas
> While men and women talk in the
> Canteens of Raleigh and the Red October,
> At evening by the lights of Netherfield-Dubovka
> Walk similar embankments and announce their love
> To rivers snaking over peacetime faces.[46]

MAPPING AND MODERNITY

To emphasise the mapping impulse in Sillitoe's work and life and its pre-war roots is to revise the conventional interpretation of his writing. Sillitoe is concerned to accurately document local characters and their environment but he cannot simply be grouped with consciously English, realist contemporaries like Larkin, Amis and Osborne.[47] In its continental allusions, cosmopolitan vantage point, and mythological register, Sillitoe's writing may be situated in an earlier modernist tradition, one which includes authors he esteems: Hugo, Lawrence, Conrad and Joyce.

The very conventions of mapping which help to fix Nottingham's geography also release the author and his subject from purely local, vernacular associations, and they coordinate Nottingham to other cities and their cultural traditions. Sillitoe exploits both the documentary aspect of mapping and its metaphorical aspect, the transposition of cultural meanings and associations from one place to another. Mapped onto the modernisation of Nottingham, the upheaval and reconstruction of its urban fabric, are epic geographies of insurgent Paris and Stalingrad.

In Sillitoe's Nottingham novels, as in *Les Misérables,* the process of surveying proceeds vertically as well as horizontally in excavations or transections of the urban underworld. Sillitoe quotes from Hugo's novel in characterising the authorial view as stratigraphic, both documenting, as if from a mountain top, the 'external facts' of culture and, as if in the depths of a cavern, its 'hearts and souls.'[48] This vertical axis has long been a central trope in European literature. In Ovid's *Metamorphoses* it is the separation of the world of the labyrinth occupied by the Minatour, the beast-man, and that of the air occupied by Dedalus, the bird-man. The development of ballooning, the building of skyscapers and the invention of the aeroplane activated this vertical axis as a defining trope of modernism. As authors upheld a civilised superstructure of spirit and vision, populated by figures like Joyce's Stephen Dedalus or Geddes' heroic aviator, so they also excavated a primitive substructure of unreason and bodiliness, populated by figures like Hugo's *les misérables* or D. H. Lawrence's coal miners.[49]

Sillitoe's main characters in his Nottingham novels are variously positioned on this vertical axis. While Brian Seaton transcends Nottingham to achieve a cerebral, cosmopolitan vision, one vested like Sillitoe's in maps and air-mindedness, his brother Arthur remains local and visceral, prowling the warren of streets. Dedalus and Minatour. The third character Frank Dawley never achieves a fully aerial view. After speculating on 'what Nottingham looked like from the air, he fell like a stoned and frozen bird back near the middle of it.'[50] But Dawley does escape the city on an internationalist underground quest, as a guerilla fighter in North Africa.

As Alison Light has pointed out, there is a distinctly masculine positioning and scope to this radical mode of literary modernism, in its heroic, worldly visions of free movement, political liberation, sexual autonomy and economic independence.[51] Such visions were occasionally awarded to women, in the airmindedness of some of Virginia Woolf's free-spirited female characters[52] and in the educated, panoramic visions of some of D. H. Lawrence's. The opening of Lawrence's *The Rainbow* (1915) finds men archaic and earthbound, women modern and outward looking:

> The women looked out from the heated, blind intercourse of farm life, to the spoken world beyond . . . She (*sic*) stood to see the far-off world of cities and governments and the active scope of men, the magic land to her, where secrets were made known and desires fulfilled . . . to discover what was beyond, to enlarge their own scope and freedom.[53]

Sillitoe's Nottingham novels are, by contrast, comprehensively masculine, and are structured almost entirely on the expression or repression of male desire, whether in its more visceral or more educated forms. Indeed what aligns Sillitoe's novels with the gritty realism of his English contemporaries is the hardness of their male positioning and address, their aggressive, misogynistic heroes, individuated largely by running battles with women.

The very belligerence of Sillitoe's heroes, and the portrayal of Nottingham as a sexual battleground, does at least make his women characters a force to be reckoned with. There is a local context for this. The prevailing mythology of modern Nottingham is feminine. The industrialisation in the city of the lace, hosiery and clothing industries, with a conspicuous increase of female workers, was accompanied by a new urban folklore of formidable, independent women, economically, politically and sexually.[54] This was famously mobilised by D. H. Lawrence in *Sons and Lovers* (1913) in the figure of the hero's lover, lace worker Clara Dawes, a ten-year veteran of the women's move-ment. Moreover the myth was incorporated in the regal figure which imaged the 'City Beautiful' modernism in official civic publicity, 'Queen of the Midlands.' Guidebooks used this feminine image to promote Nottingham as progressively pure and healthy, free from the grime and drabness usually associated with coalfield areas.[55] All local manufacturing industries employed a large proportion of women, and promotional literature was keen to show them working in bright, spacious surroundings. In contrast, Sillitoe's novels evoke a harsher, grimier, more masculine world, the carboniferous industrialisation which shadows both Lawrence's novels and city guides. The factory floor, and work generally, is represented almost entirely as a male preserve, as are most public spaces in the novels. It is not just that Sillitoe's male characters rebel against the authority of women. The texts of his Nottingham novels rebel against authoritative texts of the city.

Angry Young Man

Saturday Night and Sunday Morning charts a year in the life of Arthur Seaton, machinist in a Nottingham bicycle factory, and young urban rebel. The longer part of the novel, 'Saturday Night,' describes Arthur's work and, more extensively, his escapes from work, his drinking bouts, sexual conquests, street fights, fishing trips and belligerent fantasies. The brief and more reflective 'Sunday Morning' finds Arthur recovering from one Saturday night's excess and contemplating, reluctantly, the 'safe and rosy path' to marriage, family and suburban life.

Saturday night was 'one of the fifty-two holidays in the slow-turning Big Wheel of the year.'[56] The Big Wheel is the driving structure of the novel. It figures as a carnivalesque Big Wheel which eventually appears in the episode at the huge Goose Fair in central Nottingham, at the giddy climax of the novel's and the city's recreational calendar. The novel is also geared to an industrial Big-Wheel, the imperative of factory work driving men and machines. The cycle of the seasons is subordinate to the urban Big-Wheel: 'As spring merged into summer or autumn became winter Arthur glimpsed the transitional mechanisms of each season only at the weekend, on Saturday or Sunday, when he straddled his bike and rode along the canal bank into the country to fish.'[57] Correspondingly, there is little organic development in the novel's narrative. Each chapter (and most were originally drafted as separate pieces) is a largely discrete component in the circular structure. In both its industrial and recreational expressions the Big-Wheel of ***Saturday Night and Sunday Morning*** is fixed, offering little escape from the city and its culture, even in the form of the bicycles that Arthur Seaton's factory produces. Movement in the novel is circumscribed, largely vertical. Reading the novel is like riding the Big-Wheel. At some points readers and, on occasion, characters achieve a panoramic view of the city and its surroundings, before being plunged into its lower depths.

First published in 1958, ***Saturday Night and Sunday Morning*** helped to frame its cultural moment. It appeared at the time of a spate of accounts of urban working-class life by academics, playwrights, novelists and documentary film makers. Many were concerned with the effect of a burgeoning consumer culture on working-class life. The very idea of 'community' was counterpointed by the emergence of a new working-class affluence and individualism.[58] The most notable ethnography of the time is Richard Hoggart's *The Uses of Literacy,* an account, largely a reminiscence, of working-class life in Hunslet first published in 1957 and issued by Penguin the following year. Like Sillitoe, Hoggart was an exile from his working-class upbringing, but a more academically educated scholarship boy, with a greater sense of Englishness and a frankly sentimental sense of the homeliness and neighbourliness of his upbringing. He charts the traditions of working-class culture and their corruption by the 'admass' world of 'chain-store modernisimus,' pin-ups, pop music and pulp fiction. Hoggart reserves particular scorn for the 'juke-box boys,' with 'drape suits, picture ties and an American slouch.'[59]

Saturday Night and Sunday Morning was aligned to a male-centred genre of plays and novels, including John Osborne's *Look Back in Anger* (1956) and John Braine's *Room at the Top* (1957), authored by and largely featuring so-called 'Angry Young Men.'[60] In contrast to politely accented literature set in the Oxbridge-London belt and its overseas outliers, the Angries' work was riveted in lower-class quarters of provincial towns and cities and largely articulated by aggressive, straight talking, often foul-mouthed, male heroes. The Angries' world seemed at the time shockingly visceral, short on wit and irony, and long on sex and violence and general bodiliness. ***Saturday Night and Sunday Morning*** opens with Arthur Seaton in a drinking match, knocking-back seven gins and ten pints of beer in quick succession, falling down the pub stairs and vomiting over a nicely dressed middle-aged man and his wife. ***Saturday Night and Sunday Morning*** made John Braine's *Room at the Top* 'look like a vicarage tea-party' announced the *Daily Telegraph*; it was, claimed the *New Statesman,* 'very much the real thing.'[61]

The popular reputation of ***Saturday Night and Sunday Morning*** was established with the release in 1960 of a film of the novel.[62] Scripted by Alan Sillitoe and directed by Karel Reisz, it starred Albert Finney as Arthur Seaton and featured the Nottingham streets, factories, pubs, canals and housing estates described in the novel. Switching between high-angled long-shots and darker, short-focused scenes, sometimes accompanied by Arthur's thoughts, the film opened up the gap between the panoramic and labyrinthine worlds of the text. This was, as Terry Lovell notes, 'a point of enunciation' in a number of British films and television programmes of working-class life of the time, one especially suited to the position of the adult working-class male looking back on the world he had left. 'Within the familiar landscape, such a viewer is offered a potent figure of identification in the young, sexually active male worker, because he may identify in him a fantasy projection of the self he might have become had he remained.'[63]

Tied into the film's release was a million selling paperback edition of the novel. This was issued by Pan (regarded, in contrast to Penguin, as a distinctly low-brow publisher), marketed in the lurid 'sex-and-violence' style associated with American pulp fiction, and largely sold from the racks of newsagents. The front cover features an illustration of a tough looking Arthur Seaton against the mean streets of Nottingham. The back cover shows a still from the film of Arthur seducing a workmate's wife and, in the wake of the controversial publication of *Lady Chatterley's Lover,* the announcement of a new author 'from Lawrence country . . . who might well have startled Lawrence himself.' Readers were promised 'a raw and uninhibited story of a working-class district of Nottingham and the people who live, love, laugh and fight there.' In giving a trans-atlantic gloss to the novel, Pan made connections with American works with rebellious male heroes, like Jack Kerouac's *On the Road* which they issued in 1958—although there was no disguising that Arthur Seaton was a very English rebel, a rebel without a car.[64]

Saturday Night and Sunday Morning does not dwell on material deprivation, moral improvement or community spirit. In a world of accelerated industrial production, full employment and rising wages, the novel traces the pursuit of pleasure and a new consumer passion among the working-class. The bicycle factory is booming, with the introduction of piece-work and streamlined production. The thousands who work there take home good wages.

> No more short-time like before the war, or getting the sack if you stood ten ten minutes in the lavatory reading your *Football Post*—if the gaffer got on to you now you could always tell him where to put the job and go somewhere else . . . With the wages you got you could save up for a motor-bike or even an old car, or you could go for a ten-day binge and get rid of all you'd saved.[65]

Television aerials are 'hooked on to almost every chimney, like a string of radar stations, each installed on the never-never.' Seaton's father has sufficient money to chain-smoke Woodbines in front of the television all evening, his mother to hold her head high in the Co-op and nonchalantly demand 'a pound of this and a pound of that,' now 'she had access to week after week of solid wages that stopped worry at the source.' The new affluence has not subdued the 'empty-bellied pre-war battles'; it has aggravated and enlarged them: 'feuds merged, suppressed ones became public.'[66]

Arthur Seaton spends much of his wage-packet on himself. For a weekend night out he chooses from 'a row of suits, trousers, sports jackets, shirts, all suspended in colourful drapes and designs, good-quality tailor-mades, a couple of hundred quid's worth, a fabulous wardrobe.'[67] Described as a Teddy boy, Arthur seems to fit the newly affluent image of working-class youth which alarmed commentators of both Right and Left.[68] He comes close to Raymond Williams' contemporary definition of a 'consumer,' a word with imagery drawn from 'the furnace or the stomach' which 'materializes as an individual figure (perhaps monstrous in size but individual in behaviour).'[69] Yet in many ways Arthur is a traditional, even anti-modern urban delinquent, the bloody-minded freeborn-Englishman which left-wing writers recruited as makers of the English working-class.[70] Arthur's leisure pivots on the pub: 'I'm a six foot pit prop that wants a pint of ale.' He is contemptuous of many modern commodities, notably television with its implications of passive, domesticated manhood,[71] and cars, with their associations of suburban living. Indeed, he physically attacks the only car to appear in the novel. The consumer good that Arthur values most is the one he helps to produce, the bicycle.[72]

Arthur Seaton is confident, 'cocksure.'[73] He has a mind to take on all figures of authority, 'fighting every day until I die . . . fighting with mothers and wives, landlords and gaffers, coppers, army, government,'[74] and all monuments of authority, the factory in which he works, the city hall, the castle which broods over the city. Arthur is against all authority, except the authority of men over women.[75] In this he has a local ancestry in D. H. Lawrence's working-class heroes, notably the men in *Nottingham and the Mining Country* (1930), figures whose roving 'physical, instinctive' masculinity, cultivated at work underground, is trapped and tamed by women no less than by schools, cinemas or machines.[76] But Arthur also has a more contemporary connection in the comic-strip culture of the time, in the war comics of rugged individualists taking on the enemy single-handed and in the tough, street-wise boy-heroes of the *Beano* and *Dandy,* forever in scrapes with authority figures: teachers, policemen, and strong-armed mothers.[77]

Arthur Seaton's world is a labyrinthine zone, recurrently described as a 'jungle' or 'maze.' Arthur prowls the back-streets of the city, or the footpaths of the adjacent country, part guerilla, part predatory beast 'caught in a game of fang-and-claw.'[78] At the fairground, Arthur passes up the aerial thrill of the Big-Wheel for the subterranean thrill of the Ghost Train. 'Assailed by black darkness and horrible screams from Hell,' Arthur tangles with Death in the form of 'the luminous bones of a hanging skeleton,' 'kicking and pummelling until his arms emerged from the heavy black cover, glistening skeleton bones looking like tiger-streaks over his back, head, and shoulders.'[79] Each outing was 'an expedition in which every corner had to be turned with care, every pub considered for the ease of tactical retreat in terms of ambush.'[80] Known and successfully navigated, the streets offer warm security.

> Walking the streets on winter nights kept him warm . . . stars hid like snipers, taking aim now and again when clouds gave them a loophole. Winter was an easy time for him to hide his secrets, for each dark street patted his shoulder and became a friend, and the gaseous eye of each lamp glowed unwinking as he passed. Houses lay in rows and ranks, a measure of safety in such numbers, and those within were snug and grateful fugitives from the broad track of bleak winds that brought rain from the Derbyshire mountains and snow from the Lincolnshire Wolds.[81]

On the way home from a night's skirmishing with his brother:

> The maze of streets sleeping between tobacco factory and bicycle factory drew them into the enormous spread of its suburban bosom and embraced them in sympathetic darkness. Beyond the empires of new red-bricked houses lay fields and woods that rolled on to the Erewash valley and the hills of Derbyshire.[82]

In charting the moral order of the city, Sillitoe is careful to distinguish the warmth of the old industrial suburb where Arthur lives from both the bleakness of the new residential suburbs on the outer heights of the city and the dankness of a low-lying slum area called The Meadows by the river near the city centre. The Meadows is presented as a dark, decayed, chaotic district, inhabited by drunks and prostitutes and Arthur's Aunt Ada. After a life of 'dole, boozing, bailiffs' Aunt Ada had 'the personality of a promiscuous barmaid.' Her 'horde of children' are, in contrast to Arthur's rebellious posturing, ferocious, almost feral figures, 'always escaping, on the run, in hiding, living with whores, thieving for food and money because they had neither ration books nor employment cards,' fending for themselves 'in such a wild free manner that Borstal had been their education and a congenial jungle their only hope.'[83]

If Arthur haunts the streets of *Saturday Night and Sunday Morning,* it is because domestic interiors are a woman's realm, inhabited by his mother, aunt, mistresses and fiancé, in which men are either absent or marginalised. A formidable female challenge to Arthur's authority, and a main target of his abuse, is a more public figure who surveys the streets. Stationed at the end of his yard, *en route* to the factory, is the gossip Mrs Bull, 'ready to level with foresight and backsight at those that crossed her path in the wrong direction':

> Deep-set beady eyes traversed the yard's length from streets to factory, were then swivelled back from the factory wall to where she was standing, ranging along upstairs and downstairs windows, no point of architecture or human movement escaping her. It was rumoured that the government had her name down for a reconnaissance unit in the next war.[84]

Mrs Bull controls networks of knowledge which Arthur can barely discern. Her 'malicious gossip travelled like electricity through a circuit, from one power-point to another, and the surprising thing was that a fuse was so rarely blown.'[85] Arthur attempts to sabotage the system. Playing the role of sniper, he shoots Mrs Bull with an air rifle, bruising her cheek, stinging her into wild gesticulation, confirming her as the slapstick figure of boy's comics.

'Once a rebel, always a rebel,' Arthur Seaton pleads at the end of the novel before he dons 'suit, collar, and tie' to meet his fiancé Doreen one cold spring Sunday morning 'on the outskirts of the housing estate' where they are destined to live.[86] If Arthur's industrial neighbourhood offered him a measure of snug security, the new modern estates on the edge of the city are bleak, aerial landscapes. '[Up] Broxtowe, on the estate, I like living in them nice new houses,' announces Doreen. 'It's a long way from the shops, but there's plenty of fresh air.' 'My sister married a man in the air force . . . and they've got a house up Wollaton. She's expecting a baby next week.'[87] Arthur and Doreen 'take a long walk back to her house, by the boulevard that bordered the estate,' the 'safe and rosy path' to domesticity.[88] To a disinterested observer they 'seemed like a loving and long-engaged couple only kept back from marriage by the housing shortage.' But to Arthur the 'new pink-walled houses gave an even gloomier appearance than the black dwellings of Radford.' The very image of 'the modern city' in official publicity, the spacious new housing estate, is, for Arthur, a trap:

> Arthur remembered seeing an aerial photo of it: a giant web of roads, avenues and crescents, with a school like a black spider lurking in the middle.[89]

New Man

In a 1965 sequel to *Saturday Night and Sunday Morning, The Death of William Posters,* Frank Dawley, a political extension of Arthur Seaton, rebel turned revolutionary, strives to break out of Arthur's world and his view of it.[90] Through twelve years of factory work and marriage Dawley 'had brooded and built up the Bill Posters legend,'[91] the legend of a local social bandit:

> There's been a long line of William Posters, a family of mellow lineage always hoved up in some cellar of Nottingham Streets. His existence explains many puzzles. Who was General Ludd? None other than the shadowy William Posters, stockinger, leading on his gallant companies of Nottingham lads to smash all that machinery . . . Who set fire to Nottingham Castle during the Chartist riots? Later, who spat in Lord Roberts' face when he led the victory parade in Nottingham after the Boer War. Who looted those shops in the General Strike?[92]

Frank 'wondered what Nottingham looked like from the air, but fell like a stoned and frozen bird back near the middle of it.'[93] He eventually breaks out of the labyrinth of Nottingham, or rather, through its demolition during redevelopment, has it broken for him:

> One street funnelled him into space, a view across rubble that a few months ago had been a populous ghetto of back-to-backs and narrow streets. He lit a fag, to absorb the sight of all these acres cleared of people, smashed down and dragged to bits. It wasn't unpleasant, this stalingrad of peace.[94]

As the labyrinth had been cleared, so William Posters had been unearthed, exposed and destroyed. 'Bill Posters, thank God, had died at last in the ruins of Radford-Stalingrad . . . crushed to death under the slabs and bricks, beams and fireplaces.'[95]

> [Dawley] walked into space, few paces taking him across a clearly marked street plan on which as a kid

> each moss-dewed corner and double entry had seemed miles from each other . . . Streets in all directions had been clawed and grabbed and hammered down, scooped up, bucketed, piled, sorted and carted off. Where had all the people gone? Moved onto new estates, all decisions made for them, whereas he also wanted to uproot himself but must make his own moves.[96]

'Exploding out of life so far,' Dawley leaves 'wife, home, job, kids' and the place 'where he had been born, bred and spiritually nullified.'[97] First he heads east for the Lincolnshire wolds. 'His mind had changed with the landscape since leaving Nottingham; surprising him at times by its breadth.'[98] Dawley's broadmindedness is framed by the copy of *Dr. Zhivago* he carries, its evocation of the 'big country' and 'wide open spaces' of Russia[99] and enlarged by his affair with a middle-class woman and his introduction to her library.

Criss-crossing the country like a fugitive, Dawley heads south, for north London, and another conquest of another middle-class wife, Myra Bassingfield. As Dawley's horizons expand, those of the jilted husband, George, close in. George Bassingfield is a professional geographer, lecturer at the London School of Economics, author of *New Aspects of Geography.* 'Few people knew the land of England as well as George, or had a deeper feeling for it . . . the subtleties of land and people were profoundly fascinating, and George was lord of all he surveyed when their composite reactions to land and air tied in with his knowledge and sympathy.' But in middle-age 'his visionary eyes did not seek harmony any more, but fixity into which people and the three elements slotted with neatness and safety.'[100] Indeed, Frank and Myra

> left him standing, looking into the tall drawn curtains that opened onto the back garden . . . Life had always seemed a straight road, and he hadn't even been foxed by a simple dead-end or caught in a false cul-de-sac. Instead he was now trapped in an unsurveyable maze of footpaths darkened by tall hedges. Such a labyrinth was extreme torment for a mind that could exist only on order and calm, which wanted everything measured and shaped, reduced to a beautiful design and set down on paper. The last few days had drawn him into the labyrinth, like a doomed fly fixed in helplessness until the spider-god came out for him.[101]

Frank and Myra leave the cramped world of England, heading south for France, Spain, Morocco, eventually Algeria. Here Dawley enlists as a guerrilla fighter with the FLN during the War of Independence.

This novel and its sequel, *A Tree on Fire* (1967), appear to be shaped by Sillitoe's reading of the theory and practice of guerrilla warfare, some in preparation for his script for a projected film on Che Guevara.[102] The spatiality of guerrilla warfare, 'drifting and subtle . . . arabesques,' 'the spider's web of revolution'[103] characterise Frank Dawley's tactics throughout his journeying. His quest evokes Che Guevara's notion of the socialist 'new man,' evolving from the 'wolfman' of capitalist competition,[104] and also the high-tech ideology of Khruschev's Soviet Union. Dawley envisages a modernist, machine-tooled utopia:

> All I believe in is houses and factories, food and power stations, bridges and coalmines and death, turning millions of things out on a machine that people can use. It's no use harping back to poaching rights and cottage industries. We've got to forget all that and come to terms with cities and machines and moon landings. We're going to become new men, whether we like it or not, and I know I am going to like it.[105]

AIRMAN

It is Brian Seaton, Arthur's eldest brother, who acquires an airborne cartographic view of the world in ***Key to the Door*** (1961) and its sequel ***The Open Door*** (1989). The course of Brian Seaton's life parallels Alan Sillitoe's own, from factory work in Nottingham, to National Service in Malaya to embarking, as a writer, for the south of France. It is these novels which challenge the prevailing stereotype of Sillitoe's Nottingham as a 'northern' province of a London-centred nationalist culture. For Brian Seaton 'London didn't exist,'[106] it was a place you passed over in a more global vision. South of the river Trent is not southern England but southern Europe, the Trent is a 'magic band of water' separating 'oak from olive, mildew from hot pines and baking rock.'[107]

Key to the Door begins in 1930s Nottingham with the destitute Seaton family on the run from the bailiffs and the slum clearance programme of 'a demolishing council.' While some slum dwellers take 'the benefit of new housing estates,' father Harold Seaton 'clung to the town centre because its burrow was familiar.'[108] Eventually they are forced out by the bulldozers, and bombardment from the air. One area of 'broken and derelict maze' is set aside 'to be the target of bombs from buzzing two-winged aeroplanes, the sideshow of a military tattoo whose full glory lay on the city's outskirts.'[109] The Seaton family take refuge in a cottage in a still-rough, semi-rural, warren-like area at the edge of the city. It is a frontier zone about to feel the turbulent force of modernisation, to be turned into a 'tipscape,' filled with rubble from the old slums, levelled and developed. 'Then they'll make an aerodrome,' Brian speculates, 'to bomb old houses like ourn was on Albion Yard.'[110]

What they actually make is a bright new estate, lit by electricity, 'magically blessed' with a mains water-supply, marked out with broad boulevards, and the first new houses:

> Pink houses of new estates were spilling into the countryside. Men with black and white poles and notebooks came across the new boulevards into lanes and fields; they set theodolites and dumpy levels pointing in sly angles at distant woods . . . invading Brian's hideouts, obliterating his short-cuts and concealed tracks.[111]

Brian is enthralled with the men and machines.

Instead of woods and fields, houses would appear along new roads, would transform the map in his mind. The idea of it caught at him like fire.[112]

Brian Seaton grows up with Alan Sillitoe's passion for books and maps. 'Moulded by an addiction to *Les Misérables*' he envisages war in the streets of Nottingham with barricades and sandbag parapets. On a huge war-map of Europe he follows the progress of the Red Army on the eastern front. Brian Seaton works in a claustrophobic factory world, in the 'underground burrow' of the boiler room, having to dig out soot from flues.

> Having to work in the dark set him thinking of coalmines and pit ponies, and the fact that he would go crackers if he didn't get out and prove he wasn't buried a thousand feet underground. Jean Valjean traipsing through the sewers was better than this, though I expect Edmond Dantes in *his* tunnels didn't feel too good either . . . This is how you get TB he thought, by breathing black dust like this for hour after hour.[113]

Brian pulls himself out of this subterranean world, to join the airforce as a wireless operator in Malaya, and a life of 'morse and mapmaking,' doing guard duty in a 'worn out part of the British empire.'[114]

The Open Door (1989) finds Brian Seaton negotiating the labyrinth of the Malayan jungle. It was 'a place where you could be as much at home as in any maze of streets' but for Seaton, the imperial outsider, it remains intractable, a heart of darkness. 'The jungle had inflicted a deadly bite by drawing him through the valley of the shadow.'[115] With map and compass, he struggles unsuccessfully through this predatory world towards the summit of a 4,000 foot peak, Gunong Barat. And writing it up, from his diary notes, he remains gripped by the experience. 'Unable to sleep, he dreamed of creepers and decomposing trees, and blades of water waving down cliff-faces enlarged my memory's infallible magnifying glass.'[116]

Returning to Nottingham, Seaton deploys his cartographic intelligence on a more pliant subject, the woman he seduces by tracing 'a map upon her back.' He also embarks on an exotic travelogue, 'looking at the Beautiful Horizon, plodding through Bangkok, eating the Sandwich Islands, swimming off Madagascar, trekking the five-fingered forests of Gunong Barat . . ..'[117] He tries it on his younger brother Arthur too, in offering the lad the kind of educated, reflective prospect of Nottinghamshire that Arthur will, as the rebellious youth in ***Saturday Night and Sunday Morning,*** never achieve. Brian takes Arthur on a bus-ride beyond the city for a spot of fraternal bonding on Misk Hill.

> 'Who showed yer where it was?'
>
> 'I found it on a map. The top's over five hundred feet above sea level.'
>
> 'Will I be able to breathe? He ran on to the plateau of a large field, arms in front like pistons . . .

Suburbs started three miles away, houses and factories under mountainous cloud. Faint haze emphasised the rich squalor of memorable dreams, his past in a semicircle from north to south . . .

'It's smashin' up 'ere.' Arthur hurled a stick . . .

A shunting train was pinpointed by feathers of smoke. Brian held him tight. 'Don't ever leave it. It's your hill.'

'Eh, fuck off!' Arthur broke away. 'Are yo' trying to fuck me, or summat?'

Brian laughed. 'Come on loony, let's get down.'[118]

EAST MIDLAND GEOGRAPHIES

In this chapter we have presented Sillitoe's novels as a field of different, sometimes conflicting forms of geographical knowledge and experience. To do this we have shown how the narratives of the novels are interleaved with a variety of discourses on Nottingham and its region, on other modernising cities, on an internationalist politics of citizenship, and, pre-eminently, on geography, specifically maps and map-reading. In this exercise we hope to further the recent broadening of the history of geography beyond the usual internal, linear, professional histories, to take account of 'lateral associations and social relations of geographical knowledge.'[119]

Sillitoe's novels chart the modernisation of Nottingham in a way which combines and competes with official, commercial and academic geographies of the city and its region.

In the period covered by the novels, the city corporation's publications represent Nottingham as a model 'modern city.' Through careful planning, economic and social development was orderly and integrated, creating the framework for a prosperous, enlightened city and citizenry. From 1954 this progressive view was endorsed, and extended to the city's hinterland by the regional journal, *The East Midland Geographer.* Under the founding editorship of K. C. Edwards, himself active in local regional planning and policy making, the journal charted infrastructural developments in the city and its region: the modernisation of the mining industry, the rationalisation of the railways, the building of municipal estates, the construction of motorways.[120] The region's representativeness in landscape and human activity made it 'an epitome of the English scene.' 'Its importance in the economic development of the country moreover is continually growing and is likely to increase vastly in the future.'[121] This was not just a forward-looking view; developments in the past were narrated as part of the same progressive story. In a series of public lectures on the development of Nottingham, from the mid-1930s to mid-1960s, Edwards charted the expansion and consolidation of the city into 'a coherent, closely-knit economic and social entity.'[122]

1958, the year that K. C. Edwards told this story of Nottingham in his address at Nottingham University to the conference of the Institute of British Geographers, the first instalment of Alan Sillitoe's *Saturday Night and Sunday Morning* was published. Like professional planners and geographers, Sillitoe framed land and life in terms of maps, but he charted a different, darker story. Sillitoe's image of the city and its citizenry is not one of coherence and continuity, of community building, but of conflict and upheaval, explosive physical and social change. As on a military map, the city is envisaged as a field of battle. There are, as we have shown, many mediations in this vision, including representations of insurgent Stalingrad, Petrograd, Paris and Nottingham itself during the Luddite and Reform riots. If official and academic versions of Nottingham's geography were written in that progressive, optimistic, enlightened discourse of modernism, Sillitoe's version was written in modernism's counter-discourse of violence, oppression and exclusion.[123]

It is not surprising that City officials responded cooly to the international success of *Saturday Night and Sunday Morning,* and accused Sillitoe moreover of stirring up the sort of trouble that the novel described.[124] Now both parties stand condemned. The City Corporation is accused of pulling down 'Victorian and Edwardian treasures' to make way for 'modern monstrosities,' and Sillitoe is condemned for tarnishing the world that remained standing. The renovation of Nottingham's derelict textile district, the Lace Market, as a heritage spectacle promised a more stylish future. 'Ten years ago the Queen of the Midlands had a slightly dowdy look [now] it is no longer the dirty city of Alan Sillitoe's *Saturday Night and Sunday Morning.*'[125] It is too soon to say if post-industrial planning will erase the memory of Arthur Seaton, or the mythology which sustained him. As recently as the summer of 1993, Albert Finney's scowling portrait of Arthur Seaton was spotted, printed on the t-shirts of protesters against the closure of local collieries.

Notes

We wish to thank Alan Sillitoe for his co-operation. Robert Bartram, Zena Forster, John Giggs, John Lucas and David Matless offered helpful comments on earlier drafts of this chapter.

1. J. A. Kestner, *The Spatiality of the Novel* (Detroit, 1978); Yi Fu Tuan, 'Literature and Geography' in David Ley and Marwyn Samuels (eds.), *Humanistic Geography: Prospects and Problems* (1978), pp. 194–206; John Barrell, 'Geographies of Hardy's Wessex,' *Journal of Historical Geography,* vol. 8 (1982), pp. 347–61 (reprinted in the present volume); Edward Said, 'Jane Austen and Empire,' in Terry Eagleton (ed.), *Raymond Williams: Critical Perspectives* (Cambridge), pp. 150–64.

2. J. Bender, *Imagining the Penitentiary: Fiction and Architecture of Mind in Eighteenth Century England* (Chicago, 1987), p. 65.

3. Simon Varey, *Space and the Eighteenth-century English Novel* (Cambridge, 1990); Nicholas Alfrey

and Stephen Daniels (eds.), *Mapping the Landscape: Essays on Art and Cartography* (Nottingham, 1990); Stephen Daniels, 'Re-visioning Britain: Mapping and Landscape Painting, 1750–1830,' in Katherine Baetjer, *Glorious Nature: British Landscape Painting, 1750–1850* (New York, 1993), pp. 61–72.

4. Ian Watt, *The Rise of the Novel* (Harmondsworth, 1957); Raymond Williams, *The Country and the City* (London, 1973); Malcolm Bradbury, 'The Cities of Modernism,' in Malcolm Bradbury and James Mcfarlane (eds.), *Modernism* (Harmondsworth, 1976), pp. 96–104; Michael Seidel, *Epic Geography: James Joyce's Ulysses* (Princeton, 1976); Marshall Berman, *All That is Solid Melts Into Air: The Experience of Modernity* (London, 1983); Edward Said, *Culture and Imperialism* (New York, 1993).

5. Sillitoe's many works are catalogued in David E. Gerard, *Alan Sillitoe: A Bibliography* (London, 1988) along with many works of criticism and commentary. This has proved a valuable resource for this chapter. Also valuable is the Sillitoe collection at the Central Library, Nottingham, especially the file of newspaper cuttings on his early career. The most comprehensive work of criticism on Sillitoe is Stanley S. Atherton, *Alan Sillitoe: A Critical Assessment* (London, 1979). A study of Sillitoe with points of connection with this article is H. M. Daleski, 'The Novelist as Map Maker' in Hedwig Bock and Albert Werthein (eds.), *Essays on the Contemporary British Novel* (Frankfurt, 1986).

6. An edited transcript of this interview is provided in Simon Rycroft, *Ordinance and Order in Alan Sillitoe's Fictional Topography,* Working Paper, no. 13, Department of Geography, University of Nottingham, 1991.

7. Douglas C. D. Pocock (ed.), *Humanistic Geography and Literature* (London, 1981); William E. Mallory and Paul Simpron-Housely (eds.), *Geography and Literature: A Meeting of the Disciplines* (Syracuse, 1987).

8. Trevor J. Barnes and James S. Duncan (eds.), *Writing Worlds: Discourse, Text and Metaphor in the Representation of Landscape* (London, 1992); Felix Driver, 'Geography's Empire: Histories of Geographical Knowledge,' *Society and Space,* vol. 10 (1992), pp. 23–40; Stephen Daniels, *Fields of Vision: Landscape Imagery and National Identity in England and the United States* (Cambridge and Princeton, 1993); Edward Said, *The World, the Text and the Critic* (London, 1983); John Barrell (ed.), *Painting and the Politics of Culture: New Essays on British Art* (Oxford, 1992).

9. Alan Sillitoe, 'We all start from home,' *Bulletin de la Société des Anglicistes de l'Enseignment Supérieur,* September 1987, pp. 6–16.

10. Alan Sillitoe, *Alan Sillitoe's Nottinghamshire* (London, 1987), p. 3.

11. Alan Sillitoe, 'Mountains and Caverns,' in *Mountains and Caverns,* pp. 152–60 (p. 156); Sillitoe, 'We All Start from Home,' p. 12; Alan Sillitoe, 'The Long Piece' in *Mountains and Caverns,* p. 12.

12. David Kempe, *Living Underground: A History of Cave and Cliff Dwelling* (London, 1988).

13. Victor Hugo, *Les Misérables* (Harmondsworth, 1982), esp. pp. 399–410.

14. David Pinkney, *Napoleon III and the Rebuilding of Paris* (Princeton, 1958); T. J. Clark, *The Painting of Modern Life: Paris in the Art of Manet and his Followers* (London, 1984).

15. Hugo, *Les Misérables,* pp. 945–7, 208.

16. Nottingham Corporation, *Nottingham: Queen City of the Midlands. The Official Guide* (Cheltenham, 1927), pp. 25, 35–7, 62–5; British Association for the Advancement of Science, *A Scientific Survey of Nottingham* (London, 1937), pp. 9–18; J. D. Chambers, *Modern Nottingham in the Making* (Nottingham, 1945).

17. Robert Mellors, *Old Nottingham Suburbs: Then and Now* (Nottingham, 1914), pp. 25–60; Chambers, *Modern Nottingham,* pp. 47–8; C. J. Thomas, 'Some Geographical Aspects of Council Housing in Nottingham,' *East Midland Geographer,* vol. 4 (1966), pp. 88–98; C. J. Thomas, 'The Growth of Nottingham Since 1919,' *East Midland Geographer,* vol. 5 (1971), pp. 119–132; R. Silburn, 'People in their Places' in *One Hundred Years of Nottingham* (Nottingham, 1981), pp. 16–35.

18. Alan Sillitoe, 'The Death of Frankie Butler' in *The Loneliness of the Long-Distance Runner* (London, 1985), pp. 154–74 (p. 156).

19. Alan Sillitoe, *Raw Material* (London, 1972), p. 98.

20. Rycroft, *Ordinance and Order,* pp. 11–12; Alan Sillitoe, 'Maps' in Sillitoe, *Mountains and Caverns,* pp. 62–3.

21. Sillitoe, *Raw Material,* pp. 98–9.

22. Rycroft, *Ordinance and Order,* pp. 11–12; Sillitoe, 'Maps,' p. 68; Sillitoe, 'We All Start from Home,' p. 9.

23. Alan Sillitoe, 'The Long Piece' in *Mountains and Caverns,* pp. 9–49 (p. 17).

24. Alan Sillitoe, Foreward to G. H. Bowden, *The Story of the Raleigh Cycle* (London, 1975), p. 9.

25. David Matless, 'The English Outlook' in Alfrey and Daniels, *Mapping the Landscape,* pp. 28–30; David Matless, 'Regional Surveys and Local Knowledges: The Geographical Imagination in Britain, 1918–39,' *Transactions of the Institute of British Geographers,* vol. 17 (1992), pp. 464–80 (p. 469).

26. Sillitoe, 'Maps,' p. 70; Sillitoe, 'We All Start from Home,' p. 10. For more details of his air training,

Alan Sillitoe, 'A Cadet Remembers,' *Air Cadet News,* March 1981, p. 5.

27. D. L. Linton, *The Interpretation of Air Photographs* (London, 1947), p. 3.

28. *Ibid.,* p. 5.

29. E. G. R. Taylor, *Geography of an Air Age* (London, 1945).

30. Alan Sillitoe, 'National service' in *Mountains and Caverns,* pp. 50–8 (p. 56).

31. Sillitoe, 'The Long Piece,' p. 24.

32. *Ibid.,* pp. 21, 24.

33. Sillitoe, 'Maps,' pp. 71–2.

34. Sillitoe, 'The Long Piece,' p. 26.

35. Sillitoe, 'The Long Piece,' p. 10.

36. David Mellor, *A Paradise Lost: The Neo-Romantic Imagination in Britain, 1935–55* (London, 1987), pp. 69–70.

37. Sillitoe, 'The Long Piece,' pp. 19–33.

38. Alan Sillitoe, 'Alan Sillitoe,' *Author* (Autumn 1983), pp. 28–30 (p. 30).

39. Rycroft, *Ordinance and Order,* pp. 16–17; Sillitoe, 'Maps,' p. 70; Sillitoe, 'We All Start from Home,' p. 13.

40. Alan Sillitoe, 'Lawrence and District,' in *Mountains and Caverns,* pp. 128–144 (quotations on pp. 133, 131, 141).

41. Sillitoe, *Raw Material,* pp. 174–5.

42. Sillitoe, 'Maps,' p. 68; Rycroft, *Ordinance and Order,* pp. 13–15.

43. Sillitoe's political sympathies shifted in the 1970s from the Soviet Union to Israel, although his sense of citizenship remained fairly constant. See Alan Sillitoe, 'Iron in the sand,' *Geographical Magazine,* November 1978, pp. 137–42; Alan Sillitoe, 'My Israel,' *New Statesman,* 20 December 1974, pp. 890–2.

44. Alan Sillitoe, *Road to Volgograd* (London, 1964), p. 81.

45. *Ibid.,* p. 41.

46. Alan Sillitoe, *A Falling Out of Love and Other Poems* (London, 1964).

47. David Lodge, *The Modes of Modern Writing: Metaphor, Metonymy and the Typology of Modern Literature* (Ithaca, New York, 1977), p. 213.

48. Sillitoe, 'Mountains and Caverns,' p. 152.

49. Michael Grant, *Myths of the Greeks and Romans* (London, 1989), pp. 385–6; Merrill Schleier, *The Skyscraper in American Art, 1890–1930* (New York, 1986), pp. 5–68; Stephen Kern, *The Culture of Space and Time, 1880–1914* (Cambridge Mass., 1983), pp. 242–7; Valentine Cunningham, *British Writers of the Thirties* (Oxford, 1988), pp. 168–73, 241–65; David Matless, 'Preservation, Modernism and the Nature of the Nation,' *Built Environment,* vol. 16 (1990), pp. 179–91; Wendy B. Faris, 'The Labyrinth as Sign' in Mary Ann Caws, *City Images: Perspectives from Literature, Philosophy and Film* (New York, 1991), pp. 33–41; Rosalind Williams, *Notes on the Underground: An Essay on Technology, Society and the Imagination* (Cambridge MA, 1990), pp. 51–81.

50. Alan Sillitoe, *The Death of William Posters* (London, 1965), p. 73.

51. Alison Light, *Forever England: Femininity, Literature and Conservatism between the Wars* (London, 1991), p. 24.

52. Gillian Beer, 'The Island and the Aeroplane' in Homi Bhaba (ed.), *Nation and Narration* (London, 1990).

53. D. H. Lawrence, *The Rainbow* (Harmondsworth, 1989), pp. 42–3.

54. Emrys Bryson, *Portrait of Nottingham* (London, 1983), pp. 150–61.

55. Nottingham Corporation, *Nottingham 'The Queen City of the Midlands.'*

56. Alan Sillitoe, *Saturday Night and Sunday Morning* (London, 1976), p. 9.

57. *Ibid.,* p. 133.

58. Robert Hewison, *In Anger: Culture in the Cold War* (London, 1981), pp. 163–80; Tim Price, 'The Politics of Culture: *Saturday Night and Sunday Morning,*' unpublished Ph.D. thesis, University of Nottingham, 1987.

59. Richard Hoggart, *The Uses of Literacy* (Harmondsworth, 1958), pp. 24, 40–1, 46–7, 50.

60. Atherton, *Alan Sillitoe,* pp. 15–21; Peter Hitchcock, *Working-Class Fiction in Theory and Practice: A Reading of Alan Sillitoe* (London, 1989), pp. 22–49.

61. Arthur Marwick, '*Room at the Top, Saturday Night and Sunday Morning* and the "Cultural Revolution" in Britain,' *Journal of Contemporary History,* vol. 19 (1984), pp. 127–52; Lynne Segal, 'Look Back in Anger: Men in the Fifties,' in Rowena Chapman and Jonathan Rutherford (eds.), *Male Order: Unwrapping Masculinity* (London, 1988), pp. 68–96.

62. Alan Sillitoe, 'Saturday Night and Sunday Morning' screenplay, in *Masterworks of the British Cinema* (London, 1974), pp. 267–328.

63. Terry Lovell, 'Landscapes and Stories in 1960s British Realism,' *Screen,* vol. 31 (1990), pp. 357–76.

64. Price, "The Politics of Culture,' pp. 162–5; Hitchcock, *Working-Class Fiction,* pp. 75–8.

65. Sillitoe, *Saturday Night and Sunday Morning*, p. 27.

66. *Ibid.*, pp. 26–8, 48, 130.

67. *Ibid.*, p. 174.

68. Geoffrey Pearson, *Hooligan: A History of Respectable Fears* (London, 1983), pp. 12–24.

69. Raymond Williams, *The Long Revolution* (Harmondsworth, 1965), p. 322.

70. E. P. Thompson, *The Making of the English Working Class* (New York, 1963), pp. 77–101.

71. Cf. Lynn Spigel, 'The Suburban Home Companion: Television and Neighbourhood in Postwar America,' in Beatriz Colomina (ed.), *Sexuality and Space* (Princeton, 1992), pp. 185–217.

72. Sillitoe has said that because he was out of the country for most of the Fifties, 'what I was doing, I think, was really bringing my experience from the Forties up into the Fifties.' 'An Interview with Alan Sillitoe,' *Modern Fiction Studies,* vol. 21 (1975–6), p. 176. Sillitoe's Nottingham seems in some respects more like 1960 'Worktown' (Bolton), about which Mass Observation commented:

    Despite the telly, despite increased working class car ownership, despite the whole complex of commodity fetishism which *looks* as if it is changing the way ordinary people in England live . . . the pub still persists as a social institution. Qualitatively and quantitatively. Never having had it so good doesn't mean only washing machines and holidays abroad; it is also more beer. (Tom Harrisson, *Britain Revisited.* (London, 1961), p. 194).

73. Sillitoe, *Saturday Night and Sunday Morning*, p. 45.

74. *Ibid.*, p. 224.

75. Nigel Gray, *The Silent Majority: A Study of the Working-class in Post-war British Fiction* (London, 1973), pp. 123–7; Jonathan Dollimore, 'The Challenge of Sexuality,' in Alan Sinfield (ed.), *Society and Literature, 1945–70* (London, 1983), pp. 51–85; Segal, 'Look Back in Anger,' pp. 80–1.

76. D. H. Lawrence, 'Nottingham and the Mining Country,' in *Selected Essays* (Harmondsworth, 1981), p. 117.

77. Segal, 'Look Back in Anger,' p. 87; George Perry and Alan Aldridge, *The Penguin Book of Comics: A Slight History* (Harmondsworth, 1975), p. 5.

78. Rycroft, *Ordinance and Order,* pp. 21–2; J. R. Ogersby, 'Alan Sillitoe's *Saturday Night and Sunday Morning,'* in G. R. Hibbard (ed.), *Renaissance and Modern Essays* (London, 1966), p. 217.

79. Sillitoe, *Saturday Night,* pp. 167–8.

80. *Ibid.*, p. 209.

81. *Ibid.*, p. 171.

82. *Ibid.*, p. 120.

83. *Ibid.*, pp. 78, 134, 78. Arthur's cousins are the prototype for the hero of Sillitoe's 1961 short story 'The Loneliness of the Long-Distance Runner,' in Sillitoe, *The Loneliness of the Long-Distance Runner,* pp. 9–54.

84. Sillitoe, *Saturday Night,* p. 121.

85. *Ibid.*, p. 121.

86. *Ibid.*, pp. 207, 209.

87. *Ibid.*, p. 154.

88. *Ibid.*, p. 160.

89. *Ibid.*, p. 161.

90. Rycroft, *Ordinance and Order,* pp. 20–1.

91. Sillitoe, *The Death of William Posters,* p. 16.

92. *Ibid.*, p. 18.

93. *Ibid.*, p. 73.

94. *Ibid.*, pp. 73–4.

95. *Ibid.*, p. 309.

96. *Ibid.*, p. 74.

97. *Ibid.*, p. 16.

98. *Ibid.*, p. 11.

99. *Ibid.*, pp. 38, 55.

100. *Ibid.*, pp. 199–200.

101. *Ibid.*, pp. 243–4.

102. Alan Sillitoe, '"Che" Guevara,' in *Mountains and Caverns*, pp. 121–7.

103. Sillitoe, *The Death of William Posters,* p. 308; Alan Sillitoe, *A Tree on Fire* (London, 1967), p. 427.

104. Michael Lowy, *The Marxism of Che Guevara: Philosophy, Economics and Revolutionary Warfare* (London, 1973), pp. 25–8.

105. Sillitoe, *The Death of William Posters,* p. 259.

106. Rycroft, *Ordinance and Order,* p. 9.

107. Alan Sillitoe, *The Open Door* (London, 1989), p. 335.

108. Alan Sillitoe, *Key to the Door* (London, 1989), p. 17.

109. *Ibid.*, p. 17.

110. *Ibid.*, p. 78.

111. *Ibid.*, p. 191.

112. *Ibid.*, p. 192.

113. *Ibid.*, p. 243.

114. *Ibid.*, pp. 301, 433.

115. Sillitoe, *The Open Door,* p. 75.

116. *Ibid.,* p. 74.

117. *Ibid.,* pp. 167, 174.

118. *Ibid.,* p. 291.

119. Driver, 'Geography's Empire,' p. 35.

120. T. W. Freeman, 'Twenty-Five Years of "The East Midland Geographer,"' *East Midland Geographer,* vol. 7 (1979), pp. 95–9.

121. K. C. Edwards, editorial introduction, *East Midland Geographer,* vol. 1 (1954), p. 2.

122. K. C. Edwards, 'Nottingham and its Region,' in British Association for the Advancement of Science, *A Scientific Survey of Nottingham* (London, 1937), pp. 25–38; K. C. Edwards, 'The Geographical Development of Nottingham,' in K. C. Edwards (ed.), *Nottingham and Its Region* (London, 1966), pp. 363–404; K. C. Edwards (ed.), 'Nottingham: Queen of the Midlands,' *Geographical Magazine,* September 1965, p. 347.

123. Stuart Hall and Bram Gieben, *Formations of Modernity* (Cambridge, 1993), p. 14. A collection of writings on Nottingham written in terms of this counter-discourse, to which Sillitoe contributed an article on 'Poor People,' is the theme issue of *Anarchy 38: A Journal of Anarchist Ideas,* April 1964.

124. Young, 'The Politics of Culture,' pp. 195–6; Rycroft, *Ordinance and Order,* p. 18.

125. *Nottingham Evening Post,* Supplement, 1988.

FURTHER READING

Criticism

Levin, Martin. Review of *Men, Women, and Children,* by Alan Sillitoe. *New York Times Book Review* (22 September 1974): 40.

Levin praises the individual feelings evoked by Sillitoe's stories in *Men, Women, and Children.*

Maitland, Sara. "Worthiness." *Spectator* 249, No. 8052 (6 November 1982): 29.

Maitland lauds several aspects of Sillitoe's *Her Victory,* but asserts that the work as a whole is flawed.

McCarthy, Tom. Review of *Alligator Playground,* by Alan Sillitoe. *Observer* (4 January 1998): 14.

McCarthy offers a generally favorable assessment of Sillitoe's *Alligator Playground,* but points out some stylistic problems with some of the stories.

Mewshaw, Michael. Review of *The Lost Flying Boat,* by Alan Sillitoe. *New York Times Book Review* (14 October 1984): 26.

Mewshaw complains that the characters in Sillitoe's *The Lost Flying Boat* often speak in clichés which limit the novel.

Quirk, Eugene F. "The Loneliness of the Long-Distance Runner." *Film Quarterly* 9, No. 3 (1981): 161–71.

Quirk analyzes the changes made between Sillitoe's short story "The Loneliness of the Long-Distance Runner" and his subsequent screenplay based on the story.

Hayden White
1928-

(Full name Hayden V. White) American historian, critic, essayist, and editor.

The following entry presents an overview of White's career through 2000.

INTRODUCTION

A prominent American historian, White is known for his analyses of the literary structures of the works of nineteenth- and twentieth-century historians and philosophers. In several of his works, White argues that historical studies are best understood not as accurate and objective representations of the past but as creative texts structured by narrative and rhetorical devices that shape historical interpretation. White's first major work, *Metahistory* (1973), presents a detailed outline for the study of the different narrative and rhetorical strategies found in the works of nineteenth-century European historians such as Leopold von Ranke and Jacob Burkhardt. Influenced by eighteenth-century scholar Giambattista Vico and literary critic Kenneth Burke, White proposes a theory of tropes, or symbolic modes, that constitutes the deep structure of historical thought. White elaborated and modified his arguments from *Metahistory* in two collections of essays, *Tropics of Discourse* (1978) and *The Content of the Form* (1987). Although his work has drawn criticism from historians and literary critics alike, White is widely respected for raising vital questions about the latent assumptions that inform all kinds of historical interpretation.

BIOGRAPHICAL INFORMATION

Born in Martin, Tennessee, in 1928, White received his undergraduate degree from Wayne State University in Michigan in 1951, his M.A. from the University of Michigan in 1952, and his Ph.D. in 1956. After serving as an instructor of history at Wayne State from 1955 to 1958, White worked as an assistant professor of history at the University of Rochester in Rochester, New York, in 1958. White later became professor of history at Rochester and served as the departmental chairperson from 1962 to 1964. During his tenure there, White published an early essay, "The Burden of History" (1966), which raised many of the questions about the discipline of history that would be the focus of his later works. White left the University of Rochester in 1968 to take a position as a history professor at the University of California, Los Angeles, where he remained until 1973. In collaboration with other scholars,

White served as an editor of the two-volume work *The Emergence of Liberal Humanism* (1966, 1970), *The Uses of History* (1968), and *Giambattista Vico* (1969). White's early work about Vico, an Italian scholar of history and literature, would inform his later writings on historical discourse. In 1973, White accepted a position as director for the Center for the Humanities at Wesleyan University in Connecticut, where he was named Kenan Professor from 1976 to 1978. While at Wesleyan, White produced his first major work, *Metahistory,* and continued to publish essays about problems of historical knowledge and the relations between history and literature in journals and edited volumes. White left Connecticut in 1978 to accept a position as professor of the history of consciousness at the University of California, Santa Cruz, where he has since remained. In two collections of his essays, *Tropics of Discourse* and *The Content of the Form,* White continued to explore and expand upon the issues raised in his earliest works about the writing of history, or historiography. In *Figural Realism* (1999), a collection of essays written since publication of *The Content of the Form,* White elaborates on his arguments about tropes and responds to some of his critics.

MAJOR WORKS

All of White's works share a concern with combining literary criticism and historiography in order to develop a deeper understanding of historical discourse and cultural perspective. In *Metahistory,* White sets out the interpretive framework that guides much of his later work. Arguing for a sustained examination of the figurative features of historiographical texts, White asserts the importance of four tropes of consciousness that shape the work of the historian at every stage. Following Vico's work on rhetoric, White associates these four modes of historical consciousness with four figures of speech: metaphor, metonymy, synecdoche, and irony. Each of these figures has its own characteristic way of organizing pieces of information into a larger whole. White argues that this poetics of history, and not historical evidence alone, determines in advance a historian's perspective and interpretation. Thus, for White, the power of these different modes of representation highlights the non-scientific nature of the discipline of history. If one assumes a base level of honesty and skill on the part of the historian, White finds no reason to privilege one historical account over another based only on historical evidence. White asserts that the kind of history one chooses to tell is based on moral and aesthetic values that stand in sharp contrast to some objective, neutral understanding of historical evidence alone. White's *Metahistory* reveals a relativism that collapses the distinctions not only between historiography and the philosophy of history, but also fiction and historiography. For White, fictitious and historiographical events are both conveyed through similar representational strategies and hence, at this formal level, no differences exist between these two kinds of discourse. Along with this relativism, White's arguments in *Metahistory* have been criticized for their adherence to a formal, literary structuralism and a lack of attention to historical context. In the three collections of essays published since the appearance of *Metahistory,* White has sought to elaborate and modify his approach and to respond to his critics. In *Tropics of Discourse,* White strives to develop a less relativistic stance by arguing that the deep structures that define human consciousness have a certain stability that allows for the creation of sound representations of human perceptions of reality. He also suggests that it is not possible for some pieces of historical evidence to be represented within particular tropological structures, and hence the historian needs to rely only on those modes of discourse that will most accurately reflect the evidence in question. Although White's arguments in *Tropics of Discourse* placed some distance between his work and that of poststructuralist theorists with whom he had been associated, they also raised tensions within his own approach. White's next collection of essays, *The Content of the Form,* places less emphasis on the almost existential separation between life and narrative found in his early work, emphasizing instead the role ideology plays in the representation of historical processes and events. In *Figural Realism,* White again employs his theory of tropes to examine the work of Proust and Freud, arguing that history cannot serve as neutral ground for the interpretation of varied texts. White also examines the difficulties and ethical problems posed in finding effective ways to represent the Holocaust.

CRITICAL RECEPTION

Since the publication of *Metahistory,* White's works have been criticized along fairly consistent lines. While White is widely respected as a thorough and wide-ranging scholar, many have faulted him for problems posed by his methodology. Historians have sharply criticized White for his alleged epistemological and moral relativism caused by his conflation of historical and fictional narrative, as well as his denial of the objective value of historical evidence. Some historians also have objected to White's use of literary history, and strongly contest his assertions about the impossibility of creating realistic representations of history. Critics have accused White of adhering to a rigid formalism that denies the plurality of forms of historical writing. In addition, White has been attacked by historians for his lack of attention to historical context within his own works. These and other criticisms from fellow historians have meant that White's work has limited his influence on the practice of writing history. In general, historians have not closely followed White's work since the publication of *Metahistory,* and have paid little critical

attention to his efforts to respond to charges of relativism or developments in other areas of his thought. Despite encountering opposition within the field of history, White's works have enjoyed a warmer reception among literary theorists and critics, who find his efforts to highlight the literary quality of historiography compelling. Literary theorists commend White's attention to the role of figurative language in historical writings, but some have criticized his willingness to classify texts into rigid and seemingly self-contained rhetorical or narrative categories. Other commentators have noted White's consistent lack of attention to feminist or post-colonial theories that, like his own work, seek to challenge the limits imposed on historical and cultural understanding by dominant modes of narrative. These critics argue that these and other newly emerging theories may provide White with some of the alternative forms of representation that he has argued for throughout his career. Despite these sustained critiques, White continues to be widely respected among scholars in a variety of fields and for raising thought-provoking questions that have influenced the direction of historical inquiry in the late twentieth century.

PRINCIPAL WORKS

The Emergence of Liberal Humanism: An Intellectual History of Western Europe, Volume I: *From the Italian Renaissance to the French Revolution* [with Willson H. Coates and J. Selwyn Schapio] (history) 1966

The Uses of History: Essays in Intellectual and Social History [editor] (essays) 1968

Giambattista Vico: An International Symposium [editor; with Giorgio Tagliacozzo] (nonfiction) 1969

The Emergence of Liberal Humanism: An Intellectual History of Western Europe, Volume II: *Since the French Revolution* [with Willson H. Coates and J. Selwyn Schapio] (history) 1970

The Ordeal of Liberal Humanism [editor; with Willson H. Coates] (nonfiction) 1970

The Greco-Roman Tradition (history) 1973

Metahistory: The Historical Imagination in Nineteenth-Century Europe (history) 1973

Tropics of Discourse: Essays in Cultural Criticism (essays) 1978

Representing Kenneth Burke [editor; with Margaret Brose] (nonfiction) 1982

The Content of the Form: Narrative Discourse and Historical Representation (essays) 1987

Figural Realism: Studies in the Mimesis Effect (history) 1999

CRITICISM

Phyllis Grosskurth (review date 1975)

SOURCE: A review of *Metahistory,* in *Canadian Historical Review,* Vol. LVI, 1975, pp. 192–93.

[*In the following review, Grosskurth offers a positive assessment of* Metahistory, *which she hails as a "deliberately provocative book."*]

Professor Hayden White of Wesleyan University is nothing if not bold. He has an amplitude of mind which does not quail before the expectation of offending the most formidable of foes. In an article published last year in *History and Theory,* **'Foucault Decoded: Notes from Underground,'** he pointed out the delusions under which French structuralists were deceiving themselves. Undisturbed by the murmurs of irritation, he has now in effect taken on *all* historians in a large book, *Metahistory,* whose subtitle *The Historical Imagination in Nineteenth-Century Europe* is applicable only insofar as he analyzes the work of several major historians of the period to demonstrate that since the nineteenth century 'most historians have affected a kind of wilful methodological naïvete.' This provocative phrase he had already employed in an earlier article ('**The Burden of History,**' *History and Theory,* v, 2, 1966).

From the outset—and there is a long introductory section of his explanation of procedure—he undertakes to demonstrate that historians have inherited an unsystematic, unscientific approach, a flaw that could be rectified if they recognized the limitations of the 'linguistic protocol' they were actually employing. As White defines his book, it is a '*history* of historical consciousness in nineteenth-century Europe, but it is also meant to contribute to the current discussion of the *problem of historical knowledge.*' History he defines as 'a verbal structure in the form of a narrative prose discourse that purports to be a model, or icon, of past structures and processes in the interest of *explaining what they were by representing them*' (Professor White is addicted to italics).

What in effect *Metahistory* is attempting to do is to create a methodology for history such as Northrop Frye provided for literary criticism in *The Anatomy of Criticism*—namely, to categorize and classify the types and conventions of particular literary forms. In sum, this suggests that White, like Croce, regards history as an art; but an art which should be regulated by exigent artistic laws. While most historians would probably agree with White's view that pluralistic approaches to art are desirable, it is likely that many of them would dispute his contention that language creates consciousness, a view compounded by the fact that the historian is dealing with events outside the consciousness of a particular individual. Here we encounter a chicken and egg dilemma.

In order to demonstrate his point, White analyzes the work of Hegel, Michelet, Ranke, Tocqueville, Burckhardt, Marx, Nietzsche, and Croce. Although he finds Croce the most attractive of these historians because of his aesthetic bias, he does not suggest that there has been progress in historical approaches, simply a variety of attitudes in which each figure has presented his vision of history in particular rhetorical terminology. Inevitably each stumbled into

contradictions through ignorance of a consistent mode of language to represent his vision of the past. We can assume, then, that the great historians would have been greater still if only they had had a coherent terminology to describe what they were doing.

It is a bold, fascinating, and deliberately provocative book that White has written. 'History,' I heard a student once remark, 'is a mystery.' What would White say if confronted with such—probably to him—a dismissive and unsophisticated statement? The student presumably meant that history was an elusive past from which historians made excavations to extract some facts to which in turn they attributed a personal significance. If I read him correctly, White would agree with the attitude that history can never be historiography or a quasi-science or that there is a single means of pouncing upon its elusiveness. Nevertheless, while he is prepared to accept such basic premises, at the same time he believes that historians can improve and enlarge their 'discipline' by frankly accepting the literary nature of their enterprise.

Metahistory is irritating and pretentious, and it may be that it has created more problems than it has solved. But if problems engender fresh attitudes to so-called 'disciplines,' so much the better.

Michael Ermarth (review date October 1975)

SOURCE: A review of *Metahistory,* in *American Historical Review,* Vol. 80, No. 4, October, 1975, pp. 961–63.

[*In the following review, Ermarth offers a positive assessment of* Metahistory.]

Metahistory is a daring, ingenious, and sometimes bewildering tour de force. White has produced a profoundly original "critique of historical reason," based not upon the usual fare of idealist metaphysics or the logic of predictive science but upon linguistics—a discipline that may become the *novum organon* of the twentieth century. The author presents a unified field theory of history, which takes its departure from the linguistic structures and figurative language implicit in the historical writing of the great practitioners—Michelet, Ranke, Tocqueville, Burckhardt—and theorists—Hegel, Marx, Nietzsche, Croce—of the "classical age" of history.

The novelty of the work lies not with its components but in their systematic combination and deft application to concrete issues. In fairness it must be said that White's style of exegesis is almost impossible to recapitulate in abbreviated form; one must see it at work. He acknowledges his debt to structuralism, the typology of explanations of Stephen Pepper, the literary criticism of Kenneth Burke and Northrop Frye, Karl Mannheim's sociology of knowledge, and above all, Vico's "new science" and its vision of history as a cycle of consciousness rooted in poetic tropes and figures of speech. From this formidable arsenal

White has fashioned a "poetic logic" of historical discourse that enables him to cut across (or below) the conventional categories and schools of historical thought.

The method is uniformly and unabashedly formal: White asserts that the historian confronts his data in a manner akin to that by which a grammarian approaches a new language. The historical work consists of various manifest and latent "levels of engagement": esthetic, epistemological, and ethical—but all patently linguistic in nature. The historian must employ a mode of emplotment—Romantic, Tragic, Comic, or Satirical; a mode of explanation—Formist, Mechanistic, Organicist, or Contextualist; and a mode of "ideological implication"—Anarchist, Radical, Conservative, or Liberal. Internal affinities and homologies among these modes constitute the interpretive strategy or "style" of the work. The strategies can be reduced to four "linguistic protocols," corresponding to Vico's four master tropes of Metaphor, Metonymy, Synecdoche, and Irony. These tropes provide the "deep grammar" of the historical account.

History is not a realistic transcription "wie es eigentlich gewesen ist" but a linguistic construct ("verbal icon") of figures of speech entailing vast but largely hidden assumptions. History is not *mimesis* but *poesis*. White's thesis plumbs the paradox implicit in the two senses of "literal" conveyed in the notion of a literal past: we must perforce think "in terms of our terms"—a self-evident but highly unsettling observation (White cites Nietzsche: "Our science is still the dupe of linguistic habit"). In delineating four different styles of realism, White shows that their standard of objectivity is defined by internal relations among the levels of engagement: there is no historical *Ding an sich*. Ranke's history is no more objective than Croce's, any more than the German language is "truer" than French; they are simply and irreducibly different systems of discourse.

White has taken considerable pains to avoid system-mongering, but his analysis suffers from a certain hardening of the categories. The solemnly upper-case concepts confer a somewhat vatic quality to the work. Although he admits that the best thinkers tended to mix their metaphors and figures, his tracing of homologies tends to assume an almost ritualistic predictability. We are not obliged to take at face value the historicist claims for the "diversity" and "individuality" of things, but in White's *bal démasqué* the surfaces get lost in the deeper paradigm. The tendency to see Irony lurking behind every post is sometimes more bothersome than illuminating. The resolution of dialectics into a trope—for example, in Marx's analysis of the riddle of money—is elegant but ultimately unpersuasive. White's occasionally arcane coinages—"motifically-encoded," "de-ideologized," "de-naming"—turn the latent level into plain archetypal murk. One might also be led to challenge his purely formal and ultimately reflexive model of language. To use the structuralist terms, historical discourse is *parole* as well as *langue*: it has semantic reference to an experienced world in addition to syntactic structure.

"Discourse is not life"—as the structuralists never tire of reminding us—but that does not make it nonrecitative music or symbolist poetry. However falteringly or obliquely (that is, metaphorically), historical discourse concerns itself with real existence as well as formal coherence. One wonders at White's wholesale adoption of formalism, especially in light of his own careful treatment of the objections of Hegel and Croce to precisely this position.

White avows that his book is framed in the Ironic mode—appropriate to a discipline, and epoch, which has lost its customary certainties and "historical faith." The reader cannot fail to recognize that his perspective is the residual outcome of the very doctrinal antagonisms toward which it is deployed. But there is a visionary as well as critical thrust to his thesis: after indicting academic historians for their "theoretical torpor" and complacent consensus model of historiography, he suggests that history, if conceived mythopoetically, can change the world as well as interpret it. There is a position "beyond Irony" that furnishes the grounds for a new historical consciousness liberated from its old habits and shibboleths. White has provided a comprehensive theoretical framework that transcends the *cordon sanitaire* between "history proper" and the various forms of philosophy of history. Despite a few dark and tight corners, this impressive synthesis casts a very new light.

Stanley Pierson (review date Spring 1978)

SOURCE: A review of *Metahistory*, in *Comparative Literature*, Vol. XXX, No. 2, Spring, 1978, pp. 178–81.

[*In the following review, Pierson praises* Metahistory *as "a bold and imaginative book" and outlines the book's key points of contention that will likely be debated by scholars.*]

The discipline of history has remained relatively free from the close critical scrutiny which, in recent years, has been laying bare the metaphysical and methodological foundations of such neighboring disciplines as literary criticism, philosophy, anthropology, psychology, and sociology. Significant inquiry into the nature of historical thinking has been confined largely to the pages of *History and Theory* and to works by philosophers—White, Dray, Mink, Gallie, Fain, and Danto. Serious self-scrutiny by historians has been limited to the important study by David Fischer, *Historians' Fallacies,* the works of George Iggers, and lighter efforts by Stuart Hughes and Peter Gay. Historians in general have shown little interest in investigating the nature of their craft and little awareness that many of their conventional forms of explanation have been called into question by major currents in modern thought. Historians have remained comparatively indifferent to fundamental philosophical issues despite the vital new perspectives on historical study which have been coming from the psychohistorians, the Marxists, cliometricians, and especially from the French "Annales" school.

Hayden White's **Metahistory** will make it difficult for historians to retain their philosophical innocence. White has attempted to clarify the nature of modern historical thinking, or the "received tradition," by analyzing the work of major nineteenth-century historians—Michelet, Ranke, Tocqueville, and Burkhardt—as well as the major "philosophers of history"—Hegel, Marx, Nietzsche, and Croce. His treatment of these figures is designed, in part, to show that the distinction usually made by historians between those who do history and those who seek to interpret the whole of history and arrive at a grand synthesis, is false. Historical thinking, according to White, is inescapably philosophical and metaphysical. In their efforts to marshall "facts," weave them into a meaningful pattern of narration, and discover underlying relationships, historians must rely on modes of thought which are not empirical; they adopt distinctive forms of argument and different types of emplotment and they make aesthetic and ethical judgments. Even more fundamental than these forms in the making of the historian's consciousness or "style," White maintains, is a poetic act which "prefigures" the historical field and enables the historian to begin his work. This initiating act of imagination involves the adoption of one of four possible "linguistic protocols" or "tropes"—metaphor, metonymy, synecdoche, or irony. On these "irreducible" linguistic foundations the structures of historical consciousness are built. The structures will differ according to the linguistic protocol adopted, for the protocols tend, because of certain "elective affinities," to dictate the explanatory strategies the historian employs to tell his story.

White borrows from a philosopher, a literary critic, and a sociologist in distinguishing the explanatory strategies or the forms of argument, emplotment, and ideology used by historians. Stephen Pepper's fourfold theory of truth—Formism, Mechanism, Organicism, and Contextualism—provides the basic forms of argumentation; Northrop Frye's typology—Romance, Tragedy, Comedy, and Satire—makes up the basic modes of emplotment; Karl Mannheim's classification of social belief systems—Anarchism, Radicalism, Conservatism, and Liberalism—covers the range of ideological options. Beyond these direct influences on White's choice of categories one can recognize his debt to the "structuralists," particularly Foucault and Lévi-Strauss, and to perspectives derived from Nietzsche, Marx, and Hegel. From these diverse sources White has constructed a complex and ingenious apparatus for analyzing historical writings.

Historians will encounter in **Metahistory** a terminology which is unfamiliar and rather intimidating. And they will leave to literary critics, linguists, and philosophers the task of assessing the ways in which White has developed his categories. But they will recognize that White's theory of the basic forms of historical thought has enabled him to offer fresh and illuminating interpretations of the historical thinkers with whom he deals. He displays a thorough command of their writings and if, at times, his categories take on a procrustean character, he recognizes that the greatest historical thinkers struggled to reconcile conflicting views of the historical process. His analyses of Marx and Tocqueville, in whom he sees a dialectical interplay between different tropes and differing modes of argument, emplotment, and ideology, are especially impressive.

Historians will quarrel with White's study in at least two ways. Many historians will not accept his claim that his "linguistic protocols" represent the irreducible foundation of historical thinking. The question here is not strictly speaking a historical question, but it has important methodological implications. To historians of a Marxist persuasion, or to those who believe that the social sciences provide the proper model for their discipline, White's insistence on the irreducibility of his tropes will appear to be a case of arrested analysis. They will reject the view that their "facts" are so largely the products of "tropes" or forms of consciousness and perhaps see in this feature of White's thought the antihistorical strain found in much of "structuralism." These historians will argue that the changing modes of consciousness, including those of the historian, can be understood more fully by exploring their relationships with institutions or with shifting patterns of social and economic interests.

Many historians will also disagree with White's emplotment of modern historiographical development and the lesson he draws from it. White writes with a sense of mission; his book is informed by a desire to arouse the historical profession from its dogmatic slumber—a slumber which takes, paradoxically, the hyperconscious form of irony. He argues that historical thought during the nineteenth century moved beyond the Romantic, Tragic, and Comic postures which, in their various ways, conferred meaning and dignity on the human enterprise, to an ironic outlook. The ironic posture, according to White, arises out of a sense of the impossibility of establishing any common ground for historical understanding and results in skepticism and "moral agnosticism." And while he concedes that none of the four basic "linguistic protocols" employed by historians can claim superiority in epistemological terms, White maintains that the historian can, and in fact should, make choices on ethical and aesthetic (or ideological) grounds. Indeed, he insists that the increased recognition of the ironic state of mind, to which his own study contributes, enables the historian to overcome it and renew the efforts of those nineteenth-century thinkers who sought guidance and inspiration from history.

One may accept White's claim that the dominant mode in modern historical consciousness is ironic without agreeing that such a mode necessarily destroys the capacity to judge and act in human affairs. Irony may function in various ways for the historian—as a means of reaching a relatively detached analysis, as a way of acknowledging the complexities and inescapable ambiguities of human development, or even as a mode of liberation from past institutions and belief systems. White's conception of the historian's consciousness is too simple to do justice to the ways in which the historian forms his values or relates his activities as a scholar to other aspects of life.

Moreover, White's call for ethical and aesthetic choice on the part of the historian is ambiguous. If he is simply pointing once more, as he does so effectively throughout his study, to the inescapable ideological element in historical writing and calling for greater self-consciousness on the part of the historian, few will object. But if, as seems more likely, he is offering an apology for the "engaged" historical writing which has become fashionable in recent years, and represents in fact an important qualification to his own generalization about the state of the discipline, many historians will disagree. They will be wary of premature commitments and be reluctant to abandon the effort to achieve broad perspectives which, for all the dangers of ironism, promise a wiser and perhaps a more compassionate view of the historical scene.

Still, White has given us a bold and imaginative book. At a time when much historical writing is occupied with narrow and trivial questions, he has challenged those in the discipline to consider anew the nature and purpose of their work. At the least White's study should bring historians to a new awareness of the forms of thought and imagination on which they rely. But *Metahistory* should also serve to remind historians of those perennial human concerns which make up the chief justification for their study.

Dominick LaCapra (review date December 1978)

SOURCE: A review of *Tropics of Discourse,* in *Modern Language Notes,* Vol. 93, No. 5, December, 1978, pp. 1037–43.

[*In the following positive review of* Tropics of Discourse, *LaCapra provides a close analysis of White's theoretical assertions and directs constructive criticism toward problematic aspects of White's philosophical assumptions.*]

No one writing in this country at the present time has done more to wake historians from their dogmatic slumber than has Hayden White. One cannot over-emphasize his importance for contemporary historiography in general and intellectual history in particular. In the recent past, intellectual history has departed from the rigorous if formalistic approach followed by Ernst Cassirer and Arthur O. Lovejoy. The result has often been its reduction to superficial contextual reportage of little interest to those in related disciplines. One might, without undue hyperbole, say that White's writings have helped to reopen the possibility of thought in intellectual history.

The collection of essays in *Tropics of Discourse* constitutes an invaluable supplement to White's masterwork of 1973, *Metahistory,* where he elaborated and applied the theory of tropes that serves as a leitmotif in the current volume.

The range of the essays is ambitiously broad: problems of historiography and the related disciplines of literary criticism and philosophy; the notions of the wild man and the noble savage in Western thought; Vico; Foucault; structuralism and poststructuralism. The tense unity of the book is provided by the recurrent concern with interpretation in history and with the need for historians to become apprised of more modern, experimental developments in literature, literary criticism, and philosophy. White's far-ranging hermeneutic interests transcend disciplinary boundaries and his critical observations apply beyond professional historiography, for they address more traditional methods in related areas, e.g., in the writing of literary history. Indeed White often looks to literary criticism for interpretive methods that may illuminate problems in historiography. This gesture is altogether in keeping with his insistence upon the importance of the problem of language, of rhetoric, and of theoretical self-reflection in the writing of history. His purpose is to question the invidious distinction between those who write history and those who write about writing history—a distinction that functions to reinforce theoretical "know-nothingism" among historians.

Allowing for the necessary leaven of exaggeration in all committed polemic, one will find White's criticisms of powerful tendencies in the historical profession to be quite telling. The following pastiche of quotations gives some sense of the nature of his comments about the great commonplace book of conventional historiography:

> The 'proper historian,' it is usually contended, seeks to explain what happened in the past by providing a precise and accurate reconstruction of the events reported in the documents (p. 52). History is perhaps the conservative discipline par excellence. Since the middle of the nineteenth century, most historians have affected a kind of willful methodological naiveté (p. 28). What is usually called the 'training' of the historian consists for the most part of study in a few languages, journeyman work in the archives, and the performance of a few set exercises to acquaint him with standard reference works and journals in his field. For the rest, a general experience of human affairs, reading in peripheral fields, self-discipline, and *Sitzfleisch* are all that are necessary (p. 40). Since the second half of the nineteenth century, history has become increasingly the refuge of all those 'sane' men who excel at finding the simple in the complex and the familiar in the strange (p. 30). It may well be that the most difficult task which the current generation of historians will be called upon to perform is to expose the historically conditioned character of the historical discipline, to preside over the dissolution of history's claim to autonomy among the disciplines, and to aid in the assimilation of history to a higher kind of intellectual inquiry which, because it is founded on an awareness of the *similarities* between art and science, rather than on their differences, can be properly designated as neither (p. 29).

In more specific form, White's critique is addressed both to positivism and to the unself-conscious employment of traditional narrative in the writing of history. The more elaborate positivistic understanding of science, in terms of causal "covering laws," had little effect upon the practice of historians. But the attraction of a more loosely understood "scientific" model has been of paramount importance in contemporary historiography. The comprehension of history as art—art itself being equated with traditional narrative—is still very much alive, but it exists on sufferance in the shadow of the scientific ideal. White points out a number of highly significant similarities between scientific and narrative history as they are generally practiced. *1)* Both are largely pre-modern in inspiration. The paradigm of science is late nineteenth-century, and that of art is the pre-Flaubertian novel. "When historians claim that history is a combination of science and art, they generally mean that it is a combination of *late-nineteenth century* social science and *mid-nineteenth century* art. . . . Historians continue to act as if they believed that the major, not to say the sole, purpose of art is to tell a story" (p. 43). *2)* Both share a pre-critical conception of "facts" as the indubitable, atomistic baseline of history—the ultimate "givens" of an account. *3)* Both reduce interpretation to marginal status, conceiving of it as a more-or-less plausible way of imaginatively filling in gaps in the historical record. For both, metahistory is much too speculative to live in the same neighborhood as "proper" history. *4)* Both rely in relatively unreflective fashion on tropologically based sense-making structures—the one on schematic models and metonymic causal mechanisms and the other on the emplotment of events in a chronologically arranged story.

For White, the rigid opposition of history "proper" and metahistory obscures more than it illuminates. The distinctive criterion of metahistory for him is the attempt to make interpretive and explanatory strategies—which remain implicit in traditional historiography practiced as a craft—explicit, self-conscious, and subject to criticism. In this sense, his own approach is militantly metahistorical. Interpretation is not a necessary evil in the face of an historical record that is always too full (hence the need for selection) and too empty (hence the need for auxiliary hypotheses to stop gaps). Interpretation is at the heart of historiography, for it relates to the way in which language prefigures and informs the historical field. Historians should not attempt to escape the need for interpretation through an illusory "positivistic" purity or experience this need as an exile from objective truth. On the contrary, they should inquire into its nature, implications, and positive possibilities in the reconstruction of the past.

As White develops his own program for the understanding of history, however, certain difficulties arise. In putting forth the following sympathetic criticisms of White, I would stress that my intention is to bring out and even to force certain tensions that exist in his own writings. For I think that White's own relation to traditional historiography and, more generally, to traditional philosophical assumptions is at certain points not fully thought out.

White continues to write what he conceives of as a history of consciousness (rather than, let's say, a history of texts

or of uses of language in various contexts). Language and discourse are seen predominantly as instruments or expressions of consciousness. "A discourse is itself a kind of model of the process of consciousness by which a given area of experience, originally apprehended as simply a field of phenomena demanding understanding, is assimilated by analogy to those areas of experience felt to be *already* understood as to their essential nature. . . . This process of understanding can only be tropological in nature, for what is involved in the rendering of the unfamiliar into the familiar is a troping that is generally figurative" (p. 5). This movement through the figurative toward the familiar is basic to White's own systematic effort in providing a theory of language in historiography. It is contested by the less predictable movement through which tropes move from the familiar to the unfamiliar—a process White recognizes and at times defends as necessary for renewal.

White's own systematic theory of language as an expression of consciousness is necessarily reductive of its object. It is much more indebted to Vico, Kant, and Hegel than it is to Nietzsche, Heidegger, and Derrida. (Indeed, the latter are interpreted at times quite negatively in the light of the former.) White's theory is also "constructivist" in that it affirms a "making" function of consciousness, identified with *poiesis,* in contrast to the "matching" function stressed by the mimetic epistemology common to positivism and traditional narrative. The title, ***Tropics of Discourse,*** itself refers to the pre-figurative and projective function of tropes in constituting a field of discourse. In articulating this function, White's metahistory becomes a metalanguage for historiography. The problem is that, in the systematic understanding he attempts to provide of figurative language, White assumes the mastery of "logocentric" philosophy over rhetoric. In other words, he writes from a position itself constituted and secured after an important battle has seemingly been won and without inquiring into the *causus belli.* In the process, he provides what Derrida would see as another version of White Mythology and Heidegger, as a subjectivist and voluntaristic distortion of the poetic.

For White, as for Vico, there are four Master Tropes (which function theoretically as masters of troping): metaphor, metonymy, synecdoche, and irony. These tropes are presented as the origin or fundamental ground that structures discourse and gives rise to other discursive levels (emplotment, argument, and ideology). Modal patterns further coordinate the relationships among the primary tropes and the other typological levels of discourse. White's own thought is here close to a genetic structuralism. Although the tropes are originative and basic, they are nonetheless seen as informed by narrative and dialectical patterns in a directed process of "encodation." Metaphor, metonymy, and synecdoche are related to one another cyclically as beginning, middle, end and as identity, difference, higher identity. (Thus the traditional patterns, shown out through the front door, re-enter through the back.) Irony has a paradoxical position as both one trope among others and as a trope-killer that—coming at the end of an era—effects a generalized displacement of the "tropics of discourse." White more than recognizes the importance of irony for any critical self-consciousness. But the primary sense of irony in White (especially in *Metahistory*) is what one might call epigonal irony—negative, decadent, dissolving, and destructive. This is the serious and even pious understanding of irony in Vico (although Vico himself is not without internal contestations on this, as on other counts). Given this understanding, one's ultimate goal must be to transcend irony with its cold and deadly effects. White even sees Nietzsche as attempting to transcend an ironic apprehension of the world in order to arrive at a restored metaphoric contact with reality that seems dangerously close to blind faith or mythologizing. But this very partial and largely misleading interpretation of Nietzsche is itself "prefigured" by White's own placement of irony in a narratively and dialectically informed cycle of the tropes. This placement of irony renders impossible a relationship between it and figuration that is repetitive, carnivalesque, contestatory, and affirmative—the relationship Nietzsche sought in his *gaya scienza*. It also renders White incapable of seeing the way in which Derrida's strategy of deconstruction and double inscription of traditional assumptions may be understood in the light of a "gay science" not reducible to Vico's "new science."

In fact, the only serious lapse in the high level of argument in *Tropics of Discourse* is to be found in the last essay, **"The Absurdist Moment in Contemporary Literary Theory."** Here figures as diverse as Poulet, Barthes, Foucault, and Derrida are lumped together, labelled absurdist, and discussed in a way that is at best caricatural. They have merely symptomatic significance as the most recent manifestation of Western self-doubt and the final blow-up of the modern crisis. White's harshest comments are reserved for Derrida who is presented as little more than an irresponsible "wild man." The interesting problem, I think, is how a writer of White's intelligence and perspicacity could possibly have arrived at these analyses and conclusions. There is, of course, a point at which everyone feels inclined to become Horatius at the bridge. The question is where one locates that point. I would suggest that one way to see White's reaction is as a turn toward secure "sanity" and conventional irony in the face of the "other" who actually articulates things that are "inside" White himself—but an "other" whose articulation is perhaps too disconcerting or at least too alien in formulation to be recognizable. One need not be an awe-struck Derridean or blind to the excesses of mindless "derridoodling" to recognize Derrida's importance. Derrida has raised the problem of the text and renewed the problem of rhetoric in a manner that both acknowledges the desire for systematicity, as well as the importance of the classical tradition, and furnishes the basis for a critical response to them. (It is significant that White himself observes of Vico's "new science": "The internal dynamics of the system represents a projection of the theory of the tropes and of the relationships between them that he took over entire

from classical poetics" [p. 216].) Just as the romances of chivalry would have been more easily forgotten (or repressed) had it not been for Cervantes' battles—both mock and real—so the assumptions and hopes of the metaphysical tradition would have been more peacefully laid to rest (or covertly resurrected, *faute de mieux*) had it not been for Derrida's contestation of them in both their ancient and modern forms. But Derrida's enterprise requires genuine respect for the tradition, which must be confronted in its most forceful expressions (or "inscriptions")—even reinvigorated and made more engaging through "reinscription"—for the contest to be possible. Derrida has made it less plausible to indulge in a falsely complacent oblivion of classical forms in philosophy and poetics. Indeed, through a fruitful paradox, the "founding fathers" of the tradition have taken on renewed interest because of Derrida's critical inquiry into their work and its legacy.

Another reading of Derrida might have provided White with the means to investigate more fully certain of his own internal tensions. For the things Derrida discusses *are* inside White. They relate to the problem of the relationship among history, discourse, and the text. It is curious that White's own constructivist tendencies, which construe the tropes as the informing forces of a creative consciousness, lead him at times to lend credence to the idea of an unprocessed historical record. The record is presented as the inert object to be animated by the shaping mind of the historian. This gesture, however, simply reverses the positivistic mythology of a mimetic consciousness and substitutes for it an idealistic mythology which converts the former meaningful plenum of the "record" into dead matter or even a void, thereby giving rise to another avoidance of the problem of interplay between structure and play in the text and in one's relation to it. But, at other times, a second view emerges in White's own approach to this problem. Then White astutely notices the way in which the historical record is itself a text "always already" processed in a manner that makes the historian begin as situated in the context of more-or-less vital or exhausted traditions of discourse. The very notion of an unprocessed historical record may in this light be seen as a critical fiction. What we perceive as unprocessed is actually the chronicle level in historiography. The chronicle itself is, however, not a pure, primary "given." It is derived through a critical process that attempts to disengage "facts" from their implication in story, plot, and myth. It is for this reason that chronicle may appear as both the most naive and the most ironically sophisticated level in historiography—why there may be a certain paradoxical resemblance between a medieval chronicler and Burckhardt (or, to switch genres, Beckett).

The latter understanding of the historical record contests any rigid categorical opposition between fact and fiction or between "matching" and "making" ("mirroring" and "lamping") functions in the writing of history. In addition, it points to a notion of discourse as other than the projection of consciousness, and it raises the problem of the actual uses of language in the text—or rhetoric in a sense not reducible to the four Master Tropes but certainly involving the question of figurative language. This different understanding of discourse is formulated by White himself:

> [Discourse] is both interpretive and preinterpretive; it is as much *about* the nature of interpretation itself as it is *about* the subject matter which is the manifest occasion of its own elaboration. . . . Precisely because it is aporetic, or ironic, with respect to its own adequacy, discourse cannot be governed by logic alone. Because it is always slipping the grasp of logic, constantly asking if logic is adequate to capture the essence of its subject matter, discourse tends toward metadiscursive reflexiveness.
>
> (p. 4)

White tends to resist an understanding of the text as the scene, in writing and in life, where discourse in this sense takes place. Indeed, he identifies the text with the book and accuses Derrida of fetishizing or mystifying the text. Yet what he writes of Foucault's conception of the text could be applied to his own often dominant understanding of it: "The names of individuals that do appear are merely shorthand devices for designating the texts; and the texts are in turn less important than the macroscopic configurations of formalized consciousness that they represent" (p. 238). What one at times misses in White is an analysis of the way in which the formalized schemata and patterns he elicits actually function in texts. In *Metahistory,* there was a Procrustean tendency to see texts as embodiments of patterned variables or modal sets of tropes, emplotments, arguments, and ideologies. Yet, in the present work, he himself says something which would indicate that the tense interplay among elements in the language of the text should be a focal point of historical and critical investigation:

> Now, in my view, any historian who simply described a set of facts in, let us say, metonymic terms and then went on to emplot its processes in the mode of tragedy and proceeded to explain those processes mechanistically, and finally drew explicit ideological implications from it—as most vulgar Marxists and materialistic determinists do—would not only be very uninteresting but could legitimately be labelled a *doctrinaire* thinker who had 'bent the facts' to fit a preconceived theory. The peculiar dialectic of historical discourse—and of other forms of discursive prose as well, perhaps even the novel—comes from the effort of the author to mediate between alternative modes of emplotment and explanation, which means, finally, *mediating between alternative modes of language use* or *tropological* strategies for originally describing a given field of phenomena and constituting it as a possible object of representation. . . . This aim of mediation, in turn, drives him [White is discussing Tocqueville here] toward the ironic recognition that any given linguistic protocol will obscure as much as it reveals about the reality it seeks to capture in an order of words. This *aporia* or sense of contradiction residing at the heart of language itself is present in *all* of the classic historians.

It is this linguistic self-consciousness which distinguishes them from their mundane counterparts and followers, who think that language can serve as a perfectly transparent medium of representation and who think that if one can only find the right language for describing events, the meaning of the events will *display itself* to consciousness.

(p. 130)

The question raised in this passage is precisely that of the text. I think that White is right in believing that formalized schemata are necessary for interpretation. The problem is how one is to understand them and their relation to actual discourse and texts. In this respect, one has a great deal to learn from Nietzsche, Heidegger, and Derrida. The linkage of irony and *aporia* invariably evokes the threat of infinite regress in discourse. But this linkage is itself related to a negative understanding of irony, which is of course a threat. The more affirmatively contestatory understanding of irony might be related to the possibility of endless egress and renewal, which is implied in Nietzsche's notions of *Heiterkeit* and gay science. Indeed, one sign of the intellectual vigor of White's own work is that it stimulates this kind of contestation. *Tropics of Discourse* is a book that engages one on every page. It should be of immense interest to literary critics, historians, and philosophers.

Roland A. Champagne (review date Summer 1979)

SOURCE: A review of *Tropics of Discourse,* in *World Literature Today,* Vol. 53, No. 3, Summer, 1979, p. 565.

[*In the following review of* Tropics of Discourse, *Champagne commends White's insights into history's roots in storytelling.*]

Addressed to the problem of whether historical writing can remain concerned with the past and with an objective view of facts, this collection of essays [*Tropics of Discourse*] presents history as a narrated story, a literary document with its origins in the human imagination. The title is based upon the etymology of "tropics" and "discourse" and is intent upon suggesting the "ways or manner" of "moving to and fro." The methodology beyond the title assumes a prelogical area of experience, forgotten by the present-day scientific posture of history and revived in order to establish the tropological basis of history. A basic thesis is the acceptance of Kenneth Burke's proposition that there have been four "master tropes" governing civilized discourse since the Renaissance: metaphor, metonymy, synecdoche and irony. This fourfold pattern is then discussed in various transformations from Piaget's child studies, through Freud's revelations about dreams, into E. P. Thompson's insights into the working-class consciousness.

Most of these essays have been independently published elsewhere. However, the introduction does tie them together with a perspective not always immediately obvious in such presentations as the two pieces on the "noble savage" and two others on Vico as a modern writer. The basic concern unifying the various studies is that, since the arts and sciences are now mutual handmaids, history is no longer an autonomous discipline. "History" must liberate the present moment from the burden given to it by ties to the past and tradition. Instead White's version of history is tasked with educating lessons about the nature of discontinuity and chaos in modern culture.

With his commentaries about Foucault, Derrida and other French writers presently speaking about the dissolution of literature (the "Absurdists"), White is indeed educating us about the innate discontinuity of culture. His position is that, since culture is a human product created by people, the very existence of that culture is dependent upon systems of signs and must perforce be disappointing. Despite this negative tone and a tendency to create his own terms for groups and movements, White gives us herein some valuable insights into the inherent determinism of the history of ideas because of its basis in human discourse. The arguments supporting Burke's four "major tropes" are an especially valuable contribution to the project of a "universal grammar" for all human discourse proposed by Barthes, Lotman, Todorov, Genette and others.

Richard King (review date Summer 1979)

SOURCE: "The Problem of Reading," in *Virginia Quarterly Review,* Vol. 55, No. 3, Summer, 1979, pp. 568–72.

[*In the following excerpt, King offers a positive evaluation of* Tropics of Discourse.]

It is increasingly apparent that our dominant model of theoretical self-understanding derives from linguistics and rhetoric. As in Saul Steinberg's whimsical sketches, we spin out a complexly dense fabric of sounds, letters, sentences, and paragraphs which constitute the possibility of individual and collective life. We discover ourselves in a text-world, "spoken" by a Discourse over which we have only illusory control. In the beginning was the Word, not man who is its concrete embodiment. We must decipher our world and ourselves as part of that world.

This cultural paradigm has been a while in the making. As Hayden White points out in *Tropics of Discourse,* Vico was perhaps the first modern thinker to understand the man-made world, *i.e.,* culture, through a variety of rhetorical figures. Descartes, Vico's great adversary, sought to describe the physical world mathematically, an effort which reached its culmination in modern physics' dissolution of matter into mathematical relationships. As the doctrine of the soul gave way to the problematics of the self, the solidity of personal identity disappeared into a complex web of interpersonal communications. From Hegel down to Sartre and the French Freudians, the self is understood

as a relationship. The linguistic revolution initiated by Saussure led to the contemporary emphasis on semiotics, which takes everything as part of a sign-system. Where Jung discovered fixed archetypes, Levi-Strauss sees "mythemes," bits of material which only have meaning in combination with other mythemes. There are no universal, transcultural symbols, only the combinatory mechanisms of the unconscious mind. Freud's psychoanalytic theory is now seen to be less concerned with the play of psychic forces than the translation of meaning.

If the world is understood as a text (or as analogous to a text), then the act of reading and the problem of interpretation become crucial. And it is a concern with this problem of reading which provides the common starting point for Hayden White and George Steiner in the works under review here. Both *Tropics of Discourse* and *On Difficulty* [by George Steiner] are collections of essays which elaborate upon their authors' earlier, more authoritative works: in White's case, *Metahistory*; in Steiner's *Extraterritorial* and *After Babel*. Both men are well-read in contemporary thought, but neither is overly given to the hermetic, allusive, and self-regarding diction of much advanced thought issuing primarily from France. (Though Steiner can lapse into an arch mandarin prose at times.) Nor are they intellectual bullies. They can admit doubts, appear tentative, and present opposing positions without sneering.

The bulk of White's essays concern themselves with the problem of reading history. According to White, all discourse is tropistic. It works through figures of speech which, far from serving as decoration or "mere" rhetoric, constitute the field of facts and meanings themselves.

White's approach to historiography and the philosophy of history implies two crucial changes in our ways of thinking about these disciplines. First, and most obviously, every work of "straight" history implies a philosophy of history and vice versa. More interestingly, White insists on minimizing the difference between fiction and fact, works of the imagination and works of history. To White's way of thinking, most contemporary historiography is bad science and bad art, still operating with otiose notions of value-free science and naïve realism. There is no such thing as an "innocent eye," no one "true" account of the past, no *wie es eigentlich gewesen ist*. A work of history has no truth-value in the strict sense, but must be judged on aesthetic and heuristic grounds. For historians work with certain standard modes of emplotment, explanation, ideology, and troping. *What* is said is synonymous with *how* it is said. One judges history according to its richness, coherence, density, and range of implication, description, and explanation. This is not to say that facts are unimportant or to be capriciously disregarded. But it is to say that what counts as a fact and what determines its "weight" are determined by the angle of vision which the historian brings to the data. Indeed, it is not clear whether the historian's framework is imposed upon or discovered in the empirical evidence.

Critics have already had a go at *Metahistory* where these views were developed in great detail through an analysis of 19th-century historians and philosophers of history. There White granted that the best, most satisfactory history was marked by tensions among the various modes of plotting, troping, ideological implication, and explanation and thus could be read in several ways. But why precisely these four categories and why does each break down into four parts? In *Tropics of Discourse* White suggests that the four master tropes—metaphor, metonymy, synecdoche, and irony—are psychogenetically grounded, and he advances a brief discussion of Piaget to bolster his point. According to White, what Piaget sees as the progressive unfolding of the mind from identity with the world to distantiation from it and from representation of it to self-consciousness matches his own four-fold schema of tropes. And harkening back to Vico, White suggests that cultural development can be understood in terms of this same progression. Presumably one should only accept White's theory as long as it seems useful, helpful in making sense of the world. But by anchoring his "tropology" in biological development, White asserts, albeit tentatively, a privileged position for his own efforts.

Whatever its difficulties, White's work in "reading" history is extraordinarily stimulating; and all historians, particularly those trained in this country, should be forced to confront it. Indeed, historians such as J. H. Hexter, Peter Gay, Gene Wise, and David Levin have dealt with some of these issues in their own work, though in a less sophisticated manner. This promises, one hopes, an added sophistication in the writing of history in the future. For, as White suggests, history-writing has yet to catch up with the 20th century. . . .

It is a larger irony of Steiner's thesis that precisely at the historical moment when serious reading of texts has become problematic, the culture's most advanced thinkers have begun to see the whole world as a Text. In the final essay in *Tropics of Discourse* White reflects on the structuralist critics' refusal to elevate the printed text, particularly ones which have been taken to be classics of the culture, over any other semiotic system. This, he suggests, illustrates the "awareness of the arbitrary nature of the whole cultural enterprise and, *a fortiori*, of the critical enterprise." Whatever their other differences, Steiner and White still believe in the text and thus, in a certain sense, in the possibilities of the survival of the culture.

Maurice Mandelbaum (essay date 1980)

SOURCE: "The Presuppositions of *Metahistory*," in *History and Theory,* Vol. XIX, No. 4, 1980, pp. 39–54.

[*In the following essay, Mandelbaum examines the thesis of* Metahistory *and finds flaws in White's failure to differentiate between the work of historians and philosophers of history, as well as his misconception of historical data, reductive application of linguistic tropes, and acceptance of relativism.*]

In the introductory chapter of his *Metahistory,* Hayden White explicitly sets forth the main presuppositions underlying that work. If one were to examine these presuppositions in the light of his other writings, one might uncover his reasons for accepting them. Such, however, is not my aim. I shall confine my discussion to certain of the views he explicitly embraces, selecting those which are basic to the aspects of *Metahistory* I especially wish to challenge.

As a point of entry into the closely articulated system of *Metahistory,* let me first mention the eight persons whom White has chosen as representing the various modes of historical consciousness with which he deals. Four of these he considers to have been the dominant historians of the classic period of nineteenth-century historiography; four he regards as the most important philosophers of history of that century. Michelet, Ranke, Tocqueville, and Burckhardt are the historians chosen; Hegel, Marx, Nietzsche, and Croce are the philosophers of history. To some extent, one may quarrel with these choices; this is a question to which I shall briefly return. What is initially noteworthy is not *whom* he has chosen, but the fact that historians and philosophers of history are treated together, a mode of treatment in direct opposition to the widespread assumption (held throughout the nineteenth century, and subsequently) that their aims and methods are not only fundamentally distinct, but are often opposed. His rejection of that view, and his account of what they have in common, is the first of his theses that I shall challenge. What lies behind that thesis is a particular view of what is most fundamental in the writing of history, and it is that view which I shall take as his first and perhaps most fundamental presupposition.

It is White's claim that "history proper" and "philosophies of history" grow out of a common root, differing only in emphasis, not in content: philosophers of history simply bring to the surface and systematically defend views that remain implicit in the works of historians (xi, 428). Unfortunately, White fails to specify with any degree of exactitude what he regards as the essential features in a philosophy of history.[1] If (for the time being) we construe philosophies of history as being, essentially, nothing more than reflection on a significant portion of man's past in order to determine what "meaning," if any, is to be discerned in it, then one might well say of Michelet, Ranke, Tocqueville, and Burckhardt that each did have a philosophy of history. On the other hand, were one to choose any single work of theirs (with the possible exception of Burckhardt's posthumous *Weltgeschichtliche Betrachtungen*), and were one to consider its aim and its content, one would surely not regard it as similar in these respects to the works usually taken to be representative philosophies of history.

In order to understand what may have led White to overlook or to disregard this obvious point, and therefore to hold that there is no deep difference between historians and philosophers of history, one must consider what he took to be the determining factors in all forms of historical inquiry.[2] He held that with the exception of those who are only concerned to write "monographs and archival reports" (ix), every historian creates a narrative verbal structure through selecting and arranging the primitive data contained in "the unprocessed historical records"; the elements in such a verbal structure are then arranged in a way that purports to represent and explain past processes; and, according to White, the manner in which these processes are represented reflects the historian's antecedent acceptance of one of four types of "metahistorical" paradigms. White's characterization of the nature of the four types of paradigm will concern us later. What is important to note here is that in labeling them "metahistorical," White is emphasizing the fact that they are not derived from the data with which the historian works; rather, they are "interpretative strategies" which determine to which data he will attend, and in what ways he will envision the relations among them (428, 430). In short, the narrative structure which an historian creates will have been "*prefigured*" by the particular paradigm in terms of which he sees the historical world (30–31). Since it is White's contention that exactly the same basic paradigms are to be found in the works of historians and philosophers of history, he rejects the widely-held view that the dissimilarities between the two genres are more fundamental than are their similarities.

Before examining what led White to stress what he took to be the similarity between historians and philosophers of history, let us consider some of the respects in which they do in fact differ. In the first place, White fails to note that with the possible exception of some attempts to write universal histories, every historical inquiry is limited in scope, dealing with what is recognized to be only one segment or one aspect of human history. Most philosophers of history, on the other hand, have traditionally embarked on sweeping surveys of what they have regarded as the whole of the significant past, in an effort to establish some one basic principle of explanation which would render intelligible the course it had followed.[3] Their purpose in doing so may be said to be an attempt to justify some particular evaluative attitudes toward various segments or elements in that history. One does not find even the most "philosophical" of historians committing himself to such a project. To be sure, as I have pointed out, one may say of various historians that "they have a philosophy of history," in the sense that they more or less consistently evince certain underlying evaluative attitudes toward the materials with which they deal. To that extent, White is correct in what he claims concerning Michelet, Ranke, Tocqueville, and Burckhardt. Nevertheless, it is implausible to hold that their works, taken either individually or as a whole, were written primarily for the sake of establishing the truth of a particular interpretation of the historical process; yet this is clearly what constitutes the aim of any philosophy of history. The immediate concern of historians may better be characterized in terms of attempts to understand and depict what happened at particular times and in particular places. Therefore, even though their

works often reflect a definite and distinctive view of overall characteristics to be found in the historical process, these works are *histories,* not philosophies of history.

A second and related difference between historians and philosophers of history lies in the fact that every philosopher of history seeks to find a principle of explanation, or of interpretation, which illuminates every significant aspect of the historical process. No such belief has been characteristic of historians, at least not since the mid-eighteenth century. Instead, historians have generally come to regard it as essential to preserve flexibility when dealing with different times and different peoples, rather than to expect that there is some particular principle of explanation which is equally applicable to all. Furthermore, most are inclined to employ different modes of explanation to deal with different dimensions of social life, rather than using a single set of categories when explaining the nature and changes in, say, the economic, the political, and the intellectual aspects of a society's life. Any insistence on either or both of these forms of pluralism completely undermines the legitimacy of the kind of claim that every philosopher of history must make—namely, that there is some one principle which, when adequately grasped, serves to reveal the meaning of all essential aspects of human history. For this reason, if for no other, the presuppositions of historians and of philosophers of history are strikingly opposed.

A third point at which there are fundamental differences between the aims of an historian and of a philosopher of history lies in the latter's absolute commitment to the view that there is some discernible lesson, or "meaning," in human history. Such a meaning is viewed as providing a way to assess the significance of various past events, to determine the attitude which should be adopted with respect to conflicts within the present, and to help envision what the future will ultimately bring. While philosophers of history have occasionally acknowledged that the meaning they attribute to history was derived from other sources, most have claimed that it arose directly out of an intensive study of the historical past. They have apparently also believed that the same meaning would be acknowledged by all who studied the past in equal depth and with equal intensity.

This claim has often been challenged by historians. They have argued that philosophers of history do not derive meaning *from* history, but attribute meaning *to* history as a way of justifying their own antecedent evaluative beliefs. Not only can historians cite instances in which this appears to have been true, but they can quite convincingly argue that the events of human history, taken as a whole, are far too complex and ambiguous to support the claim that there is any single meaning to be directly derived from them. A philosopher of history might possibly reply that there is no great difference in principle between this and what is involved in such interpretations of history as are to be found in Michelet, Ranke, Tocqueville, and Burckhardt, each of whom had singled out certain forces or tendencies which they regarded as dominant factors in the historical field. However, any supposed parallel between these two endeavors does not hold. Historians such as Michelet, Ranke, Tocqueville, and Burckhardt did not claim to have arrived at their understanding of these forces through a comprehensive survey of the whole past; instead, they had simply dipped successively into the historical stream at various points and were generalizing concerning significant resemblances which they found at these points.[4] Thus, instead of claiming that there is some dominant pattern running through the process as a whole, determining how each of its elements will develop, they were singling out what they took to be the important common elements in various historical situations; it was with respect to their attitudes toward these elements that they may be said to have had "a philosophy of history." This, however, only justifies characterizing them in a very loose sense as "philosophers of history." Their situation exactly parallels that in which, after examining a practicing scientist's works, one might say that he *has* "a philosophy of science," without thereby either asserting or implying that he *is* "a philosopher of science."

As we have noted, what led White to blur the distinction between the works of historians and those of philosophers of history was his view that both reflect an acceptance of one or another metahistorical paradigm which serves to organize the primary data with which they are concerned. Having noted some points at which histories and philosophies of history are obviously different, I shall now consider this presupposition which led to White's attempt to bring them exceptionally close together.

In offering his account of what he termed "the levels of conceptualization" in an historical work, White took as his starting point the data contained in "the unprocessed historical record" (5). He identified these data as the primitive elements in the historical field. The historian, he held, must first arrange such data in temporal order, thus producing "a chronicle"; he must then connect them in a way that transforms this chronicle into "a story"; this is the beginning of the odyssey that leads to the production of an historical work. This, however, is surely not the way in which any present-day historian would actually work; nor would even the earliest of historians have done so. No historian is confronted at the outset of his inquiries with an *unprocessed* historical record, with a bank of data devoid of all order, to which he must impart whatever order it is to possess. Rather, every historian will, from the outset, be confronted not by raw data but by earlier accounts of the past; embedded within those accounts will be almost all the data with which he is to work. Data not included within one account, but included within another, will lead him to alter one or the other; he must in any case fit these accounts together to obtain a larger, more consistent, and presumably more accurate "story" than any which his predecessors had produced. Nor will all of the accounts of his predecessors appear to be connected: when they deal with different times and places, large gaps may appear between them. In order to fill such gaps, the

historian must seek other accounts which will provide data that serve to connect what was previously unconnected; or he must, on his own initiative, seek out such data for himself. In either case, his awareness of the existence of gaps within what White termed "the historical record" conclusively shows that this record does not consist of unorganized raw data—data which are simply "*there*," and which have no inherent connections with one another until the historian has impressed an order upon them.

It may perhaps be objected that this criticism of White is unfair: that his analysis of the levels of conceptualization which are present in an historical work was intended to be taken as a purely analytic account, and not an attempt to trace a series of successive steps by means of which any historical work has ever actually been created. Such may indeed have been White's intention, but it would in no way alter the point of the foregoing criticism. Analytically considered, what White designates as "the primitive elements" with which historians work, and which serve as their data, are documents, legends, records, and the remains of earlier human activities, or else they are prior accounts concerning the events under investigation. If an historian is to make use of such materials for historical purposes, he cannot regard them as if they were nothing but parchment, slabs of stone, or sheaves of paper; he must view them as relating to various kinds of human activities with which he is familiar through his own direct experience, supplemented by knowledge derived from what has been said by others. Thus, the most basic level on which historical data can be interpreted will be as meaningful elements embedded in an intelligible context. Therefore, from an analytic no less than from a genetic point of view, even the simplest data with which an historian works are not unconnected atomic elements which lack all intrinsic order. What to the historian are "data"—that is, what constitutes "*the given*" for him—possess connections among themselves which exist prior to, and independently of, the ways in which he subsequently comes to order them. It is for this reason that I reject the first of White's presuppositions.

Turning to a second basic presupposition in *Metahistory,* we find White assuming, without examining alternatives, that the order bestowed by the historian on his materials represents a *poetic* act (for example, x, 4, and 30). It appears as if he took this for granted simply because when one looks at an historical work as "what it most manifestly is," one finds it to be "a verbal structure in the form of a narrative prose discourse" (2). In regarding an historical work in this light, and not considering what else it may also be, it is natural that White should turn to the theory of literature in order to identify the various metahistorical paradigms which, as he believes, control the work of historians. He finds such paradigms in four fundamental linguistic tropes. I shall not be concerned with the details of his use of these tropes, but I shall argue that White's approach leaves out of account what has generally—and, I think, rightly—been regarded as the basic intent of historical works: to discover, depict, and explain what has occurred in the past.

I wish first to take note of the fact that simply because every historical work is a verbal structure, and can be considered as such, it by no means follows that this provides the most basic level at which all of its structural aspects are to be understood. An eyewitness may, for example, give a narrative account of the sequence of events that led to an accident, a chemist may describe a series of experiments whereby he succeeded in disproving a previously held theory, a physician may trace the course of a patient's illness from its onset to his death, a traveler may tell us what befell him on his journeys before reaching his destination, and each of these would be a narrative, and would have the general structure which White (following Gallie and Danto) attributes to narratives.

To refuse to regard narratives of this sort as anything more than particular verbal structures would be capricious: as interpreted by a listener, the basic structure of each will be determined by the relationships among the events narrated, not by the manner of their narration. These relationships among the events may have been brought out clearly, or they may have been obscured in the telling, but they will have existed prior to the narration and will be independent of it. So, too, with historical works which, to some extent, these simple narrations resemble. Furthermore, White himself should not attempt to deny that the relationships depicted in an historical narrative exist prior to the act of narration, since that assumption was implicit in his characterization of an historical work. While every such work is, as he tells us, "a verbal structure in the form of narrative prose," it is more than this, for it "purports to be a model, or icon, of past structures and processes in the interest of explaining what they were by representing them" (2). Therefore, unless there is absolutely no basis for the claim that historical narratives *do* represent past structures and processes, and serve as icons which represent relationships that actually obtained, much of their structure—like the structures of the simple narratives I have cited—is not attributable to the narrator but is already present within the elements with which he has chosen to deal.

There doubtless were many reasons why White failed to raise this possibility in his discussion, but he does not suggest what they were, and I shall not speculate concerning them. Instead, it may be more fruitful to inquire what there is in the nature of an historical work itself—totally apart from any of the traditional arguments in favor of historical relativism[5]—that might make it plausible for anyone to regard the narrator as entirely responsible for the structure of his narrative. One such feature seems to me to be the historian's freedom to define the subject-matter of his inquiry in almost any way that he chooses.

Every historical work represents a particular choice of subject-matter, and in choosing his subject-matter an historian is carving out a particular segment of the past from the stream of the historical process; the definition of what constitutes that particular segment—why it does not include either more or less than it does—can be viewed as

a creative act on the part of the historian. To be sure, in some cases no genuinely creative act may be involved. For example, a run-of-the-mill historian who decides to write the history of a particular period may simply accept some conventional compartmentalization of the historical process, and work within that framework. In other cases, historians may be puzzled by problems that their predecessors failed to investigate, and their subject-matter will be defined by the particular residual problem that they have set out to solve. White would probably be inclined to place works such as these within the same general class to which "monographs and archival reports" belong; it was not with such examples that he was concerned. If, instead, one thinks of the great historians whose works he analyzed, one can see that it is entirely reasonable to regard their ways of envisioning their subject-matter as involving original, creative, expressive acts.

On White's analysis of these "precognitive," "precritical," poetic acts the whole argument of his ***Metahistory*** turns. He distinguishes three "narrative tactics" which all historians employ: an initial "emplotment," an implied form of explanatory argument, and an evaluative, ideological component (7). All of these, White claims, are packed into the historian's original creative act. It is therefore that act which not only "*pre*figures" the general shape of an historical work but determines what kinds of relationships the historian will take into account in analyzing the events with which he deals (cf. 430). As White says of such acts, they are "constitutive of the structure that will subsequently be imaged in the verbal model offered by the historian as representation and explanation of 'what *really* happened'" (31).

The various explanatory strategies which the historian can adopt are not, however, unlimited. White holds that each of the three aspects of an adopted strategy—the emplotment, explanatory argument, and ideological component—will assume one of four forms, and he relates these forms to the four fundamental linguistic tropes. He holds that the historian's use of one or another of these tropes represents the deepest level of the historical consciousness, and this is the level at which he seeks to analyze historical works (30–31). In doing so, he wishes to proceed in a purely "formalist" manner; as he says with respect to his method, "I will not try to decide whether a given historian's work is a better, or more correct, account of a specific set of events or segments of the historical process than some other historian's account of them; rather, I will seek to identify the structural components of these accounts" (3–4).

So long as he is dealing only with that particular structural component which he identifies as "emplotment," his formalism raises no special difficulties. In fact, it is his analysis of this element which gives point and substance to his claim that in the historian's original way of envisioning his subject there is already prefigured the overall form that his account will ultimately take. With respect to emplotment, White follows Northrop Frye and distinguishes four forms: Romance, Comedy, Tragedy, and Satire. These terms are not used in order to characterize distinct literary styles, nor to identify the particular types of subject-matter which are present in the works thus emplotted; rather, each refers to a basic attitude on the part of the historian toward the subject-matter with which he is to deal. In Comedy, for example, what is prefigured is the reconciliation of antagonistic forces; in Satire, the attitude is one of irony. Such attitudes are inextricably involved in how the historian envisions his subject: how the beginning of the narrative is related to its end, and which details and what changes in fortune he will emphasize.

Whether White's assimilation of these four forms of emplotment to the four fundamental tropes of poetic discourse can withstand scrutiny is not a matter with which I am concerned: the four forms of emplotment, as White has characterized them, can be accepted independently of any relations they may bear to his theory of tropes. They constitute highly relevant aspects of an historian's work, and White has made an important and suggestive contribution to the theory of historiography in having called attention to them. This cannot, however, be said of his claim that the same linguistic tropes provide the best way to understand the forms of explanatory arguments historians employ, nor the role that ideological factors play in their works. As I shall now suggest, in these cases White's formalist "tropological" account breaks down.

First consider his attempt to reduce the various types of explanatory argument to a linguistic form. Borrowing from Stephen Pepper's *World Hypotheses,* White distinguishes four types of explanatory argument: Formist, Mechanistic, Organicist, Contextualist. Let us grant that this may be an adequate typology of four characteristically different modes of explanation; let us also grant the somewhat more dubious contention that different thinkers, regardless of the subject-matter with which they deal, tend to accept one of these four types, rejecting each of the others. It would still be necessary for White to show that such a bias is not derived from some specifically *theoretical* considerations, but actually depends upon the way in which *linguistic* forms give structure to the thought of various thinkers. I suggest that when this thesis is considered in relation to the history of ideas, it will be recognized as implausible. If, for example, one examines the thought of a mechanist of the seventeenth century, or of an organicist in the later eighteenth or the nineteenth century, one discovers reasons of a specifically historical and philosophical sort why—once having chosen the subject-matter with which he was to deal—such a thinker would view his field in terms of mechanistic or organicist models. For example, in order to account for the dominance of the mechanical explanatory model in the seventeenth century, one has to look to the development of the mechanical sciences in that period; to explain organicist models in late eighteenth- and nineteenth-century thought, one must look to the anti-Newtonian views which developed out of various physical, biological, and specifically historical concerns with which the Newtonian model was unable to cope. To at-

tribute such change to whatever linguistic modes may perhaps have been dominant in the period would almost surely be an example of the hysteron-protoron fallacy, a putting of the cart before the horse: insofar as one trope rather than another was in fact dominant within the period, it was more likely to have been a reflection of the thought of the period than an independent determinant in giving structure to that thought.

Consider also the ideological and ethical stance involved in the work of any historian. White uses the concept of "ideology" in a somewhat broader than usual sense, including beliefs concerning the nature and aims of a study of society, attitudes toward historical change, and beliefs as to when and where a social ideal has been, or might be, realized (24).[6] Even when the concept is used in this extended sense, it is difficult to see how an historian's acceptance of one or another ideological stance can be clarified by relating it to one of the four linguistic tropes with which White's tropological approach is concerned. If one seeks to penetrate to what lies below the surface of the attitudes of the Anarchist, the Radical, the Conservative, or the Liberal (the four basic forms of ideology which White takes over from Mannheim), it would seem more fruitful to use other means than those provided by a linguistic analysis. In the first place, it is doubtful whether one can find any common properties determined in terms of linguistic models that would unite all who closely resemble one another in their ideologies. In the second place, it would seem imperative in any given case to try to understand the political and social situation to which the historian was exposed, and to consider his ideological stance not only with reference to it, but also in relation to those factors in his personal life which may have led him to view that situation as he did. It is surely far-fetched to interpret his view of the conflicts inherent in his own time, or his stance toward past and future, or his position regarding the possibility of creating a science of society, as if each of these were to follow from some linguistic predisposition on his part. White offers no arguments to dispel this disquietude: from the outset he has simply assumed that the structure of an historical work is to be treated as a literary structure, and that the four fundamental linguistic tropes provide the basic categories to be used in interpreting all linguistic structures.

The inflexibility of White's approach in nowhere more evident than in the manner in which he treats the history of nineteenth-century historiography. His tropological approach is fundamentally ahistorical: the possibility of organizing an historical account in terms of one of these tropes instead of another is not restricted to any one time or place, but is ever-present. Nevertheless, White attempts to trace a development in the dominant modes of historical thinking in the nineteenth century, moving from an Ironic realism in the Enlightenment through the postures of Romance, Tragedy, and Comedy, to emerge once again, at the end of the century, in a new mood of Irony which he identified with "the crisis of historicism." He failed to establish this developmental schema through any broad-ranging examination of the various lines of development to be found in the historiography of the period. He paid no attention to the impact of nationalism on historiography, to the importance of *Kulturgeschichte,* to how, if at all, evolutionary theory in biology influenced historiography, to the rise of social evolutionism among legal historians and social anthropologists, or to the ways in which a sociological interest in "the masses" affected the consciousness of historians. Nor does one find any extended treatment of many of the foremost historians of the period, of Niebuhr or of Maitland, for example. In fact, one cannot escape the impression that the historians and philosophers of history White chose to discuss were selected primarily in terms of their diversity and because of the contrasts between them. Then, having reduced the number of classic nineteenth-century historians to four, and the number of philosophers of history in the same period to four, it was not a task of great difficulty to establish a relatively clear line of development within the period. What is not evident is that the same line of development would have been discernible had White included many more historians, or had he included Comte, John Stuart Mill, and Spencer along with Hegel and Marx among his philosophers of history, or Dilthey, Rickert, Troeltsch, and Spengler along with Nietzsche and Croce.

I come now to the third and last of the presuppositions I wish to discuss: White's acceptance of relativism. In a sense, this should not be identified as one of his presuppositions, since it is a necessary consequence of his formalistic, tropological approach. Yet, had he not initially been willing to accept relativism, independently of any argumentation for it, he would have been forced to raise the question of whether an historical work can be adequately interpreted solely as a linguistic structure. Consequently, one may regard White's relativism as a basic presupposition, and one which is no less fundamental than his reasons for treating historians and philosophers of history together, or his view that what gives an historical work its structure is not the result of a careful reconstruction of the past but a creative poetic act. Actually, these presuppositions are interlocking, and I find no others that are equally fundamental in his work.

In considering White's relativism, I shall once again refuse to speculate as to how it was that he may have come to accept it; instead, I shall ask to what extent his account of the historian's work legitimates it. The first point to note is that the four historians with whom White chose to deal were engaged in very different enterprises. There was relatively little overlap in the subject-matters with which they were concerned; where such overlap existed, the scale of their inquiries differed, and the particular facets of the events with which they were concerned also differed.[7] Therefore, the question whether one of these accounts was "truer" or "more correct" than another would not naturally arise, and White was able to remain wholly within the confines of his formalistic approach. This permitted him to avoid any direct examination of the fundamental issue involved in debates concerning historical relativism:

whether it is possible, even in principle, to say of one account that it is truer, or more nearly correct, or more adequate, than another. What took the place of any such direct examination was White's assumption that the structure of every historical account is dependent upon the form which the historian impresses upon his subject-matter. Since White found that different historians had distinctively different "styles," and were therefore predisposed to use different ways of giving structure to that with which they dealt, he concluded that the only grounds on which one type of account could be given preference over another would be aesthetic or moral, rather than epistemological (xii).[8]

An entirely different situation would have arisen had he compared works concerned with the same subject-matter, which worked on the same scale, and with reference to the same aspects of that subject-matter. He would then have had to consider whether, in spite of differences in style, accounts which purported to represent the same events were congruent or incongruent, whether one or another had failed to consider certain types of data, and whether the inclusion of those data would have altered the representation of what had occurred.

To this, White might perhaps have answered that there was no need for him to enter into such discussions, since the original way in which an historian envisions any segment of the historical process will always be different from the way in which another historian does. That response, however, would be faulty in two respects. In the first place, even though White sometimes stressed the uniqueness of the structural elements in different historical works (for example, 5 and 29), the basis of his analysis lay in an acceptance of Vico's four linguistic tropes. He took these tropes to be recurrent and typical ways of organizing materials, not idiosyncratic characteristics of specific individuals. He identified the "style" of an historian with the particular combination of modes of emplotment, explanatory argument, and ideological stance which characterized that historian's work. Since, however, each of these modes derived from one or another of the four tropes, and since White acknowledged that not all of the numerically possible combinations were mutually compatible (29), the fundamental variations among historians in basic styles were limited. This is a fact which White explicitly recognized (31). Consequently, it should be both possible and meaningful for anyone examining the works of different historians to compare these works, so long as they resembled one another in their modes of emplotment, explanatory argument, and ideological implication. Since each such mode, according to White, serves to *explain* that which the historian is representing (2 and 7), one would think it possible to ask with respect to these works whether one of them is in some respects superior to another as a "model" or "icon" of the process represented. White makes no such comparisons, and obviously believed it illegitimate to try to make them (for example, xii, 3, 26–27, 432). The apparent justification for this completely relativistic commitment lay in his decision to treat an historical work solely as a linguistic structure, and so long as that point of view is strictly maintained, there is, of course, nothing against which to compare the two linguistic "models" to determine which is the more adequate representation. It was, then, his linguistic approach, and not ultimately a question of the uniqueness of each historical work, that served as justification for White's relativism.

His rejection of the possibility of comparing different historical accounts is also faulty in a second respect. It is simply not the case that the way in which one historian envisions any segment of the historical process will always be different from another historian's way. Many historians self-consciously set out to show that some account given by a predecessor is mistaken, and they attempt to produce data or arguments to establish their case. It is not that they are looking at the same segment of the past in a different way: they are contending that their predecessor misrepresented the process with which he claimed to be dealing. White failed to discuss inquiries of this sort since they were not typical of the aims and methods of the four historians whose works he had chosen as paradigms. It is even possible that he might be inclined to dismiss these and other problem-oriented types of inquiries as belonging to the class of "monographs and archival reports" (ix) or to "the kinds of disputes which arise on the reviewers' pages of professional journals" (13). This, however, would be illegitimate, since among such inquiries there are many full-scale treatments of processes that had a long and complex history, such as those which have been concerned to establish the relations between the slavery question and the American Civil War. Taking into account the fact that historians frequently engage in controversies of this sort, and finding that in some cases a consensus develops out of such controversies, White's ready acceptance of relativism is surely inadequate as a characterization of the ways in which practicing historians often view the work in which they are engaged.

On the other hand, if one turns from historical inquiries to consider the works of philosophers of history, one finds that they are almost never in agreement, either with respect to their detailed interpretations or on matters of principle. Nothing on their part in any way corresponds to the responsibility historians accept to document any challenged statement; to their commitment not to exclude from consideration any evidence that may be relevant to the material at hand; and to their recognition of an obligation to consider the criticism of those who do not share their presuppositions, so long as these criticisms directly relate to the accounts they have given of what in fact occurred in the past. We do not find the same scruples in such philosophers of history as Hegel and Marx, who sought to establish a meaning in history through a survey of the past. Instead, they selected only certain aspects of the life of society as a basis for interpreting what was truly significant in that life. They also neglected large segments of the historical past as not belonging within the province of meaningful history. Finally, each tended to take his own

interpretative presuppositions as absolute, and did not show either a willingness or an ability to find means of reconciling alternative points of view. Nor would the situation be radically altered were we to turn from those who attempt to sum up the total past in order to establish history's meaning, and consider only those who, like Croce and Nietzsche, considered themselves primarily as philosophic interpreters and critics of Western man's historical consciousness. Once again the scope of such inquiries tended to be severely limited, and the tenor of the arguments was so dogmatic that only those antecedently committed to similar philosophic presuppositions were likely to find themselves in agreement. Thus, in contrast to historical inquiries, different philosophies of history do not represent potentially compatible interpretations, nor complementary points of view. In fact, had there been as many philosophers of history as there have been historians, we would now find ourselves absolutely confounded by their babel of tongues. Because White—flying in the face of tradition—took philosophers of history to be at least as important as historians for any understanding of the historical consciousness, the wild disparities among their works tended to substantiate the relativism he was already inclined to accept.

As I have indicated, one of the basic reasons why White was so ready to accept relativism lay in the fact that he viewed every historical work as a linguistic entity whose structure wholly depended on the original poetic act which prefigured it. This, however, involved treating the statements that historians make as if they had no referents outside of their own work—as if some theory of the syntactics of poetry could supplant all questions concerning the semantics of everyday speech.[9] I find it one of the oddities of ***Metahistory*** that in spite of its "linguistic" approach, it failed to include as part of its implicit theory of language any account of how languages function with respect to their referential uses. So long as this is left out of account, one wonders how the individual statements of any historian are to be understood. Some among them refer to past occurrences whose existence is only known through inferences drawn from surviving documents; but it is not to these documents themselves, but to what they indicate concerning the past, that the historian's statements actually refer. Others among their statements depend upon what had been written in earlier accounts, but here again the object of the historian's reference is not these accounts themselves, but is to the very same entities (or to similar entities) as those to which the earlier accounts had themselves referred. Only a person treating an historical account solely as a literary document would not immediately raise the issue of reference, and with it the question of historical truth. So long as that question is not raised, I am forced to wonder in what sense White can properly characterize an historical work as a model or icon purporting to represent past structures and processes and, in doing so, as being able to explain them.

I have confined myself to some of the issues involved in White's "metahistorical" thesis; I have wholly neglected questions raised by the subtitle of his book, *The Historical Imagination in Nineteenth-Century Europe.* Such questions might be of two sorts. One would involve an assessment of what occupies by far the largest portion of the book, White's interpretations of the thought of the individual historians and philosophers of history with whom he deals. The other would be a consideration of whether the book as a whole is adequate as "a history of historical consciousness in nineteenth-century Europe" (1). In spite of a high regard for several of White's interpretations of the individuals on whom he focused attention, I find (as I have suggested in passing) that his portrayal of the scope of historical thought in the nineteenth century was far too limited; I also find unconvincing his suggestions as to the general course of development that it followed. These, however, are specifically historical issues, and it would take another and quite different paper to discuss them.

Notes

1. His closest approach to doing so, when speaking in his own voice, appears in his concluding chapter, where he identifies a philosophy of history as "a second order of consciousness in which [the philosopher of history] carries out his efforts to make sense of the historical process. [He] seeks not only to understand what happened in history but also to specify the criteria by which he can know when he has successfully grasped its meaning or significance" (428).

   The foregoing characterization covers both "critical" and "speculative" philosophies of history, as one would expect from White's linkage of Nietzsche and Croce with Hegel and Marx. Nevertheless, in most passages he explicitly refers to "speculative" philosophies of history, and he only rarely cites works that are characteristic of the extensive literature dealing with the problems of a "critical" philosophy of history.

   For my own view as to what constitutes a philosophy of history, which I presuppose in much that follows, see "Some Neglected Philosophic Problems Regarding History," *Journal of Philosophy* 49 (1952), 317–329.

2. For documentation of the following brief summary, cf. especially ix–xii, 2, 4–5, and 30–31.

3. In this respect, so-called "universal histories" often resemble philosophies of history. Nevertheless, as one can see with both Ranke and Burckhardt, historians attempt to separate themselves from philosophers of history, holding that their primary concern is with the particular and concrete, and not with events merely insofar as they are viewed as exemplifying some particular principle of explanation. On this point, cf. Ranke, *Ueber die Epochen der neueren Geschichte,* ed., with a preface, by Alfred Dove (Leipzig, 1888), vii–xi and 6–7; Burckhardt, *Force and Freedom: Reflections on History* [translation of *Weltgeschichtliche Betrachtungen,* ed. James Hastings Nichols] (New York, 1943), 80–82.

4. A few philosophers of history, such as Reinhold Niebuhr, attempt to establish their positions in essentially the same way. On the difference between Niebuhr's approach and the dominant tradition among philosophers of history, cf. my article, "Some Neglected Philosophic Problems Regarding History," cited above.

5. As we shall see, White explicitly accepts relativism, but he does not arrive at it, nor defend it, on the basis of any of the traditional arguments for it. Instead, he derives support for it from his view that when different historians give structure to the historical field, they are viewing it in terms of different tropes.

6. He tends to leave out of consideration the specific sense in which Marx and most subsequent analysts have usually used the concept of ideology.

7. For a discussion of how the concepts of "scale" and "perspectives" relate to the issue of relativism, cf. my *Anatomy of Historical Knowledge* (Baltimore, 1977), especially 151–155.

8. Here White's position differs markedly from that of Stephen Pepper, from whose doctrine of "root metaphors" he borrowed. Pepper held that the issues were fundamentally epistemological; he also believed that it is both possible and reasonable to make use of more than one of the four basic systems in our explanations. In this connection he said, "In practice, therefore, we shall want to be not rational but reasonable, and to seek, on the matter in question, the judgment supplied from each of these relatively adequate world theories. If there is some difference of judgment, we shall wish to make our decision with all these modes of evidence in mind, just as we should make any other decision where the evidence is conflicting" (*World Hypotheses* [Berkeley, 1942], 330–331).

9. This is a point also made by Michael Ermarth in his generally favorable review of *Metahistory* (*American Historical Review* 80 [1975], 961–963).

Stephen Bann (review date 7 September 1987)

SOURCE: "Hayden White and History," in *London Review of Books,* September 7, 1987, pp. 17–18.

[*In the following excerpt, Bann discusses the lasting significance of* Metahistory *and offers a positive assessment of* The Content of the Form.]

In publishing his compendious work ***Metahistory*** in 1973, Hayden White gave currency both to a term and to a programme. His subtitle, *The Historical Imagination in Nineteenth-Century Europe,* indicated the broad area of his investigations, but gave little sense of the radical originality of this programme, which was quite simply the re-examination of historiography in its written form. White had discovered a blind spot in the array of approaches to the recording of the past. While philosophers of history confined their attention to technical matters like causation, and historians of historiography elevated the individual historian at the expense of his text, the new metahistorian immersed himself willingly in the turbulent narratives of Ranke and Michelet, not to mention the discredited philosophies of history surviving from the 19th century. Using Vico's traditional battery of tropes, and Northrop Frye's more recent notion of 'emplotment' according to the patterns of tragedy and comedy, White justified his intuition that 'style' was not merely an incidental embellishment of 19th-century historical writing; it was possible to demonstrate textual patterns of a high degree of coherence and regularity which forged a connection between verbal or 'poetic' creativity and the overall world-view of particular philosophers and historians.

Defined this way, the lesson of *Metahistory* could be viewed quite differently by the various professional interests which held a stake in the study of historiography. Philosophers could turn their attention to the cognitive dimension of narrative form, and speculate on the particular grounds for the distinction between history and fiction. Historians of historiography could be redeemed (if they chose to be) from the debilitating exercise of compiling dossiers in the worst tradition of 'history of ideas,' and begin to come to terms with the intricacies of the historical text. Unfortunately, a third type of effect could also be credited to the influence of *Metahistory*: literary critics tired of tilling the exhausted soil of the 19th-century novel could discover an almost virgin territory awaiting them in the classics of historiography. This point is put pejoratively because *Metahistory*'s reputation has indeed suffered, in retrospect, from the accusation that White attempted to assimilate historiography to literature, purely and simply. It were better, no doubt, that the great Leopold von Ranke remained honoured and unread than that the literary horde picked over metaphors and metonymies in the writings of the progenitor of modern historical method!

Hayden White himself, of course, had never encouraged this dissipation of the central problem of historiography, which always maintained its irreducible difference from the narratives of fiction. Since the publication of *Metahistory,* he has not chosen to compose another overarching synthesis of the historical production of a particular period. But he has continued to gnaw away at the issues which *Metahistory* raised, and in the process his ideas have acquired a penetrating force which is undeniable. A collection of essays brought together under the title *Tropics of Discourse* was published in 1978. Here was White refining and extending his grasp of the issues of narrative structure, particularly in the essay **'The Historical Text as Literary Artifact'** (originally published the year after *Metahistory*), where the study of Frye and Collingwood was complemented by new insights from Peirce, Lévi-Strauss and Geoffrey Hartman. But the major part of this collection consisted of cultural criticism in the more

general sense. The publication of *The Content of the Form,* with eight essays dating back over the Eighties, is therefore an important event. It shows that for a long period White has been unremittingly concerned with a revaluation of the concept of narrative in the contemporary context, and that the various different intellectual stimuli which he has received have all helped to focus his intense study of the subject.

In his Preface to the collection, White locates the main problem in a development which his own earlier writings may, ironically, have helped to accentuate: this is the modern historian's withdrawal of confidence in the protocol of narrative. 'Many modern historians,' he writes, 'hold that narrative discourse, far from being a neutral medium for the representation of historical events and processes, is the very stuff of a mythical view of reality, a conceptual or pseudoconceptual "content" which, when used to represent real events, endows them with an illusory coherence and charges them with the kinds of meanings more characteristic of oneiric than of waking thought.' In taking this attitude, White suggests, the modern historian is in effect reproducing a bias which has been implicit in the process of historical reconstruction since the pioneering achievement of Herodotus: he is subscribing to the belief that 'history itself consists of a congeries of lived stories, individual and collective, and that the principal task of historians is to uncover these stories and to retell them in a narrative, the truth of which would reside in the correspondence of the story told to the story lived by real people in the past.' The crucial difference between the modern and the traditional historian is that the latter happily engages in 'stylistic embellishments' to dress up the stories that he has found, while the former wishes to expose such writerly accretions as being superfluous to the real business of historical reconstruction. The modern historian (and by this White means typically the historian of the *Annales* School) wants to denounce the mythic character of narrative, while at the same time taking for granted the implicit 'story' which it is his task to bring to light.

Can narrative be disavowed in so disingenuous a way? White thinks not, and his argument is based on the contemporary theories of discourse and ideology for which Roland Barthes served as an eloquent spokesman. His first two essays consider, from different points of view, the question of the adequacy of particular narrative forms for historical explanation. There is a conventional distinction among historians between the 'chronicle' and the history proper, which amounts to claiming that chronicles are merely imperfect, undeveloped examples of historical analysis. Yet how valid is it to impose this kind of hierarchy upon two very different types of text? White takes as his central example in the first essay not even a chronicle, but the apparently vestigial and anonymous *Annals of Saint Gall,* where the only continuing thread of the discourse is the bare succession of years. Even here, he suggests, there is no warrant for the view that the annals are defective or meaningless. 'The modern scholar seeks fullness and continuity in an order of events; the annalist has both in the sequence of years.' This leads him, in the second essay, to assert that the fully-fledged narrative history of the modern period is neither more 'literary' than the chronicle, nor more exactly attuned to the purposes of explanation (though the former interpretation would occur most readily to a literary scholar, and the latter to a professional historian). Narrativisation works 'by imposing a discursive form on the events that its own chronicle comprises by means that are poetic in nature.' A quotation from Barthes comes in handy here. 'Narrative does not *show,* does not *imitate* . . . [Its] function is not to "*represent,*" it is to constitute a spectacle.'

We are thus led back, throughout this study, to the social function of narrative history, which cannot be reduced to the terms of literary value, or scientific explanation. At the centre of White's project is a brilliantly original essay on **'The Politics of Historical Interpretation'** which re-invokes Schiller's notion of the 'historical sublime' and suggests that a positive philosophy of history can only spring from 'the pathetic spectacle of mankind wrestling with fate, the irresistible elusiveness of happiness,' and other instances of sublime disorder noted by the poet. Just as Hegel subordinated the sublime to the beautiful, so both the followers of Marx and their bourgeois counterparts have collaborated in spite of themselves in reducing history to orderliness. 'For this tradition, whatever "confusion" is displayed by the historical record is only a surface phenomenon: a product of lacunae in the documentary sources, of mistakes in ordering the archives . . .' Thus the descendants of Marx and Ranke make common cause in an aestheticism which repudiates the 'sublime,' and what is abandoned by both camps is quite simply the prospect of Utopia.

Yet White's questioning of the orderliness with which prevalent historical narratives are framed does not lead him to a cognitive nihilism. Rather it leads him to a redoubled effort in scrutinising the texts of the past. As he explains in a concluding essay which is no doubt a prologue to further investigation, the shift of attention from the content of such texts to their formal properties is not merely a vacuous stylistic exercise. What needs to be examined is the 'dynamic process of overt and covert code shifting by which a specific subjectivity is called up and established in the reader, who is supposed to entertain this representation of the world as a realistic one in virtue of its congeniality to the imaginary relationship the subject bears to his own social and cultural situation.' The concrete results of such a project can already be foreseen in the acute analysis of *The Education of Henry Adams,* by way of Denis Brogan's 1961 introduction, with which White brings this essay, and the collection as a whole, to an end.

It is quite evident that **The Content of the Form** was written under the sign of Roland Barthes, whose essay on 'The Discourse of History' is a recurring point of reference. No less evidently, *Post-Structuralism and the Question of History,* with its three editors [Derek Attridge,

Geoff Bennington, and Robert Young], and 11 contributors, goes under the sign of Jacques Derrida. The differences implicit in these two contemporary works which both deal broadly with 'the question of history' are very revealing. For White gives generous and full consideration to historical theorists whose concerns impinge upon his own: to Fredric Jameson, who still puts his faith in the 'Marxist master narrative,' to Ricoeur, who provides the philosophical arguments for seeing historical narratives as 'allegories of temporality,' and even to Foucault, who is accused of the failure to understand his own rhetorical strategies. By contrast, the contributors to the second volume choose to give themselves little room for manoeuvre. Hayden White is mentioned just in passing for his 'refined rhetorical studies'; Jameson, together with Edward Said, is attacked for holding that Derrida's method leads to the avoidance of historical issues; Foucault is prised apart from Derrida despite the efforts of Frank Lentricchia to assimilate them to one another in their 'understanding of history.' In fact, the message of most of the contributors is unequivocal. Not only is it wrong to accuse Derrida of being (as Terry Eagleton puts it) 'grossly unhistorical': but it is virtually impossible to find any thinker whose method is adequately 'historical' in the way that Derrida's is.

Suresh Raval (review date Autumn 1987)

SOURCE: "Recent Books on Narrative Theory: An Essay-Review," in *Modern Fiction Studies,* Vol. 33, No. 3, Autumn, 1987, pp. 559–70.

[*In the following excerpt, Raval offers a positive assessment of* The Content of the Form.]

Contemporary narrative theory is concerned with the analysis of narrative discourse and narrativity in order to explain the many forms and structures of storytelling in world literature and their implications. It also focuses on possible relations existing among mythic, historical, and fictional narratives, and it reflects on the possibility and implications of reconceptualizing these relations for literary, cultural, and historiographic theory. The books under review here are too diverse to allow for an integrated account that would make possible a hierarchical or some other larger context in which to place precisely and without distortion the theory presented, or the theories criticized, by each of the books in relation to one another. My attempt in the limited space here is to identify some of the central threads in each book in order to remark rather generally and all too briefly on their usefulness to narrative theory. . . .

In **Metahistory,** Hayden White sought to elaborate the strategies of what he calls tropological analysis, and in **Tropics of Discourse** he sought to refine those strategies so as to show, for instance, by an analysis of E. P. Thompson's *The Making of the English Working Class,* that even the most self-consciously antitheoretical historical study can be shown to deploy certain enabling tropo-logical strategies that make possible, in this instance, Thompson's study as a coherent, intelligent, and defensible totality. Now, in his latest book, ***The Content of the Form,*** White seems to be less concerned with pressing the claims of a systematic tropological analysis than with radicalizing the essential metahistorical and poetic insights underlying his studies of historical narratives and historical theories. This radicalizing interest figures prominently in his discus-sions of the value of narrativity in realistic representation, the politics of interpretation in modern historiography, and narrativity in historical theory. His essays on Droysen, Foucault, Jameson, and Ricoeur are models of rhetorical and conceptual deconstruction that, although employing the resources of tropological analysis, are no longer concerned with identifying dominant tropes constituting the work of these writers. The final essay on *The Educa-tion of Henry Adams* is a splendid critical exercise combin-ing the strategies of semiotics and ideological analysis.

White makes a threefold distinction among the chronicle of events, their explanation given in direct discourse as commentary, and the narrativization of the events provided by *allegoresis,* a process that enables a particular historical narrative to generate patterns of meaning not ascribable to a literal representation of facts in that narrative. Historical narrative, in other words, attempts a poetic troping of "facts" in order to endow them, in the very process of their description, with elements of the story form known as tragedy, romance, comedy, or farce, codes provided by Western literary culture. Consequently, what logical grounds there are for characterizing a historical narrative in terms of any one of these codes are provided by the logic of figuration White calls tropology. It is by probing the implications of these strategies that we can acquire a grasp of the process by which consciousness and narration enfigure specific past events into particular historical ac-counts invested with meaning and value.

One of the most interesting arguments I believe undergirds many of White's analyses is that the terms *history* and *narrative* are ambiguous and thus complicate all theoreti-cal discussions of historiography. Just as history can mean an object of study and discourse about this object, narra-tive can mean a mode of discourse and the product result-ing from the adoption of this mode of discourse. White criticizes analytic philosophers of historiography for bring-ing to their investigation the notion of explanation that rules out the importance of figurative discourse in the production of genuine knowledge. Their discussion fails to confront the process of narrativization by which a chronicle is transformed into a historical narrative. The book provides many superbly worked out illustrations to stress the point that it is important to pay attention to the narrative aspect of historical discourse, the story it tells about the events, and that it is misguided to dismiss the story a historical narrative tells about the events as mere adventitious and ornamental matter rather than an essential aspect of the discourse as a whole. ***The Content of the Form*** shows Hayden White at the top of his form, marshal-

ling the resources of rhetoric, semiology, ideological analysis, and historiographic theory. Like Ricoeur's volumes on *Time and Narrative,* White's book is a major contribution to the current advances in interdisciplinary inquiry in the humanities. . . .

For all their extraordinary diversity in viewpoint, the books reviewed here all seem to underline the centrality of the act of interpretation, however different their particular emphases by which this act is to be carried out. Both Ricoeur and White are in agreement on the importance of the interpretive act in the sense of the hermeneutics of understanding as against the scientistic aspirations underly-ing the concept of explanation; and both underline the no-tion of emplotment, though Ricoeur explicates it by link-ing it with a notion of deep temporality of experience, and White explicates it by disclosing the operations of rhetori-cal and ideological elements or codes in narrative discourse and historical theory.

Ralph Flores (review date December 1987)

SOURCE: A review of *The Content of the Form,* in *Modern Language Notes,* Vol. 102, No. 5, December, 1987, pp. 1191–196.

[*In the following review of* The Content of the Form, *Flores provides an overview of White's conceptual asser-tions, which he then applies to examples of White's own stylistic phrases in the book.*]

For most cultures, narratives are relatively unproblematic vehicles for transmitting honored traditions, and the critique or rejection of narrative (by recent historians, novelists, or theorists) may signal a cultural crisis of epochal proportions. In ***The Content of the Form*** Hayden White offers eight analytic essays on the work of several eminent theoreticians of narrative, work which both ad-dresses and may contribute to such a crisis. Among the theoreticians are Paul Ricoeur, Johann G. Droysen, Fre-deric Jameson, Michel Foucault, and the French *Annal-istes.* White is particularly sympathetic to the work of Paul Ricoeur (whose as yet unfinished *Temps et Récit* in several volumes he acclaims as our century's "most important synthesis of literary and historical theory) and to what he calls Jameson's "redemption of narrative" (170, 142). With considerable insight into their epistemological shortcom-ings, however, White is unable to give unqualified al-legiance to either of these efforts. His main endeavor, which is separate from (but constantly indebted to) that of the specific theoreticians he discusses, is to think endlessly about "narrativity," about how narratives work and what they might have to say.

In his opening essay White interestingly shows what nar-rativity accomplishes by examining the medieval German *Annals of St. Gall.* These *Annals* consist of a list of years followed by very brief entries for some (but not all) years:

"709. Hard Winter. Duke Gottfried died. / 710. Hard year and deficient in crops. / 711. / 712. Flood everywhere" (6–7). Such a scheme, according to White, is merely chronological, offering no high or low points, no explanations. What the annalist does not consider (and what later writers would consider to be "missing" in his account of events) is the question of the social context, the authority of and threats to the legal and moral system in which he writes. In other words, for St. Gall there is nothing problematic about the reality or status of the events; they are simply listed. Richerus of Rheims, by contrast, seems to write his *History of France* (ca. 998) in order "to represent . . . an authority whose legitimacy hinged upon the establishment of 'facts' of a specialized historical order" (19). Here, then, is an instance of rhetorical and semiotic force in historical narrative, a force that White will repeatedly stress: "unless at least two versions of the same set of events can be imagined, there is no reason for the historian to take upon himself the authority of giving the true account of what really happened" (20). What "really happened" is in other words arguable. Indeed it is precisely the desire to prove a point that leads a historian to the believed assumption of neutral objectivity; the ideological agenda, to be most effective, is hidden. Historians are thus advocates or rhetoricians, even when claiming the opposite; for "the appeal of historical discourse . . . [is that] it makes the real desirable, makes the real into an object of desire, and does so by its imposition, upon events that are represented as real, of the formal coherency that stories possess" (21).

Having established this much, White in his next chapter is able to attack the naive view, still held by many, that "the form of the discourse, the narrative, adds nothing to the content of the representation; rather it is a simulacrum . . . of real events" (27). This naive paradigm is no longer widely accepted, and White lists several types of theoreticians who problematize such a paradigm: the Anglo-American analytic philosophers (who critically assess the "epistemic status" of narrative), the *Annalistes* (who would substitute "scientific" studies for ideologically-loaded narrative), the semiologists (who view narrative as one code among others), the hermeneuticists (who consider narrative as a verbal manifestation of "time-consciousness"). Making use of the work of these schools, White insists, against conventional historians, that historical discourse is always more than the "literal, truth-value" level with which most historians believe themselves to be concerned. Such historians contend that tropes are mere decorations, but White argues on the contrary that to omit the figurative element from an analysis of narrative "is to miss not only its aspect as allegory but also the performance" of chronicle being transformed into narrative (48).

The notion of "performance," particularly of a communal sort, is developed by Paul Ricoeur (and closely parallels Vico's *New Science*): emplotment symbolically repeats and continues actions by past human agents who, in their actions, made worthy stories. There may thus be a making-doing-plotting-writing connection relevant to a number of

disciplines. Quite relevant, too, may be White's fine analysis (in a chapter entitled **"The Politics of Historical Interpretation"**) of the relations between politics and aesthetics. White shows how "the sublime" in Kant and Edmund Burke posed dangers to historians (including Burke himself) and thus had to be domesticated or exorcised in the interests of "practical" political and educational projects. By the same token, the notion of history as "senseless" often was and is prelude to a predictably apocalyptic, if not always sublime, visionary discourse about the future. Is "senseless" history, broken by the sublime, any more or less preferable to history as "sense"? White's conclusion is that it is not:

> One must face the fact that when it comes to apprehending the historical record, there are no grounds to be found in the historical record itself for preferring one way of construing its meaning over another. Nor can such grounds be found in any putative science of man, society, or culture. . . .
>
> (75)

The term "grounds" here seems crucial, and if one notices the first phase of this passage, one might wonder how rigorous White will be in maintaining his thesis. For his work slips back into the assumption of some sort of grounds for historical tropology, and elsewhere, when he deals with Foucault, he begins by seeking—even while admitting the impossibility of the quest—for "the grounds for [Foucault's] point of view" (34).

White needs or assumes, let us venture, some sort of ground. Consider for instance his title concept, "the content of the form." The form/content binary is a grounding concept in the history of metaphysics, and White's stress on this concept suggests a strong bias, despite disclaimers, in favor of traditional "history." To be sure, White adds a twist to the dichotomy with his content-of-the-form formula, articulated in a respectful chapter on Droysen's *Historik*:

> Droysen makes clear that he regards the content of the historian's discourse, not as the facts or events that comprise his manifest referent, but as his understanding of these facts and the moral implications he draws from their contemplation. . . . Droysen's analysis . . . allows us to speak of the 'content of the form.' . . .
>
> (90)

Whether form and content be separated or taken together, however, the form/content concept itself is never put into question, and it enables White's readings to remain comfortably ensconced within the horizon of traditional "meaning." "All the concepts," Jacques Derrida has argued, "by means of which *eidos* or *morphē* have been translated or determined refer to the theme of presence. . . . Formality is whatever aspect of the thing in general presents itself, lets itself be seen, gives itself to be thought" (*Margins of Philosophy,* trans. A. Bass [Chicago: U of Chicago P, 1982], p. 158). When White contends that the content is the form, he assumes its unproblematic intelligibility, its clear visibility. Indeed, in his endeavor of locating of tropes and emplotments, he is solidly traditional and in many ways Aristotelian.

Let us assume for the sake of argument that White's form/content formula is useful. What, we might then ask, is the content of the form of *The Content of the Form*? White's prose style, while clear and interesting, is cautious, humorless, and strictly academic. With regard to what is usually called "content," White's essays, despite their devotion to history and culture in a wide context, are at no point formed or "informed" by, say, Eastern cultures, feminist, minority or third world historians or theorists. On a more specific level, White's style is marked by a number of telling phrases. Two in particular recur with great regularity. One is "proper" taken in conjunction with "history" as a "discipline": "properly disciplined historical consciousness"; "discipline proper to itself"; "proper object of historical study"; "the socially responsible historian properly assumes"; "a historical discipline properly assessed"; "an appropriate performance in the discipline" (63, 64, 66, 71, 45, 188). The other phrase, or a version of it, usually follows a short list of names or ideas: "Lukács, Brecht, Benjamin, . . . and so on"; "Gissing, Conrad, Dreiser, and so forth"; "Machiavelli and Erasmus, and so forth"; "Comtean, Hegelian, Marxist, and so on"; "'nature,' 'atoms,' 'genes' and so forth" (143, 164, 187, 188, 187; also 112, 189, 194, 197, 204, 210). What might these stylistic turns have in common? What is the content of their forms? Granted that by "proper" White refers mostly (but not always; see p. 188) to the "discipline" as conceived by conventional historians, his repetition of the phrases betrays a certain fascination. He at any rate by no means favors a "history" or "discipline" which is much *other than* "proper," but instead seems to argue for a discourse that, with some reservations, would not be far from that of Paul Ricoeur (interestingly, perhaps, White has not as yet worked out a theory of his own). The second phrase, "and so on," or "and so forth," is a gesture of easy totalization or casual categorization, a suggestion of something he assumes himself to hold in common with the reader ("you know what I mean"; or "that sort of thing"). It could also suggest, however, that some readers are excluded and that the writer has a right to be not only vague but at the same time classificatory. The space of "the proper" which White's text assumes, especially if we attend to what that very text says about the strategies of power (as style) could be construed as a space of arrogance and usurpation. The "and so on" phrase is a presumption of categories, and is one indication among others of a certain Aristotelianism; often White simply reprocesses categories (for instance Droysen's) rather than questioning the possibility or function of the categorizations.

Despite a concern with figuration, for instance, White rarely hesitates in classifying a given text according to some basic trope, genre, or emplotment; he rarely if ever notices the complexities of texts and his readings never lead to the sorts of aporia noted by Paul de Man (whose work, incidentally, despite its relevance to White's, is

never mentioned). The commentary on Foucault is typical of much of White's work. As in *Metahistory* (1973), where White attempted to apply four basic master tropes, in conjunction with other categories, to the texts of several nineteenth-century historians, here he argues for a master trope by which to comprehend Foucault's texts. He offers no references to the extensive and often quite intelligent secondary material on Foucault, as if he wanted to "take on" Foucault's texts directly and to test out the master trope.

Foucault's work is at some distance from that of the other theorists in *The Content of the Form,* and there can be little doubt that White's tone is defensive or uneasy: Foucault's discourse is characterized by "capricious erudition, solemn disclosures . . . , aggressive redrawings of the map of cultural history" (107). The suggested tactic for reading such a text is as follows:

> We will find a clue to the meaning of his discursive style in the rhetorical theory of tropes. . . . The authority of Foucault's discourse derives primarily from its style (rather than from its factual evidence or rigor of argument); . . . this style privileges the trope of catachresis. . . .
>
> (105–06)

Note the unquestioned terms: "the meaning" (not meanings?); which "we" will "find"; "the rhetorical theory" (only one, namely "the" theory?); "derives"; "factual evidence" (earlier this was argued to be stylistic; here it is separated from "style"); "rigor of argument" (is rigor necessarily *not* stylistic?); and finally—the main insight—"catachresis." But why catachresis? How have "we" decided upon it? Is it indeed Foucault's "dominant trope" (116)—assuming, that is, that he has one? Is it even (as many have wondered) a trope at all? Catachresis is also called, as White notes, *abusio*: the "abuse" of a trope, a metaphor with no "proper" level. Thus according to White "his own discourse stands as an abuse of everything for which 'normal' or 'proper' discourse stands" (115). But what, again, of White's style? Is it by comparison less abusive or more "proper"? If so, why "everything" or "his own"—as if to locate culpability or non-propriety? Why the repeated "stands"—as if to give the impression of intense conflict? We are told in an earlier part of the same sentence that "Foucault's style . . . displays a profusion of the various figures sanctioned by this trope, such as paradox, oxymoron, chiasmus, hysteron proteron, metalepsis, prolepsis, antonomasia, paronomasia, antiphrasis, hyperbole, litotes, irony, and so on" (115). Here is yet another "and so on": the profusion must be extensive indeed, but at least the tropes have names and can be listed.

What White's list and the "and so on" fail to consider is that catachresis may be construed not only as a local abuse of tropes but as a subversion of tropology—indeed of "the" tropological system. If catachresis "sanctions" so many tropes (and our "and so on" leaves the question open), then perhaps it no longer "sanctions" anything. Indeed all tropes are to an indeterminate extent catachretic, unless "we" decide arbitrarily what is to count as the "proper"—or in this case as "the dominant trope." The problem with such a decision, however, is its easy bypassing, in the interest of its own dominance, of the text's tropological complexity. What marks, after all, some of the most challenging texts, including Foucault's, is their very lack of a "dominant trope." And to claim to "read" such a trope in the text is to fail, quite possibly, in the task of reading. It could be said, no doubt, that White is not a careful or close reader of texts. Long sections of his essays consist of paraphrases and summaries; even apart from that, he moves quickly among cited passages in order to establish or confirm some all too general thesis.

It is thus of some interest that in a concluding chapter he offers to read a text, *The Education of Henry Adams,* so as to demonstrate the shortcomings of a "'content'-oriented method" (194). The semiological reading that emerges, however, is similar in crucial ways to the thematic readings it claims to displace. The method proposes to "provide a theoretically generated reading of this text, which would give an account for every element of it" (196), and the reading is recuperative: gaps in the narrative or shifts away from the narrative mode "themselves become meaningful as message" (204). White's semiology indeed shows how a text possesses something that is proper, or its own: the text "draws attention to . . . its own processes of meaning production and makes . . . [them] its own subject matter, its own 'content'" (211). Perhaps most surprising about such a reading, explicitly modelled on Barthes' *S/Z* (196), is that it is offered as though no critiques or refinements of structuralism had as yet appeared; curiously perhaps, what is lacking in this historian's essay (first published in 1982) is a sense that the heyday of structuralist semiotics may have passed, and that something, at least, might need to be said about that. Similarly, in an attempt to explain Ricoeur's notion of history as allegory, White cites Dante's distinction in the *Convivio* between poetic and theological allegory, concluding with respect to the allegorical status of the *Commedia* (on Charles Singleton's interpretation) that "something like this, I take it, is what Ricoeur is saying in his reflections on historical narrative" (183). But surely it is not "something like this"—unless, as with yet another "and so on," we are willing to make do with a vague—and unhistorical—gesture.

White is of course under no obligation to provide a "sense of history" and on the contrary often debunks such a sense. The book, even so, is devoted to narrative theories and is sympathetic to notions of narrative as a socially significant force. Notice, then, that it would be nearly impossible to discern any sort of narrative or theoretical development in the essays in *The Content of the Form*; White's text seems to illustrate the very loss of narrative that it so articulately laments.

Giles Gunn (review date March 1988)

SOURCE: "The Kingdoms of Theory and the New Historicism in America," in *Yale Review,* Vol. 77, No. 2, March, 1988, pp. 207–36.

[*In the following excerpt, Gunn discusses trends in contemporary historical theory and issues raised by White in* The Content of the Form.]

Theory has become ubiquitous in literary and cultural studies, and it is sometimes difficult not to feel under siege. The study of verbal texts, like the study of cultural forms of almost any kind, has in many ways become a beleaguered enterprise in which the establishment of methodological and theoretical credentials now often takes precedence over all other intellectual procedures. "The aim of interpretation," as E. D. Hirsch once termed it, is more often than not to validate the system of thought that presumably serves as its premises. No longer are texts, for example, or things that can be "read" as "texts," always studied as intentional forms whose meaning can be inferred from a reconstruction of the putative conditions to which they are a response and the cognitive and affective associations to which they give rise; more and more they are being converted into "sites" for the testing of theories. What was once assumed to yield a "conflict of interpretations," in Paul Ricoeur's phrase, has given way to something that looks more like a contest of concepts, where the object is not to see what can be learned from the debate but to determine how completely the terms of discussion can be subsumed within a single discourse. The text is in danger of being displaced not by context but by metacritical templates.

Such aggressions, even if exaggerated in their depiction, have proved daunting to interpretative traditionalists of almost every stripe. The omnivorousness of theory has taken on for many humanists the enormity of a moral offense, even of religious blasphemy. So much of what earlier generations of literary and cultural interpreters once held sacred about the integrity of the object under investigation—the object, to quote Matthew Arnold, "as in itself it really is"—is now felt by many to have been profaned by this new enculturation of theory or, worse, actually desecrated, and the victims are not just texts themselves but whole traditions, indeed the entire canon of Western literature. . . .

In other words, history, too, "writes off" as well as writes in or writes down the self. If some contemporary new historicists paid closer attention to the referential subtexts of their materials, to "the context in the text"—as Hayden White calls it in his important new book, *The Content of the Form*—rather than to the rhetorical tactics that often mask such matters, they might perceive, as White observes in a discussion of Paul Ricoeur, how the "historical" (or better, "historicality") is a response or rejoinder to the tragedy of temporality. To historicize, as the better new historicists like Buell and Stephen Greenblatt have always acknowledged and as White confirms, is not to reinscribe the self in more "realistic" contexts so much as to show how those contexts are sedimented with past "forms of life" that once contributed to their realization but are now lost to us except through the text itself.

To historicize is thus to be brought up against all that the self is exposed to within time because of time—that is, to confront the odds, as Berthoff expressed earlier, against the self's continuance beyond time. No historicism, new or old, that does not acknowledge the ultimate pathos of this predicament—for example, in the social and political contexts of human resistance to it—deserves, on White's account, to be taken seriously. In addition, even if historicism is only another way of trying to get into as well as out of history, as White says of Fredric Jameson's "political unconscious," no historicism that glosses over the different tactics of historicization by which we try to do so can be regarded as other than frivolous. There are real differences, in other words, between justifying what Mircea Eliade once called the "terror of history" in the name of the kind of anti-humanism with which Foucault, in his earlier writing, attacks the collusion between modern representations of historical discourse and the reconstitution of man as a field of study and, say, Ricoeur's attempt to uncover the deep structures that compel or at least control our need to render experience narratively in order to cope with the paradox it compels us to face but cannot help us wholly overcome: the paradox of temporality and its continuance, of time and eternity.

We are thus brought back to Bishop's paradox of our knowledge of experience as historical, as "flowing, and flown." The hesitancy enforced by her comma registers the self's comprehension of the difference, a difference that makes *all the difference.* "Historicality," "historicity," "historicism," White suggests in a book far too subtle for me to do it full justice here, all refer merely to one (or more) among a variety of discursive practices for defining the odds against us, and offer us another set of terms— what Kenneth Burke would call "critical coordinates"— for, at the very least, calculating our chances, and at the most, attempting to enhance them. But the real issue isn't what we calculate our chances to be—different critical systems furnish us with different sets of calculations—or whether we can improve our margin; the crucial issue is how we go about our calculations. It all boils down—here Poirier and Berthoff oddly agree with White, Jameson, and Ricoeur—to a question of something like virtue, that is, to the "expense of spirit," to use Blackmur's phrase, that is being wagered in the process. Those works of literature that raise the stakes to the highest levels of cultural risk before making such measurements, and then make them in the face of formal and conceptual obstacles that would normally be conceived to thwart, or at least to threaten, their success, we call classics. "What the classic achieves," White says with the help of certain formulations from Jameson, "is an instantiation of the human capacity to endow lived contradictions with intimations of their possible transcendence."

Thus White is prepared to claim that what distinguishes the classic at any given time from all other similar works with which it might be compared is not the universal truths that it is sensed to contain about, say, the "human condition," but the models it provides for investigating the "human condition" and other such matters, both within the text and beyond it, when the "human condition," and the procedures for investigating it, have been rendered particularly problematic or hazardous. Hence the literary classic furnishes a particular opportunity for the expression of virtue, "not because (or only because)," to quote White again, the classic's "meaning-content is universally valid or authoritative (for that is manifestly impossible; in any event, it is a profoundly unhistorical way of looking at anything), but because it gives us insight into a process that is universal and definitive of human species-being in general, the production of meaning." But it does so, White insists with Poirier, no less than with Jameson and Ricoeur, in its own way. The difference between literary texts and all others is a function of their ability "to work up a certain knowledge (not merely a certain intuition) of the conditions of their own production and render those conditions intelligible."

It is this knowledge of literary texts not only as products of meaning but also as processes and models for producing it that is now at issue in the kingdoms of theory. How do we obtain such knowledge? Why does such knowledge matter? What does such knowledge do to our previous conceptions of literature? White's answer to this last question may not be the only answer, but it nicely converges with Poirier's thinking as well as with Jameson's, with Graff's as with Buell's and Ricoeur's:

> Insofar as art and literature, across whatever local differences in their contents occasioned by their production in concrete historical conditions, not only instantiate the human capacity for imagining a better world but also, in the universality of the forms that they utilize for the representation of vision itself, actually provide us with models or paradigms of all creative productivity of a specifically human sort, they claim an authority different in kind from that claimed by both science and politics.

Thanks to the interventions of recent theory, the critical issue that the institutions of literary study in America can no longer gloss or repress, as they once did, is what that authority amounts to, and what sorts of empowerment it makes possible.

Jeremy Tambling (review date June 1988)

SOURCE: A review of *The Content of the Form,* in *Modern Language Quarterly,* Vol. 49, No. 2, June, 1988, pp. 192–94.

[*In the following review, Tambling finds shortcomings in* The Content of the Form.]

In this compilation of essays from 1979 onward [*The Content of the Form*], Hayden White engages four recurrent themes, though they are not set out as such: the relationship between history and narrative, the relationship between historical and fictional narrative, the place that interpretation has within the writing of history, and the Nietzschean theme of the uses and disadvantages of history for life, considering, predominantly, its political and ideological uses. The essays include four on specific theorists—Michel Foucault, Fredric Jameson, Paul Ricoeur, and the post-Hegelian Droysen—and four on questions involving textuality, narrativity, and history.

The essays on Jameson and Ricoeur declare White's belief in narrativized history—narrative considered, in Jameson's *Political Unconscious,* to offer something utopian, a possibility of moving forward out of our present discontents. Literature attests to "the reality of the desire for redemption" and provides "justification for the vision of its possible realization" (p. 144). Jameson adheres to a Lukacsian model—a realist text with firm narrative form. White would agree with Jameson that there can be an understanding of events outside the framing of ideology, that, as Jameson says, "History is *not* a text, not a narrative, master or otherwise," that it "needs no particular theoretical justification: we may be sure that its alienating necessities will not forget us, however much we might prefer to ignore them" (quoted on p. 147). Nietzsche might call this a reactive statement, coming from the exploited objects of history rather than from the exploiters who make and suppress history. Although White's position establishes history as a site of conflict, it does not help to establish a sense of the past outside the text, where it can be appealed to. Indeed, by the end of White's essay the point seems almost conceded, as history appears to be (again as in Jameson, though one might also cite Stephen Dedalus) "one White, as there is in Jameson, of the alternative: of postmodernism, of Lyotard's "incredulity toward metanarratives." Utopian possibilities there remain unexplored, and White appears almost antimodernist in his belief in narrative—however aware he might be of Barthes's arguments on the force of ideology underlying the nineteenth-century realist narrative text.

If History embodies ideological struggle, a necessary question for White is "to what is the historian responsible, or rather, to what *should* one be responsible?" (p. 188), considering how even the events of the Holocaust have been doubted by "revisionist" historians (pp. 76–82). But the discussion of further implications remains inconclusive here (like much of the book, written as it is in stiffly dignified, rather dulled, safe prose) as White wrestles (*contra* Jameson) with the issue of nontextual history and history—even of the Holocaust—as perhaps "morally domesticating" (p. 78). The point recapitulates an interesting discussion (pp. 68–75) on the articulation of the beautiful and sublime with history in Burke and Schiller or Hegel, showing that the erasure of the "sublime" as a way of understanding reduces history to a succession of well-ordered, comprehensive processes that serve to blunt the radical or horrifying edge of events, to soften the visionary element needed in radical politics. Thus while he argues that history's professionalization entraps, White also sees historical thinking as a function of the political unconscious. He yokes to Jameson's notion a sense of the power of narrative, following Ricoeur: "a meaningful life is one that aspires to the coherency of a story with a plot" (p. 173), for a plot "imposes a meaning on the events that make up its story level" (p. 20).

In arguing that narrative rises when an interpretation of events is contested (p. 19), White underestimates writings such as the eighth-century *Annals of Saint Gall* (pp. 6–11). Here the citation of events and dates, with gaps going against certain years in which "nothing happened" (p. 11), is taken as an absence of narrative representation. When it originally appeared, White's position was rightly disputed by Marilyn Robinson Waldman, using Islamic historiography.[1] The main problem is that White's thesis about narrative function fails to account for non-Eurocentric models. But how would a feminist history—also an apparent record of silence—read, on White's basis? Such a question opens up the kind of issues addressed by Derrida against Foucault's attempt in *Madness and Civilization* to write the archaeology of the silence of the "mad." Derrida makes problematic Foucault's narrative text, seeing it as itself oppressive, a voice from the point of a dominant ideology. White does not point this out in his reading of Foucault. Meanwhile, deconstruction, like feminism and psychoanalysis, is ready to trouble White's rather assured sense of mainline history. White hardly refers to Derrida, and then not in contexts that suggest the power of the play of the text. He thus misses the whole issue of the failure of interpretation to stay still, to preserve its monologic character.

White's limitation is linked with his voluntaristic sense of the subject's relation to ideology. Such a relation involves "a specific kind of reading . . . subject *capable of inserting himself* into the social system that is his historically given potential field of public activity" (p. 86; my italics). White takes his account of ideology from Jameson (p. 232, n. 14), whose reading of Althusser nevertheless reduces it to "a kind of false consciousness."[2]

But it is unnecessary to bring back all Althusser to see that White's account of ideology, involuntarily positioning the subject, results in a consideration of discourse that frames and creates the subject, making the split between narrative representation and the real event nontenable. Assuming the possession of choice of narrative method or guiding trope—the "alternative ways that one might legitimately write different accounts of the same set of historical events" (p. 88)—also assumes the free subject, i.e., the ideal historian, one not caught within a discursive formation. It emphasizes what White called the "Kantian element in my thought,"[3] seriously limiting any use a historian could put to poststructuralism, and very seriously underestimating discourse theory.

Notes

1. "'The Otherwise Unnoteworthy Year 711': A Reply to Hayden White," *CritI,* 7 (1981): 784–92.

2. To use Jerry Aline Flieger's term (in "The Prison House of Ideology," *Diacritics,* 12 [1982]: 54). Flieger's article appeared with White's essay in an issue of *Diacritics* that was devoted to Jameson. To agree with Flieger's position (or with that of Terry Eagleton, who also appeared in this issue) is to suggest that ideology in White reduces to a system of beliefs that obtain in a given society—beliefs that may be dispelled in the name of a purer historicism.

3. *Tropics of Discourse: Essays in Cultural Criticism* (Baltimore: Johns Hopkins University Press, 1978), p. 22.

David S. Gross (review date Summer 1988)

SOURCE: A review of *The Content of the Form,* in *World Literature Today,* Vol. 62, No. 3, Summer, 1988, p. 516.

[*In the following review of* The Content of the Form, *Gross commends White's insightful ideas, but suggests that his "dense" and "formidable" prose may limit his audience.*]

Hayden White begins **"Foucault's Discourse: The Historiography of Anti-Humanism,"** the longest of the eight substantial essays in **The Content of the Form,** with the observation that the work of Michel Foucault "is extraordinarily difficult to deal with in any short account." The same is certainly true of White's own work. White describes his book as "some of the work I have done over the last seven years in historiography and theory of narrative and on the problem of representation in the human sciences." The essays are sophisticated theoretically, informed throughout by contemporary continental critics and philosophers. Like Foucault, Ricoeur, Jameson—some of the writers discussed at length here—White's own writing can be rather formidable, so dense as to be almost impenetrable. Certainly a problem in his book is that the practitioners of the dominant positivist, empiricist, antitheoretical school of historiography with whom he wants to argue are not likely to read very far, to listen to much of his argument.

That is a shame, because White connects many different insights of modern critical theory in ways which illuminate both historical practice and the practice of the historian. White is usually seen as a "formalist," and indeed one way of characterizing **The Content of the Form,** like his earlier work, is in terms of the attention paid to the form as opposed to the content in historical narratives. White seeks consistently to foreground the effects, the constitutive character, of discourse itself. Thus his typical rhetorical or tropological analysis.

White is concerned here with "systems of meaning production" in culture, with the *function* of any discursive

information, as it is produced and interpreted in any given context. Of all the thinkers whose work he considers, White seems to agree most with Foucault; he sums up that thinker's position as follows: "What is always at work in discourse—as in everything else—is 'desire and power.'" White agrees, and he argues persuasively that the discourse of knowledge, of education, always masks its relations to power and presents itself as dealing only with neutral, objective truth. A central function of the discipline of history, according to White, has been to discipline desire, to banish from historical narration radical discontent with the present and commitment to a fundamentally different future. Throughout his book White uses his familiarity and facility with modern theory to demystify notions of transparency or objectivity in intellectual discourse and to fix our attention squarely on the process of meaning production in all its complex and contradictory unfolding.

William H. Dray (review date October 1988)

SOURCE: A review of *The Content of the Form,* in *History and Theory,* Vol. XXVII, No. 3, October, 1988, pp. 282–87.

[*In the following review of* The Content of the Form, *Dray commends White's book but objects to his view of history as political propaganda.*]

[**The Content of the Form**] brings together eight of White's essays published between 1979 and 1985, all concerned in one way or another with theory of narrative and the problem of representation in the human sciences. It is thus a sequel to, or an updating of, his reflections on the same range of topics in **Tropics of Discourse,** and earlier in **Metahistory.** Four of the essays deal directly with problems raised by the nature of narrative: its epistemic authority, its cultural function, and its general social significance. The other four approach the same issues more obliquely through discussions of the work of Droysen, Foucault, Jameson, and Ricoeur. Only three of the papers have been substantially revised. For readers familiar with White's earlier work the collection offers few surprises. It does, however, provide welcome elaboration on a number of controversial points, a few changes of emphasis, and even an occasional retraction; and its more serene tone suggests the increasing satisfaction of a daring and original, if also highly syncretistic, thinker with the intellectual habitation he has been constructing over a number of years. The general impression one gets is nevertheless one of being made privy, not to a finished system, but to work still enthusiastically in progress; and even those who find themselves with serious reservations about much of what White has to say may take considerable pleasure in being swept up, if only momentarily, in the intellectual currents through which he navigates with such elan.

As might be expected with a group of essays written at different times and for different purposes, there are some overlaps in content, some incongruities of style, and more issues addressed than can conveniently be noted in a short review. Of special interest are a lengthy discussion of annals as an historiographical form in its own right, to be contrasted with chronicle as well as with narrative proper, and an exploration of the different approaches to the question of narrative legitimacy taken by *Annales* historians, certain analytic philosophers of history, linguistic theorists holding structuralist and post-structuralist views, philosophers with an interest in hermeneutics, and traditional historians who see narrative as essentially a craft. Much to be welcomed also is White's probing, yet respectful, critique of Ricoeur's attempt to ground narrative in human time-consciousness—here he is at his best as an interpreter of another's text. The central thrust of the book, however, like that of much of White's previous work, is the elaboration and defense of an extreme constructionist view of narrative in historical writing, the real function of which, he insists, is moral and political, not epistemological, and certainly not representational. This central position—although it may seem ungrateful to say it of a book which is so wonderfully well-informed, always thought-provoking, and frequently illuminating—seems to me to be frustratingly underargued.

A recurring problem is White's tendency, when his constructionist thesis is put in question, to let rhetoric rather than logical argument assume too much of the burden of its defense. "What wish is enacted, what desire is gratified, by the fantasy that real events are properly represented when they can be shown to display the formal coherency of a story?" he asks early in **"The Value of Narrativity in the Representation of Reality"** (4)—as if the explanation of someone's holding such a belief were alone problematic, not the claim that the belief is in fact a fantastic one to hold. That history "may be" meaningless is "a possibility that should never be ruled out," he cautions us in **"The Politics of Historical Interpretation"** (82)—going on then at other points simply to take the realization of this possibility for granted. Transitions are too easily made from what certain considerations allegedly lead one to "suspect" to what can be taken undoubtedly to be the case; the idea that the real world could, like narrative, exhibit a coherent structure is repeatedly written off as "illusion"; and sheer paradox is treated as almost magically supportive, as when a social attitude is said to be "present" in a narrative "by virtue of its absence." White's penchant for rather figurative modes of expression also makes it difficult at times to elicit a clear structure of argument from what he has to say. Nor is he above occasionally caricaturing the realist position he wishes to attack, as when he interprets the notion of events speaking for themselves as implying that, like the mythical column of Memnon, they actually give tongue (3).

Any sober assessment of White's case for claiming that narrative cannot represent reality must look carefully at what, in his view, *does* succeed in representing it. The contrast which he sometimes seems to have in mind is between offering full-blown narrative and merely reporting discrete events—perhaps with all the cultural, or even human, significance strained out of them, as seems implied by his remark that "a refusal of narrative indicates an absence or refusal of meaning itself" (2). More characteristically, non-representational narrative is set over against representational annals or chronicle. In fact, in conceding the claims of realism with regard to the latter, White considerably undermines the case for denying a representative function to narrative; for he admits that it incorporates these simpler forms. In any case, reports of discrete historical events seldom strain away all the human meaning of what is said to have happened, even annals, as illustrated by White himself, containing humanly meaningful claims like "Hard year, deficient in crops." This makes it implausible to claim, as White sometimes seems to do, that narratives go "beyond" reality merely because they typically express distinctively human perspectives, for example, value judgments. Clearly, for him, the allegedly non-representational character of narratives must be traced to features making possible a *contrast* with annals and chronicles. The feature he most emphasizes in this connection is their displaying "closure": a beginning-middle-end structure. By contrast, he says, chronicles simply terminate; and annals do not even record continuities capable of termination except in the sense of being structured by a continuous series of dates.

Why does White believe that closure opens an impassable gulf between the way the world—the human world—was, and the way narratives represent it? A consideration which he seems to think relevant is that no sequence of real events "actually comes to an end" (23), it following that "real events do not offer themselves as stories" (4). The way the objection is put, however, surely begs the question. It is true that the events which we might normally refer to collectively as the First World War do not come to an end in the sense that the end of the war is the end of the world; things go on happening. The point, however, is that none of these further happenings can be regarded as further events *of the war*. The sequence of events which it would make sense to regard as constitutive of the First World War *does* come to an end. Is that because to conceive events as First-World-War-constituting is to "impose" upon them (White's term) an interpretive concept which simply expresses the historian's "poetic" judgment? Are events rendered "imaginary" (again White's own term) by being brought under colligatory concepts which, like "First World War," ensure their being considered from a standpoint that takes account of their human meaning and value? Even if this were conceded, it could not be the point White really wants to make, since it would leave unsupported his contention that it is closure *as a formal feature of narration* that opens a hiatus between events as narrated and a real historical past. It would trace the problem for realism not to narratives' (necessary) form but to its (accidental) content. Some attention by White to beginning-middle-end structures in natural history might have been salutary in this connection, since he seems generally to assume that the study of nature is free from the problems supposedly raised for realism by the employment of narrative in *human* history. But more attention to some kinds of human history might also have been useful. A history of the bow and arrow as an implement of warfare, for example, or of the stagecoach as a means of transportation, would require closure as much as, say, a history of a revolution-turned-farce (White's example). It would be a good deal harder to discern the role of "poetic" judgment in its determination, however.

White's overdependence on rhetoric shows itself in many other ways: for example, in remarks he makes about the connection between narrative and politics. He does make it clear, in criticizing the "jejune" way narrative was rejected by *Annales* historians, that he doesn't think that writing narrative commits historians also to writing political history. Where *Annales* historians apparently envisaged a necessary connection between the two types of enterprise, White sees only an historical one. Yet he insists that narrative, as such, has a political function—that, by virtue of its very form, it is bound up with the support of *authority*. Indeed, he goes so far as to say at one point that narrative history "is, by its very nature, the representational practice best suited to the production of the 'law-abiding' citizen" (82), this apparently because it necessarily searches out continuity and wholeness in a subject matter. From an author who concedes that Marx, for example, wrote narrative history, neither the aim nor the actual effect of which was the encouragement of political and social quietism, this is surely a far-fetched judgment, which might have seemed less tempting if the question had been asked: "Continuity and wholeness of what?" But White does not always take the position that narrative is by its very nature conservative in the ordinary political sense of the term. He sometimes contends only that its aim is always to shore up some authority or other: in the case of professional history, perhaps only the authority of the discipline. Since he explicitly links the idea of the political with that of power, and even of force (58–59), he might easily be taken here as having in mind a literally coercive, professional use of narrative paradigms. In a concessive footnote, however, he observes that all this may be interpreted "metaphorically" (225). In the end, not much seems to be left of his stress upon narration as a political enterprise beyond the idea that typical historical narratives express, and thus may help to entrench, the systems of values (conservative or otherwise) held by those who construct them. Why it seemed necessary to make such heavy weather with the idea of "the politics of narrativity" in order finally to make such a widely accepted point is not easy to see.

White is to be admired for the breadth of his interest and for his willingness to range across diverse authors, traditions, and disciplines, driven, it seems, by a genuine belief that something of value may be learned from all of them. Not all those to whom he pays compliment in this way, however, will be satisfied with the use he makes of their work; and analytical philosophers of history, in particular, may well feel that, both on particular points of doctrine and in matters of philosophical technique, White does not always learn from them what they intended to teach. For

example, although he gives the impression of wishing to give due consideration to well-known analytical discussions of the logical structure of explanation in history, the view of such explanation which he generally incorporates without argument into his own broader theory of narrative understanding is the crudest version of the nomological theory. To cite a single instance, when he lists what he considers the chief structural features of narrativity, he includes "necessary connection" (6)—as if Morton White's conception of explanatory narrative as, ideally, the tracing of a causal chain had been the only paradigm of connectedness to emerge from four decades of dispute. Those familiar with recent analytical writings on narrative will also be puzzled by the friendliness shown by White towards a retrospective "narratological" (150) idea of causation, derived from Jameson, and discussed as if some such idea were an obvious product of the emphasis placed on hindsight by analytical narrativists like Danto and Mink. The idea of retrospective *significance* is easy enough to grasp, with its implication that the actual significance of a past event, and not just people's judgments about it, may change with the passage of time. But is White here suggesting that narrative historians should accept the idea of past causal relations similarly changing with time? If so, a good deal more needs to be said about how precisely such an idea can coherently be entertained.

The need for more extensive analysis may also be illustrated by White's claim that a narrative which really conveys understanding must show a story's ending to have been "immanent" (20) in its beginning. If all this means is that a narrative account may, from the outset, draw attention to a significance that events will attain with the passage of time, and which, by courtesy of hindsight, both narrator and reader may know in advance, no objection need be raised beyond impatience with a rather misleading mode of expression. But if it means that a fully satisfactory narrative must represent its beginning in such a way that its ending can be seen to follow from it necessarily, two senses in which an ending may be said to be "necessary" need to be clearly contrasted: that of causal inevitability, given certain antecedent conditions, and that of accomplished and therefore unchangeable fact (even if belonging to a future that is now past). Greater willingness to employ analytical modes of argument might also have discouraged White from claiming that the "ideological" nature of narrative history is to be discovered *both* by studying what historians have written and by analyzing the character of narrativity. For if its possessing such a nature is a conceptual truth of narratology, what room is there for asking whether it is an empirical fact?

What will give most of White's critics pause, however, is less what he says on such points of detail than the position he appears to take on the central issue of the book. He comes very close indeed to claiming that everything in an historical narrative that goes beyond sheer chronicle (or even, perhaps, beyond the mere statement of discrete facts) is somehow "invented" (ix) by the historian. In resisting such a view, there is no need to argue that, on the contrary, everything is "read off" past reality, veridical narrative simply recording what was originally perceived, as it was perceived, if not by the historian, then at least by the historical agents. Indeed, White himself would seem to concede more to historical realism than he should when, in contrasting full-blown narrative with mere chronicle, he sometimes allows that chronicle, unlike narrative, does convey what is or might have been perceived. Neither in chronicling nor in narrating, however, is it the historian's job to add something invented to something perceived; it is to *think about* something perceived with a view to discovering forms which it exemplifies. Since there is no analogue of this in the construction of fictional narrative, it is difficult to understand White's insistence that narrative history and fiction can no more be contrasted with respect to their content than they can with respect to their form (27).

In constantly emphasizing the supposedly poetic rather than factual nature of narrative emplotment in history, White seems to want to represent the historical imagination as free—as having "the facts" very much at its disposal. According to him, for example, "any given set of real events can be emplotted in a number of ways," no sequence of such events "is intrinsically tragic, comic, farcical, and so on" (44). As in previous writings, candor nevertheless forces him to admit that it may not be possible to emplot a given series of events in just any way at all. He even speaks at one point of the need for "testing" emplotments. Without a good deal more on what he thinks such testing would consist in, however, and a much more extensive analysis of narrative form itself than is offered in the present book, White is all too easily read as holding that historians can emplot the past pretty much as they like. They can have better or worse reasons for emplotting as they do, but since these, *ex hypothesi,* cannot be theoretical reasons, they must be practical, that is, "ideological," ones. What White offers in the end is a version of the pragmatic theory of history, the awful consequences of which he honestly, if somewhat chillingly, accepts in a remark he makes about a Zionist interpretation of the Holocaust. The truth of such an interpretation, he says, "consists in its effectiveness in justifying a wide range of current Israeli political policies." Such a reduction of history to the status of political propaganda ought surely to be resisted, no matter how worthy the cause ostensibly served. White's book, for all its many merits, offers too few resources for resisting it.

Dominick LaCapra (review date October 1988)

SOURCE: A review of *The Content of the Form,* in *American Historical Review,* Vol. 93, No. 4, October, 1988, pp. 1007–08.

[In the following review, LaCapra offers a positive assessment of The Content of the Form.*]*

The present book might be considered the third part of a trilogy whose two earlier installments were *Metahistory*

(1973) and *Tropics of Discourse* (1978). *Metahistory* took the form of a systematic treatise that laid down the principles for Hayden White's poetics of historiography. *Tropics of Discourse* was a collection of essays that played significant variations on those thematic principles. *The Content of the Form* is another collection of essays in which still further and at times more significant variations are in evidence.

The essay may be the best form with which to investigate the complex, controverted methodological and theoretical bases of historiography. In any case White is clearly a master of this form. In the present collection he examines such important topics as the value of narrativity in the representation of reality, the role of narrative in contemporary historical theory, the political dimensions of historical interpretation, Johann Gustav Droysen's *Historik,* Michel Foucault's discursive style, Fredric Jameson's Marxist rehabilitation of narrative, Paul Ricoeur's metaphysics of narrativity, and the general issue of method and ideology in intellectual history. The essays, written over the last seven years, have all appeared elsewhere, but it is extremely valuable to have them assembled between the covers of one book. One hopes that a paperback edition will soon appear to make the book more available for use in courses.

Narrative is the obvious leitmotif of these essays, but it is complemented and supplemented by a strong concern for ideological and political dimensions of historical inquiry. White's role has been central in focusing attention on the problem of narrative in historiography and literary criticism, and he has provided one of the most influential and provocative theories of narrative in contemporary thought. It is impossible to do justice to the richness of White's reflections in a short review. I would simply indicate what would seem to be some significant developments or even departures with reference to his earlier views.

In partial contrast to his well-known earlier emphasis on the conditioning if not determining role of tropes, White's recent insistence on the axial role of ideology in the writing of history is especially prominent in his essay on Droysen, which is subtitled "Historical Writing as a Bourgeois Science." Somewhat ironically, White praises Droysen's *Historik* as being "unique among nineteenth-century tracts on historical thinking inasmuch as it openly embraces this ideological function as an aim or purpose" (p. 88). The ideological function in question, which "dominant social groups will . . . favor," is the fundamentally legitimating one of producing a reading subject who is imbued with the mentality of a "law-abiding" citizen. Thus, White focuses attention on the problem of the kind of reading subject a form of discourse may be argued to produce. Historiography—at least historiography of a conventional sort—is for White particularly adapted to the production of the "law-abiding" citizen "because in its featuring of narrativity as a favored institutional practice, it is especially well suited to the production of notions of continuity, wholeness, closure, and individuality that every 'civilized' society wishes to see itself as incarnating, against the chaos of a merely 'natural' way of life" (p. 87). When this ideological function becomes covert or is simply institutionalized in the operating assumptions of a profession, it becomes less open to question and more insidious than it was in Droysen. The obvious issue White leaves to his readers is that of the extent to which historiography in our own time embodies the ideological function that he has analyzed with the aid of Louis Althusser's conception of ideology as crucial in the production of a certain kind of society, particularly in and through the role of conventional narrative.

White's discussion of Ricoeur's recent work on narrative may be challenged as an interpretation of Ricoeur. But it is significant for what it indicates about mutations in White's own views. Earlier, White, in rather familiar "existential" terms, conceived of a sharp divide between "life" and "narrative" whereby life itself was considered to be intrinsically chaotic and meaningless while narrative was viewed as a purely fictive reconstruction that endowed life with meaning and value. The historical record was taken to be an unprocessed datum more or less analogous to life itself.

In his discussion of Ricoeur, White emphasizes precisely what diverges from the conception of the relation between life and narrative White himself at one time espoused, and by implication he indicates the general but differential role of ideology as a mediating force. Now narrative codes, which are in White's conception favored conduits for ideology, are seen to be common to both life and discourse, and "actions are in effect lived narrativizations" (p. 54). A focus of attention is "transcoding," a process whereby overdetermined complexities are introduced into a specific text or artifact. Conversely, a chronicle, which may seem to be close to a mere reflection of the unprocessed documentary record, is itself a product of representational procedures that are now argued to be protonarrative in nature. Hence, White tends to stress the continuity between elements that he earlier saw in terms of a sharp dichotomy. He also becomes more nuanced and more urgent in stressing the role of ideological forces in the way we represent the past. Particularly forceful (and controversial) is **"The Politics of Historical Interpretation,"** in which he treats the problem of representations of the Holocaust in terms of the role of ideological or political constraints and commitments.

One may argue with certain of White's emphases and specific interpretations. But he has clearly made significant advances in laying a foundation for a better understanding of the intricate interaction between narrative representation and what it purports to represent in both history and literature. Although he may at times both exaggerate the role of the narrative imagination in history and underemphasize the way certain approaches to narrative may contest as well as convey ideologies, White has enabled us to appreciate better not only the significant place narrative indeed has but also the broader network of ideological forces in which it is implicated. More generally, he has helped raise historiography to a point where it may enter more fully as a critical "voice" in the contemporary debate over discursive and interpretive issues of interdisciplinary importance.

Brook Thomas (review date Winter 1989)

SOURCE: "Narrative Questions," in *Novel: A Forum on Fiction,* Vol. 22, No. 2, Winter, 1989, pp. 247–49.

[*In the following review of* The Content of the Form, *Thomas finds shortcomings in White's rhetorical style and habit of positing significant questions that he has not fully resolved and cannot adequately answer.*]

Although a historian, or perhaps because he is a historian, Hayden White has gained authority with literary critics, especially students of the novel, because his explorations into the relationship between narrative and historical representation have forced them to reconsider traditionally accepted distinctions between literary and historical discourse. Indeed, his work has been most consistently praised for its capacity to force historians and literary scholars alike to consider important questions. *The Content of the Form* is topical in that it touches on many prominent questions that shape current critical squabbles. The book consists of eight essays, four on specific topics and four on individuals, three contemporary figures (Foucault, Jameson, and Ricoeur) and the nineteenth-century historian Johann Gustav Droysen. White's main concern remains narrative and historical representation, but he also takes up questions about the politics of interpretation, questions about what constitutes a classic in intellectual history, and questions about the relation between text and context. The questions he raises about historiography should speak not only to historians but to those intent on rewriting literary history by making them more self-conscious about their own narrative strategies.

Questions abound in White's work. His answers, unfortunately, are not as satisfactory as we would expect from a scholar with his reputation. I'll focus on one example of interest to readers of *Novel.* In the essay on Droysen and **"The Politics of Historical Interpretation"** White provocatively combines a Foucauldian analysis of disciplines with a Barthean notion that realism supports bourgeois ideology in order to link the nineteenth-century's "disciplinization" of historical studies with the rise of realistic discourse. This occurs because "historical reflection is disciplined to understand history in such a way" that "it is removed from any connection with a visionary politics and consigned to a service that will always be antiutopian in nature" (73). Providing "nothing less than an explication of the theoretical principles of bourgeois ideology in its national-industrial phase" (86), Droysen's *Historik* offers a case study in "realist" ideology.

For Droysen, White argues, history becomes a science when it can produce a "realistic" representation of facts, realism being determined by the "criterion, not of truth, but of plausibility" (93). The realism produced by the disciplinization of history "promotes a feeling of satisfaction for 'things as they are' in any given 'present' by showing that whatever they are, they have their necessary reasons for being this way and not another" (98). White goes on to declare that "the authority of this model of discourse is surely what underlies the assertions made by a host of nineteenth-century realistic novelists, of which Balzac and Flaubert were foremost, that they were writing 'history' in their novels. It was the historical discourse that they emulated that made them 'realistic' in their own eyes" (101).

What, then, are we to make of White's argument in the same essay that "Art and literature become 'revolutionary' or at least socially threatening, not when they set forth specific doctrines of revolt or depict sympathetically revolutionary subjects, but precisely when they project—as Flaubert did in *Madame Bovary*—a reading subject alienated from the social system of which the prospective reader is a member" (87)? How can Flaubert be so "revolutionary" when he emulates realism, which according to White is a "writing activity" that engenders a "reading subject who will identify with the moral universe incarnated in 'the Law'" (86) of bourgeois society?

It is possible to explain this seeming contradiction, but not if one retains White's formalist assumptions that make an inevitable link between realism and bourgeois ideology. Further, White does not even seem aware of the potential contradiction he has raised. For instance, after summarizing Barthes' argument about realism's ideology, he concludes, "This seems plausible to me" (81), a statement that would seem to undercut itself given White's connection between realism and the criterion of plausibility.

But perhaps I am asking too much. Maybe all we can ask of a critic is that he raise important questions. Indeed, in the last essay of *Tropics of Discourse,* White distinguishes between Absurdist critics (Foucault, Barthes, Derrida) and Normal critics (most others). His final paragraph lists a series of questions and concludes, "The Absurdist critics ask these questions, and in asking them, put the Normal critics in the position of having to provide answers which they themselves cannot imagine." In *The Content of the Form,* the raising of questions becomes part of White's style. Three essays end with questions; three other with implied questions. The humility implied by this rhetoric of questioning is, however, at odds with another noticeable aspect of White's style—a rhetoric of finality. Relentlessly bombarded by "must," "only," "always," "never," I begin to suspect that all too often White's rhetoric of questioning is actually a device for presenting rhetorical questions. For instance, look at the use of "always" and "finally" in this concluding question: "Is it not possible that the question of narrative in any discussion of historical theory is always finally about the function of the imagination in the production of a specifically human truth" (57)?

I might be nit-picking by looking closely at White's style, but he invites such scrutiny. "No more vexed—and

mystifying—notion appears in the theory of historical writing than that of the historian's 'style'" (227, n. 19). The tension between White's styles of questioning and authoritarian assertion is, I think, a symptom of a historical dilemma facing critics today. On the one hand, we recognize and even celebrate "the death of the great 'master narratives'" (xi). On the other, we feel compelled to display our mastery over a field of knowledge, in White's case, a mastery over theories of narrative. This need to display mastery over the field of theory, which Paul de Man argued resists such mastery, too often produces awkward moments like the following. "For all of these [Levi-Strauss, Lacan, Althusser, Foucault]—as well as for Jacques Derrida and Julia Kristeva—history in general and narrativity specifically were *merely* representational practices by which society produced a human subject peculiarly adapted to the conditions of life in the modern *Rechtsstaat.* Their arguments on behalf of this view are too *complex* to be represented here, but . . ." (35; my emphasis except for *Rechtsstaat*).

If the need to assert mastery over the field of theory manifests itself in White's style, the fear of master narratives manifests itself in the form of the book. As is increasingly the case in the field of theory, White's book is a collection of essays. Rather than presenting a sustained elaboration of a central thesis as in *Metahistory,* White presents us with a variety of attempts to try out ideas. The tentative form of the essay allows White to suggest a number of provocative possibilities. The problem, however, has to do with the tentative nature of the collection as a whole, for it puts on display a critic trying out ideas before he has taken the proper time to integrate them with past assumptions. White's early work drew first upon Northrop Frye and then French semiotics. That influence, especially the latter, remains. As my citations indicate, he seems to share Barthes' almost anarchistic distrust of narrative. Frequently, we hear about narrative "imposing" a formal coherence on events that are represented as real. But in parts of *The Content of the Form* White has, belatedly, seriously engaged the competing tradition of phenomenological hermeneutics. He is especially taken with Ricoeur. If in one essay he finds Barthes' position "plausible," in another he declares that Ricoeur's "seems right to me" (183). Thus, creeping into White's discourse are phrases that challenge the notion that narrative is merely a code imposing form upon history that may be "meaningless 'in itself'" (82). Instead, White entertains the possibility that "It is the success of narrative in *revealing* the meaning, coherence, or significance of events that attests to the legitimacy of its practice in historiography" (54, my emphasis).

From my point of view, White's engagement with Ricoeur is welcome, and I recommend his essay on Ricoeur. What is not welcome is a collection of essays in which the tensions between White's earlier assumptions and what seem to be new ones are merely set before us rather than systematically pursued. My dissatisfaction is reinforced by White's attempt to define a classic in the last essay. Using

The Education of Henry Adams as an example, he relies on his earlier semiotic model to declare that for intellectual history a text is important insofar as it "fixes us directly before the process of meaning production" (209). So, whereas some critics have faulted *The Education*'s narrative gaps, its switching of codes, its hesitancies and duplicities, White argues that such "flaws" make it a classic by drawing attention to its own processes of meaning production and making "of these processes its own subject matter, its own 'content'" (211).

Developed this far, White's definition, which emphasizes the number of a text's codes and levels of encodation (42), reminds me of what a freshman composition student once told me. Having never been taught the notion of a thesis, she had been instructed that the best essay was one that packed in the most ideas. What is missing in White's definition is something to which Henry Adams paid great attention. Conscious of the impossibility of his task—to "mix narrative and didactic purpose and style"—Adams, nonetheless, believed that "the form is never arbitrary" and struggled to get the form of his *Education* right. That impossible struggle to find the proper form to weave together competing codes has evoked various labels in contemporary criticism. Paul de Man called it "rigor," Bakhtin the "artistic" rendering of heteroglossia. Without it, *The Content of the Form* has its share of codes, switching of codes, and gaps, but it will not, I think, despite suggestive moments, achieve classical status.

Richard H. King (review date April 1989)

SOURCE: A review of *The Content of the Form,* in *Journal of American Studies,* Vol. 23, No. 1, April, 1989, p. 180.

[*In the following review, King offers a positive assessment of* The Content of the Form.]

Over the last twenty years the philosophy of history has seen a radical shift in focus. No longer is the main point of contention whether history is a science; now it is whether and to what extent history and fiction are more alike than they are different from each other. The person most responsible for this is Hayden White, beginning with his magisterial *Metahistory* (1974) and continuing in his first collection of essays, *Tropics of Discourse* (1978).

The Content of the Form also collects essays written by White since the appearance of *Tropics* and it also takes as its concern the problem of history's relationship on the one hand to "reality" and on the other hand to "fictionality." But if not an entirely new departure, it represents a narrowing of focus and a fresh emphasis on White's part. Put succinctly, White has moved away from his elaborate and sometimes too schematic categorizations of tropes, plots, ideological positions and world-views and now emphasizes the act/fact of narrativity in history and implicitly all non-fiction. Secondly, his most powerful es-

says in *The Content of the Form* address the question of the political and social, i.e. ideological, implications of the act of constructing narratives altogether. Indeed, **"The Value of Narrativity in the Representation of Reality"** and **"The Politics of Historical Interpretation: Discipline and De-Sublimation"** are "masterful" in the genuine meaning of that term. They demand reading—and rereading—not because one agrees with everything White offers, but because he has a knack for asking the profoundly right question and raising the cogent issue.

Shorn of all qualification, White's position seems to be grounded in the following claims. First, contrary to Paul Ricoeur's work, to which White devotes a careful and respectful essay, White claims that we construct narratives *for* rather than finding them *in* events. Secondly, a given political and social order is maintained precisely by being narrativized. Indeed, it is from within a dominant narrative that we acquire the form of "individual" subjectivity needed to maintain that order. Narratives do not reflect reality so much as they establish the condition of its possibility. Finally, though less clearly, White seems to share what is ultimately a Romantic view that it is art rather than science or history that "instantiates the human capacity for imagining a better world"—a view congenial to followers of the Frankfurt School and in a strange way to the American New Critics as well.

White's work can be challenged on many points but this book confirms that it should not be ignored, particularly by historians.

Pamela McCallum (review date Summer 1989)

SOURCE: "Narrative and History," in *University of Toronto Quarterly,* Vol. 58, No. 4, Summer, 1989, pp. 538–39.

[*In the following review, McCallum offers a positive assessment of* The Content of the Form.]

No one who has read Hayden White's two previous books—*Metahistory: The Historical Imagination in Nineteenth-Century Europe* and *Tropics of Discourse*—can doubt his contribution to the reconceptualization of history. In *Metahistory* White drew on the formulations of narrative tropes in the literary theories of Northrop Frye and Kenneth Burke to examine the discursive strategies which underpinned a series of nineteenth-century histories by such divergent writers as Carlyle, Michelet, Marx, and Ranke. *Tropics of Discourse* expanded and extended these investigations into an engagement with the post-structuralist theories of Michel Foucault and Jacques Derrida. White's new book, *The Content of the Form: Narrative Discourse and Historical Representation,* brings together a number of essays which are generally thematized around the problem of narrativity in the writing of history. It both re-engages his previous work and takes up the ongoing debates about the status of historical discourse.

According to White, the study of historiographical narration is a particularly crucial area for investigation because the writing of history will inevitably generate tension or conflict between the imaginative coherence of the story-telling form and the disparate fragmentation of historical contingencies. 'It is here,' he comments, 'that our desire for the imaginary, the possible, must contest with the imperatives of the real, the actual.' Thus, for White, these tensions can be located in even such rudimentary forms of historical narration as *The Annals of St. Gall,* an account of the eighth century. To a modern reader the annalist's cryptic notions of a world of scarcity, floods, famine, wars—'Hard year and deficient in crops' is the entry for 710—seem hardly to comprise a narration of history. No connections are drawn, no explanations given, no characters delineated. However, in White's analysis, the coherence of the narrative inheres in the succession of dates: the list of the years, *anno domini,* designates, over and against the earthly world of deprivation, a time filled with the promise of Christ's second coming. The narrative which White discovers within *The Annals of St. Gall* is the conflict between the suffering of life on earth (the 'events' recorded by the annalist) and the promise of spiritual fulfilment (the 'desire' implied by *anno domini*).

Seen in this way, there can be no resolution between the narrative which the historian creates and the occurrences which are narrated. As White puts it in a striking formulation, 'this value attached to narrativity in the representation of real events arises out of a desire to have real events display the coherence, integrity, fullness and closure of an image of life that is and can only be imaginary.' The content, then, will always exist in, at best, an uneasy compromise with the form. Indeed, in White's view, the ideology of nineteenth-century historiography is to be situated in the refusal to acknowledge such a gap, in the claim that narrativity is implicit in both events and discourse. He therefore welcomes the increasing self-consciousness about the 'tissue of ambiguities and equivocations' in which history and its narration are inevitably entangled. *The Content of the Form* offers no solution but rather tries to think through the implications of the various discursive strategies presented by narratives of history.

One of the most suggestive and intriguing chapters of the book is White's analysis of Fredric Jameson's provocative study, *The Political Unconscious.* As he views it, Jameson's book (and, indeed, the whole of his *oeuvre*) is an attempt to restore to Marxism the utopian vision which had been gradually eroded by the pressures towards more 'scientific' and 'economistic' theories in the twentieth century. What *The Political Unconscious* emphasizes is the secret longing for a collective, transindividual moment which lies inscribed in the unconscious of narrative. In such a formulation, Jameson can be seen to articulate a contradiction between narrative and history that is strikingly similar to the tensions White describes in the opening chapters of *The Content of the Form*: narrative is a space in which human desire for a coherence or plenitude, for an imaginative resistance to the contingencies of his-

tory, can be constructed and represented. It may be that White's reading of Jameson places too much stress on the visionary, utopian dimension of his thought. For it seems to me that Jameson, like the annalist of St Gall, has always been all too aware of history's 'force of circumstance' which limits and restricts human desire. Still here, as elsewhere throughout *The Content of the Form,* White offers insightful reflections on the problems of narration and history. Those readers who are already familiar with his writings will welcome the opportunity to engage the essays presented here; others will find it a useful introduction to what is unquestionably a significant body of work in contemporary narrative theory.

Terry Engebretsen (review date Fall 1989)

SOURCE: A review of *The Content of the Form,* in *Southern Humanities Review,* Vol. XXIII, No. 4, Fall, 1989, pp. 377–79.

[*In the following positive review, Engebretsen summarizes White's theoretical analyses and assertions in* The Content of the Form.]

The eight essays in [*The Content of the Form*] will be familiar to White's readers, since all have appeared previously. Together, however, they provide more than a convenient collection of White's recent writing; they continue the argument developed in *Tropics of Discourse* and applied so successfully in *Metahistory* that history (and the human sciences generally) is thoroughly rhetorical. Rather than stylistic embellishment, the rhetorical code we employ is indistinguishable from our interpretation of events. But these essays focus the issues more particularly. The typologies of trope, emplotment, argument, and ideology from the earlier works here give way to the argument that "narrative, far from being merely a form of discourse that can be filled with different contents . . . already possesses a content prior to any given actualization of it in speech or writing." That prior content turns out to be ideological. White quotes Hegel approvingly on the connections between politics and nineteenth-century narrative history: "It is the state that first presents a subject matter that not only is *adapted* to the prose of history but involves the production of such history in the very progress of its own being." These essays illustrate the connection between narrative history and ideology—particularly nineteenth-century bourgeois ideology—and also examine the role of narrative and ideology in the work of three major contemporary theorists.

The first three essays in the collection demonstrate the political significance of narrative in the writing of history. **"The Value of Narrativity in the Representation of Reality"** examines the biases that have led modern historians to treat both annals and chronicles as deficient, pre-historical forms of historical writing because they fail to achieve narrativity. White argues that both annals and chronicles reflect radically different world views from the world view shaping nineteenth-century historiography. The reason historians have not detected the "plot" in the annals or chronicles is that neither form focuses on the growth and development of the state. In the annals the mysterious forces of nature, the droughts, the floods, the harvests, count for as much as foreign invasions and the deaths of princes. Only the orderly march of years gives the annals coherence, and only Christ's return at the end of time can provide closure for the annalist. The chronicles, in which events are given a clear plot, fail to provide narrative closure because they fail to provide a moral judgment on the events. Only narrative history, with the state as its reference point, gives narrative closure to the events.

Though earlier historical writing has been judged deficient in so far as it lacks narrativity, the status of narrative in contemporary historiography is by no means clear. In **"The Question of Narrative in Contemporary Historical Theory,"** White traces the outlines of the debate. Members of the *Annales* school reject narrative—seen as novelistic, dramatizing and, therefore, pre-scientific—for the "scientific" analysis of long-range political, demographic, and economic trends. Semiotic theorists see narrative as merely one code among a number of possible codes that might be deployed in a discourse. Analytical philosophers, especially Paul Ricoeur, have sought to establish the "epistemic" value of narrative. Questions about the role of narrative in historical studies may be, White notes, "about the function of imagination in the production of a specifically human truth." For White, narrative is a source of legitimate knowledge of the world.

But if narrative is a source of knowledge, it is not a neutral source. In **"The Politics of Historical Interpretation: Discipline and De-Sublimation,"** White demonstrates the specific ideological content of historical narrative and the role of narrative in allowing history to achieve the status of a discipline. The discipline of history arose to assess the claims of radical and reactionary ideologies by evaluating the philosophies of history that justified them. First, however, history had to separate from rhetoric since, as a branch of rhetoric, history could be made to bear any interpretation wit could devise. To effect this separation, historians imposed stylistic limitations on the imagination: the aesthetic of the sublime was excluded in favor of the aesthetic of the beautiful. Narrative eliminated the mysterious and the uncontrollable from history. Since, White argues, utopian ideologies of both the left and right require a sublime view of history, the disciplinization of history had already neutralized them; sublime interpretations appear unrealistic, and "realistic" interpretations are anti-utopian. Even Marxism, so far as it relies on an understandable, orderly philosophy of history, is no more utopian than its bourgeois counterpart.

Having clearly established the epistemological value and ideological content of the narrative form, White turns, in the next four essays, to theorists who confront the problem of narrative in history. The article on Droysen continues

the argument advanced in the previous essay by providing a careful analysis of the theory of historical practice Droysen offered in *Historik* (1858). Alone among the great nineteenth-century theorists, Droysen argued that historical writing not only constructed the historical record but also was shaped profoundly by present concerns. More important, Droysen's analysis of historical narrative led him to recognize that historical discourse served an ideological function, inserting "readers within the circle of moral conceptions" that impelled them "to affirm this circle of moral conceptions as the reality that they could offend only at the risk of their 'humanity.'"

For contemporary theorists whose political purposes are at odds with bourgeois values, the theory and practice of narrative history have once again become a problem. White begins his discussion of the problem of narrative in contemporary theory with an essay on Foucault. **"Foucault's Discourse"** provides a companion piece to White's earlier essay on Foucault, **"Foucault Decoded: Notes from Underground."** In that earlier essay, White analyzed Foucault's characterization of the four epistèmes. Each epistème can, White shows, be characterized by one dominant tropological strategy, and the development from the seventeenth century (a development characterized by a series of ruptures rather than by smooth progress) as a move from metaphor, through metonymy and synecdoche, to irony. In the essay included here, White analyzes the figurative strategy that characterizes Foucault's own discourse. Rather than emplotting his histories as conventional narratives, Foucault structures his discourse by catachresis. This analysis of Foucault's style is important for two reasons. First, the style is intimately related to the stories Foucault's histories present. Second, style is the only ground of authority that Foucault has not rejected, according to White.

"Getting Out of History: Jameson's Redemption of Narrative" demonstrates how Jameson's analysis of narrativity, together with the interpretative model he proposed in "On Interpretation," the introduction to *The Political Unconscious,* help to heal the split in Marxist theory between the scientific Marxists, whose goal is to explain history, and the visionary Marxists, whose concern is to transform the future. As scientific Marxism has gained the ascendancy, the utopian side of Marxism has been left to artists and critics. But scientific history can only illuminate the necessity that governs the present. Narrative returns to history its utopian and moral power by adding to mechanical causation another level of causation—the present as fulfillment of the potential of the past and as potential for future fulfillment. In addition, by relating events to the larger master narrative (in this case, the Marxist philosophy of history), narrative endows history with moral meaning as part of the struggle to wrest a realm of freedom from the realm of necessity. The breakdown of narrative, then, signals a culture's exhaustion, its attempt to repress politics. White admires Jameson's theory and his "strong" readings of texts charting the decline of the bourgeois world view, yet White questions Jameson's master narrative. The Marxist narrative provides a way into history (from false history to a true one). But the history Jameson recommends, and the return to politics it implies, may, White suggests, be outdated. Rather than returning to narrative history and politics, we may need to escape from them. Narrative history and classical, bourgeois politics are still intimately connected, and perhaps both need to be transcended.

The essays on major theorists culminate in White's essay on Paul Ricoeur's *Time and Narrative*. Ricoeur's "magisterial" work provides the first theory of historical narrative that takes into account the variety and complexity of narrative while providing a detailed argument for the epistemological value of narrative. For Ricoeur, narrative is a "true allegory" of temporality. Human intentionality causes individuals to strive to give their lives meaning by giving them the coherence of a plot, and the historian's narrative is meaningful because it mirrors the productive activity of human agents. In this respect it is different from fictional narrative which is the product of "imaginative freedom." But all narrative, both historical and fictional, reflects the human experience of temporality and symbolically suggests that the human experience of time is essentially tragic. Eventually, as his plan for the work demonstrates, Ricoeur will go on to argue that historical narrative provides an allegory of "deep temporality," our experience of the link between death and eternity.

The collection's final essay can be seen as a practical application of the arguments developed earlier in the work, although this essay deals less explicitly than the others with the problems of narrative. In this essay White demonstrates how a semiotic reading of the codes and the code shifts within a text provides one way of handling the major methodological problems in intellectual history. Currently, intellectual history is beset by three interrelated theoretical problems: the breakdown of the text-context relationship, the breakdown of the distinction between the classic and the merely documentary text, and the breakdown of the distinction between the transparent and the ideological text. Using as an example *The Education of Henry Adams*, White suggests the ways a careful semiotic reading can illuminate the text and then argues that this careful semiotic analysis provides a response to the methodological problems he has outlined. The classic text continues to fascinate us because it shows clearly the human attempt to produce meaning. And by focusing on the use of semiotic codes and code shifts within the text's narrative, White argues that the historical and ideological contexts are made a part of the text.

Individually, the eight essays in this book offer much to the reader: analyses of major theorists like Jameson and Ricoeur, a perceptive reading of *The Education of Henry Adams*, and insights into the history of narrative in historical writing. Together they build a convincing argument that narrative history (as well as the rejection of narrative in historical writing) is ideological; the choice to emplot an historical account as a narrative becomes itself a

significant part of the content of the historical interpretation. Once again, White has convincingly demonstrated the connection between contemporary theory and historical practice, reminding his readers that the structure and style of the historian are not neutral vehicles for conveying an objective content. *The Content of the Form* makes an important contribution to contemporary historiography. Even readers unwilling to accept White's central argument should find this work well worth reading.

Ann Rigney (review date Fall 1991)

SOURCE: "Narrativity and Historical Representation," in *Poetics Today*, Vol. 12, No. 3, Fall, 1991, pp. 591–605.

[*In the following excerpt, Rigney examines questions of narrativity in* The Content of the Form *and concludes that White's historiographic interpretation does not sustain a persuasive argument.*]

In an exuberant passage written in 1966, Roland Barthes celebrated the universality of narrative (*le récit*). Narrative may be manifested in any number of different forms, he wrote, and may be communicated through any number of different media (film, painting, theatre), but it is to be found in every culture, at every period, in every place: "international, transhistorique, transculturel, le récit est là, comme la vie" (1977 [1966]: 8). The recognition that "narrative" is a cultural phenomenon extending far beyond the realm of literary genres opens up exciting prospects for narratological exploration. But the price of such narratological expansionism may be a corresponding difficulty in defining the specific object of study. If narrative is as pervasive as human life itself, then where does one draw the line between what belongs to the phenomenon "narrative" and what does not? . . .

Hayden White, author of *Metahistory,* 1973, and *Tropics of Discourse* (1978), is the theorist who has done more, perhaps, than anyone else within the English-speaking world to stimulate the *narrativist* recognition that historical representation, since it takes place through language, is always a semiotic activity and not merely a reproductive one (see Ankersmit 1986). With the Rankean myth as his principal opponent, he has argued forcefully and successfully that historical works are not mirrors held up to reality, but "verbal artifacts" which generate new meanings (White 1978: 122). A key figure bridging two disciplines, White has helped to open up history-writing as a field of discursive studies. At the same time, he has undoubtedly played an important role in what Berkhofer (1988) calls the "challenge of poetics to (normal) historical practice," contributing to the greater awareness shown by present-day historians of language's role in the writing of history and in the constitution of the primary record (see, e.g., LaCapra 1985; Struever 1985).

Central to White's approach to historical works as "verbal artifacts" is his controversial claim in *Metahistory* that historical interpretation is always "tropologically" grounded in one of the four principal tropes (metaphor, metonymy, synecdoche, or irony). But another important aspect of his approach is its concern with the semiotic function of narrative structures or, more precisely, of "modes of emplotment." White has argued that nineteenth-century historians, in representing chronologically related events, gave them the aspect of stories with beginnings, middles, and ends, and furthermore, shaped them into one of the four master plots which, according to Frye, are dominant in our literary culture (tragedy, comedy, romance, satire). It is this question of narrative form which has taken center stage in White's most recent collection of essays: *The Content of the Form: Narrative Discourse and Historical Representation.*

The eight essays making up this collection reflect the evolution in White's thinking over the past ten years and his response to theoretical developments in both historiography and literary studies. Some of the essays are reviews of particular works (e.g., Ricoeur's *Temps et récit,* 1983–85, or Jameson's *The Political Unconscious,* 1981); others take the form of a critical introduction to a particular theorist (e.g., Droysen or Foucault) or to a theoretical debate (**"The Question of Narrative in Contemporary Historical Theory"**); still others are original discussions of particular theoretical issues (**"The Value of Narrativity in the Representation of Reality"** and **"The Politics of Historical Interpretation"**). The dialogic form of many of the essays makes it difficult to disentangle White's own standpoint from that of the other theorists whose work he is considering, and not much has been done to streamline the different essays for republication in book form. As a result, it is difficult to outline a single argument or thesis in the book as a whole, and the reader is sometimes left to struggle with shifts of terminology and perspective.

But what undoubtedly links the different essays together is a recurring concern with the nature and, above all, the ideological *function* of narrative form in the representation of historical processes. As White explains in his preface, he starts from the fact that historical works are "semiological apparatuses" (p. x) and that narrative representation offers particular means for the production of meaning. He goes on to suggest, furthermore, that narrative offers a particularly effective means for the production of ideology; in other words, that when narrative is used in the writing of history, it is not only a way to produce meaning of a specifically social kind, but it also has a particular rhetorical force that guarantees the individual subject's acceptance of that meaning. It is this specifically ideological function of narrative which White sets out to investigate under the umbrella title, "the content of the form" (p. xi). Adapting Althusser's definition of ideology and invoking the authority of semiological theories of discourse (especially Kristeva's), White proposes that narrative is

> a particularly effective system of discursive meaning production by which individuals can be taught to live a distinctively "imaginary relation to their real conditions of existence," that is to say, an unreal but meaningful

relation to the social formations in which they are indentured to live out their lives and realize their destinies as social subjects.

> (P. x)

In thus proposing that there is a privileged link between the use of narrative in historical representation and the production of ideology, White places enormous weight on the "content of the form" of narrative communication. As initially formulated in the preface, then, his proposal raises a number of related questions to which the rest of the book could be expected to provide an answer: (1) How does narrative in general, and historical narrative in particular, function as a system of meaning production? (2) If narrative is a "particularly effective means" for the production of ideology, then *how* is this effect to be explained, that is, on the basis of its subject matter, the form of the content, the form of the representation, or a combination of all of these? (3) To what extent is this effect endemic to the use of narrative as such, or to what extent is it bound up with the application of narrative conventions to the representation of real events of collective significance? (4) Are all narrative histories necessarily effective in the same way or to the same extent? (5) If so, then what alternatives, if any, are open to historians?

Echoing a number of other theorists (notably, Mink 1978), White insists that events in themselves are "meaningless" and without structure, that they "do not offer themselves as stories" (p. 4) which naturally form coherent, temporal wholes with a beginning, middle, and end. Instead, he argues, the same set of events may be emplotted in any number of ways, depending on the repertoire of story types available to the historian (p. 44). If a partnership between "narrative" and "historiography" is inevitable, then, this cannot be due to the "story-like" nature of the events which are the historian's object; any such partnership would seem to spring from the conventions of historiographical discourse or from what White sees as our natural "impulse to narrate" (p. 1). Yet, if we have a natural impulse to narrate, the evidence presented by White also suggests that this narrative impulse has not always been exercised in relation to real events or put to the service of the historiographical function (a function which White, along with Ricoeur, seems to link to our making sense of temporality). For, in the opening essay, **"The Value of Narrativity in the Representation of Reality,"** some alternative modes for making sense of temporal experience are considered: namely, the annals and chronicles which preceded the development of modern narrative history ("history proper"). In the same essay and in the following one, White also briefly refers to certain modern historians and modern "annalists" who have looked for other alternatives and "refused narrative" (p. 2).

Although White thus seems to suggest that alternatives to narrative were possible in the past and are theoretically possible in the future, he is generally not very clear on the real nature of the choices open to the historian. And at least part of the problem lies in the uncertainty surrounding White's central category, "narrative." As White uses it, the term's meaning seems to range from the very general and inclusive to the very specific: from meaning production in general ("a refusal of narrative indicates an absence or refusal of meaning itself" [p. 2]), to the representation of a well-made story (see p. 24), to the representation of a well-made story emplotted according to one of the master plots or story types (see p. 44). The uncertainties surrounding the term "narrative" can perhaps best be illustrated by his treatment of those historians who "refused" narrative:

> Tocqueville, Burckhardt, Huizinga, and Braudel, to mention only the most notable masters of modern historiography, refused narrative in certain of their historiographical works, presumably on the assumption that the meaning of the events with which they wished to deal did not lend itself to representation in the narrative mode. They refused to tell a story about the past, or rather, they did not tell a story with well-marked beginning, middle, and end phases; they did not impose upon the processes that interested them the form that we normally associate with storytelling. While they certainly narrated their accounts of the reality that they perceived, or thought they perceived, to exist within or behind the evidence they had examined, they did not narrativize that reality, did not impose upon it the form of a story. And their example permits us to distinguish between a historical discourse that narrates and a discourse that narrativizes, between a discourse that openly adopts a perspective that looks out on the world and reports it and a discourse that feigns to make the world speak itself and speak itself as a story.
>
> (p. 2)

What are the defining boundaries of "narrative" here? Although Tocqueville et al. are introduced as examples of those who rejected "narrative," the actual object of their refusal—and hence the nature of narrative—becomes less and less clear in the subsequent elaboration of this idea. In refusing narrative, these historians refused "to tell a story" or, more specifically, to tell "a story with well-marked beginning, middle, and end." In fact, White goes on, they did "narrate," but they did not "narrativize"; that is to say, they did not feign "to make the world speak itself and speak itself as a story." The conclusion which this passage suggests to me is that if all historical representations are narratives, then some are more narrative than others; in other words, that the "narrativity" of certain texts might be conceived of in quantitative terms according to the degree to which they are dominated by those features considered typical of *fully formed* "narrativizing" narratives: a well-made story (i.e., a set of closely connected events forming a temporal whole with a well-marked beginning and end), presented as if "telling itself" without the mediation of a retrospective narrator. White himself, however, does not explicitly draw these conclusions, with the result that his discussion leaves those historical works which do not tend towards a maximum degree of narrativity hanging in a sort of theoretical limbo, between narrative and non-narrative. Leaving Tocqueville et al. on the periphery of his discussion, White's general consideration of historical representa-

tion is centered on the way historians have catered to our persistent desire to have real events seem to take the form of stories: "to have real events display the coherence, integrity, fullness, and closure of an image of life that is and can only be imaginary" (p. 24). This desire, he suggests, was institutionalized in the ideals of nineteenth-century professional historiography, where a maximum degree of narrativity came to function paradoxically as a sign of the realism of a representation and of the "discipline" of the historian; where narrative order served to reassure the public and distract it from the sublime contemplation of historical meaninglessness.

By insisting that events are in reality meaningless, White stimulates reflection on the means through which events can actually be invested with an imaginary coherence. How is the desire to have real events display coherence, integrity, and closure actually realized in the practice of representation? The coherence is "put there by narrative techniques," White writes (p. 21), pointing the way toward research into how those narrative techniques function in practice. (It would also be interesting to know the extent to which the choice of *topic* is important in this production of coherence.) White's argument further stimulates reflection on the question of whether real events can ever actually be invested with the same degree of developmental coherence that we are accustomed to find in the imaginary events of fictional narratives, at least of the traditional kind. White himself acknowledges the fact that the historian, unlike the fiction writer, is constrained by his claim to speak with the "authority of reality itself" (p. 20); yet his general treatment of narrative representation leaves one with the impression that the historian can quite freely impose his own structure on events, without much resistance either from the events themselves or from rival historians. At one point, he does make the interesting suggestion that historians "test" historical reality against the ability of traditional plot genres to give form to them (p. 44), but he does not elaborate on the way in which this "testing" is actually perceptible in the final communicative product or "semiological apparatus."

In practice, White's primary concerns are less with the specific discursive means through which real events are invested with coherence and meaning for a reader than with the ideological and rhetorical function of that coherence once it has been achieved or approximated. In addressing this topic, White takes into account not only the specificity of historical discourse as a representation of real (vs. imaginary) events, but also its socializing function as a representation of the collective heritage, however broadly or narrowly defined: "our history." His discussion of Droysen's *Historik* is of particular interest in this regard, in that it shows a nineteenth-century historian self-consciously reflecting on the socializing function of historical representation and its role in the education of citizens. That historical representation does fulfill an important socializing function has been recognized by other theorists (Lübbe 1979; De Certeau 1982: 23; Rüsen 1987: 89); the originality of White's contribution lies in his attempt to link this socializing function to the narrativity of the representation: more precisely, to what he sees as narrative's moralizing function and its rhetorical appeal.

Provocatively reinterpreting a traditional issue in historiography, White explains the emergence of "proper" narrative history from annals and chronicles not as a function of an increasingly complex awareness of time (Topolski 1987), or as a topological change (Scholes and Kellogg 1966: 210f.), but as a function of the development of both the modern state and the belief in the existence of a central collective subject with a continuous past, present, and future. But why should this ideological change have led to the adoption of *narrative*? In a leap-frogging argument (which he himself presents more as "an enabling presupposition" than as something verifiable or falsifiable [p. 13]), White suggests (a) that the choice of narrative form for the representation of collective history was motivated by the need to resolve disputes over authority within the state, since (b) it may be impossible to separate narrative from questions of legitimacy: "The reality that lends itself to narrative representation is the conflict between desire and the law. Where there is no rule of law, there can be neither a subject nor the kind of event that lends itself to narrative representation" (pp. 12–13).

This sweeping historical hypothesis implies a definition of narrative according to the nature of its story content (the conflict between desire and law) and not merely according to the form of its content (a coherent set of events with a beginning and an end). And it is on the basis of this story content that White goes on to propose that the desire to narrativize in history-writing stems from the desire to "moralize" reality, "that is, to identify it with the social system that is the source of any morality that we can imagine" (p. 14). The rhetorical *appeal* of narrativized/moralized reality is then explained by reference to its formal coherence and closure: we are willing to participate as social beings in a reality which seems so ordered.

All of this is highly suggestive, but also highly generalized and abstract, more thought provoking than actually persuasive. What precisely are we to understand, for example, by narrative "closure" and by the "moralization of reality"? To be sure, a historical narrative could close with the resolution of a conflict and the establishment of a new moral order; but a narrative "closure" might also signal the tragic *failure* of a particular moral order to come to power. And in that case, the narrative resolution could presumably lead to a sense of dissatisfaction with the actual course of events rather than to a willingness to participate in the "coherent" moral order which they established. In other words, White's "enabling presupposition" would need to be followed up by a more detailed consideration of the different possible relations of continuity and/or discontinuity between the *past* reality that is represented and the *present* social realities to which the historian's reading public belongs. A useful starting point here might be Jörn Rüsen's (1987) typology of historical narratives (traditional, exemplary, critical, genetical), classified according to the way they function in constituting latter-day social identities and in upholding *or* criticizing the existing order.

In considering the "appeal" of narrativity in historical representation, White refers almost exclusively to the imaginary coherence with which events are invested. This seems an overly formalistic approach—an impression reinforced by his assertion that a reader will have grasped the meaning of a historical narrative when s/he recognizes the genre to which its plot belongs (p. 43). Although coherence and approximation to literary models may indeed be appealing to the reader of a historical work, it would be interesting to consider other possible explanations for the rhetorical force of narrative representations. Narrativity, for example, may facilitate persuasion by encouraging a reader to suspend his or her critical disbelief in expectation of a story's outcome; or, if indeed narrative always involves a conflict between desire and law, it may also provoke the reader's empathy with particular actorial subjects. Turning away from the question of narrative form as such, it would also be interesting to consider the appeal of other aspects of historical representation—its aura of authenticity, for example. The fact that it focuses on the everyday life of "real-life" individuals is surely one of the reasons for the popular success of a work like *Montaillou,* where otherwise the story line is not very dominant and where the presence of the latter-day narrator is foregrounded (see Ankersmit 1989: 30–35; Bann 1981: 381–82).

The Content of the Form explores the seductions of narrativity for historians and their public and, in doing so, points to the social stakes involved in our understanding of the forms and functions of narrative. But, even more immediately, White's work points to the need to clarify the basic concepts on which such an understanding can be based. Do all representations of "sequences of nonrandomly connected events" involve the production of "well-made stories" or of "plots"? Do all plots involve a conflict between desire and law, or, to recall Scholes, do they involve issues of human value? Do all plots fit into one of four types? Or do all of the above simply represent features which are characteristic of fully formed narratives, but which may or may not be exploited in particular instances? If White is correct in attributing so much power to narrative, then it becomes all the more urgent to understand its particular semiotic mechanisms. In that way, we could also more clearly identify its limits and hence the nature of the choices open to the historian.

To write a history is necessarily to produce meaning: events may be meaningless, but a "meaningless" historical representation is a contradiction in terms. In their production of meaning, however, have historians no option but to feign "to make the world . . . speak itself as a story"? Although White explores the seductions of narrativity in historical representation, he is much less clear or assertive about the critical alternatives to it: his work is modelled on nineteenth-century historiography and tends to consider modern experiments negatively in terms of a refusal or a failure to narrativize reality. Yet, recent historiographical practices (and eighteenth-century ones) show that it is in fact possible to write histories with a lesser degree of narrativity, histories which may engage the critical faculties of the reader and not merely appeal to an uncritical desire for imaginary coherence.

References

Ankersmit, Frank R. "The Dilemma of Contemporary Anglo-Saxon Philosophy of History," *History and Theory,* 25 (1986): 1–27.

————. *The Reality Effect in the Writing of History: The Dynamics of Historiographical Topology* (Amsterdam: Koninklijke Nederlandse Akademie van Wetenschappen) 1989.

Bal, Mieke. *Narratology: Introduction to the Theory of Narrative,* translated by Christine van Boheemen (Toronto: University of Toronto Press) 1985.

Bann, Stephen. "Towards a Critical Historiography: Recent Works in Philosophy," *Philosophy* 56 (1981): 365–86.

Barthes, Roland, et al. "Introduction à l'analyse structurale des récits," in *Poétique du récit,* 7–57 (Paris: Seuil) 1977 [1966].

Berkhofer, Robert F. "The Challenge of Poetics to (Normal) Historical Practice," *Poetics Today* 9(2) (1988): 435–52.

Braudel, Fernand. *La Méditerranée et le monde méditerranéen à l'époque de Philippe II,* 2 vols. (Paris: Armand Colin) 1966 [1949].

Carbonell, Charles-Olivier. "Histoire narrative et histoire structurelle dans l'historiographie positiviste du XIXème siècle," *Histoire de l'historiographie* 10 (1986): 153–61.

Chatman, Seymour. "What Novels Can Do That Films Can't (and Vice Versa)," in *On Narrative,* edited by W. J. T. Mitchell, 117–36 (Chicago: University of Chicago Press) 1981.

De Certeau, Michel. "L'Histoire, science et fiction," in *La Philosophie de l'histoire et la pratique historienne d'aujourd'hui/Philosophy of History and Contemporary Historiography,* edited by David Carr et al., 19–39 (Ottawa: University of Ottawa Press) 1982.

Furet, François. *L'Atelier de l'histoire* (Paris: Flammarion) 1982.

Hobsbawm, Eric J. "The Revival of Narrative: Some Comments," *Past and Present* 86 (1980): 3–8.

Kellner, Hans. "Narrativity in History: Post-Structuralism and Since," *History and Theory* 26 (1987): 1–29.

Kocka, Jürgen, and Thomas Nipperdey, eds. *Theorie und Erzählung in der Geschichte.* Beiträge zur Historik, Band 3 (Munich: DTV) 1982.

Koselleck, Reinhart, and Wolf-Dieter Stempel, eds. *Geschichte-Ereignis und Erzählung.* Poetik und Hermeneutik 5 (Munich: Wilhelm Fink) 1973.

LaCapra, Dominick. *History and Criticism* (Ithaca: Cornell University Press) 1985.

Le Goff, Jacques. "After Annales: The Life as History," *Times Literary Supplement* (14–20 April 1989): 394–405.

Lübbe, Hermann. "Zur Identitätspräsentationsfunktion der Historie," in *Identität,* edited by O. Marquard and K. Stierle, 277–92. Poetik und Hermeneutik 8 (Munich: Wilhelm Fink) 1979.

Martin, Wallace. *Recent Theories of Narrative* (Ithaca: Cornell University Press) 1986.

Mink, Louis O. "Narrative Form as a Cognitive Instrument," in *The Writing of History: Literary Form and Historical Understanding,* edited by Robert Canary and Henry Kozicki, 129–49 (Madison: University of Wisconsin Press) 1978.

Orr, Linda. "The Revenge of Literature: A History of History," *New Literary History* 18(1) (1986): 1–22.

Prince, Gerald. *Narratology: The Form and Functioning of Narrative.* Janua Linguarum, Series Maior 108 (Amsterdam: Mouton) 1982.

Quandt, S., and H. Süssmuth, eds. *Historisches Erzählen: Formen and Funktionen* (Göttingen: Vandenhoeck and Ruprecht) 1982.

Reill, Peter Hanns. "Narration and Structure in Late Eighteenth-Century Historical Thought," *History and Theory* 25 (1986): 286–98.

Reizov, Boris. *L'Historiographie romantique française 1815–1830.* Authorized translation (Moscow: Editions en langues étrangères).

Ricoeur, Paul. *Temps et récit,* 3 vols. (Paris: Seuil) 1983–85.

Rimmon-Kenan, Shlomith. *Narrative Fiction: Contemporary Poetics* (London: Methuen) 1983.

Rüsen, Jörn. "Historical Narration: Foundation, Types, Reason," *History and Theory* 26 (1987): 87–97.

Scholes, Robert. "Language, Narrative, and Anti-Narrative," in *On Narrative,* edited by W. J. T. Mitchell, 200–208 (Chicago: University of Chicago Press) 1980.

————. *Semiotics and Interpretation* (New Haven: Yale University Press) 1982.

Scholes, Robert, and Robert Kellogg. *The Nature of Narrative* (Oxford: Oxford University Press) 1966.

Stone, Lawrence. "The Revival of Narrative: Reflections on a New Old History," *Past and Present* 85 (1979): 3–24.

Struever, Nancy. "Historical Discourse," in *Handbook of Discourse Analysis.* Vol. 1, edited by Teun van Dijk, 249–71 (London: Academic Press) 1985.

Toolan, Michael J. *Narrative: A Critical Linguistic Introduction* (London: Routledge) 1988.

Topolski, Jerzy. "Historical Narrative: Towards a Coherent Structure," *History and Theory* 26 (1987): 75–86.

Veyne, Paul. *Comment on écrit l'histoire: Essai d'épistémologie* (Paris: Seuil) 1971.

White, Hayden. *Tropics of Discourse: Essays in Cultural Criticism* (Baltimore: Johns Hopkins University Press) 1978.

L. B. Cebik (essay date Spring 1992)

SOURCE: "Fiction and History: A Common Core?," in *International Studies in Philosophy,* Vol. XXIV, No. 1, Spring, 1992, pp. 47–63

[*In the following essay, Cebik examines the philosophical basis for conflating historical writing and literary fiction, as suggested by White's theoretical model of historical discourse and typological schema.*]

In the last decade, a fad has swept across philosophic discussion of narrative discourse. In boldest terms, the fad consists of treating historical and fictional narrative on a par. Each has equal standing before the bar of human knowledge; each has equal if not identical epistemic standing.

The fad has many roots. Deconstruction's casual dismissal of the text releases every set of narrative sentences for subjective interpretation by the reader, making every act of reading one of artistic creation also. Ricoeur attempted to show the "precedence of our narrative understanding in the epistemological order" in his reconstruction of narrative into a metaphysics of time.[1] Whether or not he merely follows the leads of the structuralistic movement or responds to a longer standing impulse stemming from Bergson we may leave to another day's speculation.

The Indistinguishability of History and Fiction

In this country, the chief proponent of equating historical and fictional narrative has been Hayden White, the father of a significant school of vociferous offspring. Relying upon the same structuralistic heritage as Ricoeur and the deconstructionists, e.g., Jakobson, Halle, Levi-Strauss, and Lacan, White reaches in his own style the same result. This result has not been overtly intentional, since White has placed numerous disclaimers into his essays. In the *Metahistory,* White separates fiction from history via the inability to distinguish in fiction between chronicle and story, a fundamental distinction for White in history. Oddly, this distinction appears in merely a footnote.[2] In *Tropics of Discourse,* White elevates the distinction to a place in the text.[3]

Still, the basic thrust of White's efforts rests on a willful insistence upon treating the historical text as a literary artifact and as that alone.[4] He dismisses differences in a sentence, e.g., "I wish to grant at the outset that historical events differ from fictional events in the ways that it has been conventional to characterize their differences since Aristotle."[5] Having granted this much, White then proceeds to his main thesis, one underlying the earlier *Metahistory* and the later essays as well:

> Viewed simply as verbal artifacts histories and novels are indistinguishable from one another. We cannot easily distinguish between them on formal grounds unless we approach them with specific preconceptions about the kinds of truths that each is supposed to deal in. But the aim of the writer of a novel must be the same as that of a writer of a history. Both wish to provide a verbal image of "reality."[6]

This little passage contains a good bit of mischief. On the surface, we find a claim of total indistinguishability immediately qualified by a disclaimer that the distinction is simply not easily made. More significantly, we encounter seemingly illicit activities contained in trying to distinguish between novels and histories: namely, that we must approach them with certain preconceptions.

Disregarding for the moment White's view of the type of preconceptions with which we must approach histories and novels, we can surely ask whether the need to approach such narratives with preconceptions is illicit or inappropriate in any way. Bruce Waters long ago wrestled with similar questions, writing before the ascendancy of the structuralists and their jargon, but after the ascendancy of the positivists and their jargon. He concluded that "It is possible [by political and other means] completely to fictionize history," for example, to make Sartoris rather than Forrest the Confederate cavalry leader at Shiloh. "In history," wrote Waters, "we can never get beyond assent."[7] Therefore, to see history as in principle different from fiction is to come to history with something in mind: for Waters, a theory or philosophy of history, for White a preconception.

We may grant that both White and Waters have recognized the rapids of having both fiction and history in the mainstream of narrative discourse. Because they are indistinguishable as verbally and visually similar linguistic products, only our approach to a given product makes the difference between them. Indeed, it is not implausible to suggest that at root we do not discover that a work is fiction or that it is history; instead, we decide that question as we approach a work. A book's dust cover may in some cases prompt us. In other cases, we may scrutinize the contents and compare them with much that we learn from other sources. The decision is not arbitrary; neither is it always easy. However, a preponderance of evidence may compel a certain decision. The evidence that a work is history, however, is not identical with the evidence for the history it contains. In the former case, we are deciding between two categorizations for a narrative; in the latter, we are determining the truth or falseness of the history's statements (among other matters).

However we come to decide whether a work is history or fiction, we decide much more than a label. We decide in fact the entire cluster of questions we can pose to the narrative. Some questions we may ask of both fictional and historical narratives. Is it well written? What metaphors occur? Does the narrative hang together with proper connectives? Other questions befit one or the other but not both types of narratives. As Macdonald noted in the 60s, "nothing can count as evidence in favor of a fictional story. And what no fact can confirm none can disconfirm, either."[8] Therefore, confirmation of the events of the story is an illicit question to pose to fictional narratives, although it remains central to history. In contrast, we may ask whether the characters of a novel achieve verisimilitude, although the same question put to a history would likely only hide an ironic criticism.

Given this much alone, we are in a position to question the next step of White's argument, namely that we approach fictional and historical narratives with specific preconceptions about the kinds of truths in which each is supposed to deal. In *The Content of the Form,* White tried to do away with this part of his formula by transferring his focus from truth to reality. Real events "offered as the proper content of historical discourse" are real "not because they occurred but because, first, they were remembered and, second, they are capable of finding a place in a chronologically ordered sequence." Fiction, by contrast, has no chronology (or was not remembered) and is thus incapable of yielding both a chronological and a narrative version of the same set of events.[9]

This evasive maneuver, fueled by the time-worn appeal to a chronology and to memory, allows Waters' potential falsification of history to alter reality. However, the point has seeming weight only so far as we exclude the possibility of there being evidence for the occurrence of events, along with methods for the evaluation of evidence. To date, Collingwood has perhaps explicated best the relationship of questions, evidence, and answers.[10] Claims as to the reality of events are, of course, no more than claims to the effect that they occurred, claims requiring (upon demand or dispute) an array of acceptable evidence. Histories, therefore, necessarily deal in questions of truths, however difficult they may be to answer satisfactorily.

In contrast, fictional sentences necessarily presuppose truths, but not as questions.[11] Fictional sentences have sense just because they are instances of generalizations whose truth is not in question relative to the fictional text. Thus, for history it is correct to say that it should deal in truth, where "should" indicates that there is an activity to perform. We cannot say the same for fiction, for its relationship to truth is not an activity, in just the manner that presupposing is not an action, but a logical condition of action.

To be involved in or with truth is not at all the same as being involved in the production of "a verbal image of 'reality.'" In fact, it is questionable whether the writer of history or the writer of fiction can be correctly described as providing a verbal image at all, let alone one of reality. Certainly, it is hardly ever if at all the intention of either kind of writer to provide verbal images except as matters of style enter into their project. Either may say or think, one imagines, that a writer wishes to choose precisely the right words to create a vivid and unforgettable image of what they are presenting. But that is but one possible thought among many. Their respective projects are not limited by style or to style. White's description of creating a narrative would, by contrast, precisely limit both tasks to matters of style.

The history writer reports, records, interprets and argues, among other things. The story he tells, if he chooses to tell what he tells as a story, is not an image of reality; it is reality. In so far as we are dealing here not with an artifact, but with a human activity, the historian tells us not an image of what happened, but simply what happened. The fiction writer creates his characters and his story. Whether either constitutes a reality is one of the writer's options. Likewise, that we take his work as an image of reality—or of unreality—is one of our options as readers. We may argue with a historian. We may also willfully refuse to believe him or her. But we do not have such options with the fiction writer, even though he or she may write with varying degrees of believability. Moreover, a historian who writes what we take to be unbelievable is not a bad stylist or bad storyteller; he or she has said something we cannot accept as true.

Any accurate description, then, of either history or of fiction cannot survive solely at the level of the literary artifact. This conclusion does not deny any of the stylistic or rhetorical facets White has found in 19th century histories. Instead it affirms that these facets are just that: facets and not the entirety of the work. History cannot be taken as solely a literary artifact except as philosophy or metahistory may restrict themselves to ignorance. The ignorance is not merely whether certain historical facts, findings, and techniques are correct. There must also be ignorance of whether we may have history at all. Then, and only then, would it be the case that we merely tell stories, we merely narrate, and this just to impress at one or another level the hearer or reader.

Both history and fiction, as narratives in a world that recognizes both kinds, are complexes of activities that defy on pain of senseless distortion such restrictive description. As such, they require treatment as activities, not as a collection of literary artifacts. Perhaps the structuralist and post-structuralist turn of thought has failed to realize what other philosophical approaches to language have realized for decades: language is not everything, and language artifacts are even less.

THE PRECONCEPTUAL AND THE AESTHETIC

To take White to task so for his excesses would seem almost fatuous, for he is easy pickings in the stream of counterargument. After all, he is predominantly a historian and not a philosopher given to care in phrasing arguments. Excepting his influence, all this analysis would be otiose did it not reveal a worthier thesis to examine, one presupposed by the passage in question. If history and fiction as literary artifacts are indistinguishable, if they purport to present verbal images of "reality," and if they have equal epistemic status, why the reduction of history to fiction rather than an equivalent reduction of fiction to history?

White explained the direction of his choice in the Preface to *Metahistory* and has not changed his central view since:

> . . . I have been forced to postulate a deep level of consciousness on which a historical thinker chooses conceptual strategies by which to explain or represent his data. On this level, I believe, the historian performs an essentially *poetic* act, in which he *pre*figures the historical field and constitutes it as a domain upon which to bring to bear the specific theories he will use to explain "what is *really* happening" in it.

White expands this theme by noting that the prefigurative act is poetic because it is precognitive and precritical in the historian's consciousness, because it is constitutive of the structure of the emergent history, and because it is constitutive of the concepts used to identify objects and relationships.[12] The most interesting question here is where we may root the idea that such prefiguring is in fact a poetic act. The answer—or an answer—lies in White's adoption of a Nietzschean perspective.

Nietzsche is neither the ultimate nor the proximate source of White's poetization of narrative prefiguration. The idea grows throughout the 19th century, with roots in both German and English Romanticism. Closer to White, as he generously recounts in an extensive footnote, Jakobson, Benveniste, and others collapse distinctions that would leave poetry distinguished from other rhetorical modes of discourse under a unifying collection of "poetic tropes."[13] Neither ultimate nor proximate, Nietzsche nevertheless serves as a focal source. He enunciates a view which—as interpreted by White and others—captures the core of the thesis in question. If Nietzsche is wrong, then so too are his followers and successors who would subsume the epistemic under the artistic or aesthetic.

White's analysis of Nietzsche in the *Metahistory* indeed foretells much of his own perspective on history. White sees Nietzsche has having changed the linguistic rules of the historiographic game through a critique of its artistic component. The goal is for history to become once more an art.[14]

> To Nietzsche the form, meaning, and content of all science and all religion were aesthetic in origin, products of a human need to flee from reality into a dream, to *impose* order on experience in the absence of any substantive meaning or content. He held all "truths" to be perversions of the original aesthetic impulse . . .[15]

What is needed by Nietzsche, as filtered through the eyes of White, is an art aware of its metaphysical purpose, which is not to imitate nature, but to supplement it and overcome it.[16] Even the impulse behind philosophy is an aesthetic one; that is, it has its origins in the desire to impose form on the world.[17]

Where White draws a line distinguishing himself from Nietzsche is in the German's attempt to release aesthetic sensibility from morality and wed it to the will. Thereby, claims White, we turn "life itself away from that knowledge of the world without which it cannot produce anything of practical benefit to anyone."[18] Instead, White envisions historians freed to conceptualize history "in whatever modality of consciousness is most consistent with their own moral and aesthetic aspirations."[19] However, if the foundation of all constructs, including historical constructs, is aesthetic, then moral freedom and whimsy are indistinguishable. Moreover, if the motivation for dream creation is escape from reality, then all histories are rebellious or revolutionary in the senses developed by Camus in *The Rebel,* or they are mere fantasies. Despite these consequences, White views without variance the construction of prefiguring conceptual structures for historical narratives as sheerly aesthetic, poetic, artistic: a function of some deeper consciousness of the historian.

Calling the prefiguring of narrative structure a function of a deeper consciousness presents problems of its own. As literary artifacts, histories (and narrative fictions) have structures of event presentation and connection that we may say the narrative presupposes. But as earlier noted, presuppositions are logical conditions of making sense; they are not necessarily the product of conscious (or unconscious) effort. Only if, like Nietzsche, we view them as functions of will do we make them products of individual thought and activity. It is in this context that Nietzsche posed the following question: "Suppose we want truth: *why not rather* untruth? and uncertainty? even ignorance?"[20] From here it is an easy step to the declaration that "the falseness of a judgment is for us not necessarily an objection to a judgment. . . ."[21]

As a figure of speech, Nietzsche's counterpoise of "untruth" to "truth" might be interpreted as merely neutralizing the entire category of "truth" from applicability to foundational preconceptions. If this is all Nietzsche is after, then the point is unexceptionable. For Nietzsche to be wrong, we must take his remarks very literally, so literally that epistemic consequences flow from his remarks. White reads him just this way.

However, prefiguring or imposing form upon nature or history occurs at a level that logically precedes the actual investigation of nature or history. The level is indicated in the mode of criticism White applies to it: it results in benefit or detriment for humankind or human individuals. There are no methods of investigation, no possible evidence to tell us that a given formulation is true or false. If "truth" applies at all, it is at best in the Heideggerian sense of truths of Alethera, which have no opposition of falsity.

What Nietzsche—and Heidegger, for that matter—are wrestling with here is a way to formulate the notion of fundamental constructs that inform perception itself, let alone description and explanation. Depending upon whom one reads, we have greater or lesser freedom in creating these constructs. For the problem at hand, the philosophic difficulty stems from calling these constructs art. They are not fictions in the way that a novel about outer space or dragons is a fiction. They are not stories just to the degree they may be able to establish and limit the shape stories may have. They are not poetry just to the degree that they defy being set aside like poetry. They are not truth, untruth, or falseness just to the degree they may determine what propositions can possibly qualify as being true or false.

In short, preconceptual constructions of this order are and can be neither art nor nonart: they logically precede the distinction. Nietzsche's and White's importation of the language of art, the aesthetic, and rhetoric to this level of preconceptual construction is as misleading as Heidegger's attempt to preserve the language of truth within the same arena. Preconceptual constructions are neither truth nor untruth, neither fictions nor nonfictions. If in fact Nietzsche viewed them as art, then he was as trapped in his own metaphor as all those who have followed him, White included.

Dropping the terms "art," "aesthetic," and "poetry" from the category labels for preconceptual constructs carries with it the elision of innumerable implications drawn almost strictly from those terms. The reality-forming function of such constructs does not carry over into fictional narratives just because they also happen to be artistic fictions. The question of whether novels or other narrative fictions have any necessary reality-forming functions remains open to be settled on its own ground.

Likewise, the question of history's epistemic status remains its own and not tied to the fortunes of fictional narrative. It is neither prima facie true nor reflectively evident that "the aim of the writer of a novel must be the same as that of a writer of a history."[22] The respective aims of each type of writer may be—and usually are—as complex as the particular projects which engage them. All that remains true of both of them is that they employ narrative.

The ultimate confusion, common to White and Ricoeur, that produces a morass of misconception lies in thinking that all elements of narrative form are preconceptual constructions. Constructions many may be, but hardly preconceptual. What is preconceptual—or more correctly presupposed by any narrative construction—is narrative discourse and its requirements for simultaneous temporal and content relations built into sentential structures. To say this, however, is no more than to say that the logic of narrative discourse is presupposed by any actual narrative discourse.

In contrast, to the very extent that we can analyze narrative forms into rhetorical types—whether or not we agree

with White's particular list—we can also consciously and rationally choose the rhetorical form for our narrative. That possibility makes the selection of rhetorical form, if not purposive, at least functional.

Functionality subjects rhetorical form to criteria, not of truth, but of evaluation and judgment. We may evaluate a narrative form relative to its content as effective, adequate, complete, and cogent to any degree from negligibly to wholly so. We may judge narrative forms as good or bad, as right or wrong for us as individuals, as communities, as a people. What we can choose, evaluate, and judge according to function we can also teach others how to use. Choosing a narrative form, then, is not either preconceptual or aesthetic in the requisite sense precisely because it is functional and therefore can be purposive.

Indeed, White's Nietzsche can call the imposition of order aesthetic in origin only if he can postulate a prearticulate—and indeed, prenarrative—activity of conjuring informed worlds. Although Nietzsche's attempt to relate Homeric epic poetry to dreaming suggests that at least early on he may have believed such a view,[23] it explains virtually nothing in narrative literature. As Macdonald noted, "Like the content of dreams, the objects of fiction may presuppose, but do not compete with, those of ordinary life. Unlike those of dreams, however, they are deliberately contrived."[24] Not only may the objects of fiction be deliberately contrived, so too may be the rhetorical structures. Contrarily, the impulse to dream, to order reality in sleep pleasantly or otherwise, is not aesthetic. It simply is, if it is an impulse at all.[25]

More recently, White has tried to avoid the language he coined in *Metahistory*, opting instead to "dissolve the distinction between realistic and fictional discourses" by dropping ontological presumptions about their respective "referents." White now prefers to adhere to the body of semiological theory that encloses language within a "systematic substitution of signifieds (conceptual contents)," thereby yielding a "system of meaning production" so that individuals can live in an imaginary—an "unreal but meaningful"—relation to "their real conditions of existence."[26] No less self-contradictory than his earlier formulations—in this case, with respect to whatever may be real—White's new foundational statement simply transfers the problem of vacuous contrast to different terms.

First, it will not do to substitute "realistic" for "historical" in naming types of discourse, since the realistic is the feigned, and this label prejudices the case before any justification for the label begins. Second, and more significantly, terms like "imaginary" and "unreal" become as illicit as the term "aesthetic." A theory that eliminates any possible justification for calling something real equally loses reason for terming anything unreal. Likewise, without grounds for determining that something is nonimaginary, we cannot warrant any claim that something is imaginary. Meaningful relations "to social formations" generally require that we be able to sort out, however imperfectly, the erroneous from the correct, the real from the feigned, the natural from the imaginary. Thus, White's socialized individuals either live inherently meaningless lives or the terms of the theory carry nothing of their everyday content into their theoretic employment. At the theoretic or foundational level, activity is no more imaginary than it is aesthetic or poetic.

In the end, White's three reasons for labeling so-called prefigurative acts poetic turn out to be reasons for nothing at all. To the degree that such acts are preconceptual—constitutive of concepts used to identify objects and relationships—they can be neither conscious nor aesthetic, and to the degree they are aesthetic, they cannot be preconceptual. Even if some aspects of the imposition of rhetorical form are also constitutive of the emergent history, the process is one of overt selection and not precognitive constitution: it is a thoroughly conscious, functional, and often purposeful act. At this level, White's four quartets of historical rhetoric reduce to a simple heuristic typology, useful but devoid of profound theory.

THE STRUCTURE OF NARRATIVE THEORY

The fad of equating history and fiction as rhetorical and therefore artistic, poetic, or imaginative enterprises flounders upon the simple bad habit of tossing everything not susceptible of truth into the barrel of art and the barrenness of the aesthetic. That practice only gives art and the aesthetic a bad name, if not a like smell. The number of things and activities unrelated to truth is legion. Most are not art. Most are not metaphysical. Most are important, or at least interesting. Some are useful to boot. The rhetoric of narrative falls somewhere within the latter categories on this list.

Free of the bias to split our world into things susceptible of truth and those not susceptible of truth, we may take a quite different view of the various ways of looking at narrative. The following outline represents one sort of prolegomena to future narrative theory. It is not the only sort; rather, this particular outline serves the present purpose of trying better to understand the role of the preconceptual and the presuppositional in several of the facets of narrative. To that end, we may employ the language of types, perhaps even of Weberian ideal types.

Initially, we may constitute fiction and history as two types along a continuum of types in a methodological typing of narratives. Within the methodological typing of narrative arise many of the considerations regarding truth that we have had occasion to note in reviewing White's conflation of the rhetorical and the epistemic. However, methodology includes many more problems: for example, the nature and justification of historical constructs and the nature and use of conceptual evidence in history and in fiction.[27] The huge range of historical constructs from the level of the assertion of the ordinary facts to the level of what Ankersmit calls *narratios* begs for a common methodological

language that transcends the simple idea of true statements and leans more toward Dewey's notion of warranted assertability.[28] Similarly, the question of "conceptual evidence," a phrase coined by Danto, is only partially concerned with the truth of our claims; it is equally, if not more significantly, concerned with the use of such evidence in both history and fiction.[29]

By treating paradigmatic history and paradigmatic fiction as types on a continuum, we achieve the ability to eliminate false methodological problems occasioned by mixed types. Historical fiction, such as *War and Peace*, and fictionalized history, such as *I, Claudius* have proper places on the continuum. We cannot view them merely as extensions of fiction on the simplistic grounds that they employ the findings of history and contribute nothing to the ongoing doing of history. Indeed, writing such an intermediate type of work may involve doing history as much as it involves the creation of a fiction. Only a superiority complex that might deny merit to the contributions made by amateur and local historians would also deny the label of doing history to certain activities of those we call novelists. Methodologically, such disputes are irrelevant.

As noted earlier, the methodological distinction between history and fiction consists in the collection of sensible questions we may bring to the work—either as an activity in which we are engaged or as a product which we read. Collingwood noticed that, although we may raise questions about certain questions in the course of questioning (relative presuppositions), questioning others (absolute presuppositions) ends the inquiry by putting its sense in jeopardy.[30] The decision to treat a work as history or as fiction can be conscious and for reason, but relative to that decision, the collection of questions constituting historical and literary inquiries is presupposed as one condition of making the decision sensible, as an absolute presupposition of the decision. Only in the process of actual inquiry may we sensibly question the questions we put to history or to fiction, for only then have we the possible means of answering them in terms of better questions for which we can have evidence. We still have far to go in sorting out the methodological presuppositions of narrative.

One advantage of calling this typology methodological rather than epistemic is that the label places questions of truth and knowledge within the framework of the activities that go into producing historical and fictional narratives. Giving priority to questions of truth and knowledge, on the other hand, has often bent the practices of both history and fiction to the requirements of a preset theory. Thus arose the unnecessary concerns for history's inability to meet correspondence requirements for truth and equally otiose concerns that somehow fictional narrative might be a form of lying. Many such spurious anxieties disappear when one gives priority to the nature of the activity.

We may also typologically distinguish argumentative forms of narrative or arguments within narrative, as most notably did Dray.[31] The argumentative typology treats the narrative as a vehicle of explanation. Dray inherited the attempt to transform all written history into disguised or overt attempts to explain why events occurred by subsuming them under general laws, however loosely or probabilistically they might be formulated. His rejoinder, often misinterpreted as an anti-covering-law bias, was to expand the number of types of explanations making use of the narrative form.

Among Dray's types were explanations showing the rationale of actions, explanations showing how events could have occurred contrary to first appearance, and explanations of what events were or amounted to as an exercise in "colligation." Passmore expanded the list of explanatory types—at least for "everyday life"—and argued that such explanatory types occurred in history more usually than covering law explanations.[32] The function of an explanation, on Passmore's ordinary language account, is to clear up a puzzlement. An explanation can only occur, therefore, if a puzzlement—a question of a certain order—preexists the account, and the account succeeds if the puzzlement disappears. The type of explanation required corresponds to the nature of the puzzlement involved.

At first sight, any explanatory typology seems fit only for historical narratives. First, as Collingwood and many others have noted, history begins with questions—at least one, but usually more. History answers questions—puzzlements, if one likes—by adducing evidence from among the relics of the past. Second, the requisite puzzlement presumes logically that one already knows something of what happened, enough to raise the puzzle in the first place. Indeed, philosophical questions concerning explanation have largely focused upon the presuppositions of historical explanations and the situations that call for an explanation of one sort or another.

First sight yields an illusion. Historical narrative is not the narrative of historians, but any narrative utilizing the methods of question, evidence, and answer to settle puzzlements. When a Sidney Sheldon apprentices himself for three years to learn the life and ways of Italian sculptors in preparation for his novel on Michelangelo, his efforts constitute an explanatory investigation (within limitations of sculpting in the modern era) to answer the puzzle of what life would have been like for the Renaissance artist. How Sheldon presented his findings departs from the norm for historical writings, but then his work never pretended unto Library of Congress cataloging with history books.

Likewise, we may mistakenly treat mixed narratives as excessively historical. Many early readers of Malraux's *La condition humaine* treated the work as principally historical, down to the existence of his characters. Only later did we discover that Malraux's involvement in Chinese revolutionary movements in the 1920s did not extend to the details of the Shanghai insurrection: he had not even visited the city when he wrote the novel. The historicity of

a novel's details is open to questions for which evidence may permit an answer. Malraux's novel, so it turns out, was not a historical explanation for the insurrection's failure. Nonetheless it may well be an explanation of the mentalities of revolutionaries.

Besides showing the relevance of explanatory types throughout the methodological spectrum, the examples also demonstrate the distinction between typologies. Although there may be no absolute separation between the methodological and explanatory typologies, one may deal with explanatory types without necessarily addressing matters of methodology or of rhetoric. Moreover, truth is significant only within certain types of explanations: it fails to be a fundamental concern or presupposition of explanatory narrative in general. The criteria for explanations include accuracy, adequacy, and relevance; and truth is but a part of one of them (accuracy).[33] The consequences of the explanatory typology thus do not compete with those of methodology.

WHITE'S RHETORICAL TYPOLOGY

We may also, as did White, distinguish rhetorical types among narratives without ever invoking the distinction between history and fiction. We may overlook that distinction simply because the typology we are addressing is not methodological. As was the case with the explanatory typology, a rhetorical typology does not compete with the methodological.

White wishes to think, however, that the rhetorical typology competes with the explanatory. He characterizes emplotment, formal argument, and ideological implication as modes of "explanation." It turns out, nonetheless, that emplotment simply identifies "a story of a particular kind."[34] Argumentation consists not in actual modes of argumentation, but favoring certain sorts of narrative connectives among the many sorts to be found. Indeed, only White's mechanistic (cause-effect), organicist (teleological), and contextualist (colligatory) modes specify types of connectives. If no one type dominates over others, White calls the work "formist."[35] Dray and others have enumerated far more connectives than White envisions, and the formist catch-all cannot do justice to them.

Ideological implication, to the degree that it is ideological, also fails to meet the explanatory requirement of answering to a puzzlement. In fact, a narrative (or other piece of writing) becomes ideological only after any puzzles have been solved. White's own account of Marx's "grammar" illustrates the point unambiguously. If Marx had a puzzle about the nature of human existence, then—according to White—he solved it out of pieces that were not historical. Rather, they were elements of the human condition: "the impulse to satisfy needs," "the capacity to reproduce," and "the constitution of modes of production."[36] Only thereafter does White's Marx write his "histories" through these principles. His histories show these principles in action: the essence of ideological writing or, less kindly, propaganda.

None of these criticism invalidate White's categories as rhetorical types. They only reduce their scope from an overarching and all-encompassing theory of historical and fictional narrative to simply one among many typologies applicable to narrative. Whether the well-worn derivative quartet of category quartets provides the best set of ideal types for the analysis of rhetorical functions is open to question, just as are the types within the other typologies.

Without the excess baggage of preconceptual and precritical deep poetic consciousness at work, the rhetorical typology has some promise of showing what is presupposed by each identifiable type. Rhetoric's constitutive function of concept selection with respect to object identity and relationship characterization does not require appeal to poetry.[37] Instead, it requires attention—as noted earlier—to function, purpose, and achievement.

Moreover, not everything constitutive is either preconceptual or presuppositional. Some constitutive matters concern simply the formative rules of an enterprise.[38] Unlike formal games, such as baseball and chess, many human activities have no rule books. Nonetheless, we can explicate rules that govern activities, or as Rawls calls them, practices. Indeed, without the practice of baseball, one may throw a ball, run, etc., but one may not balk or steal a base.[39] The act of stealing a base or balking presupposes the rules that constitute the practice (or game) of baseball, but the game or practice does not presuppose a particular set of rules. To enter the game is to enter the rule-governed practice which, in part, gives sense to the very language within which we describe objects, events, and relations. Just as we may consciously and for reason decide to enter a game of baseball, so we may consciously and for reason enter into the task of creating a tragic, mechanistic, radical narrative (even if we do not know these particular type-words).

What gives the enterprise an air of unconscious (or deep conscious) choice is that on occasion, we may give this aspect of the work no thought at all. We just write our narrative and the result turns out to be tragic, mechanistic, and radical. No recourse to hidden consciousness is required by such situations. Such narratives may emerge because over the directions that each category represents, they are the only directions one has habitually used, that one has been taught, or that one knows. Alternatively, the subject matter itself might suggest them, or our theoretical commitments might dictate them.

In what sense, then, do the rules of rhetoric prefigure the resultant narrative? Were all narratives the consequence of active, rational, strategic decisions, then prefiguration would constitute a temporal term. Since they are not, White resorts to an appeal to the deep consciousness of the narrativist to perform a poetic act. Of course, no act at all is required (even if one may on occasion be performed because such an act is possible). Rather, the elements of prefiguration are no more than the rules presupposed by the nature of the particular type of narrative one writes,

that is, the rules regarding emplotment, preferred connective, and (if any) ideological implication. Whether we intend to write or have already written a narrative showing how past events led up to the present situation, the rules specify the use of narrative connectives such as "cause-effect," "forcing," "influencing," "prompting," "reacting to," and a host of others.[40]

To the degree that we can adduce and formulate the rules for making narratives with certain functions, we cannot classify such rules as preconceptual, but only as presupposed. The preconceptual indicates a level of formative operation that determines the logic of concepts and conceptions. To see with Marx the human being or human society as essentially economic alters what it is to be human and social. Any analysis of the change presumes (or discovers) a premarxian concept of what is human and what is social and also tracks the alterations necessitated by Marx's works (and by postmarxian writings as well). Such an analysis may be historical in the sense of tracing the significant changes in the ways in which we use these concepts and find them meaningful before and after Marx. Equally, such an analysis in the heat of debating Marx may also serve to provide reasons for favoring adoption or rejection of the proposed changes. Sometimes we make changes in concepts by working out the implications of proposals that do not seem initially conceptual, as in the continuing western social unrest that accompanies the development of what follows from declaring all men or humans to be equal. As well, we emplace such changes through convincing rhetoric, the sanction of "science," and the refusal to consider any other foundational principles, as did Marx in his writings and debates. 1989 events in China suggest that we may even enforce a narrative account by social *ad baculum* measures. To the degree that any such account may include conceptual proposals, an enforced proposal may revise the very way in which we conceive experience itself. Missionaries backed by soldiers showed remarkable success in making for some the inconceivable believable.

CONCLUSION

What emerges most clearly from this examination of narrativist fallacies is that, contrary to White, the prefiguring of a narrative is not a matter of deep consciousness or even unconsciousness. Nor is it necessarily a poetic act—nor even an act. Shaping a narrative may be simply (but not merely) the process of making strategic decisions about choosing the narrative form that will best accomplish the purpose of the narrative. Whether or not chosen, the very act of writing a narrative presupposes (within the rhetorical typology) rules of emplotment, connection, and implication. Except for cases of conceptual or conceptualization proposals, none of this activity need occur at a preconceptual level.

If anything, structuralist linguistics obscures the merits of the rhetorical typology by shifting attention to unnecessary special appeals. We gain nothing in appreciating the artistry of Michelet by subsuming all of history under the aesthetic. Perhaps we may even lose a good bit, as we confuse the power to convince readers alogically, i.e., rhetorically, with the aesthetic, which includes much that is mundane and not designed to convince. As with history, only the rarest of art has ever succeeded in altering the way that even some people see and experience the world.

Moreover, tropic theory and typology has and requires other than artistic or aesthetic grounds for determining the success of its ventures, especially in the realm of tracking the history of literary and historical styles. Nothing in linguistic theory can decide among the various typological foundations for portraying the sweep and shifts of style, foundations which include Jakobson's diadic metaphoric-metonymic poles, White's more kantian preference for quartets, or Brady's more hegelian triadic and dialectical scheme.[41] Independently of each other, White and Brady adopt their larger collections of basic tropes for their power to overcome anomalies of fit created by a mere dualism. Contrary to normal applications of fundamental theory, structuralist poetics and philosophy of history find that the successful fit of tropic categories with the facts of literary and historical style (respectively) provides the criteria for selecting and evaluating theoretic foundations.

In the end, one common core to history and to fiction, as they are often but not exclusively written, is narrative discourse. Without recourse to confusions between history and fiction, especially with respect to their epistemic status, the typologies suggested here largely correct some of the errors inherent in White's misentropic treatment of narrative's rhetoric. One fears, however, that fads of theory—like common colds—run their course in their own time. The best cure may not be therapy but patience.

Notes

1. Paul Ricoeur, *Time and Narrative,* Vol. 2, Chicago, Chicago University Press, 1985, p. 7. See White's appreciation of Ricoeur in his essay "The Metaphysics of Narrativity" in *The Content of the Form,* Baltimore, The Johns Hopkins University Press, 1987, pp. 169–184.

2. Hayden White, *Metahistory,* Baltimore, The Johns Hopkins University Press, 1973, p. 6.

3. Hayden White, *Tropics of Discourse,* Baltimore, The Johns Hopkins University Press, 1978, p. 82.

4. *Ibid.,* pp. 81–100.

5. *Ibid.,* p. 121.

6. *Ibid.,* p. 122.

7. Bruce Waters, "The Past and the Historical Past," *The Journal of Philosophy* 52, 1955, pp. 266–269.

8. Margaret Macdonald, "The Language of Fiction," in *Philosophy of Art and Aesthetics,* ed. F. Tillman and S. Cahn, New York, Harper & Row, Publishers, 1969, p. 622.

9. White, *The Content of the Form,* p. 20.

10. See my "Collingwood: Action, Re-enactment, and Evidence," *The Philosophical Forum,* 2, 1970, pp. 68–89, for a review of Collingwood's ruminations on questions, evidence, and answers in history.

11. See my *Fictional Narrative and Truth,* Lanham, MD, University Press of America, 1984, especially pp. 111–126.

12. White, *Metahistory,* p. x. See also White's more extensive remarks on pp. 30–31.

13. *Ibid.,* pp. 31–33, n. 13.

14. *Ibid.,* pp. 277 and 279.

15. *Ibid.,* p. 332.

16. *Ibid.,* p. 343.

17. *Ibid.,* p. 368.

18. *Ibid.,* p. 374.

19. *Ibid.,* p. 434.

20. Friedrich Nietzsche, *Beyond Good and Evil,* trans. W. Kaufmann, New York, Vintage Books, 1966, Paragraph 1.

21. *Ibid.,* Para. 4.

22. White, *Tropics of Discourse,* p. 122.

23. For example see Nietzsche's remark, "At this stage artistic urges are satisfied directly, on the one hand through the imagery of dreams. . . . ; on the other hand, through an ecstatic reality . . ." *The Birth of Tragedy,* trans. F. Golffing, Garden City, NY, Doubleday Anchor Books, 1956, p. 24.

24. Macdonald, "The Language of Fiction," p. 625. White's own attempt to deal with differences between everyday or historical treatments of objects and stories and of fictional counterparts is too weak to require noting within the text. He bases his remarks on the distinction between a historian "finding" stories and a fiction writer "inventing" stories. Then he notes how much "invention" plays a role in the historian's attempt to tell a story. If one begins with a silly distinction, such as that between finding and inventing, of course the result can get no further. *Metahistory,* pp. 6–7.

25. Curiously, for White's Nietzsche (although perhaps not Nietzsche's Nietzsche), the dream urge is functional ("a human need to flee from reality") and not free. And freedom from function remained to Nietzsche's day a prerequisite for the artistic and the aesthetic.

26. White, *The Content of the Form,* p. x.

27. For remarks on the former problem, see my "Understanding Narrative Theory," *History and Theory,* 25,

1986, pp. 65–70; and on the latter question, see *Fictional Narrative and Truth,* pp. 116–119.

28. See John Dewey, *Logic: The Theory of Inquiry,* New York, Henry Holt and Company, 1938, pp. 3–22.

29. Arthur Danto, *Analytical Philosophy of History,* Cambridge, The University Press, 1965), pp. 122–123.

30. R. G. Collingwood, *An Essay on Metaphysics,* Oxford, Clarendon Press, 1940, p. 31. See also my *Concepts, Events, and History,* Washington, D.C., The University Press of America, 1978, pp. 87–88.

31. See William Dray, *Laws and Explanation in History,* Oxford, Oxford University Press, 1957, especially Chapters V and VI, as well as Chapter 2 of his *Philosophy of History.* Englewood Cliffs, NJ, Prentice Hall, 1964, for a summary of his work to 1964. Note his remarks on explanatory and descriptive histories, pp. 29–32, and compare them to Frank Ankersmit's idea of a *narratio* in *Narrative Logic,* The Hague, Martinus Nijhoff, 1983. See also Dray's "Colligation Under Appropriate Conceptions" in *Substance and Form in History,* ed. L. Pompa and W. Dray, Edinburgh, University of Edinburgh Press, 1981, pp. 156–170.

32. John Passmore, "Explanations in Everyday Life, in Science, and in History," in *Studies in the Philosophy of History,* ed. G. Nadel, New York, Harper and Row, Publishers, 1965, pp. 17–18.

33. Michael Scriven, "Truisms as the Grounds for Historical Explanations," in *Theories of History,* ed. P. Gardiner, New York, The Free Press, 1959, p. 446. Accuracy involves many things in addition to truth.

34. *Metahistory,* p. 12.

35. *Ibid.,* pp. 14–21.

36. *Ibid.,* pp. 297–299.

37. *Ibid.,* p. 31.

38. The notion of constitutive rules, of course, owes to the work of Rawls, "Two Concepts of Rules," *The Philosophical Review,* 64 (1955), pp. 25–29) and Searle ("How to Derive 'Ought' from 'Is'," *The Philosophical Review,* 73 1964, pp. 55–56).

39. Rawls, "Two Concepts of Rules," p. 25.

40. Mercifully, the rhetoricians of history do not, as did the covering law theorists, try to reduce all narrative connections to causes and effects. Unmercifully, they subject us to the monotony of metonymy.

41. Compare the justifications for altering Jakobson's dualism in White, *Ibid.,* pp. 32–33 (plus the preceding pages devoted to quartets of differing levels of "explanatory affect.") and in Patrick Brady, *Structuralist Perspectives in Criticism of Fiction.* Berne, Peter Lang, 1978, pp. 105–106. Despite their interests in differing literatures and centuries, the explanation for differences between the White and Brady schemes lie elsewhere. Whether or not White's more synchronic orientation toward the 19th century as a sort of unit and Brady's diachronic interests in the movements within 18th century literature hold the key to their respective kantian and hegelian perspectives is beyond the scope of this essay to decide. However, it is of interest to note that Brady does not reject the Jakobson dualism for the purposes of criticizing individual works, but only for the sake of placing the Rococo (contra Durand) between Baroque Classicism and Romanticism in a temporal schema of "affirmation/negation/reversal." Compare *Ibid.,* pp. 100–101.

Wulf Kansteiner (essay date October 1993)

SOURCE: "Hayden White's Critique of the Writing of History," in *History and Theory,* Vol. 32, No. 3, October, 1993, pp. 273–95.

[*In the following essay, Kansteiner examines the development of White's theoretical perspective, methodology, and postulations in* Metahistory, Tropics of Discourse, *and* The Content of the Form, *while discussing the critical reception of White's work among historians and literary theorists.*]

I

Recently, in the pages of this journal, F. R. Ankersmit has developed a postmodernist perspective on the writing of history.[1] He argues that history always displays some postmodern characteristics because it is based on unsolvable paradoxes. Despite the claim to one single truth, historical writing only arises from the competition between different versions of the past which are simultaneously supported and called into question by "the other" within the same discipline. Ankersmit also holds that the traditional dichotomy of language versus reality has become untenable. Language has acquired the same opacity as objects in reality which themselves have become more and more language-like. Because of this convergence, historiography assumes a fundamentally aesthetic character based on the interplay between different codes "which nowhere intersect the domain of the past."[2] For Ankersmit, Hayden White is the foremost advocate and self-reflexive practitioner of postmodern historiography.

The enthusiasm with which critics like Ankersmit and Linda Hutcheon welcome the advent of postmodern historiography in White's writing has remained in stark contrast to the determined criticism his approach has received from many historians, most recently from Carlo Ginzburg.[3] Ginzburg argues that White's work suffers from a debilitating moral dilemma caused by the conflation of the categories of historical truth and political effectiveness. He holds that because of his relativist position White is forced to sanction any historical representation as truthful which legitimizes favored political positions regardless of its factual accuracy. For Ginzburg, White's arguments echo the ruthless pragmatics of fascist politics; they deprive him of any recourse to the rules of evidence as safeguards against distortions of the past, fascist or otherwise. Against White's methodological skepticism Ginzburg insists that the referential dimension of historiographical discourse can be brought under control through diligent textual criticism. "Evidence," he writes, "could be compared to a distorted glass." Therefore, "the analysis of its inherent distortions (the codes according to which it has been constructed and/or it must be perceived)" can yield an accurate historical reconstruction.[4]

To my mind both approaches miss the focal point of White's work. Ginzburg's fails to differentiate between moral and epistemological relativism, and it simplifies the complex processes which take part in the production of narrative history. At least in contemporary history there exists a considerable indeterminacy between different types of historical knowledge, a widely agreed upon repertoire of factual knowledge on the one hand and different narrative accounts written from incompatible theoretical and political positions on the other. But Ginzburg and others have pointed to an important practical problem which White cannot solve: How can we write history successfully, for example, effectively displace unwanted emplotments of the past, without recourse to the concept of historical truth?

Ankersmit, on the other hand, has mistakenly counted White among the postmodern critics. At least until recently White's has remained a structuralist project, the displacement of meaning from the level of referentiality to a level of secondary signification, in this case the underlying narrative structures of historical discourse. As a comparison, and especially in order to illustrate this last point, I will first analyze Barthes's critique of historical discourse. Subsequently, I will trace the development of Hayden White's theory of historical writing from the publication of *Metahistory* (1973) to the present.[5] In addition to a detailed critique I offer an outline of the reception of his work among historians and literary critics. Both groups have responded to and influenced White's interdisciplinary project. Finally, in the last part of the paper I focus on the question of the historiographical representation of Nazism which White has recently addressed and which allows clarification of some shortcomings in his approach.

II

In his essay "The Discourse of History" published in 1967, Barthes offers a structuralist critique of the representational strategies which sustain the illusion of a direct link between past reality and its historiographical representation.[6] Barthes argues that the transparency effect is primarily based on the absence of any signs of the author in the text. Thus the textual form appears to be immediately related to the extradiscursive referent. This impersonal style diverts attention from the limits of the specific textual perspective and produces the paradox that the historical fact which exists only as discourse is treated as a phenomenon of the nondiscursive domain of the real. For Barthes, historical narratives are merely imaginary elaborations, webs of signifiers and signifieds projected onto the referent, the structures of which move between the two possible extremes of metaphorical and metonymic style.[7]

On the basis of this critique Barthes urges us to rethink the relationship between fiction and history. Both forms of discourse are affected by what he termed on another occasion the "totalitarian ideology of the referent."[8] He strives to keep the discursive and non-discursive strictly apart and therefore welcomes a development in fiction which repositions the agent of writing and expands the discursive space at the expense of the illusory instance of realistic representation. He relates this form of what he calls "intransitive writing" to modernist fiction which has reintroduced the question of language as a literary topic and by implication exposed the illusions and conventions of historical writing.[9]

At the beginning of the 1970s Barthes radicalized his position with regard to the possibility of a systematic study of language. The turning point is commonly associated with the publication of *S/Z* which helped to undermine the structuralist project that Barthes himself had originally helped to define.[10] Barthes tries to show now that an analysis of literary and historiographical texts would reveal the multiple codes involved in their construction; each transcription, presented in the respective metalanguage of rhetoric, linguistics, hermeneutics, and so on, contains its own conceptual framework that enables and authorizes a specific approach. Thus any interpretation implies a process of infinite regress which, with each step, presents another discursive form but never pinpoints a final content (signified), let alone a distinct referent. Moreover, due to the reversal of conceptual content and discursive form with each translation, it is impossible consistently to differentiate between systems of form and systems of content.[11]

The poststructuralist turn in Barthes's thinking was superseded by a return to questions of the constitution of the subject and referentiality in language and photography in light of the earlier structuralist and poststructuralist approaches. In *The Pleasure of the Text* Barthes tries to think towards a materialist account of reading which privileges the body as an authentic resonance board of experience, discursive and non-discursive alike.[12] Finally, in photography he claims to have found a medium that at times dissolves the distance between the referent and the spectator, a form of writing encoded by nature that attests to the facticity of past objects.[13]

With one exception,[14] Barthes's name is surprisingly absent from *Metahistory*; indeed, in 1976 White criticized him among others for fetishizing the text and thus undermining all meaningful criticism. But since the beginning of the 1980s he has referred to Barthes favorably, especially in order to support and focus his own relativist critique of historical knowledge. For both critics the question of the referent comes to the forefront at a later point in their careers. But while Barthes in his later writings combines and juxtaposes different protocols of meaning production—referential, structuralist, and poststructuralist—White has consistently favored a structuralist approach emphasizing the primacy of secondary signification in historical writing. Only recently has he altered his method, arguing that the language of modernism and postmodernism has to be understood as a response to the events which characterize our century, in particular the extermination of the Jews of Europe.

III

In *Metahistory* White proposes a systematic study of the figurative aspects in historiographical writing in order to reveal the preconceptual layers of historical consciousness within the very structure of the historiographical text. He argues for the primacy of four distinct tropes of consciousness which are intrinsic to our language and guide the various stages of the historian's work, from the initial research to the final text. White characterizes these four modes of historical consciousness through the different figures of speech which organize the semantic dimensions of the respective tropes. Metaphor, metonymy, synecdoche, and irony represent the basic categories which predetermine the secondary, conceptual level of the historian's representational framework. On this secondary level White identifies three modes of explanation which are embodied in the narrative techniques, the formal argumentation, and the ethical position developed in historiographical discourse. Each of these subcategories tends to correlate with the underlying dominant trope of the respective work of history. Thus, White's analytical grid comprises sixteen positions on four levels which to his mind suffice to grasp the essential attributes of any given study and individual style.[15]

White uses this model to analyze the evolution of historiographical style. He assumes a cyclical development through the different tropes which successively fail to establish their exclusive claim to realistic representation. White argues that average academic writing stays within the parameters delineated by the respective dominant trope. He is most interested in the texts which exemplify the margin between two tropes, the classics of historiography and philosophy of history which prepare the shift from one dominant trope to the next and negotiate between diverging explanatory strategies and different concepts of reality.[16]

For White, the competitive relationship between different modes of representation attests to the non-scientific or proto-scientific nature of the discipline of history. Without a generally agreed upon linguistic protocol, historiography always generates a variety of mutually exclusive historical

accounts which appear equally plausible from a metahistorical perspective. He argues that there are no limits inherent to the historical record which reduce the interpretative choices of the historian for the interpretation of past events. Any such limits are strictly structural and heuristic.[17]

White's epistemological relativism collapses philosophy of history and historiography. They only differ in that the former highlights the underlying epistemological, aesthetic, or political principles which determine the generation of the text, whereas the latter displays them in the implicit structure of "realistic" narratives. Similarly, White converges fiction and historiography. Historiographic and fictitious events are rendered meaningful through the same representational strategies which insert the single event into an overarching narrative structure. Thus White strives to sever any link between the reality of past events and their semantic position within the historiographical text.[18]

Metahistory displays a strong didactic agenda. White hoped that in systematically mapping out all possible explanatory combinations, he would provide historians with a manual of tropology. Thus he could reveal the epistemological arbitrariness of any figurative preferences and make historians aware of their commitment to preconceptual prefigurations of their subject matter. He argued that on the basis of this insight they could rethink their representational choices in light of their political and aesthetic commitments. He also hoped that they would overcome the limitations of the ironic trope which dominates current historical writing.

IV

Historians, especially intellectual historians, occasionally praised White's case studies of nineteenth-century historiography and philosophy of history but in general they firmly rejected his methodology because of its relativist stance. In his work following *Metahistory,* in part published in *Tropics of Discourse,* White sought to answer and contain this criticism in two ways.[19] First, he emphasized the stability of the deep structures of human consciousness which suggest the possibility of developing a consistent and reliable representation not of reality itself but of the human mind's perspective on reality. Second, White tried rather unsuccessfully to argue a middle ground between the position of the "normal" historian and the more radical representatives of poststructuralist thought by incorporating the notion of historical proof into his theory of historical writing.

White's first strategy consists in relating his categories of historical consciousness to Freud's ideas about the mechanisms of dreamwork and Piaget's transformational patterns of conceptual thought. Thus, he plays with the idea of raising the theory of tropes to the level of an onto-genetic category which is reflected in the structure of language. Viewed from this perspective, tropology reveals the strategies at our disposal in any attempt to relate self to other problematical domains of experience. But White pulls back from a universal phenomenology. He wants this homology understood only as a convention in the discourse about consciousness. Unfortunately, he does not elaborate further on the historical dimension of this convention, and therefore we learn little about the epistemological status of this aggregate total vision of the world which could be developed once the transformational patterns between different tropes and paradigms have been found.[20]

As a second strategy to counter his critics White seeks to establish an epistemological middle ground which integrates the dichotomies of proof and figuration, fact and fiction. He allows that the data may resist representation in a given mode and therefore require a different tropological structure. He argues that the representational framework is simultaneously imposed and found in the historical record and consequently asks historians to abide by the rules of evidence and to abandon any metaphor which insufficiently reflects the data at hand.[21]

These arguments represent an important departure from White's position outlined in *Metahistory.* White seems to imply now that there are some correlations between the structure of the historical record—in its unprocessed or prefigured form—and the structure of historiographical discourse. But these ideas remain rather vague and in other passages of *Tropics of Discourse* White denies any such interdependence between the three conceptual levels he identifies (unprocessed material, chronicle, final account). He again insists that all tropes are equally suited or unsuited to represent the primary material which he consistently describes as unstructured and chaotic.[22]

At times these inconsistencies lead to obvious contradictions between the different texts collected in *Tropics of Discourse.* At one point White proposes the criterion of logical consistency to differentiate between good and bad historiography, while he simultaneously argues that the historian who stays within the same tropological framework through all explanatory levels of his discourse might be accurately termed a doctrinaire thinker who "'bends the facts' to fit a preconceived theory."[23] Moreover, White still acknowledges that the most interesting works of history negotiate between diverging tropological structures. These tensions might be best appreciated as deviations from the rules of logic.[24]

The shortcomings of White's attempt to establish a twofold methodology for the study and assessment of historical writing become most apparent when he discusses critics who share many of his presuppositions about the arbitrariness of the historical record and the importance of figurative aspects in scientific discourse, but who assume a more radical position with regard to the self-referentiality of language. In the essay on Foucault, and especially in the polemic about the "absurdist moment" in contemporary literary criticism, White develops a threefold matrix in which he positions himself halfway between the poststructuralists (represented by Foucault, Barthes, and Derrida) and the assumed position of the "normal" critic/historian.[25]

In White's view, the latter trust in an unproblematic relationship between reality and representation where language serves as a transparent medium to express the meaning inherent in any past or present facts. The perceived order in the world is reflected in the ordered system of language which evolves in direct dependence on changes in reality. White contrasts this naive position with the hypercritical perspective of poststructuralism which, in his mind, proves equally one-dimensional because it combines the assumption of an utterly meaningless existence with the belief in the total arbitrariness of any sign system. For White, this position reflects a fetishization of the text and is caused by a refusal to leave the text's surface in search for its underlying structures.[26]

White aims at a compromise between these two positions when he combines the presupposition of a manifest chaos in the primary material with the notion of stable and well-structured parameters of human consciousness as expressed in his theory of tropology. White finds the presumed opacity of language less troublesome because he trusts the relative stability of the tropological structures of consciousness. He argues that, on the one hand, we have to come to terms with an inexpungible element of relativity in every discursive field which has not reached a consensus about its legitimate representational techniques. But, on the other hand, any conceptual representation *qua* representation assumes one or several of the tropes as its guiding principle(s) which ensure the text's communicability and internal cohesion.[27]

But White's dissociation of reality and representation carries the radical implications of "absurdist" criticism. His insistence on the stability of the deep structures of human consciousness and his attempts to think through the notion of an independent faculty of perception which could help to differentiate between accurate and inaccurate histories remain too vague and inconsistent in the context of his radical critique of historical discourse. Thus, in the end it remains unclear which conceptual transformation introduces the inexpungible relativism into the final historical account. Should the tropes be considered as preconceptual figures of thought which already determine the initial processing of the material, or are they more adequately described as master concepts which only guide the writing process proper, the actual emplotting of the facts?[28]

While the essays presented in *Tropics of Discourse* do not present an integrated revision of White's original methodology, they introduce a new theme which has become an important aspect of his most recent work. White in part rejects consistently stylized histories because they fail to acknowledge the initial arbitrariness found on the level of the unprocessed data. Thus he introduces the notion of negative transparency which requires historians never to exclude completely undecidability from their writing, thereby attesting to the possibility of alternative emplotments.

V

The Content of the Form includes essays published between 1979 and 1985. The volume presents a twofold shift in White's theory. On the one hand he radicalizes his critique of the discipline of history and comes closer to the position of the poststructuralists whose "absurdist" stance he dismissed in *Tropics of Discourse.* White himself now regards language as "simply another among those things that populate the human world, but more specifically a *sign system,* that is, a code bearing no necessary, or 'motivated,' relation to that which it signifies."[29] On the other hand, he proposes a definition of the historical fact which establishes a marginal but well defined space for the procedures of factual evidence. Through this move White can combine two seemingly contradictory steps. On the level of narrative structure he undercuts any traditional epistemology. The selection and development of the representational code is in principle an arbitrary decision independent of the primary material at hand and in practice immediately dependent on the social context of text production. On the level of factual representation he integrates but at the same time marginalizes the concern of historians for independent epistemological categories according to which the factual accuracy of any given account can be measured.

The unresolved discussion about the relationship between the real and the imaginary which characterized *Tropics of Discourse* is now more clearly defined under the supremacy of the latter and put in more precise terminology. White differentiates between the primary and secondary referent of historical writing. The former refers to the past events, the latter to the vision of reality upheld by the conceptual repertoire which is used to incorporate the facts into meaningful narratives. He holds that questions of adequate and truthful representation between contending versions of the past can only be resolved on the level of the singular existential statement. But White points out that history proper only starts when the established facts are fabricated into full-scale narratives for purely presentist concerns.[30]

In the two essays **"The Politics of Historical Interpretation: Discipline and De-Sublimation"** and **"Droysen's *Historik*: Historical Writing as a Bourgeois Science,"** White formulates his most radical critique of historical discourse. First he describes the inherent conservatism of history. Since historiography claims to deal with the real its methods of representation legitimate a specific standard for the conceptualization of reality, past and present alike. Thus, White argues, historiography serves to project a type of subjectivity on the audience which accepts the formal structures of the text as the sole criterion of "the real" and almost by definition undercuts radical politics as unrealistic.[31]

White claims that historiography succeeds in constituting the subject in this specific moral and political position due to its supposedly intermediary, "uncanny" position between

the possible and the imaginary. Distinct from the "possible" which is the realm of science, and the "imaginary" which is the referent for art and literature, history deals in the "plausible," the verisimilar. The plausible, according to White, is the result of the conflict between the current social constraints expressed in the totality of the symbolic system of a given society on the one hand, and the imaginary, set into being by libido and instincts, on the other. Therefore, White argues, the "plausible" is in a sense more real for the individual than the truth of science because it relates its desires to the social context and offers a compromise which allows safe orientation and positioning. Thus, White concludes, historiography is empirical and speculative at the same time, but its ultimate referent remains the social practice of the citizen who negotiates his or her own position with regard to social authorities.[32]

In a second step, White historicizes and narrativizes his concept of history in his reflections on the origins of historiography as an academic discipline. He argues that the premodern version of historical studies viewed past reality as in principle chaotic and allowed all kinds of contradictory and mutually exclusive interpretations. History was subordinated to rhetoric and openly political or confessional. The professionalization of historical studies in the nineteenth century took the form of a narrow aestheticization for decidedly political ends. The philosophy of history brought forth by German idealism linked historical studies to the aesthetics of the beautiful and facilitated the conceptualization of history as an independent discipline. White argues that for the first time the past appeared *a priori* as a well-formed entity which could be revealed by the historian through the application of the rules of evidence. This domestication restricted history to the mode of the middle style and excluded all kinds of religious and irrational events from the historical sphere proper. The matters of the state became the reference point for history, thereby limiting the spectrum of potential facts. For White, only the deideologization of historical studies through the exclusion of the sublime transformed history into a discipline and an efficient political tool.[33]

Ultimately, White charges, the discipline of history as it developed in the nineteenth century was based on a dangerous misrepresentation, an untruth of projecting order where none is to be found. Therefore, he urges historians to recognize the sublimity of reality in order to induce a shift in emphasis from the factual basis of historiography to the conceptual and political implications of the structural format of representation.[34] But the paradigmatic shift from the control of the data as proof to the control of the conceptual strategies which White proposes could itself be considered a more efficient, self-reflexive suppression of the sublime, a further disciplinization of history based on an awareness of the responsibilities and potentials involved in the manipulation of the representational framework. In this respect, White's structuralism only projects the referential illusion onto the secondary level of signification, the structures of historical narratives.[35]

This aspect is very well demonstrated through the discrepancy between White's own style and his ideas about the characteristics of subversive writing. White holds that any discursive practice becomes potentially destabilizing with regard to the status quo not through its allegiance to doctrines of revolt but through the projection of a subject position which alienates the audience from identification with its social context. He points out that Foucault's aim of the reversed style which cancels itself in its articulation could be understood as an intensification of diegetic pleasure dissolving in the moment of gratification, a veritable return of the sublime.[36] Or to put it differently: the idea of the reversed style is based on the insight that in cases in which the structures of knowledge and language form the main concern of the text (primary referent), it is crucial to destabilize these assumptions through the mode of representation (secondary referent) in order to prevent an unproblematic resubjectification of the audience. This strategy destabilizes the very dichotomy of primary versus secondary referent, and practices a continuum of form and content instead. White himself stays within the limits of academic writing trying to delineate and fix a subject position within the parameters of narratology. In this he differs most distinctly from the theorists/practitioners of postmodernism who—as I have tried to show for Barthes—attempt to juxtapose a number of different epistemologies in such way that none of them appears as a privileged repository of the truth.

The different essays in *The Content of the Form* propose an intricate, threefold epistemology. On the level of the single event/fact White retains an element of positivist stability which stands in contrast to the epistemological arbitrariness that he posits on a second level, the level of the conceptual framework of the historical writing. But on a third level, a higher level of reflexivity, White introduces a new criterion for accuracy in historical writing, albeit in a negative form. He tends to be most appreciative of historians or theoreticians who acknowledge the chaos of the primary historical field and take this meaninglessness as a challenge to construct history in a politically and socially responsible fashion without completely erasing the traces of this construction in their texts. In this view too much transparency as to the chaotic nature of the past leads to the fallacy of deconstruction, the celebration of meaninglessness for its own sake, while too little skepticism about the possibility of referential certainty gives rise to the illusions of positivist historiography.

VI

In recent years White has focused more on narrativity in literature and on problems of literary criticism. This is in part a reaction to the increased interest his work has received among literary critics. White has responded to their criticism and tried to reformulate the relationship between fact and figuration as a continuous space framed by the two extremes of factual and fictional speech. In this context he has reconsidered the relationship between historical events and their representation. He argues that

literary modernism (exemplified in the writing of authors like Virginia Woolf and James Joyce) and its more recent counterpart postmodernism have to be understood as responses to and the source of the most truthful and accurate representational techniques for such typically modernist events as the Holocaust, the two World Wars, and other catastrophes of the twentieth century.[37]

But White's reconceptualization of the relationship of literal and figurative speech, referential and non-referential language, and factual and fictional prose which he now defines as "the poles of a linguistic continuum between which speech must move in the articulation of any discourse" sometimes runs into obvious contradictions.[38] While he reaffirms the argument that "convention may limit the range of types of plot structures deemed suitable for the representation of the types of events being dealt with,"[39] he argues at the same time "that the choice of a farcical style, for the representation of some kinds of historical events would constitute, not only a lapse in taste, but also a distortion of the truth about them."[40] Apparently, the relationship between event and story includes now an aspect of necessity which undermines White's earlier relativism.

In fact, White argues that modernist literature has thus far provided the only adequate representation of the particular modern experience of life through such stylistic innovations as the abandonment of one authoritative point of view, the recovery of the middle voice, and the general predominance of a tone of doubt and questioning. This new correlation between a historical period and its paradigmatic sense of representation has succeeded the earlier homology between nineteenth-century realism and its historical context. Therefore, White criticizes historians who adhere to anachronistic, nineteenth-century forms of representation and their subsequent failure to participate in the task of making sense of our contemporary experiences—which is the only help we can realistically expect from historians.[41]

Through his latest interventions White has repositioned himself within the poststructuralist context, albeit in an ambivalent way. He now rejects the arguments of Barthes, Sande Cohen, Julia Kristeva, and Jean-François Lyotard who have problematized the use of narrative for its inherent ideological and disintellective function. White argues for the redemption of narrative on the ground that narrative as much as language is a cultural universal whose truthfulness can only be assessed within its specific social context. "Therefore," he concludes, "it is absurd to suppose that, because a historical discourse is cast in the mode of narrative, it must be mythical, fictional, substantially imaginary or otherwise 'unrealistic' in what it tells us about the world."[42] This dissociation of historical and imaginary discourse, the very combination White used in *The Content of the Form* to characterize the middle style of historical writing, indicates a turning point in his thought. But while on the one hand defending narrative as a possible form of knowledge—and in this respect rejecting the postmodern critique—White argues on the other hand that the conventional historical narrative is an anachronistic form of knowledge: "It seems to me that the kinds of anti-narrative non-stories produced by literary modernism [and postmodernism] offer the only prospect for adequate representation of the kind of unnatural events that mark our era and distinguish it absolutely from all of the 'history' that has come before it."[43]

White's decision to introduce a more dialectical element into his structuralist methodology implies a renegotiation of the status of the fact with regard to the plot structures of the historical text. Once the strict separation of the two levels is canceled, his earlier radical epistemological relativism is undermined. The proposed continuum can be interpreted all the way towards the pole of factual accuracy. Thus the possibility of representational transparency, shown out the front door, returns through the back. When White reconceptualizes the relationship between text and reality as a multi-dimensional, processual unfolding under both discursive and non-discursive restrictions he reduces his control over his own subject matter, the structure of historical consciousness.

VII

The sometimes surprising developments in White's work have in part been a response to his critics. So a proper understanding of them requires examining responses to his thought. Roughly three groups have to be considered here: historians, intellectual historians and historiographers, and literary critics.

For the average historian White's name symbolizes the use of unnecessary theoretical jargon, a debilitating relativism, and the denial of evidence and the possibility of realistic representation in history. Historians have thus rarely taken notice of the development of White's thought, be it his defense against the charge of relativism, his radical structuralist critique of the 1980s, or his most recent attempts to introduce a more flexible terminology and to rethink the question of referentiality. A typical assessment of White from this side is the following from Lawrence Stone: "I agree in denouncing the appalling corruption of style in the writing of history by social science jargon and linguistic and grammatical obfuscation. I also agree that we should fight to preserve from the attacks by extreme relativists, from Hayden White to Derrida, the hard-won professional expertise in the study of evidence that was worked out in the late nineteenth century."[44] So historians have insisted on past reality as the first cause of their writing,[45] or argued in favor of the conception of historical truth as a collectively produced, intersubjectively valid epistemological category.[46] Moreover, they have maintained that historians do not deal with unprocessed historical data. In their mind the source material contains the narrative rationalization of past agents which represents one relevant version of the past and which through the hindsight and the questions of the historian can be rendered into a historically relevant and truthful account.[47] Philoso-

phers of history and Marxist critics have in general followed the historians' critique, albeit for different reasons. The former have insisted on the differences between history and philosophy of history,[48] while the latter have dismissed White's idealism, in their eyes presented in the ideological mode of academic liberal humanism.[49]

White has been most harshly criticized by historians and even former collaborators for his relativism, which critics have consistently interpreted as a combination of epistemological and moral relativism. Lionel Gossman has expressed this concern very succinctly: "I am now concerned that the current tendency to conflate 'historical' and 'fictional' narrative and the new emphasis on the 'poetics' of history . . . may be promoting a facile and irresponsible relativism which will leave many who espouse it defenseless before the most dangerous myths and ideologies, incapable of justifying any stand."[50] This reaction shows that White has struck a widely held, sensitive consensus about the political and social functions of historical writing: the task to render justice and to provide political orientation on the grounds of facticity. The charge of relativism has limited his practical influence among historians, and at times unified a fragmented discipline against White's critique. But it has also kept the interest in his work alive; in twenty years the "challenge of poetics to (normal) historical practice" has persisted.[51]

That few scholars have imitated White is in part to be explained by the characteristic of his approach. White's original and idiosyncratic methodology defies imitation.[52] The historians who have taken up his challenge, mostly in the fields of historiography and intellectual history, are among his most astute critics.[53] Three points of criticism stand out in this context. First is the claim that White has built his critique on some basic assumptions which he shares with "normal" historians but which he cannot take for granted. The traditional dichotomy of scientific versus non-scientific discourse which allows White to posit the non-scientificity and relativism of historical discourse has become questionable in light of the development in the history and sociology of science since Kuhn. Similar reservations have been brought forth regarding White's distinction between literal and figurative language. Second, critics have attacked the rigidity of White's formalism, emphasizing the plurality of forms in historical writing against his assumption of dominant tropes. They have insisted on the dynamic interaction between text and context, writer and audience to replace White's image of the historian who can independently choose his method once he is aware of the system of tropes. Last, they admonished in particular the lack of any historical dimension in White's analysis of narrative discourse.[54] In particular they have criticized the ahistoricity of placing tropology firmly in the realm of the "real," as a science of history which guarantees the stability of the discipline.[55] The disregard for the context of historical writing and its historical dimension has been attributed to White's adherence to the "imperialist criticism" of deconstruction which led him to reduce rhetoric to style and over-emphasize the self-referentiality of the text.[56]

Literary critics have found the same shortcomings in White's work as have the theoretically interested historians.[57] But here the application of his method has been more diverse and fruitful. White's tropology has been transformed into a phenomenology of tropes, first proposed by White himself in *Tropics of Discourse,* to improve its epistemological grounding.[58] Others have tried to reformulate narratology as a theory of communication to emphasize the historical and social context of narrative discourse which White had not sufficiently considered.[59] And even literary critics have criticized the relativist implications of White's thought, especially in the context of teaching literature and history.[60] But in general White's work has become an important theoretical reference point for them in questions of history and narrativity.[61]

We can now see more clearly the importance of the dialogue between White and his critics for the development of his thought. Its twists and turns can be understood in part as White's attempt to revise his approach in the light of the criticism it has received. Through the late 1970s White was still interested in a more substantial and productive debate with "normal" historians. Therefore he responded to their concerns about inadequate epistemological grounding and the relativistic implications of tropology. In addition, he sought to establish a method for the analysis of narrative history which remained independent of the predominant brands of discourse analysis in poststructuralism and deconstruction, as demanded by some of his colleagues in historiography and intellectual history. In the early 1980s White radicalized his critique and opened it to broader questions of narrativity, possibly because of historians' lack of interest and the growing responses from literary critics. These criticisms have in turn contributed to general concern about the difficulties of responding effectively to right-wing political challenges by means of structuralist, poststructuralist, or deconstructive reading techniques, especially because some critics have identified disturbing affinities between the representational tactics of right revisionism and postmodernism. So recently White has tried less successfully to integrate two opposing demands in the theoretical community, to develop a more flexible repertoire for the analysis of history which avoids the shortcomings of structuralism but at the same time does not offer any support to projects of historical revisionism. Through this effort White inadvertently destabilized his original critique of historical writing.

The close reading of White's work shows that he has still not found a repertoire for textual analysis which proceeds in a historically responsible way, that is, lives up to our concept of historical truth and satisfies our theoretical expectations. As Peter De Bolla put it, "We lack a technology of reading in the past, in, not against history, which would enable us to locate specifically historical textualities, and allow us to follow the transformation of discourses over time and between cultures and societies. The overwhelming tendency of the powerful presentist reading technology is to reduce all history to the present."[62]

VIII

The strength and weaknesses in White's approach reveal themselves with particular clarity in two essays he has written about the historiography of Nazism. In the first, **"The Politics of Historical Interpretation: Discipline and De-Sublimation,"** included in *The Content of the Form,* White proposes some provocative thoughts about the characteristics of the revisionist and the conventional versions of the National Socialist past, the relationship between the disciplinization of the historical consciousness in nineteenth-century historiography and the rise of fascist politics in the 1930s, and the correlation between his own philosophy of history and a fascist understanding thereof. White maneuvers very carefully on these grounds because he does not want to destabilize a political position which he in principle supports, although it might be based on illusory epistemological assumptions. The resulting arbitrariness in his terminology and arguments have at times obfuscated the issues and caused considerable misunderstanding.

Thus, White considers the revisionists' claim that the Holocaust never happened to be "as morally offensive as it is intellectually bewildering."[63] The latter judgment results from his endorsement of historiographical methodology on the microlevel of the single event. The former marks White's fundamental rejection of the revisionists' political ends. But his overall argument implies that the political danger of revisionism has been exaggerated. In trying to deny the facts of the "Final Solution," revisionists question the only aspect of historiography which deals with the actual past and is based on stable epistemological ground. But more importantly, since they limit their endeavor to the question of facticity, especially to an attempt to deny established facts, they fail to recognize the main purpose of historiography in that they take the pretenses of historians at face value. Revisionists remain marginal because the presentation of negative proof, however accurate or inaccurate it may be, always falls short of the meaningful narrative web which historians are expected to produce.[64]

At this stage, White attempts to keep the epistemology and ethics of representation clearly separated. For him, the ethics of representation are negotiated exclusively on the conceptual level and depend only on the intellectual and political context. But it follows from this that a Nazi version of the history of the "Final Solution" which acknowledges the facts would have under certain conditions (for example, a revival of Nazism) the same validity as our conventional histories about the topic today or the Zionist interpretation of the Holocaust in Israel, an example White himself refers to in *The Content of the Form.*[65] All of them would represent in their respective contexts morally responsible reactions to the meaninglessness of history not refutable on the grounds of any rules of evidence.

Finally, White speculates that the success and very existence of the volatile fascist ideologies of the twentieth century are at least in part to be explained through the disciplinization and covert politicization of historical consciousness in the last century. From his perspective the ideologies of fascist regimes appear as a backlash against the overly ambitious attempts to establish historiography as a bourgeois science in the powerful disguise of a value-free discipline. White finds himself in partial agreement with this fascist notion of history because he reads it as proof of the indeterminacy of the primary historical field and a recognition of the discontinuity between the ethical and epistemological dimension of historical consciousness. This implies that the real shortcoming of our desublimated historiography lies in its failure to take the political challenge of fascism seriously, inventing a version of the past which could be equally effective but morally responsible rather than vainly pretending to counteract fascism with representations of "the true past."

White's tragic account of the suppression of the sublime and the development of history as a discipline raises many questions which have remained highly controversial. How important are fascist ideologies for the success of fascism, and how significant is their notion of history for their ideology? What is the relationship between philosophers and philosophies, which have been utilized or implicated in fascism and the nature of fascist politics, especially the politics of extermination? But for our purposes it is more important that White never elaborates how to develop liberal counterhistories which refrain from utilizing the appeal of the real in their attempt to design a politically effective response to the historical vision of Nazism.

But White's interventions helped to expose the frail epistemological basis of the postwar consensus about the exceptionality of Nazism and its crimes in today's social context. Thus, he preempted the most recent developments in the historiography of the Nazi period in particular in Germany by redirecting our attention towards a more serious kind of revisionism which leaves the facts of the matter intact but repositions the phenomenon of Nazism and fascism within the overall history of the twentieth century. Ultimately, such revisions which were brought forth during the *Historikerstreit* may prove more damaging than a mere denial of National Socialist crimes. But even this conclusion needs further qualification. As Henry Rousso has recently shown in his study of the representation of Vichy and the German occupation in postwar France, the Faurisson affair occurred at a moment when Jewish memories of the war period resurfaced and French society was arguing about the recovery of such unpleasant facts and their position in the accounts of that past which would be handed down to the next generation.[66] Under these circumstances the differences between factual and theoretical claims, or in White's terms, primary and secondary referent, are more difficult to ascertain because the repressed facts and voices retain an immediate emotional and political value that will fade only with time. In such a historical moment a denial of the unpleasant past, including its very basic factual record, might indeed adversely affect the constitution of its history. At least for a short period the facts, their emplotment, and their political meaning seem inextricably linked.

The second essay in which White addresses the problem of a truthful representation of Nazism follows closely the methodological position outlined in White's 1989 essay on the relationship between literary theory and historical writing.[67] He repeats his assessment that historical representations display an inexpungible relativism because there is no necessary connection between the factual statements and the means of emplotment which are employed to craft the narrative. But he concludes that "[i]n the case of an emplotment of the events of the Third Reich in a 'comic' or 'pastoral' mode, we would be eminently justified in appealing to 'the facts' in order to dismiss it from the lists of 'competing narratives' of the Third Reich."[68] In light of the initial affirmation of his relativist position the apparent contradiction leaves the reader in a state of methodological uncertainty. One can interpret the term "the facts" in quotation marks as a reference to the current scholarly consensus which assumes the story form of tragedy inherent in the factual record of the Nazi period and therefore rejects any comic emplotment as improper in the sense of untruthful (or better, inappropriate). One could furthermore interpret White's move towards the referential pole within the earlier proposed continuum of figural and literal discourse as implicit support for the political and moral agenda in Holocaust studies. However, while this might please historians, it considerably weakens White's argument in favor of an inexpungible relativism in historical writing.

This revision is paralleled in White's return to the theme of a new type of discursive transparency manifest in the language of modernism. As we have seen, White assumes now that the representational framework has changed in response to events like the "Final Solution, total war, nuclear contamination, mass starvation and ecological suicide."[69]

IX

White's is one of few attempts to develop a phenomenology of historical thought and historical representation. It is equaled in scope only by Johann G. Droysen's *Historik* and Jörn Rüsen's *Grundzüge einer Historik* and shares with Nietzsche's *The Use and Abuse of History* the hope to lay the foundation for a new, creative, life-serving historiography.[70] In this White so far has had little success. Few historians have followed his appeal and even fewer have applied his methods. Among historians whose texts he has analyzed he has been most influential as a negative foil. These historians have considered his work the most tangible manifestation of a vaguely perceived postmodern challenge. White's insight into the narrative structures of historical discourse has only temporarily destabilized their professional self-image. For the theoretically inclined historians who have studied White as a representative of the new intellectual history and the literary critics who have been interested in his theory of narrativity, the methodology proposed in *Metahistory* soon appeared outdated. Both groups have grown more and more suspicious of any closed theoretical system and have preferred the more flexible and self-reflexive discursive modes of poststructuralism and deconstruction. As a result White has been widely read but has also been placed outside the narrowly defined parameters of the respective academic disciplines. The two most frequent criticisms of White's work—its relativism and formalism—mark the respective borders and illustrate White's peculiar position within American academe.

The different strategies that White has employed to counter the charges of relativism and formalism have been unsuccessful because they have destabilized his original critique without delineating any consistent new critical position. This applies to his attempts to graft the tropological system onto an ontological base and to incorporate the notion of a veto power of historical facts vis-à-vis certain emplotments. White is equally unconvincing when he argues for a correlation between modernist events and modernist representations and when he tries to introduce a more flexible dialectical element in his structuralist approach to the study of narrative. It is most remarkable, however, that these revisions and contradictions have gone unnoticed. For the most part White's work has been considered as a monolithic block, dismissed in its entirety. This also explains why there have been few productive debates about *Metahistory* since it was first published twenty years ago.

What is most clearly missing in White's work is a *systematic* revision of his critique of the writing of history in light of the criticism his approach has received since *Metahistory,* focusing especially on the modes of emplotment which characterize historical writing in the twentieth century. Thus far neither White nor his critics have been able convincingly to refute the argument that White developed most succinctly in his essay **"The Politics of Historical Interpretation: Discipline and De-Sublimation."** The narrative strategies which we employ to make sense of our past evolve independently of the established protocols for gaining and asserting historical facts. This circumstance applies to all historical representations but is most disturbing when considered in the context of the representation of Nazism.

Notes

1. F. R. Ankersmit, "Historiography and Postmodernism," *History and Theory* 28 (1989), 137–153; Perez Zagorin's critique and Ankersmit's reply in *History and Theory* 29 (1990), 263–296; compare to Peter De Bolla, "Disfiguring History," *Diacritics* (Winter 1986), 49–57.

2. Ankersmit, "Historiography and Postmodernism," 145. Ankersmit concludes his essay with the conciliatory statement "I am not saying that historical truth and reliability are of no importance or are even obstacles on the road to a more meaningful historiography" (152). This, however, is difficult to reconcile with the notion that the language of historiography never intersects with the past.

3. Linda Hutcheon, *A Poetics of Postmodernism: History, Theory, Fiction* (New York, 1988), 15, 96, 121, 143; F. R. Ankersmit, "The Dilemma of Contemporary Anglo-Saxon Philosophy of History" in *Knowing and Telling History: The Anglo-Saxon Debate* (*History and Theory* 25 [1986]), 1–27. Carlo Ginzburg, "Just One Witness" in *Probing the Limits of Representation: Nazism and the "Final Solution,"* ed. Saul Friedlander (Cambridge, Mass., 1992), 82–96.

4. Carlo Ginzburg, "Checking the Evidence: The Judge and the Historian," *Critical Inquiry* 18 (1991), 79–92, quote from 84.

5. Hayden White, *Metahistory: The Historical Imagination in Nineteenth-Century Europe* (Baltimore, 1973). For an analysis of White's earlier work in comparison to *Metahistory* and subsequent publications, see Hans Kellner, *Language and Historical Representation: Getting the Story Crooked* (Madison, Wisc., 1989), especially chapter 8, "A Bedrock of Order: Hayden White's Linguistic Humanism" (first published in *History and Theory* 19 [1980], 1–29); and Paul A. Roth, "Hayden White and the Aesthetics of Historiography," *History of the Human Sciences* 5 (1992), 17–35.

6. Roland Barthes, "The Discourse of History," in *Comparative Criticism* 3 (1981), 7–20. For a contextualization of "The Discourse of History" see Stephen Bann, "Introduction: Barthes' Discourse," *Comparative Criticism* 3 (1981), 3–6, and Geoff Bennington and Robert Young, "Introduction: Posing the Question," in *Post-structuralism and the Question of History,* ed. Derek Attridge, Goeff Bennington, and Robert Young (Cambridge, Eng., 1987), 1–11. For further discussion and application of Barthes's concepts see Stephen Bann, *The Inventions of History: Essays on the Representation of the Past* (Manchester, Eng., 1990), 40, 57–60.

7. In 1962 in "The Imagination of the Sign" included in *A Barthes Reader,* ed. Susan Sontag (New York, 1982), 211–217, Barthes had proposed a different, tripartite analysis of the sign. Here he differentiates between the internal relation between signifier and signified which he calls symbolic and the two external relations between the sign and its context, the paradigmatic and syntagmatic relations. For further discussion see James M. Mellard, *Doing Tropology: Analysis of Narrative Discourse* (Urbana, Ill., 1987), 4–6.

8. Roland Barthes, "To Write: An Intransitive Verb," in *The Rustle of Language* (New York, 1986), 11–21, essay first published in 1966.

9. *Ibid.,* 20.

10. *S/Z,* transl. Richard Miller [1970] (New York, 1974). *S/Z* has been read both as a structuralist and poststructuralist work of criticism; see Jonathan Culler,

Barthes, 2nd ed. (London, 1990), 88, and Mary Bittner Wiseman *The Ecstasies of Roland Barthes* (New York, 1989), 41, 95–97.

11. Roland Barthes, "Style and Its Image," in *Literary Style,* ed. Seymour Chatman (London, 1971), 3–10.

12. Roland Barthes, *The Pleasure of the Text* [1973] (New York, 1989).

13. White, *Metahistory,* 3, #4.

14. "Photography never lies: or rather, it can lie as to the meaning of things, being by nature tendentious, never as to its existence." Roland Barthes, *Camera Lucida: Reflections on Photography* [1980] (New York, 1991), 87.

15. Hayden White, *Metahistory,* 29. For a detailed discussion of White's grid see Kellner, *Language and Historical Representation,* 221–225, and David Konstan, "The Function of Narrative in Hayden White's *Metahistory,*" *Clio* 11 (1981), 65–78; for a comparative analysis of White's tropology see Wallace Martin, "Floating an Issue of Tropes," *Diacritics* 12 (1982), 75–83, esp. 77, and compare to Donald Ostrowski, "A Metahistorical Analysis: Hayden White and Four Narratives of Russian History," *Clio* 19 (1990), 215–236, esp. 236, and Robert F. Berkhofer, "The Challenge of Poetics to (Normal) Historical Practice," *Poetics Today* 9 (1988), 435–452. On White's terminology, in particular on "story" and "plot" see Paul Ricoeur, *Time and Narrative* (Chicago, 1984), I, 161–174 and compare to Hayden White, "The Structure of Historical Narrative," *Clio* 1 (1972), 5–20.

16. *Metahistory,* 432.

17. *Ibid.,* 4, 20, 26. Like Barthes, White uses the difference between chronicles and histories to support his argument. On the level of the chronicle, historians select different facts because they apply incompatible criteria to differentiate between relevant and irrelevant data. But only the second level of historical conceptualization, the casting of the events in proper stories, produces radical incompatibility because each event assumes a specific meaning through its position within the overall textual structure. Barthes, "The Discourse of History," 15; White, *Metahistory,* 5–7.

18. White, *Metahistory,* x, 427.

19. Hayden White, *Tropics of Discourse: Essays in Cultural Criticism* (Baltimore, 1978).

20. *Ibid.,* 6, 12–13, 19, 22, 117. See also White's arguments in favor of a general theory of language in literary criticism in "The Problem of Change in Literary History," *New Literary History* 7 (1975), 97–111, esp. 106.

21. Hayden White argues here for a "continuity between error and truth." *Tropics of Discourse,* 21; compare

to 1, 47, 97 and Hayden White, "Ethnological 'Lie' and Mythical 'Truth,'" *Diacritics* (Spring 1978), 2–9, esp. 8.

22. *Tropics of Discourse,* 84.

23. *Ibid.,* 129.

24. In a similar passage White seeks to separate historiography from propaganda and ideology, while his own objective to have historians decide on their representational techniques with regard to their aesthetic and political preferences might itself pass as an apt definition of propagandistic writing in the absence of clear standards of historical truth. *Tropics of Discourse,* 99.

25. Hayden White, "The Absurdist Moment in Contemporary Literary Theory," in *Tropics of Discourse,* 261–282.

26. *Ibid.,* 263, 278, 280–281. See also Hayden White, "Criticism as Cultural Politics," *Diacritics* (Fall 1976), 8–13, esp. 10.

27. This is true even for those texts which systematically frustrate the reader's tropological expectations. They gain coherence through the negation of the standard tropological practices. But to White this gesture of irony remains within the overall scope of figurative language as one of the four basic attitudes towards representation. To include their writings in his tropological scheme White reduces the texts of such "sectarian" and hermetic critics as Foucault and Derrida to the figure of irony which he identifies as the deep structure of their texts. *Tropics of Discourse,* 255, 259, 267.

28. Dominick LaCapra argues that the "absurdist" critics "actually articulate things that are 'inside' White himself." *Rethinking Intellectual History: Texts, Contexts, Language* (Ithaca, 1983), 78.

29. Hayden White, *The Content of the Form: Narrative Discourse and Historical Representation* (Baltimore, 1987), 189.

30. *Ibid.,* 40, 43, 45. See also Hayden White, "Historical Pluralism," *Critical Inquiry* 12 (1986), 480–502, esp. 486–487.

31. White illustrates the conciliatory and domesticating capacities of history through the causality principle which explains and justifies the status quo. To subscribe to the rules of history always implies that one assumes good reasons for things to be the way they are. *The Content of the Form,* 57, 85.

32. *Ibid.,* 87, 89, 93. This radical critique of the discipline of history has been further developed by Sande Cohen, *Historical Culture: On the Recoding of an Academic Discipline* (Berkeley, 1987).

33. White, *The Content of the Form,* 66–67, 72. White concedes that this type of historical consciousness

might be the single most important reason for the relative success of the concept of social responsibility in Western democracies. But at the same time the suppression of the sublime, based on the illusion that we partake in a well-formed historical process, opens a dangerous void in the very moment that this illusion loses its power of conviction. White argues that fascism could be understood as a reaction formation, which imposes a meaning on past and present reality in the moment of a general legitimation crisis, as a negative recuperation of the sublime which acknowledges and exploits the meaninglessness of history. Therefore from White's perspective, fascist politics cannot be resisted by insisting on the proper historiographical methodology. Rather, we have to take the apparent meaninglessness of history as a challenge for the construction of a more humane vision of history. *Ibid.,* 75.

34. White's text on this point is worth quoting: "If you are going to 'go to history,' you had better have a pretty good notion as to whether it is hospitable to the values you carry into it. This is the function of theory in general—that is to say, to provide justification of a stance vis-à-vis the materials being dealt with that can render it plausible." *The Content of the Form,* 164.

35. Therefore Sande Cohen has argued that White's critique of historical writing has to be understood not as an attack but a new justification, a specific recoding of historical thinking. Sande Cohen, *Historical Culture,* 81–87.

36. *Ibid.,* 139–140.

37. The following essays by Hayden White will be considered here: "The Rhetoric of Interpretation," *Poetics Today* 9 (1988), 253–279; "Introduction" to the issue of the *Stanford Literature Review* on "History and Memory in European Romanticism" (6; 1989), 5–14; "New Historicism: A Comment" in *The New Historicism,* ed. H. Aram Veeser (New York, 1989), 293–302; "'Figuring the nature of the times deceased': Literary Theory and Historical Writing," in *The Future of Literary Theory,* ed. Ralph Cohen (New York, 1989), 19–43: "Historical Emplotment and the Question of Truth" in *Probing the Limits of Representation: Nazism and the "Final Solution,"* ed. Saul Friedlander (Cambridge, Mass., 1992), 37–53; "Writing in the Middle Voice," in *Writing, Schrift, Ecriture,* ed. Hans Gumbrecht (forthcoming); "The Fact of Modernism: The Fading of the Historical Event," AFI lecture delivered at UCLA on April 8, 1992.

38. White, "'Figuring the nature of the times deceased,'" 34. See also "The Rhetoric of Interpretation," 254–255.

39. White, "'Figuring the nature of the times deceased,'" 27.

40. *Ibid.,* 30.

41. *Ibid.,* 43. When White stresses the interdependencies and correlations between twentieth-century events and modern representational techniques in opposition to earlier forms of historical knowledge, we are led to conclude that there existed a similar causal relationship between nineteenth-century events and the contemporary historiographical repertoire.

42. *Ibid.,* 39.

43. "The Fact of Modernism," AFI Lecture, UCLA April 8, 1992.

44. Lawrence Stone, "Dry Heat, Cool Reason: Historians under Siege in England and France," *TLS* (January 31, 1992).

45. Michael Ermarth, "Review of *Metahistory,"* *American Historical Review* 80 (1975), 961–963; Adrian Kuzminski, "A New Science," *Comparative Studies in Society and History* 18 (1976), 129–143, esp. 140; Christopher Browning, "German Memory, Judicial Interrogation, and Historical Reconstruction: Writing Perpetrator History from Postwar Testimony" in Friedlander, ed., *Probing the Limits,* 22–36, esp. 31–32. For a contextualization of White within the American historical profession, see in particular Peter Novick, *That Noble Dream: The Objectivity Question and the American Historical Profession* (Cambridge, Eng., 1988), 599–607.

46. Martin Jay, "Of Plots, Witnesses, and Judgements" in *Probing the Limits,* 97–107; see also Lionel Gossman, *Between History and Literature* (Cambridge, Mass., 1990), 316–320.

47. Andrew Ezergailis, "Review of *Metahistory,"* *Clio* 5 (1976), 235–245, esp. 244; Amos Funkenstein, "History, Counterhistory, Narrative" in *Probing the Limits,* 66–81, 66; this point has been argued in detail by Leon Pompa, "Narrative Form, Significance and Historical Knowledge" in *La philosophie de l'histoire et la pratique historienne d'aujourd'hui,* ed. David Carr (Ottawa, 1982), 143–157. See also Noel Carroll, "Interpretation, History, and Narrative," *Monist* 73 (1990), 134–166, esp. 143, 161.

48. William H. Dray, *On History and Philosophers of History* (Leiden, 1989), 133–162, and William H. Dray, "Review of *The Content of the Form,"* *History and Theory* 27 (1988), 282–287; see in particular Maurice Mandelbaum, "The Presuppositions of *Metahistory,"* *History and Theory* 19 (1980), 39–54; compare to Louis Mink, "Narrative Form as a Cognitive Instrument" in *The Writing of History: Literary Form and Historical Understanding,* ed. Robert H. Canary and Henry Kozicki (Madison, Wisc., 1978), 129–141, esp. 140, where he explicitly supports White.

49. Terry Eagleton, "Review of *Tropics of Discourse,"* *Notes and Queries* 27 (1980), 478; Frederic Jameson, "Figural Relativism, or the Poetics of Historiography" *Diacritics* (Spring 1976), 2–9; 6, 9. See in

addition Perry Anderson, "On Emplotment: Two Kinds of Ruin," in *Probing the Limits,* 54–65, esp. 63.

50. Gossman, *Between History and Literature,* 303. See also Carlo Ginzburg, "Just One Witness"; Arnaldo Momigliano, "The Rhetoric of History and the History of Rhetoric: On Hayden White's Tropes," *Comparative Criticism* 3 (1981), 259–268, esp. 261–262; Arnaldo Momigliano, "Biblical and Classical Studies: Simple Reflections upon Historical Method," *Annali della Scuola Normale Superiore di Pisa* 11 (1981), 25–32; Eugene Golob, "The Irony of Nihilism," *History and Theory* 19 (1980), 55–65, esp. 65; and William H. Dray, "Review of *The Content of the Form,*" 287; and most recently Russell Jacoby, "A New Intellectual History?" *American Historical Review* 97 (1992), 405–424. See in addition Lloyd S. Kramer, "Literature, Criticism, and Historical Imagination: The Literary Challenge of Hayden White and Dominick LaCapra" in *The New Cultural History,* ed. Lynn Hunt (Berkeley, 1989), 97–129; 122ff.

51. Robert F. Berkhofer, "The Challenge of Poetics."

52. William M. Johnston, "Review of *Tropics of Discourse,*" *Journal of Modern History* 52 (1980), 122–124, 122.

53. See esp. Stephen Bann, *The Clothing of Clio: A Study of the Representation of History in Nineteenth-Century Britain and France* (Cambridge, Eng., 1984); Stephen Bann, *The Inventions of History*; Stephen Bann, "Towards a Critical Historiography," *Philosophy* 56 (1981), 365–385; Hans Kellner, *Language and Historical Representation*; Suzanne Gearhart, *The Open Boundary of History and Fiction: A Critical Approach to the French Enlightenment* (Princeton, N.J., 1984); Linda Orr, *Headless History: Nineteenth-Century French Historiography of the Revolution* (Ithaca, N.Y., 1990); Nancy Struever, "Topics in History," *History and Theory* 19 (1980), 66–79; and in particular, Sande Cohen, *Historical Culture.*

54. Gearhart, *The Open Boundary,* 61–63; Wilda Anderson, "Dispensing with the Fixed Point: Scientific Law as Historical Event," *History and Theory* 22 (1983), 264–277. Kellner, *Language and Historical Representation,* 212, 219; Paul A. Roth, "Hayden White and Historiography," 17. Lionel Gossman takes this as an opportunity to base the rationality of history on complex, and as yet not fully understood, intersubjective criteria for evidence and reasoning that facilitate a high degree of accountability in historical practice. Gossman, "The Rationality of History," 311, 316, 319–320. See also Noel Carroll, "Interpretation, History, and Narrative," 147–148.

55. Struever, "Topics in History," 67; Gossman, "The Rationality of History," 286; Gearhart, *The Open Boundary,* 18; Dominick LaCapra, "A Poetics of

Historiography," 76–77. See also Brian Vickers, *In Defense of Rhetoric* (Oxford, 1989), 441–442.

56. Nancy S. Struever, "Topics in History," esp. 66–67 and 75–76.

57. On the problematic position of irony in White's tropology and its reductive and idealistic elements see David Carroll, "On Tropology: The Forms of History," *Diacritics* (Fall 1976), 58–64, and Stanley Pierson, "Review of *Metahistory,*" *Comparative Literature* 30 (1978), 178–181. On irony in White compare to Philip Pomper, "Typologies and Cycles in Intellectual History," *History and Theory* 19 (1980), 30–38; John S. Nelson, "Review of *Metahistory,*" *History and Theory* 14 (1975), 74–91; Gearhart, "Open Boundaries," 62. On the problematic epistemological grounding of White's tropes and a critique of White's academic style, see Ralph Flores, "Review of *The Content of the Form,*" *MLN* 102 (1987), 1191–1196.

58. James M. Mellard, *Doing Tropology,* 19–20, 32–34.

59. Didier Coste, *Narrative as Communication* (Minneapolis, 1989). See especially the foreword by Wlad Godzich, ix–xvii and 15–17, 30–32.

60. Christopher Norris argued recently that such approaches might leave the students without defense against right-wing revisionist historians who could create "a massively falsified consensus, brought about by the misreading or manipulative use of evidence, the suppression of crucial facts and the creation of a certain selective amnesia in those whose memory might otherwise go far enough back." Christopher Norris, *Deconstruction and the Interests of Theory* (Norman, Okla., 1989), 16.

61. See for instance, Jonathan Culler, *Framing the Sign* (Norman, Okla., 1988), 208–210; David Perkins, *Is Literary History Possible?* (Baltimore, 1992), 11, 34, 42, 108, 125; Herbert Lindenberger, *The History in Literature: On Value, Genre, Institution* (New York, 1990), 17, 221, 234. Renewed interest in narrative structures and especially plot structures among literary theorists might also further the reception of White's work. See Ruth Ronen, "Paradigm Shift in Plot Models: An Outline of the History of Narratology," *Poetics Today* 11 (1990), 817–842.

62. Peter De Bolla, "Disfiguring History," 56.

63. *Ibid.,* 76. In respect to Nazism the term revisionism refers to a group of writers who doubt the event of the "Final Solution." They argue that functioning gas chambers never existed in any of the Nazi camps and that the evidence for their existence was fabricated by the Allies after the war. Their position is commonly identified with Robert Faurisson, who received considerable public attention when the French daily *Le Monde* published one of his programmatic texts in December 1978. On the Faurisson affair and revisionism see Pierre Vidal-Naquet, "A Paper Eich-

mann?" *Democracy* (April, 1981), 67–95; Nadine Fresco, "The Denial of the Dead," *Dissent* (Fall 1981), 467–483; Lucy Dawidowicz, "Lies about the Holocaust." *Commentary* 70 (December, 1980), 31–47; Roger Eatwell, "The Holocaust Denial: A Study in Propaganda Technique," in *Neo-Fascism in Europe,* ed. Luciano Cheles (London, 1991), 120–146; and especially, Henry Rousso, *The Vichy Syndrome: History and Memory in France since 1944* (Cambridge, Mass., 1991), 151–169.

64. A similar lack of clarity is to be found in White's discussion of the difference between a lie and an untruth in historical discourse. Based on his differentiation between singular existential statements and larger narrative constructions, he first defines the difference between a lie and an untruth. The former represents a denial of the historiographical facts whereas the latter applies to cases where historians draw "false conclusions from reflections on events whose reality remains attestable on the level of 'positive' historical inquiry" (*The Content of the Form,* 78). But he immediately destabilizes the definition of untruth and, with reference to the Zionist interpretation of the "Final Solution," argues that any historiographical representation gains legitimacy and purpose from its compatibility with its political and conceptual context. Therefore he finds it misleading to talk about truth, which implies an underlying stable epistemology, when all one can attest to is the effectiveness or ineffectiveness of any given historiographical account in its immediate social framework.

65. *The Content of the Form,* 80.

66. Rousso, *The Vichy Syndrome,* 156–157.

67. Hayden White, "Historical Emplotment and the Problem of Truth," in *Probing the Limits,* 37–53.

68. *Ibid.,* 40.

69. *Ibid.,* 52.

70. Johann Gustav Droysen, *Historik,* ed. Peter Leyh (Stuttgart, 1977); Jörn Rüsen's *Grundzüge einer Historik* is in three volumes: *Historische Vernunft: Die Grundlagen der Geschichtswissenschaft* (Göttingen, 1983); *Rekonstruktion der Vergangenheit: Die Prinzipien der historischen Forschung* (Göttingen, 1986); and *Lebendige Geschichte: Formen und Funktionen des historischen Wissens* (Göttingen, 1989). See also Jörn Rüsen, *Zeit und Sinn: Strategien historischen Denkens* (Frankfurt, 1990); Friedrich Nietzsche, *The Use and Abuse of History,* transl. Adrian Collins (Indianapolis, 1957).

Wulf Kansteiner (essay date January 1996)

SOURCE: "Searching for an Audience: The Historical Profession in the Media Age—A Comment on Arthur Mar-

wick and Hayden White," in *Journal of Contemporary History,* Vol. 31, No. 1, January, 1996, pp. 215–19.

[*In the following essay, Kansteiner discusses the different historiographic perspectives of Marwick and White, and suggests that a new historiographic approach is needed to deal with questions raised by popular visual media, notably films and documentaries.*]

The exchange of arguments between Arthur Marwick and Hayden White, published in recent issues of this Journal, is certainly not remarkable for having introduced new perspectives into the debate about the relationship between academic historiographical practice, postmodern theory, and the possibility or threat of a vaguely conceived postmodern historiography. During the two decades that historians and critics have discussed these issues, little progress in terms of clarification and mutual enlightenment has been made. Most of the exchanges are noteworthy for their polemics and imprecise terminology, in the present case as pronounced as ever.[1] Obviously, any short interjection cannot displace these frustrating continuities of twenty years. Nevertheless, I would like to offer a new perspective on one of the issues under debate, a perspective which leads away from the history/fiction dichotomy and its discursive focus and raises the question of the representation of the past in different media.

The intensity of past and present debates about postmodernism and academic history suggests powerful motives, one of which is the concern for the integrity of the discipline as reflected in the works of future historians. For Marwick and many other critics of poststructuralist anti-epistemology, the responsibility for teaching the next generation of historians is one of the touchstones of their critique. Marwick shares this concern with theoreticians like Christopher Norris and Lionel Gossman, who have qualified their support for postmodern theories and White's structuralist critique of historical writing in light of their teaching experiences and responsibilities.[2] Considering that there are few history departments which give credence to poststructuralism as a historiographical tool, it is improbable that the next generation of historians will be markedly influenced by postmodern theory. But the concern with the discipline's future reflects a more serious problem. In my opinion, the polemics about postmodern historiography are partly fuelled by a growing awareness of the social and political insignificance of historical scholarship in contemporary Western societies. Since the end of the second world war, the social task of orienting society and especially its élites vis-à-vis the past has passed from the historical profession to other ways of imagining the past, most importantly to the electronic media. In this sense, I would like to challenge what Marwick repeatedly argues in his piece and what he considers common ground, that is, that we 'only know the human past through the works of historians' (*JCH*, January 1995, p. 28, see also pp. 8, 9, 11, 12, 29).

Unfortunately for us historians, few members of contemporary Western societies derive information about the past from sources based upon or compatible with professional historical scholarship. From our perspective the discipline of history might 'fulfil a necessary social function'—as Marwick puts it—(p. 9) but today it is hardly a popular one. More than ever before, 'society's need to understand particular aspects of the human past' (p. 8) is met by visual media, such as television, the tabloids, and historical museums, which are not rivalled by scholarship's widespread but not necessarily popular nor influential derivative, the textbook. Unlike textbooks, media representations of the past are mostly produced without the involvement of historians and they distribute information about the past in ways incompatible with academic, discursively-fixed scholarship. These sources might not provide what Marwick calls 'serious knowledge' of the past (p. 11). They might be closer to 'family gossip, old photographs, folk memories, old buildings, museums, pageants' which Marwick lists as non-professional sources of historical information (p. 11). He mistakenly assumes, however, that these sources merely attest to the existence of the past. In their own way they provide interpretations and orientation, especially if we add the electronic media to the list. I want to illustrate this point by referring to an example which I witnessed recently.

During the first half of 1995, German society was swept up in a wave of anniversary festivities which commemorated the end of the second world war fifty years ago, mostly in terms of the liberating effect of this event on German society but at times also mourning the defeat of the German army and state. In the wake of this media outpouring, a generation of Germans who had had, thus far, little exposure to the history of nazi Germany—being too young to remember media events like 'Holocaust' and the debates surrounding it—were confronted for the first time with images of the liberation of the camps, the German capitulation, and the immediate postwar period. Few of these representations in documentaries, TV films, and movies can live up to scholarly standards and all of them function on levels outside the scope of even the most popular history books.

In their attempts to assemble material for the current anniversaries, TV journalists sometimes consulted historians for prestigious projects—a co-operation which often ends in frustration—but most of the time their choices of how to represent the end of Nazism was determined by what historians would consider unfortunate factors, i.e. by what material is easily available in the station's archives, what copyrights the station holds at the moment, how many minutes and seconds are available in the evening broadcast, and what might be efficient ways of beating the competition in the ratings. As a result, the audience was often faced with the type of representations of the past which Marwick has rightly rejected for historians: simplistic, imprecise, abstract, metaphorical language combined with highly suggestive footage. Thus, for instance, the undue emphasis on Hitler's last days in the bunker, which have been the focus of many media stories during the commemorations, is certainly not a reflection of the historical

discipline's most important or most recent achievements.[3] Even more importantly, the many shows combined have assumed a life of their own. The sombre, at times listless faces of the German politicians who reflected upon the liberation of the camps in official, live broadcast ceremonies between January and April 1995, lit up when they commemorated 8 May in carefully crafted, tentatively optimistic speeches.[4] In the same period, the gruesome images of the camps gave way to films about the peace celebrations which invariably ended with references to the imminent economic miracle. Although we still know very little about historical identity formation and the dynamics of collective memory—topics which have only recently begun to interest historians—I assume that these simple but powerful stories, produced collectively by the media within a period of less than six months, are very influential for the development of the historical consciousness of teenagers growing up in Germany today.

From this vantage point, the polemics between Marwick and White mark the differences between a particular kind of intellectual history and a particular, more widely-practised type of social history, both of which are located well within the parameters of the academic tradition for the study and representation of the past. Marwick's and White's concern for the future audience and social relevance of historical scholarship which, I suggest, has influenced the letter and the spirit of their exchange, has to be met by other strategies than 'history as usual'—as proposed by Marwick—or the development of modernist historical writing in the tradition of literary modernism—which White favours. Rather, the growing insignificance of traditional historiography indicates the need to focus on different, in practical and theoretical terms more challenging questions, for instance on the problem of bridging the gap between scholarly historical narratives and the kind of sweeping, imprecise, visually-based narratives about the past that find the interest of larger audiences; or on the problem of how scholarly protocols for the writing of truthful histories can be transferred to visual media, that is, how histories can be responsibly narrated in images. Such projects would entail an understanding of the metaphysics and metahistories of the media and in this respect would make use of some of the more productive aspects of the discussions on postmodern historiography. Such projects are also more pressing and rewarding than attempts to unravel the intricacies of the discursive protocols of two relatively closely associated ways of doing history and providing historical knowledge, especially if these attempts are partly triggered by concerns about the discipline's marginality. Finally, they might help us 'to conceive a way of doing history to meet the needs of our audiences' (White ['**Response to Arthur Marwick**'], *JCH*, April 1995, p. 244), or to find them in the first place.

Notes

1. The most recent in a long line of debates features a conventionally polemic critique of the perceived postmodern threat followed by an unusually thoughtful response. See K. Barkin, 'Bismarck in a Post-

modern World,' *German Studies Review,* 28, 2 (May 1995), 241–51, and M. Geyer/K. H. Jarausch, 'Great Men and Postmodern Ruptures: Overcoming the "Belatedness" of German Historiography,' *German Studies Review,* 28, 2 (May 1995), 253–73.

2. For Norris's and Gossman's critique of White and the general reception of White's work see W. Kansteiner, 'Hayden White's Critique of the Writing of History,' *History and Theory,* 32 (1993), 273–95, esp. 286–90. The question of teaching and graduate training in history is also an important reference point in the above-cited exchange between Barkin and Geyer/Jarausch. See especially Geyer/Jarausch, op. cit., 254–5 and 257–9.

3. The focus on Hitler was particularly apparent in two documentaries aired by the two German national public television stations, the ARD and the ZDF, on 23 April 1995. From a historiographical perspective the ZDF's 'Hitlers Ende: Was geschah im Führerbunker?' (23/4/95) and the ARD's more critical 'Hitler und die Deutschen' (23/4/95) still compare favourably with the few shows broadcast by the commercial stations; see, for instance, RTL's 'Nachtjournal Spezial: Die Stunde Null: Hitlers Ende—Deutschlands Anfang' (30/4/95 and 7/5/95). See also the cover story of *Der Spiegel* of 3/4/1995 entitled 'Hitlers letzte Tage.'

4. In this respect, it is revealing to compare the official ceremony of the Federal Republic on 8 May which was broadcast live on a *national* public television station (ARD 'Staatsakt der Bundesrepublik Deutschland,' 8/5/95) with the numerous ceremonies broadcast on the occasion of the liberation of the camps, most of which were aired live only on *regional* channels of the public broadcasting network of the ARD; see, for example, Hessen 3, 'Gedenkveranstaltung live aus Ravensbrück,' 23/4/95, and MDR, 'Buchenwald—50 Jahre danach live,' 9/4/95.

Geoffrey Roberts (essay date January 1996)

SOURCE: "Narrative History as a Way of Life," in *Journal of Contemporary History,* Vol. 31, No. 1, January, 1996, pp. 221–28.

[In the following essay, Roberts examines the opposing theoretical positions of White and Arthur Marwick and defends Marwick's perspective of narrative history.]

Hayden White writes [in the essay **'Response to Arthur Marwick,'**]: 'Historians have systematically built into their notion of their discipline hostility or at least a blindness to theory and the kind of issues that philosophers have raised about the kind of knowledge they have produced.'[1] His explanation for this blindness seems to be in terms of a set of personal failings shared by historians: their simplistic assertion that only empirical research re-

ally matters; their mistaken belief that understanding what historians do is a matter of practical knowledge available only to fellow professionals; their inability to theorize their own discourse and the suppression of the philosophical dimensions of their craft and discipline.

Such attitudes are indeed widespread among historians. But I want to suggest a much more profound reason for the anti-theoretical tradition in history: most historians feel no need for a self-conscious, separate and distinct theoretical analysis of their discipline because the dominant discourse of knowledge in history is coterminous with the common sense discourse of modern everyday life. As John Passmore has argued: 'For the most part . . . there is nothing much to say about historical explanation; nothing that cannot be said about explanation in everyday life. . . . No wonder historians are often puzzled to know what philosophers are fussing about!'[2]

'Narrative' historians like myself, and most other historians,[3] work mainly within the framework of a human action account of the past.[4] History is viewed as a field of human action and action as the result of individual and collective reasoning in particular circumstances under the impact of a variety of social, political, economic, ideological and cultural influences (themselves contexts of action composed of and created by other human agents). The task of historians is to reconstruct the reasons for past actions. They do this by reference to surviving evidence of past human thinking, whose meaning they interpret in connection with decisions and action. This human action approach to the study of history emphasizes the freedom of individuals to act, the importance of reconstructing what happened from the actor's point of view, and the role of accident, miscalculation and unintended consequences in shaping historical outcomes.

Involved here, too, is what some writers call a philosophical anthropology of humanity: the view that human beings have certain properties, powers and predispositions. Arising out of these is the rational-purposive and self-reflective nature of human action and its intentional and intelligible character. The intelligibility of action and its expression in language—its reason-based, linguistic character—makes it possible to interpret and communicate the meaning of action.[5]

In narrative history the results of research are written up in the form of stories about connected sequences of thought and action. These narratives of action will include various descriptions relevant to the story, may include political and moral judgments about what happened, and, possibly, generalizations about past actions which ascribe to them meanings and patterns relevant to contemporary concerns. But the explanatory content of the story will be some reason-giving account of why past actors did what they did. The validity of this kind of account of the past rests on its correspondence with the direct and indirect evidence of the perceptions, motivations, goals, calculations and intentions which result in specific decisions and actions.[6]

The idea that people do things for a reason, that their individual and collective actions are the stuff of history and that it is possible to construct an evidence-based account of why past actors acted as they did is, for most of us, plain common sense. It is a set of assumptions that harmonizes with our intuition of what the world is like, corresponds with our own experience as historical actors, and forms the basis of our interaction with other human beings.

Narrative historians have been successfully practising their craft for generations, producing, within the terms of reason-giving human action accounts, an accumulation of grounded knowledge. Internal coherence and practical success, however, is no guarantee of validity and the neglect of deeper philosophical scrutiny leaves the field open to alternative (usually obfuscatory and confusing) conceptions of the nature of history. The assumptions underlying narrative history require elaboration and argument beyond the common sense propositions outlined above.

Contrary to the impression given by some philosophers and social scientists, a large and sophisticated set of theoretical resources are available to narrative historians wishing to defend their craft. These resources include:

1. The debates on individualism in the social sciences. Of particular interest to historians are efforts to validate an ontological individualism. The claim that what happens in the human world is the result of action, that the agency of action is the individual, and that while action may be constrained and influenced in various ways individuals are free to choose is of critical importance to narrative historians.[7]

2. The Collingwood school in the philosophy of history which seeks in various ways to defend and elaborate Collingwood's argument in *The Idea of History* that history is the history of human thought and action and that the accurate recovery of thought-action in the present is possible.[8]

3. The discussion among philosophers of the concept of action. Narrative histories rest on reason-giving explanations. For these to be valid, action must be volitional and intentional and intentions connected to reasons.[9]

4. The efforts of sociologists, particularly those working within the hermeneutic tradition, to produce a theory of action which links rational and individual action to its social dimension and context and provides an account of continuity and change in diverse human societies.[10]

5. The phenomenological account of the identity of form and content in narrative reconstructions of past action. Narrative historians tell stories about the past because human beings are narrative creatures and action is narrative in character. The narrative character of human existence arises out of the character of human consciousness and language.[11] The stories told by historians (if they are good

enough) correspond to those that have been played out and lived in the past. The idea that there is a correspondence between narrative and life has been brilliantly explored by some of White's philosopher colleagues who provide a coherent alternative to his view that historians produce the narratives that they do out of linguistic necessity. Their critique of White is far more effective than Marwick's polemics and denunciations—and far more useful to historians seeking a philosophical underpinning of what they do by instinct, tradition and common sense.[12]

Where does Marwick stand on the human action account of history? Although he lays claim to a defence of the 'historical' approach, at times his views seem more in tune with some kind of quasi-social scientific approach. For example, in his article he comments:

> Postmodernists . . . show no familiarity with the modes of explanation historians actually use, which certainly do not concentrate exclusively on the actions of individuals, but involve a varying balance, depending on topic and focus, between short-term human agency, contingency and convergence, and longer-term structural, ideological and institutional movements and constraints.[13]

What Marwick seems to be endorsing here is a weak version of the 'structuration' or 'social scientific realist' approach popular among some sociologists.[14] The basic concept of history informing this view is that what happens in the human world is the result of a combination of agency (human action/will) and autonomous conditioning, constraining and enabling forces and structures. The truth and usefulness of this concept of history rests ultimately on a set of ontological and epistemological claims—that the human world is like this, that it consists of two different kinds of objects (individual and social), and can be known and shown to be so. In other words, it requires validation by reference to a set of metaphysical assumptions which run counter to those of narrative history. Assuming that he could overcome his disdain for anything smacking of the metaphysical, would Marwick be prepared to defend an agency-structure account of history? The answer, on balance of the evidence, is no. In Marwick's *The Nature of History* one can find similar statements to that quoted above, but these are counter-balanced by a clear appreciation of the past as a site of human thoughts, activities and products, by his view that 'in a very profound sense, what happens is the consequence of the actions of individuals,' and his final reminder in the book that structural and ideological 'forces' 'are in fact created by the activities of multitudes of human beings.'[15]

Reclaiming Marwick for History is not, of course, the end of the discussion with the structurationists,[16] or anyone else for that matter, but it is necessary in order to clarify what the argument between historians and their opponents is really all about. In the article, and in his other writings on the nature of historical knowledge, Marwick, as I understand him, seeks to defend a traditional approach to the study of the past. He does this, firstly, by explaining and defending the research practices of historians and, secondly, by attempting to puncture the theoretical pretensions of White & co. Almost all of what Marwick has to say I, as a historian, agree and identify with. But missing from Marwick's account is the crucial dimension of a presentation and exploration of the metaphysical basis of historical practise. Like anyone else, historians have reasons for the kind of research they conduct and the type of statements and truth-claims they make. The historical approach is not in opposition to the metaphysical approach: the historical approach is as metaphysical as that of any other discipline. The fact that historians prefer to practise their metaphysics rather than talk about them does not mean they cannot and should not be discussed and defended.

Notes

1. H. White, 'Response to Arthur Marwick,' *Journal of Contemporary History* 30, 2 (April 1995), 244.

2. J. Passmore, 'Explanation in Everyday Life, in Science, and in History,' *History and Theory,* 2, 2 (1962), 122, 123.

3. The purest narrative history is to be found in the works of traditional diplomatic and political historians, but narrative accounts are to be found in every field of the discipline. Indeed, even in the writings of historians explicitly hostile to the traditionalist view espoused here one often finds a crucial, defining narrative component (e.g. Eric Hobsbawm's *The Age of Extremes,* London 1994). This is because practically all historians share a common interest in human actors and their impact on the world and admit the importance of the connection between belief and action.

4. The most sustained defence of a human action approach to history may be found in the works of Geoffrey Elton: *The Practice of History* (Sydney 1967), *Political History: Principles and Practice* (London 1970), *Which Road the Past? Two Views of History* (with R. W. Fogel Yale 1983), and *Return to Essentials: Some Reflections on the Present State of Historical Study* (Cambridge 1991). A less well-known, but equally important, and more philosophically rigorous, advocate of the human action approach (albeit on methodological rather than substantive grounds) is the British International Relations specialist Charles Reynolds: *Theory and Explanation in International Politics* (London 1973), *Modes of Imperialism* (London 1981), *The Politics of War* (London 1989) and *The World of States* (London 1992). Noteworthy here, too, is a detectable drift in the social sciences towards the human action approach long defended by historians. See, e.g., the contributions by Vayda, McCay, Eghenter and Searle in *Philosophy of the Social Sciences,* 21, 3 (September 1991).

5. To sustain the formulation about language in this paragraph would require a further argument that words have determinate meaning in relation to things, actions and ideas and that this meaning can be exchanged by speakers. The postmodernist—deconstructionist alternative—that words have meaning only in relation to other words and meaning is, therefore, ambiguous and ungraspable—is criticized by, among others, the Marxist theoretician A. Callinicos, *Against Modernism* (London 1989).

6. The notion of causality deployed here is that of reasons as causes. There are, of course, alternative conceptions of causality in history, most of them based on the notion that causation in human affairs is, in some sense, akin to that in nature. For the reasons as causes argument see, e.g., W. H. Dray, *Philosophy of History* (Prentice-Hall 1964); D. M. Taylor, *Explanation and Meaning* (Cambridge 1970); and A. R. Louch, *Explanation and Human Action* (Oxford 1966). To my mind the most useful discussion of causes in history remains Elton, *Political History,* chap. 4.

7. For a thorough and highly enlightening review of the relevant debates see R. Bhargava, *Individualism in Social Science* (Oxford 1992). While the author reveals the power of ontological, as opposed to other forms of individualism, he himself ultimately rejects it in favour of what he calls contextualism, i.e. a weak variation of the claim that there are some things in the human world irreducible to individuals.

8. R. G. Collingwood, *The Idea of History* (Oxford 1961). On the Collingwood school see F. R. Ankersmit, 'The Dilemma of Contemporary Anglo-Saxon Philosophy of History,' *History and Theory,* 25, 1986, and other contributors in the same issue. Important contributions/commentaries in this tradition include: R. Martin, *Historical Explanation* (Cornell 1977); W. H. Dray, *Laws and Explanation in History* (London 1957); G. H. von Wright, *Explanation and Understanding* (Cornell 1971); L. J. Goldstein, 'Collingwood's Theory of Historical Knowing,' *History and Theory,* IX, 1, 1970, *Historical Knowing* (Austin 1976) and 'Collingwood on the Constitution of the Historical Past' in M. Krausz (ed.), *Critical Essays on the Philosophy of R. G. Collingwood* (Oxford 1972); P. Q. Hirst, 'Collingwood, Relativism and the Purposes of History' in his *Marxism and Historical Writing* (London 1985); L. O. Mink, 'Collingwood's Dialectic of History,' *History and Theory,* 7, 1, 1968; A. Donagan, 'Historical Explanation: The Popper-Hempel Theory Reconsidered,' *History and Theory,* 4, 1, 1964 and W. B. Gallie, 'The Historical Understanding,' *History and Theory,* 3, 2, 1964.

9. For a review of these debates see C. J. Moya, *The Philosophy of Action* (London 1990). Moya's conclusions are commensurate with the commonsense, practical concept of intentional action utilized by historians. The debate on free will is also relevant here. For a summary of that discussion see D. J. O'Connor, *Free Will* (London 1971) and, for a

relevant pro-free will case, J. R. Lucas, *The Freedom of the Will* (Oxford 1970). I am aware that here are raised issues of unintentional action, of the unconscious, and the role of emotion as well as reason in human affairs.

10. Of particular interest is Jürgen Habermas's *The Theory of Communicative Action,* 2 vols (London 1989). Habermas's views are summarized by J. Bohman, *New Philosophy of Social Science* (London 1991), who also reviews other sociological theories of action. An alternative account of action is that proposed by various rational-choice theorists, whose starting-point are the models of economic behaviour developed by neo-classical economic theory. Their views are ably summarized and criticized by B. Hindess, *Choice, Rationality and Social Theory* (London 1988).

11. In relation to this point see Paul Hirst's summary of the views of Julian Jaynes in 'The Evolution of Consciousness: Identity and Personality in Historical Perspective,' *Economy and Society,* 23, 1 (February 1994).

12. See David Carr's *Time, Narrative, and History* (Indiana 1986) and 'Narrative and the Real World: An Argument for Continuity,' *History and Theory,* vol. 15, 1986, and Frederick Olafson *The Dialectic of Action* (Chicago 1979) and 'Narrative History and the Concept of Action,' *History and Theory,* 9, 3, 1970. Also: W. H. Dray, 'Narrative and Historical Realism' in his *On History and Philosophers of History* (New York 1989) and A. P. Norman, 'Telling It Like It Was: Historical Narratives on Their Own Terms,' *History and Theory,* vol. 30 1991. An important, recent contributor to this argument is M. C. Lemon, *The Discipline of History and the History of Thought* (London 1995). Hayden White is obviously aware of this alternative view of historical discourse—that it is driven by the nature of human action, experience, and thought—but he never seems to confront and criticize it directly. This is true, for example, of the essays published in *The Content of the Form* (Baltimore 1987), including the one on the work of Paul Ricoeur, who espouses a version of the narrative is life argument.

13. A. Marwick, 'Two Approaches to Historical Study: The Metaphysical (Including "Postmodernism") and the Historical,' *Journal of Contemporary History,* 30, 1 (January 1995), 16.

14. See A. Giddens, *Central Problems in Social Theory* (London 1979) espec. chap. 2, 'Agency, Structure'; R. Bhaskar, *The Possibility of Naturalism* (Brighton 1979); A. Sayer, *Method in Social Science: A Realist Approach* (London 1992); L. Doyal and R. Harris, *Empiricism, Explanation and Rationality* (London 1986); and A. Callinicos, *Making History* (London 1987). Giddens's particular approach is defended and elaborated by the historian W. H. Sewell: 'A Theory

of Structure: Duality, Agency, and Transformation,' *American Journal of Sociology,* 98, 1 (July 1992) and 'How Classes are Made: Critical Reflections on E. P. Thompson's Theory of Working-Class Formation' in H. J. Kaye and K. McClelland, *E. P. Thompson: Critical Perspectives* (London 1990).

15. A. Marwick, *The Nature of History* (3rd edn, London 1989). The quotes are from pp. 247 and 381.

16. See my 'Agency and Structure in the New History of the Stalinist Terror: An Individualist View' (forthcoming)—a critique of structuration in the context of a historical case study.

Nancy Partner (essay date December 1997)

SOURCE: "Hayden White (And the Content and the Form and Everyone Else) at the AHA," in *History and Theory,* Vol. 36, No. 4, December, 1997, pp. 102–10.

[*In the following essay, Partner relates her observations and experiences during a January 1997 meeting of the American Historical Association devoted to the subject of Hayden White.*]

I had received the invitation to speak at the Humanities Center of Wesleyan University some weeks before the January meeting of the American Historical Association where I was going to read a paper at the session on the work of Hayden White organized by Richard Vann.[1] Since the choice of topic for this evening was entirely mine, I decided to do myself a favor and piggyback my Wesleyan paper on the AHA session—not by merely repeating that paper, which I had no intention of doing, but by using the experience to report on the "state of the art" in metahistorical theory as it would emerge in the course of the proceedings at the conference. This struck me as a singularly happy idea combining, as it did, guaranteed interesting material with gross opportunism in a highly professional manner. All I had to do was show up at the AHA, read my own paper, and then take copious notes on what everyone else had to say. I had never done anything quite like this before but it felt risk-free. I knew ahead of time that Dick Vann was going to trace the influence of Hayden White through reviews and citations, which was perfect for my purpose; and Frank Ankersmit (the other scheduled speaker) is always original and provocative, and I guessed that he would contrast his latest conception of the direct historical experience with White's ideas of linguistic mediation. Hayden White, the main attraction of the event, was going to have ample time to comment and reply as he chose, and of course the audience would supply whatever had been neglected. I was counting on questions raising the topic of postmodernism, or identity politics and national narratives, or White's views on Foucault and the historicizing of the "self"—generally bringing narrative theory up to speed with postmodern critical debates. I had no anxieties about encountering challenges to my own views; with Hayden White there, no one would ask me anything at all. I was confident in the knowledge that, thanks to Dick Vann's good planning, an unusual degree of coherence and intellectual focus was built into the structure of this session (so unlike all those shambling events at the AHA where speakers who might as well be from different planets huddle together under some tattered umbrella-rubric like "Crime and Cuisine in Premodern France and Poland: A Comparative Perspective"). All I had to do was listen, take enough notes, and then come here and report on "where we are now" in historical theory. That was the plot I intended to hold together all my material. Not a progress report, certainly, in any fatuous sense of a Whig history of theory; what I had in mind was what I provisionally planned to term a "critical taxonomy" of the state of the larger question of history as cultural artifact and as cultural practice, understood self-consciously or self-critically through the linguistic turn optic by historians themselves.

Our event began promisingly on a note of personal drama. One of the participants, Frank Ankersmit, injured himself ice-skating and was unable to travel to New York from the Netherlands where he lives; but amazingly, a substitute speaker was found at the conference with an erudite paper about *Metahistory,* and she sportingly agreed to step in at the last minute. The session itself, considered in its various parts, was quite good. It certainly met a fairly high professional standard for the AHA, all of the papers being on the announced subject; the honored guest-commentator handled the tricky pitfalls of tone and manner built into such occasions with good humor, bringing forward important matters without being self-important; we had attracted a noticeably "upscale" audience (an idea I leave to your competent imaginations to fill in), and a large enough one (maybe 150 people). We ran at least half an hour over our scheduled time without people surreptitiously streaming out of the room. All went pretty well by an objective measure.

So . . . where is it "where we are now" in historical theory as an aspect of practice and consciousness? Don't ask me. I went to that session as if to the first day of school with an entire new pad of paper, the pen I made sure would write, and came away some two and a half hours later with a few illegible doodles on the margin of one page which I seem to have lost. I'm afraid that I've had to replace the high-concept "critical taxonomy" with something more like an autopsy report.

The three papers arrange themselves logically, from empirical to philosophic analysis. Starting the session with the most empirical research paper, Dick Vann stated baldly and with complete supporting evidence that Hayden White's work had had virtually no discernible influence on its most salient intended audience—historians—as measured by the only objective criteria we have: reviews and citations. Maintaining a courteous and sympathetic tone (a diplomatic *tour de force* in the circumstances), Dick Vann traced a relentless course of obscurity for all of

Hayden White's work among professional historians. Inadequately read, rarely reviewed in journals read by historians, infrequently cited, little discussed, and then routinely and grossly misunderstood, is the short version of Dick Vann's well-supported research on the White corpus. Most notable is the fact that what minuscule attention White has been given by his fellow historians has been devoted entirely to *Metahistory,* even now, with the far more nuanced, subtle, and historically pertinent formulations of his later essays in *Tropics of Discourse* and *The Content of the Form* remaining massively and impassively neglected. Casting as it did a shadow of unreality and grotesque humor over the occasion, Dick Vann's paper was a revelation and total surprise to me, I admit, and made me feel rather uneasy, or disconcerted is the more precise word, about what I had come prepared to say.

My own paper occupied a certain middle distance in approach. Partly contextual, partly interpretive, I proceeded on the confident assumption that Hayden White's work is important, is widely known, has had a pervasive impact in the historical discipline, and that its core insights and mode of analysis are far from being exhausted in their potential uses, especially for certain questions addressed to historical epistemology opened by postmodernism. I ignored *Metahistory* entirely, as an early provocative book which had done its work, as it were, choosing to concentrate on *The Content of the Form* whose refinement of insight into narrative structure I consider much more salient and suggestive for historians, especially in the wake of the epistemological upheavals of semiotics and deconstruction. I did note a certain persistent reluctance to pay serious attention to formal analysis among American academics who are endemically impatient with form, genre analysis, rhetoric, tropology, and the like, but I declared myself convinced that narrative theory, as offered by Hayden White, had somehow forced historians to acknowledge the superior potency of "textual intention" superseding the naive reading and writing strategies of authorial intention. I also proposed a clever and amusingly pointed rereading of what I took to be a patently well-known section from an essay in *The Content of the Form* which Dick Vann had just demonstrated might have been known by perhaps two people in the audience. (I hope they enjoyed it.)

The third paper, by a Polish graduate student, Ewa Domańska, who was in the United States on a Fulbright scholarship, was the most philosophical in method and presuppositions. She had written a densely reasoned argument based on a highly sophisticated encounter with *Metahistory* which assumed, as its deep premise, that White's ideas are part of a living, ongoing stream of intellectual life in which certain people (by implication, all historians and cultural critics) are fully and unapologetically engaged. She certainly spoke from a position which assumed that all contributions to this ongoing project of philosophic engagement with the foundational conditions of history are interesting and intelligible to the kind of people who might be, say, members of the American Historical Association, although I can't say that the polite audience gave much sign of it.

I cannot begin to speculate on what all this self-devouring discourse sounded like to Hayden White who exhibited an imperturbable courtesy or perhaps resignation throughout, but his practical decision to ignore all of it in his extended response struck me as a happy impulse. White began by proposing that his ideas not be regarded abstractly, but rather, that his work should be historicized, as we now say, or "situated," his preferred term, in its "moment of production" (also his phrase, I think), and he started the process by acknowledging his early fascination with structuralism and suggested that **Metahistory** resulted from his experiment with applying structuralism to nineteenth-century historical writing. But he chose to devote the majority of his comments to variant restatements of his personal, long-standing, and continuing loyalty to Marxism which he regards as superior for its critique of social structures and for other reasons, although the relation of Marxist theory to all, or indeed any, of his work on historiography remains obscure to me. In fact, neglecting utterly by that time to take any notes, all of Hayden White's Marxist thought remains obscure to me. The only clear memory I retain of that part of the program is Dick Vann murmuring approval from his seat to my left.

Just time enough remained for audience interventions to tie up any loose ends. One person asked if the use of the first-person pronoun were acceptable historiographic practice. An eminent foreign professor made a lengthy and mysterious, albeit learned, speech obliquely related to the proceedings which someone later confided to me comprised about 20% of the paper he was scheduled to read the next day. Dominick LaCapra suggested that we might regard narrative as a neurotic compensatory reaction-formation, or perhaps we shouldn't. And finally Michael Roth asked an actual question concerning the historian's freedom to emplot events: namely, when or at what point in historical work the imposition of a plot, Marxist emplotment, for example, or any other, is possible. By this time (5:00 at least) we had run long past our schedule, the room was in demand, the audience restive, and so we ended in the traditional tidal surge to the nearest bars. I have so often fantasized that the life of the mind, in its performative aspects, bears a deep structural affinity to vaudeville.

So Hayden White never addressed the one question actually related to his work in narrative theory—but I would like to. One problem that historians encounter in trying to think cogently about emplotment is having nothing useful to think about. Thinking abstractly about hypothetical sequence-structures for unknown events is not productive (at least not for historians), and all the historical events we know about in common are always already firmly emplotted, which makes thinking about alternate "plots" feel overstrained and unreal. So I suggest we consider the events I have just narrated, in both their potential emplotments and the one I chose. Given the ordinariness and

inconsequence of the episode "Hayden White at the AHA," we (including myself) are better able to think freely about whether I was successful enough in my narrative strategy to make the plot I used feel "found," not imposed, a convincing rendering of the meaning *immanent in* the event which I registered and recorded, not invented, as for a rather bad academic novel. [Note: the only version of the event most of you can know is the one I gave, but that is the case with all historical evidence at some level, and at the Center for the Humanities, I would, at least, have one other first-hand witness, as reliable or unreliable as myself, just as Thucydides required.]

Given that I had committed myself to narrating a certain public event of some modest complexity and finite duration, my task was to emplot the materials, use some criterion of selection that would allow me to produce the impression of sufficient fullness (the mimesis of real time) without reproducing the real-time two-and-one-half hours, and in the course of that *narratio* define a coherent idea or theme as the summary "meaning" of the conflated, multiplex event and make my audience (you) aware of it as if it inhered in, and emerged from, the events themselves, not as if it proceeded whimsically or tendentiously from me alone. And I had to do this within the implicit constraints of the protocol of historicity, that system of mostly unspecified but nonetheless specifiable permissions and denials (operating through syntax and semiotics via pronouns, verb tense, quotation, reference, and so forth) which constitute "truth-claim" in prose. I am not pretending to have done anything especially noteworthy or original here. Every narrative of an event has to be manipulated through the basic devices of selective inclusion, aroused expectation and foreshadowing, comparison and contrast, metaphor and other tropological shaping. Choices have to be made and basic decisions related to *hypotaxis*—giving or withholding priority to detail, indicating relations of causal or temporal subordination—determine what a narrative is "about." (In contrast to *parataxis* in which all separate narrative elements are equal: A and B and C and D and then . . . and then . . .).

In this case, my little endeavor was to infuse a normally narrative-resistant event—the academic conference session which has its simple, well-known linear sequence but no particular story—with the tropological condensation required by "meaningfulness" and the "sense of an ending" (à la Frank Kermode) in its sequence logic that are crucial to what we mean by emplotment. And it doesn't much matter if you don't think I was very successful. In fact, bad books, or formulaic genres, are often better to think with about these matters than idiosyncratic brilliant writing. The non-story of one more AHA session had to borrow its narrativity from an outside source, by regarding it as a summary episode [alias: the trope of synecdoche, or condensation in the related terminology of dream interpretation] of the career of a unified protagonist: here, not exactly Hayden White himself, but White's narrative theory as embodied in his books, in its progress through the definable world of academic history. As we all know, once an array of data can be configured into a unified subject, a world with institutions and rules, and a goal-oriented sequence of actions, the elements of a plot are in place. But what plot? *Pilgrim's Progress*? (Comedy); *Portrait of the Artist*? (Romance); *Portrait of a Lady*? (Tragedy).

I used the rudimentary but dependable device of thwarted or reversed expectation (alias: ironic outcome) to give expressive significance to my micro-narrative. I sketched in the initial wished-for plot of coherence, my announced intention to discern in the proceedings some harmonious convergence of thought on its way (implicitly in a forward direction) toward some clearer resolution or refinement: the rather pretentious "critical taxonomy" of history as cultural artifact and self-conscious practice. That provisional structure resembles Romance, I think, but it doesn't matter because its plot function was to serve as a counterpoint, a projected shadow-structure against which the events I narrate acquire their meaning, in a kind of slow-motion pratfall of accumulating disappointments and reversals of expectation registered by myself, the somewhat faux-naif narrator. There seems to be no way to avoid a certain pretentiousness in discussing these simple maneuvers, but that is part of the reason that explicit narrative theory meets a pervasive resistance: it feels so "natural" to do or to register, and sounds so insultingly contrived (to both writer and reader/listener alike) when conceptually unpacked.

I have also forced myself into a corner by invoking irony. Irony—considered one of the major tropes because it is a large-scale figure of thought like synecdoche, metonymy, and metaphor, not a small-scale ornament like anaphora, isocolon, or catachresis—is a problem. Irony is a trope of meaning expressed through verbal structure but without specified formal determinants. It always involves doubling of some sort, expressing two thoughts at the same time; and it is often reduced to some causal or intentional sequence of events having an outcome that is precisely what was to be avoided, eliciting the conversational punctuation: How ironic! The presence of irony is often indicated by tone or expression that comments on and renders the literal meaning of words self-defeating or self-deflating, or acknowledges that human behavior is a poor, inadequate lever for shifting the massive forces of malign reality. In those senses, irony can easily be a trope of cheap effect. On a large scale, irony resides in the mind of the observer who sees the many ways in which human endeavor grinds blindly toward unforeseen and undesired ends which yet express and expose the disguises of other kinds of desire. Rather messy as tropes go, irony suits modern and postmodern attitudes of coolness, knowingness, detachment, and self-observation. It certainly works well enough for an intellectual event approached with some optimistic expectation that is systematically undermined, even almost parodied, by its own unfolding reality.

The question I wanted to address, however, was Michael Roth's canny question about "when" this, or any, emplot-ment incarnates itself in and through the array of events "to be narrated?" Or to phrase this in the negative, with respect to the mind of the author, when do other potential choices get eliminated? If one is, as Hayden White insists of himself, "a Marxist," does one consciously and always think Marxist thoughts, or are one's thoughts and feelings merely always colored by whatever it is on a deeper level that makes one "a Marxist" in the first place? I admit, for example, that my own thoughts about vaudeville in relation to aspects of academic life long predate the 1997 AHA meeting, and that this recurring fantasy, although one of self-satire, is also persistently colored by desire, not revulsion. Naturally enough I have never seen a vaudeville show but I associate such events with people like Jack Benny and Mae West, the Marx brothers (a Marxism I subscribe to), and a certain raw daring of self-exposure, a boldness and risk in life, and a certain kind of nervy and wild comedy, none of which describe academe. Therefore, I admit to a half-buried longing for the glamour of "vaudevillian" excess to manifest itself in the academic world I actually inhabit. And this may well explain in part my emplotment (the ironic pratfall) of the Hayden White session which I was only too willing to see as a prolonged semi-sane episode of imploding and self-satirizing intellectual intentions doing their acts—on a stage, before an audience, with an imagined scoffer in the wings with a hooked stick.

But at what point did I begin to conceive of this formulation? When did other formulations get discarded? *I cannot remember* . And that is a substantive and important answer, the answer any author would honestly give. A choice was made (was it during Dick Vann's paper? perhaps) but it did not feel like a choice but a recognition. It has to be obvious that the process of reducing an event stretching in uninterrupted articulate speech over two-and-a-half hours to a very few pages involves severe condensation and tropological manipulation. In its primary meaning, "emplotment" is not a term derived from narrative theory but from the process of writing in prose. I think there is still a massive confusion over how and when the process of emplotment takes place. Described after the fact (which is the only metaphorical "place" from which description can take place) emplotment is a rationalizing and organizing activity which follows logically upon the collection and contemplation of the "events to be narrated." So described, any discussion of emplotment unavoidably suggests that authors do collect a mass of facts and then (in actual chronological sequence) consider what they mean in the set of relations we call narrative.

In actuality, this virtually never happens. The narrativizing process is in action prior to and all during the "research," recognizing and recording what may count as salient "facts," and it never feels as if anything so artificial as emplotment is taking place—although it is. The metahistorical process of analysis is an after-the-fact dissection of mental events that must feel spontaneous, inevitable, and self-generated while they are taking place. The act of emplotment is synonymous with the finding of meaning in reality, and thus reaches too far down into unconscious reservoirs of desire and fear (much deeper even, need I say, than vaudeville fantasies) for conscious recuperation. At a certain basic level plots are made from the same materials and using the same processes of symbolization as dreams are constructed: and plots feel "found" in the same way that dreams feel "given." But both are made.

There are, of course, major differences. The plots of truth-claim narratives are subject to a severe and extensive reality-check, to modification and self-criticism, to enlightening or painful processes of rational correction or verification. That complicated behavior is where aspects of formulated adult mental life enter the process and modify its outcome. But emplotment never starts from a blank or amoebic state of unformed contemplation of discrete units of reality. The act of apprehension of narratable elements involves very complex and deeply informed mental responses, already well on their way toward larger configurations of meaning. Emplotment seems to take place exactly at the meeting point where unconscious demands on reality confront disciplined recognitions of the larger contexts and constraints that control meaning—a point of frequent unpredictable slippages and lapses of control, and also of originality, penetration, and mental discipline. I am describing the mental "place" where we *think with* what we have learned. Everyone has experienced this; it comes in the form of "discovering what I think as I write it" or "by writing it." That common experience is our intuitive access to the mental fulcrum point between unconscious and conscious ideas. It is where narrative happens.

Anyone who has written any fiction (as I have privately, and would recommend to everyone interested in critical theory) knows the quite paradoxical feeling that fiction feels found. The actual mental experience of inventing words and gestures for non-existent characters is predominantly one of summoning those characters to mind and observing them, virtually eavesdropping on them, and recording their lives. Fictional invention feels like discovery. The classical rhetorical concept of *inventio* involves finding or discovering the specific contents of meaning, and that underlies our modern sense of "invention" as searching the imagination for meaning. Nonfictional discovery is a process closely related to fictional invention—but subject to multiple, public constraints under a protocol for truth-claim. It is no wonder that the theory of such a complex behavior of origination and revision participates in a certain slippage.

I felt that I would eventually have to introduce the explosive topic of fiction into a discussion of Hayden White's purported influence on the historical discipline. The issue here connected with my ironic plot for the AHA session is related to the occasional fictionality of reality, and the kind of decisions we make when hovering between realism and verisimilitude. In narrating the Hayden White session, I purposely omitted any description of its location—a room in the Sheraton Hotel called the Princess

Ballroom. I decided to omit that description precisely because the actual physical circumstances seemed to conspire with my ironic emplotment to frame it in a spatial metaphor so perfect that it struck me as too "novelistic" for truth-claim persuasion.

Of course now I have to attempt it: this room called a ballroom was appropriately circular, and perhaps 50 feet in diameter, with a raised platform in front of draped windows. But no one would dare dance in this room, as the free circulation of even immaterial objects is thwarted by two rows of square columns, comprising eight columns, each four-feet square, trisecting the room. Furthermore, each of the eight columns is mirrored on its four sides, so that virtually every sight line in the room leads directly to a large mirrored surface. The ceiling was low and made lower by immense crystal chandeliers which seemed to absorb the dim ambient light and multiply themselves in the mirrored columns. From the speakers' platform, one could look directly down the narrow channel of seats unobstructed by the mirrored columns or else look at oneself in a mirror; the acoustics and the microphone were dull; the lectern light was dead; the room seemed to be in shadow. The audience was unavoidably segmented, from itself and from the speakers, confronted with its own faces and the distant enhanced sound of sentences read by speakers many of them couldn't see.

What to do with this wealth of actuality clamoring to be rendered as spatial metaphor of noncommunication, intellectual disconnection, the inert absorption of ideas into a deadening atmosphere of obsessional self-regard and false light? In terms of truth-claim narrative, would I be going too far in the direction of a tropological fictionality if I described the Princess Ballroom as the material mirror-image frame for an event marked, as I perceived it, by intellectual frustration and the non-circulation of ideas? Even if I merely described the physical features of the room without comment, I would still be implicitly asking the audience to draw the significance of a ballroom where no one could dance. We are so adroit at these poetic registrations that life resolutely seems to imitate fiction. I actually found myself making the odd decision that actuality had not been subtle enough and that I wanted my ironic narratio modulated to a lower key. Verisimilitude demanded that I censor reality. And so I conclude on this note of superadded irony: that the chief conscious decision I was aware of making in the course of constructing a narrative involved filtering actuality through a standard of verisimilitude derived from realist fiction and finding reality in need of repair.

Note

1. This paper was written for the occasion of a lecture and seminar at the Wesleyan University Humanities Center (17–18 February 1997) and was intended to reflect on the Hayden White session in its entirety at the annual meeting of the American Historical Association in New York City on 4 January 1997. This account of my experience of the AHA session

provoked some extremely interesting and characteristically sharp-witted discussion among Wesleyan faculty and Humanities Center visitors: I have not altered the paper I read to this very special audience, but their acute conversation has emphatically been "good to think with," as we say.

Richard T. Vann (essay date May 1998)

SOURCE: "The Reception of Hayden White," in *History and Theory,* Vol. 37, No. 2, May, 1998, pp. 143–61.

[*In the following essay, Vann provides a quantitative analysis of White's critical reception among professional historians and discusses aspects of White's work that have drawn criticism, notably his terminology and alleged relativism.*]

The publication in 1973 of Hayden White's **Metahistory,** Brian Fay has recently written, marked a decisive turn in philosophical thinking about history.[1] White might demur that he has no "philosophy of history," since he, notoriously, has bracketed considerations of historical knowledge, as he has bracketed treatments of the referentiality of language. More plausibly, he might repeat his argument that there is no essential difference between history and metahistory; thus all practicing historians—and White still practices occasionally—have a philosophy of history whether they know it or not. However this may be, Louis Mink, writing only a few weeks after the publication of **Metahistory,** declared it was "the book around which all reflective historians must reorganize their thoughts on history."[2]

A quarter century later, we can see to what extent Mink's mandate has been heeded. White's challenge to conventional academic history, however, was not confined to **Metahistory,** though it is the work most often quoted. He fired off his first salvo in **"The Burden of History"** (1966)[3] and as late as 1992[4] was still expanding on and in fact changing some of his views. White is perhaps the premier academic essayist of our times, and he uses essays in the fashion of Montaigne, the inventor of the genre—to try things out no less than to inform and to provoke. **Tropics of Discourse: Essays in Cultural Criticism** (Baltimore, 1978) reprints **"The Burden of History"** and eleven other essays, some—like **"The Forms of Wildness: Archaeology of an Idea"** and **"The Noble Savage Theme as Fetish"**—more or less unrelated to the theory of historical writing, and some contemporary with and closely related to **Metahistory. "The Historical Text as Literary Artifact,"** one of three most often cited articles, is the best short statement of the theoretical import of **Metahistory**; but in the introduction which White wrote for the collection, he gives intimations of moving beyond the stance he offered there. In particular, the moral stance of existential humanism, so marked in **"The Burden of History"** and still implicit in **Metahistory,**[5] seems to have receded, and

while there is still much about tropes and narrative, there are now also discussions of narrativity and of discourse. These become more important in the eight essays republished in **The Content of the Form: Narrative Discourse and Historical Representation** (Baltimore, 1987), of which the first three and the eighth are entirely devoted to theoretical issues in historiography. (The other four, theoretically informed to be sure, are devoted to Droysen, Jameson, Ricoeur, and Foucault.)[6] In this collection the fruits of a decade of reflection since *Metahistory* are presented, with new emphasis, in particular, falling on the ideological and political import of historical narratives and on what White called "the historical sublime."

Apparently not all White's essays turned out to his satisfaction, since some were omitted from the collections. One of these, however, **"The Problem of Change in Literary History,"**[7] has had a long afterlife. And he has continued to publish, with undiminished energy, since 1987, although there has not been a third volume of collected essays.[8]

White's oeuvre is thus various and extensive, so any consideration of the reception of his work raises the prior and insistent question: "Which White?" Although (I would argue) he is generally free of the cruder sorts of inconsistency and incoherence, his thought has always been on the move. Furthermore, in stating his basic positions in a number of different contexts and to different implied readers, he has avoided repeating himself *verbatim,* with the consequence that various formulations of these positions—and not always cautious ones—have appeared. White has given much less attention to this than have his would-be exegetes, as he almost invariably declines invitations to explain what he meant by a given passage and as a rule does not defend against attacks on his views (or what are taken to be his views).

One way to study the reception of Hayden White is to make a quantitative study of the reactions, by historians—reflective or otherwise—and others, to the various pieces which White has written about historiography and the theory of history over the past thirty-odd years. My *Rezeptionsgeschichte* is based on citations of these works in the journals listed in the *Social Science Citation Index* and the *Arts and Humanities Citation Index* for the period 1973 to 1993.[9] This essay reports on those citations, suggests what they can tell us about White's work, and concludes with some of the important and still unresolved questions which White has raised.

To be truly comprehensive such a study would have to include all the comments made about White in books, but this is not feasible. There is of course no way to discover what views, if any, were held by people who never cited or wrote about him. This has not prevented several writers from characterizing such views. Most of them say that White has persuaded only a few eccentric historians. Amusingly, it is social-science-oriented historians, who should be most wary of venturing generalizations unsupported by comprehensive survey research, who are willing to say, as does Eric H. Monkkonen, "I suspect that only the tiniest handful of historians would concur" with White.[10] Only Hans Kellner detected the "enthusiastic reception *Metahistory* has had among many historians."[11] It is a good deal easier to find such comments as that the book is "irritating and pretentious" and amounts to "a systematic denuding of the historical consciousness" which constitutes "the most damaging undertaking ever performed by a historian on his profession."[12]

Nobody has attempted to estimate how many philosophers or literary critics White has persuaded. It seems clear, though, that the sample constituted by references in journals must overstate the extent and favorability of responses to White's work, at least among historians and literary scholars. These are much more likely to make reference to works they generally approve of, whereas philosophers do their jobs by criticizing the views of those they cite.

There are well over a thousand citations of White's work in philosophy of history in those twenty years. That averages over fifty a year; but the series starts very small (only one in 1974, and still only eighteen in 1978) and rises to close to a hundred per year in the late 1980s and early 1990s. Carl Schorske has pointed out that *Metahistory* "generated" no fewer than fourteen articles just in *History and Theory*, and a *Beiheft* as well.[13] Although this work was mentioned more often in *History and Theory* than in any other journal, yet, as might be expected from such a large number of citations, the diversity of journals in which the work of White has been cited is extraordinary. *Clio* and, more recently, the *American Historical Review* are the obvious ones, but also *ELH, ESQ,* and *MLN, Arcadia, Belfagor, Chasqui,* and *Fabula, Paragraph, Poetica, Salmagundi, Semeia,* and *Semiotica*—not to forget *Crane Bag, Sur,* and *Neophilologicus.* There are quite a few comments in German (into which all three of White's books have been translated),[14] Italian (the first language into which *Metahistory* was translated), and Spanish (also based on a Spanish translation of *Metahistory*). There are also a few in Dutch, Russian, Portuguese, and—thanks to the indefatigable Paul Ricoeur—in French, into which none of White's books has been translated. The array includes journals in administration science, anthropology, art history, biography, communications, film studies, geography, law, psychoanalysis, and theater. But to arrange the journals by discipline is misleading, not only because there are so many comments on White's work in journals of general interest (like *Partisan Review*) but also because the writers are seldom readily classifiable by their own disciplines. In fact it was usually necessary to look them up in various academic directories in order to find out in which departments they were officially rostered. Philosophers conversant with literature, the occasional historian interested in philosophy, and—especially—literary scholars disposing, or purporting to dispose of, all these fields were the ones who found reason to draw on White's writings. Furthermore, scholars interested in White have shown a tendency to migrate from one department to

another—as indeed White himself did. The out-migration from history departments has been particularly noticeable; a tabulation of commentators by discipline would look somewhat different if Hans Kellner, who has written more about White than has anyone else, is classified as a historian—as he started out being—or as a professor of English—as he now is.

A diachronic analysis reveals which disciplines confronted White's work, and when. There were, by my count, seventeen reviews of *Metahistory,* half of them in such eminently respectable journals as the *American, Canadian,* and *Pacific Historical Review, History,* and the *Journal of Modern History,* as well as interdisciplinary journals with a substantial historical content like *Clio, Comparative Studies in Society and History,* and *History and Theory.*[15] On the other hand, there were fewer than half as many reviews of *Tropics of Discourse,* and these appeared in *MLN, Nineteenth-Century French Studies, Virginia Quarterly Review, Notes & Queries, Southern Review,* and *Contemporary Sociology.* The *Journal of Modern History* was the only historical journal to review it (in a joint review with a book called *Culture as Polyphony: An Essay on the Nature of Paradigms,* which the reviewer judged as the more important of the two books).[16] *The Content of the Form* was more widely reviewed, but once again, in such serials as *British Journal of Aesthetics, Yale Review, University of Toronto Quarterly, Political Theory, Modern Languages Quarterly, Novel,* and *Partisan Review.* The only historical journals to review it were the *American Historical Review* and (bundling it with several other books) the *Journal of the History of Ideas.*

Historians took a particularly active part in the early response to *Metahistory.* About forty percent of the earliest notices of it and the early articles were made by historians, who were most of the earlier reviewers; but as these works began to attract the attention of others, especially literary scholars, the relative and even the absolute numbers of mentions by historians began to decline. Over all, fewer than fifteen percent of the comments on White that I found were made by historians, while the majority were made by literary scholars—more in English, as might be expected, but a surprising number in Spanish and German.

The purely statistical picture, then, would suggest that some historians read *Metahistory* and some of the earlier articles and found occasions to refer to them, but few indeed devoted the same attention to *Tropics of Discourse* or *The Content of the Form.* They would have had little opportunity to hear of these books, since there were so few reviews in professional journals. White became much less of a presence in historical circles, regularly preferring to attend Modern Language Association conventions rather than those of the American Historical Association (these used to be held at the same time). In 1987 Allan Megill referred to him as "something close to a *bête noire* within the [historical] discipline"; in later years some people began to refer to him as "outside of the profession" or as a "literary critic."[17]

German historians were less inclined to excommunicate White, and once his three books were translated, a number of them wrote appreciatively about him. Even an English historian, Antony Easthope, acknowledged that discussions of the "linguistic turn," largely owing to White's "magisterial intervention," had begun there.[18] Easthope's article is primarily about an old article by Lawrence Stone called "The Inflation of Honours." This reading of Stone informed by White dramatizes how abstract the discussion of his views has become in the almost complete absence of any historically informed participants. If historians have missed out on White's work, it has also missed historians.

The statistically inclined may wonder whether my figure for the declining, indeed almost disappearing, percentage of historians citing White is not in part a statistical artifact. Since there are so many more literary scholars than historians, there are that many more people "at risk," as statisticians say, of having read and cited White. I cannot think of any statistical technique to eliminate this possibility, but neither can I think of a plausible argument that what the statistics suggest is not real. The work of Hayden White has had a remarkable influence outside the profession, making him perhaps the most widely quoted historian of our time. But historians have almost entirely tuned out, especially historians in the United States (if it were not for the interest in White in the German historical profession from the late 1980s, the anemic figures for historians would have been even more unimpressive). Furthermore, even when American historians have quoted White in the last few years, they are still quoting *Metahistory,* rather than the essays which make up *Tropics of Discourse* and especially *The Content of the Form.* And within *Metahistory,* they are disproportionately attracted to those bits which discuss the great nineteenth-century historians.

Except for those who take particular pleasure in tabulations or catalogues, the main interest in surveying the reception of Hayden White is observing the variety not just of responses, but of borrowings, adaptations, and attempted paraphrases. The first review of *Metahistory* enunciated a position, if not an argument, that recurred frequently in the observations of historians.[19] Its author was Gordon Leff, the author of *The Tyranny of Concepts* (University, Ala., 1969). Leff begins, a bit surprisingly, by saying that "few would now dispute" that there is an "indispensable metahistorical foundation in all historical thinking." He identifies the novelty and interest of the book as White's location of this, beyond any particular ideological standpoint, "in the very linguistic or poetic image which 'prefigures' all conceptualization." Historical discourse thus "owes its modes to the particular linguistic imagery in which historical events are initially depicted." This sentence is not free of difficulties, but we may assume that "linguistic imagery" is a translation of "tropes" and that the "initial depiction" here is that of historians rather than the evidence about the events with which they must work.[20] Leff here avoids a common tendency to emphasize White's adaptation of Northrop Frye's four plot-types, often to the exclusion of his more radical view

of the underlying tropes. Leff then gives his critique: "the historical reader" will find in confronting White's treatment of actual nineteenth-century historians that "latent skepticism" will likely "turn to manifest disbelief." The problem is that White has taken a good idea "beyond what most historians would regard as its legitimate limits" and "reduced history to a species of poetics or linguistics." Even as a formal analysis, he concludes, *Metahistory* leaves out too much, "not least the criteria which govern historical knowledge and what is peculiar to it."

It would be unfair to demand substantiation of these claims from a short book review, but its rhetorical moves do require some notice. The most obvious is the invocation of "*the* historical reader" and "most historians" as authoritative. Then there is the reference to the unspecified supplement that history has which species of "poetics" and "linguistics" do not. White's application of the word "poetic" to historical thought, as we shall see, caused considerable offense; Leff is however unusual in claiming that history was thus "reduced" to poetics (rather than poetry). It is perfectly fair to note that White has omitted reference to "criteria governing historical knowledge"— and apparently only historical knowledge. However, even supposing that White or anyone else knows exactly what these are, his manifest purpose was to understand the great historical works of the nineteenth century not as bundles of truth claims (many of which have long since been falsified) but as books still worth reading, having "died into art."

Two other early reviewers, John Clive and Peter Burke, added a count to historians' indictments of White: obscurity. It is very unlikely that these were the only ones who had difficulty understanding *Metahistory*; but Burke went so far as to claim that White was writing "like his heroes Vico and Frye [!] . . . in what is very nearly a private language."[21] Clive complained that its style "lacks lucidity and elegance to a degree" and calls its frequent neologisms "monstrosities."[22] What is remarkable in Clive's review, however, is its openness to White's case. Whereas Burke had asserted that for White "the historical work" was "essentially the same as a work of fiction, in that it is a verbal structure which represents reality," Clive warned against too rash a rejection of the book's principal thesis, that "what is crucial to works of history, no less than works of fiction, is the mode of 'emplotment' chosen by the author," which in turn depends on the prefigurative language—once again the word "trope" is avoided—that historians "bring to facts and events as they seek them out, that is, before they even begin the task of casting them into a finished narrative." This is surely a better account of White's thesis than that offered either by Leff or Burke. Clive goes on to make more concessions: that historians have to use language to relate the results of research; that there is a relationship (perhaps partly unconscious) between form and content; and even that "ordinary as well as great historians" are "quite capable of presenting 'the same events' not only from different ideological points of view but also from different literary modes—as for example, tragically or ironically." Other than treatments by historians who were White's students, this is probably the most sympathetic account he received from his fellow professionals.

We may admire Clive's generosity while wondering whether he had either time or space in a timely short book review to spot some of the tensions and difficulties in *Metahistory*—tensions and difficulties which historians, as well as philosophers and literary critics, began to investigate. The most problematic areas were White's view of the tropes and his conception of facts and events, which led Louis Mink to characterize his position as "the New Rhetorical Relativism."[23]

One reason why early reviewers may have avoided using the word "tropes" is they did not understand what they were. If so, they had plenty of company. Scholars as well acquainted with literary theory as Fredric Jameson and Dominick LaCapra confessed themselves uncertain about how "deep" in consciousness the tropes are; their relationship to emplotments, modes of argument, and ideological implications; and whether they form any necessary historical or logical sequence. Others wondered whether the tropes are really analytically distinguishable. Metonymy and synecdoche, for example, can slide into one another,[24] and both can be seen as species of metaphor. Irony always threatens to burst any bounds and become a "super-trope," either engulfing the others or undercutting the entire typology.[25] John Nelson has argued that tropes as White saw them were not mere linguistic figures (as most early reviewers assumed) but modes of consciousness. If this is so, are they attitudes or artifacts of psychology? Moods—in both the grammatical and psychological sense of this word? Directions of imagination? Or are they overtly tied to actions (and thus not entirely distinguishable from ideologies)?[26]

No one doubts that whatever their depth, tropes as White conceives them are deeper than emplotments, modes of explanation, and ideological implications. It was not clear to his readers, however, whether the tropes operate largely or entirely unconsciously. If not, is it appropriate to characterize them as forming a "deep structure"? If so, how can White's emancipatory program, urging the historian to act as a "free artist"[27] and choose some trope other than irony, be implemented?

White's version of a Fourfold Path allows sixty-four possible combinations; but some have an "elective affinity" with one another and others appear unfeasible. It appears to be impossible to deduce the operative trope from the mode of emplotment, which may indeed be the most superficial level of a historical text.[28] The reason for this is that only the least imaginative historians (such as Ranke) line up everything according to the elective affinities. It is apparently the element of tension introduced by discordant elements which accounts for the literary power of the greatest historical texts; but inevitably this makes any claim about the relationships among them, or the priority

of the tropes, tenuous. This is curiously illustrated by an attempted "empirical" test of tropology by Daniel Ostrowski in respect of four Russian historians.[29] Ostrowski had great difficulty with the tropes, since "the rhetorical devices do not provide any clue to the trope." He nevertheless succeeds by lining up the tropes with their "elective affinities" in showing that the theory "works" for three of the four historians "tested."[30]

Inevitably, historically minded critics were tempted to speculate, as did Fredric Jameson, about what "mechanisms of historical selection" assure that some combinations of elements in his *combinatoire,* but not all, come into existence.[31] Such speculations seem to be authorized when White presents what look for all the world like historical explanations for developments in nineteenth-century historiography, especially the effect of the professionalization of history. He also traces a cycle of tropes from eighteenth-century irony (with Gibbon as chief representative), through metonymy (Marx), metaphor (Nietzsche), and finally irony again (Croce). While philosophers exemplify the succession of tropes (except for synecdoche, for which no representative was found worthy), the historians are treated in terms of emplotments: Michelet (Romance), Ranke (Comedy), Tocqueville (Tragedy), and Burckhardt (Satire). These are hard to array in neat chronological order, since Ranke was born three years before Michelet, but both were writing a decade before Tocqueville, whose *Democracy in America* was written some twenty-five years before the publication of Burckhardt's *Civilization of the Renaissance in Italy.* White's decision not to present the historians in terms of their determining tropes further complicates the question how they are related to emplotments, explanation, and ideology.

Another, eventually more fruitful, approach to explaining the tropes was suggested by historian Philip Pomper. Pomper, surveying the uncertainties surrounding the choice and succession of tropes, argued that White must have had an implicit psychological theory accounting for the occurrence (or recurrence) of tropes. If this trope were to be made explicit, he suggested, it would be found to rest on the trope of irony.[32] White never denied that his own stance was ironic, but he did suggest a psychological version of the origin and succession of tropes. The theory he adapts is Piaget's account of the stages of the intellectual development of children. Vico, Rousseau, and Nietzsche, he reminds us, felt that a kind of "poetic logic" was typical of children and "primitive" people. In the first year and a half of life, Piaget asserted, infants have a sensorimotor existence which, although it could not be characterized as metaphorical thinking, nevertheless constituted "living of the mode of similitude." After this "metaphorical" experience, the developing child conceives the world successively in ways which could be seen as metonymical, then synecdochic, and finally reaches the stage of rational thought, which is inevitably ironic. "If Piaget has provided an ontogenetic base for this pattern" of the succession of tropes, White concludes, "he adds another more positivistic confirmation of its archetypal nature." But, lest White be thought to be seeking positivistic support for his position, he quickly adds that he only claims for it "the force of a convention in the discourse about consciousness and, secondarily, the discourse about discourse itself, in the modern Western tradition."[33] And this is the last systematic word he has to say about tropes.

The other set of claims by White, about what "facts," "events," and "data" mean in historical discourse, although obviously related to the theory of tropes, could more readily be understood, and attacked, by analytical philosophy, whether wielded by historians or philosophers. Some quickly noted that a presupposition of ***Metahistory*** is that what White once called the "raw" or "unprocessed" historical record bore a striking resemblance to the "powder of facts" which Langlois and Seignobos in the heyday of positivism called upon the historian to fit to the laws governing them—unless sociologists had to do this job for them.[34] White, while rejecting the positivist program for endowing this absurd welter of facts with meaning, was just as convinced that "the historical record" had no meaning in itself. However, one of the first reviews of ***Metahistory*** already suggested that White was thus treating the "data" of history—a word which he does frequently use, in spite of its being a translation of "givens"—as analogous to those of science. But, says Andrew Ezergailis, the data of history have already been "touched by the purposes of men [and women]." Even though these purposes sometimes miscarry, so that history is littered with the unintended consequences of actions, Ezergailis regards these purposes as already "prefiguring" the data.[35] This rather cryptic statement foreshadows much more developed arguments by David Carr and Paul Ricoeur.

A similar point was made by Dominick LaCapra, who drew attention to White's "at times" lending credence to the idea of an unprocessed historical record presented as "an inert object to be animated by the shaping mind of the historian." This, he claims, ignores the degree to which the historical record is already processed and simply substitutes an idealistic event for a positive one.[36] Eugene O. Golob remarked that one of White's most notorious contentions, that different historians can stress different aspects of "the same historical field" or the "same set or sequence of events," suggests a quasi-positivist sense of events "out there" to be "observed" by the historian.[37]

These criticisms come from quite different philosophical stances. Golob chides White for not having sufficiently attended to the philosophy of R. G. Collingwood; LaCapra believes that in ***Tropics of Discourse*** White was repressing knowledge of discoveries by Derrida which were actually "inside" him.[38] Carr and Ricoeur (and perhaps Ezergailis) write from a phenomenological standpoint. From yet another, and in some ways opposite, position Alfred Louch argued for the existence of historical "facts" independent of any discourse or theory about them or of any narrative presentation of them. These would seem to be the very facts "out there" which other critics detected

as a lingering vestige of positivism in White's thought. For Louch, however, White is a consistent believer that historical "facts" are shaped by the structure of historical discourse and thus historical writing is not to be judged by its representation but by its "form of execution."[39] For White, the importance of the tropes is that through them the historian "prefigures the historical field" and decides what shall count as facts. But, Louch objects, this is to conclude that "facts are theory-dependent because our theory makes it clear what counts as relevant evidence." However this doesn't account for the existence of the fact or evidence. He illustrates the point as follows: "If we are working on a murder and have a theory about the gun involved, and then find the gun, it counts as evidence because of the theory, but doesn't exist because of the theory. 'Pass the salt' doesn't bring a salt-cellar into existence, nor is passing the pepper just a linguistic error."[40]

On a certain level this seems undeniable, and White would surely not be so daft as to deny it. He might have made it clearer that he does not suppose any such silly thing. But—leaving aside the obvious consideration that guns and saltcellars pose different hermeneutic challenges than the texts historians usually have to deal with—Louch starts his analysis at a point when a murder investigation has already been decided upon (inadvertently making a perfect connection between narrativization and power). White can afford to stop his analysis at that point, because his interest is in what makes historians decide what sort of investigation they are embarked upon; and Louch cannot claim that seeing guns always implies murder investigations.

The most under-analyzed term White uses is "event." Although he talks about "the same set of events" ensconced in different narrative accounts of them, he does not clarify what he means by "event." Louis Mink asks what an event is: "A horse throws a shoe, which cannot be nailed on quickly enough, and a kingdom is lost. Are both of these 'events'? Is the Renaissance an 'event'? Are there basic or unit events, which cannot be divided into smaller events?" He goes on to recapitulate Arthur Danto's point that "we cannot refer to events as such, but only to events *under a description*."[41] But if this is so, it is hard to see how historians could be equally well-warranted in writing about the very same "event" in different ways. White is apparently saying that there are indefinitely many ways of redescribing events, but he has not produced any argument that there is a substrate of unit or basic events that can exhibit some sort of sameness no matter how variously they are redescribed.

I know of no example where more than one account has ever been offered of exactly the same set of events—no matter how events are conceived. Ann Rigney has offered an analysis of various historical treatments of what she defines as a single event—Louis XVI's flight to Varennes in 1791. Aware of Mink's treatment of this topic, she notes how different historians have included more or less detail (about "events" that made up the larger event). Though events could figure in different stories, there was no consensus on the redescription of even this one "event"; and the historians were constrained not only by the evidence, but also, importantly, by what previous historians had said about the subject. This makes the likelihood of historians emplotting differently the same *set* of events even more remote.[42]

Few historians would be surprised by this outcome; but most would also wish for some escape from the relativistic conclusions that White draws. The problem with his position is that although there may be indefinitely many redescriptions of events, how do we determine the criteria for discrimination among them—an activity in which historians frequently engage? But the problem for the historical realist, or the advocate of "faithfulness to the facts" as a criterion, is how to defend the position that there is only one accurate description or redescription of events and only one way to select all the pertinent evidence and exclude everything else. The problem of the historian's selectivity, and its relationship to the issue of objectivity, has been curiously neglected in the philosophical literature.[43] If he had done nothing else, White would be notable for the boldness with which he thrust this to the center of his work.

The years after the appearance of *Tropics of Discourse* in 1978 saw the remarkable extension of White's influence far beyond the relatively small number of historians, philosophers, and literary critics who had quickly recognized its importance. In the years from 1973 to 1980 serious critiques predominated; from that time onward White's turn towards narrativity and his demonstration of the features shared by histories and novels were picked up by hundreds of literary critics and others interested in what became a veritable "narrative turn" in the human sciences. A good many of these references were extremely superficial; *Metahistory,* in particular, would be listed among "works cited" in a bibliography at the end of an article—but it wasn't. Quite a few of his readers evidently were introduced to Northrop Frye's plot-types and Kenneth Burke's and Vico's tropes through White. The titles of his articles were mixed up (granted, many do sound similar); his first name was misspelled (Haydn being my favorite); and more seriously, he was characterized both as a structuralist and a post-structuralist and put into the same bed as all those "absurdist" critics he had criticized in the last essay of *Tropics of Discourse.*

There is an undercurrent of satisfaction among White's literary readers to see history among the mighty cast down from their seats. Its epistemological privileges and scientific pretensions seemed to be exposed; literature's truth claims were at last taken as seriously as those of history. Some, it is true, were peeved that historians had to be recognized as imaginative and the literary artist put on the same footing as the grubber in the archives. However the overwhelming impression from these hundreds of citations is that students of the novel in many languages—and to a much lesser extent, of the theater—found White's work

comprehensible, provocative, and useful. For everyone whose attitude towards *Metahistory* seems to have been "Here is a book about narratives that I ought to show people that I know about" there were several who gave evidence of thoughtful reading and judicious appropriation. And even the namedroppers, on the periphery of White's influence, testify to the degree to which his work had become a cultural icon (except of course to historians).

Much of the interest in White's later work has focused on two essays in *The Content of the Form*: **"The Value of Narrativity in the Representation of Reality"** and **"The Politics of Historical Interpretation: Discipline and De-Sublimation."** The first, in spite of its title, gave rise to renewed charges that White does not believe in a "real" past or "real events."[44] The second placed such an emphasis on the political or ideological import of narrative form, without providing any foundation for rejecting any interpretation, that White was attacked for licensing odious interpretations of history, and condemned for inattentiveness to the relationship of emplotment and truth in historiography.

White's discussion of the referentiality of historical narratives led some readers to concur with Gabrielle Spiegel that he, like Barthes and Frank Kermode, "sees historical narrative as intrinsically no different than fictional narrative, except in its pretense to objectivity and referentiality."[45] This was not White's position in 1975, when he wrote that "historical discourse should be viewed as a sign system which points in two directions simultaneously: first, toward the set of events it purports to describe and second, toward the generic story form to which it tacitly likens the set in order to disclose its formal coherence. . . ."[46] A year later he was even more explicit, beginning **"The Fictions of Factual Representation"** by granting that historical events differ from fictional events "in the ways that it has been conventional to characterize their differences since Aristotle."[47] As for the reality of the past, of course there is no conclusive answer to Bertrand Russell's famous argument that the cosmos might have come into existence five minutes ago, complete with fossils and yesterday's copy of *The Times*; however this is an argument that only solipsists could love. But the "real past" cannot be known to be such by unmediated acquaintance; "in any narrative account of real events . . . these events are real not because they occurred but because, first, they were remembered and second, they are capable of finding a place in a chronologically ordered sequence."[48] Had White inserted "just" after "not" in this sentence, it would have been a truism. We could never have any evidence of something nobody remembered (at least long enough to write down something about it) and in a historical narrative there must be at least an implicit chronological sequence. However, as it stands the sentence leaves open the possibility that an event need not have occurred to figure in a historical narrative.

This raises again the specter of textual or linguistic determinism (or else utter relativism) which White in his early work usually tried to guard against. In **"Historical Pluralism"** (1986) White sketches a "pantextualist pluralist" position in which "the whole problem of truth is set aside in favor of a view of historical representation which leaves it virtually indistinguishable from fiction." Characterizations such as "virtually indistinguishable from fiction" readily slide into the position that there is no difference at all; but White takes pains to deny that he is saying that certain "events"—like English Romanticism!—never occurred; their occurrence is "hardly to be doubted." However, he argues, "specifically *historical* inquiry is born less of the necessity to establish *that* events occurred than of the desire to determine what certain events might *mean* for a given group."[49] For "events" like English Romanticism, this is surely true, but not for all investigations. Yet despite his lack of interest in the question of how historians might establish that events occurred, White has never abandoned the view that the contents of historical narratives are as much invented as found (which also means as much found as invented). And the more obvious the fact thrown in the face of the relativist—"You surely can't deny that John Kennedy was assassinated on November 22, 1963?"—the more weight falls on the meaning of that event for different groups.

"The Value of Narrativity" is the most often cited of all White's essays. It afforded a splendid introduction to narratology while at the same time staking out a provocative set of propositions. It also left many questions for historians to think about. How is the ideological production effected by narrative—the central theme of *Content of the Form*—achieved? (By subject matter? By the form of the content, or the content of the form? By the form of the representation? Or all of these?) Are all narrative histories equally effective? If not, what grounds are there for preferring one to another—a judgment historians make all the time? How do systems of meaning production in historical narratives get "tested against the capacity of any set of 'real' events to yield to such systems"?[50] White's attitude towards these questions, however, seems to be "Quod scripsi, scripsi"; his interests have moved on.

His critics, however, have not. To them White's emphasis on the real elements in historical narratives—shouldn't it be 90% found and only 10% invented?—and indeed his growing suspicion about narrativizing could assume alarming implications in the light of what White was saying about the ideological and moral import of historical interpretation. Narrativizing, he argues, is necessarily associated with the exercise of political power and inherently moralizes historical discourse.

In a complex and unusually adventurous argument, White draws out the political implications of much of his previous work. Part of the **"Politics of Historical Interpretation"** is, among other things, a historical explanation of what happened to historical thought once history was naturalized in the academy. The politics of this "disciplinization" consisted of a "set of negatives" operating to repress any sort of utopian thinking and thereby any

revolutionary politics, of either Left or Right, insofar as it made any claim to authority from a knowledge of history. (It goes without saying that rhetoric was also repressed in the disciplinizing process.[51])

In terms of eighteenth-century aesthetics, this development represented the suppression of the "sublime" in the interests of the "beautiful." The "beautiful," in historiography, is the construction of histories so well emplotted that they give intellectual satisfaction and aesthetic pleasure to the reader. The "sublime" is the point of view towards history which Schiller describes as arising from contemplation of "the uncertain anarchy of the moral world." He evokes "the terrifying spectacle of change which destroys everything and creates it anew, and destroys again" and "the pathetic spectacle of mankind wrestling with fate, the irresistible elusiveness of happiness, confidence betrayed, unrighteousness triumphant and innocence laid low; of these history supplies ample instances, and tragic art imitates them before our eyes."[52] Evidently only tragic art is capable of representing the historical sublime. For White the sublime is the sheer meaninglessness of history, and any historiography that deprives history of that meaninglessness—whether Marxist or bourgeois—deprives history "of the kind of meaninglessness that alone can goad living human beings to make their lives different for themselves and their children, which is to say, to endow their lives with a meaning for which they alone are fully responsible."[53]

Here again is the Nietzschean White. It is often overlooked, he says, "that the conviction that one can make sense of history stands on the same level of epistemic plausibility as the conviction that it makes no sense whatsoever." Now if each conviction is equally plausible, should commitment to one be simply left to a coin toss, or to a choice that can only be arbitrary? A visionary politics, which White obviously prefers, "can proceed only on the latter conviction."[54]

At this point White takes the argument further, confronting the hardest challenge historians could pose against his theories: Nazism and its politics of genocide as "a crucial test case for determining the ways in which any human or social science may construe its 'social responsibilities' as a discipline productive of a certain kind of knowledge." He admits that ideas of historical sublimity like those of Schiller and Nietzsche are conventionally associated with fascist regimes—with philosophers like Heidegger and Gentile and the "intuitions of Hitler and Mussolini." But this should not lead to rejecting it through guilt by association, since "[o]ne must face the fact that . . . there are no grounds to be found in the historical record itself for preferring one way of construing its meaning over another."[55]

White then proceeds to state the questions about formalism and relativism which some of his critics were quick to pose.[56] How, for one, to counter the "revisionist" argument that the Holocaust never occurred—"a claim . . . as morally offensive as it is intellectually bewildering [because the "revisionists" used all the apparatus of historical scholarship]"? Despite the claims of Pierre Vidal-Naquet, not by following the same "rules of historical method" that the "revisionists" ostentatiously imitate, nor by stigmatizing as an "untruth" rather than a lie the "quite scandalous exploitation" of the Holocaust that Vidal-Naquet attributes to Zionist ideologists, who represent the Holocaust as the inevitable result of living in the Diaspora, thus claiming that its victims would have become Israeli citizens. Vidal-Naquet calls this an "untruth" instead of a lie because it leaves the "reality" of the Holocaust intact. White defends it as true as a historical conception, because it justifies policies conceived by Israelis as crucial to their security and even survival. Who is to say that the "totalitarian, not to say fascist, aspects of Israeli treatment of Palestinians on the West Bank" is a result of a distorted conception of Jewish or European history? It is a morally responsible response to the meaninglessness of history, just as an effective Palestinian political response, entailing a new interpretation of *their* history, would be equally morally responsible.[57]

Would it, however, be morally responsible (rather than offensive) to impute a meaning to history that justified Nazi racial politics and found the Holocaust either desirable or nonexistent? The essay concludes without offering more than a hint of what the answer might be. Conventional academic history is whacked again; the alternative to it, which "seems plausible" to White, is a refusal to attempt a narrativist mode for the representation of its—history's?—truth. Such an approach might recuperate the "historical sublime" and conceive the historical record "not as a window through which the past 'as it really was' can be apprehended but rather a wall that must [be] broken through if the "terror of history" is to be directly confronted and the fear it induces dispelled."[58]

What source of terror lurks behind this wall? Why would it be easier to confront and overcome without any knowledge which we might gain from the historical record? The rhetorical questions and metaphors which crowd the last page and a half of this essay suggest an argument in the embryonic stage of formulation, not to mention substantiation. Suggestive as they are, it is scarcely surprising that they would hardly satisfy those who demanded firmer grounds from which to refute the "revisionists." These demands amount to the most recent episode in the reception of Hayden White—not because they raised any new arguments or ones not anticipated by White himself, but because they elicited from him, for the first time, reflection on the relationship between emplotment and historical truth.

This, however, was carried out with his usual élan. Those who stopped reading after the fourth page of his essay **"Emplotment and Truth"** would note that he had added pastoral and farce to the possible emplotments, and that "We would be eminently justified" in rejecting a pastoral or comic emplotment of the events of the Third Reich by "appealing to 'the facts' in order to dismiss it from the list

of 'competing narratives.'"[59] To that extent they would be justified in speaking of a retraction of some of his previous claims. White however seems to have little interest in this issue, which is soon dropped. His chief effort is to evaluate the position that the Holocaust cannot be represented in a narrative at all, or only in a narrative which somehow totally avoided figurative language. He recasts the problem, using works by Barthes and Derrida, as a question of what voice historians' prose should use in writing about such events; and he argues that it is not impossible to make a realistic representation of them, if it is a modernist realism employing a "middle voice" (neither active or passive), and requiring a narrative without a narrator of objective facts, not taking any viewpoint outside the events it describes, exhibiting a tone of doubt about the interpretation of events seemingly described, open to a wide variety of literary devices (like interior monologues) and reconceiving conventional notions of time so that, for example, events can be seen not as successive episodes of a story, but as random occurrences. Such a modernism "is still concerned to represent reality 'realistically,' and it still identifies reality with history. But the history which modernism confronts is not the history envisaged by nineteenth-century realism. And that is because the social order which is the subject of this history has undergone a radical transformation. . . ."[60] This is hardly the "realism" that realists are seeking; for White it is both very new and very old. He is now clearly trying out a post-modernist idea; yet this is much of what he called for twenty-six years earlier in **"The Burden of History."**

So the question "Which White?" remains salient in the story of his reception. Historians who read him may find little that assists them in the practice of their everyday "craft." Extracting from him—or imposing upon him—a systematic philosophy of history is impossible, and it may seem that he is only ushering the flies into new fly-bottles. His forte is fecundity, not fixity, of thought; as Stephen Bann has written, "White's techniques of analysis are not beyond criticism; indeed their fertility in generating argument and counter-argument must be held to be strongly in their favour."[61] But nobody looking back at what was available to the "reflective historian" in 1973 can miss the great sea-change which White, more than anybody else, has created. One measure of White's impact can be seen in two statements. In 1980 John Cannon, editor of *The Historian at Work* (London, 1980), recommended Herbert Butterfield's *The Whig Interpretation of History* as "perhaps the best introduction to modern historiography."[62] And an eminent philosopher of history, Leon Goldstein, could discuss history purely in epistemological terms; all that mattered was for historians to find out what happened. After they had done that, all that remained was the unproblematic process of "writing up." If nobody, even in England, could write that way today, we have Hayden White to thank.

Notes

1. Editorial introduction to *Contemporary History and Theory: The Linguistic Turn and Beyond,* ed. Brian

Fay, Philip Pomper, and Richard T. Vann (forthcoming from Blackwell).

2. *Historical Understanding,* ed. Brian Fay, Eugene O. Golob, and Richard T. Vann (Ithaca, 1987), 22.

3. In *History and Theory* 5 (1966), 111–134.

4. Most notably in "Historical Emplotment and the Problem of Truth," in *Probing the Limits of Representation,* ed. Saul Friedländer (Cambridge, Mass., 1992), 37–53, in part a response to Carlo Ginzburg, "Just One Witness," in *ibid.,* especially 88–94. See also Ginzburg, "Ekphrasis and Quotation," *Tijdschrift voor Filosofie* 50 (1988), 4.

5. Hans Kellner was especially perceptive to detect this in *Metahistory*; see his "A Bedrock of Order: Hayden White's Linguistic Humanism," *History and Theory* 19 (1980), 1–29.

6. White's two essays on Foucault, "Foucault Decoded: Notes from Underground," *History and Theory* 12 (1973), 23–54 (reprinted in *Tropics*) and "Foucault's Discourse: The Historiography of Anti-Humanism," in *Structuralism and Since: From Lévi Strauss to Derrida,* ed. John Sturrock (Oxford, 1979), 81–115 (expanded and reprinted in *Content*) have been frequently cited. Allan Megill credits him with the major role in introducing Foucault to American historians, with a review of *Surveiller et punir* in the *American Historical Review* in 1977 ("The Reception of Foucault by Historians," *Journal of the History of Ideas* 48 [1987], 127). Judging from the influence of these articles, the same might be said for large sections of the American academy generally. It must be said that White provides a rather idiosyncratic view of Foucault.

7. *New Literary History* 7 (1975), 97–111. Other essays which failed to make the cut are "The Structure of Historical Narrative," *Clio* 1 (1972), 5–20; "The Tasks of Intellectual History," *The Monist* 58 (1969), 606–630; "The Politics of Contemporary Philosophy of History," *Clio* 3 (1973), 35–53 (with critique by W.H. Dray, *ibid.,* 53–76); "The Problem of Style in Realistic Representation: Marx and Flaubert," in *The Concept of Style,* ed. Berel Lang (Philadelphia, 1979), 213–229; (with Frank Manuel), "Rhetoric and History," in *Theories of History: Papers of the Clark Library Seminar,* ed. Peter Reill (Los Angeles, 1978), 1–25; and "Historical Pluralism," *Critical Inquiry* 12 (1986), 480–493.

8. Among these later essays are "The Rhetoric of Interpretation," *Poetics Today* 9 (1988), 253–279; "New Historicism: A Comment," in *The New Historicism,* ed. H. Aram Veeser (New York, 1989), 293–302; "'Figuring the Nature of the Times Deceased': Literary Theory and Historical Writing," in *The Future of Literary Theory,* ed. Ralph Cohen (New York, 1989), 19–43; "The Metaphysics of Narrativity: Time and Symbol in Ricoeur's Philosophy of History," in *On Paul Ricoeur,* ed. David C. Wood (London, 1991); "Emplotment and Truth," in *Probing the Limits of Representation,* ed. Friedländer; and "Writing in the Middle Voice," in *Schrift,* ed. Hans Ulrich Gumbrecht and Karl Ludwig Pfeiffer (Munich, 1993). Some of these are considered in Wolf Kansteiner, "Hayden White's Critique of the Writing of History," *History and Theory* 32 (1993), 273–295.

9. The *SSCI* began publication in 1973, the year in which *Metahistory* was published; the *AHCI* in 1976. For historical articles there is considerable but unfortunately not perfect overlap in the coverage of the two indexes, so both must be utilized. The terminal date, 1993, is somewhat arbitrary, but assures that all journals cited are accessible. Coverage of foreign-language journals in *AHCI* and especially *SSCI* is incomplete, but has steadily improved in more recent years.

10. "The Challenge of Quantitative History," *Historical Methods* 17 (1984), 86–94. But then the proposition with which so few would concur is "There is no difference between history and fiction." Monkkonen goes on to note that "in the philosophical literature, only a handful have actually put forth a counterargument." The view he attributes to White could much more appropriately be located in Barthes; but, bizarrely, Monkkonen does not believe that Barthes questions "the epistemological belief of the historian."

11. Kellner, "White's Linguistic Humanism," 13.

12. Phyllis Grosskurth, review of *Metahistory* in *Canadian Historical Review* 56 (1975), 193; Andrew Ezergailis, review of *Metahistory* in *Clio* 5 (Winter 1976), 240. Grosskurth was not totally hostile, although she believed that White wished to impose "exigent artistic laws" on historical writing, while Ezergailis, who called the work a tour de force, was on the whole favorable.

13. "History and the Study of Culture," *New Literary History* 21 (Winter, 1990), 417; (reprinted in *History and . . . : Histories within the Human Sciences,* ed. Ralph Cohen and Michael S. Roth [Charlottesville, Va., 1995], 382–395).

14. A peculiarity of the German reception of White is that his books were not translated in the order in which they originally appeared; the order was *Auch Dichtet Klio oder die Fiktion des Faktischen* (Stuttgart, 1986) followed by *Die Bedeutung der Form: Erzählstrukturen in der Geschichtsschreibung* (Frankfurt am Main, 1990) and finally *Metahistory: Die historische Einbildungskraft im 19. Jahrhundert in Europa* (Frankfurt am Main, 1991).

15. *Metahistory* (in its German translation) was reviewed as late as 1991 in *Zeitschrift für Geschichtswissenschaft,* which was the official East German historical periodical. Although it had been mentioned in previ-

ous articles in that journal while it was directed by the Marxist East German academic establishment, this lengthy and fair-minded review is one small indicator of *glasnost* in the former DDR.

16. *Journal of Modern History* 52 (1980), 124.

17. Megill, "Reception of Foucault," 127.

18. "Romancing the Stone: History-Writing and Rhetoric," *Social History* 18 (1993), 235–249.

19. Review of *Metahistory* in *Pacific Historical Review* 43 (1974), 598–600.

20. Another difficulty is the ambiguity of "initially depicted." As Arthur Danto usefully reminds us, historical events *always* come to us already "under some description." This would make the "initial depiction" reside in the sources, rather than in the historian's poetic imagination.

21. Review of *Metahistory* in *History* 60 (1975), 83.

22. Review of *Metahistory* in *Journal of Modern History* 47 (1975), 642–43. Sometimes yesterday's monstrosity quickly becomes acceptable, like White's coinage "emplotment."

23. "Philosophy and Theory of History," in *International Handbook of Historical Studies,* ed. Georg Iggers and Harold T. Parker (Westbrook, Conn., 1979), 25.

24. Kenneth Burke, one of the two authors most influential in White's thinking about tropes, acknowledges this difficulty (*A Grammar of Motives* [1945] [Berkeley, 1969], 503), cited in David Carroll, "On Tropology: The Forms of History" [a review of *Metahistory*], *Diacritics* 6 (Fall 1976), 58–64.

25. The best discussion of these issues is Hans Kellner, "The Inflatable Trope as Narrative Theory: Structures or Allegory," *Diacritics* (Spring 1981), 14–28.

26. See John S. Nelson, "Tropal History and the Social Sciences: Reflections on [Nancy] Struever's Remarks," *History and Theory* 19 (1980), 80–101. Struever's essay was "Topics in History," *ibid.,* 66–79.

27. *Metahistory,* 372.

28. Carroll, "On Tropology" argues that the four levels are nested as follows: first emplotment, then mode of explanation, by which the historian explains in a deductive-nomological argument what the point of the emplotment is. Then comes ideological implication, which combines elements of the first two. The tropes are on the deepest level.

29. "A Metatheoretical Analysis: Hayden White and Four Narratives of 'Russian' History," *Clio* 19 (1990), 215–235. Ostrowski thinks it a "lapse" in the response to White's book that nobody had tried such an empirical test before.

30. *Ibid.,* 227. The four historians include Richard Pipes and the "Short Course" of the Soviet Communist Party.

31. "Figural Relativism, or the Poetics of Historiography [review of *Metahistory*]," *Diacritics* 6 (1976), 2–9.

32. "Typologies and Cycles in Intellectual History," *History and Theory* 19 (1980), 30–38.

33. "Introduction," *Tropics,* 7–13. White acknowledges that Piaget "would not appreciate being put in this line of thinking."

34. The reference to the "raw, unprocessed" record is from "Structure of Historical Narrative."

35. Review of *Metahistory* in *Clio,* 245.

36. Review of *Tropics, MLN* 93 (1978), 1037–1043, especially 1042.

37. "The Irony of Nihilism," *History and Theory* 19 (1980), 55–68. He refers to *Metahistory,* 274.

38. LaCapra refers specifically to the essay "The Absurdist Moment in Contemporary Literary Theory," which criticizes—he says "caricatures"—the thought of Georges Poulet, Barthes, Foucault, and Derrida.

39. "The Discourse of Subversion," *Humanities in Society* 2 (1979), 34.

40. *Idem.*

41. *Historical Understanding,* 23.

42. "Toward Varennes," *New Literary History* 18 (1986), 77–98, especially 87.

43. An exception is the remarkable article by J.L. Gorman, "Objectivity and Truth in History," *Inquiry* 17 (1974), 373–397.

44. L. B. Cebik in "Fiction and History: A Common Core?" *International Studies in Philosophy* 24 (1992), 47–63 treats this as White's true position, disregarding all his qualifications and disclaimers. The article is a tirade against White.

45. "Social Change and Literary Language: The Textualization of the Past in Thirteenth-Century Old French Historiography," *Journal of Medieval and Renaissance Studies* 17 (1987), 139 n. 2.

46. *Tropics,* 106.

47. *Ibid.,* 121.

48. "The Value of Narrativity in the Representation of Reality," in *Content,* 20.

49. "Historical Pluralism," *Critical Inquiry* 12 (1986), 484–487.

50. "The Question of Narrative in Contemporary Historical Theory," in *The Content of the Form,* 44. Several of the questions I have asked are pointed out by Ann Rigney in her excellent "Narrativity and Historical Representation," *Poetics Today* 12 (1991), 591–605.

51. "Politics of Historical Interpretation," *Content,* 62–63.

52. Quoted in *ibid.,* 68–69.

53. *Ibid.,* 72. It is curious that children seem to be capable of inheriting the meanings for which their parents "alone are fully responsible."

54. *Ibid.,* 73. In fn. 12 to this article (p. 227) White "registers" an item of personal belief: that revolutions "always misfire" (an apparent covering law) and that in advanced industrial societies, they are likely only to strengthen oppressive powers. The "socially responsible" interpreter, he continues, "can do two things: (1) expose the fictitious nature of any political program based on an appeal to what 'history' supposedly teaches and (2) remain adamantly 'utopian' in any criticism of political 'realism.'" Commenting on a shorter version of this paper (and others) at the AHA meeting in New York in January 1997 White declared himself a Marxist (perhaps utopian after 1989)—certainly a moral commitment rather than an endorsement of the Marxian master historical narrative.

55. *Ibid.,* 74–76.

56. Besides Ginzburg (fn. 4) see Aviezer Tucker, "A Theory of Historiography as a Pre-Science," *Studies in History and Philosophy of Science* 24 (1993), 656, fn. 48 and Gregory F. Goekjian, "Genocide and Historical Desire," *Semiotica* 83 (1991), 212–215. Jean-François Lyotard raises the ante in this debate by concluding, after a discussion of "revisionist" historians, that the historian "must then break with the monopoly over history granted to the cognitive regimen of phrases, and he must venture forth by lending his ear to what is not presentable under the rules of knowledge. . . . [Auschwitz's] name marks the confines wherein historical knowledge sees its competence impugned." ("The Differend, the Referent, and the Proper Name," *Diacritics* 14 [1984], 4–14.)

57. *Content,* 80.

58. *Ibid.,* 80–81.

59. "Emplotment and Truth," 40.

60. *Ibid.,* 50–51.

61. "Towards a Critical Historiography: Recent Work in Philosophy of History," *Philosophy* 56 (1981), 370.

62. Cited by Bann, *ibid.,* 367.

Philippe Carrard (review date Winter 2000)

SOURCE: A review of *Figural Realism,* in *Clio,* Vol. 29, No. 2, Winter, 2000, pp. 229–32.

[*In the following review, Carrard provides an overview of the topics addressed by White in* Figural Realism. *Carrard expresses disapproval over White's decision to forego a unifying prefatory essay in the volume.*]

Figural Realism collects essays written by Hayden White between 1988 and 1997, that is, after the publication of ***The Content of the Form*** in 1987. The oxymoronic title points to two of White's most basic theses: namely, that figurative language refers to reality "as faithfully and much more effectively than any putatively literalist idiom or mode of discourse might do" (vii); and, conversely, that seemingly "realistic" modes of representation like historiography include elements of "literariness" (ix), as they are grounded in the "four general types of trope" comprised of metaphor, metonymy, synecdoche, and irony (11). Let us recall that White's "tropes" differ from the "figures" of traditional rhetoric insofar as they do not pertain to the linguistic surface of texts. When Marcel Proust, in a passage that White comments on at length in chapter 7 of ***Figural Realism,*** describes the drops of water that become suspended at the top of a fountain in the Guermantes's garden as a "nuage humide" (literally: a wet cloud) (129), he connects two different realms through a metaphor in the "traditional" sense, substituting one phrase for another according to a technique he himself explains (and celebrates) in a famous section of "Le temps retrouvé." For White, in contrast, "tropes" are among the models that provide texts with a configuration in their deep structures. Therefore, "tropology" does not concern itself with individual utterances; it focuses on ways of associating words and thoughts with one another "across an entire discourse," allowing the critic to characterize the structure of that discourse "as a whole" in rhetorical terms (11). Thus—to return to the same example—White does not seek to identify the numerous figures of speech that Proust uses in his description of the fountain. Emphasizing the turns from one tropological "type" to the other, he argues that the passage unfolds in four successive stages, "cast respectively in the modes of metaphor, metonymy, synecdoche, and irony" (131).

Several of the essays in ***Figural Realism*** proceed along the same lines, advancing the view that tropes shape all discourses, whether they are referential or fictional. Chapter 1 thus argues for the relevance of literary theory to the analysis of the historiography, which—being written according to rhetorical conventions just like literature is—can no longer be regarded as an "unproblematical, neutral container of a content supposedly given in its entirety by a reality that lies beyond its confines" (25). Chapters 3 and 5 explore the notion of "context" in literary history and literary theory, showing how scholars (e.g., the new historicists, to whom White devotes an extensive analysis in chapter 3) have turned to history for the "kind of knowledge" it is supposed to provide (64), only to discover that there is not one but a "variety" of historical approaches (66). Focused on *The Interpretation of Dreams,* chapter 6 submits that Freud has "reinvented, rediscovered, or simply recalled" the theory of tropes found in nineteenth-century rhetoric (124), contributing a "terminology" for characterizing the moves of nonlogical thinking as well as a "psychology" of figurative discourse (125). As for the chapter on *A la recherche du temps perdu,* it demonstrates that rhetoric and narrative can have a theoretical function, Proust, at any rate, adopting them to "interpret" (141) things as diverse as sexual preference, social attitudes, social class, and works of art.

For the readers who have followed White's output since *Metahistory* (1973), the most provocative among the essays in *Figural Realism* are probably the ones in which White tests his conceptual apparatus in unfamiliar territories. Chapter 2, for example, is to my knowledge the only text in which White considers the representations of the Holocaust in historiography and literature. Addressing the issue of "truth" in those representations, White asks whether some styles, forms, or genres are more suited to the facts than others, and whether specific tropes or plots must be excluded because of the very nature of the subject. According to him, the Holocaust is not "any more unrepresentable than any other event in human history" (42), but archival and aesthetic constraints restrict the way(s) that it can be described. Thus, it is illegitimate to emplot it in a "comic" or "pastoral" mode, if that plot is presented as "literal" (rather than "figurative"), and as "inherent" in the facts (rather than "imposed" upon them) (30). On the other hand, there is nothing wrong about setting forth the Shoah in those modes, if the goal is to make a "metacritical comment not so much on the facts as on the versions of the facts emplotted in a comic or pastoral way" (30). White thus praises Art Spiegelman's *Maus: A Survivor's Tale* (1986) for casting the Holocaust in the medium of the comic book and in a mode of "bitter satire" (31). Indeed, by mixing a low genre with events of the utmost significance, Spiegelman successfully challenges the idea that a "serious theme . . . demands a noble genre" (31), and he manages to raise "all the crucial issues" regarding the limits of representation in general, of the representation of real, traumatic events in particular (32). The last chapter in *Figural Realism,* **"Form, Reference, and Ideology in Musical Discourse,"** takes White even further away from his turf. A long comment about the papers edited by Steven Paul Scher as *Music and Text: Critical Inquiries* (1992), it deals with the relations between musicology and literary theory. White, to be sure, claims no expertise in the area of music, and he presents the essay as a "test case for assessing the critical grasp that discourse theory might provide for cultural critics working at the interface of two or more disciplines" (197). But he asks interesting layman's questions, for instance, while discussing a paper by Ruth Solie, whether it is documented that "major always denoted positive and minor negative," or at least "was presumed to have been apprehensible as such," at the time when Schumann composed his *Frauenliebe* songs (161). More generally, he brilliantly assesses the difficulties confronting "efforts to construe musical works on the analogy to literary texts," also showing how attempts to relate both of these to their historical context(s)—White here returns to (for him) more familiar grounds—require "a full theorization of what is meant by history itself" (175). ·

In his preface, White signals that he intended to write a long introduction relating the essays in *Figural Realism* to one another as well as to essays he published earlier, but that he soon gave up, leaving the texts to "stand by themselves" (vi). Readers certainly can understand how attempts at synthesis might "bore" (as White puts it) even their authors (vi). They can also understand how theorists are now wary of "totalizing systems of thought" that privilege the whole at the expenses of the parts (viii). Yet they may still regret the absence of a preamble of some sort, in which White would if not defend the wholeness and coherence of his system, at least self-consciously define his current positions and look back at certain aspects of his work. To take just one example, it would be intriguing to see how White responds to the critics who challenge his thesis of the nondifferentiation between fictional and historical discourses from a formalist perspective. Indeed, White has made a specialty of refuting the views of the critics who oppose his conception of historiography as a "literary artifact" (the title of a chapter in *Tropics of Discourse*) in the name of "realism," and he again devotes several pages (13–16) to answering those critics' renewed attacks. Yet he does not engage with the theorists who—like Dorrit Cohn—argue that if fiction and historiography are both literary constructs, they do include textual features that unquestionably set them apart (Cohn's *The Distinction of Fiction* appeared like *Figural Realism* in 1999, but Cohn has been publishing on the subject since the early 1980s). As a friendly amendment to White's preface, we might thus add that there is nothing rhetorically or epistemologically objectionable to the fact that established scholars should periodically revisit—and reassess—their past productions. Such metacritical considerations, moreover, are not necessarily "boring." Whether the reader is familiar with the author or just interested in the issues, they may be among the most inspiring elements of a study.

Allan Megill (review date September 2000)

SOURCE: A review of *Figural Realism,* in *Journal of Modern History,* Vol. 72, No. 3, September, 2000, pp. 777–78.

[*In the following review of* Figural Realism, *Megill finds flaws in White's rhetorical approach and the interpretative "multiplicity" of his historical perspective.*]

Figural Realism: Studies in the Mimesis Effect is the fourth book by Hayden White in a series that began with the raw, ungainly, and brilliantly suggestive *Metahistory: The Historical Imagination in Nineteenth-Century Europe* (Baltimore, 1973). Taken together, White's books and essays have done much to alter the theory of history. Although his focus on trope and narrative is far from what most historians are interested in, they are all aware of his work. This does not mean that it has been carefully read, but it does mean that in some slightly perverse way it now registers as part of the discipline's "cultural capital," getting cited in such otherwise unlikely contexts as American Historical Association presidential addresses. Who would have figured it in 1973? But it seems to be so, and perhaps in retrospect it is not surprising.

Most of the essays in *Figural Realism* will be of only marginal interest to most historians, although parts of the book ought to be of interest at some level to all. White's preoccupations in the collection are heavily literary. The book is best approached if one sees it for what it mainly is—an attempt to make sense of literary modernism's apprehension of history. Of least interest for historians are chapters 6, 7, and 8. Chapters 6 and 7 analyze, respectively, Freud's theory of the dream-work and a passage from Proust's *Sodome et Gomorrhe,* in the light of the four "master tropes" of metaphor, metonymy, synecdoche, and irony; chapter 8 reflects on the applicability (or not) of literary theory to music. More interesting for historians is chapter 1, **"Literary Theory and Historical Writing,"** which amounts to an excellent brief overview and defense of White's approach to the theory of history. Chapter 2, **"Historical Emplotment and the Problem of Truth in Historical Representation,"** is the one essay in this collection that many historians will already be familiar with: it was originally published in Saul Friedlander's collection, *Probing the Limits of Representation: Nazism and the Final Solution* (Cambridge, Mass., 1992). Here White discusses the problem of how the Holocaust is to be represented in language. Chapter 3 discusses formalist and contextualist strategies of explanation. Chapter 4 explores the alleged tendency of literary modernism to "derealize" the notion of the singular, specific event, which, White suggests, melts away under the combined pressure of modernist narrative techniques and a surfeit of documentation. Chapter 5 brilliantly discusses Erich Auerbach's *Mimesis: The Representation of Reality in Western Literature* (1946), which White regards as an exemplification of a specifically modernist historicism.

I shall content myself with making two general points. The first has to do with White's nimbleness and daring (some would say foolhardiness). Time and again White has undertaken to investigate intellectual objects and materials lying far beyond any technical field of competence that he might claim. He is able to do so because he has mastered a nontechnical field of expertise: he is a rhetorician, in the classical sense of a person who has learned how to produce speech that is appropriate to every particular occasion. The rhetorician holds in mind sets of rhetorical commonplaces or topoi (e.g., the master tropes) that are potentially available to be brought to bear on whatever matter lies at hand. The rhetorician also generally does not reject but, instead, works within the conceptual framework of the audience that he or she is addressing. Thus the distinction between formalism and contextualism in chapter 3 came from conference organizers. In chapter 4 White begins with a "commonplace" of contemporary literary criticism, namely, that modernism dissolves away the event. In chapter 6 psychoanalysis is

never questioned. And so on. With his topoi and with his willingness to meet his audiences far more than halfway, White is able to speak fluently and interestingly on an astonishingly wide variety of matters.

This way of proceeding has both defects and virtues. On the one hand, rhetorical topoi do seem to embody an inherited wisdom: at any rate, one is quite often surprised at how much they actually do illuminate the objects and discourses to which they are applied. One can also learn from exploring the discursive structure of positions without questioning the positions themselves. On the other hand, one is here engaged in the pursuit of something close to what Giambattista Vico called "vulgar wisdom" (in the sense of "common" or "popular" wisdom). Admittedly, White's vulgar wisdom is often the wisdom of modernist intellectuals, but it is still "vulgar" in the sense that the question of its validity is more or less self-consciously held in abeyance. Thus White proceeds as if the formalist/contextualist distinction were adequate, as if what modernists say about the dissolution of the event were true, and as if Freud's theory of the dream-work actually holds up under empirical scrutiny. White sometimes expresses reservations about these conceptions, but he does not throw them out, because if he did that the speech-generating machine would grind to a halt.

My second point has to do less with White's project than with historiography. White sees historiography itself as an embodiment of vulgar wisdom. Another way of putting this is to say that White is concerned with historiography in its interpretive aspect (and with its descriptive and explanatory aspects insofar as they are matters of interpretation). He leaves aside the argumentative or justificatory aspect, whereby historians, engaging in extended dialectical debate, seek to infer to the best descriptions or explanations. At one point White notes offhandedly that "the precise nature of the relation between arguments and narrativizations in histories is unclear" (p. 182, n. 1). White is interested in the narrativizations (or interpretations) of the past that we offer from the perspective of our constantly changing present perspectives. These narrativizations are multiple, for they involve a continual and potentially infinite "retroactive re-alignment of the Past," to use Arthur Danto's phrase (*Analytical Philosophy of History* [New York, 1965], p. 168). White helps us to see both the possibility and the interest of the multiplicity. But on both epistemological and ethical grounds such multiplicity also needs to be winnowed down. One of the roles of the historian (which White, in his sunny optimism and sublime exuberance, is not much interested in exploring) is to engage in such a winnowing.

Noël Carroll (review date October 2000)

SOURCE: "Tropology and Narration," in *History and Theory,* Vol. 39, No. 3, October, 2000, pp. 396–404.

[*In the following review of* Figural Realism, *Carroll explores the shortcomings in White's application of tropes to narrative history and objects to the suggestion that historical writing is essentially indistinguishable from literary fiction.*]

Figural Realism: Studies in the Mimesis Effect by Hayden White is a selection of his articles published between 1988 and 1996. Like his previous, frequently cited anthologies—*Tropics of Discourse* and *The Content of the Form*—it is primarily concerned with narrative and figural discourse (or tropes), especially as the latter appear in unexpected places, such as historiography. As in his other writing, *Figural Realism* shows White to be a person of great learning, at ease with the classics—of literature, history, and much else—as well as conversant with current debates within that interdisciplinary animal referred to as Theory (with a capital "T").

After a very brief but extremely polemical Preface (more on that anon), White begins *Figural Realism* with an essay entitled **"Literary Theory and Historical Writing."** This essay is probably the one that will attract the most interest from philosophers of history. In it, White sounds his oft-rehearsed leitmotif: inasmuch as history (historical writing in contrast to historical research) is a distinctive kind of written discourse, literary theory is relevant to the theory and practice of historiography *and* the philosophy of history. That is, history (history writing) is first and foremost a verbal artifact and, therefore, an apt object of scrutiny from the perspective of literary theory. Perhaps predictably for readers familiar with White's work, the dimension of literary theory that most preoccupies him is tropology, the study of figurative discourse (or figuration).

Given White's commitment to the notion that historical writing is, in important respects, both representational and figurative, and given his additional belief that the tropological nature of history entails that any event is susceptible to different forms of emplotment, White is particularly interested in certain claims about narrating the Holocaust, notably: that the Holocaust is unrepresentable, that it must be narrated literally (not figuratively or aesthetically), and that there should be one and only one narrative of it. Thus, in his second article—**"Historical Emplotments and the Problem of the Truth in Historical Representation"**—he critically examines these claims about the historical representation of the Holocaust. At the same time that he challenges these allegations, he also concedes that the Holocaust may confront the historian with special problems and, in order to solve them, he recommends that historians might negotiate them by adopting the literary form of the modernist antinarrative.

The modernist antinarrative also makes an appearance in the fourth article of the book, **"The Modernist Event,"** where White suggests that the appropriate literary form for treating the unique, unprecedented events of our times (so-called "modernist events," such as the Holocaust) is the modernist antinarrative. Indeed, one comes away from *Figural Realism* with the impression that White is convinced that historical writing should catch up with the advanced techniques of twentieth-century fictional writing. Thus, *Figural Realism* is not only committed to the relevance of literary theory to history writing, but also to the relevance of the practice of literature itself to history.

The third chapter—**"Formalist and Contextualist Strategies in Historical Explanation"**—seems to me to be primarily concerned with New Historicism whose achievement White locates in its advancement of a cultural or historical poetics (61). That is, for instance, by juxtaposing information from arcane legal procedures with canonical plays, the New Historicist breaks with, revises, or weakens the prevailing ways of thinking about the historical record creatively in a way such that the emergent, contingent, exotic, abject or uncanny aspects of the historical record are disclosed (61). Insofar as the New Historicists are poetic (in the sense of creative), one surmises that White is favorably disposed to them as an example of scholars who make history writing more explicitly like literary writing (in a very broad construal of that term).

New Historicism, of course, is primarily a creature of literary history; and White is interested in exploring the relevance of the writing of literary history for the writing of history in general. Consequently, he includes a chapter entitled **"Auerbach's Literary History"** in which he interrogates Auerbach's concept of this practice, as exemplified by his masterpiece *Mimesis*. White argues that what is distinctively historicist *and* modernist about Auerbach's approach is the idea of figural causation (particularly the narrative of prefiguration and fulfillment), which White believes has ramifications not only for literary history but for history in general (87).

In **"Freud's Tropology of Dreaming,"** White unravels the relation between Freud's account of the transformative processes of the dreamwork—condensation, displacement, representation, and secondary revision—to the various tropes used by rhetoricians to catalogue the articulation of figurative language. White argues, persuasively I think, that Freud, in this case, rediscovered or reinvented neoclassical tropology in order to theorize the dreamwork, though, White points out, whereas tropes function generally to clarify thought in figurative discourse, their function in the dreamwork is to disguise it.

"Narrative, Description and Tropology in Proust" performs a very close reading of a segment of Proust's *Sodome et Gomorrhe*—the scene of Marcel's interpretation of Robert's fountain. White is interested in this interlude for two related reasons: for what it reveals about the relation of interpretation in general to tropology (maybe unsurprisingly, he contends that interpretation, like narrative and interpretation-as-narrative, is tropological or tropic through and through); and for what it indicates about the ways in which tropes are concatenated in texts (how one trope leads to, yields to, or is connected to antecedent and subsequent tropes).

White rounds off the volume with **"Form, Reference, and Ideology in Musical Discourse."** In this article, White comments as an outsider (a nonmusicologist) on a series of papers by music theorists that explore the narrative dimension of music. The connection between this essay and the rest of the book is, of course, narrative, and White undoubtedly was invited to play the role of commentator here because, as a recognized narratologist, he is well-placed to assess the strengths and weaknesses of attempts to import narrative concepts to the study of music.

Though White, it seems to me, is usefully critical and reserved about many of the tendencies in the new musicology, nevertheless, I think that he is still not critical enough, especially when it comes to attempts to attribute a narrative dimension to pure instrumental or absolute music. For if we are speaking of pure instrumental music, there is the continuing issue of whether it makes sense to call music discourse, let alone narrative discourse. Unfortunately, White seems to presume uncritically that it does and as a result many of his claims in this chapter involving pure instrumental music appear simply to beg the most vexing theoretical question in this domain of inquiry.

As already indicated, **"Literary Theory and Historical Writing"** is probably the essay in the volume of greatest interest to philosophers of history. There White advances the view that history does not have a distinctive method, but rather is a distinctive kind of written discourse (1). It is an assertion that he iterates several times in this volume. Nevertheless, he does not really account adequately for what he believes is distinctive about historical writing, since, though he alludes to tropes and figures repeatedly, he also suggests that figuration is a feature of all discourse (17). So we are unfortunately left with the question of why White believes that historical writing is a distinctive mode of writing.

Surely White is right that most historical exposition is verbal and that, therefore, literary analysis might be pertinent to it. Nevertheless, the phrase White uses is "literary theory." If this conjures up images of *contemporary* literary theory in readers' minds, however, they are bound to be disappointed, since the literary apparatus to which White most frequently resorts is the tropology of *neoclassical* rhetoricians (which some might claim is less a theory than an arguably messy, though pragmatically serviceable, descriptive taxonomy). This, of course, is not really a problem, because everyone should be willing to admit that historical writing often involves figures of speech, such as metaphor, synecdoche, metonymy, and irony. Were that White's claim, it would be unexceptionable.

However, the use of figures of speech or tropes in historical writing portends larger epistemological issues for White. The language of a historian is not, on his view, a transparent container, nor is the historian's use of tropes a neutral, dispensable form of ornamentation that can be paraphrased away without remainder. Tropes contribute to the content of historical writing—hence, White's notion of the content of form. White believes that tropes have content because he associates them with narrative structures.

Though White does not discuss the connection here at great length, readers familiar with his other writings will recall that the relevant narrative structures are of the order of comedy, tragedy, romance, epic, and so on. Since it makes an integral difference to the content (the meaning) of a piece of historical writing whether it emplots a sequence of events as a tragedy or as a farce, if we consider the structure of historical narration to be intimately connected to the historian's choice of tropes, then tropes contribute to the content of historical narratives.

Despite the fact that, to my mind, White has never satisfactorily spelt out in compelling detail the nature of the connection of tropes to narrative structure, nor shown that all historical narratives are, necessarily, tropological in form, the epistemological work he wishes these controversial presuppositions to do is quite clear. If historical narratives are inescapably tropic, if the choice of tropes renders the shape of any historical narrative figurative, and if said figuration is part of the content of a historical narrative, then there is a dimension of meaningful content in historical texts that remains to be assessed after all the fact-stating sentences in the historical discourse have been evaluated atomistically for their literal truth content. But how are we to assess this additional content?

Not, according to White, in terms of literal truth, since the relevant content in question is allegedly always figurative. Thus, White suggests we might think of this dimension of the narrative history as being true in the way that metaphors are true, where it is understood that so-called metaphorical truths and literal truths are assessed differently from the epistemic point of view (6–9). In this regard, historical narratives would be evaluated in the standard, literal way with respect to their fact-stating sentences and by the criteria of metaphorical truth with respect to their emplotment.

This epistemic ploy, however, is not conclusive, since White has failed to scotch the still defensible view, first broached by Aristotle, that metaphors are just abbreviated similes, and, therefore, amenable, once expanded, to the same literal standards of truth that other fact-stating utterances are. Of course, White may be able to refute this view of metaphor, but, as of now, the burden of proof belongs to him, if he wants to continue using this epistemological gambit.

Another suggestion that White makes is that the putatively special kind of truth that pertains to the tropological content of historical narratives might be understood on the model of fictional truth (9–13). That is, we typically believe that fictions can disclose truths about the world, though not literal truths, since fictions are made up. At the same time, historical writing and fictional writing share many of the same tropological and narrative structures. So might we not say that in virtue of these shared devices that history has a fictional dimension—that the distinction between literal history and fiction is not as implacable as members of the AHA suppose—and that histories, as well as being, in part, literally true, are also, in part, fictionally true, that is, true in the way that fictions are true of the world?

White does not attempt to deconstruct utterly the boundary between the literal and the fictional with respect to historical writing, though he does suggest that historical writing has an inexpungible fictional dimension in virtue of its tropic structures, whose content is best assessed in the way that we assess what might be called fictional truth.

Many historians will be unhappy to learn that their writing is fictional, even if White attempts to console them epistemologically by reassuring them that fictions can tell us about the world. I share their misgivings. Moreover, I do not think that they should be swayed by White's argument, since I think that it rests on a mistaken view of the distinction between fiction and nonfiction, the category to which historical writing belongs.

White appears to assume that since historical writing and fictional writing share tropological devices and narrative structures, one is entitled to say that history writing, or a dimension thereof, is fictional. This, in turn, presupposes that the way in which one distinguishes fiction is in terms of its formal devices and structures. But this is a view that has been abandoned by philosophers of fiction for the simple reason that, as White himself believes, fictions and nonfictions can share formal and narrative features. For example, the same point-of-view editing structure used in narrative fiction films can be used in a documentary film without compromising the nonfiction status of the documentary film.

What distinguishes fiction from nonfiction, according to theorists like Kendall Walton and Gregory Currie, is the intended stance that the author mandates the audience to take toward the propositional content of his discourse. With nonfiction, the author intends the reader to *believe* the propositional content of the discourse; with fiction, the author merely intends the reader to imagine or to entertain the propositional content of the work. Historians, it is fair to say, intend the audience to believe the content of their work—to believe that it applies to the historical past—and in that sense their writing is squarely nonfictional, even if it shares certain formal expositional structures with fictional writing. The realist political historian who projects a tragic viewpoint toward the history of the Balkans is not writing fiction in this sense, no matter how fond he might be of synecdoches, because he intends readers to believe literally the content of his discourse. Unless White can undermine this sort of approach to the identification of fiction, he is not warranted in asserting that history writing, or a dimension thereof, is fictional and, therefore, to be assessed in terms of a different epistemic standard than that appropriate to all literal nonfictions.

White's tropological/fictional approach to historical writing is well known and has, as one would expect, garnered its share of criticism. In **"Literary History and Historical Writing"** White addresses a number of those criticisms, some more successfully than others. Possibly the most threatening charge leveled at White is that his position is self-refuting. That is, White appears to believe that all discourse is tropological. Consequently, the critic suggests, White's own metahistorical discourse must be tropological. White appears to concede as much (17–18), but then goes on to respond that this is not a problem because it does not detract from the seriousness of a discourse that it has tropological features. The possession of figuration, and even of figurative content, does not, White insists, imply frivolousness.

True enough. But nevertheless I think that White has missed the point of his critic here. I take the critic to be charging that if White's theory is tropological in the way he concedes, then it is fictional. If it is fictional, then we are not intended to believe it. But surely White wants us to believe his theory. Therefore, his concessions are self-undermining. To protest, as White does, that his theories are serious—perhaps serious fiction—is simply to change the subject. For if they are fictional, then they are not presented as objects to be believed. But since, presumably, White intends them to be believed, then he does not intend them to be fictional. This is, I think, the trap in which White's critic wishes to ensnare him, and I do not see that White's invocation of *seriousness* sets him free of it.

Throughout White's writings, he seems to presuppose that all the plot structures or narrative connectives used in historical writing are figurative; that is why he attributes a metaphorical and/or fictional aspect to history writing, alleging that it is not straightforwardly reducible to assessment in terms of literal truth. I have never been convinced by this generalization. Rather, it seems to me that most often (typically) the narrative connectives in historical writings involve causal networks—though not necessarily fully deterministic ones—such as lines of influence, agent causation, and so on (which can be assessed in terms of a straightforward, literal conception of truth). Thus I, at least, do not feel the pressure White does to arrive at some alternative standard of truth for the assessment of the narrative linkages in historical writing.

White takes up the issue of literal causation versus figurative causation in his essay **"Auerbach's Literary History."** For White, Auerbach's history of Western literature has the form of a prefiguration narrative. Just as theologians once found prefigurations of Christ in the Old Testament Adam, so, White maintains, Auerbach finds prefigurations of later developments in Western literature in earlier ones. Thus, it is the trope of similarity—metaphor—that supplies the connective tissue in Auerbach's story. For that reason, White dubs this connective "figural causation," which contrasts with literal causation, since, for example, there need be no really significant genetic link between the prefiguring events or persons and the prefigured ones; the former may anticipate the latter without playing any literal role in the latter's actual causal history.

Whether White's interpretation of Auerbach is correct is, I conjecture, of less interest to readers of this journal than his notion of figural causation. How extensive is it and how important is it for the practice of historical writing, not only literary history, but history in general? Undeniably, some histories secure coherence tropically in the way that White suggests—by unifying their subjects by means of the narrative figure of prefiguration/fulfillment. But I suspect that most modern historians would be wary of narratives told this way, unless a line of influence can be traced between the earlier events and persons and the later ones.

Moreover, if a line of influence can be traced between, say, one author and an earlier one, then we are not dealing with figural causation, but with literal causation. That is, the work of the earlier author is a causal condition, though not a fully deterministic one, for the work of the later author. Furthermore, if we distinguish narratives of influence from prefigurative narratives, my guess is that the incidence of prefigurative narratives (and the accompanying reliance on figural causation), though perhaps not totally negligible, is not widely pervasive either in the practice of contemporary history writing, literary or otherwise.

Of course, one apparent deviation from my maybe overly confident estimate here is the tendency of history writers to analogize one period with another—to say things like the 1990s are just like the 1890s. Is this a matter of figural causation? One reason not to think so is that historians who speak this way often do so with the unstated presupposition that the similarities they note are underwritten by causal regularities, laws, tendencies, or probabilities.

That is, the events or periods in question are similar because they are thought to be subject to similar causal processes, and the comparison between them is warranted since the genesis and outcome of the earlier events and periods may illuminate causally the direction of the evolving events at a later time. This does not show a commitment to figural causation, but an attempt at a familiar type of causal explanation, rooted in the faith that we can glean some causal regularities—though not necessarily laws—in the historical process. But even if this faith were ill-advised, such attempts are not thereby matters of figural causation, but rather, at worst, misguided, though literal, essays in causal explanation.

My objections in this case are based on my sense of the contemporary practice of history writing. But in *Figural Realism,* White is not just concerned to limn that practice; he also wants to change it. He not only argues that history writing is already literary, in ways generally unacknowledged by practitioners, but that they should become self-consciously literary and avail themselves energetically of the strategies of modernist fiction writers. For example, he recommends that the most effective way for history writers to grapple with the supposedly unprecedented events of the twentieth century is to embrace the techniques of the modernist antinarrative.

Though I admit that the events of the twentieth century are often different from events of earlier times—frequently due to the hyper-organization and interconnectedness afforded by modern developments (for example, totalitarianism, globalization—including global war—and so on)—I do worry that uniqueness claims for modern times may be exaggerated. But even if White is right that we are today confronted by events of a different and historically distinctive order than anything confronted by past epochs, I still find troublesome his recommendation of the modernist antinarrative as the solution to the problem of how to represent modern events.

My primary reservation has to do with my feeling that White has not really given us much of an idea of what a modernist antinarrative historical text would be like. Almost all his examples are fictional, including not only literature and film, but also the cartoon novel *Maus.* But it is difficult for the historian to take up White's programmatic suggestion without concrete historical exemplars. The only example that White mentions that seems to approach historical writing is Primo Levi's *Il Sistema periodico,* but unfortunately White does not say enough about it to provide a working historian with an instructive model. Thus, White's advice for historians of our times is pretty thin and airy. One wonders whether White would count the recent Reagan biography *Dutch* as the sort of narrative that he has in mind, since it, like modernist writing, blurs the distinction between fiction and fact. But that, of course, would hardly be a rousing testimonial for White's program.

White does propose that we might think of Auerbach's *Mimesis* as a modernist text because Auerbach himself suggests that his method approximates Virginia Woolf's (100). However, White recognizes that at the manifest level of technique *Mimesis* does not satisfy even Auerbach's own list of modernist strategies. So even if *Mimesis* is truly a modernist text, it provides little guidance for the working historian in search of a new mode of writing.

White's own writing in *Figural Realism* is often dense. I think the reason for this is his preoccupation with tropology. He is out to find tropes everywhere. But in order to do this, his conception of figuration is rather loose. It can apply literally to figures of speech, though unfortunately White does not define them rigorously and, as a result, sometimes his application of the category of one figure rather than another seems arbitrary. Moreover, the notion of figures or tropes can be extended metaphorically (or associatively) to narrative structures and to modes of thought. Indeed, some figures can be used to explain other figures. Thus, at the level of writing, the reader, or, at least, this reader is often confused by the unmarked, shifting senses of how one is to understand White's central concepts.

This may also be a case, to steal one of White's favorite themes, where form becomes a matter of content. Because White's use of the notion of tropes is so slippery, it is no accident that he can pile up so many examples. But this then raises the question of whether the extent of troping he finds in historical discourse isn't really a function of the slackness of his category. In that case, White's discovery of troping in unexpected places is not as surprising as a magician pulling a rabbit out of a hat. It is more like the magician moving the hat from one hand to the other.

Finally, some comment on White's Preface is in order. It is very short and it has the flavor of a "Here-I-Stand" manifesto. A number of White's pronouncements seem predicated on giving the faint of heart, like me, the jitters. Three especially stand out. First, White maintains that there is no active thought outside of theory; "to think that one can think outside of theory is a delusion" (viii). I can only think (actively) that White must have a pretty inflated idea of what counts as a theory. I thought that my car wouldn't start this morning, but I had no theory. Second, White contends that theory puts in abeyance the distinction between true and false, fact and fiction (viii). This hardly seems (dare I say it) true of scientific theory, most philosophical theory, social-scientific theory, and so on; White can't be advancing an empirical generalization. Also, as far as fact and fiction go, theoretical physicists are not likely to invite Arthur C. Clark to deliver a technical paper on plasma dynamics anytime in the near future.

Of course, if theories are not evaluated in terms of truth and falsity (or truth indicativeness and falsity indicativeness), how are they to be assessed? White suggests the criterion for evaluating theories should be their utility in promoting the moral and political aims, goals, and ends of the human species at large (viii–ix). Not only do I wonder how this will be done without considerations of truth and falsity, but I fear it mires White in the same kind of problems that bedevil classical utilitarians, namely, how can anyone conceivably perform these utility calculations?

Since these rather incendiary assertions do not seem to me to play a major or even explicit role in the essays that follow, I don't imagine that there is much point in making a big deal about them. Maybe the Preface is just White's way of getting unadventurous folks like me to sit up and take notice. Perhaps, following White's preferred mode of exegesis, we should read the Preface tropologically. It certainly sounds like hyperbole, and, I, at least, hope that it may be irony.

Jeffrey J. Folks (review date Fall 2000)

SOURCE: A review of *Figural Realism,* in *College Literature,* Vol. 27, No. 3, Fall, 2000, p. 171.

[*In the following review, Folks regards* Figural Realism *as "an eloquent effort" in defense of poststructuralism.*]

Building upon his previous studies *Metahistory: The Historical Imagination in Nineteenth-Century Europe* (1973) and *Tropics of Discourse: Essays in Cultural Criticism* (1978), White's latest book, *Figural Realism: Studies in the Mimesis Effect,* is an eloquent effort to defend an earlier tradition of poststructuralism that has come to seem less and less relevant to the social and historical issues that occupy contemporary critical practice. Drawing on the mid-century criticism of Auerbach, Barthes, Derrida, de Man, and Ricoeur and aligning himself with modernist literary culture, White defends a perspective that has been challenged by New Historical, neo-Marxist, and social agenda critics.

From a historicist perspective, a major difficulty with poststructuralist theory lies in its inability to make distinctions between historical events which, in and of themselves, are significant and those which are not, and in its obscuring of the grounds for historical causation and development. For those who attempt to understand the astounding scale of human destruction in the Holocaust, for example, does that event's "meaning" rest only in its incomprehensibility, or does its meaning lie in the literal events themselves? In attempting to refute the arguments of those, such as Berel Lang and George Steiner, who regard the Holocaust in the terms of realist historiography, as an event that requires our scrupulous attention to literal truth, White resorts to a familiar poststructuralist argument, but one that seems inadequate in a discussion of historical events of such a great order. Since the historical event itself can only be expressed in language, its "reality" is linguistic rather than literal, and thus only a figural presentation of historical events—no matter how "real" they may seem—can add to our understanding of history. The aesthetic or intellectual value of such "figural realism" rests in its self-conscious and inventive use of form and language rather than in its probing of the "reasons" for historical events. For example, White posits as "much more critically self-conscious" a work like Art Spiegelman's *Maus: A Survivor's Tale* "which presents the event of the Holocaust in the medium of the (black and white) comic book and in a mode of bitter satire" (31–32). *Maus* exemplifies "the modernist version of the realist project," that is, a questioning, obscuring, or rejecting of the grounds of "objective reality" and obliterating of a sense of purposeful or "linear" development of historical chronology (40).

Maus may or may not be more self-conscious than historical accounts and memoirs by Primo Levi, Elie Wiesel, and a host of others, but the weakness of White's position follows directly from the assumption that, given the absence of meaning and order within experiential reality, only narrative that in its form embodies this absence is significant. Narrative that "only" adds to our knowledge of facts or which proposes causes for historical events fails White's standard of self-consciousness; narrative that achieves a self-conscious level is meaningful, even if, as a realistic account, it is trite or highly speculative (as is Oliver

Stone's *JFK,* a film White finds more appropriate to our postmodern sensibilities than nineteenth and twentieth century works of classic realism).

White's most detailed application of tropological theory occurs in a chapter on **"Narrative, Description, and Tropology in Proust."** Focusing on a paragraph from *Sodome et Gomorrhe* in Proust's *A la recherche du temps perdu,* White attempts to demonstrate that "all genuinely interpretative discourse" involves a "play" of tropological figures and "an allegorization of the act of interpreting itself" (128). The paragraph in question describes (but in describing also interprets the surrounding text) the fountain by Hubert Robert in the Guermantes's palace garden. Proust's description of the fountain is an interpretive narrative that affords a reading of proxemic events in the narrative and that views these events, as White would have it, as a "chaotic and senseless . . . stream of life" (135). At the end of this chapter White discloses that all narrative emplotments must be understood as having a single intention: "the meaning of which is nothing but the process of linguistic figuration itself" (144).

It should be stressed that limitation of narrative meaning to the play of four classical tropes (metaphor, metonymy, synecdoche, and irony) amounts not only to a method of productive reading but also to a restriction of reading: even as it clarifies the tropological basis of narrative emplotment, it closes off the reading of narrative as primarily referential or manifestly historical. It is important to consider further just what, in the practice of figural reading, has been excluded from discussion—just what sorts of "meaning" are left out: in essence, all readings that would discover order or purpose, rather than devastation and confusion, in ordinary existence. In an piquant coda to his reading of the fountain passage, White notes Proust's recognition (in his insertion of the figure of Hubert Robert, the painter and architect whose fascination with ruins occasioned the nickname "Robert des ruines") of the inherent condition of "ruin" of experiential reality—"its impression of solidity and beauty and its real nature as a chaos as senseless as" the fountain itself (146). This reading of the fountain passage seems a remote and melancholy characterization, but one that is mirrored in the essays in White's new book.

FURTHER READING

Criticism

Ankersmit, F. R. "Hayden White's Appeal to the Historians." *History and Theory* 37, No. 2 (May 1998): 182–93.

Ankersmit discusses the animosity of historians toward philosophers of history—particularly that of Arthur Marwick toward White—and defends White's theoretical inquiries into the nature of historical reality and historical writing.

Carroll, Noël. "Interpretation, History, and Narrative." *Monist* 73, No. 2 (April 1990): 134–66.

Carroll provides analysis of White's complex theory of historical discourse as interpretive narrative writing. Carroll finds the "philosophical considerations" and "empirical theses" of White's argument unpersuasive.

Clive, John. Review of *Metahistory,* by Hayden White. *Journal of Modern History* 47, No. 3 (September 1975): 542–43.

Clive judges *Metahistory* to be "an immensely ambitious undertaking," though he admits that the book's central thesis will cause disagreements among historians.

Domańska, Ewa. "Hayden White: Beyond Irony." *History and Theory* 37, No. 2 (May 1998): 173–81.

Domańska examines White's theoretical position in *Metahistory* and discusses the significance of the ironic mode as an attempt to come to terms with the postmodern "prison house of language."

Golob, Eugene O. "The Irony of Nihilism." *History and Theory* XIX, No. 4 (1980): 55–65.

Golob examines aspects of positivism and idealism in *Metahistory,* and argues against White's application of structural linguistics and positivist assumptions to the field of historical writing.

Leff, Gordon. Review of *Metahistory,* by Hayden White. *Pacific Historical Review* XLIII (1974): 598–600.

Leff commends White's theoretical formulation in *Metahistory,* but finds flaws in its application to nineteenth-century historiography.

Partner, Nancy. "Hayden White: The Form of the Content." *History and Theory* 37, No. 2 (May 1998): 162–72.

Partner discusses White's problematic reception among historians, the underlying humor of his analysis of the *Annals of St. Gall* in *The Content of the Form,* and affinities between the work of White and philosopher Paul Ricoeur, whom White has criticized.

Pomper, Philip. "Typologies and Cycles in Intellectual History." *History and Theory* XIX, No. 4 (1980): 30–38.

Pomper praises White's contribution in *Metahistory,* but finds flaws in his typological framework, particularly the ironic mode.

Southgate, Beverly. "History and Metahistory: Marwick Versus White." *Journal of Contemporary History* 31, No. 1 (January 1996): 209–13.

Southgate discusses the opposing theoretical positions of White and Arthur Marwick, addressing inadequacies in Marwick's views and the unwillingness of traditional historiographers to engage newer developments.

Wellek, René. "The Politics of Interpretation." *Partisan Review* LV, No. 2 (1988): 334–37.

An essay in which Wellek criticizes White's arguments in *The Content of the Form.*

Additional coverage of White's life and career is contained in the following sources published by the Gale Group: *Contemporary Authors,* **Vol. 128; and** *Literature Resource Center.*

C. K. Williams
1936-

(Full name Charles Kenneth Williams; has also written under the pseudonym K) American poet, critic, and memoirist.

The following entry presents an overview of Williams's career through 2000. For further information on his life and works, see *CLC,* Volumes 33 and 56.

INTRODUCTION

A Pulitzer-prize winning poet, Williams is recognized by critics and readers alike as a keen observer of the subjective states of awareness and the urban and civic scenes, which he relates in distinctive long lines and colloquial language. Sociopolitical concerns are often at the heart of Williams's works. Williams is known for his belief that all experience—even the most profane and degraded—is a viable topic for poetry. Vignettes of contemporary urban life, subconscious reactions to tragedies both large and small, and the interaction of reason and emotion are represented in his work. Credited by some for reintroducing philosophy into contemporary American poetry, Williams believes that poetry expresses truth in ways that other forms of literature cannot.

BIOGRAPHICAL INFORMATION

Born in Newark, New Jersey, to Paul Bernard and Dossie Williams, Williams was educated at Bucknell University and the University of Pennsylvania, where he completed his B.A. in 1959. Williams's friend, poet Anne Sexton, convinced him to publish his first volume of poetry, *Lies,* in 1969. The last poem in this collection, "A Day for Anne Frank," had been published separately a year earlier. His next volume, *I Am the Bitter Name* (1972), contains "In the Heart of the Beast," written in response to the killing of four student Vietnam war protestors by the Ohio National Guard at Kent State University in 1970. *The Sensuous President,* a collection including previously unpublished work, was also published in 1972. Williams married Sarah Jones in 1966, but divorced her in 1975. He then married Catherine Mauger, an editor. Williams's second wife and their son, Jed, became the subjects of several of his better known poems. Williams held academic appointments as a writing professor at Columbia University in New York and a literature professor at George Mason University in Virginia during the 1980s and 1990s. Williams also held a number of visiting professorships at other universities, including the University of California at Irvine, Boston University, Brooklyn College, and the University of California at Berkeley. Since 1996 Williams has been a lecturer at Princeton University. Williams also has won a number of awards throughout his career. *Flesh and Blood* (1987) won the National Book Critics Circle Award, and *Repair* (1999) won both the Pulitzer Prize and the *Los Angeles Times* award for poetry. Williams divides his time between residences in France and the United States.

MAJOR WORKS

Williams's trademark style is known for its long succession of lines of twenty to thirty-five syllables. It is also noted for descriptions of mundane scenes from urban America, and narratives that leap from specific to universal experiences. Williams found his populist, storyteller voice in *With Ignorance* (1977), his first collection to contain poems with long lines and a conversational voice. One of the poems from this collection, "Sanctity," employs only a few lines to effectively describe the dual sides of a working man's personality. The man is completely in control of himself—even jovial—at work, but at home he sulks and becomes violent. The title poem of *Tar* (1983), Williams's next volume focuses on a crew of roofers working during the Three-Mile Island nuclear crisis in Harrisburg, Pennsylvania, in 1979, and comments on humanity's ability to cope with uncertainty and potentially harmful effects of technology. A poetic memorial to a colleague and friend, *Flesh and Blood,* is an eighteen-part work tracing Williams's grief process and his attempt to savor a friendship with someone who is dying. The final section, which is titled "Le Petit Salvié," is an elegy to poet Paul Zweig. The collection *Poems, 1963–1983* (1988) contains selections from *Lies* and *I Am the Bitter Name,* and all of the poems from *Tar* and *Flesh and Blood. A Dream of Mind* (1992) explores the machinations of thought and the relationship between reason (conscious thought) and dreams (subconscious thought). Williams's subjects continue to be linked to urban life—particularly the urban street scene—with sociopolitical statements appearing throughout the narratives. The collection is anchored by two long poems, "Some of the Forms of Jealousy," and "A Dream of Mind." The first poem consists of vignettes that focus on the miseries and doubts caused by jealousy, while the second poem, in part a philosophical essay, attempts to transcribe those fleeting moments when unconscious thought rises to the conscious level. The work is technically complex and includes a juxtaposition of long and short lines to form rhythmic units.

Selected Poems (1994) contains thirteen new poems in addition to verses from *Flesh and Blood,* and *A Dream of Mind. The Vigil* (1996) builds on themes from "A Dream of Mind," moving towards a preoccupation with psychological analysis in Williams's work. The three-stanza poems in *The Vigil* are structured with the first two stanzas describing a scene and the third providing a moral or psychological analysis of what has been observed. The poems in *Repair* initiate unanswerable, open-ended queries, and prompt readers to consider questions from a wide variety of stances. Williams also has translated or adapted a number of works, most notably *The Lark. The Thrush. The Starling.* (1983), an adaptation (rather than a direct translation) of verse by Japanese poet Kobayashi Issa. Whether collaborating with a scholar or working with other translated copies of works, Williams transforms foreign-language verse into his own interpretations, speaking to contemporary concerns. "Hercules, Deinira, Nessus," found in *Selected Poems,* is a direct translation of Ovid, in which Williams's characteristic long line structure resembles Ovid's hexameters. Williams also has written the memoir *Misgivings* (2000), and a major work of criticism, *Poetry and Consciousness* (1998).

CRITICAL RECEPTION

Although Williams has earned the respect and admiration of several reviewers, many believe he has yet to receive the recognition that he deserves. Despite his literary achievements, some critics find fault in the content rather than the structure and diction of his poetry. Others, however, praise his gift for organization and form, commending the energy and dramatic tension found in his poetry. Some reviewers consider Williams's first two volumes, *Lies,* and *I Am the Bitter Name,* dated due to their topical concerns. Many commentators feel that Williams found his true voice in *With Ignorance,* the collection where he began to experiment with expansive lines. This signature line structure—frequently compared to the blank verse of Walt Whitman—is extolled by many critics as evidence of Williams's poetic virtuosity. Others, however, find Williams's long lines limiting and relentless, noting that his later work has suffered from a degree of self-absorption. Williams's middle volumes, especially *Tar, Flesh and Blood,* and *A Dream of Mind,* continue to receive critical praise and are considered fine examples of late twentieth-century American poetry.

PRINCIPAL WORKS

A Day for Anne Frank (poetry) 1968
Lies (poetry) 1969
I Am the Bitter Name (poetry) 1972
The Sensuous President (poetry) 1972
With Ignorance (poetry) 1977
*The Lark. The Thrush. The Starling. (poetry) 1983
Tar (poetry) 1983
Flesh and Blood (poetry) 1987
Poems, 1963–1983 (poetry) 1988
Helen (poetry) 1991
A Dream of Mind (poetry) 1992
Selected Poems (poetry) 1994
New and Selected Poems (poetry) 1995
The Vigil (poetry) 1996
Poetry and Consciousness (criticism) 1998
Repair (poetry) 1999
Misgivings: My Mother, My Father, Myself (memoirs) 2000
Love about Love (poetry) 2001

*This work is an adaptation, not a direct translation, of verse by Japanese poet Kobayashi Issa.

CRITICISM

Peter Stitt (review date Winter 1983)

SOURCE: "A Variegation of Styles: Inductive, Deductive, and Linguistic," in *Georgia Review,* Vol. XXXVII, No. 4, Winter, 1983, pp. 894–905.

[*In the following excerpt, Stitt concludes that* Tar *is Williams's "best book," noting that the poet is at his finest when observing the concrete external world, and at his worst when looking inward at the psyche.*]

The sentence has increased our awareness of how the meaning of a thing may be changed by the manner of saying it. Life is transformed into style, and we are no longer at the mercy of accidents—the infidelity of a mistress, the treachery of a friend.

—Louis Simpson

I.

In the passage I have chosen for an epigraph, Louis Simpson notes how "the meaning of a thing may be changed by the manner of saying it. Life is transformed into style. . . ." The first clause is clear and accurate; the second is a bit fuzzy, and for a semantic reason: the word "style" is too close in meaning to the phrase "the manner of saying it." I don't wish to take exception to the first statement, but I do suggest that the second would be more accurate if we were to substitute some other word for "style"—say, "fiction," or "idea." Literature does alter life—it gives it a form and a meaning which are generally lacking within the rawness of reality. And the agency which is used to bring about this transformation is what we call *style,* the author's "manner of saying it."

At least, this is one way a writer has of proceeding; because the movement it describes is from the multiplicity of experience towards the unity of understanding, we might call it the inductive method. Two of the writers in the present group of five work this way: C. K. Williams and Roland Flint both write from an immersion within a ragged and unpredictable universe; by applying the methods of poetry, they manage to give order to this world, make it comprehensible, remove some of its sting. Two others might be said to move in the opposite direction: Frank Bidart and Jorie Graham seem to begin their writing with a general idea in mind, an idea which is then applied to experience, tested against it, in an attempt to understand the multiplicity of reality. Their method is deductive. Bill Knott, the fifth of these writers, follows yet a third way; for him, style is all—he is willing to change both experience and idea for the sake of a better word.

II.

In C. K. Williams' fourth book, *Tar,* it is style that gives the world beauty and love and makes it comprehensible. The setting of these poems is the urban landscape of the northeastern United States; before his discovery of the transforming power of language, the speaker finds it a grimy, grungy, soulless, loveless world: "Slumped on my friend's shoulder, I watch the relentless, *wordless* misery of the route twenty-two sky / that seems to be filming my face with a grainy oil I keep trying to rub off or in" [emphasis added]. The lines are from **"The Gas Station,"** the closest thing to an ars poetica in the book. The speaker tells a story from his adolescence, from "before I'd read

Nietzsche. Before Kant or Kierkegaard, even before Whitman and Yeats. / I don't think there were three words in my head yet." In the story which the poem tells, the speaker has been up all night with his friends; among other adventures, they had visited a prostitute who had agreed to "take care of us." By the end of the poem, the speaker has found at least a few words that might make a difference:

. . . Maybe the right words were there all along.
Complicity. Wonder.
How pure we were then, before Rimbaud, before
Blake. *Grace. Love. Take care of us. Please.*

Besides expressing that disconcerting brand of brotherly love one occasionally encounters on city streets, Williams' best poems are packed with specific details and concrete images, are vigorous in language, and have a strong narrative flow (thanks to the engaging voice of the man who speaks to us). For example, the opening poem of the volume, called **"From My Window,"** contains these narrative lines:

A girl in a gym suit jogged by a while ago, some kids
    passed, playing hooky, I imagine,
And now the paraplegic Vietnam vet who lives in a
    half-converted warehouse down the block
and the friend who stays with him and seems to help
    him out come weaving towards me,
their battered wheelchair lurching uncertainly from
    one edge of the sidewalk to the other.

The rest of the poem centers on these two characters, their relationship, the frustrations which the speaker imagines are felt by the caretaker, the walking friend of the paraplegic. At the end of the poem we see him again, trying to trace a figure eight at night in a vacant lot during a snowstorm: "but the race was lost, his prints were filling faster than he made them." Finally, "In the morning, nothing: every trace of him effaced, all the field pure white, / its surface glittering, the dawn, glancing from its gaze, oblique, relentless, unadorned." The speaker is touched by the hopelessness of this man's life; his words express the anonymous and distant affection of the ghetto.

In his best poems, Williams is an observer, the man in the upstairs window looking out at the action, describing it, turning its phrase. In his weaker poems, he forsakes the window in favor of a mirror, the better to analyze himself. I once had a friend who described another friend as "the kind of guy who likes to begin every conversation with the phrase, 'I'm the kind of guy who . . .'" C. K. Williams is similarly addicted, and loves to say things like: "I was at loose ends, and, although I didn't like admitting it, chronically adrift and lonely." Unfortunately, the poem which is by far the worst in this regard is the longest in the volume; **"One of the Muses"** is full of passages like this one:

She had come to me . . . *She* to *me* . . . I know that,
    I knew it then, however much, at the end,
trying so to hang on to it, to keep something of what
    by then was nothing, I came to doubt,

to call the memory into question, that futile irreducible of what had happened and stopped happening.

(p. 52)

When he gazes so relentlessly inward, Williams loses one
of the most important characteristics of his style—his use
of specific details, concrete images. Apparently these are
easier for him to find in the world at large than in the
recesses of the psyche. Thus this fifteen-page poem, all of
which is like the lines I have quoted, is the worst in the
book. Happily, it is also an atypical performance. Nearly
all the other poems in *Tar* are like **"From My Window"**
in their use of detail and an outward-looking narrator. And
it is for that reason that *Tar* is Williams' best book.

Robert McDowell (review date Spring 1984)

SOURCE: "Recombinative Poetry," in *Hudson Review*,
Vol. XXXVII, No. 1, Spring, 1984, pp. 115–31.

[*In the following excerpt, McDowell comments on the narrative modes of contemporary poetry and offers a favorable assessment of* Tar.]

If poets today are up to anything it may be this: recombinations of traditional strategies (or impulses) that define
anew our relationships to timeless subjects—love, death,
isolation, God and His godless double, anxiety, fear.
Whether the poets know it or not, this recombinant impulse
has its roots in what happened to narrative after the epic
tradition waned.

Nearly twenty years ago, Robert Scholes and Robert
Kellogg[1] called our attention to narrative's post-epic division into two antithetical types: *empirical,* or realistic, narrative; and *fictional,* or idealistic, narrative. Furthermore,
these branches could be subdivided: empirical narrative
into the *historical* and the *mimetic*; fictional narrative into
the *romantic* and the *didactic*. Though Scholes and Kellogg
employed this framework to arrive ultimately at an explication of the modern novel, its application also provides a
compelling historical context for reading contemporary
poetry. It is clear, to this reader, that the narrative types, or
recombinations of them, listed above are everywhere
present and necessary in the volumes I will consider here.

Believe this and you must believe, as I do, that all poetry
begins with a narrative impulse. That is not to say that all
poetry—even all good poetry—is narrative. The popular
contemporary essay-in-verse demonstrates that the above
types can be recombined so that narrative vanishes
altogether. Like other strategies, this is sometimes successful, sometimes not. Recognition of this recombinant
impulse, more than anything else, provides the key to
unlock what is happening in contemporary poetry. It allows us to reject the application to poetry of erroneous
popular labels like *formlessness* and *chaos*. It encourages
us to see the work itself. Informed scrutiny of an individual

text will enable a reader to make judgments, but the reader
must be aware of the larger historical context in which the
text inevitably exists. Awareness of this context sweeps the
reader far beyond snap judgments and personal bias and
enhances appreciation. . . .

More than anyone writing today, Bidart legitimizes the notion of a visual prosody. His poems are proof that lines *on
the page* create *visual* rhythms accurately conveying the
sense of hesitations in speech and the gestures and expressions accompanying them. This poetry is meant for the
eye as well as for the ear. It enlarges and enhances
understanding of our world.

I can reverse my concluding statement about Bidart to
express my only reservation about *Tar* by C. K. Williams.
His long, long lines are not so much prosodically relentless as relentlessly long. In other words, the reader of *Tar*
must be prepared to deal with an acute sensation of visual
monotony. However, he ought to be prepared to overcome
it by trusting his ear.

C. K. Williams succeeds in compressing and depicting the
convoluted nature of conversation, the rambling qualities
of letters to intimate friends. Decked out in elegant repetitions and the adjectival necklaces of Robert Lowell, these
poems yearn for peace of mind—the state of grace before
paradox, doubt, and loss of faith started working, keeping
one up all night, every night. In **"My Mother's Lips,"** the
speaker remembers his mother's habit of lip-synching his
words as he spoke to her.

> when I was saying something to her, something
>   important, she would move her lips as I was speak-
>   ing
> so that she seemed to be saying under her breath the
>   very words I was saying as I was saying them.
>
> Or, even more disconcertingly—wildly so now that
>   my puberty had erupted—*before* I said them.
> When I was smaller, I must just have assumed that
>   she was omniscient. Why not?
> She knew everything else—when I was tired, or lying;
>   she know I was ill before I did.
> I may even have thought—how could it not have come
>   into my mind?—that she *caused* what I said.

Coming back to the present, to the fact of his own parent-
hood, the speaker recognizes "the edge of anxiety in it, the
wanting to bring you along out of the silence, / the compulsion to lift you again from those blank caverns of
namelessness we encase." His paranoia is transformed,
becoming the ability to recognize a graceful and compassionate gesture. This is the moment Williams is after, and
his talent in rendering it sets him apart from the standard
fare of incomplete details, shoddy transitions and sensational assertions. This poet is always in service to his
subjects. Through fierce observation he becomes the story
he is telling, allowing it gradually to reveal itself through
him.

Note

1. *The Nature of Narrative,* Oxford University Press.

David Lehman (review date Summer 1985)

SOURCE: "The Prosaic Principle," in *Partisan Review,* Vol. LII, No. 3, Summer, 1985, pp. 302–08.

[In the following excerpt, Lehman comments on the prose quality of contemporary poetry and offers a tempered assessment of Tar. *According to Lehman, Williams's long lines are often well-suited to the poet's subject, but occasionally come off as "plodding" and needlessly elaborate.]*

Marianne Moore recommended that we read poetry "with a perfect contempt for it." Sensible advice, especially these days when, from the swelling ranks of MFA poetry programs, every Tom, Dick, and Harry—not to mention Jane, Judy, and Janice—seems to have a volume in the offing. To these competitors for our attention, we would be wise to offer strenuous resistance, at least initially, and as much in self-defense as in the earnest desire to distinguish the genuine from the spurious article. Perhaps no period before ours has set such great store by originality and authenticity as values; and how, except by an act of nerve, are we to evaluate the putatively original, the assertedly authentic? In the absence of any kind of objective criterion—it being generally conceded that command of the old techniques of verse reveals a reactionary temperament—what else can the reader rely on but his impatience with vanity, his truculence in the face of so many assertions put forth on the basis of so little evidence?

In one important respect, the contemporary critic's task has been simplified by contemporary poetic trends. T. S. Eliot stated the case in "Reflections on Vers Libre": "When the comforting echo of rhyme is removed, success or failure in the choice of words, in the sentence structure, in the order, is at once more apparent. Rhyme removed, the poet is at once held up to the standards of prose. Rhyme removed, much ethereal music leaps up from the word, music which has hitherto chirped unnoticed in the expanse of prose. Any rhyme forbidden, many Shagpats were unwigged."

A number of our poets do indeed insist that we hold them up to the standards of prose. Some among them are so emphatically committed to a prosaic principle that they seem intent on rewriting the verse of the past as prose—without, however, justifying the right margin. "Meredith is a prose Browning, and so is Browning," wrote Oscar Wilde, but the same remark applied to, say, Robert Bly would have its wit overwhelmed by its Wahrheit. . . .

To be fair, not all practitioners of the prosaic principle operate with so arrogant a notion of the purviews of contemporary parlance. C. K. Williams, in *Tar,* wisely puts his versified prose at the service of experiences for which it is a suitable measure. Here's the opening of **"My Mother's Lips"**:

> Until I asked her to please stop doing it and was
> astonished to find that she not only could

but from the moment I asked her in fact would stop
doing it, my mother, all through my childhood,
when I was saying something to her, something
important, would move her lips as I was speaking
so that she seemed to be saying under her breath the
very words I was saying as I was saying them.

If there is something both charming and genuine about these lines, and I think there is, it follows from the impassioned urgency effected by the rhythmic repetitions—so that we feel a pleasurable rush when we get to "the very words I was saying as I was saying them." This is, again to quote Miss Moore (quoting somebody else this time), "prose with a sort of heightened consciousness."

Reading it, however, with a perfect contempt for it, we find not only a place for the genuine but a relentless sameness of tone that can prove deadening when the aim is straight narrative. Where James Schuyler, in the long, prosey lines of his justly praised "Morning of the Poem," freely espouses, digresses, and leaps from incident to reflection, Williams gives the impression of plodding solemnly ahead in a straight line. We suspect that the means are too elaborate for the ends—and that the moment of revelation is needlessly postponed—in such a poem as **"Combat."**

C. K. Williams with Lynn Keller (interview date 21 November 1985)

SOURCE: "An Interview with C. K. Williams," in *Contemporary Literature,* Vol. XXIX, No. 2, Summer, 1988, pp. 157–76.

[In the following interview, originally conducted on November 21, 1985, Williams discusses the political role of poetry, his literary influences and preferred poets, his approach to writing and aesthetic concerns, his work as a translator, and his thoughts on contemporary poetry.]

C. K. Williams recalls, in his poem **"My Mother's Lips,"** that throughout his childhood his mother had mouthed his words whenever he attempted to communicate "something important." As recreated in the poem, the evening in his adolescence when he asked her not to do so—and for the first time felt himself having to find his own words and go on speaking by himself—marked his entry into poetry as well as adulthood. The poems that came to the lips of the solitary young man continued the speech he had previously directed toward his mirroring mother; they were efforts to reach within himself to "the blank caverns of namelessness we encase." Yet the lines of the beginning artist were also reaching outward toward an embrace of otherness; thus, at the close of **"My Mother's Lips,"** the poet speaks with the "sweet, alien air against [him] like a kiss." In his published work, C. K. Williams has pursued with ferocious intensity both the impulse to look deep within his own darkness and the impulse to confront, as lovingly as possible, the alien world, the situations and feelings of others.

His first volume, *Lies* (1969), is the most inward and obscure of his collections. With strange, terrifying metaphors and a sometimes thunderous but colloquial voice, Williams explores the bestial and subconscious impulses within himself. The twisted world of these sur-realistic fables conveys the "moral terror" Williams experiences witnessing the evil and destructive urges of all humankind. With *I Am the Bitter Name* (1972), Williams opens his poetry more fully and explicitly to immediate political events. Disjunctive and largely short-lined like the poems of *Lies,* these lyrics rage bitterly against the insanity of recent historical events.

The poems in *With Ignorance* (1977) differ strikingly from those collected earlier. Prosaic, casual speech and a generously inclusive manner replace the telegraphic cries of the preceding volumes. Long lines permit the relaxed unfolding of personal memories and dialogic meditations. The discursiveness of *With Ignorance* and of the succeeding collection, *Tar* (1983), allows Williams space to explore the ethical and intellectual complexities surrounding the questions he poses. "Are we commended to each other to alleviate our terror of solitude and annihilation and that's all?" "[H]ow much of my anxiety is always for myself[?]" These questions are voiced directly; others, about the origins of brutality, the dangers of nostalgia, the possibilities of transcendence, the powers of love, implicitly drive the poems. Only partially analytic and propositional, Williams's questioning often takes the form of narrative and description. He interrogates a situation by recalling or imagining its unfolding in ample graphic detail.

The subjects of his narratives are often saddening, sometimes hideous or distasteful: a boy overhearing drunken neighbors fight, a paraplegic Vietnam veteran losing his pants as he falls from his wheelchair, a dog with an intestinal blockage shrieking as he tries to defecate. They inhabit a run-down urban setting of boarded tenements and glass-littered parks, where drunks lounge on the sidewalks and long-time losers brag in bars. Sometimes they are stranded in even more desolate country towns, America's "great, naked wastes of wrack and spill." While Williams's stance is often the observer's, he manages to watch compassionately without distancing himself as outsider. He does not hold himself above any degradation. Yet he does not attempt to claim others' experience as his own. Avoiding appropriations that would be emotionally manipulative or intellectually suspect, Williams's portraits of people who are impoverished, oppressed, broken, or nearly broken do not pretend to speak from within that deprivation. Rather, the poems suggest that seeing is itself a crucial political act in our crowded world, for what we refuse to see we will not attempt to change.

Although the people Williams portrays are partially crippled by holding in cries of anguish, they nonetheless embody small, essential triumphs of the human spirit—and this qualified triumph is the emphasis of Williams's recent work. The paraplegic vet's companion determinedly tracks the figure of infinity even if the falling snow inevitably obliterates that image; a has-been grocer continues to make his bed and sweep his condemned apartment; models posing for pornographic photos are imagined sharing a moment of tenderness. Thus Williams's description of Jim Daniels's poetic achievement could just as well describe his own: "He has captured and enacted the blind and sad anguish of souls so trapped that they have ceased to know how to speak even to themselves, but he has never lost sight of the remarkable dignity, humor, and spiritual resilience which at the end are what redeems our passion and our hope."

In addition to the four volumes of poetry that had appeared before this interview took place, Williams has published a translation of Sophocles' *Women of Trachis* (1978) as part of the Greek Tragedy in New Translations project edited by the late William Arrowsmith for Oxford University Press and *The Lark. The Thrush. The Starling.* (1983), in lovely limited edition from Burning Deck, which contains twenty-four "poems from Issa." Williams's most recent collection of poems, *Flesh and Blood,* won the 1987 National Book Critics Circle Award. His translation of Euripides' *The Bacchae* is forthcoming.

This interview was conducted on November 21, 1985, in conjunction with a reading supported by the Wisconsin Union Directorate Ideas and Issues Committee and by the English Department of the University of Wisconsin, Madison. Our thanks to them and to Professor Ron Wallace for arrangements that made the interview possible.

[Keller:] Since you are here in Madison partly because you were the final judge for this year's Brittingham poetry prize, I'll start with questions prompted by your introduction to the book you selected. In introducing Jim Daniels's Places/Everyone, *you praise the volume's political engagement. In Latin America and countries in extreme political turmoil, poets' voices have real political power. Do they have any here?*

[Williams:] I'm not sure that poets in other countries have that much political power either, or not much *direct* power. In places like Latin America and Eastern Europe, where there's a clear social emergency, then the recourse to poetry becomes more common. In America, since the Civil War anyway, one of the prevalent political tactics has been for those in power to pretend that there is no emergency, even when there clearly is. What we're going through in America now, with a realignment of class, of economic expectation, with a continuing unemployment and poverty problem, would in most places be considered a sociopolitical emergency, but here we regard it as a wave in the economic cycle. I don't think, though, that poetry has much to offer in a programmatic sense. Whether poetry has a particular political agenda isn't nearly as important as the fact that it promulgates by its very essence basic human decency, basic values, and a shared vision of community. When there is an emergency that people feel, or are allowed to feel, is real, then they tend to go looking for poetry, for the solaces it offers and for the heightened moral consciousness it presupposes. That's what happened during the Vietnam war, when first the college kids and then many other people realized that poetry could speak, and was already speaking, for them.

While it's obviously valuable, it can be awkward for someone in the comfortable middle class to be proclaiming emergency or trying to speak for the destitute and oppressed. Sometimes in your work you bring to the fore a sense of the guilt experienced by the privileged and by the survivors. That's the case in, say, **"The Beginning of April"** *or in some of your poems referring to the Nazi Holocaust. Do poems help you deal with that discomfort of being relatively free and strong and prosperous?*

Yes. That's an excellent question. I think I'm more radically political than I ever was in terms of the intensity of feeling I have about political issues now. At the same time, I have less sense of what a political program would be that would avoid the various shoals all the existing political systems tend to run aground on. In the sixties and the seventies when there seemed to be the possibility for some activism—for a way to really act, to go into the street . . . All the illusions we had then, or maybe they weren't illusions, maybe they were just lost hopes . . . I suffered a great deal then from the feeling that I wasn't doing enough. The real activists would say, "Put your body on the line," and I had no wish to do that. I went to the demonstrations and the readings, but I didn't feel comfortable with that sort of activism, and I still don't. I feel less lively guilt about it now, partly because going to the streets would be like running around in circles, and secondly, because I'm a little more certain of the function that poetry—what I do spend all my time at—does fulfill. I'm more sure that there's a task for the poet that doesn't involve putting down poetry and grabbing a gun or grabbing the lecturn or whatever you would grab. But the discomfort you speak of is still one of the main emotions I feel just living in the middle class in America, especially living in New York. If I ever leave New York, it will be because of the tensions I feel, the discrepancy between my life and the life that I have to see around me. And "I have to see" is the part that I often write about, because that's the middle class emotion: watching people who are condemned to live the way they do and feeling there's nothing you can do about it, especially at such a reactionary time as we're going through now.

What political writers do you particularly admire?

I've been studying a book by Robert Bellah and his four co-authors, *Habits of the Heart: Individualism and Commitment in American Life.* It's a wonderful book. Over the last five years I've studied a lot of economics just to try to figure how the world works—nothing systematic, unfortunately. I've read a lot of Albert Hirschman, who is a great economist; a book of his, *Shifting Involvements: Private Interest and Public Action,* contains very good studies of how people move politically, what makes them stay with an idea or an institution or abandon it. And now I'm reading more—I'm starting Tocqueville who I somehow never read and some of the people who Bellah and his people referred to, notably Alasdair MacIntyre.

What about political poets or people who have written political poems?

During the sixties I did most of my reading in that. There isn't all that much in America, although there's quite a bit from other countries. No, that's not fair to say—I think for instance of Whitman, who was a big influence on all American poets. When I first read him he was a major political influence on me. Yeats, who is probably my aesthetic model as far as making a poem, to me is a very important political poet. During the sixties I read a lot of the Latin Americans and Spaniards, as most poets here did: Neruda, Vallejo, Lorca, Hernández, Machado. And also during that period all the Eastern European poets, particularly the Polish poets, who were a very strong influence not just on me but on the several generations of postwar poets writing then. Milosz did a book called *Postwar Polish Poetry* which was like a secret text only the poets knew about, and through that we got into a lot of the Eastern European poets who have to live in that state of emergency we spoke of before, and who tend to write out of a much more direct sense of being in history and who have a much more direct *access* to history. They feel little compunction about locating themselves in historical situations in their poems. There's something in the American political character that makes us feel as though we're being hubristic when we speak that way: again, except in emergencies, we tend to be shy about making the first person the real enactor of history. Even somebody like Lowell who wrote a lot about history—and wrote wonderfully—except in a very few poems wrote almost as a historian rather than as a poet who was the legitimate embodiment of history.

What about Ginsberg? He's obviously in the Whitman tradition, and when I was reading your early works, the forward rush of some of the poems with their accumulation of surrealistic images and their black humor often made me think of early Ginsberg.

I admire *Howl,* I admire *Kaddish,* but I was never influenced by him. The concept of energy intrigues me. I remember once coming across a book of Charles Olson's, *Reading at Berkeley.* I was really impressed with the force of the energy of Olson's language, and I remember at the time brooding over that, trying to find out how he had access to that kind of power. If there was anybody from that school that I did get some of that from, it would have been Olson rather than Ginsberg.

You mentioned Lowell. That makes me think of the confessional and of your poem **"The Gas Station."** *The speaker* *in that poem asks some difficult questions about the confessional mode: "what am I, doing this, telling this, on her, on myself, / hammering it down, cementing it, sealing it in, but a machine?" The poem goes on to mention Augustine, apparently an allusion to the* Confessions. *Is a confessional writer a machine? And how do you place yourself in relation to that scene?*

It's funny, because when I wrote that poem I really didn't think of it at all in that sense. Yet it obviously does refer rather overtly to confessionalism, about which I have mixed feelings. I was a friend of Anne Sexton's. She helped me get my first book published and was a general source of support for me. But I was never a great fan of the confessional stance as such. When you come down to it, there are really only three confessional poets of any note: Sexton, Plath, and Lowell.

You don't count Berryman?

I don't think so—somewhat, but really only in the "Dream Songs," and there he wasn't so much a confessional poet as a narcissistic poet. The great "Dream Songs," the first seventy-seven, were hardly at all confessional except in very splendid, broad, abstract ways, but then when he kept going on the poems, they became quite self-indulgent. For me the confessional presents a great quandary because Lowell over the last few years—or Bishop and then Lowell—in some sense has been my technical model, to the degree that I've had to start pulling away from him somewhat. But his unscrupulous use of his own and other people's experience really troubles me. I recently read some letters that were written to him—I think it was Bishop who wrote them—telling him that he really didn't have to do that and shouldn't, and I would agree.[1] There are two issues to being a poet: there's the issue of making or trying to make great poems (and certainly Lowell did that) and there's the issue of *being* a poet (which is very mysterious for a poet) and the fact that other people can value your very existence. It's something you never believe in. You can never believe in it about yourself, but at the same time you know that when you fall in love with a poem there is something about the poet, too, that you love. Last week I was with Galway [Kinnell] and we were talking about Rilke. He said he had made the mistake of reading a biography of Rilke and Rilke had been somewhat diminished in his eyes. With Lowell, then, there is that question: was he in fact attending adequately to that part of the poet's function, or was he misusing it in order to produce his poems? The paradox is that you *can* write a poem about anything; ideally that's what a voice is, it's being able to deal with anything. So he was dealing with what was his truth, *but* . . .

You mention Bishop. I did think very much of her work when reading **Tar** *because one of the ways you achieve a talky quality there is through lots of interruptions—digressions and questions and parenthetical remarks—a strategy typical of Bishop.*

She was a big influence on *Tar.* For about half the time I was writing it, I was studying her work very closely. But I

don't think it was primarily her talkiness that influenced me. I certainly was affected by her subtle use of language rhythms, but I think that it was her purity of vision that was more important to me: the absolute rightness of her figures and the precision of her details. Also, the real analytic rigor in her work: she does it so deftly that you hardly notice it. I was with a well-known poet the other night who said he doesn't particularly care for her. I was trying to read some poems to convince him—I read that wonderful epistemological section of "In the Waiting Room"—but he didn't really hear her, and I understood because I didn't either for a long time. I felt just what my friend did: here's somebody using ordinary language to talk about ordinary things and what's the big deal? Then one day I was in the Boston Public Library with my son, there was a pile of paperback books on a table, and I picked up—I think it was *Geography III*—and just about fell over. I started reading and kept reading for three or four years.

Something else you and she have in common is your skill as visual artists. I've seen your drawings in American Poetry Review *and then of course on the cover of the Issa book. Did you ever think of becoming a visual artist?*

Too late. There are times I have regretted not being a visual artist—because of the money, for one thing, and the involvement of the body. Poetry is so much a mental activity that when things are bad you feel as though your mind is just going to crack. You could be like one of H. G. Wells's time creatures, this little white slug with a brain. And painters aren't that. They work with their hands, their eyes, their whole bodies. Actually when I started out writing poetry I never had an inkling I would have done something so unlikely. All my friends were architects, and if I had said something even *more* unlikely, "I'm going to be a painter," they would have laughed me out of the room. "What do you mean you're going to be a painter; you have to have some skill," but I had as much, probably more skill, actually, as a painter than as a poet.

Let's talk about your four volumes. There seems to be a dramatic split between the first two and the second two. Would you comment on whether you think that's true, and if so, what the essence of that development is?

It is true. I have talked a lot about this. I did stop and start again for very personal reasons. I didn't stop for long, though it seemed at the time long enough. I stopped and I started, and I started somehow with this new voice that allowed me to go on. I think if I hadn't found a new voice, I would have stopped writing poetry.

One of the big changes that I see is in your approach to syntax, and I'm curious about that. In some of the early short-lined poems, syntax almost seems to be in control; it's the forward drive of the syntax that carries the poem. But then in the later volumes you're controlling syntax and using it to burrow into your subject. Was that a conscious strategy?

I didn't think of it in terms of syntax; I thought of it in terms of extended intellectual units. The long line came first. I didn't really know what I was doing when I started with the long line. I just started writing it and felt that it was right. What I felt intuitively was that I could deal with larger units of meaning than I had. Once you begin to work with larger units of meaning, then syntax does become a greater issue because the organization of the elements of language becomes more important. It also then becomes one of the technical felicities that you try to enact in the poetry.

It's not only your lines that are getting longer—your poems seem to be growing longer as well. If you look, for instance, at the long poems that end each of your volumes, **"One of the Muses"** *is by far the longest yet.*

Though my next book [**Flesh and Blood**] is going to be all eight-line poems.

Oh, interesting! Even so, I want to ask you about **"One of the Muses."** *Most of the reviewers commented on how different it was from the rest of the volume, how abstract it was in comparison to the very grounded specificity, the physical nitty-gritty of the other poems. How did you come to write* **"One of the Muses"** *that way?*

I was trying to deal with a very fugitive emotional and mental state that required that kind of analytic approach. The whole poem is the analysis of one emotion, in a sense, which is the emotion of loss. I haven't really ever thought of it in secondary terms this way, but I would say it's the emotion of loss, the problem of how we recover from loss. What the poem says is that there's some sort of rupture that allows us to recover from loss. I guess that trying to redeem or account for or come to terms with that sort of experience required a different kind of attack, and although the poem is much longer than the others, in terms of experience it really isn't. It's just that the experience took more time to get at. I wasn't sure whether to put it last in the book. It isn't meant to be last the way the Anne Frank poem in the first book is meant to be last because it's really a culmination, as is **"In the Heart of the Beast"** in the second book. In fact, all the first three books have last poems that are more extensive workings out of the style, although they weren't necessarily written last. **"One of the Muses"** was different in that it allowed me to let my style try things it hadn't yet.

Yet many of your works deal with some sort of fugitive emotional state, and in them you found some nonabstract embodiment. You have lines about that in one of the poems in **With Ignorance**: *"Sometimes the universe inside us can assume the aspect of places we've been / so that instead of emotions we see trees we knew or touched or a path, / and instead of the face of a thought, there'll be an unmade bed, a car nosing from an alley"* [**"Bread"**]. *It seems to me that many of your poems that use memory are really giving some physical aspect to a fleeting emotion or to some transitory psychological state.*

I think that's true, but I actually wrote the poems upside-down from that: I used memory as the skeleton in which the events, "the face of the thoughts," could occur. So in a way the memories are incidental; they're just devices. When the poems are called "memory poems" I always feel a little squeamish because I realize I could have written them in another way.

What is the relation between your titles and your poems? Especially in your early work, sometimes I wasn't able to make a connection.

That's what Anne Sexton said too. Titles for poems just come to me. I think in the first few books I was working so much with disjunction that sometimes what would please me would just be a title that clearly seemed to have nothing to do with the poem but that I knew really added on an unconscious level to the resonance of the poem.

I want to ask you about the comic element in your work, and maybe I can ground this in **"Soldiers,"** *the poem that you sent for the broadside.[2] When I first read the poem, Ron Wallace asked me what I thought and I said, "I think it's spooky," and he said, "Oh, I think it's funny." So we discussed where we got our views. Ron said, "He takes this almost Jamesian nuance and blows it up until it's completely ridiculous." And Ron was—understandably— chuckling over lines like "My . . . hungry mouth hefts the morsels of its sustenance over its firmament." But the lines Ron was chortling over were lines I found chilling because a supposed presentness and hereness is presented in terms of such abstraction that at the end when the speaker is saying, "I'm here," there's really a denial of being here. It's as if the only way to be sane is not to be here.*

I'd like you to comment first on that poem and then more generally on the comic elements in your work.

In **"Soldiers,"** I meant to do both. I did mean the elements of the poem to be funny, but at the same time, what the poem is dealing with is, as you say, chilling. The perceptions in the poem are very tense, almost unbearably so, but the mind in the poem deals so desperately with the evident sadnesses there that the absurdity of the images and the metaphors, and the comic element, became for me the most real embodiment of the lengths consciousness will go to to retain "normality" in the face of anguish. As for the comic in general, it's a tricky thing to talk about. People have mentioned to me that they find elements in the poems funny, but I've never really systematically tried to put humor into them. The way I seem to come up with what later can appear funny is more through a sort of exuberance, a delight in what the poem can in the most unlikely way do. It's always nice that it's noticed, but it feels as though I shouldn't talk about it too much: I might spook the beast.

I think humor has been there all along in your work, but I'm curious if it plays into the shift between the two pairs of volumes. My sense is that there is almost a shift in your view of human nature, or more accurately, a shift in emphasis: the murderousness of humanity is more a central preoccupation in the early books. That doesn't disappear— it's certainly still there in **"The Last Deaths,"** *say, the one with your daughter watching television. But there seems to be a shift. The epitome of the change might be a poem like* **"Floor,"** *the pornographic post card poem, where the emphasis is on these unaccountable tendernesses and wondrous transcendencies. Where does your humor fit into that?*

I don't connect those with humor. I think there's a lot of humor in the first two books. I think your perception is right about the general trend of the books, but I don't think that would be where the comic would be implicated.

One other thing in your development I want to ask about is translation. I think your Women of Trachis *is very powerful. Do you have anything to say about the affinities between your own world view and Sophocles' in that play?*

When I was doing the translation I became fascinated with the fact that the *Women of Trachis* is really about civilization, about what [Norbert] Elias called "the civilizing process"—the moment at which we become civilized. Herakles is the pivotal figure; he's from the world of precivilization, but he's the agent of civilization. He's the civilizer, but he never really quite civilizes himself. I've always been fascinated with that phenomenon as it occurs in the individual. Freud calls it the relation between the id and the ego or the id and the superego. One of the constant themes of my adult consciousness has been the struggle between instinct and reason, if you would call it reason and if you'd call it instinct. I'm not sure either term in fact is adequate. In a way the play is the enactment of the same drama. The other thing that interested me was that when I was a kid my father used to tell me bedtime stories when I was sick, and my favorites were the labors of Hercules, and so when I began to do the play, it had a double meaning for me.

In discussing the choruses in the "Translator's Comments" you make a distinction between music with its organic connectedness on the one hand and poetry with its intellectual meaning on the other. Do you remember that? What do you see as the role of music in your own work?

Those are two different questions. I was speaking about actual music, the fact that the Greek choruses were actually sung to music. I've said somewhere how unfortunate it is that the only term we have when we speak of what happens in poetry is "music." It all becomes very confusing. The splendor of real music is its disconnection from human experience, the fact that it is a totally human artifice, while the music of poetry has to do just with its connectedness to our real situation and plight.

In the poetic music of a play like that, the various metrical shifts would have been significant for a classical audience, I assume—various conventions would be associated with

particular meters. As a modern writer, you can't rely on that. What do you feel are substitutes? Does that seem like an impoverishment to you?

No, there is a different set of necessities, that's all. When you really get into trying to translate anything, you realize it's a pretty hopeless project. With something as grand as a Greek tragedy, the attempt can seem pretty absurd. At the same time, you do it. You find rigors of syntax and rhythm to try to make an equivalent for the formal demands of the original. Greek verse is based on vowel length, ours on stress patterns—the best you can do is approximate. Art is really always a working out of various necessities, conventions, forms, whatever, and the freedoms of consciousness: you just try to keep enough necessities going so that you're not oversimplifying.

In your commentary you mention the constraints of the translator's cultural and literary milieu, and this would certainly be one of them. What else were you particularly aware of as a constraint for you?

That part doesn't have so much to do with constraint. It's almost a sense of squeamishness because you realize that you are really rewriting history. What happens in our minds in reading the play isn't what happened in the minds of the Greeks. So every aesthetic decision you make about the intensity of a word, the intensity of a moment, the intensity of a scene and the reasons for it is an alteration of what the Greeks would have experienced. I'm reading Robert Darnton, a great historian, and that kind of shift is one of the things he takes off from. Clifford Geertz, who is another favorite of mine, an anthropologist, talks about the same thing, about how we have to do that. Darnton uses as an example the interpretation of fairy tales. He shows how Fromm and Bettelheim interpret "Little Red Riding Hood," and then he goes back to the original and realizes that they're interpreting a "Little Red Riding Hood" that wasn't even there. And so in a sense, although they're pretending to say something about the universal and timeless in the human soul, they're in fact wrong about the very people who generated the story. When you go to something like Greek tragedy you take that to heart. What are you doing here, daring to touch cultural monuments? But at the same time you know you're giving something to your own culture. Translation is a very shifty activity anyway, a little bit like grave robbing. The truth of the matter, though, is that you end up with something, and hopefully it gets to the museum, but you have ransacked and violated something too.

Where did you get your interest in translating Issa?

I had loved the haiku for a long time. I was reading a translation of some and felt, "These are so silly." I realized these people are *really* ransacking: they're ransacking both Japanese and English because just trying to make a poem in English in seventeen syllables is absurd, because a syllable means something different in Japanese. So I said, "Well, I'll really make these into English poems," and I got really going in it. Actually, I did them a long time before they were published, and I was never sure whether to publish them. I did a great many while I was writing **With Ignorance.**

Do you know Japanese at all?

No, I just looked at existing translations. When I did the Greek things I didn't have Greek either. I worked with a classicist and I would get all the other versions I could, even a good French version. But with this I was just having fun. That's why I call them **"Poems from Issa."** I don't even call them versions. They're not versions. They're poems that take an image or an epiphany of Issa's and try to bring it into being in American poetry.

How do you think being a translator has affected the rest of your writing?

I suppose not much after all, except that being so deeply exposed to anything has to affect you somehow.

What about your generation? You talked earlier about your generation reading all sorts of people you wouldn't have been reading if they weren't being translated. But do you feel that the activity of translation, which has been so popular, has affected your poetic generation?

Poets have always been intrigued with translation, with bringing things across cultural boundaries. It's also a very, very complex subject. When I was at Boston University, there was a professors' seminar in translation that I became very active in; they brought up all sorts of people who were speculating and theorizing about translating. I think the most interesting thing I realized is that there seem to be periods in cultures in which the literature suddenly turns and begins looking for its poetry in other languages. It happened in England of course during the Renaissance, and it happened to us during the sixties. It must have something to do with culture in crisis, with the feeling that the resources of your own society have been used up, somehow. I remember that there was a good period when I very rarely read any poems that had originally been written in English. Everything I was learning was coming from other poetries.

It's easy to see the fifties as a very stifled time in poetry. Do you think translation was a way to get out of a kind of deadened modernism?

I don't know about that. I didn't really start writing until near the end of the fifties, so it would be hard for me to say if it was as bad as they say. I was really by myself in the beginning, doing it on my own. I didn't go to graduate school or anything, and I was groping along by myself. My main poets were Rilke and Yeats; I didn't know any other poets and for some reason I didn't feel compelled to read the poetry that was around, until I began to meet other poets. Whether the fifties were all that bad a time for poetry is another question. There were certainly some

great poems written then. Maybe moving from one stylistic period to another entails rejecting much of the poetry that came before. Maybe it's just that we're always filtering out the bad poetry in our vision of a period, and the combination of the shift toward looser forms in the sixties and that filtering process made everything more dramatic.

The word God *appears in your work frequently.*

Not so much now.

OK. But I was bewildered, as I read your work, by what this God was.

When I was working on my first two books, I felt as though much poetry had a sort of conceptual politeness about it that seemed to me to omit a lot of human experience. Of course this is one of those egomaniacal things a young poet can say to himself—"Poetry is such and such"—not even knowing half the poetry in the world yet. But at any rate I did feel very intensely that the way we actually experience concepts like God, soul, death has a much rawer tone and edge to it than we generally acknowledge. So in those first books I very consciously tried to make a God who would be the kind of God children experience, very simply and directly, with a kind of primitiveness about it. Adults perhaps can never re-experience God that way, as simply Him, It, She, in a very direct sensual-mental apprehension, but that's what I was trying for. There was another God in those poems, the God of theodicy, the allower or even perpetrator of evil. I think that God had a lot to do with my becoming aware of what the Holocaust had been. In the best sense, the God I conceived of was descended from some of Buber's ideas. God as something the collective human soul experiences, God as what happens between our psyches, but I think that the theodicy issue more or less overwhelmed that part of it. I've written a poem about all this recently.

W. H. Auden has said that it's the poet's role to maintain the sacredness of language. Does that mean anything to you?

Yes, of course, that's what being a poet is, finally. You don't think that when you start out. It's the kind of thing that someone who is hard into middle age would come to, because when you're young you think poetry has much more to do with experience, and language is just the means you use to deal with experience. By the time you have written a lot, you realize that really poetry is at base language enacting itself. You are the medium of enactment, which is both humbling and exalting; I guess that's what any experience of sacredness is—the sense that you are being acted through rather than just acting yourself.

When you were judging the Brittingham contest, why did you choose Daniels's book, or, to make the question more general, what do you look for in new writing?

This book was an anomaly; it's a very odd book. It doesn't really fit into any categories. The culling process at

Wisconsin had brought the selection down to about a dozen books, and there were some very good books among those. There were some that had individual poems that were as good as or better than anything in Jim's book, and when I first read the book I almost dismissed it—it seemed so simple-minded and so clunky. But I found it was the book I kept coming back to to read with genuine interest. I have not been systematic at all in my poetry contest judging. I did one contest in which I really wanted to pick someone whose poetry wasn't like mine so I could overcome my subjective limitations, and that wasn't such a good idea finally. I don't think in that case I really picked the best book. So it changes; you just try to be responsible to whatever you're feeling about poetry and young poets at that moment. It's such a difficult thing to be a young poet anyway—even if everything works out great, it's difficult. But with Jim's book I was glad and also very relieved at how many people loved it; everybody who saw it really liked it, and I thought, "Well, it's not only me."

About the contemporary scene more generally, do you think there's an avant-garde today?

I think I've become a little dubious about the whole notion of an avant-garde. We've somehow become used to assuming that what happened around 1910, with Pound, Eliot, dada, et cetera, is the model of the way cultural history happens, but I'm beginning to think that the moment of the birth of modernism had more to do with historical phenomena than cultural. The world had changed radically over the decades before that; people were realizing it had, but we were still using intellectual equipment that came from the eighteenth century, and I think that it had become clear that the age of revolution and industrial capitalism, besides the development of modern physics and the working out of the implications of Darwin, demanded a different set of cultural forms. The artists were the first—as they often are, or always—to sense the cultural and emotional implications of it all. Once you accept that that kind of world-revising moment is the model for the normal evolution of art, though, you begin to create disruptions and disjunctions in cultural history that are really grounded in nothing but marketing, and you get all sorts of people simply proposing themselves as the avant-garde, with not much substance to their claim either culturally or aesthetically. The Language poets, for instance, go to great theoretical lengths to certify themselves as avant-garde, but when you actually read their work, their connection to any kind of cultural necessity seems really quite retrograde. Maybe I'm wrong, but I just don't see any other instances of anything approaching an avant-garde other than the birth of modernism. The romantic poets responded to the French Revolution with a new kind of poetry, but it wasn't nearly so radical in its formal shift as we like to think, and if what they were doing was dismissed at first, that dismissal really had to do with attempting to deny the consciousness they were enacting; the critics hadn't moved into the new age with them yet.

Do you think being in a postnuclear age has meant any sort of dramatic shift in consciousness?

God, it has to. I don't know that I could trace it, though. Certainly we suffer from it terribly. When you look at what's happening in New York in painting, with these young brutal painters, I suppose it could be traced to that—almost the rush to get something done before extinction. The apparently rushed quality of the paint, the way the paint is put on the canvas, is an expression of something that intense. Whether it's happening in poetry or not I don't know. Or whether it's happening anywhere I don't know. It might be that humanity has finally come up with something so enormous that all you can do is repress it; how can you possibly deal with your own extinction? And when we do try, like that television movie *The Day After,* things become absurd, and trivial. I seem to have contradicted what I said a moment ago, haven't I?

It seems to me that a lot of your work carries an end-of-the-world sense that may be associated with the Nazi Holocaust as much as a nuclear holocaust, but it's very strong. I wonder whether the poet reflecting on that is doing anything different for the reader than the poet traditionally confronting mortality—or whether that's even possible.

That's a very interesting way to look at it. I don't know. I think that I write under this image, a compelling image. I have a poem in my new book [*Flesh and Blood*] called **"The Dream"** about a dream that I had when I was a kid about the atomic bomb, and I'm very tempted to title my next book *The Dream,* even though it's only one of 150 poems, just because you *can* say that in a sense we are living a dream, the dream of our own survival. Writers generally are weird about manuscripts, about unpublished work. I realized one day, "My God, I've got thirty-five poems here and I don't have copies of them." And then I had this image of an atomic bomb coming and blowing all my poetry up. My God, what an absurd thought, what repression!

That's the level at which we can conceive it.

Exactly. But there has to be some enormous cultural repression, especially when you have a madman in the White House. Clearly you have madmen in both countries, but no sane person would say, "Let's have Star Wars. Let's add a whole new layer of weapons onto the weapons that are already going to kill us."

You are a poet very much associated with the urban scene, and of course ours is a nation becoming increasingly urban. Do you see that as something that is going to become more predominant in poetry? And what do you think are the limitations of that? Or the strengths of it?

The strengths of it are obvious: the city is where our culture happens. For good or ill, mostly ill, although that's not always so. I don't really know that there are any limitations. The urban poet always can leave and go to the land. On the other hand, the poets who have stayed on the land, the poets who do write of the land, Gary Snyder, Wendell

Berry—I can't make a list—obviously do bring us news that is still crucial for us. With Berry the news can be rather dire: that the land is not what it used to be, that we are consuming the land just as quickly as we consume people. But for me, obviously, the urban matrix is absolutely necessary. When I was a kid I was a nature freak; I wanted to be a cowboy and I wanted to live out of the city. We lived in Newark and I was always trying to convince my parents to move to the country; obviously they couldn't. The switch in my attitude was so radical that sometimes I wonder what happened—I think maybe I should try to go back to do a little more of the country again, but somehow it never happens. And my wife is even more urban than I am. She's Parisian, and she doesn't have any truck with anything but fleeting visits to "nature."

It's not as if you turn to nature for some sort of celebratory vision or comfort in your poems.

No, I think the age of nature romanticism is over for us. Nature pantheism, natural mysticism, whatever. Except for isolated individuals—Snyder would be one. At the same time, though, what people such as Snyder and Berry do for us is to remind us that there are basic human necessities that can't be violated, that we are a part of nature, however much havoc we wreak with it. To go back to where we started, it does seem as though we're in a time of great emergency in many ways, in almost every way, and to speak with any kind of false nostalgia about nature would be the ultimate joke we could play on ourselves.

Notes

1. A letter Elizabeth Bishop wrote to Lowell protesting his use of Elizabeth Hardwick's letters in *The Dolphin* appears in Ian Hamilton, *Robert Lowell: A Biography* (New York: Random, 1982) 422–23.

2. For Williams's reading at the University of Wisconsin, Madison, Silver Buckle Press produced a broadside of this uncollected poem.

Ashley Brown (review date Winter 1989)

SOURCE: A review of *Flesh and Blood,* in *World Literature Today,* Vol. 63, No. 1, Winter, 1989, pp. 104–05.

[*In the following review of* Flesh and Blood, *Brown commends the distinctiveness and accessibility of Williams's poetry.*]

C. K. Williams is a rather curious case among contemporary American poets. Aside from some interesting work in translation, he has published five collections of verse since 1969. They have been well reviewed in a number of journals, and in 1987 he won the National Book Critics Circle Award for Poetry. He is thus known in the quarters where literary reputations are made. However, he is not discussed by fashionable critics or included in influential anthologies, and one would not easily "place" him in the current scene. He simply has not emerged as a literary personality, the kind of poet about whom readers have immediate opinions. Still, the impression of a strong personality is on every page of his new collection. Although we do not know where he lives (probably New York City), he is certainly an urban poet who delights in the incongruities of a great city. Most of the poems are vignettes about people observed at a close angle of vision. There is little artifice, almost no literary borrowing.

Williams's verse medium is unusual. He has evolved a very long line (up to twenty-five syllables) with which he feels comfortable. The lines necessarily run over and are frequently sentences in themselves. In *Flesh and Blood* all the poems consist of eight lines; there are always two to a page. One could hardly call them parts of a sequence, but here and there little groups are unified by a thematic center (**"Reading," "Suicide," "Love,"** et cetera); and finally there is a group of eighteen called **"Le Petit Salvié,"** an elegy on the death of the poet Paul Zweig that is the finest thing in the book. Here Williams moves beyond the vignette to a meditation that engages much more than the sympathetic eye which controls the main group of poems. Here the poet commits himself to a view of life and death which was only implied earlier. He is a very accessible poet, and one can see why he has appealed to the nation's book critics.

J. D. McClatchy (review date April 1989)

SOURCE: "Masks and Passions," in *Poetry,* Vol. CLIV, No. 1, April, 1989, pp. 29–48.

[*In the following excerpt, McClatchy praises Williams's collected work in* Poems, 1963–1983, *drawing attention to Williams's distinct style and social consciousness.*]

To accompany C. K. Williams's prize-winning 1987 collection, *Flesh and Blood,* his new publisher has now gathered his four earlier books into a comprehensive volume. *Poems, 1963–1983* includes the long out-of-print *Lies* (1969), minus two poems; *I Am the Bitter Name* (1971), from which three poems have been deleted, and the order of its first and second (of four) groupings of poems reversed; then a chapbook of translations from Issa called *The Lark. The Thrush. The Starling,* first published in 1983 but actually written in the mid-seventies and so placed between his two early and his two mature books; and finally, complete, the remarkable *With Ignorance* (1977) and *Tar* (1983), the best work of his career to date, the work whose distinctive style and brooding tone announced a singular presence in American poetry.

From the start, Williams has been above all a stylist. Here, almost chosen at random, is a stanza from his first book, from a poem called **"Twice More"**:

> understand me please there's no man underneath
> there's

no woman no dog no opening what happens in the
   first
place is hunger is silence a cold
mathematical thumb-mark and
every time I hurt I didn't mean it
and when the shame quit closing its little mouth lock-
   ing
its feet down melting what happened
was that they didn't care they ticked
a night off they counted
me up they threw my name back. . . .

The emphasis is on voice, its flat affect set off by lurid details, and thereby wrenching rather than winning from the reader a fascinated attention. The example of W. S. Merwin's *The Lice,* say, is behind Williams's method, though Merwin's apocalyptic strain always sounded more hieratic and elegant. In contrast with Merwin, Williams was always more interested in society than the soul, and with the underside of a society or a psyche—its pain and confusion, its hopeless mess of wounds and absences. And as he puts it in a later poem, "sometimes when you go to speak about life it's as though your mouth's full of nails." His tone is angry, keening, the violence of his material matched by a violence in the spill-over lines themselves. *I Am the Bitter Name* is essentially a continuation of *Lies,* though the Vietnam War, at home and abroad, erects a kind of barbed wire fence that runs through the book and into **"In the Heart of the Beast,"** the long final poem whose subtitle alone, "May 1970: Cambodia, Kent State, Jackson State," predicts its anguished accusations.

The pertinent question is: how does all this read today? Undoubtedly because of their very timeliness these early poems seemed more striking then than now, and stronger in effect than in conception. But Williams's struggle with style continued. "The problem in one's own poems," he once told an interviewer, "is to find ways to get more of the world in." That meant a more inclusive style, more rhetorically flexible. He hit upon the loping, overlapping Whitmanian line that has since become a kind of trade-mark. At one point he refers to these later poems as "dithyrambs," and that's a proper term for their sprawling, passionate, elevated manner. Though his subjects remain the sex and violence, despair and horror in everyday life, Williams writes about them in an "elevated" (though never sublime) way, from the mediated distance that reflection and a vivid, though sometimes overheated, even fussy rhetoric demand, as in **"The Race of the Flood"**:

   Or this. Messages, codes; the way he, the next one,
      the way he pins them all over himself,
   on his clothes, on his skin, and then walks through the
      street like a signpost, a billboard;
   the way there are words to his wife and words to his
      kids, words even to god so our lord
   is over his eyes and our father over his belly and the
      history of madness and history of cliffs;
   the way there's no room now, the way every word in
      the world has stuck to the skin
   and is used up now, and his eyes move, roll, spin up
      to the top of his head

the way the eyes of those fish who try to see god or
   the lid of the water roll, like dice,
so me, within me again: I cover myself with my own
   scrawl and wait in the shallow,
I face the shallow and wait like a fin and I ripple the
   membrane of scrawl like water. . . .

Williams himself realizes that "style is both self-sustaining and self-consuming," that "you can become trapped in a style, so that you're fulfilling the demands of a style, rather than the style working for *you*." Reading page after page of this can be as wearying as reading alexandrines; and the structure of the poems grows a little formulaic—something in the world juxtaposed with something in his life, the outer with the inner, objective with subjective. Still, their Proustian method, whereby sensations recall memories and image invokes image, works through the hardbitten, downbeat nature of his material towards genuine enlightenment. "One's moral structures tended to be air unless you grounded them in real events," he says in the poem **"Combat."** The "real events" mostly involve stories (and narrative itself is a moral structure), and stories about women, children, cripples, teenagers—all of them projections of the vulnerable or victimized yearnings of the poet himself. And, by moral extension, of the reader. Williams's extraordinary patience with his material, and his canny way of taking the reader into his confidence, including him in his anger and sympathy, succeeds in creating powerful effects. Where his early work is content merely to shock, the later poems use shock in order to jolt the reader, to keep him off-guard while the poet then sets about recomposing the "moral structure" of things. I'm not convinced *jolting* is the best way to accomplish this; it is too self-conscious and too often sensationalistic. But there is no denying Williams's superior talent for sending an electric current through his reader. Reading this book has reminded me of just how many of his poems have never left my mind after my first stunned encounter with them. They stay in the mind not because they shock (they can only do that once) but because they continue to haunt, and because his way of speaking—hovering, tender, overbearing—sounds like nothing else in American poetry today.

Michael Leddy (review date Autumn 1989)

SOURCE: A review of *Poems, 1963–1983,* in *World Literature Today,* Vol. 63, No. 4, Autumn, 1989, p. 685.

[*In the following review of* Poems, 1963–1983, *Leddy comments that he finds Williams's later poetry in* With Ignorance *and* Tar *richer than that of his earliest volumes.*]

Poems, 1963–1983 collects C. K. Williams's first four volumes of poetry—*Lies* (1969), *I Am the Bitter Name* (1972), *With Ignorance* (1977), and *Tar* (1983)—along with *The Lark. The Thrush. The Starling* (1983), translations of the Japanese poet Issa. The four volumes reveal a marked development, as Williams moves from the ominous abstractions and assured invective of his earlier poems to more concrete, less certain considerations of particular human conditions.

The earlier poems of *Lies* and *I Am the Bitter Name* do not wear well; too often they are made of extremes of emotion and diction whose causes remain unclear; they abound in disjunctive syntax and images of scabs, scars, tumors, and genitalia that seem intended to force the reader's assent that the poems are genuine. Williams at times resorts to embarrassing declarations: "I am going to rip myself down the middle into two pieces" (**"Halves"**), or "this poem is an onion / for you . . . because / I want tears from you now" (**"A Poem for the Governments"**). The poem **"Yours"** captures the uneasy commerce of poet and reader, as Williams declares his desire to write poems for "everyone" while calling his sincerity into question: "you are a wonder of soul spirit intelligence one for every one."

With Ignorance and *Tar* are much more rewarding volumes. They represent a departure, as Williams attends to particular people, scenes, and memories: a paralyzed veteran, a city storefront, an adolescent sexual encounter. Form becomes newly significant: these poems are virtually all narratives, employing an extremely long line (up to thirty syllables) that accommodate hesitation, clarification, and digression. It is a pleasure to follow a sentence through four or five such lines, casting tangents in several directions before coming to rest, as in the following poem about a child waking.

> Though I say nothing, don't move, gradually, far down
> within, he, or rather not *he* yet,
> something, a presence, an element of being, becomes
> aware of me: there begins a subtle
> very gentle alteration in the structure of the face, or
> maybe less than that, more elusive,
> as though the soft distortions of sleep-warmth radiat-
> ing from his face and flesh,
> those essentially unreal mirages in the air between us,
> were modifying, dissipating.
>
> (**"Waking Jed"**)

Williams indeed writes in these later two volumes with ignorance, with uncertainty, finding no easy lessons in the narratives he presents. Several of the poems in which he observes city life from an apartment window are exceptionally rich in their play upon the tenuous distinction between spectator and participant (reminiscent of Alfred Hitchcock's *Rear Window*) and in the ways they implicate the poet in the dramas he witnesses.

Sherod Santos (review date 1990)

SOURCE: "The Disparates Fuse," in *Parnassus*, Vol. 16, No. 1, 1990, pp. 115–35.

[*In the following review of* Flesh and Blood *and* Poems, 1963–1983, *Santos examines the development of Williams's distinct poetic voice and style from the 1960s to present.*]

1

After two decades of wrestling by turns with discursive and dramatic modes—a struggle chronicled in *Poems, 1963–1983*—C. K. Williams developed a voice almost instantly identifiable; and in *Flesh and Blood*, his fifth collection, he has devised a form supple enough to accommodate both tendencies. Each of its 147 eight-line poems is set in a highly alliterative, double pentameter line—normally ten strong stresses played against an unpredictable number of syllables—that recalls Old English or Hopkins's sprung rhythm. To anchor that line, and to save it from bombast, Williams employs a gritty, streetwise realism that assumes the character—and charged vernacular—of the common man. This overlay of the colloquial onto the line's innate oratorical sweep gives his poems uncanny tonal range, mimetic of the mind reeling in flux between the worlds of experience and contemplation.

In fact, it may be no exaggeration to say that Williams has done for the long line what William Carlos Williams did for the short one: recast it in such a way that a reader discovers within it an activity of the mind, a correlation of eye and ear, heart and intellect, that is completely new and yet strangely familiar, as though the humdrum world were suddenly infused with a wildly invigorated energy. More often than not, the feel of these poems is like a ride on a roller coaster: Once you get on, you don't get off, and the thrill comes from the slow, tantalizing rise to a height from which you plunge in a blinding swirl of syntactic reversals, rhythmic shifts, dialectical turns, all leading headlong to some dizzying, epiphanic brink:

> They're at that stage where so much desire streams
> between them, so much frank need and want,
> so much absorption in the other and the self and the
> self-admiring entity and unity they make—
> her mouth so full, breast so lifted, head thrown back
> *so* far in her laughter at his laughter,
> he so solid, planted, oaky, firm, so resonantly factual
> in the headiness of being craved so,
> she almost wreathed upon him as they intertwine
> again, touch again, cheek, lip, shoulder, brow,
> every glance moving toward the sexual, every glance
> away soaring back in flame into the sexual—
> that just to watch them is to feel again that hitching in
> the groin, that filling of the heart,
> the old, sore heart, the battered, foundered, faithful
> heart, snorting again, stamping in its stall.
>
> (**"Love: Beginnings"**)

That almost manic insistence to William's line gives ordinary moments a stupefying psychological power, an Orphic music. With a microscopic eye that notch by notch closes in on its subject, he magnifies the book's innumerable vignettes through a mass of adjectives, adverbs, and nouns, through pell-mell pacing and the studied uses of repetition: "so much . . . so much . . . so much . . . ," she "so full . . . so lifted . . . *so* far . . . ," "every glance moving . . . ," "every glance away . . . ," etc. And like a photographic blowup, this process of magnification tests reality's surfaces—"he so solid, planted, oaky, firm," "she almost wreathed upon him as they intertwine"—until they finally yield what lies beneath: in this case, a heady brew of vanity and sex. Interestingly enough, since Williams lays claim to a deep social conscience, it is not in the arena of human behavior, but in that underworld of motive and impulse that he most often discovers the ineradicable stain of our common identity: "just to watch them is to feel again that hitching in the groin, that filling of the heart, / the old, sore heart, the battered, foundered, faithful heart, snorting again, stamping in its stall."

This poem contains all the signature elements of Williams's mature style: the extended, refracted line; the perceptive sense tuned like an aerial to the daily round; the explicit gloss on some commonplace scene; the universal story suddenly revealed underpinning the individual moment. While this latter preoccupation haunts his work from the very start, in the first two books those verbal leaps to significance—couched as they are in a style ill-suited to discourse or analysis—rarely sound like anything more than didactic dreams. As Williams said in an interview in 1986, "I like Yeats's remark about his having realized that everything he ever thought and did was already implicit in him when he was eighteen, that all he had to do was to work it all out" (*The Missouri Review*, volume IX, no. 1, p. 151). To grasp the magnitude of labor required for Williams "to work it all out," one need only browse through the first two books in his watershed collection, *Poems, 1963–1983*: *Lies* (1969) and *I Am the Bitter Name* (1972).

2

In *Lies,* Williams takes as his distinctive gesture the hyped-up rhetorical question, often angrily addressed to an angry God, on subjects ranging from moral decay to world hunger, and couched in the lingo of a corrupt sexual appetite. The central images—ash, debris, rot, spillage—all serve as generalized indictments of the sleazy spirit of the modern age. The following, spoken by a garrulous, if fiendish, trash collector, typifies that impulse:

> What do they do with kidneys and toes
> in hospitals? And where did your old dog go
> who peed on the rug and growled?
> They are at my house now, and what grinds
> in your wife's teeth while she sleeps
> is mine. She is chewing
> on embryos, on the eyes of your lover,
> on your phone book and the empty glass
> you left in the kitchen. And in your body,
> the one who died there and rots
> secretly in the fingers of your spirit,
> she is hauling his genitals out, basket
> after basket
> and mangling all of it in the crusher.
>
> (from **"Trash"**)

From the details in the poem we may infer that the "you" is a male, probably suburban, middle-class American (that

arch-villain of the sixties), whose inner life "rots / secretly," and whose inadequacies and apparent infidelities have transformed his wife, if only in her dreams, into a monstrous, cannibalistic machine. Pitted against them, the trash collector functions as the nightmare voice of the subconscious world, the one who both hoards and exposes our vilest cast-off selves. But something childish, something even cartoonlike and funny negates the squalor of this grisly scene. The details are almost extravagantly gratuitous (especially the "basket / after basket" of "his genitals"—wouldn't the normal measure of his anatomy be enough?). And since we never really learn why the "you" has sunk to such depravities, we can't help wondering: Is it truly as bad as all that?

Images of mangled man and woman-as-ball-breaker come up again and again in *Lies*. Sex is never invoked without grotesquerie and violence, the sexual drive is never playful or procreative but always destructive, the sexual organs are never erotic but always horrifying and tumescent: "genitals swell like tumors" and "men / . . . ooze their penises out like snail / feet" (**"Saint Sex"**); people think of "raw spots at the root / of the penis and the pimple that grows / inwards" (**"Three Seasons and a Gorilla"**), and so on. I suppose we're urged to trust that the speaker's nausea symptomatically registers his disgust with the world (North America in particular), though we're never told what precise circumstances provoke that reaction—America's war in Vietnam? Mississippi's vicious repression of voter registration drives? Los Angeles's police action in Watts? Since Williams rarely ventures beyond generalities, we're left with a despair unpleasantly summoned for the sake of the poem, and a poem divorced from history—a response, one suspects, largely at odds with his intentions.

In *I Am the Bitter Name* the grotesque grows less obsessive, though scabrous elements still linger: "if you told him god lived in his own penis / he'd bite into it" (**"They Warned Him Then They Threw Him Away"**); "I am nailed in like a root / meat" (**"What Must I Do To Be Lost"**), etc. But a broader subject matter enters the poems, as does some clearer conception of the issues at stake: Money, commerce, and government stand in as worldly, oppressive forces; the poor, the alienated, the disenfranchised as their hapless victims. Passing references invoke the poor of Biafra, Bengal, Harlem, and Rio, and a gnarled list of crimes threads its way through the poems, as if the list were a noose and we, the reader-subject-accused, were slowly closed in its cinch.

Perhaps inevitably, questions of personal responsibility begin to intrude, though even here excesses test a reader's credulity. The sexual guilt so obsessive in *Lies* now serves as a disturbing emblem of Williams's feelings of political impotence and frustration. **"The Beginning of April,"** for example, attempts to link the worlds of the private and public self in yet another moment of animated self-arousal, when the poet feels "I could smash bricks . . . / or screw / until I was half out of my mind":

the only trouble
jesus the only trouble
is I keep thinking about a kid I saw starving on television
last night from biafra he was unbearably fragile
his stomach puffed up arms and legs sticks eyes distorted
what if I touched somebody like that when I was this way?

This mawkish self-accusation serves as a moral equivalent to the first book's debasement of the sexual passions. The central proposition—how can he be full of lust when African children are starving?—not only figures as a dubious piece of introspection, but grossly exploits the Biafran child. His conclusion strikes me as equally embarrassing: "I promise I won't feel myself like this ever again / it's just the spring it doesn't mean anything please." An indefatigable moralist, Williams, at this stage in his career, veers too often into false pieties or, worse, overexcited sexual fantasies (in **"Innings,"** "somebody keeps track of how many times / I make love don't you god don't you?"). Too often the informing grief has the unreal air of the healthy regarding the sick at a vast remove.

3

Poems, 1963–1983 retains forty-five poems from ***Lies*** and forty-nine from ***I Am the Bitter Name.*** Although an author's note tells us that "several poems" have been omitted here (***With Ignorance*** and ***Tar*** remain intact), the book would have gained from a more judicious selection. The first two volumes betray a lingering attachment to the fashions of their time: A blurry, imported surrealism dominates the imagery, and a poetic posturing (forgivable if still tedious in the young) suspends the poems in a glumly shortsighted idealism. Williams has acknowledged his early debt to Vallejo, Neruda, and Miguel Hernandez, but more than any stylistic traits or political affinities, what appears to have crossed over into his work is the picturesque—the turbulence, animation, quixotic ardors their poems project—a seductive alternative to the ennui of a middle-class life he loathes. But young poets soon learn from their foreign influences that the literal or psychological landscape of another country resists transplanting to one's native soil. With Neruda, no matter how surreal the text, the United Fruit Company and the right-wing forces in the Spanish Civil War loom immediately as presences in Chile or Barcelona. With Williams, examples of oppression (like the Biafran child on television) seem to come to him secondhand. The net effect is to convince us of his desire—even if, for the moment, it lacks the backing of experience—to emulate the inspired conscientiousness of those poets.

Starting with his third book, Williams appears to fall under a different and more compatible influence: Walt Whitman. Certainly we feel the presence of Whitman's ropy lines, his abundant realism, his hearty erotics and studied inclusion of all the social classes, and his profound rootedness in the landscape and experience of North America, what

Whitman called "the large unconscious scenery of my land." The sensationalist of the first two books now begins to work in more covert ways:

> In the first two books I think I was trying to take the issues head-on, as raw as I could. . . . In *With Ignorance* and *Tar,* I quite intentionally tried to bury anything that looked like a message in the unconscious of the poem, the part of the poem that would work more subtly, more subliminally, if that's the word, on the reader.

(*The Missouri Review,* op. cit.)

The upshot of that decision is remarkable. Between the publication of ***I Am the Bitter Name*** in 1972 and ***With Ignorance*** in 1977, Williams's poems take a giant stride forward in vision, voice, attitude, and style. We notice the change in the book's opening lines:

> The men working on the building going up here have got these great,
> little motorized wheelbarrows that're supposed to be for lugging bricks and mortar
> but that they seem to spend most of their time barrel-assing up the street in,
> racing each other or trying to con the local secretaries into taking rides in the bucket.
> I used to work on jobs like that and now when I pass by the skeleton of the girders
> and the tangled heaps of translucent brick wrappings, I remember the guys I was with then
> and how hard they were to know.

(from **"The Sanctity"**)

In place of the studied mannerisms of the previous two collections, Williams now adopts a blithely natural tone. We hear it in the way the lines mimic the jaunty colloquialisms—"that're," "barrel-assing," "con," and "guys"—of the construction workers; the way the preposition suspended until the end of line three is grammatically awkward yet conversationally true; the way the sentence unfolds down the page in the cadences of a tavern bard. The parti-colored strains of American speech will play across every line Williams writes in the years to come. From a lachrymose New-World Job venting his sufferings in the language of abuse to this deft, street-talking populist—so complete an act of self-revision leaves one wondering how and why, and in the face of what knotty disavowals.

During this period, Williams was working on a translation (with Gregory W. Dickerson) of Sophocles's *Women of Trachis.* One might speculate that, in coming to terms with the formal demands of the play, he felt the powerful allure of the narrative, for he shifts from a conception of the poem as a hermetic unit to a conception of it as a vehicle for storytelling and rumination. Because narrative is more accessible to the common reader, something in Williams's proletarian leanings must have felt more at home in its structures; more momentously, narrative provided contexts—personal, historical, imagined—to ground his habitual speculative side. It turns out that Williams has a lot to say, and in **With Ignorance** he begins to say it.

Accordingly, in the next three books Williams turns more directly to the actual and historic for his material, all the while abjuring the mystifications—or more ornate embellishments—of poetry. He now asks that his poems be judged, not by some abstract idea of poetic beauty, but by the urgency with which they seem wrested from life. The following passage from **"Spit"** presents as its frame the story of a Nazi who begins to spit into a Rabbi's mouth "*so that the Rabbi could continue to spit on the Torah*":

> War, that happens and stops happening but is always
>   somehow right there, twisting and hardening us;
> then what we make of God—words, spit, degradation,
>   murder, shame; every conceivable torment.
> All these ways to live that have something to do with
>   how we live
> and that we're almost ashamed to use as metaphors
>   for what goes on in us
> but that we do anyway, so that love is battle and we
>   watch ourselves in love
> become maddened with pride and incompletion, and
>   God is what it is when we're alone
> wrestling with solitude and everything speaking in our
>   souls turns against use like His fury
> and just facing another person, there is so much terror
>   and hatred that yes,
> spitting in someone's mouth, trying to make him defile
>   his own meaning,
> would signify the struggle to survive each other and
>   what we'll enact to accomplish it.

One might say that the enormity of the horror has overwhelmed the poet's faculties. Certainly Williams would have us believe that in this situation it would be inappropriate, even unethical, to speak in a more artful, more "written" language. And by conceding that there are things "we're almost ashamed to use as metaphors for what goes on in us," he licenses himself to engage—like a rabbi in the Midrash interpreting a sacred text—this woolly homily on the brutal text of the Nazi's spitting. Until now, he has viewed human events as a range of tropes for his own interior life; but an atrocity like "spitting in someone's mouth, trying to make him defile his own meaning" calls such easy correspondences into question. To the moral dilemma, is it right to turn extreme suffering into private lyric excursion, he gives an implicit no. And yet, he declares, "we do anyway." And the reason we do—which locates us collectively in the figure of the Nazi—resides devastatingly in "the struggle to survive each other and what we'll enact to accomplish it."

That Williams sees this moment not as an isolated act of individual cruelty, but as one of those "ways to live that have something to do with how we live" points to the deepening consciousness he now brings to a poem. And though the Darwinian conjecture about "the struggle to survive" may seem too neat, in the act of questioning poetry's responsibilities he argues for a more lucid understanding of his own relationship to the poem. Rather than beginning with the self and searching for incidents to illustrate its confusions (an almost literal definition of the egoist), he now treats events as texts of their own, as Darwin treated the idea of species. Compare the Biafran child who spoiled a gleeful sexual moment in *I Am the Bitter Name* to a similar situation in **"The Last Deaths,"** a poem which could be read as a corrective to that earlier one:

> A few nights ago I was half-watching the news on
>   television and half-reading to my daughter.
> The book was about a boy who makes a zoo out of
>   junk he finds in a lot—
> I forget exactly; a horse-bottle, a bedspring that's a
>   snake, things like that—
> and on the news they were showing a film about the
>   most recent bombings.
> There was a woman crying, tearing at her hair and
>   breasts, shrieking incomprehensibly
> because her husband and all her children had been
>   killed the night before
> and just when she'd flung herself against the legs of
>   one of the soldiers watching her,
> Jessie looked up and said, "What's the matter with
>   her? Why's she crying?"

The quicksilver backing has faded from Williams's TV screen, for it's no longer just himself he finds reflected there. Instead, in seeing the war through the eyes of his daughter—and in seeing through her the careful balance between the storybook boy making a world out of rubble and the woman whose world has been reduced to rubble— the reader experiences, as does the father, that harrowing silence behind the daughter's unanswerable questions.

Williams's awareness of the ground he's breaking is suggested in the book's title, a phrase from Kierkegaard ("With ignorance begins a knowledge the first characteristic of which is ignorance"). If ignorance here means the willed sacrifice of some former self, then knowledge begins in the meticulous process of reimagining that self. In many poems the narrative anecdote alone illustrates that change; but in a significant number of others, Williams's heightened language allows him to examine the implications of his own conscious self-invention. The title poem, a series of charged, rhetorical X-rays, exposes the underlying psychic motives that the narrative (here called "history") sets in motion:

> And then back, from the dread, from locution and
>   turn, from whatever history reflects us,
> the self grounds itself again in itself and reflects itself,
>   even its loss, as its own,
> and back again, still holding itself back, the certainty
>   and belief tearing again,
> back from the edge of that one flood of surrender
>   which, given space, would, like space itself,
> rage beyond any limit, the flesh itself giving way in
>   its terror, and back from that,
> into love, what we have to call love, the one moment
>   before we move onwards again,
> toward the end, the life again of the self-willed, self-
>   created, embodied, reflected again.

It could certainly be argued that this passage is as abstract or prone to sensation as anything in the earlier poems. But the ear catches a movement across the line—the breathless sentence mediated by a nervous tonal patterning—which leads, on its own, to a singular experience of the spectacle it describes. Frost's phrase for it was "the sound of sense," like a conversation one overhears through a closed door: Though the words are unintelligible, the mood and spirit still come clear. In the passage above, Williams's long, oscillating line imitates the way the mind under pressure badgers, cajoles, interrogates itself, an anxiety one hears in the willed confusion of repeated words: "the self grounds itself again in itself and reflects itself, even its loss, as its own, / and back again, still holding itself back." Even without clues sufficient to decode the complex cipher of those lines, we still quail a little at the audible self-erasure of those obsessive words.

Williams's interest in the link between the behavioral and psychological has been mirrored all along in his discrete uses of figurative and discursive language. But this new sanction to speak about abstract things in abstract terms calls up an old quandary which form itself cannot resolve: how to make a poem that unites the worlds of plot and rumination while still maintaining the linear insistence of poetry. As the marked differences in the last two quoted poems show, Williams tended to work in the two modes separately. In *Tar,* however, he begins, experimentally, to weave the two together; and given the huge demands of that ambition, it comes as no surprise that the book's true muse derives less from poetry than from Dostoyevski, whose capacious novels so colossally embody that struggle:

> . . . I think it's probably been Dostoyevski more than anyone else who's been the deep novelistic influence. I've always been in great awe of him, of his inexhaustible moral energy. No matter how much you disagree with his world-vision, in a way you *have* to come to terms with his thoroughness, with the way he is always in touch with the larger questions, and most importantly, with the way his characters exist with so much curiosity and conviction and willingness to risk. He's also for me the philosophical novelist: his characters live out the quandaries and paradoxes of post-revolutionary, post-Kantian humanity in the most naked possible way.
>
> (*The Missouri Review,* op. cit.)

It is easy to see what in Dostoyevski so attracted Williams's interest; and though, for better or worse, that interest has been there all along, not until *Tar* does he succeed in creating a persona who can "philosophize"—or, by turns, psychologize—and still exist full-bodied as a character. Like Dostoyevski's Underground Man, who declares "that to be conscious is an illness—a real thoroughgoing illness," Williams sets out to dramatize consciousness itself, to set it in direct confrontation with an often unconscious world. Predictably, the poems take on a more disturbing sense of "the malleable, / mazy, convoluted matter of the psyche" (**"One of the Muses"**), that tarlike core of human nature. Near the end of **"Com-**

bat"—the most darkly unrelenting example in the book—we see the poet with his miner's lamp winding through a labyrinth of instincts and motivations. Looking back on a frustrated romance carried out in the apartment and under the watchful eye of his girlfriend's mother—a German refugee whose husband, a former Nazi, killed himself after a failed plot to assassinate Hitler—Williams comes slowly to this observation:

> These revisions of the past are probably even less trustworthy than our random, everyday assemblages
> and have most likely even more to do with present unknowables, so I offer this almost in passing,
> with nothing, no moral distillation, no headily pressing imperatives meant to be lurking beneath it.
> I wonder, putting it most simply, leaving out humiliation, anything like that, if I might have been their Jew?
> I wonder, I mean, if I might have been an implement for them, not of atonement—I'd have nosed that out—
> but of absolution, what they'd have used to get them shed of something rankling—history, it would be:
> they'd have wanted to be categorically and finally shriven of it, or of that part of it at least
> which so befouled the rest, which so acutely contradicted it with glory and debasement.
> The mother, what I felt from her, that bulk of silence, that withholding that I read as sorrow:
> might it have been instead the heroic containment of a probably reflexive loathing of me?

Like someone prefacing a personal remark by saying "I don't mean this to sound personal," Williams clearly intends us to doubt those opening qualifications, to trust this particular revision of the past, indeed to see it as a "moral distillation," a "headily pressing imperative." It is nothing if not headiness that we hear in the propulsive rhythm of the lines, and in the religious echoes of "atonement," "absolution," "shriven," "befouled," "glory," and "debasement." Yet while the tone is rapt, the method is psychoanalytic, and the accuracy of analysis depends less on eloquence than on the care and thoroughness it brings to "the facts." And so, like a clinician presenting a case study, Williams, 102 lines earlier, documents those details upon which his conclusion is based. The poem opens with Williams, yet again seated in front of a TV set, being reminded (by a boxer's face) of a former lover ("Moira was her name") and the lover's mother, who

> . . . was so white, not all that old but white: everything, hair, skin, lips, was ash,
> except her feet, which Moira would often hold on her lap to massage and which were a deep,
> frightening yellow, the skin thickened and dense, horned with calluses and chains of coarse, dry bunions,
> the nails deformed and brown, so deeply buried that they looked like chips of tortoiseshell.

Those lines illustrate the poem's "other," novelistic side, the side by which characters and settings assume memorable identities. The old woman's jaundiced feet are so palpably gross that the analytic sections that deal with her prove forceful and precise. Williams's unflagging ability to make those correspondences lends to *Tar* an extraordinary richness as narrative poetry, the sense that not *only* a story (or, conversely, *only* analysis) is at stake.

Another sign of Williams's maturation lies in his growing refusal of poetic closure. The early poems almost always end with the finality of a slammed door. In *With Ignorance,* those moments sound far less concussive, though an emotional tidying up still takes place. In *Tar,* rarely does the "story" that begins a poem also end it, and often a large time shift signifies some unresolved distance from the subject. At its best, the poem rushes not to conclusion, but to the verge of some harsh, unspeakable knowledge, which in turn leads back to the oddly unaltered day-to-day. Recalling his down-and-out years, when he walked into a grim, drug-stunned party in a run-down apartment, Williams writes:

> There was something almost maniacally mindless
>   about it, but at the same time it was like a battle,
> that intense, that lunatic, and, hesitating in the
>   doorway, something made me realize just how much
> without noticing I'd come to be of that, to want or
>   need it, and I swear I must have swayed,
> the way, over their imaginary chaos, Manfred must
>   have swayed, and Faust, before it swallowed them.
>
> There's park there now. The morning I came back, I
>   wandered by and stopped to sit awhile.
> Why, after all the fuss, a park, I don't know, but at
>   any rate, it's not a pleasant place . . .
>
>   (from **"Flight"**)

This final stanza goes on to notice "unpleasant" details from the present-day neighborhood, an out-of-order drinking fountain, the "bleak concrete mostly"; then the poet's attention falls on "Two busloads of retarded kids . . . playing with their teachers on the asphalt ball field," the smallest ones wearing plastic football helmets stencilled with eagles and "GIANTS." It is a touching moment, but Williams doesn't insist on the pathos or attempt to exploit the obvious ironic connection with the people at the "mindless" party. Instead, the children are left in the cloister of that sunny moment, and the poem ends with the poet closing his eyes, dozing and dreaming, "listening to the children." After that stormy entrance as Manfred, the poet's peaceful exit leaves a reader heartened and subdued, as though a momentary triumph over chaos had been effected—not by the stubborn counterforce of some Byronic hero, but by the cheerful endurance of the retarded children, "twittering with glee and shrieking as they lumbered from home plate to center field and back."

4

In a 1987 essay, **"Poetry and Consciousness"** (*American Poetry Review,* vol. 16, no. 1), Williams reflects on the way the mind receives, translates into language, and organizes experience. The emotion that finally results from the process is as much a product of the mind as it is a consequence of experience:

> Whatever the experience . . . emotion arises from, the mind will have to process it. During this processing, there will also be images generated into consciousness, some dictated by the experience itself, some with very little or nothing to do with it. There will also be the participation of the senses, of language, as it comments, criticizes, reflects, plus there will be an awareness that the equation which all of this makes, the emotion, is something that is not a normal moment of passing consciousness.

The passage says a lot about Williams's evolving interest in a poetry that simulates the mind's chaotic methods. If we think of "experience" as the subject that initiates a poem, and "emotion" as the effect that follows it, then the poem becomes the "consciousness" responsible for "processing" the one into the other—a process that allows for arbitrariness, interpolation, caprice, digression, things generally thought to be anathema to poetry. For all the satisfactions that must have come with *Tar,* Williams has continued to push toward a more faithful enactment of that process. In *Flesh and Blood,* he resolves again to reform his poem, to capture the way the mind's currents arc between those poles of experience and emotion.

While the long line remains, the poem's fixed length precludes certain habits of the extended narratives: the elaboration of dramatic action, his exhaustive attention to character and setting, those prolonged passages of excited speculation, etc. But Williams doesn't do away altogether with any of those things; instead, he finds a method for reactivating them by narrowing the poem's temporal range. In this he lights upon certain tactics akin to haiku—e.g., the flash of insight—like those which Lowell acknowledged were crucial to the writing of his sonnets. While *Tar* returns like memory to revise and make sense of the past, *Flesh and Blood,* like an unblinking eye, convenes the disorderly present tense—the impression, if not the fact, of experience played out before us:

> The way she tells it, they were in the Alps or
>   somewhere, tall, snow-capped mountains anyway,
> in their hotel, a really nice hotel, she says, they'd
>   decided that for once they'd splurge.
> They'd just arrived, they were looking from their ter-
>   race out across a lake or bay or something.
> She was sitting there, just sitting there and thinking to
>   herself how pleasant it all looked,
> like a postcard, just the way for once it's supposed to
>   look, clean and pure and cool,
> when his hand came to her shoulder and he asked her
>   something, "Don't you think it's lovely?"
> then something else, his tone was horrid; there was
>   something that he wanted her to say—
> how was *she* to know what he wanted her to say?—
> and he *shook* her then, until she ached.
>
>   (**"The Marriage"**)

We see here something of the manner by which Williams scales down his earlier narratives. In the first clause, he quickly fixes the event: a story the married woman has confided to the narrator, and one the narrator in turn confides to the reader. (And, given Williams's bent for autobiography, we might reasonably assume that initial conversation happened once.) Next, he filters her story through the narrator's consciousness, which extracts the most resonant features: The "Alps or somewhere," and "a lake or bay or something" are muted in favor of essences, "the way for once it's supposed to look, clean and pure and cool." Like a portraitist blurring background detail to examine his subject more carefully, Williams obscures everything around the troubled wife. That scrutiny grows so intense that in the last three lines the narrator's voice merges with hers. Certainly the quote is the woman's, as is, it seems, the word "horrid." And don't we hear *her* emphasis in that last line? By such acts of concentration a reader enters the rising craziness of that ruthless moment: "how was *she* to know what he wanted her to say?—and he *shook* her then, until she ached."

Williams's dogged interest in states of mind (typically moments of psychic extremity) materializes nowhere more fully than in *Flesh and Blood.* Nor does his flair for discourse. The constraints of the eight-line form permit him to place abstract thoughts on a stage of their own, freed of the apparatus of narrative. Still, the lessons of twenty years have not been lost; he now knows the abstract depends on the concrete for substance, as the concrete depends on the abstract for significance. And the success of this book's countless meditations—on everything from anger, conscience, suicide, and love to reading, mothers, and dreams—derives in large part from Williams's gift for metaphor:

> It is the opposite or so of the friendly gossip from
>   upstairs who stops by every other evening.
> It's the time she comes in once too often, or it's more
>   exactly in the middle of her tête-à-tête,
> when she grows tedious beyond belief, and you real-
>   ize that unless an etiquette is violated
> this will just go on forever, the way, forever, rain
>   never comes, then comes, the luscious opposite,
> the shock of early drops, the pavements and the
>   rooftops drinking, then the scent, so heady with
>   release
> it's almost overwhelming, thick and vaginal, and then
>   the earth, terrified that she'd bungled it,
> that she'd dwelt too long upon the problems of the
>   body and the mind, the ancient earth herself,
> like someone finally touching pen to page, breathes
>   her languid, aching suspiration of relief.

("**End of Drought**")

Just as **"The Marriage"** demonstrates the novelistic amplitude possible still in this sonnetlike form, **"End of Drought"** shows the poet's imaginative gamut when he sets his sights on more abstract game. The luxuriance in the arrival of that longed-for rain reaches us through a series of adroitly interwoven tropes: the thrice-qualified metaphor of the gossip; a simile comparing the rain's arrival to the end of the gossip's tireless monologue; the personification of the earth, which (linking it backward to

the gossip and forward to the poet) fears it "dwelt too long upon the problems of the body and the mind." Perhaps not until a second or third reading do we realize that the body of the poem is just one extended image of the gossip. As if on their own momentum, Williams's "abstract" poems cut a path back to their titles through lush, unpredictable terrain, and the sensibility which maps that course forces us to feel—even before we understand—the rough topography of the subjects it covers.

The overall impression of *Flesh and Blood* is kaleidoscopic, the world broken into a thousand fine, luminous fragments which cohere in a crazed, elaborate design, forming and being formed, as one poem tells us, by "the circles of community that intersect within us" ("**Le Petit Salvié**"). It is also enormously inclusive, taking in the poor, the leisured, the middle-class, the intellectual and illiterate, the healthy and insane—"of old and young, of the foolish as much as the wise," as Whitman said. But unlike Whitman, who views everything with a certain divine secular love, Williams is a moralist who registers more acutely his own angers, fears, and judgments:

> *Vas en Afrique! Back to Africa!* the butcher we used
>   to patronize in the rue Cadet market,
> beside himself, shrieked at a black man in an argu-
>   ment the rest of the import of which I missed
> but that made me anyway for three years walk an
>   extra street to a shop of definitely lower quality
> until I convinced myself that probably I'd misunder-
>   stood that other thing and could come back.
> Today another black man stopped, asking something
>   that again I didn't catch, and the butcher,
> who at the moment was unloading his rotisserie, slip-
>   ping the chickens off their heavy spit,
> as he answered—how get this right?—casually but ac-
>   curately *brandished* the still-hot metal,
> so the other, whatever he was there for, had subtly to
>   lean away a little, so as not to flinch.

("**Racists**")

"Racists" strikes a critical balance between two separate incidents, each held up as a proposition in an ethical argument which, if only the poet can "get this right," the reader can comprehend. In this case getting it right depends on his choice of "brandishing," for with that word comes an unmistakable judgment. (Consider, for example, the different sense called up by a word like *waving.*) Williams throws into the argument his own lack of moral rigor: Three years after the first incident, "I convinced myself that probably I'd misunderstood," so he could again patronize the better market. Williams realizes we not only form our language, but our language forms us; and we may presume that his resolve in choosing the word "brandishing" has less to do with accuracy than it does with enforcing that moral rigor. With *that* word in mind, he won't be able to go back again.

This simple moral lesson aside, **"Racists"** raises one of the technical difficulties in any book-length sequence in a fixed form. The poem treads a fine line between the lyric and anecdotal, and, with too many poems like it grouped together, one could be tempted to scrap the form (the physical tug of the narrative) and read for the anecdote alone (that prosy ground from which the narrative is launched). Perhaps Williams has so shrewdly alternated between abstract and dramatic poems in order to create a secondary rhythm which itself ensures that lyric surge. It may be possible to draw a connection between this discontinuous technique and that of the modernists, but his style is much less one of a design moving toward fragmentation than of fragments moving toward design. In that way the book more closely resembles the Alexandrian art of the idyll—a series of little pictures whose narrative links are suppressed, and whose dramatic effect is gained by the juxtaposition of scenes. And since, in poetry, sound is more crucial than story or idea, we must listen for Williams's "sound" not only in the line and poem, but in those swings of emphasis from one poem to the next.

All five of Williams's volumes end in poem cycles, but not until **Flesh and Blood** does one effectively duplicate the book's larger motifs. **"Le Petit Salvié,"** an eighteen-poem elegy for Williams's friend, the poet Paul Zweig, is an act of portraiture, homage, self-scrutiny, and extended speculation on the meaning of death. And in the manner of Yeats's "In Memory of Major Robert Gregory," it is also a calling up of presences (as if "Beside a fire of turf in th' ancient tower"): remembered visits between the two families (Zweig's and Williams's); touchingly private moments between the two men alone; an imagined meeting (in "something like heaven") between Zweig, his "guru," and another of Williams's friends recently dead, all of them "glowing, grinning down at me from somewhere in the heart of being, / ablaze with wonder and a child's relief that this after all is how astonishingly it finishes."

From those "covenants of affection we embody," Williams gleans whatever provisional solace he can, a solace made grander by the gravity of the questions he undauntedly asks: "Are we to be redeemed? When? How? After so much disbelief, will something be beyond us to receive us?" And: "What if after, though, there is something else, will there be judgment then, will it be retributive, / and if it is, if there is sin, will you have to suffer some hellish match with what your wrongs were?" Pursuing these questions leads him to his own dark night of the soul, and out of one such night he brings back the tentative affirmation that Zweig himself embodies:

> Our last night, though, I strolled into the moonless
>   fields, it might have been a thousand centuries ago,
> and something suddenly was with me: just beyond the
>   boundaries of my senses presences were threatening,
> something out of childhood, mine or humankind's; I
>   felt my fear, familiar, unfamiliar, fierce,
> might freeze me to the dark, but I looked back—I
>   wasn't here alone, your house was there,
> the zone of warmth it made was there, you yourself
>   were there, circled in the waiting light.

>   (from **"Le Petit Salvié"**)

That moment of timeless jeopardy might have led Williams earlier in his career to some grandiose conclusion, but with the ripening of his talents has come a chastened modesty before the rituals of human experience. Like a soldier who has gone off to war filled with heroic visions of battle—only to return home with the simple knowledge of human suffering—Williams has learned that the Furies' hearts hold secrets blacker than he imagined. As readers, our indebtedness to him perhaps begins in that boyish fervor to open himself to experience; but it's sustained in his tough, often heart-stopping candor, his flat refusal to turn away, even in the hardest hours, and even in *those* to remain essentially life-affirming. In that alone he distinguishes himself from most of his contemporaries.

The vicissitudes of a restless, headstrong mind are Williams's trademark, but the evolution of his work is more aptly characterized by the thresholds in his development: from the early self-absorbed, self-dramatizing poet to the outward-looking Dostoyevskian narrator, to the immediate, unblinking detective-witness of **Flesh and Blood.** For readers who ask little more of poetry than personal testimonial or an attentive eye, Williams's work may seem disturbingly heterogeneous, for it willfully disregards the contemporary dictum about segregating ideas and things. And, stepping back from the work as a whole, even a sympathetic reader may find it a little unbuttoned with all its philosophical and psychological shoptalk. But in Williams's cosmology ideas *are* things—real, substantial, fully formed—and since they take their place among our everyday furnishings, they are also knocked about and taken for granted. The point is, they are *used,* not as fragile antique display pieces closeted from reach until the guests come by, but as those glued, patched, timeworn objects on which we eat, sleep, study, make love, those obdurate structures on which our daily lives depend so resolutely.

That one generally feels equal to those ideas (and part of their appeal *is* their accessibility) we must attribute to the virtues of Williams's later style: its shrewd blend of the dramatic and discursive, its blunt refusal to refine the human figure out of its unkempt form. If the cultivation of that style has exacted a price in terms of self-revisions and repudiations, its achievement has brought sure, though sobering, rewards. One can almost imagine that the closing lines of section sixteen of **"Le Petit Salvié"** are spoken by the poet as he, too, looks back—from the welcome landfall of these last two books—across the clarifying sea of his collected poems:

> There are no consolations, no illuminations, nothing
>   of that long-awaited flowing toward transcendence.
> There is, though, compensation, the simple certainty
>   of having touched and having been touched.
> The silence and the speaking come together, grief and
>   gladness come together, the disparates fuse.

Michael Collier (review date Summer 1991)

SOURCE: "Poetic Voices," in *Partisan Review,* Vol. LVIII, No. 3, Summer, 1991, pp. 565–69.

[*In the following excerpt, Collier praises aspects of Williams's more mature work, but finds his early poetry marred by too much raw emotion.*]

C. K. Williams's *Poems, 1963–1983* brings back into print his first four books of poems (*Lies,* 1969; *I Am the Bitter Name,* 1971; *With Ignorance,* 1977; and *Tar,* 1983). The volume also includes lovely versions of the late-eighteenth-century Japanese poet Kobayashi Issa. Although the Issa versions were published in 1983, Williams places them between *I Am the Bitter Name* and *With Ignorance.* As such the Issa serves as both a divider and bridge between the early and later work.

With Ignorance and *Tar* are characterized by long-lined narratives dramatized by elliptical and anecdotal meditations. The diction is colloquial, conversational; its rhythms wind through the length of a poem rather than being fenced off by line breaks and caesuras. The poems, with titles like **"Spit," "Neglect," "The Dog,"** are inclusive and expansive, almost Whitmanesque in their eagerness to declare all experience a suitable domain for poetry. Williams writes in **"With Ignorance"**: "Imagine a space prepared for with hunger, with dread, with power and / the power / over dread which is dread, and the love, with no space for itself, no / power for itself, / a moment, a silence, a rising, the terror for that, the space for that. / Imagine love."

In contrast to this speculative "imagining" and prose-like discursiveness, which controls and presents a poem's passion and emotion, C. K. Williams's early work—*Lies* and *I Am the Bitter Name*—is imagistic, often syntactically fragmented, and is filled with an emotional anger and violence, petulance and self-laceration. "I am going to rip myself down the middle into two pieces," he writes in **"Halves,"** and in **"Downwards,"** ". . . I am rolling, fragile as a bubble in the upstream spin, / battered by carcasses, drawn down by the lips of weeds / to the terrible womb of torn tires and children's plastic shoes / and pennies and urine. I am no more, and what is left, / baled softly with wire, floating / like a dark pillow in the hold of the brown ship, is nothing."

It would be too easy to say that Williams's work changes because his own character matures, though certainly this is true. In a poem from *Tar,* he writes, "What else did I have then? Not very much: being alone most of the time, / retrospectively noble, / but bitter back then, brutal, abrasive, corrosive—I was wearing away / with it like a tooth." As **"Halves"** and **"Downwards"** show, the early work does not lack substance or turbulence and is, in a raw emotive way, extremely powerful, but a reader will feel that the idiom and diction of Williams's early style allowed him to express passion and emotion without transforming and transcending them. As a result one feels that Williams is trapped not only within the violent prison of the self but also within an imprisoning idiom. Williams finds in the long lines of his later poems a way to escape the self, a way to examine his experience and find in it not only the rage and anger, the injustice and arbitrariness of

life but also its mercy and forgiveness. Williams writes, again from **"With Ignorance,"** "Self and other the self within other and the self still moved through its / word, / consuming itself, still, and consuming, still being rage, war, the fear, the / aghast, / but bless, bless still, even the fear, the loss, the gutting of word, the / gutting even of hunger, / but still to bless and bless, even the turn back, the refusal, to bless and / to bless and to bless."

C. K. Williams comes to accept this mercy and forgiveness by making an act of faith in the power of words. This acceptance is a triumph, human and poetic, and it is this triumph that makes *Poems, 1963–1983* a remarkable and important poetic document.

C. K. Williams with Keith S. Norris (interview date 30 October 1991)

SOURCE: "An Interview with C. K. Williams," in *New England Review,* Vol. 17, No. 2, Spring, 1995, pp. 127–40.

[*In the following interview, originally conducted on October 30, 1991, Williams discusses the function of poetic form in his own work, the historical and narrative aspects of poetry, trends in contemporary poetry, criticism, and writing programs, and the role of poetry as a moral force and mode of shared consciousness.*]

The interview was conducted on 30 October 1991, at the University of Tennessee, and was revised by C. K. Williams in 1992 and 1993.

[*Norris:*] *I'd like to begin with what seems almost a digression. What kind of effect do you think has living in Paris had on how you view social situations, on how you write? Has living in France and having to conduct so much of the ordinary business of life in another language affected your relationship to English?*

[Williams:] There's no question there are advantages to having distance from your home place; you can see certain things more clearly if you're not involved in them every day. I was reading an article this morning which was talking about something I'd already realized, which is that Americans tend to be more attached to cultural than to political issues. Americans don't argue, for instance, about the fact that the last ten years have seen a huge proportion of the national wealth taken away from the lower and middle classes and given over to the rich. Something that momentous would be the subject of heated debate in Europe, but in America, it barely seems to catch people's attention. Many Americans are passionately absorbed, though, in abortion, which is really a cultural issue, but which is debated in the political arena. The country, when you see things like that, is frighteningly divided: the libertarians versus the puritans, the religionists versus the secularists, not even to speak of the various racial tensions. But again, many of these divisions are expressed as political rather than cultural questions, and they tend to crowd out the real social-political decisions which are being made without people even noticing. Most American working people should be, by definition, liberal Democrats; you would have to be if you have any hope of getting your share of the society's economic pie, but this is obscured by appeals to people's cultural fears. How does being away, and how does coming back to America affect my writing? I think things like that are easier to see when you become more familiar with how other cultures deal with them. On the other hand, I realized recently that my new book is much more introspective than the others; I thought at first that probably this was just a time in my life when I wanted a more intense kind of inward attention, but then I realized that maybe I've been more introspective because I'm no longer a member of the American community the way I used to be. I certainly consider myself an American, and have always resisted the idea of being an expatriate; I just want to be an American who happens to live in Paris. My audience is American, and so am I, and I've been careful not to set too many poems in Paris. Although I've been going to Paris off and on for a long time, and have written a number of poems there, I've often changed the setting of those poems. I'd see some situation being manifested in some way in Paris, but I'd realize that it was something that was common to both cultures, so I'd move the action back to the States. A few poems I'd leave set in Paris, because I realized it could also be an effective strategy to let the reader believe they're involved in something that's rather exotic, and then have to realize that it's all actually part of their own struggle, their own identity. There's a poem in *Flesh and Blood* called **"Racists"** that does that quite clearly.

I wanted to start off talking about an essay you published in The American Poetry Review, **"Poetry and Consciousness."** *I thought we might discuss narrative a little, which is a subject I'm pursuing myself, the idea of narrative and fantasy in the mind of a poet, how that translates onto the page, and how it might become a political act for the poet.*

It sounds as though you're asking three questions, about things that are usually pretty separate. Do you mean fantasy, as distinct from imagination, in Coleridge's terms?

I'm defining it the way you do in the **"Poetry and Consciousness"** *essay, as the narrative the mind pursues on its own.*

That essay was originally a talk I delivered to a convention of psychiatrists, and I was using the term "fantasy" in the way they use it, to describe the little dramas the mind constantly produces, which they interpret as expressing the tensions of the unconscious. I don't know whether in a literary conversation I'd call them narratives, although I suppose they are. I find fantasy, in both the way the psychiatrists use it, and the way Coleridge did, a terrifically useful mechanism, and I imagine everyone who writes does. What we call memory isn't really distinct in substance and quality, in the vivid and elusive way it comes to us, from fantasy.

In your poetry, for example in **"From My Window,"** *the poem's subject matter often includes many different narratives, recounted from the poet's point of view. Is this an inherently political act? Are you assuming an Archimedean point in the poems, and creating narratives to evolve a personal political space?*

That's an interesting thought. **"From My Window,"** is, as you say, about different life-narratives, and it does imply, certainly, different points of view. I suppose once you begin accumulating narratives in that way, the poem has to become political or social in some sense of those words because you're trying to deal with more than your own world. All of that might actually be a good description of what the poem is about. I once was asked to write about the poem at some length, and I came to similar conclusions, although when I was writing the poem, all the thematic matter wasn't that premeditated. But what you're saying might be a way to amplify the idea of why one would use narrative in the first place, because you can begin to feel limited by your own narrative situation, and once you decide to expand it, you have to move to a kind of mind-set which includes other people, and out of that follows a different sort of poetic consciousness.

I'll take a little detour and ask about your long line. Do you find expressing this kind of narrative consciousness easier in the long-lined poem?

Yes, I think that's really one of the main reasons I started using the long line, so I'd be able to include that kind of objective narrative material, although I have to say I never actually thought of the term narrative per se when I began to write those poems. The word seemed to arrive after I published **With Ignorance,** the first book in which I used the line. People remarked a lot on the narrative identity of the poems, but really most of the poems in the book aren't narrative at all. In fact, most of the poems I've written in long lines haven't really been narratives, although many of them use narrative elements. It's a shame—I've said this before—that the word "anecdote" has been debased. Anecdote for us tends to mean something superficial, even trivial, but anecdotal material has always been one of the core resources of lyric poetry. Many lyric poems depend on an anecdote which is embodied and then reflected upon. I think that in all the long-lined poems I've been trying to loosen up what I felt were the constraints the lyric had placed on me. I've always felt that almost all my poems were primarily lyric, and to have the word *narrative* applied to the poems seems to undercut what I was trying to do. Even **"From My Window,"** which does include, as you say, strips of narrative, really has no story the way we usually mean it when we speak of narrative. These guys are going along the street, somebody falls down, I'm looking out the window and see them. The poem really has more to do with various kinds of vision, and the epiphanies that happen in terms of vision.

I guess I was using the word narrative because in much of the literary theory that's been written lately, not much has been done with poetry. Much contemporary literary theory has dealt with fiction, often using the term "narrative" as a basis for evaluating the political actions in the text. I was wondering if we could begin to apply some of the same standards, some of the same ways of looking at experience, to poetry?

I'm trying to write an essay now about that. I think one of the great shortcomings of contemporary criticism is that for the most part it looks so single-mindedly to fiction for its experiential matter. I think the reason is because many readers, even critics, even teachers of literature, have become mistrustful, or apprehensive, or, to be frank, ignorant, of the function form plays in art and in experience. Compared to poetry, fiction is essentially a formless genre, in the sense that it doesn't have the artifice, the purely artificial layer of necessity that poetry takes upon itself. There are exceptions, of course, but it's certainly true of what we could call the generic novel. When you subtract form from subject-matter, you're always subtracting from potential experience. I don't want to go into this too much, because, as I say, I'm writing about it, but I think people are getting a little tired of the novel, and are going to begin to turn to poetry again; I think many young people already have.

About contemporary criticism—much of it is historical, or historicist, or economically inquisitive in some way, trying to get a political handle on the work it discusses. Can a poem deal with history in a way a novel can't?

This is a nice coincidence, because for the last few weeks, during my time at George Mason, I've been giving a seminar-workshop on just that theme. When I do my classes there, I find that I can use the short time I have more profitably by studying poems from the canon with some idea in mind, and then looking at the workshop participants poems in the same way, and this last session has been on myth and history. We studied Keats and the way he uses myth in some of his poems, then we looked at Yeats and Lowell and the way they used history in some of theirs. The poem we studied most closely was "For the Union Dead," and when you begin to analyze it from an historical point of view, it's really quite astonishing. Just the different periods of history that are dealt with in the poem; it moves from the time the poem was written, in the late Fifties, back to Lowell's childhood, then to the Civil War, then to the colonial era, then to after the Civil War, when the St. Gauden's memorial sculpture was dedicated, then to the Second World War, and the advent of the nuclear age with Hiroshima, then back to the present, which included the Civil Rights marches, the beginning of the reshaping of the American cities, etc. All in an amazingly condensed lyric structure that concentrates the experience in a completely unpolemical way, and attaches itself to our own lives in a way I don't think fiction would be able to. The precision with which poems deal with time makes a different demand on consciousness compared to the more amorphous, flowing sense of time in fiction. The moments of a poem are very intense, very discrete and vivid; you're moved through them, and through time, in a formal way, with a kind of double consciousness that makes you very aware of other realms, the moral, the ethical and political.

Do poems create a new sense of time? Can they create a new history, a safer history that tells a new story?

Rather than "safer," I'd prefer to say "more reliable." For people who are experienced in the language of poetry, going into a poem means going into a different sense of time. That's one of the reasons you go to poetry. What might be "new" in the story, and that poetry has as one of its essential resources, is the story of itself. Through its form, poetry recounts the way it manages time and consciousness. Once you move into the kind of consciousness poetry evokes, you move into a special kind of mental space. It's like being in a church, or in prayer. You pay attention to what's happening to you differently from the way you ordinarily do. When you move into the space of a poem, you're attentive to your consciousness, you expect different things of it, and in that way the poet has access to the mind of the reader in a way very little else does, I think.

*In **"Poetry and Consciousness,"** again, you mention that ability of consciousness to do several things simultaneously as almost in itself creating a moral sense; we combine different elements of consciousness into the single creation we call a poem.*

It might be that attentiveness to consciousness is the beginning of any moral reflection or act, at least for a modern liberal. Most religions, or, I probably should say, most fundamentalist interpretations of religions, demand quite a different attitude. For them, what goes on in consciousness, its intentions and its reflections, are essentially incidental. What's important is what's asked of consciousness by the community of believers; the individual's consciousness has to be revised and reshaped to fit that. In liberalism, of any age, starting with the Greeks, what happens in the mind of the individual matters excruciatingly. We presume that out of our reflections will come self-truths that will allow us a more sensitive social awareness and richer kinds of moral actions.

You mentioned form earlier. Sometimes in your poetry it seems as though you're following an almost Charles Olson-like conception, with the syllable as a unit of meaning, and the line taking care of the whole breath, so that the line can seem to comprise many small ideas, while it's still a whole breath, a complete unit, a single musical phrase. Is that similar to the way you conceive your particular idea of line?

I haven't thought about Olsen much lately, although there was a period in which I found something fascinating in the sheer energy he gave off in his writing, more in his prose than in his poetry. I never really felt a deep sympathy with the project of his poetry. About my own work: I don't conceive of my line as related especially to the breath, but though technically it isn't metrical, in that it isn't accountable in any regular way, I do consider it a definite musical unit, albeit one that I vary quite a bit.

Do you think that it's the poet's responsibility to try to achieve meaning in the poem? Is it the poet's responsibility to bring the music and the sense together in a cohesive meaning, or should we tolerate meaninglessness? If so, how far can we let meaninglessness go? What about the Language Poets? Are the Language Poets irresponsible in attempting to achieve a meaning translatable to the reader?

I find the Language Poets trivial rather than irresponsible. Certainly in their polemic and rhetoric, they speak a great deal of responsibility, of the commitment of art to social ideals, and so forth, but you certainly don't see much of it in their work. From a technical point of view, if they're willing to sacrifice the meaning of language to its potential as music, they certainly could be doing a lot more interesting things with the music than they are. If they're trying to develop a new system of meaning, they're not doing anything much different from what the Dadaists did, and they're much less interesting and inspiring than the Dadaists or Surrealists. I feel they're mostly driven by a passion for novelty, by the desire to be out ahead of everybody else, to be more "avant garde," but they're giving away an awful lot in that way. Of course, I might be speaking of some poets I don't mean to; someone like Leslie Scallopino, who I often find fascinating: I've heard her mentioned along with the Language Poets, although I don't find much similarity between her work and the poets who are the hard core of the movement. Certainly poetry is always an expression, or at least an embodiment of meaning, because if you put two words together, language will evoke something of meaning out of them, no matter how badly you might want it not to. The issue I've been struggling with over the last years has had more to do with the level of *discursive* meaning a poem can hold. We all know there are many different ways a poem can mean something; it can move from being almost wholly connotative, to being much closer to what I'm calling the discursive. It seems our moment of poetry has mostly been committed to connotative kinds of meaning, and I've been working with trying to push myself towards the other end of the scale. I've been exploring, at least for myself, how much you can say of what you'd mean in other modes of language, in what we might crudely call the philosophical mode, for example. Poems that are very formally complex, formally attentive, on the surface don't seem to have to have as high a degree of denotative meaning to be satisfying, they work in more freely connotative ways, but it seems to me that we should be able to put our intellects to use, and our more overtly analytic mental operations, and still have our poems be formally and musically satisfying. In my new book, *A Dream of Mind,* I've been trying to find ways to be even more directly discursive than I have been before, while not sacrificing anything of the musical interest I think a poem should have.

Does this mean that we leave the idea of the objective correlative behind entirely?

Without over-simplifying too much, I think that what Eliot meant by the objective correlative is pretty close to what we call now the image. The objective correlative is one of the characteristic methods of what I've been calling connotative meaning. It's always in poetry, it's almost the very substance of poetry. What we do around it is what changes in the evolution, or I should say shifting, of styles. I guess the more discursive kinds of poetic events don't have titles yet, although you could probably find some good ones in old books of rhetoric.

If we follow the idea of discursive thinking or discursive poetry, do you simply follow the way your mind takes you when you're writing a poem, or is there more of a sense of purpose?

I wish it were so neat. Usually the purpose of the poem, along with its meaning, evolves as I work on it. In some poems, it can seem as though the meaning is evident, and all I'm doing is following along after it, but that's very rare. Generally, there's a sort of fusion of purpose and play. It's one of the more interesting things about writing poetry, that fusion. For the reader, what's most noticeable as an element of play is the music; there's really no reason for music to exist in language, it's arbitrary and artificial, and that's quite evident. But the fact that the eyes and mind attach to a particular image or a particular happening can also be regarded as arbitrary, as playful. Why one thing rather than another? There's really no reason. What we call the purpose, the moral element of the poem, the apparatus which evokes that purpose, seems at first the opposite of playful: it's deadly serious. But when the poem is realized in the mind, the purposeful and playful, the moral and the musical come together. There are two ways of looking at the poem. You can say what the purpose is that's been imposed on the poem, which might really have been quite incidental in the composition, and what is the moral truth that evolves from all these fusions, these dances between play and purpose.

I guess that leads us back to form. I want to address the distinction between Post-modern poetry and Post-modern fiction. Do we distinguish between the two by saying that post-modern poetry can have that sort of dance in it, a sort of purposeful playfulness that fiction can't?

No, fiction can be playful, too, but in a different sense. Poetry has a much higher consciousness of form, and play and form aren't at all the same thing. I suppose you can attach a kind of scale to form. All art has it to one degree or another, but in the literary arts, the novel has the least commitment to form, and poetry the greatest. The style of a novel, of the prose, can be very energetic, very playful, and the voice of the novelist in this sense can play as much as the poet. But the poem has the extra layer of formal attentiveness that's not in the novel, by definition.

Do you think that there is a post-modern form to poetry? A few years ago, Jonathan Holden wrote an essay on post-

modern form, saying that poetic form is no longer based on epistemological anxiety, and that it isn't inherently organic, but that it is now analogical. Forms are based on meaning placed on a continuum ranging from confessional to what he calls "primal scream." Do you think it's helpful to devise such a post-modern form?

I hadn't heard that idea. I'm not terribly interested in the concept of post-modernism; it seems as though the word began to be used as a catch-all and remains a catch-all. It originally came up in architecture, to describe the next stage in the evolution of architectural style after what was called Modernism, and I think it was a very useful term, for architecture, not for everything in the world. On the other hand, I think that what Holden says is interesting. I don't think, though, that it's post-modernism that he's speaking of, if you apply it to poetry. I think that he's describing the evolution of free verse, of what you could call functional verse, in which the form of the verse is generated at a level much closer to the meaning than in the forms of non-free verse. In Holden's terms, Walt Whitman would have to be called a post-modernist, because who better developed a form that came out of its meaning than he did? Alan Shapiro has written a very strong essay on all this. I don't want to give away his ideas before he publishes them, but he postulates two quite different visions of the world that are implied in the use of free verse and in the use of metrical verse. He points out that each has a different vision of history and time, and of human potentiality within history and time, and I think that's true.

What about the conscious choice of poets to use traditional forms? We've talked about various forms, Language poetry probably being the lack of any controlling form, except perhaps that they have the lack of form as intent. What about your choices of form, the eight-line poem of **Flesh and Blood.** *Is this a choice for form? And, if so, why a choice to operate in that one form? Is it limiting, or particularly helpful?*

It was something I blundered on. When I finished *Tar,* I had a lot of poems left over. One, in eight-line stanzas I'd been struggling with for a few years, and one day I was working on it and realized it was never going to be a poem. But when I looked at one of the stanzas, I realized it could stand by itself, that with a few changes it could work as a poem that I found quite satisfying. I began to go through the poems that were left over, and to find stanzas that could be shaped into poems, and I went on from there. I've written about this before somewhere, but non-artists tend to think of form as a limiting thing; they think you have to hammer experience into a form, but in fact form is generative, it helps you create. If, for instance, you're committed to writing six-line stanzas in a poem, and you come up with an idea that takes up only four lines, you're forced to find two more lines, and often you'll come up with something unexpected that you wouldn't have found without that formal compulsion. It's the same thing with the music of a poem; the need to satisfy the formal demands of the music often takes you where you wouldn't

have otherwise gone, on the most detailed as well as the most general level. That's what happened with the eight line poems. Once I became committed to them, their form became terrifically liberating, and I began to deal with themes I don't think I would have otherwise, and to use language in ways I never had. The problem with that kind of form, though, is that you consume it, you have to be careful because it can become automatic, and empty. The first seventy-seven of Berryman's *Dream Songs,* for example, were marvelous, and made an astonishing book. But then he went on, and the next three hundred of the poems were for the most part, on a much lower level; I think many of them shouldn't have existed at all; they actually seemed to dilute the power of the first group. The same thing happened to a lesser degree with Lowell in his *Notebook* and *History.* Although I think Lowell had a greater genius for that kind of expansiveness than Berryman did, you still get a sense by the end that he's sometimes trivializing his own talent by aiming it at themes and subjects that aren't worthy of him, just because it became so easy. With me, towards the end of writing **Flesh and Blood,** I felt I could make a poem out of almost anything. There was an amazing feeling of freedom, as though my imagination had finally found the perfect way to work, and it was also very seductive; form has its traps, too. When I finished the book, I had another fifty poems, finished or nearly. When the book was in production, I remember I finished one last poem and brought it to my editor Jon Galassi. He began to proof read it, I was looking at it over his shoulder, and I suddenly realized it wasn't a real poem; it was hollow, it rang false to me; I took it back, and put the rest of the poems in a file.

Have you pretty much left that form behind, then? The latest poem I saw in The New Yorker, *"***When,***" didn't take the eight-line form.*

Yes. It used a four-line stanza poem. I've given up the eight-line stanza as a form for complete poems, but I still usually, although not always, like to work in regular stanzas of one length or another. As I say, I find the kind of rigor it demands important for me in going as far as I can with an idea.

We talked earlier about the ability of the poem to teach. When you're teaching poetry, do you try to teach traditional forms, or to teach discovery of a form? When we're learning how to write poetry, how to put meaning into a poem, figuring out what poems can say; how do you teach that? Do you try and teach through forms?

As I think I've said here, if you're teaching poetry, you have to be teaching form. Poetry is form. If your students are primarily writing in free verse, you try to teach them the formal necessities free verse entails, of which there are just as many as in the more conventional forms; they're harder to talk about, because in traditional forms you count, and counting seems much more rational than working with musical elements that are more closely tied to the way language moves when it's not being counted. I believe very much in learning to use traditional forms and meters. When I started writing, one of the first things I did was a sonnet sequence of about fifty sonnets; each poem had a different rhyme scheme; I used full rhymes and slant rhymes and para-rhymes. I ended up throwing the whole thing away, but it was very important to me. I wrote mostly in meters in those days, and then one day something made me begin to write in free verse, and I felt very liberated. I didn't so much make a conscious decision to give up meters, I just began experimenting with free verse, and kept going. When I'm teaching, I find I try to encourage some students to be freer, to move out into areas of experience which might make them write more expansively, with less encumbrances, while I try to get others to impose stricter limits on themselves, to give them shapes to work in. Most often what you're trying to do, though, is find what a student has done without quite being aware of what they were doing, and then to try to show them how to go farther in the direction they're already moving. As far as the difference between free verse and meter, I think there's a very active dialectic between the traditional forms and those that I've called the more functional ones. Even poets who write only free verse by necessity have to spend a great deal or most of their time reading and studying poems in meters, since that's the greater part of our tradition. I think that's one of the misapprehensions of the so-called New Formalists, who are fundamentalists in the same way religious fundamentalists are: they say there's only one way to see the world, through various kinds of authority, and everything else is suspect at best, and value-less at worst. There are some people who feel as strongly the other way; that any kind of meter or rhyme is intolerable, and I think they're just as wrong. There are always exchanges going on between various notions of form; the conventional forms are still there to be used, and since the entire tradition in some ways is implicit in any poem, you can always find traces of the metrical tradition in a good free-verse poem. I've been using rhymes in my translations these days, and who knows, I might start using them in my poems. One of the delights of being an artist is in moving into areas where you wouldn't have ever thought you'd go.

So you're saying that the New Formalists have no real generative tension in their poetry?

No, I don't say that at all. I have nothing intrinsically against their poems. Some are good, some bad, just as some free verse poems are good and some bad. What I often find reprehensible are their polemics. They're like the Language Poets in the way they mix up so crudely their aesthetics with their politics. They claim to be conservative in the good sense of the term; they want to conserve old values, but they never articulate what the broader implications of the values they're trying to save or resurrect might be, except for their one aesthetic obsession. To impose an aesthetic point of view on reality is a very complex matter, especially if you're going also to be cranky about it. I think that after a century of watching how polemics can turn on human beings, how that sort of

passionate certainty can be put to uses one would never have dreamed of, we have to be careful of any gesture anybody makes that first tries to make of someone else an opponent, and then tries, in whatever way, to wipe that opponent out. The revolutionary polemics at the end of the nineteenth century and the beginning of the twentieth were trying to break down social forms, and they had a very clear, and very certain idea, at least for awhile, of how the social and aesthetic were woven together, which they are. Things certainly did break down, to our chagrin, but we're in a period of trying to put things back together; the social forms we've inherited are at best incomplete, they leave too many people out, and at worst totally malignant. When you have people ranting, and they do rant, about somebody else's vision of poetry, what becomes important isn't the particular vision, because a vision will reveal itself for good and ill in the poems it generates, but the rant.

Let's talk about what has been termed "workshop poetry." Is there a problem with the poetry that university programs produce?

That term is a misnomer, and it's an unfair attack on a lot of well-meaning and hard-working people. If you use the term "workshop poetry" to describe what's actually written in the writing programs, you have to take into account that it's being written by poets who are in the process of realizing themselves. Although this isn't always true, what's produced is really a kind of apprentice poetry, and you can't expect apprentice poetry to be terribly exalting. The problem is that the term is also used, wrongly, to describe a particular style that has evolved over the past few decades, a very loose, often talky kind of free verse poetry that doesn't have anything particularly interesting about it in terms of its perceptions, its music, or the movement of its thought. There's no question that it's a very mediocre kind of poetry, and that it's the prevalent mode of our time. But if you take the trouble to look closely, the prevalent mode of any literary moment is always rather appalling. We get so used to reading in anthologies that we don't notice how rigorously selective they are, how much pure *drek* has been left behind. If you try to read the vast majority of poems that came out of the Romantic movement, you'd die of boredom, and the fact that the poems were written in meters doesn't help at all. I started writing in the Fifties, and although I had no confidence whatsoever in my aesthetic capacities, I felt instinctively that most of the poems I read were empty, dead, and when I go back now and read them, I know I was right. The fact that many of the poets now who are perpetrating bad poetry come out of the writing programs is just an historical accident. Poets will always come out of something, agorae or coffee houses or universities. The *good* poems that are being written now, the ones that aren't in the prevalent mode, that aren't mediocre in any way, are also, for the most part, being written by people from the programs.

Earlier, you mentioned the poet's toolbox. Do you consider the university an effective place for the poet to learn to use that?

Yes, I think there are elements of the composition of poetry that can be taught. I also think there are things, important things, that you pick up by osmosis. Of course most of the equipment you have in your toolbox you pick up by reading other poets. But you can only absorb something when you're ready to, when you've struggled through to the point where you're ready to understand how to do it; in a way, you don't even notice the thing until then. I think that the workshop can accelerate all of this, at least for many people. For some people it doesn't do anything, but nothing would; they drop out and stop trying to be poets, or at least professional poets. One hopes they go on reading and writing, and as far as I can tell, they often do. For the people who keep at it, the workshop helps them to understand the principles behind various poetic practices. I think that's important, being able to ask yourself more clearly what's involved in what you're trying to do, what you can only dream of doing, or of what's right there as the next thing to try. How can you generate out of your own system of composition what you admire in other poetry? We always feel we're working by trial and error; we don't have to think about what we know how to do well. It's moving into the unknown that requires labor, working at the front end of your conceptual apparatus, and this requires, often, the kind of articulation of principle I'm talking about. I find being in the workshop can often be exhilarating; there's a real feeling of discovery, and when one of the participants breaks through, into their own voice, into that first poem that's a real *poem*, it's very exciting. I'm always intrigued, too, by the delicate mix of competition and cooperation in the workshops. Everyone's pushing themselves, they're aware of what all their friends are doing, but you hardly ever see anything but delight when somebody does something well. That might be a good lesson against the insane competitiveness of much of our society, if nothing else.

About poetry in the general university education—what role do you see contemporary poetry playing in educating students? It seems as though we have found a place in the curriculum for the historical modes of poetry; we know how to teach Romanticism or Modernism, for example. But outside of the workshop, what do you think is the role of teaching contemporary poetry?

I like to give readings at colleges where the audience consists of mostly students who are coerced into being there. It's an intriguing challenge to try to show the kids that poetry can be something that doesn't exist only in the classroom, and that it isn't as forbidding as they think it is, as they're taught to think it is, that it might even have something to do with their lives. You say we know how to teach Romantic and modern poetry, but do we really? How do we teach Romantic poetry to a freshman or a sophomore who's never voluntarily read a poem? I know some terrific teachers, I'm often awed by how good they are at teaching poetry to younger students, but for the most part what goes on in the classroom is a little sad, because the kids come out feeling that all they've done is finished a course, taken an exam, and they never look at a poem again. Once someone becomes an English major, of course, and becomes a specialist in literature, then we're pretty sure we know how to teach them, although I'm not even sure of that. But before that, what are we teaching? I feel very strongly that contemporary poetry is, or could be, the best possible introduction to poetry in general. If you expose people to the poems that are *their* poems, that are written for them, for them in their moment of history, and show them that you don't need to read a history of literature to understand them, you just have to listen and let them happen to you, then you can go on to show them how poems from the past can work in similar ways in illuminating themselves to themselves, and can even give pleasure. We could use the analogy of music. You don't introduce kids to music by playing them Bach fugues. First you hear the lullabies your mother sings, then you hear popular music, and you learn very quickly what music is. Then if you want to go on to classical music, you do; there's no need to study musical theory, and even if you stay with popular music, you're in that realm, you're in *music,* and that's important. I think poetry can be learned the same way, and in fact I think it is, to a great extent; you hear nursery rhymes, you hear childrens' poems, and everything's all right until someone starts to teach you what poetry *really* is, and how you have to study it, and you immediately let yourself fall away from it. I think it's a wonderful thing, which to a great extent has grown out of the graduate programs, that so many poets are brought to universities to give readings. When I went to college there were almost never poetry readings; in my years at Penn, we had one reading, by e. e. cummings. I think that reading to a university audience is good for the poets, too. Somehow in our recent past, the study of poetry began to be regarded as the history of poetry. When the Romantics were writing, they were certainly conscious of their tradition, but so was their audience, and both they and the audience were acutely aware that the poetry was speaking for the issues they were living, and for the kind of sensibilities they were interested in. There was a period in American poetry, at least in what was then thought of as the mainstream, when people actually believed they were writing for the canon, that awful, but I suppose useful concept—I used it myself a few minutes ago—as though what you were doing when you wrote a poem was sort of tacking it onto the front end of this great historical locomotive called literature. But that's not what poetry is at all.

We've often been accused, as poets, of talking only to other poets, or writing only for other poets. When you speak to a general audience, or even to a class of nonpoets, what does a poem educate in the general audience? You've said that poetry can educate emotion. In what ways can poetry educate the emotion of the general audience?

When you give a reading to a group of people who aren't experienced in poetry, at least a reading that goes well, several things happen. First, partway into the reading, there's a feeling of relief that comes from the audience, that this isn't as bad as they thought it was going to be, that it'll be an hour they might get through without dying of boredom. Then, if things go really well, there's a kind of excitement that begins to set in. Not that anybody's dancing on the chairs, but you can sense that the kids are with you, that they're really listening, and that they understand what the poems are saying. It doesn't happen every time and it certainly doesn't happen to every kid, but you can tell, and afterwards a few of them will sometimes overcome their shyness and come up to thank you, which is wonderful. I remember the first time I was reading to high school students—this was in the early seventies—a group of kids came up afterwards and asked if I'd like to write some lyrics for their rock group. I thought that was a terrific compliment. There's no question that the kids can hear they're being spoken to, that something in them is being spoken for. What that something is is probably terribly complicated. You used the expression "educating the emotions . . . of the audience," and I think that's very germane. That's really what education is about, at least on the highest level; teaching us the part that what I'll call our moral imagination plays in our emotions. That's what a poem does, it bridges a gap, it makes people aware that their everyday emotions, the feelings they have as they move through their own experiences, are a part of a realm they aren't usually conscious of. Poetry, or good poetry, necessarily deals with moral questions, if nothing else with questions of truth, and it deals at the same time with the most common emotions; it puts the two together in a way that can be immediately grasped. There's something else, too. I tried to talk before about how the moral realm and formal realm come together in poems, and I think that this is something that happens to an audience, too, although they're not necessarily entirely conscious of it. When a poem is speaking to someone, I should say singing to someone, they begin to realize that their own experience can be a part of the formal realm, too. They can hear themselves being sung to themselves, the way Odysseus was in the *Odyssey*. It's an amazing thing. And you can see that this can go back to what I was saying about the use of contemporary poetry in education. To find yourself being sung into a formal universe, you have to realize that what's being sung is an identity different and greater from the one you believed you had. We usually conceive of our identities, however involved with them we are, as entities that just plod through the world, but to hear your experience moved into form, into a poetry that both sings and implies a fuller, more vivid consciousness, has to give you a different vision of yourself. As I say, I wouldn't want to have to say how much of this is conscious in kids who aren't experienced in poetry, or even to people who are, but I think it must be something like this that happens when a poem moves us.

Let's clarify the term "moral imagination" as it relates to poetry. Do you mean an individual's moral imagination or a greater moral imagination?

In the simplest sense, you could say that it's just the individual's consciousness of participating in an imagination that's greater than his or her own. As long as a person

believes that he or she is only an individual sensibility, with an insular imagination, there's no reason to be anything but solipsistic, egoistic, self-protective. I think the basic force of community depends on members of a group participating in a shared imagination. That's a rather basic definition of culture. When this starts to break down, when the imagination is neglected, or perverted, and people don't have any sense of participating in the real moral life of the group, then the community itself begins to suffer. You can see this happening in Yugoslavia now, where people are defining themselves ethnically rather than culturally, or, even more interestingly from the point of view of poetry, in relation to their identities in language, because that's often the way people experience their social identity most intensely. Communism offered a shared image of society; the problem of course was that the image was imposed, it didn't grow out of the actual cultural imagination of the people, and so when communism collapsed, everyone ran as quickly as possible to other identities, other imaginations of community, with the chaos we see now. I suppose we could say the same thing about the split in American society between various social groups. We tend to see the divisive issues in America in terms of race, and race certainly plays a key role in our social anguish, but I think that the breakdown of our educational system, and so of any kind of shared imagination, is even more frightening, and will finally cause us more pain.

Do poets disturb the moral identity or the moral imagination? So are we talking here about a kind of ethical action on the part of poetry?

There's no question that poetry is, or can be, an ethical act. And as far as poetry disturbing the moral identity, as I said before, I think there are times when it does, when it should, and times perhaps where it might have different functions. Right now, we seem to be at the end of a period in which one of the primary functions of poetry was to break down what were conceived to be oppressive or inhibiting social forms. Poetry in that what already seems ancient epoch was constantly trying to explode received identities, received ideas of imagination. It seems now, though, that we might be going into a time when what poetry and art has to do is to emphasize the essential community of people. Since we don't have any grand ideas anymore of ways to perfect societies, maybe our task is to try to make the social shapes we already have more viable, more just. I don't know how this all might manifest itself in poetry, or whether it might have manifested itself already, but clearly we're in a moment of terrific historical change, and one way or another our poetry and our art is going to enact all of that.

Charles Altieri (essay date Summer 1992)

SOURCE: "Contemporary Poetry as Philosophy: Subjective Agency in John Ashbery and C. K. Williams," in *Contemporary Literature,* Vol. XXXIII, No. 2, Summer, 1992, pp. 214–42.

[In the following excerpt, Altieri examines the philosophical notion of subjective agency and its manifestation in the poetry of Williams and John Ashbery as an alternative to poststructural theory.]

If one teaches contemporary poetry in the academy there seems no way to avoid engaging the tangled question of its relation to literary theory, now more imperially dubbed simply "theory." And if one engages the question, there seem only two basic options: one can try to show how theory composes frameworks far too crude for the intricacies of lyric sensibility, or one can evaluate poets in terms of the degree to which they address, or even subscribe to, the "sophisticated" intellectual life which theory now composes. Faced with this binary, one has little choice but to opt for both, seeking a rapprochement that puts intellectual pressure on the poets and demands more intricately contoured thinking from the theorists. However, this opting for both cannot suffice. One must decide on priorities. Is theory to determine which poets matter, or is there some possible independent position from which we can say that certain poets address the theorists' issues more richly than the theorists do? This of course requires our deciding who will decide on the criteria for judging relative richness. But that question may be finessable if we take the time to adapt our concepts to what the poets do. That will give us concrete cases to judge, where we can hope to find terms for assessment more general than those developed by either side.

In this spirit I will take up the issue of subjective agency in order to argue that some of the best contemporary poetry provides modes of thinking at once more subtle and more conceptually provocative than we find in the prevailing theoretical stances. All the theoretical instruments seem to agree that our culture must develop versions of agency that neither return to romantic notions of a deep-buried and alienated self desperate for expression nor replace that inwardness by reducing subjectivity to subjection within linguistic and social codes. Yet, as I have argued on other occasions, contemporary theory has become so dependent on poststructural concepts that it lacks the resources to develop an adequate third choice on this issue. Given its biases, this theorizing can do little more than return to the ironies of subjection, idealize a heterogeneity whose interactions it cannot account for, and produce claims about resisting hegemonic orders that by now seem little more than a rhetorical antidialectic already swallowed up within the play of market simulacra.[1] Our poets do better, I will argue, because they envision subjective agency in positive terms as a specific mode of dynamic intentionality inseparable from how we inhabit the sentences we speak. Developing in their own way lines of thinking explored by Nietzsche and by Wittgenstein, these poets offer a perspective that frees us from having to locate subjectivity in any specific image or narrative account. For they realize that such projections entail chains of substitutions and displacements that keep deferring that self until it can only appear a deeply buried and alienated principle.

My central figures will be John Ashbery and C. K. Williams because I find their work the fullest contemporary efforts to develop this alternative view of subjective agency (which we might call "deictic intentionality," for reasons that I hope become clear). Where their predecessors sought strong images as locales for positing identities, these poets explore the subjective force projected in deictics and other shifters, hoping that how one establishes one's relation to utterances and situations provides a sufficient grounding for the range of identities and identifications that constitutes subjective life. Taking my lead from Wittgenstein, I will stress their self-conscious foregrounding of the operators "now" and "this" (and their correlates) to establish expressive energies and assume responsibilities that cannot be treated simply as ideological functions subjecting what projects itself as subject. Instead "now" and "this" prove fundamentally relational, locating agency in the specific ways that persons apply the range of sentences they have learned to speak. Personal agency then resides not in some deep underlying content for the self but in paths that emerge through what the sentences carry as desire and how they come to define basic commitments shaping future paths and relationships. Ashbery will be our poet defining the resources of the lyric "really now," an expression that enables desire to resist those alienating idealizations that occur when lovers seek images of their own relationship. Then Williams becomes our poet of the "this": his long line defines through time how the will gives affirmative qualities to the now, so the line becomes an image of dynamic subjectivity working through what would subject it if it turned from relational activity to more specular self-reflexive states. . . .

I do not think any philosopher gives us as fully developed a rendering of subjective agency immanent to the indexical uses of language, yet thereby capable of establishing long-term aspects of identity for the agents. But in order to understand and provide a context for this achievement we must turn to the history of ideas so as to clarify the specific pressures on contemporary sensibilities that Ashbery is responding to and to indicate some of the conceptual possibilities that he extends into specific imaginative figures. Then we will shift to what Ashbery's work can be said to have enabled, poetically and psychologically, in the recent poetry of C. K. Williams, where the "really now" becomes the basic active principle for a full range of subjective states, including those that involve duration.

There is a sense in which the basic traits of Ashberyan agency—its awareness of the will's inseparability from multiple affective states, its attaching of intentionality to bodily dispositions, its developing expressive capacities not bound to self-images or concepts, and its aligning the psyche's mobility with a complex temporality fundamental to any rich sense of what love demands—fits the best poststructural thinking on the subject. This stems from his carrying out a fundamentally Nietzschean project. But unlike even Derrida, who remains caught in an impasse fundamental to that poststructural theory, Ashbery can activate the full implications of that project. Before we can develop those implications, however, we must get clear on the dilemma within poststructural accounts of subjective agency.

Poststructuralist thinkers break from structuralism in large part because they recognize the need to speak of singular expressive versions of the "really now," but the analytic terms they continue from structuralism afford them no positive means by which to envision that "now" as a way for that subjectivity to achieve full articulation. Instead the entire enterprise is haunted by the models of subjection developed by Lacan and by Althusser—the one in terms of family romance, the other in terms of the interpellation that gives agents a place in the social order. Both perspectives prove disturbingly essentialist, asserting necessary structures for the psyche which divide subjective agency from itself and force it to live its imaginative life in thrall to some other that it internalizes as the means of attributing to itself powers of subjectivity. Lacan stresses the mirroring function of the mother, which gives the child a sense of an inner life tragically dependent on its outer reflections. And Althusser makes the feeling of subjectivity depend on our internalizing identities embedded in social roles by hegemonic ideological structures. Derrida and Foucault are more abstract, but perhaps also even more trapped, since for them the depersonalizing force is a property of all categories: categories and hence concepts force third-person frameworks necessary for intelligibility on first-person states and thus necessarily banish subjective agency to the margins of a public world. So the best that poststructural theory can do is preserve this sense of singularity by locating it exclusively in what might be termed a working negativity—in Lacan's speaking subject kept distinct from the ego, in Foucault's emphasis on creating a life that is beautiful to contemplate for itself, and in Derrida's emphasis on a singular "yes" articulated by a working that parasitically plays itself against all determinate meaning. Any more ambitious claims seem blocked by the very structure of semantic form and psychic development. So while modes of subjection change over time, the fact of subjection constantly subsuming subjective negativity remains constant. . . .

This is where Wittgenstein must enter our story. While he shares Nietzsche's sense of will as immanent to situations and as too directly involved in action-orientations to be subject to scrutiny by the reason, Wittgenstein's own asceticism enables him to purify these ideas so that there is no possibility of projecting fantasies of one's own power on to the public order (in part because such fantasies betray a misunderstanding of both the privacy of will and the structures forming public order). Then Wittgenstein will lead us to the full import of C. K. Williams's extending the "really now" into a mobile and fluent controlling line that gives subjective agency a duration and a gathering power without having to attribute to it any mysterious inner life.

Wittgenstein can achieve a more radical and more workable sense of subjective agency than Nietzsche in part because he manages to reverse Nietzsche's perspectivism. Where Nietzsche collapses the knowing subject who takes responsibility for propositions into the willing subject constructing the world in accord with specific values, Wittgenstein proposes a sharp distinction between the willing and the knowing subject. There are domains in which the ego shrinks to an extensionless point, its agency subsumed under the task of description or under the rules of language games. In such cases one can imagine the I as an eye that takes in a visual field but that also understands itself enclosed within what it sees. At the other pole there is a willing subject that as will cannot be enclosed within the visual field: how the eye feels about what it sees and how it gives significance or projections to that field does not appear within the scene. Rather, developing Nietzsche's sense of will's immanence within behavioral orientations, Wittgenstein locates the force of will in what frames everything that can be described. Willing is not a specular projection so much as an overall disposition, measured by how one engages the "now," not by who one imagines oneself to be.

It is not easy to grasp a sense of the agent as at once attentive to the objective and irreducibly a locus of subjective will. But we get considerable help from the figure of boundary conditions that Wittgenstein uses to connect ethics and aesthetics to the transcendental nature of logical form. In each of these domains we must allow sharp distinctions between what can be said and what must be shown. What can be said presupposes certain lines of connection between language and the world. But we cannot speak about those containing frames because any claim we made about them would have to presuppose exactly what it purported to describe. Logic provides the most striking example of the two conditions. Logic gives the form of propositions, which means there cannot be meaningful propositions about logic itself; there can only be displays of what logical form does in its establishing boundary conditions for what can count as truths. Ethics and aesthetics rely on analogous distinctions, but there the nature of individual wills takes the place of the boundary force of logical form. In aesthetics the framing condition requires treating the object as "seen *sub specie aeternitatis* from outside" rather than from within the midst of other objects, so that one perceives it together with space and time rather than in space and time. In ethics, on the other hand, the boundary condition becomes the state of the subject as the force which composes values for its specific moment in space and time:

> Things acquire "significance" only through their relation to my will. As my idea is the world, in the same way my will is the world-will. The will is an attitude of the subject to the world.
>
> (Wittgenstein, *Notebooks* 83–88)
>
> If good or bad acts of the will do alter the world, it can only be the limits of the world that they alter, not the facts, not what can be expressed by means of language.
>
> In short their effect must be that it becomes an altogether different world. It must, so to speak, wax and wane as a whole.

The world of the happy man is a different one from that of the unhappy man.

(Wittgenstein, *Tractatus* 6.43)

This version of the willing subject now allows us a conceptual framework for showing how an agent's "really now" can bear values and offer a sense of identity and connection even though there can be no adequate descriptive account of such actions. What cannot be thematized can nonetheless be recognized in the intensities that engage descriptions and in the ways agents take responsibility for their actions. In lyric poetry it then becomes possible to imagine the line itself as this bounding condition, at once displaying the contours defining our intensities and providing an expressive register that establishes a sense of public responsibility for how one engages the now. Or so we are led to believe by the working of C. K. Williams's long, sinuous line in his *Flesh and Blood.* Here Ashbery's "really now" must play out its values in a much less interpersonal, much less gentle reflective space. In Williams, this "now" begins as a site of intense demand, often accompanied by a painful and irreducible sense of his own anguish, alienated both from others and from his own efforts to get his passions under the control of his judgments. Yet it proves to be precisely this sense of risk and pain that drives Williams to a fuller articulation of the elements of that "really now" which poetry can capture, and which in turn can give poetry alternatives to the endless displacements that accompany all efforts at specular self-representation. The long line allows a naturalness of conversation folded into the intimacy of internal dialogue, so that lyric speech even at its most expansive seems entirely rooted in momentary observations and reflections on the implications of those observations. Williams's long line affords an expressive register combining a remarkable mobility of investments with a naturalness allowing poetry to seem simply ordinary speech at its most articulate, and hence giving the lyric will a sense of being grounded despite the restless urgencies of reflective consciousness.[2] Putting the same observations in philosophical terms, we might say that this line renders a Wittgensteinian model of subjective agency because it comes to manifest a force, something like Spinoza's *conatus,* which cannot be made the object of an image or of imaginary projections but which nonetheless makes continually present the contours of an insistent expressive will inseparable from a knowing subject bound entirely to the facts of a shareable world. By tracking where will can be "really now" as the mind tries to contour itself to the facts of his world (including facts about how his mind works), Williams's poems exemplify a struggle to prevent overdetermining those facts by interpretive constructs, and thus underdetermining personal agency by trapping itself within the vacancies of self-consciousness.

All this abstraction requires examples. Let us begin with the tensions that lead Williams to appreciate fully how he might locate subjective agency within fundamentally Wittgensteinian parameters. Insistent on acknowledging the mind's inescapable self-divisions while refusing himself any consoling images or abstract beliefs, Williams finds himself facing at one extreme the infinite regresses of a radical insecurity, at the other a fierce lust for the very self his need keeps displacing. This is the insecurity at its most intense:

> as though you'd lost possession of the throat and then
>   the voice or what it is that wills the voice
> to carry thoughtlessly the thought through tone and
>   word, and then the thoughts themselves are lost
> and the mind that thought the thoughts begins to lose
>   itself, despairing of itself and of its voice,
> this infected voice that infects itself with its despair,
>   this voice of terror that won't stop,
> that lays the trap of doubt, this pit of doubt, this voice-
>   less throat that swallows us in doubt.

(68)

The long line's apparently endless doubling of all the key terms makes it seem as if language could eat away at itself endlessly, destroying the voice that one desires it to mediate. But the greater the doubt, the greater our "fiercest lust of self toward self," here defined in relation to resentment, that most Nietzschean of subjects:

> What is there which so approaches an art form in its
>   stubborn patience, its devotion to technique,
> to elegant refinement: that relentless searching for
>   receptacles to capture content and expression?
>   . . . . .
> My slights, affronts: how I shuffle and reshuffle them,
>   file them, index, code, and collate.
> Justification, accusation: I permutate, elaborate,
>   combine, condense, refocus, re-refine.

(16)

Now what threatens the ego also calls forth constructive energies so intense that the lyric line must take on tortuous extensions of its own traditional capacities. The rush of feelings generated by resentment proliferates verbs, eventually isolating them from nouns and pushing the verse against the margin so that it must rely on syllabic breaks normally found only in prose. Yet we gradually gain substantial rewards for such energy, since the line affords so complex a frame that the demands of consciousness become almost comic, without losing their intensity. Thus the risk of losing a composed voice becomes the means for finding another by mocking one's own efforts to find a righteous pose. On one level then the analogy to art is ironic. Resentment elicits the perversely formal energies of the artist while refusing it any content adequate to the self's inordinate responses to what it feels as threat. But on another level that lust for self discovers what must be its necessary principle of investment—not in any specific content but in how the line as expressive force contours itself to (and perhaps *as*) the psychic movements generated by the need for a self-image. The line takes on the task of providing continuity as a dynamic drive maintaining the will's investments, while at the same time it makes visible the threats continually haunting those efforts: what promises expression also keeps undoing itself in its greed to capture and balance all the elements informing its own productive energies.

When Williams brings these opposite impulses together, he manages to establish the full thematic significance for his own sense of line as emblem for style, quintessentially in the ways that "Conscience" once again engages a central Nietzschean theme:

> That moment when the high-wire walker suddenly
>   begins to falter, wobble, sway, arms flailing,
> that breathtakingly rapid back-and-forth aligning-
>   realigning of the displaced center of gravity,
> weight thrown this way, no, too far; that way, no, too
>   far again, until the movements themselves
> of compensation have their rhythms established so
>   that there's no way possibly to stop now . . .
> that very moment, wheeling back and forth, back and
>   forth, appeal, repeal, negation,
> just before he lets it go and falls to deftly catch himself
>   going by the wire, somersaulting up,
> except for us it never ceases, testing moments of the
>   mind-weight this way, back and back and forth,
> no re-establishing of balance, no place to start again,
>   just this, this force, this gravity and fear.
>
>   (67)

By opening with this sudden emergence of the moment, Williams beautifully defines the issues by establishing the force of unpredictable events as the threat to voice that drives conscience to its full intensity. Thus the analogy to the high-wire walker's beginning to falter takes on a double role. It establishes a dramatic focus for reflection, and it calls attention to the mind's need for determinate content, hence for some analogy in order to suture the wound that the sudden eruption of events opens up. Yet the sense of time's pressure will not relent. Notice the repeated "that," which displays a mind seeking to fix itself by setting reference points as its boundary conditions. In the very effort to fix stationary points, however, each "that" phrase collapses because of the weight it must bear, both within the analogy and in relation to the demand for analogy. Nonetheless, by facing this risk of falling, the poem ultimately discovers its own way of "somersaulting up," since it manages to shift from those "thats" to a sense of rhythm within the balancing that gives conscience its access to a constantly shifting "now." This sense requires surrendering any hope for specific stopping points (which I take to be figures for the ego's desires for specific images of itself), so that one can reconcile oneself to the irreducible and inescapable demands of conscience. Even the analogy must collapse, destroyed by that painful "except us" marking the mind's difference from any satisfying allegorical representations of itself. Unable then to rely on images, self-reflection finds itself forced back on the pun in "gravity" as the ironic price exacted by the effort to take oneself seriously. Personal identity founded on demands like these cannot be separated from a constant sense of fear, a sense left beautifully indeterminate at and as the poem's conclusion: "no re-establishing of balance, no place to start again, just this, this force, this gravity and fear."

At the heart of this indeterminacy, however, we find a determining directional force that may suffice for handling that inescapable fear. The repetition of "this," grounded in an intricate syntactic balance and following a string of negations, locates in simple assertion a responsiveness to the motions of mind and shifts in its contents far more supple than any analogy. At first these repeated negations insist on the return of doubt's voiceless throat as the analogy collapses. Dreaming of gravity seems inseparable from having a constant fear of falling. For taking identity as a serious issue and allowing conscience its nagging voices submits all ideas about the self to judgments about truth that lack any possible grounds for making the necessary assessments. Not only does gravity then elicit direct fear, it also opens the possibility that conscience makes fools of us all by producing the ironic suspicion that the fears we feel are themselves only stage props in a circus act we create in order to claim that consciousness had some determining power in our struggles.[3] But there remains a referent for "this" which is not under the regime of truth, since there remains its relationship to the actual and metaphoric force of the line's ability to contour itself even to such gravities because it does not rely on images of itself. Instead the line literally constitutes a gravity in its own activity as it attaches to destructive forces, establishing at least an intimacy and directness sharply opposed to the mind's efforts earlier in the poem to make the repeated "that" sustain a distanced balance. Thus there may be no need for a place elsewhere from which one might start again. While the effort to negotiate the mind's desires for gravity and the fears which this generates may strip away all projected stabilities, there remains available a Cartesian response to the poem's version of Cartesian doubt: the poem cannot doubt its own passionate investment in the process of defining those doubts. Yet it need not follow Descartes's way of locating the "I am" purely in some inner process. Here the cogito finds a home within the activity of language, in the justness of how that concluding string of deictics adapts to the mind's desperation. Here too a new level of metaphoric thinking opens up, one based not on analogy but on the interpretation of the very processes undergone within the poem. There need be no place from which to begin, since the tracking of beginnings takes us beyond abstract possibilities to a place continually in the making. Where William Carlos Williams idealized no ideas about the thing but the thing itself, this Williams locates the necessary alternative to ideas in the mind's coming to feel the force of the gravity it constantly produces.

Not all of the later Williams is as grim as this, or as Cartesian. Once a principle of gravity is discovered, the poet is free to explore the workings of desire that the line makes articulate, and to celebrate the modes of thinking that the line protects from self-defensive ironies. So we might say that the strength of his view of agency depends on finding an ethics within his aesthetics, or better, of discovering how ethical possibilities are woven into his understanding of lyrical intensities. To elaborate this I will conclude by developing what I take to be the four basic features of subjective agency that Williams makes vital within his poetry and therefore makes vital as emblems for reflecting on how we dispose of our investments in every sphere of life.

First, Williams's line offers intricate and diverse means of extending the "really now" from thematic statement into an actual condition of lyric investments in a wide range of situations. In its struggling against the Cartesianism that calls it into being, this line becomes the linguistic bearer of a dynamic intentionality locating values and a sense of identity not in concepts or in images but only in the qualities of engagement its utterances establish. And intentionality itself becomes so intimately involved in linguistic activity that there can be a strong sense of subjectivity with only minimal needs to project a deep inner life for that subject, and thus to pursue an authenticity based on self-reflection. Instead, both immediate desires and long-term identifications become inseparable from the specific ways that verbs heap up on one another, that complex syntactic balances develop, or that descriptions move through supple ranges of register—all freed from the need for supplementary allegories.

A second important feature of *Flesh and Blood* emerges in relation to this freedom from allegorical supplements. Because there is so little need to go beyond the life of words in situations, and so powerful a means of establishing significance without relying on general interpretive schema, Williams recuperates an old power rendered problematic in romanticism, the power to make eloquent discursive statement guarded against the need for irony simply by the cleanness of the assertion and the sense of character which it carries. Rather than lament the abstractness of discursive expressions (opposed by romanticism to a concreteness that makes the allegorizing impulse defensible because it can be transformed into living symbols), the poet is free to treat discursiveness as simply one of the ways that this mobile line organizes its investments so that we can engage the considerable desires that we invest directly in processes of abstract reflection. So long as we focus on the movement of desire, discursiveness is as concrete as images, since both are simply aspects of what Williams calls "vehicles" of mental life. Moreover, Williams's best poems, like **"Failure"** (23), make that discursiveness seem itself the mind's most complex tonal register, since it can play the clarity of precise psychological analysis against a range of second-order emotions that occur as one tries to come to terms with the success of one's descriptions: "Less love, yes, but what was love: a febrile, restless, bothersome trembling to continue to possess / what one was only partly certain was worth wanting anyway, and if the reservoir of hope is depleted. . . ." The more the poet accommodates himself to the loss of love, the more despondent he becomes about the only alternative available to him, even as he testifies to its power.

Third, Williams's supple discursiveness seems to me crucial to contemporary poetry because of the relationship to subject matter that his version of subjective agency al-

lows. This point can be most clearly developed by a negative example. It seems obvious to many of us now that the pastoral lyricism so prevalent in the past two decades marked a crisis in poetic content. Committed to satisfying romantic emotions and exalting lyrical sensibility, poetry found itself unable to handle urban and political materials. Only scenic renderings of moods or natural analogues for states of feeling seemed to allow expressive energies that did not collapse into self-defensive irony or melodramatic bombast. And even these preserves for lyricism seemed to require the supplement of vague metaphysical yearnings, sustained mostly by a vocabulary of stars, stones, and associated darknesses. Ashbery provided one vein of relief from that situation, only to become absorbed by his own somewhat narrow self-reflexive lyricism. Williams provides a better way because he shifts the burden of lyricism from what the content offers or how metaphors bind the psyche to aspects of the world to a concern for how the line's shifting affects can nonetheless engage a full range of subjects and thereby establish a fully ranging subjectivity.

The resulting sense of art as a greed for the world, and an exercise in complex digestive mechanisms for satisfying that greed, tempts one to draw analogies between Williams's work and the ambitions of contemporary photography. But Williams's line can continually comment on and qualify its own needs as well as develop intimate attachments with what it engages. Probably his richest commentary on this hunger for the world consists in the elegant gesture of finding that as he tracks a simple scene of his wife going out into the snow he needs a second poem, as if not even the long line could gather in one poem the range of feelings that she elicits in this context (31). For another, more elaborately self-conscious staging of the line as carrying investment within an omnivorous, attentive sensibility we can turn to **"Dawn,"** Williams's signature version of a secular nature lyric fully responsive to modernist concerns for the sentence as a medium, yet also profoundly committed to making that medium a mode of accepting the quotidian constraints that were modernism's deadly enemy:

> The first morning of mist after days of draining,
>   unwavering heat along the shore: *a breath*:
> a plume of sea fog actually visible, coherent, intact,
>   with all of the quieter mysteries
> of the sea implicit in its inconspicuous, unremarkable
>   gathering in the weary branches
> of the drought-battered spruce on its lonely knoll; it
>   thins now, sidles through the browning needles,
> is penetrated sharply by a sparrow swaying precipi-
>   tously on a drop-glittering twiglet,
> then another bird, unseen, is there, a singer, chatter-
>   ing, and another, long purls of warble,
> which also from out of sight insinuate themselves into
>   that dim, fragile, miniature cloud,
> already now, almost with reluctance, beginning its dis-
>   sipation in the overpowering sunlight.
>
>   (50)

As in most of Williams, every moment of pleasure or shape is on the verge of disappearance. But the long line provides an intricate gravity for that flux, holding it before the eye, then treasuring all the modifications that time produces. Look again at what happens to the breath here as it first transforms into fog, then allows fog to modulate into a range of its properties; then, as the sense of "now" intensifies, the line can shift from attending to a single sparrow into a state in which it yields to the slow unfolding of unseen but equally real and equally intense presences, mysterious not for what they suggest metaphorically or symbolically but for how they reveal the complex contours of a representative effort to have one's words open into one's actual situation. Finally the poem's single sentence comes to rest in an observation that could also serve as a perfect accounting for its own powers: given the light it sheds, the line can accept its own dissipation while yielding to a world whose mystery it has managed to echo in its own movements.

Finally, Williams manages to make his experiments in agency ultimately sustain an overall model of value, defined most fully in the elegy for Paul Zweig that concludes *Flesh and Blood.* **"Le Petit Salvié"** faces what is by now the standard issue for all elegies—how can one find means of giving meaning to death and continuity to one's own life in a culture deprived of all consoling stories? How can one honor the imperatives to mourn without succumbing to the death in life that is melancholia? The first half of the sequence develops three basic features of this mourning that the poem must come to terms with. From the very beginning Williams calls attention to fundamental opposites within human temporality that become in escapably oppressive as one faces the death of someone one loves. At one pole the encounter with death proceeds excruciatingly slowly, as attention fixes on each feature of the person and his illness. But given the quickness of life's passing, nothing can be slow enough. Second, such elemental paradoxes tempt one to accept transcendental resolutions for that pain, only to force one to a double dilemma. There can be no such escape for us: the transcendental is mere fantasy. And even this yielding to secular truth brings none of the comfort once imagined by Enlightenment thinkers. While clear-sightedness may afford us a sense of truth, it cannot bring conviction to that truth, and hence it cannot help us align the will to the one world we have (poem 7). Then, in the central poem of the entire sequence, that failure to find a place for will opens strong temptations to turn to the consolations of romantic inwardness, since at the least one can identify with the intensity of a divided self: "Now we have the air, transparent, and the lucid psyche, and gazing inward, always inward, to the wound" (77).

For my purposes it is crucial that we see how dead the line becomes in these central poems. The line still contains the complex play of mind, but it cannot provide any direction for mind by sustaining complex syntactic figures or opening into intricate, expansive relations. For example, when Williams registers the failure of the secular intel-

lectual position to bring conviction, the line breaks down into ellipses and repetitions. Similarly, the line I have just quoted can do no more than struggle with paratactic connections bound to the pain of repetition. And even when the second half of the poem turns from that inwardness to alternative imaginative frameworks, the line remains relatively dead, often caught up in abstraction and able at best to name details without putting them into intricate motions. (Williams's poems on Zweig's wife seem especially paralyzed, probably because the speaking voice is trapped into attempting to resolve through another what it has not yet been able to handle for itself.)

Gradually two basic strategies emerge for alleviating that stiffness, each a way of learning to say once again, "Here's where we are." One way leads back to Zweig in memories, now become a mode of speaking to the present; the other requires developing a transformed version of the relation between "slowly" and "quickly," now understood as the fusing of grief and gladness about what was powerful enough in life to elicit the grief (poem 16). On that basis Williams tries a summary poem in which the line is once again allowed its full gathering power, as we see in the following example:

> the circles of community that intersect within us, hold
>   us, touch us always with their presence,
> even as, today, mourning, grief, themselves becoming
>   memory, there still is that within us which endures,
> not in possession of the single soul in solitude, but in
>   the covenants of affection we embody,
> the way an empty house embodies elemental pres-
>   ences, and the way, attentive, we can sense them.
> Breath held, heart held, body stilled, we attend, and
>   they are there, covenant, elemental presence,
> and the voice, in the lightest footfall, the eternal wind,
>   leaf and earth, the constant voice.
>
>   (81)

But neither strategy quite suffices, primarily because the resolving voice here comes too much from the outside, from the will to adapt rather than from an actual shifting of concrete alignments. So the sequence needs one more poem, not to contradict or resist the thematic resolution but to extend it into the line's full voicing in its own right. And by acknowledging that challenge Williams finally brings together the full powers of subjective agency whose various facets this volume had been exploring:

> "The immortalities of the moment spin and expand;
>   they seem to have no limits, yet time passes.
> These last days here are bizarrely compressed, busy,
>   and yet full of suppressed farewells . . ."
> The hilly land you loved, lucerne and willow, the fields
>   of butterfly and wasp and flower.
> Farewell the crumbling house, barely held together by
>   your ministrations, the shed, the pond.
> Farewell your dumb French farmer's hat, your pads of
>   yellow paper, your joyful, headlong scrawl.
> The coolness of the woods, the swallow's swoop and
>   whistle, the confident call of the owl at night.
> Scents of dawn, the softening all-night fire, char, ash,
>   warm embers in the early morning chill.

The moment holds, you move across the path and go,
the light lifts, breaks: goodbye, my friend, farewell.

(82)

"Farewell" cannot simply be thought or rationalized or even quoted, as this poem initially attempts. Instead Williams stakes his entire sequence on its capacity to mark a substantial difference between quoting and voicing. Actually two fundamental differences emerge. The first is marked by the movement from suppressed farewell to its repeated utterance, to its final statement where, oddly, we first grasp the full etymological force of the word, as if only the repeated voicing that memorializes the particularity of *this* friendship could evoke the full ritual force of this piece of public language. That union of particular and abstract then gets reinforced by the second difference, set in motion by the direct addresses that modulate from the "you" to a series of highly particularized apostrophes. Here the long line's capacity to hold what continues to flow takes the form of returning to the "you," a "you" after its apostrophes, but now also a "you" that can be a form of self-address. The entire elegiac process brings the speaker's grief so intimately into alignment with both the setting and the resources of language that the speaker can in effect also let himself go. He is able to speak the full good wishes of "farewell" because he can at the same time live out the richness of his memories while loosening their hold on him. There is no other route to conviction, because there is no other way that the moment can hold so as to align the speaking subject with the full import of his language.[4] But once that moment does hold, the poem's farewell also becomes a way of sublating the dreams of lyrical inwardness that for romanticism had to supplement a conception of language from which they could not but be alienated.

Notes

1. See especially chapter 7 of my *Canons and Consequences,* which takes up both the academic scene represented by Paul Smith's *Discerning the Subject* and the philosophical work of Foucault and Derrida. In addition one will find a good deal more material, handled brilliantly, insisting that poststructural thinking is bound to negative views of the subject in Mikkel Borch-Jacobsen's *Lacan: The Absolute Master.* Marjorie Perloff is the critic perhaps most sensitive to the implications of the split between theory and sensibility, and she offers a good critique of romantic models of lyrical subjectivity as they affect contemporary poetry in her *Poetic License,* esp. 63. Also important for my case in a somewhat different way is Charles Bernstein's "Optimism and Critical Excess (Process)." Bernstein's model for a contemporary poetry and poetics informed by "theory" is certainly sophisticated in its own right, but it pays a substantial price for that sophistication by being unable to get beyond the limitations of the prevailing modes within that theory. Bernstein ends up with another version of Derridean errant singularity. Recognizing this helps open the way to realizing that

it may not be the most experimental contemporary poets who provide the richest engagement in distinctively contemporary intellectual issues.

2. The importance of Williams's line emerges most clearly if we see how he at once takes up and extends an ambition I think fundamental to much of the best contemporary American poetry, an ambition involving experiments on a much subtler and more resonant level than those experiments by the Language poets which lead in an opposite, and to me less promising, direction. This ambition is to make the "really now" of the lyric voice also a "really now" for the personal energies of the poet. Thus we find a very different sense of conversation from William Carlos Williams's emphasis on a spoken American diction, from the cult of breath urgencies in Charles Olson and Robert Creeley, from Allen Ginsberg's irrepressible theatricality, and from the tin intimacies in Richard Hugo's letters. None of these suffice to make the lyric activity an exemplary anchoring for full personal presence. That requires a more urgent and more capacious intimacy blended with a sense of dynamic intelligence sustaining a fluid intensity that needs only a minimum degree of melodrama or claims on a deep, tormented psychological inwardness—for example in the direct speech of Adrienne Rich's recent work, or Tess Gallagher's narratives, or Ashbery's fluid conversation, or, quintessentially the way Robert Hass's *Human Wishes* handles divorce almost entirely by tonal control of specific descriptions.

In my view, Hass sets the ideal of lyric character which Williams tries to realize in a more elemental stylistic way, so that the principle of voice is less dependent on charm and more aware of its underlying principles for expressing personal singularity. Think of Hass's reading style and imagine being a traditional poet who must follow him. The traditional poet would find himself or herself seeming at best a master of craft making isolated artifacts that are offered for judgment and consumption. Hass, on the other hand, makes his poems seem actual speech within a life, so that the reading becomes testimony to the forms of personal activity, in reflection and in public relations, that poetry can carry. And then we realize that for the past thirty years our poetry has been trying to find its way out of the dominance of the artifact codified by the poetry and the criticism of what we might call the New Critical years. It seems our task then is to carry this revolution as far as it can go by testing the degree to which art can be made continuous with life, not as a reductive realism but as a means of elaborating personal desires and of demonstrating the forms of communication and community that speech can establish. Hass does this by voice, Ashbery by intricate mobile intelligence, Rich by an aura of simple directness. Williams, I shall argue, wants his line to become the philosophical emblem for those aspects of agency necessary for and satisfied within this project.

3. For an explicit rendering of this kind of suspicion, see "Vehicle: Violence" (Williams 70).

4. For very similar attitudes toward elegy's relation to the grammatical resources of the language, see Ann Lauterbach's "Vernal Elegy" 62. I develop that sense of language in my "Jorie Graham and Ann Lauterbach: Towards a Contemporary Poetics of Eloquence."

Works Cited

Altieri, Charles. "Ashbery as Love Poet." *Verse* 8 (1991): 8–15.

———. *Canons and Consequences: Reflections on the Ethical Force of Imaginative Ideals.* Evanston: Northwestern UP, 1990.

———. "Jorie Graham and Ann Lauterbach: Towards a Contemporary Poetics of Eloquence." *Cream City Review* 12 (1988): 45–72.

Ashbery, John. *Selected Poems.* New York: Viking, 1985.

Bernstein, Charles. "Optimism and Critical Excess (Process)." *Critical Inquiry* 16 (1990): 830–56.

Borch-Jacobsen, Mikkel. *Lacan: The Absolute Master.* Stanford: Stanford UP, 1991.

Lauterbach, Ann. *Before Recollection.* Princeton: Princeton UP, 1987.

Nietzsche, Friedrich. *Beyond Good and Evil.* New York: Vintage, 1966.

———. *On the Genealogy of Morals.* New York: Vintage, 1989.

Perloff, Marjorie. *Poetic License: Essays on Modernist and Postmodernist Lyric.* Evanston: Northwestern UP, 1990.

Smith, Paul. *Discerning the Subject.* Minneapolis: U of Minnesota P, 1987.

Staten, Henry. *Nietzsche's Voice.* Ithaca: Cornell UP, 1990.

Williams, C. K. *Flesh and Blood.* New York: Farrar, 1987.

Wittgenstein, Ludwig. *Ludwig Wittgenstein Notebooks, 1914–16.* Trans. G. E. M. Anscombe. New York: Harper, 1961.

———. *Tractatus Logicus-Philosophicus.* Trans. D. F. Pears and B. F. McGuiness. London: Routledge, 1961.

Edward Hirsch (review date 17–24 August 1992)

SOURCE: "Walking the Line," in *New Republic*, August 17–24, 1992, pp. 46–48.

[*In the following review of* A Dream of Mind, *Hirsch examines the development of Williams's poetic style and thematic concerns.*]

C. K. Williams is a poet of disquietudes, of the mind aggressively questioning and requestioning its own workings, brooding upon the fluctuating data of consciousness, quarreling with itself. No other contemporary poet, except perhaps John Ashbery, has given us a more textured or pressurized rendering of what it feels like to think—to try to think—through a situational or mental problem moment by moment: to bring the unconscious into the available light of language, to anatomize the psyche with a continual tally of internal and external evidence.

Behind the acute, painstaking self-consciousness of this work there is a sense that the burden of poetry is to discover the darkest inner truth, to confront the secret that can no longer be sublimated, that forces itself to be known. "The return of the repressed," Williams names it in his poem **"Child Psychology,"** and the phrase reverberates throughout the rest of his new book. In *A Dream of Mind* he has taken his candid and inclusive poetry of agonistic consciousness even further in the direction of interiority and discursiveness, as if literalizing the dictum of the baroque Jesuit poet Tommaso Ceva that poetry is "a dream dreamed in the presence of reason."

Williams has always been a poet of psychological extremes, the sorrows of a diligent, self-reflexive consciousness his initiating subject. In his first two books, *Lies* (1969) and *I Am the Bitter Name* (1971), however, he was less interested in exploring linkages and associations, the mind's obsessive thirst for connection, than in tracking what he has called "varieties of disjunctive consciousness." His early work, influenced by Artaud and Vallejo, intentionally subverted logical connectives and struggled to enact the movement of the mind as it swoops, hovers, and starts in at least three different directions at once.

Unsparingly honest and violently self-divided ("I am going to rip myself down the middle into two pieces," he wrote in **"Halves"**), his poems were also motivated by a furious political consciousness, almost breaking apart with frustration and rage over the outright lies of the social and political world. Some rail against a perversely absent God (**"A Day for Anne Frank," "The Next to the Last Poem about God"**); others storm against government (**"A Poem for the Governments," "Another Dollar"**). The furies peak in **"In the Heart of the Beast,"** a long unpunctuated poem that responded to May 1970 (Cambodia, Kent State, Jackson State) at the level of a howl. These single-minded assaults shouldn't be dismissed; they were biographically and historically necessary. Still, in retrospect Williams's poetry seems hampered by the protest mode, the uncapitalized directness ("this is fresh meat right mr. nixon?") of the late '60s.

Throughout his new book, Williams uses with great effectiveness the flexible, rangy, and capacious long line that he first discovered in *With Ignorance* (1977), refined in *Tar* (1983), and adapted to a group of eight-line poems in *Flesh and Blood* (1987). If emotion, for the lyric poet, is necessarily predicated on technique, then the decisive moment in Williams's development was when he began to enlarge and to extend his lineation even further than Whitman's free verse line, to see how far he could push and shape that line before it faltered or became prose. By using the line as the largest possible rhythmic unit, he forced himself to put things into his poems rather than to leave them out, to break the abbreviated rhetorical code—the lyric shorthand for emotion—that seems to characterize so much of the poetry of any period. As if heeding Frost's directive to dramatize, Williams also became an insistent storyteller, burying his social message deeper in the substance and the political unconscious of his poems.

The fourteen poems in *With Ignorance* have a powerful narrative propulsion and velocity. They are raw, colloquial, out-sized. Here was a starkly confessional, democratic, ambitious lyric poet who had crossed William Carlos Williams and Robert Lowell with Dostoevsky, whose poems had a streetwise urban intelligence—

> If you put in enough hours in bars, sooner or later you get to hear every imaginable kind of bullshit.
>
> **("Bob")**

a canny psychological sense of other people—

> I think most people are relieved the first time they actually know someone who goes crazy.
>
> **("The Cave")**

and an outlandish, almost biblical sense of outrage—

> It stinks. It stinks and it stinks and it stinks and it stinks.
>
> **("Hog Heaven")**

One is keyed to the underlying existential quest and paradoxical nature of Williams's enterprise by the quotation from Kierkegaard that gives the book its title: "With ignorance begins a knowledge the first characteristic of which is ignorance." There is a tremendous amount of social information in Williams's work, but it is animated and subsumed by the hungers of consciousness repeatedly circling back and striving to know itself.

In *Tar,* Williams refined his storytelling gift and perfected the long line he had invented in *With Ignorance,* transforming it into a more sinuous and symmetrical unit, an instrument for speeding up or slowing down narrative, for modulating, correcting, and intensifying thought. His music can be as supple as a needle pulling thread or as pounding as a hammer coming down on metal. Copiousness of detail, a commanding narrative scope and energy, and an unremitting psychological intensity characterize such poems as **"From My Window," "My Mother's Lips," "On Learning of a Friend's Illness,"** and **"Com-**

bat." These poems not only tell dramatic stories—seeing two Vietnam vets, one in a wheelchair, careening haphazardly down the street; remembering his mother mouthing his words even as he spoke them—but they also think critically about those stories, doggedly pursuing human motivation, implicating and convicting the self as both actor and narrator, transfiguring the anecdotal into the mythical and archetypal. Perhaps most telling for William's new work is the concluding twenty-five-part poem, **"One of the Muses."** This highly abstract, non-narrative poem evokes and traces his tormenting struggle to conceptualize and to bring into language a presence who at one time visited him, an evasive, nameless, bodiless spirit, possibly an inner construction, an almost palpable figure, a Platonic muse, a dream of mind.

The 130 poems of *Flesh and Blood* have the feeling of a contemporary sonnet sequence. Like Berryman's *Dream Songs* or Lowell's *Notebooks,* Williams's long-lined short poems are shapely and yet open-ended and self-generative, loosely improvisational though with an underlying formal necessity. Many present single extended moments intently observed: a girl with an artificial hand stepping onto the subway, a bum scribbling in a battered notebook in the public library. Others are miniature short stories, sudden fictions. Still others take meditative stabs at ideas of "nostalgia" or "the past" or "failure." All of these poems present people in situations in which they are vulnerable, exposed, on the edge.

The poems in *Flesh and Blood* have a thick naturalistic surface and a fast narrative current. But a philosopher lurks behind the sociologist. The poems in the second section, for example, are structured as urban parables. They take a general idea—"reading" or "love" or "the good mother"—and yoke it to a specific story: a man fixing his car in bitter cold stops to read a newspaper or a bored couple "perversely" persist in kissing each other. In these poems, the general is exemplified by the particular and the individual vignette aspires to the exemplum. In the eighteen-part elegy that concludes the book, Williams not only eulogizes his friend Paul Zweig but also charts the contours of consciousness as it tries to hold onto a friend even as it must let him go.

A *Dream of Mind* is Williams's most varied and challenging work so far. It, too, is about "thinking thought," thought it is also about the ways in which thought—or, more precisely, dream—thinks us, how a complex of unconscious desires, fantasies, and projections stream through and motivate our actions. One recurrent subject of this five-part book is how the psyche constitutes and reconstitutes itself—beset by a steady stream of impressions and mental images, obsessed by the wounds and fissures of memory, the tormenting routes of self-consciousness, the continual gap and flow we experience between our conceptions of ourselves and what we actually see and experience in the world. An old man badgers his family to help him commit suicide, but then asks not to be told when (**"When"**); the poet recalls the traumatic project of remaking himself as a writer during his 20s ("**She, Though**"); an aged Paris broods upon the dying Helen of Troy ("**Helen**"): the poems in this volume remind us how hard it is to remain one person, how painful it is to see ourselves and others clearly, how radically unstable and uncertain is our knowing.

Williams's poems are nothing if not extreme. Relentless, urban, invasive—like city life itself, they are not for the faint-hearted. One of his characteristic strategies is to dramatize the turbulence of the mind at work under terrific duress; that is, in the presence of others at moments of their greatest social weakness and vulnerability, moments when the fabric of daily life is torn open and someone is profoundly exposed. The speaker is an inadvertent voyeur—self-conscious, self-critical—who sees something suppressed or forbidden, often something offensive. He discovers another person simultaneously observing what he observes, ascertaining what he is avoiding or avoiding what he is compelled to acknowledge, and thereby sees his own reactions in an obverse mirror. He catches himself looking, looking away, knowing. Many of the poems are structured precisely around this process of perception, resistance and denial, and recognition.

The poem "**Harm**," for example, recounts the memory of a local homeless person—familiar, usually inoffensive—who recently "stepped abruptly out between parked cars, / undid his pants, and, not even bothering to squat, sputtered out a noxious, almost liquid stream." It is not only that the speaker must stare at the man's bony shanks, stained buttocks, and scarlet, diseased testicles, but also

> that a slender adolescent girl from down the block
>   happened by right then, and looked,
> and looked away, and looked at me, and looked away
>   again, and made me want to say to her,
>
> because I imagined what she must have felt, It's not
>   like this, really, it's not this,
> but she was gone, so I could think, But isn't it like
>   this, isn't this just what it is?

The burden of this poem is the knowledge of the soiled and sordid, the comprehension that cannot be evaded, rationalized, or denied.

One hears in these poems the inner voice of the mind not only lacerating itself but also coming up against the blunt reality of other people. Thus, in the emblematic encounter "**Child Psychology**," the repressed returns in the form of a worker who had been mucking about in the sewer—"those viscous, unforgiving depths"—and fished out some keys that the speaker very much wanted to forget losing. The agent of his self-knowledge has arrived, his punishment postponed but now swift and inexorable. In such ways other people often become the external correlative for a demonic internal force, embodying the shunned or refused self. "No wonder my fascination turned to those as lost as me, the drugged, the drunk, the mad," the poet writes in "**The Loneliness**": "Like ancient wounds they

were, punctured with their solitude and sorrow, suppurating, stinking: / I'd recoil from what the soul could come to, but I knew within my soul that they were me."

A Dream of Mind is dominated by two complementary long poems. The fourteen-part sequence "**Some of the Forms of Jealousy**" both dramatizes and investigates the forms of consciousness obsessed by sexual betrayal. In a series of vignettes and meditations the poet painstakingly recreates the degrading miseries of jealousy, the cells of doubt that expand into full-fledged torments, the unrelenting anxiety that inevitably involves and implicates others, the "terrific agitation" and "scalding focus," the "desperate single-mindedness" and "odious dependency" that takes over the jealous mind. "This is so exhausting: when will it relent?" the speaker asks in "**The Silence**," and immediately answers his own question: "It seems never, not as long as consciousness exists." Obsessive jealousy is consciousness run amok, the mind humiliating and annihilating itself, not knowing that "what we're living isn't ever what we think we are."

The sequence "**A Dream of Mind**" also takes up the subject of "the mind in its endless war with itself," but here it becomes an idea of poetic method, a struggle to illuminate the themes of being by clarifying various tremulous epistemological states, to solidify the fluidity of a self that at times seems no more than a field of interchanges. There is a nearly endless regress as the dreamer tries to know himself ("Always in the dream I seemed conscious of myself having the dream even as I dreamed it"), and the poet vigilantly tries to transcribe and shape the unconscious wave passing through him ("It almost seems that this is what dream is about, to think what's happening as it's happening"). "**A Dream of Mind**" is Williams at his most complex, abstract, and discursive, the poet "deciphering and encoding," thinking through and being thought.

"Poetry confronts in the most clear-eyed way just those emotions which consciousness wishes to slide by," Williams wrote in his essay "**Poetry and Consciousness**," and in *A Dream of Mind* he has voraciously struggled to clarify that sliding, to unmask what is most painful and hidden in our psyches, and to embody that unmasking in the processes of lyric.

Robert Michaels (review date December 1992)

SOURCE: A review of *A Dream of Mind*, in *American Journal of Psychiatry*, Vol. 149, No. 12, December, 1992, pp. 1745–47.

[*In the following positive review of* A Dream of Mind, *Michaels concludes that Williams is "an important poet."*]

"I couldn't put it down" is a phrase not often associated with a volume of poetry. [*A Dream of Mind*] is an exception. C. K. Williams, who won the 1988 National Book

Critics Circle award, is one of the nation's most gifted poets. He writes about the themes that tend to interest psychiatrists—sex, love, jealousy, anger, aging, disease, and dying. Like many psychiatrists, he is also interested in the workings of the mind, turning his attention inward and creating a sort of poetic metapsychology of dreams, meditation, prayer, and abstractions about mental life. His genius is most striking when he observes and communicates the moment, the incident, the image of a person. For example, in **"When,"** he describes a dying man,

> he wanted out of the business, out of the miserable
>   game, and he told whoever would listen,
> whenever they'd listen, wife, family, friends, that he'd
>   do it himself but how could he,
> without someone to help, unable to walk as he was,
>   get out of bed or up from the toilet himself?

In **"Harm,"** he sees that a homeless vagrant relieves himself in the street,

> and that a slender adolescent girl from down the block
>   happened by right then, and looked,
> and looked away, and looked at me, and looked away
>   again, and made me want to say to her,
> because I imagined what she must have felt, It's not
>   like this, really it's not this,
> but she was gone, so I could think, But isn't it like
>   this, isn't this just what it is?

In **"Child Psychology,"** Williams speaks of latency and libido, of oedipal adventures and the return of the repressed, when

> we were going somewhere and without telling him I
>   took my father's keys and went outside to wait.
> House, car, office keys: how proud I was to be the
>   keeper of that weighty, consequential mass.
> I stood there, tossing it from hand to hand, then, like
>   my father, high into the air.
> And then I missed, and saw it fall, onto the narrow
>   grating of a storm sewer, and then in.

In **"The Cautionary"** (my favorite poem in the volume), which was first published in *The Times Literary Supplement,* Williams writes about a man and his attractive, somewhat younger wife:

> he decides that it's not he himself, as himself, his wife
>   desires, but that she simply *desires.*
> He comes to think he's incidental to this desire, which
>   is general, unspecific, without object,
> almost, in its intensity and heat, without a subject: she
>   herself seems secondary to it,
> as though the real project of her throaty, heaving pas-
>   sion was to melt her mindlessly away.

In **"Helen,"** Paris says of the dying Helen,

> The next night her cough was worse, with a harsher
>   texture, the spasms came more rapidly,
> and they'd end with a deep, complicated emptying,
>   like the whining flattening of a bagpipe.

> The whole event seemed to need more labor: each
>   cough sounded more futile than the last,
> as though the effort she'd made and the time lost mak-
>   ing it had added to the burden of illness.

Williams is introspective and self-reflective. In **"She, Though,"** narrated by a writer, he speaks of the dedication of an artist:

> That dedication, or obsession, or semblance of obses-
>   sion, counted for much in those days.
> For most of us it was all we had, struggling through
>   our perplexed, interminable apprenticeships.
> We were trying to create identities as makers and as
>   thinkers, and that entailed so much.

When he writes about people or events, this self-awareness leads to a double consciousness of what was and of what the poet saw and felt and thought about what was. We have access to a vivid representation of the world and at the same time share a privileged participation in his personal view of it. This self-awareness works less well when it is directed only inward. A third of this book is occupied by the cycle of 16 poems providing the title for the volume. The cycle starts with **"The Method"**:

> A dream of method first, in which mind is malleable,
>   its products as revisable as sentences,
> in which I'll be able to extract and then illuminate the
>   themes of being as I never have.
> I'm intrigued—how not be?—but I soon realize that
>   though so much flexibility is tempting—
> whole zones of consciousness wouldn't only be
>   reflected or referred to, but embodied, as themselves.

Later, in **"Vocations,"** he explains,

> they can be considered in a way that implies conse-
>   quence, what I come to call the dream's "meaning."
> Although I can't quite specify how this ostensible
>   meaning differs from the sum of its states,
> it holds an allure, *solutions* are implied, so I keep
>   winding the dream's filaments onto its core.
> The problem is that trying to make the recalcitrant
>   segments of the dream cohere is distracting.

In **"The Gap,"** he adds,

> So often and with such cruel fascination I have
>   dreamed the implacable void that contains dream.
> The space there, the silence, the scrawl of trajectories
>   tracked, traced, and let go.

He also says, in **"The Fear,"**

> In my dream of unspecific anxiety, nothing is what it
>   should be, nothing acts as it should;
> everything shifts, shudders, won't hold still long
>   enough for me to name or constrain it.
> The fear comes with no premonition, no flicker in the
>   daily surges and currents of dream.

I read these impatiently, eager to get back to narratives with plots and characters. Williams' gift of language is immense and apparent, but without the content of real people and concrete events, his view of mind and mental life failed to hold me.

Of course, poetry is the music of language as much as the meaning, and Williams is a virtuoso of words. His style is quite distinctive; his lines are said to be the longest of any poet writing today. This permits, or perhaps demands, that he include all of the possibilities inherent in each thought, each moment. He turns to runs of words in which the same consonant is used repeatedly when he wants to carry us with him through an image and then shifts to short, almost clipped syllables when he wants us to pause and consider. For example, in my favorite, **"The Cautionary,"** we have "a man who's married," who broods "fretfully on her faithfulness," and observes with a "degree of detachment" until the flow is disrupted as "it dawns on him in a shocking and oddly exciting insight."

The impact of this is subliminal: one must study closely to discern how Williams achieves his effects, but the impact is nonetheless powerful. Others who attempt to use language to communicate ideas with emotional impact might well consider their use of language as carefully.

Williams deserves a wide audience. He is an important poet and a first-rate psychologist as well.

David Herd (review date 4 December 1992)

SOURCE: "House Guests," in *New Statesman & Society*, December 4, 1992, pp. 39–40.

[*In the following excerpt, Herd offers a favorable assessment of* A Dream of Mind.]

At one point in the title poem of C. K. Williams' *A Dream of Mind,* the poet's rigorous speculations carry him to the edge of Ashbery's world. "How even tell who I am now, how know if I'll ever be more than the field of these interchangings?" Here, however, the comparison ends, as Williams draws back from the conclusion Ashbery so gladly entertains.

A Dream of Mind is written in the long, double pentameter line Williams has used exclusively since the mid-1970s. This form, which owes more to late 18th-century blank verse than to Whitman, is the site for sharply different kinds of poems. The first is an unflinching description of the brutalities of urban America.

For instance, **"Harm,"** in which a vagrant defecates so horribly in front of an "adolescent girl" that even Charles Bukowski might have turned his eye. The long line drags out such experiences to the threshold of tolerance. It is, however, as it sustains Williams' extended enquiries into human motivation that its full value is realised.

In the sequences **"Some of the Forms of Jealousy"** and **"A Dream of Mind,"** the poet encounters a series of ethical and epistemological problems. Never departing from the syntax of ordinary speech, the poetry moves at the pace of the thought, through a process of intelligent questioning towards heightened understanding. What this displays is a faith in the power of an alert, often highly metaphorical language to arbitrate and persuade.

This is not a sentimental, but an earnest faith that flows from the poet's belief in "that healing accord" which "must precede or succeed dream." Williams has too often been passed over by American academic criticism. *A Dream of Mind* deserves to be read.

John Saunders (review date Winter 1993)

SOURCE: "Recent Poetry," in *Stand Magazine,* Vol. 35, No. 1, Winter, 1993, pp. 77–84.

[*In the following excerpt, Saunders offers a generally positive assessment of* A Dream of Mind, *while noting that Williams's long lines and ordinary language occasionally fall flat.*]

Doubters who think [John] Ashbery reduces mental activity to a kind of effete daydreaming could try C. K. Williams's latest collection *A Dream of Mind.* Here the title sequence investigates 'this mind streaming through me, its turbulent stillness, its murmur, inexorable, beguiling' but at least sets out with 'a dream of method,' however intractable its potential application. He still believes that 'these parcels of experience have a significance beyond their accumulation. . . . solutions are implied' and is prepared to 'butt in' (**'Vocations'**) to distil a kind of faith from 'the fearful demands consciousness makes for linkage, coherence, congruence.' The faith can only be 'partial, imperfect,' threatened by 'imperious laws of doubt and denial,' closer indeed to 'dread' in contemplating 'the sad molecule of the self in its chunk of duration' (**'The Gap'**). The self may be 'fleeting, dissolving,' 'my character has become the function of its own revisions,' yet he can entertain the hypothesis of its being 'more than the field of these interchangings' (**'Shadows'**). The series moves towards **'Light,'** title of the final poem, though nightmare always lurks in the darkness at the edge of the dream, the nightmare of 'having so little power, even over my own consciousness,' but drawing on mental powers beyond analysis he can recapture an innocence stronger than despair: 'I imagine myself in that healing accord I still somehow believe must precede or succeed dream.'

There may be a certain amount of camouflaged theology here, in contrast with Ashbery's resolutely secular drift. The dream can be a kind of ethical project, involving the imagination and the heart: 'Heart' he wonders in **'Shells,'** 'ever unworthy of you, lost in you, will I ever truly dream you, or dream beyond you?' It is a question which preoccupies him through the book, especially in the second section **'Some of the Forms of Jealousy,'** where we meet precise notation and an awareness of other people and situations, though 'this unsavoury, unsilent solitude of self' remains locked in unending soliloquy, sometimes comic in tone, like the anguished articulate self-tormentors of Bellow or Heller, sometimes witty and detached. In **'Signs,'** dinner with a friend whose wife he comes to feel must have a lover, signalled by 'complex inward blushes of accomplishment, achievement, pride' though perhaps unsuspected by her husband leads into an extended, Titanic metaphor as the social forms are maintained whatever the stresses and strains below the surface: 'I ply my boilers too; my workers hum: light the deck lamps, let the string quartet play.' In **'The Cautionary'** the husband's mad logic leaves Othello standing as his suspicious scrutiny colludes in its own sadly self-fulfilling prophesy: 'Yes. No. Yes. He knows he should stop all this: but how can he without going to the end?' In the last of them, **'Soliloquies'** it seems this world of overwhelming and unspoken questions might be grounded in 'a more radical uncertainty.' If love 'with its promise of certainties the only answer to these doubts' cannot hold its own against the melancholy long with-drawing roar Arnold heard on Dover Beach, is God too 'potentially beloved other . . . who already has sufficient knowledge of our fate to heal us, but may well decide not to do so'?

If Williams's habitual long line occasionally sags, the language a little ordinary, in the title sequence sometimes smacking of rejected passages from *Four Quartets,* he is more often rigorous and alert, with the American knack of modulating from the informal and prosaic to a commanding rhetoric, as in **'The Insult'** which seems to link both Stevens and Frost. He can tell a good story too, whether the Freudian anecdote of **'Child Psychology,'** or **'Allies: According to Herodotus,'** where the affronted Xerxes en route for Greece chops his host's son in two and marches his army between the halves. I'm less sure about **'She, Though,'** the extended narrative of love among the artists maybe with autobiographical elements which makes up the third section, a kind of 'groping dialectic' about art and death. The protagonist, perhaps a Stephen Dedalus to the mature Williams's Joyce, comes to understand that 'what art needed at the end / was an acceptance of what's muddled and confused in us' rather than 'the mastery of expression' supposedly attained by his antagonist, the girl he once rejected. There's more muddle than I can accept and for more than a hundred years the novelists have been refining these nuances with greater lucidity. In the final piece, **'Helen'** he does regain the unflinching clarity of shorter poems like **'Harm'** and **'Scar'** in contemplating the last illness of his (it reads as autobiography though distanced by the third person) wife. The subject is really not unlike Poe's 'Ligeia' without the note of hysteria, the death of a beautiful woman providing a near-mystical climax:

'she had entered death, he was with her in it.
Death was theirs, she'd become herself again; her final,

searing loveliness had been revealed.'

Lawrence Norfolk (review date 12 February 1993)

SOURCE: "A Leap Backwards," in *Times Literary Supplement,* February 12, 1993, p. 11.

[*In the following review of* A Dream of Mind, *Norfolk praises Williams's "masterly" technical skill and his "extraordinary, magisterial" approach to unanswered philosophical questions.*]

C. K. Williams's work has never flinched from the difficulties and complications of American life. As his readership dips a cautious toe in the pleasant ambience of President Clinton's mysterious policies, Williams offers a vision of capability and purpose. This is poetry that can cope, it seems to say, that can deal with the uncertainties of its time. He is also being advocated as the latest answer to the perennial and destructive query, "Where, today, is American poetry at?" In *A Dream of Mind,* that question may have met its match.

Williams's sixth collection is divided into five parts which seem at first sight to bear little relation to each other. The first consists of a number of short poems serving up uncomfortable or harrowing realities; a remembered insult, a child's burned face, a man's son sawn in half, a tramp excreting in the street watched by a horrified girl and watched in turn by the poet, who wants to tell her, "It's not like this, really it's not this,—but she was gone, so I could think. But isn't it like this, isn't this just what it is?" Other poems end similarly, fading out rather than concluding, as though the poetic muscle which has rendered these scenes atrophies when it comes to rendering them meaningful. Sometimes there is no attempt made at all. In **"Allies: According to Herodotus"** the reader is simply left to grapple with the image of Xerxes' army marching off to war between the severed halves of a body. What to do?

Williams's personae lay themselves open to such assaults, but somehow avoid permanent damage. At the core of these poems is a stubbornness or refusal to turn away, which proves itself a match (and no more) for the batterings meted out by reality. Between the poet and his material, there is an abrasive stand-off.

Two longer, narrative poems locate this difficult reality with more insistence among other people. **"She, Though"** unpicks and weighs the incidents of a bizarrely elaborate revenge taken on the poet (Williams appears *in propria persona*) by a young woman whose advances he has refused. Her attack, by an oblique thrust, is on Williams's role as an artist: "No, it wasn't me she hated and wanted vengeance from, it was art." At some level either not fully grasped by the poem or allowed to run unchecked, this is about the larger antagonism between humanity and art. "She—how specify her now?" Williams asks dismissively of his, and his art's, erstwhile tormentor. But the poet and his art, and their enemy, remain tangled in each other. Their crossfire is correspondingly confusing. Is the girl someone whom Williams, all too human, simply doesn't like, or an element too virulent for the poem to include, or is she proof of her own contention that poetry is inhumane, somehow alien to life as it is lived?

"**Helen,**" a husband's account of his wife's decline and death, examines these relations quite differently. Poetry is ostensibly the hero of the piece, recouping and compensating for the impending loss. But by resisting its own central fact—the wife's death—the poem inevitably suffers periodic collapses, "Then he couldn't hold it, couldn't keep it, it was all illusion, a confection of his sorrow." The poet darts about, salvaging, recording, but he can never be quite quick enough for the sudden thrusts and overwhelmings of his experience. This could easily turn into a familiar and arid argument about the ultimate inadequacy of poetry, but Williams refuses to blame his tools. Instead he does something quite startling.

Two further groups of poems make up the collection. "**Some of the Forms of Jealousy**" plants the green-eyed monster in a succession of personae, then sits back to watch the results. Jealous minds, Williams demonstrates, play all kinds of obsessive tricks on themselves. There is social comedy too, but the mind's internal movements are the real focus. Jealousy itself functions as a kind of catalyst. Half-thought, half-emotion, lacking any real object, jealousy is a mental goad to excite the minds of his personae and direct them in upon themselves. He concludes, "Might jealousy finally suggest that what we're living isn't ever what we think we are?" Williams uses jealousy partly as a test case, partly as a mechanism to establish some broad parameters. "Living," "thinking," "being," what are the relations, left so provocatively unresolved in the above quotation, between these three? The title-poem of "**A Dream of Mind**" sets itself no lesser task than describing them.

The dream is, and is of, consciousness. It has little or no content, this being both an account and an enactment of its operations, which are fleeting and evanescent; half-thoughts, wishes, fears, murmurs, intimations of others. There are few metaphors—what can consciousness itself be *like*?—and little imagery, although, when Williams is forced to it, it is Blakean in its intensity and strangeness; other presences in the dream are "beasts, captives of fear and hunger" and "angels, nearly on fire." Most difficult of all, being both account and enactment, the poem's status is problematic, always somehow in the way of what Williams is attempting, something to be continually got rid of.

As a result, the poem's more overt rhetorical energies are necessarily suppressed. Its vocabulary is restricted, ambiguities very carefully controlled. Because Williams's whole method depends on his being at once within and without the dream, both observer and observed, grammar and syntax are placed under extraordinary strain.

> The dream is of beings like me, assembled, sur-
> rounded, herded like creatures, driven, undone.
> And beings like me, not more like me but like me, as-
> semble and herd them, us; undo us.

Williams's trademark—the long line—is crucial to the enterprise, giving him time to follow a notion through its range of aspects, amplifying, redirecting, sometimes allowing it to run unchecked for a stanza, sometimes reversing it mid-line with a caesura which can fall like a guillotine, or intervene with the briefest of pauses. The technical control exerted over these lines in masterly.

It needs to be. "**A Dream of Mind**" does not gesture at consciousness as some taken-as-read precondition of poetry, it traces, refuses everything but, and in a sense is, the act itself. In terms of poetry, it is analogous to Heidegger's return to the ur-question of Being which was left unanswered in the prehistory of philosophy; a foundation that should have been built, but never was. Whence and how these abrasions of experience, these unresolved knots of memory? Why cannot poetry deal better with all this? In answer to such questions, Williams has taken an extraordinary, magisterial leap *back*.

The contention lying behind, and beyond the remit of, this poem, is that the most basic tool of poetry, its workbench perhaps, has been taken as mysterious, mystical even, when its understanding is in fact crucial. Put crudely, the reason there is so much wilfully obscure poetry is not that modern experience is overwhelming, but that the consciousness it meets has been wrongly characterized as unknowable and is thus ill-prepared. These are implications that Williams does not draw, but "**A Dream of Mind**" is none the less restorative. Part philosophical essay, part dramatization, part confession, it is also an intensely human poem. Its centre and edges are pervaded alike by the dreamer who is both pure observer and complicit creator, fascinated, appalled, attracted, repulsed, beholding and beheld by "this and streaming through me, its turbulent stillness, its murmur, inexorable, beguiling."

Bernard F. Dick (review date Spring 1993)

SOURCE: A review of *A Dream of Mind*, in *World Literature Today*, Vol. 67, No. 2, Spring, 1993, p. 387.

[*In the following review, Dick offers a positive assessment of* A Dream of Mind, *noting that the collection is an important work of poetry.*]

Using his familiar combination of long and short lines, C. K. Williams has arranged his latest collection so that it culminates in "**Helen,**" a summary poem in which are fused his main themes of death, dream, and memory. Death haunts *A Dream of Mind*, beginning with the very first poem, "**When,**" in which children help their terminally ill father end his life with dignity, and concluding with "**Helen,**" in which the speaker argues that to achieve union with the dead, the living must enter death themselves—not literally, but in a dream state where death is truly the mother of beauty, restoring the dead to the pure form of which the act of dying has robbed them.

Technically, Williams is in top form, creating two-line combinations that are not so much distichs, where the shorter line is a response to the longer (or simply has a foot less than the longer), but rhythmic units, where the shorter line forces the reader to stop, pause, or reflect. Sometimes the transition is rough, when the long line ends with a preposition or the definite article (e.g., "I protest, but the violence goes on, I cry out, but the pain, the rage, the / rancor continue"). Separation of article and noun jolts the reader into the poet's emotional state.

The title derives from a sequence of sixteen poems, the fourth section of the collection, that explore the nature of dream as both personal and cosmic. One might even speak of the epistemology of dream, since Williams is questioning the knowledge derived from dream (not in the sense of the nonwaking state but closer to what Coleridge would have called the secondary imagination). At times reminiscent of the *Four Quartets,* these are the only poems in the collection that can be called intermittently successful. Williams's talent lies in the confessional and the observational; when he becomes speculative, his wonderful clarity clouds over, sometimes resulting in opacity. Still, *A Dream of Mind* is a major work by a major poet, whose insights the reader feels privileged to have shared.

Judith Kitchen (review date Fall 1993)

SOURCE: "Skating on Paper," in *Georgia Review,* Vol. XLVII, No. 3, Fall, 1993, pp. 578–95.

[*In the following excerpt, Kitchen offers a mixed assessment of* A Dream of Mind.]

"Poetry in motion!"—the announcer bursts forth with the old cliché as soon as the skaters hit the ice. I am instantly on the defensive. But, resist as I will, the skaters win. Three hours of Brian Boitano, of Mark Mitchell or Lu Chen, of the dancers Klimova and Ponomarenko, the Duchesnays, Torvill and Dean, three hours of the electric Viktor Petrenko and I am convinced that I know the source of the cliché and that, as is often the case, the source resides in what is most true.

The spotlight catches one figure dressed completely in black, including a hooded mask. Faceless, he is all body—tall and fluid. Through the sound system: the odd beat of a drum, an occasional rasp of flute, a tinkle, a shimmer—nothing that could be called a tune. Against this "music," the body jerks into syncopated motion, begins a wide sweep, a truncated spin. The skates resist the ice, making a sound. Shhhkk. And the ice resists the body, stops it mid-movement. Forces it back on itself. The flashing strobe light momentarily illuminates, then conceals, segmenting

motion into separate frames. Faceless, the body reveals the way each jump or spin is made up of a specific sequence of individual moves. Watching this, I understand how those moves go together to make a completed figure. I have *felt* the shape of the line.

The faceless figure turns out to have a name—Gary Beacom of Canada. He returns in white pants, turquoise shirt, yellow tie. His face is expressive; the skating is seamless once more. But I'm haunted by the body that is no longer before me, the skeletal shape that revealed the poem. It's Beacom, not Petrenko, who has taken me to the secret of Petrenko's most amazing leap: the presence of a vision. Petrenko knows what he's reaching for; his face relaxes even before he lands, flashes a quick smile. This is choreography: each line by itself displays amazing skill, yet each is essential to the construction of a whole. The poem has been set in motion.

Too much contemporary poetry is pyrotechnics, manner, attitude. It displays skill—even, in bursts, imagination—yet is lacking in any sense of a whole, a sustaining purpose which gives meaning to the skill displayed. This is not a simple matter. I am convinced that it is possible to learn to write a poem in the same way it is possible to learn to skate, by practicing the individual moves over and over. I am also convinced that the result will look like, even act like, a poem. But it will not be a poem until it is impelled by something beyond the desire to have written a poem. I'd name it *yearning* except that a friend's anecdote comes so quickly to mind: *A graduate student said a poem had moved him. "Moved?" said the professor. "That word has no place in our discussion."* But why not refute the professors who refuse to begin the discussion with emotion? Why not look for poems that embody the need to fly?

Looking over the many books sent to me to consider for this review, I see that they fall essentially into two categories: those where the line is predominant (that is, the line seems to drive the poem and creates the tone or cadence, even the *meaning*) and those where the overall vision seems to determine the line and the way it will function in the poem. Of course the reader cannot know exactly how a poem came into being, but this latter category consists of poems which could be described as those whose shape was felt before the act of articulation began. Some poems, explicitly or implicitly, raise the question of line versus vision; it becomes part of the drama in reading. It's similar to the way a spectator at an ice show can be involved in moment-to-moment risks the performer takes—will she make it? will he fall?—all the while building toward the hoped-for recognition of a perfectly completed shape. We watch poets bend and extend their lines in interesting ways and we may go with them for the moment, even admire the daring or subtlety, but in the end we need to see that the flashes of brilliance have been in the service of something more complex.

At any rate, that's the sort of concern I bring with me as a reader to six new books of poetry. The line is extremely personal to the poet. It orchestrates individual voice, and poets today are feeling quite free to experiment with how best to capture this personal element. I'm going to pay attention not only to the characteristic line of each poet, but to what that line *does,* how it serves the articulation of the larger vision.

C. K. Williams has developed a deliberately elongated line (almost every one is over twenty syllables) that is instantly recognizable to readers of contemporary poetry. *A Dream of Mind,* his latest collection, uses that line to serve its title. Williams' long lines not only launch the narrative, they also allow enough room for a kind of internal equivocation. They flow more easily when read quietly to oneself than when read aloud. The rhythms are the rhythms of thought—actually, of reason—so that the reader is constantly aware of the mind at work, twisting back on itself in order to fix and define what is otherwise ambiguous. In this way, Williams' lines allow him to become so obsessive about getting it right that the poems often unfold as an unending scrutiny of nuance. For example, the fourteen poems of the second section, entitled **"Some of the Forms of Jealousy,"** let the reader know from the beginning what they are all "about." The meaning, therefore, resides in the process, as can be seen by the opening lines of **"Signs"**:

> My friend's wife has a lover; I come to this conclu-
>   sion—not suspicion, mind, conclusion,
> not a doubt about it, not a hesitation, although how I
>   get there might be hard to track;
> a blink a little out of phase, say, with its sentence,
>   perhaps a word or two too few;
> a certain tenderness of atmosphere, of aura, almost
>   like a pregnancy, with less glow, perhaps,
> but similar complex inward blushes of accomplish-
>   ment, achievement, pride—during dinner,
> as she passes me a dish of something, as I fork a
>   morsel of it off, as our glances touch.

By the time we reach the end, we've been caught up in the psychology of the poem's persona, worrying away at the minor details that make up the major portion of our lives. And the fun in the reading is to use our own knowledge of human nature, enough to follow the speaker's logic through to its conclusion and simultaneously reserve judgment so that the speaker might be—definitely *could* be—wrong about everything. **"Jealousy"** is the ostensible subject, but the intricacies of the mind—its ability to deliberate to the point of utter self-consciousness—are what fascinate the reader, and probably the poet as well.

The expansive lines give sustenance to **"She, Though,"** the eleven-page poem that comprises the middle section, by establishing a *spoken* voice—that of someone telling an anecdote, someone maddeningly literal and, at the same time, fascinating in his fanatic precision. The poem opens with the peculiar vagaries of speech, all its qualifications and ambiguities: "Her friend's lover was dying, or not 'friend,' they weren't that yet, if they ever really were;

. . ." The reader is able to maintain an interest in the primary "story," but the real interest is in how the speaker reacts to the "she" of the title. In analyzing a particular woman's response to her roommate's tragedy as well as that woman's relationship to her art, he finds himself enmeshed in his own crisis of identity. This poem is indicative of Williams' characteristic achievement. He is able to render something like the full complexity of consciousness—typically that of an observer catching himself in the act of observation.

If the first half of the book calls attention to the mind at work, the sixteen discrete poems of the title section shift the emphasis slightly from the "mind" to the "dream," with varying connotations, including the imaginary, the insubstantial, the illusory, the pensive, and the visionary. Williams uses the mind and its convoluted forays into logic to decipher the meaning of dream, what he terms "ideas of dreams." But the treacherous mind often ends the speculation with a question mark. In dream, where the mind can make "something out of nothing," the shadowy figures or the reincarnated dead are understood only in abstractions. More often than not, those abstractions lead to even more abstruse questions, as in **"Light"**:

> And if this isn't the case, wouldn't the alternative be
>   as bad; that each element of the dream
> would contain its own entailment so that what came
>   next would just do so for no special reason?

"Reason" is at the heart of *A Dream of Mind,* and yet dream resists reason. It leads, so often, to truly unanswerable questions.

The culminating concern of so many of the poems in the title sequence is that of death, of its place in the human order, of what we are to make of it. **"Helen,"** the long final poem that comprises the fifth section, is the account of one man's experience of his wife's final days. As an observer, he is able to *will* an attitude toward death—that he could keep "all the person she had been" inside himself so she would go on living. But the dream cannot hold. Death is recognized for what it is—a singular event—and he must give her over to it, knowing he couldn't retain the illusion. The poem pushes on from this point, though, in the way of human willfulness, to a closure where the speaker feels that he has entered death with her, has bridged the gap of separation. Unfortunately, the last two stanzas ring false. Grief is not identical to death. This reader, at least, is left stymied by something that does not mesh with her experience.

The long lines that allow Williams to explore this particular kind of consciousness also seem to imprison him in their very flexibility. He almost acknowledges this in **"The Method"** when he states, "I dream a dream of method, comprehending little of the real forces or necessities of dream, / and find myself entangled in the dream, entrapped, already caught in what the dream contrived, / in what it made, of my ambitions, or of what it itself aspired to. . . ." Substitute the word "line" for all but the first "dream" and you discover his problem: the line seems to have a life of its own; it dictates tone; it limits the eventual conclusion. In fact, most of Williams' lines end with a period, a semicolon or, at the very least, a comma, thus completing their function before he goes on. Coupled with the abstract nature of the argument itself, Williams' line demarcates what the reader can easily hold intact in the head. One reads to the end of the line, comprehends the fullness of thought, then readies oneself for the next.

Williams' strength is his limitation: his means are so self-conscious that they inevitably become a stance rather than an exploration. Because these lines represent thought chiefly as a verbal process, there are few images on which readers can focus. We are expected to enter the abstract discourse of the poem rather than bring our own worlds with us. The effect is both stimulating and frustrating. There is serious pleasure in matching one's mind to that of the writer, in seeing things through his eyes—or rather, voice. This is especially true for the humorous poems such as **"The Vessel"** and **"Child Psychology."** The frustration comes when there is simply too much of what might be a good thing, as though the lines were stamped out by machine, one after the other, all of a kind. In the book as a whole, their aggregate weight seems to drain energy from the individual pieces. It's a bit like eating a very large Caesar salad. At first the palate is pleased by the sharp sensation, the blend of distinctive tastes. But all too soon the flavor is familiar and there's still so much lettuce on the plate.

Williams' poems are at their best when read individually in *The New Yorker.* There, they have wit and energy. Their "vision" is discernable and their line seems more a mark of virtuosity rather than a mere compulsory figure.

Ben Howard (review date December 1993)

SOURCE: "Masters of Transience," in *Poetry,* Vol. CLXIII, No. 3, December, 1993, pp. 158–70.

[*In the following review of* A Dream of Mind, *Howard concludes that Williams's shorter poems mitigate the shortcomings of his longer poems in "this uneven collection."*]

"The poems flow from the hand unbidden," writes Derek Mahon, "and the hidden source is the watchful heart." C. K. Williams has called his tenth collection *A Dream of Mind,* and to an extent rare in contemporary poetry his new poems enact the dialectics and tease out the nuances of analytical thought. But these are also poems of the watchful heart, in which the poet's insecurities, his fear of death and his yearning for religious belief, come under the scrutiny of intuitive awareness, and the less admissible feelings are made known. Thus, in **"The Insult,"** as the narrator walks in the forest, he recalls an insult incurred "a continent and years away." "[S]immering and stinging,"

the memory impels him faster down the path, even as it prompts his intellect to question. "Are there deeper wounds in us than we know," he asks; "might grief itself be communion and solace?"

One of William's subtlest poems situates the narrator at a dinner party, where he becomes aware that his friend's wife has taken a lover:

> My friend's wife has a lover; I come to this conclu-
>   sion—not suspicion, mind, conclusion,
> not a doubt about it, not a hesitation, although how I
>   get there might be hard to track;
> a blink a little out of phase, say, with its sentence,
>   perhaps a word or two too few;
> a certain tenderness of atmosphere, of aura, almost
>   like a pregnancy, with less glow, perhaps,
> but similar complex inward blushes of accomplish-
>   ment, achievement, pride—during dinner,
> as she passes me a dish of something, as I fork a
>   morsel of it off, as our glances touch.
>
>   **"Signs"**

As the poem progresses, the narrator's intuition deepens ("Something in the wifely glance tells me now she knows I know"), and his discomfort grows. Focusing intently on his food, he defends his innocence and privacy against the wife's unwelcome confession:

> The wife smiles yet again, I smile, too, but what I'm
>   saying is if what she means is so,
> I have no wish to know; more, I never did know;
>   more, if by any chance I might have known,
> I've forgotten, absolutely, yes: if it ever did come into
>   my mind it's slipped my mind.
> In truth, I don't remember anything; I eat, I drink, I
>   smile; I hardly even know I'm there.

Here, as in many of Williams's poems, intuition and awareness play the dominant roles, ferreting out the truth and tracking the narrator's emotional response. Analysis is secondary, and moral judgment is, at most, implied.

At their strongest, Williams's shorter poems work much in the manner of **"Signs,"** setting up a tense situation and limning its dynamics. Williams's subjects include a dying man begging for euthanasia, a guilt-ridden son, a man on the verge of bankruptcy, and an adolescent girl exposed to a homeless man's indecency. An entire section of his book, entitled **"Some of the Forms of Jealousy,"** examines the travails of lovers and spouses, finding more fear than affection, more treachery than fulfillment. In **"The Caution-ary,"** a husband's suspicions drive his wife toward betrayal; in **"The Call,"** an abandoned lover salves his wounds by "dutifully forgiving everyone" and wondering "what kind of realignment could possibly redeem so much despair?" In **"The Image,"** an unfaithful wife endures her husband's brutal reprisal:

> It must have almost starved in him, she thinks, all
>   those years spent scenting out false stimuli,
> all that passive vigilance, secreting bitter enzymes of
>   suspicion, ingesting its own flesh;

> he must have eaten at himself, devouring his own soul
>   until his chance had finally come.
> But now it had and he had driven fangs in her and
>   nothing could contain his terrible tenacity.
> She let the vision take her further; they had perished,
>   both of them, there they lay, decomposing,
> one of them drained white, the other bloated, gorged,
>   stale blood oozing through its carapace.
> Only as a stupid little joke, she thought, would
>   anybody watching dare wonder which was which.

Not all of Williams's explorations are so graphic as **"The Image"**—or so compelling. A group of poems entitled **"A Dream of Mind"** describes its own enterprise as a "frenzied combing of the countries of mind / where I always believed I'd find safety and solace but where now are confusion and fear / and a turmoil so total that all I have known or might know drags me with it towards chaos." In their encounters with fear in general and the dread of death in particular, these poems carry no little power, but too often they dilute their own urgencies with obsessive questioning:

> What do I mean by nightmare itself, though? Wouldn't
>   that imply a mind here besides mine?
> But how else explain all the *care,* first to involve me,
>   then to frighten me out of my wits?
> Mustn't something with other agendas be shaping the
>   dream; don't all the enticements and traps
> suggest an intention more baleful than any I'd have
>   for visiting such mayhem on myself?

Rather than evoke the watchful witness, these lines bring to mind the compulsive worrier. Intelligent though they are, the poet's rhetorical questions distance both narrator and reader from the horrors of the "nightmare," which is itself only vaguely described.

Williams has included two long narrative poems, one of them recounting a beautiful woman's decline and death, as witnessed by her husband, and the other examining the destructive element in art, its "evasions" and "grievous cosmic flinchings from reality." Williams's narrative skills are considerable, and his speculations gain immediacy from their embodiment in concrete narrative detail. But on balance it is Williams's shorter poems, employing dramatic rather than narrative devices, that sustain this uneven collection. In these poems (of which **"Signs," "Scar,"** and **"Chapter Eleven"** are the most remarkable examples) the poet's long lines explore the tensions of the moment, and his complex syntax, replete with antitheses and reversals, unfolds the contradictions of his heart and mind.

Ross Feld (review date 1995)

SOURCE: "Timing and Spacing the As If: Poetic Prose and Prosaic Poetry," in *Parnassus,* Vol. 20, Nos. 1–2, 1995, pp. 11–31.

[*In the following excerpt, Feld discusses distinctions between prose and poetry, and offers a favorable assess-ment of Williams's* Selected Poems, *drawing attention to the use and effect of Williams's long line.*]

Where it starts as well as ends, Roman Jakobson told us, is with the etymologies. Prose: *oratio prosa < prorsa < proversa* (speech turned straightforward) and Poetry: *versus* (return). He'd have us keep in mind, too, Gerard Manley Hopkins' early insistence, historically difficult to argue with, that the spine of so many master poems from the Bible onward is parallelism, doubling, interior resurrection. Prose, on the other hand, isn't asked to curl itself back; instead it stops dead in time, something which the genre of the story requires in no vague manner, either. "The death of another lends an appetite for novels," Walter Benjamin wrote in his essay "The Storyteller." "What draws the reader to the novel is the hope of warming his shivering life with a death he reads about." A character's *character* can be foreshadowed by the quality of that person's eventual end-in-time: "How do the characters make him understand that death is already waiting for them—a very definite death and at a very definite place? That is the question which feeds the reader's consuming interest in the events of a novel."

Churning inside their polishing mechanisms, forms of art do seem to develop real attractions for each other—or for each other's myth. These attractions aren't questioned much, seeming to matter only as much as art itself matters at any given moment. You can take it merely as a form of cross-platform flattery, reciprocal advertisement; or, on another, more blue-note level, as the disheartening privacy of art—that no one will know, therefore much care, if Cousin A sneaks into Cousin B's room at night.

Yet despite the fact that a true hermaphroditism is as rarely found in literature as it is in human biology, the daydream that this is otherwise keeps growing. Poetry that doesn't want to be read as poetry and fictional prose that would prefer not to be read as fiction—these never really received much self-conscious boost from switch-hitters like Pushkin or Poe, from Hugo or Hardy or Meredith. Andrei Biely's *St. Petersburg* or Virginia Woolf's *The Waves* sometimes are set out as markers, but whichever the progenitor, the recurrent temptation to render prose as poetry's biography, and poetry as prose's thing-in-itself, seems to be of recent vintage. It makes you wonder if it isn't as much a shift in the *anthropology* of literary form as one of technical refinement.

Four current striking examples easily come to hand. C. K. Williams' poems are hallmarked by the room they take up on the page—one very long line followed by a very short one. A poetry reader subconsciously feels that he or she is getting good value here: a lot of plain nouns, not too crowded or pinched; Williams sprawling with his elbows out but also knowing when to tuck them back in, his poems rolling and stopping along this tracking scheme of expansion and contraction. Whitmanesque in that they frequently deal with life in the distressed city—deal, that is to say, in a distressed poet nakedly in a distressed place—these loquacious narrative poems *look* appropriate. Post-industrial dreck causes Williams first to watch, then deliver:

> An old hill town in northern Pennsylvania, a missed
>   connection for a bus, an hour to kill.
> For all intents and purposes, the place was uninhabited;
>   the mine closed years before—
> anthracite too dear to dig, the companies went west to
>   strip, the miners to the cities—
> and now, although the four-lane truck route still went
>   through—eighteen wheelers pounding past—
> that was almost all: a shuttered Buick dealer, a
>   grocery, not even a McDonald's

(from "Neglect")

Williams' long line heaps detail, the short one cauterizes by specificity. From behind a counter a drab woman serves coffee, a kid is scanning dirty man / man magazines at the news rack, and the dinginess and the smoke of the "violated, looted country, the fraying fringes / of the town / those gutted hills, hills by rote, hills by permission, great, naked wastes / of wrack and spill," hardly leaves the poet unhappy to see his bus finally come, only a little guilty.

But what the long line increases isn't always discrete. Often there will be cumulative rephrasings:

> It would feel less like desperation, being driven down,
>   ground down, and much more like a reflex, almost
>   whim,
> as though the pestering forces of inertia that for so
>   long had held you back had ebbed at last,
> and you could slip through now, not to peace particu-
>   larly, not even to escape, but to completion

(from "Suicide: Anne")

Set above the off-center fulcrum of the short lines, these planks of rephrasing give the sensation of an avid, agonized, psychologically venturesome poet-character, someone a little like one of the petty-devil desperadoes in Dostoevsky's *Demons*. But the poem's basis continues to be parallelism, a kind of parquet. Williams' earliest poems using the long line didn't have the rhythm quite set yet—

> This is going to get a little nutty now, maybe because
>   everything was a little nutty for me back then.
> Not a little. I'd been doing some nice refining. No
>   work, no woman, hardly any friends left.
> The details don't matter. I was helpless, self-pitying,
>   angry, inert, and right now
> I was flying to Detroit to interview for a job I knew I
>   wouldn't get. . . .

(from "Bob")

—but they had already worked out a role for the short line. A touch of self-pity makes every other line somewhat bowl-shaped, depressed.

> In the Colonial Luncheonette on Sixth Street they
>   know everything there is to know, the shits.
> Sam Terminidi will tell you how to gamble yourself at
>   age sixty from accountant to bookie

and Sam Finkel will tell you more than anyone cares
    to hear how to parlay an ulcer into a pension . . .

(from "The Regulars")

Not a lot separates this from being a Jimmy Breslin column in verse. Williams employs the second line—"the shits"—to set us straight on his apartness, as well as showing his skill with a lasso ("accountant to bookie" and "an ulcer into a pension"). As the luncheonette's regulars go on to dissect the inevitable failure of an immigrant-owned business that has opened across the street, tightening themselves into mean-spirited "angles," they do so largely in terms of Williams' paraphrase and swallowed counterargument:

> Sam T can tell you the answer to
>   anything in the world
> in one word and Sam F prefaces all his I-told-you-
>   so's with "you don't understand, it's complex."
> "It's simple," Sam T says, "where around here is
>   anyone going to get money for toys?" The end.
> Never mind the neighborhood's changing so fast that
>   the new houses at the end of the block
> are selling for twice what the whole block would have
>   five years ago, that's not the point.
> Business shits, right? Besides, the family—what's that
>   they're eating—are wrong, right?
> Not totally wrong, what are they, Arabs or something?
>   but still, wrong enough, that's sure.

Calling the two Sams by name extends to them a friendliness they don't offer the toystore owners. Still, the poem, too, seems slightly infected by bad faith. In a novel, these dumb opinions, spoken words, could be contextualized beyond immediate, shocking use; in a poem there's no time for that: They have to be called smartly to center-stage right away, where they will be contrasted or italicized. This functions as the *poet's* "angle," if you will. The poet comes into the luncheonette often enough to name its denizens, and be known by them—the democratic sub-assumption—but unless this is brand-new behavior by the Sams (which of course it isn't), the poet somehow is too bound by habit or fug to stop going in there: the self-pity. The drum of Whitman's long line, and even Ginsberg's, keeps coming at you, but the relentlessness of Williams' line keeps letting it all come at *him*. In a shorter-lined poem this kind of welcome afforded to humiliation would quickly seem arch, a bone in the throat. But the long, prosy-looking line buffers.

Williams has to be admired for his white knuckles, for how hard he hangs on. One engrossing sequence of poems addresses jealousy, for instance; and Williams' iron grasp is shown most fully in a long sad memorial poem to his close friend Paul Zweig, as well as one on the theme of a wife's wasting death. In these, the previously sexy thrusts of the first long lines now in tired acceptance match that of the small second ones, which in turn read like the rhythmical amens heard in a black church. Death's escape becomes the poetic, and this is where prosiness serves Williams better than it did before: The poet making up his mind about it all is a more justifiably elongated process than anything "the shits" can allow.

> A flat, cool, dawn light washed in on her: how pale
> her skin was, how dull her tangled hair.
> So much of her had burned away, and what was left
> seemed draped listlessly upon her frame.
> It was her eye that shocked him most, though; he
> could only see her profile, and the eye in it,
> without fire or luster, was strangely isolated from her
> face, and even from her character.
>
> For the time he looked at her, the eye existed not as
> her eye, his wife's, his beloved's eye,
> but as *an* eye, an object, so emphatic, so pronounced,
> it was separate both from what it saw
> and from who saw with it: it could have been a
> creature's eye, a member of that larger class
> which simply indicated sight and not that essence
> which her glance had always brought him.

Often Williams' short lines come where, conventionally, a new paragraph would be spaced on a typewriter or word-processor. But these late poems are made of stanzas. With a modal shift, the beginning of a paragraph leaves the one atop it behind the way no verse stanza quite manages to do. The stanza equals a double breath, a recuperative gentling; the prose paragraph, granted no such defined interlude, is simply another marker-cairn passed on its march.

March to where? To its end. The most common modern charge against fiction is determinism, but surely what galls us as much is that, after so much time spent with a novel, the damn thing so blithely just ends. Despite its illusory congregations of so many voices, authorial masks, its last word as a form is no more than the time it has demanded we spend with it. Poems, on the other hand, are entitled to picture themselves as pure Middles: Their last word switches on, waiting, as soon as the very first one is uttered.

If Williams' long lines, held back by their instinct for embellishment, can't really approach prose, they nevertheless establish for themselves a laudably romantic *capacity*.

Ashley Brown (review date Summer 1995)

SOURCE: A review of *Selected Poems,* in *World Literature Today,* Vol. 69, No. 3, Summer, 1995, pp. 589–90.

[*In the following review, Brown offers a positive assessment of Williams's* Selected Poems.]

Selected Poems represents C. K. Williams very well at the height of his career. He has become known for his poems in long lines (up to twenty-five syllables) that run across the page and necessarily carry over. Reading him is an unusually active process; the eye follows the lines with a kind of fascination; what are they leading to? At times the

process of reading almost seems an end in itself. However, Williams is not concerned merely with the virtuosity of lines much longer than those normally written in English. Among the thirteen new poems in this collection there is a remarkable version of the story of Hercules, Deianira, and Nessus from Ovid's *Metamorphoses,* book 9. Williams here comes close to reproducing Ovid's hexameters. It is a small masterpiece of translation; in which frequent present participles (mostly trochees) give the verse much of its energy. One could easily imagine the entire *Metamorphoses* being rendered by this poet, and it would probably be more readable than Golding's famous Elizabethan version, highly recommended by Ezra Pound but perhaps too rich in its texture for long stretches. The effect of reading Williams for half an hour is something like the effect one gets from Ovid, and since many of his poems are vignettes, the comparison makes sense. Like almost any poet since Wordsworth, Williams has had to compose his mythology out of his own experience, domestic or otherwise, with the usual risk that these personal details won't be sufficiently representative for his readership.

As a late-twentieth-century poet, Williams has learned from Proust how to make the power of memory operate to maximum effect. One of the finest poems in the collection is a new one, **"Time: 1976,"** concerned with exactly that theme: the power of involuntary memory. The situation involves nothing more than the poet, a woman named Catherine, and a small child, Jed. Bach's *Musical Offering* is playing on the phonograph; Catherine is coaxing the child toward a book: "Voilà le chateau, voilà Babar." The relationship between the three is not exactly stated, but the situation is fixed in the poet's memory long after Catherine and Jed seem to have disappeared. Catherine's little phrase occurs three times in the poem and gives it a certain unity; at the end it goes. "Voilà Babar, voilà la vieille dame." The following poem, **"Time: 1978,"** continues the effort to retain the fleeting past. Now there is even less to retain: Jed on Catherine's lap, and the child's new sneakers, the focal point of the central image. The poet is trying to perpetuate it by writing it down; his pen scratching on the paper is part of the larger scene, his "eyes rushing to follow the line," exactly as the reader is doing.

Since *Selected Poems* is a substantial selection of Williams's work over thirty years, one can observe more variety in his oeuvre here than in some of his recent single collections. **"Interrogation II,"** another late poem, this one in five sections, has some interesting meditations in short lines. And **"Villanelle of the Suicide's Mother"** is a powerful formal poem that reminds one of Elizabeth Bishop's "One Art." This poet has been honored in recent years, but he still is not as well known as he should be.

Thomas M. Disch (review date Summer 1995)

SOURCE: "Poetry Chronicle," in *Hudson Review,* Vol. XLVIII, No. 2, Summer, 1995, pp. 339–49.

[In the following excerpt, Disch offers a positive assessment of Williams's Selected Poems.]

Readers with only a casual, or dutiful, interest in poetry seek out poets they can be comfortable with. Shades of the schoolhouse begin to close round such readers when poems require too much deciphering. So, according to their temperaments, they will gravitate to poets of amiability or moral earnestness, whose work they will reward with a knowing chuckle or an approving nod. . . .

Of all the collections reviewed here, C. K. Williams' *Selected Poems* was the one I kept returning to most often, as I might phone a friend who's always home, always welcoming, and always has a new angle on What's Happening. Williams' signature long, long (eight to ten beat) lines and looping syntax seem to be generated more by a liking for lucidity than a lyrical impulse, yet one never feels, as one does with [Galway] Kinnell or [Andrew] Hudgins, that his poems are simply inspired conversation. They have the force, rather, of the best journalism—human interest stories, editorials, news flashes from around the world and across the street, all of it rendered in a level tone that one is surprised to find so surprising.

> Here was my relation with the woman who lived all
>   last autumn and winter day and night
> on a bench in the Hundred and Third Street subway
>   station until finally one day she vanished:
>
> we regarded each other, scrutinized one another: me
>   shyly, obliquely, trying not to be furtive;
> she boldly, unblinkingly, even pugnaciously; wrathfully even, when her bottle was empty.

So begins **"Thirst,"** a poem that puzzles over "the dance of our glances" for six more stanzas that are notable less for their rhetorical energy (though it suffices) than for the poet's determination to imagine an inner life for a figure we all know and dread to think of. For [Mary Jo] Salter she would be a "ghost" among the crack vials of drive-thru slums; for [Marilyn] Hacker and [David] Wojahn a comrade at the barricades. For Williams she is one among literally hundreds of characters whom he has imagined as intensely as Pattiann Rogers has imagined her red-spotted toads.

The dramatic gift is not a requirement for writing good poetry. Some poets, like Ann Lauterbach, lack it entirely; their mental horizon stops at their own hairlines. Others, like Rita Dove, aspire to drama, but have no gift for speaking in other voices than their own, so that "characters" can speak only in the clockwork accents of received wisdom.

But those poets fortunate enough to possess a dramatic gift, like Williams or Robert Browning or Richard Howard, live in a larger and more blessed universe, a fact reflected in the largeness, psychological complexity, and variety of their oeuvres. **"Thirst"** is a single poem among some 150 that bulk out 279 pages of a book that is most notable for its social and discursive range. Poetry, Williams would

seem to be saying, between his lines, can be *about* something. It can matter.

Keith Jeffery (review date 8 December 1995)

SOURCE: A review of *New and Selected Poems,* in *Times Literary Supplement,* December 8, 1995, p. 28.

[In the following review, Jeffery offers a positive assessment of New and Selected Poems, *though he regrets its small selection from Williams's early volumes, which are unavailable in Britain.]*

C. K. Williams is one of the most important poets currently using and recharging the English language. Hitherto he's been very much a poet's poet, enjoying the lively respect of his peers both in Britain and in his native America; this book should accelerate the dissemination of his work into the literary culture at large.

New and Selected Poems replaces and partly replicates *Poems, 1963–1983.* Excerpts from his first books, *Lies* and *I Am the Bitter Name,* have been heavily curtailed to make way for extensive selections from the most recent, *Flesh and Blood* and *A Dream of Mind.* Although this results in a comprehensive compilation, it actually reduces the scope of his available work, since his last two volumes are the only ones published in Britain; it would be a shame if the origins of his art were mislaid. His early poetry establishes at a crucial distance the hard facts and a subjective experience of history, with topics ranging from the annihilation of Anne Frank to Three Mile Island and the "unquenchable agony" of Vietnam. Later work strikes a more refined balance between social and individual responsibilities, weighing the interpersonal (for instance, **"Some of the Forms of Jealousy"**) with the intrapersonal (the title poem of *A Dream of Mind*).

To read Williams's work is to be aware of the continuous process of revision and annotation which is taking place. Texts overlap, and ideas of community are redefined—"It was as though some soft herd-alarm, a warning signal for the species, had been permanently tripped." This type of extra-sensory networking is expressed with uncommon simplicity in **"Interrogations II,"** the most notable of the thirteen new poems included here: "The human soul, the soul (solidus) / we share, the single soul." It's something of a stylistic departure, as is **"Villanelle for a Suicide's Mother,"** but his voices remain recognizable: the rewarding perils of fatherhood, a rephrased Classicism, the B-movie demise of one Sid Mizraki. The book ends with **"Thirst,"** in which the disappearance of a homeless woman closes a circle which began with Anne Frank: "holocaust: host on host of ill, injured presences, squandered, consumed. / Her vigil, somewhere, I know, continues: her occupancy, her absolute, faithful attendance; / the dance of our glances: challenge, abdication, effacement; the perfume of our consternation."

William Logan (review date December 1996)

SOURCE: "Old Guys," in *New Criterion,* Vol. 15, No. 4, December, 1996, pp. 61–68.

[In the following excerpt, Logan offers an unfavorable assessment of The Vigil.*]*

Sigmund Freud of voyeurs, analyst and analysand of complex states of watching, C. K. Williams has accepted the labor of observation with an almost religious devotion. We look to religion for words like *passion,* which has infected our image of love with a theology of suffering. In *The Vigil,* as in his recent books, Williams has turned the long verse line of Whitman, that brawny lover of men, of laborers and loungers, into the medium of modern urban anxiety, of naked souls in the naked city. It is not without religious instinct that such densely neurotic notation of the inner life has been called *confession.*

Williams is a smalltown, Sinclair Lewis busybody about the lives of others—a store clerk murdered in a hold-up, his dying caught on camera; an old acquaintance beaten to death in an alley; a retarded woman given a peanut to eat before a little audience of ladies; a neighbor who keeps a wretched menagerie in her apartment:

> Her five horrid, deformed little dogs, who incessantly
>   yap on the roof under my window;
> her cats, god knows how many, who must piss on her
>   rugs—her landing's a sickening reek. . . .

If you're not squeamish, Williams makes you *want* to be squeamish. Soon that poor old woman is not just mad, she's Medea. Williams's gift, if it is a gift, is to turn the most loathsome observations against himself: the ravaged presence of this woman is shadowed by memories of a lover he'd once been cruel to—as if, in some Borgesian reality, they might be the same woman. They're not, and he knows they're not, but at the center of his disgust is a kind of erotic longing. His own sins are the first to be written.

Unfortunately, Williams also has other designs upon the reader. He loves the extra gush of significance that places his poems high in the annals of bathos: "the true history I inhabit, its sea of suffering, its wave to which I am froth, scum" or "Quickly, never mind death, never mind mute, oblivious, onrushing time: wake, hold me!" or "the leaves quake, and Oh, I throw myself this way, the trees say, then that way, I tremble, / I moan, and still you don't understand the absence I'll be in the void of unredeemable time."

Such lines confirm your worst fears—that the poet is a little too aroused by his own nakedness. Many of these poems are anatomy lessons (you feel Williams would like to buy a textbook and take out his own appendix). The poet watches himself, watches those around him (in a way that must be excruciating to those around him), watches the poems that will never relieve him of responsibility for what he observes. Here and there, in **"Hawk"** and **"Insight"** and **"The Lover,"** Williams achieves a passionate despair that rivals Edwin Arlington Robinson's lesson in neurotic psychology, "Eros Turannos."

> . · . . at first she thinks it's just coincidence; after all,
>   she knows she's sometimes wrong,
> everyone is sometimes wrong, but with him now all
>   there seem to be are sides, she's always wrong;
> even when she doesn't know she's arguing, when she
>   doesn't care, he finds her wrong,
> in herself it seems she's wrong, she feels she should
>   apologize, to someone, anyone, to him;
> him, him, him; what is it that he wants from her:
>   remorse, contrition, should she just *die?*

The rising panic is precisely pitched on the rhyming of wrongs. At such moments the poet's loss of shame becomes a perfected form of guilt. Far too many poems, however, are like watching a dog eat its own vomit.

Williams must hope, vainly, that watching can change things, even when he knows that nothing can change (why else would he be so attracted to transformation, to poets like Ovid and Rilke?). If things could change, we would not have to die. Williams's poetry seeks absolution, and confession must always come before absolution. You leave his poems, as you leave most rituals, feeling more soiled than ever.

Bruce Murphy (review date May 1997)

SOURCE: "The Big Poem," in *Poetry,* Vol. CLXX, No. 2, May, 1997, pp. 90–100.

[In the following review, Murphy offers a positive assessment of Selected Poems, *drawing attention to Williams's effective use of the long line.]*

The "big line" of C. K. Williams somehow invites the assumption that bigger must mean fuller, more capacious, even encyclopedic—that a big line makes a big poem. Certainly this is the thrust of the comments of Edward Hirsch, Michael Hoffman, and Robert Pinsky on the back of the **Selected Poems.** Williams did not discover the long line (think of Hopkins, or Langland, without it). It is not true that, because he chooses a big line, Williams can fit more of what thinking is into his poems, nor that the unconscious (which must be very big) is subjected to more "available light of language." Thought has no size.

So, what is the big deal about the big line? It is the *quality* of Williams's line, not its length. Take, for example, the poems from **A Dream of Mind**; nothing could be less dream-like than Williams's manner of exposition, but then his approach is not mimetic but interpretive, or analytical:

> How dream away these tireless reflexes of self-
>   protection that almost define heart
> and these sick startles of shame at confronting again
>   the forms of fear the heart weaves,

the certitudes and the hatreds, the thoughtless fortifica-
tions of scarred, fearful self? . . .

How can I dream the stripping away of the petrified
membranes muffling the tremulous heart?
I reach towards the heart and attain only heart's stores
of timidity, self-hatred, and blame.

"Shells"

The heart, like a shell, is made up of layers of excretions,
the dead matter that an amorphous, vulnerable blob
excretes to protect itself. But the exposure of the layers is
endless; is there anything really there? The poem might
continue thus:

And you see behind every face the mental emptiness
deepen
Leaving only the growing terror of nothing to think
about;
Or when, under ether, the mind is conscious but
conscious of nothing—

"East Coker"

Williams's similarity to Eliot comes as something of a
shock. Beyond the anglophilia, conservatism, and orthodoxy that are so hard to swallow, there is an incredible
transparency of mind. Williams is, in a way, what Eliot
might have been if he had stayed in St. Louis. He is one
of the least romantic poets now writing. He does not give
us the dream in its first outburst, "spontaneously"; it appears, instead, as a moment in a larger dialogue of self-
reflection. The dream is not given, but emerges into visibility only through the effort to comprehend what it
means. Remarkably, Williams has brought philosophy back
into poetry. Philosophy, of course, is more about searching
for truth than finding it. The hackneyed exhortation to
"show, don't tell" may have killed off a lot of bogus
pontificating, but also led to a predilection for giving the
experience in a white-hot lump, assuming that what we
feel about it in the moment must be true. Williams, attending to "the murmur of multitudes" within, asks "How even
tell who I am now, how know if I'll ever be more than the
field of these interchangings?" If we cannot even know
ourselves, that which we seem (but only seem) to be closest to, then the only intelligent attitude is skepticism,
another quite rare quality that Williams shares with Eliot
("There is, it seems to us, / At best, only a limited value /
In the knowledge derived from experience" he said in
Four Quartets).

In the face of those "reflexes of self-protection," the
"certitudes and the hatreds," what can we claim really to
know? If we can't know the mind, how can we claim to
know the world we know *with* it? Thinking is an endless
journey; what we know may be only the falsehoods we
have exposed and laid aside.

The long line could be seen as part of the modern confusion over (or abandonment of) the line itself as a significant
unit. At some point, the line disappears into the sentence.
The line, "What, though, would more require our love,

being loved, our vow of faithfulness and faith?," in its
"though," makes use of the resources of prose. What is
amazing is that the long line does have an economy; it is
not just a form for the concrete to be poured into. While it
is sometimes essayistic, and Johnsonian when it faces ethics, at other times it recalls quite different forebears:

The dance of our glances, the clash: pulling each other
through our perceptual punctures;
then holocaust, holocaust: host on host of ill, injured
presences squandered, consumed.

"Thirst"

With repetition, assonance and alliteration, the long line
expands into the taut net of Hopkins:

Disremembering, disremembering all now. Heart, you
round me right
With: Our evening is over us; our night whelms,
whelms, and will end us.

"Spelt From Sibyl's Leaves"

Williams's poetry is a thinking, rather than a talking, out
loud. Very few poets develop a voice that is also a form.
As with Dickinson, here it is a question not of how much
can be crammed into the available space, but of how much
the tool of the form can liberate from unintelligibility
without breaking. Whether he is thinking about torture
("Interrogation II"), the possibility that a fly is the
reincarnation of a dead friend ("My Fly"), or corrosive
desire ("The Game"), Williams neither betrays his line
nor is he betrayed by it.

Frederick Pollack (review date Spring–Summer 1997)

SOURCE: "Axis of Passion," in *Salmagundi*, Nos. 114–
115, Spring–Summer, 1997, pp. 205–27.

[*In the following excerpt, Pollack offers a tempered evaluation of* The Vigil. *While noting the great achievement of*
A Dream of Mind, *Pollack finds shortcomings in Williams's subsequent inability to balance idealistic and
objective elements in* The Vigil.]

Imagine an axis, not of realism per se, but of poets' degrees
of commitment to mimesis. At one pole, the "empirical,"
poetry is *about something*. At the opposite, "idealist" pole,
it exists only to call attention to itself or to the mind that
wrote it; subject-matter of any sort, from nymphs to
warfare, is a pretext. Since the Romantics, lyric poetry has
been inherently idealist—although Imagists, Futurists,
Objectivists, and Brechtian constructivists have tried to
subordinate word to thing or mind to world. Even Surrealists and Projectivists have attempted, through various associative techniques, to escape conventional modes of
subjectivity and the constricting poetic personae based on
them. The net effect of these attempts, however, has been
to sustain an old ideology with new styles. The concerns
of most contemporary poets fill only a segment of the axis

we have outlined. Most contemporary poems are not about the world but about the poet's feelings, which may involve no other reality.

Difficulties arise when those feelings are insipid, contradictory, or embarrassing. If one role of the "complexity" of modern verse has been to reflect real ambivalence, another has been to conceal irresolution, emotionalism, and mental laziness. To make matters worse, both necessary and self-serving obscurities can inhabit one poem.

Some readers will object that it is old-fashioned to speak of "reality," or to describe poems as being "about" anything. To this we may say that many if not most poets think their poems are about something, and this belief is patent in their work. Others will claim that a poem's reality need not be the world, but God, the imagination, a private vision or metaphysics. Such visions, however, manifest themselves in images drawn from the world. These are more or less strongly felt, and so array themselves along our axis.

The three poets [C. K. Williams, John Peck, and Debora Gregor] under review range from the otherworldly to the intensely worldly, and struggle variously to distinguish real from conventional (or convenient) ambivalence. . . .

Of our three poets, C. K. Williams is the most passionately mimetic: the one for whom breadth and intensity of response to the world are most valued and most linked. Towards the end of **"Grief,"** an elegy for his mother in his new book, he states his theme and credo:

> grief for the flesh and the body and face, for the eyes
> that can see only into the world,
> and the mind that can only think and feel what the
> world gives it to think and to feel.

To understand the challenges Williams confronts in **The Vigil,** we must place it in the context of his work. In **Tar** (1983), Williams perfected the long line and narrative structure that allow him to think and feel what the world gives him. In **Flesh and Blood** (1987), he accepted further discipline: the length of poems dropped from several pages to a consistent eight lines. (The long elegy for Paul Zweig is in eight-line sections.) The tone, at its best, continued to balance elegy and reportage: whether the self was the subject or observer of a story, guilt and anguish were subordinated to accuracy. **A Dream of Mind** (1992) began with a few page-long or two-page narratives, then astonished us with two *tours de force*: a long study of jealousy whose drama occurred at the subtlest psychological level; and the title poem, a study of imagination or consciousness at work. (The terms are not really distinct for Williams.) This poem raises two issues that remain important in **The Vigil**: the degree of control that consciousness has over itself, and its complicity in the evil it observes:

> I dreamed I protested, I dreamed I cried out: I was
> mute, there was only an inarticulate moan.

> What deceived me to think I'd objected when really
> I'd only cowered, embraced myself, moaned?
> My incompetent courage deceived me, my too-timid
> hopes for the human, my qualms, my doubts.

We may note, in passing, a paradox. John Peck, the most "idealist" of our three poets—the most committed to imaginative transcendence and a metaphysics of process—feels he must invoke real life (artists' biographies, ecological problems, etc.). Sometimes he does so superficially. Williams, our most "empirical" poet, feels he must observe (and be able to answer for) *how* he observes, and detours into his own idealism: a phenomenology of creativity. I believe that **"A Dream of Mind"** will be a classic of American poetry. But its presence athwart Williams' work creates problems for him in **The Vigil.** Specifically: by increasing his self-consciousness it threatens the balance of subjective and objective elements—of elegy and reportage.

A sequence entitled **"Symbols"** is most obviously an attempt to extend the "method"—a term Williams plays with—of **"A Dream of Mind."** One of these symbols is **"Dog"**:

> Howl after pitiful, aching howl: an enormous, efficiently muscular doberman pinscher
> has trapped itself in an old-fashioned phone booth, the door closed firmly upon it,
> but when someone approaches to try to release it, the howl quickens and descends,
>
> and if someone in pity dares anyway lean on and crack open an inch the obstinate hinge,
> the quickened howl is a snarl, the snarl a blade lathed in the scarlet gape of the gullet,
> and the creature powers itself towards that sinister slit, ears flattened, fangs flashing,
>
> the way, caught in the deepest, most unknowing cell of itself, heart's secret, heart's wound,
> decorous usually, seemly, though starving now, desperate, will turn nonetheless, raging,
> ready to kill, or die, to stay where it is, to maintain itself just as it is, decorous, seemly.

If the final stanza were dropped and the others slightly extended, the poem would belong in **Flesh and Blood.** The last three lines negate the suggestiveness, the polysemousness, of the central image. That is, they impose a tone distinct from the tone of the facts, and they impose a meaning.

One speculates that Williams now has an "agenda" that clouds his intuitions. That agenda is to live up to **"A Dream of Mind."** The genuine phenomenological detachment that poem possessed—the stepping back from one's own thoughts and feelings—is difficult, and the poet is tempted to force this detachment, to pretend to it. The results, in many poems, are 1) an impression of *too little* detachment, and 2) an imposed meaning, whose language hovers between those of self-analysis and moralism.

Between half and two-thirds of *The Vigil* escapes the agenda. Escape depends on how intensely a subject reminds the poet of himself.

Among the **"Symbols,"** **"Guitar"** escapes:

> For long decades the guitar lay disregarded in its case,
>   unplucked and untuned,
> then one winter morning, the steam heat coming on
>   hard, the maple neck swelling again,
> the sixth, gravest string, weary of feeling itself submis-
>   sively tugged to and fro
>
> over the ivory lip of the bridge, could no longer bear
>   the tension preceding release,
> and, with a faint thud and a single, weak note like a
>   groan stifled in a fist, it gave way,
> its portions curling agonizingly back on themselves
>   like sundered segments of worm.
>
> . . . The echoes abruptly decay; silence again, the
>   other strings still steadfast, still persevering,
> still feeling the music potent within them, their convic-
>   tion of timelessness only confirmed,
> of being essential, elemental, like earth, fire, air, from
>   which all beauty must be evolved.

Here, the third, moralizing or psychologizing stanza grows from the rest. Identification is subsumed in description; it does not appear as an extraneous element. Breakdown, loneliness, abandonment, idealistic perseverance—these themes, while painful, are not personally painful. Williams is able to play with them, and they remain polysemous.

The book contains many similar contrasts. **"Grief,"** Williams' elegy for his mother, is unsuccessful. We are given no sense of her personality or of their relationship. The pitiful vanity (or commendable pride) with which the dying woman applies her makeup inspires

> grief for all women's faces, applied, created, trying to
>   manifest what the soul seeks to be;
> grief for the faces of all human beings, our own faces
>   telling us so much and no more,
> offering pain to all who behold them, but which when
>   they turn to themselves, petrify, pose.

The poem, in other words, justifies its own generalization (and evasion) of particulars, not only of the person and the relationship, but of this grief itself. (One could say that a classical elegy—Milton's "Lycidas," for example—also evades particulars; but "Lycidas" has many themes besides the poet's grief.)

In strong contrast is **"My Fly,"** a delightful quasi-elegy for the sociologist Erving Goffman, himself a keen phenomenologist of interpersonal relations. A big green fly has appeared above Williams' desk and the poet imagines it's his friend:

> Joy! To be together, even for a time! Yes, tilt your
>   fuselage, turn it towards the light,
> aim the thousand lenses of your eyes back up at me:
>   how I've missed the layers of your attention,

how often been bereft without your gift for sniffing out pretentiousness and moral sham.

To **"Grief"** we can also juxtapose **"The Coma,"** dedicated "to the memory of S. J. Marks." Marks apparently expressed in person the sort of self-blame that fills Williams' poems. Phrases included "My character wound," "my flaw," "I've been discarded but I've earned it," "My weak, hopeless, incompetent reparations," "It's my fault, my arrogant doubt, my rage," etc. In **"The Coma"** Williams battles poignantly with his late friend. The title implies not just Marks' final physical condition but his blindness to

> the virtues his ruined past had never let
>   him believe in,
> his gifts for sympathy, kindness, compassion (. . .)
> not "my malaise, my destructive neurosis": let him
>   have known for himself his purity and his warmth;
> not "my crippled, hateful disdain": let have come to
>   him, in his last lift away from himself,
> his having wanted to heal the world he'd found so
>   wounded in himself; let him have known,
> though his sorrow wouldn't have wanted him to, that,
>   in his love and affliction, he had.

The point is not that Williams should be as kind to himself as he is to Marks. Rather, **"The Coma"** succeeds because of qualities lacking in more autobiographical poems. Chief among these are detachment from the subject, and a willingness to draw conclusions rather than impose them.

Another way of stating the problem is as follows: though Williams is interested in **"Symbols,"** his tendency is to allegorize, and the meaning of his allegories is himself. In **"Hawk"** (I wonder if Williams was thinking of Jeffers, and if so, *what* he was thinking), the dying, struggling bird makes him think of his own inadequacies ("I knew what to do, but, child of the city, I couldn't: there was no one to help me; / I could only—forgive me—retreat . . ."); then of his father's death and of similar emotions it inspired: "then, too, something was asked and I wasn't who I wanted to be." Of course, such emotions are commonplace; but the poem, by evading a subject (the hawk? the father?), replicates without transcending the state it describes. In contrast, **"The Hovel"** elaborates one interesting symbol (an utterly decrepit hut and oppressed life), and universalizes a private emotion ("the true history I inhabit, its sea of suffering, its wave to which I am froth, scum"). There are also many poems that display selfless sympathy; they include the Marks and Goffman elegies, and **"Instinct,"** a heartbreaking portrait of a drunken, loving, teenaged father.

Apart from what I interpret as the challenge of **"A Dream of Mind,"** Williams in *The Vigil* is beset by being sixty. In a number of poems he looks back on life with his son Jed and his wife Catherine, regrets mistakes, recalls successes, gives thanks for joy and love. Some of these poems are "moving"—very much so—but they do not transcend their situation: they have the warmth and immediacy that non-intellectuals mistake for, or prefer to, art. My image of Jed and Catherine will remain defined by the eight-line **"Two: Resurrections"** in *Flesh and Blood.* This judgment is obviously as informed by a *taste* for irony and detachment as by any literary value; other readers might rank these poems differently.

But irony and detachment remain strong in *The Vigil.* **"Insight"** is a short phenomenological study in the style of **"A Dream of Mind"** or **"Some of the Forms of Jealousy."** Its situation is almost the inverse of the latter's. A certain bemused and/or browbeaten female figure appears often in Williams' poems. Sometimes she dies; in "Insight," she perhaps escapes:

> Such matters end, there are healings, breakings-free;
>   she tells herself they end, but still,
> years later, when the call she'd dreaded comes, when
>   he calls, asking why she hasn't called,
> as though all those years it wasn't her who'd called,
>   then stopped calling and began to wait,
> then stopped waiting, healed, broke free, so when he
>   innocently suggests they get together,
> she says absolutely not, but feels uncertain—is she
>   being spiteful? small?—and then she knows:
> after this he'll cause her no more pain, though no
>   matter how she wished it weren't, this is pain.

This emotional precision extends from the personal to the political; as in *Tar,* moral outrage makes use of, rather than annuls, detachment and irony. **"In Darkness"** dissects a company goon who shot down miners in Harlan County. In six lines and one good metaphor **"The Demagogue"** does justice to its subject, and **"Money"** brings a vast abstraction home:

> We asked soul to be huge, encompassing, sensitive,
>   knowing, all-knowing, but not this (. . .)
> not joy become calculation, life counting itself,
>   compounding itself like a pocket of pebbles:
> sorrow, it feels like; a weeping, unhealable wound, an
>   affront at all costs to be avenged.

Finally, the poem I quote when recommending *The Vigil* is **"Secrets."** This story of the sad life and cruel death of Sid Mizraki hearkens back to the narratives of *Tar.* Sid, formerly an acquaintance of the poet's, works for the city. Driven mad by his boss, he hires two burglars to kill him, paying them with rich people's addresses. "Then suddenly he was transferred, got a friendlier boss, forgot the whole witless affair"—but the thieves are caught and turn him in.

> He got off with probation, but was fired, of course,
>   and who'd hire him with that record?
> He worked as a bartender, went on relief, drifted, got
>   into drugs, some small-time dealing.
>
> Then he married—"the plainest woman on earth,"
>   someone told me—but soon was divorced:
> more drugs, more dealing, run-ins with cops, then his
>   unthinkable calvary in that alley.

The poet had liked Sid but had lost track of him. He learns of Sid's death the way he learns too many things: late.

"[D]o people hide things from me to protect me?" he cries, before telling Sid's story. "Do they mistrust me?" Towards the end, addressing Sid's ghost, he says: "to come so close to a life and not comprehend it, acknowledge it, truly know it is life"—a line that, unusually for Williams, can be read two ways. Here the referral of another's experience to the self, and the search for its meaning in the self, is neither arbitrary, ungenerous, nor successful: *"Poor poet,* you'd tell me, *poor sheltered creature: if you can't open your eyes, at least stay still."*

Having long since recognized Williams' greatness, I realize that, like other great poets—like Frost or Auden—he can appeal in different ways to different values. My own values should by now be clear. I want, not reportage at the expense of elegy, not mimesis that precludes idealism, but a convincing fusion. Peck, Greger, and Williams all strive for this fusion; given the difficulties, it is unsurprising that none of them is wholly successful. One of the difficulties is the obscurity of the "ideal" in our culture, its disappearance into subjectivism and sensibility. This obvious fact helps me rationalize my preference for "reportage" in poetry; poets can derive values from facts, though philosophers cannot. Such, at least, is the faith I sense behind *Tar* and *Flesh and Blood.*

Jamie McKendrick (review date 3 October 1997)

SOURCE: "The World's Violences," in *Times Literary Supplement,* October 3, 1997, p. 25.

[*In the following review, McKendrick commends Williams's intensity and empathy in* The Vigil, *but finds shortcomings in his tendency to allegorize and to employ dubious shifts of perspective in this volume.*]

The long lines and short poems of the American poet C. K. Williams's *Flesh and Blood* (1988) combined the leisure of a *flâneur* with the urgency of a frontline reporter. His next book, *A Dream of Mind* (1992), although it contained some poems of the same extraordinary quality, turned inwards (at least in the long title sequence), quarrying the psyche, and was rewarded by grim, unwieldy slabs of abstraction. *The Vigil* is somewhere between the two.

Here, too, as in both preceding books, there is a poem about a vagrant which attends unflinchingly to infirmity and terminal squalor. In this latest example, **"Thirst,"** it is Williams's perceptions, from the first phrase, that hold the foreground of the story. "Here was my relation with the woman who lived all last autumn and winter day and night / on a beach in the Hundred and Third Street subway. . . ." The "shocking seethe of her stench" is a feral protest the poet recoils from but can't escape: "how rich, I would think, is the lexicon of our self-absolving, / how enduring our bland, fatal assurance that reflection is righteousness being accomplished." This goes further than the earlier poems by accusing consciousness, and implicitly Williams's own poetry, of complacency for merely not having averted its gaze. The poem then lurches into an inferno of empathy: "then holocaust, holocaust: host on host of ill, injured presences squandered, consumed.— / Her vigil, somewhere, I know, continues. . . ." If Williams sometimes hovers like a cleric at the deathbed, his calling as a poet of mortal anguish is not in doubt.

This collection also explores the distance as well as the proximity of the gazed-upon. His powerful version from Ovid records its belatedness: "In our age of scrutiny and dissection we know Deinira's mind better than she does herself." This distinguishes Williams from the Adamic imagination of Whitman, whose long lines his own superficially resemble, in the way his work acknowledges the secondary manner through which at least in part we come to know the world and its violences with a knowledge that sometimes seems illicit. In this respect *The Vigil* exercises in its voyeurism a kind of vigilance. In **"Fragment,"** a murdered shopkeeper's last moments, relayed on the video system, are retold with excruciated empathy. **"In Darkness"** re-enacts a violent scene from "That old documentary about the miners' strike in Harlan Country . . . ." Williams draws an explicit political analogy from the snarling strike-breaker who "posed, strutted . . . the way, now, so many in power assuming that same stance of righteous rectitude and rage / snarl their contempt at those who'd dare hold differing notions of governance and justice." Yet even for those of us in sympathy with Williams's political stance, both the language and the shift of perspective ("the way") have a kind of imaginative fatigue about them which suggest that his use of these longer lines may have outlived its creative purpose. This instant allegorizing is characteristic of the volume. In **"Fire,"** for example, the description of a burnt house is immediately translated for us: "Like love ill and soiled, like affection, affinity, passion, misused and consumed. . . ." Somehow the nouns are too cursory and indistinct to convince us, and the cadences too monotonously doleful. Williams has often been willing to sacrifice subtlety for intensity. The urgency and clamour of his style can be mawkish, but it also makes available to him as a writer tracts of the psyche which are overlooked by other poets. What is unusual is Williams's visceral empathy with others, with moments *in extremis* when the civilized mask drops and the human face with all its psychic lacerations and marks of woe appears before us.

In **"The Game,"** another kind of vigilance is seen, when, contemplating the outset of an affair, he asks "What difference if she was married, and perhaps mad (both only a little, I thought wrongly)"? The poem's last line, however, abruptly switches from acute psychological observation to a vertiginous, cosmic perspective: "beneath me a planet possessed: cycles of transfiguration and soaring, storms crossing." Because of his almost forensic attention to detail, his heaping up of evidenciary images, the reader is inclined to believe these rhetorical shifts, and yet they also feel calculatedly intensified. **"The Hovel,"** however, though written entirely in this visionary register, finds an arresting emblem for the soul: "Slate scraps, split stone, third hand splintering timber; rusted nails and sheet tin. . . ." This is Plato's cave installed with the faulty plumbing of nightmares.

"My Neighbour" proceeds via an ungainly cortège of possessed gerundives that shelve into present participles: "my holding the door, her crossing the fragmented tiles, faltering at the step to the street / droning, not looking at me," which all insist on the actual now of perception. And yet this poem, which brings together the poet's repelled surveillance of his neighbour and the memory of a relationship, requires of us a sudden leap of faith when, out of nowhere, "the god of frenzied, inexhaustible love says, rising in bloody splendour: *Behold me.*" Many of these poems functions as parables and exempla in which the meticulously recorded everyday occurrences are denuded and then hurtled into a realm where they become "cycles of transfiguration." The redemptive urge behind these poems makes them compelling, but the manner in which their perspectives shift can seem like the arrival of a *deus ex machina.*

Ashley Brown (review date Autumn 1997)

SOURCE: A review of *The Vigil,* in *World Literature Today,* Vol. 71, No. 4, Autumn, 1997, p. 794.

[*In the following review, Brown offers a positive assessment of* The Vigil.]

The Vigil follows C. K. Williams's *Selected Poems* by only three years. The poet has published seven volumes since 1969, and perhaps a review should note that ten of the forty-four poems in the new collection were published in the *Selected Poems,* where they appeared among a group designated as "New Poems." Since there are no textual changes in the poems as reprinted, one can only suppose that the poet wishes to emphasize their importance in his oeuvre. And indeed, at least five of these poems are among his finest: **"Interrogation II," "Time: 1976"** and its successor **"Time: 1978,"** and especially **"Villanelle of the Suicide's Mother"** and **"Hercules, Deianira, Nessus."** The last is a splendid version of the story in Ovid's *Metamorphoses,* book 9, in which Williams's characteristic long lines (up to twenty-five syllables) resemble Ovid's hexameters.

The recent poems in *The Vigil* are composed in these longish lines in every case. As I have already suggested, reading them is a quite active process, since the eye, which cannot take in the entirety of a line at once, is virtually directed to follow it to the end and then over. The poet is frequently a kind of observer whose wide-ranging glance takes in a lot; the technique is almost cinematic, as in the first line of **"The Hovel":** "Slate scraps, split stone, third hand splintering timber; rusted nails and sheet-tin." This is energetic poetry; surely twelve of the seventeen syllables are stressed, and the auditory effect accompanies the vigor of the images. But a reader can hardly keep up this effect for very long, and perhaps it is just as well that the poem runs to only nine lines. It is rather different from such a cinematic poem as Auden's famous "Consider This and in Our Time," where the blank verse easily carries the reader through sixty or so lines.

A number of the new poems are linked to those in the 1994 volume. For instance, we now have **"Time: 1975"** and **"Time: 1972"** to go along with the pair of "Time" poems carried over from the *Selected Poems*. Of these two, the 1972 **"Time"** has some lovely phrasing, but it lacks the particularity of the earlier pair, where the small child, Jed, and his mother Catherine are the center of attention in a memorable sequence. In **"1975"** we have Jed, only three weeks old and asleep but the focus for the meditation that concerns Catherine, her mother Renée, and "the music of the women's voices." Catherine, to whom *The Vigil* is dedicated, is now identified as the poet's wife, a matter that was not altogether clear in the earlier poems. **"Time: 1976"** is the masterpiece of this group; Williams's gift for organization is most apparent here, and the power of memory operates at full effect. Perhaps Williams is following the late James Merrill in his series called "Days of 1964" and so on, in turn suggested by poems from Cavafy. In general, Williams's poems gain something when they do not depend on their Latinate diction as much as on their particularity.

Carol Muske (review date October 1999)

SOURCE: "Poetry in Review," in *Yale Review,* Vol. 87, No. 4, October, 1999, pp. 154–64.

[*In the following excerpt, Muske offers a positive assessment of* Repair. *According to Muske, "These poems demand everything of the reader, and thus they are political and social in the most profound reconfigurative sense."*]

What is often said about C. K. Williams is that he is "Whitmanesque"—he's got that Whitman-like long line, that Whitmanish turn of phrase, the expansive vision. It would be pointless to deny Walt's influence on this work, but finally, the comparison yields little in terms of getting under the skin of the poems. Williams's new book, *Repair,* again situates him in America (or an American's Europe) once again—and again the reader prepares to enter the holy precincts of the Bible—Psalms—Whitman—Ginsberg—where pious homage is paid to the Long Line, that great big democratic yak-vista.

Frankly, the long line holds less interest for me than the nature of "address"—or the introspection that becomes a kind of extroverted style, a style that insists on the reader's sympathetic ear. Whitman feels entitled to our attention: that interests me. Williams, too, feels entitled to our atten-

tion, and for some of the same reasons. Not the reasons that stoked the fires of the Puritan jeremiad or ran William Jennings Bryan's mouth from a cross-country caboose; Williams's argument for his expansiveness eschews what is didactic or rhetorical-egalitarian.

In fact, as Williams himself puts it in an essay in *Poetry and Consciousness*: "I wanted to write poems and imply existences that subverted—or at least, circumvented—conceptual fanaticism." Further, "I was trying to find ways to embody political and social realities by structuring and figuring poems in ways that went beyond apparent limits or logical connectiveness."

What he's struggling against, then, is "logic" in thought (and speech)—the template of preconception that is pressed onto our thought impressions to make them "whole." Yet he's not necessarily interested in "stream of consciousness" or tiresome "subjectless" poems. There is always a unifying context in Williams. It's a matter of epistemology: *The lyric stance* does not have to be passive." And: "Lyrics worked by compression, omission. I wanted to expand."

This is hardly an attack on the tight-lipped lyric; rather, it's a restructuring, a reeducating of the reader's attention, the reader's way of listening to the lyric, which includes consciousness of one's manner of reading—and of formulating thought. Like Miles and Wright, the vicissitudes of speech capture his imagination, but Williams is passionately loyal to *one* voice—the voice within the mind, the voice of consciousness. As he writes in *Poetry and Consciousness*: "Choosing to enact oneself in the first person implies a belief that the person so evoked will have a connection to reality in ways that are spiritually essential and productive, but in fact there is no way of knowing, no matter how scrupulously one tries to oversee one's solipsism, that the matters one is struggling with aren't ultimately idiosyncratic."

Here we have *Repair,* the title implying less actual fixing or healing than human attempts to fix or heal, to restore. In **"Last Things,"** one of the most startling and disturbing poems in the collection, the "speaker" recounts how, while visiting a photographer-friend's darkroom, he discovers a "curled up photo of his son the instant after his death, / his glasses still on, a drop of blood caught at his mouth." The reader is informed that the photographer-friend has published a book "to commemorate this son" and that it closes with a picture of the son taken the day *before* he died, with a caption identifying it as the "last photo of Alex." Then Williams reaches out and draws the reader into the poem as a participant; he notes that he'll have to ask his friend's "permission" to "show this."

> If you're reading it, you'll know my friend pardoned me,
> that he found whatever small truth his story might embody
> was worth the anguish of remembering that reflexive moment

The "reflexive moment" is (presumably) the moment in which the man, who has photographed "everything" for "fifty years" and has grown used to "bringing reality into himself through a lens" could not stop himself from capturing unflinchingly his son's face in death.

Williams ends the poem abruptly, leaving the reader in a state of complicitous confusion. Why *did* the man take this picture and why does he keep it in his darkroom? The questions keep coming—without answers. No enormities about Art and Life are hinted at, yet the mind quickly moves to these issues. The "lyric" has been expanded to include all that lies outside the frame. And outside the frame of the "conceptual," the "photographable," the lens, is the unanswerable. So here is the image that "immortalizes" or haunts, the "repair" of art (or *documentation*) versus the random destruction of life. It hardly seems sufficient simply to attribute the photograph to a reflexive impulse. Williams knows this, and he knows the reader will go on, enlarging the frame of the poem. Why did he take that photograph? What can it mean and how can it alleviate or exacerbate his suffering? What is a furtive act, an unconscious act, or a deliberate creation of a "death mask"?

All of these poems—as figures of "repair"—confront impossible questions, making real healing seem unlikely. Yet Williams does believe in the saving experience of the poem. Like Miles and Wright, who introduce speech that "enlarges" the field, Williams gives us the poem itself as proactive diction, as the experience *in itself.* The questions we ask ourselves reading **"Last Things"** are part of the process of (as the title of another poem about three old women, Fates at the loom, has it) "invisible mending."

We enter a poem about a frightened man on a city street, accidentally striking a beggar who has come up, unexpectedly, behind him to ask for change, we enter a poem (**"King"**) about an individual's experience with racism in the 1960s, we enter each outpouring of transformative reflection like unsuspecting rafters suddenly plunged into white water. Where are we going, where is the poem taking us?

No poem is meant to provide answers. Williams has an astonishing gift for creating poems that *seem* to be answers, seem to be large-lined explanations, meditations on the familiar, wide grassy vistas of contemplation, but that are in fact phenomenological questions that move as the mind moves, that are in fact *forces* that move us out of familiar contexts and into intense acts of attention. These poems demand everything of the reader, and thus they are political and social in the most profound reconfigurative sense. Williams intends nothing less than a change in how we perceive our world. With the poems of **Repair,** he seems to be asking something further: that we investigate ways to forgive and try to heal the past by finding a way to "end" what is endless. Or, as he puts it in **"Invisible Mending,"** describing the crones at their work:

> And in your loneliness you'd notice

> how really very gently they'd take
> the fabric to its last, with what
> solicitude gather up worn edges
> to be bound, and with what severe
> but kind detachment wield
> their amputating shears:
> forgiveness, and repair.

William Logan (review date 10 March 2000)

SOURCE: "The Guilty Party," in *Times Literary Supplement,* March 10, 2000, p. 23.

[*In the following review of* Repair, *Logan objects to Williams's mawkish and self-serving studies of human suffering and tragedy.*]

C. K. Williams is the guilt-ridden Peeping Tom of American poetry. His meandering long-lined poems have a distinctive shape and distinctive moral air: for two decades, beginning in **With Ignorance** (1977), he has been drawn to the underside of the human condition. He watches with an intensity almost prurient in its particulars. Williams is rarely shocked by what he sees (though the poems long to shock the reader); but if shocked, he invokes his tattered humanity.

When a poem in his new collection, **Repair,** introduces an unnamed dictator who murdered his enemies by having nails hammered into their brains, it is hard to know the poetic purpose. As an object lesson, it fails in specificity and might as well refer to some barbaric torture practised by ancient Gauls. As a reminder that the brutality of the past survives in the present, that something immutably cruel is written in human DNA, it must compete with the daily news. Williams sometimes seems to write only to beat his breast and rend his tunic—he wants his horrors to confront us with the knowledge that "it's we who do such things," as if this were somehow a surprise.

Repair suffers from having, not too many occasions for such operatic guilts, but too few. Williams's longer lines are still the medium of his moral thinking, his new experiments with short lines oddly without imaginative pressure. When Williams discovered the long line (meaning one of up to thirty-five syllables), it freed him from lyric burden and lyric obligation. He took confessional poetry back to the psychiatrist's couch, where every story seemed half a dream remembered, half a sin to be purged—and one very impatient to be analysed.

Imaginations are not just indebted to their forms; they are partly invented by forms. Williams's lines are pretty in a way Whitman's never were; they are calculated, even precious, where Whitman's tumbled over themselves in democratic abandon (the shaggy line and shaggy poem are American ideals). But length sustains Williams's slightly sadistic habits of observation, and longer lines capture the nervous sweep of the voyeur's eye—Williams is not just greedy for experience, but greedy to be the experience, to play Boswell to every petty failing he uncovers.

The poems in *Repair* struggle in the quiet squalor of their sentiment. A reminiscence of a half-mad street poet drags to mawkish conclusion:

> I never found out what he came to in the end;
> I've always kept him as "Bobby the poet."
> I only hope he didn't suffer more rue, that the
> Muse kept watch on her innocent stray.

More rue? The Muse has fallen out of some Christmas carol.

Williams the old-line liberal is full of Freudian anguish and anxiety, guilty over privilege but never honest about the nature of his privilege. He is best when capturing (he is less a camera than a camcorder) the self-satisfied anxieties of the middle class. In a mortally funny poem, he tries to interpret a disturbing dream about his wife, using all Freud's gimcrack machinery to reassure himself. It doesn't work, and in such poems Williams turns a slightly hapless *schlemiel*, his guilts either lachrymose or bellicose. He can observe his own mother with pitiless fascination, in a kind of mortal disgust, but can't help himself from turning soppy over her in the end. Even a visit to Auschwitz becomes a visit to the poet's private theme park of opportune guilt.

The bearing of witness is often prosecutorial. Deep in his divided consciousness, where the poet is given to staring at mirrors, given to "that passion to be other," lies the coarse psychological motive: if the other is so terrible, the self is not so guilty—even if needy, indulgent, salving itself over the hurt of consciousness. Williams loves to give *faux*-rhetorical weight to his poems, and more than a third end with the hammer blows of a repeated or echoed phrase: "*Mad dreams! Mad love!*"; "Or she to me? / *Oh, surely she to me!*"; "Drop it. *Drop it! Drop it! Drop it!*" Distracted from his long-winded homilies on, for example, race relations, the poet can describe with tender wit and charm a pair of shoes abandoned on a window sill, describe them and make the reader feel they couldn't have been rendered by a more sympathetic imagination—not even by Williams's namesake William Carlos, the one who wrote in *short* lines about plums and wheelbarrows.

C. K. Williams is still a dealer in the repulsive, though less in this book than others—a poem may end with a beloved horse, though it starts with an old lady farting in a doctor's waiting-room. In his eagerness to push the poetic subject into the creature discomforts of modern life, there is bleak knowledge of shame; the poet finds a photo concealed by a friend, a photographer: a photo of the man's son taken just after the boy's death:

> Is telling about it a violation of confidence?
> Before I show this to anyone else, I'll have to ask his
>   permission.
> If you're reading it, you'll know my friend pardoned
>   me, that he found whatever small truth his story
>   might embody was worth the anguish . . .

It is a pity that a poet who knows the moody faults and moral falterings of being human tries, in the crudest way, to make the reader party to (and victim of) such complicity. What are sometimes delicate explorations of motive and doubt too often become the vain, and vanity-ridden, search for repentance in the sin that is the world. Williams stares into the abyss with a damp handkerchief, and wants the reader to pat him on the back.

Elizabeth Lund (review date 10 August 2000)

SOURCE: "A Plunge into the Still, Cold Lake of Self," in *Christian Science Monitor,* August 10, 2000, p. 20.

[*In the following review of* Repair, *Lund agrees with Williams's status as a "major poet," but finds the volume "inconsistent."*]

Some poets are perfect for reading at the beach. Others are better beside a still lake. C. K. Williams is the latter.

Williams's work is not something one can breeze through. His long, dense lines force readers to slow down and let the language seep into their skin. It's a bit like wading into very cold water. The movement is inch by inch, ankle to knee to hip. The poems must be unpacked layer by layer.

Williams's approach has not changed in *Repair,* his eighth book, which won this year's Pulitzer Prize in poetry. Readers must still lower themselves gingerly into his poems. Take, for example, these lines from the book's opener, **"Ice"**:

> The astonishing thing that happens when you crack a
>   needle-awl into a block of ice:
> the way a perfect section through it crazes into gleam-
>   ing fault-lines, fractures, facets;
> dazzling silvery deltas that in one too-quick-to-capture
>   instant madly complicate the cosmos of its innards.

Williams has not made it easy for someone to dive in, but as the work progresses, one often finds the cold inviting. And there are a few warm springs. A poem to his grandson, **"Owen: Seven Days,"** is a good example:

> . . . when I
> look into his eyes
> darkish grayish blue
>
> a whole tone
> lighter
> than his mother's
>
> I feel myself almost
> with a *whoosh*
> dragged
>
> into his consciousness
> and processed
> processed processed

his brows knit
I'm in there now
I don't know

in what form but
his gaze hasn't
faltered an instant

Williams's concerns, despite his sometimes difficult surfaces, are fairly universal: He writes of self-doubt, isolation, of trying to find his place in the world. *Repair* is about bridging the gap between what we are and what we want to be. It's about the lifelong process of accepting the face we were given instead of the one that will never be. From **"Glass"**:

Is how we live or try to live supposed to embellish
    us?
All I see is the residue of my other, failed faces.

But maybe what we're after is just a less abrasive
    regard:
not "It's still not there," but something like "Come in,
    be still."

Repair has some strong poems, including **"The Train"** and the lovely, lyrical **"Droplets."** At his best, Williams is insightful, vulnerable, unblinking. He explores the hidden mental realms behind people's outward actions, and he leads us fearlessly behind the mind's closed doors. Often his poems are hauntingly stark, but the collection itself is a bit inconsistent.

At times the language becomes too abstract, too esoteric, as if the speaker can't get outside of his own thoughts. In other places the work becomes too self-absorbed, too unconvincing, as in the long poem **"The Poet,"** where Williams wonders about a long-lost acquaintance.

Some readers will be quick to say that *Repair* is not Williams's best book. What he says about love is a bit too pat, and his familiar themes have appeared in sharper, more memorable poems.

Repair does not invigorate as much as it could, but it does give ample glimpses into why Williams has become a major poet. His work, like an early-morning dip in icy water, does make the nerves and skin tingle.

Brian Phillips (review date 18 September 2000)

SOURCE: "Plainly, but with Flair," in *New Republic,* September 18, 2000, pp. 42–45.

[*In the following review, Phillips objects to Williams's overly explanatory verse in* Repair *and suggests that the long lines are essentially indistinguishable from prose, and thus do not serve any aesthetic purpose.*]

"Didactic poetry," Shelley declares in the preface to *Prometheus Unbound,* "is my abhorrence; nothing can be equally well expressed in prose that is not tedious and supererogatory in verse." The poems of C. K. Williams are not quite didactic, but neither are they quite undidactic. His long poetic line often dips its toe testingly into the waters of the prosaic, and his inspections of motive and meaning seem more fit to offer moral instruction than to summon aesthetic intensity.

Too often, the second half of a Williams stanza devolves into critical commentary on the event of the first half, swerving casually from the fictional scene it has been sketching into speculation on what that fiction means for "us," as though the duty of the poet were not only to propose the metaphor, but also to supervise its interpretation. In these moments Williams does not make art of the process by which the mind arrives at explanation; he simply explains, never describing so much as a housedress without also informing the housewife that

I see the dresses also as a proclamation: that in your
    dim kitchen,
your laundry, your bleak concrete yard, what you
    revealed of yourself was a fabulation;
your real sensual nature, veiled in those sexless vest-
    ments, was utterly your dominion.

Williams has a real skill for scrutinizing intentions, his own and those of the characters, real and fictional, who inhabit his poetic narratives. His best poems, including many from his successful collections of the late '80s and early '90s, limit themselves to a kind of privileged observation, confining their self-commentary to strict, short psychological underscorings. His worst poems, including some from *Repair,* reveal too much of themselves. When Williams restrains his urge to tell us exactly what his characters are thinking and exactly what his metaphors mean, he is capable of real sensibility; but when he gives full vent to his talent for perceptive explanation, he achieves the strange effect of obscuring his subjects beneath layers of clarification.

In this vein Williams follows his resonant, if verbose, description of cracking "a needle-awl into a block of ice"—"the way a perfect section through it crazes into gleaming fault-lines, fractures, facets; / dazzling silvery deltas that in one too-quick-to-capture instant madly complicate the cosmos of its innards"—with an immediate aside about how the activity is also "a metaphor, like Kafka's frozen sea within." And in **"Archetypes,"** he follows an obvious metaphor for the essential separateness of individuals—one sleeping lover jerking inexplicably away from the other—with an essay into the mind of the wakeful lover: "I felt again how separate we all are from one another, how even our passions / . . . heal only the most benign divisions."

There is something a little patronizing about this sort of elucidation, as Williams shepherds the reader away from direct aesthetic experience and into the fold of comprehension. It would be one thing if he worked the process of understanding—of the mind coming to grips with meaning—into the unfoldings of his poems, so that the block of ice and the sleeping lover were simply two starting points for his poems' real subject, which is thought; but he does not do this. Instead he seems to jump-cut between the subject of a poem and a conclusory commentary on that subject, sharply demarcating his cuts with phrases like "And I realized" and "Isn't it this way for us, too?"

Thought is almost never Williams's real subject, and his poems almost never take the shape of thought. Like Lowell, he is his feelings' historian rather than their rhapsode, and the subjects of his poems are almost always exactly what he says they are: separation, loneliness, the memory of old wounds, emotional healing. (This last is the most common subject of *Repair*.) The sort of verse that Williams has undertaken to write is patient, somewhat pedagogical, and in love with clarity; many of his poems seem designed to do the work of the reader as well as the work of the writer, and one feels that they are meant to succeed by convincing that Williams's reasons for selecting a particular metaphor are sound, rather than by shocking the reader into feeling the way the poet has felt.

Thus a poem called **"Depths"** equates a child's fear of falling from his father's shoulders, where he sits looking down from the roof of a building, with a young man's fear of being disappointed in love:

> Even now I feel a frost of fear
> to think I might not have found you,
> my love, or not believed in you,
> but still be reeling on another roof.

But the single word devoted in the poem to the evocation of fear—calling the feeling a "frost"—evokes nothing; there is no fear in the poem, there is only the reference to fear, and the subsequent explanation of the equation. The metaphor, insufficiently expressed, sputters; the work of poetry, strictly speaking, has been left unfinished.

Williams operates within a narrow linguistic range and with a constricted formal imagination. As *Repair* shows, his register is casual, prizing simplicity; but Williams is no populist. His language is conversational rather than academic, but his range of reference is often quite the opposite. He uses the diction of common speech to describe simple events and narratives, but his simple narratives often allude to sources ranging from Greek mythology, one of his favorite sources for metaphor, to English Romanticism and the work of the French symbolists. His line recalls Whitman and Ginsberg in length and shape, and his delivery recalls the uncluttered, easy manner of Elizabeth Bishop (I can imagine a Williams poem beginning "I caught a tremendous fish"), but his influences are in some ways as European as they are American. His work reflects the moral self-questioning of Herbert, the plain-spokenness and the yearning toward nature of Wordsworth, the foul rag-and-bone shop of the heart of the later Yeats.

Like Yeats, Williams takes the responsibilities of verse very seriously. He is dedicated to its ardors rather than to its pleasures, which may explain his exegetical inclination: if he ensures that the reader understands what he means in a poem, he has saved his work from the threat of self-indulgence. And yet he often indulges his reader, glossing every potential difficulty, and in this way he leaves his reader curiously vacant of ardor. In **"House,"** Williams begins by introducing his metaphor, the reconstruction of a ruined house around its existing frame:

> The way you'd renovate a ruined house, keeping the
>   "shell," as we call it, brick, frame or stone,
> and razing the rest: the inside walls—partitions, we
>   say—then stairs, pipes, wiring, commodes,
> saving only . . . no, saving nothing this time; take the
>   self-shell down to its emptiness, hollowness, void.

There is skill in that procession of nouns indicating absence—from emptiness through hollowness to void, from simple absence through essential absence to nothingness. But the passage's self-conscious flirtation with the diction of the renovating workmen ("shell,' as we call it . . . partitions, we say") is distracting, and already the not-terribly-complicated metaphor is receiving authorial explanation ("the self-shell").

In the second stanza—the finest stanza in the poem and one of the finest passages in *Repair*—Williams enacts the demolition of the house, getting down to the essentials beneath it:

> Down to the scabrous plaster, down to the lining bricks
>   with mortar squashed through their joints,
> down to the eyeless windows, the forlorn doorless
>   doorways, the sprung joists powdery with rot;
> down to the slab of the cellar, the erratically stuccoed
>   foundation, the black earth underneath all.

The lively description in this stanza (the mortar squashed through the joints of the bricks, the joints powdery with rot) is perfectly clear on its own; the Yeatsian clearing-away of the rotten and the ruined, and the rediscovery of the black earth on which the "self-shell" rests, requires no further elucidation.

But in the third stanza, Williams acts like one of those eyeless windows, and makes things utterly transparent:

> Down under all to the ancient errors, indolence, envy,
>   pretension, the frailties as though in the gene;
> down to where consciousness cries, "Make me new,"
>   but pleads as pitiably, "Cherish me as I was."
> Down to the swipe of the sledge, the ravaging bite of
>   the pick; rubble, wreckage, vanity: the abyss.

The "surprise" in this stanza is that the black earth does not represent, as the nature-image often does in this kind of poem, the desirable or the good, but rather the "ancient errors" on which, in this poem, the self is grounded. But why not make this assignation a subject for portrayal, rather than for explication? Why not describe the black earth in such a way as to make its function clear? Why zoom abruptly out of the metaphor at the start of the third stanza into an explanation of what it means, only to zoom as abruptly back into it at the close of the poem? After all, this kind of house is old as the hills—it was familiar to Shakespeare ("O, what a mansion have those vices got, / Which for their habitation chose out thee") and to Descartes, who devoted a long passage in the *Discourse on Method* to a metaphor equating home reconstruction and philosophical self-improvement.

When it is incorporated into aesthetic experience, of course, the authorial negotiation of metaphor has an ancient and serious history in English poetry, both in its disclosures (the Everyman tradition, Spenserian allegories, Petrarchan love-conceits) and in its concealments (the Anglo-Saxon kenning, the metaphysical tangles of Donne and Herbert). Williams is often acutely aware of the poetic traditions that precede him—his poem **"The Island"** alludes to Shakespeare, Wordsworth, Coleridge, Yeats, and Hopkins in just over a page—but his lapses of metaphoric rigor never seem figured into any such tradition. He seems to feel that his poems require their mini-commentaries in order to make their point, as though making a point were, well, the point of a poem.

It does not help that Williams's long, wordy line and his occasional looseness with language imply a prose style as much as his compacted multisyllabics and his occasional care with language imply a poetic style. Consider the opening of **"The Poet,"** from *Repair,* and see if you can guess where the line breaks should go when it is transcribed in prose:

> I always knew him as "Bobby the poet," though whether he was one or not, someone who lives in words, making a world from their music, might be a question. In those strange years of hippiedom and "people-power," saying you were an artist made you one, but at least Bobby acted the way people think poets are supposed to. He dressed plainly, but with flair, spoke little, yet listened with genuine attention, and a kind of preoccupied, tremulous seriousness always seemed to absorb him.

Compare this character sketch, written in Williams's "poetic" language, with a similar sketch from Williams's affecting new prose memoir, *Misgivings: My Mother, My Father, Myself*:

> I remember them dancing like that at their fiftieth wedding anniversary party: everyone's watching them, they both look dashing. My mother has on a beautiful new dress, and she's just beaming with pleasure, as though my father had just wonderfully surprised her with some new step, and my father looks, unless you'd known him before, healthy, physically impressive, tanned, graceful.

The styles are virtually indistinguishable, with the same reliance on long sentences made up of many short clauses, the same use of rhythmic punctuation, and the same dependence on strings of adjectives and adverbs to carry descriptive freight ("plainly, but with flair"; "healthy, physically impressive").

Of course, there may be something slightly unfair about invoking this likeness between prose style and poetic style critically, simply because to do so is to ignore the work of the line break as a material component of the poem. If the basic difference between poetry and prose is not a difference in attitude, subject, or rhetorical register, then there is nothing reductive or lazy about identifying it as material, formal, or even typographical. The mere presence of the line break, with the pressure that it places on language, can imbue a block of text with aesthetic possibilities that are vastly different from those available to the same text written with no line break. A great many extraordinary poems would seem as bafflingly unpoetic as Williams's, if they were written out as prose: "As the cat climbed over the top of the jamcloset, first the right forefoot, carefully, then the hind, stepped down into the pit of the empty flowerpot." In the same way, it may be that Williams's particular use of line breaks in that passage from **"The Poet"** transforms it in some way, or distinguishes it aesthetically from its prose incarnation.

The question, then, is to what effect Williams's line breaks work. Here is the passage written with his lineation intact:

> I always knew him as "Bobby the poet," though
>   whether he ever was one or not,
> someone who lives in words, making a world from
>   their music, might be a question.
>
> In those strange years of hippiedom and "people-
>   power," saying you were an artist
> made you one, but at least Bobby acted the way people
>   think poets are supposed to.
>
> He dressed plainly, but with flair, spoke little, yet
>   listened with genuine attention,
> and a kind of preoccupied, tremulous seriousness
>   always seemed to absorb him.

A few things are immediately obvious. There are three stanzas, each containing a single sentence of the prose fragment, so that three of the six line breaks occur after a period. Two of the remaining three occur after a comma, at a natural moment of pause. The remaining break, that separating "saying you were an artist" from "made you one" in the middle stanza, is the only standout, balancing a moment of gentle wit across a break that works elegantly to maintain the line-length insisted upon syntactically elsewhere in the poem. Other than in that middle line, the breaks seem primarily organizational, gathering large thoughts into sentences preserved as individual stanzas, and breaking those large thoughts in half at moments indicating subtle shifts in subject: the third stanza, for instance, is devoted to the physical description of Bobby the Poet, and separates the idea of Bobby's "preoccupied, tremulous seriousness" from the shorter characterizations grouped in the previous line.

This is a clear-headed and efficient way of presenting ideas, but it cannot be said to have much of a felt impact on the aesthetic experience of reading the poem. Apart from the break after "artist," the lineation feels designed mainly to separate elements of the subject into segments of equal length; but given that the line breaks fall after punctuation in almost every case, the lineation does not even have a pronounced effect on the rhythm of our reading. And given that the poem's style so closely resembles Williams's prose style, and that it is actually somewhat ungainly in any form ("those strange years of hippiedom and 'people-power'"), one wonders why it was not written in prose to begin with, where it would at least not find Williams violating his own commandment that poets must "live in words, making a world from their music."

This complaint can be made about every long-lined poem in *Repair.* Even when Williams summons impressive language ("the nail which is the axis upon which turns the brutal human world upon the world"), and even when he writes about chaos, pain, or fear, his lineation is almost always the whisk broom of his consciousness, sweeping his thoughts into well-proportioned piles. From time to time he does experiment with other deployments; occasionally there are poems with far shorter and more frequently enjambed lines, whose enactment of spectacular violence in agitated verbs and adjectives recalls Ted Hughes, Geoffrey Hill, and the school of the Anglo-Saxon Awfuls:

> Furiously a crane
> in the scrapyard out of whose grasp
> a car it meant to pick up slipped,
> lifts and lets fall, lifts and lets fall
> the steel ton of its clenched pincers
> onto the shuddering carcass
> which spurts fragments of anguished glass
> until it's sufficiently crushed
> to be hauled up and flung onto
> the heap . . .

These lines (from **"Shock"**) are virtuosic—but even here Williams covertly relies on clausal organizations (*onto* the shuddering carcass / *which* spurts fragments . . . / *until* it's sufficiently crushed) to spruce up the wreck.

What happens when Williams weds his explicit, precise self-explorations to unadorned prose? In recent years he has tried the union twice, first in 1998 with the loftily titled and mostly unlofty book of essays *Poetry and Consciousness,* and now with his memoir. In some ways, *Misgivings* is Williams's most satisfying book. It is written in a form (short, tightly focused chapters, each dealing with a particular memory or observation) and about a subject (his parents, whom he calls "the conspiracy that made me who I am") to which his talents as a writer— even his talents as a poet—are perfectly matched. In his memoir, Williams plumbs few deep truths, but he emerges as one of the most authoritative psychologists (or pop-psychologists) in contemporary prose.

Many of the poems in *Repair* are also about Williams's parents; but the very sobering *Misgivings* seems to undo the argument of many of those poems. The most commonly sounded theme of the poems is that love, however painfully, heals psychological wounds; but in the memoir, love inflicts more psychological damage than it mends, and the emphasis is squarely off the mending—characters barely have time to forgive one another before they die.

The précis is simple: Williams's father, an egocentric businessman, hardens with time and loses touch emotionally with his wife, a long-suffering, narcissistic housewife, and poet son, leading to complication and to confrontation documented in plentiful detail. Williams's method is to sketch scenes based on memories of his parents, both now deceased, and then to question them sharply. The resulting forays into the interrogative mode sometimes become overlong, query piled upon query with towering abandon:

> My father's oath never to say he was sorry: what does it mean when you decide you'll never again, to anyone, even to your wife, even to any of your children, apologize, about anything? Is it an ethical decision? Something that comes out of a long consideration of moral necessities and imponderables? Is it the logical conclusion of one's vision of a cosmos which includes self, beyond-self, other selves, and a God, or some semblance of a God? And how does one arrive at a conclusion so coherent and compelling that anything else seems a positive affront to your belief system?
>
> Or is making such a decision, a resolution of such inclusiveness, more of a psychological realization? The perception that when one wounds or offends someone else, there's already pain in having to admit that you have, and an apology would only add to the total quotient of misery between offender and offended?
>
> Or does it have something to do with the sense of one's self-making, with coming to believe that self-creation isn't a continuing, indeterminate process, but that it has an end, comes to fruition and stops; that one can, must say, "I'm finished, the identity I have evolved is no longer open to negotiation, change is no longer an option"?

No, no, no, no, yes, arrogantly, and no, the reader thinks; but Williams never offers an answer, preferring instead to explore nuance through the sheer accumulation of perplexity. This threatens to become tedious, and by the end of the book, it does; even if the sifting ambiguities are a welcome change from the overexplanatory poetry, we eventually want a resolution.

As the book progresses, however, Williams creates an increasingly vivid portrait of both parents, who become fully realized and plausible human beings; and it is impossible to deny that, in this way he handsomely fulfills the mandate of descriptive memoir. When he leaves his questioning behind and focuses on narrative recollection, Williams often finds little diamonds, brighter and more instantly right than the little discourses in the poetry: "When I picture my father on my horse, inelegant and graceless, it comes to me to think of him in a car as well, because there he was another person entirely." This goes on:

My father is wearing a suit and the business hat he still sported in those days, and he drives with a deft, athletic, unselfconscious ease. As he does, he peels an orange—his breakfast—manipulating the steering wheel with the delicate pressure against it of one slightly raised knee; the fingers of his right hand curve and without him looking at the fruit his nails insert themselves into the skin at precisely the most efficacious point for it to be cleanly stripped, then he throws out the peels and segments the orange, one section at a time going neatly into his mouth.

Passages such as this are lovely to read, and they are even helpful in life; and when Williams writes, just a few sentences later, that his father's failing vision made him a nervous and accident-prone driver in his old age, the effect is chilling. Let her paint an inch thick, to this favor she must come.

It is a small luxury to watch a writer construct character as skillfully as Williams does at these moments, and the narrative is sometimes very moving. But it is weirdly static as well. The book is not a novel, and so it lacks a well-shaped plot. Williams has tried to circumvent this difficulty by flashing quickly between scenes, but once the characters are created, they do little that is exceedingly interesting to watch. So the pleasures of the memoir are mainly incidental pleasures, taken from brief moments of life made visible, such as the description of the father eating the orange. In this way, oddly enough, the pleasures of Williams's prose are poetic pleasures. Just as Williams's poems often tailspin into the prosaic, his writing comes to life poetically when it stretches out in the (comparative) aesthetic relaxation of prose.

This is interesting, because aesthetics is precisely what seems to be at stake in a great deal of Williams's writing, or rather a sort of uneasy truce with the idea of aesthetics that Williams feels continually tempted to break. Especially when it comes to his poetry, something in Williams's mind seems to distrust the idea that what he says should be judged by how he says it; that expressive quality, rhetorical power, formal ability, metaphorical aptitude, and linguistic artfulness might be called upon to establish his themes or be seen as primary to his subjects. His poems often seem determined to test the limits of aesthetic duty, as though Williams wants to see just how un-aesthetic poetry can become and still be poetry. The result is his tendency toward clear, discursive language and heavy explanation. It may be impossible, he seems to be saying, to write a poem about lovers that does not become a metaphor for love; but at least I can explicitly unmask the hidden term of the metaphor, and leave no doubt as to what I mean. In the end, this is an artist who deeply mistrusts art.

The problem that haunts this verse is that aesthetic complexity may be the first (and even the only) absolute requirement of successful poetry. Largely because of the pressure exerted upon language by the inescapable sectionalizing of the line break, it is impossible for a poem to be successful unless it is first aesthetically successful, no matter how smart, important, or personal its ideas and themes. Kant could not have been a poet; and there are great poets who have produced poems with very little to say. At some level, Williams seems to know this: his preoccupation with poetic metaphor is a concession to aesthetics not found in the prose. Yet the poems chafe against it; they ask to be admired for the seriousness of their content rather than for the achievements of their structure and their diction.

Williams is a trenchant observer and a dedicated examiner of mind and motive. But those qualities are not, by themselves, sufficient to the requirements of poetry. This may be why his memoir seems so much more actualized than his verse. The form of memoir is aesthetic only at second-hand; its art is merely the blush of the historical. Here, instead of resisting the generalizing aesthetic essence of his form, Williams is free to give the particular truth the weight that the particular truth always seems to warrant in his mind. Instead of balancing art with exegesis, and burdening painted ornament with skeletal organization, he is free to give full rein to his analytical abilities, employing art at his discretion to enliven and to illustrate his argument, and to keep his readers reading.

At one moment in his memoir, Williams writes that

> I'm writing of my parents as though they were emblematic of something, as though there were some aura of meaning about them that transcended the small stories—and I realize they are small stories—that contain them.

This simple, frank, admission is one of the saving graces of Williams's book. There are moments, and registers of speech, for which poetry is unnecessary. Sometimes just being honest is enough.

FURTHER READING

Criticism

Dickerson, Debra. "The Parent Trap." *Washington Post Book World* (23 July 2000): 6.
    Dickerson discusses Williams's recollection of his parents and upbringing in *Misgivings.*

Gunderson, Elizabeth. Review of *Selected Poems,* by C. K. Williams. *Booklist* (1 October 1994): 232.
    Gunderson offers a positive assessment of *Selected Poems,* calling the work a "complete and thoughtful collection."

Kirby, David. Review of *Misgivings: My Mother, My Father, Myself,* by C. K. Williams. *Library Journal* (1 March 2000): 92.
    Kirby offers a positive assessment of *Misgivings.*

Kizer, Carolyn. "Poetry." *Washington Post Book World* (9 October 1983): 8.

In this positive review of *Tar,* Kizer focuses on the poem "Combat" to illustrate the "splendor" of Williams's style and authentic American voice.

Logan, William. "Angels, Voyeurs, and Cooks." *New York Times Book Review* (15 November 1992): 15.

Logan offers a mixed assessment of *A Dream of Mind.*

McKee, Louis. Review of *A Dream of Mind,* by C. K. Williams. *Library Journal* (1 May 1992): 86.

McKee offers a positive assessment of *A Dream of Mind,* and calls Williams "one of the few truly original voices of this generation."

Muratori, Fred. Review of *Love about Love,* by C. K. Williams. *Library Journal* (1 January 2001): 112.

Muratori offers a mixed assessment of *Love about Love,* comparing Williams's poetry to the confessional poets of the 1960s.

Olson, Ray. Review of *The Vigil,* by C. K. Williams. *Booklist* (1 December 1996): 640.

Olson offers a positive assessment of *The Vigil.*

Ratner, Rochelle. Review of *Repair,* by C. K. Williams. *Library Journal* (1 June 1999): 120.

Ratner offers a brief positive assessment of *Repair,* and states that the short-lined poems in the collection may be "his finest works to date."

"Sentiment without Sentimentality." *Economist* (6 September 1997): 19.

The critic offers a positive assessment of *The Vigil.*

"Whose Voice Is It Anyway?" *Economist* (18 March 2000): 14.

The critic offers a positive assessment of *Repair.*

Williamson, Alan. "Poems Including Politics." *American Poetry Review* 23, No. 3 (May–June 1994): 17–20.

Williamson discusses problematic aspects of American protest poetry and presents Williams's poem "Tar" as an exemplar of the genre for its evocation of personal and political experience.

Woods, Frances. Review of *A Dream of Mind,* by C. K. Williams. *Booklist* (15 June 1992): 1803.

Woods offers a positive evaluation of *A Dream of Mind.*

Additional coverage of Williams's life and career is contained in the following sources published by the Gale Group: *Contemporary Authors,* **Vols. 37–40R;** *Contemporary Authors Autobiography Series,* **Vol. 26;** *Contemporary Authors New Revision Series,* **Vol. 57;** *Contemporary Poets; Dictionary of Literary Biography,* **Vol. 5;** *DISCovering Authors Module: Poets;* **and** *Literature Resource Center.*

How to Use This Index

The main references

Calvino, Italo
1923-1985 .... CLC 5, 8, 11, 22, 33, 39,
73; SSC 3

list all author entries in the following Gale Literary Criticism series:

BLC = *Black Literature Criticism*
CLC = *Contemporary Literary Criticism*
CLR = *Children's Literature Review*
CMLC = *Classical and Medieval Literature Criticism*
DA = *DISCovering Authors*
DAB = *DISCovering Authors: British*
DAC = *DISCovering Authors: Canadian*
DAM = *DISCovering Authors: Modules*
    DRAM: *Dramatists Module;* **MST:** *Most-Studied Authors Module;*
    MULT: *Multicultural Authors Module;* **NOV:** *Novelists Module;*
    POET: *Poets Module;* **POP:** *Popular Fiction and Genre Authors Module*
DC = *Drama Criticism*
HLC = *Hispanic Literature Criticism*
LC = *Literature Criticism from 1400 to 1800*
NCLC = *Nineteenth-Century Literature Criticism*
NNAL = *Native North American Literature*
PC = *Poetry Criticism*
SSC = *Short Story Criticism*
TCLC = *Twentieth-Century Literary Criticism*
WLC = *World Literature Criticism, 1500 to the Present*

The cross-references

See also CANR 23; CA 85-88;
obituary CA116

list all author entries in the following Gale biographical and literary sources:

AAYA = *Authors & Artists for Young Adults*
AITN = *Authors in the News*
BEST = *Bestsellers*
BW = *Black Writers*
CA = *Contemporary Authors*
CAAS = *Contemporary Authors Autobiography Series*
CABS = *Contemporary Authors Bibliographical Series*
CANR = *Contemporary Authors New Revision Series*
CAP = *Contemporary Authors Permanent Series*
CDALB = *Concise Dictionary of American Literary Biography*
CDBLB = *Concise Dictionary of British Literary Biography*
DLB = *Dictionary of Literary Biography*
DLBD = *Dictionary of Literary Biography Documentary Series*
DLBY = *Dictionary of Literary Biography Yearbook*
HW = *Hispanic Writers*
JRDA = *Junior DISCovering Authors*
MAICYA = *Major Authors and Illustrators for Children and Young Adults*
MTCW = *Major 20th-Century Writers*
SAAS = *Something about the Author Autobiography Series*
SATA = *Something about the Author*
YABC = *Yesterday's Authors of Books for Children*

Literary Criticism Series
Cumulative Author Index

20/1631
See Upward, Allen

A/C Cross
See Lawrence, T(homas) E(dward)

Abasiyanik, Sait Faik 1906-1954
See Sait Faik
See also CA 123

Abbey, Edward 1927-1989 .... **CLC 36, 59**
See also CA 45-48; 128; CANR 2, 41; DA3; MTCW 2; TCWW 2

Abbott, Lee K(ittredge) 1947- .... **CLC 48**
See also CA 124; CANR 51, 101; DLB 130

Abe, Kobo 1924-1993 ...... **CLC 8, 22, 53, 81; DAM NOV**
See also CA 65-68; 140; CANR 24, 60; DLB 182; MJW; MTCW 1, 2; SFW

Abelard, Peter c. 1079-c. 1142 ...... **CMLC 11**
See also DLB 115, 208

Abell, Kjeld 1901-1961 .... **CLC 15**
See also CA 191; 111; DLB 214

Abish, Walter 1931- .... **CLC 22; SSC 44**
See also CA 101; CANR 37; CN; DLB 130, 227

Abrahams, Peter (Henry) 1919- .... **CLC 4**
See also BW 1; CA 57-60; CANR 26; CN; DLB 117, 225; MTCW 1, 2; RGEL; WLIT 2

Abrams, M(eyer) H(oward) 1912- ... **CLC 24**
See also CA 57-60; CANR 13, 33; DLB 67

Abse, Dannie 1923- .... **CLC 7, 29; DAB; DAM POET**
See also CA 53-56; CAAS 1; CANR 4, 46, 74; CBD; CP; DLB 27; MTCW 1

Abutsu 1222(?)-1283 .... **CMLC 46**
See also DLB 203

Achebe, (Albert) Chinua(lumogu) 1930- ...... **CLC 1, 3, 5, 7, 11, 26, 51, 75, 127; BLC 1; DA; DAB; DAC; DAM MST, MULT, NOV; WLC**
See also AAYA 15; AFW; BPFB 1; BW 2, 3; CA 1-4R; CANR 6, 26, 47; CLR 20; CN; CP; CWRI; DA3; DLB 117; DNFS; EXPN; EXPS; LAIT 2; MAICYA; MTCW 1, 2; NFS 2; RGEL; RGSF; SATA 38, 40; SATA-Brief 38; SSFS 3; WLIT 2

Acker, Kathy 1948-1997 .... **CLC 45, 111**
See also CA 117; 122; 162; CANR 55; CN

Ackroyd, Peter 1949- .... **CLC 34, 52, 140**
See also BRWS 6; CA 123; 127; CANR 51, 74, 99; CN; DLB 155, 231; HGG; INT 127; MTCW 1; RHW

Acorn, Milton 1923-1986 .... **CLC 15; DAC**
See also CA 103; CCA 1; DLB 53; INT 103

Adamov, Arthur 1908-1970 .... **CLC 4, 25; DAM DRAM**
See also CA 17-18; 25-28R; CAP 2; GFL 1789 to the Present; MTCW 1; RGWL

Adams, Alice (Boyd) 1926-1999 .. **CLC 6, 13, 46; SSC 24**
See also CA 81-84; 179; CANR 26, 53, 75, 88; CN; CSW; DLB 234; DLBY 86; INT CANR-26; MTCW 1, 2

Adams, Andy 1859-1935 .... **TCLC 56**
See also TCWW 2; YABC 1

Adams, Brooks 1848-1927 .... **TCLC 80**
See also CA 123; DLB 47

Adams, Douglas (Noel) 1952-2001 .. **CLC 27, 60; DAM POP**
See also AAYA 4, 33; BEST 89:3; CA 106; CANR 34, 64; CPW; DA3; DLBY 83; JRDA; MTCW 1; NFS 7; SATA 116; SFW

Adams, Francis 1862-1893 .... **NCLC 33**

Adams, Henry (Brooks) 1838-1918 .... **TCLC 4, 52; DA; DAB; DAC; DAM MST**
See also AMW; CA 104; 133; CANR 77; DLB 12, 47, 189; MTCW 1; NCFS 1

Adams, Richard (George) 1920- ... **CLC 4, 5, 18; DAM NOV**
See also AAYA 16; AITN 1, 2; BPFB 1; BYA 5; CA 49-52; CANR 3, 35; CLR 20; CN; FANT; JRDA; LAIT 5; MAICYA; MTCW 1, 2; NFS 11; SATA 7, 69; YAW

Adamson, Joy(-Friederike Victoria) 1910-1980 .... **CLC 17**
See also CA 69-72; 93-96; CANR 22; MTCW 1; SATA 11; SATA-Obit 22

Adcock, Fleur 1934- .... **CLC 41**
See also CA 25-28R, 182; CAAE 182; CAAS 23; CANR 11, 34, 69, 101; CP; CWP; DLB 40; FW

Addams, Charles (Samuel) 1912-1988 .... **CLC 30**
See also CA 61-64; 126; CANR 12, 79

Addams, Jane 1860-1945 .... **TCLC 76**
See also AMWS 1; FW

Addison, Joseph 1672-1719 .... **LC 18**
See also CDBLB 1660-1789; DLB 101; RGEL; WLIT 3

Adler, Alfred (F.) 1870-1937 .... **TCLC 61**
See also CA 119; 159

Adler, C(arole) S(chwerdtfeger) 1932- .... **CLC 35**
See also AAYA 4, 41; CA 89-92; CANR 19, 40, 101; JRDA; MAICYA; SAAS 15; SATA 26, 63, 102; YAW

Adler, Renata 1938- .... **CLC 8, 31**
See also CA 49-52; CANR 95; CN; MTCW 1

Adorno, Theodor W(iesengrund) 1903-1969 .... **TCLC 111**
See also CA 89-92; 25-28R; CANR 89; DLB 242

Ady, Endre 1877-1919 .... **TCLC 11**
See also CA 107

A.E. .... **TCLC 3, 10**
See also Russell, George William

Aelfric c. 955-c. 1010 .... **CMLC 46**
See also DLB 146

Aeschines c. 390B.C.-c. 320B.C. .... **CMLC 47**
See also DLB 176

Aeschylus 525(?)B.C.-456(?)B.C. .. **CMLC 11; DA; DAB; DAC; DAM DRAM, MST; DC 8; WLCS**
See also DFS 5, 10; DLB 176; RGWL

Aesop 620(?)B.C.-560(?)B.C. .... **CMLC 24**
See also CLR 14; MAICYA; SATA 64

Affable Hawk
See MacCarthy, Sir (Charles Otto) Desmond

Africa, Ben
See Bosman, Herman Charles

Afton, Effie
See Harper, Frances Ellen Watkins

Agapida, Fray Antonio
See Irving, Washington

Agee, James (Rufus) 1909-1955 ...... **TCLC 1, 19; DAM NOV**
See also AITN 1; AMW; CA 108; 148; CDALB 1941-1968; DLB 2, 26, 152; LAIT 3; MTCW 1; RGAL

Aghill, Gordon
See Silverberg, Robert

Agnon, S(hmuel) Y(osef Halevi) 1888-1970 .... **CLC 4, 8, 14; SSC 30**
See also CA 17-18; CANR 60; CAP 2; MTCW 1, 2; RGSF; RGWL

Agrippa von Nettesheim, Henry Cornelius 1486-1535 .... **LC 27**

Aguilera Malta, Demetrio 1909-1981
See also CA 111; 124; CANR 87; DAM MULT, NOV; DLB 145; HLCS 1; HW 1

Agustini, Delmira 1886-1914
See also CA 166; HLCS 1; HW 1, 2

Aherne, Owen
See Cassill, R(onald) V(erlin)

Ai 1947- .... **CLC 4, 14, 69**
See also CA 85-88; CAAS 13; CANR 70; DLB 120

Aickman, Robert (Fordyce) 1914-1981 .... **CLC 57**
See also CA 5-8R; CANR 3, 72, 100; HGG; SUFW

Aiken, Conrad (Potter) 1889-1973 .... **CLC 1, 3, 5, 10, 52; DAM NOV, POET; PC 26; SSC 9**
See also AMW; CA 5-8R; 45-48; CANR 4, 60; CDALB 1929-1941; DLB 9, 45, 102; EXPS; HGG; MTCW 1, 2; RGAL; RGSF; SATA 3, 30; SSFS 8

Aiken, Joan (Delano) 1924- .... **CLC 35**
See also AAYA 1, 25; CA 9-12R, 182; CAAE 182; CANR 4, 23, 34, 64; CLR 1, 19; DLB 161; FANT; HGG; JRDA; MAI-

CYA; MTCW 1; RHW; SAAS 1; SATA 2, 30, 73; SATA-Essay 109; WYA; YAW

Ainsworth, William Harrison 1805-1882 .... **NCLC 13**
See also DLB 21; HGG; RGEL; SATA 24

Aitmatov, Chingiz (Torekulovich) 1928- .... **CLC 71**
See also CA 103; CANR 38; MTCW 1; RGSF; SATA 56

Akers, Floyd
See Baum, L(yman) Frank

Akhmadulina, Bella Akhatovna 1937- .... **CLC 53; DAM POET**
See also CA 65-68; CWP; CWW 2

Akhmatova, Anna 1888-1966 ..... **CLC 11, 25, 64, 126; DAM POET; PC 2**
See also CA 19-20; 25-28R; CANR 35; CAP 1; DA3; MTCW 1, 2; RGWL

Aksakov, Sergei Timofeyvich 1791-1859 .... **NCLC 2**
See also DLB 198

Aksenov, Vassily
See Aksyonov, Vassily (Pavlovich)

Akst, Daniel 1956- .... **CLC 109**
See also CA 161

Aksyonov, Vassily (Pavlovich) 1932- .... **CLC 22, 37, 101**
See also CA 53-56; CANR 12, 48, 77; CWW 2

Akutagawa Ryunosuke 1892-1927 .... **TCLC 16; SSC 44**
See also CA 117; 154; DLB 180; MJW; RGSF; RGWL

Alain 1868-1951 .... **TCLC 41**
See also CA 163; GFL 1789 to the Present

Alain-Fournier .... **TCLC 6**
See also Fournier, Henri Alban
See also DLB 65; GFL 1789 to the Present; RGWL

Alarcon, Pedro Antonio de 1833-1891 .... **NCLC 1**

Alas (y Urena), Leopoldo (Enrique Garcia) 1852-1901 .... **TCLC 29**
See also CA 113; 131; HW 1; RGSF

Albee, Edward (Franklin III) 1928- . **CLC 1, 2, 3, 5, 9, 11, 13, 25, 53, 86, 113; DA; DAB; DAC; DAM DRAM, MST; DC 11; WLC**
See also AITN 1; AMW; CA 5-8R; CABS 3; CAD; CANR 8, 54, 74; CD; CDALB 1941-1968; DA3; DFS 2, 3, 8, 10, 13; DLB 7; INT CANR-8; LAIT 4; MTCW 1, 2; RGAL; TUS

Alberti, Rafael 1902-1999 .... **CLC 7**
See also CA 85-88; 185; CANR 81; DLB 108; HW 2; RGWL

Albert the Great 1193(?)-1280 ...... **CMLC 16**
See also DLB 115

Alcala-Galiano, Juan Valera y
See Valera y Alcala-Galiano, Juan

Alcayaga, Lucila Godoy
See Godoy Alcayaga, Lucila

Alcott, Amos Bronson 1799-1888 .... **NCLC 1**
See also DLB 1, 223

Alcott, Louisa May 1832-1888 . **NCLC 6, 58, 83; DA; DAB; DAC; DAM MST, NOV; SSC 27; WLC**
See also AAYA 20; AMWS 1; BPFB 1; BYA 2; CDALB 1865-1917; CLR 1, 38; DA3; DLB 1, 42, 79, 223, 239, 242; DLBD 14; FW; JRDA; LAIT 2; MAI-CYA; NFS 12; RGAL; SATA 100; YABC 1; YAW

Aldanov, M. A.
See Aldanov, Mark (Alexandrovich)

Aldanov, Mark (Alexandrovich) 1886(?)-1957 .... **TCLC 23**
See also CA 118; 181

Aldington, Richard 1892-1962 .... **CLC 49**
See also CA 85-88; CANR 45; DLB 20, 36, 100, 149; RGEL

Aldiss, Brian W(ilson) 1925- . **CLC 5, 14, 40; DAM NOV; SSC 36**
See also CA 5-8R; CAAE 190; CAAS 2; CANR 5, 28, 64; CN; DLB 14; MTCW 1, 2; SATA 34; SFW

Alegria, Claribel 1924- .... **CLC 75; DAM MULT; HLCS 1; PC 26**
See also CA 131; CAAS 15; CANR 66, 94; CWW 2; DLB 145; HW 1; MTCW 1

Alegria, Fernando 1918- .... **CLC 57**
See also CA 9-12R; CANR 5, 32, 72; HW 1, 2

Aleichem, Sholom .... **TCLC 1, 35; SSC 33**
See also Rabinovitch, Sholem

Aleixandre, Vicente 1898-1984 ... **TCLC 113; HLCS 1**
See also CANR 81; HW 2; RGWL

Alepoudelis, Odysseus
See Elytis, Odysseus
See also CWW 2

Aleshkovsky, Joseph 1929-
See Aleshkovsky, Yuz
See also CA 121; 128

Aleshkovsky, Yuz .... **CLC 44**
See also Aleshkovsky, Joseph

Alexander, Lloyd (Chudley) 1924- ... **CLC 35**
See also AAYA 1, 27; BPFB 1; BYA 5; CA 1-4R; CANR 1, 24, 38, 55; CLR 1, 5, 48; CWRI; DLB 52; FANT; JRDA; MAI-CYA; MAICYAS; MTCW 1; SAAS 19; SATA 3, 49, 81; SUFW; WYA; YAW

Alexander, Meena 1951- .... **CLC 121**
See also CA 115; CANR 38, 70; CP; CWP; FW

Alexander, Samuel 1859-1938 .... **TCLC 77**

Alexie, Sherman (Joseph, Jr.) 1966- .... **CLC 96; DAM MULT**
See also AAYA 28; CA 138; CANR 95; DA3; DLB 175, 206; MTCW 1; NNAL

Alfau, Felipe 1902-1999 .... **CLC 66**
See also CA 137

Alfieri, Vittorio 1749-1803 .... **NCLC 101**
See also RGWL

Alfred, Jean Gaston
See Ponge, Francis

Alger, Horatio, Jr. 1832-1899 .... **NCLC 8, 83**
See also DLB 42; LAIT 2; RGAL; SATA 16; TUS

Algren, Nelson 1909-1981 ..... **CLC 4, 10, 33; SSC 33**
See also BPFB 1; CA 13-16R; 103; CANR 20, 61; CDALB 1941-1968; DLB 9; DLBY 81, 82; MTCW 1, 2; RGAL; RGSF

Ali, Ahmed 1908-1998 .... **CLC 69**
See also CA 25-28R; CANR 15, 34

Alighieri, Dante
See Dante

Allan, John B.
See Westlake, Donald E(dwin)

Allan, Sidney
See Hartmann, Sadakichi

Allan, Sydney
See Hartmann, Sadakichi

Allard, Janet .... **CLC 59**

Allen, Edward 1948- .... **CLC 59**

Allen, Fred 1894-1956 .... **TCLC 87**

Allen, Paula Gunn 1939- .... **CLC 84; DAM MULT**
See also AMWS 4; CA 112; 143; CANR 63; CWP; DA3; DLB 175; FW; MTCW 1; NNAL; RGAL

Allen, Roland
See Ayckbourn, Alan

Allen, Sarah A.
See Hopkins, Pauline Elizabeth

Allen, Sidney H.
See Hartmann, Sadakichi

Allen, Woody 1935- .... **CLC 16, 52; DAM POP**
See also AAYA 10; CA 33-36R; CANR 27, 38, 63; DLB 44; MTCW 1

Allende, Isabel 1942- . **CLC 39, 57, 97; DAM MULT, NOV; HLC 1; WLCS**
See also AAYA 18; CA 125; 130; CANR 51, 74; CWW 2; DA3; DLB 145; DNFS; FW; HW 1, 2; INT 130; LAIT 5; MTCW 1, 2; NCFS 1; NFS 6; RGSF; SSFS 11; WLIT 1

Alleyn, Ellen
See Rossetti, Christina (Georgina)

Alleyne, Carla D. .... **CLC 65**

Allingham, Margery (Louise) 1904-1966 .... **CLC 19**
See also CA 5-8R; 25-28R; CANR 4, 58; CMW; DLB 77; MSW; MTCW 1, 2

Allingham, William 1824-1889 ...... **NCLC 25**
See also DLB 35; RGEL

Allison, Dorothy E. 1949- .... **CLC 78**
See also CA 140; CANR 66; CSW; DA3; FW; MTCW 1; NFS 11; RGAL

Alloula, Malek .... **CLC 65**

Allston, Washington 1779-1843 .... **NCLC 2**
See also DLB 1, 235

Almedingen, E. M. .... **CLC 12**
See also Almedingen, Martha Edith von
See also SATA 3

Almedingen, Martha Edith von 1898-1971
See Almedingen, E. M.
See also CA 1-4R; CANR 1

Almodovar, Pedro 1949(?)- .... **CLC 114; HLCS 1**
See also CA 133; CANR 72; HW 2

Almqvist, Carl Jonas Love 1793-1866 .... **NCLC 42**

Alonso, Damaso 1898-1990 .... **CLC 14**
See also CA 110; 131; 130; CANR 72; DLB 108; HW 1, 2

Alov
See Gogol, Nikolai (Vasilyevich)

Alta 1942- .... **CLC 19**
See also CA 57-60

Alter, Robert B(ernard) 1935- .... **CLC 34**
See also CA 49-52; CANR 1, 47, 100

Alther, Lisa 1944- .... **CLC 7, 41**
See also BPFB 1; CA 65-68; CAAS 30; CANR 12, 30, 51; CN; CSW; GLL 2; MTCW 1

Althusser, L.
See Althusser, Louis

Althusser, Louis 1918-1990 .... **CLC 106**
See also CA 131; 132; DLB 242

Altman, Robert 1925- .... **CLC 16, 116**
See also CA 73-76; CANR 43

Alurista
See Urista, Alberto H.
See also DLB 82; HLCS 1

Alvarez, A(lfred) 1929- .... **CLC 5, 13**
See also CA 1-4R; CANR 3, 33, 63, 101; CN; CP; DLB 14, 40

Alvarez, Alejandro Rodriguez 1903-1965
See Casona, Alejandro
See also CA 131; 93-96; HW 1

Alvarez, Julia 1950- .... **CLC 93; HLCS 1**
See also AAYA 25; AMWS 7; CA 147; CANR 69, 101; DA3; MTCW 1; NFS 5, 9; WLIT 1

Alvaro, Corrado 1896-1956 .... **TCLC 60**
See also CA 163

Amado, Jorge 1912-2001 ... **CLC 13, 40, 106; DAM MULT, NOV; HLC 1**
See also CA 77-80; CANR 35, 74; DLB 113; HW 2; MTCW 1, 2; RGWL; WLIT 1

Ambler, Eric 1909-1998 .... **CLC 4, 6, 9**
See also BRWS 4; CA 9-12R; 171; CANR 7, 38, 74; CMW; CN; DLB 77; MTCW 1, 2

Ambrose, Stephen E(dward) 1936- .... **CLC 145**
See also CA 1-4R; CANR 3, 43, 57, 83; NCFS 2; SATA 40

Amichai, Yehuda 1924-2000 .. **CLC 9, 22, 57, 116**
See also CA 85-88; 189; CANR 46, 60, 99; CWW 2; MTCW 1

Amichai, Yehudah
See Amichai, Yehuda

Amiel, Henri Frederic 1821-1881 .... **NCLC 4**

Amis, Kingsley (William) 1922-1995 ...... **CLC 1, 2, 3, 5, 8, 13, 40, 44, 129; DA; DAB; DAC; DAM MST, NOV**
See also AITN 2; BPFB 1; BRWS 2; CA 9-12R; 150; CANR 8, 28, 54; CDBLB 1945-1960; CN; CP; DA3; DLB 15, 27, 100, 139; DLBY 96; HGG; INT CANR-8; MTCW 1, 2; RGEL; RGSF; SFW

Amis, Martin (Louis) 1949- .... **CLC 4, 9, 38, 62, 101**
See also BEST 90:3; BRWS 4; CA 65-68; CANR 8, 27, 54, 73, 95; CN; DA3; DLB 14, 194; INT CANR-27; MTCW 1

Ammons, A(rchie) R(andolph) 1926-2001 ...... **CLC 2, 3, 5, 8, 9, 25, 57, 108; DAM POET; PC 16**
See also AITN 1; CA 9-12R; 193; CANR 6, 36, 51, 73; CP; CSW; DLB 5, 165; MTCW 1, 2; RGAL

Amo, Tauraatua i
See Adams, Henry (Brooks)

Amory, Thomas 1691(?)-1788 .... **LC 48**

Anand, Mulk Raj 1905- .. **CLC 23, 93; DAM NOV**
See also CA 65-68; CANR 32, 64; CN; MTCW 1, 2; RGSF

Anatol
See Schnitzler, Arthur

Anaximander c. 611B.C.-c. 546B.C. .... **CMLC 22**

Anaya, Rudolfo A(lfonso) 1937- ...... **CLC 23, 148; DAM MULT, NOV; HLC 1**
See also AAYA 20; BYA 13; CA 45-48; CAAS 4; CANR 1, 32, 51; CN; DLB 82, 206; HW 1; LAIT 4; MTCW 1, 2; NFS 12; RGAL; RGSF; WLIT 1

Andersen, Hans Christian 1805-1875 .... **NCLC 7, 79; DA; DAB; DAC; DAM MST, POP; SSC 6; WLC**
See also CLR 6; DA3; MAICYA; RGSF; RGWL; SATA 100; YABC 1

Anderson, C. Farley
See Mencken, H(enry) L(ouis); Nathan, George Jean

Anderson, Jessica (Margaret) Queale 1916- .... **CLC 37**
See also CA 9-12R; CANR 4, 62; CN

Anderson, Jon (Victor) 1940- . **CLC 9; DAM POET**
See also CA 25-28R; CANR 20

Anderson, Lindsay (Gordon) 1923-1994 .... **CLC 20**
See also CA 125; 128; 146; CANR 77

Anderson, Maxwell 1888-1959 .... **TCLC 2; DAM DRAM**
See also CA 105; 152; DLB 7, 228; MTCW 2; RGAL

Anderson, Poul (William) 1926-2001 .... **CLC 15**
See also AAYA 5, 34; BPFB 1; BYA 6; CA 1-4R, 181; CAAE 181; CAAS 2; CANR 2, 15, 34, 64; CLR 58; DLB 8; FANT; INT CANR-15; MTCW 1, 2; SATA 90; SATA-Brief 39; SATA-Essay 106; SCFW 2; SFW; SUFW

Anderson, Robert (Woodruff) 1917- .... **CLC 23; DAM DRAM**
See also AITN 1; CA 21-24R; CANR 32; DLB 7

Anderson, Roberta Joan
See Mitchell, Joni

Anderson, Sherwood 1876-1941 ..... **TCLC 1, 10, 24; DA; DAB; DAC; DAM MST, NOV; SSC 1, 46; WLC**
See also AAYA 30; AMW; BPFB 1; CA 104; 121; CANR 61; CDALB 1917-1929; DA3; DLB 4, 9, 86; DLBD 1; EXPS; GLL 2; MTCW 1, 2; NFS 4; RGAL; RGSF; SSFS 4, 10, 11

Andier, Pierre
See Desnos, Robert

Andouard
See Giraudoux, Jean(-Hippolyte)

Andrade, Carlos Drummond de ..... **CLC 18**
See Drummond de Andrade, Carlos
See also RGWL

Andrade, Mario de 1893-1945 .... **TCLC 43**
See also RGWL; WLIT 1

Andreae, Johann V(alentin) 1586-1654 .... **LC 32**
See also DLB 164

Andreas Capellanus fl. c. 1185- .... **CMLC 45**
See also DLB 208

Andreas-Salome, Lou 1861-1937 ... **TCLC 56**
See also CA 178; DLB 66

Andress, Lesley
See Sanders, Lawrence

Andrewes, Lancelot 1555-1626 .... **LC 5**
See also DLB 151, 172

Andrews, Cicily Fairfield
See West, Rebecca

Andrews, Elton V.
See Pohl, Frederik

Andreyev, Leonid (Nikolaevich) 1871-1919 .... **TCLC 3**
See also CA 104; 185

Andric, Ivo 1892-1975 .... **CLC 8; SSC 36**
See also CA 81-84; 57-60; CANR 43, 60; DLB 147; MTCW 1; RGSF; RGWL

Androvar
See Prado (Calvo), Pedro

Angelique, Pierre
See Bataille, Georges

Angell, Roger 1920- .... **CLC 26**
See also CA 57-60; CANR 13, 44, 70; DLB 171, 185

Angelou, Maya 1928- .... **CLC 12, 35, 64, 77; BLC 1; DA; DAB; DAC; DAM MST, MULT, POET, POP; PC 32; WLCS**
See also AAYA 7, 20; AMWS 4; BPFB 1; BW 2, 3; BYA 2; CA 65-68; CANR 19, 42, 65; CDALBS; CLR 53; CP; CPW; CSW; CWP; DA3; DLB 38; EXPN; EXPP; LAIT 4; MTCW 1, 2; NCFS 2; NFS 2; PFS 2, 3; RGAL; SATA 49; YAW

Anna Comnena 1083-1153 .... **CMLC 25**

Annensky, Innokenty (Fyodorovich) 1856-1909 .... **TCLC 14**
See also CA 110; 155

Annunzio, Gabriele d'
See D'Annunzio, Gabriele

Anodos
See Coleridge, Mary E(lizabeth)

Anon, Charles Robert
See Pessoa, Fernando (Antonio Nogueira)

Anouilh, Jean (Marie Lucien Pierre) 1910-1987 .... **CLC 1, 3, 8, 13, 40, 50; DAM DRAM; DC 8**
See also CA 17-20R; 123; CANR 32; DFS 9, 10; EW; GFL 1789 to the Present; MTCW 1, 2; RGWL

Anthony, Florence
See Ai

Anthony, John
See Ciardi, John (Anthony)

Anthony, Peter
See Shaffer, Anthony (Joshua); Shaffer, Peter (Levin)

Anthony, Piers 1934- .... **CLC 35; DAM POP**
See also AAYA 11; BYA 7; CA 21-24R; CANR 28, 56, 73; CPW; DLB 8; FANT; MTCW 1, 2; SAAS 22; SATA 84; SFW; YAW

Anthony, Susan B(rownell) 1820-1906 .... **TCLC 84**
See also FW

Antoine, Marc
See Proust, (Valentin-Louis-George-Eugene-)Marcel

Antoninus, Brother
See Everson, William (Oliver)

Antoninus, Marcus Aurelius 121-180 .... **CMLC 45**
See also AW

Antonioni, Michelangelo 1912- .... **CLC 20, 144**
See also CA 73-76; CANR 45, 77

Antschel, Paul 1920-1970
See Celan, Paul
See also CA 85-88; CANR 33, 61; MTCW 1

Anwar, Chairil 1922-1949 .... **TCLC 22**
See also CA 121

Anzaldua, Gloria (Evanjelina) 1942-
See also CA 175; CSW; CWP; DLB 122; FW; HLCS 1; RGAL

Apess, William 1798-1839(?) .... **NCLC 73; DAM MULT**
See also DLB 175; NNAL

Apollinaire, Guillaume 1880-1918 .. **TCLC 3, 8, 51; DAM POET; PC 7**
See also CA 152; GFL 1789 to the Present; MTCW 1; RGWL; WP

Appelfeld, Aharon 1932- ... **CLC 23, 47; SSC 42**
See also CA 112; 133; CANR 86; CWW 2; RGSF

Apple, Max (Isaac) 1941- .... **CLC 9, 33**
See also CA 81-84; CANR 19, 54; DLB 130

Appleman, Philip (Dean) 1926- .... **CLC 51**
See also CA 13-16R; CAAS 18; CANR 6, 29, 56

Appleton, Lawrence
See Lovecraft, H(oward) P(hillips)

Apteryx
See Eliot, T(homas) S(tearns)

Apuleius, (Lucius Madaurensis) 125(?)-175(?) .... **CMLC 1**
See also AW; DLB 211; RGWL; SUFW

Aquin, Hubert 1929-1977 .... **CLC 15**
See also CA 105; DLB 53

Aquinas, Thomas 1224(?)-1274 ..... **CMLC 33**
See also DLB 115; EW

Aragon, Louis 1897-1982 .. **CLC 3, 22; DAM NOV, POET**
See also CA 69-72; 108; CANR 28, 71; DLB 72; GFL 1789 to the Present; GLL 2; MTCW 1, 2; RGWL

Arany, Janos 1817-1882 .... **NCLC 34**

Aranyos, Kakay 1847-1910
See Mikszath, Kalman

Arbuthnot, John 1667-1735 .... **LC 1**
See also DLB 101

Archer, Herbert Winslow
See Mencken, H(enry) L(ouis)

Archer, Jeffrey (Howard) 1940- ...... **CLC 28; DAM POP**
See also AAYA 16; BEST 89:3; BPFB 1; CA 77-80; CANR 22, 52, 95; CPW; DA3; INT CANR-22

Archer, Jules 1915- .... **CLC 12**
See also CA 9-12R; CANR 6, 69; SAAS 5; SATA 4, 85

Archer, Lee
See Ellison, Harlan (Jay)

Archilochus c. 7th cent. B.C.- .... **CMLC 44**
See also DLB 176

Arden, John 1930- .... **CLC 6, 13, 15; DAM DRAM**
See also BRWS 2; CA 13-16R; CAAS 4; CANR 31, 65, 67; CBD; CD; DFS 9; DLB 13; MTCW 1

Arenas, Reinaldo 1943-1990 . **CLC 41; DAM MULT; HLC 1**
See also CA 124; 128; 133; CANR 73; DLB 145; GLL 2; HW 1; MTCW 1; RGSF; WLIT 1

Arendt, Hannah 1906-1975 .... **CLC 66, 98**
See also CA 17-20R; 61-64; CANR 26, 60; DLB 242; MTCW 1, 2

Aretino, Pietro 1492-1556 .... **LC 12**
See also RGWL

Arghezi, Tudor .... **CLC 80**
See also Theodorescu, Ion N.
See also CA 167; DLB 220

Arguedas, Jose Maria 1911-1969 .... **CLC 10, 18; HLCS 1**
See also CA 89-92; CANR 73; DLB 113; HW 1; RGWL; WLIT 1

Argueta, Manlio 1936- .... **CLC 31**
See also CA 131; CANR 73; CWW 2; DLB 145; HW 1

Arias, Ron(ald Francis) 1941-
See also CA 131; CANR 81; DAM MULT; DLB 82; HLC 1; HW 1, 2; MTCW 2

Ariosto, Ludovico 1474-1533 .... **LC 6**
See also EW; RGWL

Aristides
See Epstein, Joseph

Aristophanes 450B.C.-385B.C. .... **CMLC 4; DA; DAB; DAC; DAM DRAM, MST; DC 2; WLCS**
See also DA3; DFS 10; DLB 176; RGWL

Aristotle 384B.C.-322B.C. ...... **CMLC 31; DA; DAB; DAC; DAM MST; WLCS**
See also DA3; DLB 176; RGEL

Arlt, Roberto (Godofredo Christophersen) 1900-1942 .... **TCLC 29; DAM MULT; HLC 1**
See also CA 123; 131; CANR 67; HW 1, 2; LAW

Armah, Ayi Kwei 1939- .... **CLC 5, 33, 136; BLC 1; DAM MULT; POET**
See also BW 1; CA 61-64; CANR 21, 64; CN; DLB 117; MTCW 1; WLIT 2

Armatrading, Joan 1950- .... **CLC 17**
See also CA 114; 186

Arnette, Robert
See Silverberg, Robert

Arnim, Achim von (Ludwig Joachim von Arnim) 1781-1831 ..... **NCLC 5; SSC 29**
See also DLB 90

Arnim, Bettina von 1785-1859 .... **NCLC 38**
See also DLB 90; RGWL

Arnold, Matthew 1822-1888 ..... **NCLC 6, 29, 89; DA; DAB; DAC; DAM MST, POET; PC 5; WLC**
See also CDBLB 1832-1890; DLB 32, 57; EXPP; PAB; PFS 2; WP

Arnold, Thomas 1795-1842 .... **NCLC 18**
See also DLB 55

Arnow, Harriette (Louisa) Simpson 1908-1986 .... **CLC 2, 7, 18**
See also BPFB 1; CA 9-12R; 118; CANR 14; DLB 6; FW; MTCW 1, 2; RHW; SATA 42; SATA-Obit 47

Arouet, Francois-Marie
See Voltaire

Arp, Hans
See Arp, Jean

Arp, Jean 1887-1966 .... **CLC 5**
See also CA 81-84; 25-28R; CANR 42, 77

Arrabal
See Arrabal, Fernando

Arrabal, Fernando 1932- ... **CLC 2, 9, 18, 58**
See also CA 9-12R; CANR 15

Arreola, Juan Jose 1918- ... **CLC 147,; DAM MULT; HLC 1; SSC 38**
See also CA 113; 131; CANR 81; DLB 113; DNFS; HW 1, 2; RGSF

Arrian c. 89(?)-c. 155(?) .... **CMLC 43**
See also DLB 176

Arrick, Fran .... **CLC 30**
See also Gaberman, Judie Angell
See also BYA 6

Artaud, Antonin (Marie Joseph) 1896-1948 . **TCLC 3, 36; DAM DRAM; DC 14**
See also CA 104; 149; DA3; EW; GFL 1789 to the Present; MTCW 1; RGWL

Arthur, Ruth M(abel) 1905-1979 ..... **CLC 12**
See also CA 9-12R; 85-88; CANR 4; CWRI; SATA 7, 26

Artsybashev, Mikhail (Petrovich) 1878-1927 .... **TCLC 31**
See also CA 170

Arundel, Honor (Morfydd) 1919-1973 .... **CLC 17**
See also CA 21-22; 41-44R; CAP 2; CLR 35; CWRI; SATA 4; SATA-Obit 24

Arzner, Dorothy 1900-1979 .... **CLC 98**

Asch, Sholem 1880-1957 .... **TCLC 3**
See also CA 105; GLL 2

Ash, Shalom
See Asch, Sholem

Ashbery, John (Lawrence) 1927- .. **CLC 2, 3, 4, 6, 9, 13, 15, 25, 41, 77, 125; DAM POET; PC 26**
See also Berry, Jonas
See also AMWS 3; CA 5-8R; CANR 9, 37, 66; CP; DA3; DLB 5, 165; DLBY 81; INT CANR-9; MTCW 1, 2; PAB; PFS 11; RGAL; WP

Ashdown, Clifford
See Freeman, R(ichard) Austin

Ashe, Gordon
See Creasey, John

Ashton-Warner, Sylvia (Constance) 1908-1984 .... **CLC 19**
See also CA 69-72; 112; CANR 29; MTCW 1, 2

Asimov, Isaac 1920-1992 ..... **CLC 1, 3, 9, 19, 26, 76, 92; DAM POP**
See also AAYA 13; BEST 90:2; BPFB 1; BYA 4; CA 1-4R; 137; CANR 2, 19, 36, 60; CLR 12; CMW; CPW; DA3; DLB 8; DLBY 92; INT CANR-19; JRDA; LAIT 5; MAICYA; MTCW 1, 2; RGAL; SATA 1, 26, 74; SCFW 2; SFW; YAW

Assis, Joaquim Maria Machado de
See Machado de Assis, Joaquim Maria

Astell, Mary 1666-1731 .... **LC 68**
See also FW

Astley, Thea (Beatrice May) 1925- .. **CLC 41**
See also CA 65-68; CANR 11, 43, 78; CN

Aston, James
See White, T(erence) H(anbury)

Asturias, Miguel Angel 1899-1974 .... **CLC 3, 8, 13; DAM MULT, NOV; HLC 1**
See also CA 25-28; 49-52; CANR 32; CAP 2; DA3; DLB 113; HW 1; LAW; MTCW 1, 2; RGWL; WLIT 1

Atares, Carlos Saura
See Saura (Atares), Carlos

Atheling, William
See Pound, Ezra (Weston Loomis)

Atheling, William, Jr.
See Blish, James (Benjamin)

Atherton, Gertrude (Franklin Horn) 1857-1948 .... **TCLC 2**
See also CA 104; 155; DLB 9, 78, 186; HGG; RGAL; SUFW; TCWW 2

Atherton, Lucius
See Masters, Edgar Lee

Atkins, Jack
See Harris, Mark

Atkinson, Kate .... **CLC 99**
See also CA 166; CANR 101

Attaway, William (Alexander) 1911-1986 .... **CLC 92; BLC 1; DAM MULT**
See also BW 2, 3; CA 143; CANR 82; DLB 76

Atticus
See Fleming, Ian (Lancaster); Wilson, (Thomas) Woodrow

Atwood, Margaret (Eleanor) 1939- ... **CLC 2, 3, 4, 8, 13, 15, 25, 44, 84, 135; DA; DAB; DAC; DAM MST, NOV, POET; PC 8; SSC 2, 46; WLC**
See also AAYA 12; BEST 89:2; BPFB 1; CA 49-52; CANR 3, 24, 33, 59, 95; CN; CP; CPW; CWP; DA3; DLB 53; EXPN; FW; INT CANR-24; LAIT 3; MTCW 1, 2; NFS 4, 12; PFS 7; RGSF; SATA 50; SSFS 3; YAW

Aubigny, Pierre d'
See Mencken, H(enry) L(ouis)

Aubin, Penelope 1685-1731(?) .... **LC 9**
See also DLB 39

Auchincloss, Louis (Stanton) 1917- .. **CLC 4, 6, 9, 18, 45; DAM NOV; SSC 22**
See also AMWS 4; CA 1-4R; CANR 6, 29, 55, 87; CN; DLB 2; DLBY 80; INT CANR-29; MTCW 1; RGAL

Auden, W(ystan) H(ugh) 1907-1973 . **CLC 1, 2, 3, 4, 6, 9, 11, 14, 43, 123; DA; DAB; DAC; DAM DRAM, MST, POET; PC 1; WLC**
See also AAYA 18; AMWS 2; BRW; CA 9-12R; 45-48; CANR 5, 61; CDBLB 1914-1945; DA3; DLB 10, 20; EXPP; MTCW 1, 2; PAB; PFS 1, 3, 4, 10; WP

Audiberti, Jacques 1900-1965 .... **CLC 38; DAM DRAM**
See also CA 25-28R

Audubon, John James 1785-1851 . **NCLC 47**

Auel, Jean M(arie) 1936- .... **CLC 31, 107; DAM POP**
See also AAYA 7; BEST 90:4; BPFB 1; CA 103; CANR 21, 64; CPW; DA3; INT CANR-21; NFS 11; RHW; SATA 91

Auerbach, Erich 1892-1957 .... **TCLC 43**
See also CA 118; 155

Augier, Emile 1820-1889 .... **NCLC 31**
See also DLB 192; GFL 1789 to the Present

August, John
See De Voto, Bernard (Augustine)

Augustine, St. 354-430 .... **CMLC 6; DA; DAB; DAC; DAM MST; WLCS**
See also DA3; DLB 115; EW; RGWL

Aunt Belinda
See Braddon, Mary Elizabeth

Aurelius
See Bourne, Randolph S(illiman)
See also RGWL

Barbour, John c. 1316-1395 .... **CMLC 33**
See also DLB 146

Barbusse, Henri 1873-1935 .... **TCLC 5**
See also CA 105; 154; DLB 65; RGWL

Barclay, Bill
See Moorcock, Michael (John)

Barclay, William Ewert
See Moorcock, Michael (John)

Barea, Arturo 1897-1957 .... **TCLC 14**
See also CA 111

Barfoot, Joan 1946- .... **CLC 18**
See also CA 105

Barham, Richard Harris
1788-1845 .... **NCLC 77**
See also DLB 159

Baring, Maurice 1874-1945 .... **TCLC 8**
See also CA 105; 168; DLB 34; HGG

Baring-Gould, Sabine 1834-1924 ... **TCLC 88**
See also DLB 156, 190

Barker, Clive 1952- ...... **CLC 52; DAM POP**
See also AAYA 10; BEST 90:3; BPFB 1;
CA 121; 129; CANR 71; CPW; DA3;
HGG; INT 129; MTCW 1, 2

Barker, George Granville
1913-1991 .... **CLC 8, 48; DAM POET**
See also CA 9-12R; 135; CANR 7, 38; DLB
20; MTCW 1

Barker, Harley Granville
See Granville-Barker, Harley
See also DLB 10

Barker, Howard 1946- .... **CLC 37**
See also CA 102; CBD; CD; DLB 13, 233

Barker, Jane 1652-1732 .... **LC 42**

Barker, Pat(ricia) 1943- ...... **CLC 32, 94, 146**
See also BRWS 4; CA 117; 122; CANR 50,
101; CN; INT 122

Barlach, Ernst (Heinrich)
1870-1938 .... **TCLC 84**
See also CA 178; DLB 56, 118

Barlow, Joel 1754-1812 .... **NCLC 23**
See also AMWS 2; DLB 37; RGAL

Barnard, Mary (Ethel) 1909- .... **CLC 48**
See also CA 21-22; CAP 2

Barnes, Djuna 1892-1982 .... **CLC 3, 4, 8, 11,
29, 127; SSC 3**
See also Steptoe, Lydia
See also AMWS 3; CA 9-12R; 107; CAD;
CANR 16, 55; CWD; DLB 4, 9, 45; GLL
1; MTCW 1, 2; RGAL

Barnes, Julian (Patrick) 1946- .... **CLC 42,
141; DAB**
See also BRWS 4; CA 102; CANR 19, 54;
CN; DLB 194; DLBY 93; MTCW 1

Barnes, Peter 1931- .... **CLC 5, 56**
See also CA 65-68; CAAS 12; CANR 33,
34, 64; CBD; CD; DFS 6; DLB 13, 233;
MTCW 1

Barnes, William 1801-1886 .... **NCLC 75**
See also DLB 32

Baroja (y Nessi), Pio 1872-1956 ..... **TCLC 8;
HLC 1**
See also CA 104; EW

Baron, David
See Pinter, Harold

Baron Corvo
See Rolfe, Frederick (William Serafino
Austin Lewis Mary)

Barondess, Sue K(aufman)
1926-1977 .... **CLC 8**
See also Kaufman, Sue
See also CA 1-4R; 69-72; CANR 1

Baron de Teive
See Pessoa, Fernando (Antonio Nogueira)

Baroness Von S.
See Zangwill, Israel

Barres, (Auguste-)Maurice
1862-1923 .... **TCLC 47**
See also CA 164; DLB 123; GFL 1789 to
the Present

Barreto, Afonso Henrique de Lima
See Lima Barreto, Afonso Henrique de

Barrett, Andrea 1965- .... **CLC 150**
See also CA 156; CANR 92

Barrett, Michele .... **CLC 65**

Barrett, (Roger) Syd 1946- .... **CLC 35**

Barrett, William (Christopher)
1913-1992 .... **CLC 27**
See also CA 13-16R; 139; CANR 11, 67;
INT CANR-11

Barrie, J(ames) M(atthew)
1860-1937 .... **TCLC 2; DAB; DAM
DRAM**
See also BRWS 3; BYA 4; CA 104; 136;
CANR 77; CDBLB 1890-1914; CLR 16;
CWRI; DA3; DFS 7; DLB 10, 141, 156;
FANT; MAICYA; MTCW 1; SATA 100;
SUFW; WCH; WLIT 4; YABC 1

Barrington, Michael
See Moorcock, Michael (John)

Barrol, Grady
See Bograd, Larry

Barry, Mike
See Malzberg, Barry N(athaniel)

Barry, Philip 1896-1949 .... **TCLC 11**
See also CA 109; DFS 9; DLB 7, 228;
RGAL

Bart, Andre Schwarz
See Schwarz-Bart, Andre

Barth, John (Simmons) 1930- ... **CLC 1, 2, 3,
5, 7, 9, 10, 14, 27, 51, 89; DAM NOV;
SSC 10**
See also AITN 1, 2; AMW; BPFB 1; CA
1-4R; CABS 1; CANR 5, 23, 49, 64; CN;
DLB 2, 227; FANT; MTCW 1; RGAL;
RGSF; RHW; SSFS 6

Barthelme, Donald 1931-1989 ... **CLC 1, 2, 3,
5, 6, 8, 13, 23, 46, 59, 115; DAM NOV;
SSC 2**
See also AMWS 4; BPFB 1; CA 21-24R;
129; CANR 20, 58; DA3; DLB 2, 234;
DLBY 80, 89; FANT; MTCW 1, 2;
RGAL; RGSF; SATA 7; SATA-Obit 62;
SSFS 3

Barthelme, Frederick 1943- ...... **CLC 36, 117**
See also CA 114; 122; CANR 77; CN;
CSW; DLBY 85; INT 122

Barthes, Roland (Gerard)
1915-1980 .... **CLC 24, 83**
See also CA 130; 97-100; CANR 66; EW;
GFL 1789 to the Present; MTCW 1, 2

Barzun, Jacques (Martin) 1907- ..... **CLC 51,
145**
See also CA 61-64; CANR 22, 95

Bashevis, Isaac
See Singer, Isaac Bashevis

Bashkirtseff, Marie 1859-1884 .... **NCLC 27**

Basho, Matsuo
See Matsuo Basho
See also RGWL; WP

Basil of Caesaria c. 330-379 .... **CMLC 35**

Bass, Kingsley B., Jr.
See Bullins, Ed

Bass, Rick 1958- .... **CLC 79, 143**
See also CA 126; CANR 53, 93; CSW;
DLB 212

Bassani, Giorgio 1916-2000 .... **CLC 9**
See also CA 65-68; 190; CANR 33; CWW
2; DLB 128, 177; MTCW 1; RGWL

Bastian, Ann .... **CLC 70**

Bastos, Augusto (Antonio) Roa
See Roa Bastos, Augusto (Antonio)

Bataille, Georges 1897-1962 .... **CLC 29**
See also CA 101; 89-92

Bates, H(erbert) E(rnest)
1905-1974 . **CLC 46; DAB; DAM POP;
SSC 10**
See also CA 93-96; 45-48; CANR 34; DA3;
DLB 162, 191; EXPS; MTCW 1, 2;
RGSF; SSFS 7

Bauchart
See Camus, Albert

Baudelaire, Charles 1821-1867 . **NCLC 6, 29,
55; DA; DAB; DAC; DAM MST,
POET; PC 1; SSC 18; WLC**
See also DA3; GFL 1789 to the Present;
RGWL

Baudouin, Marcel
See Peguy, Charles Pierre

Baudouin, Pierre
See Peguy, Charles Pierre

Baudrillard, Jean 1929- .... **CLC 60**

Baum, L(yman) Frank 1856-1919 ... **TCLC 7**
See also CA 108; 133; CLR 15; DLB 22;
JRDA; MAICYA; MTCW 1, 2; SATA 18,
100

Baum, Louis F.
See Baum, L(yman) Frank

Baumbach, Jonathan 1933- .... **CLC 6, 23**
See also CA 13-16R; CAAS 5; CANR 12,
66; CN; DLBY 80; INT CANR-12;
MTCW 1

Bausch, Richard (Carl) 1945- .... **CLC 51**
See also AMWS 7; CA 101; CAAS 14;
CANR 43, 61, 87; CSW; DLB 130

Baxter, Charles (Morley) 1947- .... **CLC 45,
78; DAM POP**
See also CA 57-60; CANR 40, 64; CPW;
DLB 130; MTCW 2

Baxter, George Owen
See Faust, Frederick (Schiller)

Baxter, James K(eir) 1926-1972 .... **CLC 14**
See also CA 77-80

Baxter, John
See Hunt, E(verette) Howard, (Jr.)

Bayer, Sylvia
See Glassco, John

Baynton, Barbara 1857-1929 .... **TCLC 57**
See also DLB 230; RGSF

Beagle, Peter S(oyer) 1939- .... **CLC 7, 104**
See also BPFB 1; BYA 9; CA 9-12R;
CANR 4, 51, 73; DA3; DLBY 80; FANT;
INT CANR-4; MTCW 1; SATA 60;
SUFW; YAW

Bean, Normal
See Burroughs, Edgar Rice

Beard, Charles A(ustin)
1874-1948 .... **TCLC 15**
See also CA 115; 189; DLB 17; SATA 18

Beardsley, Aubrey 1872-1898 .... **NCLC 6**

Beattie, Ann 1947- ..... **CLC 8, 13, 18, 40, 63,
146; DAM NOV, POP; SSC 11**
See also AMWS 5; BEST 90:2; BPFB 1;
CA 81-84; CANR 53, 73; CN; CPW;
DA3; DLBY 82; MTCW 1, 2; RGAL;
RGSF; SSFS 9

Beattie, James 1735-1803 .... **NCLC 25**
See also DLB 109

Beauchamp, Kathleen Mansfield 1888-1923
See Mansfield, Katherine
See also CA 104; 134; DA; DA3; DAC;
DAM MST; MTCW 2

Beaumarchais, Pierre-Augustin Caron de
1732-1799 . **LC 61; DAM DRAM; DC 4**
See also GFL Beginnings to 1789; RGWL

Beaumont, Francis 1584(?)-1616 .... **LC 33;
DC 6**
See also CDBLB Before 1660; DLB 58, 121

Beauvoir, Simone (Lucie Ernestine Marie Bertrand) de 1908-1986 .... **CLC 1, 2, 4, 8, 14, 31, 44, 50, 71, 124; DA; DAB; DAC; DAM MST, NOV; SSC 35; WLC**
See also BPFB 1; CA 9-12R; 118; CANR 28, 61; DA3; DLB 72; DLBY 86; EW; FW; GFL 1789 to the Present; MTCW 1, 2; RGSF; RGWL

Becker, Carl (Lotus) 1873-1945 ..... **TCLC 63**
See also CA 157; DLB 17

Becker, Jurek 1937-1997 .... **CLC 7, 19**
See also CA 85-88; 157; CANR 60; CWW 2; DLB 75

Becker, Walter 1950- .... **CLC 26**

Beckett, Samuel (Barclay) 1906-1989 .. **CLC 1, 2, 3, 4, 6, 9, 10, 11, 14, 18, 29, 57, 59, 83; DA; DAB; DAC; DAM DRAM, MST, NOV; SSC 16; WLC**
See also BRWS 1; CA 5-8R; 130; CANR 33, 61; CBD; CDBLB 1945-1960; DA3; DFS 2, 7; DLB 13, 15, 233; DLBY 90; GFL 1789 to the Present; MTCW 1, 2; RGSF; RGWL; WLIT 4

Beckford, William 1760-1844 .... **NCLC 16**
See also BRW; DLB 39,213; HGG; SUFW

Beckman, Gunnel 1910- .... **CLC 26**
See also CA 33-36R; CANR 15; CLR 25; MAICYA; SAAS 9; SATA 6

Becque, Henri 1837-1899 .... **NCLC 3**
See also DLB 192; GFL 1789 to the Present

Becquer, Gustavo Adolfo 1836-1870
See also DAM MULT; HLCS 1

Beddoes, Thomas Lovell 1803-1849 .... **NCLC 3; DC 15**
See also DLB 96

Bede c. 673-735 .... **CMLC 20**
See also DLB 146

Bedford, Donald F.
See Fearing, Kenneth (Flexner)

Beecher, Catharine Esther 1800-1878 .... **NCLC 30**
See also DLB 1

Beecher, John 1904-1980 .... **CLC 6**
See also AITN 1; CA 5-8R; 105; CANR 8

Beer, Johann 1655-1700 .... **LC 5**
See also DLB 168

Beer, Patricia 1924- .... **CLC 58**
See also CA 61-64; 183; CANR 13, 46; CP; CWP; DLB 40; FW

Beerbohm, Max
See Beerbohm, (Henry) Max(imilian)
See also BRWS 2; FANT

Beerbohm, (Henry) Max(imilian) 1872-1956 .... **TCLC 1, 24**
See also CA 104; 154; CANR 79; DLB 34, 100

Beer-Hofmann, Richard 1866-1945 .... **TCLC 60**
See also CA 160; DLB 81

Beg, Shemus
See Stephens, James

Begiebing, Robert J(ohn) 1946- .... **CLC 70**
See also CA 122; CANR 40, 88

Behan, Brendan 1923-1964 ...... **CLC 1, 8, 11, 15, 79; DAM DRAM**
See also BRWS 2; CA 73-76; CANR 33; CBD; CDBLB 1945-1960; DFS 7; DLB 13, 233; MTCW 1, 2

Behn, Aphra 1640(?)-1689 .... **LC 1, 30, 42; DA; DAB; DAC; DAM DRAM, MST, NOV, POET; DC 4; PC 13; WLC**
See also BRWS 3; DA3; DLB 39, 80, 131; FW; WLIT 3

Behrman, S(amuel) N(athaniel) 1893-1973 .... **CLC 40**
See also CA 13-16; 45-48; CAD; CAP 1; DLB 7, 44; IDFW 3; RGAL

Belasco, David 1853-1931 .... **TCLC 3**
See also CA 104; 168; DLB 7; RGAL

Belcheva, Elisaveta 1893-1991 .... **CLC 10**
See also Bagryana, Elisaveta

Beldone, Phil "Cheech"
See Ellison, Harlan (Jay)

Beleno
See Azuela, Mariano

Belinski, Vissarion Grigoryevich 1811-1848 .... **NCLC 5**
See also DLB 198

Belitt, Ben 1911- .... **CLC 22**
See also CA 13-16R; CAAS 4; CANR 7, 77; CP; DLB 5

Bell, Gertrude (Margaret Lowthian) 1868-1926 .... **TCLC 67**
See also CA 167; DLB 174

Bell, J. Freeman
See Zangwill, Israel

Bell, James Madison 1826-1902 ... **TCLC 43; BLC 1; DAM MULT**
See also BW 1; CA 122; 124; DLB 50

Bell, Madison Smartt 1957- ...... **CLC 41, 102**
See also BPFB 1; CA 111, 183; CAAE 183; CANR 28, 54, 73; CN; CSW; MTCW 1

Bell, Marvin (Hartley) 1937- ...... **CLC 8, 31; DAM POET**
See also CA 21-24R; CAAS 14; CANR 59; CP; DLB 5; MTCW 1

Bell, W. L. D.
See Mencken, H(enry) L(ouis)

Bellamy, Atwood C.
See Mencken, H(enry) L(ouis)

Bellamy, Edward 1850-1898 ...... **NCLC 4, 86**
See also DLB 12; RGAL; SFW

Belli, Gioconda 1949-
See also CA 152; CWW 2; HLCS 1

Bellin, Edward J.
See Kuttner, Henry

Belloc, (Joseph) Hilaire (Pierre Sebastien Rene Swanton) 1870-1953 ...... **TCLC 7, 18; DAM POET; PC 24**
See also CA 106; 152; CWRI; DLB 19, 100, 141, 174; MTCW 1; SATA 112; WCH; YABC 1

Belloc, Joseph Peter Rene Hilaire
See Belloc, (Joseph) Hilaire (Pierre Sebastien Rene Swanton)

Belloc, Joseph Pierre Hilaire
See Belloc, (Joseph) Hilaire (Pierre Sebastien Rene Swanton)

Belloc, M. A.
See Lowndes, Marie Adelaide (Belloc)

Bellow, Saul 1915- . **CLC 1, 2, 3, 6, 8, 10, 13, 15, 25, 33, 34, 63, 79; DA; DAB; DAC; DAM MST, NOV, POP; SSC 14; WLC**
See also AITN 2; AMW; BEST 89:3; BPFB 1; CA 5-8R; CABS 1; CANR 29, 53, 95; CDALB 1941-1968; CN; DA3; DLB 2, 28; DLBD 3; DLBY 82; MTCW 1, 2; NFS 4; RGAL; RGSF; SSFS 12

Belser, Reimond Karel Maria de 1929-
See Ruyslinck, Ward
See also CA 152

Bely, Andrey .... **TCLC 7; PC 11**
See also Bugayev, Boris Nikolayevich
See also MTCW 1

Belyi, Andrei
See Bugayev, Boris Nikolayevich
See also RGWL

Benary, Margot
See Benary-Isbert, Margot

Benary-Isbert, Margot 1889-1979 .... **CLC 12**
See also CA 5-8R; 89-92; CANR 4, 72; CLR 12; MAICYA; SATA 2; SATA-Obit 21

Benavente (y Martinez), Jacinto 1866-1954 .... **TCLC 3; DAM DRAM, MULT; HLCS 1**
See also CA 106; 131; CANR 81; GLL 2; HW 1, 2; MTCW 1, 2

Benchley, Peter (Bradford) 1940- . **CLC 4, 8; DAM NOV, POP**
See also AAYA 14; AITN 2; BPFB 1; CA 17-20R; CANR 12, 35, 66; CPW; HGG; MTCW 1, 2; SATA 3, 89

Benchley, Robert (Charles) 1889-1945 .... **TCLC 1, 55**
See also CA 105; 153; DLB 11; RGAL

Benda, Julien 1867-1956 .... **TCLC 60**
See also CA 120; 154; GFL 1789 to the Present

Benedict, Saint c. 480-c. 547 .... **CMLC 29**

Benedict, Ruth (Fulton) 1887-1948 .... **TCLC 60**
See also CA 158

Benedikt, Michael 1935- .... **CLC 4, 14**
See also CA 13-16R; CANR 7; CP; DLB 5

Benet, Juan 1927-1993 .... **CLC 28**
See also CA 143

Benet, Stephen Vincent 1898-1943 . **TCLC 7; DAM POET; SSC 10**
See also CA 104; 152; DA3; DLB 4, 48, 102; DLBY 97; HGG; MTCW 1; RGAL; RGSF; WP; YABC 1

Benet, William Rose 1886-1950 .... **TCLC 28; DAM POET**
See also CA 118; 152; DLB 45; RGAL

Benford, Gregory (Albert) 1941- ..... **CLC 52**
See also BPFB 1; CA 69-72, 175; CAAE 175; CAAS 27; CANR 12, 24, 49, 95; CSW; DLBY 82; SCFW 2; SFW

Bengtsson, Frans (Gunnar) 1894-1954 .... **TCLC 48**
See also CA 170

Benjamin, David
See Slavitt, David R(ytman)

Benjamin, Lois
See Gould, Lois

Benjamin, Walter 1892-1940 .... **TCLC 39**
See also CA 164; DLB 242

Benn, Gottfried 1886-1956 .. **TCLC 3; PC 35**
See also CA 106; 153; DLB 56; RGWL

Bennett, Alan 1934- .... **CLC 45, 77; DAB; DAM MST**
See also CA 103; CANR 35, 55; CBD; CD; MTCW 1, 2

Bennett, (Enoch) Arnold 1867-1931 .... **TCLC 5, 20**
See also BRW; CA 106; 155; CDBLB 1890-1914; DLB 10, 34, 98, 135; MTCW 2

Bennett, Elizabeth
See Mitchell, Margaret (Munnerlyn)

Bennett, George Harold 1930-
See Bennett, Hal
See also BW 1; CA 97-100; CANR 87

Bennett, Hal .... **CLC 5**
See also Bennett, George Harold
See also DLB 33

Bennett, Jay 1912- .... **CLC 35**
See also AAYA 10; CA 69-72; CANR 11, 42, 79; JRDA; SAAS 4; SATA 41, 87; SATA-Brief 27; YAW

Bennett, Louise (Simone) 1919- ...... **CLC 28; BLC 1; DAM MULT**
See also BW 2, 3; CA 151; DLB 117

Benson, E(dward) F(rederic) 1867-1940 .... **TCLC 27**
See also CA 114; 157; DLB 135, 153; HGG; SUFW

Benson, Jackson J. 1930- .... **CLC 34**
See also CA 25-28R; DLB 111

Benson, Sally 1900-1972 .... **CLC 17**
See also CA 19-20; 37-40R; CAP 1; SATA 1, 35; SATA-Obit 27

Blacklin, Malcolm
See Chambers, Aidan

Blackmore, R(ichard) D(oddridge)
1825-1900 .... **TCLC 27**
See also CA 120; DLB 18; RGEL

Blackmur, R(ichard) P(almer)
1904-1965 .... **CLC 2, 24**
See also AMWS 2; CA 11-12; 25-28R;
CANR 71; CAP 1; DLB 63

Black Tarantula
See Acker, Kathy

Blackwood, Algernon (Henry)
1869-1951 .... **TCLC 5**
See also CA 105; 150; DLB 153, 156, 178;
HGG; SUFW

Blackwood, Caroline 1931-1996 .... **CLC 6, 9,
100**
See also CA 85-88; 151; CANR 32, 61, 65;
CN; DLB 14, 207; HGG; MTCW 1

Blade, Alexander
See Hamilton, Edmond; Silverberg, Robert

Blaga, Lucian 1895-1961 .... **CLC 75**
See also CA 157; DLB 220

Blair, Eric (Arthur) 1903-1950
See Orwell, George
See also CA 104; 132; DA; DA3; DAB;
DAC; DAM MST, NOV; MTCW 1, 2;
SATA 29

Blair, Hugh 1718-1800 .... **NCLC 75**

Blais, Marie-Claire 1939- .... **CLC 2, 4, 6, 13,
22; DAC; DAM MST**
See also CA 21-24R; CAAS 4; CANR 38,
75, 93; DLB 53; FW; MTCW 1, 2

Blaise, Clark 1940- .... **CLC 29**
See also AITN 2; CA 53-56; CAAS 3;
CANR 5, 66; CN; DLB 53; RGSF

Blake, Fairley
See De Voto, Bernard (Augustine)

Blake, Nicholas
See Day Lewis, C(ecil)
See also DLB 77

Blake, William 1757-1827 .... **NCLC 13, 37,
57; DA; DAB; DAC; DAM MST,
POET; PC 12; WLC**
See also CDBLB 1789-1832; CLR 52;
DA3; DLB 93, 163; EXPP; MAICYA;
PAB; PFS 2; 12; SATA 30; WLIT 3; WP

Blanchot, Maurice 1907- .... **CLC 135**
See also CA 117; 144; DLB 72

Blasco Ibanez, Vicente
1867-1928 .... **TCLC 12; DAM NOV**
See also BPFB 1; CA 110; 131; CANR 81;
DA3; EW; HW 1, 2; MTCW 1

Blatty, William Peter 1928- .... **CLC 2; DAM
POP**
See also CA 5-8R; CANR 9; HGG

Bleeck, Oliver
See Thomas, Ross (Elmore)

Blessing, Lee 1949- .... **CLC 54**
See also CAD; CD

Blight, Rose
See Greer, Germaine

Blish, James (Benjamin) 1921-1975 . **CLC 14**
See also BPFB 1; CA 1-4R; 57-60; CANR
3; DLB 8; MTCW 1; SATA 66; SCFW 2;
SFW

Bliss, Reginald
See Wells, H(erbert) G(eorge)

Blixen, Karen (Christentze Dinesen)
1885-1962
See Dinesen, Isak
See also CA 25-28; CANR 22, 50; CAP 2;
DA3; MTCW 1, 2; NCFS 2; SATA 44

Bloch, Robert (Albert) 1917-1994 .... **CLC 33**
See also AAYA 29; CA 5-8R, 179; 146;
CAAE 179; CAAS 20; CANR 5, 78;
DA3; DLB 44; HGG; INT CANR-5;
MTCW 1; SATA 12; SATA-Obit 82; SFW;
SUFW

Blok, Alexander (Alexandrovich)
1880-1921 .... **TCLC 5; PC 21**
See also CA 104; 183; EW; RGWL

Blom, Jan
See Breytenbach, Breyten

Bloom, Harold 1930- .... **CLC 24, 103**
See also CA 13-16R; CANR 39, 75, 92;
DLB 67; MTCW 1; RGAL

Bloomfield, Aurelius
See Bourne, Randolph S(illiman)

Blount, Roy (Alton), Jr. 1941- .... **CLC 38**
See also CA 53-56; CANR 10, 28, 61;
CSW; INT CANR-28; MTCW 1, 2

Bloy, Leon 1846-1917 .... **TCLC 22**
See also CA 121; 183; DLB 123; GFL 1789
to the Present

Blume, Judy (Sussman) 1938- .. **CLC 12, 30;
DAM NOV, POP**
See also AAYA 3, 26; BYA 1; CA 29-32R;
CANR 13, 37, 66; CLR 2, 15, 69; CPW;
DA3; DLB 52; JRDA; MAICYA; MAIC-
YAS; MTCW 1, 2; SATA 2, 31, 79; WYA;
YAW

Blunden, Edmund (Charles)
1896-1974 .... **CLC 2, 56**
See also CA 17-18; 45-48; CANR 54; CAP
2; DLB 20, 100, 155; MTCW 1; PAB

Bly, Robert (Elwood) 1926- .... **CLC 1, 2, 5,
10, 15, 38, 128; DAM POET**
See also AMWS 4; CA 5-8R; CANR 41,
73; CP; DA3; DLB 5; MTCW 1, 2; RGAL

Boas, Franz 1858-1942 .... **TCLC 56**
See also CA 115; 181

Bobette
See Simenon, Georges (Jacques Christian)

Boccaccio, Giovanni 1313-1375 ... **CMLC 13;
SSC 10**
See also RGSF; RGWL

Bochco, Steven 1943- .... **CLC 35**
See also AAYA 11; CA 124; 138

Bodel, Jean 1167(?)-1210 .... **CMLC 28**

Bodenheim, Maxwell 1892-1954 .... **TCLC 44**
See also CA 110; 187; DLB 9, 45; RGAL

Bodker, Cecil 1927- .... **CLC 21**
See also CA 73-76; CANR 13, 44; CLR 23;
MAICYA; SATA 14

Boell, Heinrich (Theodor)
1917-1985 ..... **CLC 2, 3, 6, 9, 11, 15, 27,
32, 72; DA; DAB; DAC; DAM MST,
NOV; SSC 23; WLC**
See Boll, Heinrich
See also CA 21-24R; 116; CANR 24; DA3;
DLB 69; DLBY 85; EW; MTCW 1, 2

Boerne, Alfred
See Doeblin, Alfred

Boethius c. 480-c. 524 .... **CMLC 15**
See also DLB 115; RGWL

Boff, Leonardo (Genezio Darci)
1938- .... **CLC 70; DAM MULT; HLC 1**
See also CA 150; HW 2

Bogan, Louise 1897-1970 .... **CLC 4, 39, 46,
93; DAM POET; PC 12**
See also AMWS 3; CA 73-76; 25-28R;
CANR 33, 82; DLB 45, 169; MTCW 1,
2; RGAL

Bogarde, Dirk
See Van Den Bogarde, Derek Jules Gaspard
Ulric Niven

Bogosian, Eric 1953- .... **CLC 45, 141**
See also CA 138; CAD; CD

Bograd, Larry 1953- .... **CLC 35**
See also CA 93-96; CANR 57; SAAS 21;
SATA 33, 89

Boiardo, Matteo Maria 1441-1494 .... **LC 6**

Boileau-Despreaux, Nicolas 1636-1711 . **LC 3**
See also GFL Beginnings to 1789; RGWL

Bojer, Johan 1872-1959 .... **TCLC 64**
See also CA 189

Bok, Edward W. 1863-1930 .... **TCLC 101**
See also DLB 91; DLBD 16

Boland, Eavan (Aisling) 1944- .. **CLC 40, 67,
113; DAM POET**
See also BRWS 5; CA 143; CANR 61; CP;
CWP; DLB 40; FW; MTCW 2; PFS 12

Boll, Heinrich
See Boell, Heinrich (Theodor)
See also BPFB 1; RGSF; RGWL

Bolt, Lee
See Faust, Frederick (Schiller)

Bolt, Robert (Oxton) 1924-1995 ...... **CLC 14;
DAM DRAM**
See also CA 17-20R; 147; CANR 35, 67;
CBD; DFS 2; DLB 13, 233; LAIT 1;
MTCW 1

Bombal, Maria Luisa 1910-1980 ...... **SSC 37;
HLCS 1**
See also CA 127; CANR 72; HW 1; RGSF

Bombet, Louis-Alexandre-Cesar
See Stendhal

Bomkauf
See Kaufman, Bob (Garnell)

Bonaventura .... **NCLC 35**
See also DLB 90

Bond, Edward 1934- .... **CLC 4, 6, 13, 23;
DAM DRAM**
See also BRWS 1; CA 25-28R; CANR 38,
67; CBD; CD; DFS 3,8; DLB 13; MTCW
1

Bonham, Frank 1914-1989 .... **CLC 12**
See also AAYA 1; BYA 1; CA 9-12R;
CANR 4, 36; JRDA; MAICYA; SAAS 3;
SATA 1, 49; SATA-Obit 62; TCWW 2;
YAW

Bonnefoy, Yves 1923- .. **CLC 9, 15, 58; DAM
MST, POET**
See also CA 85-88; CANR 33, 75, 97;
CWW 2; GFL 1789 to the Present; MTCW
1, 2

Bontemps, Arna(ud Wendell)
1902-1973 ..... **CLC 1, 18; BLC 1; DAM
MULT, NOV, POET**
See also BW 1; CA 1-4R; 41-44R; CANR
4, 35; CLR 6; CWRI; DA3; DLB 48, 51;
JRDA; MAICYA; MTCW 1, 2; SATA 2,
44; SATA-Obit 24; WCH; WP

Booth, Martin 1944- .... **CLC 13**
See also CA 93-96; CAAE 188; CAAS 2;
CANR 92

Booth, Philip 1925- .... **CLC 23**
See also CA 5-8R; CANR 5, 88; CP; DLBY
82

Booth, Wayne C(layson) 1921- .... **CLC 24**
See also CA 1-4R; CAAS 5; CANR 3, 43;
DLB 67

Borchert, Wolfgang 1921-1947 .... **TCLC 5**
See also CA 104; 188; DLB 69, 124

Borel, Petrus 1809-1859 .... **NCLC 41**
See also GFL 1789 to the Present

Borges, Jorge Luis 1899-1986 ... **CLC 1, 2, 3,
4, 6, 8, 9, 10, 13, 19, 44, 48, 83; DA;
DAB; DAC; DAM MST, MULT; HLC
1; PC 22, 32; SSC 4, 41; WLC**
See also AAYA 26; BPFB 1; CA 21-24R;
CANR 19, 33, 75; DA3; DLB 113; DLBY
86; DNFS; HW 1, 2; MTCW 1, 2; RGSF;
RGWL; SFW; SSFS 4,9; TCLC 109;
WLIT 1

Borowski, Tadeusz 1922-1951 .... **TCLC 9**
See also CA 106; 154; RGSF

Borrow, George (Henry)
1803-1881 .... **NCLC 9**
See also DLB 21, 55, 166

Bosch (Gavino), Juan 1909-
See also CA 151; DAM MST, MULT; DLB
145; HLCS 1; HW 1, 2

Bosman, Herman Charles
1905-1951 .... **TCLC 49**
See also Malan, Herman
See also CA 160; DLB 225; RGSF

Bosschere, Jean de 1878(?)-1953 ... **TCLC 19**
See also CA 115; 186

Boswell, James 1740-1795 ...... **LC 4, 50; DA; DAB; DAC; DAM MST; WLC**
See also CDBLB 1660-1789; DLB 104, 142; WLIT 3

Bottomley, Gordon 1874-1948 ..... **TCLC 107**
See also CA 120; 192; DLB 10

Bottoms, David 1949- .... **CLC 53**
See also CA 105; CANR 22; CSW; DLB 120; DLBY 83

Boucicault, Dion 1820-1890 .... **NCLC 41**

Boucolon, Maryse
See Conde, Maryse

Bourget, Paul (Charles Joseph)
1852-1935 .... **TCLC 12**
See also CA 107; DLB 123; GFL 1789 to the Present

Bourjaily, Vance (Nye) 1922- .... **CLC 8, 62**
See also CA 1-4R; CAAS 1; CANR 2, 72; CN; DLB 2, 143

Bourne, Randolph S(illiman)
1886-1918 .... **TCLC 16**
See also Aurelius
See also AMW; CA 117; 155; DLB 63

Bova, Ben(jamin William) 1932- ...... **CLC 45**
See also AAYA 16; CA 5-8R; CAAS 18; CANR 11, 56, 94; CLR 3; DLBY 81; INT CANR-11; MAICYA; MTCW 1; SATA 6, 68; SFW

Bowen, Elizabeth (Dorothea Cole)
1899-1973 . **CLC 1, 3, 6, 11, 15, 22, 118; DAM NOV; SSC 3, 28**
See also BRWS 2; CA 17-18; 41-44R; CANR 35; CAP 2; CDBLB 1945-1960; DA3; DLB 15, 162; EXPS; FW; HGG; MTCW 1, 2; RGSF; SSFS 5; SUFW; WLIT 4

Bowering, George 1935- .... **CLC 15, 47**
See also CA 21-24R; CAAS 16; CANR 10; DLB 53

Bowering, Marilyn R(uthe) 1949- .... **CLC 32**
See also CA 101; CANR 49; CP; CWP

Bowers, Edgar 1924-2000 .... **CLC 9**
See also CA 5-8R; 188; CANR 24; CP; CSW; DLB 5

Bowie, David .... **CLC 17**
See also Jones, David Robert

Bowles, Jane (Sydney) 1917-1973 ..... **CLC 3, 68**
See also CA 19-20; 41-44R; CAP 2

Bowles, Paul (Frederick) 1910-1999 . **CLC 1, 2, 19, 53; SSC 3**
See also AMWS 4; CA 1-4R; 186; CAAS 1; CANR 1, 19, 50, 75; CN; DA3; DLB 5, 6; MTCW 1, 2; RGAL

Bowles, William Lisle 1762-1850 . **NCLC 103**
See also DLB 93

Box, Edgar
See Vidal, Gore
See also GLL 1

Boyd, Nancy
See Millay, Edna St. Vincent
See also GLL 1

Boyd, Thomas (Alexander)
1898-1935 .... **TCLC 111**
See also CA 111; 183; DLB 9; DLBD 16

Boyd, William 1952- .... **CLC 28, 53, 70**
See also CA 114; 120; CANR 51, 71; CN; DLB 231

Boyle, Kay 1902-1992 .... **CLC 1, 5, 19, 58, 121; SSC 5**
See also CA 13-16R; 140; CAAS 1; CANR 29, 61; DLB 4, 9, 48, 86; DLBY 93; MTCW 1, 2; RGAL; RGSF; SSFS 10

Boyle, Mark
See Kienzle, William X(avier)

Boyle, Patrick 1905-1982 .... **CLC 19**
See also CA 127

Boyle, T. C.
See Boyle, T(homas) Coraghessan
See also AMWS 8

Boyle, T(homas) Coraghessan
1948- .... **CLC 36, 55, 90; DAM POP; SSC 16**
See also Boyle, T. C.
See also BEST 90:4; BPFB 1; CA 120; CANR 44, 76, 89; CN; CPW; DA3; DLBY 86; MTCW 2

Boz
See Dickens, Charles (John Huffam)

Brackenridge, Hugh Henry
1748-1816 .... **NCLC 7**
See also DLB 11, 37; RGAL

Bradbury, Edward P.
See Moorcock, Michael (John)
See also MTCW 2

Bradbury, Malcolm (Stanley)
1932-2000 .... **CLC 32, 61; DAM NOV**
See also CA 1-4R; CANR 1, 33, 91, 98; CN; DA3; DLB 14, 207; MTCW 1, 2

Bradbury, Ray (Douglas) 1920- .... **CLC 1, 3, 10, 15, 42, 98; DA; DAB; DAC; DAM MST, NOV, POP; SSC 29; WLC**
See also AAYA 15; AITN 1, 2; AMWS 4; BPFB 1; BYA 4; CA 1-4R; CANR 2, 30, 75; CDALB 1968-1988; CN; CPW; DA3; DLB 2, 8; EXPN; EXPS; HGG; LAIT 3, 5; MTCW 1, 2; NFS 1; RGAL; RGSF; SATA 11, 64, 123; SCFW 2; SFW; SSFS 1; SUFW; YAW

Braddon, Mary Elizabeth
1837-1915 .... **TCLC 111**
See also Aunt Belinda; White, Babington
See also CA 108; 179; CMW; DLB 18, 70, 156; HGG

Bradford, Gamaliel 1863-1932 .... **TCLC 36**
See also CA 160; DLB 17

Bradford, William 1590-1657 .... **LC 64**
See also DLB 24, 30; RGAL

Bradley, David (Henry), Jr. 1950- ... **CLC 23, 118; BLC 1; DAM MULT**
See also BW 1, 3; CA 104; CANR 26, 81; CN; DLB 33

Bradley, John Ed(mund, Jr.) 1958- . **CLC 55**
See also CA 139; CANR 99; CN; CSW

Bradley, Marion Zimmer
1930-1999 .... **CLC 30; DAM POP**
See also Chapman, Lee; Dexter, John; Gardner, Miriam; Ives, Morgan; Rivers, Elfrida
See also AAYA 40; BPFB 1; CA 57-60; 185; CAAS 10; CANR 7, 31, 51, 75; CPW; DA3; DLB 8; FANT; FW; MTCW 1, 2; SATA 90; SATA-Obit 116; SFW; YAW

Bradshaw, John 1933- .... **CLC 70**
See also CA 138; CANR 61

Bradstreet, Anne 1612(?)-1672 ...... **LC 4, 30; DA; DAC; DAM MST, POET; PC 10**
See also AMWS 1; CDALB 1640-1865; DA3; DLB 24; EXPP; FW; PFS 6; RGAL; WP

Brady, Joan 1939- .... **CLC 86**
See also CA 141

Bragg, Melvyn 1939- .... **CLC 10**
See also BEST 89:3; CA 57-60; CANR 10, 48, 89; CN; DLB 14; RHW

Brahe, Tycho 1546-1601 .... **LC 45**

Braine, John (Gerard) 1922-1986 . **CLC 1, 3, 41**
See also CA 1-4R; 120; CANR 1, 33; CD-BLB 1945-1960; DLB 15; DLBY 86; MTCW 1

Bramah, Ernest 1868-1942 .... **TCLC 72**
See also CA 156; CMW; DLB 70; FANT

Brammer, William 1930(?)-1978 ...... **CLC 31**
See also CA 77-80

Brancati, Vitaliano 1907-1954 .... **TCLC 12**
See also CA 109

Brancato, Robin F(idler) 1936- .... **CLC 35**
See also AAYA 9; BYA 6; CA 69-72; CANR 11, 45; CLR 32; JRDA; MAICYAS; SAAS 9; SATA 97; WYA; YAW

Brand, Max
See Faust, Frederick (Schiller)
See also BPFB 1; TCWW 2

Brand, Millen 1906-1980 .... **CLC 7**
See also CA 21-24R; 97-100; CANR 72

Branden, Barbara .... **CLC 44**
See also CA 148

Brandes, Georg (Morris Cohen)
1842-1927 .... **TCLC 10**
See also CA 105; 189

Brandys, Kazimierz 1916-2000 .... **CLC 62**

Branley, Franklyn M(ansfield)
1915- .... **CLC 21**
See also CA 33-36R; CANR 14, 39; CLR 13; MAICYA; SAAS 16; SATA 4, 68

Brathwaite, Edward (Kamau)
1930- ...... **CLC 11; BLCS; DAM POET**
See also BW 2, 3; CA 25-28R; CANR 11, 26, 47; CP; DLB 125

Brautigan, Richard (Gary)
1935-1984 .... **CLC 1, 3, 5, 9, 12, 34, 42; DAM NOV**
See also BPFB 1; CA 53-56; 113; CANR 34; DA3; DLB 2, 5, 206; DLBY 80, 84; FANT; MTCW 1; RGAL; SATA 56

Brave Bird, Mary
See Crow Dog, Mary (Ellen)
See also NNAL

Braverman, Kate 1950- .... **CLC 67**
See also CA 89-92

Brecht, (Eugen) Bertolt (Friedrich)
1898-1956 .... **TCLC 1, 6, 13, 35; DA; DAB; DAC; DAM DRAM, MST; DC 3; WLC**
See also CA 104; 133; CANR 62; DA3; DFS 4, 5, 9; DLB 56, 124; EW; IDTP; MTCW 1, 2; RGWL

Brecht, Eugen Berthold Friedrich
See Brecht, (Eugen) Bertolt (Friedrich)

Bremer, Fredrika 1801-1865 .... **NCLC 11**

Brennan, Christopher John
1870-1932 .... **TCLC 17**
See also CA 117; 188; DLB 230

Brennan, Maeve 1917-1993 .... **CLC 5**
See also CA 81-84; CANR 72, 100

Brent, Linda
See Jacobs, Harriet A(nn)

Brentano, Clemens (Maria)
1778-1842 .... **NCLC 1**
See also DLB 90; RGWL

Brent of Bin Bin
See Franklin, (Stella Maria Sarah) Miles (Lampe)

Brenton, Howard 1942- .... **CLC 31**
See also CA 69-72; CANR 33, 67; CBD; CD; DLB 13; MTCW 1

Breslin, James 1935-1996
See Breslin, Jimmy
See also CA 73-76; CANR 31, 75; DAM NOV; MTCW 1, 2

Breslin, Jimmy .... **CLC 4, 43**
See also Breslin, James
See also AITN 1; DLB 185; MTCW 2

Bresson, Robert 1901(?)-1999 .... **CLC 16**
See also CA 110; 187; CANR 49

Breton, Andre 1896-1966 .. **CLC 2, 9, 15, 54; PC 15**
See also CA 19-20; 25-28R; CANR 40, 60; CAP 2; DLB 65; GFL 1789 to the Present; MTCW 1, 2; RGWL; WP

Cervantes (Saavedra), Miguel de
1547-1616 .. LC 6, 23; DA; DAB; DAC;
DAM MST, NOV; HLCS; SSC 12;
WLC
See also BYA 1; EW; LAIT 1; NFS 8;
RGSF; RGWL

Cesaire, Aime (Fernand) 1913- . CLC 19, 32,
112; BLC 1; DAM MULT, POET; PC
25
See also BW 2, 3; CA 65-68; CANR 24,
43, 81; DA3; GFL 1789 to the Present;
MTCW 1, 2; WP

Chabon, Michael 1963- .... CLC 55, 149
See also CA 139; CANR 57, 96

Chabrol, Claude 1930- .... CLC 16
See also CA 110

Challans, Mary 1905-1983
See Renault, Mary
See also CA 81-84; 111; CANR 74; DA3;
MTCW 2; SATA 23; SATA-Obit 36

Challis, George
See Faust, Frederick (Schiller)
See also TCWW 2

Chambers, Aidan 1934- .... CLC 35
See also AAYA 27; CA 25-28R; CANR 12,
31, 58; JRDA; MAICYA; SAAS 12;
SATA 1, 69, 108; YAW

Chambers, James 1948-
See Cliff, Jimmy
See also CA 124

Chambers, Jessie
See Lawrence, D(avid) H(erbert Richards)
See also GLL 1

Chambers, Robert W(illiam)
1865-1933 .... TCLC 41
See also CA 165; DLB 202; HGG; SATA
107; SUFW

Chamisso, Adelbert von
1781-1838 .... NCLC 82
See also DLB 90; RGWL

Chandler, Raymond (Thornton)
1888-1959 .... TCLC 1, 7; SSC 23
See also AAYA 25; AMWS 4; BPFB 1; CA
104; 129; CANR 60; CDALB 1929-1941;
CMW; DA3; DLB 226; DLBD 6; MSW;
MTCW 1, 2; RGAL

Chang, Eileen 1921-1995 .... SSC 28
See also CA 166; CWW 2

Chang, Jung 1952- .... CLC 71
See also CA 142

Chang Ai-Ling
See Chang, Eileen

Channing, William Ellery
1780-1842 .... NCLC 17
See also DLB 1, 59, 235; RGAL

Chao, Patricia 1955- .... CLC 119
See also CA 163

Chaplin, Charles Spencer
1889-1977 .... CLC 16
See also Chaplin, Charlie
See also CA 81-84; 73-76

Chaplin, Charlie
See Chaplin, Charles Spencer
See also DLB 44

Chapman, George 1559(?)-1634 .... LC 22;
DAM DRAM
See also BRW 1; DLB 62, 121; RGEL

Chapman, Graham 1941-1989 .... CLC 21
See also Monty Python
See also CA 116; 129; CANR 35, 95

Chapman, John Jay 1862-1933 .... TCLC 7
See also CA 104; 191

Chapman, Lee
See Bradley, Marion Zimmer
See also GLL 1

Chapman, Walker
See Silverberg, Robert

Chappell, Fred (Davis) 1936- ..... CLC 40, 78
See also CA 5-8R; CAAS 4; CANR 8, 33,
67; CN; CP; CSW; DLB 6, 105; HGG

Char, Rene(-Emile) 1907-1988 .... CLC 9, 11,
14, 55; DAM POET
See also CA 13-16R; 124; CANR 32; GFL
1789 to the Present; MTCW 1, 2; RGWL

Charby, Jay
See Ellison, Harlan (Jay)

Chardin, Pierre Teilhard de
See Teilhard de Chardin, (Marie Joseph)
Pierre

Charlemagne 742-814 .... CMLC 37

Charles I 1600-1649 .... LC 13

Charriere, Isabelle de 1740-1805 .. NCLC 66

Chartier, Emile-Auguste
See Alain

Charyn, Jerome 1937- .... CLC 5, 8, 18
See also CA 5-8R; CAAS 1; CANR 7, 61,
101; CMW; CN; DLBY 83; MTCW 1

Chase, Adam
See Marlowe, Stephen

Chase, Mary (Coyle) 1907-1981 .... DC 1
See also CA 77-80; 105; CAD; CWD; DFS
11; DLB 228; SATA 17; SATA-Obit 29

Chase, Mary Ellen 1887-1973 .... CLC 2
See also CA 13-16; 41-44R; CAP 1; SATA
10

Chase, Nicholas
See Hyde, Anthony
See also CCA 1

Chateaubriand, Francois Rene de
1768-1848 .... NCLC 3
See also DLB 119; EW; GFL 1789 to the
Present; RGWL

Chatterje, Sarat Chandra 1876-1936(?)
See Chatterji, Saratchandra
See also CA 109

Chatterji, Bankim Chandra
1838-1894 .... NCLC 19

Chatterji, Saratchandra .... TCLC 13
See also Chatterje, Sarat Chandra
See also CA 186

Chatterton, Thomas 1752-1770 ..... LC 3, 54;
DAM POET
See also DLB 109; RGEL

Chatwin, (Charles) Bruce
1940-1989 . CLC 28, 57, 59; DAM POP
See also AAYA 4; BEST 90:1; BRWS 4;
CA 85-88; 127; CPW; DLB 194, 204

Chaucer, Daniel
See Ford, Ford Madox
See also RHW

Chaucer, Geoffrey 1340(?)-1400 .. LC 17, 56;
DA; DAB; DAC; DAM MST, POET;
PC 19; WLCS
See also BRW 1; CDBLB Before 1660;
DA3; DLB 146; LAIT 1; PAB; RGEL;
WLIT 3; WP

Chavez, Denise (Elia) 1948-
See also CA 131; CANR 56, 81; DAM
MULT; DLB 122; FW; HLC 1; HW 1, 2;
MTCW 2

Chaviaras, Strates 1935-
See Haviaras, Stratis
See also CA 105

Chayefsky, Paddy .... CLC 23
See also Chayefsky, Sidney
See also CAD; DLB 7, 44; DLBY 81;
RGAL

Chayefsky, Sidney 1923-1981
See Chayefsky, Paddy
See also CA 9-12R; 104; CANR 18; DAM
DRAM

Chedid, Andree 1920- .... CLC 47
See also CA 145; CANR 95

Cheever, John 1912-1982 ..... CLC 3, 7, 8, 11,
15, 25, 64; DA; DAB; DAC; DAM
MST, NOV, POP; SSC 1, 38; WLC
See also AMWS 1; BPFB 1; CA 5-8R; 106;
CABS 1; CANR 5, 27, 76; CDALB 1941-
1968; CPW; DA3; DLB 2, 102, 227;
DLBY 80, 82; EXPS; INT CANR-5;
MTCW 1, 2; RGAL; RGSF; SSFS 2

Cheever, Susan 1943- .... CLC 18, 48
See also CA 103; CANR 27, 51, 92; DLBY
82; INT CANR-27

Chekhonte, Antosha
See Chekhov, Anton (Pavlovich)

Chekhov, Anton (Pavlovich)
1860-1904 .... TCLC 3, 10, 31, 55, 96;
DA; DAB; DAC; DAM DRAM, MST;
DC 9; SSC 2, 28, 41; WLC
See also CA 104; 124; DA3; DFS 1, 5, 10,
12; EW; EXPS; LAIT 3; RGSF; RGWL;
SATA 90; SSFS 5

Cheney, Lynne V. 1941- .... CLC 70
See also CA 89-92; CANR 58

Chernyshevsky, Nikolai Gavrilovich
See Chernyshevsky, Nikolay Gavrilovich

Chernyshevsky, Nikolay Gavrilovich
1828-1889 .... NCLC 1
See also DLB 238

Cherry, Carolyn Janice 1942-
See Cherryh, C. J.
See also CA 65-68; CANR 10; FANT; SFW;
YAW

Cherryh, C. J. .... CLC 35
See also Cherry, Carolyn Janice
See also AAYA 24; BPFB 1; DLBY 80;
SATA 93

Chesnutt, Charles W(addell)
1858-1932 .. TCLC 5, 39; BLC 1; DAM
MULT; SSC 7
See also AFAW 1, 2; BW 1, 3; CA 106;
125; CANR 76; DLB 12, 50, 78; MTCW
1, 2; RGAL; RGSF; SSFS 11

Chester, Alfred 1929(?)-1971 .... CLC 49
See also CA 33-36R; DLB 130

Chesterton, G(ilbert) K(eith)
1874-1936 . TCLC 1, 6, 64; DAM NOV,
POET; PC 28; SSC 1, 46
See also BRW; CA 104; 132; CANR 73;
CDBLB 1914-1945; CMW; DLB 10, 19,
34, 70, 98, 149, 178; FANT; MTCW 1, 2;
RGEL; RGSF; SATA 27; SUFW

Chiang, Pin-chin 1904-1986
See Ding Ling
See also CA 118

Ch'ien Chung-shu 1910- .... CLC 22
See also CA 130; CANR 73; MTCW 1, 2

Chikamatsu Monzaemon 1653-1724 ... LC 66
See also RGWL

Child, L. Maria
See Child, Lydia Maria

Child, Lydia Maria 1802-1880 .. NCLC 6, 73
See also DLB 1, 74; RGAL; SATA 67

Child, Mrs.
See Child, Lydia Maria

Child, Philip 1898-1978 .... CLC 19, 68
See also CA 13-14; CAP 1; RHW; SATA
47

Childers, (Robert) Erskine
1870-1922 .... TCLC 65
See also CA 113; 153; DLB 70

Childress, Alice 1920-1994 .. CLC 12, 15, 86,
96; BLC 1; DAM DRAM, MULT,
NOV; DC 4
See also AAYA 8; BW 2, 3; BYA 2; CA 45-
48; 146; CAD; CANR 3, 27, 50, 74; CLR
14; CWD; DA3; DFS 2,8; DLB 7, 38;
JRDA; LAIT 5; MAICYA; MTCW 1, 2;
RGAL; SATA 7, 48, 81; YAW

Chin, Frank (Chew, Jr.) 1940- ...... **CLC 135;
DAM MULT; DC 7**
See also CA 33-36R; CANR 71; CD; DLB
206; LAIT 5; RGAL

Chislett, (Margaret) Anne 1943- ...... **CLC 34**
See also CA 151

Chitty, Thomas Willes 1926- .... **CLC 11**
See also Hinde, Thomas
See also CA 5-8R; CN

Chivers, Thomas Holley
1809-1858 .... **NCLC 49**
See also DLB 3; RGAL

Choi, Susan .... **CLC 119**

Chomette, Rene Lucien 1898-1981
See Clair, Rene
See also CA 103

Chomsky, (Avram) Noam 1928- ..... **CLC 132**
See also CA 17-20R; CANR 28, 62; DA3;
MTCW 1, 2

Chopin, Kate . **TCLC 5, 14; DA; DAB; SSC
8; WLCS**
See also Chopin, Katherine
See also AAYA 33; AMWS 1; CDALB
1865-1917; DLB 12, 78; EXPN; EXPS;
LAIT 3; NFS 3; RGAL; RGSF; SSFS 2

Chopin, Katherine 1851-1904
See Chopin, Kate
See also CA 104; 122; DA3; DAC; DAM
MST, NOV; FW

Chretien de Troyes c. 12th cent. - . **CMLC 10**
See also DLB 208; RGWL

Christie
See Ichikawa, Kon

Christie, Agatha (Mary Clarissa)
1890-1976 .... **CLC 1, 6, 8, 12, 39, 48,
110; DAB; DAC; DAM NOV**
See also AAYA 9; AITN 1, 2; BPFB 1;
BRWS 2; CA 17-20R; 61-64; CANR 10,
37; CBD; CDBLB 1914-1945; CMW;
CPW; CWD; DA3; DFS 2; DLB 13, 77;
MSW; MTCW 1, 2; NFS 8; RGEL; RHW;
SATA 36; YAW

Christie, (Ann) Philippa
See Pearce, Philippa
See also CA 5-8R; CANR 4; CWRI; FANT

Christine de Pizan 1365(?)-1431(?) .... **LC 9**
See also DLB 208; RGWL

Chubb, Elmer
See Masters, Edgar Lee

Chulkov, Mikhail Dmitrievich
1743-1792 .... **LC 2**
See also DLB 150

Churchill, Caryl 1938- .... **CLC 31, 55; DC 5**
See also BRWS 4; CA 102; CANR 22, 46;
CBD; CWD; DFS 12; DLB 13; FW;
MTCW; RGEL

Churchill, Charles 1731-1764 .... **LC 3**
See also DLB 109; RGEL

Churchill, Sir Winston (Leonard Spencer)
1874-1965 .... **TCLC 113**
See also CA 97-100; CDBLB 1890-1914;
DA3; DLB 100; DLBD 16; LAIT 4;
MTCW 1, 2

Chute, Carolyn 1947- .... **CLC 39**
See also CA 123

Ciardi, John (Anthony) 1916-1986 . **CLC 10,
40, 44, 129; DAM POET**
See also CA 5-8R; 118; CAAS 2; CANR 5,
33; CLR 19; CWRI; DLB 5; DLBY 86;
INT CANR-5; MAICYA; MTCW 1, 2;
RGAL; SAAS 26; SATA 1, 65; SATA-
Obit 46

Cibber, Colley 1671-1757 .... **LC 66**
See also DLB 84; RGEL

Cicero, Marcus Tullius
106B.C.-43B.C. .... **CMLC 3**
See also AW; DLB 211; RGWL

Cimino, Michael 1943- .... **CLC 16**
See also CA 105

Cioran, E(mil) M. 1911-1995 .... **CLC 64**
See also CA 25-28R; 149; CANR 91; DLB
220

Cisneros, Sandra 1954- . **CLC 69, 118; DAM
MULT; HLC 1; SSC 32**
See also AAYA 9; AMWS 7; CA 131;
CANR 64; CWP; DA3; DLB 122, 152;
EXPN; FW; HW 1, 2; LAIT 5; MTCW 2;
NFS 2; RGAL; RGSF; SSFS 3; WLIT 1;
YAW

Cixous, Helene 1937- .... **CLC 92**
See also CA 126; CANR 55; CWW 2; DLB
83, 242; FW; MTCW 1, 2

Clair, Rene .... **CLC 20**
See also Chomette, Rene Lucien

Clampitt, Amy 1920-1994 .... **CLC 32; PC 19**
See also CA 110; 146; CANR 29, 79; DLB
105

Clancy, Thomas L., Jr. 1947-
See Clancy, Tom
See also CA 125; 131; CANR 62; CPW;
DA3; DLB 227; INT 131; MTCW 1, 2

Clancy, Tom .... **CLC 45, 112; DAM NOV,
POP**
See also Clancy, Thomas L., Jr.
See also AAYA 9; BEST 89:1, 90:1; BPFB
1; BYA 10; CMW; MTCW 2

Clare, John 1793-1864 ... **NCLC 9, 86; DAB;
DAM POET; PC 23**
See also DLB 55, 96; RGEL

Clarin
See Alas (y Urena), Leopoldo (Enrique
Garcia)

Clark, Al C.
See Goines, Donald

Clark, (Robert) Brian 1932- .... **CLC 29**
See also CA 41-44R; CANR 67; CBD; CD

Clark, Curt
See Westlake, Donald E(dwin)

Clark, Eleanor 1913-1996 .... **CLC 5, 19**
See also CA 9-12R; 151; CANR 41; CN;
DLB 6

Clark, J. P.
See Clark Bekederemo, J(ohnson) P(epper)
See also DLB 117

Clark, John Pepper
See Clark Bekederemo, J(ohnson) P(epper)
See also CD; CP; RGEL

Clark, M. R.
See Clark, Mavis Thorpe

Clark, Mavis Thorpe 1909- .... **CLC 12**
See also CA 57-60; CANR 8, 37; CLR 30;
CWRI; MAICYA; SAAS 5; SATA 8, 74

Clark, Walter Van Tilburg
1909-1971 .... **CLC 28**
See also CA 9-12R; 33-36R; CANR 63;
DLB 9, 206; LAIT 2; RGAL; SATA 8

Clark Bekederemo, J(ohnson) P(epper)
1935- .. **CLC 38; BLC 1; DAM DRAM,
MULT; DC 5**
See also Clark, J. P.; Clark, John Pepper
See also BW 1; CA 65-68; CANR 16, 72;
DFS 13; MTCW 1

Clarke, Arthur C(harles) 1917- .... **CLC 1, 4,
13, 18, 35, 136; DAM POP; SSC 3**
See also AAYA 4, 33; BPFB 1; BYA 13;
CA 1-4R; CANR 2, 28, 55, 74; CN; CPW;
DA3; JRDA; LAIT 5; MAICYA; MTCW
1, 2; SATA 13, 70, 115; SCFW; SFW;
SSFS 4; YAW

Clarke, Austin 1896-1974 ... **CLC 6, 9; DAM
POET**
See also CA 29-32; 49-52; CAP 2; DLB 10,
20; RGEL

Clarke, Austin C(hesterfield) 1934- .. **CLC 8,
53; BLC 1; DAC; DAM MULT; SSC
45**
See also BW 1; CA 25-28R; CAAS 16;
CANR 14, 32, 68; CN; DLB 53, 125;
DNFS; RGSF

Clarke, Gillian 1937- .... **CLC 61**
See also CA 106; CP; CWP; DLB 40

Clarke, Marcus (Andrew Hislop)
1846-1881 .... **NCLC 19**
See also DLB 230; RGEL; RGSF

Clarke, Shirley 1925-1997 .... **CLC 16**
See also CA 189

Clash, The
See Headon, (Nicky) Topper; Jones, Mick;
Simonon, Paul; Strummer, Joe

Claudel, Paul (Louis Charles Marie)
1868-1955 .... **TCLC 2, 10**
See also CA 104; 165; DLB 192; EW; GFL
1789 to the Present; RGWL

Claudian 370(?)-404(?) .... **CMLC 46**
See also RGWL

Claudius, Matthias 1740-1815 .... **NCLC 75**
See also DLB 97

Clavell, James (duMaresq)
1925-1994 .. **CLC 6, 25, 87; DAM NOV,
POP**
See also BPFB 1; CA 25-28R; 146; CANR
26, 48; CPW; DA3; MTCW 1, 2; NFS 10;
RHW

Clayman, Gregory .... **CLC 65**

Cleaver, (Leroy) Eldridge
1935-1998 . **CLC 30, 119; BLC 1; DAM
MULT**
See also BW 1, 3; CA 21-24R; 167; CANR
16, 75; DA3; MTCW 2; YAW

Cleese, John (Marwood) 1939- .... **CLC 21**
See also Monty Python
See also CA 112; 116; CANR 35; MTCW 1

Cleishbotham, Jebediah
See Scott, Sir Walter

Cleland, John 1710-1789 .... **LC 2, 48**
See also DLB 39; RGEL

Clemens, Samuel Langhorne 1835-1910
See Twain, Mark
See also CA 104; 135; CDALB 1865-1917;
DA; DA3; DAB; DAC; DAM MST, NOV;
DLB 11, 12, 23, 64, 74, 186, 189; JRDA;
MAICYA; SATA 100; YABC 2

Clement of Alexandria
150(?)-215(?) .... **CMLC 41**

Cleophil
See Congreve, William

Clerihew, E.
See Bentley, E(dmund) C(lerihew)

Clerk, N. W.
See Lewis, C(live) S(taples)

Cliff, Jimmy .... **CLC 21**
See also Chambers, James
See also CA 193

Cliff, Michelle 1946- .... **CLC 120; BLCS**
See also BW 2; CA 116; CANR 39, 72;
DLB 157; FW; GLL 2

Clifton, (Thelma) Lucille 1936- .... **CLC 19,
66; BLC 1; DAM MULT, POET; PC
17**
See also AFAW 2; BW 2, 3; CA 49-52;
CANR 2, 24, 42, 76, 97; CLR 5; CP;
CSW; CWP; CWRI; DA3; DLB 5, 41;
EXPP; MAICYA; MTCW 1, 2; PFS 1;
SATA 20, 69; WP

Clinton, Dirk
See Silverberg, Robert

Clough, Arthur Hugh 1819-1861 ... **NCLC 27**
See also DLB 32; RGEL

Clutha, Janet Paterson Frame 1924-
See Frame, Janet
See also CA 1-4R; CANR 2, 36, 76; MTCW
1, 2; SATA 119

Clyne, Terence
See Blatty, William Peter

Cobalt, Martin
See Mayne, William (James Carter)

Cobb, Irvin S(hrewsbury)
1876-1944 .... **TCLC 77**
See also CA 175; DLB 11, 25, 86
Cobbett, William 1763-1835 .... **NCLC 49**
See also DLB 43, 107, 158; RGEL
Coburn, D(onald) L(ee) 1938- .... **CLC 10**
See also CA 89-92
Cocteau, Jean (Maurice Eugene Clement)
1889-1963 .... **CLC 1, 8, 15, 16, 43; DA;
DAB; DAC; DAM DRAM, MST, NOV;
WLC**
See also CA 25-28; CANR 40; CAP 2;
DA3; DLB 65; EW; GFL 1789 to the
Present; MTCW 1, 2; RGWL
Codrescu, Andrei 1946- .... **CLC 46, 121;
DAM POET**
See also CA 33-36R; CAAS 19; CANR 13,
34, 53, 76; DA3; MTCW 2
Coe, Max
See Bourne, Randolph S(illiman)
Coe, Tucker
See Westlake, Donald E(dwin)
Coen, Ethan 1958- .... **CLC 108**
See also CA 126; CANR 85
Coen, Joel 1955- .... **CLC 108**
See also CA 126
The Coen Brothers
See Coen, Ethan; Coen, Joel
Coetzee, J(ohn) M(ichael) 1940- ...... **CLC 23,
33, 66, 117; DAM NOV**
See also AAYA 37; AFW; BRWS 6; CA 77-
80; CANR 41, 54, 74; CN; DA3; DLB
225; MTCW 1, 2; WLIT 2
Coffey, Brian
See Koontz, Dean R(ay)
Coffin, Robert P(eter) Tristram
1892-1955 .... **TCLC 95**
See also CA 123; 169; DLB 45
Cohan, George M(ichael)
1878-1942 .... **TCLC 60**
See also CA 157; RGAL
Cohen, Arthur A(llen) 1928-1986 ...... **CLC 7,
31**
See also CA 1-4R; 120; CANR 1, 17, 42;
DLB 28
Cohen, Leonard (Norman) 1934- ...... **CLC 3,
38; DAC; DAM MST**
See also CA 21-24R; CANR 14, 69; CN;
CP; DLB 53; MTCW 1
Cohen, Matt(hew) 1942-1999 .... **CLC 19;
DAC**
See also CA 61-64; 187; CAAS 18; CANR
40; CN; DLB 53
Cohen-Solal, Annie 19(?)- .... **CLC 50**
Colegate, Isabel 1931- .... **CLC 36**
See also CA 17-20R; CANR 8, 22, 74; CN;
DLB 14, 231; INT CANR-22; MTCW 1
Coleman, Emmett
See Reed, Ishmael
Coleridge, Hartley 1796-1849 .... **NCLC 90**
See also DLB 96
Coleridge, M. E.
See Coleridge, Mary E(lizabeth)
Coleridge, Mary E(lizabeth)
1861-1907 .... **TCLC 73**
See also CA 116; 166; DLB 19, 98
Coleridge, Samuel Taylor
1772-1834 . **NCLC 9, 54, 99; DA; DAB;
DAC; DAM MST, POET; PC 11; WLC**
See also BYA 4; CDBLB 1789-1832; DA3;
DLB 93, 107; EXPP; PAB; PFS 4, 5;
RGEL; WLIT 3; WP
Coleridge, Sara 1802-1852 .... **NCLC 31**
See also DLB 199
Coles, Don 1928- .... **CLC 46**
See also CA 115; CANR 38; CP
Coles, Robert (Martin) 1929- .... **CLC 108**
See also CA 45-48; CANR 3, 32, 66, 70;
INT CANR-32; SATA 23

Colette, (Sidonie-Gabrielle)
1873-1954 . **TCLC 1, 5, 16; DAM NOV;
SSC 10**
See also Willy, Colette
See also CA 104; 131; DA3; DLB 65; EW;
GFL 1789 to the Present; MTCW 1, 2;
RGWL
Collett, (Jacobine) Camilla (Wergeland)
1813-1895 .... **NCLC 22**
Collier, Christopher 1930- .... **CLC 30**
See also AAYA 13; BYA 2; CA 33-36R;
CANR 13, 33; JRDA; MAICYA; SATA
16, 70; WYA; YAW 1
Collier, James Lincoln 1928- .... **CLC 30;
DAM POP**
See also AAYA 13; BYA 2; CA 9-12R;
CANR 4, 33, 60; CLR 3; JRDA; MAI-
CYA; SAAS 21; SATA 8, 70; WYA; YAW
1
Collier, Jeremy 1650-1726 .... **LC 6**
Collier, John 1901-1980 .... **SSC 19**
See also CA 65-68; 97-100; CANR 10;
DLB 77; FANT
Collingwood, R(obin) G(eorge)
1889(?)-1943 .... **TCLC 67**
See also CA 117; 155
Collins, Hunt
See Hunter, Evan
Collins, Linda 1931- .... **CLC 44**
See also CA 125
Collins, (William) Wilkie
1824-1889 .... **NCLC 1, 18, 93**
See also BRWS 6; CDBLB 1832-1890;
CMW; DLB 18, 70, 159; MSW; RGEL;
RGSF; SUFW; WLIT 4
Collins, William 1721-1759 . **LC 4, 40; DAM
POET**
See also DLB 109; RGEL
Collodi, Carlo .... **NCLC 54**
See also Lorenzini, Carlo
See also CLR 5; WCH
Colman, George
See Glassco, John
Colt, Winchester Remington
See Hubbard, L(afayette) Ron(ald)
Colter, Cyrus 1910- .... **CLC 58**
See also BW 1; CA 65-68; CANR 10, 66;
CN; DLB 33
Colton, James
See Hansen, Joseph
See also GLL 1
Colum, Padraic 1881-1972 .... **CLC 28**
See also BYA 4; CA 73-76; CANR
35; CLR 36; CWRI; MAICYA; MTCW
1; RGEL; SATA 15
Colvin, James
See Moorcock, Michael (John)
Colwin, Laurie (E.) 1944-1992 .... **CLC 5, 13,
23, 84**
See also CA 89-92; 139; CANR 20, 46;
DLBY 80; MTCW 1
Comfort, Alex(ander) 1920-2000 .... **CLC 7;
DAM POP**
See also CA 1-4R; 190; CANR 1, 45; CP;
MTCW 1
Comfort, Montgomery
See Campbell, (John) Ramsey
Compton-Burnett, I(vy)
1892(?)-1969 .... **CLC 1, 3, 10, 15, 34;
DAM NOV**
See also BRW; CA 1-4R; 25-28R; CANR
4; DLB 36; MTCW 1; RGEL
Comstock, Anthony 1844-1915 ...... **TCLC 13**
See also CA 110; 169
Comte, Auguste 1798-1857 .... **NCLC 54**
Conan Doyle, Arthur
See Doyle, Sir Arthur Conan
See also BPFB 1; BYA 4

Conde (Abellan), Carmen 1901-
See also CA 177; DLB 108; HLCS 1; HW
2
Conde, Maryse 1937- .... **CLC 52, 92; BLCS;
DAM MULT**
See also BW 2, 3; CA 110; CAAE 190;
CANR 30, 53, 76; CWW 2; MTCW 1
Condillac, Etienne Bonnot de
1714-1780 .... **LC 26**
Condon, Richard (Thomas)
1915-1996 ...... **CLC 4, 6, 8, 10, 45, 100;
DAM NOV**
See also BEST 90:3; BPFB 1; CA 1-4R;
151; CAAS 1; CANR 2, 23; CMW; CN;
INT CANR-23; MTCW 1, 2
Confucius 551B.C.-479B.C. .. **CMLC 19; DA;
DAB; DAC; DAM MST; WLCS**
See also DA3
Congreve, William 1670-1729 .... **LC 5, 21;
DA; DAB; DAC; DAM DRAM, MST,
POET; DC 2; WLC**
See also BRW 2; CDBLB 1660-1789; DLB
39, 84; RGEL; WLIT 3
Connell, Evan S(helby), Jr. 1924- . **CLC 4, 6,
45; DAM NOV**
See also AAYA 7; CA 1-4R; CAAS 2;
CANR 2, 39, 76, 97; CN; DLB 2; DLBY
81; MTCW 1, 2
Connelly, Marc(us Cook) 1890-1980 . **CLC 7**
See also CA 85-88; 102; CANR 30; DFS
12; DLB 7; DLBY 80; RGAL; SATA-Obit
25
Connor, Ralph .... **TCLC 31**
See also Gordon, Charles William
See also DLB 92; TCWW 2
Conrad, Joseph 1857-1924 .... **TCLC 1, 6, 13,
25, 43, 57; DA; DAB; DAC; DAM
MST, NOV; SSC 9; WLC**
See also AAYA 26; BPFB 1; BYA 2; CA
104; 131; CANR 60; CDBLB 1890-1914;
DA3; DLB 10, 34, 98, 156; EXPN; EXPS;
LAIT 2; MTCW 1, 2; NFS 2; RGEL;
RGSF; SATA 27; SSFS 1, 12; WLIT 4
Conrad, Robert Arnold
See Hart, Moss
Conroy, Pat
See Conroy, (Donald) Pat(rick)
See also BPFB 1; LAIT 5; MTCW 2
Conroy, (Donald) Pat(rick) 1945- ... **CLC 30,
74; DAM NOV, POP**
See also Conroy, Pat
See also AAYA 8; AITN 1; CA 85-88;
CANR 24, 53; CPW; CSW; DA3; DLB 6;
MTCW 1
Constant (de Rebecque), (Henri) Benjamin
1767-1830 .... **NCLC 6**
See also DLB 119; EW; GFL 1789 to the
Present
Conybeare, Charles Augustus
See Eliot, T(homas) S(tearns)
Cook, Michael 1933-1994 .... **CLC 58**
See also CA 93-96; CANR 68; DLB 53
Cook, Robin 1940- .... **CLC 14; DAM POP**
See also AAYA 32; BEST 90:2; BPFB 1;
CA 108; 111; CANR 41, 90; CPW; DA3;
HGG; INT CA-111
Cook, Roy
See Silverberg, Robert
Cooke, Elizabeth 1948- .... **CLC 55**
See also CA 129
Cooke, John Esten 1830-1886 .... **NCLC 5**
See also DLB 3; RGAL
Cooke, John Estes
See Baum, L(yman) Frank
Cooke, M. E.
See Creasey, John
Cooke, Margaret
See Creasey, John

Ellison, Harlan (Jay) 1934- ... **CLC 1, 13, 42, 139; DAM POP; SSC 14**
See also AAYA 29; BPFB 1; CA 5-8R; CANR 5, 46; CPW; DLB 8; HGG; INT CANR-5; MTCW 1, 2; SCFW 2; SFW; SUFW

Ellison, Ralph (Waldo) 1914-1994 .... **CLC 1, 3, 11, 54, 86, 114; BLC 1; DA; DAB; DAC; DAM MST, MULT, NOV; SSC 26; WLC**
See also AAYA 19; AFAW 1, 2; AMWS 2; BPFB 1; BW 1, 3; BYA 2; CA 9-12R; 145; CANR 24, 53; CDALB 1941-1968; CSW; DA3; DLB 2, 76, 227; DLBY 94; EXPN; EXPS; LAIT 4; MTCW 1, 2; NFS 2; RGAL; RGSF; SSFS 1, 11; YAW

Ellmann, Lucy (Elizabeth) 1956- ..... **CLC 61**
See also CA 128

Ellmann, Richard (David) 1918-1987 .... **CLC 50**
See also BEST 89:2; CA 1-4R; 122; CANR 2, 28, 61; DLB 103; DLBY 87; MTCW 1, 2

Elman, Richard (Martin) 1934-1997 .... **CLC 19**
See also CA 17-20R; 163; CAAS 3; CANR 47

Elron
See Hubbard, L(afayette) Ron(ald)

Eluard, Paul .... **TCLC 7, 41**
See also Grindel, Eugene
See also GFL 1789 to the Present; RGWL

Elyot, Thomas 1490(?)-1546 .... **LC 11**
See also RGEL

Elytis, Odysseus 1911-1996 .... **CLC 15, 49, 100; DAM POET; PC 21**
See also Alepoudelis, Odysseus
See also CA 102; 151; CANR 94; CWW 2; MTCW 1, 2; RGWL

Emecheta, (Florence Onye) Buchi 1944- .. **CLC 14, 48, 128; BLC 2; DAM MULT**
See also AFW; BW 2, 3; CA 81-84; CANR 27, 81; CN; CWRI; DA3; DLB 117; FW; MTCW 1, 2; NFS 12; SATA 66; WLIT 2

Emerson, Mary Moody 1774-1863 .... **NCLC 66**

Emerson, Ralph Waldo 1803-1882 . **NCLC 1, 38, 98; DA; DAB; DAC; DAM MST, POET; PC 18; WLC**
See also AMW; CDALB 1640-1865; DA3; DLB 1, 59, 73, 223; EXPP; LAIT 2; PFS 4; RGAL; WP

Eminescu, Mihail 1850-1889 .... **NCLC 33**

Empson, William 1906-1984 ... **CLC 3, 8, 19, 33, 34**
See also BRWS 2; CA 17-20R; 112; CANR 31, 61; DLB 20; MTCW 1, 2; RGEL

Enchi, Fumiko (Ueda) 1905-1986 ..... **CLC 31**
See also CA 129; 121; DLB 182; FW; MJW

Ende, Michael (Andreas Helmuth) 1929-1995 .... **CLC 31**
See also BYA 5; CA 118; 124; 149; CANR 36; CLR 14; DLB 75; MAICYA; MAIC-YAS; SATA 61; SATA-Brief 42; SATA-Obit 86

Endo, Shusaku 1923-1996 ..... **CLC 7, 14, 19, 54, 99; DAM NOV**
See also CA 29-32R; 153; CANR 21, 54; DA3; DLB 182; MTCW 1, 2; RGSF; RGWL

Engel, Marian 1933-1985 .... **CLC 36**
See also CA 25-28R; CANR 12; DLB 53; FW; INT CANR-12

Engelhardt, Frederick
See Hubbard, L(afayette) Ron(ald)

Engels, Friedrich 1820-1895 .... **NCLC 85**
See also DLB 129

Enright, D(ennis) J(oseph) 1920- .. **CLC 4, 8, 31**
See also CA 1-4R; CANR 1, 42, 83; CP; DLB 27; SATA 25

Enzensberger, Hans Magnus 1929- .... **CLC 43; PC 28**
See also CA 116; 119

Ephron, Nora 1941- .... **CLC 17, 31**
See also AAYA 35; AITN 2; CA 65-68; CANR 12, 39, 83

Epicurus 341B.C.-270B.C. .... **CMLC 21**
See also DLB 176

Epsilon
See Betjeman, John

Epstein, Daniel Mark 1948- .... **CLC 7**
See also CA 49-52; CANR 2, 53, 90

Epstein, Jacob 1956- .... **CLC 19**
See also CA 114

Epstein, Jean 1897-1953 .... **TCLC 92**

Epstein, Joseph 1937- .... **CLC 39**
See also CA 112; 119; CANR 50, 65

Epstein, Leslie 1938- .... **CLC 27**
See also CA 73-76; CAAS 12; CANR 23, 69

Equiano, Olaudah 1745(?)-1797 .... **LC 16; BLC 2; DAM MULT**
See also DLB 37, 50; WLIT 2

Erasmus, Desiderius 1469(?)-1536 ...... **LC 16**
See also RGWL

Erdman, Paul E(mil) 1932- .... **CLC 25**
See also AITN 1; CA 61-64; CANR 13, 43, 84

Erdrich, Louise 1954- .... **CLC 39, 54, 120; DAM MULT, NOV, POP**
See also AAYA 10; AMWS 4; BEST 89:1; BPFB 1; CA 114; CANR 41, 62; CDALBS; CN; CP; CPW; CWP; DA3; DLB 152, 175, 206; EXPP; LAIT 5; MTCW 1; NFS 5; NNAL; RGAL; SATA 94; TCWW 2

Erenburg, Ilya (Grigoryevich)
See Ehrenburg, Ilya (Grigoryevich)

Erickson, Stephen Michael 1950-
See Erickson, Steve
See also CA 129; SFW

Erickson, Steve .... **CLC 64**
See also Erickson, Stephen Michael
See also CANR 60, 68

Ericson, Walter
See Fast, Howard (Melvin)

Eriksson, Buntel
See Bergman, (Ernst) Ingmar

Ernaux, Annie 1940- .... **CLC 88**
See also CA 147; CANR 93

Erskine, John 1879-1951 .... **TCLC 84**
See also CA 112; 159; DLB 9, 102; FANT

Eschenbach, Wolfram von
See Wolfram von Eschenbach

Eseki, Bruno
See Mphahlele, Ezekiel

Esenin, Sergei (Alexandrovich) 1895-1925 .... **TCLC 4**
See also CA 104; RGWL

Eshleman, Clayton 1935- .... **CLC 7**
See also CA 33-36R; CAAS 6; CANR 93; CP; DLB 5

Espriella, Don Manuel Alvarez
See Southey, Robert

Espriu, Salvador 1913-1985 .... **CLC 9**
See also CA 154; 115; DLB 134

Espronceda, Jose de 1808-1842 ..... **NCLC 39**

Esquivel, Laura 1951(?)- ... **CLC 141; HLCS 1**
See also AAYA 29; CA 143; CANR 68; DA3; DNFS; LAIT 3; MTCW 1; NFS 5; WLIT 1

Esse, James
See Stephens, James

Esterbrook, Tom
See Hubbard, L(afayette) Ron(ald)

Estleman, Loren D. 1952- ..... **CLC 48; DAM NOV, POP**
See also AAYA 27; CA 85-88; CANR 27, 74; CMW; CPW; DA3; DLB 226; INT CANR-27; MTCW 1, 2

Euclid 306B.C.-283B.C. .... **CMLC 25**

Eugenides, Jeffrey 1960(?)- .... **CLC 81**
See also CA 144

Euripides c. 484B.C.-406B.C. .... **CMLC 23; DA; DAB; DAC; DAM DRAM, MST; DC 4; WLCS**
See also DA3; DFS 1, 4, 6; DLB 176; LAIT 1; RGWL

Evan, Evin
See Faust, Frederick (Schiller)

Evans, Caradoc 1878-1945 ... **TCLC 85; SSC 43**

Evans, Evan
See Faust, Frederick (Schiller)
See also TCWW 2

Evans, Marian
See Eliot, George

Evans, Mary Ann
See Eliot, George

Evarts, Esther
See Benson, Sally

Everett, Percival
See Everett, Percival L.
See also CSW

Everett, Percival L. 1956- .... **CLC 57**
See also Everett, Percival
See also BW 2; CA 129; CANR 94

Everson, R(onald) G(ilmour) 1903-1992 .... **CLC 27**
See also CA 17-20R; DLB 88

Everson, William (Oliver) 1912-1994 .... **CLC 1, 5, 14**
See also CA 9-12R; 145; CANR 20; DLB 212; MTCW 1

Evtushenko, Evgenii Aleksandrovich
See Yevtushenko, Yevgeny (Alexandrovich)
See also RGWL

Ewart, Gavin (Buchanan) 1916-1995 .... **CLC 13, 46**
See also BRWS 7; CA 89-92; 150; CANR 17, 46; CP; DLB 40; MTCW 1

Ewers, Hanns Heinz 1871-1943 ..... **TCLC 12**
See also CA 109; 149

Ewing, Frederick R.
See Sturgeon, Theodore (Hamilton)

Exley, Frederick (Earl) 1929-1992 .... **CLC 6, 11**
See also AITN 2; BPFB 1; CA 81-84; 138; DLB 143; DLBY 81

Eynhardt, Guillermo
See Quiroga, Horacio (Sylvestre)

Ezekiel, Nissim 1924- .... **CLC 61**
See also CA 61-64; CP

Ezekiel, Tish O'Dowd 1943- .... **CLC 34**
See also CA 129

Fadeyev, A.
See Bulgya, Alexander Alexandrovich

Fadeyev, Alexander .... **TCLC 53**
See also Bulgya, Alexander Alexandrovich

Fagen, Donald 1948- .... **CLC 26**

Fainzilberg, Ilya Arnoldovich 1897-1937
See Ilf, Ilya
See also CA 120; 165

Fair, Ronald L. 1932- .... **CLC 18**
See also BW 1; CA 69-72; CANR 25; DLB 33

Fairbairn, Roger
See Carr, John Dickson

Fairbairns, Zoe (Ann) 1948- .... **CLC 32**
See also CA 103; CANR 21, 85; CN

Fairman, Paul W. 1916-1977
  See Queen, Ellery
  See also CA 114; SFW

Falco, Gian
  See Papini, Giovanni

Falconer, James
  See Kirkup, James

Falconer, Kenneth
  See Kornbluth, C(yril) M.

Falkland, Samuel
  See Heijermans, Herman

Fallaci, Oriana 1930- .... **CLC 11, 110**
  See also CA 77-80; CANR 15, 58; FW;
  MTCW 1

Faludi, Susan 1959- .... **CLC 140**
  See also CA 138; FW; MTCW 1

Faludy, George 1913- .... **CLC 42**
  See also CA 21-24R

Faludy, Gyoergy
  See Faludy, George

Fanon, Frantz 1925-1961 ... **CLC 74; BLC 2;
  DAM MULT**
  See also BW 1; CA 116; 89-92; WLIT 2

Fanshawe, Ann 1625-1680 .... **LC 11**

Fante, John (Thomas) 1911-1983 ..... **CLC 60**
  See also CA 69-72; 109; CANR 23; DLB
  130; DLBY 83

Farah, Nuruddin 1945- .. **CLC 53, 137; BLC
  2; DAM MULT**
  See also BW 2, 3; CA 106; CANR 81; CN;
  DLB 125; WLIT 2

Fargue, Leon-Paul 1876(?)-1947 .... **TCLC 11**
  See also CA 109

Farigoule, Louis
  See Romains, Jules

Farina, Richard 1936(?)-1966 .... **CLC 9**
  See also CA 81-84; 25-28R

Farley, Walter (Lorimer)
  1915-1989 .... **CLC 17**
  See also CA 17-20R; CANR 8, 29, 84; DLB
  22; JRDA; MAICYA; SATA 2, 43; YAW

Farmer, Philip Jose 1918- .... **CLC 1, 19**
  See also AAYA 28; BPFB 1; CA 1-4R;
  CANR 4, 35; DLB 8; MTCW 1; SATA
  93; SFW

Farquhar, George 1677-1707 ... **LC 21; DAM
  DRAM**
  See also BRW 2; DLB 84; RGEL

Farrell, J(ames) G(ordon)
  1935-1979 .... **CLC 6**
  See also CA 73-76; 89-92; CANR 36; DLB
  14; MTCW 1; RGEL; RHW; WLIT 4

Farrell, James T(homas) 1904-1979 . **CLC 1,
  4, 8, 11, 66; SSC 28**
  See also AMW; BPFB 1; CA 5-8R; 89-92;
  CANR 9, 61; DLB 4, 9, 86; DLBD 2;
  MTCW 1, 2; RGAL

Farrell, Warren (Thomas) 1943- ...... **CLC 70**
  See also CA 146

Farren, Richard J.
  See Betjeman, John

Farren, Richard M.
  See Betjeman, John

Fassbinder, Rainer Werner
  1946-1982 .... **CLC 20**
  See also CA 93-96; 106; CANR 31

Fast, Howard (Melvin) 1914- .. **CLC 23, 131;
  DAM NOV**
  See also AAYA 16; BPFB 1; CA 1-4R; 181;
  CAAE 181; CAAS 18; CANR 1, 33, 54,
  75, 98; CMW; CN; CPW; DLB 9; INT
  CANR-33; MTCW 1; RHW; SATA 7;
  SATA-Essay 107; TCWW 2; YAW

Faulcon, Robert
  See Holdstock, Robert P.

Faulkner, William (Cuthbert)
  1897-1962 .... **CLC 1, 3, 6, 8, 9, 11, 14,
  18, 28, 52, 68; DA; DAB; DAC; DAM
  MST, NOV; SSC 1, 35, 42; WLC**
  See also AAYA 7; AMW; AMWR; BPFB 1;
  BYA 5; CA 81-84; CANR 33; CDALB
  1929-1941; DA3; DLB 9, 11, 44, 102;
  DLBD 2; DLBY 86, 97; EXPN; EXPS;
  LAIT 2; MTCW 1, 2; NFS 4, 8; RGAL;
  RGSF; SSFS 2, 5, 6, 12

Fauset, Jessie Redmon
  1882(?)-1961 .... **CLC 19, 54; BLC 2;
  DAM MULT**
  See also AFAW 2; BW 1; CA 109; CANR
  83; DLB 51; FW; MAWW

Faust, Frederick (Schiller)
  1892-1944(?) .... **TCLC 49; DAM POP**
  See also Austin, Frank; Brand, Max; Challis, George; Dawson, Peter; Dexter, Martin; Evans, Evan; Frederick, John; Frost,
  Frederick; Manning, David; Silver, Nicholas
  See also CA 108; 152

Faust, Irvin 1924- .... **CLC 8**
  See also CA 33-36R; CANR 28, 67; CN;
  DLB 2, 28; DLBY 80

Fawkes, Guy
  See Benchley, Robert (Charles)

Fearing, Kenneth (Flexner)
  1902-1961 .... **CLC 51**
  See also CA 93-96; CANR 59; CMW; DLB
  9; RGAL

Fecamps, Elise
  See Creasey, John

Federman, Raymond 1928- .... **CLC 6, 47**
  See also CA 17-20R; CAAS 8; CANR 10,
  43, 83; CN; DLBY 80

Federspiel, J(uerg) F. 1931- .... **CLC 42**
  See also CA 146

Feiffer, Jules (Ralph) 1929- ..... **CLC 2, 8, 64;
  DAM DRAM**
  See also AAYA 3; CA 17-20R; CAD; CANR
  30, 59; CD; DLB 7, 44; INT CANR-30;
  MTCW 1; SATA 8, 61, 111

Feige, Hermann Albert Otto Maximilian
  See Traven, B.

Feinberg, David B. 1956-1994 .... **CLC 59**
  See also CA 135; 147

Feinstein, Elaine 1930- .... **CLC 36**
  See also CA 69-72; CAAS 1; CANR 31,
  68; CN; CP; CWP; DLB 14, 40; MTCW
  1

Feke, Gilbert David .... **CLC 65**

Feldman, Irving (Mordecai) 1928- ..... **CLC 7**
  See also CA 1-4R; CANR 1; CP; DLB 169

Felix-Tchicaya, Gerald
  See Tchicaya, Gerald Felix

Fellini, Federico 1920-1993 .... **CLC 16, 85**
  See also CA 65-68; 143; CANR 33

Felsen, Henry Gregor 1916-1995 ..... **CLC 17**
  See also CA 1-4R; 180; CANR 1; SAAS 2;
  SATA 1

Felski, Rita .... **CLC 65**

Fenno, Jack
  See Calisher, Hortense

Fenollosa, Ernest (Francisco)
  1853-1908 .... **TCLC 91**

Fenton, James Martin 1949- .... **CLC 32**
  See also CA 102; CP; DLB 40; PFS 11

Ferber, Edna 1887-1968 .... **CLC 18, 93**
  See also AITN 1; CA 5-8R; 25-28R; CANR
  68; DLB 9, 28, 86; MTCW 1, 2; RGAL;
  RHW; SATA 7; TCWW 2

Ferdowsi, Abu'l Qasem 940-1020 . **CMLC 43**
  See also RGWL

Ferguson, Helen
  See Kavan, Anna

Ferguson, Niall 1964- .... **CLC 134**
  See also CA 190

Ferguson, Samuel 1810-1886 .... **NCLC 33**
  See also DLB 32; RGEL

Fergusson, Robert 1750-1774 .... **LC 29**
  See also DLB 109; RGEL

Ferling, Lawrence
  See Ferlinghetti, Lawrence (Monsanto)

Ferlinghetti, Lawrence (Monsanto)
  1919(?)- .... **CLC 2, 6, 10, 27, 111; DAM
  POET; PC 1**
  See also CA 5-8R; CANR 3, 41, 73;
  CDALB 1941-1968; CP; DA3; DLB 5,
  16; MTCW 1, 2; RGAL; WP

Fern, Fanny
  See Parton, Sara Payson Willis

Fernandez, Vicente Garcia Huidobro
  See Huidobro Fernandez, Vicente Garcia

Fernandez-Armesto, Felipe .... **CLC 70**

Fernandez de Lizardi, Jose Joaquin
  See Lizardi, Jose Joaquin Fernandez de

Ferre, Rosario 1942- ...... **CLC 139; HLCS 1;
  SSC 36**
  See also CA 131; CANR 55, 81; CWW 2;
  DLB 145; HW 1, 2; MTCW 1; WLIT 1

Ferrer, Gabriel (Francisco Victor) Miro
  See Miro (Ferrer), Gabriel (Francisco
  Victor)

Ferrier, Susan (Edmonstone)
  1782-1854 .... **NCLC 8**
  See also DLB 116; RGEL

Ferrigno, Robert 1948(?)- .... **CLC 65**
  See also CA 140

Ferron, Jacques 1921-1985 .... **CLC 94; DAC**
  See also CA 117; 129; CCA 1; DLB 60

Feuchtwanger, Lion 1884-1958 .... **TCLC 3**
  See also CA 104; 187; DLB 66

Feuillet, Octave 1821-1890 .... **NCLC 45**
  See also DLB 192

Feydeau, Georges (Leon Jules Marie)
  1862-1921 .... **TCLC 22; DAM DRAM**
  See also CA 113; 152; CANR 84; DLB 192;
  EW; GFL 1789 to the Present; RGWL

Fichte, Johann Gottlieb
  1762-1814 .... **NCLC 62**
  See also DLB 90

Ficino, Marsilio 1433-1499 .... **LC 12**

Fiedeler, Hans
  See Doeblin, Alfred

Fiedler, Leslie A(aron) 1917- .. **CLC 4, 13, 24**
  See also CA 9-12R; CANR 7, 63; CN; DLB
  28, 67; MTCW 1, 2; RGAL

Field, Andrew 1938- .... **CLC 44**
  See also CA 97-100; CANR 25

Field, Eugene 1850-1895 .... **NCLC 3**
  See also DLB 23, 42, 140; DLBD 13; MAI-
  CYA; RGAL; SATA 16

Field, Gans T.
  See Wellman, Manly Wade

Field, Michael 1915-1971 .... **TCLC 43**
  See also CA 29-32R

Field, Peter
  See Hobson, Laura Z(ametkin)
  See also TCWW 2

Fielding, Helen 1959(?)- .... **CLC 146**
  See also CA 172; DLB 231

Fielding, Henry 1707-1754 ..... **LC 1, 46; DA;
  DAB; DAC; DAM DRAM, MST, NOV;
  WLC**
  See also CDBLB 1660-1789; DA3; DLB
  39, 84, 101; RGEL; WLIT 3

Fielding, Sarah 1710-1768 .... **LC 1, 44**
  See also DLB 39; RGEL

Fields, W. C. 1880-1946 .... **TCLC 80**
  See also DLB 44

Fierstein, Harvey (Forbes) 1954- .... **CLC 33;
  DAM DRAM, POP**
  See also CA 123; 129; CAD; CD; CPW;
  DA3; DFS 6; GLL

Figes, Eva 1932- .... **CLC 31**
See also CA 53-56; CANR 4, 44, 83; CN; DLB 14; FW

Finch, Anne 1661-1720 .... **LC 3; PC 21**
See also DLB 95

Finch, Robert (Duer Claydon) 1900- .... **CLC 18**
See also CA 57-60; CANR 9, 24, 49; CP; DLB 88

Findley, Timothy 1930- . **CLC 27, 102; DAC; DAM MST**
See also CA 25-28R; CANR 12, 42, 69; CCA 1; CN; DLB 53; FANT; RHW

Fink, William
See Mencken, H(enry) L(ouis)

Firbank, Louis 1942-
See Reed, Lou
See also CA 117

Firbank, (Arthur Annesley) Ronald 1886-1926 .... **TCLC 1**
See also BRWS 2; CA 104; 177; DLB 36; RGEL

Fish, Stanley
See Fish, Stanley Eugene

Fish, Stanley E.
See Fish, Stanley Eugene

Fish, Stanley Eugene 1938- .... **CLC 142**
See also CA 112; 132; CANR 90; DLB 67

Fisher, Dorothy (Frances) Canfield 1879-1958 .... **TCLC 87**
See also CA 114; 136; CANR 80; CLR 71,; CWRI; DLB 9, 102; MAICYA; YABC 1

Fisher, M(ary) F(rances) K(ennedy) 1908-1992 .... **CLC 76, 87**
See also CA 77-80; 138; CANR 44; MTCW 1

Fisher, Roy 1930- .... **CLC 25**
See also CA 81-84; CAAS 10; CANR 16; CP; DLB 40

Fisher, Rudolph 1897-1934 .. **TCLC 11; BLC 2; DAM MULT; SSC 25**
See also BW 1, 3; CA 107; 124; CANR 80; DLB 51, 102

Fisher, Vardis (Alvero) 1895-1968 ...... **CLC 7**
See also CA 5-8R; 25-28R; CANR 68; DLB 9, 206; RGAL; TCWW 2

Fiske, Tarleton
See Bloch, Robert (Albert)

Fitch, Clarke
See Sinclair, Upton (Beall)

Fitch, John IV
See Cormier, Robert (Edmund)

Fitzgerald, Captain Hugh
See Baum, L(yman) Frank

FitzGerald, Edward 1809-1883 .... **NCLC 9**
See also DLB 32; RGEL

Fitzgerald, F(rancis) Scott (Key) 1896-1940 .. **TCLC 1, 6, 14, 28, 55; DA; DAB; DAC; DAM MST, NOV; SSC 6, 31; WLC**
See also AAYA 24; AITN 1; AMW; AMWR; BPFB 1; CA 110; 123; CDALB 1917-1929; DA3; DLB 4, 9, 86; DLBD 1, 15, 16; DLBY 81, 96; EXPN; EXPS; LAIT 3; MTCW 1, 2; NFS 2; RGAL; RGSF; SSFS 4

Fitzgerald, Penelope 1916-2000 . **CLC 19, 51, 61, 143**
See also BRWS 5; CA 85-88; 190; CAAS 10; CANR 56, 86; CN; DLB 14, 194; MTCW 2

Fitzgerald, Robert (Stuart) 1910-1985 .... **CLC 39**
See also CA 1-4R; 114; CANR 1; DLBY 80

FitzGerald, Robert D(avid) 1902-1987 .... **CLC 19**
See also CA 17-20R; RGEL

Fitzgerald, Zelda (Sayre) 1900-1948 .... **TCLC 52**
See also CA 117; 126; DLBY 84

Flanagan, Thomas (James Bonner) 1923- .... **CLC 25, 52**
See also CA 108; CANR 55; CN; DLBY 80; INT 108; MTCW 1; RHW

Flaubert, Gustave 1821-1880 .... **NCLC 2, 10, 19, 62, 66; DA; DAB; DAC; DAM MST, NOV; SSC 11; WLC**
See also DA3; DLB 119; EXPS; GFL 1789 to the Present; LAIT 2; RGSF; RGWL; SSFS 6

Flavius Josephus
See Josephus, Flavius

Flecker, Herman Elroy
See Flecker, (Herman) James Elroy

Flecker, (Herman) James Elroy 1884-1915 .... **TCLC 43**
See also CA 109; 150; DLB 10, 19; RGEL

Fleming, Ian (Lancaster) 1908-1964 . **CLC 3, 30; DAM POP**
See also AAYA 26; BPFB 1; CA 5-8R; CANR 59; CDBLB 1945-1960; CMW; CPW; DA3; DLB 87, 201; MSW; MTCW 1, 2; RGEL; SATA 9; YAW

Fleming, Thomas (James) 1927- ...... **CLC 37**
See also CA 5-8R; CANR 10; INT CANR-10; SATA 8

Fletcher, John 1579-1625 .... **LC 33; DC 6**
See also BRW 2; CDBLB Before 1660; DLB 58; RGEL

Fletcher, John Gould 1886-1950 .... **TCLC 35**
See also CA 107; 167; DLB 4, 45; RGAL

Fleur, Paul
See Pohl, Frederik

Flooglebuckle, Al
See Spiegelman, Art

Flora, Fletcher 1914-1969
See Queen, Ellery
See also CA 1-4R; CANR 3, 85

Flying Officer X
See Bates, H(erbert) E(rnest)

Fo, Dario 1926- .... **CLC 32, 109; DAM DRAM; DC 10**
See also CA 116; 128; CANR 68; CWW 2; DA3; DLBY 97; MTCW 1, 2

Fogarty, Jonathan Titulescu Esq.
See Farrell, James T(homas)

Follett, Ken(neth Martin) 1949- ..... **CLC 18; DAM NOV, POP**
See also AAYA 6; BEST 89:4; BPFB 1; CA 81-84; CANR 13, 33, 54; CMW; CPW; DA3; DLB 87; DLBY 81; INT CANR-33; MTCW 1

Fontane, Theodor 1819-1898 .... **NCLC 26**
See also DLB 129; RGWL

Fontenot, Chester .... **CLC 65**

Foote, Horton 1916- .... **CLC 51, 91; DAM DRAM**
See also CA 73-76; CAD; CANR 34, 51; CD; CSW; DA3; DLB 26; INT CANR-34

Foote, Mary Hallock 1847-1938 .. **TCLC 108**
See also DLB 186, 188, 202, 221

Foote, Shelby 1916- ..... **CLC 75; DAM NOV, POP**
See also AAYA 40; CA 5-8R; CANR 3, 45, 74; CN; CPW; CSW; DA3; DLB 2, 17; MTCW 2; RHW

Forbes, Esther 1891-1967 .... **CLC 12**
See also AAYA 17; BYA 2; CA 13-14; 25-28R; CAP 1; CLR 27; DLB 22; JRDA; MAICYA; RHW; SATA 2, 100; YAW

Forche, Carolyn (Louise) 1950- .... **CLC 25, 83, 86; DAM POET; PC 10**
See also CA 109; 117; CANR 50, 74; CP; CWP; DA3; DLB 5, 193; INT CA-117; MTCW 1; RGAL

Ford, Elbur
See Hibbert, Eleanor Alice Burford

Ford, Ford Madox 1873-1939 ... **TCLC 1, 15, 39, 57; DAM NOV**
See Chaucer, Daniel
See also CA 104; 132; CANR 74; CDBLB 1914-1945; DA3; DLB 162; MTCW 1, 2; RGEL

Ford, Henry 1863-1947 .... **TCLC 73**
See also CA 115; 148

Ford, John 1586-1639 .... **LC 68; DAM DRAM; DC 8**
See also BRW 2; CDBLB Before 1660; DA3; DFS 7; DLB 58; IDTP; RGEL

Ford, John 1895-1973 .... **CLC 16**
See also CA 187; 45-48

Ford, Richard 1944- .... **CLC 46, 99**
See also AMWS 5; CA 69-72; CANR 11, 47, 86; CN; CSW; DLB 227; MTCW 1; RGAL; RGSF

Ford, Webster
See Masters, Edgar Lee

Foreman, Richard 1937- .... **CLC 50**
See also CA 65-68; CAD; CANR 32, 63; CD

Forester, C(ecil) S(cott) 1899-1966 ... **CLC 35**
See also CA 73-76; 25-28R; CANR 83; DLB 191; RGEL; RHW; SATA 13

Forez
See Mauriac, Francois (Charles)

Forman, James Douglas 1932- .... **CLC 21**
See also AAYA 17; CA 9-12R; CANR 4, 19, 42; JRDA; MAICYA; SATA 8, 70; YAW

Fornes, Maria Irene 1930- . **CLC 39, 61; DC 10; HLCS 1**
See also CA 25-28R; CAD; CANR 28, 81; CD; CWD; DLB 7; HW 1, 2; INT CANR-28; MTCW 1; RGAL

Forrest, Leon (Richard) 1937-1997 .. **CLC 4; BLCS**
See also AFAW 2; BW 2; CA 89-92; 162; CAAS 7; CANR 25, 52, 87; CN; DLB 33

Forster, E(dward) M(organ) 1879-1970 ... **CLC 1, 2, 3, 4, 9, 10, 13, 15, 22, 45, 77; DA; DAB; DAC; DAM MST, NOV; SSC 27; WLC**
See also AAYA 2, 37; BRW; CA 13-14; 25-28R; CANR 45; CAP 1; CDBLB 1914-1945; DA3; DLB 34, 98, 162, 178, 195; DLBD 10; EXPN; LAIT 3; MTCW 1, 2; NCFS 1; NFS 3, 10, 11; RGEL; RGSF; SATA 57; SUFW; WLIT 4

Forster, John 1812-1876 .... **NCLC 11**
See also DLB 144, 184

Forster, Margaret 1938- .... **CLC 149**
See also CA 133; CANR 62; CN; DLB 155

Forsyth, Frederick 1938- .... **CLC 2, 5, 36; DAM NOV, POP**
See also BEST 89:4; CA 85-88; CANR 38, 62; CMW; CN; CPW; DLB 87; MTCW 1, 2

Forten, Charlotte L. 1837-1914 .... **TCLC 16; BLC 2**
See also Grimke, Charlotte L(ottie) Forten
See also DLB 50, 239

Foscolo, Ugo 1778-1827 .... **NCLC 8, 97**

Fosse, Bob .... **CLC 20**
See also Fosse, Robert Louis

Fosse, Robert Louis 1927-1987
See Fosse, Bob
See also CA 110; 123

Foster, Hannah Webster 1758-1840 .... **NCLC 99**
See also DLB 37, 200; RGAL

Foster, Stephen Collins 1826-1864 .... **NCLC 26**
See also RGAL

Fuller, Margaret 1810-1850
See Ossoli, Sarah Margaret (Fuller)
See also AMWS 2; DLB 239

Fuller, Roy (Broadbent) 1912-1991 ... **CLC 4, 28**
See also BRWS 7; CA 5-8R; 135; CAAS 10; CANR 53, 83; CWRI; DLB 15, 20; RGEL; SATA 87

Fuller, Sarah Margaret
See Ossoli, Sarah Margaret (Fuller)

Fulton, Alice 1952- .... **CLC 52**
See also CA 116; CANR 57, 88; CP; CWP; DLB 193

Furphy, Joseph 1843-1912 .... **TCLC 25**
See also CA 163; DLB 230; RGEL

Fuson, Robert H(enderson) 1927- .... **CLC 70**
See also CA 89-92

Fussell, Paul 1924- .... **CLC 74**
See also BEST 90:1; CA 17-20R; CANR 8, 21, 35, 69; INT CANR-21; MTCW 1, 2

Futabatei, Shimei 1864-1909 .... **TCLC 44**
See also CA 162; DLB 180; MJW

Futrelle, Jacques 1875-1912 .... **TCLC 19**
See also CA 113; 155; CMW

Gaboriau, Emile 1835-1873 .... **NCLC 14**
See also CMW

Gadda, Carlo Emilio 1893-1973 .... **CLC 11**
See also CA 89-92; DLB 177

Gaddis, William 1922-1998 ... **CLC 1, 3, 6, 8, 10, 19, 43, 86**
See also AMWS 4; BPFB 1; CA 17-20R; 172; CANR 21, 48; CN; DLB 2; MTCW 1, 2; RGAL

Gaelique, Moruen le
See Jacob, (Cyprien-)Max

Gage, Walter
See Inge, William (Motter)

Gaines, Ernest J(ames) 1933- ...... **CLC 3, 11, 18, 86; BLC 2; DAM MULT**
See also AAYA 18; AFAW 1, 2; AITN 1; BPFB 2; BW 2, 3; BYA 6; CA 9-12R; CANR 6, 24, 42, 75; CDALB 1968-1988; CLR 62; CN; CSW; DA3; DLB 2, 33, 152; DLBY 80; EXPN; LAIT 5; MTCW 1, 2; NFS 5, 7; RGAL; RGSF; RHW; SATA 86; SSFS 5; YAW

Gaitskill, Mary 1954- .... **CLC 69**
See also CA 128; CANR 61

Galdos, Benito Perez
See Perez Galdos, Benito

Gale, Zona 1874-1938 .... **TCLC 7; DAM DRAM**
See also CA 105; 153; CANR 84; DLB 9, 78, 228; RGAL

Galeano, Eduardo (Hughes) 1940- . **CLC 72; HLCS 1**
See also CA 29-32R; CANR 13, 32, 100; HW 1

Galiano, Juan Valera y Alcala
See Valera y Alcala-Galiano, Juan

Galilei, Galileo 1564-1642 .... **LC 45**

Gallagher, Tess 1943- ...... **CLC 18, 63; DAM POET; PC 9**
See also CA 106; CP; CWP; DLB 212

Gallant, Mavis 1922- .. **CLC 7, 18, 38; DAC; DAM MST; SSC 5**
See also CA 69-72; CANR 29, 69; CCA 1; CN; DLB 53; MTCW 1, 2; RGEL; RGSF

Gallant, Roy A(rthur) 1924- .... **CLC 17**
See also CA 5-8R; CANR 4, 29, 54; CLR 30; MAICYA; SATA 4, 68, 110

Gallico, Paul (William) 1897-1976 ..... **CLC 2**
See also AITN 1; CA 5-8R; 69-72; CANR 23; DLB 9, 171; FANT; MAICYA; SATA 13

Gallo, Max Louis 1932- .... **CLC 95**
See also CA 85-88

Gallois, Lucien
See Desnos, Robert

Gallup, Ralph
See Whitemore, Hugh (John)

Galsworthy, John 1867-1933 .... **TCLC 1, 45; DA; DAB; DAC; DAM DRAM, MST, NOV; SSC 22; WLC**
See also CA 104; 141; CANR 75; CDBLB 1890-1914; DA3; DLB 10, 34, 98, 162; DLBD 16; MTCW 1; RGEL; SSFS 3

Galt, John 1779-1839 .... **NCLC 1**
See also DLB 99, 116, 159; RGEL; RGSF

Galvin, James 1951- .... **CLC 38**
See also CA 108; CANR 26

Gamboa, Federico 1864-1939 .... **TCLC 36**
See also CA 167; HW 2

Gandhi, M. K.
See Gandhi, Mohandas Karamchand

Gandhi, Mahatma
See Gandhi, Mohandas Karamchand

Gandhi, Mohandas Karamchand 1869-1948 .... **TCLC 59; DAM MULT**
See also CA 121; 132; DA3; MTCW 1, 2

Gann, Ernest Kellogg 1910-1991 ..... **CLC 23**
See also AITN 1; BPFB 2; CA 1-4R; 136; CANR 1, 83; RHW

Garber, Eric 1943(?)-
See Holleran, Andrew
See also CANR 89

Garcia, Cristina 1958- .... **CLC 76**
See also CA 141; CANR 73; DNFS; HW 2

Garcia Lorca, Federico 1898-1936 . **TCLC 1, 7, 49; DA; DAB; DAC; DAM DRAM, MST, MULT, POET; DC 2; HLC 2; PC 3; WLC**
See also Lorca, Federico Garcia
See also CA 104; 131; CANR 81; DA3; DFS 10; DLB 108; HW 1, 2; MTCW 1, 2

Garcia Marquez, Gabriel (Jose) 1928- .... **CLC 2, 3, 8, 10, 15, 27, 47, 55, 68; DA; DAB; DAC; DAM MST, MULT, NOV, POP; HLC 1; SSC 8; WLC**
See also AAYA 3, 33; BEST 89:1, 90:4; BPFB 2; BYA 12; CA 33-36R; CANR 10, 28, 50, 75, 82; CPW; DA3; DLB 113; DNFS; EXPN; EXPS; HW 1, 2; LAIT 2; LAW; MTCW 1, 2; NFS 1, 5, 10; RGSF; RGWL; SSFS 1, 6; WLIT 1

Garcilaso de la Vega, El Inca 1503-1536
See also HLCS 1

Gard, Janice
See Latham, Jean Lee

Gard, Roger Martin du
See Martin du Gard, Roger

Gardam, Jane 1928- .... **CLC 43**
See also CA 49-52; CANR 2, 18, 33, 54; CLR 12; DLB 14, 161, 231; MAICYA; MTCW 1; SAAS 9; SATA 39, 76; SATA-Brief 28; YAW

Gardner, Herb(ert) 1934- .... **CLC 44**
See also CA 149; CAD; CD

Gardner, John (Champlin), Jr. 1933-1982 ...... **CLC 2, 3, 5, 7, 8, 10, 18, 28, 34; DAM NOV, POP; SSC 7**
See also AITN 1; AMWS 2; BPFB 2; CA 65-68; 107; CANR 33, 73; CDALBS; CPW; DA3; DLB 2; DLBY 82; FANT; MTCW 1; NFS 3; RGAL; RGSF; SATA 40; SATA-Obit 31; SSFS 8

Gardner, John (Edmund) 1926- ...... **CLC 30; DAM POP**
See also CA 103; CANR 15, 69; CMW; CPW; MTCW 1

Gardner, Miriam
See Bradley, Marion Zimmer
See also GLL 1

Gardner, Noel
See Kuttner, Henry

Gardons, S. S.
See Snodgrass, W(illiam) D(e Witt)

Garfield, Leon 1921-1996 .... **CLC 12**
See also AAYA 8; BYA 1; CA 17-20R; 152; CANR 38, 41, 78; CLR 21; DLB 161; JRDA; MAICYA; SATA 1, 32, 76; SATA-Obit 90; YAW

Garland, (Hannibal) Hamlin 1860-1940 .... **TCLC 3; SSC 18**
See also CA 104; DLB 12, 71, 78, 186; RGAL; RGSF; TCWW 2

Garneau, (Hector de) Saint-Denys 1912-1943 .... **TCLC 13**
See also CA 111; DLB 88

Garner, Alan 1934- ..... **CLC 17; DAB; DAM POP**
See also AAYA 18; BYA 3; CA 73-76, 178; CAAE 178; CANR 15, 64; CLR 20; CPW; DLB 161; FANT; MAICYA; MTCW 1, 2; SATA 18, 69; SATA-Essay 108; YAW

Garner, Hugh 1913-1979 .... **CLC 13**
See also Warwick, Jarvis
See also CA 69-72; CANR 31; CCA 1; DLB 68

Garnett, David 1892-1981 .... **CLC 3**
See also CA 5-8R; 103; CANR 17, 79; DLB 34; FANT; MTCW 2; RGEL; SFW

Garos, Stephanie
See Katz, Steve

Garrett, George (Palmer) 1929- .. **CLC 3, 11, 51; SSC 30**
See also AMWS 7; BPFB 2; CA 1-4R; CAAS 5; CANR 1, 42, 67; CN; CP; CSW; DLB 2, 5, 130, 152; DLBY 83

Garrick, David 1717-1779 .... **LC 15; DAM DRAM**
See also DLB 84; RGEL

Garrigue, Jean 1914-1972 .... **CLC 2, 8**
See also CA 5-8R; 37-40R; CANR 20

Garrison, Frederick
See Sinclair, Upton (Beall)

Garro, Elena 1920(?)-1998
See also CA 131; 169; CWW 2; DLB 145; HLCS 1; HW 1; WLIT 1

Garth, Will
See Hamilton, Edmond; Kuttner, Henry

Garvey, Marcus (Moziah, Jr.) 1887-1940 ...... **TCLC 41; BLC 2; DAM MULT**
See also BW 1; CA 120; 124; CANR 79

Gary, Romain .... **CLC 25**
See also Kacew, Romain
See also DLB 83

Gascar, Pierre .... **CLC 11**
See also Fournier, Pierre

Gascoyne, David (Emery) 1916- .... **CLC 45**
See also CA 65-68; CANR 10, 28, 54; CP; DLB 20; MTCW 1; RGEL

Gaskell, Elizabeth Cleghorn 1810-1865 .... **NCLC 5, 70, 97; DAB; DAM MST; SSC 25**
See also BRW; CDBLB 1832-1890; DLB 21, 144, 159; RGEL; RGSF

Gass, William H(oward) 1924- . **CLC 1, 2, 8, 11, 15, 39, 132; SSC 12**
See also AMWS 6; CA 17-20R; CANR 30, 71, 100; CN; DLB 2, 227; MTCW 1, 2; RGAL

Gassendi, Pierre 1592-1655 .... **LC 54**
See also GFL Beginnings to 1789

Gasset, Jose Ortega y
See Ortega y Gasset, Jose

Gates, Henry Louis, Jr. 1950- .... **CLC 65; BLCS; DAM MULT**
See also BW 2, 3; CA 109; CANR 25, 53, 75; CSW; DA3; DLB 67; MTCW 1; RGAL

Gautier, Theophile 1811-1872 .. **NCLC 1, 59; DAM POET; PC 18; SSC 20**
See also DLB 119; GFL 1789 to the Present; RGWL

Gawsworth, John
See Bates, H(erbert) E(rnest)

Gay, John 1685-1732 .. **LC 49; DAM DRAM**
See also DLB 84, 95; RGEL; WLIT 3

Gay, Oliver
See Gogarty, Oliver St. John

Gaye, Marvin (Pentz, Jr.)
1939-1984 .... **CLC 26**
See also CA 112

Gebler, Carlo (Ernest) 1954- .... **CLC 39**
See also CA 119; 133; CANR 96

Gee, Maggie (Mary) 1948- .... **CLC 57**
See also CA 130; CN; DLB 207

Gee, Maurice (Gough) 1931- .... **CLC 29**
See also CA 97-100; CANR 67; CLR 56; CN; CWRI; RGSF; SATA 46, 101

Gelbart, Larry (Simon) 1928- .... **CLC 21, 61**
See also Gelbart, Larry
See also CA 73-76; CANR 45, 94

Gelbart, Larry 1928-
See Gelbart, Larry (Simon)
See also CAD; CD

Gelber, Jack 1932- .... **CLC 1, 6, 14, 79**
See also CA 1-4R; CAD; CANR 2; DLB 7, 228

Gellhorn, Martha (Ellis)
1908-1998 .... **CLC 14, 60**
See also CA 77-80; 164; CANR 44; CN; DLBY 82, 98

Genet, Jean 1910-1986 .. **CLC 1, 2, 5, 10, 14, 44, 46; DAM DRAM**
See also CA 13-16R; CANR 18; DA3; DFS 10; DLB 72; DLBY 86; GFL 1789 to the Present; GLL 1; MTCW 1, 2; RGWL

Gent, Peter 1942- .... **CLC 29**
See also AITN 1; CA 89-92; DLBY 82

Gentile, Giovanni 1875-1944 .... **TCLC 96**
See also CA 119

Gentlewoman in New England, A
See Bradstreet, Anne

Gentlewoman in Those Parts, A
See Bradstreet, Anne

Geoffrey of Monmouth c.
1100-1155 .... **CMLC 44**
See also DLB 146

George, Jean
See George, Jean Craighead

George, Jean Craighead 1919- .... **CLC 35**
See also AAYA 8; BYA 2; CA 5-8R; CANR 25; CLR 1; DLB 52; JRDA; MAICYA; SATA 2, 68, 124; YAW

George, Stefan (Anton) 1868-1933 . **TCLC 2, 14**
See also CA 104; 193; EW

Georges, Georges Martin
See Simenon, Georges (Jacques Christian)

Gerhardi, William Alexander
See Gerhardie, William Alexander

Gerhardie, William Alexander
1895-1977 .... **CLC 5**
See also CA 25-28R; 73-76; CANR 18; DLB 36; RGEL

Gerstler, Amy 1956- .... **CLC 70**
See also CA 146; CANR 99

Gertler, T. .... **CLC 134**
See also CA 116; 121

Ghalib .... **NCLC 39, 78**
See also Ghalib, Asadullah Khan

Ghalib, Asadullah Khan 1797-1869
See Ghalib
See also DAM POET; RGWL

Ghelderode, Michel de 1898-1962 ..... **CLC 6, 11; DAM DRAM; DC 15**
See also CA 85-88; CANR 40, 77

Ghiselin, Brewster 1903- .... **CLC 23**
See also CA 13-16R; CAAS 10; CANR 13; CP

Ghose, Aurabinda 1872-1950 .... **TCLC 63**
See also CA 163

Ghose, Zulfikar 1935- .... **CLC 42**
See also CA 65-68; CANR 67; CN; CP

Ghosh, Amitav 1956- .... **CLC 44**
See also CA 147; CANR 80; CN

Giacosa, Giuseppe 1847-1906 .... **TCLC 7**
See also CA 104

Gibb, Lee
See Waterhouse, Keith (Spencer)

Gibbon, Lewis Grassic .... **TCLC 4**
See also Mitchell, James Leslie
See also RGEL

Gibbons, Kaye 1960- .... **CLC 50, 88, 145; DAM POP**
See also AAYA 34; CA 151; CANR 75; CSW; DA3; MTCW 1; NFS 3; RGAL; SATA 117

Gibran, Kahlil 1883-1931 .... **TCLC 1, 9; DAM POET, POP; PC 9**
See also CA 104; 150; DA3; MTCW 2

Gibran, Khalil
See Gibran, Kahlil

Gibson, William 1914- .. **CLC 23; DA; DAB; DAC; DAM DRAM, MST**
See also CA 9-12R; CAD 2; CANR 9, 42, 75; CD; DFS 2; DLB 7; LAIT 2; MTCW 2; SATA 66; YAW

Gibson, William (Ford) 1948- ... **CLC 39, 63; DAM POP**
See also AAYA 12; BPFB 2; CA 126; 133; CANR 52, 90; CN; CPW; DA3; MTCW 2; SCFW 2; SFW

Gide, Andre (Paul Guillaume)
1869-1951 . **TCLC 5, 12, 36; DA; DAB; DAC; DAM MST, NOV; SSC 13; WLC**
See also CA 104; 124; DLB 65; EW; GFL 1789 to the Present; MTCW 1, 2; RGSF; RGWL

Gifford, Barry (Colby) 1946- .... **CLC 34**
See also CA 65-68; CANR 9, 30, 40, 90

Gilbert, Frank
See De Voto, Bernard (Augustine)

Gilbert, W(illiam) S(chwenck)
1836-1911 .... **TCLC 3; DAM DRAM, POET**
See also CA 104; 173; RGEL; SATA 36

Gilbreth, Frank B(unker), Jr.
1911-2001 .... **CLC 17**
See also CA 9-12R; SATA 2

Gilchrist, Ellen (Louise) 1935- .. **CLC 34, 48, 143; DAM POP; SSC 14**
See also BPFB 2; CA 113; 116; CANR 41, 61; CN; CPW; CSW; DLB 130; EXPS; MTCW 1, 2; RGAL; RGSF; SSFS 9

Giles, Molly 1942- .... **CLC 39**
See also CA 126; CANR 98

Gill, Eric 1882-1940 .... **TCLC 85**

Gill, Patrick
See Creasey, John

Gillette, Douglas .... **CLC 70**

Gilliam, Terry (Vance) 1940- .... **CLC 21, 141**
See also Monty Python
See also AAYA 19; CA 108; 113; CANR 35; INT 113

Gillian, Jerry
See Gilliam, Terry (Vance)

Gilliatt, Penelope (Ann Douglass)
1932-1993 .... **CLC 2, 10, 13, 53**
See also AITN 2; CA 13-16R; 141; CANR 49; DLB 14

Gilman, Charlotte (Anna) Perkins (Stetson)
1860-1935 .... **TCLC 9, 37; SSC 13**
See also BYA 11; CA 106; 150; DLB 221; EXPS; FW; HGG; LAIT 2; MAWW; MTCW 1; RGAL; RGSF; SFW; SSFS 1

Gilmour, David 1949- .... **CLC 35**
See also CA 138, 147

Gilpin, William 1724-1804 .... **NCLC 30**

Gilray, J. D.
See Mencken, H(enry) L(ouis)

Gilroy, Frank D(aniel) 1925- .... **CLC 2**
See also CA 81-84; CAD; CANR 32, 64, 86; CD; DLB 7

Gilstrap, John 1957(?)- .... **CLC 99**
See also CA 160; CANR 101

Ginsberg, Allen 1926-1997 .... **CLC 1, 2, 3, 4, 6, 13, 36, 69, 109; DA; DAB; DAC; DAM MST, POET; PC 4; WLC**
See also AAYA 33; AITN 1; AMWS 2; CA 1-4R; 157; CANR 2, 41, 63, 95; CDALB 1941-1968; CP; DA3; DLB 5, 16, 169, 237; GLL 1; MTCW 1, 2; PAB; PFS 5; RGAL; WP

Ginzburg, Eugenia .... **CLC 59**

Ginzburg, Natalia 1916-1991 .... **CLC 5, 11, 54, 70**
See also CA 85-88; 135; CANR 33; DLB 177; MTCW 1, 2; RGWL

Giono, Jean 1895-1970 .... **CLC 4, 11**
See also CA 45-48; 29-32R; CANR 2, 35; DLB 72; GFL 1789 to the Present; MTCW 1; RGWL

Giovanni, Nikki 1943- .... **CLC 2, 4, 19, 64, 117; BLC 2; DA; DAB; DAC; DAM MST, MULT, POET; PC 19; WLCS**
See also AAYA 22; AITN 1; BW 2, 3; CA 29-32R; CAAS 6; CANR 18, 41, 60, 91; CDALBS; CLR 6, 73; CP; CSW; CWP; CWRI; DA3; DLB 5, 41; EXPP; INT CANR-18; MAICYA; MTCW 1, 2; RGAL; SATA 24, 107; YAW

Giovene, Andrea 1904- .... **CLC 7**
See also CA 85-88

Gippius, Zinaida (Nikolayevna) 1869-1945
See Hippius, Zinaida
See also CA 106

Giraudoux, Jean(-Hippolyte)
1882-1944 .... **TCLC 2, 7; DAM DRAM**
See also CA 104; DLB 65; EW; GFL 1789 to the Present; RGWL

Gironella, Jose Maria 1917-1991 ..... **CLC 11**
See also CA 101; RGWL

Gissing, George (Robert)
1857-1903 .... **TCLC 3, 24, 47; SSC 37**
See also BRW; CA 105; 167; DLB 18, 135, 184; RGEL

Giurlani, Aldo
See Palazzeschi, Aldo

Gladkov, Fyodor (Vasilyevich)
1883-1958 .... **TCLC 27**
See also CA 170

Glanville, Brian (Lester) 1931- .... **CLC 6**
See also CA 5-8R; CAAS 9; CANR 3, 70; CN; DLB 15, 139; SATA 42

Glasgow, Ellen (Anderson Gholson)
1873-1945 .... **TCLC 2, 7; SSC 34**
See also AMW; CA 104; 164; DLB 9, 12; MAWW; MTCW 2; RGAL; RHW; SSFS 9

Glaspell, Susan 1882(?)-1948 . **TCLC 55; DC 10; SSC 41**
See also AMWS 3; CA 110; 154; DFS 8; DLB 7, 9, 78, 228; RGAL; SSFS 3; TCWW 2; YABC 2

Glassco, John 1909-1981 .... **CLC 9**
See also CA 13-16R; 102; CANR 15; DLB 68

Glasscock, Amnesia
See Steinbeck, John (Ernst)

Glasser, Ronald J. 1940(?)- .... **CLC 37**

Glassman, Joyce
See Johnson, Joyce

Gleick, James (W.) 1954- .... **CLC 147**
See also CA 131; 137; CANR 97; INT CA-
137

Glendinning, Victoria 1937- .... **CLC 50**
See also CA 120; 127; CANR 59, 89; DLB
155

Glissant, Edouard 1928- . **CLC 10, 68; DAM
MULT**
See also CA 153; CWW 2

Gloag, Julian 1930- .... **CLC 40**
See also AITN 1; CA 65-68; CANR 10, 70;
CN

Glowacki, Aleksander
See Prus, Boleslaw

Gluck, Louise (Elisabeth) 1943- .. **CLC 7, 22,
44, 81; DAM POET; PC 16**
See also AMWS 5; CA 33-36R; CANR 40,
69; CP; CWP; DA3; DLB 5; MTCW 2;
PFS 5; RGAL

Glyn, Elinor 1864-1943 .... **TCLC 72**
See also DLB 153; RHW

Gobineau, Joseph-Arthur
1816-1882 .... **NCLC 17**
See also DLB 123; GFL 1789 to the Present

Godard, Jean-Luc 1930- .... **CLC 20**
See also CA 93-96

Godden, (Margaret) Rumer
1907-1998 .... **CLC 53**
See also AAYA 6; BPFB 2; BYA 2; CA
5-8R; 172; CANR 4, 27, 36, 55, 80; CLR
20; CN; CWRI; DLB 161; MAICYA;
RHW; SAAS 12; SATA 3, 36; SATA-Obit
109

Godoy Alcayaga, Lucila
1899-1957 .... **TCLC 2; DAM MULT;
HLC 2; PC 32**
See also Mistral, Gabriela
See also BW 2; CA 104; 131; CANR 81;
DNFS; HW 1, 2; MTCW 1, 2

Godwin, Gail (Kathleen) 1937- ..... **CLC 5, 8,
22, 31, 69, 125; DAM POP**
See also BPFB 2; CA 29-32R; CANR 15,
43, 69; CN; CPW; CSW; DA3; DLB 6,
234; INT CANR-15; MTCW 1, 2

Godwin, William 1756-1836 .... **NCLC 14**
See also CDBLB 1789-1832; CMW; DLB
39, 104, 142, 158, 163; HGG; RGEL

Goebbels, Josef
See Goebbels, (Paul) Joseph

Goebbels, (Paul) Joseph
1897-1945 .... **TCLC 68**
See also CA 115; 148

Goebbels, Joseph Paul
See Goebbels, (Paul) Joseph

Goethe, Johann Wolfgang von
1749-1832 ...... **NCLC 4, 22, 34, 90; DA;
DAB; DAC; DAM DRAM, MST,
POET; PC 5; SSC 38; WLC**
See also DA3; DLB 94; RGWL

Gogarty, Oliver St. John
1878-1957 .... **TCLC 15**
See also CA 109; 150; DLB 15, 19; RGEL

Gogol, Nikolai (Vasilyevich)
1809-1852 . **NCLC 5, 15, 31; DA; DAB;
DAC; DAM DRAM, MST; DC 1; SSC
4, 29; WLC**
See also DFS 12; DLB 198; EW; EXPS;
RGSF; RGWL; SSFS 7

Goines, Donald 1937(?)-1974 . **CLC 80; BLC
2; DAM MULT, POP**
See also AITN 1; BW 1, 3; CA 124; 114;
CANR 82; CMW; DA3; DLB 33

Gold, Herbert 1924- .... **CLC 4, 7, 14, 42**
See also CA 9-12R; CANR 17, 45; CN;
DLB 2; DLBY 81

Goldbarth, Albert 1948- .... **CLC 5, 38**
See also CA 53-56; CANR 6, 40; CP; DLB
120

Goldberg, Anatol 1910-1982 .... **CLC 34**
See also CA 131; 117

Goldemberg, Isaac 1945- .... **CLC 52**
See also CA 69-72; CAAS 12; CANR 11,
32; HW 1; WLIT 1

Golding, William (Gerald)
1911-1993 ..... **CLC 1, 2, 3, 8, 10, 17, 27,
58, 81; DA; DAB; DAC; DAM MST,
NOV; WLC**
See also AAYA 5; BPFB 2; BRWS 1; BYA
2; CA 5-8R; 141; CANR 13, 33, 54; CD-
BLB 1945-1960; DA3; DLB 15, 100;
EXPN; HGG; LAIT 4; MTCW 1, 2; NFS
2; RGEL; RHW; SFW; WLIT 4; YAW

Goldman, Emma 1869-1940 .... **TCLC 13**
See also CA 110; 150; DLB 221; FW;
RGAL

Goldman, Francisco 1954- .... **CLC 76**
See also CA 162

Goldman, William (W.) 1931- ...... **CLC 1, 48**
See also BPFB 2; CA 9-12R; CANR 29,
69; CN; DLB 44; FANT; IDFW 3, 4

Goldmann, Lucien 1913-1970 .... **CLC 24**
See also CA 25-28; CAP 2

Goldoni, Carlo 1707-1793 .... **LC 4; DAM
DRAM**
See also RGWL

Goldsberry, Steven 1949- .... **CLC 34**
See also CA 131

Goldsmith, Oliver 1730-1774 . **LC 2, 48; DA;
DAB; DAC; DAM DRAM, MST, NOV,
POET; DC 8; WLC**
See also BRW; CDBLB 1660-1789; DFS 1;
DLB 39, 89, 104, 109, 142; IDTP; RGEL;
SATA 26; TEA; WLIT 3

Goldsmith, Peter
See Priestley, J(ohn) B(oynton)

Gombrowicz, Witold 1904-1969 .... **CLC 4, 7,
11, 49; DAM DRAM**
See also CA 19-20; 25-28R; CAP 2; RGWL

Gomez de la Serna, Ramon
1888-1963 .... **CLC 9**
See also CA 153; 116; CANR 79; HW 1, 2

Goncharov, Ivan Alexandrovich
1812-1891 .... **NCLC 1, 63**
See also DLB 238; EW; RGWL

Goncourt, Edmond (Louis Antoine Huot) de
1822-1896 .... **NCLC 7**
See also DLB 123; EW; GFL 1789 to the
Present; RGWL

Goncourt, Jules (Alfred Huot) de
1830-1870 .... **NCLC 7**
See also DLB 123; EW; GFL 1789 to the
Present; RGWL

Gontier, Fernande 19(?)- .... **CLC 50**

Gonzalez Martinez, Enrique
1871-1952 .... **TCLC 72**
See also CA 166; CANR 81; HW 1, 2

Goodison, Lorna 1947- .... **PC 36**
See also CA 142; CANR 88; CP; CWP;
DLB 157

Goodman, Paul 1911-1972 ..... **CLC 1, 2, 4, 7**
See also CA 19-20; 37-40R; CAD; CANR
34; CAP 2; DLB 130; MTCW 1; RGAL

Gordimer, Nadine 1923- ...... **CLC 3, 5, 7, 10,
18, 33, 51, 70, 123; DA; DAB; DAC;
DAM MST, NOV; SSC 17; WLCS**
See also AAYA 39; BRWS 2; CA 5-8R;
CANR 3, 28, 56, 88; CN; DA3; DLB 225;
EXPS; INT CANR-28; MTCW 1, 2; NFS
4; RGEL; RGSF; SSFS 2; WLIT 2; YAW

Gordon, Adam Lindsay
1833-1870 .... **NCLC 21**
See also DLB 230

Gordon, Caroline 1895-1981 . **CLC 6, 13, 29,
83; SSC 15**
See also AMW; CA 11-12; 103; CANR 36;
CAP 1; DLB 4, 9, 102; DLBD 17; DLBY
81; MTCW 1, 2; RGAL; RGSF

Gordon, Charles William 1860-1937
See Connor, Ralph
See also CA 109

Gordon, Mary (Catherine) 1949- .... **CLC 13,
22, 128**
See also AMWS 4; BPFB 2; CA 102;
CANR 44, 92; CN; DLB 6; DLBY 81;
FW; INT 102; MTCW 1

Gordon, N. J.
See Bosman, Herman Charles

Gordon, Sol 1923- .... **CLC 26**
See also CA 53-56; CANR 4; SATA 11

Gordone, Charles 1925-1995 .... **CLC 1, 4;
DAM DRAM; DC 8**
See also BW 1, 3; CA 93-96; 180; 150;
CAAE 180; CAD; CANR 55; DLB 7; INT
93-96; MTCW 1

Gore, Catherine 1800-1861 .... **NCLC 65**
See also DLB 116; RGEL

Gorenko, Anna Andreevna
See Akhmatova, Anna

Gorky, Maxim .... **TCLC 8; DAB; SSC 28;
WLC**
See also Peshkov, Alexei Maximovich
See also DFS 9; MTCW 2

Goryan, Sirak
See Saroyan, William

Gosse, Edmund (William)
1849-1928 .... **TCLC 28**
See also CA 117; DLB 57, 144, 184; RGEL

Gotlieb, Phyllis Fay (Bloom) 1926- .. **CLC 18**
See also CA 13-16R; CANR 7; DLB 88;
SFW

Gottesman, S. D.
See Kornbluth, C(yril) M.; Pohl, Frederik

Gottfried von Strassburg fl. c.
1170-1215 .... **CMLC 10**
See also DLB 138; RGWL

Gould, Lois .... **CLC 4, 10**
See also CA 77-80; CANR 29; MTCW 1

Gourmont, Remy(-Marie-Charles) de
1858-1915 .... **TCLC 17**
See also CA 109; 150; GFL 1789 to the
Present; MTCW 2

Govier, Katherine 1948- .... **CLC 51**
See also CA 101; CANR 18, 40; CCA 1

Goyen, (Charles) William
1915-1983 .... **CLC 5, 8, 14, 40**
See also AITN 2; CA 5-8R; 110; CANR 6,
71; DLB 2; DLBY 83; INT CANR-6

Goytisolo, Juan 1931- .... **CLC 5, 10, 23, 133;
DAM MULT; HLC 1**
See also CA 85-88; CANR 32, 61; CWW
2; GLL 2; HW 1, 2; MTCW 1, 2

Gozzano, Guido 1883-1916 .... **PC 10**
See also CA 154; DLB 114

Gozzi, (Conte) Carlo 1720-1806 .... **NCLC 23**

Grabbe, Christian Dietrich
1801-1836 .... **NCLC 2**
See also DLB 133; RGWL

Grace, Patricia Frances 1937- .... **CLC 56**
See also CA 176; CN; RGSF

Gracian y Morales, Baltasar
1601-1658 .... **LC 15**

Gracq, Julien .... **CLC 11, 48**
See also Poirier, Louis
See also CWW 2; DLB 83; GFL 1789 to
the Present

Grade, Chaim 1910-1982 .... **CLC 10**
See also CA 93-96; 107

Graduate of Oxford, A
See Ruskin, John

Grafton, Garth
See Duncan, Sara Jeannette

Graham, John
See Phillips, David Graham

Graham, Jorie 1951- .... **CLC 48, 118**
See also CA 111; CANR 63; CP; CWP;
DLB 120; PFS 10

Harson, Sley
   See Ellison, Harlan (Jay)
Hart, Ellis
   See Ellison, Harlan (Jay)
Hart, Josephine 1942(?)- .... **CLC 70; DAM POP**
   See also CA 138; CANR 70; CPW
Hart, Moss 1904-1961 .... **CLC 66; DAM DRAM**
   See also CA 109; 89-92; CANR 84; DFS 1; DLB 7; RGAL
Harte, (Francis) Bret(t) 1836(?)-1902 ... **TCLC 1, 25; DA; DAC; DAM MST; SSC 8; WLC**
   See also AMWS 2; CA 104; 140; CANR 80; CDALB 1865-1917; DA3; DLB 12, 64, 74, 79, 186; EXPS; LAIT 2; RGAL; RGSF; SATA 26; SSFS 3
Hartley, L(eslie) P(oles) 1895-1972 ... **CLC 2, 22**
   See also BRWS 7; CA 45-48; 37-40R; CANR 33; DLB 15, 139; HGG; MTCW 1, 2; RGEL; RGSF; SUFW
Hartman, Geoffrey H. 1929- .... **CLC 27**
   See also CA 117; 125; CANR 79; DLB 67
Hartmann, Sadakichi 1869-1944 ... **TCLC 73**
   See also CA 157; DLB 54
Hartmann von Aue c. 1170-c. 1210 .... **CMLC 15**
   See also DLB 138; RGWL
Haruf, Kent 1943- .... **CLC 34**
   See also CA 149; CANR 91
Harwood, Ronald 1934- .... **CLC 32; DAM DRAM, MST**
   See also CA 1-4R; CANR 4, 55; CBD; CD; DLB 13
Hasegawa Tatsunosuke
   See Futabatei, Shimei
Hasek, Jaroslav (Matej Frantisek) 1883-1923 .... **TCLC 4**
   See also CA 104; 129; EW; MTCW 1, 2; RGSF; RGWL
Hass, Robert 1941- ... **CLC 18, 39, 99; PC 16**
   See also AMWS 6; CA 111; CANR 30, 50, 71; CP; DLB 105, 206; RGAL; SATA 94
Hastings, Hudson
   See Kuttner, Henry
Hastings, Selina .... **CLC 44**
Hathorne, John 1641-1717 .... **LC 38**
Hatteras, Amelia
   See Mencken, H(enry) L(ouis)
Hatteras, Owen .... **TCLC 18**
   See also Mencken, H(enry) L(ouis); Nathan, George Jean
Hauptmann, Gerhart (Johann Robert) 1862-1946 .... **TCLC 4; DAM DRAM; SSC 37**
   See also CA 104; 153; DLB 66, 118; EW; RGSF; RGWL
Havel, Vaclav 1936- ..... **CLC 25, 58, 65, 123; DAM DRAM; DC 6**
   See also CA 104; CANR 36, 63; CWW 2; DA3; DFS 10; DLB 232; MTCW 1, 2
Haviaras, Stratis .... **CLC 33**
   See also Chaviaras, Strates
Hawes, Stephen 1475(?)-1529(?) .... **LC 17**
   See also DLB 132; RGEL
Hawkes, John (Clendennin Burne, Jr.) 1925-1998 .. **CLC 1, 2, 3, 4, 7, 9, 14, 15, 27, 49**
   See also BPFB 2; CA 1-4R; 167; CANR 2, 47, 64; CN; DLB 2, 7, 227; DLBY 80, 98; MTCW 1, 2; RGAL
Hawking, S. W.
   See Hawking, Stephen W(illiam)
Hawking, Stephen W(illiam) 1942- . **CLC 63, 105**
   See also AAYA 13; BEST 89:1; CA 126; 129; CANR 48; CPW; DA3; MTCW 2

Hawkins, Anthony Hope
   See Hope, Anthony
Hawthorne, Julian 1846-1934 .... **TCLC 25**
   See also CA 165; HGG
Hawthorne, Nathaniel 1804-1864 ... **NCLC 2, 10, 17, 23, 39, 79, 95; DA; DAB; DAC; DAM MST, NOV; SSC 3, 29, 39; WLC**
   See also AAYA 18; AMW; BPFB 2; BYA 3; CDALB 1640-1865; DA3; DLB 1, 74, 223; EXPN; EXPS; HGG; LAIT 1; NFS 1; RGAL; RGSF; SSFS 1, 7, 11; YABC 2
Haxton, Josephine Ayres 1921-
   See Douglas, Ellen
   See also CA 115; CANR 41, 83
Hayaseca y Eizaguirre, Jorge
   See Echegaray (y Eizaguirre), Jose (Maria Waldo)
Hayashi, Fumiko 1904-1951 .... **TCLC 27**
   See also CA 161; DLB 180
Haycraft, Anna (Margaret) 1932-
   See Ellis, Alice Thomas
   See also CA 122; CANR 85, 90; MTCW 2
Hayden, Robert E(arl) 1913-1980 . **CLC 5, 9, 14, 37; BLC 2; DA; DAC; DAM MST, MULT, POET; PC 6**
   See also AFAW 1, 2; AMWS 2; BW 1, 3; CA 69-72; 97-100; CABS 2; CANR 24, 75, 82; CDALB 1941-1968; DLB 5, 76; EXPP; MTCW 1, 2; PFS 1; RGAL; SATA 19; SATA-Obit 26; WP
Hayek, F(riedrich) A(ugust von) 1899-1992 .... **TCLC 109**
   See also CA 93-96; 137; CANR 20; MTCW 1, 2
Hayford, J(oseph) E(phraim) Casely
   See Casely-Hayford, J(oseph) E(phraim)
Hayman, Ronald 1932- .... **CLC 44**
   See also CA 25-28R; CANR 18, 50, 88; CD; DLB 155
Hayne, Paul Hamilton 1830-1886 . **NCLC 94**
   See also DLB 3, 64, 79; RGAL
Haywood, Eliza (Fowler) 1693(?)-1756 .... **LC 1, 44**
   See also DLB 39; RGEL
Hazlitt, William 1778-1830 ...... **NCLC 29, 82**
   See also DLB 110, 158; RGEL
Hazzard, Shirley 1931- .... **CLC 18**
   See also CA 9-12R; CANR 4, 70; CN; DLBY 82; MTCW 1
Head, Bessie 1937-1986 .... **CLC 25, 67; BLC 2; DAM MULT**
   See also BW 2, 3; CA 29-32R; 119; CANR 25, 82; DA3; DLB 117, 225; EXPS; FW; MTCW 1, 2; RGSF; SSFS 5; WLIT 2
Headon, (Nicky) Topper 1956(?)- ..... **CLC 30**
Heaney, Seamus (Justin) 1939- ..... **CLC 5, 7, 14, 25, 37, 74, 91; DAB; DAM POET; PC 18; WLCS**
   See also BRWS 2; CA 85-88; CANR 25, 48, 75, 91; CDBLB 1960 to Present; CP; DA3; DLB 40; DLBY 95; EXPP; MTCW 1, 2; PAB; PFS 2, 5, 8; RGEL; WLIT 4
Hearn, (Patricio) Lafcadio (Tessima Carlos) 1850-1904 .... **TCLC 9**
   See also CA 105; 166; DLB 12, 78, 189; HGG; RGAL
Hearne, Vicki 1946- .... **CLC 56**
   See also CA 139
Hearon, Shelby 1931- .... **CLC 63**
   See also AITN 2; AMWS 8; CA 25-28R; CANR 18, 48; CSW
Heat-Moon, William Least .... **CLC 29**
   See also Trogdon, William (Lewis)
   See also AAYA 9
Hebbel, Friedrich 1813-1863 .... **NCLC 43; DAM DRAM**
   See also DLB 129; RGWL

Hebert, Anne 1916-2000 .... **CLC 4, 13, 29; DAC; DAM MST, POET**
   See also CA 85-88; 187; CANR 69; CCA 1; CWP; CWW 2; DA3; DLB 68; GFL 1789 to the Present; MTCW 1, 2
Hecht, Anthony (Evan) 1923- ...... **CLC 8, 13, 19; DAM POET**
   See also CA 9-12R; CANR 6; CP; DLB 5, 169; PFS 6; WP
Hecht, Ben 1894-1964 .... **CLC 8**
   See also CA 85-88; DFS 9; DLB 7, 9, 25, 26, 28, 86; FANT; IDFW 3, 4; RGAL; TCLC 101
Hedayat, Sadeq 1903-1951 .... **TCLC 21**
   See also CA 120; RGSF
Hegel, Georg Wilhelm Friedrich 1770-1831 .... **NCLC 46**
   See also DLB 90
Heidegger, Martin 1889-1976 .... **CLC 24**
   See also CA 81-84; 65-68; CANR 34; MTCW 1, 2
Heidenstam, (Carl Gustaf) Verner von 1859-1940 .... **TCLC 5**
   See also CA 104
Heifner, Jack 1946- .... **CLC 11**
   See also CA 105; CANR 47
Heijermans, Herman 1864-1924 .... **TCLC 24**
   See also CA 123
Heilbrun, Carolyn G(old) 1926- .... **CLC 25**
   See also Cross, Amanda
   See also CA 45-48; CANR 1, 28, 58, 94; CMW; CPW; FW
Heine, Heinrich 1797-1856 .... **NCLC 4, 54; PC 25**
   See also DLB 90; RGWL
Heinemann, Larry (Curtiss) 1944- .. **CLC 50**
   See also CA 110; CAAS 21; CANR 31, 81; DLBD 9; INT CANR-31
Heiney, Donald (William) 1921-1993
   See Harris, MacDonald
   See also CA 1-4R; 142; CANR 3, 58; FANT
Heinlein, Robert A(nson) 1907-1988 . **CLC 1, 3, 8, 14, 26, 55; DAM POP**
   See also AAYA 17; BPFB 2; BYA 4; CA 1-4R; 125; CANR 1, 20, 53; CPW; DA3; DLB 8; EXPS; JRDA; LAIT 5; MAICYA; MTCW 1, 2; RGAL; SATA 9, 69; SATA-Obit 56; SCFW; SFW; SSFS 7; YAW
Helforth, John
   See Doolittle, Hilda
Hellenhofferu, Vojtech Kapristian z
   See Hasek, Jaroslav (Matej Frantisek)
Heller, Joseph 1923-1999 . **CLC 1, 3, 5, 8, 11, 36, 63; DA; DAB; DAC; DAM MST, NOV, POP; WLC**
   See also AAYA 24; AITN 1; AMWS 4; BPFB 2; BYA 1; CA 5-8R; 187; CABS 1; CANR 8, 42, 66; CN; CPW; DA3; DLB 2, 28, 227; DLBY 80; EXPN; INT CANR-8; LAIT 4; MTCW 1, 2; NFS 1; RGAL; YAW
Hellman, Lillian (Florence) 1906-1984 .. **CLC 2, 4, 8, 14, 18, 34, 44, 52; DAM DRAM; DC 1**
   See also AITN 1, 2; AMWS 1; CA 13-16R; 112; CAD; CANR 33; CWD; DA3; DFS 1, 3; DLB 7, 228; DLBY 84; FW; LAIT 3; MAWW; MTCW 1, 2; RGAL
Helprin, Mark 1947- .... **CLC 7, 10, 22, 32; DAM NOV, POP**
   See also CA 81-84; CANR 47, 64; CDALBS; CPW; DA3; DLBY 85; FANT; MTCW 1, 2
Helvetius, Claude-Adrien 1715-1771 .. **LC 26**
Helyar, Jane Penelope Josephine 1933-
   See Poole, Josephine
   See also CA 21-24R; CANR 10, 26; SATA 82

Hunt, Violet 1866(?)-1942 .... **TCLC 53**
See also CA 184; DLB 162, 197
Hunter, E. Waldo
See Sturgeon, Theodore (Hamilton)
Hunter, Evan 1926- .... **CLC 11, 31; DAM POP**
See also AAYA 39; BPFB 2; CA 5-8R; CANR 5, 38, 62, 97; CMW; CN; CPW; DLBY 82; INT CANR-5; MTCW 1; SATA 25; SFW
Hunter, Kristin (Eggleston) 1931- .... **CLC 35**
See also AITN 1; BW 1; BYA 3; CA 13-16R; CANR 13; CLR 3; CN; DLB 33; INT CANR-13; MAICYA; SAAS 10; SATA 12; YAW
Hunter, Mary
See Austin, Mary (Hunter)
Hunter, Mollie 1922- .... **CLC 21**
See also McIlwraith, Maureen Mollie Hunter
See also AAYA 13; BYA 6; CANR 37, 78; CLR 25; DLB 161; JRDA; MAICYA; SAAS 7; SATA 54, 106; YAW
Hunter, Robert (?)-1734 .... **LC 7**
Hurston, Zora Neale 1891-1960 .. **CLC 7, 30, 61; BLC 2; DA; DAC; DAM MST, MULT, NOV; DC 12; SSC 4; WLCS**
See also AAYA 15; AFAW 1, 2; BW 1, 3; BYA 12; CA 85-88; CANR 61; CDALBS; DA3; DFS 6; DLB 51, 86; EXPN; EXPS; FW; LAIT 3; MTCW 1, 2; NFS 3; RGAL; RGSF; SSFS 1, 6, 11; YAW
Husserl, E. G.
See Husserl, Edmund (Gustav Albrecht)
Husserl, Edmund (Gustav Albrecht) 1859-1938 .... **TCLC 100**
See also CA 116; 133
Huston, John (Marcellus) 1906-1987 .... **CLC 20**
See also CA 73-76; 123; CANR 34; DLB 26
Hustvedt, Siri 1955- .... **CLC 76**
See also CA 137
Hutten, Ulrich von 1488-1523 .... **LC 16**
See also DLB 179
Huxley, Aldous (Leonard) 1894-1963 .... **CLC 1, 3, 4, 5, 8, 11, 18, 35, 79; DA; DAB; DAC; DAM MST, NOV; SSC 39; WLC**
See also AAYA 11; BPFB 2; BRW; CA 85-88; CANR 44, 99; CDBLB 1914-1945; DA3; DLB 36, 100, 162, 195; EXPN; LAIT 5; MTCW 1, 2; NFS 6; RGEL; SATA 63; SCFW 2; SFW; YAW
Huxley, T(homas) H(enry) 1825-1895 .... **NCLC 67**
See also DLB 57
Huysmans, Joris-Karl 1848-1907 ... **TCLC 7, 69**
See also CA 104; 165; DLB 123; EW; GFL 1789 to the Present; RGWL
Hwang, David Henry 1957- .. **CLC 55; DAM DRAM; DC 4**
See also CA 127; 132; CAD; CANR 76; CD; DA3; DFS 11; DLB 212; INT 132; MTCW 2; RGAL
Hyde, Anthony 1946- .... **CLC 42**
See also Chase, Nicholas
See also CA 136; CCA 1
Hyde, Margaret O(ldroyd) 1917- ..... **CLC 21**
See also CA 1-4R; CANR 1, 36; CLR 23; JRDA; MAICYA; SAAS 8; SATA 1, 42, 76
Hynes, James 1956(?)- .... **CLC 65**
See also CA 164
Hypatia c. 370-415 .... **CMLC 35**
Ian, Janis 1951- .... **CLC 21**
See also CA 105; 187

Ibanez, Vicente Blasco
See Blasco Ibanez, Vicente
Ibarbourou, Juana de 1895-1979
See also HLCS 2; HW 1
Ibarguengoitia, Jorge 1928-1983 ...... **CLC 37**
See also CA 124; 113; HW 1
Ibsen, Henrik (Johan) 1828-1906 ... **TCLC 2, 8, 16, 37, 52; DA; DAB; DAC; DAM DRAM, MST; DC 2; WLC**
See also CA 104; 141; DA3; DFS 1, 6, 8, 10, 11; EW; LAIT 2; RGWL
Ibuse, Masuji 1898-1993 .... **CLC 22**
See also CA 127; 141; DLB 180
Ichikawa, Kon 1915- .... **CLC 20**
See also CA 121
Ichiyo, Higuchi 1872-1896 .... **NCLC 49**
See also MJW
Idle, Eric 1943-2000 .... **CLC 21**
See also Monty Python
See also CA 116; CANR 35, 91
Ignatow, David 1914-1997 .... **CLC 4, 7, 14, 40; PC 34**
See also CA 9-12R; 162; CAAS 3; CANR 31, 57, 96; CP; DLB 5
Ignotus
See Strachey, (Giles) Lytton
Ihimaera, Witi 1944- .... **CLC 46**
See also CA 77-80; CN; RGSF
Ilf, Ilya .... **TCLC 21**
See also Fainzilberg, Ilya Arnoldovich
Illyes, Gyula 1902-1983 .... **PC 16**
See also CA 114; 109; DLB 215; RGWL
Immermann, Karl (Lebrecht) 1796-1840 .... **NCLC 4, 49**
See also DLB 133
Ince, Thomas H. 1882-1924 .... **TCLC 89**
See also IDFW 3, 4
Inchbald, Elizabeth 1753-1821 ...... **NCLC 62**
See also DLB 39, 89; RGEL
Inclan, Ramon (Maria) del Valle
See Valle-Inclan, Ramon (Maria) del
Infante, G(uillermo) Cabrera
See Cabrera Infante, G(uillermo)
Ingalls, Rachel (Holmes) 1940- .... **CLC 42**
See also CA 123; 127
Ingamells, Reginald Charles
See Ingamells, Rex
Ingamells, Rex 1913-1955 .... **TCLC 35**
See also CA 167
Inge, William (Motter) 1913-1973 ..... **CLC 1, 8, 19; DAM DRAM**
See also CA 9-12R; CDALB 1941-1968; DA3; DFS 1, 5, 8; DLB 7; MTCW 1, 2; RGAL
Ingelow, Jean 1820-1897 .... **NCLC 39**
See also DLB 35, 163; FANT; SATA 33
Ingram, Willis J.
See Harris, Mark
Innaurato, Albert (F.) 1948(?)- ... **CLC 21, 60**
See also CA 115; 122; CAD; CANR 78; CD; INT CA-122
Innes, Michael
See Stewart, J(ohn) I(nnes) M(ackintosh)
Innis, Harold Adams 1894-1952 .... **TCLC 77**
See also CA 181; DLB 88
Ionesco, Eugene 1912-1994 ... **CLC 1, 4, 6, 9, 11, 15, 41, 86; DA; DAB; DAC; DAM DRAM, MST; DC 12; WLC**
See also CA 9-12R; 144; CANR 55; CWW 2; DA3; DFS 4, 9; GFL 1789 to the Present; MTCW 1, 2; RGWL; SATA 7; SATA-Obit 79
Iqbal, Muhammad 1877-1938 .... **TCLC 28**
Ireland, Patrick
See O'Doherty, Brian
Irenaeus St. 130- .... **CMLC 42**
Iron, Ralph
See Schreiner, Olive (Emilie Albertina)

Irving, John (Winslow) 1942- ... **CLC 13, 23, 38, 112; DAM NOV, POP**
See also AAYA 8; AMWS 6; BEST 89:3; BPFB 2; CA 25-28R; CANR 28, 73; CN; CPW; DA3; DLB 6; DLBY 82; MTCW 1, 2; NFS 12; RGAL
Irving, Washington 1783-1859 . **NCLC 2, 19, 95; DA; DAB; DAC; DAM MST; SSC 2, 37; WLC**
See also AMW; CDALB 1640-1865; DA3; DLB 3, 11, 30, 59, 73, 74, 186; EXPS; LAIT 1; RGAL; RGSF; SSFS 1, 8; YABC 2
Irwin, P. K.
See Page, P(atricia) K(athleen)
Isaacs, Jorge Ricardo 1837-1895 ... **NCLC 70**
See also LAW
Isaacs, Susan 1943- .... **CLC 32; DAM POP**
See also BEST 89:1; BPFB 2; CA 89-92; CANR 20, 41, 65; CPW; DA3; INT CANR-20; MTCW 1, 2
Isherwood, Christopher (William Bradshaw) 1904-1986 .. **CLC 1, 9, 11, 14, 44; DAM DRAM, NOV**
See also BRW; CA 13-16R; 117; CANR 35, 97; DA3; DLB 15, 195; DLBY 86; MTCW 1, 2; RGAL; RGEL; WLIT 4
Ishiguro, Kazuo 1954- . **CLC 27, 56, 59, 110; DAM NOV**
See also BEST 90:2; BPFB 2; BRWS 4; CA 120; CANR 49, 95; CN; DA3; DLB 194; MTCW 1, 2; WLIT 4
Ishikawa, Hakuhin
See Ishikawa, Takuboku
Ishikawa, Takuboku 1886(?)-1912 ... **TCLC 15; DAM POET; PC 10**
See also CA 113; 153
Iskander, Fazil 1929- .... **CLC 47**
See also CA 102
Isler, Alan (David) 1934- .... **CLC 91**
See also CA 156
Ivan IV 1530-1584 .... **LC 17**
Ivanov, Vyacheslav Ivanovich 1866-1949 .... **TCLC 33**
See also CA 122
Ivask, Ivar Vidrik 1927-1992 .... **CLC 14**
See also CA 37-40R; 139; CANR 24
Ives, Morgan
See Bradley, Marion Zimmer
See also GLL 1
Izumi Shikibu c. 973-c. 1034 .... **CMLC 33**
J .... **CLC 10, 36, 86; DAM NOV; SSC 20**
See also CA 97-100; CANR 36, 50, 74; DA3; DLB 182; DLBY 94; MTCW 1, 2
J. R. S.
See Gogarty, Oliver St. John
Jabran, Kahlil
See Gibran, Kahlil
Jabran, Khalil
See Gibran, Kahlil
Jackson, Daniel
See Wingrove, David (John)
Jackson, Helen Hunt 1830-1885 .... **NCLC 90**
See also DLB 42, 47, 186, 189; RGAL
Jackson, Jesse 1908-1983 .... **CLC 12**
See also BW 1; CA 25-28R; 109; CANR 27; CLR 28; CWRI; MAICYA; SATA 2, 29; SATA-Obit 48
Jackson, Laura (Riding) 1901-1991
See Riding, Laura
See also CA 65-68; 135; CANR 28, 89; DLB 48
Jackson, Sam
See Trumbo, Dalton
Jackson, Sara
See Wingrove, David (John)

Kesselring, Joseph (Otto)
1902-1967 .... **CLC 45; DAM DRAM, MST**
See also CA 150

Kessler, Jascha (Frederick) 1929- ...... **CLC 4**
See also CA 17-20R; CANR 8, 48

Kettelkamp, Larry (Dale) 1933- .... **CLC 12**
See also CA 29-32R; CANR 16; SAAS 3; SATA 2

Key, Ellen (Karolina Sofia)
1849-1926 .... **TCLC 65**

Keyber, Conny
See Fielding, Henry

Keyes, Daniel 1927- ...... **CLC 80; DA; DAC; DAM MST, NOV**
See also AAYA 23; BYA 11; CA 17-20R, 181; CANR 10, 26, 54, 74; DA3; EXPN; LAIT 4; MTCW 2; NFS 2; SATA 37; SFW

Keynes, John Maynard
1883-1946 .... **TCLC 64**
See also CA 114; 162, 163; DLBD 10; MTCW 2

Khanshendel, Chiron
See Rose, Wendy

Khayyam, Omar 1048-1131 .... **CMLC 11; DAM POET; PC 8**
See also Omar Khayyam
See also DA3

Kherdian, David 1931- .... **CLC 6, 9**
See also CA 21-24R; CAAE 192; CAAS 2; CANR 39, 78; CLR 24; JRDA; LAIT 3; MAICYA; SATA 16, 74; SATA-Essay 125

Khlebnikov, Velimir .... **TCLC 20**
See also Khlebnikov, Viktor Vladimirovich
See also RGWL

Khlebnikov, Viktor Vladimirovich 1885-1922
See Khlebnikov, Velimir
See also CA 117

Khodasevich, Vladislav (Felitsianovich)
1886-1939 .... **TCLC 15**
See also CA 115

Kielland, Alexander Lange
1849-1906 .... **TCLC 5**
See also CA 104

Kiely, Benedict 1919- .... **CLC 23, 43**
See also CA 1-4R; CANR 2, 84; CN; DLB 15

Kienzle, William X(avier) 1928- ..... **CLC 25; DAM POP**
See also CA 93-96; CAAS 1; CANR 9, 31, 59; CMW; DA3; INT CANR-31; MTCW 1, 2

Kierkegaard, Soren 1813-1855 ..... **NCLC 34, 78**

Kieslowski, Krzysztof 1941-1996 .... **CLC 120**
See also CA 147; 151

Killens, John Oliver 1916-1987 .... **CLC 10**
See also BW 2; CA 77-80; 123; CAAS 2; CANR 26; DLB 33

Killigrew, Anne 1660-1685 .... **LC 4**
See also DLB 131

Killigrew, Thomas 1612-1683 .... **LC 57**
See also DLB 58; RGEL

Kim
See Simenon, Georges (Jacques Christian)

Kincaid, Jamaica 1949- ..... **CLC 43, 68, 137; BLC 2; DAM MULT, NOV**
See also AAYA 13; AFAW 2; AMWS 7; BRWS 7; BW 2, 3; CA 125; CANR 47, 59, 95; CDALBS; CLR 63; CN; DA3; DLB 157, 227; DNFS; EXPS; FW; MTCW 2; NCFS 1; NFS 3; SSFS 5, 7; YAW

King, Francis (Henry) 1923- .... **CLC 8, 53, 145; DAM NOV**
See also CA 1-4R; CANR 1, 33, 86; CN; DLB 15, 139; MTCW 1

King, Kennedy
See Brown, George Douglas

King, Martin Luther, Jr.
1929-1968 .... **CLC 83; BLC 2; DA; DAB; DAC; DAM MST, MULT; WLCS**
See also BW 2, 3; CA 25-28; CANR 27, 44; CAP 2; DA3; LAIT 5; MTCW 1, 2; SATA 14

King, Stephen (Edwin) 1947- .... **CLC 12, 26, 37, 61, 113; DAM NOV, POP; SSC 17**
See also AAYA 1, 17; AMWS 5; BEST 90:1; BPFB 2; CA 61-64; CANR 1, 30, 52, 76; CPW; DA3; DLB 143; DLBY 80; HGG; JRDA; LAIT 5; MTCW 1, 2; RGAL; SATA 9, 55; SUFW; WYAS 1; YAW

King, Steve
See King, Stephen (Edwin)

King, Thomas 1943- ... **CLC 89; DAC; DAM MULT**
See also CA 144; CANR 95; CCA 1; CN; DLB 175; NNAL; SATA 96

Kingman, Lee .... **CLC 17**
See also Natti, (Mary) Lee
See also SAAS 3; SATA 1, 67

Kingsley, Charles 1819-1875 .... **NCLC 35**
See also DLB 21, 32, 163, 190; FANT; RGEL; YABC 2

Kingsley, Sidney 1906-1995 .... **CLC 44**
See also CA 85-88; 147; CAD; DLB 7; RGAL

Kingsolver, Barbara 1955- .... **CLC 55, 81, 130; DAM POP**
See also AAYA 15; AMWS 7; CA 129; 134; CANR 60, 96; CDALBS; CPW; CSW; DA3; DLB 206; INT CA-134; LAIT 5; MTCW 2; NFS 5, 10, 12; RGAL

Kingston, Maxine (Ting Ting) Hong
1940- .... **CLC 12, 19, 58, 121; AAL; DAM MULT, NOV; WLCS**
See also AAYA 8; BPFB 2; CA 69-72; CANR 13, 38, 74, 87; CDALBS; CN; DA3; DLB 173, 212; DLBY 80; FW; INT CANR-13; LAIT 5; MAWW; MTCW 1, 2; NFS 6; RGAL; SATA 53; SSFS 3

Kinnell, Galway 1927- ..... **CLC 1, 2, 3, 5, 13, 29, 129; PC 26**
See also AMWS 3; CA 9-12R; CANR 10, 34, 66; CP; DLB 5; DLBY 87; INT CANR-34; MTCW 1, 2; PAB; PFS 9; RGAL; WP

Kinsella, Thomas 1928- .... **CLC 4, 19, 138**
See also BRWS 5; CA 17-20R; CANR 15; CP; DLB 27; MTCW 1, 2; RGEL

Kinsella, W(illiam) P(atrick) 1935- . **CLC 27, 43; DAC; DAM NOV, POP**
See also AAYA 7; BPFB 2; CA 97-100; CAAS 7; CANR 21, 35, 66, 75; CN; CPW; FANT; INT CANR-21; LAIT 5; MTCW 1, 2; RGSF

Kinsey, Alfred C(harles)
1894-1956 .... **TCLC 91**
See also CA 115; 170; MTCW 2

Kipling, (Joseph) Rudyard
1865-1936 ...... **TCLC 8, 17; DA; DAB; DAC; DAM MST, POET; PC 3; SSC 5; WLC**
See also AAYA 32; BRW; BYA 4; CA 105; 120; CANR 33; CDBLB 1890-1914; CLR 39, 65; CWRI; DA3; DLB 19, 34, 141, 156; EXPS; FANT; LAIT 3; MAICYA; MTCW 1, 2; RGEL; RGSF; SATA 100; SFW; SSFS 8; SUFW; WCH; WLIT 4; YABC 2

Kirkland, Caroline M. 1801-1864 . **NCLC 85**
See also DLB 3, 73, 74; DLBD 13

Kirkup, James 1918- .... **CLC 1**
See also CA 1-4R; CAAS 4; CANR 2; DLB 27; SATA 12

Kirkwood, James 1930(?)-1989 .... **CLC 9**
See also AITN 2; CA 1-4R; 128; CANR 6, 40; GLL 2

Kirshner, Sidney
See Kingsley, Sidney

Kis, Danilo 1935-1989 .... **CLC 57**
See also CA 109; 118; 129; CANR 61; DLB 181; MTCW 1; RGSF; RGWL

Kissinger, Henry A(lfred) 1923- ..... **CLC 137**
See also CA 1-4R; CANR 2, 33, 66; MTCW 1

Kivi, Aleksis 1834-1872 .... **NCLC 30**

Kizer, Carolyn (Ashley) 1925- ... **CLC 15, 39, 80; DAM POET**
See also CA 65-68; CAAS 5; CANR 24, 70; CP; CWP; DLB 5, 169; MTCW 2

Klabund 1890-1928 .... **TCLC 44**
See also CA 162; DLB 66

Klappert, Peter 1942- .... **CLC 57**
See also CA 33-36R; CSW; DLB 5

Klein, A(braham) M(oses)
1909-1972 . **CLC 19; DAB; DAC; DAM MST**
See also CA 101; 37-40R; DLB 68; RGEL

Klein, Norma 1938-1989 .... **CLC 30**
See also AAYA 2, 35; BPFB 2; BYA 6; CA 41-44R; 128; CANR 15, 37; CLR 2, 19; INT CANR-15; JRDA; MAICYA; SAAS 1; SATA 7, 57; YAW

Klein, T(heodore) E(ibon) D(onald)
1947- .... **CLC 34**
See also CA 119; CANR 44, 75; HGG

Kleist, Heinrich von 1777-1811 ...... **NCLC 2, 37; DAM DRAM; SSC 22**
See also DLB 90; RGSF; RGWL

Klima, Ivan 1931- .... **CLC 56; DAM NOV**
See also CA 25-28R; CANR 17, 50, 91; CWW 2; DLB 232

Klimentov, Andrei Platonovich
1899-1951 .... **TCLC 14; SSC 42**
See also CA 108

Klinger, Friedrich Maximilian von
1752-1831 .... **NCLC 1**
See also DLB 94

Klingsor the Magician
See Hartmann, Sadakichi

Klopstock, Friedrich Gottlieb
1724-1803 .... **NCLC 11**
See also DLB 97; RGWL

Knapp, Caroline 1959- .... **CLC 99**
See also CA 154

Knebel, Fletcher 1911-1993 .... **CLC 14**
See also AITN 1; CA 1-4R; 140; CAAS 3; CANR 1, 36; SATA 36; SATA-Obit 75

Knickerbocker, Diedrich
See Irving, Washington

Knight, Etheridge 1931-1991 . **CLC 40; BLC 2; DAM POET; PC 14**
See also BW 1, 3; CA 21-24R; 133; CANR 23, 82; DLB 41; MTCW 2; RGAL

Knight, Sarah Kemble 1666-1727 .... **LC 7**
See also DLB 24, 200

Knister, Raymond 1899-1932 .... **TCLC 56**
See also CA 186; DLB 68; RGEL

Knowles, John 1926- . **CLC 1, 4, 10, 26; DA; DAC; DAM MST, NOV**
See also AAYA 10; BPFB 2; BYA 3; CA 17-20R; CANR 40, 74, 76; CDALB 1968-1988; CN; DLB 6; EXPN; MTCW 1, 2; NFS 2; RGAL; SATA 8, 89; YAW

Knox, Calvin M.
See Silverberg, Robert

Knox, John c. 1505-1572 .... **LC 37**
See also DLB 132

Knye, Cassandra
See Disch, Thomas M(ichael)

Koch, C(hristopher) J(ohn) 1932- .... **CLC 42**
See also CA 127; CANR 84; CN

Koch, Christopher
 See Koch, C(hristopher) J(ohn)
Koch, Kenneth 1925- .... CLC 5, 8, 44; DAM POET
 See also CA 1-4R; CAD; CANR 6, 36, 57, 97; CD; CP; DLB 5; INT CANR-36; MTCW 2; SATA 65; WP
Kochanowski, Jan 1530-1584 .... LC 10
 See also RGWL
Kock, Charles Paul de 1794-1871 . NCLC 16
Koda Rohan
 See Koda Shigeyuki
Koda Shigeyuki 1867-1947 .... TCLC 22
 See also CA 121; 183; DLB 180
Koestler, Arthur 1905-1983 ... CLC 1, 3, 6, 8, 15, 33
 See also BRWS 1; CA 1-4R; 109; CANR 1, 33; CDBLB 1945-1960; DLBY 83; MTCW 1, 2; RGEL
Kogawa, Joy Nozomi 1935- ..... CLC 78, 129; DAC; DAM MST, MULT
 See also CA 101; CANR 19, 62; CN; CWP; FW; MTCW 2; NFS 3; SATA 99
Kohout, Pavel 1928- ....:........ CLC 13
 See also CA 45-48; CANR 3
Koizumi, Yakumo
 See Hearn, (Patricio) Lafcadio (Tessima Carlos)
Kolmar, Gertrud 1894-1943 .... TCLC 40
 See also CA 167
Komunyakaa, Yusef 1947- .... CLC 86, 94; BLCS
 See also AFAW 2; CA 147; CANR 83; CP; CSW; DLB 120; PFS 5; RGAL
Konrad, George
 See Konrad, Gyorgy
 See also CWW 2
Konrad, Gyorgy 1933- .... CLC 4, 10, 73
 See also Konrad, George
 See also CA 85-88; CANR 97; CWW 2; DLB 232
Konwicki, Tadeusz 1926- .... CLC 8, 28, 54, 117
 See also CA 101; CAAS 9; CANR 39, 59; CWW 2; DLB 232; IDFW 3; MTCW 1
Koontz, Dean R(ay) 1945- .... CLC 78; DAM NOV, POP
 See also AAYA 9, 31; BEST 89:3, 90:2; CA 108; CANR 19, 36, 52, 95; CMW; CPW; DA3; HGG; MTCW 1; SATA 92; SFW; YAW
Kopernik, Mikolaj
 See Copernicus, Nicolaus
Kopit, Arthur (Lee) 1937- ..... CLC 1, 18, 33; DAM DRAM
 See also AITN 1; CA 81-84; CABS 3; CD; DFS 7; DLB 7; MTCW 1; RGAL
Kops, Bernard 1926- .... CLC 4
 See also CA 5-8R; CANR 84; CBD; CN; CP; DLB 13
Kornbluth, C(yril) M. 1923-1958 .... TCLC 8
 See also CA 105; 160; DLB 8; SFW
Korolenko, V. G.
 See Korolenko, Vladimir Galaktionovich
Korolenko, Vladimir
 See Korolenko, Vladimir Galaktionovich
Korolenko, Vladimir G.
 See Korolenko, Vladimir Galaktionovich
Korolenko, Vladimir Galaktionovich 1853-1921 .... TCLC 22
 See also CA 121
Korzybski, Alfred (Habdank Skarbek) 1879-1950 .... TCLC 61
 See also CA 123; 160

Kosinski, Jerzy (Nikodem) 1933-1991 .... CLC 1, 2, 3, 6, 10, 15, 53, 70; DAM NOV
 See also AMWS 7; BPFB 2; CA 17-20R; 134; CANR 9, 46; DA3; DLB 2; DLBY 82; HGG; MTCW 1, 2; NFS 12; RGAL
Kostelanetz, Richard (Cory) 1940- .. CLC 28
 See also CA 13-16R; CAAS 8; CANR 38, 77; CN; CP
Kotlowitz, Robert 1924- .... CLC 4
 See also CA 33-36R; CANR 36
Kotzebue, August (Friedrich Ferdinand) von 1761-1819 .... NCLC 25
 See also DLB 94
Kotzwinkle, William 1938- ..... CLC 5, 14, 35
 See also BPFB 2; CA 45-48; CANR 3, 44, 84; CLR 6; DLB 173; FANT; MAICYA; SATA 24, 70; SFW; YAW
Kowna, Stancy
 See Szymborska, Wislawa
Kozol, Jonathan 1936- .... CLC 17
 See also CA 61-64; CANR 16, 45, 96
Kozoll, Michael 1940(?)- .... CLC 35
Kramer, Kathryn 19(?)- .... CLC 34
Kramer, Larry 1935- .. CLC 42; DAM POP; DC 8
 See also CA 124; 126; CANR 60; GLL 1
Krasicki, Ignacy 1735-1801 .... NCLC 8
Krasinski, Zygmunt 1812-1859 .... NCLC 4
 See also RGWL
Kraus, Karl 1874-1936 .... TCLC 5
 See also CA 104; DLB 118
Kreve (Mickevicius), Vincas 1882-1954 .... TCLC 27
 See also CA 170; DLB 220
Kristeva, Julia 1941- .... CLC 77, 140
 See also CA 154; CANR 99; DLB 242; FW
Kristofferson, Kris 1936- .... CLC 26
 See also CA 104
Krizanc, John 1956- .... CLC 57
 See also CA 187
Krleza, Miroslav 1893-1981 .... CLC 8, 114
 See also CA 97-100; 105; CANR 50; DLB 147; RGWL
Kroetsch, Robert 1927- . CLC 5, 23, 57, 132; DAC; DAM POET
 See also CA 17-20R; CANR 8, 38; CCA 1; CN; CP; DLB 53; MTCW 1
Kroetz, Franz
 See Kroetz, Franz Xaver
Kroetz, Franz Xaver 1946- .... CLC 41
 See also CA 130
Kroker, Arthur (W.) 1945- .... CLC 77
 See also CA 161
Kropotkin, Peter (Aleksieevich) 1842-1921 .... TCLC 36
 See also CA 119
Krotkov, Yuri 1917-1981 .... CLC 19
 See also CA 102
Krumb
 See Crumb, R(obert)
Krumgold, Joseph (Quincy) 1908-1980 .... CLC 12
 See also BYA 1; CA 9-12R; 101; CANR 7; MAICYA; SATA 1, 48; SATA-Obit 23; YAW
Krumwitz
 See Crumb, R(obert)
Krutch, Joseph Wood 1893-1970 ..... CLC 24
 See also CA 1-4R; 25-28R; CANR 4; DLB 63, 206
Krutzch, Gus
 See Eliot, T(homas) S(tearns)
Krylov, Ivan Andreevich 1768(?)-1844 .... NCLC 1
 See also DLB 150

Kubin, Alfred (Leopold Isidor) 1877-1959 .... TCLC 23
 See also CA 112; 149; DLB 81
Kubrick, Stanley 1928-1999 .... CLC 16
 See also AAYA 30; CA 81-84; 177; CANR 33; DLB 26; TCLC 112
Kueng, Hans 1928-
 See Kung, Hans
 See also CA 53-56; CANR 66; MTCW 1, 2
Kumin, Maxine (Winokur) 1925- ..... CLC 5, 13, 28; DAM POET; PC 15
 See also AITN 2; AMWS 4; ANW; CA 1-4R; CAAS 8; CANR 1, 21, 69; CP; CWP; DA3; DLB 5; EXPP; MTCW 1, 2; PAB; SATA 12
Kundera, Milan 1929- . CLC 4, 9, 19, 32, 68, 115, 135; DAM NOV; SSC 24
 See also AAYA 2; BPFB 2; CA 85-88; CANR 19, 52, 74; CWW 2; DA3; DLB 232; MTCW 1, 2; RGSF; SSFS 10
Kunene, Mazisi (Raymond) 1930- ... CLC 85
 See also BW 1, 3; CA 125; CANR 81; DLB 117
Kung, Hans .... CLC 130
 See also Kueng, Hans
Kunikida, Doppo 1869(?)-1908 ...... TCLC 99
 See also DLB 180
Kunitz, Stanley (Jasspon) 1905- .. CLC 6, 11, 14, 148; PC 19
 See also AMWS 3; CA 41-44R; CANR 26, 57, 98; CP; DA3; DLB 48; INT CANR-26; MTCW 1, 2; PFS 11; RGAL
Kunze, Reiner 1933- .... CLC 10
 See also CA 93-96; CWW 2; DLB 75
Kuprin, Aleksander Ivanovich 1870-1938 .... TCLC 5
 See also CA 104; 182
Kureishi, Hanif 1954(?)- .... CLC 64, 135
 See also CA 139; CBD; CD; CN; DLB 194; GLL 2; IDFW 4; WLIT 4
Kurosawa, Akira 1910-1998 .... CLC 16, 119; DAM MULT
 See also AAYA 11; CA 101; 170; CANR 46
Kushner, Tony 1957(?)- .... CLC 81; DAM DRAM; DC 10
 See also CA 144; CAD; CANR 74; CD; DA3; DFS 5; DLB 228; GLL 1; LAIT 5; MTCW 2; RGAL
Kuttner, Henry 1915-1958 .... TCLC 10
 See also CA 107; 157; DLB 8; FANT; SFW
Kuzma, Greg 1944- .... CLC 7
 See also CA 33-36R; CANR 70
Kuzmin, Mikhail 1872(?)-1936 ...... TCLC 40
 See also CA 170
Kyd, Thomas 1558-1594 .... LC 22; DAM DRAM; DC 3
 See also BRW 1; DLB 62; IDTP; RGEL; TEA; WLIT 3
Kyprianos, Iossif
 See Samarakis, Antonis
La Bruyere, Jean de 1645-1696 .... LC 17
 See also GFL Beginnings to 1789
Lacan, Jacques (Marie Emile) 1901-1981 .... CLC 75
 See also CA 121; 104
Laclos, Pierre Ambroise Francois 1741-1803 .... NCLC 4, 87
 See also EW; GFL Beginnings to 1789; RGWL
Lacolere, Francois
 See Aragon, Louis
La Colere, Francois
 See Aragon, Louis
La Deshabilleuse
 See Simenon, Georges (Jacques Christian)
Lady Gregory
 See Gregory, Isabella Augusta (Persse)
Lady of Quality, A
 See Bagnold, Enid

Lucas, Hans
See Godard, Jean-Luc

Lucas, Victoria
See Plath, Sylvia

Lucian c. 125-c. 180 .... **CMLC 32**
See also DLB 176; RGWL

Ludlam, Charles 1943-1987 .... **CLC 46, 50**
See also CA 85-88; 122; CAD; CANR 72, 86

Ludlum, Robert 1927-2001 .... **CLC 22, 43; DAM NOV, POP**
See also AAYA 10; BEST 89:1, 90:3; BPFB 2; CA 33-36R; CANR 25, 41, 68; CMW; CPW; DA3; DLBY 82; MTCW 1, 2

Ludwig, Ken .... **CLC 60**
See also CAD

Ludwig, Otto 1813-1865 .... **NCLC 4**
See also DLB 129

Lugones, Leopoldo 1874-1938 ...... **TCLC 15; HLCS 2**
See also CA 116; 131; HW 1

Lu Hsun .... **TCLC 3; SSC 20**
See also Shu-Jen, Chou

Lukacs, George .... **CLC 24**
See also Lukacs, Gyorgy (Szegeny von)

Lukacs, Gyorgy (Szegeny von) 1885-1971
See Lukacs, George
See also CA 101; 29-32R; CANR 62; DLB 242; EW; MTCW 2

Luke, Peter (Ambrose Cyprian)
1919-1995 .... **CLC 38**
See also CA 81-84; 147; CANR 72; CBD; CD; DLB 13

Lunar, Dennis
See Mungo, Raymond

Lurie, Alison 1926- .... **CLC 4, 5, 18, 39**
See also BPFB 2; CA 1-4R; CANR 2, 17, 50, 88; CN; DLB 2; MTCW 1; SATA 46, 112

Lustig, Arnost 1926- .... **CLC 56**
See also AAYA 3; CA 69-72; CANR 47; CWW 2; DLB 232; SATA 56

Luther, Martin 1483-1546 .... **LC 9, 37**
See also DLB 179; RGWL

Luxemburg, Rosa 1870(?)-1919 ..... **TCLC 63**
See also CA 118

Luzi, Mario 1914- .... **CLC 13**
See also CA 61-64; CANR 9, 70; CWW 2; DLB 128

L'vov, Arkady .... **CLC 59**

Lyly, John 1554(?)-1606 .... **LC 41; DAM DRAM; DC 7**
See also BRW 1; DLB 62, 167; RGEL

L'Ymagier
See Gourmont, Remy(-Marie-Charles) de

Lynch, David (K.) 1946- .... **CLC 66**
See also CA 124; 129

Lynch, James
See Andreyev, Leonid (Nikolaevich)

Lyndsay, Sir David 1485-1555 .... **LC 20**
See also RGEL

Lynn, Kenneth S(chuyler)
1923-2001 .... **CLC 50**
See also CA 1-4R; CANR 3, 27, 65

Lynx
See West, Rebecca

Lyons, Marcus
See Blish, James (Benjamin)

Lyotard, Jean-Francois
1924-1998 .... **TCLC 103**
See also DLB 242

Lyre, Pinchbeck
See Sassoon, Siegfried (Lorraine)

Lytle, Andrew (Nelson) 1902-1995 ... **CLC 22**
See also CA 9-12R; 150; CANR 70; CN; CSW; DLB 6; DLBY 95; RGAL; RHW

Lyttelton, George 1709-1773 .... **LC 10**
See also RGEL

Lytton of Knebworth
See Bulwer-Lytton, Edward (George Earle Lytton)

Maas, Peter 1929-2001 .... **CLC 29**
See also CA 93-96; INT CA-93-96; MTCW 2

Macaulay, Catherine 1731-1791 .... **LC 64**
See also DLB 104

Macaulay, (Emilie) Rose
1881(?)-1958 .... **TCLC 7, 44**
See also CA 104; DLB 36; RGEL; RHW

Macaulay, Thomas Babington
1800-1859 .... **NCLC 42**
See also CDBLB 1832-1890; DLB 32, 55; RGEL

MacBeth, George (Mann)
1932-1992 .... **CLC 2, 5, 9**
See also CA 25-28R; 136; CANR 61, 66; DLB 40; MTCW 1; PFS 8; SATA 4; SATA-Obit 70

MacCaig, Norman (Alexander)
1910-1996 .... **CLC 36; DAB; DAM POET**
See also BRWS 6; CA 9-12R; CANR 3, 34; CP; DLB 27; RGEL

MacCarthy, Sir (Charles Otto) Desmond
1877-1952 .... **TCLC 36**
See also CA 167

MacDiarmid, Hugh .... **CLC 2, 4, 11, 19, 63; PC 9**
See also Grieve, C(hristopher) M(urray)
See also CDBLB 1945-1960; DLB 20; RGEL

MacDonald, Anson
See Heinlein, Robert A(nson)

Macdonald, Cynthia 1928- .... **CLC 13, 19**
See also CA 49-52; CANR 4, 44; DLB 105

MacDonald, George 1824-1905 .... **TCLC 9, 113**
See also BYA 5; CA 106; 137; CANR 80; CLR 67; DLB 18, 163, 178; FANT; MAI-CYA; RGEL; SATA 33, 100; SFW

Macdonald, John
See Millar, Kenneth

MacDonald, John D(ann)
1916-1986 .. **CLC 3, 27, 44; DAM NOV, POP**
See also BPFB 2; CA 1-4R; 121; CANR 1, 19, 60; CMW; CPW; DLB 8; DLBY 86; MTCW 1, 2; SFW

Macdonald, John Ross
See Millar, Kenneth

Macdonald, Ross ..... **CLC 1, 2, 3, 14, 34, 41**
See also Millar, Kenneth
See also AMWS 4; BPFB 2; DLBD 6; RGAL

MacDougal, John
See Blish, James (Benjamin)

MacDougal, John
See Blish, James (Benjamin)

MacDowell, John
See Parks, Tim(othy Harold)

MacEwen, Gwendolyn (Margaret)
1941-1987 .... **CLC 13, 55**
See also CA 9-12R; 124; CANR 7, 22; DLB 53; SATA 50; SATA-Obit 55

Macha, Karel Hynek 1810-1846 .... **NCLC 46**

Machado (y Ruiz), Antonio
1875-1939 .... **TCLC 3**
See also CA 104; 174; DLB 108; EW; HW 2; RGWL

Machado de Assis, Joaquim Maria
1839-1908 ..... **TCLC 10; BLC 2; HLCS 2; SSC 24**
See also CA 107; 153; CANR 91; RGSF; RGWL; WLIT 1

Machen, Arthur .... **TCLC 4; SSC 20**
See also Jones, Arthur Llewellyn
See also CA 179; DLB 36, 156, 178; RGEL

Machiavelli, Niccolo 1469-1527 ..... **LC 8, 36; DA; DAB; DAC; DAM MST; WLCS**
See also EW; LAIT 1; NFS 9; RGWL

MacInnes, Colin 1914-1976 .... **CLC 4, 23**
See also CA 69-72; 65-68; CANR 21; DLB 14; MTCW 1, 2; RGEL; RHW

MacInnes, Helen (Clark)
1907-1985 .... **CLC 27, 39; DAM POP**
See also BPFB 2; CA 1-4R; 117; CANR 1, 28, 58; CMW; CPW; DLB 87; MSW; MTCW 1, 2; SATA 22; SATA-Obit 44

Mackenzie, Compton (Edward Montague)
1883-1972 .... **CLC 18**
See also CA 21-22; 37-40R; CAP 2; DLB 34, 100; RGEL

Mackenzie, Henry 1745-1831 .... **NCLC 41**
See also DLB 39; RGEL

Mackintosh, Elizabeth 1896(?)-1952
See Tey, Josephine
See also CA 110; CMW

MacLaren, James
See Grieve, C(hristopher) M(urray)

Mac Laverty, Bernard 1942- .... **CLC 31**
See also CA 116; 118; CANR 43, 88; CN; INT CA-118; RGSF

MacLean, Alistair (Stuart)
1922(?)-1987 .. **CLC 3, 13, 50, 63; DAM POP**
See also CA 57-60; 121; CANR 28, 61; CMW; CPW; MTCW 1; SATA 23; SATA-Obit 50; TCWW 2

Maclean, Norman (Fitzroy)
1902-1990 .... **CLC 78; DAM POP; SSC 13**
See also ANW; CA 102; 132; CANR 49; CPW; DLB 206; TCWW 2

MacLeish, Archibald 1892-1982 ... **CLC 3, 8, 14, 68; DAM POET**
See also AMW; CA 9-12R; 106; CAD; CANR 33, 63; CDALBS; DLB 4, 7, 45; DLBY 82; EXPP; MTCW 1, 2; PAB; PFS 5; RGAL

MacLennan, (John) Hugh
1907-1990 . **CLC 2, 14, 92; DAC; DAM MST**
See also CA 5-8R; 142; CANR 33; DLB 68; MTCW 1, 2; RGEL

MacLeod, Alistair 1936- .... **CLC 56; DAC; DAM MST**
See also CA 123; CCA 1; DLB 60; MTCW 2; RGSF

Macleod, Fiona
See Sharp, William
See also RGEL

MacNeice, (Frederick) Louis
1907-1963 .... **CLC 1, 4, 10, 53; DAB; DAM POET**
See also BRW; CA 85-88; CANR 61; DLB 10, 20; MTCW 1, 2; RGEL

MacNeill, Dand
See Fraser, George MacDonald

Macpherson, James 1736-1796 .... **LC 29**
See also Ossian
See also DLB 109; RGEL

Macpherson, (Jean) Jay 1931- .... **CLC 14**
See also CA 5-8R; CANR 90; CP; CWP; DLB 53

MacShane, Frank 1927-1999 .... **CLC 39**
See also CA 9-12R; 186; CANR 3, 33; DLB 111

Macumber, Mari
See Sandoz, Mari(e Susette)

Madach, Imre 1823-1864 .... **NCLC 19**

Madden, (Jerry) David 1933- .... **CLC 5, 15**
See also CA 1-4R; CAAS 3; CANR 4, 45; CN; CSW; DLB 6; MTCW 1

Maddern, Al(an)
See Ellison, Harlan (Jay)

Madhubuti, Haki R. 1942- . CLC 6, 73; BLC
  2; DAM MULT, POET; PC 5
  See also Lee, Don L.
  See also BW 2, 3; CA 73-76; CANR 24,
  51, 73; CP; CSW; DLB 5, 41; DLBD 8;
  MTCW 2; RGAL
Maepenn, Hugh
  See Kuttner, Henry
Maepenn, K. H.
  See Kuttner, Henry
Maeterlinck, Maurice 1862-1949 ... TCLC 3;
  DAM DRAM
  See also CA 104; 136; CANR 80; DLB 192;
  GFL 1789 to the Present; RGWL; SATA
  66
Maginn, William 1794-1842 .... NCLC 8
  See also DLB 110, 159
Mahapatra, Jayanta 1928- .... CLC 33; DAM
  MULT
  See also CA 73-76; CAAS 9; CANR 15,
  33, 66, 87; CP
Mahfouz, Naguib (Abdel Aziz Al-Sabilgi)
  1911(?)-
  See Mahfuz, Najib (Abdel Aziz al-Sabilgi)
  See also BEST 89:2; CA 128; CANR 55,
  101; CWW 2; DA3; DAM NOV; MTCW
  1, 2; RGWL; SSFS 9
Mahfuz, Najib (Abdel Aziz al-Sabilgi)
  .... CLC 52, 55
  See also Mahfouz, Naguib (Abdel Aziz Al-
  Sabilgi)
  See also DLBY 88; RGSF; WLIT 2
Mahon, Derek 1941- .... CLC 27
  See also BRWS 6; CA 113; 128; CANR 88;
  CP; DLB 40
Maiakovskii, Vladimir
  See Mayakovski, Vladimir (Vladimirovich)
  See also RGWL
Mailer, Norman 1923- ... CLC 1, 2, 3, 4, 5, 8,
  11, 14, 28, 39, 74, 111; DA; DAB;
  DAC; DAM MST, NOV, POP
  See also AAYA 31; AMW; BPFB
  2; CA 9-12R; CABS 1; CANR 28, 74, 77;
  CDALB 1968-1988; CN; CPW; DA3;
  DLB 2, 16, 28, 185; DLBD 3; DLBY 80,
  83; MTCW 1, 2; NFS 10; RGAL
Maillet, Antonine 1929- .. CLC 54, 118; DAC
  See also CA 115; 120; CANR 46, 74, 77;
  CCA 1; CWW 2; DLB 60; INT 120;
  MTCW 2
Mais, Roger 1905-1955 .... TCLC 8
  See also BW 1, 3; CA 105; 124; CANR 82;
  DLB 125; MTCW 1; RGEL
Maistre, Joseph 1753-1821 .... NCLC 37
  See also GFL 1789 to the Present
Maitland, Frederic William
  1850-1906 .... TCLC 65
Maitland, Sara (Louise) 1950- .... CLC 49
  See also CA 69-72; CANR 13, 59; FW
Major, Clarence 1936- . CLC 3, 19, 48; BLC
  2; DAM MULT
  See also AFAW 2; BW 2, 3; CA 21-24R;
  CAAS 6; CANR 13, 25, 53, 82; CN; CP;
  CSW; DLB 33
Major, Kevin (Gerald) 1949- . CLC 26; DAC
  See also AAYA 16; CA 97-100; CANR 21,
  38; CLR 11; DLB 60; INT CANR-21;
  JRDA; MAICYA; SATA 32, 82; WYA;
  YAW
Maki, James
  See Ozu, Yasujiro
Malabaila, Damiano
  See Levi, Primo
Malamud, Bernard 1914-1986 .. CLC 1, 2, 3,
  5, 8, 9, 11, 18, 27, 44, 78, 85; DA;
  DAB; DAC; DAM MST, NOV, POP;
  SSC 15; WLC
  See also AAYA 16; AMWS 1; BPFB 2; CA
  5-8R; 118; CABS 1; CANR 28, 62;
  CDALB 1941-1968; CPW; DA3; DLB 2,

28, 152; DLBY 80, 86; EXPS; LAIT 4;
  MTCW 1, 2; NFS 4, 9; RGAL; RGSF;
  SSFS 8
Malan, Herman
  See Bosman, Herman Charles; Bosman,
  Herman Charles
Malaparte, Curzio 1898-1957 .... TCLC 52
Malcolm, Dan
  See Silverberg, Robert
Malcolm X .... CLC 82, 117; BLC 2; WLCS
  See also Little, Malcolm
  See also LAIT 5
Malherbe, Francois de 1555-1628 .... LC 5
  See also GFL Beginnings to 1789
Mallarme, Stephane 1842-1898 ...... NCLC 4,
  41; DAM POET; PC 4
  See also GFL 1789 to the Present; RGWL
Mallet-Joris, Francoise 1930- .... CLC 11
  See also CA 65-68; CANR 17; DLB 83;
  GFL 1789 to the Present
Malley, Ern
  See McAuley, James Phillip
Mallowan, Agatha Christie
  See Christie, Agatha (Mary Clarissa)
Maloff, Saul 1922- .... CLC 5
  See also CA 33-36R
Malone, Louis
  See MacNeice, (Frederick) Louis
Malone, Michael (Christopher)
  1942- .... CLC 43
  See also CA 77-80; CANR 14, 32, 57
Malory, Sir Thomas 1410(?)-1471(?) . LC 11;
  DA; DAB; DAC; DAM MST; WLCS
  See also BRW 1; CDBLB Before 1660;
  DLB 146; EFS 2; RGEL; SATA 59;
  SATA-Brief 33; SUFW; WLIT 3
Malouf, (George Joseph) David
  1934- .... CLC 28, 86
  See also CA 124; CANR 50, 76; CN; CP;
  MTCW 2
Malraux, (Georges-)Andre
  1901-1976 .... CLC 1, 4, 9, 13, 15, 57;
  DAM NOV
  See also BPFB 2; CA 21-22; 69-72; CANR
  34, 58; CAP 2; DA3; DLB 72; EW; GFL
  1789 to the Present; MTCW 1, 2; RGWL
Malzberg, Barry N(athaniel) 1939- ... CLC 7
  See also CA 61-64; CAAS 4; CANR 16;
  CMW; DLB 8; SFW
Mamet, David (Alan) 1947- .. CLC 9, 15, 34,
  46, 91; DAM DRAM; DC 4
  See also AAYA 3; CA 81-84; CABS 3;
  CANR 15, 41, 67, 72; CD; DA3; DFS 2,
  3, 6, 12; DLB 7; IDFW 4; MTCW 1, 2;
  RGAL
Mamoulian, Rouben (Zachary)
  1897-1987 .... CLC 16
  See also CA 25-28R; 124; CANR 85
Mandelshtam, Osip
  See Mandelstam, Osip (Emilievich)
  See also RGWL
Mandelstam, Osip (Emilievich)
  1891(?)-1943(?) .... TCLC 2, 6; PC 14
  See also Mandelshtam, Osip
  See also CA 104; 150; EW; MTCW 2
Mander, (Mary) Jane 1877-1949 ... TCLC 31
  See also CA 162; RGEL
Mandeville, John fl. 1350- .... CMLC 19
  See also DLB 146
Mandiargues, Andre Pieyre de .... CLC 41
  See also Pieyre de Mandiargues, Andre
  See also DLB 83
Mandrake, Ethel Belle
  See Thurman, Wallace (Henry)
Mangan, James Clarence
  1803-1849 .... NCLC 27
  See also RGEL
Maniere, J.-E.
  See Giraudoux, Jean(-Hippolyte)

Mankiewicz, Herman (Jacob)
  1897-1953 .... TCLC 85
  See also CA 120; 169; DLB 26; IDFW 3, 4
Manley, (Mary) Delariviere
  1672(?)-1724 .... LC 1, 42
  See also DLB 39, 80; RGEL
Mann, Abel
  See Creasey, John
Mann, Emily 1952- .... DC 7
  See also CA 130; CAD; CANR 55; CD;
  CWD
Mann, (Luiz) Heinrich 1871-1950 ... TCLC 9
  See also CA 106; 164, 181; DLB 66, 118;
  EW; RGWL
Mann, (Paul) Thomas 1875-1955 ... TCLC 2,
  8, 14, 21, 35, 44, 60; DA; DAB; DAC;
  DAM MST, NOV; SSC 5; WLC
  See also BPFB 2; CA 104; 128; DA3; DLB
  66; EW; GLL 1; MTCW 1, 2; RGSF;
  RGWL; SSFS 4, 9
Mannheim, Karl 1893-1947 .... TCLC 65
Manning, David
  See Faust, Frederick (Schiller)
  See also TCWW 2
Manning, Frederic 1887(?)-1935 ... TCLC 25
  See also CA 124
Manning, Olivia 1915-1980 .... CLC 5, 19
  See also CA 5-8R; 101; CANR 29; FW;
  MTCW 1; RGEL
Mano, D. Keith 1942- .... CLC 2, 10
  See also CA 25-28R; CAAS 6; CANR 26,
  57; DLB 6
Mansfield, Katherine .... TCLC 2, 8, 39;
  DAB; SSC 9, 23, 38; WLC
  See also Beauchamp, Kathleen Mansfield
  See also BPFB 2; DLB 162; EXPS; FW;
  GLL 1; RGEL; RGSF; SSFS 2,8,10,11
Manso, Peter 1940- .... CLC 39
  See also CA 29-32R; CANR 44
Mantecon, Juan Jimenez
  See Jimenez (Mantecon), Juan Ramon
Mantel, Hilary (Mary) 1952- .... CLC 144
  See also CA 125; CANR 54, 101; CN;
  RHW
Manton, Peter
  See Creasey, John
Man Without a Spleen, A
  See Chekhov, Anton (Pavlovich)
Manzoni, Alessandro 1785-1873 ... NCLC 29,
  98
  See also RGWL
Map, Walter 1140-1209 .... CMLC 32
Mapu, Abraham (ben Jekutiel)
  1808-1867 .... NCLC 18
Mara, Sally
  See Queneau, Raymond
Marat, Jean Paul 1743-1793 .... LC 10
Marcel, Gabriel Honore 1889-1973 . CLC 15
  See also CA 102; 45-48; MTCW 1, 2
March, William 1893-1954 .... TCLC 96
Marchbanks, Samuel
  See Davies, (William) Robertson
  See also CCA 1
Marchi, Giacomo
  See Bassani, Giorgio
Marcus Aurelius
  See Antoninus, Marcus Aurelius
Marguerite
  See de Navarre, Marguerite
Marguerite de Navarre
  See de Navarre, Marguerite
  See also RGWL
Margulies, Donald .... CLC 76
  See also DFS 13; DLB 228
Marie de France c. 12th cent. - ..... CMLC 8;
  PC 22
  See also DLB 208; FW; RGWL

Marie de l'Incarnation 1599-1672 ...... **LC 10**
Marier, Captain Victor
    See Griffith, D(avid Lewelyn) W(ark)
Mariner, Scott
    See Pohl, Frederik
Marinetti, Filippo Tommaso
    1876-1944 .... **TCLC 10**
    See also CA 107; DLB 114
Marivaux, Pierre Carlet de Chamblain de
    1688-1763 .... **LC 4; DC 7**
    See also GFL Beginnings to 1789; RGWL
Markandaya, Kamala .... **CLC 8, 38**
    See also Taylor, Kamala (Purnaiya)
    See also BYA 13
Markfield, Wallace 1926- .... **CLC 8**
    See also CA 69-72; CAAS 3; CN; DLB 2, 28
Markham, Edwin 1852-1940 .... **TCLC 47**
    See also CA 160; DLB 54, 186; RGAL
Markham, Robert
    See Amis, Kingsley (William)
Marks, J
    See Highwater, Jamake (Mamake)
Marks-Highwater, J
    See Highwater, Jamake (Mamake)
Markson, David M(errill) 1927- .... **CLC 67**
    See also CA 49-52; CANR 1, 91; CN
Marley, Bob .... **CLC 17**
    See also Marley, Robert Nesta
Marley, Robert Nesta 1945-1981
    See Marley, Bob
    See also CA 107; 103
Marlowe, Christopher 1564-1593 ...... **LC 22, 47; DA; DAB; DAC; DAM DRAM, MST; DC 1; WLC**
    See also BRW 1; CDBLB Before 1660; DA3; DFS 1, 5, 13; DLB 62; EXPP; RGEL; WLIT 3
Marlowe, Stephen 1928- .... **CLC 70**
    See also Queen, Ellery
    See also CA 13-16R; CANR 6, 55; CMW; SFW
Marmontel, Jean-Francois 1723-1799 .. **LC 2**
Marquand, John P(hillips)
    1893-1960 .... **CLC 2, 10**
    See also AMW; BPFB 2; CA 85-88; CANR 73; CMW; DLB 9, 102; MTCW 2; RGAL
Marques, Rene 1919-1979 ..... **CLC 96; DAM MULT; HLC 2**
    See also CA 97-100; 85-88; CANR 78; DLB 113; HW 1, 2; RGSF
Marquez, Gabriel (Jose) Garcia
    See Garcia Marquez, Gabriel (Jose)
Marquis, Don(ald Robert Perry)
    1878-1937 .... **TCLC 7**
    See also CA 104; 166; DLB 11, 25; RGAL
Marric, J. J.
    See Creasey, John
Marryat, Frederick 1792-1848 .... **NCLC 3**
    See also DLB 21, 163; RGEL
Marsden, James
    See Creasey, John
Marsh, Edward 1872-1953 .... **TCLC 99**
Marsh, (Edith) Ngaio 1899-1982 .... **CLC 7, 53; DAM POP**
    See also CA 9-12R; CANR 6, 58; CMW; CPW; DLB 77; MTCW 1, 2; RGEL
Marshall, Garry 1934- .... **CLC 17**
    See also AAYA 3; CA 111; SATA 60
Marshall, Paule 1929- .. **CLC 27, 72; BLC 3; DAM MULT; SSC 3**
    See also AFAW 1, 2; BPFB 2; BW 2, 3; CA 77-80; CANR 25, 73; CN; DA3; DLB 33, 157, 227; MTCW 1, 2; RGAL
Marshallik
    See Zangwill, Israel
Marsten, Richard
    See Hunter, Evan

Marston, John 1576-1634 .... **LC 33; DAM DRAM**
    See also BRW 2; DLB 58, 172; RGEL
Martha, Henry
    See Harris, Mark
Marti (y Perez), Jose (Julian)
    1853-1895 ...... **NCLC 63; DAM MULT; HLC 2**
    See also HW 2; LAW; RGWL; WLIT 1
Martial c. 40-c. 104 .... **CMLC 35; PC 10**
    See also DLB 211; RGWL
Martin, Ken
    See Hubbard, L(afayette) Ron(ald)
Martin, Richard
    See Creasey, John
Martin, Steve 1945- .... **CLC 30**
    See also CA 97-100; CANR 30, 100; MTCW 1
Martin, Valerie 1948- .... **CLC 89**
    See also BEST 90:2; CA 85-88; CANR 49, 89
Martin, Violet Florence
    1862-1915 .... **TCLC 51**
Martin, Webber
    See Silverberg, Robert
Martindale, Patrick Victor
    See White, Patrick (Victor Martindale)
Martin du Gard, Roger
    1881-1958 .... **TCLC 24**
    See also CA 118; CANR 94; DLB 65; GFL 1789 to the Present; RGWL
Martineau, Harriet 1802-1876 .... **NCLC 26**
    See also DLB 21, 55, 159, 163, 166, 190; FW; RGEL; YABC 2
Martines, Julia
    See O'Faolain, Julia
Martinez, Enrique Gonzalez
    See Gonzalez Martinez, Enrique
Martinez, Jacinto Benavente y
    See Benavente (y Martinez), Jacinto
Martinez de la Rosa, Francisco de Paula
    1787-1862 .... **NCLC 102**
Martinez Ruiz, Jose 1873-1967
    See Azorin; Ruiz, Jose Martinez
    See also CA 93-96; HW 1
Martinez Sierra, Gregorio
    1881-1947 .... **TCLC 6**
    See also CA 115
Martinez Sierra, Maria (de la O'LeJarraga)
    1874-1974 .... **TCLC 6**
    See also CA 115
Martinsen, Martin
    See Follett, Ken(neth Martin)
Martinson, Harry (Edmund)
    1904-1978 .... **CLC 14**
    See also CA 77-80; CANR 34
Marut, Ret
    See Traven, B.
Marut, Robert
    See Traven, B.
Marvell, Andrew 1621-1678 .. **LC 4, 43; DA; DAB; DAC; DAM MST, POET; PC 10; WLC**
    See also BRW 2; CDBLB 1660-1789; DLB 131; EXPP; PFS 5; RGEL; WP
Marx, Karl (Heinrich) 1818-1883 . **NCLC 17**
    See also DLB 129
Masaoka, Shiki .... **TCLC 18**
    See also Masaoka, Tsunenori
Masaoka, Tsunenori 1867-1902
    See Masaoka, Shiki
    See also CA 117; 191
Masefield, John (Edward)
    1878-1967 ..... **CLC 11, 47; DAM POET**
    See also CA 19-20; 25-28R; CANR 33; CAP 2; CDBLB 1890-1914; DLB 10, 19, 153, 160; EXPP; FANT; MTCW 1, 2; PFS 5; RGEL; SATA 19

Maso, Carole 19(?)- .... **CLC 44**
    See also CA 170; GLL 2; RGAL
Mason, Bobbie Ann 1940- ... **CLC 28, 43, 82; SSC 4**
    See also AAYA 5; AMWS 8; BPFB 2; CA 53-56; CANR 11, 31, 58, 83; CDALBS; CN; CSW; DA3; DLB 173; DLBY 87; EXPS; INT CANR-31; MTCW 1, 2; NFS 4; RGAL; RGSF; SSFS 3,8; YAW
Mason, Ernst
    See Pohl, Frederik
Mason, Hunni B.
    See Sternheim, (William Adolf) Carl
Mason, Lee W.
    See Malzberg, Barry N(athaniel)
Mason, Nick 1945- .... **CLC 35**
Mason, Tally
    See Derleth, August (William)
Mass, Anna .... **CLC 59**
Mass, William
    See Gibson, William
Massinger, Philip 1583-1640 .... **LC 70**
    See also DLB 58; RGEL
Master Lao
    See Lao Tzu
Masters, Edgar Lee 1868-1950 .... **TCLC 2, 25; DA; DAC; DAM MST, POET; PC 1, 36; WLCS**
    See also AMWS 1; CA 104; 133; CDALB 1865-1917; DLB 54; EXPP; MTCW 1, 2; RGAL; WP
Masters, Hilary 1928- .... **CLC 48**
    See also CA 25-28R; CANR 13, 47, 97; CN
Mastrosimone, William 19(?)- .... **CLC 36**
    See also CA 186; CAD; CD
Mathe, Albert
    See Camus, Albert
Mather, Cotton 1663-1728 .... **LC 38**
    See also AMWS 2; CDALB 1640-1865; DLB 24, 30, 140; RGAL
Mather, Increase 1639-1723 .... **LC 38**
    See also DLB 24
Matheson, Richard (Burton) 1926- .. **CLC 37**
    See also AAYA 31; CA 97-100; CANR 88, 99; DLB 8, 44; HGG; INT 97-100; SCFW 2; SFW
Mathews, Harry 1930- .... **CLC 6, 52**
    See also CA 21-24R; CAAS 6; CANR 18, 40, 98; CN
Mathews, John Joseph 1894-1979 .. **CLC 84; DAM MULT**
    See also CA 19-20; 142; CANR 45; CAP 2; DLB 175; NNAL
Mathias, Roland (Glyn) 1915- .... **CLC 45**
    See also CA 97-100; CANR 19, 41; CP; DLB 27
Matsuo Basho 1644-1694 .... **LC 62; DAM POET; PC 3**
    See also Basho, Matsuo
    See also PFS 2, 7
Mattheson, Rodney
    See Creasey, John
Matthews, (James) Brander
    1852-1929 .... **TCLC 95**
    See also DLB 71, 78; DLBD 13
Matthews, Greg 1949- .... **CLC 45**
    See also CA 135
Matthews, William (Procter, III)
    1942-1997 .... **CLC 40**
    See also CA 29-32R; 162; CAAS 18; CANR 12, 57; CP; DLB 5
Matthias, John (Edward) 1941- .... **CLC 9**
    See also CA 33-36R; CANR 56; CP
Matthiessen, F(rancis) O(tto)
    1902-1950 .... **TCLC 100**
    See also CA 185; DLB 63

Matthiessen, Peter 1927- ... **CLC 5, 7, 11, 32, 64; DAM NOV**
See also AAYA 6, 40; AMWS 5; BEST 90:4; BPFB 2; CA 9-12R; CANR 21, 50, 73, 100; CN; DA3; DLB 6, 173; MTCW 1, 2; SATA 27

Maturin, Charles Robert
1780(?)-1824 .... **NCLC 6**
See also DLB 178; HGG; RGEL

Matute (Ausejo), Ana Maria 1925- .. **CLC 11**
See also CA 89-92; MTCW 1; RGSF

Maugham, W. S.
See Maugham, W(illiam) Somerset

Maugham, W(illiam) Somerset
1874-1965 ... **CLC 1, 11, 15, 67, 93; DA; DAB; DAC; DAM DRAM, MST, NOV; SSC 8; WLC**
See also BPFB 2; BRW; CA 5-8R; 25-28R; CANR 40; CDBLB 1914-1945; CMW; DA3; DLB 10, 36, 77, 100, 162, 195; LAIT 3; MTCW 1, 2; RGEL; RGSF; SATA 54

Maugham, William Somerset
See Maugham, W(illiam) Somerset

Maupassant, (Henri Rene Albert) Guy de
1850-1893 . **NCLC 1, 42, 83; DA; DAB; DAC; DAM MST; SSC 1; WLC**
See also DA3; DLB 123; EW; EXPS; GFL 1789 to the Present; LAIT 2; RGSF; RGWL; SSFS 4; SUFW; TWA

Maupin, Armistead (Jones, Jr.)
1944- .... **CLC 95; DAM POP**
See also CA 125; 130; CANR 58, 101; CPW; DA3; GLL 1; INT 130; MTCW 2

Maurhut, Richard
See Traven, B.

Mauriac, Claude 1914-1996 .... **CLC 9**
See also CA 89-92; 152; CWW 2; DLB 83; GFL 1789 to the Present

Mauriac, Francois (Charles)
1885-1970 .... **CLC 4, 9, 56; SSC 24**
See also CA 25-28; CAP 2; DLB 65; EW; GFL 1789 to the Present; MTCW 1, 2; RGWL

Mavor, Osborne Henry 1888-1951
See Bridie, James
See also CA 104

Maxwell, William (Keepers, Jr.)
1908-2000 .... **CLC 19**
See also CA 93-96; 189; CANR 54, 95; CN; DLBY 80; INT 93-96

May, Elaine 1932- .... **CLC 16**
See also CA 124; 142; CAD; CWD; DLB 44

Mayakovski, Vladimir (Vladimirovich)
1893-1930 .... **TCLC 4, 18**
See also Maiakovskii, Vladimir; Mayakovsky, Vladimir
See also CA 104; 158; EW; MTCW 2; SFW

Mayakovsky, Vladimir
See Mayakovski, Vladimir (Vladimirovich)
See also WP

Mayhew, Henry 1812-1887 .... **NCLC 31**
See also DLB 18, 55, 190

Mayle, Peter 1939(?)- .... **CLC 89**
See also CA 139; CANR 64

Maynard, Joyce 1953- .... **CLC 23**
See also CA 111; 129; CANR 64

Mayne, William (James Carter)
1928- .... **CLC 12**
See also AAYA 20; CA 9-12R; CANR 37, 80, 100; CLR 25; FANT; JRDA; MAICYA; SAAS 11; SATA 6, 68, 122; YAW

Mayo, Jim
See L'Amour, Louis (Dearborn)
See also TCWW 2

Maysles, Albert 1926- .... **CLC 16**
See also CA 29-32R

Maysles, David 1932-1987 .... **CLC 16**
See also CA 191

Mazer, Norma Fox 1931- .... **CLC 26**
See also AAYA 5, 36; BYA 1; CA 69-72; CANR 12, 32, 66; CLR 23; JRDA; MAICYA; SAAS 1; SATA 24, 67, 105; YAW

Mazzini, Guiseppe 1805-1872 .... **NCLC 34**

McAlmon, Robert (Menzies)
1895-1956 .... **TCLC 97**
See also CA 107; 168; DLB 4, 45; DLBD 15; GLL 1

McAuley, James Phillip 1917-1976 .. **CLC 45**
See also CA 97-100; RGEL

McBain, Ed
See Hunter, Evan

McBrien, William (Augustine)
1930- .... **CLC 44**
See also CA 107; CANR 90

McCabe, Patrick 1955- .... **CLC 133**
See also CA 130; CANR 50, 90; CN; DLB 194

McCaffrey, Anne (Inez) 1926- .... **CLC 17; DAM NOV, POP**
See also AAYA 6, 34; AITN 2; BEST 89:2; BPFB 2; BYA 5; CA 25-28R; CANR 15, 35, 55, 96; CLR 49; CPW; DA3; DLB 8; JRDA; MAICYA; MTCW 1, 2; SAAS 11; SATA 8, 70, 116; SFW; WYA; YAW

McCall, Nathan 1955(?)- .... **CLC 86**
See also BW 3; CA 146; CANR 88

McCann, Arthur
See Campbell, John W(ood, Jr.)

McCann, Edson
See Pohl, Frederik

McCarthy, Charles, Jr. 1933-
See McCarthy, Cormac
See also CANR 42, 69, 101; CN; CPW; CSW; DA3; DAM POP; MTCW 2

McCarthy, Cormac .... **CLC 4, 57, 59, 101**
See also McCarthy, Charles, Jr.
See also AMWS 8; BPFB 2; CA 13-16R; CANR 10; DLB 6, 143; MTCW 2; TCWW 2

McCarthy, Mary (Therese)
1912-1989 .. **CLC 1, 3, 5, 14, 24, 39, 59; SSC 24**
See also AMW; BPFB 2; CA 5-8R; 129; CANR 16, 50, 64; DA3; DLB 2; DLBY 81; FW; INT CANR-16; MAWW; MTCW 1, 2; RGAL

McCartney, (James) Paul 1942- . **CLC 12, 35**
See also CA 146

McCauley, Stephen (D.) 1955- .... **CLC 50**
See also CA 141

McClaren, Peter .... **CLC 70**

McClure, Michael (Thomas) 1932- ... **CLC 6, 10**
See also CA 21-24R; CAD; CANR 17, 46, 77; CD; CP; DLB 16; WP

McCorkle, Jill (Collins) 1958- .... **CLC 51**
See also CA 121; CSW; DLB 234; DLBY 87

McCourt, Frank 1930- .... **CLC 109**
See also CA 157; CANR 97; NCFS 1

McCourt, James 1941- .... **CLC 5**
See also CA 57-60; CANR 98

McCourt, Malachy 1932- .... **CLC 119**

McCoy, Horace (Stanley)
1897-1955 .... **TCLC 28**
See also CA 108; 155; CMW; DLB 9

McCrae, John 1872-1918 .... **TCLC 12**
See also CA 109; DLB 92; PFS 5

McCreigh, James
See Pohl, Frederik

McCullers, (Lula) Carson (Smith)
1917-1967 .... **CLC 1, 4, 10, 12, 48, 100; DA; DAB; DAC; DAM MST, NOV; SSC 9, 24; WLC**
See also AAYA 21; AMW; BPFB 2; CA 5-8R; 25-28R; CABS 1, 3; CANR 18; CDALB 1941-1968; DA3; DFS 5; DLB 2, 7, 173, 228; EXPS; FW; GLL 1; LAIT 3, 4; MAWW; MTCW 1, 2; NFS 6; RGAL; RGSF; SATA 27; SSFS 5; YAW

McCulloch, John Tyler
See Burroughs, Edgar Rice

McCullough, Colleen 1938(?)- .... **CLC 27, 107; DAM NOV, POP**
See also AAYA 36; BPFB 2; CA 81-84; CANR 17, 46, 67, 98; CPW; DA3; MTCW 1, 2; RHW

McDermott, Alice 1953- .... **CLC 90**
See also CA 109; CANR 40, 90

McElroy, Joseph 1930- .... **CLC 5, 47**
See also CA 17-20R; CN

McEwan, Ian (Russell) 1948- .... **CLC 13, 66; DAM NOV**
See also BEST 90:4; BRWS 4; CA 61-64; CANR 14, 41, 69, 87; CN; DLB 14, 194; HGG; MTCW 1, 2; RGSF

McFadden, David 1940- .... **CLC 48**
See also CA 104; CP; DLB 60; INT 104

McFarland, Dennis 1950- .... **CLC 65**
See also CA 165

McGahern, John 1934- ... **CLC 5, 9, 48; SSC 17**
See also CA 17-20R; CANR 29, 68; CN; DLB 14, 231; MTCW 1

McGinley, Patrick (Anthony) 1937- . **CLC 41**
See also CA 120; 127; CANR 56; INT 127

McGinley, Phyllis 1905-1978 .... **CLC 14**
See also CA 9-12R; 77-80; CANR 19; CWRI; DLB 11, 48; PFS 9; SATA 2, 44; SATA-Obit 24

McGinniss, Joe 1942- .... **CLC 32**
See also AITN 2; BEST 89:2; CA 25-28R; CANR 26, 70; CPW; DLB 185; INT CANR-26

McGivern, Maureen Daly
See Daly, Maureen

McGrath, Patrick 1950- .... **CLC 55**
See also CA 136; CANR 65; CN; DLB 231; HGG

McGrath, Thomas (Matthew)
1916-1990 ..... **CLC 28, 59; DAM POET**
See also CA 9-12R; 132; CANR 6, 33, 95; MTCW 1; SATA 41; SATA-Obit 66

McGuane, Thomas (Francis III)
1939- .... **CLC 3, 7, 18, 45, 127**
See also AITN 2; BPFB 2; CA 49-52; CANR 5, 24, 49, 94; CN; DLB 2, 212; DLBY 80; INT CANR-24; MTCW 1; TCWW 2

McGuckian, Medbh 1950- .... **CLC 48; DAM POET; PC 27**
See also BRWS 5; CA 143; CP; CWP; DLB 40

McHale, Tom 1942(?)-1982 .... **CLC 3, 5**
See also AITN 1; CA 77-80; 106

McIlvanney, William 1936- .... **CLC 42**
See also CA 25-28R; CANR 61; CMW; DLB 14, 207

McIlwraith, Maureen Mollie Hunter
See Hunter, Mollie
See also SATA 2

McInerney, Jay 1955- .... **CLC 34, 112; DAM POP**
See also AAYA 18; BPFB 2; CA 116; 123; CANR 45, 68; CN; CPW; DA3; INT 123; MTCW 2

McIntyre, Vonda N(eel) 1948- .... **CLC 18**
See also CA 81-84; CANR 17, 34, 69; MTCW 1; SFW; YAW

McKay, Claude .... **TCLC 7, 41; BLC 3;**
DAB; PC 2
  See also McKay, Festus Claudius
  See also AFAW 1, 2; DLB 4, 45, 51, 117;
  EXPP; GLL 2; LAIT 3; PAB; PFS 4;
  RGAL; WP
McKay, Festus Claudius 1889-1948
  See McKay, Claude
  See also BW 1, 3; CA 104; 124; CANR 73;
  DA; DAC; DAM MST, MULT, NOV,
  POET; MTCW 1, 2; WLC
McKuen, Rod 1933- .... **CLC 1, 3**
  See also AITN 1; CA 41-44R; CANR 40
McLoughlin, R. B.
  See Mencken, H(enry) L(ouis)
McLuhan, (Herbert) Marshall
    1911-1980 .... **CLC 37, 83**
  See also CA 9-12R; 102; CANR 12, 34, 61;
  DLB 88; INT CANR-12; MTCW 1, 2
McMillan, Terry (L.) 1951- .... **CLC 50, 61,**
  112; BLCS; DAM MULT, NOV, POP
  See also AAYA 21; BPFB 2; BW 2, 3; CA
  140; CANR 60; CPW; DA3; MTCW 2;
  RGAL; YAW
McMurtry, Larry (Jeff) 1936- .. **CLC 2, 3, 7,**
  11, 27, 44, 127; DAM NOV, POP
  See also AAYA 15; AITN 2; AMWS 5;
  BEST 89:2; BPFB 2; CA 5-8R; CANR
  19, 43, 64; CDALB 1968-1988; CN;
  CPW; CSW; DA3; DLB 2, 143; DLBY
  80, 87; MTCW 1, 2; RGAL; TCWW 2
McNally, T. M. 1961- .... **CLC 82**
McNally, Terrence 1939- ... **CLC 4, 7, 41, 91;**
  DAM DRAM
  See also CA 45-48; CAD; CANR 2, 56; CD;
  DA3; DLB 7; GLL 1; MTCW 2
McNamer, Deirdre 1950- .... **CLC 70**
McNeal, Tom .... **CLC 119**
McNeile, Herman Cyril 1888-1937
  See Sapper
  See also CA 184; CMW; DLB 77
McNickle, (William) D'Arcy
    1904-1977 .... **CLC 89; DAM MULT**
  See also CA 9-12R; 85-88; CANR 5, 45;
  DLB 175, 212; NNAL; RGAL; SATA-
  Obit 22
McPhee, John (Angus) 1931- .... **CLC 36**
  See also AMWS 3; ANW; BEST 90:1; CA
  65-68; CANR 20, 46, 64, 69; CPW; DLB
  185; MTCW 1, 2
McPherson, James Alan 1943- .. **CLC 19, 77;**
  BLCS
  See also BW 1, 3; CA 25-28R; CAAS 17;
  CANR 24, 74; CN; CSW; DLB 38;
  MTCW 1, 2; RGAL; RGSF
McPherson, William (Alexander)
    1933- .... **CLC 34**
  See also CA 69-72; CANR 28; INT
  CANR-28
McTaggart, J. McT. Ellis
  See McTaggart, John McTaggart Ellis
McTaggart, John McTaggart Ellis
    1866-1925 .... **TCLC 105**
  See also CA 120
Mead, George Herbert 1873-1958 . **TCLC 89**
Mead, Margaret 1901-1978 .... **CLC 37**
  See also AITN 1; CA 1-4R; 81-84; CANR
  4; DA3; FW; MTCW 1, 2; SATA-Obit 20
Meaker, Marijane (Agnes) 1927-
  See Kerr, M. E.
  See also CA 107; CANR 37, 63; INT 107;
  JRDA; MAICYA; MTCW 1; SATA 20,
  61, 99; SATA-Essay 111; YAW
Medoff, Mark (Howard) 1940- ... **CLC 6, 23;**
  DAM DRAM
  See also AITN 1; CA 53-56; CAD; CANR
  5; CD; DFS 4; DLB 7; INT CANR-5
Medvedev, P. N.
  See Bakhtin, Mikhail Mikhailovich

Meged, Aharon
  See Megged, Aharon
Meged, Aron
  See Megged, Aharon
Megged, Aharon 1920- .... **CLC 9**
  See also CA 49-52; CAAS 13; CANR 1
Mehta, Ved (Parkash) 1934- .... **CLC 37**
  See also CA 1-4R; CANR 2, 23, 69; MTCW
  1
Melanter
  See Blackmore, R(ichard) D(oddridge)
Melies, Georges 1861-1938 .... **TCLC 81**
Melikow, Loris
  See Hofmannsthal, Hugo von
Melmoth, Sebastian
  See Wilde, Oscar (Fingal O'Flahertie Wills)
Meltzer, Milton 1915- .... **CLC 26**
  See also AAYA 8; BYA 2; CA 13-16R;
  CANR 38, 92; CLR 13; DLB 61; JRDA;
  MAICYA; SAAS 1; SATA 1, 50, 80;
  SATA-Essay 124; YAW
Melville, Herman 1819-1891 ..... **NCLC 3, 12,**
  29, 45, 49, 91, 93; DA; DAB; DAC;
  DAM MST, NOV; SSC 1, 17, 46; WLC
  See also AAYA 25; AMW; CDALB 1640-
  1865; DA3; DLB 3, 74; EXPN; EXPS;
  LAIT 1, 2; NFS 7, 9; RGAL; RGSF;
  SATA 59; SSFS 3
Membreno, Alejandro .... **CLC 59**
Menander c. 342B.C.-c. 293B.C. ... **CMLC 9;**
  DAM DRAM; DC 3
  See also DLB 176; RGWL
Menchu, Rigoberta 1959-
  See also CA 175; DNFS; HLCS 2; WLIT 1
Mencken, H(enry) L(ouis)
    1880-1956 .... **TCLC 13**
  See also AMW; CA 105; 125; CDALB
  1917-1929; DLB 11, 29, 63, 137, 222;
  MTCW 1, 2; RGAL
Mendelsohn, Jane 1965- .... **CLC 99**
  See also CA 154; CANR 94
Mercer, David 1928-1980 .... **CLC 5; DAM**
  DRAM
  See also CA 9-12R; 102; CANR 23; CBD;
  DLB 13; MTCW 1; RGEL
Merchant, Paul
  See Ellison, Harlan (Jay)
Meredith, George 1828-1909 .. **TCLC 17, 43;**
  DAM POET
  See also CA 117; 153; CANR 80; CDBLB
  1832-1890; DLB 18, 35, 57, 159; RGEL
Meredith, William (Morris) 1919- .... **CLC 4,**
  13, 22, 55; DAM POET; PC 28
  See also CA 9-12R; CAAS 14; CANR 6,
  40; CP; DLB 5
Merezhkovsky, Dmitry Sergeyevich
    1865-1941 .... **TCLC 29**
  See also CA 169
Merimee, Prosper 1803-1870 ... **NCLC 6, 65;**
  SSC 7
  See also DLB 119, 192; EXPS; GFL 1789
  to the Present; RGSF; RGWL; SSFS 8
Merkin, Daphne 1954- .... **CLC 44**
  See also CA 123
Merlin, Arthur
  See Blish, James (Benjamin)
Merrill, James (Ingram) 1926-1995 .. **CLC 2,**
  3, 6, 8, 13, 18, 34, 91; DAM POET; PC
  28
  See also AMWS 3; CA 13-16R; 147; CANR
  10, 49, 63; DA3; DLB 5, 165; DLBY 85;
  INT CANR-10; MTCW 1, 2; PAB; RGAL
Merriman, Alex
  See Silverberg, Robert
Merriman, Brian 1747-1805 .... **NCLC 70**
Merritt, E. B.
  See Waddington, Miriam

Merton, Thomas 1915-1968 ..... **CLC 1, 3, 11,**
  34, 83; PC 10
  See also AMWS 8; CA 5-8R; 25-28R;
  CANR 22, 53; DA3; DLB 48; DLBY 81;
  MTCW 1, 2
Merwin, W(illiam) S(tanley) 1927- ... **CLC 1,**
  2, 3, 5, 8, 13, 18, 45, 88; DAM POET
  See also AMWS 3; CA 13-16R; CANR 15,
  51; CP; DA3; DLB 5, 169; INT CANR-
  15; MTCW 1, 2; PAB; PFS 5; RGAL
Metcalf, John 1938- .... **CLC 37; SSC 43**
  See also CA 113; CN; DLB 60; RGSF
Metcalf, Suzanne
  See Baum, L(yman) Frank
Mew, Charlotte (Mary) 1870-1928 .. **TCLC 8**
  See also CA 105; 189; DLB 19, 135; RGEL
Mewshaw, Michael 1943- .... **CLC 9**
  See also CA 53-56; CANR 7, 47; DLBY 80
Meyer, Conrad Ferdinand
    1825-1905 .... **NCLC 81**
  See also DLB 129; RGWL
Meyer, Gustav 1868-1932
  See Meyrink, Gustav
  See also CA 117; 190
Meyer, June
  See Jordan, June
  See also GLL 2
Meyer, Lynn
  See Slavitt, David R(ytman)
Meyers, Jeffrey 1939- .... **CLC 39**
  See also CA 73-76; CAAE 186; CANR 54;
  DLB 111
Meynell, Alice (Christina Gertrude
    Thompson) 1847-1922 .... **TCLC 6**
  See also CA 104; 177; DLB 19, 98; RGEL
Meyrink, Gustav .... **TCLC 21**
  See Meyer, Gustav
  See also DLB 81
Michaels, Leonard 1933- .... **CLC 6, 25; SSC**
  16
  See also CA 61-64; CANR 21, 62; CN;
  DLB 130; MTCW 1
Michaux, Henri 1899-1984 .... **CLC 8, 19**
  See also CA 85-88; 114; GFL 1789 to the
  Present; RGWL
Micheaux, Oscar (Devereaux)
    1884-1951 .... **TCLC 76**
  See also BW 3; CA 174; DLB 50; TCWW
  2
Michelangelo 1475-1564 .... **LC 12**
Michelet, Jules 1798-1874 .... **NCLC 31**
  See also GFL 1789 to the Present
Michels, Robert 1876-1936 .... **TCLC 88**
Michener, James A(lbert)
    1907(?)-1997 .... **CLC 1, 5, 11, 29, 60,**
  109; DAM NOV, POP
  See also AAYA 27; AITN 1; BEST 90:1;
  BPFB 2; CA 5-8R; 161; CANR 21, 45,
  68; CN; CPW; DA3; DLB 6; MTCW 1,
  2; RHW
Mickiewicz, Adam 1798-1855 .. **NCLC 3, 101**
  See also RGWL
Middleton, Christopher 1926- .... **CLC 13**
  See also CA 13-16R; CANR 29, 54; DLB
  40
Middleton, Richard (Barham)
    1882-1911 .... **TCLC 56**
  See also CA 187; DLB 156; HGG
Middleton, Stanley 1919- .... **CLC 7, 38**
  See also CA 25-28R; CAAS 23; CANR 21,
  46, 81; CN; DLB 14
Middleton, Thomas 1580-1627 .... **LC 33;**
  DAM DRAM, MST; DC 5
  See also BRW 2; DLB 58; RGEL
Migueis, Jose Rodrigues 1901- .... **CLC 10**
Mikszath, Kalman 1847-1910 .... **TCLC 31**
  See also CA 170

Montale, Eugenio 1896-1981 ... **CLC 7, 9, 18; PC 13**
See also CA 17-20R; 104; CANR 30; DLB 114; MTCW 1; RGWL

Montesquieu, Charles-Louis de Secondat 1689-1755 .... **LC 7, 69**
See also GFL Beginnings to 1789

Montessori, Maria 1870-1952 ...... **TCLC 103**
See also CA 115; 147

Montgomery, (Robert) Bruce 1921(?)-1978
See Crispin, Edmund
See also CA 179; 104; CMW

Montgomery, L(ucy) M(aud) 1874-1942 .... **TCLC 51; DAC; DAM MST**
See also AAYA 12; BYA 1; CA 108; 137; CLR 8; DA3; DLB 92; DLBD 14; JRDA; MAICYA; MTCW 2; RGEL; SATA 100; WYA; YABC 1

Montgomery, Marion H., Jr. 1925- .... **CLC 7**
See also AITN 1; CA 1-4R; CANR 3, 48; CSW; DLB 6

Montgomery, Max
See Davenport, Guy (Mattison, Jr.)

Montherlant, Henry (Milon) de 1896-1972 ..... **CLC 8, 19; DAM DRAM**
See also CA 85-88; 37-40R; DLB 72; EW; GFL 1789 to the Present; MTCW 1

Monty Python
See Chapman, Graham; Cleese, John (Marwood); Gilliam, Terry (Vance); Idle, Eric; Jones, Terence Graham Parry; Palin, Michael (Edward)
See also AAYA 7

Moodie, Susanna (Strickland) 1803-1885 .... **NCLC 14**
See also DLB 99

Moody, Hiram F. III 1961-
See Moody, Rick
See also CA 138; CANR 64

Moody, Rick .... **CLC 147**
See also Moody, Hiram F. III

Moody, William Vaughan 1869-1910 .... **TCLC 105**
See also CA 110; 178; DLB 7, 54; RGAL

Mooney, Edward 1951-
See Mooney, Ted
See also CA 130

Mooney, Ted .... **CLC 25**
See also Mooney, Edward

Moorcock, Michael (John) 1939- ...... **CLC 5, 27, 58**
See also Bradbury, Edward P.
See also AAYA 26; CA 45-48; CAAS 5; CANR 2, 17, 38, 64; CN; DLB 14, 231; FANT; MTCW 1, 2; SATA 93; SFW; SUFW

Moore, Brian 1921-1999 ... **CLC 1, 3, 5, 7, 8, 19, 32, 90; DAB; DAC; DAM MST**
See also Bryan, Michael
See also CA 1-4R; 174; CANR 1, 25, 42, 63; CCA 1; CN; FANT; MTCW 1, 2; RGEL

Moore, Edward
See Muir, Edwin
See also RGEL

Moore, G. E. 1873-1958 .... **TCLC 89**

Moore, George Augustus 1852-1933 .... **TCLC 7; SSC 19**
See also BRW; CA 104; 177; DLB 10, 18, 57, 135; RGEL; RGSF

Moore, Lorrie .... **CLC 39, 45, 68**
See also Moore, Marie Lorena
See also DLB 234

Moore, Marianne (Craig) 1887-1972 .... **CLC 1, 2, 4, 8, 10, 13, 19, 47; DA; DAB; DAC; DAM MST, POET; PC 4; WLCS**
See also AMW; CA 1-4R; 33-36R; CANR 3, 61; CDALB 1929-1941; DA3; DLB 45;

DLBD 7; EXPP; MAWW; MTCW 1, 2; PAB; RGAL; SATA 20; WP

Moore, Marie Lorena 1957-
See Moore, Lorrie
See also CA 116; CANR 39, 83; CN; DLB 234

Moore, Thomas 1779-1852 .... **NCLC 6**
See also DLB 96, 144; RGEL

Moorhouse, Frank 1938- .... **SSC 40**
See also CA 118; CANR 92; CN; RGSF

Mora, Pat(ricia) 1942-
See also CA 129; CANR 57, 81; CLR 58; DAM MULT; DLB 209; HLC 2; HW 1, 2; SATA 92

Moraga, Cherrie 1952- .... **CLC 126; DAM MULT**
See also CA 131; CANR 66; DLB 82; FW; GLL 1; HW 1, 2

Morand, Paul 1888-1976 .... **CLC 41; SSC 22**
See also CA 184; 69-72; DLB 65

Morante, Elsa 1918-1985 .... **CLC 8, 47**
See also CA 85-88; 117; CANR 35; DLB 177; MTCW 1, 2; RGWL

Moravia, Alberto .... **CLC 2, 7, 11, 27, 46; SSC 26**
See also Pincherle, Alberto
See also DLB 177; MTCW 2; RGSF; RGWL

More, Hannah 1745-1833 .... **NCLC 27**
See also DLB 107, 109, 116, 158; RGEL

More, Henry 1614-1687 .... **LC 9**
See also DLB 126

More, Sir Thomas 1478-1535 .... **LC 10, 32**
See also BRWS 7; RGEL

Moreas, Jean .... **TCLC 18**
See also Papadiamantopoulos, Johannes
See also GFL 1789 to the Present

Morgan, Berry 1919- .... **CLC 6**
See also CA 49-52; DLB 6

Morgan, Claire
See Highsmith, (Mary) Patricia
See also GLL 1

Morgan, Edwin (George) 1920- .... **CLC 31**
See also CA 5-8R; CANR 3, 43, 90; CP; DLB 27

Morgan, (George) Frederick 1922- .. **CLC 23**
See also CA 17-20R; CANR 21; CP

Morgan, Harriet
See Mencken, H(enry) L(ouis)

Morgan, Jane
See Cooper, James Fenimore

Morgan, Janet 1945- .... **CLC 39**
See also CA 65-68

Morgan, Lady 1776(?)-1859 .... **NCLC 29**
See also DLB 116, 158; RGEL

Morgan, Robin (Evonne) 1941- .... **CLC 2**
See also CA 69-72; CANR 29, 68; FW; GLL 2; MTCW 1; SATA 80

Morgan, Scott
See Kuttner, Henry

Morgan, Seth 1949(?)-1990 .... **CLC 65**
See also CA 185; 132

Morgenstern, Christian (Otto Josef Wolfgang) 1871-1914 .... **TCLC 8**
See also CA 105; 191

Morgenstern, S.
See Goldman, William (W.)

Mori, Rintaro
See Mori Ogai
See also CA 110

Moricz, Zsigmond 1879-1942 .... **TCLC 33**
See also CA 165

Morike, Eduard (Friedrich) 1804-1875 .... **NCLC 10**
See also DLB 133; RGWL

Mori Ogai 1862-1922 .... **TCLC 14**
See also CA 164; DLB 180; TWA

Moritz, Karl Philipp 1756-1793 .... **LC 2**
See also DLB 94

Morland, Peter Henry
See Faust, Frederick (Schiller)

Morley, Christopher (Darlington) 1890-1957 .... **TCLC 87**
See also CA 112; DLB 9; RGAL

Morren, Theophil
See Hofmannsthal, Hugo von

Morris, Bill 1952- .... **CLC 76**

Morris, Julian
See West, Morris L(anglo)

Morris, Steveland Judkins 1950(?)-
See Wonder, Stevie
See also CA 111

Morris, William 1834-1896 .... **NCLC 4**
See also BRW; CDBLB 1832-1890; DLB 18, 35, 57, 156, 178, 184; FANT; RGEL; SFW; SUFW

Morris, Wright 1910-1998 .. **CLC 1, 3, 7, 18, 37**
See also AMW; CA 9-12R; 167; CANR 21, 81; CN; DLB 2, 206; DLBY 81; MTCW 1, 2; RGAL; TCLC 107; TCWW 2

Morrison, Arthur 1863-1945 .... **TCLC 72; SSC 40**
See also CA 120; 157; CMW; DLB 70, 135, 197; RGEL

Morrison, Chloe Anthony Wofford
See Morrison, Toni

Morrison, James Douglas 1943-1971
See Morrison, Jim
See also CA 73-76; CANR 40

Morrison, Jim .... **CLC 17**
See also Morrison, James Douglas

Morrison, Toni 1931- . **CLC 4, 10, 22, 55, 81, 87; BLC 3; DA; DAB; DAC; DAM MST, MULT, NOV, POP**
See also AAYA 1, 22; AFAW 1, 2; AMWS 3; BPFB 2; BW 2, 3; CA 29-32R; CANR 27, 42, 67; CDALB 1968-1988; CN; CPW; DA3; DLB 6, 33, 143; DLBY 81; EXPN; FW; LAIT 4; MTCW 1, 2; NFS 1, 6, 8; RGAL; RHW; SATA 57; SSFS 5; YAW

Morrison, Van 1945- .... **CLC 21**
See also CA 116; 168

Morrissy, Mary 1958- .... **CLC 99**

Mortimer, John (Clifford) 1923- ..... **CLC 28, 43; DAM DRAM**
See also CA 13-16R; CANR 21, 69; CD; CDBLB 1960 to Present; CMW; CN; CPW; DA3; DLB 13; INT CANR-21; MSW; MTCW 1, 2; RGEL

Mortimer, Penelope (Ruth) 1918-1999 .... **CLC 5**
See also CA 57-60; 187; CANR 45, 88; CN

Morton, Anthony
See Creasey, John

Mosca, Gaetano 1858-1941 .... **TCLC 75**

Mosher, Howard Frank 1943- .... **CLC 62**
See also CA 139; CANR 65

Mosley, Nicholas 1923- .... **CLC 43, 70**
See also CA 69-72; CANR 41, 60; CN; DLB 14, 207

Mosley, Walter 1952- .... **CLC 97; BLCS; DAM MULT, POP**
See also AAYA 17; BPFB 2; BW 2; CA 142; CANR 57, 92; CMW; CPW; DA3; MTCW 2

Moss, Howard 1922-1987 ...... **CLC 7, 14, 45, 50; DAM POET**
See also CA 1-4R; 123; CANR 1, 44; DLB 5

Mossgiel, Rab
See Burns, Robert

Motion, Andrew (Peter) 1952- .... **CLC 47**
See also BRWS 7; CA 146; CANR 90; CP; DLB 40

Ortiz, Simon J(oseph) 1941- . **CLC 45; DAM MULT, POET; PC 17**
See also AMWS 4; CA 134; CANR 69; CP; DLB 120, 175; EXPP; NNAL; PFS 4; RGAL

Orton, Joe .... **CLC 4, 13, 43; DC 3**
See also Orton, John Kingsley
See also BRWS 5; CBD; CDBLB 1960 to Present; DFS 3, 6; DLB 13; GLL 1; MTCW 2; RGEL; WLIT 4

Orton, John Kingsley 1933-1967
See Orton, Joe
See also CA 85-88; CANR 35, 66; DAM DRAM; MTCW 1, 2

Orwell, George .... **TCLC 2, 6, 15, 31, 51; DAB; WLC**
See also Blair, Eric (Arthur)
See also BPFB 3; BYA 5; CDBLB 1945-1960; CLR 68; DLB 15, 98, 195; EXPN; LAIT 5; NFS 3, 7; RGEL; SCFW 2; SFW; SSFS 4; WLIT 4; YAW

Osborne, David
See Silverberg, Robert

Osborne, George
See Silverberg, Robert

Osborne, John (James) 1929-1994 .... **CLC 1, 2, 5, 11, 45; DA; DAB; DAC; DAM DRAM, MST; WLC**
See also BRWS 1; CA 13-16R; 147; CANR 21, 56; CDBLB 1945-1960; DFS 4; DLB 13; MTCW 1, 2; RGEL

Osborne, Lawrence 1958- .... **CLC 50**
See also CA 189

Osbourne, Lloyd 1868-1947 .... **TCLC 93**

Oshima, Nagisa 1932- .... **CLC 20**
See also CA 116; 121; CANR 78

Oskison, John Milton 1874-1947 .. **TCLC 35; DAM MULT**
See also CA 144; CANR 84; DLB 175; NNAL

Ossian c. 3rd cent. - .... **CMLC 28**
See also Macpherson, James

Ossoli, Sarah Margaret (Fuller) 1810-1850 .... **NCLC 5, 50**
See also Fuller, Margaret; Fuller, Sarah Margaret
See also CDALB 1640-1865; DLB 1, 59, 73, 183, 223, 239; FW; SATA 25

Ostriker, Alicia (Suskin) 1937- .... **CLC 132**
See also CA 25-28R; CAAS 24; CANR 10, 30, 62, 99; CWP; DLB 120; EXPP

Ostrovsky, Alexander 1823-1886 .. **NCLC 30, 57**

Otero, Blas de 1916-1979 .... **CLC 11**
See also CA 89-92; DLB 134

Otto, Rudolf 1869-1937 .... **TCLC 85**

Otto, Whitney 1955- .... **CLC 70**
See also CA 140

Ouida .... **TCLC 43**
See also De La Ramee, (Marie) Louise
See also DLB 18, 156; RGEL

Ouologuem, Yambo 1940- .... **CLC 146**
See also CA 111; 176

Ousmane, Sembene 1923- ... **CLC 66; BLC 3**
See also Sembene, Ousmane
See also BW 1, 3; CA 117; 125; CANR 81; CWW 2; MTCW 1

Ovid 43B.C.-17 . **CMLC 7; DAM POET; PC 2**
See also DA3; DLB 211; RGWL; WP

Owen, Hugh
See Faust, Frederick (Schiller)

Owen, Wilfred (Edward Salter) 1893-1918 .... **TCLC 5, 27; DA; DAB; DAC; DAM MST, POET; PC 19; WLC**
See also CA 104; 141; CDBLB 1914-1945; DLB 20; EXPP; MTCW 2; PFS 10; RGEL; WLIT 4

Owens, Rochelle 1936- .... **CLC 8**
See also CA 17-20R; CAAS 2; CAD; CANR 39; CD; CP; CWD; CWP

Oz, Amos 1939- ...... **CLC 5, 8, 11, 27, 33, 54; DAM NOV**
See also CA 53-56; CANR 27, 47, 65; CWW 2; MTCW 1, 2; RGSF

Ozick, Cynthia 1928- .... **CLC 3, 7, 28, 62; DAM NOV, POP; SSC 15**
See also AMWS 5; BEST 90:1; CA 17-20R; CANR 23, 58; CN; CPW; DA3; DLB 28, 152; DLBY 82; EXPS; INT CANR-23; MTCW 1, 2; RGAL; RGSF; SSFS 3, 12

Ozu, Yasujiro 1903-1963 .... **CLC 16**
See also CA 112

Pacheco, C.
See Pessoa, Fernando (Antonio Nogueira)

Pacheco, Jose Emilio 1939-
See also CA 111; 131; CANR 65; DAM MULT; HLC 2; HW 1, 2; RGSF

Pa Chin .... **CLC 18**
See also Li Fei-kan

Pack, Robert 1929- .... **CLC 13**
See also CA 1-4R; CANR 3, 44, 82; CP; DLB 5; SATA 118

Padgett, Lewis
See Kuttner, Henry

Padilla (Lorenzo), Heberto 1932-2000 .... **CLC 38**
See also AITN 1; CA 123; 131; 189; HW 1

Page, Jimmy 1944- .... **CLC 12**

Page, Louise 1955- .... **CLC 40**
See also CA 140; CANR 76; CBD; CD; CWD; DLB 233

Page, P(atricia) K(athleen) 1916- ...... **CLC 7, 18; DAC; DAM MST; PC 12**
See also Cape, Judith
See also CA 53-56; CANR 4, 22, 65; CP; DLB 68; MTCW 1; RGEL

Page, Stanton
See Fuller, Henry Blake

Page, Stanton
See Fuller, Henry Blake

Page, Thomas Nelson 1853-1922 .... **SSC 23**
See also CA 118; 177; DLB 12, 78; DLBD 13; RGAL

Pagels, Elaine Hiesey 1943- .... **CLC 104**
See also CA 45-48; CANR 2, 24, 51; FW

Paget, Violet 1856-1935
See Lee, Vernon
See also CA 104; 166; GLL 1; HGG

Paget-Lowe, Henry
See Lovecraft, H(oward) P(hillips)

Paglia, Camille (Anna) 1947- .... **CLC 68**
See also CA 140; CANR 72; CPW; FW; GLL 2; MTCW 2

Paige, Richard
See Koontz, Dean R(ay)

Paine, Thomas 1737-1809 .... **NCLC 62**
See also AMWS 1; CDALB 1640-1865; DLB 31, 43, 73, 158; LAIT 1; RGAL; RGEL

Pakenham, Antonia
See Fraser, (Lady)Antonia (Pakenham)

Palamas, Kostes 1859-1943 .... **TCLC 5**
See also CA 105; 190; RGWL

Palazzeschi, Aldo 1885-1974 .... **CLC 11**
See also CA 89-92; 53-56; DLB 114

Pales Matos, Luis 1898-1959
See also HLCS 2; HW 1

Paley, Grace 1922- .... **CLC 4, 6, 37, 140; DAM POP; SSC 8**
See also AMWS 6; CA 25-28R; CANR 13, 46, 74; CN; CPW; DA3; DLB 28; EXPS; FW; INT CANR-13; MTCW 1, 2; RGAL; RGSF; SSFS 3

Palin, Michael (Edward) 1943- .... **CLC 21**
See also Monty Python
See also CA 107; CANR 35; SATA 67

Palliser, Charles 1947- .... **CLC 65**
See also CA 136; CANR 76; CN

Palma, Ricardo 1833-1919 .... **TCLC 29**
See also CA 168

Pancake, Breece Dexter 1952-1979
See Pancake, Breece D'J
See also CA 123; 109

Pancake, Breece D'J .... **CLC 29**
See also Pancake, Breece Dexter
See also DLB 130

Panchenko, Nikolai .... **CLC 59**

Pankhurst, Emmeline (Goulden) 1858-1928 .... **TCLC 100**
See also CA 116; FW

Panko, Rudy
See Gogol, Nikolai (Vasilyevich)

Papadiamantis, Alexandros 1851-1911 .... **TCLC 29**
See also CA 168

Papadiamantopoulos, Johannes 1856-1910
See Moreas, Jean
See also CA 117

Papini, Giovanni 1881-1956 .... **TCLC 22**
See also CA 121; 180

Paracelsus 1493-1541 .... **LC 14**
See also DLB 179

Parasol, Peter
See Stevens, Wallace

Pardo Bazan, Emilia 1851-1921 .... **SSC 30**
See also FW; RGSF; RGWL

Pareto, Vilfredo 1848-1923 .... **TCLC 69**
See also CA 175

Paretsky, Sara 1947- .. **CLC 135; DAM POP**
See also AAYA 30; BEST 90:3; CA 125; 129; CANR 59, 95; CMW; CPW; DA3; INT 129; RGAL

Parfenie, Maria
See Codrescu, Andrei

Parini, Jay (Lee) 1948- .... **CLC 54, 133**
See also CA 97-100; CAAS 16; CANR 32, 87

Park, Jordan
See Kornbluth, C(yril) M.; Pohl, Frederik

Park, Robert E(zra) 1864-1944 ..... **TCLC 73**
See also CA 122; 165

Parker, Bert
See Ellison, Harlan (Jay)

Parker, Dorothy (Rothschild) 1893-1967 .... **CLC 15, 68; DAM POET; PC 28; SSC 2**
See also CA 19-20; 25-28R; CAP 2; DA3; DLB 11, 45, 86; EXPP; MTCW 1, 2

Parker, Robert B(rown) 1932- .... **CLC 27; DAM NOV, POP**
See also AAYA 28; BEST 89:4; BPFB 3; CA 49-52; CANR 1, 26, 52, 89; CMW; CPW; INT CANR-26; MTCW 1

Parkin, Frank 1940- .... **CLC 43**
See also CA 147

Parkman, Francis, Jr. 1823-1893 .. **NCLC 12**
See also AMWS 2; DLB 1, 30, 186, 235; RGAL

Parks, Gordon (Alexander Buchanan) 1912- .... **CLC 1, 16; BLC 3; DAM MULT**
See also AAYA 36; AITN 2; BW 2, 3; CA 41-44R; CANR 26, 66; DA3; DLB 33; MTCW 2; SATA 8, 108

Parks, Tim(othy Harold) 1954- ...... **CLC 147**
See also CA 126; 131; CANR 77; DLB 231; INT CA-131

Parmenides c. 515B.C.-c. 450B.C. .... **CMLC 22**
See also DLB 176

Parnell, Thomas 1679-1718 .... **LC 3**
See also DLB 94; RGEL

Perutz, Leo(pold) 1882-1957 .... **TCLC 60**
See also CA 147; DLB 81
Peseenz, Tulio F.
See Lopez y Fuentes, Gregorio
Pesetsky, Bette 1932- .... **CLC 28**
See also CA 133; DLB 130
Peshkov, Alexei Maximovich 1868-1936
See Gorky, Maxim
See also CA 105; 141; CANR 83; DA;
DAC; DAM DRAM, MST, NOV; MTCW
2
Pessoa, Fernando (Antonio Nogueira)
1898-1935 .... **TCLC 27; DAM MULT;
HLC 2; PC 20**
See also CA 125; 183; EW; RGWL; WP
Peterkin, Julia Mood 1880-1961 ...... **CLC 31**
See also CA 102; DLB 9
Peters, Joan K(aren) 1945- .... **CLC 39**
See also CA 158
Peters, Robert L(ouis) 1924- .... **CLC 7**
See also CA 13-16R; CAAS 8; CP; DLB
105
Petofi, Sandor 1823-1849 .... **NCLC 21**
See also RGWL
Petrakis, Harry Mark 1923- .... **CLC 3**
See also CA 9-12R; CANR 4, 30, 85; CN
Petrarch 1304-1374 .... **CMLC 20; DAM
POET; PC 8**
See also DA3; RGWL
Petronius c. 20-66 .... **CMLC 34**
See also DLB 211; EW; RGWL
Petrov, Evgeny .... **TCLC 21**
See also Kataev, Evgeny Petrovich
Petry, Ann (Lane) 1908-1997 ... **CLC 1, 7, 18**
See also AFAW 1, 2; BPFB 3; BW 1, 3;
BYA 2; CA 5-8R; 157; CAAS 6; CANR
4, 46; CLR 12; CN; DLB 76; JRDA;
LAIT 1; MAICYA; MAICYAS; MTCW
1; RGAL; SATA 5; SATA-Obit 94; TCLC
112
Petursson, Halligrimur 1614-1674 .... **LC 8**
Peychinovich
See Vazov, Ivan (Minchov)
Phaedrus c. 15B.C.-c. 50 .... **CMLC 25**
See also DLB 211
Phelps (Ward), Elizabeth Stuart
See Phelps, Elizabeth Stuart
See also FW
Phelps, Elizabeth Stuart
1844-1911 .... **TCLC 113**
See also Dickinson, Mrs.Herbert Ward
See also DLB 74
Philips, Katherine 1632-1664 .... **LC 30**
See also DLB 131; RGEL
Philipson, Morris H. 1926- .... **CLC 53**
See also CA 1-4R; CANR 4
Phillips, Caryl 1958- . **CLC 96; BLCS; DAM
MULT**
See also BRWS 5; BW 2; CA 141; CANR
63; CBD; CD; CN; DA3; DLB 157;
MTCW 2; WLIT 4
Phillips, David Graham
1867-1911 .... **TCLC 44**
See also CA 108; 176; DLB 9, 12; RGAL
Phillips, Jack
See Sandburg, Carl (August)
Phillips, Jayne Anne 1952- .... **CLC 15, 33,
139; SSC 16**
See also BPFB 3; CA 101; CANR 24, 50,
96; CN; CSW; DLBY 80; INT CANR-24;
MTCW 1, 2; RGAL; RGSF; SSFS 4
Phillips, Richard
See Dick, Philip K(indred)
Phillips, Robert (Schaeffer) 1938- .... **CLC 28**
See also CA 17-20R; CAAS 13; CANR 8;
DLB 105
Phillips, Ward
See Lovecraft, H(oward) P(hillips)

Piccolo, Lucio 1901-1969 .... **CLC 13**
See also CA 97-100; DLB 114
Pickthall, Marjorie L(owry) C(hristie)
1883-1922 .... **TCLC 21**
See also CA 107; DLB 92
Pico della Mirandola, Giovanni
1463-1494 .... **LC 15**
Piercy, Marge 1936- .... **CLC 3, 6, 14, 18, 27,
62, 128; PC 29**
See also BPFB 3; CA 21-24R; CAAE 187;
CAAS 1; CANR 13, 43, 66; CN; CP;
CWP; DLB 120, 227; EXPP; FW; MTCW
1, 2; PFS 9; SFW
Piers, Robert
See Anthony, Piers
Pieyre de Mandiargues, Andre 1909-1991
See Mandiargues, Andre Pieyre de
See also CA 103; 136; CANR 22, 82; GFL
1789 to the Present
Pilnyak, Boris .... **TCLC 23**
See also Vogau, Boris Andreyevich
Pincherle, Alberto 1907-1990 .... **CLC 11, 18;
DAM NOV**
See also Moravia, Alberto
See also CA 25-28R; 132; CANR 33, 63;
MTCW 1
Pinckney, Darryl 1953- .... **CLC 76**
See also BW 2, 3; CA 143; CANR 79
Pindar 518(?)B.C.-438(?)B.C. .... **CMLC 12;
PC 19**
See also DLB 176; RGWL
Pineda, Cecile 1942- .... **CLC 39**
See also CA 118; DLB 209
Pinero, Arthur Wing 1855-1934 ... **TCLC 32;
DAM DRAM**
See also CA 110; 153; DLB 10; RGEL
Pinero, Miguel (Antonio Gomez)
1946-1988 .... **CLC 4, 55**
See also CA 61-64; 125; CAD; CANR 29,
90; HW 1
Pinget, Robert 1919-1997 .... **CLC 7, 13, 37**
See also CA 85-88; 160; CWW 2; DLB 83;
GFL 1789 to the Present
Pink Floyd
See Barrett, (Roger) Syd; Gilmour, David;
Mason, Nick; Waters, Roger; Wright, Rick
Pinkney, Edward 1802-1828 .... **NCLC 31**
Pinkwater, Daniel Manus 1941- .... **CLC 35**
See also Pinkwater, Manus
See also AAYA 1; BYA 9; CA 29-32R;
CANR 12, 38, 89; CLR 4; CSW; FANT;
JRDA; MAICYA; SAAS 3; SATA 46, 76,
114; SFW; YAW
Pinkwater, Manus
See Pinkwater, Daniel Manus
See also SATA 8
Pinsky, Robert 1940- .... **CLC 9, 19, 38, 94,
121; DAM POET; PC 27**
See also AMWS 6; CA 29-32R; CAAS 4;
CANR 58, 97; CP; DA3; DLBY 82, 98;
MTCW 2; RGAL
Pinta, Harold
See Pinter, Harold
Pinter, Harold 1930- .. **CLC 1, 3, 6, 9, 11, 15,
27, 58, 73; DA; DAB; DAC; DAM
DRAM, MST; DC 15; WLC**
See also BRWS 1; CA 5-8R; CANR 33, 65;
CBD; CD; CDBLB 1960 to Present; DA3;
DFS 3, 5, 7; DLB 13; IDFW 3, 4; MTCW
1, 2; RGEL
Piozzi, Hester Lynch (Thrale)
1741-1821 .... **NCLC 57**
See also DLB 104, 142
Pirandello, Luigi 1867-1936 ...... **TCLC 4, 29;
DA; DAB; DAC; DAM DRAM, MST;
DC 5; SSC 22; WLC**
See also CA 104; 153; DA3; DFS 4, 9;
MTCW 2; RGSF; RGWL

Pirsig, Robert M(aynard) 1928- ... **CLC 4, 6,
73; DAM POP**
See also CA 53-56; CANR 42, 74; CPW 1;
DA3; MTCW 1, 2; SATA 39
Pisarev, Dmitry Ivanovich
1840-1868 .... **NCLC 25**
Pix, Mary (Griffith) 1666-1709 .... **LC 8**
See also DLB 80
Pixerecourt, (Rene Charles) Guilbert de
1773-1844 .... **NCLC 39**
See also DLB 192; GFL 1789 to the Present
Plaatje, Sol(omon) T(shekisho)
1878-1932 .... **TCLC 73; BLCS**
See also BW 2, 3; CA 141; CANR 79; DLB
225
Plaidy, Jean
See Hibbert, Eleanor Alice Burford
Planche, James Robinson
1796-1880 .... **NCLC 42**
See also RGEL
Plant, Robert 1948- .... **CLC 12**
Plante, David (Robert) 1940- ...... **CLC 7, 23,
38; DAM NOV**
See also CA 37-40R; CANR 12, 36, 58, 82;
CN; DLBY 83; INT CANR-12; MTCW 1
Plath, Sylvia 1932-1963 ..... **CLC 1, 2, 3, 5, 9,
11, 14, 17, 50, 51, 62, 111; DA; DAB;
DAC; DAM MST, POET; PC 1; WLC**
See also AAYA 13; AMWS 1; BPFB 3; CA
19-20; CANR 34, 101; CAP 2; CDALB
1941-1968; DA3; DLB 5, 6, 152; EXPN;
EXPP; FW; LAIT 4; MTCW 1, 2; NFS 1;
PAB; PFS 1; RGAL; SATA 96; WP; YAW
Plato c. 428B.C.-347B.C. .... **CMLC 8; DA;
DAB; DAC; DAM MST; WLCS**
See also DA3; DLB 176; LAIT 1; RGWL
Platonov, Andrei
See Klimentov, Andrei Platonovich
Platt, Kin 1911- .... **CLC 26**
See also AAYA 11; CA 17-20R; CANR 11;
JRDA; SAAS 17; SATA 21, 86
Plautus c. 254B.C.-c. 184B.C. ...... **CMLC 24;
DC 6**
See also DLB 211; RGWL
Plick et Plock
See Simenon, Georges (Jacques Christian)
Plieksans, Janis
See Rainis, Janis
See also CA 170; DLB 220
Plimpton, George (Ames) 1927- .... **CLC 36**
See also AITN 1; CA 21-24R; CANR 32,
70; DLB 185, 241; MTCW 1, 2; SATA 10
Pliny the Elder c. 23-79 .... **CMLC 23**
See also DLB 211
Plomer, William Charles Franklin
1903-1973 .... **CLC 4, 8**
See also AFW; CA 21-22; CANR 34; CAP
2; DLB 20, 162, 191, 225; MTCW 1;
RGSF; SATA 24
Plotinus 204-270 .... **CMLC 46**
See also DLB 176
Plowman, Piers
See Kavanagh, Patrick (Joseph)
Plum, J.
See Wodehouse, P(elham) G(renville)
Plumly, Stanley (Ross) 1939- .... **CLC 33**
See also CA 108; 110; CANR 97; CP; DLB
5, 193; INT 110
Plumpe, Friedrich Wilhelm
1888-1931 .... **TCLC 53**
See also CA 112
Po Chu-i 772-846 .... **CMLC 24**
Poe, Edgar Allan 1809-1849 ..... **NCLC 1, 16,
55, 78, 94, 97; DA; DAB; DAC; DAM
MST, POET; PC 1; SSC 1, 22, 34, 35;
WLC**
See also AAYA 14; AMW; BPFB 3; BYA 5;
CDALB 1640-1865; CMW; DA3; DLB 3,
59, 73, 74; EXPP; EXPS; HGG; LAIT 2;

PAB; PFS 1, 3, 9; RGAL; RGSF; SATA 23; SFW; SSFS 2, 4, 7, 8; WP

Poet of Titchfield Street, The
See Pound, Ezra (Weston Loomis)

Pohl, Frederik 1919- .... **CLC 18; SSC 25**
See also AAYA 24; CA 61-64; CAAE 188; CAAS 1; CANR 11, 37, 81; CN; DLB 8; INT CANR-11; MTCW 1, 2; SATA 24; SCFW 2; SFW

Poirier, Louis 1910-
See Gracq, Julien
See also CA 122; 126; CWW 2

Poitier, Sidney 1927- .... **CLC 26**
See also BW 1; CA 117; CANR 94

Polanski, Roman 1933- .... **CLC 16**
See also CA 77-80

Poliakoff, Stephen 1952- .... **CLC 38**
See also CA 106; CBD; CD; DLB 13

Police, The
See Copeland, Stewart (Armstrong); Summers, Andrew James; Sumner, Gordon Matthew

Polidori, John William 1795-1821 . **NCLC 51**
See also DLB 116; HGG

Pollitt, Katha 1949- .... **CLC 28, 122**
See also CA 120; 122; CANR 66; MTCW 1, 2

Pollock, (Mary) Sharon 1936- .... **CLC 50; DAC; DAM DRAM, MST**
See also CA 141; DLB 60

Polo, Marco 1254-1324 .... **CMLC 15**

Polonsky, Abraham (Lincoln)
1910-1999 .... **CLC 92**
See also CA 104; 187; DLB 26; INT 104

Polybius c. 200B.C.-c. 118B.C. ...... **CMLC 17**
See also AW; DLB 176; RGWL

Pomerance, Bernard 1940- ... **CLC 13; DAM DRAM**
See also CA 101; CAD; CANR 49; CD; DFS 9; LAIT 2

Ponge, Francis 1899-1988 . **CLC 6, 18; DAM POET**
See also CA 85-88; 126; CANR 40, 86; GFL 1789 to the Present; RGWL

Poniatowska, Elena 1933- ... **CLC 140; DAM MULT; HLC 2**
See also CA 101; CANR 32, 66; DLB 113; HW 1, 2; WLIT 1

Pontoppidan, Henrik 1857-1943 .... **TCLC 29**
See also CA 170

Poole, Josephine .... **CLC 17**
See also Helyar, Jane Penelope Josephine
See also SAAS 2; SATA 5

Popa, Vasko 1922-1991 .... **CLC 19**
See also CA 112; 148; DLB 181; RGWL

Pope, Alexander 1688-1744 ..... **LC 3, 58, 60, 64; DA; DAB; DAC; DAM MST, POET; PC 26; WLC**
See also CDBLB 1660-1789; DA3; DLB 95, 101; EXPP; PAB; PFS 12; RGEL; WLIT 3; WP

Popov, Yevgeny .... **CLC 59**

Porter, Connie (Rose) 1959(?)- .... **CLC 70**
See also BW 2, 3; CA 142; CANR 90; SATA 81

Porter, Gene(va Grace) Stratton .. **TCLC 21**
See also Stratton-Porter, Gene(va Grace)
See also BPFB 3; CA 112; CWRI; RHW

Porter, Katherine Anne 1890-1980 ... **CLC 1, 3, 7, 10, 13, 15, 27, 101; DA; DAB; DAC; DAM MST, NOV; SSC 4, 31, 43**
See also AITN 2; AMW; BPFB 3; CA 1-4R; 101; CANR 1, 65; CDALBS; DA3; DLB 4, 9, 102; DLBD 12; DLBY 80; EXPS; LAIT 3; MTCW 1, 2; RGAL; RGSF; SATA 39; SATA-Obit 23; SSFS 1, 8, 11

Porter, Peter (Neville Frederick)
1929- .... **CLC 5, 13, 33**
See also CA 85-88; CP; DLB 40

Porter, William Sydney 1862-1910
See Henry, O.
See also CA 104; 131; CDALB 1865-1917; DA; DA3; DAB; DAC; DAM MST; DLB 12, 78, 79; MTCW 1, 2; YABC 2

Portillo (y Pacheco), Jose Lopez
See Lopez Portillo (y Pacheco), Jose

Portillo Trambley, Estela 1927-1998
See Trambley, Estela Portillo
See also CANR 32; DAM MULT; DLB 209; HLC 2; HW 1

Posse, Abel .... **CLC 70**

Post, Melville Davisson
1869-1930 .... **TCLC 39**
See also CA 110; CMW

Potok, Chaim 1929- ... **CLC 2, 7, 14, 26, 112; DAM NOV**
See also AAYA 15; AITN 1, 2; BPFB 3; BYA 1; CA 17-20R; CANR 19, 35, 64, 98; CN; DA3; DLB 28, 152; EXPN; INT CANR-19; LAIT 4; MTCW 1, 2; NFS 4; SATA 33, 106; YAW

Potter, Dennis (Christopher George)
1935-1994 .... **CLC 58, 86, 123**
See also CA 107; 145; CANR 33, 61; CBD; DLB 233; MTCW 1

Pound, Ezra (Weston Loomis)
1885-1972 .. **CLC 1, 2, 3, 4, 5, 7, 10, 13, 18, 34, 48, 50, 112; DA; DAB; DAC; DAM MST, POET; PC 4; WLC**
See also AMW; AMWR; CA 5-8R; 37-40R; CANR 40; CDALB 1917-1929; DA3; DLB 4, 45, 63; DLBD 15; EFS 2; EXPP; MTCW 1, 2; PAB; PFS 2, 8; RGAL; WP

Povod, Reinaldo 1959-1994 .... **CLC 44**
See also CA 136; 146; CANR 83

Powell, Adam Clayton, Jr.
1908-1972 .... **CLC 89; BLC 3; DAM MULT**
See also BW 1, 3; CA 102; 33-36R; CANR 86

Powell, Anthony (Dymoke)
1905-2000 .... **CLC 1, 3, 7, 9, 10, 31**
See also BRW; CA 1-4R; 189; CANR 1, 32, 62; CDBLB 1945-1960; CN; DLB 15; MTCW 1, 2; RGEL

Powell, Dawn 1897-1965 .... **CLC 66**
See also CA 5-8R; DLBY 97

Powell, Padgett 1952- .... **CLC 34**
See also CA 126; CANR 63, 101; CSW; DLB 234

Powell, (Oval) Talmage 1920-2000
See Queen, Ellery
See also CA 5-8R; CANR 2, 80

Power, Susan 1961- .... **CLC 91**
See also CA 160; NFS 11

Powers, J(ames) F(arl) 1917-1999 ..... **CLC 1, 4, 8, 57; SSC 4**
See also CA 1-4R; 181; CANR 2, 61; CN; DLB 130; MTCW 1; RGAL; RGSF

Powers, John J(ames) 1945-
See Powers, John R.
See also CA 69-72

Powers, John R. .... **CLC 66**
See also Powers, John J(ames)

Powers, Richard (S.) 1957- .... **CLC 93**
See also BPFB 3; CA 148; CANR 80; CN

Pownall, David 1938- .... **CLC 10**
See also CA 89-92, 180; CAAS 18; CANR 49, 101; CBD; CD; CN; DLB 14

Powys, John Cowper 1872-1963 ... **CLC 7, 9, 15, 46, 125**
See also CA 85-88; DLB 15; FANT; MTCW 1, 2; RGEL

Powys, T(heodore) F(rancis)
1875-1953 .... **TCLC 9**
See also CA 106; 189; DLB 36, 162; FANT; RGEL; SUFW

Prado (Calvo), Pedro 1886-1952 ... **TCLC 75**
See also CA 131; HW 1; LAW

Prager, Emily 1952- .... **CLC 56**

Pratt, E(dwin) J(ohn)
1883(?)-1964 .... **CLC 19; DAC; DAM POET**
See also CA 141; 93-96; CANR 77; DLB 92; RGEL

Premchand .... **TCLC 21**
See also Srivastava, Dhanpat Rai

Preussler, Otfried 1923- .... **CLC 17**
See also CA 77-80; SATA 24

Prevert, Jacques (Henri Marie)
1900-1977 .... **CLC 15**
See also CA 77-80; 69-72; CANR 29, 61; GFL 1789 to the Present; IDFW 3, 4; MTCW 1; RGWL; SATA-Obit 30

Prevost, (Antoine Francois)
1697-1763 .... **LC 1**
See also EW; GFL Beginnings to 1789; RGWL

Price, (Edward) Reynolds 1933- ... **CLC 3, 6, 13, 43, 50, 63; DAM NOV; SSC 22**
See also AMWS 6; CA 1-4R; CANR 1, 37, 57, 87; CN; CSW; DLB 2, 218; INT CANR-37

Price, Richard 1949- .... **CLC 6, 12**
See also CA 49-52; CANR 3; DLBY 81

Prichard, Katharine Susannah
1883-1969 .... **CLC 46**
See also CA 11-12; 141; CANR 31; CAP 1; MTCW 1; RGEL; RGSF; SATA 66

Priestley, J(ohn) B(oynton)
1894-1984 .... **CLC 2, 5, 9, 34; DAM DRAM, NOV**
See also BRW; CA 9-12R; 113; CANR 33; CDBLB 1914-1945; DA3; DLB 10, 34, 77, 100, 139; DLBY 84; MTCW 1, 2; RGEL; SFW

Prince 1958(?)- .... **CLC 35**

Prince, F(rank) T(empleton) 1912- .. **CLC 22**
See also CA 101; CANR 43, 79; CP; DLB 20

Prince Kropotkin
See Kropotkin, Peter (Aleksieevich)

Prior, Matthew 1664-1721 .... **LC 4**
See also DLB 95; RGEL

Prishvin, Mikhail 1873-1954 .... **TCLC 75**

Pritchard, William H(arrison)
1932- .... **CLC 34**
See also CA 65-68; CANR 23, 95; DLB 111

Pritchett, V(ictor) S(awdon)
1900-1997 ...... **CLC 5, 13, 15, 41; DAM NOV; SSC 14**
See also BPFB 3; BRWS 3; CA 61-64; 157; CANR 31, 63; CN; DA3; DLB 15, 139; MTCW 1, 2; RGEL; RGSF

Private 19022
See Manning, Frederic

Probst, Mark 1925- .... **CLC 59**
See also CA 130

Prokosch, Frederic 1908-1989 ...... **CLC 4, 48**
See also CA 73-76; 128; CANR 82; DLB 48; MTCW 2

Propertius, Sextus c. 50B.C.-c. 16B.C. .... **CMLC 32**
See also AW; DLB 211; RGWL

Prophet, The
See Dreiser, Theodore (Herman Albert)

Prose, Francine 1947- .... **CLC 45**
See also CA 109; 112; CANR 46, 95; DLB 234; SATA 101

Proudhon
See Cunha, Euclides (Rodrigues Pimenta) da

Proulx, Annie
See Proulx, E(dna) Annie
See also AMWS 7

Roelvaag, O(le) E(dvart)
1876-1931 .... **TCLC 17**
See also Rolvaag, O(le) E(dvart)
See also CA 117; 171; DLB 9

Roethke, Theodore (Huebner)
1908-1963 .... **CLC 1, 3, 8, 11, 19, 46, 101; DAM POET; PC 15**
See also AMW; CA 81-84; CABS 2; CDALB 1941-1968; DA3; DLB 5, 206; EXPP; MTCW 1, 2; PAB; PFS 3; RGAL; WP

Rogers, Samuel 1763-1855 .... **NCLC 69**
See also DLB 93; RGEL

Rogers, Thomas Hunton 1927- .... **CLC 57**
See also CA 89-92; INT 89-92

Rogers, Will(iam Penn Adair)
1879-1935 ... **TCLC 8, 71; DAM MULT**
See also CA 105; 144; DA3; DLB 11; MTCW 2; NNAL

Rogin, Gilbert 1929- .... **CLC 18**
See also CA 65-68; CANR 15

Rohan, Koda
See Koda Shigeyuki

Rohlfs, Anna Katharine Green
See Green, Anna Katharine

Rohmer, Eric .... **CLC 16**
See also Scherer, Jean-Marie Maurice

Rohmer, Sax .... **TCLC 28**
See also Ward, Arthur Henry Sarsfield
See also DLB 70

Roiphe, Anne (Richardson) 1935- .. **CLC 3, 9**
See also CA 89-92; CANR 45, 73; DLBY 80; INT 89-92

Rojas, Fernando de 1475-1541 .... **LC 23; HLCS 1**
See also RGWL

Rojas, Gonzalo 1917-
See also HLCS 2; HW 2

Rojas, Gonzalo 1917-
See also CA 178; HLCS 2

Rolfe, Frederick (William Serafino Austin Lewis Mary) 1860-1913 .... **TCLC 12**
See also Corvo, Baron
See also CA 107; DLB 34, 156; RGEL

Rolland, Romain 1866-1944 .... **TCLC 23**
See also CA 118; DLB 65; GFL 1789 to the Present; RGWL

Rolle, Richard c. 1300-c. 1349 ...... **CMLC 21**
See also DLB 146; RGEL

Rolvaag, O(le) E(dvart)
See Roelvaag, O(le) E(dvart)
See also DLB 212; NFS 5; RGAL

Romain Arnaud, Saint
See Aragon, Louis

Romains, Jules 1885-1972 .... **CLC 7**
See also CA 85-88; CANR 34; DLB 65; GFL 1789 to the Present; MTCW 1

Romero, Jose Ruben 1890-1952 .... **TCLC 14**
See also CA 114; 131; HW 1

Ronsard, Pierre de 1524-1585 . **LC 6, 54; PC 11**
See also GFL Beginnings to 1789; RGWL

Rooke, Leon 1934- . **CLC 25, 34; DAM POP**
See also CA 25-28R; CANR 23, 53; CCA 1; CPW

Roosevelt, Franklin Delano
1882-1945 .... **TCLC 93**
See also CA 116; 173; LAIT 3

Roosevelt, Theodore 1858-1919 ..... **TCLC 69**
See also CA 115; 170; DLB 47, 186

Roper, William 1498-1578 .... **LC 10**

Roquelaure, A. N.
See Rice, Anne

Rosa, Joao Guimaraes 1908-1967 ... **CLC 23; HLCS 1**
See also CA 89-92; DLB 113; WLIT 1

Rose, Wendy 1948- .. **CLC 85; DAM MULT; PC 13**
See also CA 53-56; CANR 5, 51; CWP; DLB 175; NNAL; RGAL; SATA 12

Rosen, R. D.
See Rosen, Richard (Dean)

Rosen, Richard (Dean) 1949- .... **CLC 39**
See also CA 77-80; CANR 62; CMW; INT CANR-30

Rosenberg, Isaac 1890-1918 .... **TCLC 12**
See also CA 107; 188; DLB 20; PAB; RGEL

Rosenblatt, Joe .... **CLC 15**
See also Rosenblatt, Joseph

Rosenblatt, Joseph 1933-
See Rosenblatt, Joe
See also CA 89-92; CP; INT 89-92

Rosenfeld, Samuel
See Tzara, Tristan

Rosenstock, Sami
See Tzara, Tristan

Rosenstock, Samuel
See Tzara, Tristan

Rosenthal, M(acha) L(ouis)
1917-1996 .... **CLC 28**
See also CA 1-4R; 152; CAAS 6; CANR 4, 51; CP; DLB 5; SATA 59

Ross, Barnaby
See Dannay, Frederic

Ross, Bernard L.
See Follett, Ken(neth Martin)

Ross, J. H.
See Lawrence, T(homas) E(dward)

Ross, John Hume
See Lawrence, T(homas) E(dward)

Ross, Martin 1862-1915
See Martin, Violet Florence
See also DLB 135; GLL 2; RGEL; RGSF

Ross, (James) Sinclair 1908-1996 ... **CLC 13; DAC; DAM MST; SSC 24**
See also CA 73-76; CANR 81; CN; DLB 88; RGEL; RGSF; TCWW 2

Rossetti, Christina (Georgina)
1830-1894 . **NCLC 2, 50, 66; DA; DAB; DAC; DAM MST, POET; PC 7; WLC**
See also BRW; BYA 4; DA3; DLB 35, 163, 240; EXPP; MAICYA; PFS 10; RGEL; SATA 20; WCH

Rossetti, Dante Gabriel 1828-1882 . **NCLC 4, 77; DA; DAB; DAC; DAM MST, POET; WLC**
See also CDBLB 1832-1890; DLB 35; EXPP; RGEL

Rossner, Judith (Perelman) 1935- . **CLC 6, 9, 29**
See also AITN 2; BEST 90:3; BPFB 3; CA 17-20R; CANR 18, 51, 73; CN; DLB 6; INT CANR-18; MTCW 1, 2

Rostand, Edmond (Eugene Alexis)
1868-1918 .... **TCLC 6, 37; DA; DAB; DAC; DAM DRAM, MST; DC 10**
See also CA 104; 126; DA3; DFS 1; DLB 192; LAIT 1; MTCW 1

Roth, Henry 1906-1995 ..... **CLC 2, 6, 11, 104**
See also CA 11-12; 149; CANR 38, 63; CAP 1; CN; DA3; DLB 28; MTCW 1, 2; RGAL

Roth, (Moses) Joseph 1894-1939 ... **TCLC 33**
See also CA 160; DLB 85

Roth, Philip (Milton) 1933- ... **CLC 1, 2, 3, 4, 6, 9, 15, 22, 31, 47, 66, 86, 119; DA; DAB; DAC; DAM MST, NOV, POP; SSC 26; WLC**
See also AMWS 3; BEST 90:3; BPFB 3; CA 1-4R; CANR 1, 22, 36, 55, 89; CDALB 1968-1988; CN; CPW 1; DA3; DLB 2, 28, 173; DLBY 82; MTCW 1, 2; RGAL; RGSF; SSFS 12

Rothenberg, Jerome 1931- .... **CLC 6, 57**
See also CA 45-48; CANR 1; CP; DLB 5, 193

Rotter, Pat ed. .... **CLC 65**

Roumain, Jacques (Jean Baptiste)
1907-1944 ...... **TCLC 19; BLC 3; DAM MULT**
See also BW 1; CA 117; 125

Rourke, Constance (Mayfield)
1885-1941 .... **TCLC 12**
See also CA 107; YABC 1

Rousseau, Jean-Baptiste 1671-1741 ...... **LC 9**

Rousseau, Jean-Jacques 1712-1778 .... **LC 14, 36; DA; DAB; DAC; DAM MST; WLC**
See also DA3; EW; GFL Beginnings to 1789; RGWL

Roussel, Raymond 1877-1933 .... **TCLC 20**
See also CA 117; GFL 1789 to the Present

Rovit, Earl (Herbert) 1927- .... **CLC 7**
See also CA 5-8R; CANR 12

Rowe, Elizabeth Singer 1674-1737 ..... **LC 44**
See also DLB 39, 95

Rowe, Nicholas 1674-1718 .... **LC 8**
See also DLB 84; RGEL

Rowlandson, Mary 1637(?)-1678 .... **LC 66**
See also DLB 24, 200; RGAL

Rowley, Ames Dorrance
See Lovecraft, H(oward) P(hillips)

Rowling, J(oanne) K. 1966(?)- .... **CLC 137**
See also AAYA 34; CA 173; CLR 66; SATA 109

Rowson, Susanna Haswell
1762(?)-1824 .... **NCLC 5, 69**
See also DLB 37, 200; RGAL

Roy, Arundhati 1960(?)- .... **CLC 109**
See also CA 163; CANR 90; DLBY 97

Roy, Gabrielle 1909-1983 .... **CLC 10, 14; DAB; DAC; DAM MST**
See also CA 53-56; 110; CANR 5, 61; CCA 1; DLB 68; MTCW 1; RGWL; SATA 104

Royko, Mike 1932-1997 .... **CLC 109**
See also CA 89-92; 157; CANR 26; CPW

Rozanov, Vassili 1856-1919 .... **TCLC 104**

Rozewicz, Tadeusz 1921- ..... **CLC 9, 23, 139; DAM POET**
See also CA 108; CANR 36, 66; CWW 2; DA3; DLB 232; MTCW 1, 2

Ruark, Gibbons 1941- .... **CLC 3**
See also CA 33-36R; CAAS 23; CANR 14, 31, 57; DLB 120

Rubens, Bernice (Ruth) 1923- .... **CLC 19, 31**
See also CA 25-28R; CANR 33, 65; CN; DLB 14, 207; MTCW 1

Rubin, Harold
See Robbins, Harold

Rudkin, (James) David 1936- .... **CLC 14**
See also CA 89-92; CBD; CD; DLB 13

Rudnik, Raphael 1933- .... **CLC 7**
See also CA 29-32R

Ruffian, M.
See Hasek, Jaroslav (Matej Frantisek)

Ruiz, Jose Martinez .... **CLC 11**
See also Martinez Ruiz, Jose

Rukeyser, Muriel 1913-1980 . **CLC 6, 10, 15, 27; DAM POET; PC 12**
See also AMWS 6; CA 5-8R; 93-96; CANR 26, 60; DA3; DLB 48; FW; GLL 2; MTCW 1, 2; PFS 10; RGAL; SATA-Obit 22

Rule, Jane (Vance) 1931- .... **CLC 27**
See also CA 25-28R; CAAS 18; CANR 12, 87; CN; DLB 60; FW

Rulfo, Juan 1918-1986 .... **CLC 8, 80; DAM MULT; HLC 2; SSC 25**
See also CA 85-88; 118; CANR 26; DLB 113; HW 1, 2; MTCW 1, 2; RGSF; RGWL; WLIT 1

Rumi, Jalal al-Din 1207-1273 .... **CMLC 20**
See also RGWL; WP

Runeberg, Johan 1804-1877 .... **NCLC 41**

Runyon, (Alfred) Damon
1884(?)-1946 .... **TCLC 10**
See also CA 107; 165; DLB 11, 86, 171;
MTCW 2; RGAL

Rush, Norman 1933- .... **CLC 44**
See also CA 121; 126; INT 126

Rushdie, (Ahmed) Salman 1947- .... **CLC 23,
31, 55, 100; DAB; DAC; DAM MST,
NOV, POP; WLCS**
See also BEST 89:3; BPFB 3; BRWS 4;
CA 108; 111; CANR 33, 56; CN; CPW 1;
DA3; DLB 194; FANT; INT CA-111;
MTCW 1, 2; RGEL; RGSF; WLIT 4

Rushforth, Peter (Scott) 1945- .... **CLC 19**
See also CA 101

Ruskin, John 1819-1900 .... **TCLC 63**
See also BYA 5; CA 114; 129; CDBLB
1832-1890; DLB 55, 163, 190; RGEL;
SATA 24

Russ, Joanna 1937- .... **CLC 15**
See also BPFB 3; CA 5-28R; CANR 11,
31, 65; CN; DLB 8; FW; GLL 1; MTCW
1; SCFW 2; SFW

Russell, George William 1867-1935
See Baker, Jean H.
See also CA 104; 153; CDBLB 1890-1914;
DAM POET; RGEL

Russell, Jeffrey Burton 1934- .... **CLC 70**
See also CA 25-28R; CANR 11, 28, 52

Russell, (Henry) Ken(neth Alfred)
1927- .... **CLC 16**
See also CA 105

Russell, William Martin 1947- .... **CLC 60**
See also CA 164; DLB 233

Rutherford, Mark .... **TCLC 25**
See also White, William Hale
See also DLB 18; RGEL

Ruyslinck, Ward .... **CLC 14**
See also Belser, Reimond Karel Maria de

Ryan, Cornelius (John) 1920-1974 .... **CLC 7**
See also CA 69-72; 53-56; CANR 38

Ryan, Michael 1946- .... **CLC 65**
See also CA 49-52; DLBY 82

Ryan, Tim
See Dent, Lester

Rybakov, Anatoli (Naumovich)
1911-1998 .... **CLC 23, 53**
See also CA 126; 135; 172; SATA 79;
SATA-Obit 108

Ryder, Jonathan
See Ludlum, Robert

Ryga, George 1932-1987 .... **CLC 14; DAC;
DAM MST**
See also CA 101; 124; CANR 43, 90; CCA
1; DLB 60

S. H.
See Hartmann, Sadakichi

S. S.
See Sassoon, Siegfried (Lorraine)

Saba, Umberto 1883-1957 .... **TCLC 33**
See also CA 144; CANR 79; DLB 114;
RGWL

Sabatini, Rafael 1875-1950 .... **TCLC 47**
See also BPFB 3; CA 162; RHW

Sabato, Ernesto (R.) 1911- .... **CLC 10, 23;
DAM MULT; HLC 2**
See also CA 97-100; CANR 32, 65; DLB
145; HW 1, 2; LAW; MTCW 1, 2

Sa-Carniero, Mario de 1890-1916 . **TCLC 83**

Sacastru, Martin
See Bioy Casares, Adolfo

Sacastru, Martin
See Bioy Casares, Adolfo
See also CWW 2

Sacher-Masoch, Leopold von
1836(?)-1895 .... **NCLC 31**

Sachs, Marilyn (Stickle) 1927- .... **CLC 35**
See also AAYA 2; BYA 6; CA 17-20R;
CANR 13, 47; CLR 2; JRDA; MAICYA;
SAAS 2; SATA 3, 68; SATA-Essay 110;
WYA; YAW

Sachs, Nelly 1891-1970 .... **CLC 14, 98**
See also CA 17-18; 25-28R; CANR 87;
CAP 2; MTCW 2; RGWL

Sackler, Howard (Oliver)
1929-1982 .... **CLC 14**
See also CA 61-64; 108; CAD; CANR 30;
DLB 7

Sacks, Oliver (Wolf) 1933- .... **CLC 67**
See also CA 53-56; CANR 28, 50, 76;
CPW; DA3; INT CANR-28; MTCW 1, 2

Sadakichi
See Hartmann, Sadakichi

Sade, Donatien Alphonse Francois
1740-1814 .... **NCLC 3, 47**
See also EW; GFL Beginnings to 1789;
RGWL

Sadoff, Ira 1945- .... **CLC 9**
See also CA 53-56; CANR 5, 21; DLB 120

Saetone
See Camus, Albert

Safire, William 1929- .... **CLC 10**
See also CA 17-20R; CANR 31, 54, 91

Sagan, Carl (Edward) 1934-1996 .... **CLC 30,
112**
See also AAYA 2; CA 25-28R; 155; CANR
11, 36, 74; CPW; DA3; MTCW 1, 2;
SATA 58; SATA-Obit 94

Sagan, Francoise .... **CLC 3, 6, 9, 17, 36**
See also Quoirez, Francoise
See also CWW 2; DLB 83; GFL 1789 to
the Present; MTCW 2

Sahgal, Nayantara (Pandit) 1927- .... **CLC 41**
See also CA 9-12R; CANR 11, 88; CN

Said, Edward W. 1935- .... **CLC 123**
See also CA 21-24R; CANR 45, 74; DLB
67; MTCW 2

Saint, H(arry) F. 1941- .... **CLC 50**
See also CA 127

St. Aubin de Teran, Lisa 1953-
See Teran, Lisa St. Aubin de
See also CA 118; 126; CN; INT 126

Saint Birgitta of Sweden c.
1303-1373 .... **CMLC 24**

Sainte-Beuve, Charles Augustin
1804-1869 .... **NCLC 5**
See also EW; GFL 1789 to the Present

**Saint-Exupery, Antoine (Jean Baptiste
Marie Roger) de** 1900-1944 .... **TCLC 2,
56; DAM NOV; WLC**
See also BPFB 3; BYA 3; CA 108; 132;
CLR 10; DA3; DLB 72; EW; GFL 1789
to the Present; LAIT 3; MAICYA; MTCW
1, 2; RGWL; SATA 20

St. John, David
See Hunt, E(verette) Howard, (Jr.)

St. John, J. Hector
See Crevecoeur, Michel Guillaume Jean de

Saint-John Perse
See Leger, (Marie-Rene Auguste) Alexis
Saint-Leger
See also GFL 1789 to the Present; RGWL

Saintsbury, George (Edward Bateman)
1845-1933 .... **TCLC 31**
See also CA 160; DLB 57, 149

Sait Faik .... **TCLC 23**
See also Abasiyanik, Sait Faik

Saki .... **TCLC 3; SSC 12**
See also Munro, H(ector) H(ugh)
See also BRWS 6; LAIT 2; MTCW 2;
RGEL; SSFS 1

Sala, George Augustus 1828-1895 . **NCLC 46**

Saladin 1138-1193 .... **CMLC 38**

Salama, Hannu 1936- .... **CLC 18**

Salamanca, J(ack) R(ichard) 1922- .. **CLC 4,
15**
See also CA 25-28R; CAAE 193

Salas, Floyd Francis 1931-
See also CA 119; CAAS 27; CANR 44, 75,
93; DAM MULT; DLB 82; HLC 2; HW
1, 2; MTCW 2

Sale, J. Kirkpatrick
See Sale, Kirkpatrick

Sale, Kirkpatrick 1937- .... **CLC 68**
See also CA 13-16R; CANR 10

Salinas, Luis Omar 1937- ..... **CLC 90; DAM
MULT; HLC 2**
See also CA 131; CANR 81; DLB 82; HW
1, 2

Salinas (y Serrano), Pedro
1891(?)-1951 .... **TCLC 17**
See also CA 117; DLB 134

Salinger, J(erome) D(avid) 1919- .. **CLC 1, 3,
8, 12, 55, 56, 138; DA; DAB; DAC;
DAM MST, NOV, POP; SSC 2, 28;
WLC**
See also AAYA 2, 36; AMW; BPFB 3; CA
5-8R; CANR 39; CDALB 1941-1968;
CLR 18; CN; CPW 1; DA3; DLB 2, 102,
173; EXPN; LAIT 4; MAICYA; MTCW
1, 2; NFS 1; RGAL; RGSF; SATA 67;
WYA; YAW

Salisbury, John
See Caute, (John) David

Salter, James 1925- .... **CLC 7, 52, 59**
See also CA 73-76; DLB 130

Saltus, Edgar (Everton) 1855-1921 . **TCLC 8**
See also CA 105; DLB 202; RGAL

Saltykov, Mikhail Evgrafovich
1826-1889 .... **NCLC 16**
See also DLB 238:

Saltykov-Shchedrin, N.
See Saltykov, Mikhail Evgrafovich

Samarakis, Antonis 1919- .... **CLC 5**
See also CA 25-28R; CAAS 16; CANR 36

Sanchez, Florencio 1875-1910 .... **TCLC 37**
See also CA 153; HW 1

Sanchez, Luis Rafael 1936- .... **CLC 23**
See also CA 128; DLB 145; HW 1; WLIT
1

Sanchez, Sonia 1934- .... **CLC 5, 116; BLC 3;
DAM MULT; PC 9**
See also BW 2, 3; CA 33-36R; CANR 24,
49, 74; CLR 18; CP; CSW; CWP; DA3;
DLB 41; DLBD 8; MAICYA; MTCW 1,
2; SATA 22; WP

Sand, George 1804-1876 ..... **NCLC 2, 42, 57;
DA; DAB; DAC; DAM MST, NOV;
WLC**
See also DA3; DLB 119, 192; FW; GFL
1789 to the Present; RGWL

Sandburg, Carl (August) 1878-1967 . **CLC 1,
4, 10, 15, 35; DA; DAB; DAC; DAM
MST, POET; PC 2; WLC**
See also AAYA 24; AMW; BYA 1; CA
5-8R; 25-28R; CANR 35; CDALB 1865-
1917; CLR 67; DA3; DLB 17, 54; EXPP;
LAIT 2; MAICYA; MTCW 1, 2; PAB;
PFS 3, 6, 12; RGAL; SATA 8; WCH; WP;
WYA

Sandburg, Charles
See Sandburg, Carl (August)

Sandburg, Charles A.
See Sandburg, Carl (August)

Sanders, (James) Ed(ward) 1939- ... **CLC 53;
DAM POET**
See also CA 13-16R; CAAS 21; CANR 13,
44, 78; CP; DLB 16

Schuyler, James Marcus 1923-1991 .. **CLC 5, 23; DAM POET**
See also CA 101; 134; DLB 5, 169; INT 101; WP

Schwartz, Delmore (David) 1913-1966 ... **CLC 2, 4, 10, 45, 87; PC 8**
See also AMWS 2; CA 17-18; 25-28R; CANR 35; CAP 2; DLB 28, 48; MTCW 1, 2; PAB; RGAL

Schwartz, Ernst
See Ozu, Yasujiro

Schwartz, John Burnham 1965- .... **CLC 59**
See also CA 132

Schwartz, Lynne Sharon 1939- .... **CLC 31**
See also CA 103; CANR 44, 89; MTCW 2

Schwartz, Muriel A.
See Eliot, T(homas) S(tearns)

Schwarz-Bart, Andre 1928- .... **CLC 2, 4**
See also CA 89-92

Schwarz-Bart, Simone 1938- . **CLC 7; BLCS**
See also BW 2; CA 97-100

Schwitters, Kurt (Hermann Edward Karl Julius) 1887-1948 .... **TCLC 95**
See also CA 158

Schwob, Marcel (Mayer Andre) 1867-1905 .... **TCLC 20**
See also CA 117; 168; DLB 123; GFL 1789 to the Present

Sciascia, Leonardo 1921-1989 .. **CLC 8, 9, 41**
See also CA 85-88; 130; CANR 35; DLB 177; MTCW 1; RGWL

Scoppettone, Sandra 1936- .... **CLC 26**
See also Early, Jack
See also AAYA 11; BYA 8; CA 5-8R; CANR 41, 73; GLL 1; SATA 9, 92; YAW

Scorsese, Martin 1942- .... **CLC 20, 89**
See also AAYA 38; CA 110; 114; CANR 46, 85

Scotland, Jay
See Jakes, John (William)

Scott, Duncan Campbell 1862-1947 .... **TCLC 6; DAC**
See also CA 104; 153; DLB 92; RGEL

Scott, Evelyn 1893-1963 .... **CLC 43**
See also CA 104; 112; CANR 64; DLB 9, 48; RHW

Scott, F(rancis) R(eginald) 1899-1985 .... **CLC 22**
See also CA 101; 114; CANR 87; DLB 88; INT CA-101; RGEL

Scott, Frank
See Scott, F(rancis) R(eginald)

Scott, Joan .... **CLC 65**

Scott, Joanna 1960- .... **CLC 50**
See also CA 126; CANR 53, 92

Scott, Paul (Mark) 1920-1978 ...... **CLC 9, 60**
See also BRWS 1; CA 81-84; 77-80; CANR 33; DLB 14, 207; MTCW 1; RGEL; RHW

Scott, Sarah 1723-1795 .... **LC 44**
See also DLB 39

Scott, Sir Walter 1771-1832 .... **NCLC 15, 69; DA; DAB; DAC; DAM MST, NOV, POET; PC 13; SSC 32; WLC**
See also AAYA 22; BRW; BYA 2; CDBLB 1789-1832; DLB 93, 107, 116, 144, 159; HGG; LAIT 1; RGEL; RGSF; SSFS 10; SUFW; WLIT 3; YABC 2

Scribe, (Augustin) Eugene 1791-1861 ..... **NCLC 16; DAM DRAM; DC 5**
See also DLB 192; EW; GFL 1789 to the Present; RGWL

Scrum, R.
See Crumb, R(obert)

Scudery, Madeleine de 1607-1701 .. **LC 2, 58**
See also GFL Beginnings to 1789

Scum
See Crumb, R(obert)

Scumbag, Little Bobby
See Crumb, R(obert)

Seabrook, John
See Hubbard, L(afayette) Ron(ald)

Sealy, I(rwin) Allan 1951- .... **CLC 55**
See also CA 136; CN

Search, Alexander
See Pessoa, Fernando (Antonio Nogueira)

Sebastian, Lee
See Silverberg, Robert

Sebastian Owl
See Thompson, Hunter S(tockton)

Sebestyen, Ouida 1924- .... **CLC 30**
See also AAYA 8; BYA 7; CA 107; CANR 40; CLR 17; JRDA; MAICYA; SAAS 10; SATA 39; YAW

Secundus, H. Scriblerus
See Fielding, Henry

Sedges, John
See Buck, Pearl S(ydenstricker)

Sedgwick, Catharine Maria 1789-1867 .... **NCLC 19, 98**
See also DLB 1, 74, 239; RGAL

Seelye, John (Douglas) 1931- .... **CLC 7**
See also CA 97-100; CANR 70; INT 97-100; TCWW 2

Seferiades, Giorgos Stylianou 1900-1971
See Seferis, George
See also CA 5-8R; 33-36R; CANR 5, 36; MTCW 1

Seferis, George .... **CLC 5, 11**
See also Seferiades, Giorgos Stylianou
See also RGWL

Segal, Erich (Wolf) 1937- . **CLC 3, 10; DAM POP**
See also BEST 89:1; BPFB 3; CA 25-28R; CANR 20, 36, 65; CPW; DLBY 86; INT CANR-20; MTCW 1

Seger, Bob 1945- .... **CLC 35**

Seghers, Anna .... **CLC 7**
See also Radvanyi, Netty
See also DLB 69

Seidel, Frederick (Lewis) 1936- .... **CLC 18**
See also CA 13-16R; CANR 8, 99; CP; DLBY 84

Seifert, Jaroslav 1901-1986 .. **CLC 34, 44, 93**
See also CA 127; DLB 215; MTCW 1, 2

Sei Shonagon c. 966-1017(?) .... **CMLC 6**

Sejour, Victor 1817-1874 .... **DC 10**
See also DLB 50

Sejour Marcou et Ferrand, Juan Victor
See Sejour, Victor

Selby, Hubert, Jr. 1928- .... **CLC 1, 2, 4, 8; SSC 20**
See also CA 13-16R; CANR 33, 85; CN; DLB 2, 227

Selzer, Richard 1928- .... **CLC 74**
See also CA 65-68; CANR 14

Sembene, Ousmane
See Ousmane, Sembene
See also AFW; CWW 2; WLIT 2

Senancour, Etienne Pivert de 1770-1846 .... **NCLC 16**
See also DLB 119; GFL 1789 to the Present

Sender, Ramon (Jose) 1902-1982 ...... **CLC 8; DAM MULT; HLC 2**
See also CA 5-8R; 105; CANR 8; HW 1; MTCW 1; RGWL

Seneca, Lucius Annaeus c. 4B.C.-c. 65 .... **CMLC 6; DAM DRAM; DC 5**
See also AW; DLB 211; RGWL

Senghor, Leopold Sedar 1906- .... **CLC 54, 130; BLC 3; DAM MULT, POET; PC 25**
See also BW 2; CA 116; 125; CANR 47, 74; DNFS; GFL 1789 to the Present; MTCW 1, 2

Senna, Danzy 1970- .... **CLC 119**
See also CA 169

Serling, (Edward) Rod(man) 1924-1975 .... **CLC 30**
See also AAYA 14; AITN 1; CA 162; 57-60; DLB 26; SFW

Serna, Ramon Gomez de la
See Gomez de la Serna, Ramon

Serpieres
See Guillevic, (Eugene)

Service, Robert
See Service, Robert W(illiam)
See also BYA 4; DAB; DLB 92

Service, Robert W(illiam) 1874(?)-1958 .... **TCLC 15; DA; DAC; DAM MST, POET; WLC**
See also Service, Robert
See also CA 115; 140; CANR 84; PFS 10; RGEL; SATA 20

Seth, Vikram 1952- .... **CLC 43, 90; DAM MULT**
See also CA 121; 127; CANR 50, 74; CN; CP; DA3; DLB 120; INT 127; MTCW 2

Seton, Cynthia Propper 1926-1982 .. **CLC 27**
See also CA 5-8R; 108; CANR 7

Seton, Ernest (Evan) Thompson 1860-1946 .... **TCLC 31**
See also ANW; BYA 3; CA 109; CLR 59; DLB 92; DLBD 13; JRDA; SATA 18

Seton-Thompson, Ernest
See Seton, Ernest (Evan) Thompson

Settle, Mary Lee 1918- .... **CLC 19, 61**
See also BPFB 3; CA 89-92; CAAS 1; CANR 44, 87; CN; CSW; DLB 6; INT 89-92

Seuphor, Michel
See Arp, Jean

Sevigne, Marie (de Rabutin-Chantal) 1626-1696 .... **LC 11**
See also GFL Beginnings to 1789

Sewall, Samuel 1652-1730 .... **LC 38**
See also DLB 24; RGAL

Sexton, Anne (Harvey) 1928-1974 ..... **CLC 2, 4, 6, 8, 10, 15, 53, 123; DA; DAB; DAC; DAM MST, POET; PC 2; WLC**
See also AMWS 2; CA 1-4R; 53-56; CABS 2; CANR 3, 36; CDALB 1941-1968; DA3; DLB 5, 169; EXPP; FW; MAWW; MTCW 1, 2; PAB; PFS 4; RGAL; SATA 10

Shaara, Jeff 1952- .... **CLC 119**
See also CA 163

Shaara, Michael (Joseph, Jr.) 1929-1988 .... **CLC 15; DAM POP**
See also AITN 1; BPFB 3; CA 102; 125; CANR 52, 85; DLBY 83

Shackleton, C. C.
See Aldiss, Brian W(ilson)

Shacochis, Bob .... **CLC 39**
See also Shacochis, Robert G.

Shacochis, Robert G. 1951-
See Shacochis, Bob
See also CA 119; 124; CANR 100; INT 124

Shaffer, Anthony (Joshua) 1926- ..... **CLC 19; DAM DRAM**
See also CA 110; 116; CBD; CD; DFS 13; DLB 13

Shaffer, Peter (Levin) 1926- .. **CLC 5, 14, 18, 37, 60; DAB; DAM DRAM, MST; DC 7**
See also BRWS 1; CA 25-28R; CANR 25, 47, 74; CBD; CD; CDBLB 1960 to Present; DA3; DFS 5, 13; DLB 13, 233; MTCW 1, 2; RGEL

Shakey, Bernard
See Young, Neil

Shalamov, Varlam (Tikhonovich) 1907(?)-1982 .... **CLC 18**
See also CA 129; 105; RGSF

Shamlu, Ahmad 1925-2000 .... **CLC 10**
See also CWW 2

Spillane, Frank Morrison 1918-
See Spillane, Mickey
See also CA 25-28R; CANR 28, 63; DA3;
DLB 226; MTCW 1, 2; SATA 66
Spillane, Mickey .... **CLC 3, 13**
See also Spillane, Frank Morrison
See also BPFB 3; CMW; DLB 226; MTCW
2
Spinoza, Benedictus de 1632-1677 .. **LC 9, 58**
Spinrad, Norman (Richard) 1940- ... **CLC 46**
See also BPFB 3; CA 37-40R; CAAS 19;
CANR 20, 91; DLB 8; INT CANR-20;
SFW
Spitteler, Carl (Friedrich Georg)
1845-1924 .... **TCLC 12**
See also CA 109; DLB 129
Spivack, Kathleen (Romola Drucker)
1938- .... **CLC 6**
See also CA 49-52
Spoto, Donald 1941- .... **CLC 39**
See also CA 65-68; CANR 11, 57, 93
Springsteen, Bruce (F.) 1949- .... **CLC 17**
See also CA 111
Spurling, Hilary 1940- .... **CLC 34**
See also CA 104; CANR 25, 52, 94
Spyker, John Howland
See Elman, Richard (Martin)
Squires, (James) Radcliffe
1917-1993 .... **CLC 51**
See also CA 1-4R; 140; CANR 6, 21
Srivastava, Dhanpat Rai 1880(?)-1936
See Premchand
See also CA 118
Stacy, Donald
See Pohl, Frederik
Stael
See Stael-Holstein, Anne Louise Germaine
Necker
See also RGWL
Stael, Germaine de .... **NCLC 91**
See also Stael-Holstein, Anne Louise Ger-
maine Necker
See also DLB 119, 192; FW; GFL 1789 to
the Present
Stael-Holstein, Anne Louise Germaine
Necker 1766-1817 .... **NCLC 3**
See also Stael; Stael, Germaine de
See also EW; TWA
Stafford, Jean 1915-1979 .. **CLC 4, 7, 19, 68;**
SSC 26
See also CA 1-4R; 85-88; CANR 3, 65;
DLB 2, 173; MTCW 1, 2; RGAL; RGSF;
SATA-Obit 22; TCWW 2
Stafford, William (Edgar)
1914-1993 .. **CLC 4, 7, 29; DAM POET**
See also CA 5-8R; 142; CAAS 3; CANR 5,
22; DLB 5, 206; EXPP; INT CANR-22;
PFS 2, 8; RGAL; WP
Stagnelius, Eric Johan 1793-1823 . **NCLC 61**
Staines, Trevor
See Brunner, John (Kilian Houston)
Stairs, Gordon
See Austin, Mary (Hunter)
See also TCWW 2
Stairs, Gordon 1868-1934
See Austin, Mary (Hunter)
Stalin, Joseph 1879-1953 .... **TCLC 92**
Stancykowna
See Szymborska, Wislawa
Stannard, Martin 1947- .... **CLC 44**
See also CA 142; DLB 155
Stanton, Elizabeth Cady
1815-1902 .... **TCLC 73**
See also CA 171; DLB 79; FW
Stanton, Maura 1946- .... **CLC 9**
See also CA 89-92; CANR 15; DLB 120
Stanton, Schuyler
See Baum, L(yman) Frank

Stapledon, (William) Olaf
1886-1950 .... **TCLC 22**
See also CA 111; 162; DLB 15; SFW
Starbuck, George (Edwin)
1931-1996 .... **CLC 53; DAM POET**
See also CA 21-24R; 153; CANR 23
Stark, Richard
See Westlake, Donald E(dwin)
Staunton, Schuyler
See Baum, L(yman) Frank
Stead, Christina (Ellen) 1902-1983 ... **CLC 2,**
5, 8, 32, 80
See also BRWS 4; CA 13-16R; 109; CANR
33, 40; FW; MTCW 1, 2; RGEL; RGSF
Stead, William Thomas
1849-1912 .... **TCLC 48**
See also CA 167
Stebnitsky, M.
See Leskov, Nikolai (Semyonovich)
Steele, Sir Richard 1672-1729 .... **LC 18**
See also BRW; CDBLB 1660-1789; DLB
84, 101; RGEL; WLIT 3
Steele, Timothy (Reid) 1948- .... **CLC 45**
See also CA 93-96; CANR 16, 50, 92; CP;
DLB 120
Steffens, (Joseph) Lincoln
1866-1936 .... **TCLC 20**
See also CA 117
Stegner, Wallace (Earle) 1909-1993 .. **CLC 9,**
49, 81; DAM NOV; SSC 27
See also AITN 1; AMWS 4; ANW; BEST
90:3; BPFB 3; CA 1-4R; 141; CAAS 9;
CANR 1, 21, 46; DLB 9, 206; DLBY 93;
MTCW 1, 2; RGAL; TCWW 2
Stein, Gertrude 1874-1946 ... **TCLC 1, 6, 28,**
48; DA; DAB; DAC; DAM MST, NOV,
POET; PC 18; SSC 42; WLC
See also AMW; CA 104; 132; CDALB
1917-1929; DA3; DLB 4, 54, 86, 228;
DLBD 15; EXPS; GLL 1; MTCW 1, 2;
RGAL; RGSF; SSFS 5; WP
Steinbeck, John (Ernst) 1902-1968 ... **CLC 1,**
5, 9, 13, 21, 34, 45, 75, 124; DA; DAB;
DAC; DAM DRAM, MST, NOV; SSC
11, 37; WLC
See also AAYA 12; AMW; BPFB 3; BYA 2;
CA 1-4R; 25-28R; CANR 1, 35; CDALB
1929-1941; DA3; DLB 7, 9, 212; DLBD
2; EXPS; LAIT 3; MTCW 1, 2; NFS 1, 5,
7; RGAL; RGSF; RHW; SATA 9; SSFS
3, 6; TCWW 2; WYA; YAW
Steinem, Gloria 1934- .... **CLC 63**
See also CA 53-56; CANR 28, 51; FW;
MTCW 1, 2
Steiner, George 1929- .. **CLC 24; DAM NOV**
See also CA 73-76; CANR 31, 67; DLB 67;
MTCW 1, 2; SATA 62
Steiner, K. Leslie
See Delany, Samuel R(ay), Jr.
Steiner, Rudolf 1861-1925 .... **TCLC 13**
See also CA 107
Stendhal 1783-1842 .... **NCLC 23, 46; DA;**
DAB; DAC; DAM MST, NOV; SSC
27; WLC
See also DA3; DLB 119; GFL 1789 to the
Present; RGWL
Stephen, Adeline Virginia
See Woolf, (Adeline) Virginia
Stephen, Sir Leslie 1832-1904 .... **TCLC 23**
See also BRW; CA 123; DLB 57, 144, 190
Stephen, Sir Leslie
See Stephen, Sir Leslie
Stephen, Virginia
See Woolf, (Adeline) Virginia
Stephens, James 1882(?)-1950 .... **TCLC 4**
See also CA 104; 192; DLB 19, 153, 162;
FANT; RGEL
Stephens, Reed
See Donaldson, Stephen R(eeder)

Steptoe, Lydia
See Barnes, Djuna
See also GLL 1
Sterchi, Beat 1949- .... **CLC 65**
Sterling, Brett
See Bradbury, Ray (Douglas); Hamilton,
Edmond
Sterling, Bruce 1954- .... **CLC 72**
See also CA 119; CANR 44; SCFW 2; SFW
Sterling, George 1869-1926 .... **TCLC 20**
See also CA 117; 165; DLB 54
Stern, Gerald 1925- .... **CLC 40, 100**
See also CA 81-84; CANR 28, 94; CP; DLB
105; RGAL
Stern, Richard (Gustave) 1928- ... **CLC 4, 39**
See also CA 1-4R; CANR 1, 25, 52; CN;
DLBY 87; INT CANR-25
Sternberg, Josef von 1894-1969 .... **CLC 20**
See also CA 81-84
Sterne, Laurence 1713-1768 .. **LC 2, 48; DA;**
DAB; DAC; DAM MST, NOV; WLC
See also CDBLB 1660-1789; DLB 39;
RGEL
Sternheim, (William Adolf) Carl
1878-1942 .... **TCLC 8**
See also CA 105; 193; DLB 56, 118; RGWL
Stevens, Mark 1951- .... **CLC 34**
See also CA 122
Stevens, Wallace 1879-1955 ...... **TCLC 3, 12,**
45; DA; DAB; DAC; DAM MST,
POET; PC 6; WLC
See also AMW; CA 104; 124; CDALB
1929-1941; DA3; DLB 54; EXPP; MTCW
1, 2; PAB; RGAL; WP
Stevenson, Anne (Katharine) 1933- .. **CLC 7,**
33
See also BRWS 6; CA 17-20R; CAAS 9;
CANR 9, 33; CP; CWP; DLB 40; MTCW
1; RHW
Stevenson, Robert Louis (Balfour)
1850-1894 . **NCLC 5, 14, 63; DA; DAB;**
DAC; DAM MST, NOV; SSC 11; WLC
See also AAYA 24; BPFB 3; BRW; BYA 1;
CDBLB 1890-1914; CLR 10, 11; DA3;
DLB 18, 57, 141, 156, 174; DLBD 13;
HGG; JRDA; LAIT 1, 3; MAICYA; NFS
11; RGEL; RGSF; SATA 100; SUFW;
WCH; WLIT 4; WYA; YABC 2; YAW
Stewart, J(ohn) I(nnes) M(ackintosh)
1906-1994 .... **CLC 7, 14, 32**
See also CA 85-88; 147; CAAS 3; CANR
47; CMW; MTCW 1, 2
Stewart, Mary (Florence Elinor)
1916- .... **CLC 7, 35, 117; DAB**
See also AAYA 29; BPFB 3; CA 1-4R;
CANR 1, 59; CMW; CPW; FANT; RHW;
SATA 12; YAW
Stewart, Mary Rainbow
See Stewart, Mary (Florence Elinor)
Stifle, June
See Campbell, Maria
Stifter, Adalbert 1805-1868 .. **NCLC 41; SSC**
28
See also DLB 133; RGSF; RGWL
Still, James 1906-2001 .... **CLC 49**
See also CA 65-68; CAAS 17; CANR 10,
26; CSW; DLB 9; SATA 29
Sting 1951-
See Sumner, Gordon Matthew
See also CA 167
Stirling, Arthur
See Sinclair, Upton (Beall)
Stitt, Milan 1941- .... **CLC 29**
See also CA 69-72
Stockton, Francis Richard 1834-1902
See Stockton, Frank R.
See also CA 108; 137; MAICYA; SATA 44;
SFW

Swados, Harvey 1920-1972 .... **CLC 5**
See also CA 5-8R; 37-40R; CANR 6; DLB 2

Swan, Gladys 1934- .... **CLC 69**
See also CA 101; CANR 17, 39

Swanson, Logan
See Matheson, Richard (Burton)

Swarthout, Glendon (Fred)
1918-1992 .... **CLC 35**
See also CA 1-4R; 139; CANR 1, 47; LAIT 5; SATA 26; TCWW 2; YAW

Sweet, Sarah C.
See Jewett, (Theodora) Sarah Orne

Swenson, May 1919-1989 ...... **CLC 4, 14, 61, 106; DA; DAB; DAC; DAM MST, POET; PC 14**
See also AMWS 4; CA 5-8R; 130; CANR 36, 61; DLB 5; EXPP; GLL 2; MTCW 1, 2; SATA 15; WP

Swift, Augustus
See Lovecraft, H(oward) P(hillips)

Swift, Graham (Colin) 1949- ...... **CLC 41, 88**
See also BRWS 5; CA 117; 122; CANR 46, 71; CN; DLB 194; MTCW 2; RGSF

Swift, Jonathan 1667-1745 ..... **LC 1, 42; DA; DAB; DAC; DAM MST, NOV, POET; PC 9; WLC**
See also BYA 5; CDBLB 1660-1789; CLR 53; DA3; DLB 39, 95, 101; EXPN; LAIT 1; NFS 6; RGEL; SATA 19; WLIT 3

Swinburne, Algernon Charles
1837-1909 .... **TCLC 8, 36; DA; DAB; DAC; DAM MST, POET; PC 24; WLC**
See also CA 105; 140; CDBLB 1832-1890; DA3; DLB 35, 57; PAB; RGEL

Swinfen, Ann .... **CLC 34**

Swinnerton, Frank Arthur
1884-1982 .... **CLC 31**
See also CA 108; DLB 34

Swithen, John
See King, Stephen (Edwin)

Sylvia
See Ashton-Warner, Sylvia (Constance)

Symmes, Robert Edward
See Duncan, Robert (Edward)

Symonds, John Addington
1840-1893 .... **NCLC 34**
See also DLB 57, 144

Symons, Arthur 1865-1945 .... **TCLC 11**
See also CA 107; 189; DLB 19, 57, 149; RGEL

Symons, Julian (Gustave)
1912-1994 .... **CLC 2, 14, 32**
See also CA 49-52; 147; CAAS 3; CANR 3, 33, 59; CMW; DLB 87, 155; DLBY 92; MSW; MTCW 1

Synge, (Edmund) J(ohn) M(illington)
1871-1909 . **TCLC 6, 37; DAM DRAM; DC 2**
See also BRW; CA 104; 141; CDBLB 1890-1914; DLB 10, 19; RGEL; WLIT 4

Syruc, J.
See Milosz, Czeslaw

Szirtes, George 1948- .... **CLC 46**
See also CA 109; CANR 27, 61; CP

Szymborska, Wislawa 1923- .... **CLC 99**
See also CA 154; CANR 91; CWP; CWW 2; DA3; DLB 232; DLBY 96; MTCW 2

T. O., Nik
See Annensky, Innokenty (Fyodorovich)

Tabori, George 1914- .... **CLC 19**
See also CA 49-52; CANR 4, 69; CBD; CD

Tagore, Rabindranath 1861-1941 ... **TCLC 3, 53; DAM DRAM, POET; PC 8**
See also CA 104; 120; DA3; MTCW 1, 2; RGEL; RGSF; RGWL

Taine, Hippolyte Adolphe
1828-1893 .... **NCLC 15**
See also EW; GFL 1789 to the Present

Talese, Gay 1932- .... **CLC 37**
See also AITN 1; CA 1-4R; CANR 9, 58; DLB 185; INT CANR-9; MTCW 1, 2

Tallent, Elizabeth (Ann) 1954- .... **CLC 45**
See also CA 117; CANR 72; DLB 130

Tally, Ted 1952- .... **CLC 42**
See also CA 120; 124; CAD; CD; INT 124

Talvik, Heiti 1904-1947 .... **TCLC 87**

Tamayo y Baus, Manuel
1829-1898 .... **NCLC 1**

Tammsaare, A(nton) H(ansen)
1878-1940 .... **TCLC 27**
See also CA 164; DLB 220

Tam'si, Tchicaya U
See Tchicaya, Gerald Felix

Tan, Amy (Ruth) 1952- . **CLC 59, 120; AAL; DAM MULT, NOV, POP**
See also AAYA 9; BEST 89:3; BPFB 3; CA 136; CANR 54; CDALBS; CN; CPW 1; DA3; DLB 173; EXPN; FW; LAIT 5; MTCW 2; NFS 1; RGAL; SATA 75; SSFS 9; YAW

Tandem, Felix
See Spitteler, Carl (Friedrich Georg)

Tanizaki, Jun'ichiro 1886-1965 ... **CLC 8, 14, 28; SSC 21**
See also CA 93-96; 25-28R; DLB 180; MJW; MTCW 2; RGSF; RGWL

Tanner, William
See Amis, Kingsley (William)

Tao Lao
See Storni, Alfonsina

Tarantino, Quentin (Jerome)
1963- .... **CLC 125**
See also CA 171

Tarassoff, Lev
See Troyat, Henri

Tarbell, Ida M(inerva) 1857-1944 . **TCLC 40**
See also CA 122; 181; DLB 47

Tarkington, (Newton) Booth
1869-1946 .... **TCLC 9**
See also BPFB 3; BYA 3; CA 110; 143; CWRI; DLB 9, 102; MTCW 2; RGAL; SATA 17

Tarkovsky, Andrei (Arsenyevich)
1932-1986 .... **CLC 75**
See also CA 127

Tartt, Donna 1964(?)- .... **CLC 76**
See also CA 142

Tasso, Torquato 1544-1595 .... **LC 5**
See also EFS 2; RGWL

Tate, (John Orley) Allen 1899-1979 .. **CLC 2, 4, 6, 9, 11, 14, 24**
See also AMW; CA 5-8R; 85-88; CANR 32; DLB 4, 45, 63; DLBD 17; MTCW 1, 2; RGAL; RHW

Tate, Ellalice
See Hibbert, Eleanor Alice Burford

Tate, James (Vincent) 1943- ..... **CLC 2, 6, 25**
See also CA 21-24R; CANR 29, 57; CP; DLB 5, 169; PFS 10; RGAL; WP

Tauler, Johannes c. 1300-1361 ...... **CMLC 37**
See also DLB 179

Tavel, Ronald 1940- .... **CLC 6**
See also CA 21-24R; CAD; CANR 33; CD

Taviani, Paolo 1931- .... **CLC 70**
See also CA 153

Taylor, Bayard 1825-1878 .... **NCLC 89**
See also DLB 3, 189; RGAL

Taylor, C(ecil) P(hilip) 1929-1981 .... **CLC 27**
See also CA 25-28R; 105; CANR 47; CBD

Taylor, Edward 1642(?)-1729 ..... **LC 11; DA; DAB; DAC; DAM MST, POET**
See also AMW; DLB 24; EXPP; RGAL

Taylor, Eleanor Ross 1920- .... **CLC 5**
See also CA 81-84; CANR 70

Taylor, Elizabeth 1932-1975 ..... **CLC 2, 4, 29**
See also CA 13-16R; CANR 9, 70; DLB 139; MTCW 1; RGEL; SATA 13

Taylor, Frederick Winslow
1856-1915 .... **TCLC 76**
See also CA 188

Taylor, Henry (Splawn) 1942- .... **CLC 44**
See also CA 33-36R; CAAS 7; CANR 31; CP; DLB 5; PFS 10

Taylor, Kamala (Purnaiya) 1924-
See Markandaya, Kamala
See also CA 77-80; CN

Taylor, Mildred D(elois) 1943- .... **CLC 21**
See also AAYA 10; BW 1; BYA 3; CA 85-88; CANR 25; CLR 9, 59; CSW; DLB 52; JRDA; LAIT 3; MAICYA; SAAS 5; SATA 15, 70; WYA; YAW

Taylor, Peter (Hillsman) 1917-1994 .. **CLC 1, 4, 18, 37, 44, 50, 71; SSC 10**
See also AMWS 5; BPFB 3; CA 13-16R; 147; CANR 9, 50; CSW; DLBY 81, 94; EXPS; INT CANR-9; MTCW 1, 2; RGSF; SSFS 9

Taylor, Robert Lewis 1912-1998 .... **CLC 14**
See also CA 1-4R; 170; CANR 3, 64; SATA 10

Tchekhov, Anton
See Chekhov, Anton (Pavlovich)

Tchicaya, Gerald Felix 1931-1988 .. **CLC 101**
See also CA 129; 125; CANR 81

Tchicaya U Tam'si
See Tchicaya, Gerald Felix

Teasdale, Sara 1884-1933 .... **TCLC 4; PC 31**
See also CA 104; 163; DLB 45; GLL 1; RGAL; SATA 32

Tegner, Esaias 1782-1846 .... **NCLC 2**

Teilhard de Chardin, (Marie Joseph) Pierre
1881-1955 .... **TCLC 9**
See also CA 105; GFL 1789 to the Present

Temple, Ann
See Mortimer, Penelope (Ruth)

Tennant, Emma (Christina) 1937- .. **CLC 13, 52**
See also CA 65-68; CAAS 9; CANR 10, 38, 59, 88; CN; DLB 14; SFW

Tenneshaw, S. M.
See Silverberg, Robert

Tennyson, Alfred 1809-1892 ... **NCLC 30, 65; DA; DAB; DAC; DAM MST, POET; PC 6; WLC**
See also BRW; CDBLB 1832-1890; DA3; DLB 32; EXPP; PAB; PFS 1, 2, 4, 11; RGEL; WLIT 4; WP

Teran, Lisa St. Aubin de .... **CLC 36**
See also St. Aubin de Teran, Lisa

Terence c. 184B.C.-c. 159B.C. ...... **CMLC 14; DC 7**
See also DLB 211; RGWL

Teresa de Jesus, St. 1515-1582 .... **LC 18**

Terkel, Louis 1912-
See Terkel, Studs
See also CA 57-60; CANR 18, 45, 67; DA3; MTCW 1, 2

Terkel, Studs .... **CLC 38**
See also Terkel, Louis
See also AAYA 32; AITN 1; MTCW 2

Terry, C. V.
See Slaughter, Frank G(ill)

Terry, Megan 1932- .... **CLC 19; DC 13**
See also CA 77-80; CABS 3; CAD; CANR 43; CD; CWD; DLB 7; GLL 2

Tertullian c. 155-c. 245 .... **CMLC 29**

Tertz, Abram
See Sinyavsky, Andrei (Donatevich)
See also CWW 2; RGSF

Tesich, Steve 1943(?)-1996 .... **CLC 40, 69**
See also CA 105; 152; CAD; DLBY 83

Veblen, Thorstein B(unde)
1857-1929 .... **TCLC 31**
See also AMWS 1; CA 115; 165

Vega, Lope de 1562-1635 .... **LC 23; HLCS 2**
See also RGWL

Vendler, Helen (Hennessy) 1933- ... **CLC 138**
See also CA 41-44R; CANR 25, 72; MTCW
1, 2

Venison, Alfred
See Pound, Ezra (Weston Loomis)

Verdi, Marie de
See Mencken, H(enry) L(ouis)

Verdu, Matilde
See Cela, Camilo Jose

Verga, Giovanni (Carmelo)
1840-1922 .... **TCLC 3; SSC 21**
See also CA 104; 123; CANR 101; EW;
RGSF; RGWL

Vergil 70B.C.-19B.C. .... **CMLC 9, 40; DA;
DAB; DAC; DAM MST, POET; PC
12; WLCS**
See also Virgil
See also DA3; DLB 211; EFS 1

Verhaeren, Emile (Adolphe Gustave)
1855-1916 .... **TCLC 12**
See also CA 109; GFL 1789 to the Present

Verlaine, Paul (Marie) 1844-1896 .. **NCLC 2,
51; DAM POET; PC 2, 32**
See also EW; GFL 1789 to the Present;
RGWL

Verne, Jules (Gabriel) 1828-1905 ... **TCLC 6,
52**
See also AAYA 16; BYA 4; CA 110; 131;
DA3; DLB 123; GFL 1789 to the Present;
JRDA; LAIT 2; MAICYA; RGWL; SATA
21; SCFW; SFW; WCH

Verus, Marcus Annius
See Antoninus, Marcus Aurelius

Very, Jones 1813-1880 .... **NCLC 9**
See also DLB 1; RGAL

Vesaas, Tarjei 1897-1970 .... **CLC 48**
See also CA 190; 29-32R

Vialis, Gaston
See Simenon, Georges (Jacques Christian)

Vian, Boris 1920-1959 .... **TCLC 9**
See also CA 106; 164; DLB 72; GFL 1789
to the Present; MTCW 2; RGWL

Viaud, (Louis Marie) Julien 1850-1923
See Loti, Pierre
See also CA 107

Vicar, Henry
See Felsen, Henry Gregor

Vicker, Angus
See Felsen, Henry Gregor

Vidal, Gore 1925- ...... **CLC 2, 4, 6, 8, 10, 22,
33, 72, 142; DAM NOV, POP**
See also Box, Edgar
See also AITN 1; AMWS 4; BEST 90:2;
BPFB 3; CA 5-8R; CAD; CANR 13, 45,
65, 100; CD; CDALBS; CN; CPW; DA3;
DFS 2; DLB 6, 152; INT CANR-13;
MTCW 1, 2; RGAL; RHW

Viereck, Peter (Robert Edwin)
1916- .... **CLC 4; PC 27**
See also CA 1-4R; CANR 1, 47; CP; DLB
5; PFS 9

Vigny, Alfred (Victor) de
1797-1863 . **NCLC 7, 102; DAM POET;
PC 26**
See also DLB 119, 192; EW; GFL 1789 to
the Present; RGWL

Vilakazi, Benedict Wallet
1906-1947 .... **TCLC 37**

Villa, Jose Garcia 1914-1997 .... **PC 22**
See also AAL; CA 25-28R; CANR 12;
EXPP

Villarreal, Jose Antonio 1924-
See also CA 133; CANR 93; DAM MULT;
DLB 82; HLC 2; HW 1; LAIT 4; RGAL

Villaurrutia, Xavier 1903-1950 ...... **TCLC 80**
See also CA 192; HW 1

Villehardouin, Geoffroi de
1150(?)-1218(?) .... **CMLC 38**

**Villiers de l'Isle Adam, Jean Marie Mathias
Philippe Auguste** 1838-1889 ... **NCLC 3;
SSC 14**
See also DLB 123; GFL 1789 to the Present;
RGSF

Villon, Francois 1431-1463(?) . **LC 62; PC 13**
See also DLB 208; EW; RGWL

Vine, Barbara .... **CLC 50**
See also Rendell, Ruth (Barbara)
See also BEST 90:4

Vinge, Joan (Carol) D(ennison)
1948- .... **CLC 30; SSC 24**
See also AAYA 32; BPFB 3; CA 93-96;
CANR 72; SATA 36, 113; SFW; YAW

Viola, Herman J(oseph) 1938- .... **CLC 70**
See also CA 61-64; CANR 8, 23, 48, 91

Violis, G.
See Simenon, Georges (Jacques Christian)

Viramontes, Helena Maria 1954-
See also CA 159; DLB 122; HLCS 2; HW
2

Virgil
See Vergil
See also LAIT 1; RGWL; WP

Visconti, Luchino 1906-1976 .... **CLC 16**
See also CA 81-84; 65-68; CANR 39

Vittorini, Elio 1908-1966 .... **CLC 6, 9, 14**
See also CA 133; 25-28R; RGWL

Vivekananda, Swami 1863-1902 .... **TCLC 88**

Vizenor, Gerald Robert 1934- .... **CLC 103;
DAM MULT**
See also CA 13-16R; CAAS 22; CANR 5,
21, 44, 67; DLB 175, 227; MTCW 2;
NNAL; TCWW 2

Vizinczey, Stephen 1933- .... **CLC 40**
See also CA 128; CCA 1; INT 128

Vliet, R(ussell) G(ordon)
1929-1984 .... **CLC 22**
See also CA 37-40R; 112; CANR 18

Vogau, Boris Andreyevich 1894-1937(?)
See Pilnyak, Boris
See also CA 123

Vogel, Paula A(nne) 1951- .... **CLC 76**
See also CA 108; CD; RGAL

Voigt, Cynthia 1942- .... **CLC 30**
See also AAYA 3, 30; BYA 1; CA 106;
CANR 18, 37, 40, 94; CLR 13, 48; INT
CANR-18; JRDA; LAIT 5; MAICYA;
SATA 48, 79, 116; SATA-Brief 33; YAW

Voigt, Ellen Bryant 1943- .... **CLC 54**
See also CA 69-72; CANR 11, 29, 55; CP;
CSW; CWP; DLB 120

Voinovich, Vladimir (Nikolaevich)
1932- .... **CLC 10, 49, 147**
See also CA 81-84; CAAS 12; CANR 33,
67; MTCW 1

Vollmann, William T. 1959- .. **CLC 89; DAM
NOV, POP**
See also CA 134; CANR 67; CPW; DA3;
MTCW 2

Voloshinov, V. N.
See Bakhtin, Mikhail Mikhailovich

Voltaire 1694-1778 .... **LC 14; DA; DAB;
DAC; DAM DRAM, MST; SSC 12;
WLC**
See also DA3; GFL Beginnings to 1789;
NFS 7; RGWL

von Aschendrof, BaronIgnatz 1873-1939
See Ford, Ford Madox

von Daniken, Erich 1935- .... **CLC 30**
See also AITN 1; CA 37-40R; CANR 17,
44

von Daniken, Erich
See von Daeniken, Erich

von Hartmann, Eduard
1842-1906 .... **TCLC 96**

von Hayek, Friedrich August
See Hayek, F(riedrich) A(ugust von)

von Heidenstam, (Carl Gustaf) Verner
See Heidenstam, (Carl Gustaf) Verner von

von Heyse, Paul (Johann Ludwig)
See Heyse, Paul (Johann Ludwig von)

von Hofmannsthal, Hugo
See Hofmannsthal, Hugo von

von Horvath, Odon
See Horvath, Oedoen von

von Horvath, Oedoen
See Horvath, Oedoen von
See also CA 184

**von Liliencron, (Friedrich Adolf Axel)
Detlev**
See Liliencron, (Friedrich Adolf Axel) De-
tlev von

Vonnegut, Kurt, Jr. 1922- . **CLC 1, 2, 3, 4, 5,
8, 12, 22, 40, 60, 111; DA; DAB; DAC;
DAM MST, NOV, POP; SSC 8; WLC**
See also AAYA 6; AITN 1; AMWS 2; BEST
90:4; BPFB 3; BYA 3; CA 1-4R; CANR
1, 25, 49, 75, 92; CDALB 1968-1988;
CN; CPW 1; DA3; DLB 2, 8, 152; DLBD
3; DLBY 80; EXPN; EXPS; LAIT 4;
MTCW 1, 2; NFS 3; RGAL; SCFW;
SFW; SSFS 5; TUS; YAW

Von Rachen, Kurt
See Hubbard, L(afayette) Ron(ald)

von Rezzori (d'Arezzo), Gregor
See Rezzori (d'Arezzo), Gregor von

von Sternberg, Josef
See Sternberg, Josef von

Vorster, Gordon 1924- .... **CLC 34**
See also CA 133

Vosce, Trudie
See Ozick, Cynthia

Voznesensky, Andrei (Andreievich)
1933- .... **CLC 1, 15, 57; DAM POET**
See also CA 89-92; CANR 37; CWW 2;
MTCW 1

Waddington, Miriam 1917- .... **CLC 28**
See also CA 21-24R; CANR 12, 30; CCA
1; CP; DLB 68

Wagman, Fredrica 1937- .... **CLC 7**
See also CA 97-100; INT 97-100

Wagner, Linda W.
See Wagner-Martin, Linda (C.)

Wagner, Linda Welshimer
See Wagner-Martin, Linda (C.)

Wagner, Richard 1813-1883 .... **NCLC 9**
See also DLB 129

Wagner-Martin, Linda (C.) 1936- .... **CLC 50**
See also CA 159

Wagoner, David (Russell) 1926- .... **CLC 3, 5,
15; PC 33**
See also CA 1-4R; CAAS 3; CANR 2, 71;
CN; CP; DLB 5; SATA 14; TCWW 2

Wah, Fred(erick James) 1939- .... **CLC 44**
See also CA 107; 141; CP; DLB 60

Wahloo, Per 1926-1975 .... **CLC 7**
See also BPFB 3; CA 61-64; CANR 73;
CMW 1

Wahloo, Peter
See Wahloo, Per

Wain, John (Barrington) 1925-1994 . **CLC 2,
11, 15, 46**
See also CA 5-8R; 145; CAAS 4; CANR
23, 54; CDBLB 1960 to Present; DLB 15,
27, 139, 155; MTCW 1, 2

Wajda, Andrzej 1926- .... **CLC 16**
See also CA 102

Wakefield, Dan 1932- .... **CLC 7**
See also CA 21-24R; CAAS 7; CN

Wakoski, Diane 1937- ...... **CLC 2, 4, 7, 9, 11, 40; DAM POET; PC 15**
See also CA 13-16R; CAAS 1; CANR 9, 60; CP; CWP; DLB 5; INT CANR-9; MTCW 2

Wakoski-Sherbell, Diane
See Wakoski, Diane

Walcott, Derek (Alton) 1930- .... **CLC 2, 4, 9, 14, 25, 42, 67, 76; BLC 3; DAB; DAC; DAM MST, MULT, POET; DC 7**
See also BW 2; CA 89-92; CANR 26, 47, 75, 80; CBD; CD; CP; DA3; DLB 117; DLBY 81; DNFS; EFS 1; MTCW 1, 2; PFS 6; RGEL

Waldman, Anne (Lesley) 1945- .... **CLC 7**
See also CA 37-40R; CAAS 17; CANR 34, 69; CP; CWP; DLB 16

Waldo, E. Hunter
See Sturgeon, Theodore (Hamilton)

Waldo, Edward Hamilton
See Sturgeon, Theodore (Hamilton)

Walker, Alice (Malsenior) 1944- ... **CLC 5, 6, 9, 19, 27, 46, 58, 103; BLC 3; DA; DAB; DAC; DAM MST, MULT, NOV, POET, POP; PC 30; SSC 5; WLCS**
See also AAYA 3, 33; AFAW 1; AMWS 3; BEST 89:4; BPFB 3; BW 2, 3; CA 37-40R; CANR 9, 27, 49, 66, 82; CDALB 1968-1988; CN; CPW; CSW; DA3; DLB 6, 33, 143; EXPN; EXPS; FW; INT CANR-27; LAIT 3; MTCW 1, 2; NFS 5; RGAL; RGSF; SATA 31; SSFS 2, 11; YAW

Walker, David Harry 1911-1992 ...... **CLC 14**
See also CA 1-4R; 137; CANR 1; CWRI; SATA 8; SATA-Obit 71

Walker, Edward Joseph 1934-
See Walker, Ted
See also CA 21-24R; CANR 12, 28, 53; CP

Walker, George F. 1947- . **CLC 44, 61; DAB; DAC; DAM MST**
See also CA 103; CANR 21, 43, 59; CD; DLB 60

Walker, Joseph A. 1935- .... **CLC 19; DAM DRAM, MST**
See also BW 1, 3; CA 89-92; CAD; CANR 26; CD; DFS 12; DLB 38

Walker, Margaret (Abigail) 1915-1998 .... **CLC 1, 6; BLC; DAM MULT; PC 20**
See also AFAW 1, 2; BW 2, 3; CA 73-76; 172; CANR 26, 54, 76; CN; CP; CSW; DLB 76, 152; EXPP; FW; MTCW 1, 2; RGAL; RHW

Walker, Ted .... **CLC 13**
See also Walker, Edward Joseph
See also DLB 40

Wallace, David Foster 1962- ..... **CLC 50, 114**
See also CA 132; CANR 59; DA3; MTCW 2

Wallace, Dexter
See Masters, Edgar Lee

Wallace, (Richard Horatio) Edgar 1875-1932 .... **TCLC 57**
See also CA 115; CMW; DLB 70; RGEL

Wallace, Irving 1916-1990 .... **CLC 7, 13; DAM NOV, POP**
See also AITN 1; BPFB 3; CA 1-4R; 132; CAAS 1; CANR 1, 27; CPW; INT CANR-27; MTCW 1, 2

Wallant, Edward Lewis 1926-1962 ... **CLC 5, 10**
See also CA 1-4R; CANR 22; DLB 2, 28, 143; MTCW 1, 2; RGAL

Wallas, Graham 1858-1932 .... **TCLC 91**

Walley, Byron
See Card, Orson Scott

Walpole, Horace 1717-1797 .... **LC 49**
See also DLB 39, 104; HGG; RGEL

Walpole, Hugh (Seymour) 1884-1941 .... **TCLC 5**
See also CA 104; 165; DLB 34; HGG; MTCW 2; RGEL; RHW

Walser, Martin 1927- .... **CLC 27**
See also CA 57-60; CANR 8, 46; CWW 2; DLB 75, 124

Walser, Robert 1878-1956 .... **TCLC 18; SSC 20**
See also CA 118; 165; CANR 100; DLB 66

Walsh, Gillian Paton
See Paton Walsh, Gillian

Walsh, Jill Paton .... **CLC 35**
See also Paton Walsh, Gillian
See also CLR 2, 65

Walter, Villiam Christian
See Andersen, Hans Christian

Wambaugh, Joseph (Aloysius, Jr.) 1937- .... **CLC 3, 18; DAM NOV, POP**
See also AITN 1; BEST 89:3; BPFB 3; CA 33-36R; CANR 42, 65; CMW; CPW 1; DA3; DLB 6; DLBY 83; MTCW 1, 2

Wang Wei 699(?)-761(?) .... **PC 18**

Ward, Arthur Henry Sarsfield 1883-1959
See Rohmer, Sax
See also CA 108; 173; CMW; HGG

Ward, Douglas Turner 1930- .... **CLC 19**
See also BW 1; CA 81-84; CAD; CANR 27; CD; DLB 7, 38

Ward, E. D.
See Lucas, E(dward) V(errall)

Ward, Mrs. Humphry 1851-1920
See Ward, Mary Augusta
See also RGEL

Ward, Mary Augusta 1851-1920 ... **TCLC 55**
See also Ward, Mrs. Humphry
See also DLB 18

Ward, Peter
See Faust, Frederick (Schiller)

Warhol, Andy 1928(?)-1987 .... **CLC 20**
See also AAYA 12; BEST 89:4; CA 89-92; 121; CANR 34

Warner, Francis (Robert le Plastrier) 1937- .... **CLC 14**
See also CA 53-56; CANR 11

Warner, Marina 1946- .... **CLC 59**
See also CA 65-68; CANR 21, 55; CN; DLB 194

Warner, Rex (Ernest) 1905-1986 ...... **CLC 45**
See also CA 89-92; 119; DLB 15; RGEL; RHW

Warner, Susan (Bogert) 1819-1885 .... **NCLC 31**
See also DLB 3, 42, 239

Warner, Sylvia (Constance) Ashton
See Ashton-Warner, Sylvia (Constance)

Warner, Sylvia Townsend 1893-1978 .... **CLC 7, 19; SSC 23**
See also BRWS 7; CA 61-64; 77-80; CANR 16, 60; DLB 34, 139; FANT; FW; MTCW 1, 2; RGEL; RGSF; RHW

Warren, Mercy Otis 1728-1814 ..... **NCLC 13**
See also DLB 31, 200; RGAL

Warren, Robert Penn 1905-1989 .. **CLC 1, 4, 6, 8, 10, 13, 18, 39, 53, 59; DA; DAB; DAC; DAM MST, NOV, POET; SSC 4; WLC**
See also AITN 1; AMW; BPFB 3; BYA 1; CA 13-16R; 129; CANR 10, 47; CDALB 1968-1988; DA3; DLB 2, 48, 152; DLBY 80, 89; INT CANR-10; MTCW 1, 2; RGAL; RGSF; RHW; SATA 46; SATA-Obit 63; SSFS 8

Warshofsky, Isaac
See Singer, Isaac Bashevis

Warton, Thomas 1728-1790 ..... **LC 15; DAM POET**
See also DLB 104, 109; RGEL

Waruk, Kona
See Harris, (Theodore) Wilson

Warung, Price .... **TCLC 45**
See also Astley, William
See also RGEL

Warwick, Jarvis
See Garner, Hugh
See also CCA 1

Washington, Alex
See Harris, Mark

Washington, Booker T(aliaferro) 1856-1915 ...... **TCLC 10; BLC 3; DAM MULT**
See also BW 1; CA 114; 125; DA3; LAIT 2; RGAL; SATA 28

Washington, George 1732-1799 .... **LC 25**
See also DLB 31

Wassermann, (Karl) Jakob 1873-1934 .... **TCLC 6**
See also CA 104; 163; DLB 66

Wasserstein, Wendy 1950- .. **CLC 32, 59, 90; DAM DRAM; DC 4**
See also CA 121; 129; CABS 3; CAD; CANR 53, 75; CD; CWD; DA3; DFS 5; DLB 228; FW; INT 129; MTCW 2; SATA 94

Waterhouse, Keith (Spencer) 1929- . **CLC 47**
See also CA 5-8R; CANR 38, 67; CBD; CN; DLB 13, 15; MTCW 1, 2

Waters, Frank (Joseph) 1902-1995 ... **CLC 88**
See also CA 5-8R; 149; CAAS 13; CANR 3, 18, 63; DLB 212; DLBY 86; RGAL; TCWW 2

Waters, Mary C. .... **CLC 70**

Waters, Roger 1944- .... **CLC 35**

Watkins, Frances Ellen
See Harper, Frances Ellen Watkins

Watkins, Gerrold
See Malzberg, Barry N(athaniel)

Watkins, Gloria Jean 1952(?)-
See hooks, bell
See also BW 2; CA 143; CANR 87; MTCW 2; SATA 115

Watkins, Paul 1964- .... **CLC 55**
See also CA 132; CANR 62, 98

Watkins, Vernon Phillips 1906-1967 .... **CLC 43**
See also CA 9-10; 25-28R; CAP 1; DLB 20; RGEL

Watson, Irving S.
See Mencken, H(enry) L(ouis)

Watson, John H.
See Farmer, Philip Jose

Watson, Richard F.
See Silverberg, Robert

Waugh, Auberon (Alexander) 1939-2001 .... **CLC 7**
See also CA 45-48; 192; CANR 6, 22, 92; DLB 14, 194

Waugh, Evelyn (Arthur St. John) 1903-1966 .. **CLC 1, 3, 8, 13, 19, 27, 44, 107; DA; DAB; DAC; DAM MST, NOV, POP; SSC 41; WLC**
See also BPFB 3; BRW; CA 85-88; 25-28R; CANR 22; CDBLB 1914-1945; DA3; DLB 15, 162, 195; MTCW 1, 2; RGEL; RGSF; WLIT 4

Waugh, Harriet 1944- .... **CLC 6**
See also CA 85-88; CANR 22

Ways, C. R.
See Blount, Roy (Alton), Jr.

Waystaff, Simon
See Swift, Jonathan

Webb, Beatrice (Martha Potter) 1858-1943 .... **TCLC 22**
See also CA 117; 162; DLB 190; FW

Webb, Charles (Richard) 1939- .... **CLC 7**
See also CA 25-28R

Williamson, Jack .... **CLC 29**
See also Williamson, John Stewart
See also CAAS 8; DLB 8; SCFW 2

Williamson, John Stewart 1908-
See Williamson, Jack
See also CA 17-20R; CANR 23, 70; SFW

Willie, Frederick
See Lovecraft, H(oward) P(hillips)

Willingham, Calder (Baynard, Jr.)
1922-1995 .... **CLC 5, 51**
See also CA 5-8R; 147; CANR 3; CSW;
DLB 2, 44; IDFW 3, 4; MTCW 1

Willis, Charles
See Clarke, Arthur C(harles)

Willy
See Colette, (Sidonie-Gabrielle)

Willy, Colette
See Colette, (Sidonie-Gabrielle)
See also GLL 1

Wilson, A(ndrew) N(orman) 1950- .. **CLC 33**
See also BRWS 6; CA 112; 122; CN; DLB
14, 155, 194; MTCW 2

Wilson, Angus (Frank Johnstone)
1913-1991 . **CLC 2, 3, 5, 25, 34; SSC 21**
See also BRWS 1; CA 5-8R; 134; CANR
21; DLB 15, 139, 155; MTCW 1, 2;
RGEL; RGSF

Wilson, August 1945- ... **CLC 39, 50, 63, 118;**
BLC 3; DA; DAB; DAC; DAM
DRAM, MST, MULT; DC 2; WLCS
See also AAYA 16; AFAW 2; AMWS 8; BW
2, 3; CA 115; 122; CAD; CANR 42, 54,
76; CD; DA3; DFS 3,7; DLB 228; LAIT
4; MTCW 1, 2; RGAL

Wilson, Brian 1942- .... **CLC 12**

Wilson, Colin 1931- .... **CLC 3, 14**
See also CA 1-4R; CAAS 5; CANR 1, 22,
33, 77; CMW; CN; DLB 14, 194; HGG;
MTCW 1; SFW

Wilson, Dirk
See Pohl, Frederik

Wilson, Edmund 1895-1972 .. **CLC 1, 2, 3, 8,**
24
See also AMW; CA 1-4R; 37-40R; CANR
1, 46; DLB 63; MTCW 1, 2; RGAL

Wilson, Ethel Davis (Bryant)
1888(?)-1980 .... **CLC 13; DAC; DAM**
POET
See also CA 102; DLB 68; MTCW 1;
RGEL

Wilson, Harriet
See Wilson, Harriet E. Adams
See also DLB 239

Wilson, Harriet E. Adams
1827(?)-1863(?) .... **NCLC 78; BLC 3;**
DAM MULT
See also Wilson, Harriet
See also DLB 50

Wilson, John 1785-1854 .... **NCLC 5**

Wilson, John (Anthony) Burgess 1917-1993
See Burgess, Anthony
See also CA 1-4R; 143; CANR 2, 46; DA3;
DAC; DAM NOV; MTCW 1, 2

Wilson, Lanford 1937- .... **CLC 7, 14, 36;**
DAM DRAM
See also CA 17-20R; CABS 3; CAD; CANR
45, 96; CD; DFS 4, 9, 12; DLB 7

Wilson, Robert M. 1944- .... **CLC 7, 9**
See also CA 49-52; CAD; CANR 2, 41; CD;
MTCW 1

Wilson, Robert McLiam 1964- .... **CLC 59**
See also CA 132

Wilson, Sloan 1920- .... **CLC 32**
See also CA 1-4R; CANR 1, 44; CN

Wilson, Snoo 1948- .... **CLC 33**
See also CA 69-72; CBD; CD

Wilson, William S(mith) 1932- .... **CLC 49**
See also CA 81-84

Wilson, (Thomas) Woodrow
1856-1924 .... **TCLC 79**
See also CA 166; DLB 47

Wilson and Warnke eds. .... **CLC 65**

Winchilsea, Anne (Kingsmill) Finch
1661-1720
See Finch, Anne
See also RGEL

Windham, Basil
See Wodehouse, P(elham) G(renville)

Wingrove, David (John) 1954- .... **CLC 68**
See also CA 133; SFW

Winnemucca, Sarah 1844-1891 .... **NCLC 79;**
DAM MULT
See also DLB 175; NNAL; RGAL

Winstanley, Gerrard 1609-1676 .... **LC 52**

Wintergreen, Jane
See Duncan, Sara Jeannette

Winters, Janet Lewis .... **CLC 41**
See also Lewis, Janet
See also DLBY 87

Winters, (Arthur) Yvor 1900-1968 .... **CLC 4,**
8, 32
See also AMWS 2; CA 11-12; 25-28R; CAP
1; DLB 48; MTCW 1; RGAL

Winterson, Jeanette 1959- .... **CLC 64; DAM**
POP
See also BRWS 4; CA 136; CANR 58; CN;
CPW; DA3; DLB 207; FANT; FW; GLL
1; MTCW 2; RHW

Winthrop, John 1588-1649 .... **LC 31**
See also DLB 24, 30

Wirth, Louis 1897-1952 .... **TCLC 92**

Wiseman, Frederick 1930- .... **CLC 20**
See also CA 159

Wister, Owen 1860-1938 .... **TCLC 21**
See also BPFB 3; CA 108; 162; DLB 9, 78,
186; RGAL; SATA 62; TCWW 2

Witkacy
See Witkiewicz, Stanislaw Ignacy

Witkiewicz, Stanislaw Ignacy
1885-1939 .... **TCLC 8**
See also CA 105; 162; DLB 215; RGWL;
SFW

Wittgenstein, Ludwig (Josef Johann)
1889-1951 .... **TCLC 59**
See also CA 113; 164; MTCW 2

Wittig, Monique 1935(?)- .... **CLC 22**
See also CA 116; 135; CWW 2; DLB 83;
FW; GLL 1

Wittlin, Jozef 1896-1976 .... **CLC 25**
See also CA 49-52; 65-68; CANR 3

Wodehouse, P(elham) G(renville)
1881-1975 .... **CLC 1, 2, 5, 10, 22; DAB;**
DAC; DAM NOV; SSC 2
See also AITN 2; BRWS 3; CA 45-48; 57-
60; CANR 3, 33; CDBLB 1914-1945;
CPW 1; DA3; DLB 34, 162; MTCW 1, 2;
RGEL; RGSF; SATA 22; SSFS 10; TCLC
108

Woiwode, L.
See Woiwode, Larry (Alfred)

Woiwode, Larry (Alfred) 1941- ... **CLC 6, 10**
See also CA 73-76; CANR 16, 94; CN;
DLB 6; INT CANR-16

Wojciechowska, Maia (Teresa)
1927- .... **CLC 26**
See also AAYA 8; BYA 3; CA 9-12R; 183;
CAAE 183; CANR 4, 41; CLR 1; JRDA;
MAICYA; SAAS 1; SATA 1, 28, 83;
SATA-Essay 104; YAW

Wojtyla, Karol
See John Paul II, Pope

Wolf, Christa 1929- .... **CLC 14, 29, 58, 150**
See also CA 85-88; CANR 45; CWW 2;
DLB 75; FW; MTCW 1; RGWL

Wolfe, Gene (Rodman) 1931- .... **CLC 25;**
DAM POP
See also AAYA 35; CA 57-60; CAAS 9;
CANR 6, 32, 60; CPW; DLB 8; FANT;
MTCW 2; SATA 118; SCFW 2; SFW

Wolfe, George C. 1954- .... **CLC 49; BLCS**
See also CA 149; CAD; CD

Wolfe, Thomas (Clayton)
1900-1938 ...... **TCLC 4, 13, 29, 61; DA;**
DAB; DAC; DAM MST, NOV; SSC
33; WLC
See also AMW; BPFB 3; CA 104; 132;
CDALB 1929-1941; DA3; DLB 9, 102;
DLBD 2, 16; DLBY 85, 97; MTCW 1, 2;
RGAL

Wolfe, Thomas Kennerly, Jr.
1930- .... **CLC 147; DAM POP**
See also Wolfe, Tom
See also CA 13-16R; CANR 9, 33, 70;
DA3; DLB 185; INT CANR-9; MTCW 1,
2; TUS

Wolfe, Tom .... **CLC 1, 2, 9, 15, 35, 51**
See also Wolfe, Thomas Kennerly, Jr.
See also AAYA 8; AITN 2; AMWS 3; BEST
89:1; BPFB 3; CN; CPW; CSW; DLB
152; LAIT 5; RGAL

Wolff, Geoffrey (Ansell) 1937- .... **CLC 41**
See also CA 29-32R; CANR 29, 43, 78

Wolff, Sonia
See Levitin, Sonia (Wolff)

Wolff, Tobias (Jonathan Ansell)
1945- .... **CLC 39, 64**
See also AAYA 16; AMWS 7; BEST 90:2;
BYA 12; CA 114; 117; CAAS 22; CANR
54, 76, 96; CN; CSW; DA3; DLB 130;
INT CA-117; MTCW 2; RGAL; RGSF;
SSFS 4, 11

Wolfram von Eschenbach c. 1170-c.
1220 .... **CMLC 5**
See also DLB 138; RGWL

Wolitzer, Hilma 1930- .... **CLC 17**
See also CA 65-68; CANR 18, 40; INT
CANR-18; SATA 31; YAW

Wollstonecraft, Mary 1759-1797 ..... **LC 5, 50**
See also BRWS 3; CDBLB 1789-1832;
DLB 39, 104, 158; FW; LAIT 1; RGEL;
WLIT 3

Wonder, Stevie .... **CLC 12**
See also Morris, Steveland Judkins

Wong, Jade Snow 1922- .... **CLC 17**
See also CA 109; CANR 91; SATA 112

Woodberry, George Edward
1855-1930 .... **TCLC 73**
See also CA 165; DLB 71, 103

Woodcott, Keith
See Brunner, John (Kilian Houston)

Woodruff, Robert W.
See Mencken, H(enry) L(ouis)

Woolf, (Adeline) Virginia
1882-1941 .. **TCLC 1, 5, 20, 43, 56, 101;**
DA; DAB; DAC; DAM MST, NOV;
SSC 7; WLC
See also BPFB 3; BRW; CA 104; 130;
CANR 64; CDBLB 1914-1945; DA3;
DLB 36, 100, 162; DLBD 10; EXPS; FW;
LAIT 3; MTCW 1, 2; NCFS 2; NFS 8,
12; RGEL; RGSF; SSFS 4, 12; WLIT 4

Woollcott, Alexander (Humphreys)
1887-1943 .... **TCLC 5**
See also CA 105; 161; DLB 29

Woolrich, Cornell .... **CLC 77**
See also Hopley-Woolrich, Cornell George

Woolson, Constance Fenimore
1840-1894 .... **NCLC 82**
See also DLB 12, 74, 189, 221; RGAL

Wordsworth, Dorothy 1771-1855 .. **NCLC 25**
See also DLB 107

Wordsworth, William 1770-1850 .. **NCLC 12, 38; DA; DAB; DAC; DAM MST, POET; PC 4; WLC**
See also CDBLB 1789-1832; DA3; DLB 93, 107; EXPP; PAB; PFS 2; RGEL; WLIT 3; WP

Wotton, Sir Henry 1568-1639 .... **LC 68**
See also DLB 121; RGEL

Wouk, Herman 1915- ... **CLC 1, 9, 38; DAM NOV, POP**
See also BPFB 2, 3; CA 5-8R; CANR 6, 33, 67; CDALBS; CN; CPW; DA3; DLBY 82; INT CANR-6; LAIT 4; MTCW 1, 2; NFS 7

Wright, Charles (Penzel, Jr.) 1935- .. **CLC 6, 13, 28, 119, 146**
See also AMWS 5; CA 29-32R; CAAS 7; CANR 23, 36, 62, 88; CP; DLB 165; DLBY 82; MTCW 1, 2; PFS 10

Wright, Charles Stevenson 1932- ... **CLC 49; BLC 3; DAM MULT, POET**
See also BW 1; CA 9-12R; CANR 26; CN; DLB 33

Wright, Frances 1795-1852 .... **NCLC 74**
See also DLB 73

Wright, Frank Lloyd 1867-1959 .... **TCLC 95**
See also AAYA 33; CA 174

Wright, Jack R.
See Harris, Mark

Wright, James (Arlington)
1927-1980 .... **CLC 3, 5, 10, 28; DAM POET; PC 36**
See also AITN 2; AMWS 3; CA 49-52; 97-100; CANR 4, 34, 64; CDALBS; DLB 5, 169; EXPP; MTCW 1, 2; PFS 7, 8; RGAL; WP

Wright, Judith (Arundell)
1915-2000 .... **CLC 11, 53; PC 14**
See also CA 13-16R; 188; CANR 31, 76, 93; CP; CWP; MTCW 1, 2; PFS 8; RGEL; SATA 14; SATA-Obit 121

Wright, L(aurali) R. 1939- .... **CLC 44**
See also CA 138; CMW

Wright, Richard (Nathaniel)
1908-1960 .... **CLC 1, 3, 4, 9, 14, 21, 48, 74; BLC 3; DA; DAB; DAC; DAM MST, MULT, NOV; SSC 2; WLC**
See also AAYA 5; AFAW 1, 2; AMW; BPFB 3; BW 1; BYA 2; CA 108; CANR 64; CDALB 1929-1941; DLB 76, 102; DLBD 2; EXPN; LAIT 3, 4; MTCW 1, 2; NCFS 1; NFS 1, 7; RGAL; RGSF; SSFS 3, 9; YAW

Wright, Richard B(ruce) 1937- .... **CLC 6**
See also CA 85-88; DLB 53

Wright, Rick 1945- .... **CLC 35**

Wright, Rowland
See Wells, Carolyn

Wright, Stephen 1946- .... **CLC 33**

Wright, Willard Huntington 1888-1939
See Van Dine, S. S.
See also CA 115; 189; CMW; DLBD 16

Wright, William 1930- .... **CLC 44**
See also CA 53-56; CANR 7, 23

Wroth, LadyMary 1587-1653(?) .... **LC 30**
See also DLB 121

Wu Ch'eng-en 1500(?)-1582(?) .... **LC 7**

Wu Ching-tzu 1701-1754 .... **LC 2**

Wurlitzer, Rudolph 1938(?)- .... **CLC 2, 4, 15**
See also CA 85-88; CN; DLB 173

Wyatt, Sir Thomas c. 1503-1542 . **LC 70; PC 27**
See also BRW 1; DLB 132; EXPP; RGEL; TEA

Wycherley, William 1640-1716 ...... **LC 8, 21; DAM DRAM**
See also BRW 2; CDBLB 1660-1789; DLB 80; RGEL

Wylie, Elinor (Morton Hoyt)
1885-1928 .... **TCLC 8; PC 23**
See also AMWS 1; CA 105; 162; DLB 9, 45; EXPP; RGAL

Wylie, Philip (Gordon) 1902-1971 ... **CLC 43**
See also CA 21-22; 33-36R; CAP 2; DLB 9; SFW

Wyndham, John .... **CLC 19**
See also Harris, John (Wyndham Parkes Lucas) Beynon
See also SCFW 2

Wyss, Johann David Von
1743-1818 .... **NCLC 10**
See also JRDA; MAICYA; SATA 29; SATA-Brief 27

Xenophon c. 430B.C.-c. 354B.C. ... **CMLC 17**
See also DLB 176; RGWL

Yakumo Koizumi
See Hearn, (Patricio) Lafcadio (Tessima Carlos)

Yamamoto, Hisaye 1921- .... **SSC 34; AAL; DAM MULT**
See also LAIT 4

Yanez, Jose Donoso
See Donoso (Yanez), Jose

Yanovsky, Basile S.
See Yanovsky, V(assily) S(emenovich)

Yanovsky, V(assily) S(emenovich)
1906-1989 .... **CLC 2, 18**
See also CA 97-100; 129

Yates, Richard 1926-1992 ...... **CLC 7, 8, 23**
See also CA 5-8R; 139; CANR 10, 43; DLB 2, 234; DLBY 81, 92; INT CANR-10

Yeats, W. B.
See Yeats, William Butler

Yeats, William Butler 1865-1939 .... **TCLC 1, 11, 18, 31, 93; DA; DAB; DAC; DAM DRAM, MST, POET; PC 20; WLC**
See also CA 104; 127; CANR 45; CDBLB 1890-1914; DA3; DLB 10, 19, 98, 156; EXPP; MTCW 1, 2; PAB; PFS 1, 2, 5, 7; RGEL; WLIT 4; WP

Yehoshua, A(braham) B. 1936- .. **CLC 13, 31**
See also CA 33-36R; CANR 43, 90; RGSF

Yellow Bird
See Ridge, John Rollin

Yep, Laurence Michael 1948- .... **CLC 35**
See also AAYA 5, 31; BYA 7; CA 49-52; CANR 1, 46, 92; CLR 3, 17, 54; DLB 52; FANT; JRDA; MAICYA; MAICYAS; SATA 7, 69, 123; WYA; YAW

Yerby, Frank G(arvin) 1916-1991 . **CLC 1, 7, 22; BLC 3; DAM MULT**
See also BPFB 3; BW 1, 3; CA 9-12R; 136; CANR 16, 52; DLB 76; INT CANR-16; MTCW 1; RGAL; RHW

Yesenin, Sergei Alexandrovich
See Esenin, Sergei (Alexandrovich)

Yevtushenko, Yevgeny (Alexandrovich)
1933- .. **CLC 1, 3, 13, 26, 51, 126; DAM POET**
See also Evtushenko, Evgenii Aleksandrovich
See also CA 81-84; CANR 33, 54; CWW 2; MTCW 1

Yezierska, Anzia 1885(?)-1970 .... **CLC 46**
See also CA 126; 89-92; DLB 28, 221; FW; MTCW 1; RGAL

Yglesias, Helen 1915- .... **CLC 7, 22**
See also CA 37-40R; CAAS 20; CANR 15, 65, 95; CN; INT CANR-15; MTCW 1

Yokomitsu, Riichi 1898-1947 .... **TCLC 47**
See also CA 170

Yonge, Charlotte (Mary)
1823-1901 .... **TCLC 48**
See also CA 109; 163; DLB 18, 163; RGEL; SATA 17; WCH

York, Jeremy
See Creasey, John

York, Simon
See Heinlein, Robert A(nson)

Yorke, Henry Vincent 1905-1974 ..... **CLC 13**
See also Green, Henry
See also CA 85-88; 49-52

Yosano Akiko 1878-1942 .... **TCLC 59; PC 11**
See also CA 161

Yoshimoto, Banana .... **CLC 84**
See also Yoshimoto, Mahoko
See also NFS 7

Yoshimoto, Mahoko 1964-
See Yoshimoto, Banana
See also CA 144; CANR 98

Young, Al(bert James) 1939- . **CLC 19; BLC 3; DAM MULT**
See also BW 2, 3; CA 29-32R; CANR 26, 65; CN; CP; DLB 33

Young, Andrew (John) 1885-1971 ...... **CLC 5**
See also CA 5-8R; CANR 7, 29; RGEL

Young, Collier
See Bloch, Robert (Albert)

Young, Edward 1683-1765 .... **LC 3, 40**
See also DLB 95; RGEL

Young, Marguerite (Vivian)
1909-1995 .... **CLC 82**
See also CA 13-16; 150; CAP 1; CN

Young, Neil 1945- .... **CLC 17**
See also CA 110; CCA 1

Young Bear, Ray A. 1950- ..... **CLC 94; DAM MULT**
See also CA 146; DLB 175; NNAL

Yourcenar, Marguerite 1903-1987 ... **CLC 19, 38, 50, 87; DAM NOV**
See also BPFB 3; CA 69-72; CANR 23, 60, 93; DLB 72; DLBY 88; GFL 1789 to the Present; GLL 1; MTCW 1, 2; RGWL

Yuan, Chu 340(?)B.C.-278(?)B.C. . **CMLC 36**

Yurick, Sol 1925- .... **CLC 6**
See also CA 13-16R; CANR 25; CN

Zabolotsky, Nikolai Alekseevich
1903-1958 .... **TCLC 52**
See also CA 116; 164

Zagajewski, Adam 1945- .... **PC 27**
See also CA 186; DLB 232

Zalygin, Sergei -2000 .... **CLC 59**

Zamiatin, Evgenii
See Zamyatin, Evgeny Ivanovich
See also RGSF; RGWL

Zamiatin, Yevgenii
See Zamyatin, Evgeny Ivanovich

Zamora, Bernice (B. Ortiz) 1938- .. **CLC 89; DAM MULT; HLC 2**
See also CA 151; CANR 80; DLB 82; HW 1, 2

Zamyatin, Evgeny Ivanovich
1884-1937 .... **TCLC 8, 37**
See also Zamiatin, Evgenii
See also CA 105; 166; EW; SFW

Zangwill, Israel 1864-1926 ... **TCLC 16; SSC 44**
See also CA 109; 167; CMW; DLB 10, 135, 197; RGEL

Zappa, Francis Vincent, Jr. 1940-1993
See Zappa, Frank
See also CA 108; 143; CANR 57

Zappa, Frank .... **CLC 17**
See also Zappa, Francis Vincent, Jr.

Zaturenska, Marya 1902-1982 ..... **CLC 6, 11**
See also CA 13-16R; 105; CANR 22

Zeami 1363-1443 .... **DC 7**
See also RGWL

Zelazny, Roger (Joseph) 1937-1995 . **CLC 21**
See also AAYA 7; BPFB 3; CA 21-24R; 148; CANR 26, 60; CN; DLB 8; FANT; MTCW 1, 2; SATA 57; SATA-Brief 39; SCFW; SFW; SUFW

Zhdanov, Andrei Alexandrovich
1896-1948 .... **TCLC 18**
See also CA 117; 167

Literary Criticism Series
Cumulative Topic Index

This index lists all topic entries in Gale's *Classical and Medieval Literature Criticism, Contemporary Literary Criticism, Literature Criticism from 1400 to 1800, Nineteenth-Century Literature Criticism,* and *Twentieth-Century Literary Criticism.*

Topic Index

CLC Cumulative Nationality Index

Nationality Index

CLC-148 Title Index

ISBN 0-7876-5217-2

90000